Mike Holt's Illustrated Guide to

UNDERSTANDING THE NATIONAL ELECTRICAL CODE®

Volume 2

Articles 500 - 810

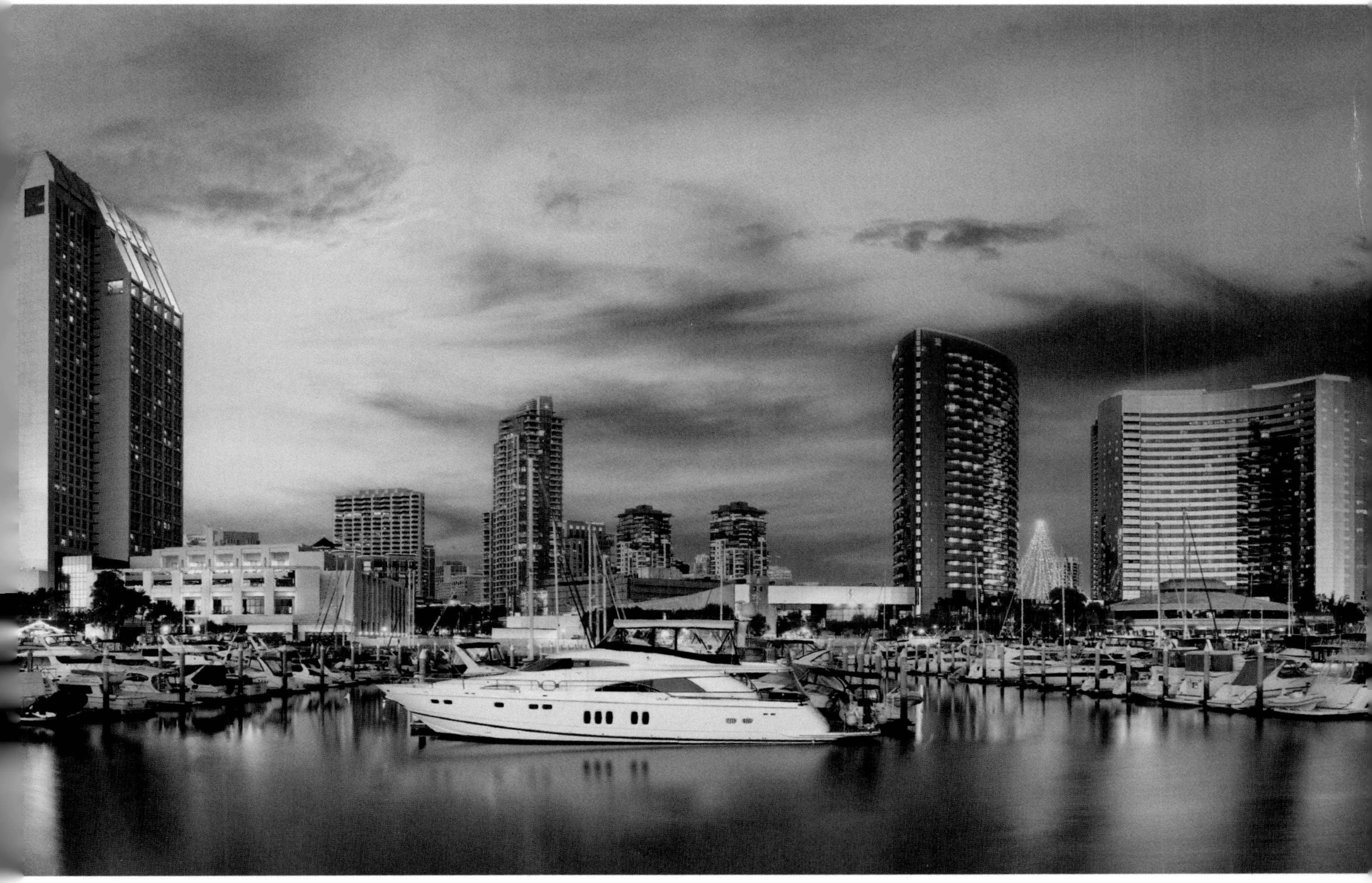

BASED ON THE

2023 NEC®

NOTICE TO THE READER

The text and commentary in this book is the author's interpretation of the 2023 Edition of NFPA 70®, *National Electrical Code®*. It shall not be considered an endorsement of or the official position of the NFPA® or any of its committees, nor relied upon as a formal interpretation of the meaning or intent of any specific provision or provisions of the 2023 edition of NFPA 70, *National Electrical Code*.

The publisher does not warrant or guarantee any of the products described herein or perform any independent analysis in connection with any of the product information contained herein. The publisher does not assume, and expressly disclaims, any obligation to obtain and include information other than that provided to it by the manufacturer.

The reader is expressly warned to consider and adopt all safety precautions and applicable federal, state, and local laws and regulations. By following the instructions contained herein, the reader willingly assumes all risks in connection with such instructions.

Mike Holt Enterprises disclaims liability for any personal injury, property or other damages of any nature whatsoever, whether special, indirect, consequential or compensatory, directly or indirectly resulting from the use of this material. The reader is responsible for relying on his or her personal independent judgment in determining safety and appropriate actions in all circumstances.

The publisher makes no representation or warranties of any kind, including but not limited to, the warranties of fitness for particular purpose or merchantability, nor are any such representations implied with respect to the material set forth herein, and the publisher takes no responsibility with respect to such material. The publisher shall not be liable for any special, consequential, or exemplary damages resulting, in whole or part, from the reader's use of, or reliance upon, this material.

Mike Holt's Illustrated Guide to Understanding the National Electrical Code® Volume 2, based on the 2023 NEC®

First Printing: April 2023
Author: Mike Holt
Technical Illustrator: Mike Culbreath
Cover Design: Bryan Burch
Layout Design and Typesetting: Cathleen Kwas

ISBN 978-1-950431-78-6

Produced and Printed in the USA

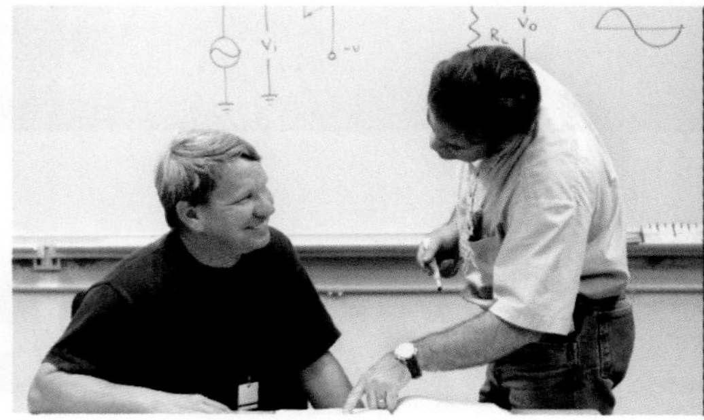

I dedicate this book to the
***Lord Jesus Christ,** my mentor and teacher.*
Proverbs 16:3

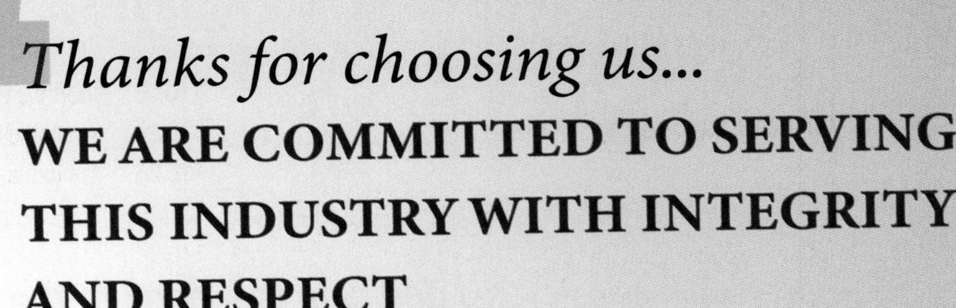
Thanks for choosing us...
WE ARE COMMITTED TO SERVING THIS INDUSTRY WITH INTEGRITY AND RESPECT

Since 1975, we have worked hard to develop products that get results, and to help individuals in their pursuit of success in this exciting industry.

From the very beginning we have been committed to the idea that customers come first. Everyone on my team will do everything they possibly can to help you succeed. I want you to know that we value you and are honored that you have chosen us to be your partner in training.

You are the future of this industry and we know that it is you who will make the difference in the years to come. My goal is to share with you everything that I know and to encourage you to pursue your education on a continuous basis. I hope that not only will you learn theory, *Code*, calculations, or how to pass an exam, but that in the process, you will become the expert in the field and the person others know to trust.

To put it simply, we genuinely care about your success and will do everything that we can to help you take your skills to the next level!

We are happy to partner with you on your educational journey.

God bless and much success,

TABLE OF CONTENTS

1st Printing

1st Printing

ABOUT THIS TEXTBOOK

Mike Holt's Illustrated Guide to Understanding the National Electrical Code, Volume 2, based on the 2023 NEC

Mike Holt's Illustrated Guide to Understanding the National Electrical Code®, Volume 2, based on the 2023 NEC®, textbook is intended to provide you with the tools necessary to understand the technical requirements of the *National Electrical Code (NEC)*, Articles 500 through 810, and is the second volume of this 2-part program.

Mike's writing style is informative, practical, easy to understand, and applicable for today's electrical professional. Just like all of Mike Holt's textbooks, this one is built around hundreds of full-color illustrations and photographs that show the requirements of the *National Electrical Code* in practical use. The images provide a visual representation of the information being discussed, helping you to better understand just how the *Code* rules are applied.

This textbook explains possible conflicts or confusing *NEC* requirements, tips on proper electrical installations, and warnings or dangers related to improper electrical installations. Sometimes a rule seems confusing or it may be difficult to understand its actual application. Where this may be the case, you will find additional content to help you to better interpret a rule in an upfront and straightforward manner. Our intention is to help the industry better understand the current *NEC*, point out areas needing refinement, and encourage all *Code* users to be a part of the change process that helps create a better *NEC* for the future.

Keeping up with the requirements of the *Code* should be the goal of everyone involved in electrical safety—whether you are an installer, contractor, inspector, engineer, or instructor. This textbook is the perfect tool to help you do so. The level of specialization and technicality of Chapters 5 through 8 of the *NEC* require a comprehensive understanding of Electrical Theory and the *Code* rules and requirements in Chapters 1 through 4, so be sure to complete Volume 1 before you dive into the text and videos that accompany this textbook. The associated videos contain in-depth commentary and explanations from a panel of industry experts that breakdown the intricacies of the *Code* Rules and where and when they're to be applied.

The Scope of This Textbook

This textbook covers those installation requirements that we consider to be important and is based on the following conditions:

1. Power Systems and Voltage. All power-supply systems are assumed to be one of the following nominal voltages or "voltage class," unless identified otherwise:

- 2-wire, single-phase, 120V
- 3-wire, single-phase, 120/240V
- 4-wire, three-phase, 120/240V Delta High-Leg
- 4-wire, three-phase, 208YY120V or 480Y/277V Wye

2. Electrical Calculations. Unless the question or example specifies three-phase, they're based on a single-phase power supply. In addition, all amperage calculations are rounded to the nearest whole number in accordance with Section 220.5(B).

3. Conductor Material/Insulation. The conductor material and insulation are copper THWN-2, unless otherwise indicated.

4. Conductor Sizing.

Circuits Rated 100A or Less. Conductors are sized to the 60°C column of Table 310.16 [110.14(C)(1)(a)(2)]. Where equipment is listed and identified for use with conductors having at least a 75°C temperature rating, the conductors can be sized to the 75°C column of Table 310.16 [110.14(C)(1)(a)(3)].

Circuits Rated Over 100A. Conductors are sized to the 75°C column of Table 310.16 [110.14(C)(1)(b)(2)].

5. Overcurrent Protective Device. The term "overcurrent protective device" refers to a molded-case circuit breaker, unless specified otherwise. Where a fuse is specified, it's a single-element type fuse, also known as a "onetime fuse," unless the text specifies otherwise.

How to Use This Textbook

This textbook is intended to help you interpret the *NEC* and is not a replacement for it, so be sure to have a copy of the 2023 *National Electrical Code* handy. You will notice that we have paraphrased a great deal of the wording, and some of the article and section titles appear different than those in the actual *Code* book. We believe doing so makes it easier to understand the content of the rule, so keep that in mind when comparing this textbook to the *NEC*.

Always compare what is being explained in this textbook to what the *Code* book says and underline or highlight pertinent rules. Get with others who are knowledgeable about the *NEC* to discuss any topics you find difficult to understand or join our free *Code* Forum at www.MikeHolt.com/Forum to post your question.

***NEC* Content.** This textbook follows the *Code* format, but it does not cover every requirement. For example, it does not include every article, section, subsection, exception, or Informational Note. So, do not be concerned if you see that the textbook contains Exception 1 and Exception 3, but not Exception 2.

Cross-References. Many *NEC* rules refer to requirements located in other sections of the *Code*. This textbook does the same with the intention of helping you develop a better understanding of how the *NEC* rules relate to one another. These cross-references are indicated by *Code* section numbers in brackets, an example of which is "[90.4]."

Informational Notes. Informational Notes contained in the *NEC* will be identified in this textbook as "Note."

Exceptions. Where shown in this textbook, Exceptions to *NEC* rules will be identified as simply "Ex" and not spelled out.

As you read through this textbook, allow yourself enough time to review the text using the graphics and follow the step-by-step examples meant to assist you in a more in-depth understanding of the *Code*.

Answer Keys

Digital answer keys are provided for all your purchases of Mike Holt textbooks, and can be found in your online account at Mike Holt Enterprises. Go to MikeHolt.com/MyAccount and log in to your account, or create one if you haven't already. If you are not currently a Mike Holt customer, you can access your answer key at MikeHolt.com/MyAK23UND2.

Watch the Videos That Accompany This Textbook

Mike, along with an expert panel, recorded videos to accompany this textbook. Watching these videos will complete your learning experience. The videos contain explanations and additional commentary that expand on the topics covered in the text. Mike and the panel discuss the nuances behind the rules, and cover their practical application in the field, in a way that is different from what can be conveyed in written format.

To watch a few video clips, scan this QR Code with a smartphone app or visit MikeHolt.com/23UN2videos for a sample selection. To get the complete video library that accompanies this book, call 888.632.2633 and let them know you want to add the videos, or visit MikeHolt.com/Upgrade23UND2.

Technical Questions

As you progress through this textbook, you might find that you don't understand every explanation, example, calculation, or comment. If you find some topics difficult to understand, they are discussed in detail in the videos that correlate to this book. You may also find it helpful to discuss your questions with instructors, co-workers, other students, or your supervisor—they might have a perspective that will help you understand more clearly. Don't become frustrated, and don't get down on yourself.

If you have additional questions that aren't covered in this material, visit MikeHolt.com/Forum, and post your question on the Code Forum for help.

Textbook Errors and Corrections

We're committed to providing you the finest product with the fewest errors and take great care to ensure our textbooks are correct. But we're realistic and know that errors might be found after printing. If you believe that there's an error of any kind (typographical, grammatical, technical, etc.) in this textbook or in the Answer Key, please visit MikeHolt.com/Corrections and complete the online Textbook Correction Form.

Textbook Format

The layout and design of this textbook incorporate special features and symbols that were designed for Mike Holt textbooks to help you easily navigate through the material, and to enhance your understanding of the content.

Formulas

$$P = I \times E$$

Formulas are easily identifiable in green text on a gray bar.

According to Article 100

Throughout the textbook, Mike references definitions that are easily identified by colored text "**According to Article 100,**" at the start of the paragraph.

Modular Color-Coded Page Layout

Chapters are color-coded and modular to make it easy to navigate through each section of the textbook.

Changes to the *Code*

Underlined text denotes changes to the *Code* from the previous 2020 cycle for the 2023 *NEC*.

> **(B) Bonding.**
>
> **(1) Specific Bonding Means.**
>
> (a) Locknuts are not suitable for bonding purposes in hazardous (classified) locations so bonding jumpers with identified fittings or other approved means of bonding must be used. Such means of bonding apply to all metal raceways between Class II locations and service disconnects or a separately derived system. ▸Figure 502–11

Additional Background Information Boxes

Where the author believes that information unrelated to the specific rule will help you understand the concept being taught, he includes these topics, easily identified in boxes that are shaded gray.

> **Dangers of Objectionable Current**
>
> Objectionable neutral current on metal parts can cause electric shock, fires, and the improper operation of electronic equipment and overcurrent protective devices such as GFPEs, GFCIs, SPGFCIs, and AFCIs.

Caution, Danger, and Warning Icons

These icons highlight areas of concern.

Caution

CAUTION: An explanation of possible damage to property or equipment.

Danger

DANGER: An explanation of possible severe injury or death.

Warning

WARNING: An explanation of possible severe property damage or personal injury.

1st Printing

Key Features

Each first level subsection of each *Code* rule is highlighted in yellow to help you navigate through the text.

Chapters are color-coded and modular to make it easy to navigate through each section of the textbook.

Author's Comments provide additional information to help you understand the context.

Detailed full-color educational graphics illustrate the rule in a real-world application.

Examples and practical application questions and answers are contained in yellow boxes.

If you see an ellipsis (● ● ●) at the bottom right corner of a page or example box, it is continued on the following page.

Fire Pumps | **695.4**

(F) Transfer of Power. Transfer of power to the fire pump controller must take place within the pump room.

695.4 Continuity of Power

(B) Connection Through Disconnect and Overcurrent Device.

(1) Number of Disconnecting Means.

(a) A single means of disconnect is permitted to be installed between the fire pump electric supply and:

(1) A listed fire pump controller, or

(2) A listed fire pump power transfer switch, or

(3) A listed combination fire pump controller/power transfer switch.

(2) Overcurrent Device Selection.

(a) Individual Sources. Overcurrent protection for individual sources must comply with the following:

(1) The overcurrent protective device(s) must have an ampere rating to carry indefinitely the sum of the locked-rotor current of the largest fire pump motor and 100 percent of the full-load current of the other pump motors and fire pump's accessory equipment. ▸Figure 695–4

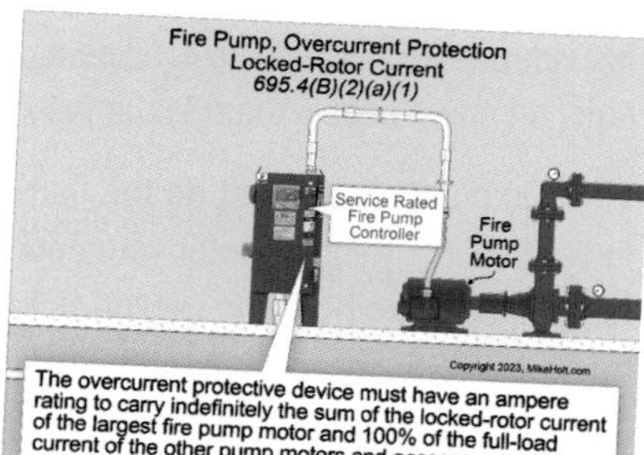

▸Figure 695–4

Author's Comment:

▸ Motor Locked-Rotor Current (LRC). If the rotating part of the motor winding (armature) becomes jammed so it cannot rotate, no counter-electromotive force (CEMF) will be produced in the motor winding. This results in a decrease in conductor impedance to the point that it is effectively a short circuit. The motor then operates at locked-rotor current (often six times the full-load ampere rating) depending on the motor's *Code* letter rating [430.7(B)]. This condition will cause the motor winding to overheat and be destroyed if the current is not quickly reduced or removed. ▸Figure 695–5

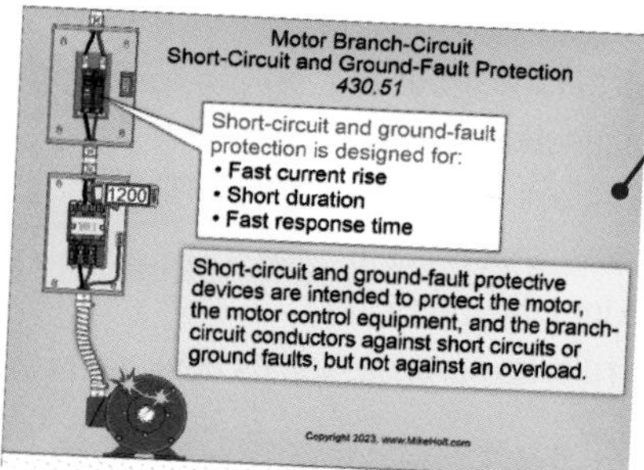

▸Figure 695–5

▸ Fire Pump Overcurrent Size Example

Question: *What size overcurrent protective device is required for a 25 hp, 460V, three-phase fire pump motor that has a locked-rotor current rating of 183A where the circuit conductors are 8 AWG?* ▸**Figure 695–6**

(a) 100A *(b) 200A* *(c) 250A* *(d) 300A*

Solution:

The overcurrent protective device(s) must be selected or set to carry indefinitely the locked-rotor current of the fire pump motor [695.4(B)(2)(a)(1) and 240.6(A)].

Locked-Rotor Current = 183A
Protection Size = 200A

Answer: *(b) 200A*

The branch-circuit conductors are sized at no less than 125 percent of the motor's FLC [695.6(B)(1)(1) and Table 430.250].

Branch-Circuit Conductor = 34A × 125%
Branch-Circuit Conductor = 42.50A

8 AWG is rated 50A at 75°C [110.14(C)(1)(a)(3) and Table 310.16].

• • •

1st Printing *Understanding the 2023 National Electrical Code, Volume 2* | MikeHolt.com | 351

ADDITIONAL PRODUCTS TO HELP YOU LEARN

Upgrade Your Textbook with the *Understanding the 2023 National Electrical Code Volume 2* Videos

One of the best ways to get the most out of this textbook is to use it in conjunction with the corresponding videos. These videos showcase dynamic discussions as Mike and his video team of industry experts deep-dive into the topics in this book. They analyze each rule, its purpose, and its application in the field.

Whether you're a visual or an auditory learner, watching the videos as you work through the textbook will enhance your knowledge and provide additional in-depth insight into each topic. Upgrade your program today, and you will broaden your understanding of the changes and their impact on your work. All upgrade purchases include the corresponding videos plus a digital copy of the textbook.

UPGRADE PACKAGE INCLUDES:

- *Understanding the 2023 National Electrical Code Volume 2 videos*

Digital answer key

Plus! A digital version of the textbook

Ready to get started? To add the videos that accompany this textbook, scan the QR code, call our office at 888.632.2633, or visit MikeHolt.com/Upgrade23UND2.

Have questions? You can e-mail info@MikeHolt.com.

Product Code: [23UND2UPGRADEVI]

Understanding the 2023 *National Electrical Code* Volume 1 Video Library

This product is Volume 1 of our best-selling Understanding the *National Electrical Code* video series. Thousands of Electricians across the United States have learned and mastered the rules of the *Code* in this easy to use program.

Volume 1 covers Articles 90 through 480 as Mike breaks them down with thousands of full-color illustrations and clear and easy-to-understand examples. The videos provide an even broader explanation of how to apply the *NEC*. Watch Mike and his video team dissect the articles as they provide important feedback on how to apply them in the field.

There is no other product on the market that provides this type of in-depth code training. Order your copy today so you can learn from *NEC* Expert Mike Holt, and get the skills and knowledge you need to apply the *Code* successfully in the field.

LIBRARY INCLUDES:

Understanding the *National Electrical Code*, Volume 1 Textbook

- *Understanding the National Electrical Code Volume 1 videos*

Understanding the *National Electrical Code* Workbook (Articles 90–480)

Bonding and Grounding Textbook

- *Bonding and Grounding videos*

Fundamental *NEC* Calculations Textbook

- *Fundamental NEC Calculations videos*

Digital answer keys

Plus! A digital version of each book

Product Code: [23UND1MM]

To order visit MikeHolt.com/Code, or call 888.632.2633.

2023 Solar Photovoltaic and Energy Storage Systems Video Program

When you think of solar photovoltaic systems and the *Code*, you typically think of Article 690. But there are many supporting articles related to solar photovoltaic systems in the *NEC*. While Article 690 covers the rules related to the wiring at the array, it doesn't cover how to connect the array to the rest of the equipment and to the grid.

Even if you're a seasoned expert, this textbook is required reading for anyone who designs, installs, services, and or inspects solar photovoltaic and energy storage systems. It not only includes the 2023 rules related to Articles 690, 625, 691, 702, 710, and 750, but also provides a complete review of the major rules that cover the installation of the related equipment, wiring, and connection to utility power.

PROGRAM INCLUDES:

Understanding *NEC* Requirements for Solar Photovoltaic and Energy Storage Systems textbook

- *Understanding NEC Requirements for Solar Photovoltaic and Energy Storage Systems videos*

Digital answer keys

Plus! A digital version of the book

Product Code: [23SOLMM]

2023 *Code* Books and Tabs

The easiest way to use your copy of the *NEC* correctly is to tab it for quick reference. Mike's best-selling tabs make organizing your *Code* book easy. Please note that if you're using it for an exam, you'll need to confirm with your testing authority that a tabbed *Code* book is allowed into the exam room.

PRODUCT INCLUDES:

NFPA Softbound *Code* Book

Mike Holt's *NEC* Tabs

Product Code: [23NECB]

To order visit MikeHolt.com/Code, or call 888.632.2633.

Notes |

HOW TO USE THE *NATIONAL ELECTRICAL CODE*

The original *NEC* document was developed in 1897 as a result of the united efforts of various insurance, electrical, architectural, and other cooperative interests. The National Fire Protection Association (NFPA) has sponsored the *National Electrical Code* since 1911.

The purpose of the *Code* is the practical safeguarding of persons and property from hazards arising from the use of electricity. It isn't intended as a design specification or an instruction manual for untrained persons. It is, in fact, a standard that contains the minimum requirements for an electrical installation that's essentially free from hazard. Learning to understand and use the *Code* is critical to you working safely; whether you're training to become an electrician, or are already an electrician, electrical contractor, inspector, engineer, designer, or instructor.

The *NEC* was written for qualified persons; those who understand electrical terms, theory, safety procedures, and electrical trade practices. Learning to use the *Code* is a lengthy process and can be frustrating if you don't approach it the right way. First, you'll need to understand electrical theory and if you don't have theory as a background when you get into the *NEC*, you're going to struggle. Take one step back if necessary and learn electrical theory. You must also understand the concepts and terms in the *Code* and know grammar and punctuation in order to understand the complex structure of the rules and their intended purpose(s). The *NEC* is written in a formal outline which many of us haven't seen or used since high school or college so it's important for you to pay particular attention to this format. Our goal for the next few pages is to give you some guidelines and suggestions on using your *Code* book to help you understand that standard, and assist you in what you're trying to accomplish and, ultimately, your personal success as an electrical professional!

Language Considerations for the *NEC*

Terms and Concepts

The *NEC* contains many technical terms, and it's crucial for *Code* users to understand their meanings and applications. If you don't understand a term used in a rule, it will be impossible to properly apply the *NEC* requirement. Article 100 defines those that are used generally in two or more articles throughout the *Code*; for example, the term "Dwelling Unit" is found in many articles. If you don't know the *NEC* definition for a "dwelling unit" you can't properly identify its *Code* requirements. Another example worth mentioning is the term "Outlet." For many people it has always meant a receptacle—not so in the *NEC*!

Article 100 contains the definitions of terms used throughout the *Code*. Where a definition is unique to a specific article, the article number is indicated at the end of the definition in parenthesis (xxx). For example, the definition of "Pool" is specific to Article 680 and ends with (680) because it applies ONLY to that article. Definitions of standard terms, such as volt, voltage drop, ampere, impedance, and resistance are not contained in Article 100. If the *NEC* does not define a term, then a dictionary or building code acceptable to the authority having jurisdiction should be consulted.

Small Words, Grammar, and Punctuation

Technical words aren't the only ones that require close attention. Even simple words can make a big difference to the application of a rule. Is there a comma? Does it use "or," "and," "other than," "greater than," or "smaller than"? The word "or" can imply alternate choices for wiring methods. A word like "or" gives us choices while the word "and" can mean an additional requirement must be met.

An example of the important role small words play in the *NEC* is found in 110.26(C)(2), where it says equipment containing overcurrent, switching, "or" control devices that are 1,200A or more "and" over 6 ft wide require a means of egress at each end of the working space. In this section, the word "or" clarifies that equipment containing any of the three types of devices listed must follow this rule. The word "and" clarifies that 110.26(C)(2) only applies if the equipment is both 1,200A or more and over 6 ft wide.

Grammar and punctuation play an important role in establishing the meaning of a rule. The location of a comma can dramatically change the requirement of a rule such as in 250.28(A), where it says a main bonding jumper shall be a wire, bus, screw, or similar suitable conductor. If the comma between "bus" and "screw" was removed, only a "bus screw" could be used. That comma makes a big change in the requirements of the rule.

Slang Terms or Technical Jargon

Trade-related professionals in different areas of the country often use local "slang" terms that aren't shared by all. This can make it difficult to communicate if it isn't clear what the meaning of those slang terms are. Use the proper terms by finding out what their definitions and applications are before you use them. For example, the term "pigtail" is often used to describe the short piece of conductor used to connect a device to a splice, but a "pigtail" is also used for a rubberized light socket with pre-terminated conductors. Although the term is the same, the meaning is very different and could cause confusion. The words "splice" and "tap" are examples of terms often interchanged in the field but are two entirely different things! The uniformity and consistency of the terminology used in the *Code*, makes it so everyone says and means the same thing regardless of geographical location.

NEC Style and Layout

It's important to understand the structure and writing style of the *Code* if you want to use it effectively. The *National Electrical Code* is organized using twelve major components.

1. Table of Contents
2. Chapters—Chapters 1 through 9 (major categories)
3. Articles—Chapter subdivisions that cover specific subjects
4. Parts—Divisions used to organize article subject matter
5. Sections—Divisions used to further organize article subject matter
6. Tables and Figures—Represent the mandatory requirements of a rule
7. Exceptions—Alternatives to the main *Code* rule
8. Informational Notes—Explanatory material for a specific rule (not a requirement)
9. Tables—Applicable as referenced in the *NEC*
10. Annexes—Additional explanatory information such as tables and references (not a requirement)
11. Index
12. Changes to the *Code* from the previous edition

1. Table of Contents. The Table of Contents displays the layout of the chapters, articles, and parts as well as the page numbers. It's an excellent resource and should be referred to periodically to observe the interrelationship of the various *NEC* components. When attempting to locate the rules for a specific situation, knowledgeable *Code* users often go first to the Table of Contents to quickly find the specific *NEC* rule that applies.

2. Chapters. There are nine chapters, each of which is divided into articles. The articles fall into one of four groupings: General Requirements (Chapters 1 through 4), Specific Requirements (Chapters 5 through 7), Communications Systems (Chapter 8), and Tables (Chapter 9).

Chapter 1—General
Chapter 2—Wiring and Protection
Chapter 3—Wiring Methods and Materials
Chapter 4—Equipment for General Use
Chapter 5—Special Occupancies
Chapter 6—Special Equipment
Chapter 7—Special Conditions
Chapter 8—Communications Systems (Telephone, Data, Satellite, Cable TV, and Broadband)
Chapter 9—Tables-Conductor and Raceway Specifications

3. Articles. The *NEC* contains approximately 160 articles, each of which covers a specific subject. It begins with Article 90, the introduction to the *Code* which contains the purpose of the *NEC*, what is covered and isn't covered, along with how the *Code* is arranged. It also gives information on enforcement, how mandatory and permissive rules are written, and how explanatory material is included. Article 90 also includes information on formal interpretations, examination of equipment for safety, wiring planning, and information about formatting units of measurement. Here are some other examples of articles you'll find in the *NEC*:

Article 110—General Requirements for Electrical Installations
Article 250—Grounding and Bonding
Article 300—General Requirements for Wiring Methods and Materials
Article 430—Motors, Motor Circuits, and Motor Controllers
Article 500—Hazardous (Classified) Locations
Article 680—Swimming Pools, Fountains, and Similar Installations
Article 725—Class 2 and Class 3 Power-Limited Circuits
Article 800—General Requirements for Communications Systems

1st Printing

4. Parts. Larger articles are subdivided into parts. Because the parts of a *Code* article aren't included in the section numbers, we tend to forget to what "part" an *NEC* rule is relating. For example, Table 110.34(A) contains working space clearances for electrical equipment. If we aren't careful, we might think this table applies to all electrical installations, but Table 110.34(A) is in Part III, which only contains requirements for "Over 1,000 Volts, Nominal" installations. The rules for working clearances for electrical equipment for systems 1,000V, nominal, or less are contained in Table 110.26(A)(1), which is in Part II—1,000 Volts, Nominal, or Less.

5. Sections. Each *NEC* rule is called a "*Code* Section." A *Code* section may be broken down into subdivisions; first level subdivision will be in parentheses like (A), (B),..., the next will be second level subdivisions in parentheses like (1), (2),..., and third level subdivisions in lowercase letters such as (a), (b), and so on.

For example, the rule requiring all receptacles in a dwelling unit bathroom to be GFCI protected is contained in Section 210.8(A)(1) which is in Chapter 2, Article 210, Section 8, first level subdivision (A), and second level subdivision (1).

Note: According to the *NEC Style Manual*, first and second level subdivisions are required to have titles. A title for a third level subdivision is permitted but not required.

Many in the industry incorrectly use the term "Article" when referring to a *Code* section. For example, they say "Article 210.8," when they should say "Section 210.8." Section numbers in this textbook are shown without the word "Section," unless they're at the beginning of a sentence. For example, Section 210.8(A) is shown as simply 210.8(A).

6. Tables and Figures. Many *NEC* requirements are contained within tables, which are lists of *Code* rules placed in a systematic arrangement. The titles of the tables are extremely important; you must read them carefully in order to understand the contents, applications, and limitations of each one. Notes are often provided in or below a table; be sure to read them as well since they're also part of the requirement. For example, Note 1 for Table 300.5(A) explains how to measure the cover when burying cables and raceways and Note 5 explains what to do if solid rock is encountered.

7. Exceptions. Exceptions are *NEC* requirements or permissions that provide an alternative method to a specific rule. There are two types of exceptions—mandatory and permissive. When a rule has several exceptions, those exceptions with mandatory requirements are listed before the permissive exceptions.

Mandatory Exceptions. A mandatory exception uses the words "shall" or "shall not." The word "shall" in an exception means that if you're using the exception, you're required to do it in a specific way. The phrase "shall not" means it isn't permitted.

Permissive Exceptions. A permissive exception uses words such as "shall be permitted," which means it's acceptable (but not mandatory) to do it in this way.

8. Informational Notes. An Informational Note contains explanatory material intended to clarify a rule or give assistance, but it isn't a *Code* requirement.

9. Tables. Chapter 9 consists of tables applicable as referenced in the *NEC*. They're used to calculate raceway sizing, conductor fill, the radius of raceway bends, and conductor voltage drop.

10. Informative Annexes. Annexes aren't a part of the *Code* requirements and are included for informational purposes only.

Annex A. Product Safety Standards
Annex B. Application Information for Ampacity Calculation
Annex C. Conduit, Tubing, and Cable Tray Fill Tables for Conductors and Fixture Wires of the Same Size
Annex D. Examples
Annex E. Types of Construction
Annex F. Availability and Reliability for Critical Operations Power Systems (COPS), and Development and Implementation of Functional Performance Tests (FPTs) for Critical Operations Power Systems
Annex G. Supervisory Control and Data Acquisition (SCADA)
Annex H. Administration and Enforcement
Annex I. Recommended Tightening Torque Tables from UL Standard 486A-486B
Annex J. ADA Standards for Accessible Design
Annex K. Use of Medical Electrical Equipment in Dwellings and Residential Board-and-Care Occupancies

11. Index. The Index at the back of the *NEC* is helpful in locating a specific rule using pertinent keywords to assist in your search.

12. Changes to the *Code*. Changes in the *NEC* are indicated as follows:

- Rules that were changed since the previous edition are identified by shading the revised text.
- New rules aren't shaded like a change, instead they have a shaded "N" in the margin to the left of the section number.
- Relocated rules are treated like new rules with a shaded "N" in the left margin by the section number.

- Deleted rules are indicated by a bullet symbol " • " located in the left margin where the rule was in the previous edition. Unlike older editions the bullet symbol is only used where one or more complete paragraphs have been deleted.
- A "Δ" represents partial text deletions and or figure/table revisions somewhere in the text. There's no specific indication of which word, group of words, or a sentence was deleted.

How to Locate a Specific Requirement

How to go about finding what you're looking for in the *Code* book depends, to some degree, on your experience with the *NEC*. Experts typically know the requirements so well that they just go to the correct rule. Very experienced people might only need the Table of Contents to locate the requirement for which they're looking. On the other hand, average users should use all the tools at their disposal, including the Table of Contents, the Index, and the search feature on electronic versions of the *Code* book.

Let's work through a simple example: What *NEC* rule specifies the maximum number of disconnects permitted for a service?

Using the Table of Contents. If you're an experienced *Code* user, you might use the Table of Contents. You'll know Article 230 applies to "Services," and because this article is so large, it's divided up into multiple parts (eight parts to be exact). With this knowledge, you can quickly go to the Table of Contents and see it lists the Service Equipment Disconnecting Means requirements in Part VI.

Author's Comment:

- The number "70" precedes all page numbers in this standard because the *NEC* is NFPA Standard Number 70.

Using the Index. If you use the Index (which lists subjects in alphabetical order) to look up the term "service disconnect," you'll see there's no listing. If you try "disconnecting means," then "services," you'll find that the Index indicates the rule is in Article 230, Part VI. Because the *NEC* doesn't give a page number in the Index, you'll need to use the Table of Contents to find it, or flip through the *Code* book to Article 230, then continue to flip through pages until you find Part VI.

Many people complain that the *NEC* only confuses them by taking them in circles. Once you gain experience in using the *Code* and deepen your understanding of words, terms, principles, and practices, you'll find it much easier to understand and use than you originally thought. With enough exposure in the use of the *NEC*, you'll discover that some words and terms are often specific to certain articles. The word "solar" for example will immediately send experienced *Code* book users to Article 690—Solar Photovoltaic (PV) Systems. The word "marina" suggests what you seek might be in Article 555. There are times when a main article will send you to a specific requirement in another one in which compliance is required in which case it will say (for example), "in accordance with 230.xx." Don't think of these situations as a "circle," but rather a map directing you to exactly where you need to be.

Customizing Your *Code* Book

One way to increase your comfort level with your *Code* book is to customize it to meet your needs. You can do this by highlighting and underlining important *NEC* requirements. Preprinted adhesive tabs are also an excellent aid to quickly find important articles and sections that are regularly referenced. However, understand that if you're using your *Code* book to prepare to take an exam, some exam centers don't allow markings of any type. For more information about tabs for your *Code* book, visit MikeHolt.com/Tabs.

Highlighting. As you read through or find answers to your questions, be sure you highlight those requirements in the *NEC* that are the most important or relevant to you. Use one color, like yellow, for general interest and a different one for important requirements you want to find quickly. Be sure to highlight terms in the Index and the Table of Contents as you use them.

Underlining. Underline or circle key words and phrases in the *Code* with a red or blue pen (not a lead pencil) using a short ruler or other straightedge to keep lines straight and neat. This is a very handy way to make important requirements stand out. A short ruler or other straightedge also comes in handy for locating the correct information in a table.

Interpretations

Industry professionals often enjoy the challenge of discussing, and at times debating, the *Code* requirements. These types of discussions are important to the process of better understanding the *NEC* requirements and applications. However, if you decide you're going to participate in one of these discussions, don't spout out what you think without having the actual *Code* book in your hand. The professional way of discussing a requirement is by referring to a specific section rather than talking in vague generalities. This will help everyone involved clearly understand the point and become better educated. In fact, you may become so well educated about the *NEC* that you might even decide to participate in the change process and help to make it even better!

Become Involved in the *NEC* Process

The actual process of changing the *Code* takes about two years and involves hundreds of individuals trying to make the *NEC* as current and accurate as possible. As you advance in your studies and understanding of the *Code*, you might begin to find it very interesting, enjoy it more, and realize that you can also be a part of the process. Rather than sitting back and allowing others to take the lead, you can participate by making proposals and being a part of its development. For the 2023 cycle, there were over 4,000 Public Inputs and 1,956 Public Comments. This resulted in several new articles and a wide array of revised rules to keep the *NEC* up to date with new technologies and pave the way to a safer and more efficient electrical future.

Here's how the process works:

STEP 1—Public Input Stage

Public Input. The revision cycle begins with the acceptance of Public Input (PI) which is the public notice asking for anyone interested to submit input on an existing standard or a committee-approved new draft standard. Following the closing date, the committee conducts a First Draft Meeting to respond to all Public Inputs.

First Draft Meeting. At the First Draft (FD) Meeting, the Technical Committee considers and provides a response to all Public Input. The Technical Committee may use the input to develop First Revisions to the standard. The First Draft documents consist of the initial meeting consensus of the committee by simple majority. However, the final position of the Technical Committee must be established by a ballot which follows.

Committee Ballot on First Draft. The First Draft developed at the First Draft Meeting is balloted. In order to appear in the First Draft, a revision must be approved by at least two-thirds of the Technical Committee.

First Draft Report Posted. First revisions which pass ballot are ultimately compiled and published as the First Draft Report on the document's NFPA web page. This report serves as documentation for the Input Stage and is published for review and comment. The public may review the First Draft Report to determine whether to submit Public Comments on the First Draft.

STEP 2—Public Comment Stage

Public Comment. Once the First Draft Report becomes available, there's a Public Comment period during which anyone can submit a Public Comment on the First Draft. After the Public Comment closing date, the Technical Committee conducts/holds their Second Draft Meeting.

Second Draft Meeting. After the Public Comment closing date, if Public Comments are received or the committee has additional proposed revisions, a Second Draft Meeting is held. At the Second Draft Meeting, the Technical Committee reviews the First Draft and may make additional revisions to the draft Standard. All Public Comments are considered, and the Technical Committee provides an action and response to each Public Comment. These actions result in the Second Draft.

Committee Ballot on Second Draft. The Second Revisions developed at the Second Draft Meeting are balloted. To appear in the Second Draft, a revision must be approved by at least two-thirds of the Technical Committee.

Second Draft Report Posted. Second Revisions which pass ballot are ultimately compiled and published as the Second Draft Report on the document's NFPA website. This report serves as documentation of the Comment Stage and is published for public review.

Once published, the public can review the Second Draft Report to decide whether to submit a Notice of Intent to Make a Motion (NITMAM) for further consideration.

STEP 3—NFPA Technical Meeting (Tech Session)

Following completion of the Public Input and Public Comment stages, there's further opportunity for debate and discussion of issues through the NFPA Technical Meeting that takes place at the NFPA Conference & Expo®. These motions are attempts to change the resulting final Standard from the committee's recommendations published as the Second Draft.

STEP 4—Council Appeals and Issuance of Standard

Issuance of Standards. When the Standards Council convenes to issue an NFPA standard, it also hears any related appeals. Appeals are an important part of assuring that all NFPA rules have been followed and that due process and fairness have continued throughout the standards development process. The Standards Council considers appeals based on the written record and by conducting live hearings during which all interested parties can participate. Appeals are decided on the entire record of the process, as well as all submissions and statements presented.

After deciding all appeals related to a standard, the Standards Council, if appropriate, proceeds to issue the Standard as an official NFPA Standard. The decision of the Standards Council is final subject only to limited review by the NFPA Board of Directors. The new NFPA standard becomes effective twenty days following the Standards Council's action of issuance.

Temporary Interim Amendment—(TIA)

Sometimes, a change to the *NEC* is of an emergency nature. Perhaps an editing mistake was made that can affect an electrical installation to the extent it may create a hazard. Maybe an occurrence in the field created a condition that needs to be addressed immediately and can't wait for the normal *Code* cycle and next edition of the standard. When these circumstances warrant it, a TIA or "Temporary Interim Amendment" can be submitted for consideration.

The NFPA defines a TIA as, "tentative because it has not been processed through the entire standards-making procedures. It is interim because it is effective only between editions of the standard. A TIA automatically becomes a Public Input of the proponent for the next edition of the standard; as such, it then is subject to all of the procedures of the standards-making process."

Author's Comment:

- Proposals, comments, and TIAs can be submitted for consideration online at the NFPA website, www.nfpa.org. From the homepage, look for "Codes & Standards," then find "Standards Development," and click on "How the Process Works." If you'd like to see something changed in the *Code*, you're encouraged to participate in the process.

ARTICLE 90

INTRODUCTION TO THE *NATIONAL ELECTRICAL CODE*

Introduction to Article 90—Introduction to the *National Electrical Code*

Article 90 describes the purpose of the *NEC*, when it applies, when it does not, who enforces the *Code*, and the arrangement of the different chapters. Although the information is valuable, this article contains no actual requirements. It only serves to provide the reader with the scope of the *National Electrical Code*.

This article stands alone outside of the chapter structure of the rest of the *Code* and has no parts because it contains no requirements. Take the time to become familiar with all nine sections of Article 90 before you begin your journey through the *NEC*. Doing so will help you better understand when and how to apply the *Code*.

90.1 Scope

Article 90 covers the use, application, arrangement, and enforcement of this *Code*. It also covers how mandatory, permissive, and nonmandatory text is expressed and provides guidance on the examination of equipment, planning wiring, and specifies the use and expression of measurements.

90.2 Use and Application of the *NEC*

(A) Purpose of the *NEC*.

Protect People and Property. The purpose of the *National Electrical Code* is to ensure electrical systems are installed in a manner that protects people and property by minimizing the risks associated with the use of electricity. ▸**Figure 90–1**

NEC Not a Specification or Instruction Manual. The *NEC* is not a design specification standard, nor is it an instruction manual for the untrained. ▸**Figure 90–2**

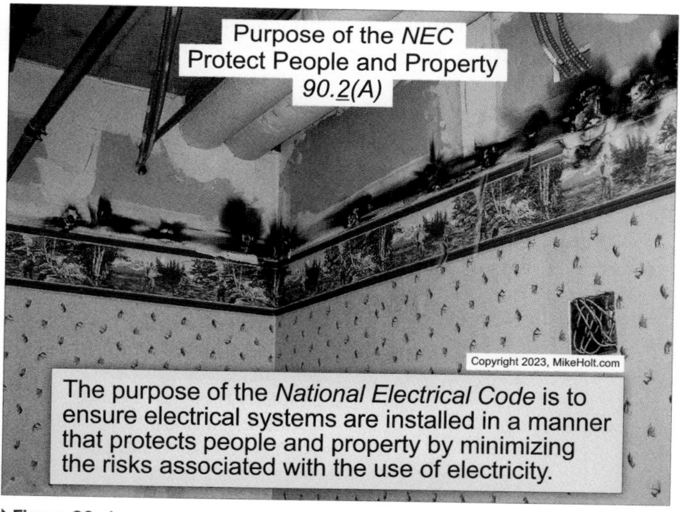
Purpose of the NEC
Protect People and Property
90.2(A)
Copyright 2023, MikeHolt.com
The purpose of the National Electrical Code is to ensure electrical systems are installed in a manner that protects people and property by minimizing the risks associated with the use of electricity.

▸**Figure 90–1**

Author's Comment:

- The *Code* is intended to be used by those who are skilled and knowledgeable in electrical theory, electrical systems, building and electrical construction, and the installation and operation of electrical equipment.

▸Figure 90–2

(B) Essentially Safe Installation.

Considered Safe. The *NEC* contains the requirements considered necessary for safety.

Essentially Free from Hazards. Installations complying with the *Code* and properly maintained are considered essentially free from electrical hazards. ▸**Figure 90–3**

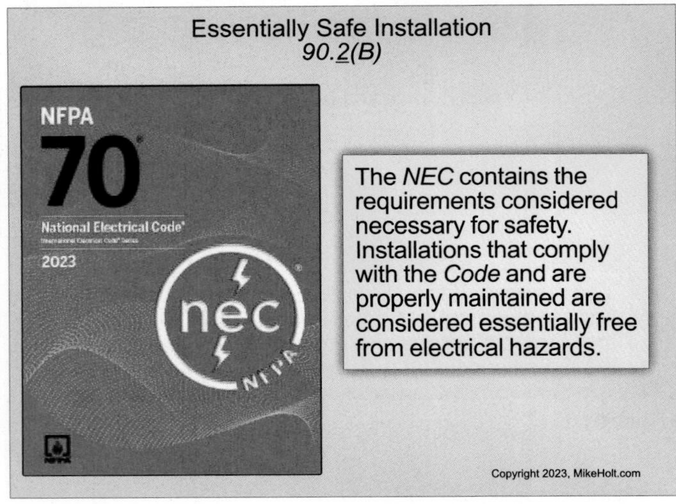

▸Figure 90–3

NEC Rules not Intended. The requirements contained in the *NEC* are not intended to ensure an electrical installation will be efficient, convenient, adequate for good service, or suitable for future expansion. ▸**Figure 90–4**

Note: Hazards often occur because the initial wiring did not provide for increases in the use of electricity resulting in wiring systems becoming overloaded. ▸**Figure 90–5**

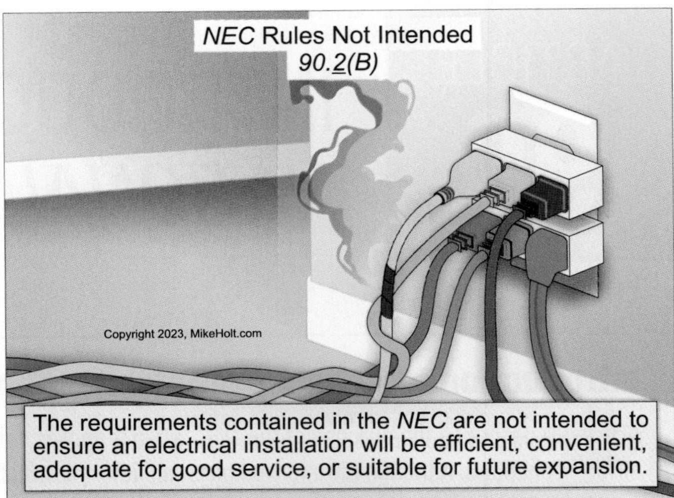

▸Figure 90–4

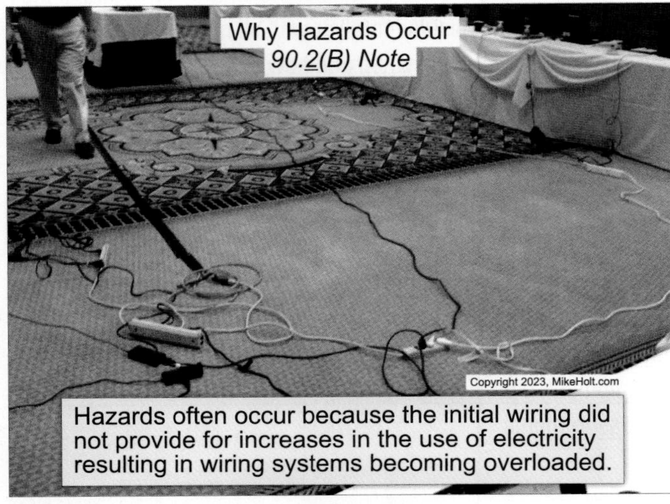

▸Figure 90–5

Author's Comment:

- The *NEC* does not require electrical systems to be designed or installed to accommodate future loads. However, consideration should be given not only to ensuring electrical safety (*Code* compliance), but also that the electrical system meets the customers' needs—both for today and in the coming years.

(C) Installations Covered by the *NEC*. The *Code* covers the installation and removal of electrical conductors, equipment, and raceways. It also covers limited-energy and communications conductors, equipment, and raceways, plus optical fiber cables for the following: ▸**Figure 90–6**

(1) Public and private premises including buildings, mobile homes, recreational vehicles, and floating buildings.

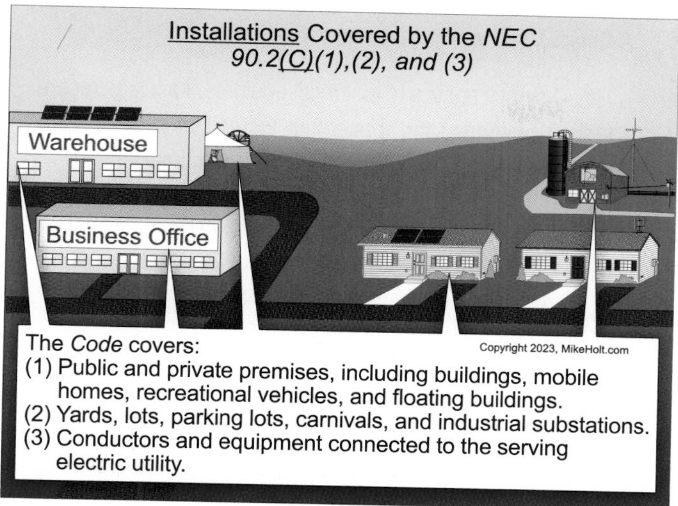
Installations Covered by the NEC
90.2(C)(1),(2), and (3)
Warehouse
Business Office
The Code covers:
(1) Public and private premises, including buildings, mobile homes, recreational vehicles, and floating buildings.
(2) Yards, lots, parking lots, carnivals, and industrial substations.
(3) Conductors and equipment connected to the serving electric utility.
Copyright 2023, MikeHolt.com

▸Figure 90–6

(2) Yards, lots, parking lots, carnivals, and industrial substations.

(3) Conductors and equipment connected to the serving electric utility.

(4) Installations used by a serving electric utility such as office buildings, warehouses, garages, machine shops, recreational buildings, and other electric utility buildings that are not an integral part of a utility's generating plant, substation, or control center. ▸Figure 90–7

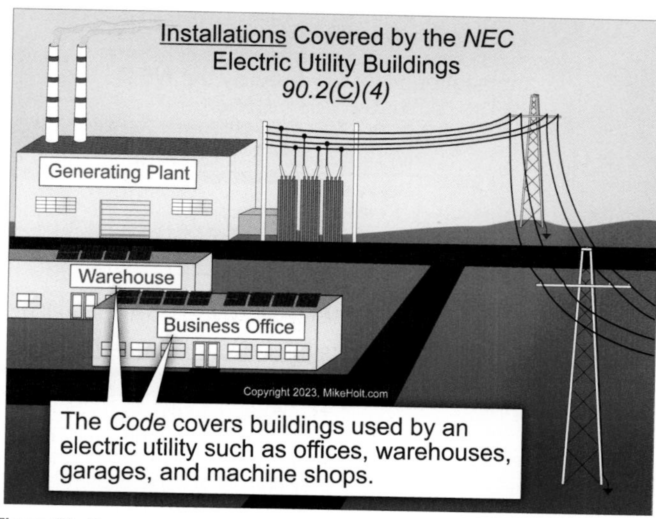
Installations Covered by the NEC
Electric Utility Buildings
90.2(C)(4)
Generating Plant
Warehouse
Business Office
Copyright 2023, MikeHolt.com
The Code covers buildings used by an electric utility such as offices, warehouses, garages, and machine shops.

▸Figure 90–7

(5) Installations supplying shore power to ships and watercraft in marinas and boatyards, including monitoring of leakage current. ▸Figure 90–8

Installations Covered by the NEC
Marina Shore Power
90.2(C)(5)
Copyright 2023, MikeHolt.com
The NEC covers installations supplying shore power to ships and watercraft in marinas and boatyards, including monitoring of leakage current.

▸Figure 90–8

Author's Comment:

- The text in 555.35(B) requires leakage detection equipment to detect leakage current from boats and applies to the load side of the supplying receptacle.

(6) Installations used to export power from vehicles to premises wiring or for bidirectional current flow. ▸Figure 90–9

Installations Covered by the NEC
Electric Vehicles
90.2(C)(6)
BI-DIRECTIONAL CHARGER
The Code covers installations used to export power from vehicles to premises wiring or for bidirectional current flow.
Copyright 2023, MikeHolt.com

▸Figure 90–9

Author's Comment:

- The battery power supply of an electric vehicle can be used "bidirectionally" which means it can be used as a backup or alternate power source to supply premises wiring circuits in the event of a power failure. The rules for this application can be found in Article 625.

(D) Installations Not Covered by the *NEC*. The *Code* does not cover installations of electrical or communications systems for:

(1) Transportation Vehicles. The *NEC* does not cover installations in ships, watercraft (other than floating buildings), aircraft, or automotive vehicles (other than mobile homes and recreational vehicles).

Author's Comment:

- An automotive vehicle is any vehicle that may be transported upon a public highway. The wiring of food trucks is not required to comply with the *NEC*, since they are considered automotive vehicles.

(2) Mining Equipment. The *Code* does not cover installations in underground mines or self-propelled mobile surface mining machinery and its attendant electrical trailing cables.

(3) Railways. The *NEC* does not cover installations for railway power, energy storage, and communications wiring.

(4) Communications Utilities. The *Code* does not cover installations of communications equipment under the exclusive control of the communications utility located outdoors or in building spaces used exclusively for these purposes. ▶Figure 90–10

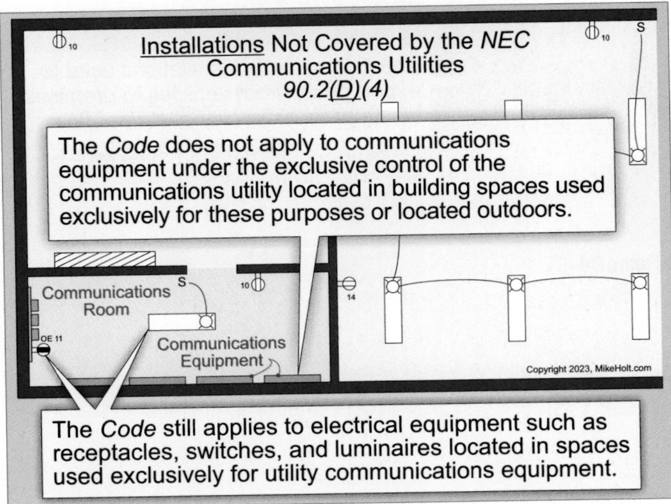

▶Figure 90–10

Author's Comment:

- The *Code* still applies to electrical equipment such as receptacles, switches, and luminaires located in spaces used exclusively for utility communications equipment.

(5) Electric Utilities. The *NEC* does not cover installations under the exclusive control of a serving electric utility where such installations:

a. Consist of service drops or service laterals and associated metering. ▶Figure 90–11 and ▶Figure 90–12

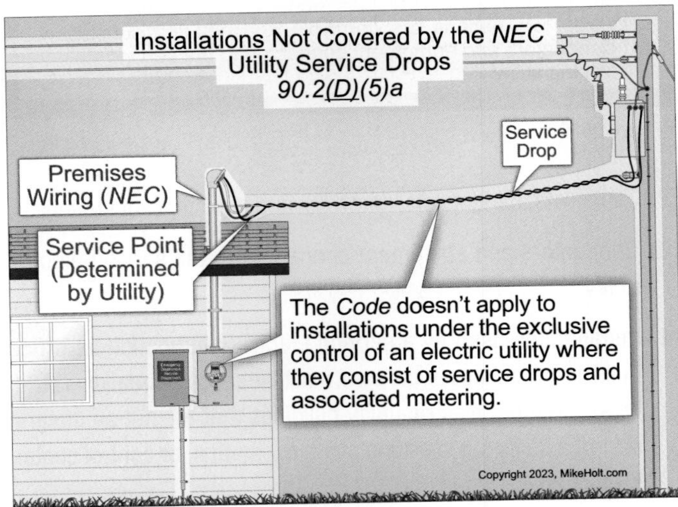

▶Figure 90–11

▶Figure 90–12

b. Are on property owned or leased by the utility for the purpose of communications, metering, generation, control, transformation, transmission, energy storage, or distribution of electrical energy. ▶Figure 90–13

1st Printing

▶Figure 90–13

c. Are in legally established easements or rights-of-way. ▶Figure 90–14

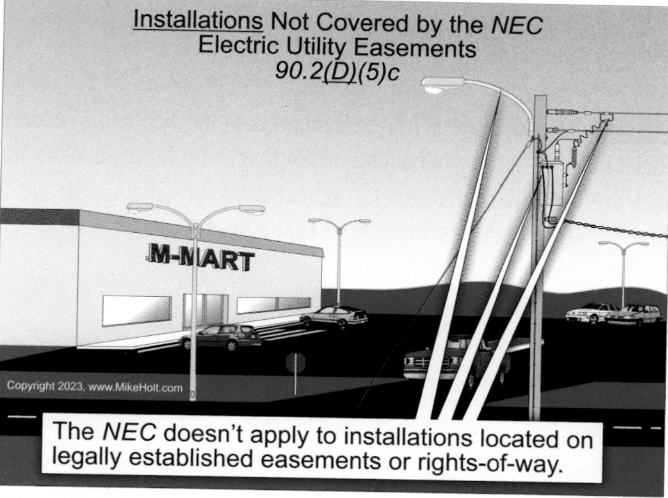

▶Figure 90–14

(E) Relation to International Standards. The requirements of the *NEC* address the fundamental safety principles contained in the International Electrotechnical Commission (IEC) Standard IEC 60364-1, *Low-Voltage Electrical Installations—Part 1: Fundamental Principles, Assessment of General Characteristics, Definitions.*

Note: IEC 60364-1, *Low-Voltage Electrical Installations—Part 1: Fundamental Principles, Assessment of General Characteristics, Definitions, Section 131*, contains fundamental principles of protection for safety that encompass protection against electric shock, thermal effects, overcurrent, fault currents, and overvoltage. All these potential hazards are addressed by the requirements in this *Code*. ▶Figure 90–15

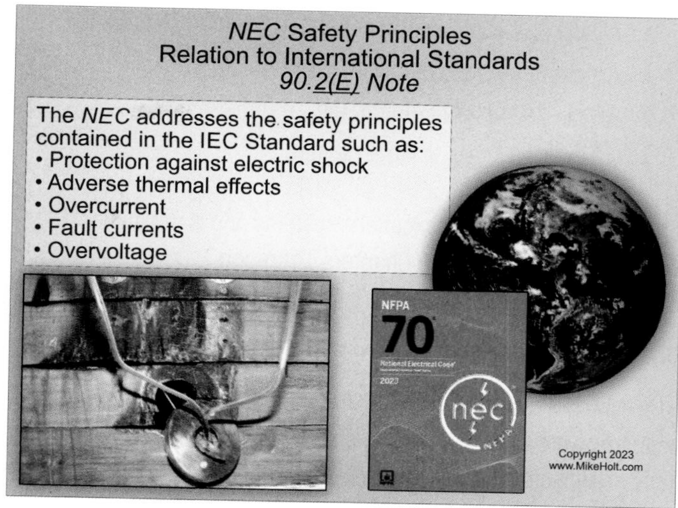

▶Figure 90–15

90.3 *Code* Arrangement

General Requirements. The *NEC* consists of an introduction and nine chapters followed by informative annexes. The requirements contained in Chapters 1, 2, 3, and 4 apply generally to all electrical installations. ▶Figure 90–16

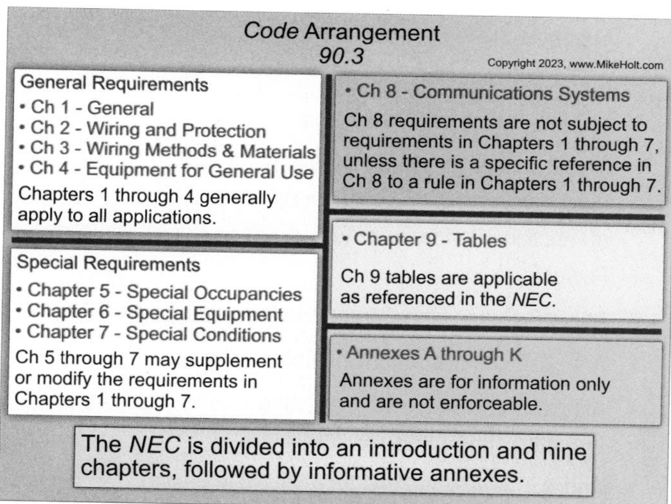

▶Figure 90–16

The requirements contained in Chapters 5, 6, and 7 apply to special occupancies, special equipment, or special conditions, which may supplement or modify the requirements contained in Chapters 1 through 7—but not Chapter 8. Chapter 7 wiring systems covered in this material include:

- Article 722—Cables for Power-Limited Circuits and Optical Fiber

- Article 724—Class 1 Power-Limited Circuits
- Article 725—Class 2 Power-Limited Circuits
- Article 760—Fire Alarm Circuits
- Article 770—Optical Fiber Circuits

Chapter 8 covers communications systems and is not subject to the requirements contained in Chapters 1 through 7, unless specifically referenced in Chapter 8.

Chapter 8 wiring systems covered in this material include:

- Article 800—General Requirements for Communications Systems
- Article 810—Radio and Television Antennas

Chapter 9 consists of tables that apply as referenced in the *NEC*. The tables are used to calculate raceway sizing, conductor fill, the radius of raceway bends, and conductor voltage drop.

Annexes are not part of the requirements of the *Code but* are included for informational purposes only. There are eleven annexes:

- Annex A. Product Safety Standards
- Annex B. Application Information for Ampacity Calculation
- Annex C. Conduit, Tubing, and Cable Tray Fill Tables for Conductors and Fixture Wires of the Same Size
- Annex D. Examples
- Annex E. Types of Construction
- Annex F. Availability and Reliability for Critical Operations Power Systems (COPS), and Development and Implementation of Functional Performance Tests (FPTs) for Critical Operations Power Systems
- Annex G. Supervisory Control and Data Acquisition (SCADA)
- Annex H. Administration and Enforcement
- Annex I. Recommended Tightening Torque Tables from UL Standard 486A-486B
- Annex J. ADA Standards for Accessible Design
- Annex K. Use of Medical Electrical Equipment in Dwellings and Residential Board-and-Care Occupancies

90.4 *NEC* Enforcement

(A) Suitable for Adoption. The *NEC* is intended to be adopted for mandatory application by governmental bodies that exercise legal jurisdiction over electrical installations. ▸**Figure 90–17**

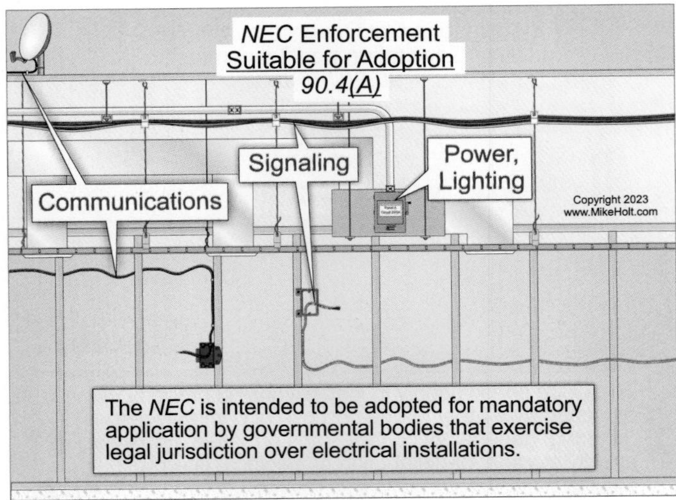

▸**Figure 90–17**

Author's Comment:

- Once adopted (in part or amended), the *National Electrical Code* becomes statutory law for the adopting jurisdiction and is thereby considered a legal document.

(B) AHJ Responsibility. The enforcement of the *NEC* is the responsibility of the "authority having jurisdiction" who is responsible for interpreting *Code* requirements, approving equipment and materials, and granting special permission. ▸**Figure 90–18**

▸**Figure 90–18**

According to Article 100, "Authority Having Jurisdiction" is defined as the organization, office, or individual responsible for approving equipment, materials, an installation, or a procedure. See 90.4 and 90.7 for more information.

According to Article 100, "Approved" is acceptable to the authority having jurisdiction, usually the electrical inspector.

(C) Waiving Requirements and Alternate Methods. By special permission, the authority having jurisdiction may waive *NEC* requirements or approve alternate methods where equivalent safety can be achieved and maintained. ▶Figure 90–19

NEC Enforcement
Waiving Requirements and Alternate Methods
90.4(C)
Okay
Inverter (Interactive)
DC Disconnect
Copyright 2023, MikeHolt.com
By special permission, the AHJ may waive *NEC* requirements or approve alternate methods where equivalent safety can be achieved and maintained.

▶Figure 90–19

According to Article 100, "Special Permission" is defined as the written consent of the AHJ.

Author's Comment:

- According to 90.4(B), the authority having jurisdiction determines the approval of equipment. This means he/she can reject an installation of listed equipment and approve the use of unlisted equipment. Given our highly litigious society, approval of unlisted equipment is becoming increasingly difficult to obtain.

(D) Waiver of Product Requirements. If the *Code* requires products, constructions, or materials that are not yet available at the time the *NEC* is adopted, the authority having jurisdiction can allow products that were acceptable in the previous *Code* that was adopted in the jurisdiction to continue to be used.

Author's Comment:

- Typically, the AHJ will approve equipment listed by a product testing organization such as Underwriters Laboratories, Inc. (UL). The *NEC* does not require all equipment to be listed, but many state and local authorities having jurisdictions do. See 90.7, 110.2, and 110.3 and the definitions for "Approved," "Identified," "Labeled," and "Listed" in Article 100.
- Sometimes it takes years for testing laboratories to establish product standards for new *NEC* product requirements. It takes time before manufacturers can design, manufacture, and distribute those products to the marketplace.

90.5 Mandatory Requirements and Explanatory Material

(A) Mandatory Requirements. The words "shall" or "shall not" indicate a mandatory requirement.

Author's Comment:

- For greater ease in reading this material, we will use the word "must" instead of "shall," and "must not" will be used instead of "shall not."

(B) Permissive Requirements. The phrases "shall be permitted" or "shall not be required" indicate the action is permitted, but not required, or there are other options or alternatives permitted.

Author's Comment:

- For greater ease in reading, the phrase "shall be permitted" (as used in the *NEC*) has been replaced in this material with "is permitted" or "are permitted."

(C) Explanatory Material. Explanatory material referencing other standards, referencing related sections to an *NEC* rule, or just providing information related to a rule, is included in this *Code* in the form of informational notes or informative annexes. These are not enforceable as *NEC* requirements, unless the standard reference includes a date, the reference is to be considered as the latest edition of the standard.

Author's Comment:

- For convenience and ease in reading this material, "Informational Notes" will simply be identified as "Note."

- A Note, while not enforceable itself, may reference an enforceable *Code* rule elsewhere in the *NEC*.

Caution

CAUTION: Informational Notes are not enforceable but notes to tables are. Within this material, we will call notes contained in a table a "Table Note."

(D) Informative Annexes. Nonmandatory information relative to the use of the *Code* is provided in informative annexes. These annexes are not enforceable as requirements of the *NEC, but* are included for informational purposes only.

90.7 Examination of Equipment for Safety

Product evaluation for *Code* compliance, approval, and safety is typically performed by a qualified electrical testing laboratory (QETL) in accordance with the listing standards.

Except to detect alterations or damage, listed factory-installed internal wiring of equipment does not need to be inspected for *NEC* compliance at the time of installation. ▸Figure 90–20

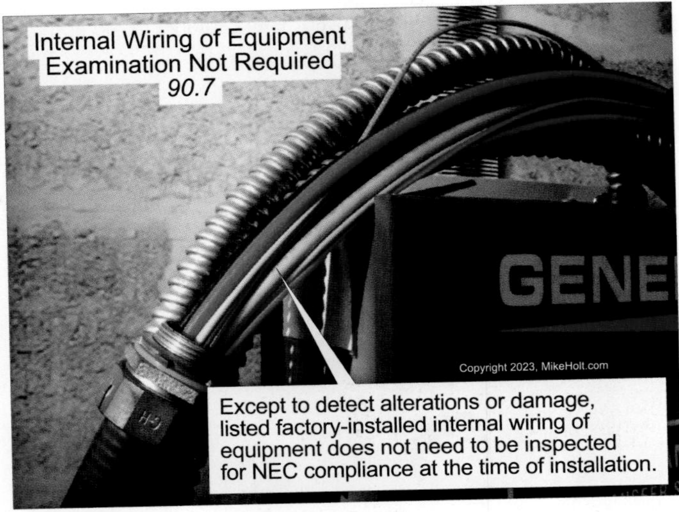
Internal Wiring of Equipment
Examination Not Required
90.7
GENE
Copyright 2023, MikeHolt.com
Except to detect alterations or damage, listed factory-installed internal wiring of equipment does not need to be inspected for NEC compliance at the time of installation.

▸Figure 90–20

Note 1: The requirements contained in Article 300 do not apply to the integral parts of electrical equipment [300.1(B)]. See 110.3 for guidance on safety examinations.

According to Article 100, "Listed" equipment or materials included in a list published by an organization acceptable to the authority having jurisdiction. The listing organization must periodically inspect the production of listed equipment or material to ensure it meets appropriate designated standards and suitable for a specified purpose.

1st Printing

ARTICLE

90 REVIEW QUESTIONS

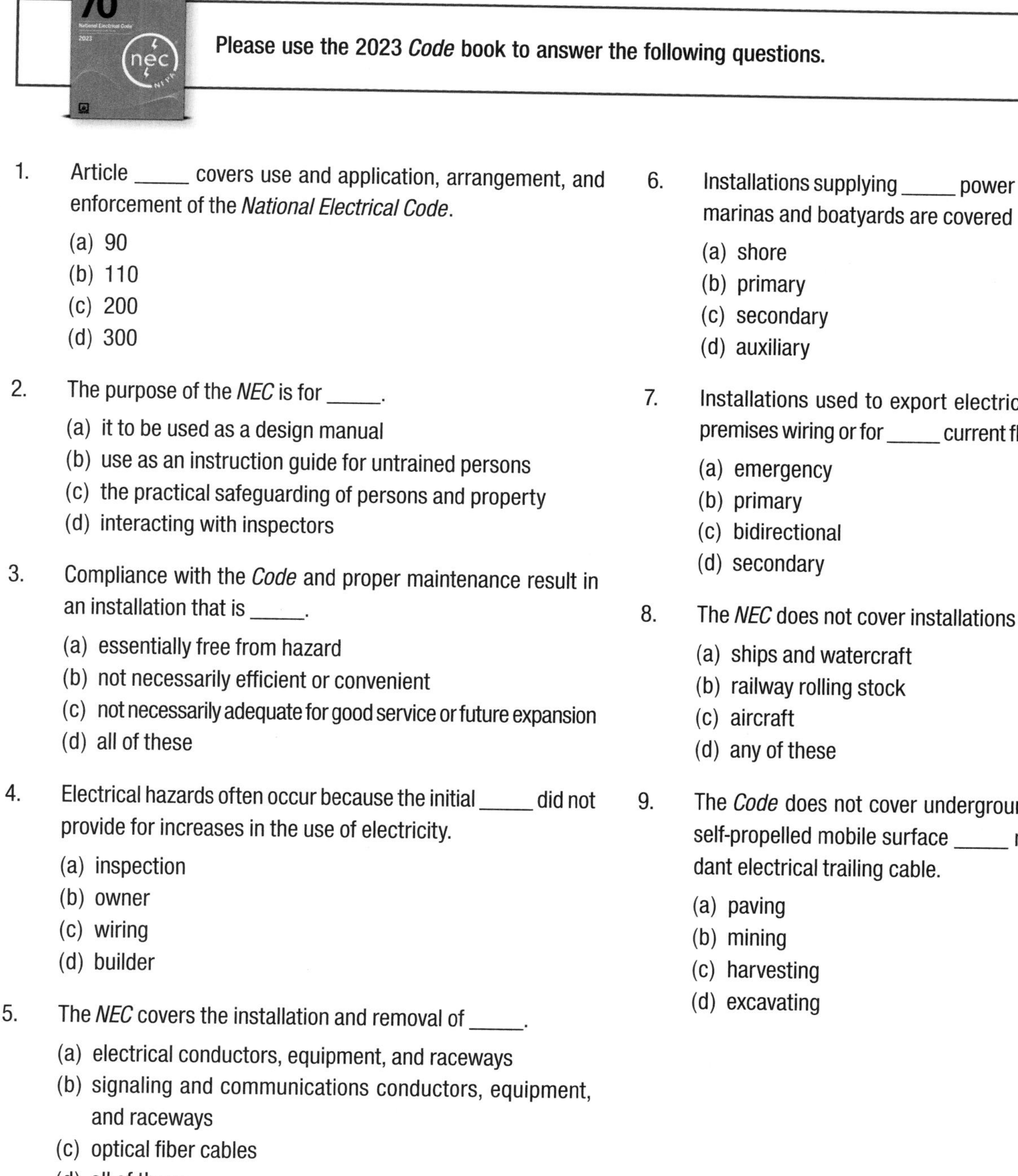

Please use the 2023 *Code* book to answer the following questions.

1. Article _____ covers use and application, arrangement, and enforcement of the *National Electrical Code*.
   (a) 90
   (b) 110
   (c) 200
   (d) 300

2. The purpose of the *NEC* is for _____.
   (a) it to be used as a design manual
   (b) use as an instruction guide for untrained persons
   (c) the practical safeguarding of persons and property
   (d) interacting with inspectors

3. Compliance with the *Code* and proper maintenance result in an installation that is _____.
   (a) essentially free from hazard
   (b) not necessarily efficient or convenient
   (c) not necessarily adequate for good service or future expansion
   (d) all of these

4. Electrical hazards often occur because the initial _____ did not provide for increases in the use of electricity.
   (a) inspection
   (b) owner
   (c) wiring
   (d) builder

5. The *NEC* covers the installation and removal of _____.
   (a) electrical conductors, equipment, and raceways
   (b) signaling and communications conductors, equipment, and raceways
   (c) optical fiber cables
   (d) all of these

6. Installations supplying _____ power to ships and watercraft in marinas and boatyards are covered by the *NEC*.
   (a) shore
   (b) primary
   (c) secondary
   (d) auxiliary

7. Installations used to export electric power from vehicles to premises wiring or for _____ current flow is covered by the *NEC*.
   (a) emergency
   (b) primary
   (c) bidirectional
   (d) secondary

8. The *NEC* does not cover installations in _____.
   (a) ships and watercraft
   (b) railway rolling stock
   (c) aircraft
   (d) any of these

9. The *Code* does not cover underground mine installations, or self-propelled mobile surface _____ machinery and its attendant electrical trailing cable.
   (a) paving
   (b) mining
   (c) harvesting
   (d) excavating

10. Installations of communications equipment under the exclusive control of communications utilities located outdoors or in building spaces used exclusively for such installations _____ covered by the *NEC*.
    (a) are
    (b) are sometimes
    (c) are not
    (d) may be

11. The *Code* does not cover installations under the exclusive control of an electric utility such as _____.
    (a) service drops or service laterals
    (b) electric utility office buildings
    (c) electric utility warehouses
    (d) electric utility garages

12. Chapters 1, 2, 3, and 4 of the *NEC* apply _____.
    (a) generally to all electrical installations
    (b) only to special occupancies and conditions
    (c) only to special equipment and material
    (d) all of these

13. Chapters 5, 6, and 7 of the *NEC* apply to _____ and may supplement or modify the requirements contained in Chapters 1 through 7.
    (a) special occupancies
    (b) special equipment
    (c) special conditions
    (d) all of these

14. Chapter 8 covers _____ systems and is not subject to the requirements of Chapters 1 through 7 unless specifically referenced in Chapter 8.
    (a) communications
    (b) fire alarm
    (c) emergency standby
    (d) sustainable energy

15. Annexes are not part of the requirements of this *Code* but are included for _____ purposes only.
    (a) informational
    (b) reference
    (c) supplemental enforcement
    (d) educational

16. The enforcement of the *NEC* is the responsibility of the authority having jurisdiction, who is responsible for _____.
    (a) making interpretations of rules
    (b) approval of equipment and materials
    (c) granting special permission
    (d) all of these

17. By special permission, the authority having jurisdiction may waive *NEC* requirements or approve alternative methods where equivalent _____ can be achieved and maintained.
    (a) safety
    (b) workmanship
    (c) installations
    (d) job progress

18. If the *Code* requires new products that may not yet be available at the time the *NEC* is adopted, the _____ can allow products that comply with the most recent previous edition of the *Code* adopted by the jurisdiction.
    (a) electrical engineer
    (b) master electrician
    (c) authority having jurisdiction
    (d) none of these

19. In the *NEC*, the word(s) "_____" indicate a mandatory requirement.
    (a) shall
    (b) shall not
    (c) shall be permitted
    (d) shall or shall not

20. When the *Code* uses "_____," it indicates the actions are allowed but not required.
    (a) shall or shall not
    (b) shall not be permitted
    (c) shall be permitted
    (d) none of these

21. Explanatory material, such as references to other standards, references to related sections of this *Code*, or information related to a *Code* rule, is included in this *Code* in the form of _____.
    (a) informational notes
    (b) footnotes
    (c) table notes
    (d) italicized text

22. Nonmandatory information relative to the use of the *NEC* is provided in informative annexes and are _____.
    (a) included for information purposes only
    (b) not enforceable requirements of the *Code*
    (c) enforceable as a requirement of the *Code*
    (d) included for information purposes only and are not enforceable requirements of the *Code*

23. Except to detect alterations or damage, qualified electrical testing laboratory listed factory-installed _____ wiring of equipment does not need to be inspected for *NEC* compliance at the time of installation.
    (a) external
    (b) associated
    (c) internal
    (d) all of these

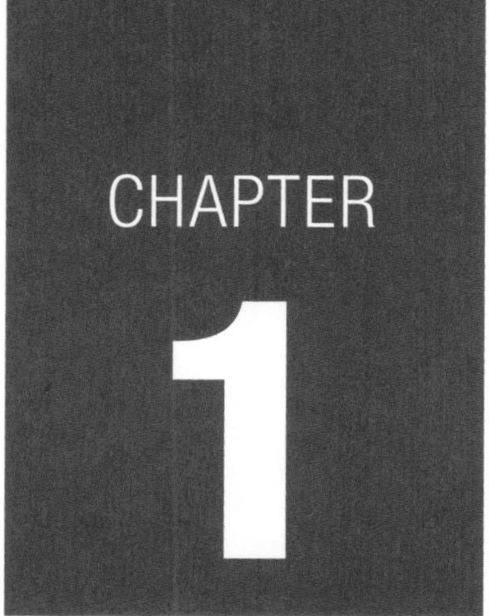

GENERAL RULES

Introduction to Chapter 1—General Rules

The *National Electrical Code* (*NEC*) is a set of standards that are used to ensure the safe installation and operation of electrical systems in the United States. The *NEC* is published by the National Fire Protection Association (NFPA) and is updated every three years. The *NEC* is not a law, but it is widely adopted by local and state governments as a regulatory standard for electrical installations in the United States. The *NEC* is also recognized as a standard for electrical installations in other countries. The value of the *NEC* lies in its role as a set of guidelines for the safe installation and operation of electrical systems, which helps to protect people and property from the dangers of electrical fires and shocks.

Chapter 1 of the *NEC* is divided into two articles. The first contains the definitions of important terms used throughout the *Code*, and the second provides the general requirements for all electrical installations. The definitions and rules in this chapter apply to all electrical installations covered by the *NEC*.

Chapter 1 is often overlooked because the rules are very broad and do not clearly apply to specific situations. Be sure you understand the rules, concepts, definitions, and requirements in Chapter 1 as doing so will make a difficult rule(s) much easier to apply. Chapter 1 articles covered by this material are:

- **Article 100—Definitions.** Article 100 contains the definitions essential to the application of this *Code. Where* terms are not defined in Article 100, the *NEC Style Manual* directs us to use *Webster's Collegiate Dictionary*, or to consult with the authority having jurisdiction.
- **Article 110—General Requirements for Electrical Installations.** This article covers the general requirements for the examination and approval, installation and use, and access to spaces around electrical equipment.

Notes

ARTICLE 100 DEFINITIONS

Introduction to Article 100—Definitions

Have you ever had a conversation with someone only to discover that what you meant and what they understood were completely different? This often happens when people have different interpretations of the words being used, and that is why the definitions of key *NEC* terms are located at the beginning of the *Code*. Definitions used out of context are a leading cause of misinterpretations of rules by people such as electricians, engineers, and inspectors. Because the *NEC* exists to protect people and property, it is important to be able to convey and comprehend the language used. Review and reference Article 100 whenever there is a possibility of an inaccurate (or incorrect) definition of a term being used in a rule.

100 Definitions

Scope. This article contains definitions essential to the application of this *Code.* Definitions of standard terms, such as volt, voltage drop, ampere, impedance, and resistance are not contained in Article 100. If the *NEC* does not define a term, then a dictionary or building code acceptable to the authority having jurisdiction should be consulted.

The *Code* does not include general or technical terms from other codes and standards. An article number in parentheses following the definition indicates that the definition only applies to that article.

Author's Comment:

- In this material, the Article 100 definitions that only apply to a specific article can also be found in that specific article.

Accessible, Readily (Readily Accessible). Capable of being reached quickly for operation, renewal, or inspection without requiring those to whom ready access is necessary to use tools (other than keys), climb over or under obstructions, remove obstacles, resort to using portable ladders, and so forth. ▸**Figure 100–1**

Note: The use of keys for locks on electrical equipment and locked doors to electrical equipment rooms and vaults is a common practice. They are permitted by the *NEC* as this is still considered as readily accessible. ▸**Figure 100–2**

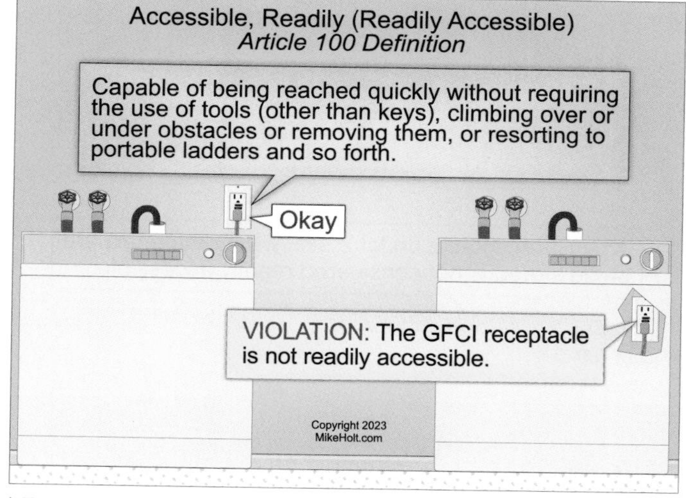

▸**Figure 100–1**

Author's Comment:

- A GFCI receptacle located in a cabinet under a sink is not readily accessible because it is not capable of being reached quickly without having to remove obstacles. ▸**Figure 100–3**

Ampacity. The maximum current, in amperes, a conductor can carry continuously under its conditions of use—without exceeding its temperature rating. ▸**Figure 100–4**

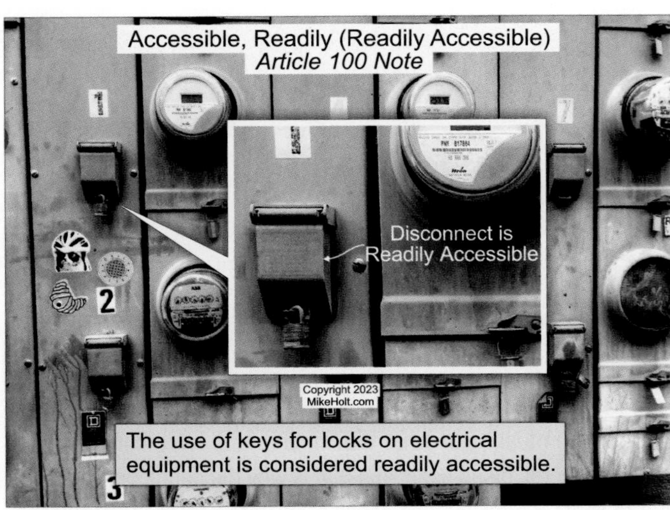

▶Figure 100–2

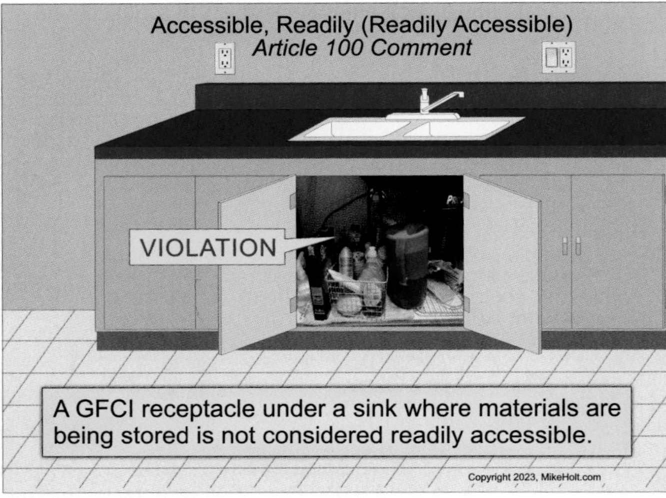

Accessible, Readily (Readily Accessible)
Article 100 Comment
VIOLATION
A GFCI receptacle under a sink where materials are being stored is not considered readily accessible.
Copyright 2023, MikeHolt.com

▶Figure 100–3

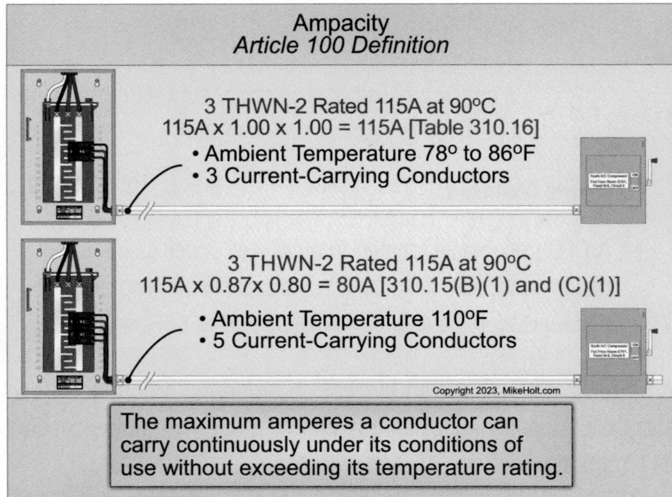

▶Figure 100–4

Author's Comment:

- See 310.14 and 310.15 for details and examples of types of conductors and cables suitable for the conditions of use, their respective temperature ratings, and the ampacity corrections and adjustments depending on the condition of use of those conductors and cables.

Ambulatory Health Care Occupancy. An occupancy used to provide services or treatment simultaneously to four or more patients that provides, on an outpatient basis, one or more of the following:

(1) Treatment for patients that renders the patients incapable of taking action for self-preservation under emergency conditions without the assistance of others.

(2) Anesthesia that renders the patient's incapable of taking action for self-preservation under emergency conditions without the assistance of others.

(3) Treatment for patients who, due to the nature of their injury or illness, are incapable of taking action for self-preservation under emerge.

Approved. Acceptable to the authority having jurisdiction (AHJ), usually the electrical inspector. ▶Figure 100–5

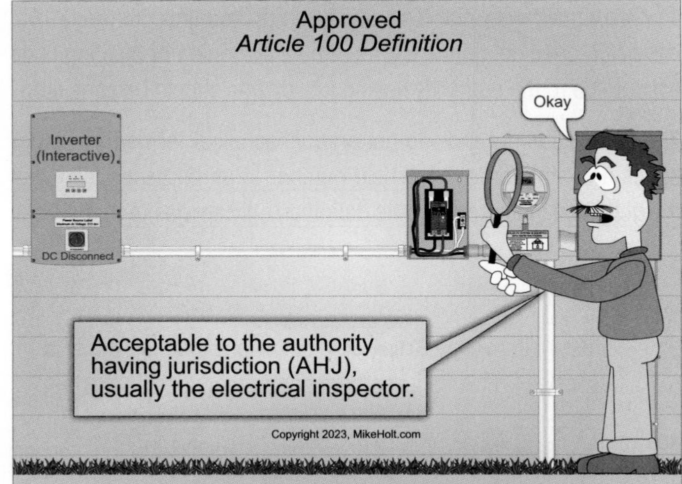

▶Figure 100–5

Author's Comment:

- Product listing does not mean the product is approved, but it can be a basis for approval. See 90.4, 90.7, and 110.2 and the definitions in this article for "Authority Having Jurisdiction," "Identified," "Labeled," and "Listed."

Attachment Plug (Plug Cap). A wiring device at the end of a flexible cord inserted into a receptacle to make an electrical connection. ▶Figure 100–6

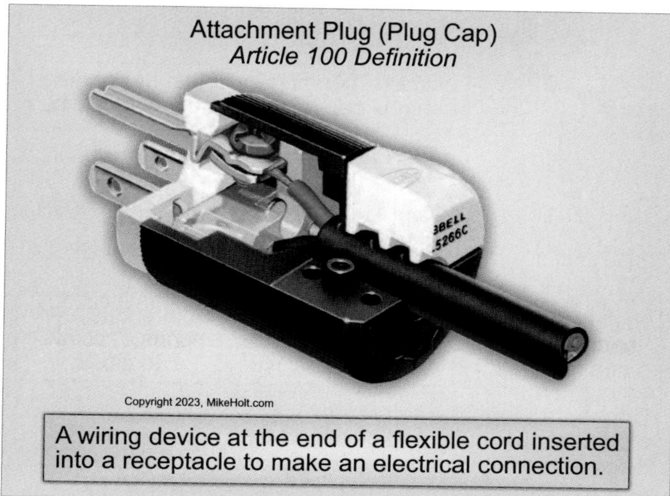

▶Figure 100–6

Authority Having Jurisdiction (AHJ). The organization, office, or individual responsible for approving equipment, materials, or installation. See 90.4 and 90.7 for more information. ▶Figure 100–7

▶Figure 100–7

Note: The authority having jurisdiction (AHJ) may be a federal, state, or local government department or individual such as a fire chief, fire marshal, chief of a fire prevention bureau, labor or health department, a building official, electrical inspector, or others having statutory authority. The utility company can also be an AHJ. In some circumstances, the property owner or his/her agent assumes the role, and at government installations, the commanding officer, or departmental official may be the AHJ.

Author's Comment:

- The AHJ is typically the electrical inspector who has legal statutory authority. In the absence of federal, state, or local regulations, the operator of the facility or his/her agent (such as an architect or engineer of the facility) can assume the role.
- Most expect the AHJ to have at least some prior experience in the electrical field, such as having studied electrical engineering or having obtained an electrical contractor's license. In a few states this is a legal requirement. Memberships, certifications, and active participation in electrical organizations such as the International Association of Electrical Inspectors (IAEI) speak to an individual's qualifications. Visit www.IAEI.org for more information about that organization.

Bathroom. An area including a sink as well as one or more toilet, urinal, tub, shower, bidet, or similar plumbing fixture. ▶Figure 100–8

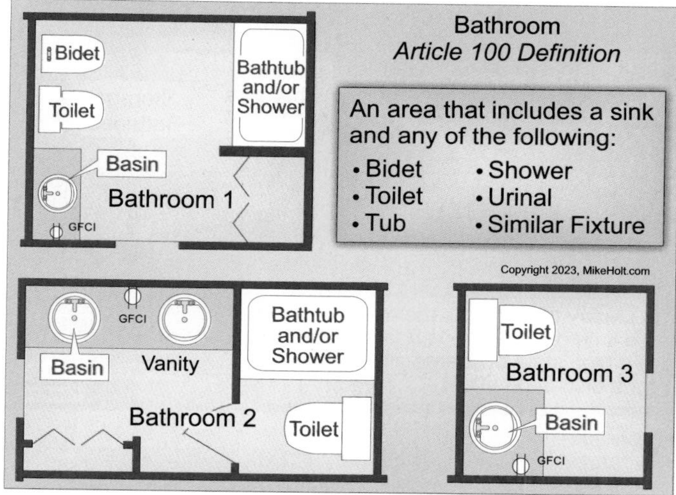

▶Figure 100–8

Battery. A single cell or a group of cells connected together electrically in series, in parallel—or a combination of both. ▶Figure 100–9

Battery, Stationary Standby. A battery that spends the majority of the time on continuous float charge or in a high state of charge, in readiness for a discharge event. ▶Figure 100–10

Note: Uninterruptible Power Supply (UPS) batteries are an example that falls under this definition.

Boatyard. A facility use for constructing, repairing, servicing, hauling from the water, storing (on land and in water), and launching of boats. ▶Figure 100–11

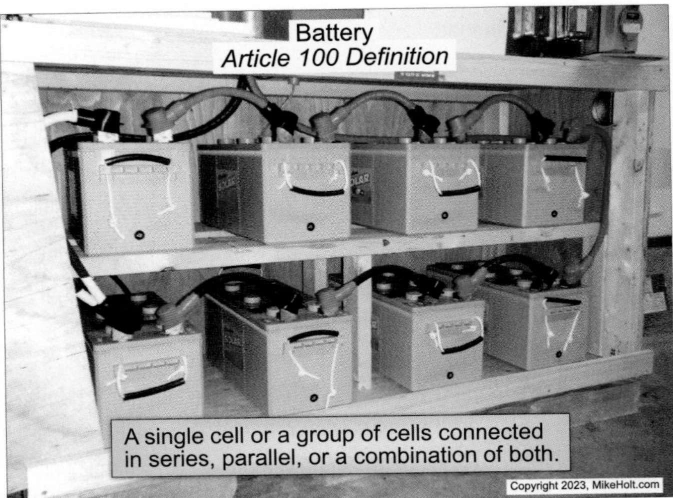

▶Figure 100–9

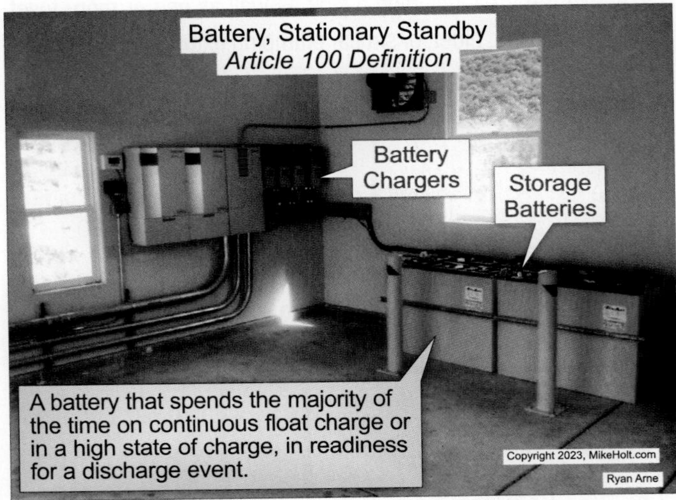

▶Figure 100–10

▶Figure 100–11

Bonded (Bonding). Connected to establish electrical continuity and conductivity. ▶Figure 100–12

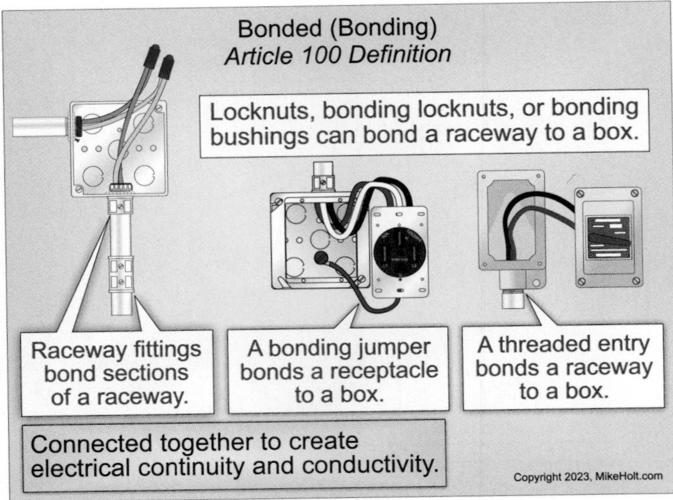

Bonded (Bonding)
Article 100 Definition
Locknuts, bonding locknuts, or bonding bushings can bond a raceway to a box.
Raceway fittings bond sections of a raceway.
A bonding jumper bonds a receptacle to a box.
A threaded entry bonds a raceway to a box.
Connected together to create electrical continuity and conductivity.
Copyright 2023, MikeHolt.com

▶Figure 100–12

Author's Comment:

- Bonding electrical equipment in accordance with 250.4(A)(3) and bonding metal parts in accordance with 250.4(A)(4) creates an effective path for ground-fault current to return to the supply source and open the overcurrent protective device.

Bonding Conductor (Bonding Jumper). A conductor that ensures electrical conductivity by connecting metal parts of equipment together. ▶Figure 100–13

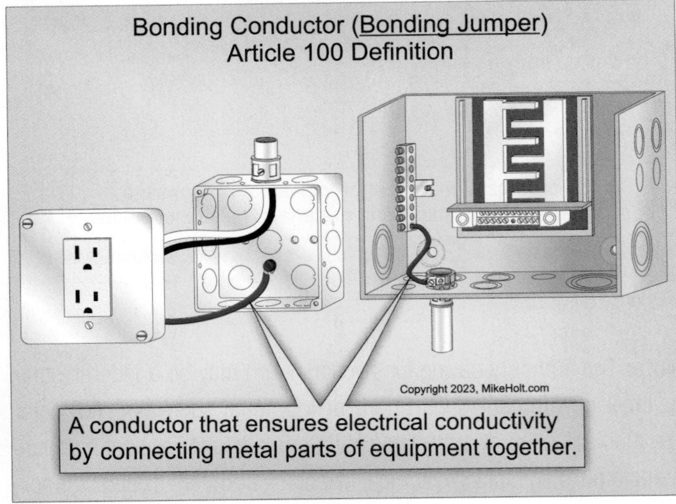

▶Figure 100–13

1st Printing

Bonding Jumper, Equipment (Equipment Bonding Jumper). A connection to ensure electrical continuity between two or more portions of the equipment grounding conductor. ▸Figure 100–14 and ▸Figure 100–15

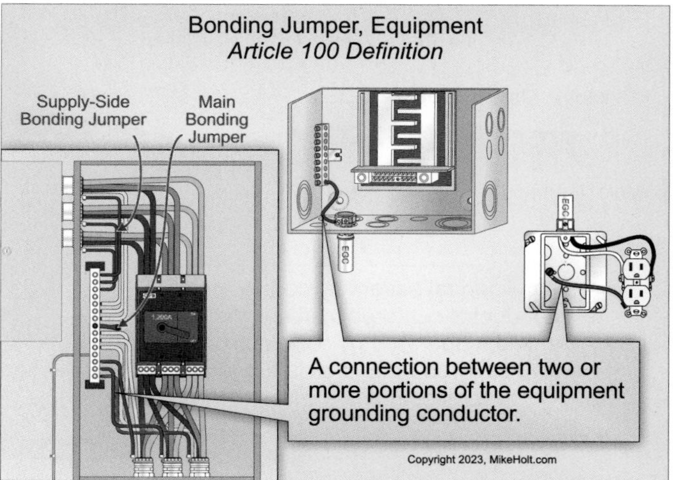
Bonding Jumper, Equipment
Article 100 Definition
Supply-Side Bonding Jumper
Main Bonding Jumper
A connection between two or more portions of the equipment grounding conductor.
Copyright 2023, MikeHolt.com

▸Figure 100–14

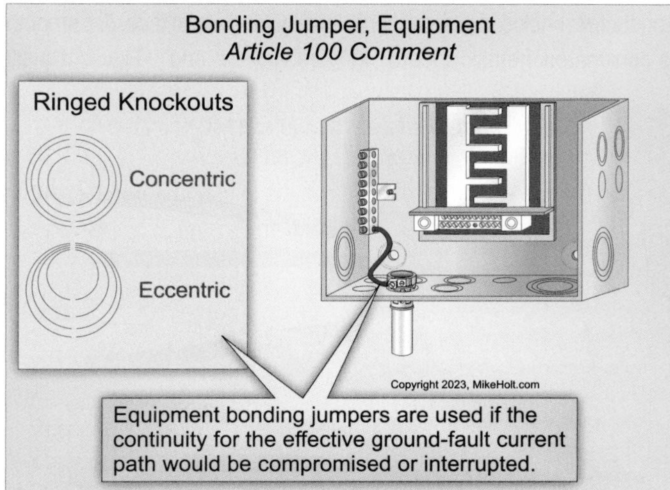
Bonding Jumper, Equipment
Article 100 Comment
Ringed Knockouts
Concentric
Eccentric
Equipment bonding jumpers are used if the continuity for the effective ground-fault current path would be compromised or interrupted.
Copyright 2023, MikeHolt.com

▸Figure 100–15

Branch Circuit. The conductors between the final overcurrent protective device and the receptacle outlets, lighting outlets, or other outlets. ▸Figure 100–16

Branch Circuit, Individual (Individual Branch Circuit). A branch circuit that supplies only one utilization equipment. ▸Figure 100–17

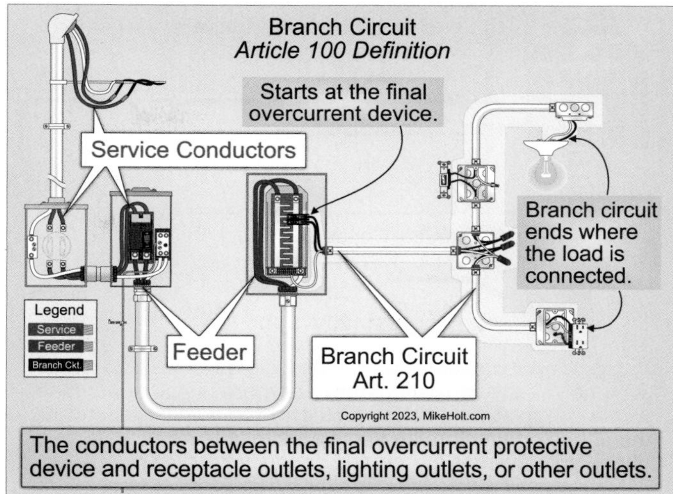
Branch Circuit
Article 100 Definition
Starts at the final overcurrent device.
Service Conductors
Branch circuit ends where the load is connected.
Legend
Service
Feeder
Branch Ckt.
Feeder
Branch Circuit Art. 210
Copyright 2023, MikeHolt.com
The conductors between the final overcurrent protective device and receptacle outlets, lighting outlets, or other outlets.

▸Figure 100–16

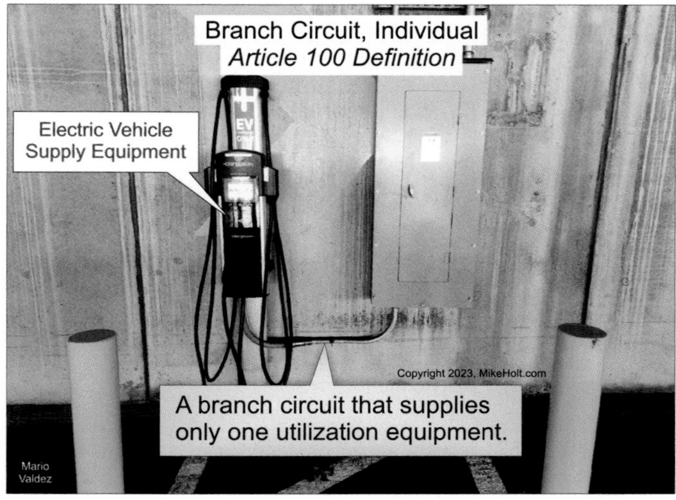
Branch Circuit, Individual
Article 100 Definition
Electric Vehicle Supply Equipment
Copyright 2023, MikeHolt.com
A branch circuit that supplies only one utilization equipment.
Mario Valdez

▸Figure 100–17

Branch Circuit, Multiwire (Multiwire Branch Circuit). A branch circuit consisting of two or more phase conductors with a common neutral conductor having a voltage between the phase conductors, and an equal voltage from each phase conductor to the neutral conductor. ▸Figure 100–18

Building. A structure that stands alone or is separated by fire walls. ▸Figure 100–19

Cable, Armored (Type AC). A fabricated assembly of conductors in a flexible interlocked metallic armor with an internal bonding strip in intimate contact with the armor for its entire length. ▸Figure 100–20

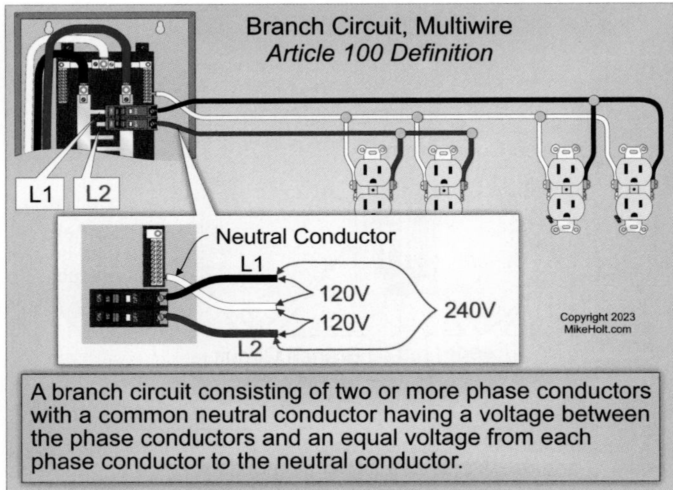
Branch Circuit, Multiwire
Article 100 Definition
L1
L2
Neutral Conductor
L1
120V
120V
240V
L2
Copyright 2023 MikeHolt.com
A branch circuit consisting of two or more phase conductors with a common neutral conductor having a voltage between the phase conductors and an equal voltage from each phase conductor to the neutral conductor.

▸Figure 100–18

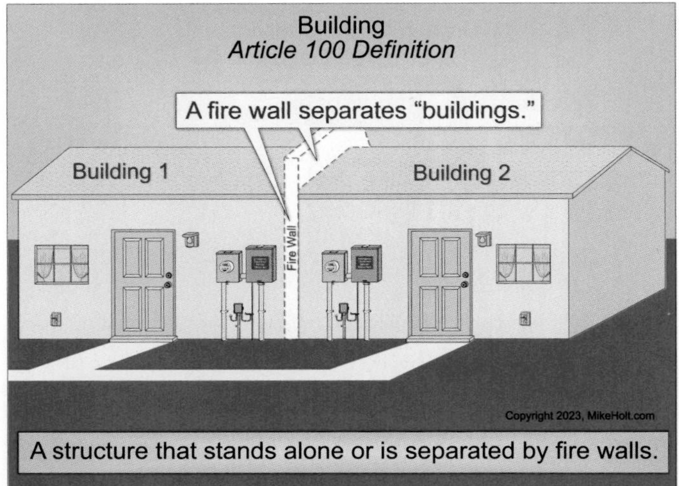
Building
Article 100 Definition
A fire wall separates "buildings."
Building 1
Building 2
Fire Wall
Copyright 2023, MikeHolt.com
A structure that stands alone or is separated by fire walls.

▸Figure 100–19

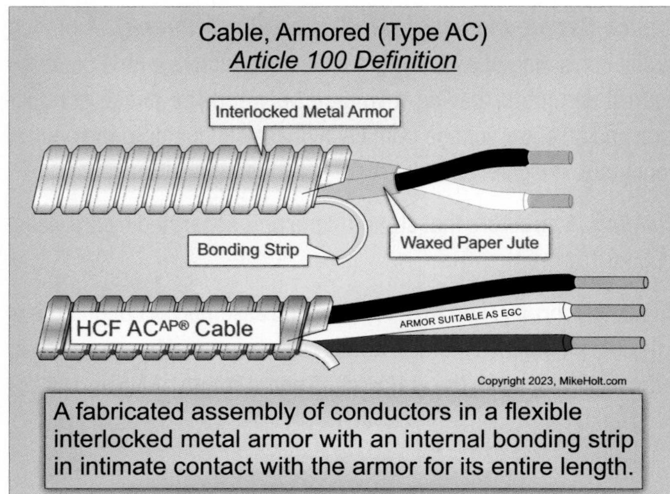
Cable, Armored (Type AC)
Article 100 Definition
Interlocked Metal Armor
Bonding Strip
Waxed Paper Jute
HCF AC AP® Cable
ARMOR SUITABLE AS EGC
Copyright 2023, MikeHolt.com
A fabricated assembly of conductors in a flexible interlocked metal armor with an internal bonding strip in intimate contact with the armor for its entire length.

▸Figure 100–20

Cable, Coaxial (Coaxial Cable). A cylindrical assembly containing a conductor centered inside a metallic shield, separated by a dielectric material, and covered by an insulating jacket. ▸**Figure 100–21**

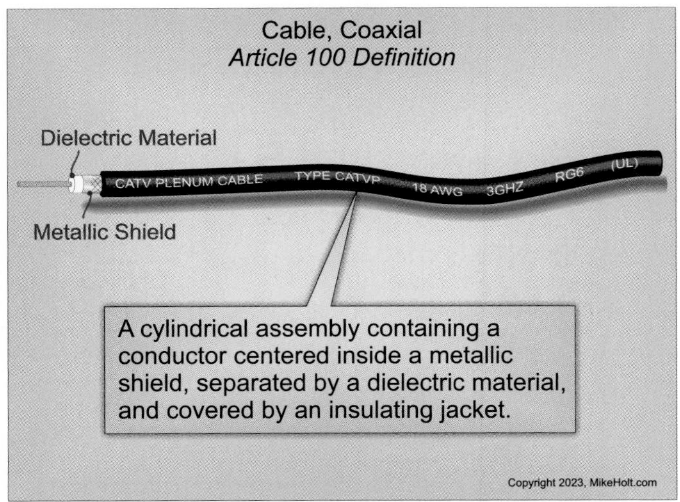
Cable, Coaxial
Article 100 Definition
Dielectric Material
Metallic Shield
CATV PLENUM CABLE TYPE CATVP 18 AWG 3GHZ RG6 (UL)
A cylindrical assembly containing a conductor centered inside a metallic shield, separated by a dielectric material, and covered by an insulating jacket.
Copyright 2023, MikeHolt.com

▸Figure 100–21

Cable, Metal-Clad (Type MC). A factory assembly of insulated circuit conductors enclosed in an armor of interlocking metal tape, or a smooth or corrugated metallic sheath. ▸**Figure 100–22** and ▸**Figure 100–23**

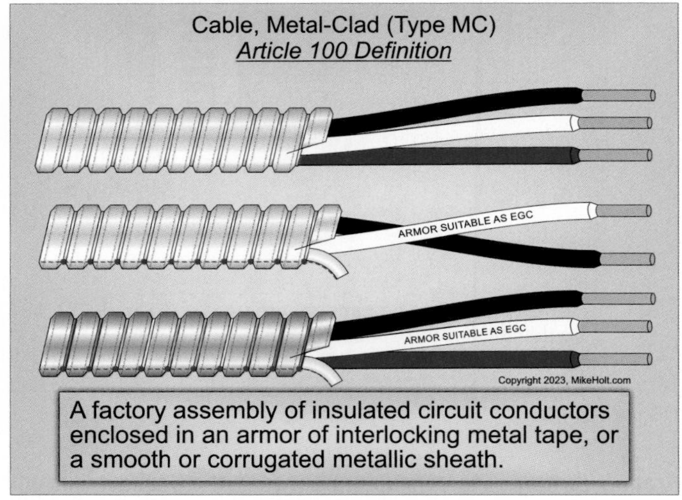
Cable, Metal-Clad (Type MC)
Article 100 Definition
ARMOR SUITABLE AS EGC
ARMOR SUITABLE AS EGC
Copyright 2023, MikeHolt.com
A factory assembly of insulated circuit conductors enclosed in an armor of interlocking metal tape, or a smooth or corrugated metallic sheath.

▸Figure 100–22

Cable, Nonmetallic-Sheathed (Type NM). A wiring method that encloses two or more insulated conductors within an outer nonmetallic jacket. ▸**Figure 100–24** and ▸**Figure 100–25**

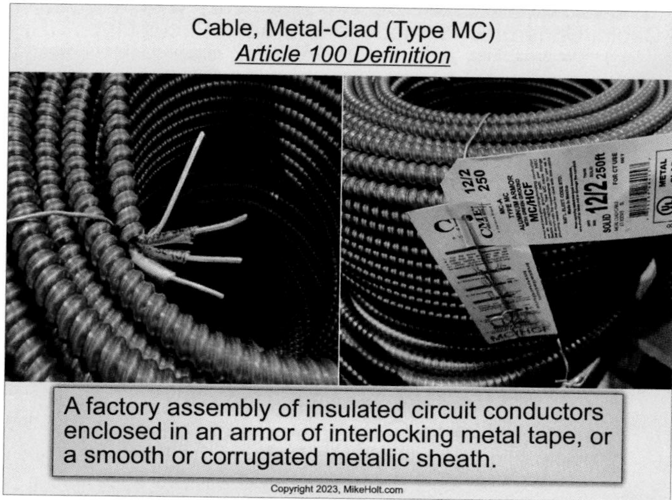
Cable, Metal-Clad (Type MC)
Article 100 Definition
A factory assembly of insulated circuit conductors enclosed in an armor of interlocking metal tape, or a smooth or corrugated metallic sheath.
Copyright 2023, MikeHolt.com

▶Figure 100–23

Cable, Nonmetallic-Sheathed (Type NM)
Article 100 Definition
NON-METALLIC SHEATHED CABLE
CME
1000 ft
300722
A wiring method that encloses two or more insulated conductors within an outer nonmetallic jacket.
Copyright 2023, MikeHolt.com

▶Figure 100–24

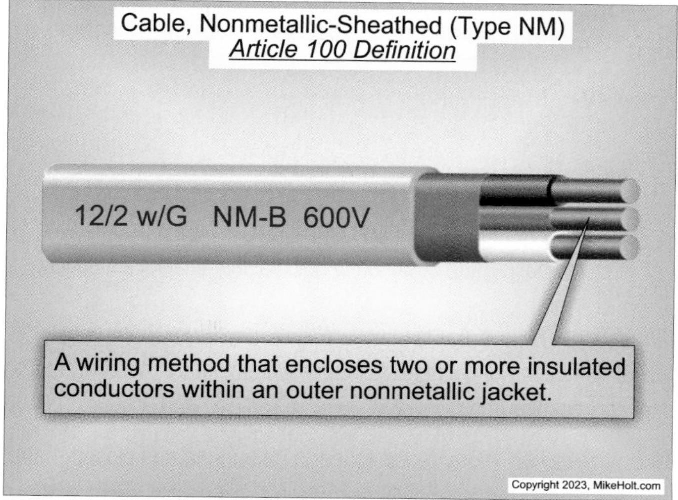
Cable, Nonmetallic-Sheathed (Type NM)
Article 100 Definition
12/2 w/G NM-B 600V
A wiring method that encloses two or more insulated conductors within an outer nonmetallic jacket.
Copyright 2023, MikeHolt.com

▶Figure 100–25

Author's Comment:

- It is the generally accepted practice in the electrical industry to call Type NM cable "Romex®," a registered trademark of the Southwire Company.

Cable, Optical Fiber (Optical Fiber Cable). An assembly of optical fibers having an overall covering. ▶Figure 100–26

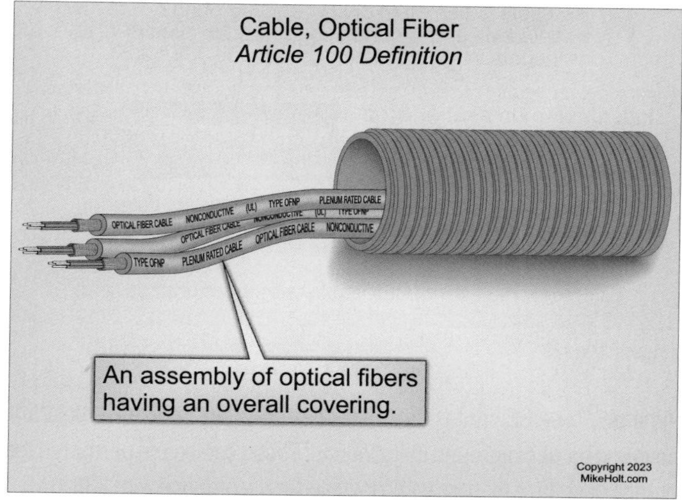
Cable, Optical Fiber
Article 100 Definition
An assembly of optical fibers having an overall covering.
Copyright 2023 MikeHolt.com

▶Figure 100–26

Note: A field-assembled optical fiber cable is an assembly of one or more optical fibers within a jacket. The jacket is installed like a raceway into which the optical fibers are inserted.

Cable, Power and Control Tray (Type TC). A factory assembly of insulated conductors with or without bare or covered equipment grounding conductors, under a nonmetallic jacket. ▶Figure 100–27

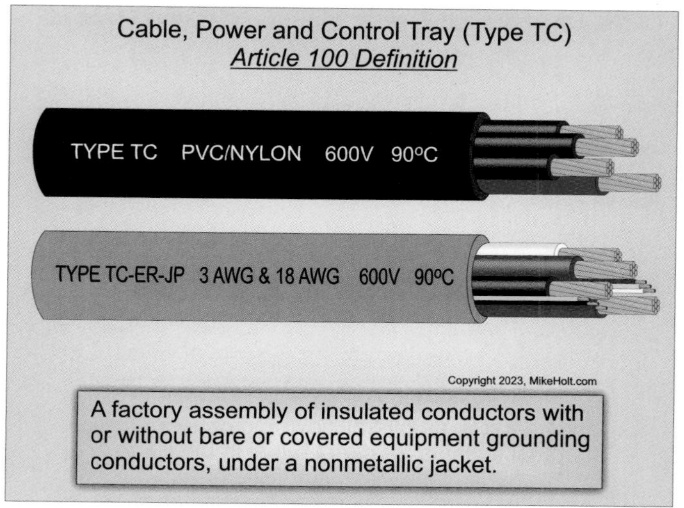
Cable, Power and Control Tray (Type TC)
Article 100 Definition
TYPE TC PVC/NYLON 600V 90°C
TYPE TC-ER-JP 3 AWG & 18 AWG 600V 90°C
Copyright 2023, MikeHolt.com
A factory assembly of insulated conductors with or without bare or covered equipment grounding conductors, under a nonmetallic jacket.

▶Figure 100–27

Cable, Service-Entrance (Types SE and USE). Service-entrance cable is a single or multiconductor cable with an overall covering. ▶Figure 100–28

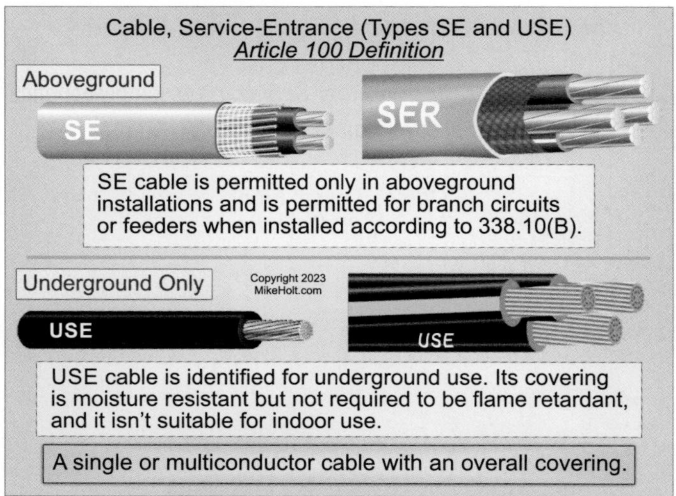

▶Figure 100–28

Type SE. Type SE cables have a flame-retardant, moisture-resistant covering for aboveground installations. These cables are permitted for branch circuits or feeders when installed in accordance with 338.10(B).

Type USE. USE cable is identified as a wiring method permitted for underground use. Its covering is moisture resistant, but not flame retardant.

Cable, Underground Feeder and Branch-Circuit (Type UF). A factory assembly of insulated conductors with an integral or overall covering of nonmetallic material suitable for direct burial in the Earth. ▶Figure 100–29 and ▶Figure 100–30

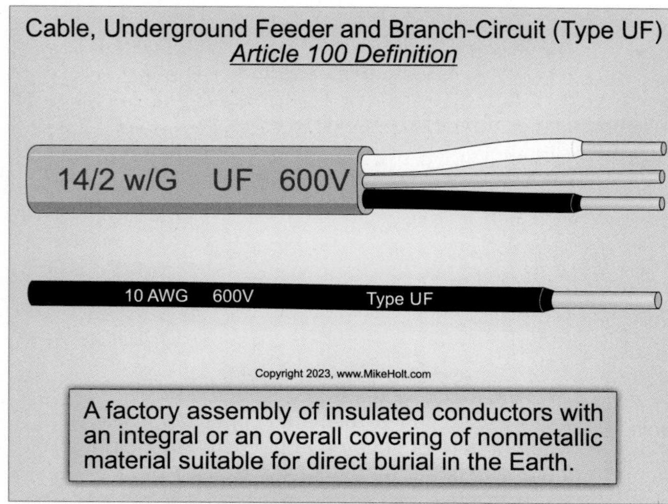

▶Figure 100–29

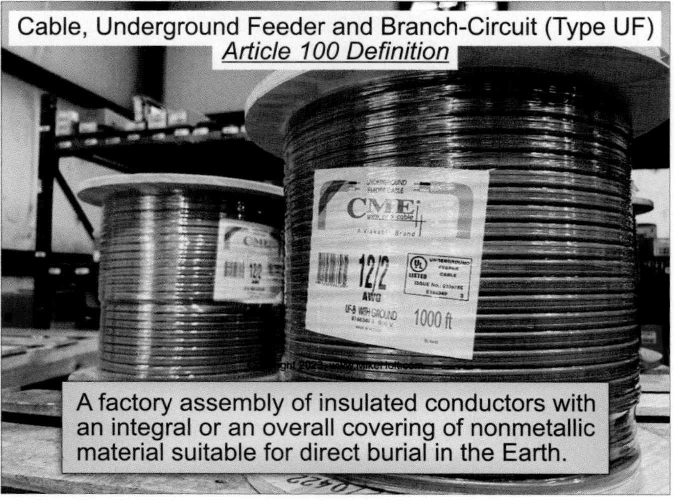

▶Figure 100–30

Cable Routing Assembly. A channel or channels (with their fittings) that support and route Class 2 power-limited, fire alarm, optical fiber, and coaxial cables. ▶Figure 100–31

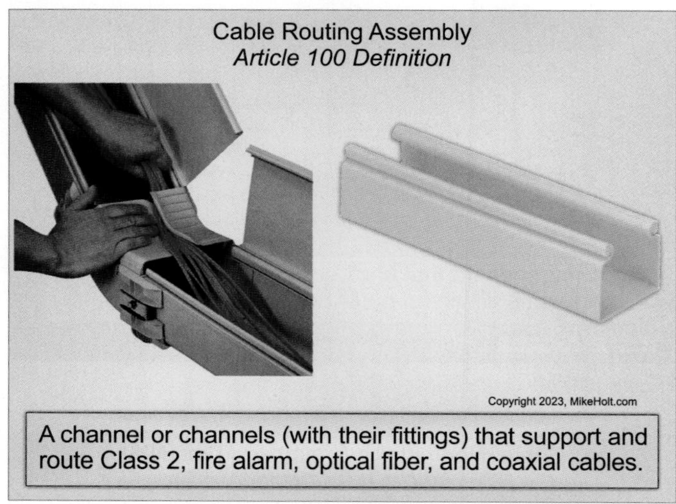

▶Figure 100–31

Author's Comment:

- A cable routing assembly is typically a U-shaped trough (with or without covers) designed to hold cables—it is not a raceway.

Cable Tray System. A unit or assembly of units or sections with associated fittings forming a rigid structural system used to securely fasten or support cables and raceways. ▶Figure 100–32 and ▶Figure 100–33

Circuit Breaker. A device designed to be opened and closed manually, but opens automatically during an overcurrent event without damage to itself. ▶Figure 100–34

1st Printing

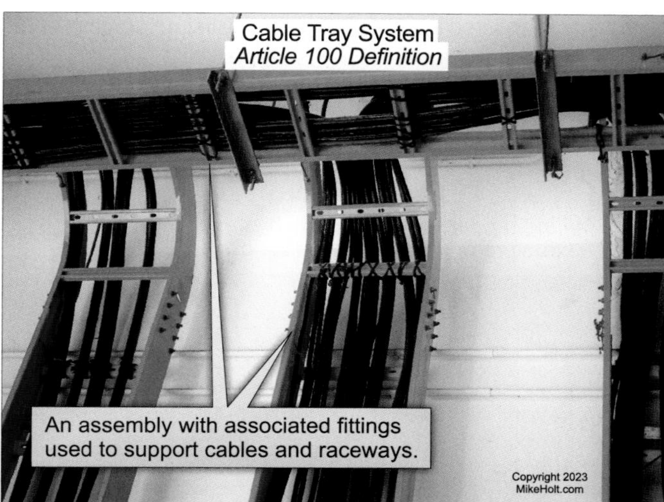
Cable Tray System
Article 100 Definition
An assembly with associated fittings used to support cables and raceways.
Copyright 2023 MikeHolt.com

▸Figure 100–32

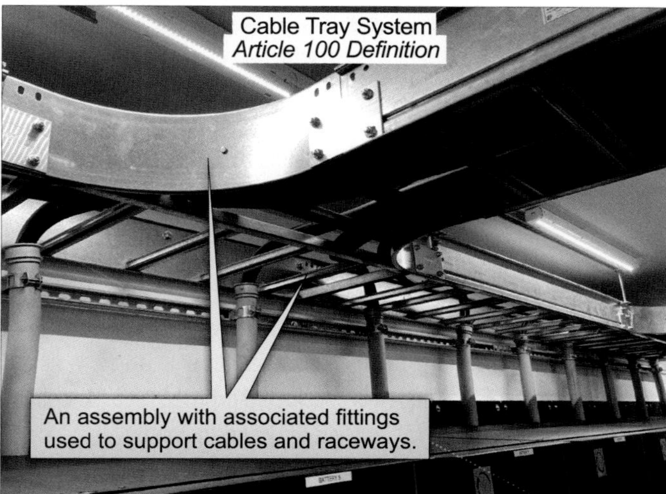
Cable Tray System
Article 100 Definition
An assembly with associated fittings used to support cables and raceways.

▸Figure 100–33

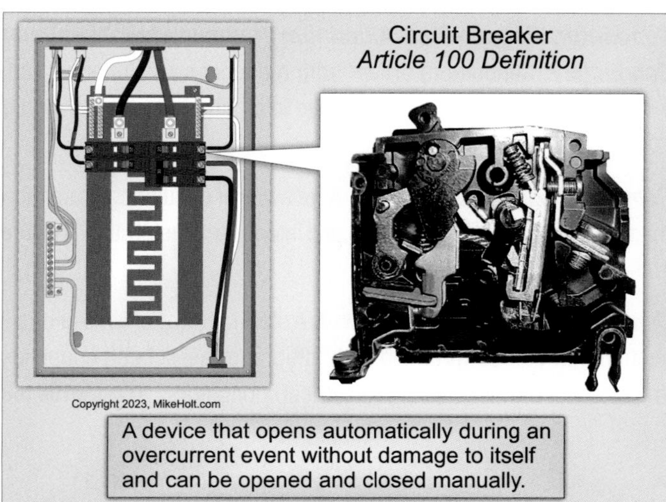
Circuit Breaker
Article 100 Definition
Copyright 2023, MikeHolt.com
A device that opens automatically during an overcurrent event without damage to itself and can be opened and closed manually.

▸Figure 100–34

Class 1 Power-Limited Circuit. The wiring system between the load side of a Class 1 power-limited power source and the connected equipment. ▸Figure 100–35

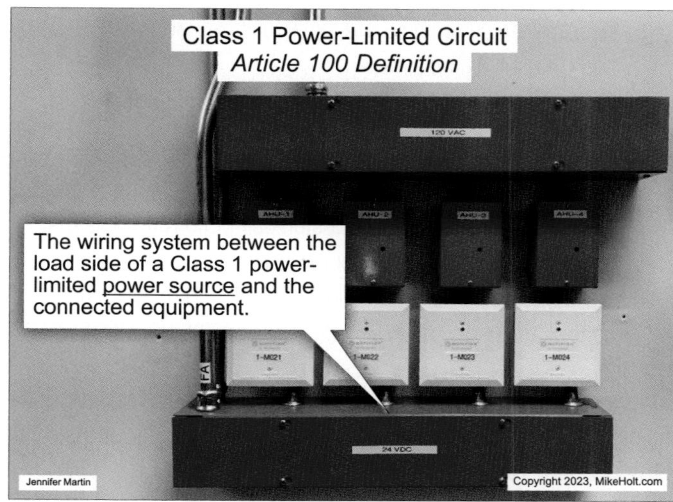
Class 1 Power-Limited Circuit
Article 100 Definition
120 VAC
The wiring system between the load side of a Class 1 power-limited power source and the connected equipment.
24 VDC
Jennifer Martin
Copyright 2023, MikeHolt.com

▸Figure 100–35

Class 2 Power-Limited Circuit. The wiring system between the load side of a power-limited power source and the connected Class 2 power-limited equipment. ▸Figure 100–36

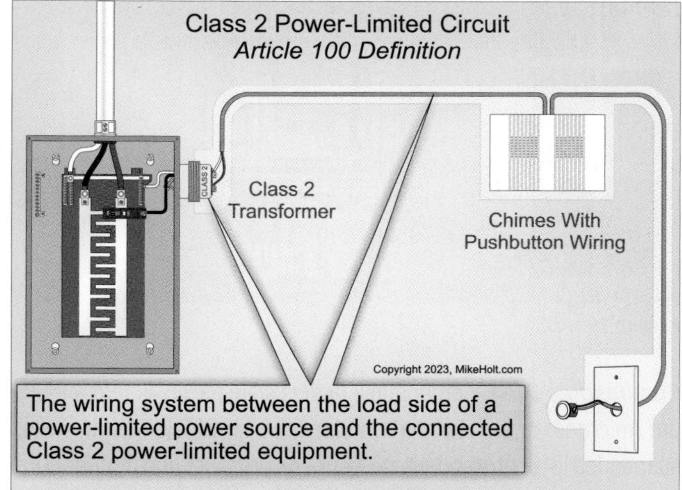
Class 2 Power-Limited Circuit
Article 100 Definition
Class 2 Transformer
Chimes With Pushbutton Wiring
Copyright 2023, MikeHolt.com
The wiring system between the load side of a power-limited power source and the connected Class 2 power-limited equipment.

▸Figure 100–36

Due to the power limitations of its power source, a Class 2 power-limited circuit is considered safe from a fire initiation standpoint and provides acceptable electric shock protection.

Author's Comment:

- Class 2 power-limited circuits are rendered safe by limiting the power source to 100 VA for circuits operating at 30V or less, and the current to 5 mA for circuits over 30V [725.60(A) and Chapter 9, Table 11(A)].
- Class 2 power-limited circuits typically include wiring for low-energy, low-voltage loads such as thermostats, programmable controllers, burglar alarms, and security systems. This type of circuit also includes twisted-pair or coaxial cable that interconnects computers for local area networks (LANs), power over ethernet applications (POEs), and programmable controller I/O circuits [725.60(A)(3) and 725.60(A)(4)].

Combiner, DC (DC Combiner). An enclosure that includes devices for the parallel connection of two or more PV system dc circuits (Article 690). ▸**Figure 100–37**

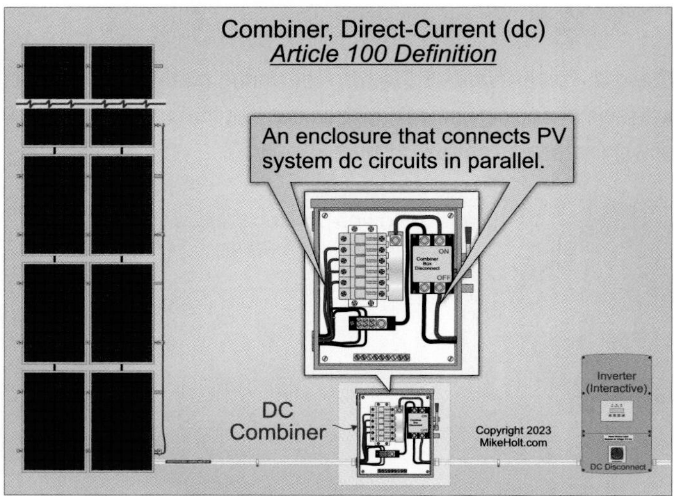
Combiner, Direct-Current (dc)
Article 100 Definition
An enclosure that connects PV system dc circuits in parallel.
DC Combiner
Inverter (Interactive)
DC Disconnect
Copyright 2023 MikeHolt.com

▸**Figure 100–37**

Combustible Dust. Combustible dust is solid particles that are 500 μm (microns) or smaller that can form an explosible mixture when suspended in air at standard atmospheric pressure and temperature.

Commissioning. The process, procedures, and testing used to set up and verify the initial performance, operational controls, safety systems, and sequence of operation of electrical devices and equipment prior to them being placed into active service.

Author's Comment:

- This term is used in Emergency Standby Power Systems 700.3, Legally Required Standby Power Systems 701.3, and Energy Storage Systems 706.7(A).

Concealed. Rendered inaccessible by the structure or finish of the building. ▸**Figure 100–38**

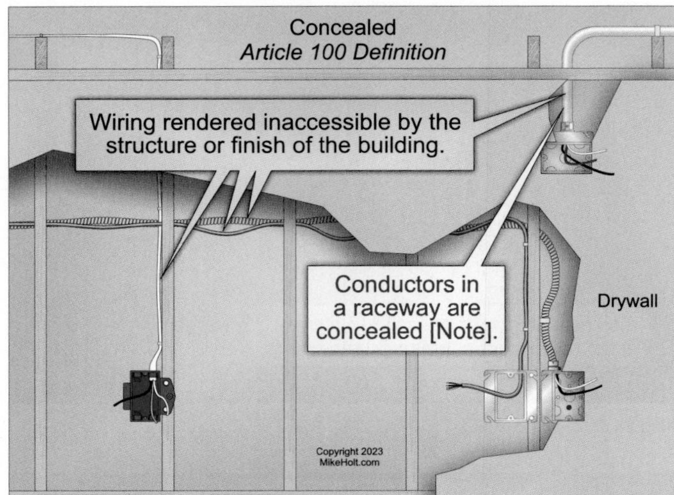
Concealed
Article 100 Definition
Wiring rendered inaccessible by the structure or finish of the building.
Conductors in a raceway are concealed [Note].
Drywall
Copyright 2023 MikeHolt.com

▸**Figure 100–38**

Note: Conductors in a concealed raceway are considered concealed even though they may be made accessible by withdrawing them from the raceway.

Author's Comment:

- Wiring behind panels designed to allow access, such as removable ceiling tile and wiring in accessible attics, is not considered concealed—it is considered exposed. See the definition of "Exposed (as applied to wiring methods)."
- Boxes are not permitted to be concealed by the finish of the building. ▸**Figure 100–39**

Conductor, Copper-Clad Aluminum (Copper-Clad Aluminum Conductor). Conductors drawn from a copper-clad aluminum rod, with the copper metallurgically bonded to an aluminum core. ▸**Figure 100–40** and ▸**Figure 100–41**

Conduit, Flexible Metal (FMC). A raceway of circular cross section made of a helically wound, formed,and interlocked metal strip. ▸**Figure 100–42**

Conduit, Intermediate Metal (IMC). A steel raceway of circular cross section that can be threaded with integral or associated couplings and listed for the installation of electrical conductors. ▸**Figure 100–43**

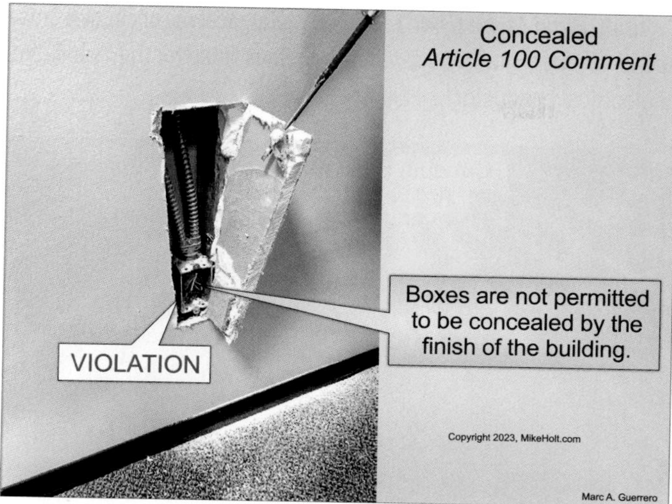
Concealed
Article 100 Comment
Boxes are not permitted to be concealed by the finish of the building.
VIOLATION
Copyright 2023, MikeHolt.com
Marc A. Guerrero

▸Figure 100–39

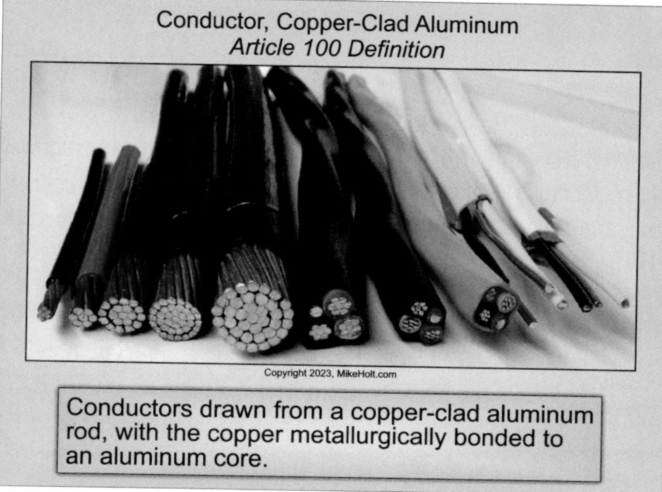
Conductor, Copper-Clad Aluminum
Article 100 Definition
Copyright 2023, MikeHolt.com
Conductors drawn from a copper-clad aluminum rod, with the copper metallurgically bonded to an aluminum core.

▸Figure 100–40

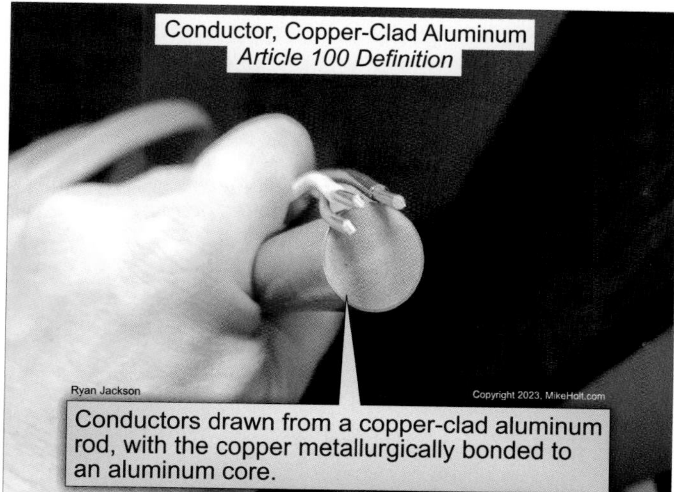
Conductor, Copper-Clad Aluminum
Article 100 Definition
Ryan Jackson
Copyright 2023, MikeHolt.com
Conductors drawn from a copper-clad aluminum rod, with the copper metallurgically bonded to an aluminum core.

▸Figure 100–41

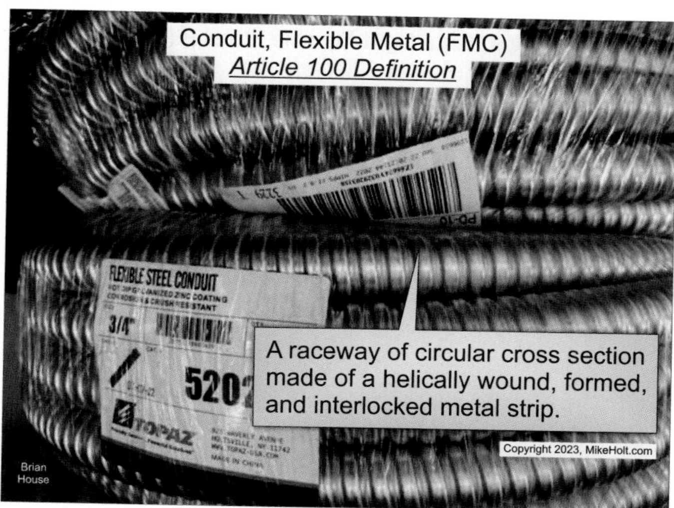
Conduit, Flexible Metal (FMC)
Article 100 Definition
FLEXIBLE STEEL CONDUIT
3/4"
520
TOPAZ
A raceway of circular cross section made of a helically wound, formed, and interlocked metal strip.
Brian House
Copyright 2023, MikeHolt.com

▸Figure 100–42

Conduit, Intermediate Metal (IMC)
Article 100 Definition
Trade Size 1/2"
Atkore
Allied Tube & Conduit
INTERMEDIATE METAL CONDUIT
MADE IN USA
CONSULT MANUFACTURER FOR PROPER INSTALLATION
©Atkore Inc. All Rights Reserved.
LISTED E58688
A listed steel circular raceway that can be threaded with integral or associated couplings.
Copyright 2023, MikeHolt.com

▸Figure 100–43

Conduit, Liquidtight Flexible Metal (LFMC). A raceway of circular cross section (having an outer liquidtight, nonmetallic, sunlight-resistant jacket over an inner flexible metal core) with associated connectors and fittings listed for the installation of electrical conductors. ▸Figure 100–44 and ▸Figure 100–45

Conduit, Liquidtight Flexible Nonmetallic (LFNC). A raceway of circular cross section (with an outer liquidtight, nonmetallic, sunlight-resistant jacket over a flexible inner core) with associated couplings, connectors, and fittings listed for the installation of electrical conductors. ▸Figure 100–46

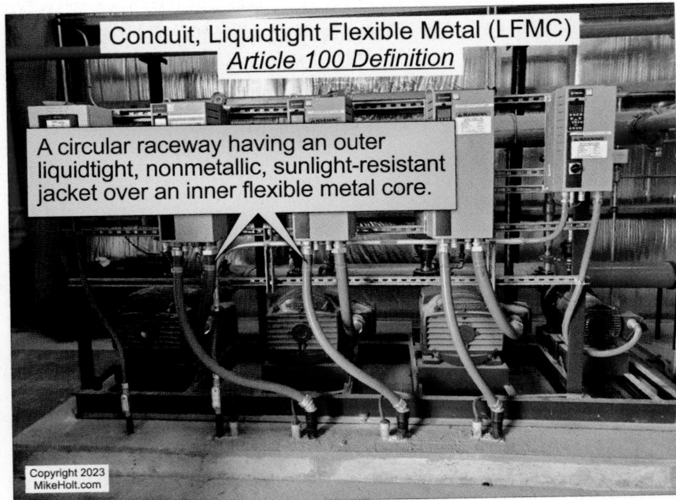
Conduit, Liquidtight Flexible Metal (LFMC)
Article 100 Definition
A circular raceway having an outer liquidtight, nonmetallic, sunlight-resistant jacket over an inner flexible metal core.
Copyright 2023 MikeHolt.com

▶Figure 100–44

Conduit, Liquidtight Flexible Metal (LFMC)
Article 100 Definition
A circular raceway having an outer liquidtight, nonmetallic, sunlight-resistant jacket over an inner flexible metal core.
Copyright 2023 MikeHolt.com

▶Figure 100–45

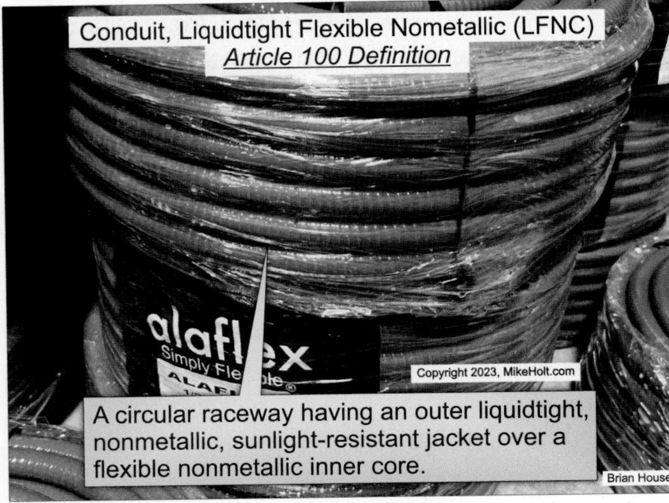
Conduit, Liquidtight Flexible Nometallic (LFNC)
Article 100 Definition
alaflex
Simply Flexible
Copyright 2023, MikeHolt.com
A circular raceway having an outer liquidtight, nonmetallic, sunlight-resistant jacket over a flexible nonmetallic inner core.
Brian House

▶Figure 100–46

Conduit, Rigid Metal (RMC). A listed metal raceway of circular cross section with integral or associated couplings listed for the installation of electrical conductors. ▶Figure 100–47

Conduit, Rigid Metal (RMC)
Article 100 Definition
A listed metal circular raceway with integral or associated couplings.
Copyright 2023, MikeHolt.com

▶Figure 100–47

Conduit, Rigid Polyvinyl Chloride (PVC). A rigid nonmetallic raceway of circular cross section with integral or associated couplings, connectors, and fittings listed for the installation of electrical conductors. ▶Figure 100–48

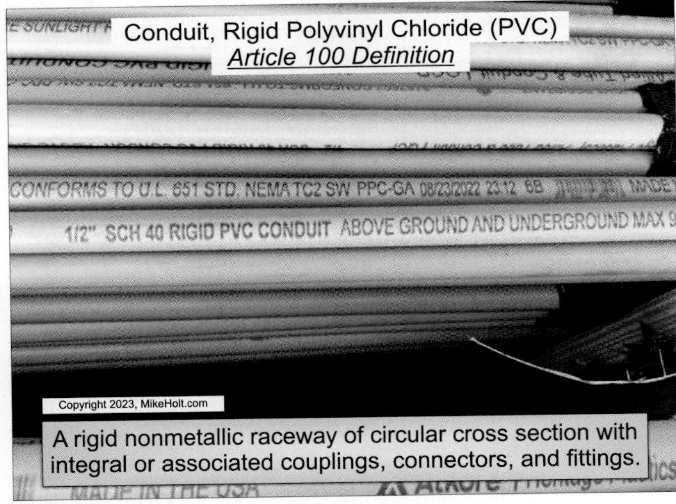
Conduit, Rigid Polyvinyl Chloride (PVC)
Article 100 Definition
CONFORMS TO U.L. 651 STD. NEMA TC2 SW PPC-GA 08/23/2022 23:12 6B
1/2" SCH 40 RIGID PVC CONDUIT ABOVE GROUND AND UNDERGROUND
Copyright 2023, MikeHolt.com
A rigid nonmetallic raceway of circular cross section with integral or associated couplings, connectors, and fittings.

▶Figure 100–48

Conduit Body. A fitting installed on a raceway that provides access to conductors through a removable cover. ▶Figure 100–49 and ▶Figure 100–50

1st Printing

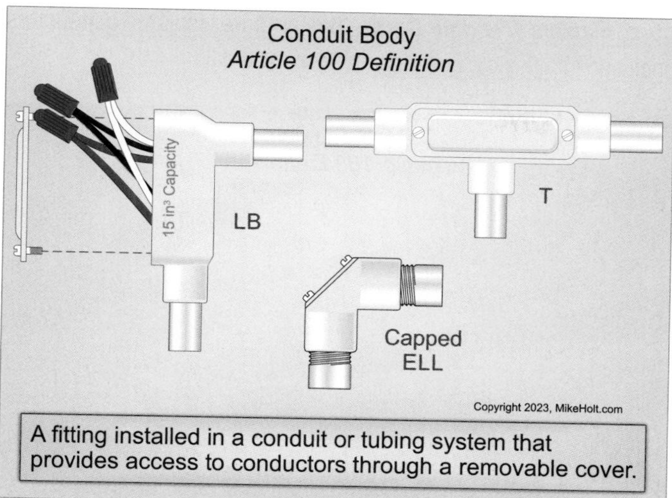
Conduit Body
Article 100 Definition
15 in³ Capacity
LB
T
Capped
ELL
Copyright 2023, MikeHolt.com
A fitting installed in a conduit or tubing system that provides access to conductors through a removable cover.

▸Figure 100–49

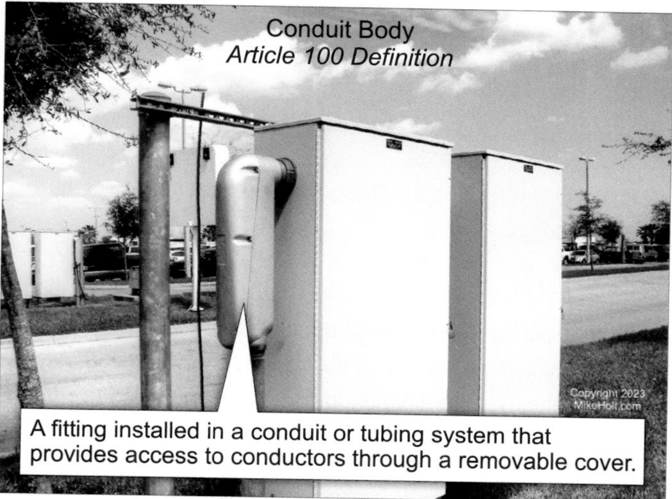
Conduit Body
Article 100 Definition
Copyright 2023 MikeHolt.com
A fitting installed in a conduit or tubing system that provides access to conductors through a removable cover.

▸Figure 100–50

Continuous Load. A load where the maximum current is expected for three hours or more continuously.

Control Circuit. The circuit of a control apparatus or system that carries the electric signals directing the performance of a controller but does not carry the main power current. ▸Figure 100–51

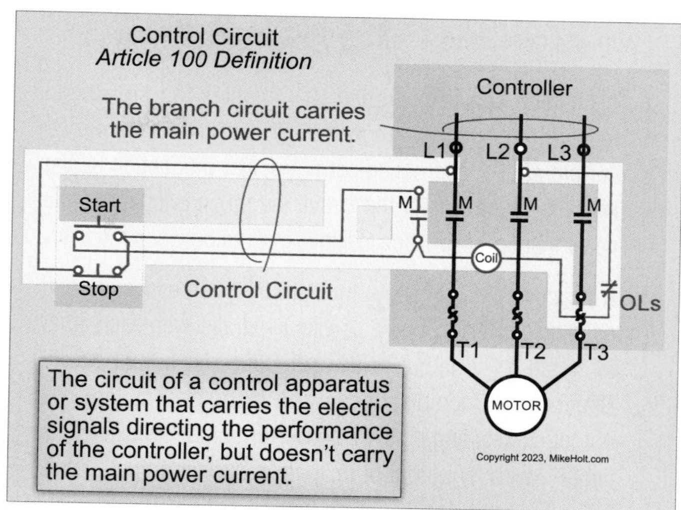
Control Circuit
Article 100 Definition
Controller
The branch circuit carries the main power current.
L1
L2
L3
Start
Stop
M
Coil
Control Circuit
OLs
T1
T2
T3
MOTOR
The circuit of a control apparatus or system that carries the electric signals directing the performance of the controller, but doesn't carry the main power current.
Copyright 2023, MikeHolt.com

▸Figure 100–51

Controller. A device that controls the electric power delivered to electrical equipment in some predetermined manner. This includes motor starters, time clocks, lighting contactors, photocells, and equipment with similar functions. ▸Figure 100–52

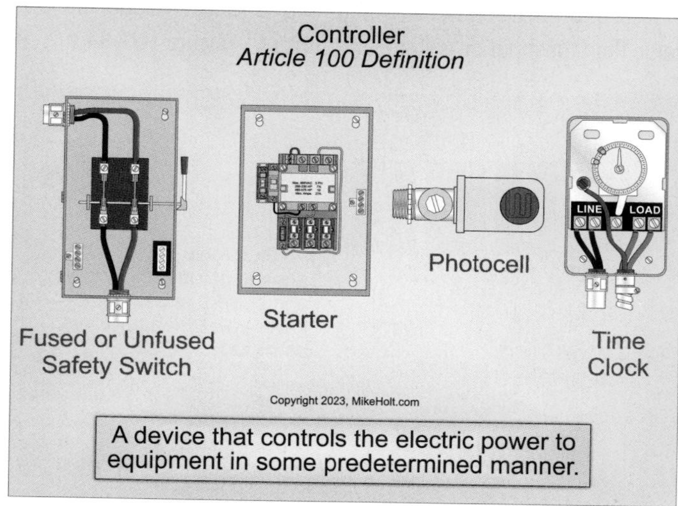
Controller
Article 100 Definition
Photocell
LINE
LOAD
Starter
Fused or Unfused Safety Switch
Time Clock
Copyright 2023, MikeHolt.com
A device that controls the electric power to equipment in some predetermined manner.

▸Figure 100–52

Converter Circuit, DC-to-DC (DC-to-DC Converter Circuit). The dc circuit conductors connected to the output of dc-to-dc converters (Article 690). ▸Figure 100–53

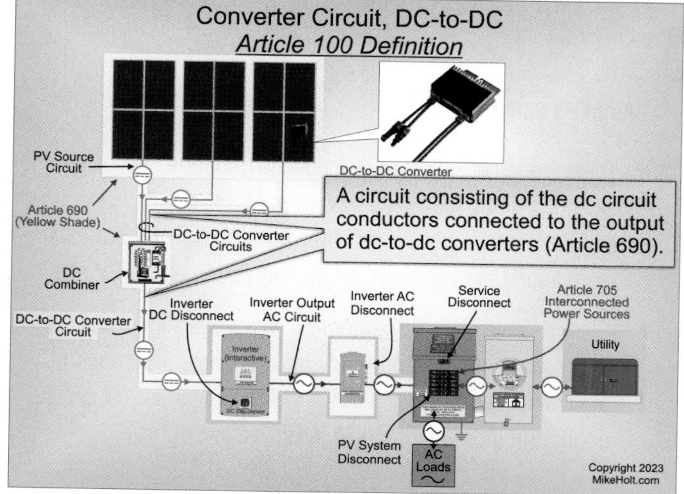
Converter Circuit, DC-to-DC
Article 100 Definition
PV Source Circuit
DC-to-DC Converter
Article 690 (Yellow Shade)
A circuit consisting of the dc circuit conductors connected to the output of dc-to-dc converters (Article 690).
DC-to-DC Converter Circuits
DC Combiner
DC-to-DC Converter Circuit
Inverter DC Disconnect
Inverter Output AC Circuit
Inverter AC Disconnect
Service Disconnect
Article 705 Interconnected Power Sources
Utility
PV System Disconnect
AC Loads
Copyright 2023 MikeHolt.com

▸Figure 100–53

Author's Comment:

- A dc-to-dc converter (optimizer)l enables the inverter to receive the circuit voltage that is maximized for direct-current and/or alternating-current power production by the inverter—regardless of the circuit length, individual module performance, or variance in light exposure between modules.
- A dc combiner connects multiple PV source circuits and dc-to-dc converter source circuits in parallel with each other to create a PV output or dc-to-dc converter output circuit. Direct-current combiners can also recombine multiple PV output circuits and dc-to-dc converter output circuits with a larger 2-wire PV output or dc-to-dc converter output circuit.

Converter, DC-to-DC (DC-to-DC Converter). An electronic device that can provide an output dc voltage and current at a higher or lower value than the input dc voltage and current. ▶Figure 100–54

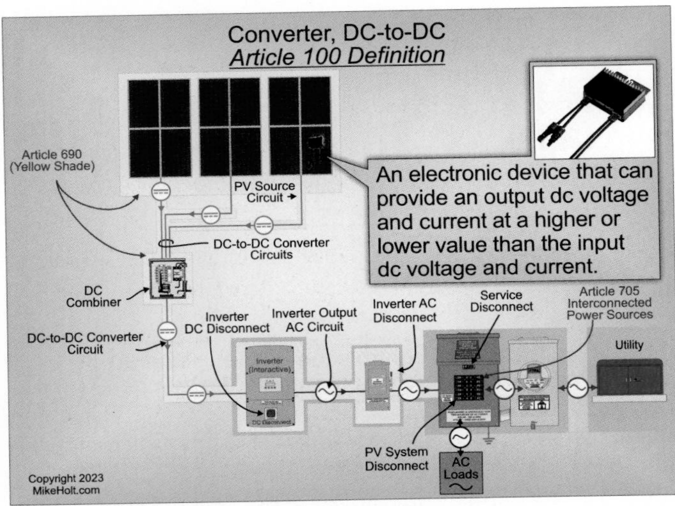

▶Figure 100–54

Author's Comment:

- The dc-to-dc converters are intended to maximize the output of independent PV modules and reduce losses due to variances between modules' outputs. They are directly wired to each module and are bolted to the module frame or the PV rack.
- A dc-to-dc converter (optimizer)l enables a PV inverter to automatically maintain a fixed circuit voltage, at the optimal point for dc/ac conversion by the inverter, regardless of circuit length and individual module performance.

Cord, Flexible (Flexible Cord). Two or more insulated conductors enclosed in a flexible covering. ▶Figure 100–55

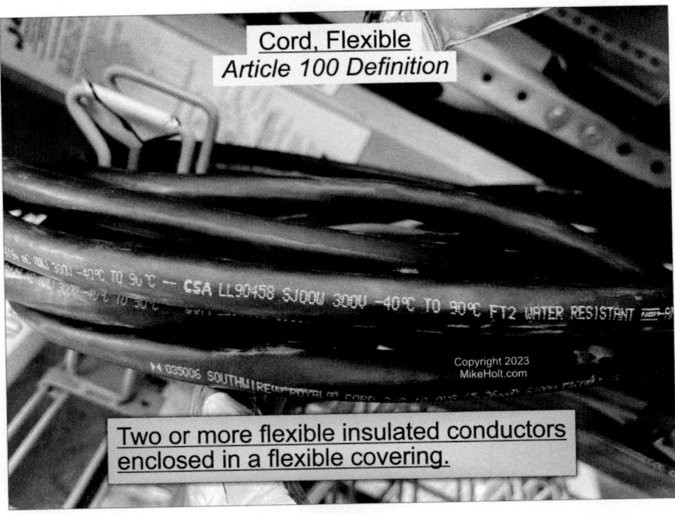

▶Figure 100–55

Author's Comment:

- Article 400 contains the primary requirements for flexible cords.

Coordination, Selective (Selective Coordination). Localization of an overcurrent condition to restrict outages to the circuit or equipment affected, accomplished by the choice of overcurrent protective devices. Selective coordination includes currents from overloads, short circuits, or ground faults. ▶Figure 100–56

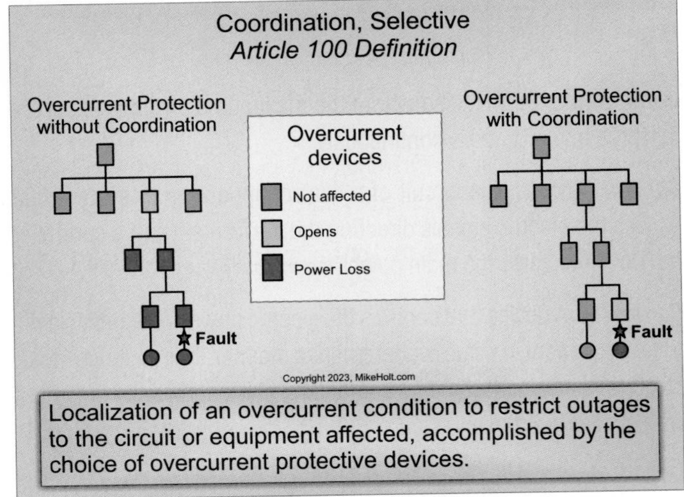

▶Figure 100–56

1st Printing

Author's Comment:

- Selective coordination means the overcurrent protection scheme confines the interruption to a specific circuit, rather than to the entire electrical system. For example, if someone plugs in a space heater and raises the total demand on a 20A circuit to 25A, or if a short circuit or ground fault occurs, with selective coordination the only breaker or fuse that will open is the one protecting just that branch circuit.

Corrosive Environment. Areas or enclosures without adequate ventilation where electrical equipment is located, and pool sanitation chemicals are stored, handled, or dispensed (Article 680). ▸Figure 100–57

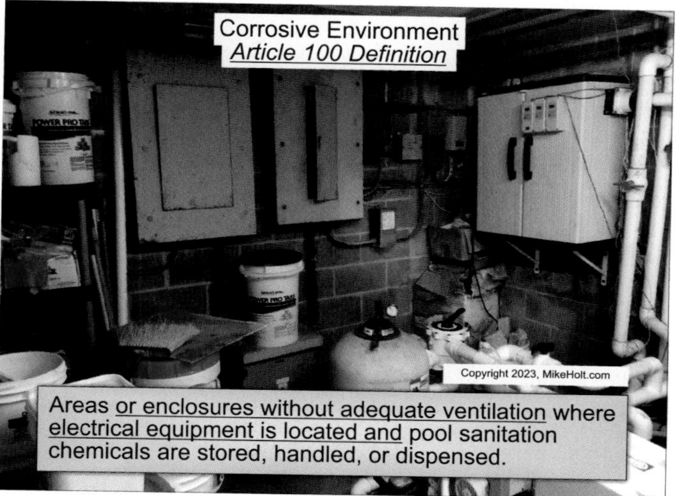

▸Figure 100–57

Note 1: Sanitation chemicals and pool water pose a risk of corrosion (gradually damaging or destroying materials) due to the presence of oxidizers (for example, calcium hypochlorite, sodium hypochlorite, bromine, and chlorinated isocyanurates) and chlorinating agents that release chlorine when dissolved in water.

Dental Office. A building or portion of a building in which the following occur:

(1) Examinations and minor treatments or procedures performed under the continuous supervision of a dental professional.

(2) Use of limited to minimal sedation and treatment or procedures that do not render the patient incapable of self-preservation under emergency conditions.

(3) No overnight stays for patients or 24-hour operations.

Device. A component intended to carry or control electric energy as its principal function. ▸Figure 100–58

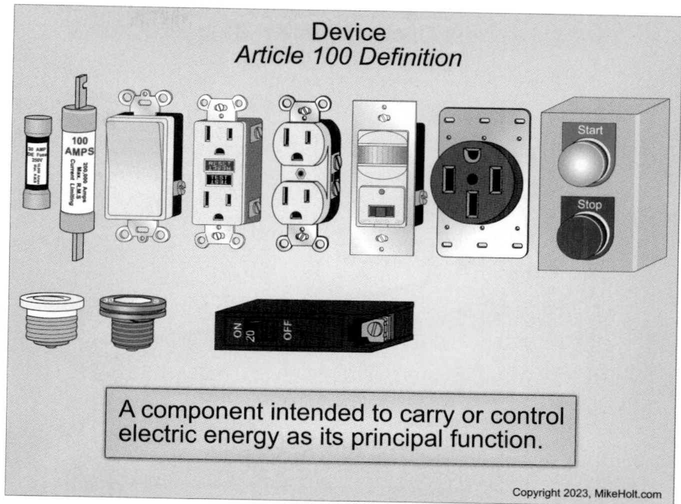

▸Figure 100–58

Author's Comment:

- Devices generally do not consume electric energy and include receptacles, switches, illuminated switches, circuit breakers, fuses, time clocks, controllers, attachment plugs, and so forth. Some (such as illuminated switches, contactors, or relays) consume very small amounts of energy and are still classified as a device based on their primary function.

Disconnecting Means (Disconnect). A device that disconnects the circuit conductors from their power source. ▸Figure 100–59

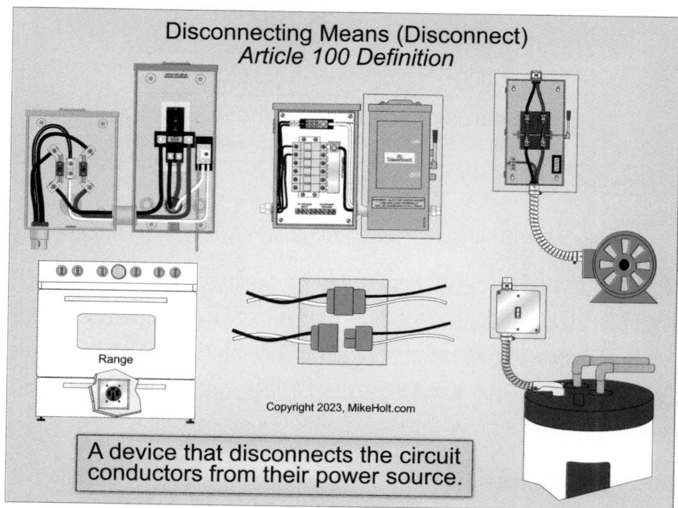

▸Figure 100–59

Docking Facility. A fixed or floating structure that provides access to the water and to which boats are secured (Article 555). ▶Figure 100–60

Docking Facility
Article 100 Definition
Copyright 2023, MikeHolt.com
Mario Valdes
A fixed or floating structure that provides access to the water and to which boats are secured.

▶Figure 100–60

Dusttight (Enclosures). Enclosures constructed so that dust will not enter under specified test conditions. ▶Figure 100–61

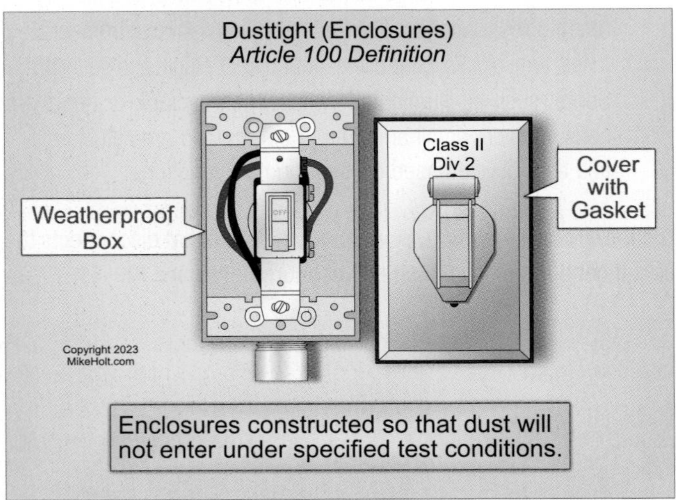
Dusttight (Enclosures)
Article 100 Definition
Class II Div 2
Cover with Gasket
Weatherproof Box
Copyright 2023 MikeHolt.com
Enclosures constructed so that dust will not enter under specified test conditions.

▶Figure 100–61

Note 2: See NEMA 250, *Enclosures for Electrical Equipment (1000 Volts Maximum)*, and ANSI/UL 50E, *Enclosures for Electrical Equipment, Environmental Considerations*, for additional information on enclosure Types 3, 3X, 3S, 3SX, 4, 4X, 5, 6, 6P, 12, 12K, and 13 that are considered dusttight.

Dust-ignitionproof Enclosures. Equipment enclosures designed to exclude dusts and will not permit arcs, sparks, or heat within the enclosure to cause the ignition of exterior dust. ▶Figure 100–62

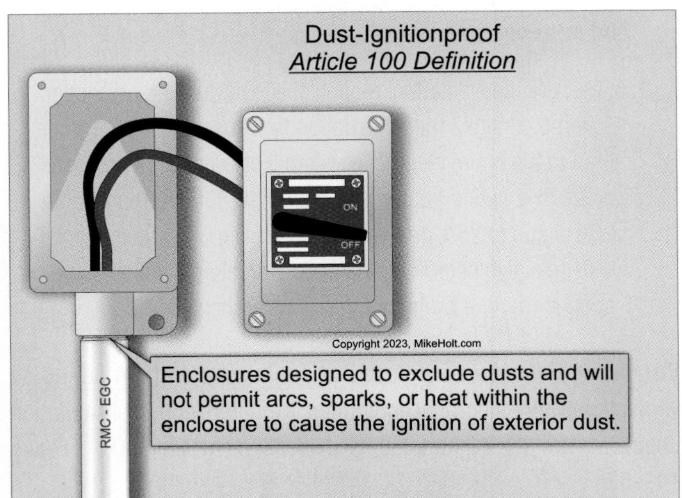
Dust-Ignitionproof
Article 100 Definition
ON
OFF
Copyright 2023, MikeHolt.com
RMC - EGC
Enclosures designed to exclude dusts and will not permit arcs, sparks, or heat within the enclosure to cause the ignition of exterior dust.

▶Figure 100–62

Dwelling, One-Family (One-Family Dwelling). A building that consists solely of one dwelling unit.

Dwelling, Two-Family (Two-Family Dwelling). A building that consists solely of two dwelling units. ▶Figure 100–63

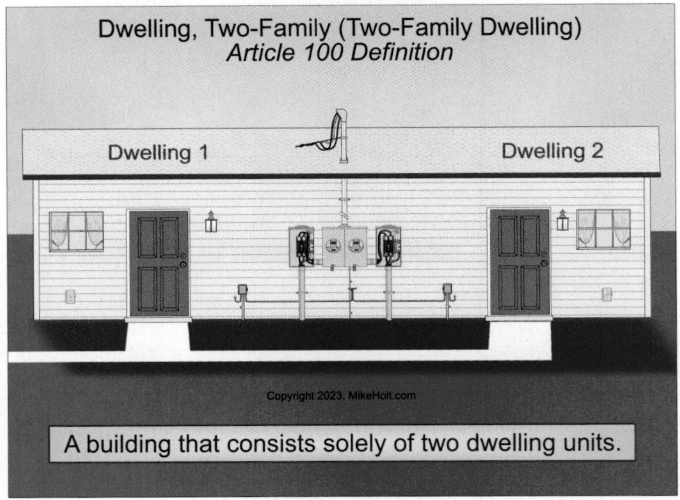
Dwelling, Two-Family (Two-Family Dwelling)
Article 100 Definition
Dwelling 1
Dwelling 2
Copyright 2023, MikeHolt.com
A building that consists solely of two dwelling units.

▶Figure 100–63

Dwelling Unit. A single unit that provides independent living facilities with permanent provisions for living, sleeping, cooking, and sanitation. ▶Figure 100–64

Electric Vehicle. An on-road use automobile, bus, truck, van, neighborhood electric vehicle, or motorcycle primarily powered by an electric motor. ▶Figure 100–65

1st Printing

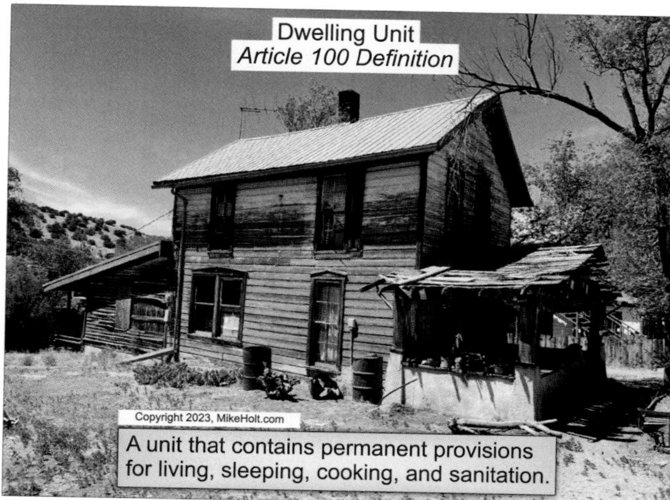
Dwelling Unit
Article 100 Definition
Copyright 2023, MikeHolt.com
A unit that contains permanent provisions for living, sleeping, cooking, and sanitation.
▶Figure 100–64

Electric Vehicle
Article 100 Definition
Copyright 2023 www.MikeHolt.com
An on-road use automobile, bus, truck, van, neighborhood vehicle, or motorcycle primarily powered by an electric motor.
▶Figure 100–65

Note: Off-road, self-propelled electric industrial trucks, hoists, lifts, transports, golf carts, airline ground support equipment, tractors, and boats are not electric vehicles for the purposes of the *NEC*. ▶**Figure 100–66**

Author's Comment:

- The portion of plug-in vehicles containing both an electric motor and a combustion engine that pertains to re-charging the electric motor is covered by Article 625.

Electric Vehicle Supply Equipment (EVSE). Connectors, attachment plugs, personnel protection systems, devices, and power outlets installed for the purpose of transferring energy between the premises wiring and an electric vehicle (Article 625). ▶**Figure 100–67** and ▶**Figure 100–68**

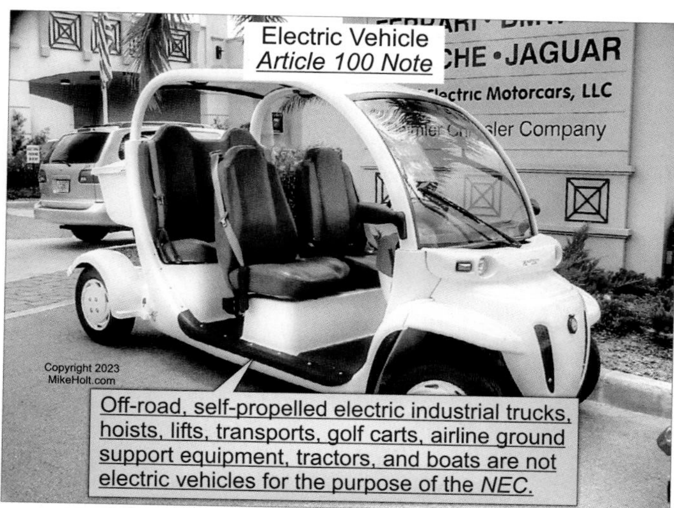
Electric Vehicle
Article 100 Note
Copyright 2023 MikeHolt.com
Off-road, self-propelled electric industrial trucks, hoists, lifts, transports, golf carts, airline ground support equipment, tractors, and boats are not electric vehicles for the purpose of the NEC.
▶Figure 100–66

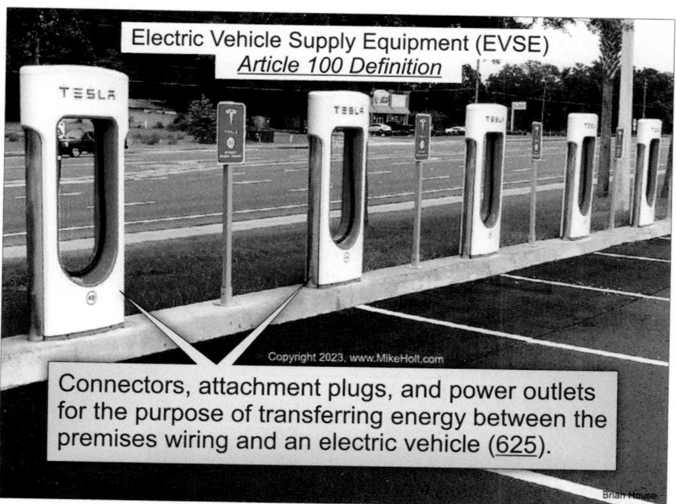
Electric Vehicle Supply Equipment (EVSE)
Article 100 Definition
TESLA
Copyright 2023, www.MikeHolt.com
Connectors, attachment plugs, and power outlets for the purpose of transferring energy between the premises wiring and an electric vehicle (625).
Brian House
▶Figure 100–67

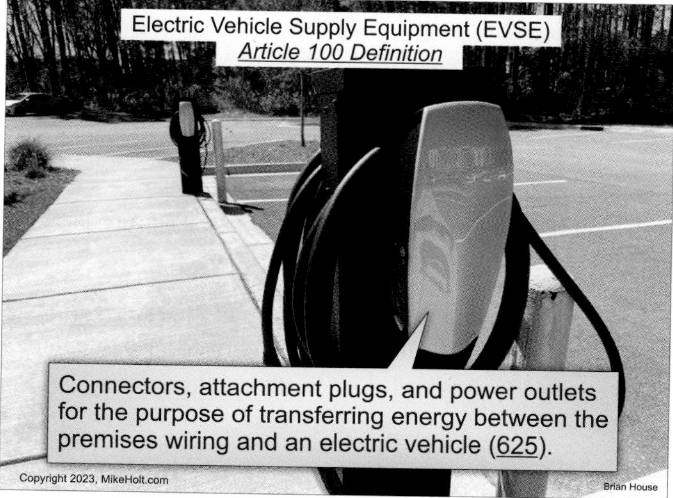
Electric Vehicle Supply Equipment (EVSE)
Article 100 Definition
Connectors, attachment plugs, and power outlets for the purpose of transferring energy between the premises wiring and an electric vehicle (625).
Copyright 2023, MikeHolt.com
Brian House
▶Figure 100–68

Electronic Power Converter. A device that uses power electronics to convert one form of electrical power into another form of electrical power. ▸Figure 100–69 and ▸Figure 100–70

Electronic Power Converter
Article 100 Definition
A device that uses power electronics to convert one form of electrical power into another form of electrical power.
Copyright 2023, MikeHolt.com
Generac

▸Figure 100–69

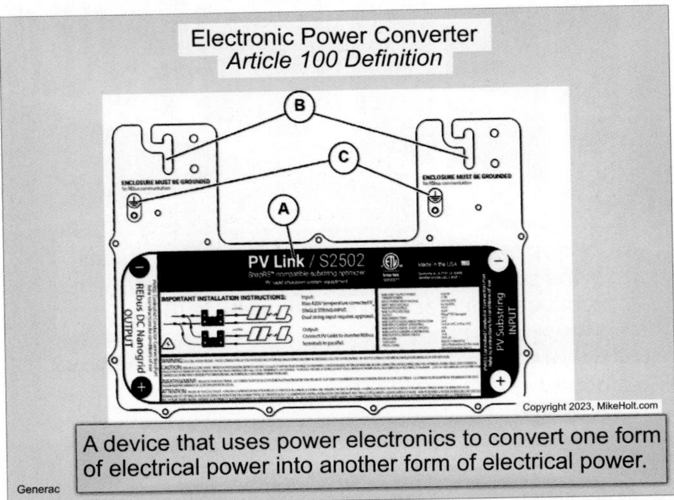
Electronic Power Converter
Article 100 Definition
B
C
A
PV Link / S2502
A device that uses power electronics to convert one form of electrical power into another form of electrical power.
Copyright 2023, MikeHolt.com
Generac

▸Figure 100–70

Note: Examples of electronic power converters include, but are not limited to, inverters and dc-to-dc converters. These devices have limited current capabilities based on the device ratings at continuous rated power.

Emergency Luminaire, Battery-Equipped (Battery-Equipped Emergency Luminaire). A luminaire with a rechargeable battery, a battery charging means, and an automatic load control relay. ▸Figure 100–71

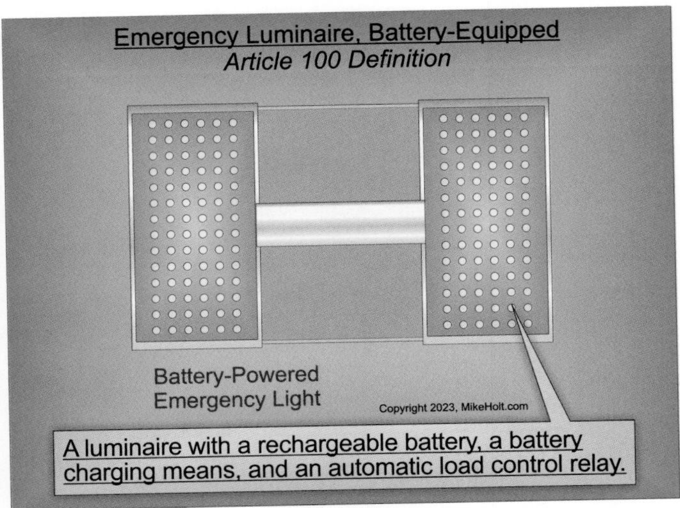
Emergency Luminaire, Battery-Equipped
Article 100 Definition
Battery-Powered
Emergency Light
Copyright 2023, MikeHolt.com
A luminaire with a rechargeable battery, a battery charging means, and an automatic load control relay.

▸Figure 100–71

Emergency Systems. Emergency power systems are those systems required and classed as emergency by a governmental agency having jurisdiction. These systems are intended to automatically supply illumination and/or power essential for safety to human life. ▸Figure 100–72

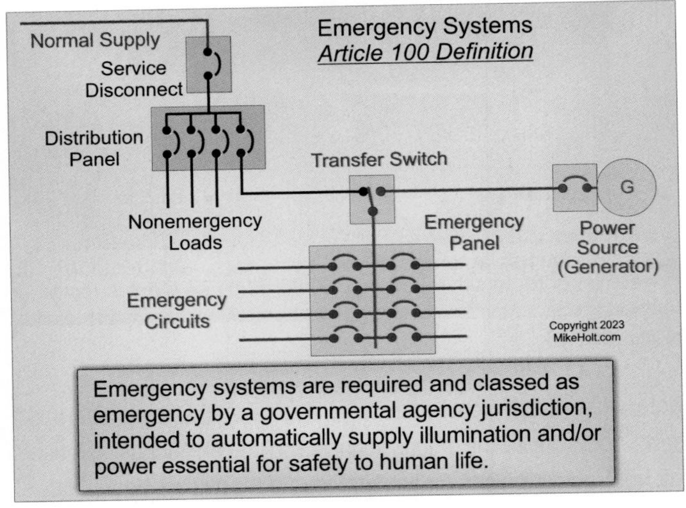
Emergency Systems
Article 100 Definition
Normal Supply
Service
Disconnect
Distribution
Panel
Transfer Switch
G
Nonemergency
Loads
Emergency
Panel
Power
Source
(Generator)
Emergency
Circuits
Copyright 2023
MikeHolt.com
Emergency systems are required and classed as emergency by a governmental agency jurisdiction, intended to automatically supply illumination and/or power essential for safety to human life.

▸Figure 100–72

Author's Comment:

- Emergency power systems may also provide power to maintain life, fire detection/alarm systems, elevators, fire pumps, public safety, industrial processes where current interruption would produce serious life safety or health hazards, and similar functions.

Energized. Electrically connected to a source of voltage. ▸Figure 100–73

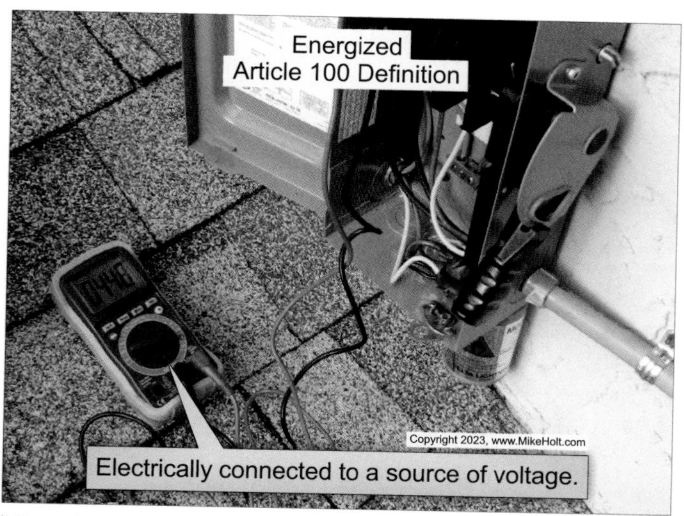

▶Figure 100–73

Energized, Likely to Become (Likely to Become Energized). Conductive material that could become energized because of the failure of electrical insulation or electrical spacing. ▶Figure 100–74

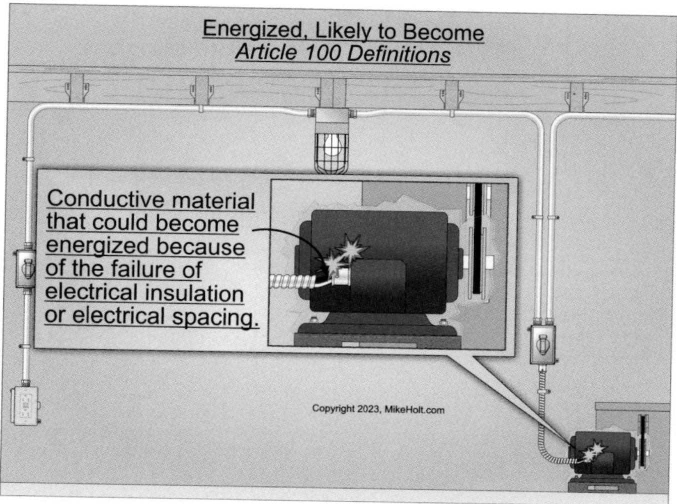

▶Figure 100–74

Energy Management System. A system consisting of monitor(s), communications equipment, controller(s), timer(s), or other device(s) that monitors and/or controls an electrical load or a power production or storage source. ▶Figure 100–75 and ▶Figure 100–76

Author's Comment:

- Article 750 contains the primary requirements for energy management systems.

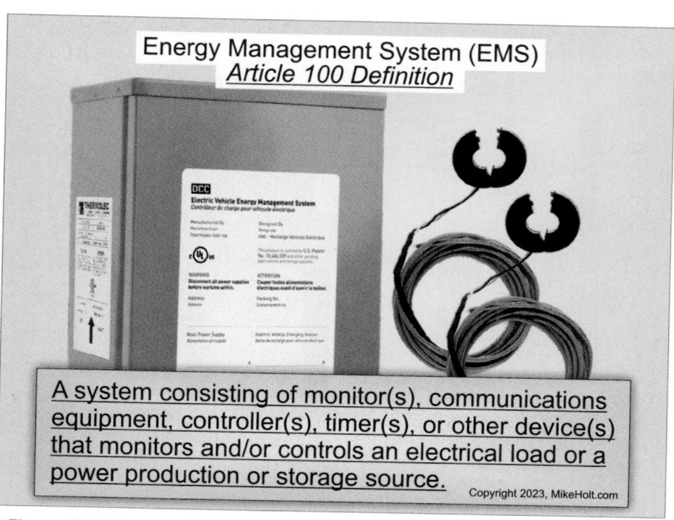

▶Figure 100–75

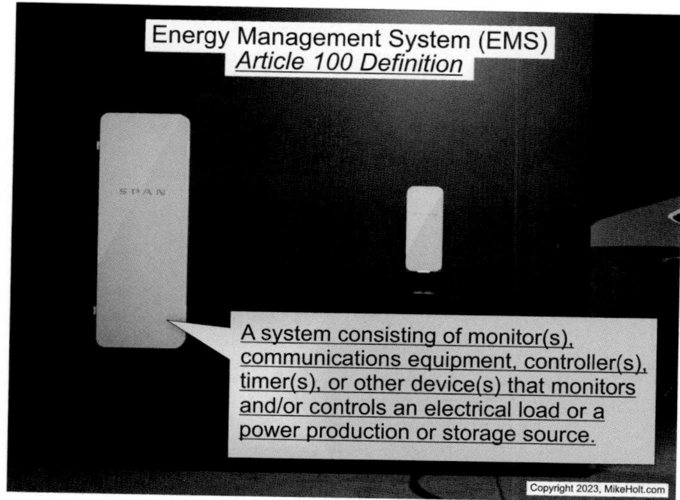

▶Figure 100–76

Energy Storage System. One or more devices installed as a system capable of storing energy and providing electrical energy to the premises wiring system. ▶Figure 100–77 and ▶Figure 100–78

Note 1: Energy storage systems can include batteries, capacitors, and kinetic energy devices such as flywheels and compressed air. Energy storage systems can include inverters or converters to change voltage levels or to make a change between an alternating-current or a direct-current system.

Author's Comment:

- Article 706 contains the primary requirements for energy storage systems.

▶Figure 100–77

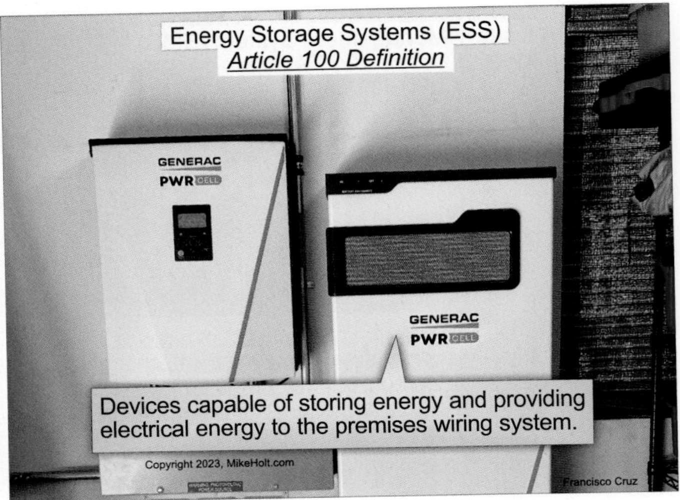

▶Figure 100–78

Equipotential Plane. Conductive elements connected together to minimize voltage differences. ▶Figure 100–79

Explosionproof Equipment. Equipment capable of withstanding and containing the force of an internal explosion and designed so the hot gases within the enclosure cool as they escape. ▶Figure 100–80

Exposed (as applied to live parts). Capable of being inadvertently touched or approached nearer than a safe distance by a person.

Note: This term applies to parts that are not suitably guarded, isolated, or insulated.

Exposed (as applied to wiring methods). On or attached to the surface of a building, or behind panels designed to allow access. ▶Figure 100–81

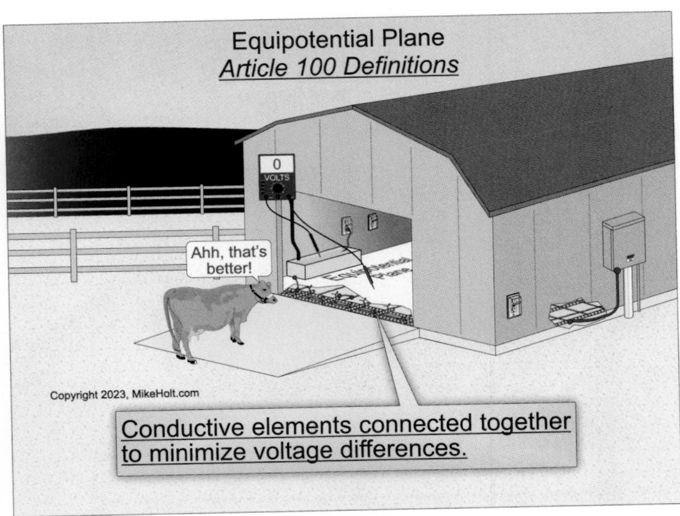

▶Figure 100–79

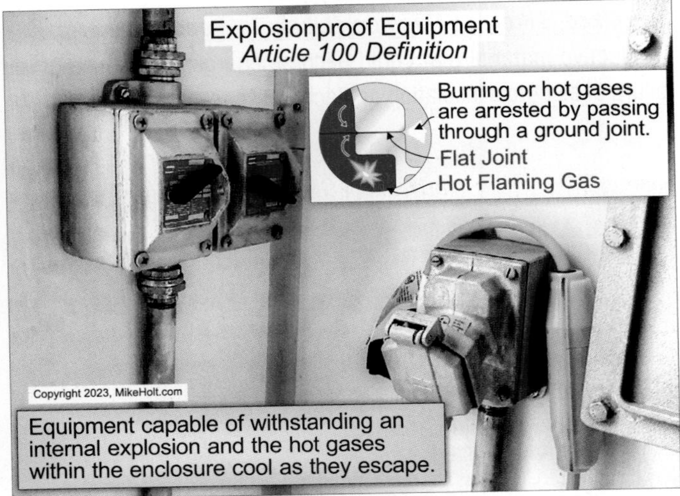

▶Figure 100–80

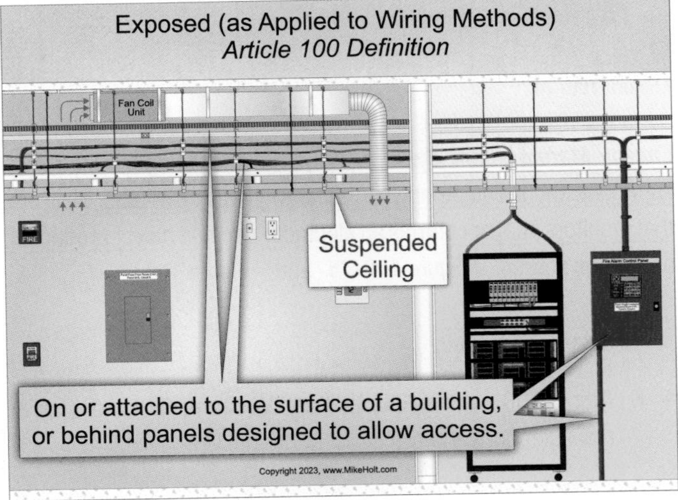

▶Figure 100–81

1st Printing

Fault Current, Available (Available Fault Current). The largest amount of current capable of being delivered at a point on the electrical system during a short-circuit condition. ▸Figure 100–82

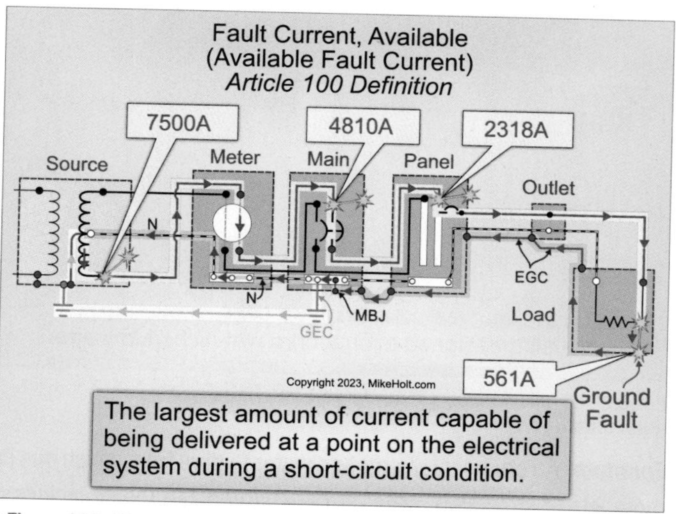

▸Figure 100–82

Feeder. The conductors between a service disconnect, transformer, generator, PV system output circuit, or other power-supply source and the branch-circuit overcurrent protective device. ▸Figure 100–83, ▸Figure 100–84, and ▸Figure 100–85

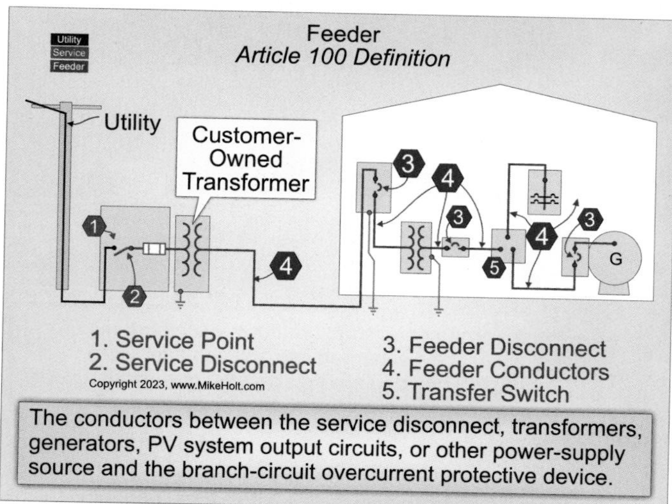

▸Figure 100–83

Fibers/Flyings, Combustible. (Combustible Fibers/Flyings). Fibers/flyings, where any dimension is greater than 500 μm in nominal size, which can form an explosive mixture when suspended in air at standard atmospheric pressure and temperature.

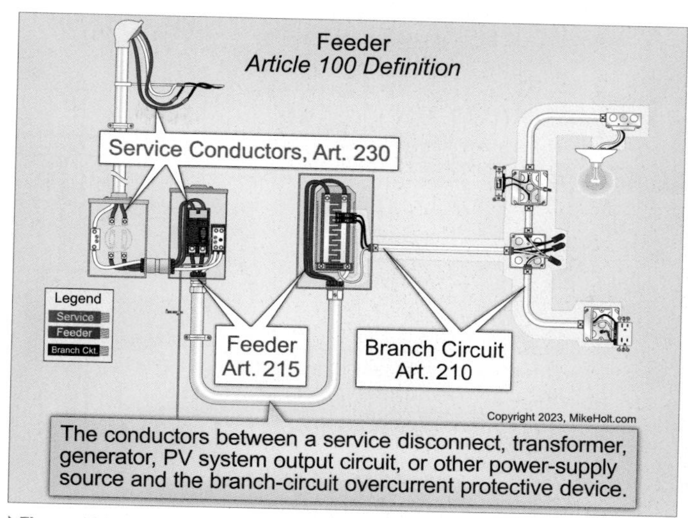

▸Figure 100–84

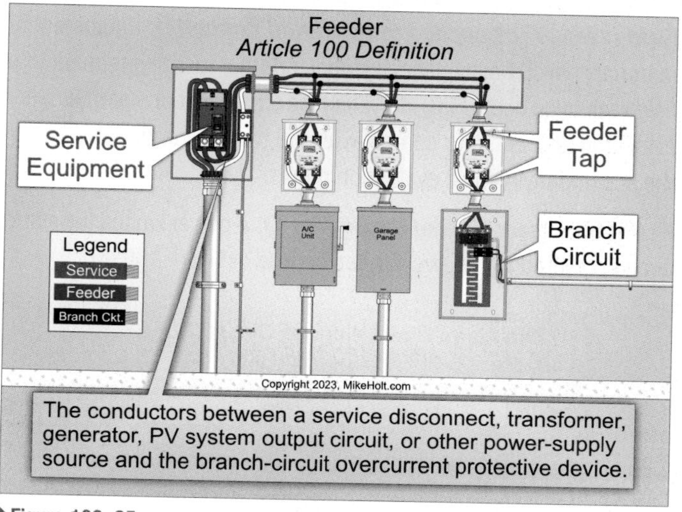

▸Figure 100–85

Fire Alarm Circuit. The wiring connected to equipment powered and controlled by the fire alarm system. ▸Figure 100–86

Author's Comment:

- Article 760 contains the primary requirements for fire alarm systems.

Field Evaluation Body (FEB). An organization (or part of an organization) that performs field evaluations of electrical equipment and materials.

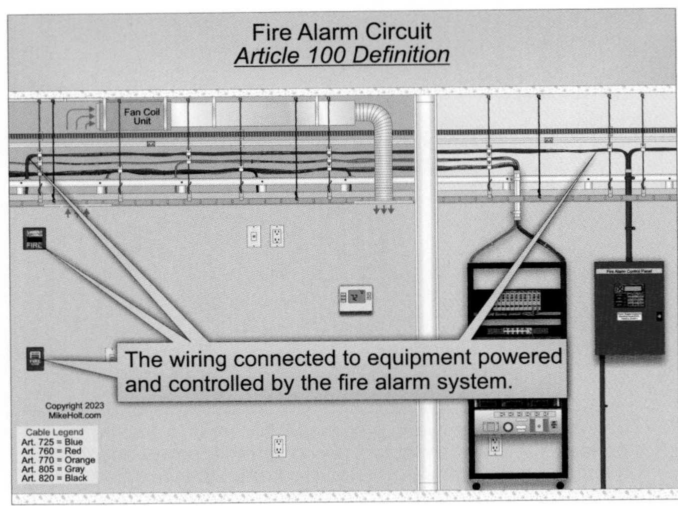

▶Figure 100–86

Field Labeled (as applied to evaluated products). Equipment or materials which have a label, symbol, or other identifying mark of a field evaluation body (FEB) indicating the equipment or materials were evaluated and found to comply with the requirements described in the accompanying field evaluation report.

Fire Alarm Power-Limited Circuit (PLFA). A power-limited fire alarm circuit powered by a power-limited source. ▶Figure 100–87

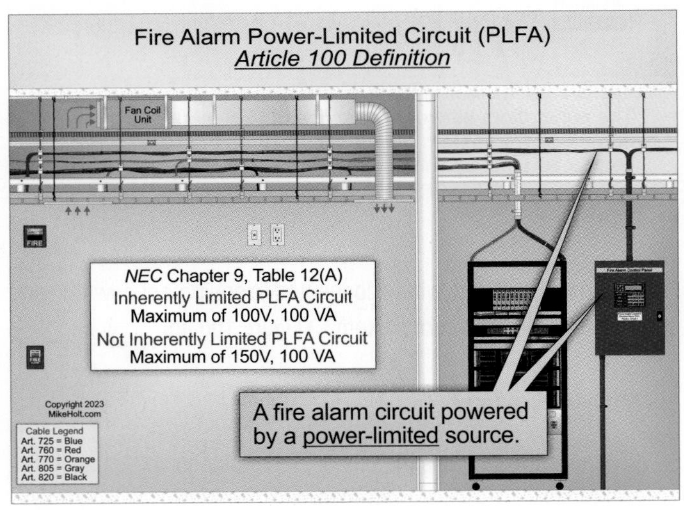

▶Figure 100–87

Note: For requirements on power-limited fire alarm circuits, see 760.121.

Forming Shell. A housing designed to support a wet-niche luminaire (Article 680). ▶Figure 100–88

▶Figure 100–88

Fountain. An ornamental structure water feature from which one or more jets or streams of water are discharged into the air including splash pads, ornamental pools, display pools, or reflection pools. This definition does not include drinking water fountains or water coolers (Article 680). ▶Figure 100–89

▶Figure 100–89

Fuse. An overcurrent protective device with a circuit-opening fusible part that is heated and severed by the passage of overcurrent. ▶Figure 100–90

Garage. A building or portion of a building in which one or more vehicles can be kept for use, sale, storage, rental, repair, exhibition, or demonstration purposes. ▶Figure 100–91

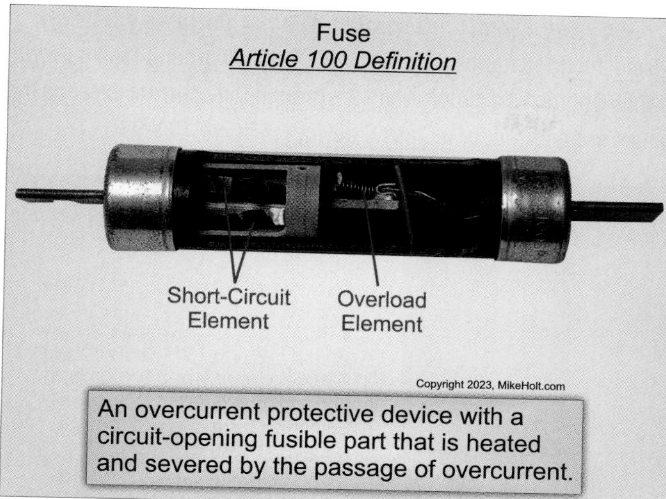
Fuse
Article 100 Definition
Short-Circuit Element
Overload Element
Copyright 2023, MikeHolt.com
An overcurrent protective device with a circuit-opening fusible part that is heated and severed by the passage of overcurrent.

▸Figure 100–90

Garage
Article 100 Definition
GRANTS SAFETY LANE
FRONT END SERVICE
BRAKE SERVICE
Copyright 2023, MikeHolt.com
A building or portion of a building in which one or more vehicles can be kept for use, sale, storage, rental, repair, exhibition, or demonstration purposes.

▸Figure 100–91

Garage, Major Repair (Major Repair Garage). A building or portions of a building where major repairs such as engine overhauls, painting, body and fender work, welding or grinding, and repairs that require draining or emptying of the motor vehicle fuel tank are performed on motor vehicles. This includes associated floor space used for offices, parking, or showrooms.

Garage, Minor Repair (Minor Repair Garage). A building or portions of a building used for lubrication, inspection, and minor automotive maintenance work such as engine tune-ups, replacement of parts, fluid changes (such as oil, antifreeze, transmission fluid, brake fluid, and air-conditioning refrigerants), brake system repairs, tire rotation, and similar routine maintenance work. This includes the associated floor space used for offices, parking, or showrooms.

Generating Capacity, Inverter (Inverter Generating Capacity). The sum of parallel-connected inverter maximum continuous output power at 40°C in watts, kilowatts, volt-amperes, or kilovolt-amperes.

Generator. A machine that converts mechanical energy into electrical energy by means of a prime mover or inverter. ▸Figure 100–92

Generator
Article 100 Definition
GENERAC
Copyright 2023 MikeHolt.com
A machine that uses a prime mover to convert mechanical energy into electrical energy.
Generac

▸Figure 100–92

Ground-Fault Circuit Interrupter (GFCI). A device intended to protect people by de-energizing a circuit when ground-fault current exceeds the value established for a Class A device. ▸Figure 100–93

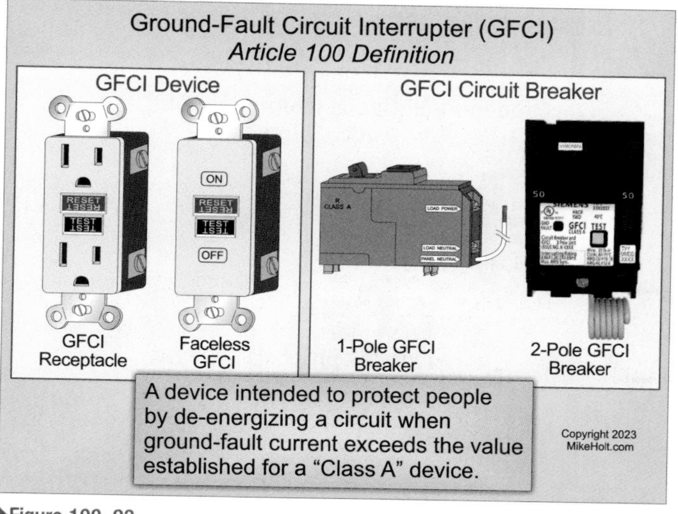
Ground-Fault Circuit Interrupter (GFCI)
Article 100 Definition
GFCI Device
GFCI Circuit Breaker
RESET
TEST
ON
OFF
GFCI Receptacle
Faceless GFCI
1-Pole GFCI Breaker
2-Pole GFCI Breaker
A device intended to protect people by de-energizing a circuit when ground-fault current exceeds the value established for a "Class A" device.
Copyright 2023 MikeHolt.com

▸Figure 100–93

Note: A GFCI opens the circuit when the ground-fault current is 6 mA or higher, and it does not open when the ground-fault current is less than 4 mA. ▸**Figure 100–94**

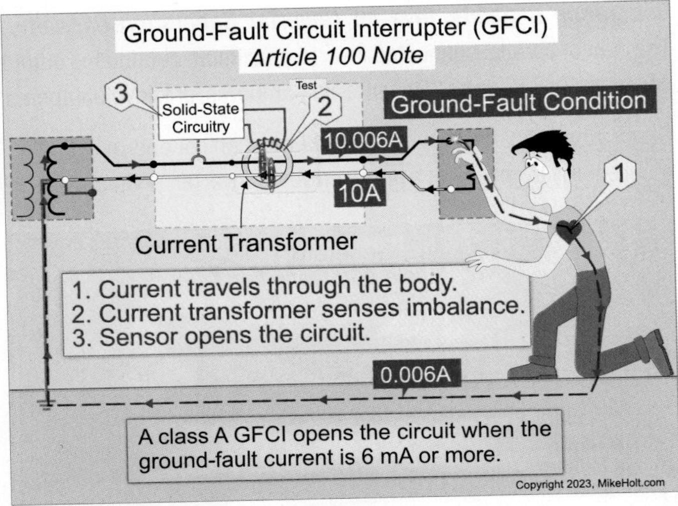
Ground-Fault Circuit Interrupter (GFCI)
Article 100 Note
Solid-State Circuitry
Test
Ground-Fault Condition
10.006A
10A
Current Transformer
1. Current travels through the body.
2. Current transformer senses imbalance.
3. Sensor opens the circuit.
0.006A
A class A GFCI opens the circuit when the ground-fault current is 6 mA or more.
Copyright 2023, MikeHolt.com

▸Figure 100–94

Author's Comment:

- A GFCI-protective device is designed to protect persons against electric shock and operates on the principle of monitoring the unbalanced current between the current-carrying circuit conductors. On a 120V circuit, the GFCI will monitor the unbalanced current between the phase and neutral conductors. On 240V circuits, monitoring is between circuit conductors. Receptacles, circuit breakers, cord sets, and other types of devices that incorporate GFCI protection are commercially available. ▸Figure 100–95

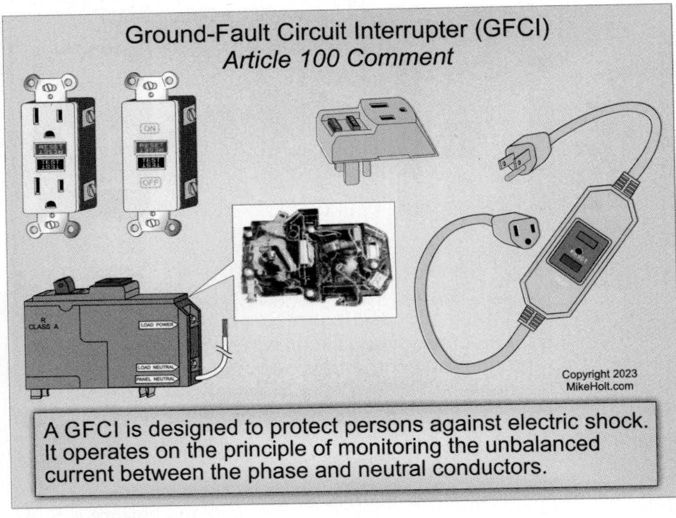
Ground-Fault Circuit Interrupter (GFCI)
Article 100 Comment
Copyright 2023 MikeHolt.com
A GFCI is designed to protect persons against electric shock. It operates on the principle of monitoring the unbalanced current between the phase and neutral conductors.

▸Figure 100–95

- GFCI devices should be tested monthly for functionality as recommended by the manufacturer's instructions.

Ground-Fault Circuit Interrupter, Special Purpose (SPGFCI). A device intended for the detection of 277/480V ground-fault currents that de-energizes a circuit when the ground-fault current exceeds the values established for a Class C device. ▸Figure 100–96

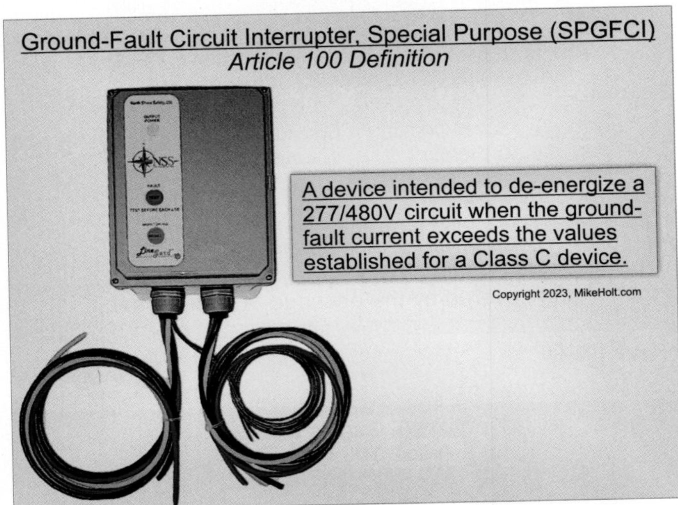
Ground-Fault Circuit Interrupter, Special Purpose (SPGFCI)
Article 100 Definition
A device intended to de-energize a 277/480V circuit when the ground-fault current exceeds the values established for a Class C device.
Copyright 2023, MikeHolt.com

▸Figure 100–96

Author's Comment:

- In accordance with "UL 943C, *Standard for Special Purpose Ground-Fault Circuit Interrupters*," SPGFCIs are engineered to interrupt leakages of 20 mA or greater to reduce the likelihood of electrocution.

Ground-Fault Current Path, Effective (Effective Ground-Fault Current Path). An intentionally constructed low-impedance conductive path designed to carry ground-fault current during a ground-fault event to the power source. The purpose of the effective ground-fault current path is to assist in opening the circuit overcurrent protective device in the event of a ground fault. ▸Figure 100–97

Author's Comment:

- The effective ground-fault current path is intended to help remove dangerous voltage from a ground fault by opening the circuit overcurrent protective device.

Ground-Fault Detector-Interrupter, dc (GFDI). A device that provides protection for PV system dc circuits by detecting a ground fault and could interrupt the fault path in the dc circuit (690).

Ground-Fault Protection of Equipment (GFPE). A device intended to provide protection of equipment from damaging ground faults. ▸Figure 100–98

1st Printing

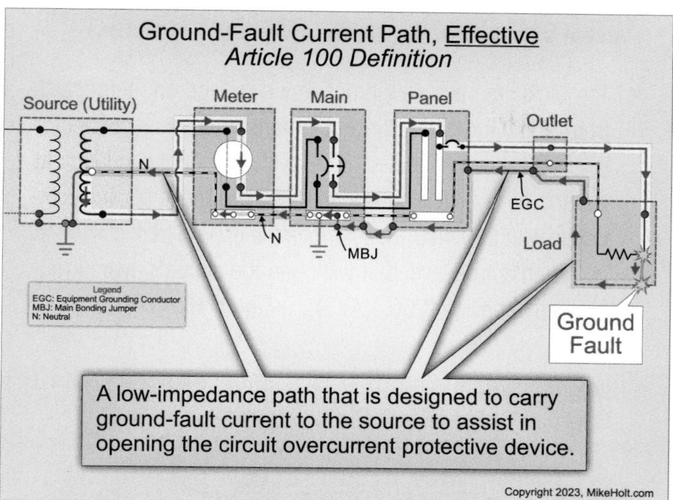
Ground-Fault Current Path, Effective
Article 100 Definition
Source (Utility)
Meter
Main
Panel
Outlet
N
EGC
N
MBJ
Load
Legend
EGC: Equipment Grounding Conductor
MBJ: Main Bonding Jumper
N: Neutral
Ground Fault
A low-impedance path that is designed to carry ground-fault current to the source to assist in opening the circuit overcurrent protective device.
Copyright 2023, MikeHolt.com

▶Figure 100–97

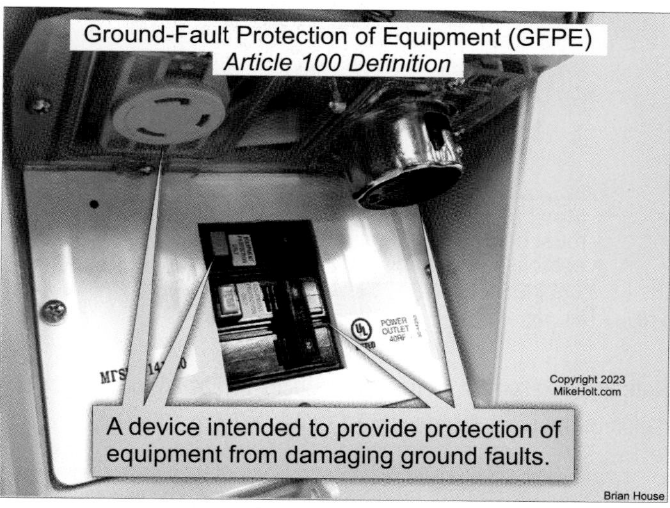
Ground-Fault Protection of Equipment (GFPE)
Article 100 Definition
Copyright 2023 MikeHolt.com
A device intended to provide protection of equipment from damaging ground faults.
Brian House

▶Figure 100–98

Author's Comment:

- This type of protective device is not intended to protect persons because its opening ground-fault trip setting is 30 mA.

Grounded, Functionally (Functionally Grounded). A functionally grounded PV system that has an electrical ground reference for operational purposes that is not solidly grounded.

Note: A functionally grounded PV system is often connected to ground through an electronic means that is internal to an inverter or charge controller which provides ground-fault protection.

Author's Comment:

- Most PV arrays are functionally grounded, the exception is usually going to be a very small, stand-alone (off-grid) PV system.

Grounded (Grounding). Connected to the Earth (ground) or to a conductive body that extends the Earth connection. ▶Figure 100–99

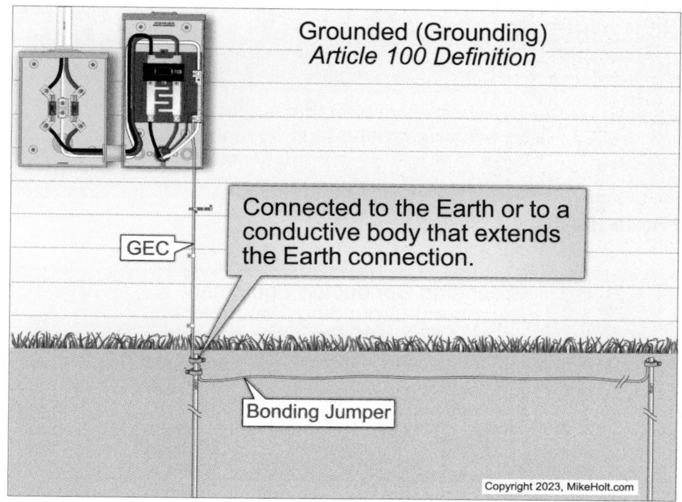
Grounded (Grounding)
Article 100 Definition
Connected to the Earth or to a conductive body that extends the Earth connection.
GEC
Bonding Jumper
Copyright 2023, MikeHolt.com

▶Figure 100–99

Author's Comment:

- An example of a "body that extends the ground (Earth) connection" is a termination to structural steel that is connected to the Earth either directly or by the termination to another grounding electrode in accordance with 250.52.

Grounding Conductor, Equipment (Equipment Grounding Conductor). The conductive path(s) that is part of an effective ground-fault current path. ▶Figure 100–100 and ▶Figure 100–101

Author's Comment:

- Metal enclosures can be part of the effective ground-fault current path. They are used to connect bonding jumpers and equipment grounding conductors but are not actually an equipment grounding conductor [250.109]. ▶Figure 100–102

Note 1: The circuit equipment grounding conductor also performs bonding.

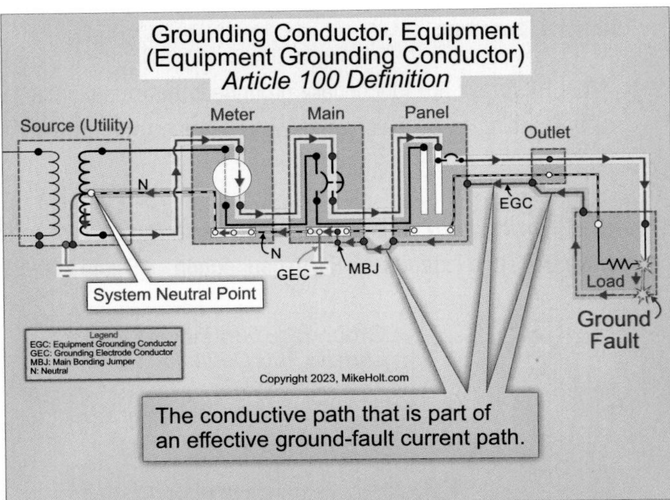

▶Figure 100–100

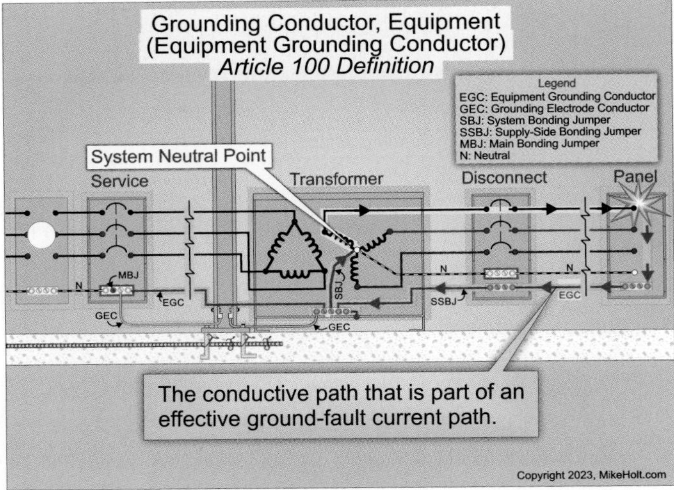

▶Figure 100–101

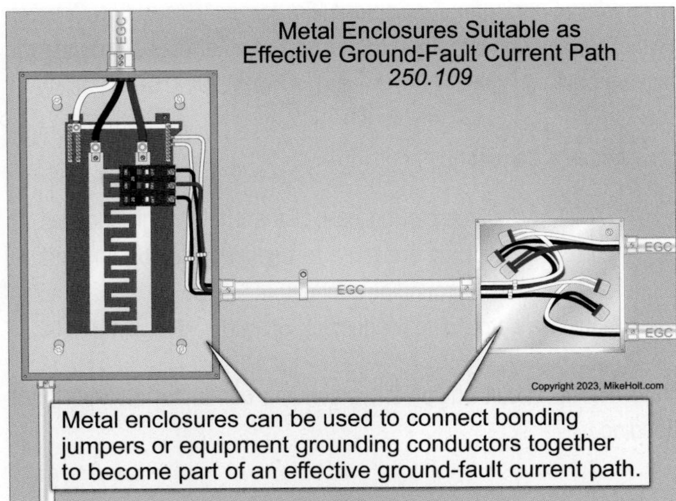

▶Figure 100–102

Author's Comment:

- To quickly remove dangerous touch voltage on metal parts from a ground fault, the equipment grounding conductor (EGC) must be connected to the system neutral conductor at the source and have sufficiently low impedance (Z), in accordance with 250.4(A). This permits the ground-fault current to quickly rise to a level that will open the circuit's overcurrent protective device [250.4(A)(3)]. ▶Figure 100–103

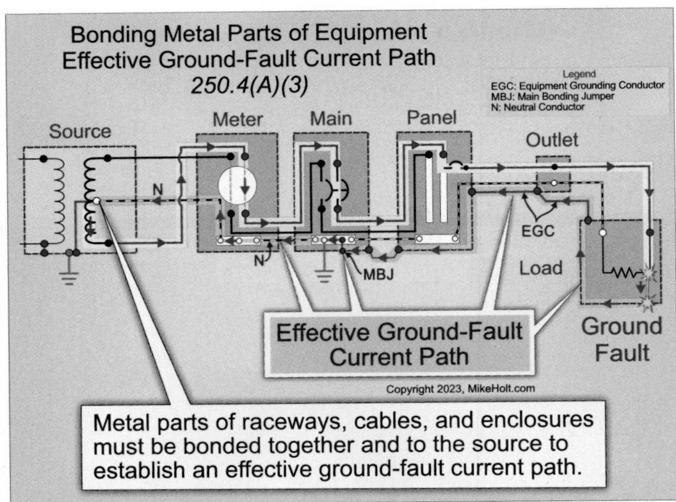

▶Figure 100–103

Note 2: An equipment grounding conductor can be any one or a combination of the types listed in 250.118(A). ▶Figure 100–104

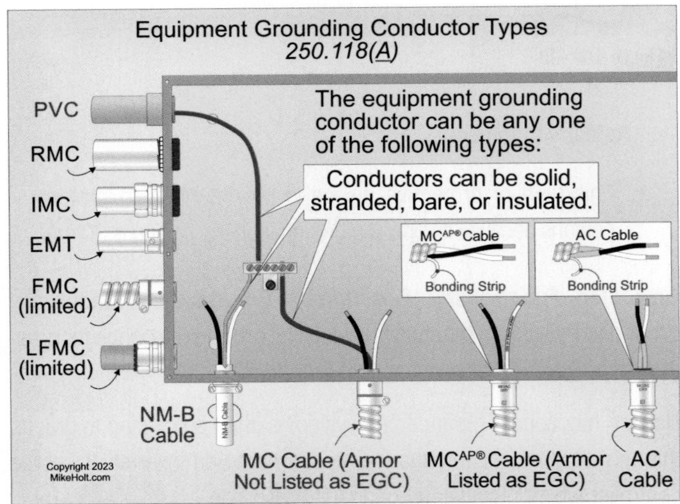

▶Figure 100–104

Author's Comment:

- Equipment grounding conductors include:
  - a bare or insulated conductor
  - rigid metal conduit
  - intermediate metal conduit
  - electrical metallic tubing
  - listed flexible metal conduit as limited by 250.118(A)(5)
  - listed liquidtight flexible metal conduit as limited by 250.118(A)(6)
  - armored cable
  - the copper metal sheath of mineral-insulated cable
  - metal-clad cable as limited by 250.118(A)(10)
  - metal cable trays as limited by 250.118(A)(11) and 392.60
  - electrically continuous metal raceways listed for grounding
  - surface metal raceways listed for grounding
  - metal enclosures

Grounding Electrode. A conducting object used to make a direct electrical connection to the Earth [250.50 through 250.70]. ▶Figure 100–105

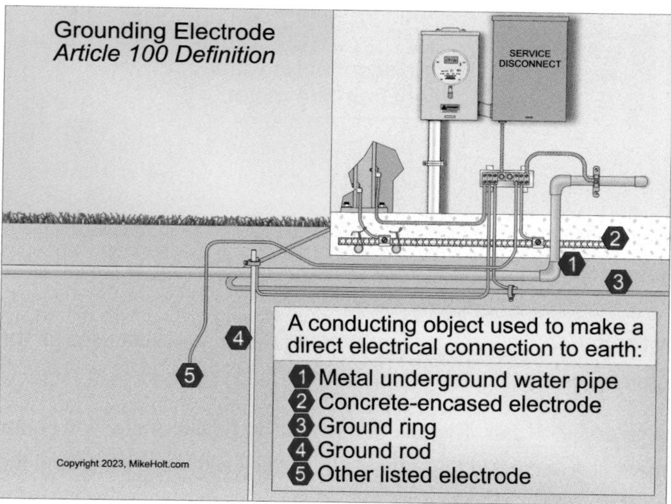

▶Figure 100–105

Grounding Electrode Conductor (GEC). The conductor used to connect the system neutral conductor, grounded-phase conductor, or the equipment to the grounding electrode system. ▶Figure 100–106

Health Care Facilities. Buildings, portions of buildings, or mobile enclosures in which medical, dental, psychiatric, nursing, obstetrical, or surgical care is provided for humans. ▶Figure 100–107

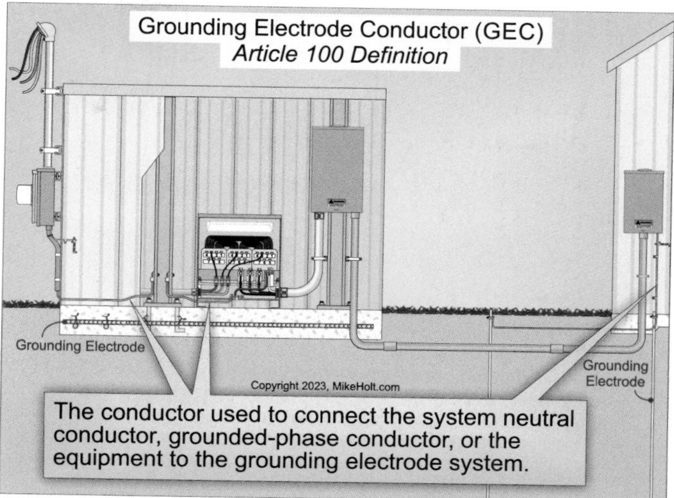

▶Figure 100–106

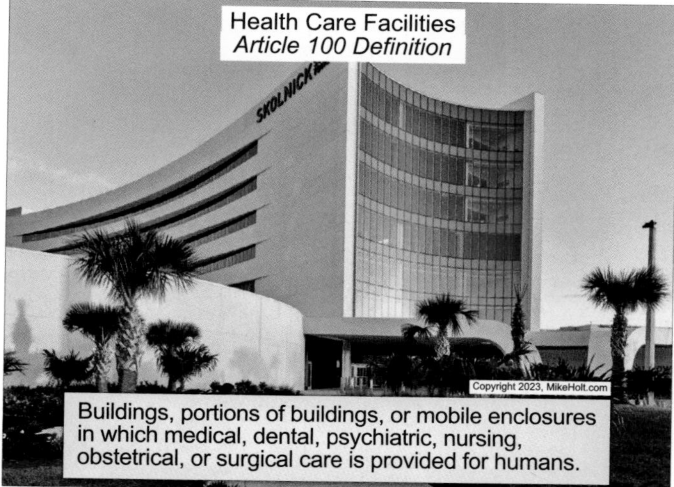

▶Figure 100–107

Note: Examples of health care facilities include, but are not limited to, hospitals, nursing homes, limited-care facilities, supervisory-care facilities, clinics, medical/dental offices, and ambulatory care facilities.

Health Care Facility's Governing Body. The person or persons who have the overall legal responsibility for the operation of a health care facility

Hospital. A building or portion thereof used on a 24-hour basis for the medical, psychiatric, obstetrical, or surgical care of four or more inpatients. ▶Figure 100–108

Hydromassage Bathtub. A permanently installed bathtub with a recirculating piping system designed to accept, circulate, and discharge water after each use (Article 680). ▶Figure 100–109

Identified (as applied to equipment). Recognized as suitable for a specific purpose, function, use, environment, or application. ▶Figure 100–110

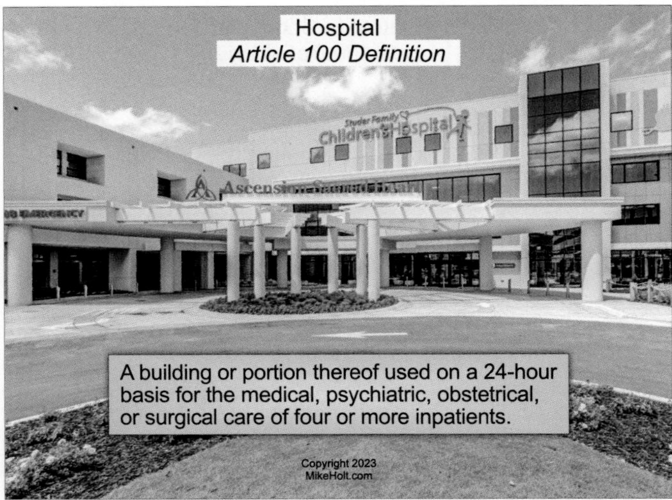
Hospital
Article 100 Definition
A building or portion thereof used on a 24-hour basis for the medical, psychiatric, obstetrical, or surgical care of four or more inpatients.
Copyright 2023 MikeHolt.com

▸Figure 100–108

Hydromassage Bathtub
Article 100 Definition
A permanently installed bathtub with a recirculating piping system designed to accept, circulate, and discharge water after each use.
Copyright 2023 MikeHolt.com

▸Figure 100–109

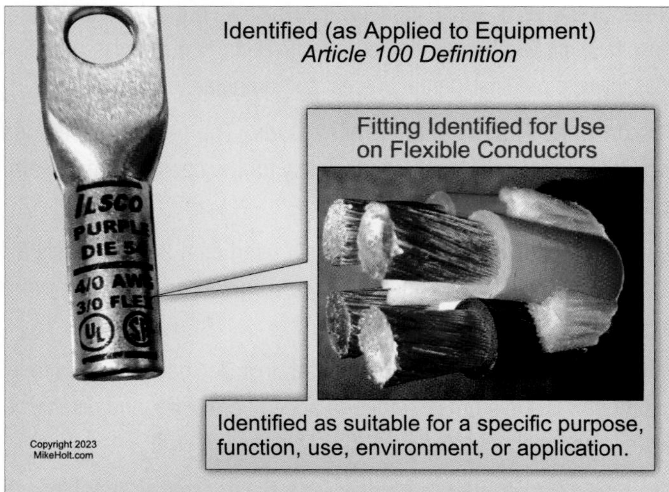
Identified (as Applied to Equipment)
Article 100 Definition
Fitting Identified for Use on Flexible Conductors
Identified as suitable for a specific purpose, function, use, environment, or application.
Copyright 2023 MikeHolt.com

▸Figure 100–110

Author's Comment:

- According to 110.3(A)(1) Note 2, "Suitability of equipment use may be identified by a description marked on, or provided with, a product to identify the suitability of the product for a specific purpose, environment, or application. Special conditions of use or other limitations may be marked on the equipment, in the product instructions, or included in the appropriate listing and labeling information. Suitability of equipment may be evidenced by listing or labeling."

In Sight From (Within Sight From). Equipment that is visible and not more than 50 ft away from other equipment is considered within sight. ▸**Figure 100–111**

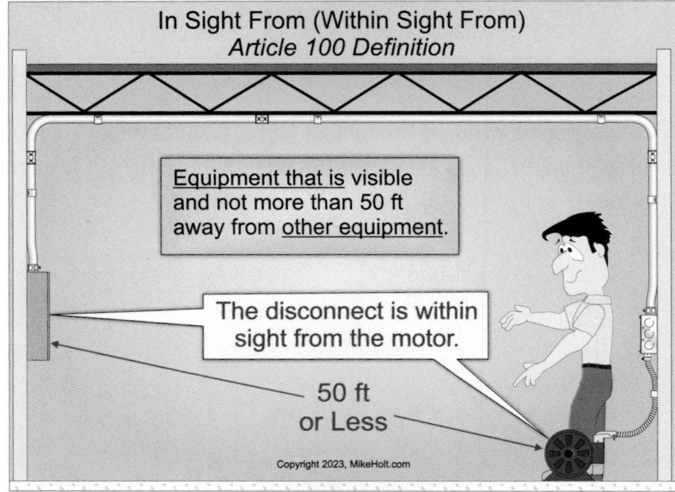
In Sight From (Within Sight From)
Article 100 Definition
Equipment that is visible and not more than 50 ft away from other equipment.
The disconnect is within sight from the motor.
50 ft or Less
Copyright 2023, MikeHolt.com

▸Figure 100–111

Information Technology Equipment (ITE). Equipment used for the creation and manipulation of data, voice, and video. ▸**Figure 100–112**

Interactive Mode. The operating mode for power production equipment or a microgrid that operate in parallel with each other and the electric utility. ▸**Figure 100–113**

Author's Comment:

- A listed interactive (grid tied) inverter automatically stops exporting power upon loss of electric utility voltage and cannot be reconnected until the voltage has been restored. Interactive (grid tied) inverters can automatically or manually resume exporting power to the electric utility once the electric utility source is restored. ▸**Figure 100–114**

 1st Printing

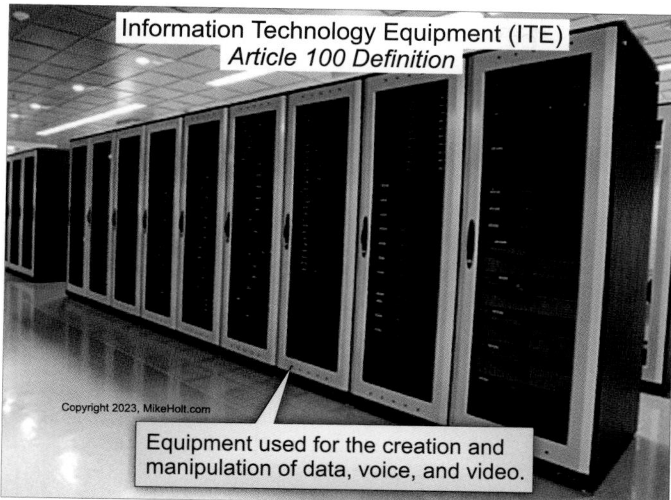
Information Technology Equipment (ITE)
Article 100 Definition
Copyright 2023, MikeHolt.com
Equipment used for the creation and manipulation of data, voice, and video.

▸Figure 100–112

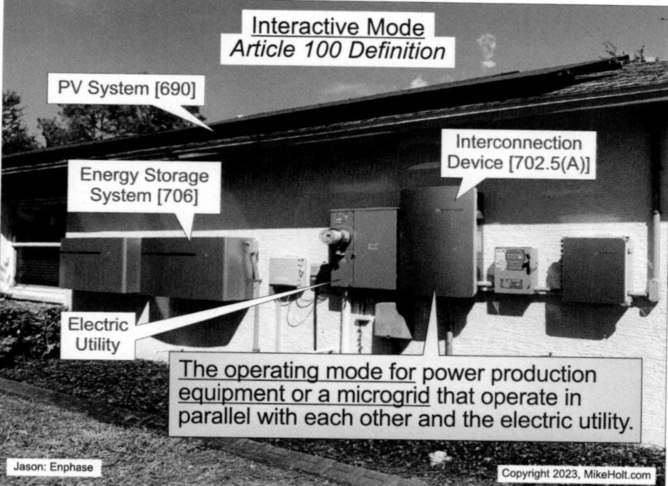
Interactive Mode
Article 100 Definition
PV System [690]
Interconnection Device [702.5(A)]
Energy Storage System [706]
Electric Utility
The operating mode for power production equipment or a microgrid that operate in parallel with each other and the electric utility.
Jason: Enphase
Copyright 2023, MikeHolt.com

▸Figure 100–113

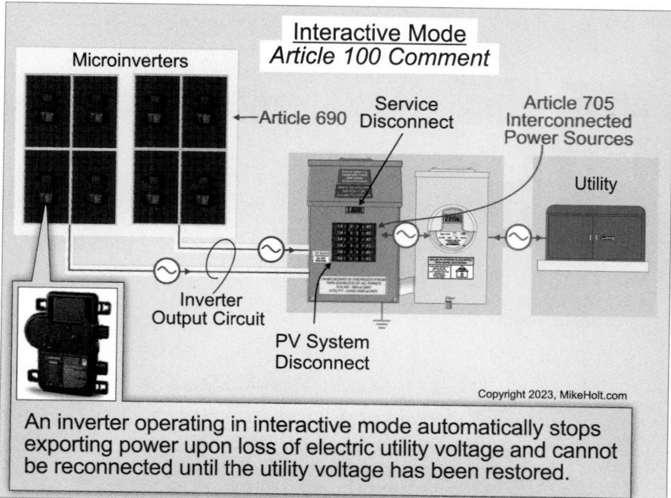
Interactive Mode
Article 100 Comment
Microinverters
Article 690
Service Disconnect
Article 705 Interconnected Power Sources
Utility
Inverter Output Circuit
PV System Disconnect
Copyright 2023, MikeHolt.com
An inverter operating in interactive mode automatically stops exporting power upon loss of electric utility voltage and cannot be reconnected until the utility voltage has been restored.

▸Figure 100–114

Interrupting Rating. The highest fault current at rated voltage the device is identified to safely interrupt under standard test conditions.

Intersystem Bonding Termination. A device that provides a means to connect intersystem bonding conductors for communications systems to the grounding electrode system in accordance with 250.94. ▸Figure 100–115

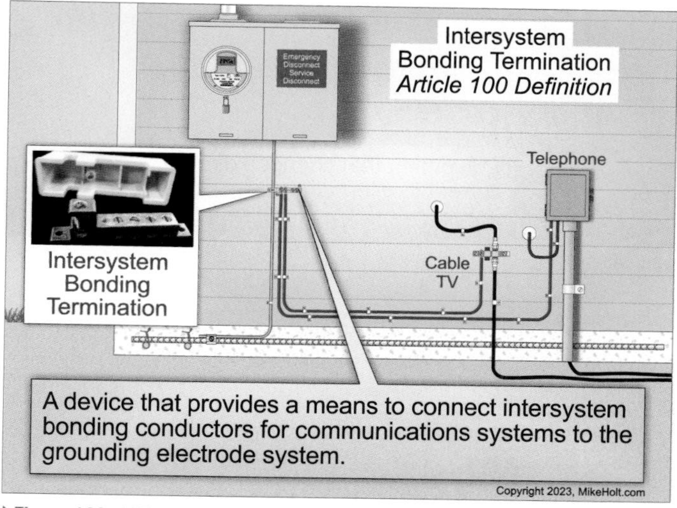
Intersystem Bonding Termination
Article 100 Definition
Telephone
Cable TV
Intersystem Bonding Termination
A device that provides a means to connect intersystem bonding conductors for communications systems to the grounding electrode system.
Copyright 2023, MikeHolt.com

▸Figure 100–115

Inverter. Equipment that changes direct current to alternating current. ▸Figure 100–116 and ▸Figure 100–117

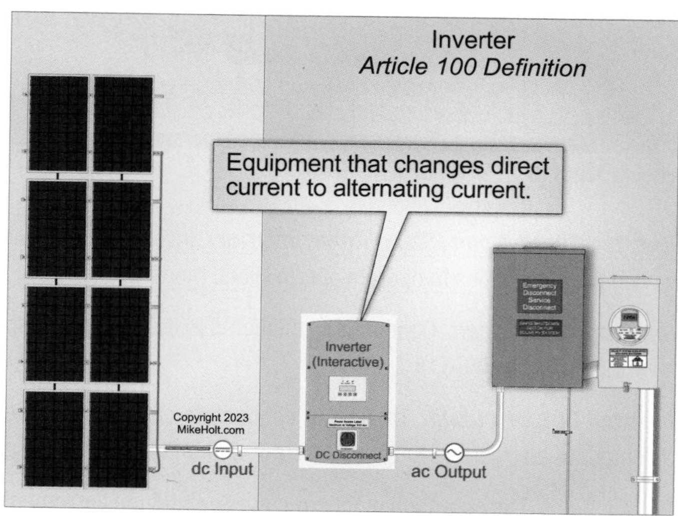
Inverter
Article 100 Definition
Equipment that changes direct current to alternating current.
Inverter (Interactive)
DC Disconnect
Copyright 2023 MikeHolt.com
dc Input
ac Output

▸Figure 100–116

Inverter, Multimode (Multimode Inverter). Multimode inverters are listed to operate in both interactive (grid tied) and island mode (off-grid). ▸Figure 100–118

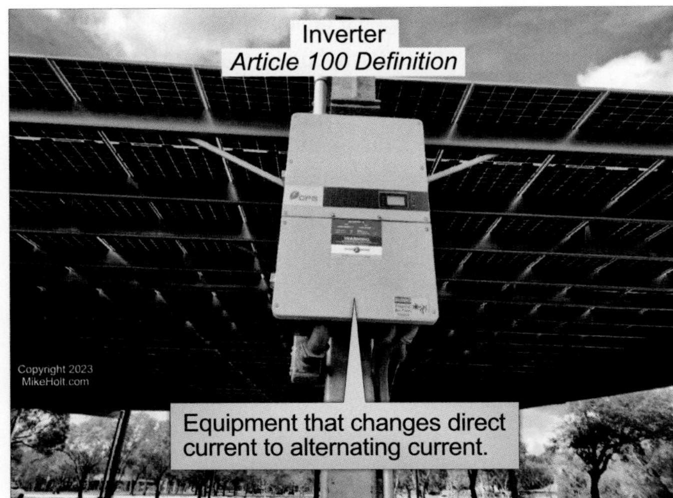

▸Figure 100–117

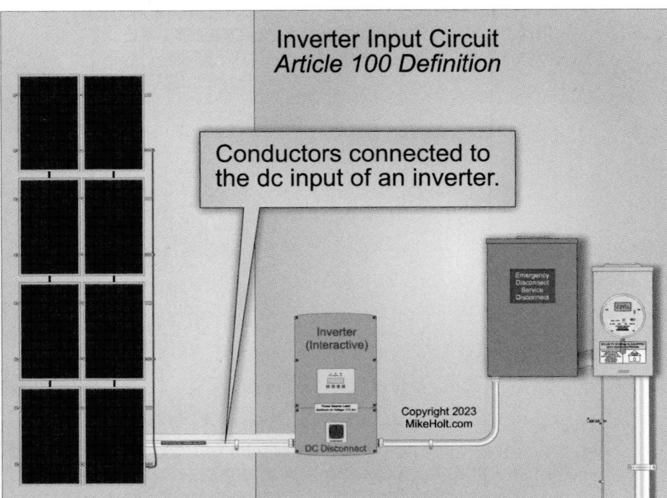

▸Figure 100–119

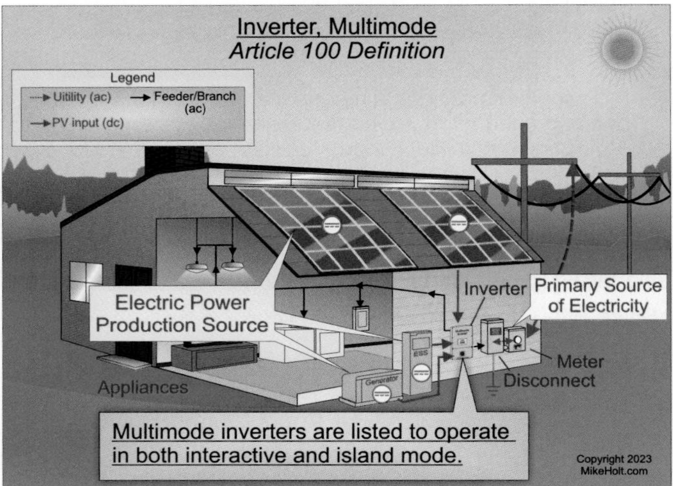

▸Figure 100–118

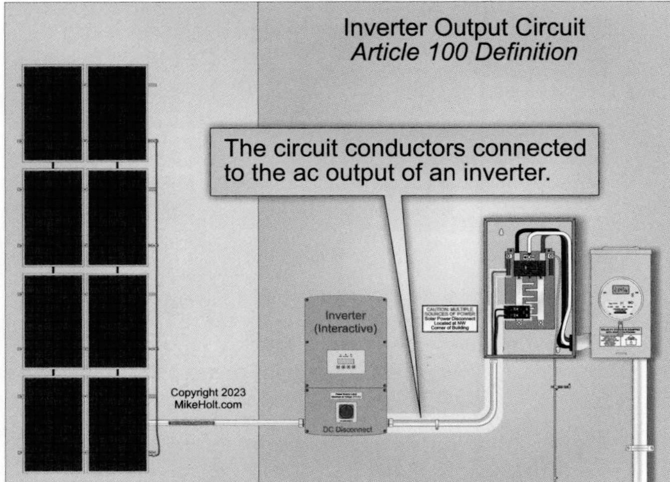

▸Figure 100–120

<u>Inverter, Stand-Alone (Stand-Alone Inverter).</u> <u>Inverter equipment having the capabilities to operate only in island mode.</u>

Inverter Input Circuit. Conductors connected to the dc input of an inverter. ▸Figure 100–119

Inverter Output Circuit. The circuit conductors connected to the ac output of an inverter. ▸Figure 100–120 and ▸Figure 100–121

<u>Island Mode.</u> The <u>operating</u> mode for power production equipment <u>or a microgrid</u> that is disconnected from an electric utility or other primary power source. ▸Figure 100–122

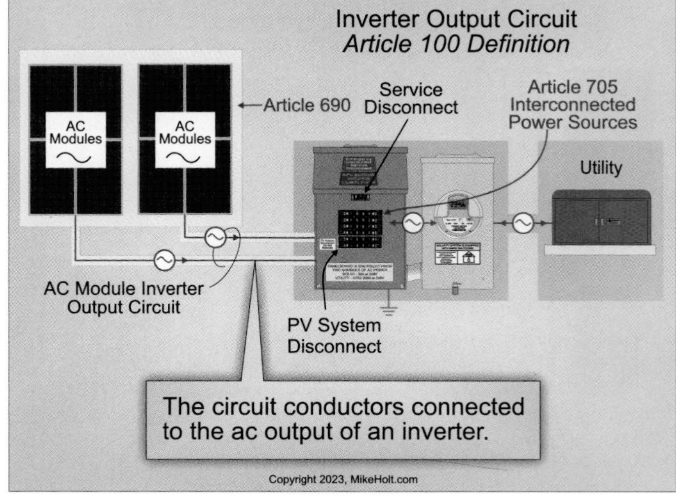

▸Figure 100–121

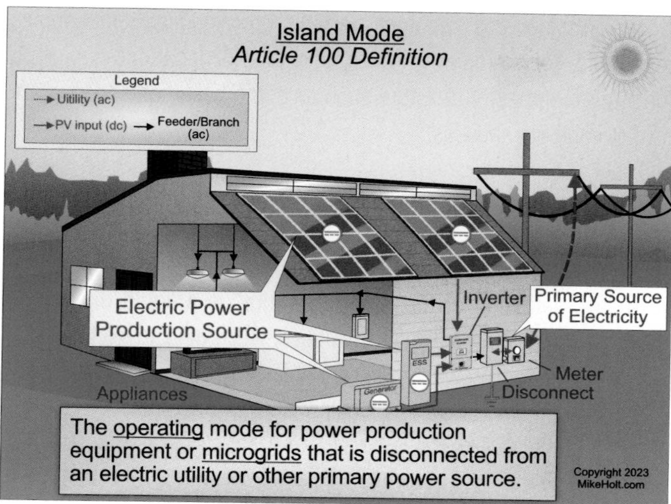
Island Mode
Article 100 Definition
Legend
Utility (ac)
PV input (dc)
Feeder/Branch (ac)
Electric Power Production Source
Inverter
Primary Source of Electricity
Meter
Disconnect
Appliances
The operating mode for power production equipment or microgrids that is disconnected from an electric utility or other primary power source.
Copyright 2023 MikeHolt.com

▶Figure 100–122

Labeled. Equipment or materials that have a label, symbol, or other identifying mark in the form of a sticker, decal, printed label, or with the identifying mark molded or stamped into the product by a recognized testing laboratory acceptable to the authority having jurisdiction. ▶Figure 100–123

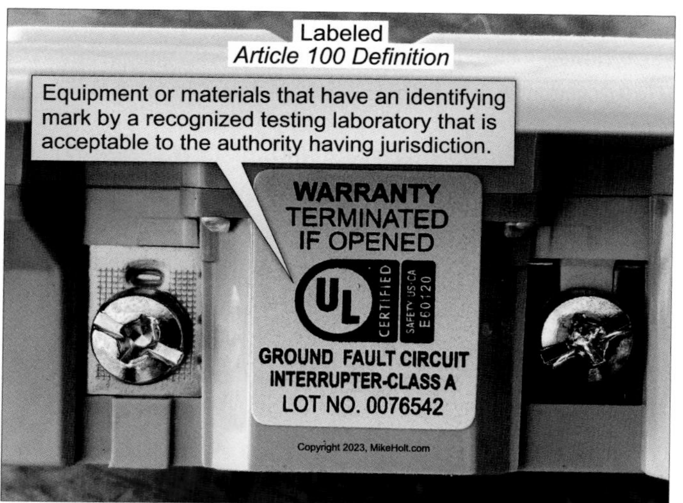
Labeled
Article 100 Definition
Equipment or materials that have an identifying mark by a recognized testing laboratory that is acceptable to the authority having jurisdiction.
WARRANTY TERMINATED IF OPENED
UL
CERTIFIED
SAFETY US-CA
E60120
GROUND FAULT CIRCUIT INTERRUPTER-CLASS A
LOT NO. 0076542
Copyright 2023, MikeHolt.com

▶Figure 100–123

Note: When a listed product is of such a size, shape, material, or surface texture that it is not possible to legibly apply the complete label to the product, it may appear on the smallest unit container in which the product is packaged.

Author's Comment:

- Labeling and listing of equipment typically provide the basis for equipment approval by the authority having jurisdiction [90.4(B), 90.7, 110.2, and 110.3].

Legally Required Standby Systems. A system, classified as legally required by a governmental agency, intended to automatically supply power to selected loads in the event of failure of the normal power source. ▶Figure 100–124

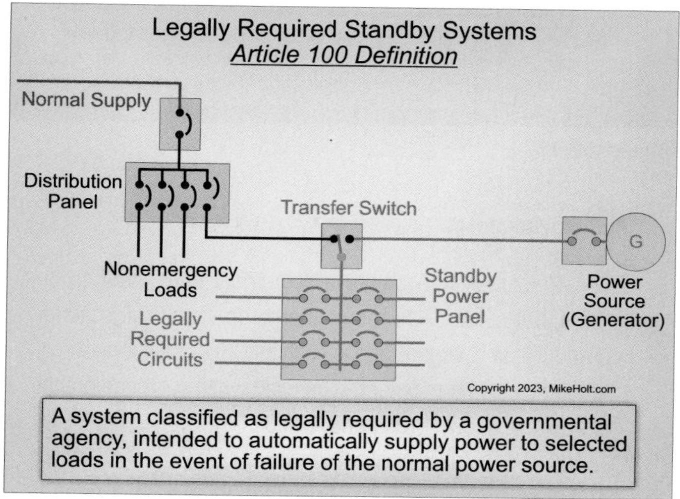
Legally Required Standby Systems
Article 100 Definition
Normal Supply
Distribution Panel
Transfer Switch
G
Nonemergency Loads
Legally Required Circuits
Standby Power Panel
Power Source (Generator)
Copyright 2023, MikeHolt.com
A system classified as legally required by a governmental agency, intended to automatically supply power to selected loads in the event of failure of the normal power source.

▶Figure 100–124

Author's Comment:

- Legally required standby systems typically supply loads such as heating and refrigeration systems, ventilation and smoke removal systems, sewage disposal, lighting systems, and industrial processes that, when stopped, could create hazards or hamper rescue or firefighting operations.

Limited-Care Facility. A building or an area of a building used for the housing, on a 24-hour basis, of four or more persons who are incapable of self-preservation because of age, physical limitations due to accident or illness, or limitations such as intellectual disability, developmental disability, mental illness, or chemical dependency (Article 517). ▶Figure 100–125

Listed. Equipment or materials included in a list published by a recognized testing laboratory acceptable to the authority having jurisdiction. The listing organization must periodically inspect the production of listed equipment or material to ensure they meet appropriate designated standards and suitable for a specified purpose.

▶Figure 100–125

Author's Comment:

- The *NEC* does not require all electrical equipment to be listed, but some *Code* requirements do specifically call for product listing. Organizations such as OSHA are increasingly requiring listed equipment to be used when such equipment is available [90.7, 110.2, and 110.3].

Live Parts. Energized conductive components.

Location, Damp (Damp Location). Locations protected from weather and not subject to saturation with water or other liquids, but subject to moderate degrees of moisture. ▶**Figure 100–126**

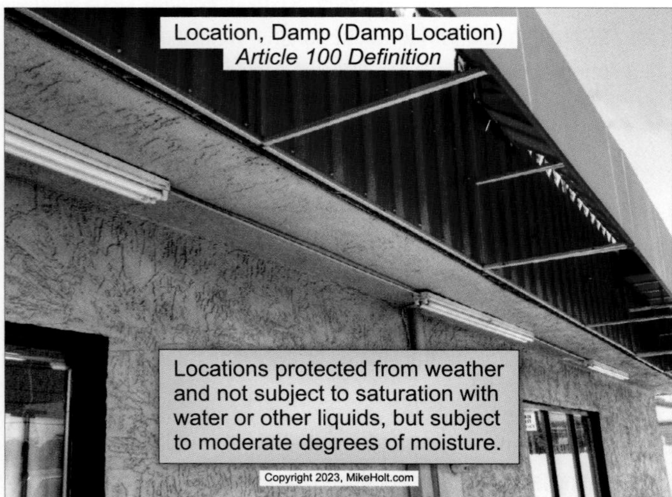

▶Figure 100–126

Note: This includes locations partially protected under canopies, marquees, roofed open porches, and interior locations subject to moderate degrees of moisture such as some basements, barns, and cold-storage warehouses.

Author's Comment:

- The key to understanding a damp location is to know that the definition of the term "moisture" is a liquid diffused or condensed in small quantities. According to Webster's Dictionary (www.merriam-webster.com), "liquid diffused or condensed in relatively small quantity."

Location, Dry (Dry Location). **An area not normally subjected to dampness or wetness, but which may temporarily be subjected to dampness or wetness, such as a building under construction.**

Author's Comment:

- Wiring methods and equipment that are listed for dry location use only are permitted to be installed in a building under construction even if the building is subject to temporary dampness or wetness, as it is still considered a dry location. However, the equipment must be protected from damage in accordance with 110.11.

Locations, Hazardous (Classified) Hazardous (Classified) Locations). Locations where fire or explosion hazards might exist due to flammable gases, flammable liquid-produced vapors, combustible liquid-produced vapors, combustible dusts, combustible fiber/flyings, or ignitible fibers/flyings. ▶**Figure 100–127**

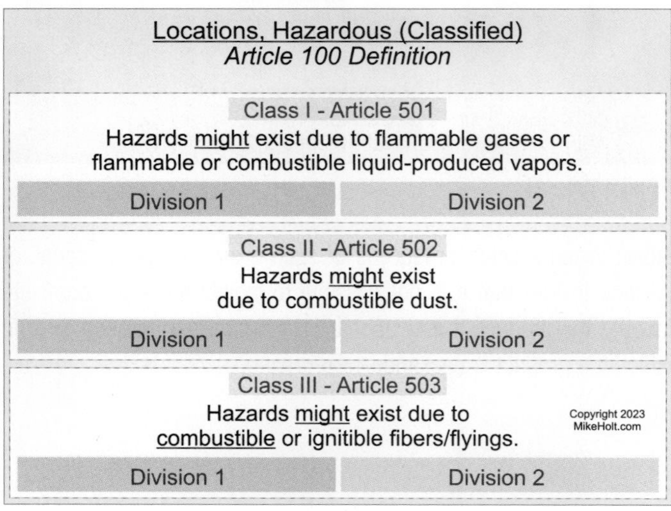

Locations, Hazardous (Classified)
Article 100 Definition
Class I - Article 501
Hazards might exist due to flammable gases or flammable or combustible liquid-produced vapors.
Division 1
Division 2
Class II - Article 502
Hazards might exist due to combustible dust.
Division 1
Division 2
Class III - Article 503
Hazards might exist due to combustible or ignitible fibers/flyings.
Copyright 2023 MikeHolt.com
Division 1
Division 2

▶Figure 100–127

Author's Comment:

- Article 500 contains important information about hazardous (classified) locations.

Location, Wet (Wet Location). A location that is one or more of the following: ▶Figure 100–128 and ▶Figure 100–129

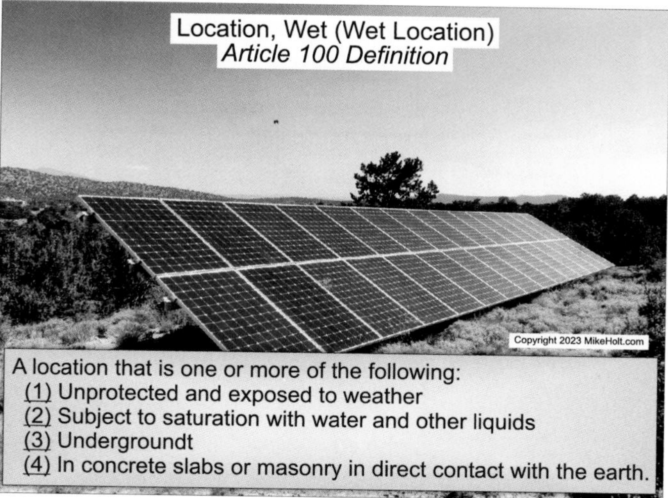

▶Figure 100–128

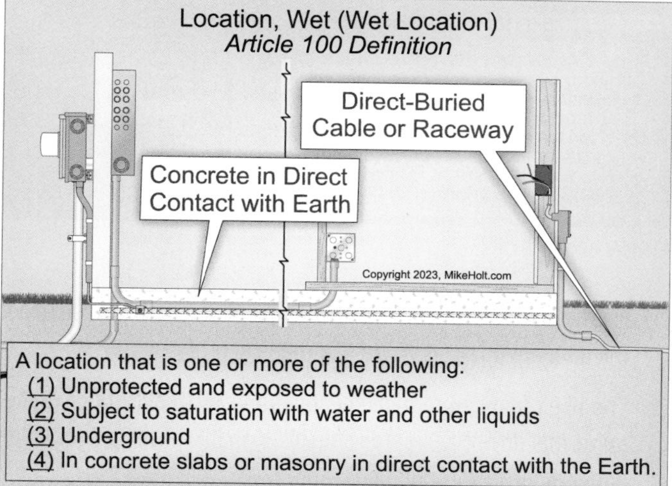

▶Figure 100–129

(1) Unprotected and exposed to weather

(2) Subject to saturation with water and other liquids

(3) Underground

(4) In concrete slabs or masonry in direct contact with the Earth

Note: A vehicle washing area is an example of a wet location saturated with water or other liquids.

Low-Voltage Contact Limit. A voltage not exceeding the following values (Article 680): ▶Figure 100–130

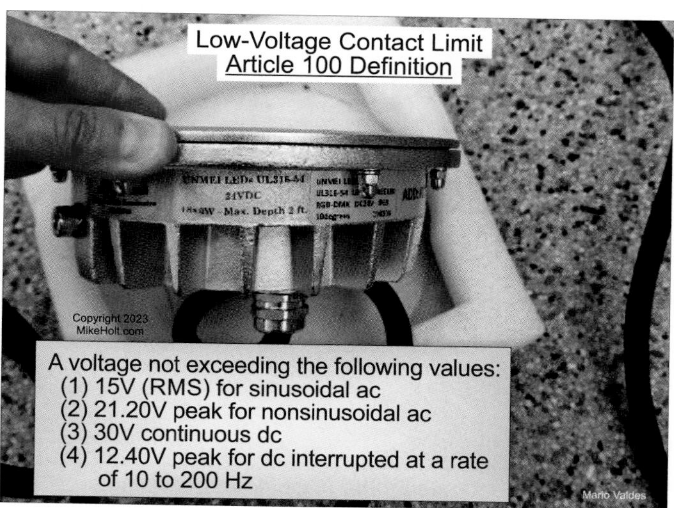

▶Figure 100–130

(1) 15V (RMS) for sinusoidal alternating current

(2) 21.20V peak for nonsinusoidal alternating current

(3) 30V for continuous direct current

(4) 12.40V peak for direct current that is interrupted at a rate of 10 to 200 Hz

Luminaire. A lighting unit consisting of parts to position, protect, and distribute the light source connected to the power supply. ▶Figure 100–131

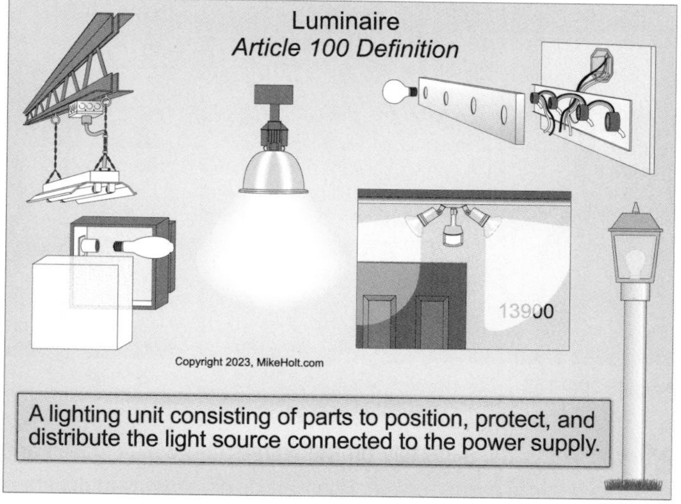

▶Figure 100–131

Luminaire, Wet-Niche (Wet-Niche Luminaire). A luminaire intended to be installed in a forming shell where it will be surrounded by water (Article 680). ▶Figure 100–132

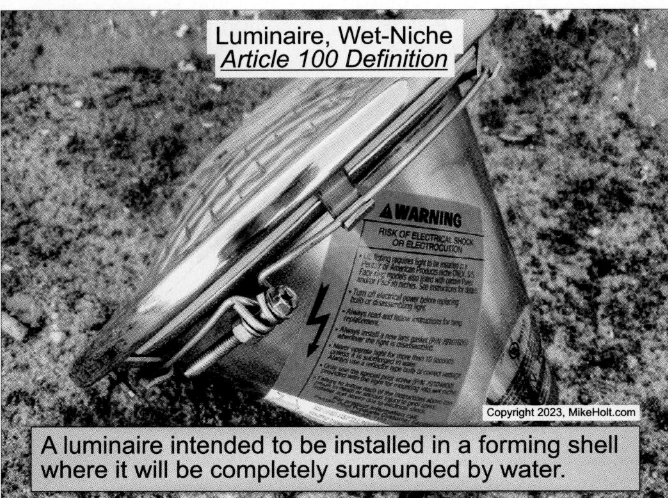
Luminaire, Wet-Niche
Article 100 Definition
Copyright 2023, MikeHolt.com
A luminaire intended to be installed in a forming shell where it will be completely surrounded by water.

▶Figure 100–132

Manufactured Wiring System. A system used for the connection of luminaires, utilization equipment, and devices that are assembled by a manufacturer with components which cannot be inspected at the building site without damage to, or destruction of, the component (Article 604). ▶Figure 100–133

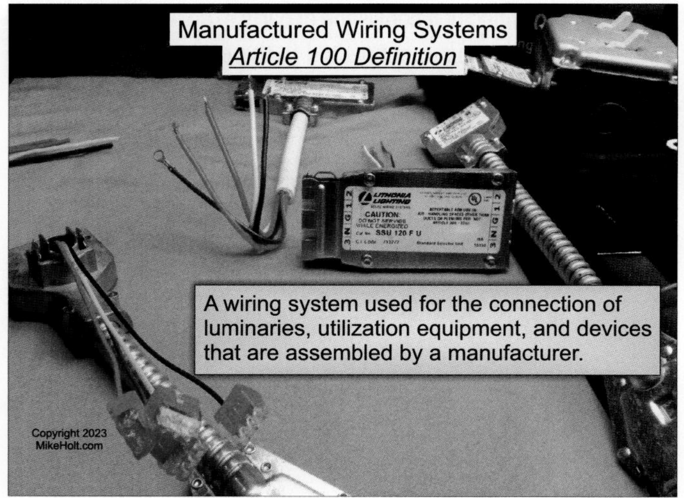
Manufactured Wiring Systems
Article 100 Definition
A wiring system used for the connection of luminaries, utilization equipment, and devices that are assembled by a manufacturer.
Copyright 2023 MikeHolt.com

▶Figure 100–133

Marina. A facility, generally on the waterfront, which stores and services boats in berths, on moorings, and in dry storage or dry stack storage (Article 555). ▶Figure 100–134

Medical Office. A building or part thereof in which the following occur: ▶Figure 100–135

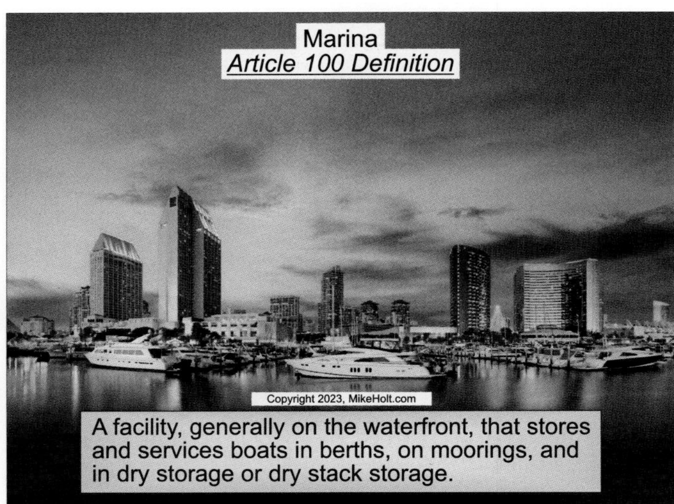
Marina
Article 100 Definition
Copyright 2023, MikeHolt.com
A facility, generally on the waterfront, that stores and services boats in berths, on moorings, and in dry storage or dry stack storage.

▶Figure 100–134

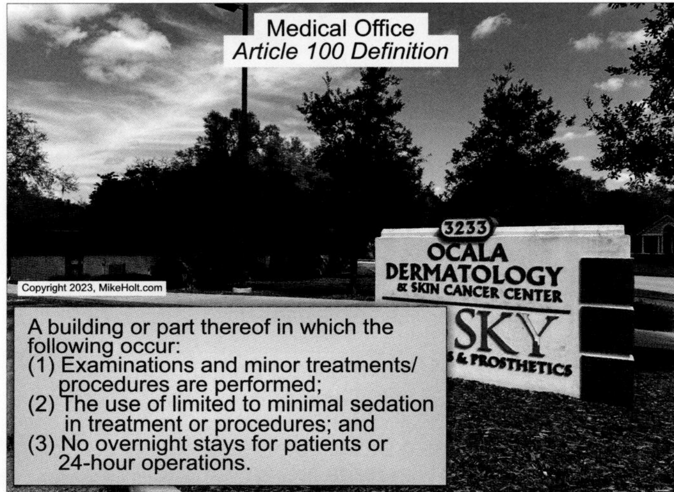
Medical Office
Article 100 Definition
3233
OCALA
DERMATOLOGY
& SKIN CANCER CENTER
Copyright 2023, MikeHolt.com
A building or part thereof in which the following occur:
(1) Examinations and minor treatments/ procedures are performed;
(2) The use of limited to minimal sedation in treatment or procedures; and
(3) No overnight stays for patients or 24-hour operations.

▶Figure 100–135

(1) Examinations and minor treatments/procedures performed under the continuous supervision of a medical professional;

(2) The use of limited to minimal sedation and treatment or procedures that do not render the patient incapable of self-preservation under emergency conditions; and

(3) No overnight stays for patients or 24-hour operations.

Microgrid. An electric power source system capable of operating in island (off-grid) or interactive (grid tied) mode with the electric utility. ▶Figure 100–136

Note 2: Examples of microgrid power sources include photovoltaic systems, energy storage systems, generators, electric vehicles that are used as a source of supply.

1st Printing

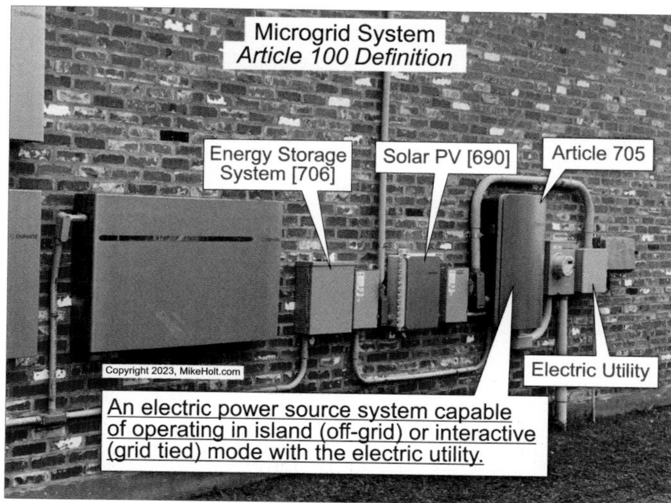
Microgrid System
Article 100 Definition
Energy Storage System [706]
Solar PV [690]
Article 705
Electric Utility
Copyright 2023, MikeHolt.com
An electric power source system capable of operating in island (off-grid) or interactive (grid tied) mode with the electric utility.

▸Figure 100–136

Microgrid Interconnect Device (MID). A device that enables a microgrid system to disconnect from and reconnect to an interconnected primary power source. ▸Figure 100–137 and ▸Figure 100–138

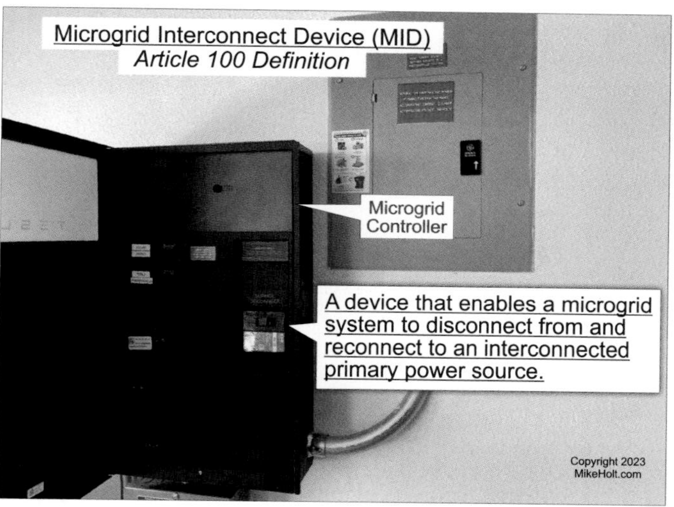
Microgrid Interconnect Device (MID)
Article 100 Definition
Microgrid Controller
A device that enables a microgrid system to disconnect from and reconnect to an interconnected primary power source.
Copyright 2023 MikeHolt.com

▸Figure 100–137

Module, Alternating-Current (Alternating-Current Module). A module consisting of solar cells, inverter, and other components designed to produce alternating-current power (Article 690). ▸Figure 100–139

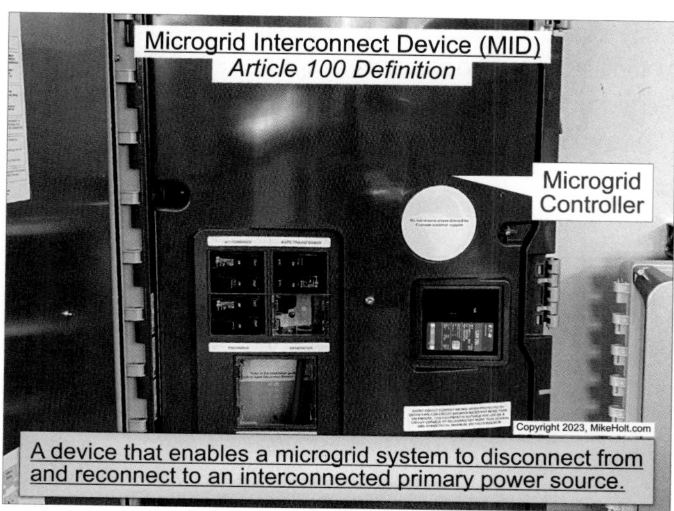
Microgrid Interconnect Device (MID)
Article 100 Definition
Microgrid Controller
Copyright 2023, MikeHolt.com
A device that enables a microgrid system to disconnect from and reconnect to an interconnected primary power source.

▸Figure 100–138

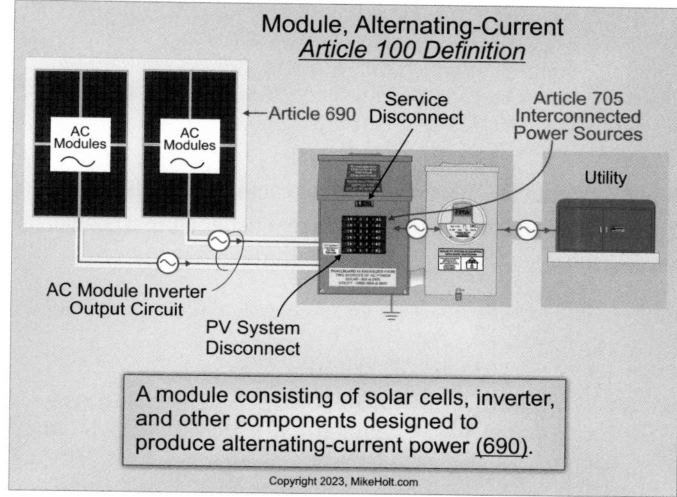
Module, Alternating-Current
Article 100 Definition
AC Modules
AC Modules
Article 690
Service Disconnect
Article 705 Interconnected Power Sources
Utility
AC Module Inverter Output Circuit
PV System Disconnect
A module consisting of solar cells, inverter, and other components designed to produce alternating-current power (690).
Copyright 2023, MikeHolt.com

▸Figure 100–139

Author's Comment:

- Alternating-current modules are connected in parallel with each other and in parallel with the electric utility in an interactive (grid tied) mode. These modules operate interactively with the electric utility, meaning the ac output current from the ac module will cease exporting power upon sensing the loss of voltage from the electric utility.
- Manufacturer's instructions for ac modules will specify the size of the dedicated branch circuit on which they are to be connected and the maximum number of ac modules permitted on the branch circuit.

Motor Fuel Dispensing Facility. That portion of a property where motor fuels are stored and dispensed from fixed equipment into the fuel tanks of motor vehicles, marine craft, or into approved containers. ▸**Figure 100–140**

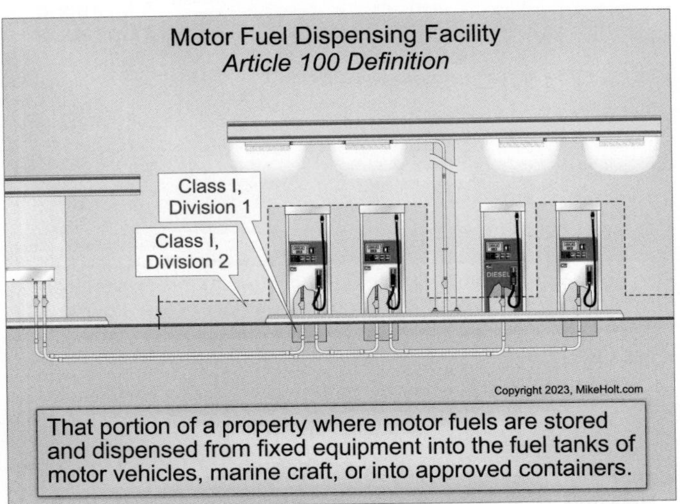

▸**Figure 100–140**

Neutral Conductor. The conductor connected to the neutral point of a system that is intended to carry current under normal conditions. ▸**Figure 100–141**

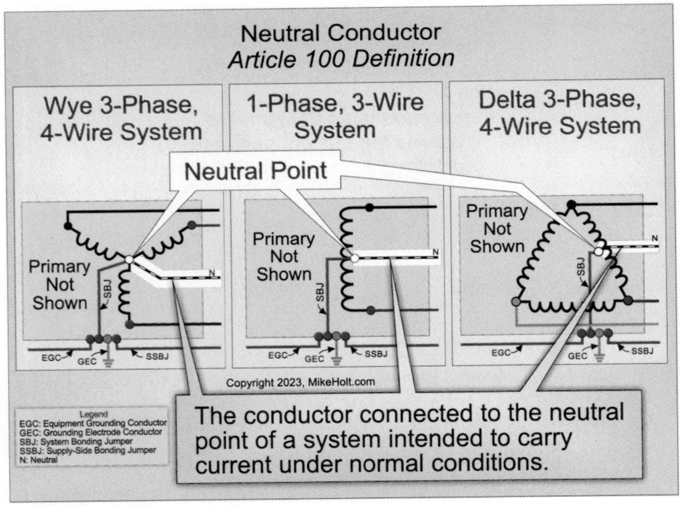

▸**Figure 100–141**

Neutral Point. The common point of a 4-wire, three-phase, wye-connected system; the midpoint of a 3-wire, single-phase system; or the midpoint of the single-phase portion of a three-phase, delta-connected system. ▸**Figure 100–142**

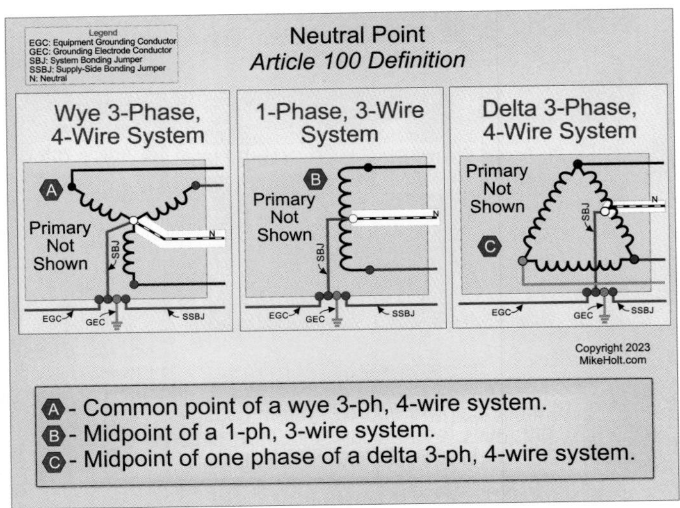

▸**Figure 100–142**

Nursing Home. A building or portion of a building used on a 24-hour basis for the housing and nursing care of four or more persons who, because of mental or physical incapacity, might be unable to provide for their own needs and safety without the assistance of another person. ▸**Figure 100–143**

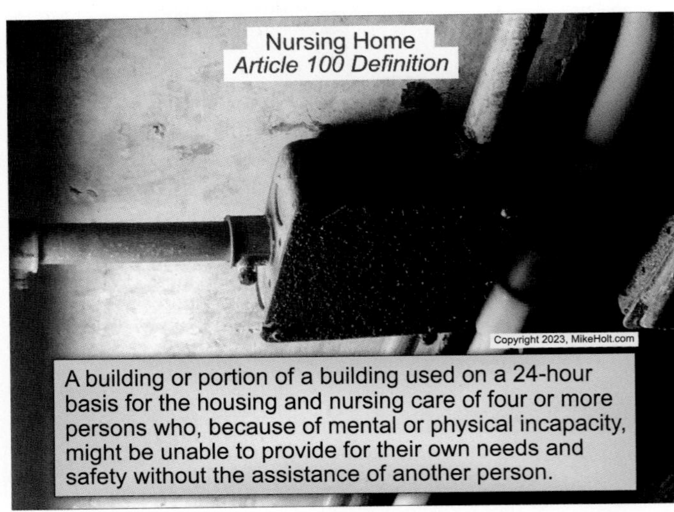

▸**Figure 100–143**

Optional Standby Systems. A system intended to supply power where life safety does not depend on the performance of the system. ▸**Figure 100–144** and ▸**Figure 100–145**

1st Printing

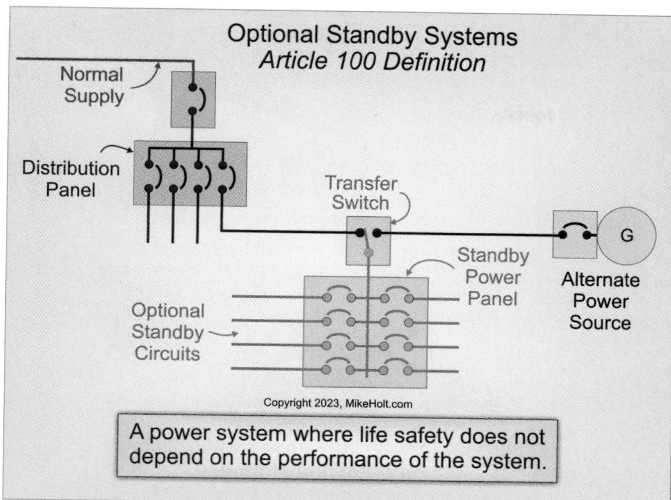

▸Figure 100–144

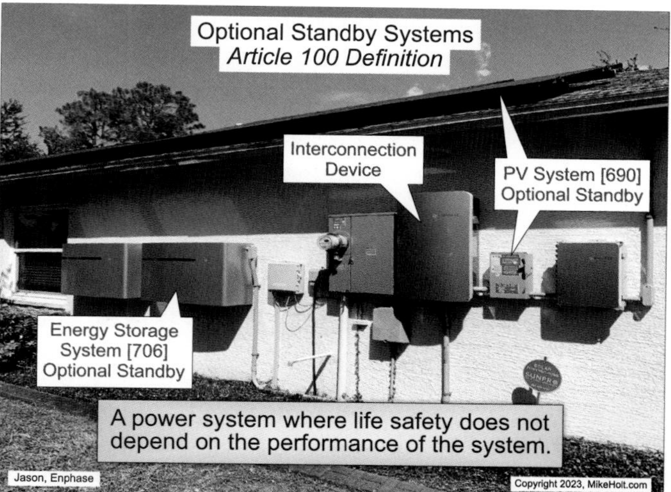

▸Figure 100–145

Author's Comment:

- Optional standby systems are typically installed to provide an alternate source of electric power for such facilities as industrial/commercial buildings, farms, and residences. It serves loads such as heating and refrigeration systems, data processing, and industrial processes that when stopped during any power outage can cause discomfort, economic loss, serious interruption of the process, damage to the product or process, or the like.

Overcurrent. Current in excess of the equipment's ampere rating or a conductor's ampacity caused by an overload, short circuit, or ground fault. ▸**Figure 100–146**

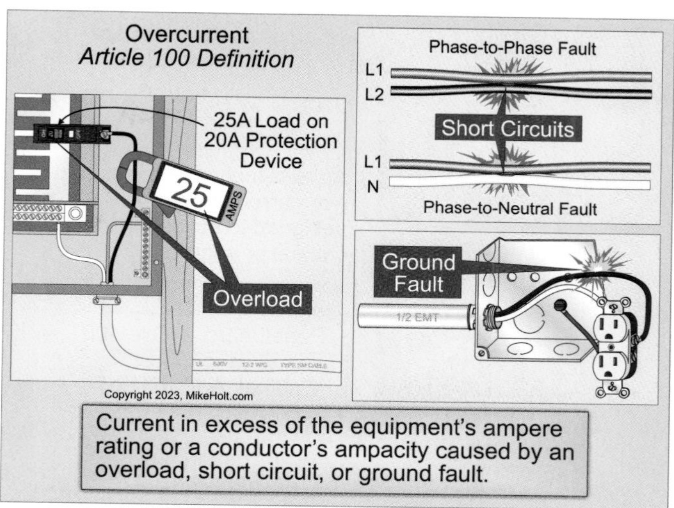

▸Figure 100–146

Overcurrent Protective Device, Branch-Circuit (Branch-Circuit Overcurrent Protective Device). A device capable of providing protection from an overload, short circuit, or ground fault for service, feeder, and branch circuits.

Overload. An overload occurs when equipment operates above its ampere rating or current in excess of a conductor's ampacity. A short circuit or ground fault is not an overload. ▸**Figure 100–147**

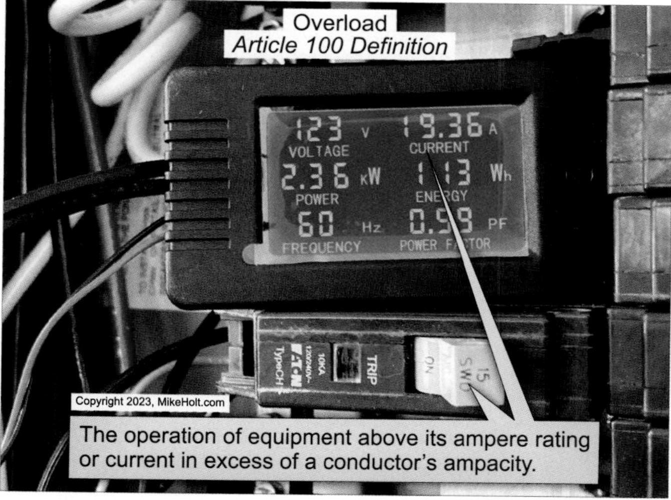

▸Figure 100–147

Panelboard. An assembly with buses and overcurrent protective devices designed to be placed in a cabinet or enclosure. ▸**Figure 100–148**

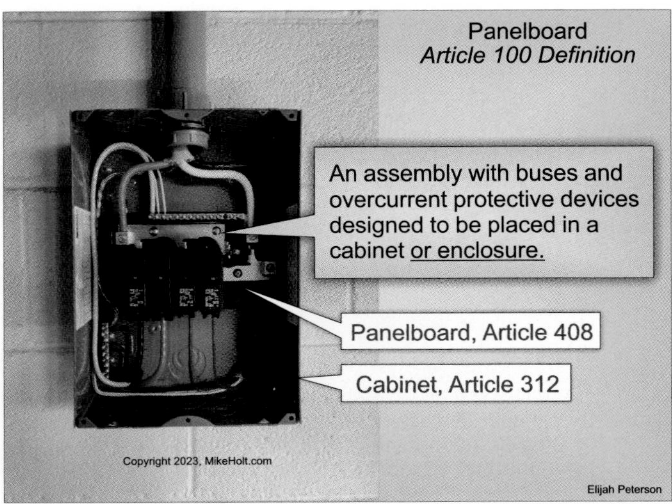

▶Figure 100–148

Author's Comment:

- The slang term in the electrical field for a panelboard is "the guts." The requirements for panelboards are contained in Article 408.

Patient Bed Location. The location of an inpatient sleeping bed of a Category 1 space (Article 517). ▶Figure 100–149

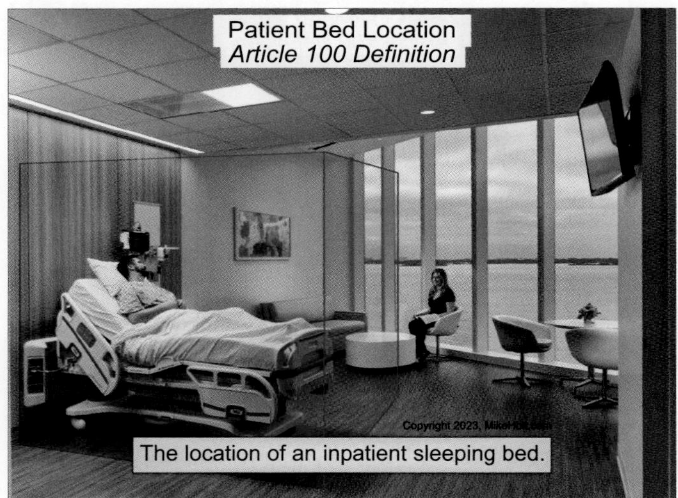

▶Figure 100–149

Patient Care Space Category. Any space of a health care facility where patients are intended to be examined or treated (Article 517). ▶Figure 100–150

Note 2: Business offices, corridors, lounges, day rooms, dining rooms, or similar areas are not classified as patient care spaces.

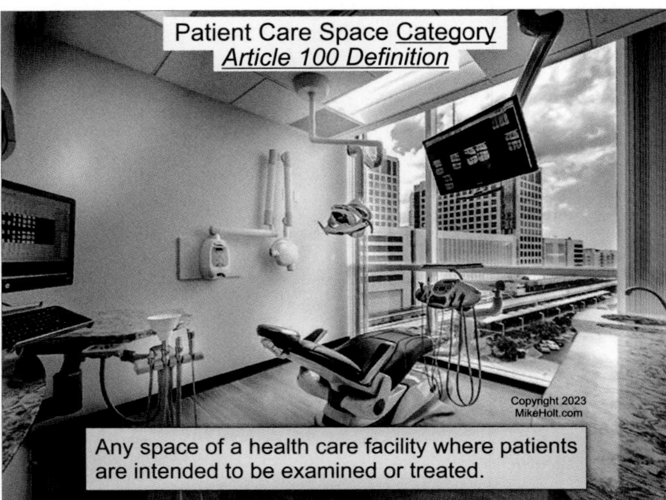

▶Figure 100–150

Patient Care Vicinity. A space extending vertically to 7 ft 6 in. above the floor and 6 ft horizontally beyond the patient bed, chair, table, treadmill or other device that supports the patient during examination and treatment (Article 517). ▶Figure 100–151

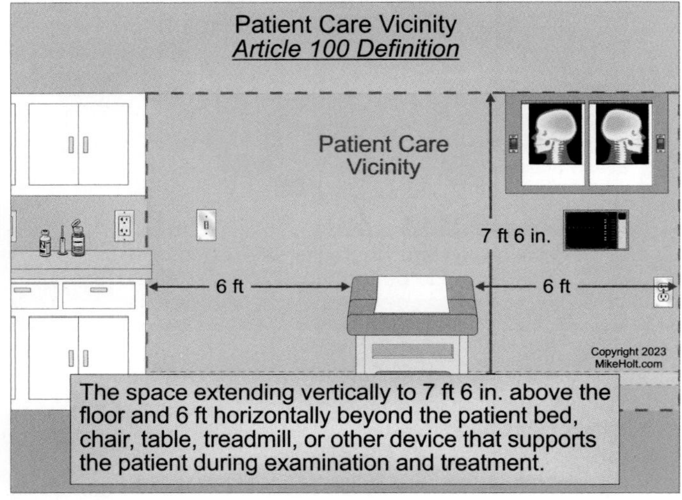

▶Figure 100–151

Pool. Manufactured or field-constructed equipment designed to contain water on a permanent or semipermanent basis and used for swimming, wading, immersion, or other purposes (Article 680). ▶Figure 100–152

Author's Comment:

- The definition of a pool includes baptisteries (immersion pools) which must comply with the requirements of Article 680.
- An aboveground pool having a maximum water depth greater than 42 in. is considered a permanent pool. See the definition of "storable pool."

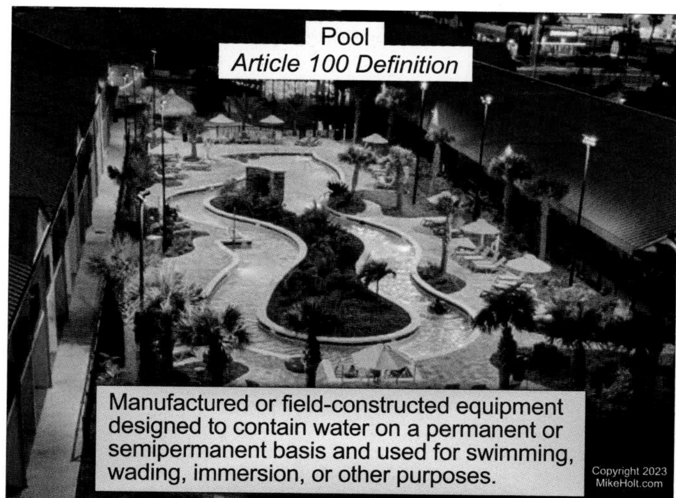
Pool
Article 100 Definition
Manufactured or field-constructed equipment designed to contain water on a permanent or semipermanent basis and used for swimming, wading, immersion, or other purposes.
Copyright 2023 MikeHolt.com

▸Figure 100–152

Pool, Immersion (Immersion Pool). A pool for the ceremonial or ritual immersion of users which is designed and intended to have its contents drained or discharged (Article 680). ▸Figure 100–153

Pool, Immersion
Article 100 Definition
A pool designed for the ceremonial or ritual immersion and intended to have its contents drained or discharged .

▸Figure 100–153

Pool, Permanently Installed (Permanently Installed Pool). Pools constructed or installed in the ground or partially in the ground, and pools installed inside of a building (Article 680). ▸Figure 100–154

Pool, Storable (Storable Pool). A pool installed entirely on or above the ground designed for ease of relocation regardless of water depth (Article 680). ▸Figure 100–155

Power Outlet, Marina (Marina Power Outlet). An enclosed assembly that can include equipment such as receptacles, circuit breakers, watt-hour meters, and panelboards (Article 555). ▸Figure 100–156

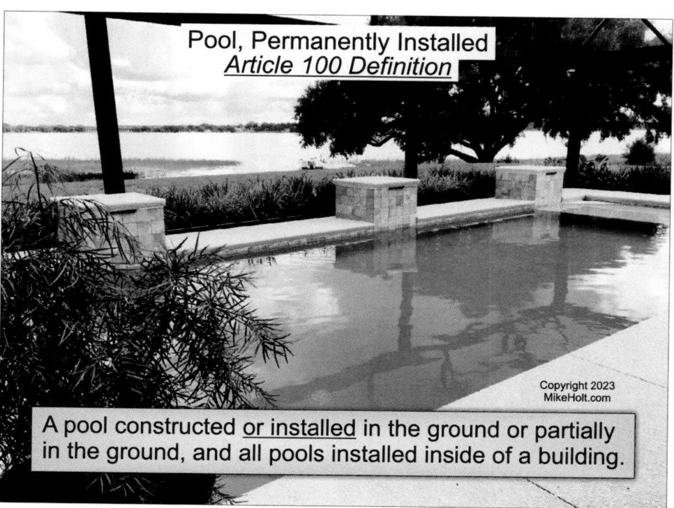
Pool, Permanently Installed
Article 100 Definition
Copyright 2023 MikeHolt.com
A pool constructed or installed in the ground or partially in the ground, and all pools installed inside of a building.

▸Figure 100–154

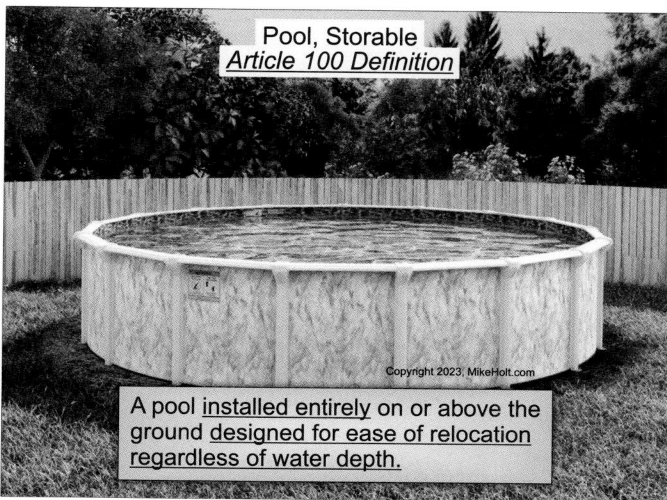
Pool, Storable
Article 100 Definition
Copyright 2023, MikeHolt.com
A pool installed entirely on or above the ground designed for ease of relocation regardless of water depth.

▸Figure 100–155

Marina Power Outlet
Article 100 Definition
An enclosed assembly that can include receptacles, circuit breakers, watt-hour meters, and panelboards.
Copyright 2023, MikeHolt.com

▸Figure 100–156

Power Production Equipment. Electrical generating equipment up to the power production system disconnect supplied by a power source other than the electric utility. ▶Figure 100–157

▶Figure 100–157

Note: Examples of power production equipment include generators, solar photovoltaic systems, and energy storage and fuel cell systems. ▶Figure 100–158

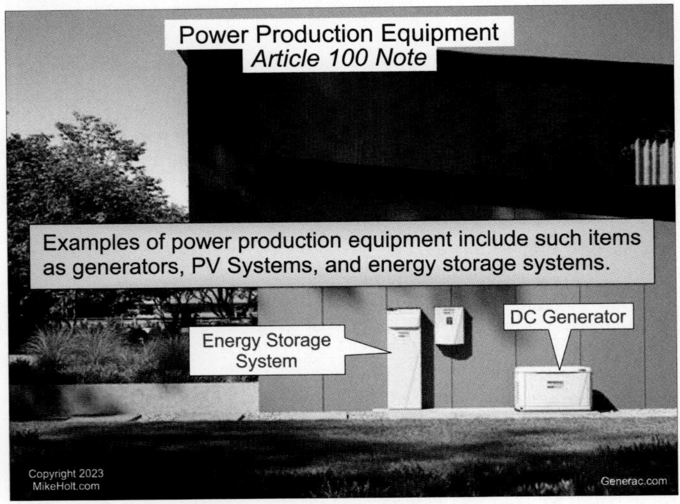

▶Figure 100–158

Power Source Output Conductors. The conductors from power production equipment to service equipment or premises wiring. ▶Figure 100–159 and ▶Figure 100–160

Power-Supply Cord. An assembly consisting of an attachment plug and a length of flexible cord connected to utilization equipment.

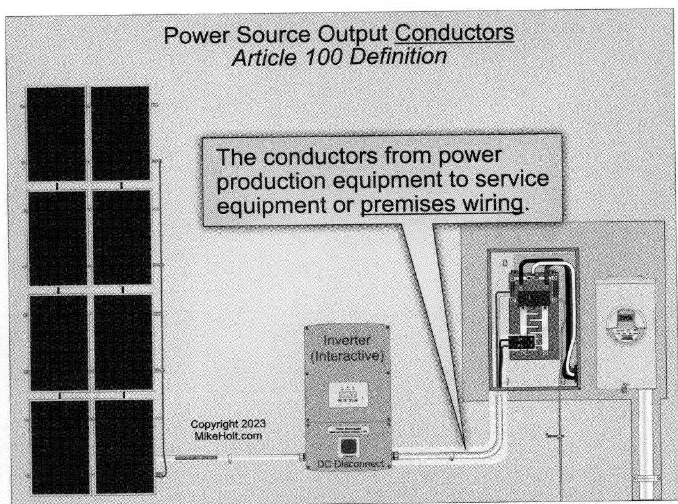

▶Figure 100–159

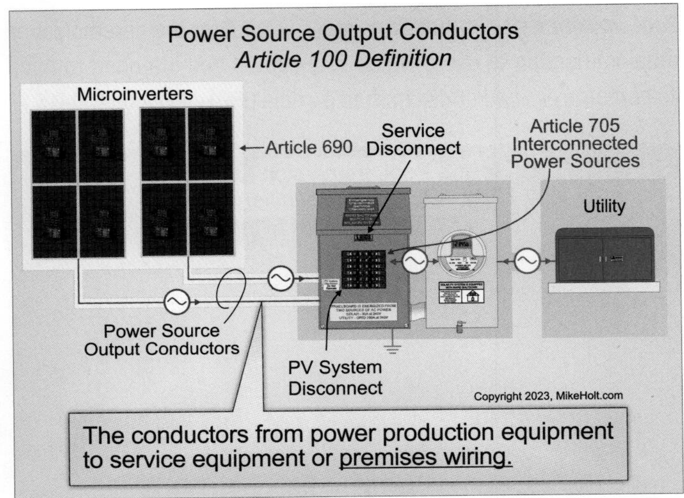

▶Figure 100–160

Author's Comment:

- Article 400 contains information on the use of power-supply cords.

Primary Source of Power. The main source of power in an electric power system, typically the electric utility.

Pier. A structure extending over the water and supported on a fixed or floating pier structure that provides access to the water. ▶Figure 100–161

PV Module. A PV module is a unit of environmentally protected solar cells and components designed to produce dc power. ▶Figure 100–162

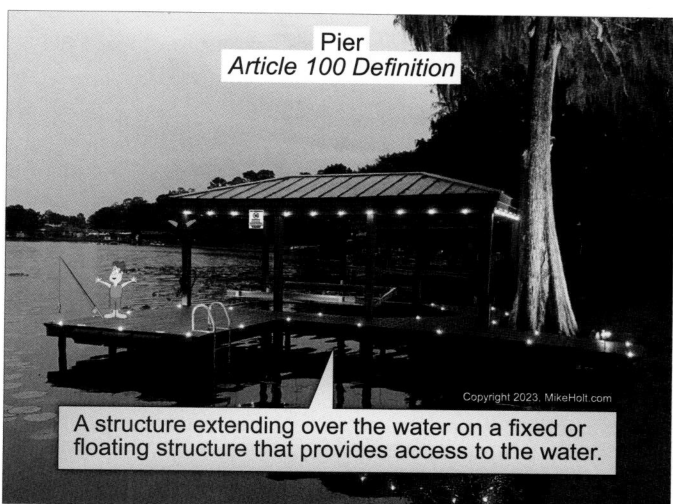
Pier
Article 100 Definition
Copyright 2023, MikeHolt.com
A structure extending over the water on a fixed or floating structure that provides access to the water.

▶Figure 100–161

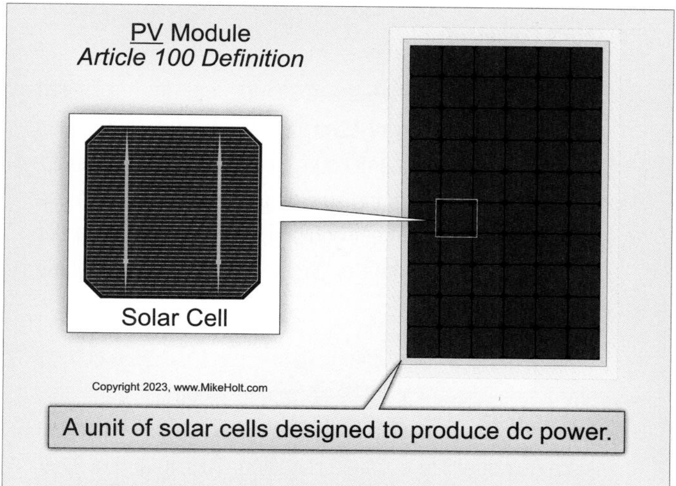
PV Module
Article 100 Definition
Solar Cell
Copyright 2023, www.MikeHolt.com
A unit of solar cells designed to produce dc power.

▶Figure 100–162

Author's Comment:

- PV modules use sunlight to generate dc electricity by using light (photons) to move electrons in a semiconductor. This is known as the "photovoltaic effect."

PV System DC Circuit. Any dc conductor in PV source circuits, PV string circuits, and PV dc-to-dc converter circuits (Article 690). ▶Figure 100–163

PV Source Circuit. The PV source circuit consists of the dc circuit conductors between modules in a PV string and from PV string circuits to dc combiners, electronic power converters, or the PV system dc disconnect (Article 690). ▶Figure 100–164

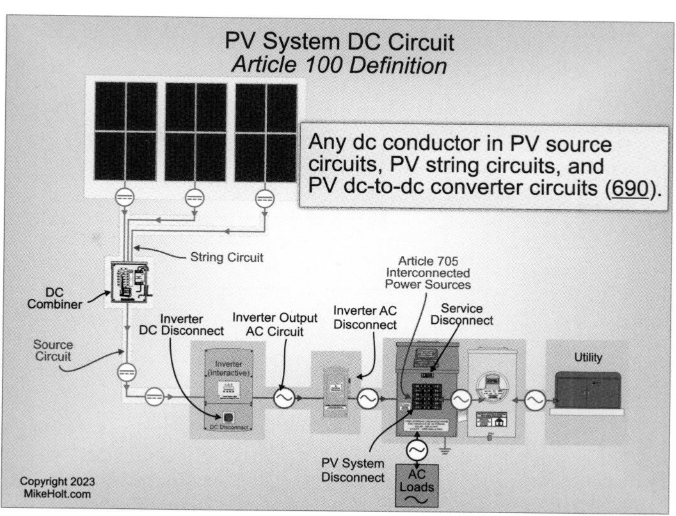
PV System DC Circuit
Article 100 Definition
Any dc conductor in PV source circuits, PV string circuits, and PV dc-to-dc converter circuits (690).
String Circuit
DC Combiner
Source Circuit
Inverter DC Disconnect
Inverter Output AC Circuit
Inverter AC Disconnect
Article 705 Interconnected Power Sources
Service Disconnect
Utility
PV System Disconnect
AC Loads
Copyright 2023 MikeHolt.com

▶Figure 100–163

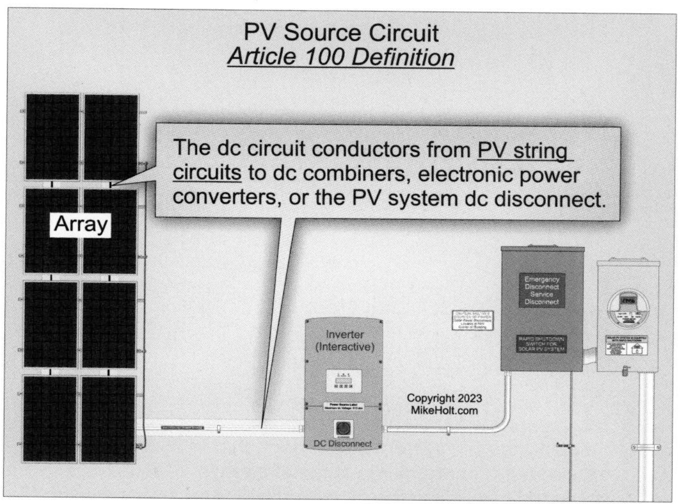
PV Source Circuit
Article 100 Definition
The dc circuit conductors from PV string circuits to dc combiners, electronic power converters, or the PV system dc disconnect.
Array
Inverter (Interactive)
DC Disconnect
Copyright 2023 MikeHolt.com

▶Figure 100–164

Author's Comment:

- The term "PV String" is the International Electrotechnical Commission term for what the *NEC* identifies as a PV Source Circuit.

PV String Circuit. The PV source circuit conductors of one or more series-connected PV modules (Article 690). ▶Figure 100–165

PV System. The components, circuits, and equipment up to and including the PV system disconnect, that in combination convert solar energy into electrical energy. ▶Figure 100–166

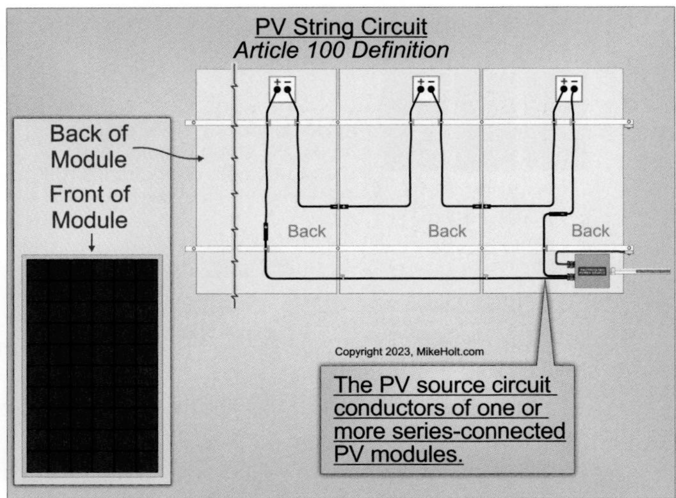
PV String Circuit
Article 100 Definition
Back of Module
Front of Module
Back
Back
Back
Copyright 2023, MikeHolt.com
The PV source circuit conductors of one or more series-connected PV modules.

▸Figure 100–165

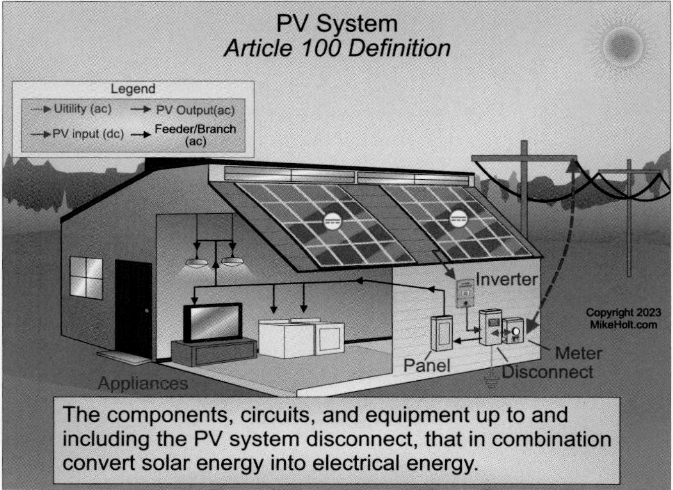
PV System
Article 100 Definition
Legend
Uitility (ac)
PV Output(ac)
PV input (dc)
Feeder/Branch (ac)
Inverter
Copyright 2023 MikeHolt.com
Panel
Meter
Disconnect
Appliances
The components, circuits, and equipment up to and including the PV system disconnect, that in combination convert solar energy into electrical energy.

▸Figure 100–166

Qualified Person. A person with skills and knowledge related to the construction and operation of electrical equipment and installations. This person must have received safety training to recognize and avoid the hazards involved with electrical systems. ▸**Figure 100–167**

Note: NFPA 70E, *Standard for Electrical Safety in the Workplace,* provides information on the safety training requirements expected of a "qualified person."

Qualified Person
Article 100 Definition
70E
Copyright 2023 MikeHolt.com
A person with skills and knowledge related to the construction and operation of electrical equipment and installations. This person must have received safety training to recognize and avoid the hazards involved with electrical systems.

▸Figure 100–167

Author's Comment:

- Examples of this safety training include, but are not limited to, training in the use of special precautionary techniques such as lockout/tagout procedures, personal protective equipment (PPE), insulating and shielding materials, and the use of insulated tools and test equipment when working on or near exposed conductors or circuit parts that can become energized.
- In many parts of the United States, electricians, electrical contractors, electrical inspectors, and electrical engineers must complete from 6 to 24 hours of *NEC* review each year as a requirement to maintain licensing. This, in and of itself, does not make one qualified to deal with the specific hazards involved with electrical systems.

Raceway. An enclosed channel designed for the installation of conductors, cables, or busbars.

Author's Comment:

- A cable tray system is not a raceway—it is a support system for cables and raceways.

Receptacle. A contact device installed at an outlet for the connection of an attachment plug, or for the connection of equipment designed to mate with the contact device. ▸**Figure 100–168**

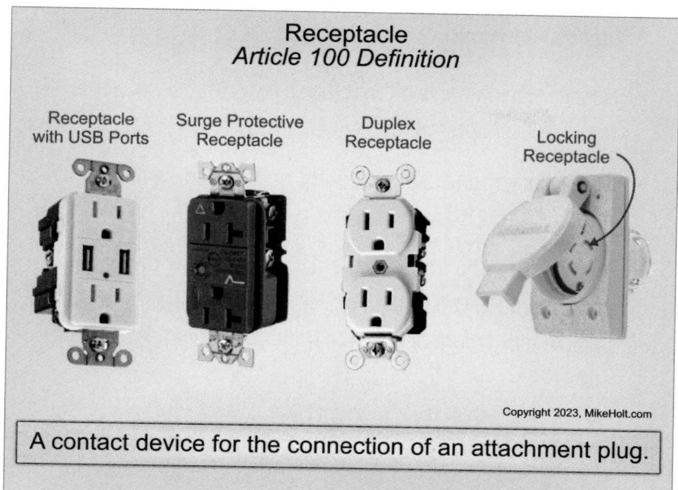

▸Figure 100–168

A single receptacle contains one contact device on the same a yoke or strap. A multiple receptacle has more than one contact device on the same yoke or strap. ▸Figure 100–169

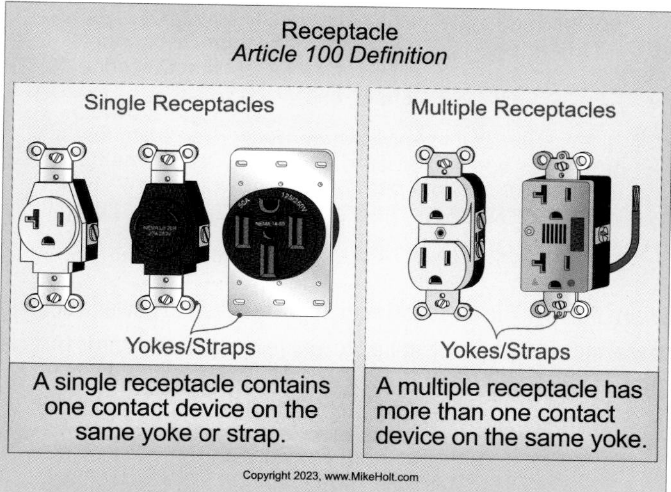

▸Figure 100–169

Author's Comment:

- A yoke (also called a "strap") is the metal mounting structure for such items as receptacles, switches, switches with pilot lights, and switch/receptacles to name a few.

Note: A duplex receptacle is an example of a multiple receptacle with two receptacles on the same yoke or strap.

Sealed [as applied to hazardous (classified) locations]. Constructed such that equipment is sealed effectively against entry of an external atmosphere and not opened during normal operation or any maintenance activities.

Author's Comment:

- Articles 501, 502, and 503 contain information on the use of the term "sealed" as it relates to hazardous (classified) locations.

Service. The conductors and equipment connecting the serving electric utility to the premises wiring system. ▸Figure 100–170

Service
Article 100 Definition
The conductors and equipment connecting the serving electric utility to the wiring system of the premises served.
Copyright 2023, www.MikeHolt.com

▸Figure 100–170

Service Conductors. The conductors from the serving electric utility service point to the service disconnect. ▸Figure 100–171

Author's Comment:

- Service conductors can include overhead service conductors, overhead service-entrance conductors, and underground service conductors. These conductors are not under the exclusive control of the serving electric utility, which means they are owned by the customer and are covered by the requirements in Article 230.

Service Equipment (Service Disconnect). Equipment such as circuit breakers or switches connected to the serving electric utility and intended to disconnect the power from the serving electric utility. ▸Figure 100–172 and ▸Figure 100–173

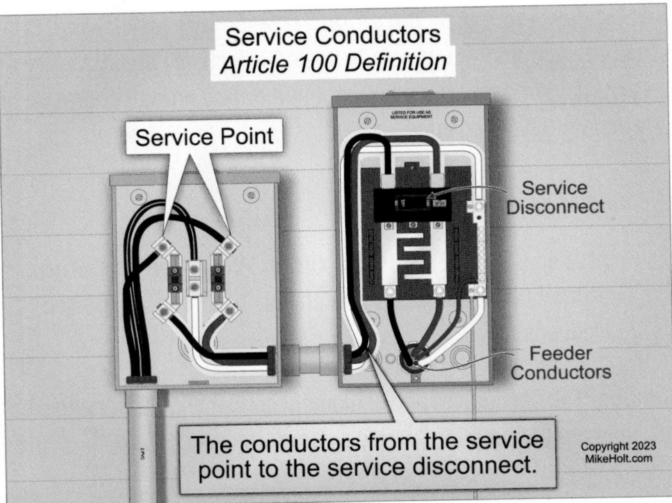

▸Figure 100–171

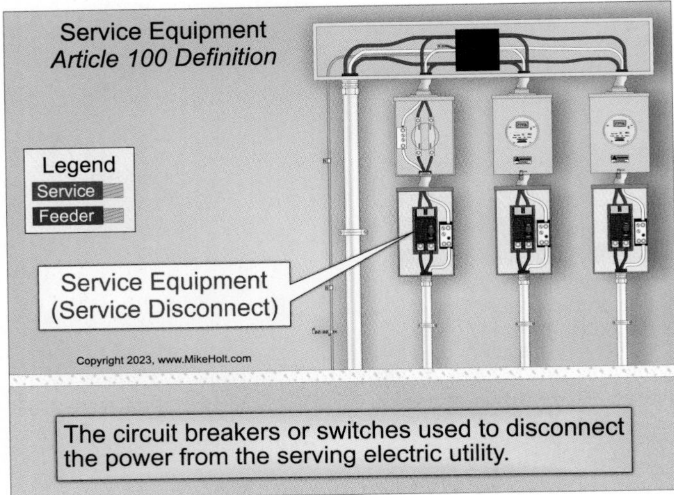

▸Figure 100–172

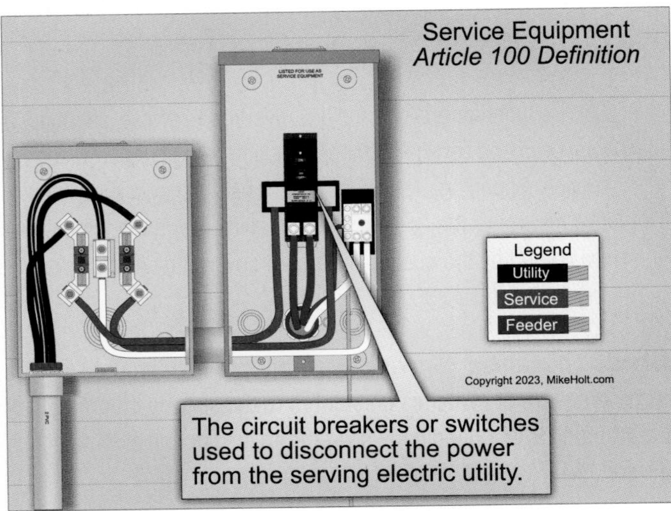

▸Figure 100–173

Author's Comment:

- Service equipment is often referred to as the "service disconnect" or "service main."
- Meter socket enclosures are not considered service equipment [230.66(B)].
- It is important to know where a service begins and where it ends to properly apply the *Code* requirements. The service can begin either before or after the metering equipment. ▸**Figure 100–174**

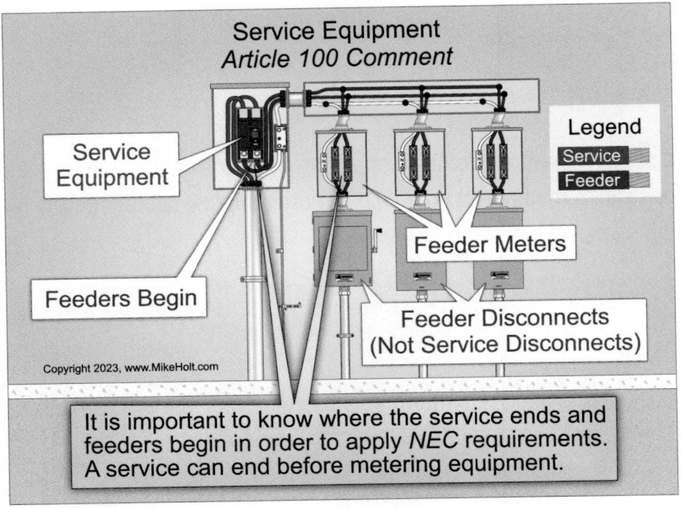

▸Figure 100–174

Shore Power. The electrical equipment required to power a floating vessel including, but not limited to, the receptacle and cords (Article 555). ▸**Figure 100–175**

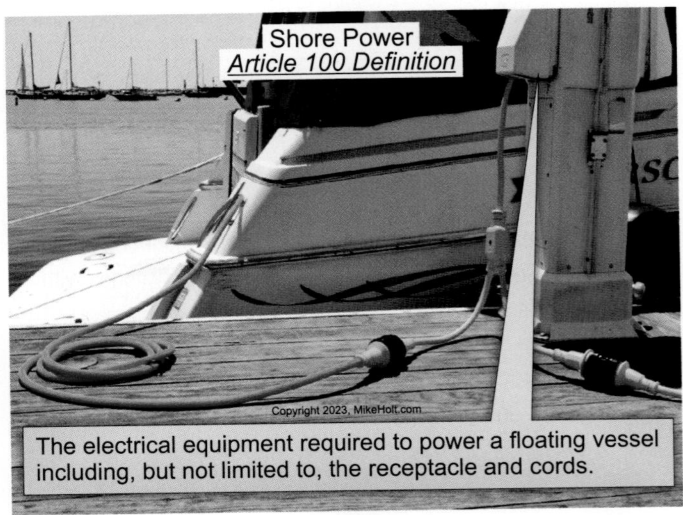

▸Figure 100–175

Short Circuit. An abnormal connection of low impedance, whether made accidentally or intentionally, between two or more points of different potential. ▶Figure 100–176

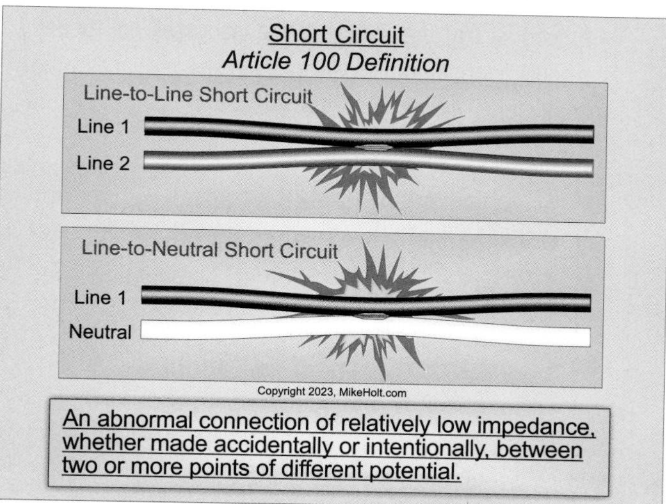
Short Circuit
Article 100 Definition
Line-to-Line Short Circuit
Line 1
Line 2
Line-to-Neutral Short Circuit
Line 1
Neutral
Copyright 2023, MikeHolt.com
An abnormal connection of relatively low impedance, whether made accidentally or intentionally, between two or more points of different potential.

▶Figure 100–176

Author's Comment:

- A short circuit occurs when there is an unintentional electrical connection between two phase conductors, or a phase conductor and neutral conductor.

Short-Circuit Current Rating. The prospective symmetrical fault current at a nominal voltage to which electrical equipment can be connected without sustaining damage exceeding defined acceptance criteria.

Spa/Hot Tub. A tub designed for recreational or therapeutic use typically not drained after each use (Article 680). ▶Figure 100–177

Special Permission. The written consent of the authority having jurisdiction.

Splash Pad. A fountain intended for recreational use by pedestrians with a water depth of 1 in. or less (Article 680). ▶Figure 100–178

Stand-Alone System. An electrical power system that is not interconnected to the electric utility.

Author's Comment:

- Although stand-alone (off-grid) systems can operate independently of the electric utility, they may include a connection to the electric utility for use when not operating in stand-alone (off-grid) mode ("island mode").

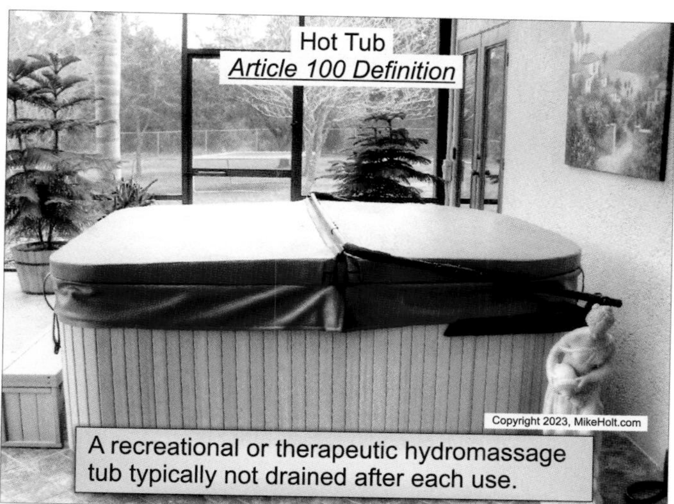
Hot Tub
Article 100 Definition
Copyright 2023, MikeHolt.com
A recreational or therapeutic hydromassage tub typically not drained after each use.

▶Figure 100–177

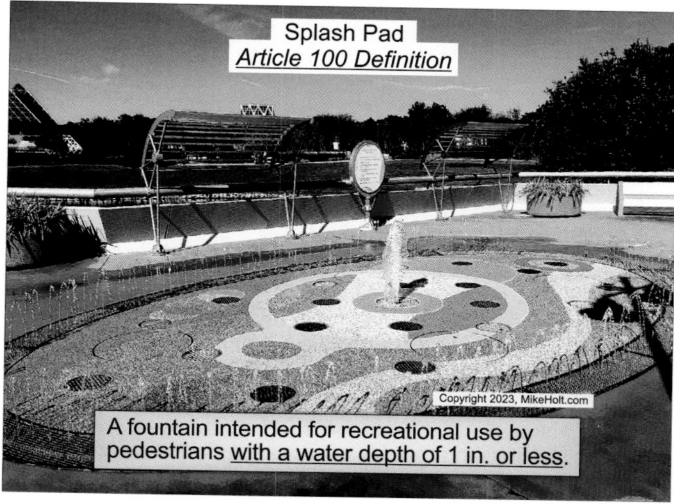
Splash Pad
Article 100 Definition
Copyright 2023, MikeHolt.com
A fountain intended for recreational use by pedestrians with a water depth of 1 in. or less.

▶Figure 100–178

Structure. That which is built or constructed, other than equipment. ▶Figure 100–179

Surge-Protective Device (SPD). A protective device intended to limit transient voltages by diverting or limiting surge current and preventing its continued flow while remaining capable of repeating these functions. ▶Figure 100–180 and ▶Figure 100–181

▶Figure 100–179

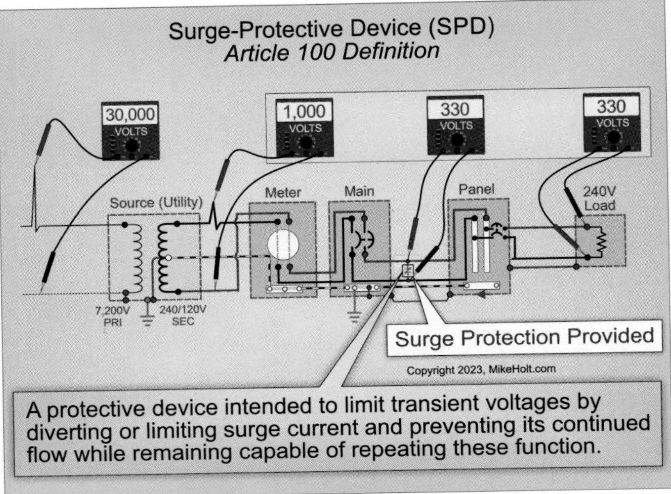

▶Figure 100–180

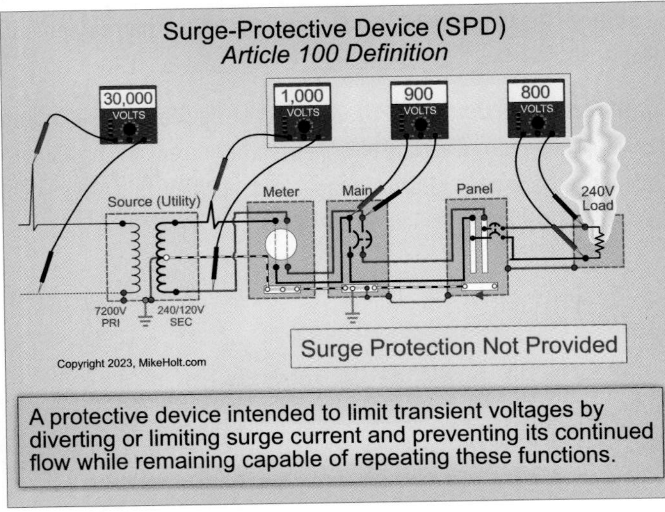

▶Figure 100–181

Author's Comment:

- Surge-protective devices are designed to shunt transient voltages away from the load to protect equipment and are arranged so that the voltage to the load does not exceed the equipment's maximum voltage rating as designed by the manufacturer. ▶**Figure 100–182**

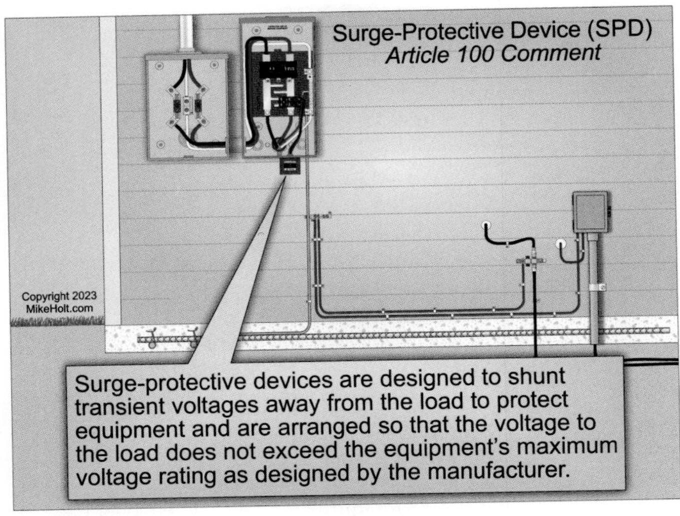

▶Figure 100–182

SPD, Type 1 (Type 1 SPD). A Type 1 surge-protective device is listed for the installation at or ahead of the service disconnect. ▶**Figure 100–183**

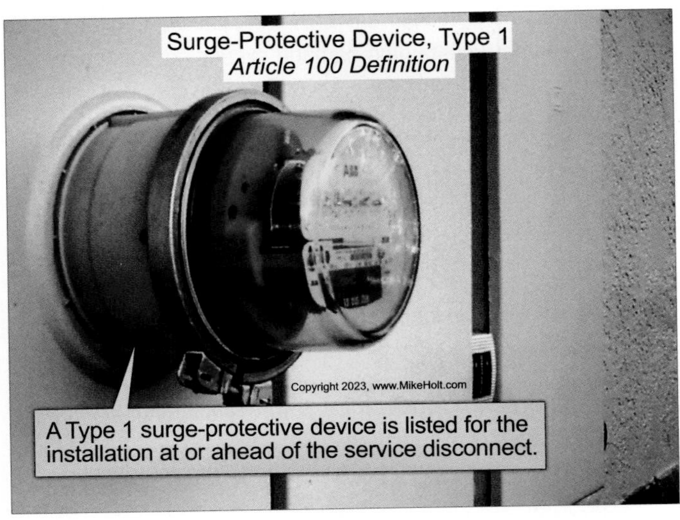

▶Figure 100–183

SPD, Type 2 (Type 2 SPD). A Type 2 surge-protective device is listed for the installation on the load side of the service disconnect. ▶**Figure 100–184**

1st Printing

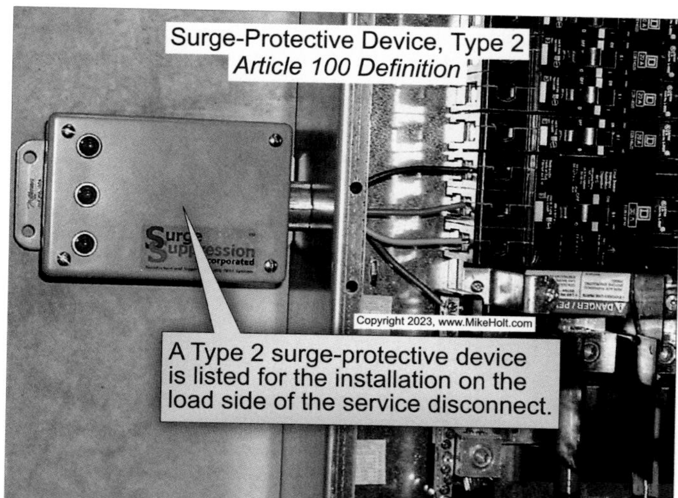
Surge-Protective Device, Type 2
Article 100 Definition
Copyright 2023, www.MikeHolt.com
A Type 2 surge-protective device is listed for the installation on the load side of the service disconnect.

▸Figure 100–184

Note: For further information, see UL 1449, *Standard for Surge-Protective Devices.*

Transfer Switch. An automatic or nonautomatic device used for transferring loads from one power source to another. ▸Figure 100–185

Transfer Switch
Article 100 Definition
Copyright 2023
MikeHolt.com
An automatic or nonautomatic device used to transfer loads from one power source to another.

▸Figure 100–185

Transformer. Equipment, either single-phase or three-phase, that uses electromagnetic induction to convert current and voltage in a primary circuit into current and voltage in a secondary circuit. ▸Figure 100–186

Author's Comment:

- Article 450 contains the primary requirements for transformers.

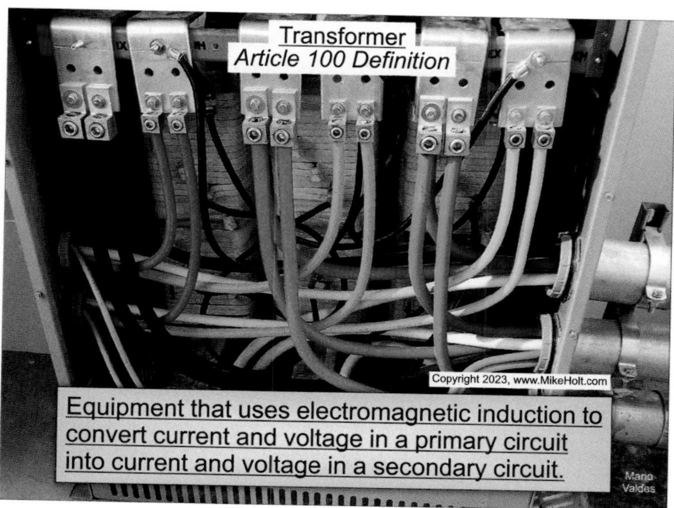
Transformer
Article 100 Definition
Copyright 2023, www.MikeHolt.com
Equipment that uses electromagnetic induction to convert current and voltage in a primary circuit into current and voltage in a secondary circuit.
Mario Valdes

▸Figure 100–186

Tap Conductors. A conductor, other than a service conductor, with overcurrent protection rated more than the ampacity of the conductor. ▸Figure 100–187

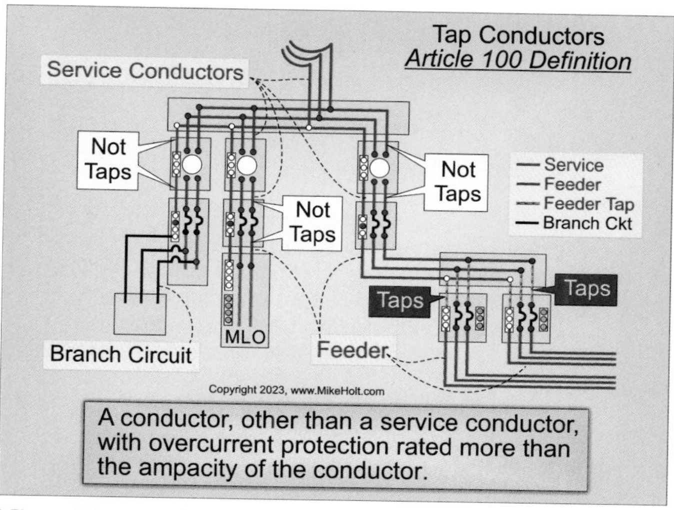
Tap Conductors
Article 100 Definition
Service Conductors
Not Taps
Not Taps
Not Taps
Service
Feeder
Feeder Tap
Branch Ckt
Taps
Taps
Branch Circuit
MLO
Feeder
Copyright 2023, www.MikeHolt.com
A conductor, other than a service conductor, with overcurrent protection rated more than the ampacity of the conductor.

▸Figure 100–187

Tubing, Electrical Metallic (EMT). An unthreaded thinwall circular metallic raceway that when joined together is a reliable effective ground-fault current path. ▸Figure 100–188

Tubing, Electrical Nonmetallic (ENT). A pliable corrugated circular raceway with couplings, connectors, and fittings composed of a material that is resistant to moisture and chemical atmospheres and is flame retardant. ▸Figure 100–189

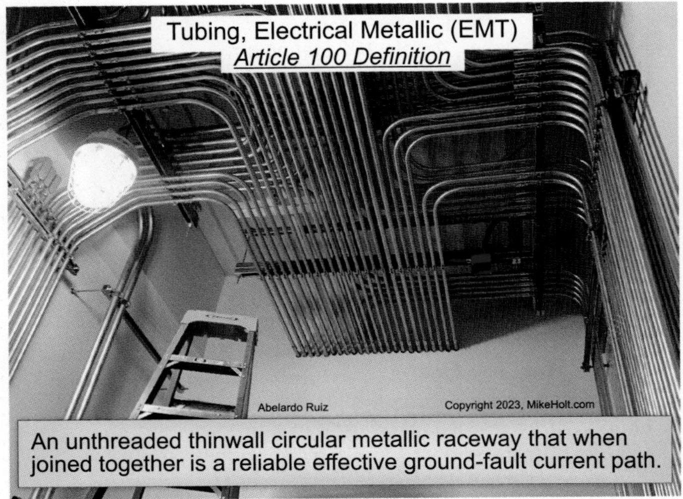
Tubing, Electrical Metallic (EMT)
Article 100 Definition
Abelardo Ruiz
Copyright 2023, MikeHolt.com
An unthreaded thinwall circular metallic raceway that when joined together is a reliable effective ground-fault current path.

▸Figure 100–188

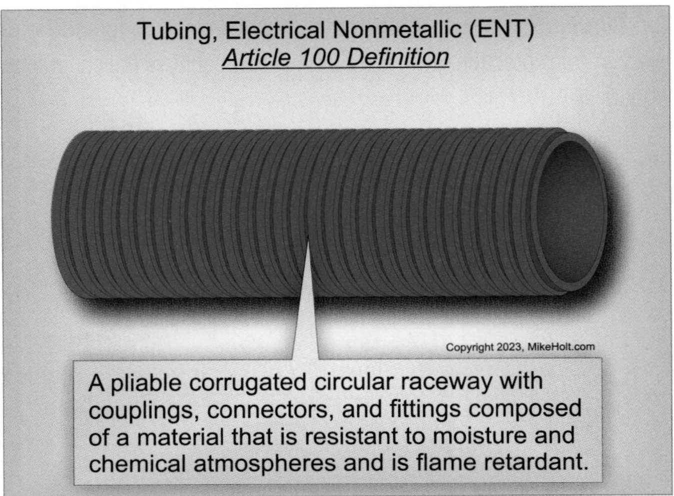
Tubing, Electrical Nonmetallic (ENT)
Article 100 Definition
Copyright 2023, MikeHolt.com
A pliable corrugated circular raceway with couplings, connectors, and fittings composed of a material that is resistant to moisture and chemical atmospheres and is flame retardant.

▸Figure 100–189

Author's Comment:

- Electrical nonmetallic tubing can be bent by hand with reasonable force and without other assistance.

Voltage, Nominal (Nominal Voltage). A value assigned for conveniently designating voltage classes. Examples include 120/240V, 120/208V, and 277/480V. ▸Figure 100–190

Note 1: The actual voltage at which a circuit operates can vary from the nominal within a range that permits satisfactory operation of equipment. ▸Figure 100–191

Voltage-to-Ground, Grounded Systems. For grounded systems, the voltage-to-ground is the voltage between any phase and neutral conductor. ▸Figure 100–192

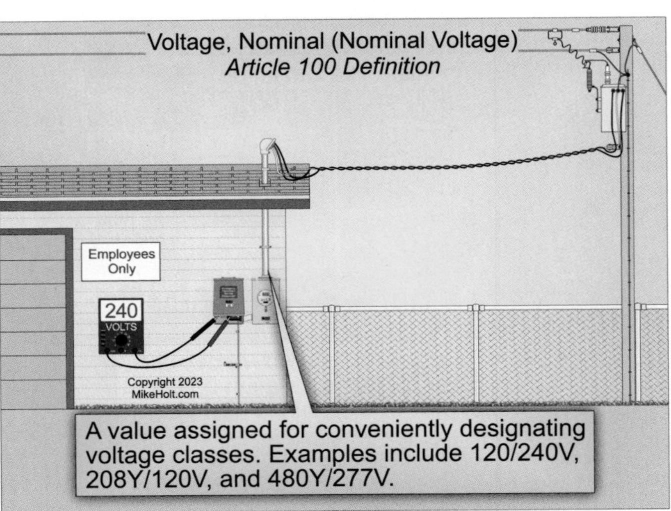
Voltage, Nominal (Nominal Voltage)
Article 100 Definition
Employees Only
240
VOLTS
Copyright 2023
MikeHolt.com
A value assigned for conveniently designating voltage classes. Examples include 120/240V, 208Y/120V, and 480Y/277V.

▸Figure 100–190

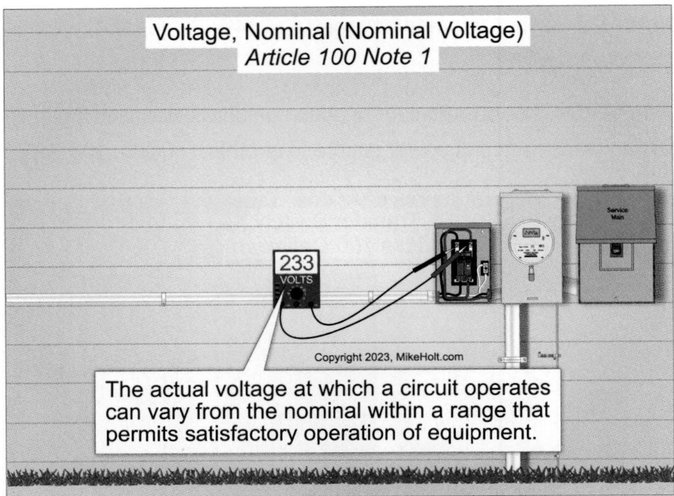
Voltage, Nominal (Nominal Voltage)
Article 100 Note 1
233
VOLTS
Copyright 2023, MikeHolt.com
The actual voltage at which a circuit operates can vary from the nominal within a range that permits satisfactory operation of equipment.

▸Figure 100–191

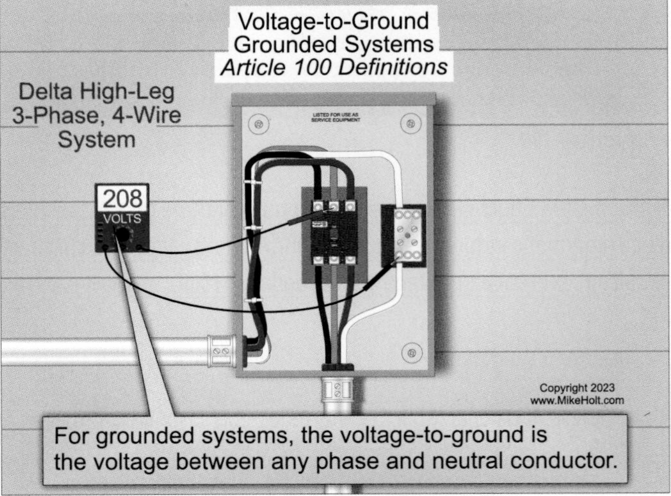
Voltage-to-Ground
Grounded Systems
Article 100 Definitions
Delta High-Leg
3-Phase, 4-Wire
System
208
VOLTS
Copyright 2023
www.MikeHolt.com
For grounded systems, the voltage-to-ground is the voltage between any phase and neutral conductor.

▸Figure 100–192

Weatherproof. Constructed or protected so exposure to the weather will not interfere with successful operation.

Wireless Power Transfer Equipment (WPTE). Equipment for the purpose of transferring energy between premises wiring and an electric vehicle without physical electrical contact (Article 625). ▶Figure 100–193

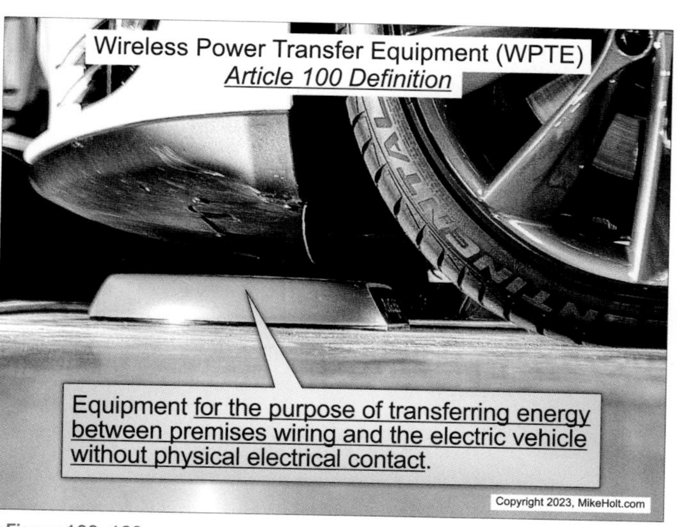

▶Figure 100–193

Wireway, Metal (Metal Wireway). A sheet metal trough with hinged or removable covers for housing and protecting electrical conductors and cable, and in which conductors are placed after the raceway has been installed. ▶Figure 100–194

▶Figure 100–194

Notes

ARTICLE 110 GENERAL REQUIREMENTS FOR ELECTRICAL INSTALLATIONS

Introduction to Article 110—General Requirements for Electrical Installations

Article 110 is the first article in the *NEC* that contains requirements as opposed to overall scope information or definitions. It contains the general rules that apply to all installations and, as such, is the foundation of the *Code*. Topics covered in our material for Article 110 include:

- How equipment is approved
- How to determine when or where equipment can be used
- How to arrange equipment so it is safe to operate and maintain for the end user
- How to identify the characteristics of the systems being installed so future alterations, service, or maintenance can be completed safely

This article is divided into five parts. The first two cover systems under 1000V, nominal and are the only parts of this article covered in this material. As you begin your journey to understanding the *NEC*, remember that many other *Code* rules were written with the understanding that you will come to Article 100 to determine the general requirements. Set yourself up for success by taking the time to read and understand each of these rules.

Part I. General Requirements

110.1 Scope

Article 110 covers the general requirements for the examination, approval, installation, use, and access to spaces around electrical equipment. ▶Figure 110–1

Author's Comment:

- Requirements for people with disabilities include things like mounting heights for switches, receptacles and the requirements for the distance that objects (such as wall sconces) protrude from a wall.

Note: For information regarding ADA accessibility design, see Annex J.

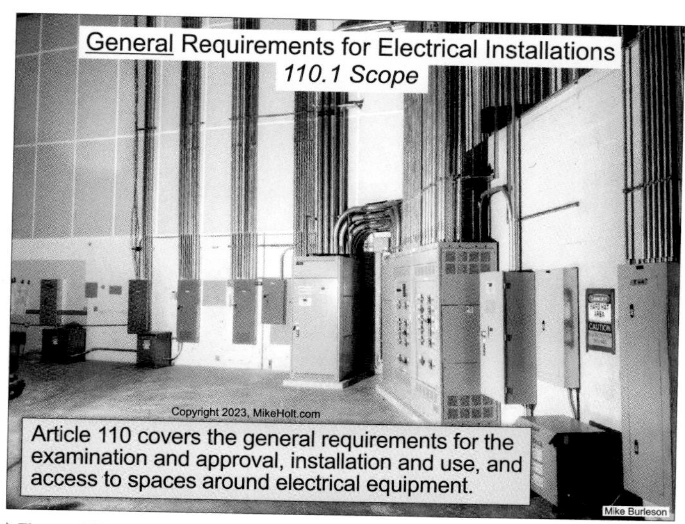
General Requirements for Electrical Installations
110.1 Scope
Copyright 2023, MikeHolt.com
Article 110 covers the general requirements for the examination and approval, installation and use, and access to spaces around electrical equipment.
Mike Burleson

▶Figure 110–1

110.2 Approval of Conductors and Equipment

The authority having jurisdiction must approve all electrical conductors and equipment. ▶Figure 110–2

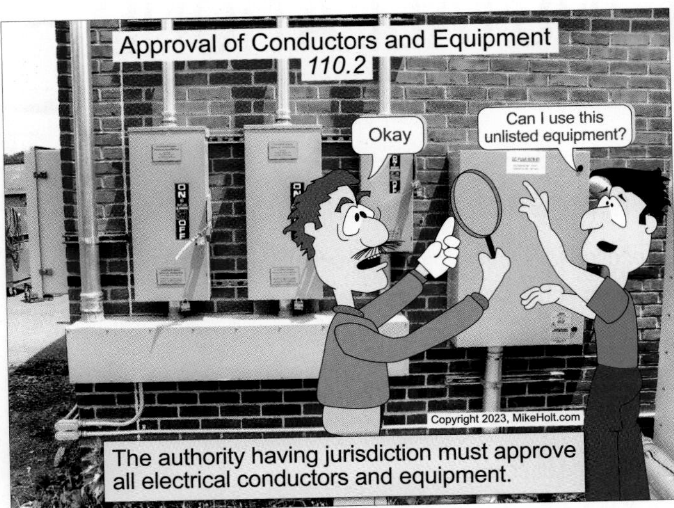

▶Figure 110–2

According to Article 100, "Approved" means acceptable to the authority having jurisdiction (AHJ), usually the electrical inspector. Product listing does not mean the product is approved, but it can be a basis for approval. ▶Figure 110–3

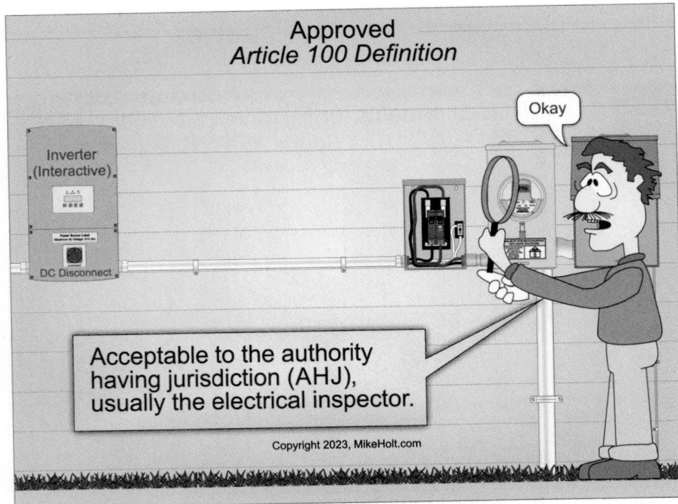

▶Figure 110–3

According to Article 100, "Authority Having Jurisdiction (AHJ)" refers the organization, office, or individual responsible for approving equipment, materials, or an installation. See 90.4 and 90.7 for more information. ▶Figure 110–4

▶Figure 110–4

110.3 Use of Equipment

(A) Guidelines for Approval. The authority having jurisdiction must approve equipment. In doing so, consideration must be given to the following:

(1) Suitability for installation and use in accordance with the *NEC*

Note 1: Equipment may be new, reconditioned, refurbished, or remanufactured.

Note 2: Suitability of equipment use may be identified by a description marked on (or provided with) a product to identify the suitability of the product for a specific purpose, environment, or application. Special conditions of use or other limitations may be marked on the equipment, in the product instructions, or included in the appropriate listing and labeling information. Suitability of equipment may be evidenced by listing or labeling.

According to Article 100, "Identified (as Applied to Equipment)" means that it is recognized as suitable for a specific purpose, function, use, environment, or application. ▶Figure 110–5

(2) Mechanical strength and durability

(3) Wire-bending and connection space

(4) Electrical insulation

(5) Heating effects under all conditions of use

(6) Arcing effects

1st Printing

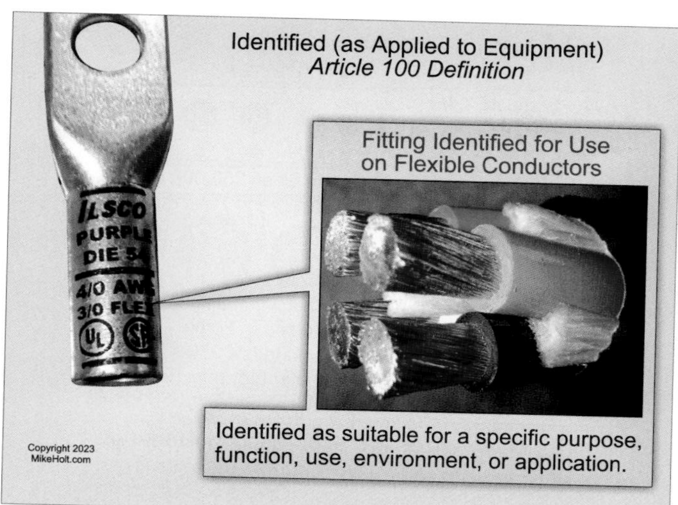
Identified (as Applied to Equipment)
Article 100 Definition
Fitting Identified for Use on Flexible Conductors
Identified as suitable for a specific purpose, function, use, environment, or application.
Copyright 2023 MikeHolt.com

▸Figure 110–5

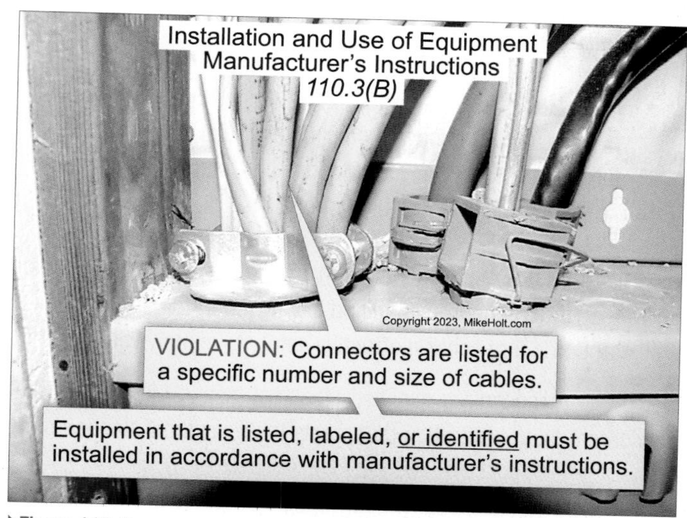
Installation and Use of Equipment
Manufacturer's Instructions
110.3(B)
VIOLATION: Connectors are listed for a specific number and size of cables.
Equipment that is listed, labeled, or identified must be installed in accordance with manufacturer's instructions.
Copyright 2023, MikeHolt.com

▸Figure 110–6

(7) Classification by type, size, voltage, current capacity, and specific use

(8) Cybersecurity for network-connected life safety equipment to address its ability to withstand unauthorized updates and malicious attacks while continuing to perform its intended life safety functionality

Note 3: See the IEC 62443 series of standards for industrial automation and control systems, the UL 2900 series of standards for software cybersecurity for network connectible products, and UL 5500, *Standard for Remote Software Updates*, which are standards that provide frameworks to mitigate current and future security cybersecurity vulnerabilities and address software integrity in systems of electrical equipment.

(9) Other factors contributing to the practical safeguarding of persons using or in contact with the equipment

(B) Installation and Use. Equipment that is listed, labeled, or identified must be installed in accordance with manufacturer's instructions. ▸**Figure 110–6**

According to Article 100, "Labeled" mean equipment or materials that have a label, symbol, or other identifying mark in the form of a sticker, decal, printed label, or with the identifying mark molded or stamped into the product by a recognized testing laboratory acceptable to the authority having jurisdiction. ▸**Figure 110–7**

Note: The installation instructions can be provided in the form of printed material, quick response (QR) code, or the address on the Internet where users can download the required instructions. ▸**Figure 110–8**

Labeled
Article 100 Definition
Equipment or materials that have an identifying mark by a recognized testing laboratory that is acceptable to the authority having jurisdiction.
WARRANTY TERMINATED IF OPENED
UL
CERTIFIED
SAFETY US-CA
E60120
GROUND FAULT CIRCUIT INTERRUPTER-CLASS A
LOT NO. 0076542
Copyright 2023, MikeHolt.com

▸Figure 110–7

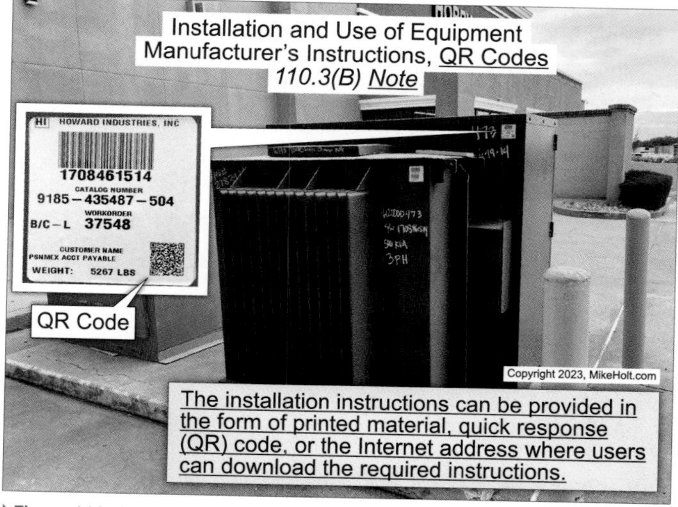
Installation and Use of Equipment
Manufacturer's Instructions, QR Codes
110.3(B) Note
HOWARD INDUSTRIES, INC
1708461514
CATALOG NUMBER
9185–435487–504
WORKORDER
B/C–L 37548
CUSTOMER NAME
PSNMEX ACCT PAYABLE
WEIGHT: 5267 LBS
QR Code
The installation instructions can be provided in the form of printed material, quick response (QR) code, or the Internet address where users can download the required instructions.
Copyright 2023, MikeHolt.com

▸Figure 110–8

Author's Comment:

- Many electricians simply throw away installation instructions, but that excuse is now becoming less valid since manufacturers are starting to use QR codes on electrical equipment, so the instructions are always readily available.

(C) Product Listing. Product testing, evaluation, and listing must be performed by a recognized qualified testing laboratory in accordance with standards that achieve effective safety to comply with the *NEC*.

Note: OSHA recognizes qualified electrical testing laboratories that provide product certification that meets their electrical standards.

110.5 Conductor Material

Conductors must be copper, aluminum, or copper-clad aluminum unless otherwise provided in this *Code*. If the conductor material is not specified in a rule, the sizes given in the *NEC* are based on a copper conductor. ▸Figure 110–9

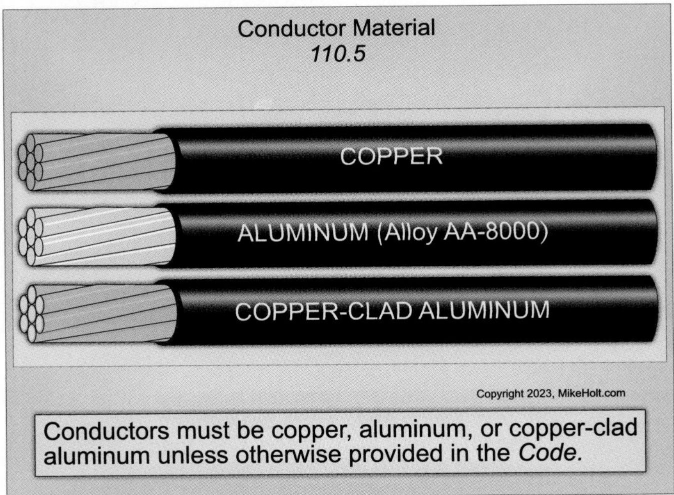

▸Figure 110–9

110.6 Conductor Sizes

Conductor sizes are expressed in American Wire Gauge (AWG) or circular mils (cmil). ▸Figure 110–10

Author's Comment:

- Chapter 9, Table 8 gives the circular mil area of AWG conductors.

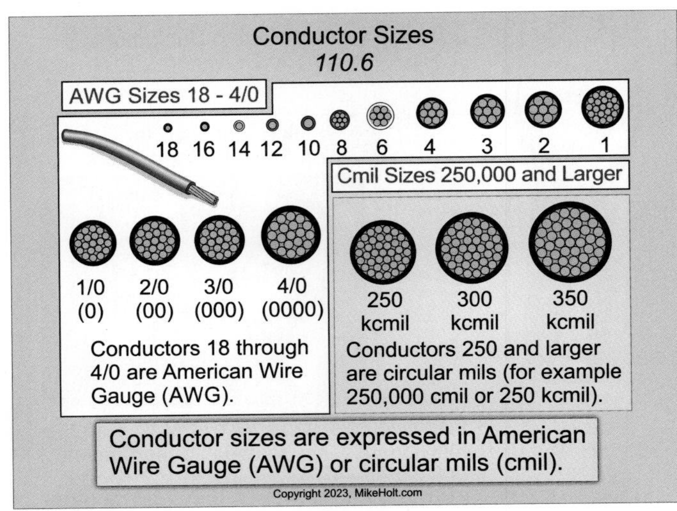

▸Figure 110–10

110.7 Wiring Integrity

Electrical installations must be free from short circuits, ground faults, or neutral to ground connections unless required or permitted by the *Code*. ▸Figure 110–11, ▸Figure 110–12, and ▸Figure 110–13

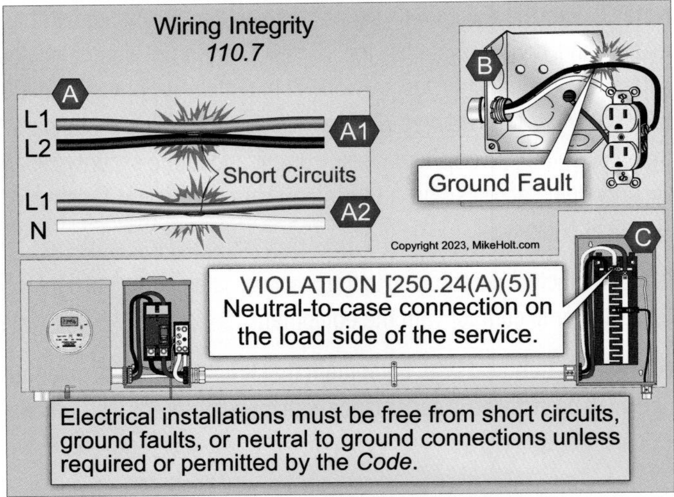

▸Figure 110–11

110.8 Suitable Wiring Methods

The only wiring methods permitted to be installed in buildings, occupancies, or premises are those recognized by the *NEC*. ▸Figure 110–14

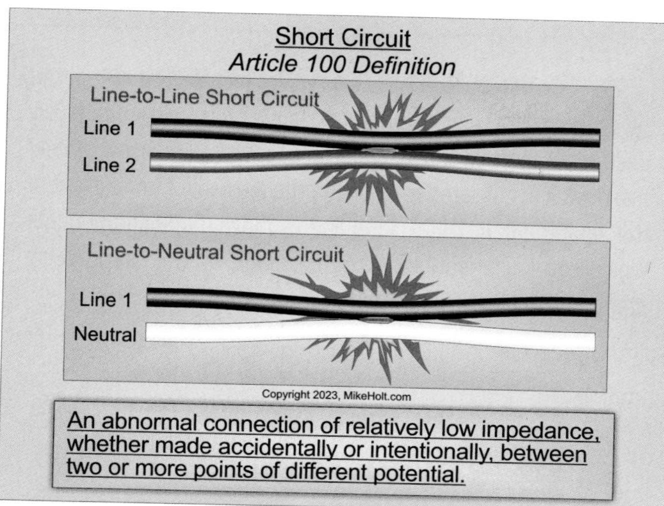

▶Figure 110–12

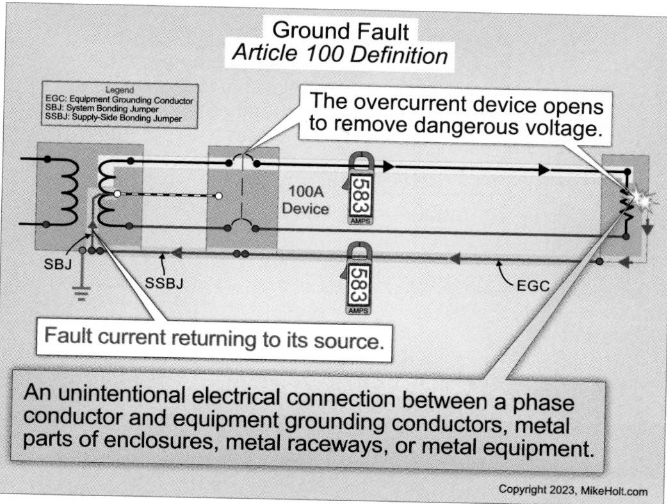

Ground Fault
Article 100 Definition
Legend
EGC: Equipment Grounding Conductor
SBJ: System Bonding Jumper
SSBJ: Supply-Side Bonding Jumper
The overcurrent device opens to remove dangerous voltage.
100A Device
583
SBJ
SSBJ
EGC
Fault current returning to its source.
An unintentional electrical connection between a phase conductor and equipment grounding conductors, metal parts of enclosures, metal raceways, or metal equipment.
Copyright 2023, MikeHolt.com

▶Figure 110–13

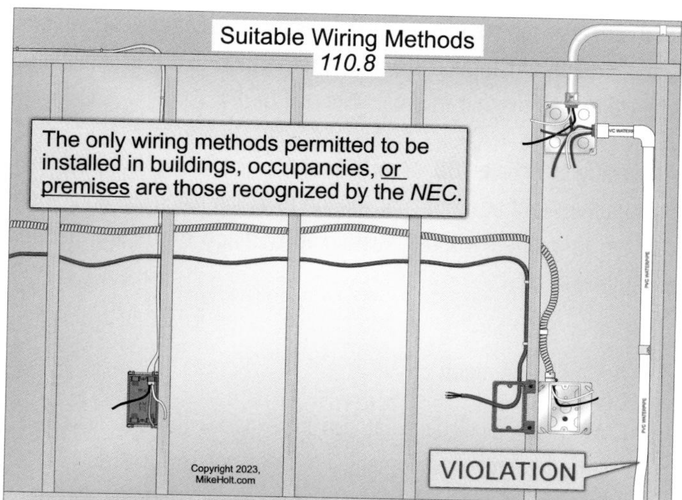

▶Figure 110–14

110.9 Interrupting Rating of Overcurrent Protective Devices

Circuit breakers and fuses must have an interrupting rating equal to or greater than the available fault current at the line terminals of the equipment. ▶Figure 110–15

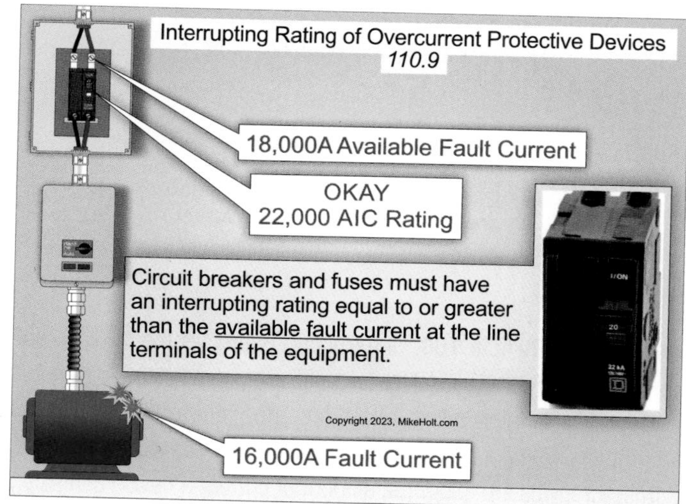

▶Figure 110–15

According to Article 100, "Circuit Breaker" is a device designed to be opened and closed manually and opens automatically during an overcurrent event without damage to itself. ▶Figure 110–16

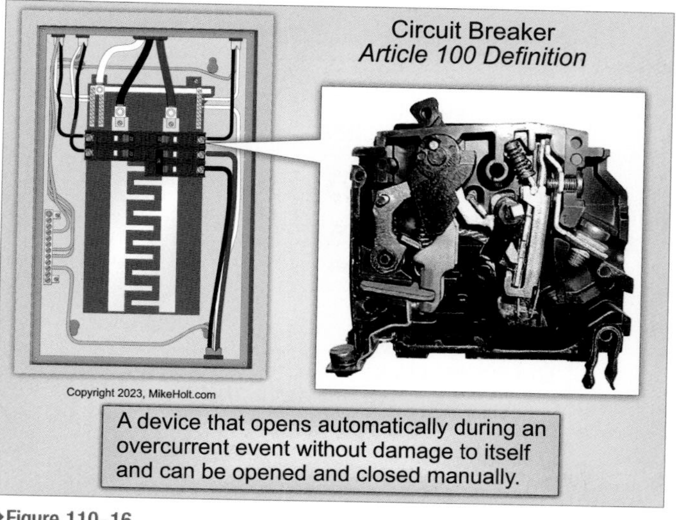

▶Figure 110–16

According to Article 100, "Fuse" is an overcurrent protective device with a circuit-opening fusible part that is heated and severed by the passage of overcurrent. ▶Figure 110–17

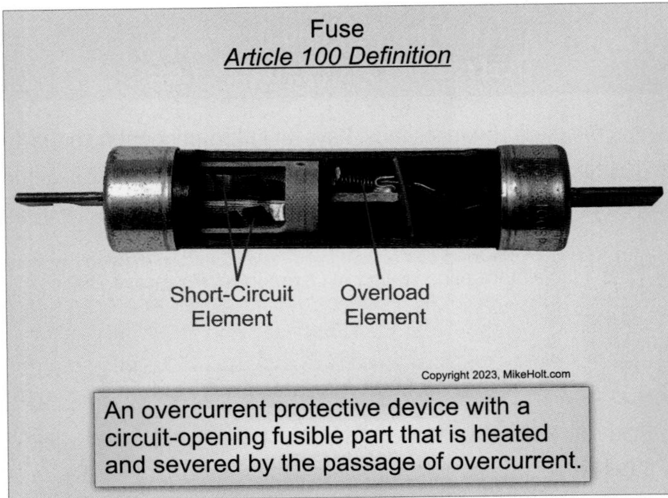
Fuse
Article 100 Definition
Short-Circuit Element
Overload Element
Copyright 2023, MikeHolt.com
An overcurrent protective device with a circuit-opening fusible part that is heated and severed by the passage of overcurrent.

▸Figure 110–17

According to Article 100, "Interrupting Rating" is the highest fault current at rated voltage a device is identified to interrupt under standard test conditions. Interrupting ratings are often referred to as "Ampere Interrupting Rating" (AIR) or "Ampere Interrupting Capacity" (AIC). Both terms/acronyms are about the amount of current a device can safely handle while clearing a fault.

"Available Fault Current" is the largest amount of current capable of being delivered at a point on the electrical system during a short-circuit condition. ▸Figure 110–18

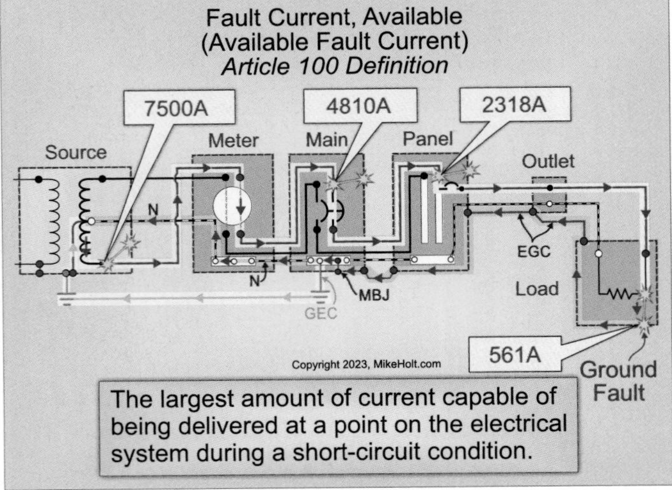
Fault Current, Available
(Available Fault Current)
Article 100 Definition
7500A
4810A
2318A
Source
Meter
Main
Panel
Outlet
N
N
EGC
Load
MBJ
GEC
561A
Ground Fault
Copyright 2023, MikeHolt.com
The largest amount of current capable of being delivered at a point on the electrical system during a short-circuit condition.

▸Figure 110–18

Caution

CAUTION: Extremely high values of fault currents caused by short circuits or ground faults produce tremendously destructive thermal and magnetic forces. If an overcurrent protective device is not rated to interrupt the available fault current at the equipment, it can explode and vaporize metal components which can cause serious injury or death, as well as property damage and electrical system down time. ▸Figure 110–19

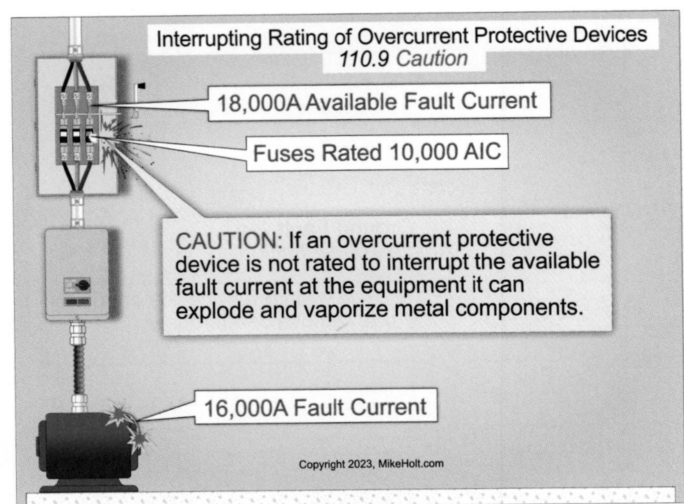
Interrupting Rating of Overcurrent Protective Devices
110.9 Caution
18,000A Available Fault Current
Fuses Rated 10,000 AIC
CAUTION: If an overcurrent protective device is not rated to interrupt the available fault current at the equipment it can explode and vaporize metal components.
16,000A Fault Current
Copyright 2023, MikeHolt.com

▸Figure 110–19

110.10 Equipment Short-Circuit Current Rating

Electrical equipment must have a short-circuit current rating that permits the circuit protective device to clear a short circuit or ground fault without extensive damage to the electrical equipment of the circuit. Listed equipment applied in accordance with its listing is considered to have met this requirement. ▸Figure 110–20

According to Article 100, "Short-Circuit Current Rating" is the symmetrical fault current at a nominal voltage to which electrical equipment can be connected without sustaining damage exceeding defined acceptance criteria.

Author's Comment:

- When the available fault current exceeds the short-circuit current rating of equipment, it can damage busbars, conductors, and equipment from excessive electromagnetic forces and heat.

1st Printing

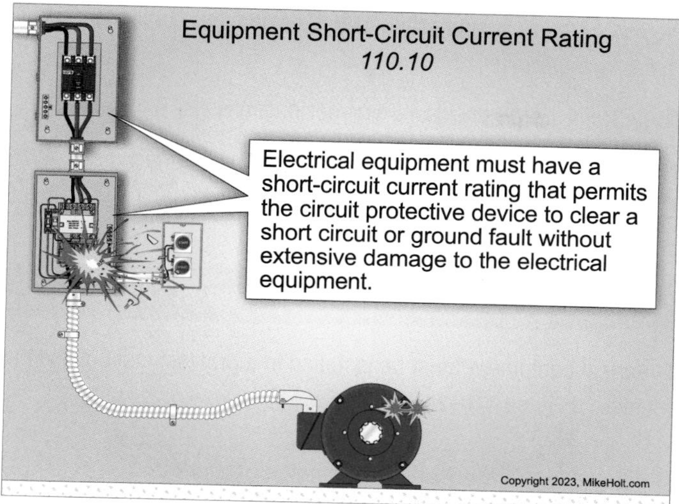
Equipment Short-Circuit Current Rating
110.10
Electrical equipment must have a short-circuit current rating that permits the circuit protective device to clear a short circuit or ground fault without extensive damage to the electrical equipment.
Copyright 2023, MikeHolt.com

▶Figure 110–20

Danger

DANGER: Equipment can explode if the available fault current exceeds the equipment short-circuit current rating, endangering persons and property. ▶Figure 110–21

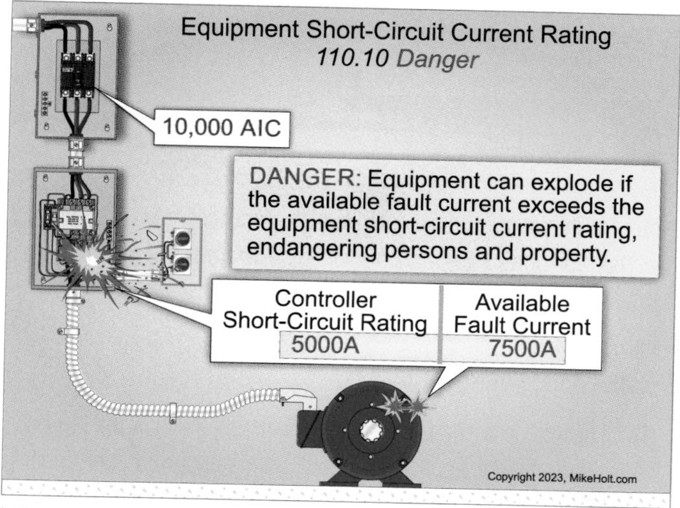
Equipment Short-Circuit Current Rating
110.10 Danger
10,000 AIC
DANGER: Equipment can explode if the available fault current exceeds the equipment short-circuit current rating, endangering persons and property.
Controller Short-Circuit Rating
5000A
Available Fault Current
7500A
Copyright 2023, MikeHolt.com

▶Figure 110–21

Available Fault Current

Sections 110.9 and 110.10 use similar sounding terms making it a bit challenging to understand the differences. Be careful not to confuse the term "interrupting rating" with "short-circuit rating."

Available fault current is the largest amount of short-circuit or ground-fault current, in amperes, available at a given point in the electrical system. It is first determined at the secondary terminals of the serving electric utility transformer, as given by the serving electric utility's engineer. After that, it is calculated at the terminals of the service disconnect, then panelboards and other equipment as various connections are made downstream from the main service. Beginning at the serving electric utility transformer, the available fault current decreases at each downstream connection point of the electrical system.

The available fault current at any point depends on the impedance of the circuit. As the circuit impedance increases, the available fault current decreases. ▶Figure 110–22

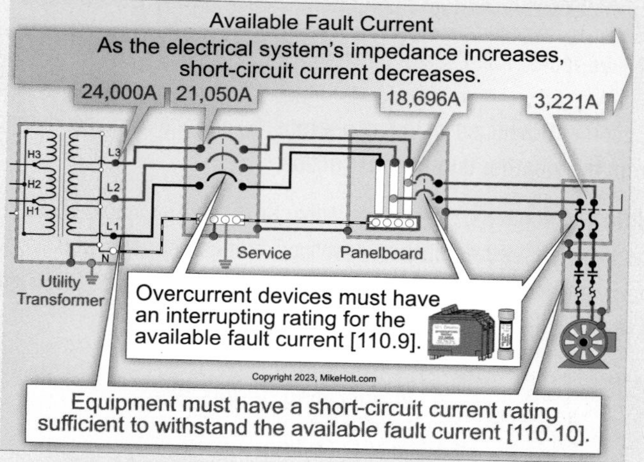
Available Fault Current
As the electrical system's impedance increases, short-circuit current decreases.
24,000A
21,050A
18,696A
3,221A
H3
H2
H1
L3
L2
L1
N
Service
Panelboard
Utility Transformer
Overcurrent devices must have an interrupting rating for the available fault current [110.9].
Copyright 2023, MikeHolt.com
Equipment must have a short-circuit current rating sufficient to withstand the available fault current [110.10].

▶Figure 110–22

Factors that affect the available fault current at the serving electric utility transformers are the system voltage, transformer kVA rating, and impedance. Properties that have an impact on the impedance of the circuit include the conductor material (copper versus aluminum), conductor size, conductor length, raceway type (metallic versus nonmetallic), ambient temperature, and motor loads.

110.11 Deteriorating Agents

Electrical equipment and conductors must be suitable for the environment and the conditions for which they will be used. Consideration must also be given to the presence of corrosive gases, fumes, vapors, liquids, or other substances that can have a deteriorating effect on conductors and equipment. ▸Figure 110–23

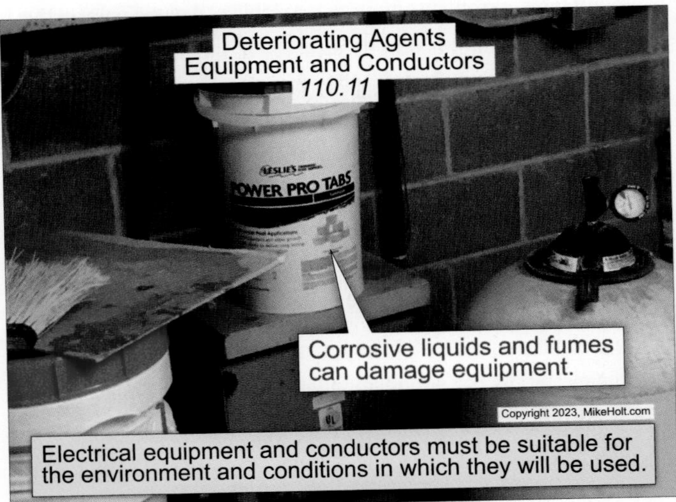

▸Figure 110–23

Equipment identified for indoor use must be protected against damage from the weather during construction.

Note 1: Raceways, cable trays, cable armor, boxes, cable sheathing, cabinets, enclosures, elbows, couplings, fittings, supports, and support hardware must be suitable for the environment. See 300.6. ▸Figure 110–24

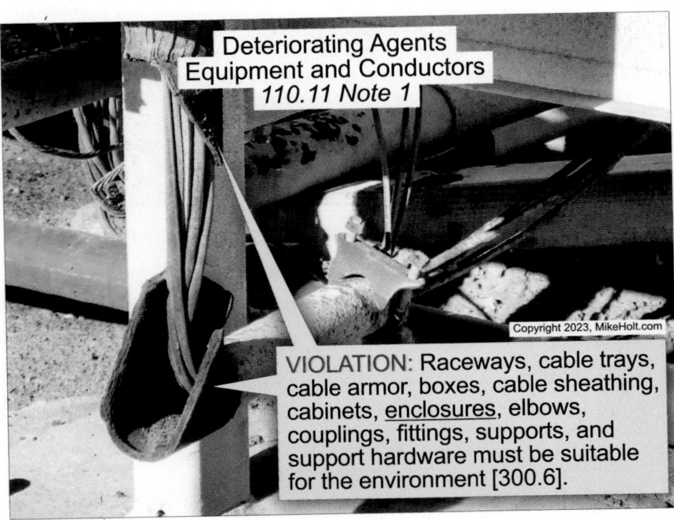

▸Figure 110–24

Note 2: Some cleaning and lubricating compounds contain chemicals that can cause plastic to deteriorate.

Note 3: For NEMA enclosure-type designations, see Table 110.28.

Note 4: For minimum flood provisions, see the *International Building Code* (IBC) and the *International Residential Code* (IRC).

110.12 Mechanical Execution of Work

Electrical equipment must be installed in a professional and skillful manner. ▸Figure 110–25

▸Figure 110–25

Note: For information on accepted industry practices, see ANSI/NECA 1, *Standard for Good Workmanship in Electrical Construction*, and other ANSI-approved installation standards. ▸Figure 110–26

Author's Comment:

- This rule is perhaps one of the most subjective of the entire *Code*, and its application is still ultimately a judgment call made by the authority having jurisdiction.

(A) Unused Openings. Unused openings (other than those used for mounting equipment or the operation of equipment), must be closed by fittings that provide protection substantially equivalent to the wall of the equipment. Unused openings that are intended for mounting the equipment are not required to be closed. ▸Figure 110–27

(B) Integrity of Electrical Equipment. Internal parts of electrical equipment must not be damaged or contaminated by foreign material such as paint, plaster, cleaners, and so forth. ▸Figure 110–28

1st Printing

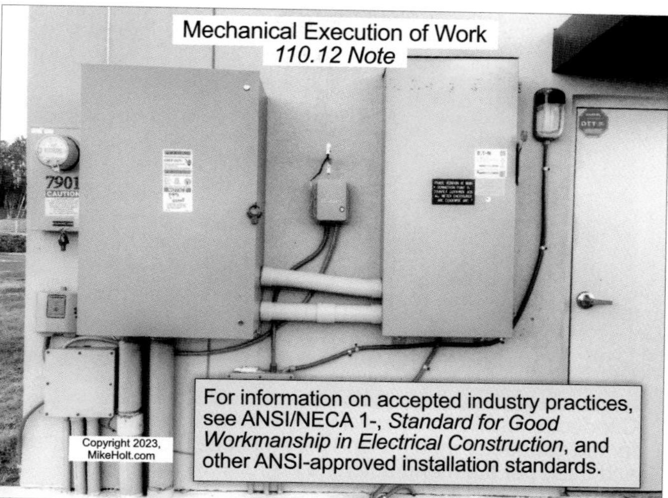

▶Figure 110–26

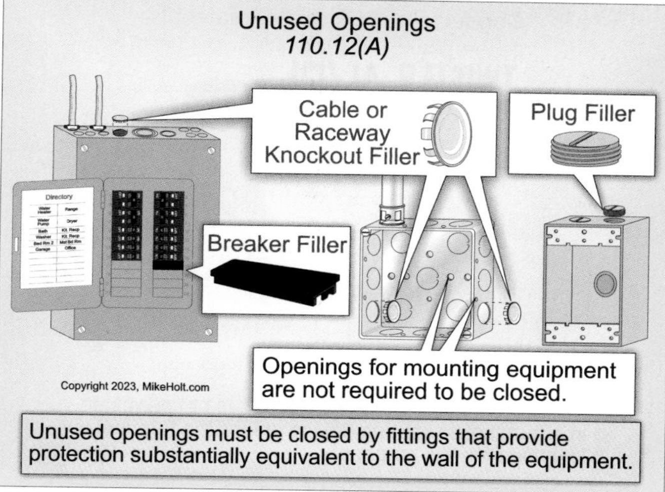

▶Figure 110–27

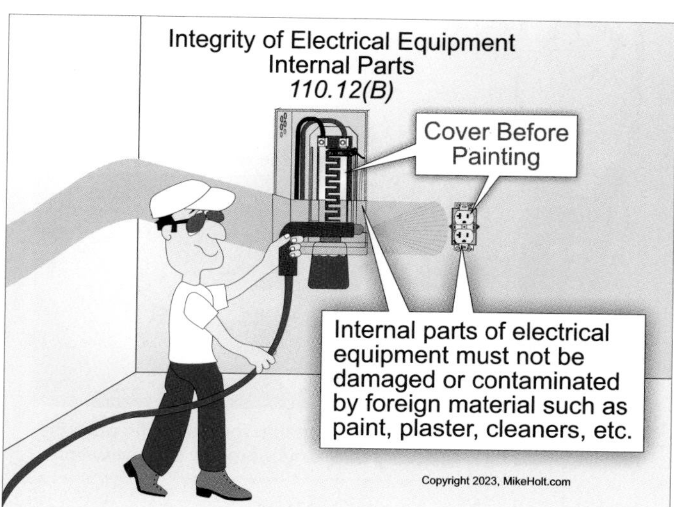

▶Figure 110–28

Author's Comment:

- Precautions must be taken to provide protection from the contamination of internal parts of panelboards and receptacles during building construction. Be sure the electrical equipment is properly masked and protected before drywall, painting, or other phases of the project that can contaminate or cause damage begins. ▶Figure 110–29

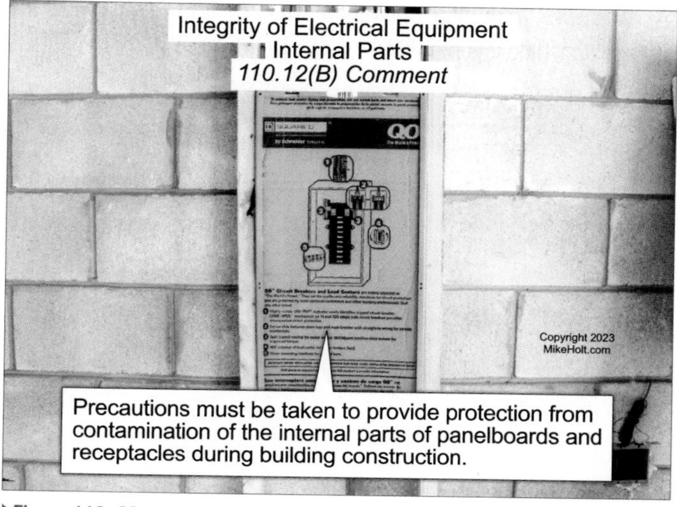

▶Figure 110–29

Electrical equipment containing damaged parts (such as items broken, bent, or cut), or those that have been deteriorated by corrosion, chemical action, or overheating are not permitted to be installed. ▶Figure 110–30

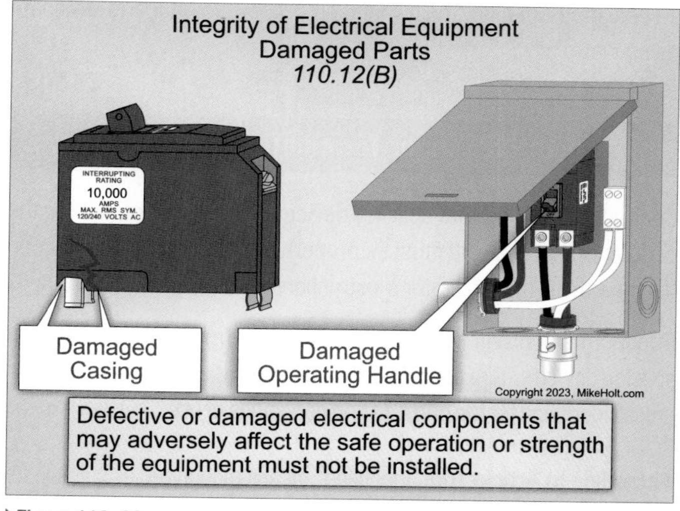

▶Figure 110–30

Author's Comment:

- Damaged parts include cracked insulators, arc shields not in place, overheated fuse clips, and damaged or missing switch handles or circuit-breaker handles.

110.13 Mounting and Cooling of Equipment

(A) Mounting. Electrical equipment must be firmly secured to the surface on which it is mounted. ▶Figure 110–31

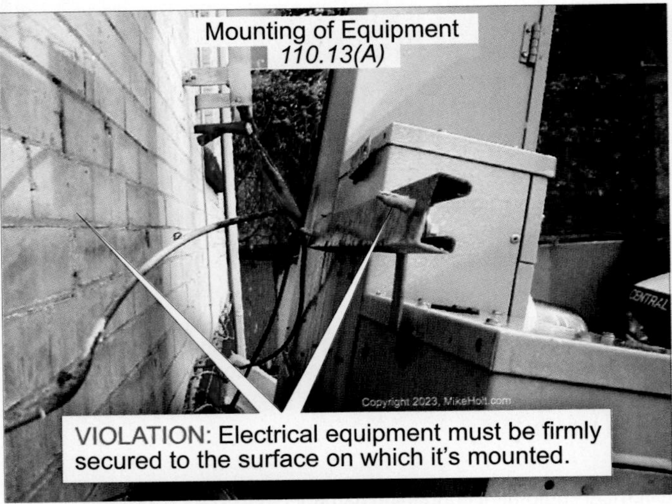

Mounting of Equipment
110.13(A)
Copyright 2023, MikeHolt.com
VIOLATION: Electrical equipment must be firmly secured to the surface on which it's mounted.

▶Figure 110–31

(B) Cooling. Electrical equipment that depends on heat dissipation must be installed in air-conditioned spaces, or if equipped with a ventilating opening, must maintain proper clearance to dissipate rising warm air.

110.14 Conductor Termination and Splicing

Conductor terminal and splicing devices must be identified for the conductor material and must be properly installed and used in accordance with the manufacturer's instructions [110.3(B)]. ▶Figure 110–32

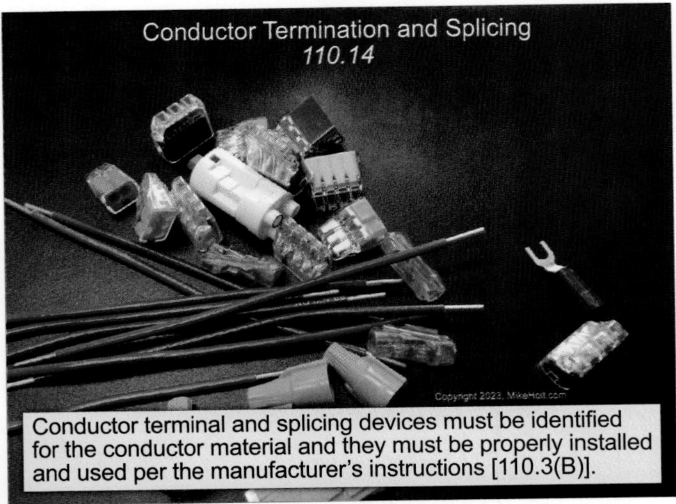

▶Figure 110–32

Conductors of dissimilar materials are not permitted in a terminal or splicing device where contact occurs between dissimilar conductors—unless identified for the purpose and conditions of use. ▶Figure 110–33

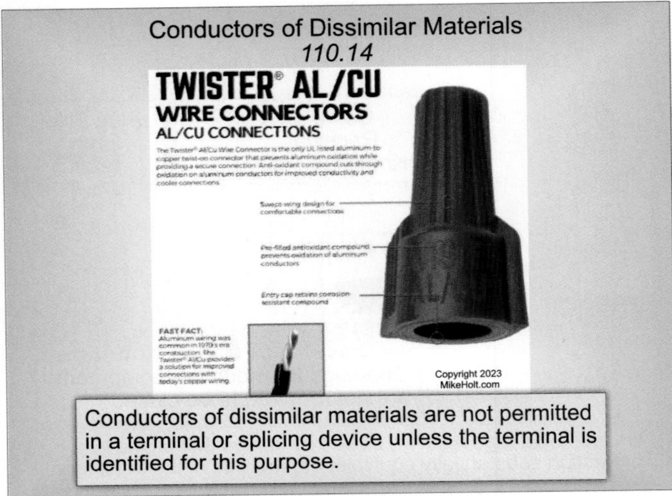

Conductors of Dissimilar Materials
110.14
TWISTER® AL/CU
WIRE CONNECTORS
AL/CU CONNECTIONS
Copyright 2023
MikeHolt.com
Conductors of dissimilar materials are not permitted in a terminal or splicing device unless the terminal is identified for this purpose.

▶Figure 110–33

According to Article 100, "Identified" means recognized as suitable for a specific purpose, function, use, environment, or application. ▶Figure 110–34

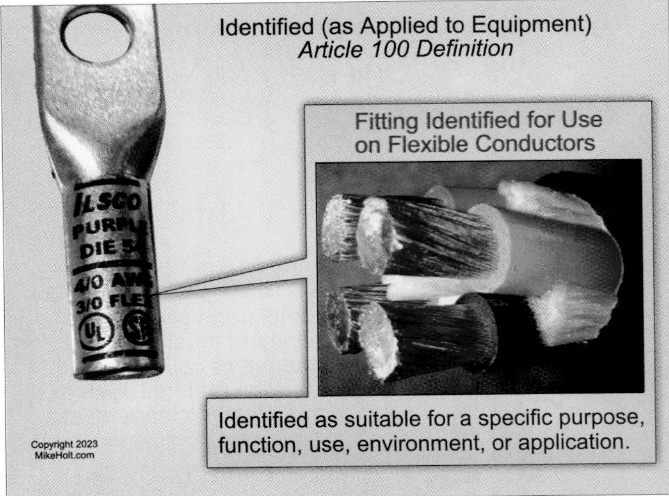

Identified (as Applied to Equipment)
Article 100 Definition
Fitting Identified for Use on Flexible Conductors
Copyright 2023
MikeHolt.com
Identified as suitable for a specific purpose, function, use, environment, or application.

▶Figure 110–34

1st Printing

Author's Comment:

- Conductor terminals suitable for aluminum wire only will be marked "AL." Those acceptable for copper wire will be marked "CU." Terminals suitable for copper, copper-clad-aluminum, and aluminum conductors will be marked "CU-AL" or "AL-CU." For 6 AWG and smaller, the markings can be printed on the container or on an information sheet inside the container. A "7" or "75" indicates a 75°C rated terminal, and a "9" or "90" indicates a 90°C rated terminal. If a terminal bears no marking, it can be used only with copper conductors. ▸Figure 110–35

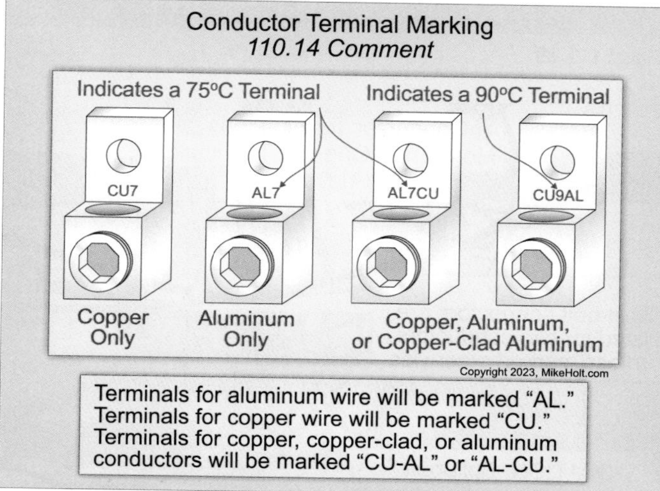

▸Figure 110–35

- Aluminum wire that was installed prior to the 1972 was the same wire used for utility power transmission lines. This aluminum wire had a major problem with oxidation at terminations and it required an antioxidant at terminations. When the antioxidant was not properly applied to the wire termination, fires were common at the termination. Since 1983, the *National Electrical Code* [310.3(B)] has required aluminum wire to be made from an aluminum alloy (AA-8000). This conductor does not require an antioxidant at terminations. ▸Figure 110–36

Connectors and terminals for conductors more finely stranded than Class B and Class C must be identified for the use of finely stranded conductors. ▸Figure 110–37

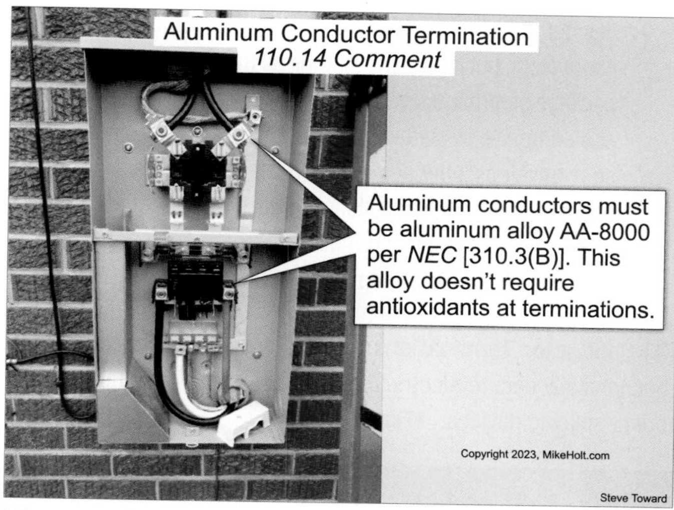

▸Figure 110–36

▸Figure 110–37

Author's Comment:

- Conductor terminations must comply with the manufacturer's instructions as required by 110.3(B). For example, if the instructions for the device are written, "Suitable for 18–12 AWG Stranded," then only stranded conductors can be used with the terminating device. If they are written, "Suitable for 18–12 AWG Solid," then only solid conductors are permitted, and if the instructions are written, "Suitable for 18–12 AWG," then either solid or stranded conductors can be used with the terminating device.

- Few terminations are listed for mixing aluminum and copper conductors, but if they are, that will be marked on the product package or terminal device. The reason copper and aluminum should not be in contact with each other is because corrosion develops between the two different metals due to galvanic action. This results in increased contact resistance at the splicing device, and increased resistance can cause the splice to overheat and result in a fire.

(A) Conductor Terminations. Conductor terminals must ensure a mechanically secure electrical connection using pressure connectors or splicing devices. ▶Figure 110–38

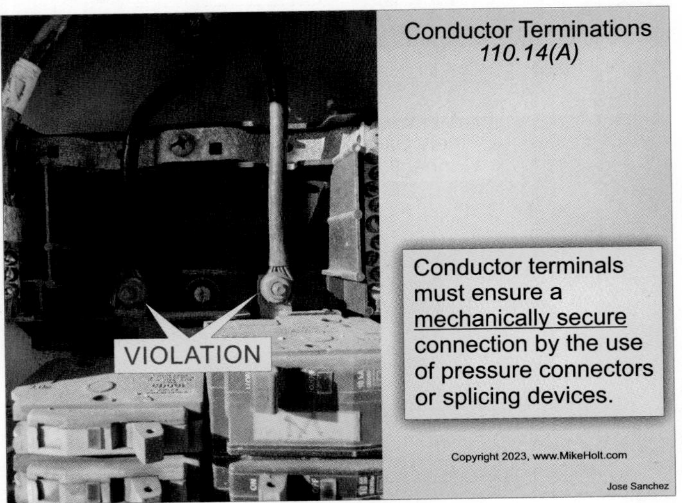

Conductor Terminations
110.14(A)
VIOLATION
Conductor terminals must ensure a mechanically secure connection by the use of pressure connectors or splicing devices.
Copyright 2023, www.MikeHolt.com
Jose Sanchez

▶Figure 110–38

Terminals are only listed for one conductor, unless marked otherwise. Terminals for more than one conductor must be identified for this purpose, either within the equipment instructions or on the terminal itself. ▶Figure 110–39

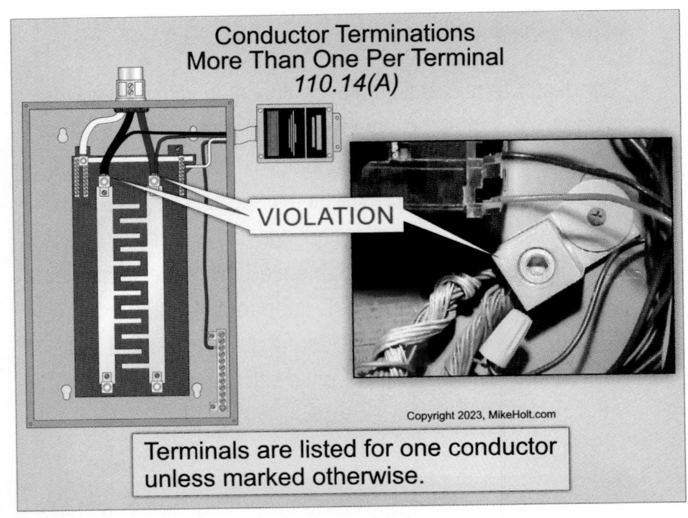

▶Figure 110–39

Author's Comment:

- Split-bolt connectors are commonly listed for only two conductors, although some are listed for three. However, it is a common industry practice to terminate as many conductors as possible within a split-bolt connector, even though this violates the *NEC*. ▶Figure 110–40

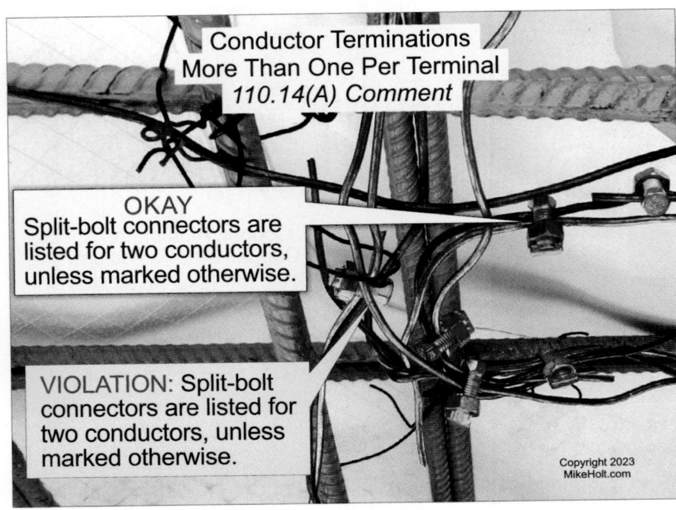

▶Figure 110–40

(B) Conductor Splices. Conductors must be spliced by a splicing device that is identified for the purpose. All splices, joints, and free ends of conductors must be covered with an identified insulating device. ▶Figure 110–41

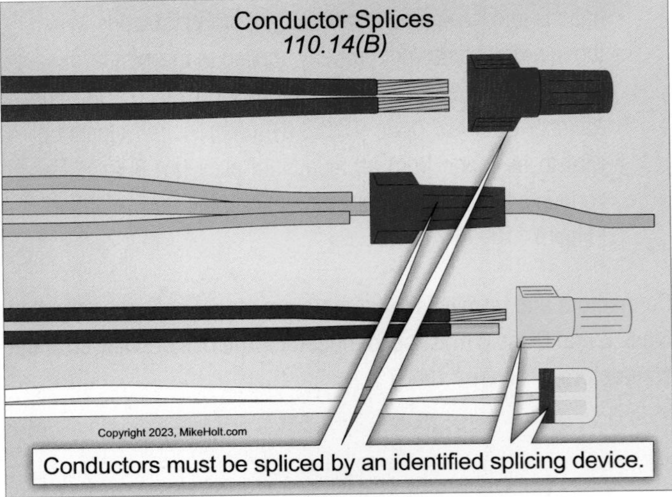

▶Figure 110–41

Author's Comment:

- To prevent an electrical hazard, the free ends of conductors must be insulated to prevent the exposed end(s) from touching energized parts. This requirement can be met by using an insulated twist-on or push-on wire connector. ▶Figure 110-42

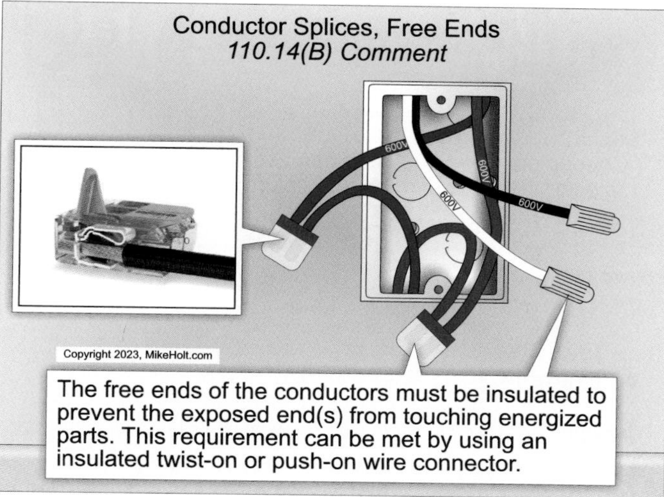

Conductor Splices, Free Ends
110.14(B) Comment
600V
Copyright 2023, MikeHolt.com
The free ends of the conductors must be insulated to prevent the exposed end(s) from touching energized parts. This requirement can be met by using an insulated twist-on or push-on wire connector.

▶Figure 110-42

- Pre-twisting conductors before applying twist-on wire connectors has been a very common practice in the field for years. The question (and subsequent debate) has always been, "Is pre-twisting required?" The *NEC* does not require that practice and, in fact, Ideal® made a statement about their Wing-Nut® twist-on connectors which said, "Pre-twisting is acceptable, but not required." Always follow the manufacturer's instructions and there will be no question [110.3(B)]. ▶Figure 110-43

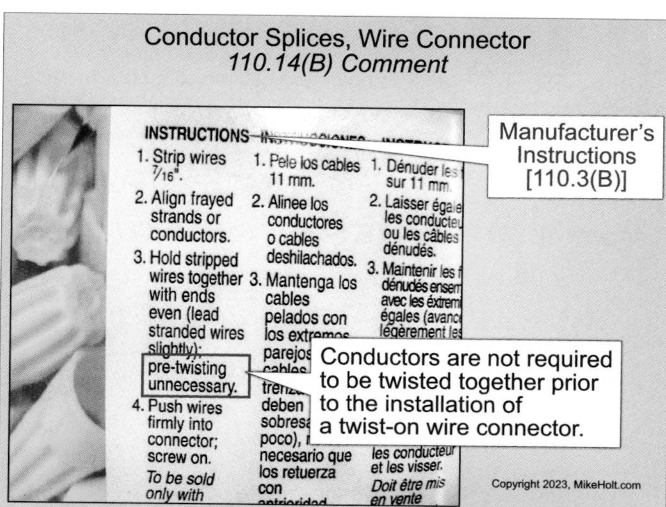

Conductor Splices, Wire Connector
110.14(B) Comment
INSTRUCTIONS
1. Strip wires 7/16".
2. Align frayed strands or conductors.
3. Hold stripped wires together with ends even (lead stranded wires slightly);
pre-twisting unnecessary.
4. Push wires firmly into connector; screw on.
To be sold only with
1. Pele los cables 11 mm.
2. Alinee los conductores o cables deshilachados.
3. Mantenga los cables pelados con los extremos parejos
deben
sobres
poco),
necesario que los retuerza con
1. Dénuder les sur 11 mm.
2. Laisser égale les conducte ou les câbles dénudés.
3. Maintenir les dénudés ensem avec les extrém égales (avanc légèrement les
les conducteur et les visser.
Doit être mis en vente
Manufacturer's Instructions [110.3(B)]
Conductors are not required to be twisted together prior to the installation of a twist-on wire connector.
Copyright 2023, MikeHolt.com

▶Figure 110-43

Single direct burial types UF or USE conductors can be spliced underground with a device listed for direct burial [300.5(E) and 300.15(G)]. ▶Figure 110-44

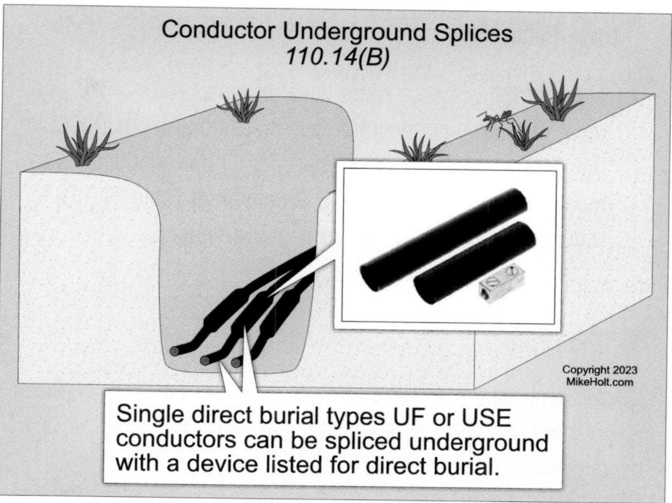

Conductor Underground Splices
110.14(B)
Copyright 2023 MikeHolt.com
Single direct burial types UF or USE conductors can be spliced underground with a device listed for direct burial.

▶Figure 110-44

The individual conductors of multiconductor UF or USE cable can be spliced underground with an underground listed splice kit that encapsulates the conductors and cable jacket.

Author's Comment:

- Electrical connection failures are the cause of many equipment and building fires. Improper terminations, poor workmanship, not following the manufacturer's instructions, and improper torquing can cause poor electrical connections. Improper electrical terminations can damage and melt conductor insulation resulting in short circuits and ground faults.

(C) Conductor Sized to Terminal Temperature Rating. Conductors terminating on equipment must be sized to the lowest terminal temperature rating in accordance with 110.14(C)(1) and (2).

(1) Equipment Terminals. Unless equipment is listed and marked otherwise, conductors are sized based on Table 310.16 in accordance with (a) or (b) as follows:

(a) Equipment Rated 100A or Less. Conductors terminating on equipment for circuits rated 100A or less, or conductors smaller than 1 AWG, must be sized as follows:

(2) Conductors rated 90°C can be used but they must be sized to the 60°C temperature column of Table 310.16.

(3) Conductors terminating on equipment rated 75°C can be sized in accordance with the ampacities in the 75°C temperature column of Table 310.16.

Author's Comment:

- Much of today's equipment have terminals rated 75°C and most of today's conductors have insulation ratings 90°C. If the equipment terminal is rated 75°C, the conductor size must be selected from the 75°C column of Table 310.16 to reduce the chance of the terminal overheating.

▶ Example 1

Question: *According to Table 310.16, what size THWN-2 conductor is required for a 50A circuit where the equipment is rated for 75°C conductors?* **▶Figure 110–45**

(a) 10 AWG *(b) 8 AWG* *(c) 6 AWG* *(d) 4 AWG*

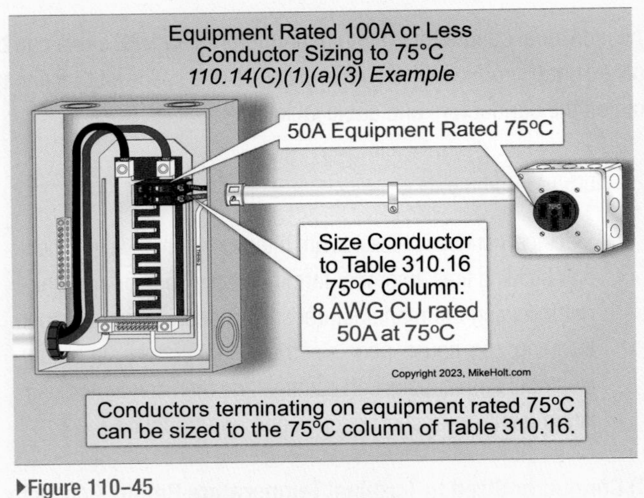

▶Figure 110–45

Answer: *(b) 8 AWG rated 50A at 75°C [110.14(C)(1)(a)(3) and Table 310.16]*

(b) Equipment Rated Over 100A. Conductors terminating on equipment for circuits rated over 100A, or conductors larger than 1 AWG, must be sized as follows:

(2) Conductors rated 90°C can be used but they must be sized to the 75°C temperature column of Table 310.16. **▶Figure 110–46**

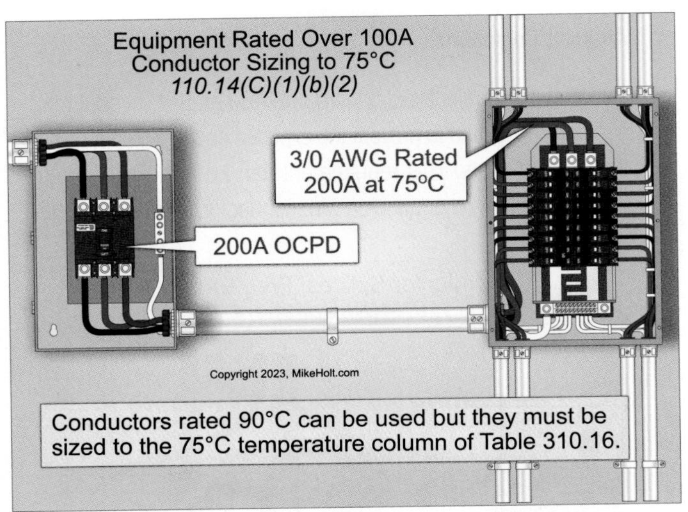

▶Figure 110–46

▶ Example 2

Question: *According to Table 310.16, what size aluminum conductor is required to supply a 200A feeder?* **▶Figure 110–47**

(a) 2/0 AWG *(b) 3/0 AWG* *(c) 4/0 AWG* *(d) 250 kcmil*

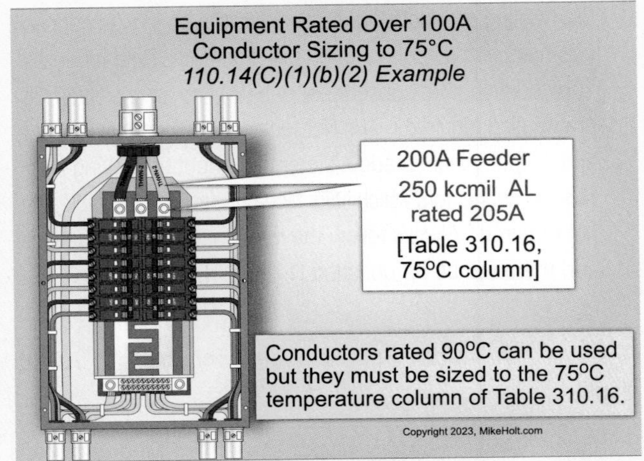

▶Figure 110–47

Answer: *(d) 250 kcmil rated 205A at 75°C [110.14(C)(1)(b)(2) and Table 310.16]*

Table 310.16 Ampacities of Insulated Conductors Based on Not More Than Three Current-Carrying Conductors and Ambient Temperature of 30°C (86°F)							
Size							Size
	60°C (140°F)	75°C (167°F)	90°C (194°F)	60°C (140°F)	75°C (167°F)	90°C (194°F)	
	TW, UF	RHW, THHW THW, THWN XHHW, USE	RHH, RHW-2 THHN, THHW THW-2, THWN-2 USE-2, XHHW XHHW-2	TW, UF	THW, THWN XHHW	THHN, THW-2 THWN-2, THHW XHHW, XHHW-2	
AWG kcmil	Copper			Aluminum/Copper-Clad Aluminum			AWG kcmil
14	15	20	25				**14**
12	20	25	30	15	20	25	**12**
10	30	35	40	25	30	35	**10**
8	40	50	55	35	40	45	**8**
6	55	65	75	40	50	55	**6**
4	70	85	95	55	65	75	**4**
3	85	100	115	65	75	85	**3**
2	95	115	130	75	90	100	**2**
1	110	130	145	85	100	115	**1**
1/0	125	150	170	100	120	135	**1/0**
2/0	145	175	195	115	135	150	**2/0**
3/0	165	200	225	130	155	175	**3/0**
4/0	195	230	260	150	180	205	**4/0**
250	215	255	290	170	205	230	**250**

(2) Separate Connector. Separately installed pressure connectors rated 90°C or more and not connected to electrical equipment, can have the conductors sized in accordance with the 90°C temperature column ampacities of Table 310.16. ▶Figure 110–48

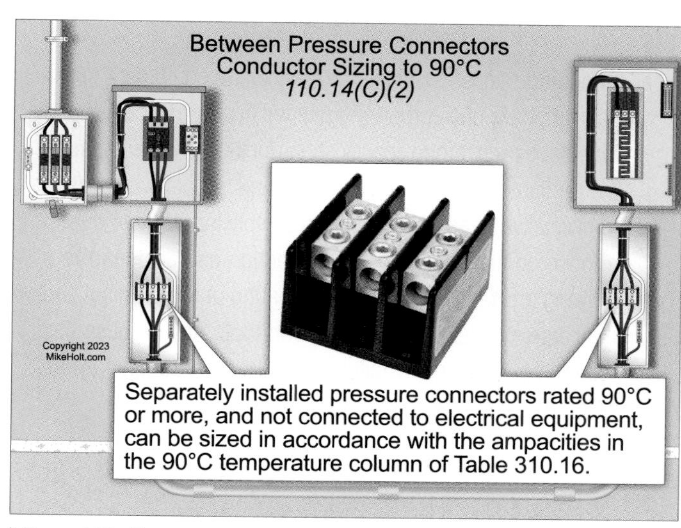

▶Figure 110–48

▶ Example 3

Question: *According to Table 310.16, what size aluminum conductor can be used to interconnect busbars protected by a 200A overcurrent protective device where the equipment is rated for 90°C conductors?*

(a) 1/0 AWG (b) 2/0 AWG (c) 3/0 AWG (d) 4/0 AWG

Answer: *(d) 4/0 AWG aluminum rated 205A at 90°C [110.14(C)(2) and Table 310.16]*

(D) Torquing of Terminal Connections. Tightening torque values for terminal connections must be as indicated on equipment or instructions. The tool or device used to achieve torque values must be approved by the authority having jurisdiction. **▶Figure 110–49**

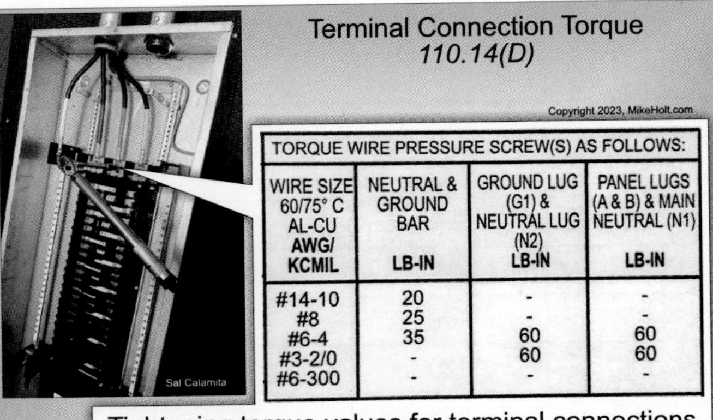

WIRE SIZE 60/75° C AL-CU AWG/ KCMIL	NEUTRAL & GROUND BAR LB-IN	GROUND LUG (G1) & NEUTRAL LUG (N2) LB-IN	PANEL LUGS (A & B) & MAIN NEUTRAL (N1) LB-IN
#14-10	20	-	-
#8	25	-	-
#6-4	35	60	60
#3-2/0	-	60	60
#6-300	-	-	-

▶Figure 110–49

Author's Comment:

- Conductors must terminate on device and equipment terminals that have been properly tightened in accordance with the manufacturer's torque specifications included with equipment instructions. Failure to torque terminals properly can result in excessive heating of terminals or splicing devices due to a loose connection. A loose connection can also lead to a glowing arc which increases the heating of the terminal and may cause a short circuit or ground fault. Any of these can result in a fire or other failure, including an arc flash event. **▶Figure 110–50** and **▶Figure 110–51**

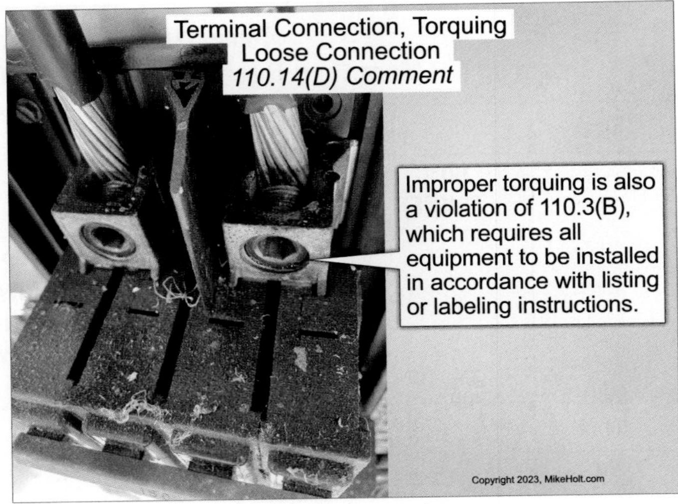

Terminal Connection, Torquing
Loose Connection
110.14(D) Comment
Improper torquing is also a violation of 110.3(B), which requires all equipment to be installed in accordance with listing or labeling instructions.
Copyright 2023, MikeHolt.com

▶Figure 110–50

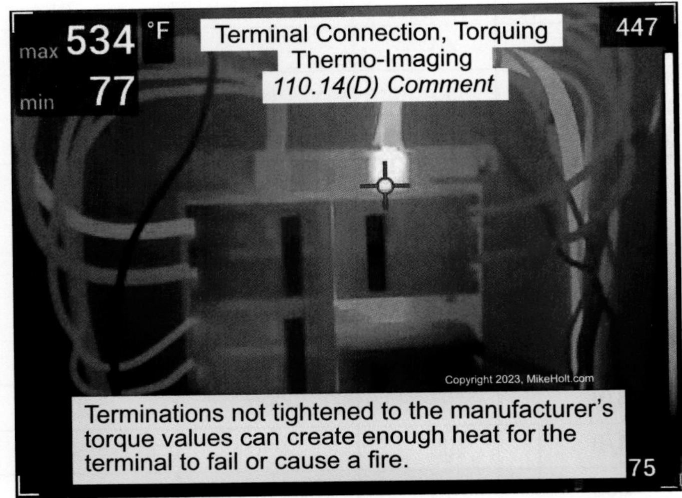

max 534 °F
min 77
447
Terminal Connection, Torquing
Thermo-Imaging
110.14(D) Comment
Copyright 2023, MikeHolt.com
Terminations not tightened to the manufacturer's torque values can create enough heat for the terminal to fail or cause a fire.
75

▶Figure 110–51

Note 1: Examples of approved means of achieving the indicated torque values include the use of torque tools or devices (such as shear bolts or breakaway-style devices) with visual indicators that demonstrate the proper torque has been applied. **▶Figure 110–52**

Note 2: In the absence of manufacturer's torque requirements, see Annex I or UL Standard 486A-486B, *Standard for Safety-Wire Connectors,* for torque values. The equipment manufacturer can be contacted if numeric torque values are not indicated on the equipment or the instructions are not available.

Note 3: For information for torquing threaded connections and terminations, see NFPA 70B, *Recommended Practice for Electrical Equipment Maintenance*, Section 8.11. **▶Figure 110–53**

1st Printing

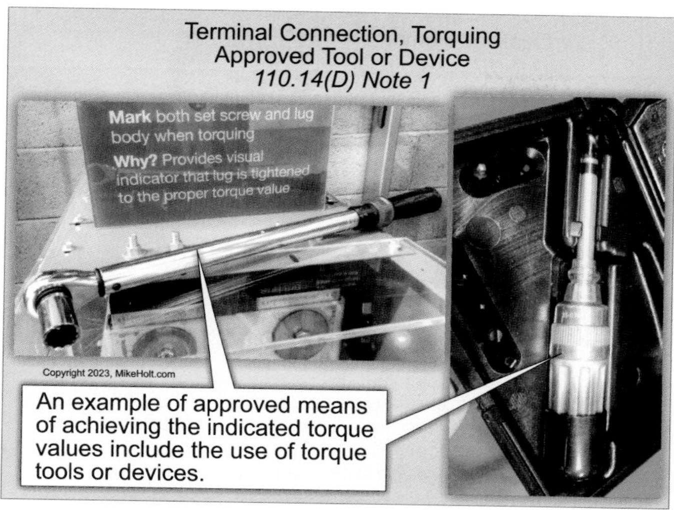

▸Figure 110–52

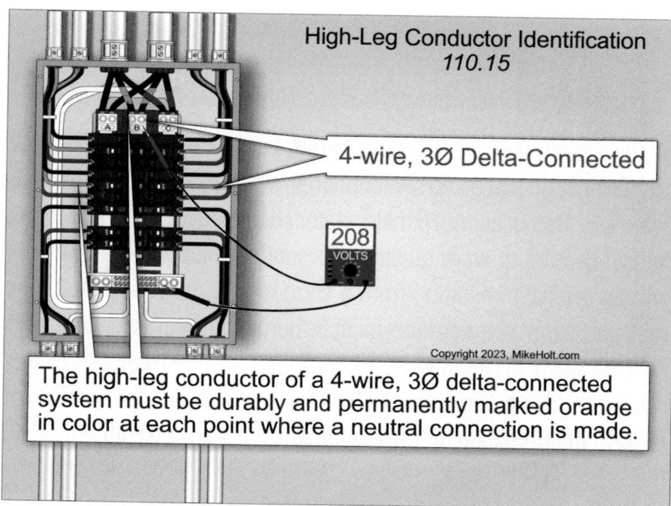

▸Figure 110–54

▸Figure 110–53

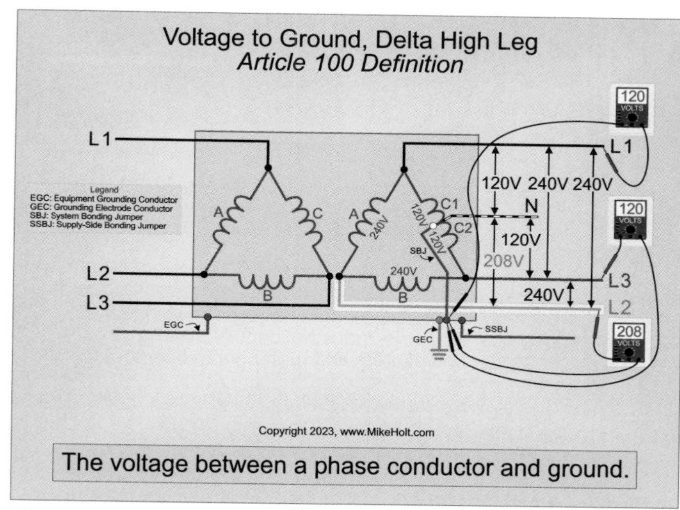

▸Figure 110–55

110.15 High-Leg Conductor Identification

On a 4-wire, delta-connected, three-phase system (where the midpoint of one phase winding of the secondary is grounded) the conductor with the resulting 208V to ground (high-leg) must be durably and permanently marked by an outer finish (insulation) that is orange in color or other effective means. Such identification must be placed at each point where a connection is made if the neutral conductor is present. ▸Figure 110–54 and ▸Figure 110–55

Author's Comment:

- The high-leg conductor is also called the "wild leg" or "stinger leg." In panelboards, the B phase busbar must be the high-leg [408.3(E)(1)], and the panelboard itself must be identified "Caution B Phase has 208V-to-Ground" [408.3(F)(1)].

110.16 Arc-Flash Hazard Warning Label, Other Than Dwelling Units

(A) Arc-Flash Hazard Warning Label. In other than dwelling units, a label must be placed on switchboards, switchgear, enclosed panelboards, industrial control panels, meter socket enclosures, and motor control centers to warn qualified persons of the danger associated with an arc flash resulting from a short circuit or ground fault. The arc-flash hazard warning label must be permanently affixed, have sufficient durability to withstand the environment [110.21(B)], and clearly visible to qualified persons before they examine, adjust, service, or perform maintenance on the equipment. ▸Figure 110–56

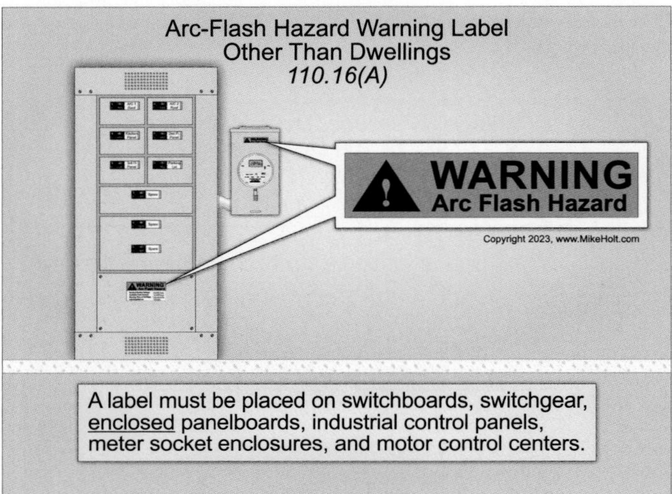
Arc-Flash Hazard Warning Label
Other Than Dwellings
110.16(A)
WARNING
Arc Flash Hazard
Copyright 2023, www.MikeHolt.com
A label must be placed on switchboards, switchgear, enclosed panelboards, industrial control panels, meter socket enclosures, and motor control centers.

▸Figure 110–56

According to Article 100, "Qualified Person" is one who has the skill and knowledge related to the construction and operation of electrical equipment and its installation. This person must have received safety training to recognize and avoid the hazards involved with electrical systems. ▸Figure 110–57

Author's Comment:

- NFPA 70E, *Standard for Electrical Safety in the Workplace*, provides information on the safety training requirements expected of a "qualified person." Examples of this safety training include training in the use of special precautionary techniques, personal protective equipment (PPE), insulating and shielding materials, and insulated tools and test equipment when working on or near exposed conductors or circuit parts that can become energized. ▸Figure 110–58

Qualified Person
Article 100 Definition
Copyright 2023
MikeHolt.com
A person with skills and knowledge related to the construction and operation of electrical equipment and installations. This person must have received safety training to recognize and avoid the hazards involved with electrical systems.

▸Figure 110–57

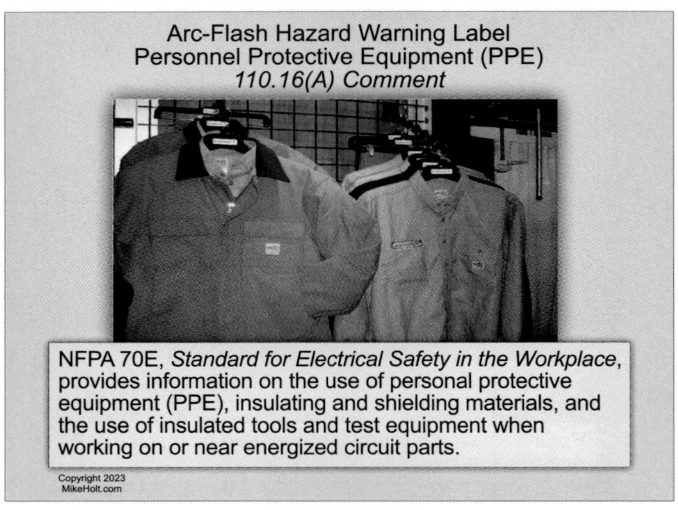
Arc-Flash Hazard Warning Label
Personnel Protective Equipment (PPE)
110.16(A) Comment
NFPA 70E, Standard for Electrical Safety in the Workplace, provides information on the use of personal protective equipment (PPE), insulating and shielding materials, and the use of insulated tools and test equipment when working on or near energized circuit parts.
Copyright 2023
MikeHolt.com

▸Figure 110–58

- In many parts of the United States, electricians, electrical contractors, electrical inspectors, and electrical engineers must complete from 6 to 24 hours of *NEC* review each year as a requirement to maintain licensing. This does not necessarily make one qualified to deal with the specific hazards involved with electrical systems.

(B) Service and Feeder Equipment. In other than dwelling units, service and feeder equipment rated 1000A or more must have an arc-flash label in accordance with applicable industry practices that includes the date the label was applied and have sufficient durability to withstand the environment. ▸Figure 110–59

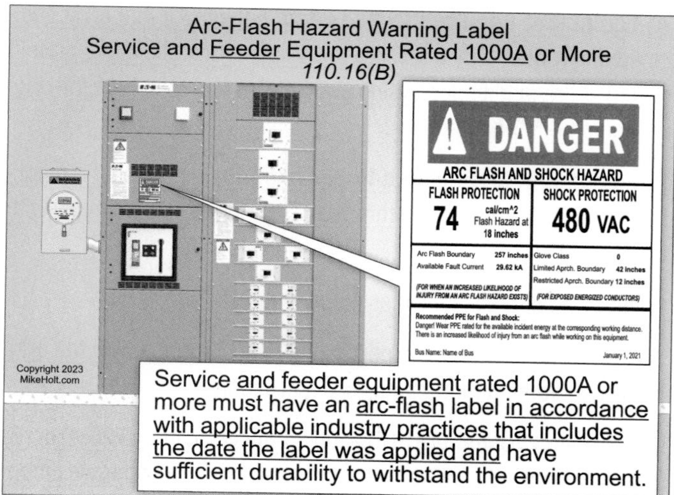

▶Figure 110–59

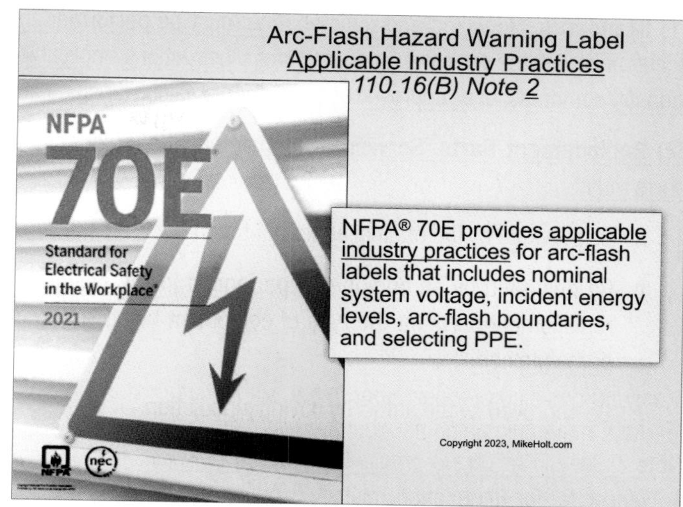

▶Figure 110–60

Author's Comment:

- Determining the available fault current on the line side of service or feeder equipment terminals requires you to know the available fault current at the secondary of the utility transformer (provided by the electric utility), conductor material, length of the conductors, and wiring method used to install conductors. With this information, you can use an app or computer software to determine the available fault current at the line terminals of service or feeder equipment.
- An arc-flash event can reach temperatures of 35,000°F, which turns metal from a solid to gas vapors, and releases molten shrapnel that pierces the skin causing severe burns—and even death. The reason the arc-flash label is not required in dwelling units is the nominal voltage will be single-phase, 120V line-to-ground (240V line-to-line), so the arc fault will self-extinguish with every zero crossing of the sinusoidal waveform. A three-phase arc fault is sustainable in accordance with IEEE-1584.

Note 2: NFPA 70E, *Standard for Electrical Safety in the Workplace*, provides applicable industry practices for developing arc-flash labels that include nominal system voltage, incident energy levels, arc-flash boundaries, and selecting personal protective equipment. ▶**Figure 110–60**

Author's Comment:

- The information required by 110.16(B) is necessary to determine the incident energy and arc-flash boundary distance by using an app or computer software to ensure the label complies with NFPA 70E, *Standard for Electrical Safety in the Workplace*, to increase safety during future work on service and feeder equipment.

110.17 Servicing and Maintenance of Equipment

Equipment servicing and maintenance is required to be performed by a qualified person trained in the servicing and maintenance of equipment and comply with the following: ▶**Figure 110–61**

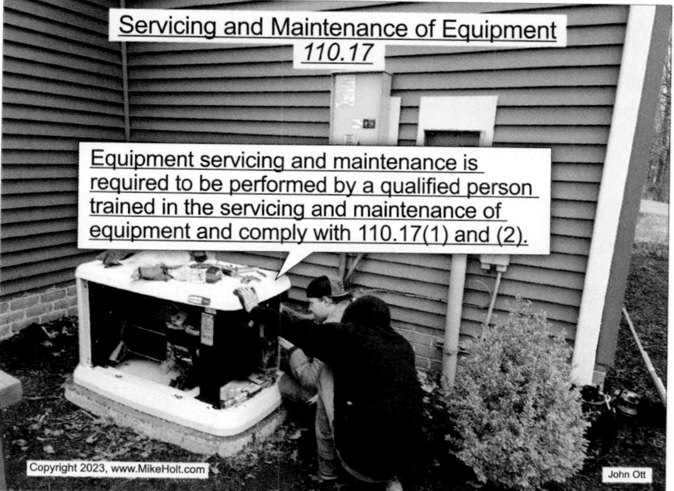

▶Figure 110–61

(1) Standards. Servicing and maintenance must be performed in accordance with the equipment manufacturer's instructions, applicable industry standards, or as approved by the authority having jurisdiction.

(2) Replacement Parts. Servicing and maintenance replacement parts must:

a. Be provided by the original equipment manufacturer.

b. Be designed by an engineer experienced in the design of replacement parts for the type of equipment being serviced or maintained.

c. Be approved by the authority having jurisdiction.

Note 2: See NFPA 70B, *Recommended Practice for Electrical Equipment Maintenance*, for information related to preventive maintenance for electrical equipment.

According to Article 100, "Servicing" means the process of following a manufacturer's instructions or industry standards to analyze, adjust, or perform maintenance and repair of equipment. ▸**Figure 110–62**

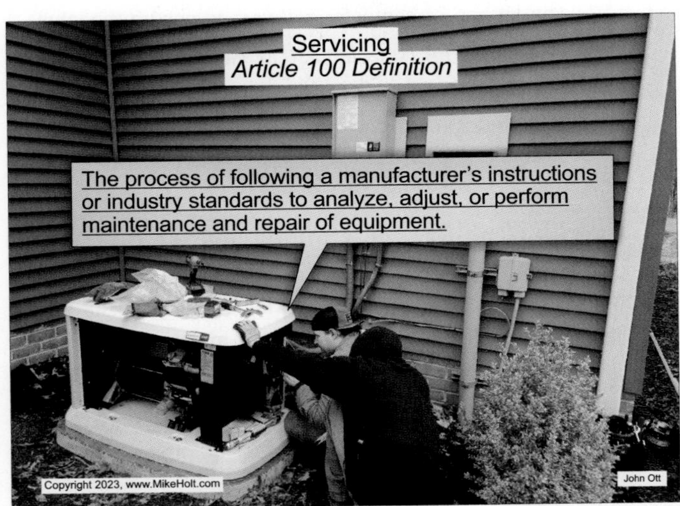
Servicing
Article 100 Definition
The process of following a manufacturer's instructions or industry standards to analyze, adjust, or perform maintenance and repair of equipment.
Copyright 2023, www.MikeHolt.com
John Ott

▸**Figure 110–62**

110.20 Reconditioned Equipment

Equipment that is restored to operating condition must be reconditioned with identified replacement parts and verified under applicable standards. These parts are either provided by the original equipment manufacturer or are designed by an engineer experienced in the design of replacement parts for the type of equipment being reconditioned.

(A) Equipment Required to Be Listed. Equipment that is reconditioned and required by this *Code* to be listed, must be listed or field labeled as "reconditioned" using available instructions from the original equipment manufacturer.

(B) Equipment Not Required to Be Listed. Equipment that is reconditioned and not required by this *Code* to be listed, must comply with one of the following:

(1) Be listed or field labeled as "reconditioned."

(2) Have the reconditioning performed in accordance with the original equipment manufacturer's instructions.

(C) Approved Equipment. If the options specified in 110.20(A) or (B) are not available, the authority having jurisdiction can approve reconditioned equipment. The reconditioner must provide the authority having jurisdiction with documentation of the changes to the product.

110.21 Hazard Markings

(B) Field-Applied Hazard Markings. Where caution, warning, or danger hazard markings are required, the markings must meet the following requirements:

(1) Field-applied hazard markings must be of sufficient durability to withstand the environment and warn of the hazards using effective words, colors, symbols, or a combination of the three. ▸**Figure 110–63**

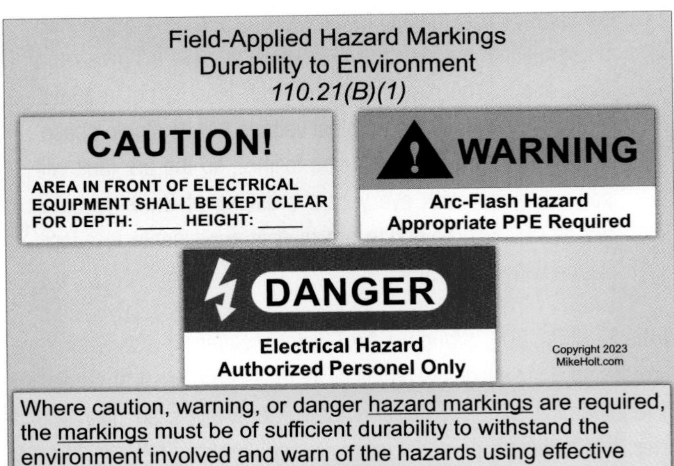
Field-Applied Hazard Markings
Durability to Environment
110.21(B)(1)
CAUTION!
AREA IN FRONT OF ELECTRICAL EQUIPMENT SHALL BE KEPT CLEAR FOR DEPTH: ____ HEIGHT: ____
WARNING
Arc-Flash Hazard
Appropriate PPE Required
DANGER
Electrical Hazard
Authorized Personel Only
Copyright 2023 MikeHolt.com
Where caution, warning, or danger hazard markings are required, the markings must be of sufficient durability to withstand the environment involved and warn of the hazards using effective words, colors, symbols, or a combination of the three.

▸**Figure 110–63**

Note: ANSI Z535.4, *Product Safety Signs and Labels,* provides guidelines for the design and durability of signs and labels.

1st Printing

(2) Field-applied hazard markings cannot be handwritten and must be permanently affixed to the equipment. ▶Figure 110-64

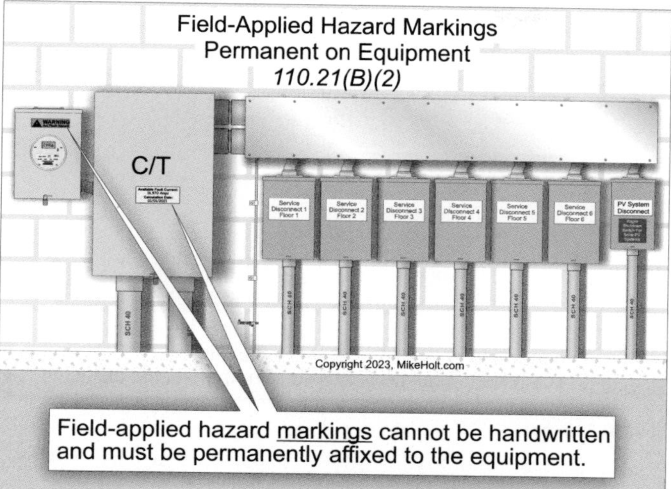

▶Figure 110-64

Ex: Markings containing information that is likely to change can be handwritten, if it is legible.

110.22 Identification of Disconnecting Means

(A) General. Each disconnect must be legibly marked to indicate its purpose unless located and arranged so the purpose is evident.

In other than one- or two-family dwelling units, the disconnect marking must include the identification and location of the circuit source that supplies the disconnect unless located and arranged so the identification and location of the circuit source is evident. The marking must be of sufficient durability to withstand the environment. ▶Figure 110-65

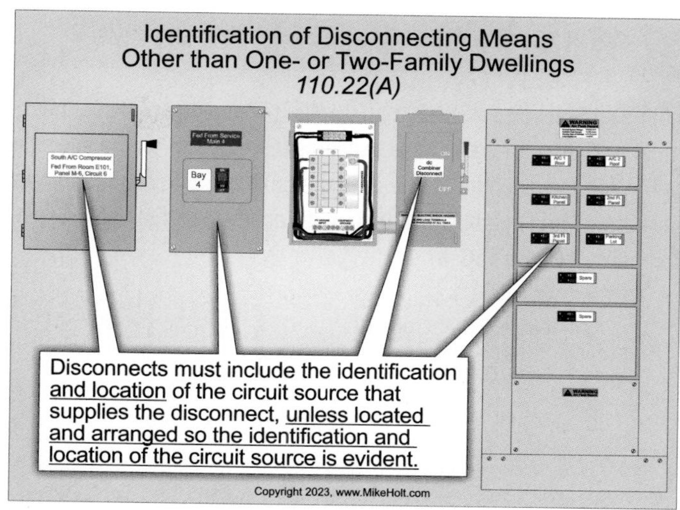

▶Figure 110-65

According to Article 100, "Disconnect" is a device that disconnects the circuit conductors from their power source. ▶Figure 110-66

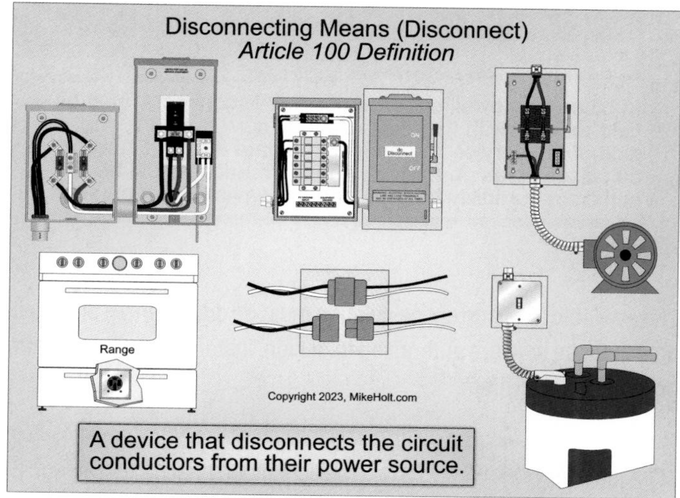

▶Figure 110-66

Author's Comment:

- See 408.4 for additional requirements for identification markings on circuit directories for switchboards and panelboards.

(C) Tested Series Combination Systems. Tested series-rated installations must be legibly field marked to indicate the equipment has been applied with a series combination rating in accordance with 240.86(B). The marking must be permanently affixed, have sufficient durability to withstand the environment in accordance with 110.21(B), and state:

CAUTION—SERIES COMBINATION SYSTEM RATED ____ AMPERES. IDENTIFIED REPLACEMENT COMPONENTS REQUIRED

110.24 Available Fault Current Marking

(A) Field Marking. In other than dwelling units, service disconnects must be field marked with the available fault current on the line side of the service disconnect, the date the fault current calculation was performed, and must be of sufficient durability to withstand the environment. ▶Figure 110-67

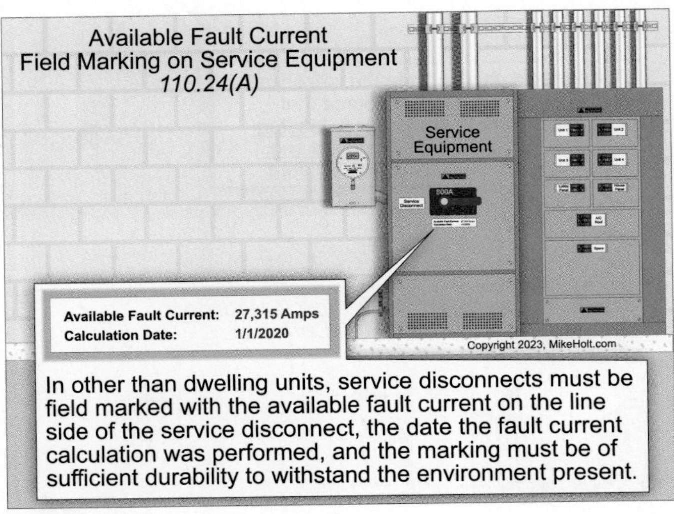
Available Fault Current
Field Marking on Service Equipment
110.24(A)
Service Equipment
Available Fault Current: 27,315 Amps
Calculation Date: 1/1/2020
Copyright 2023, MikeHolt.com
In other than dwelling units, service disconnects must be field marked with the available fault current on the line side of the service disconnect, the date the fault current calculation was performed, and the marking must be of sufficient durability to withstand the environment present.

▶Figure 110-67

The available fault current calculation must be documented and available to those who are authorized to design, install, inspect, maintain, or operate the system.

Note 1: For assistance in determining the severity of potential exposures, planning safe work practices, and selecting personal protective equipment, see NFPA 70E, *Standard for Electrical Safety in the Workplace*.

Note 2: The available fault current at the utility transformer needed to determine the available fault current at service equipment must be acquired from the electric utility. ▶Figure 110-68

(B) Modifications. When modifications to the electrical installation affect the available fault current at the service disconnect, the available fault current must be recalculated to ensure the short-circuit current ratings at the service disconnect are sufficient for the available fault current. The required field marking(s) in 110.24(A) must be adjusted to reflect the new level of available fault current.

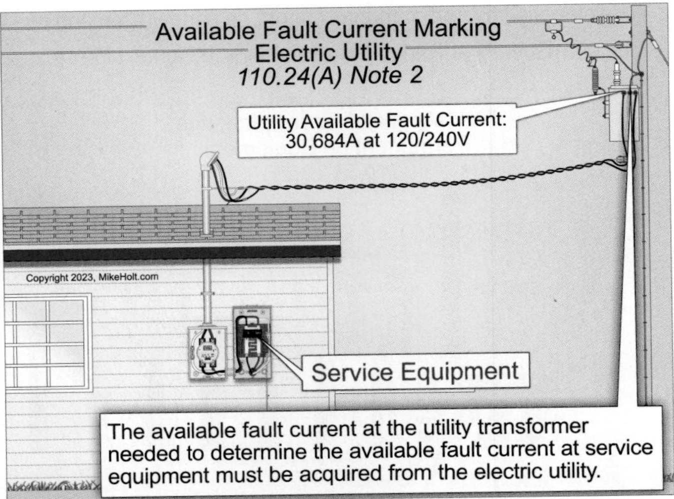
Available Fault Current Marking
Electric Utility
110.24(A) Note 2
Utility Available Fault Current:
30,684A at 120/240V
Copyright 2023, MikeHolt.com
Service Equipment
The available fault current at the utility transformer needed to determine the available fault current at service equipment must be acquired from the electric utility.

▶Figure 110-68

Author's Comment:

- It is common for electrical systems to be modified to accommodate growth. When the capacity of the system increases, either equipment is installed to increase efficiency or alternative energy systems are added. These factors can influence the available fault current if the utility transformer is changed. This increase in available fault current could end up exceeding the short-circuit current ratings of equipment in violation of 110.9 and 110.10.

110.25 Lockable Disconnecting Means

If the *Code* requires a disconnect to be lockable in the open position, the provisions for locking must remain in place whether the lock is installed or not. ▶Figure 110-69 and ▶Figure 110-70

Part II. 1000V, Nominal, or Less

110.26 Spaces Around Electrical Equipment

Working space, access to and egress from working space, must be provided and maintained around equipment to permit safe operation and maintenance of equipment. ▶Figure 110-71

1st Printing

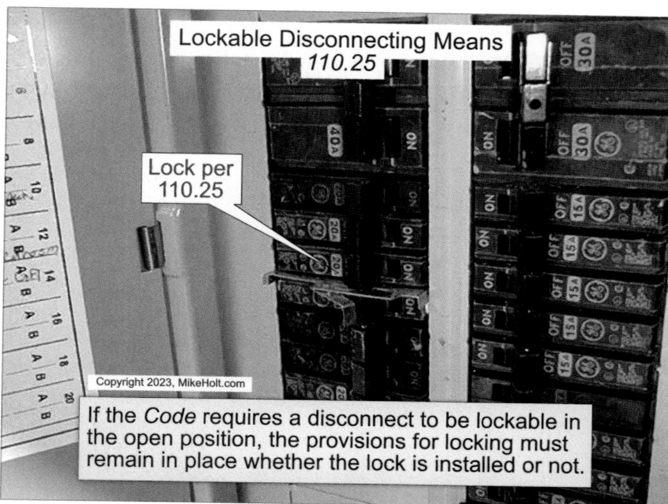

▸Figure 110–69

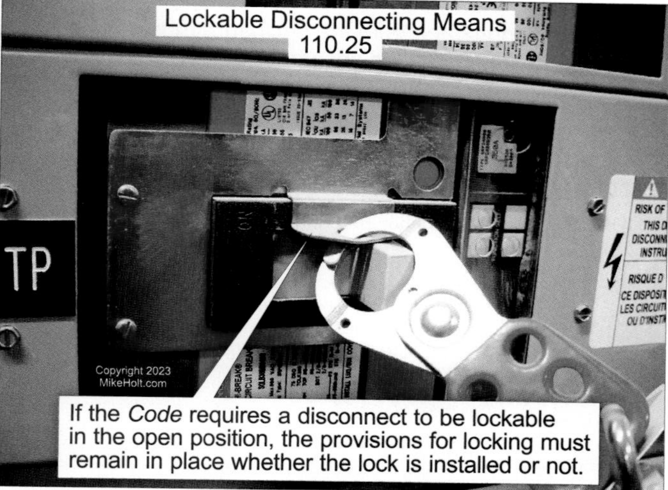

▸Figure 110–70

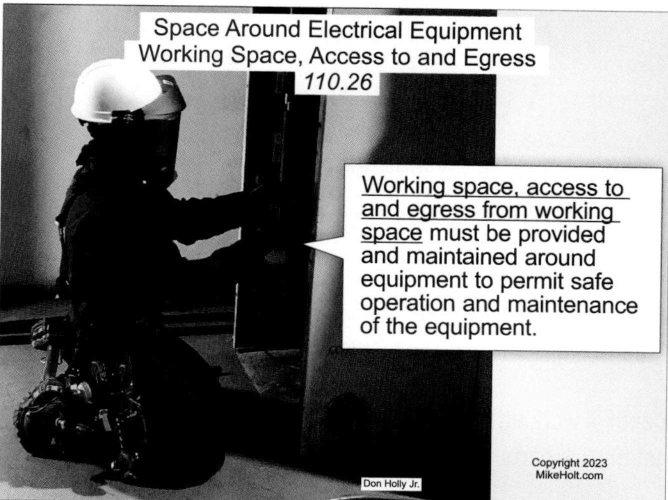

▸Figure 110–71

Open equipment doors must not impede access to and egress from the working space. Access or egress to working space is considered impeded if one or more simultaneously opened equipment doors restrict working space access to less than 24 in. wide and 6½ ft high. ▸Figure 110–72

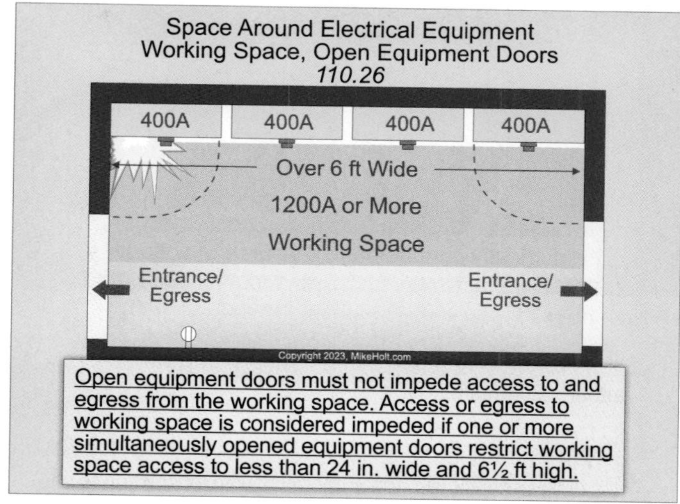

▸Figure 110–72

(A) Working Space. Equipment that is likely to need examination, adjustment, servicing, or maintenance while energized must have working space provided in accordance with 110.26(A)(1), (2), (3), and (4): ▸Figure 110–73

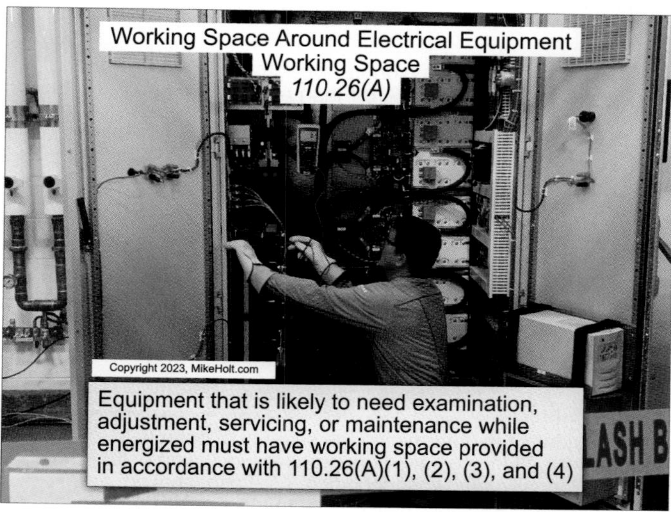

▸Figure 110–73

According to Article 100, "Energized" means electrically connected to a source of voltage. ▸Figure 110–74

Energized
Article 100 Definition
Electrically connected to a source of voltage.
Copyright 2023, www.MikeHolt.com

▶Figure 110–74

Author's Comment:

- The phrase "while energized" is the root of many debates. As always, check with the authority having jurisdiction to see what equipment he/she believes needs a clear working space.

Note: For guidance in determining the severity of potential exposure, planning safe work practices (including establishing an electrically safe work condition), arc-flash labeling, and selecting personal protective equipment see NFPA 70E, *Standard for Electrical Safety in the Workplace.* ▶Figure 110–75

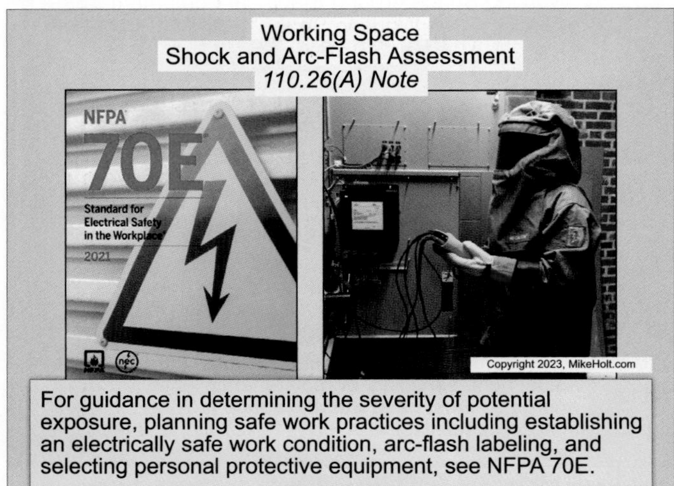

▶Figure 110–75

(1) Depth of Working Space. The depth of working space, which is measured from the enclosure front, cannot be less than the distances contained in Table 110.26(A)(1). These depths are dependent on the voltage-to-ground and three different conditions. ▶Figure 110–76

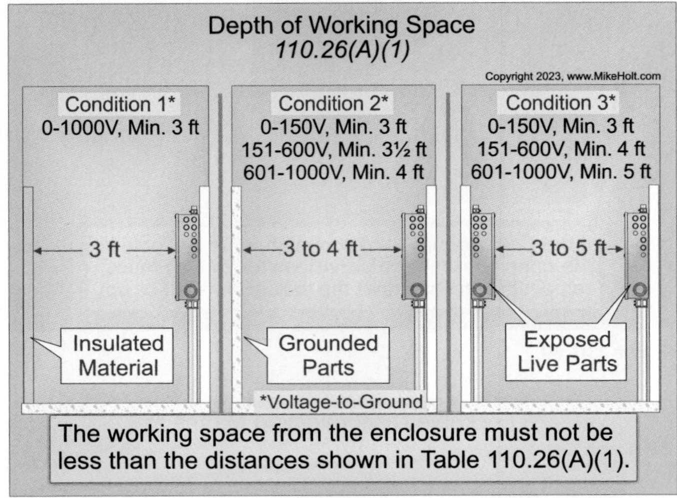

▶Figure 110–76

According to Article 100, "Voltage-to-Ground, Grounded Systems" is the voltage between any phase and neutral conductor. ▶Figure 110–77

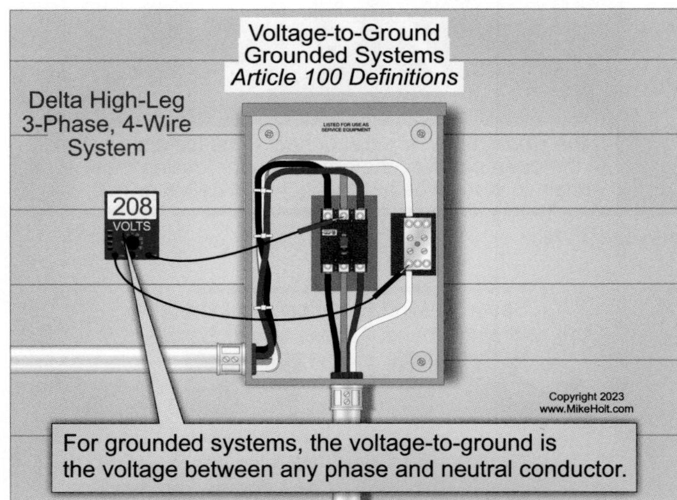

▶Figure 110–77

According to Article 100, "Voltage-to-Ground, Ungrounded Systems" is the voltage between any two phase conductors. ▶Figure 110–78

Depth of working space must be measured from the enclosure front, not the live parts. ▶Figure 110–79

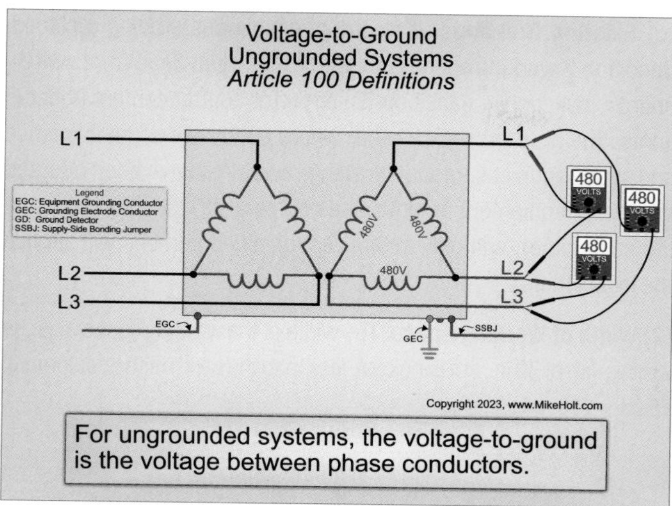

▸Figure 110–78

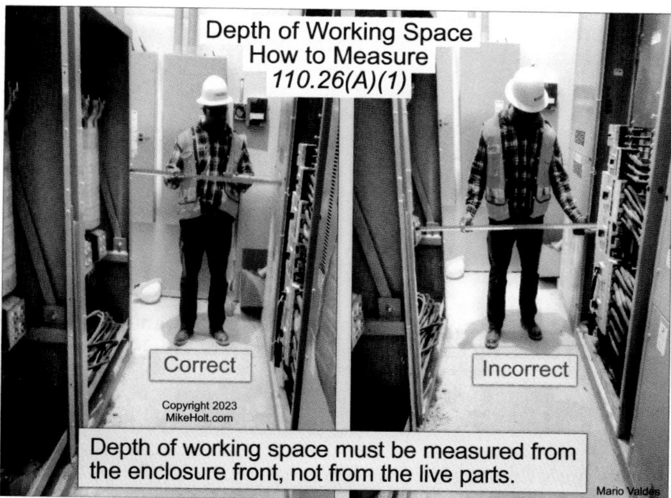

▸Figure 110–79

According to Article 100, "Live Parts" means energized conductive components.

Table 110.26(A)(1) Working Space			
Voltage-to-Ground	**Condition 1**	**Condition 2**	**Condition 3**
0–150V	3 ft	3 ft	3 ft
151–600V	3 ft	3½ft	4 ft
601–1000V	3 ft	4 ft	5 ft

▸Figure 110–80, ▸Figure 110–81, and ▸Figure 110–82

Table Note:

Condition 1: Exposed live parts on one side of the working space and no live or grounded parts (including concrete, brick, or tile walls) on the other side of the working space.

Condition 2: Exposed live parts on one side of the working space and grounded parts on the other. Concrete, brick, tile, and similar surfaces are considered grounded.

Condition 3: Exposed live parts on both sides of the working space.

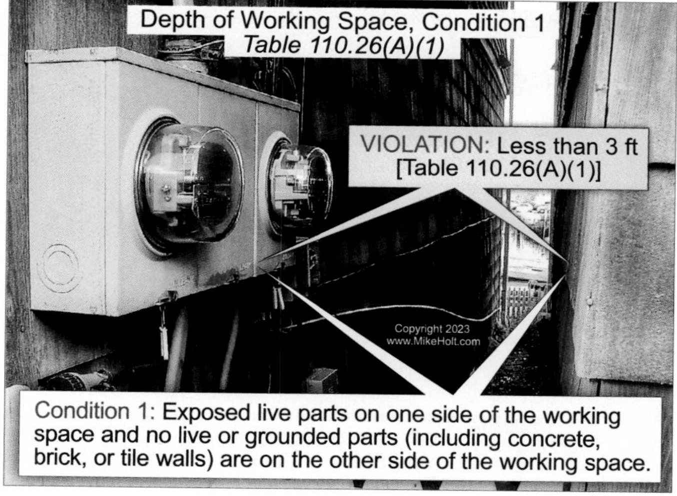

▸Figure 110–80

(a) Rear and Sides of Dead-Front Equipment. Working space is not required at the back or sides of equipment where all connections and renewable, adjustable, or serviceable parts are accessible from the front. ▸Figure 110–83

Author's Comment:

- Sections of equipment that require rear or side access to make field connections must be marked by the manufacturer on the front of the equipment. See 408.18(C).

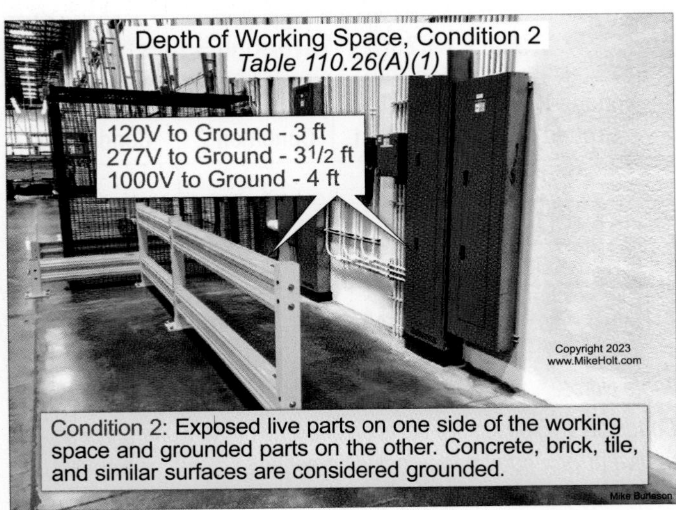
Depth of Working Space, Condition 2
Table 110.26(A)(1)
120V to Ground - 3 ft
277V to Ground - 3 1/2 ft
1000V to Ground - 4 ft
Copyright 2023
www.MikeHolt.com
Condition 2: Exposed live parts on one side of the working space and grounded parts on the other. Concrete, brick, tile, and similar surfaces are considered grounded.
Mike Burleson

▸Figure 110–81

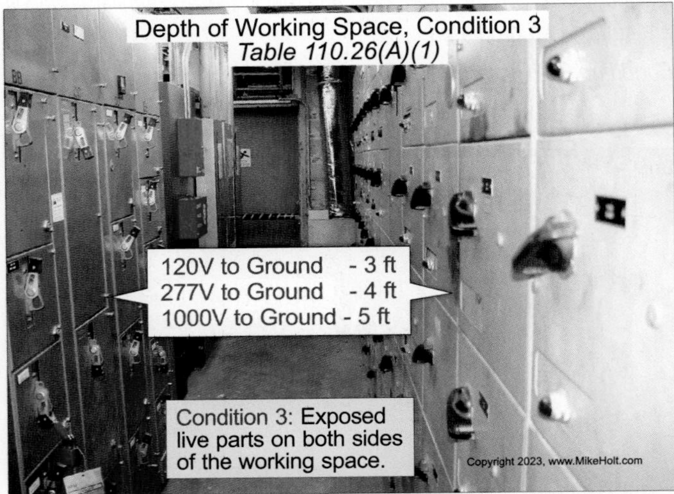
Depth of Working Space, Condition 3
Table 110.26(A)(1)
120V to Ground - 3 ft
277V to Ground - 4 ft
1000V to Ground - 5 ft
Condition 3: Exposed live parts on both sides of the working space.
Copyright 2023, www.MikeHolt.com

▸Figure 110–82

Depth of Working Space
Rear and Sides of Equipment
110.26(A)(1)(a)
Copyright 2023, www.MikeHolt.com
Working space is not required at the back or sides of equipment where all connections and all renewable, adjustable, or serviceable parts are accessible from the front.

▸Figure 110–83

(c) Existing Buildings. If electrical equipment is being replaced, Condition 2 working space is permitted between dead-front switchboards, switchgear, panelboards, or motor control centers (located across the aisle from each other where conditions of maintenance and supervision ensure that written procedures have been adopted to prohibit equipment on both sides of the aisle from being open at the same time), and only authorized, qualified persons will service the installation.

(2) Width of Working Space. The width of the working space must be a minimum of 30 in., but in no case less than the width of the equipment. ▸Figure 110–84

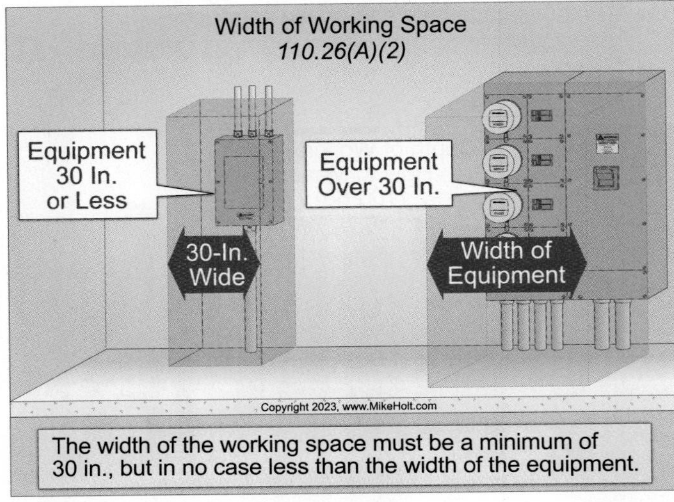
Width of Working Space
110.26(A)(2)
Equipment
30 In.
or Less
Equipment
Over 30 In.
30-In.
Wide
Width of
Equipment
Copyright 2023, www.MikeHolt.com
The width of the working space must be a minimum of 30 in., but in no case less than the width of the equipment.

▸Figure 110–84

Author's Comment:

- The width of the working space can be measured from left-to-right, from right-to-left, or simply centered on the equipment. It can overlap the working space for other electrical equipment. ▸Figure 110–85 and ▸Figure 110–86

The working space must be of sufficient width, depth, and height to permit equipment doors to open at least 90 degrees. ▸Figure 110–87

(3) Height of Working Space. The height of the working space must be clear and extend from the grade, floor, or platform to a height of 6½ ft or the height of the equipment, whichever is greater. ▸Figure 110–88

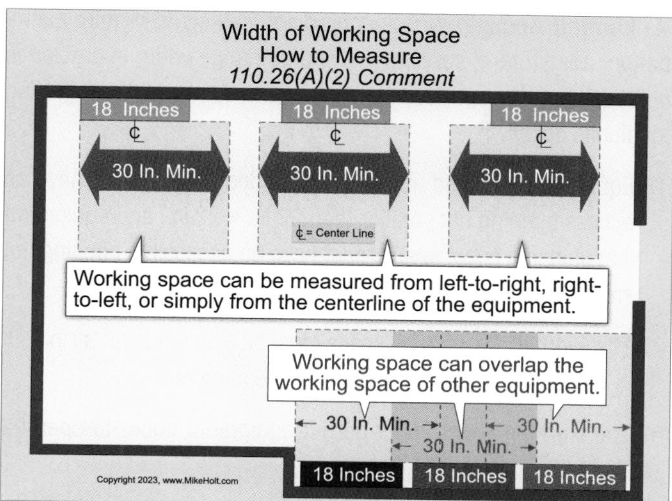

▶Figure 110–85

▶Figure 110–86

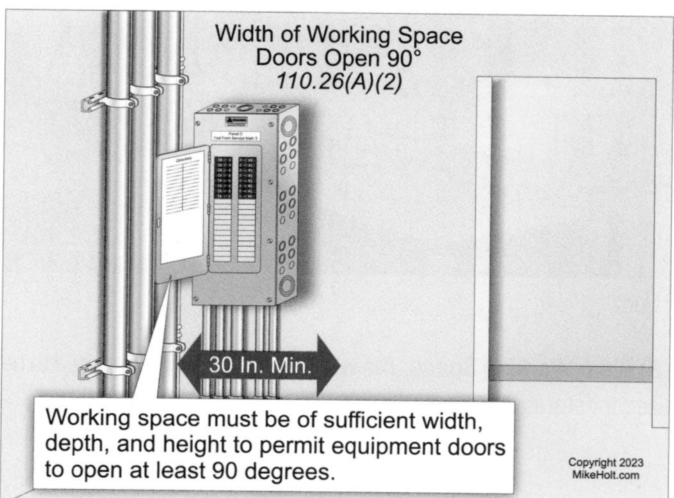

▶Figure 110–87

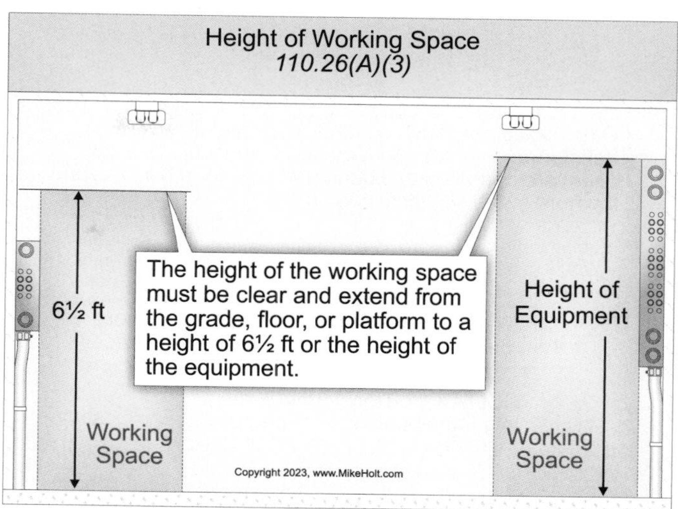

▶Figure 110–88

Other equipment such as raceways, cables, wireways, transformers, or support structures (such as concrete pads) are not permitted to extend more than 6 in. into the working space in front of the electrical equipment. ▶Figure 110–89, ▶Figure 110–90, ▶Figure 110–91, and ▶Figure 110–92

▶Figure 110–89

Ex 2: The minimum height of working space does not apply to a service disconnect or panelboards rated 200A or less located in an existing dwelling unit.

Ex 3: Meters are permitted to be installed in the required working space.

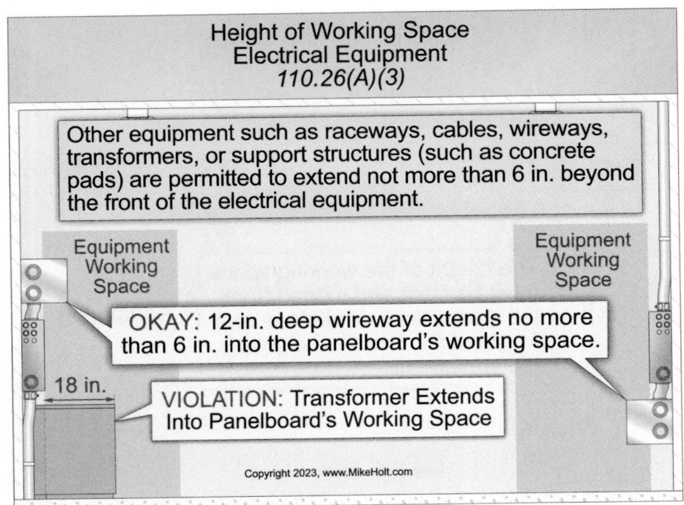

▸Figure 110–90

▸Figure 110–91

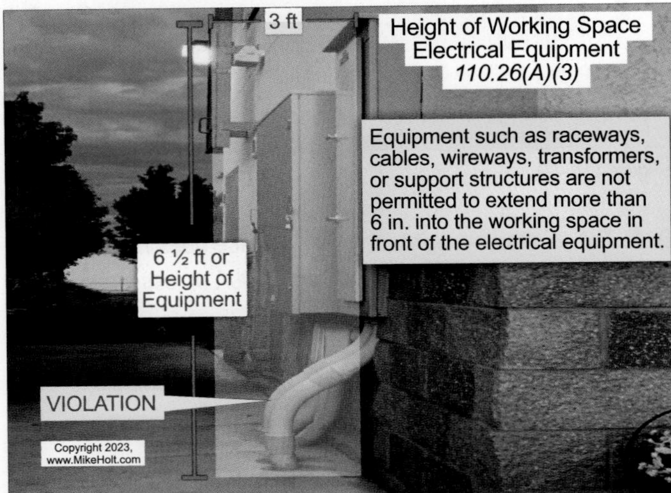

▸Figure 110–92

(4) Limited Access. Where equipment is likely to require examination, adjustment, servicing, or maintenance while energized is located above a suspended ceiling or crawl space, all the following conditions apply:

(1) Equipment installed above a suspended ceiling must have an access opening not smaller than 22 in. × 22 in., and equipment installed in a crawl space must have an accessible opening not smaller than 22 in. × 30 in.

(2) The width of the working space must be a minimum of 30 in., but in no case less than the width of the equipment.

(3) The working space must permit equipment doors to open 90 degrees.

(4) The working space in front of equipment must comply with the depth requirements of Table 110.26(A)(1) and be unobstructed to the floor by fixed cabinets, walls, or partitions. Horizontal ceiling structural members are permitted in this space provided the location of weight-bearing structural members does not result in a side reach of more than 6 in. to work within the enclosure.

(6) Grade, Floor, or Working Platform. The grade, floor, or platform for working space must be as level and flat as practical for the required depth and width of the working space. ▸Figure 110–93 and ▸Figure 110–94

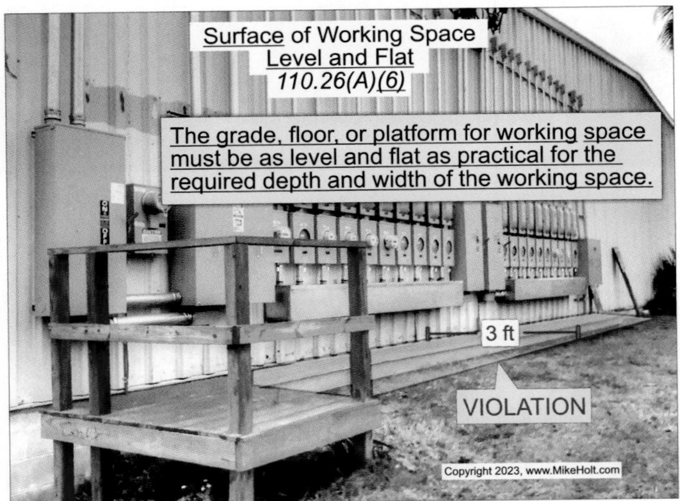

▸Figure 110–93

(B) Clear Working Space. The working space is not permitted to be used for storage. ▸Figure 110–95 and ▸Figure 110–96

1st Printing

▸Figure 110–94

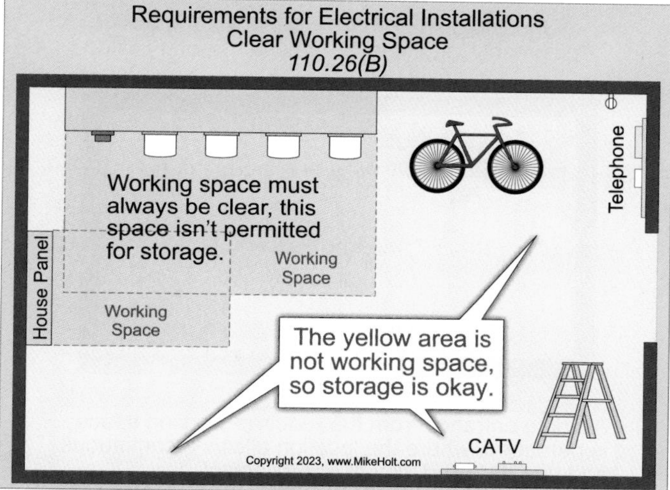

▸Figure 110–95

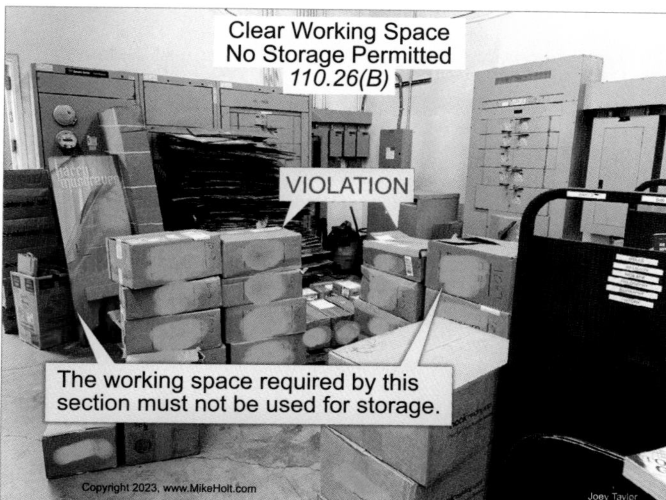

▸Figure 110–96

Caution

CAUTION: It is very dangerous to service energized parts in the first place, and unacceptable to be subjected to additional dangers by working around bicycles, boxes, crates, appliances, and other impediments.

When live parts are exposed for inspection or servicing, the working space, if in a passageway or open space, must be suitably guarded.

According to Article 100, "Exposed (to live parts)" means capable of being inadvertently touched or approached nearer than a safe distance by a person. This term applies to parts that are not suitably guarded, isolated, or insulated.

Author's Comment:

- When working in a passageway and live parts are exposed for inspection or servicing, the working space should be guarded from use by occupants. In addition, one must be mindful of a fire alarm. If one occurs, many people will need to be evacuated and might congregate while moving through the area.

(C) Entrance to and Egress from Working Space.

(1) Minimum Required. At least one entrance large enough to give access to and egress from the working space must be provided. ▸Figure 110–97

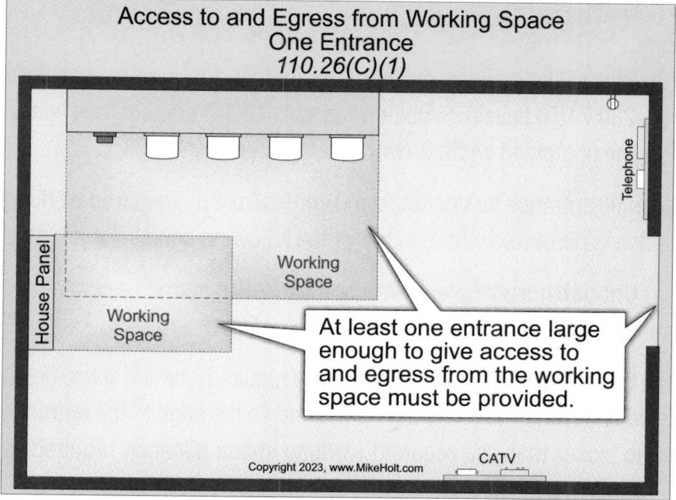

▸Figure 110–97

Author's Comment:

- Check to see what the authority having jurisdiction considers "large enough." Building codes contain minimum dimensions for doors and openings for personnel travel.

(2) Large Equipment. For large equipment containing overcurrent, switching, or control devices, an entrance to and egress from the required working space must not be less than 24 in. wide and 6½ ft high at each end of the working space. This requirement applies for either of the following conditions:

(1) Where feeder equipment is rated 1200A or more and over 6 ft wide. ▸Figure 110–98

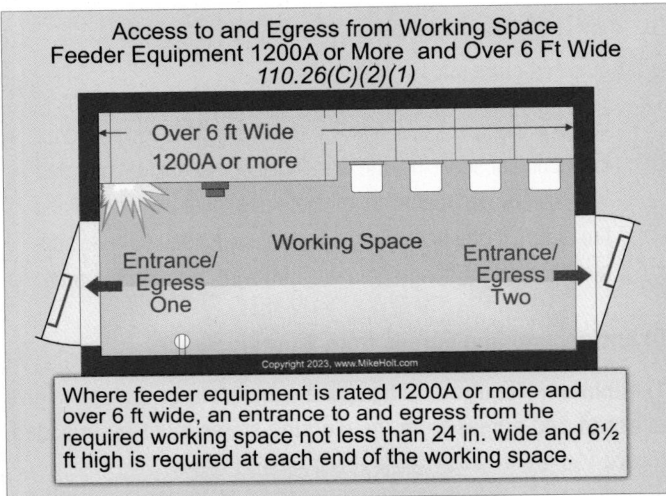

▸Figure 110–98

(2) Where the service disconnects installed in accordance with 230.71(B) have a combined rating of 1200A or more, and where the combined width is over 6 ft. ▸Figure 110–99

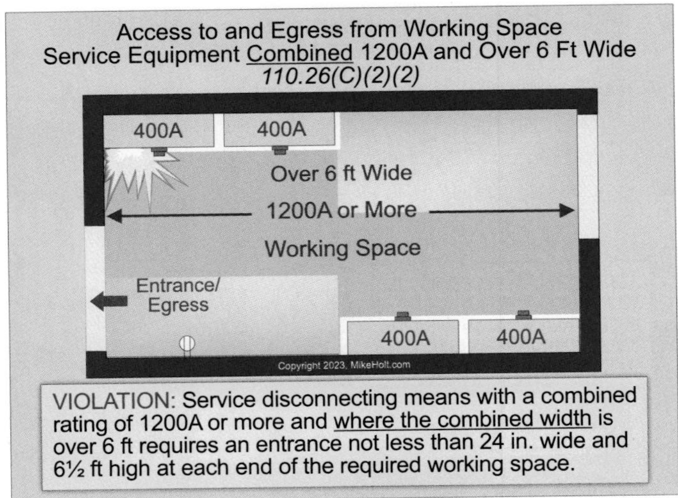

Access to and Egress from Working Space
Service Equipment Combined 1200A and Over 6 Ft Wide
110.26(C)(2)(2)
400A
400A
Over 6 ft Wide
1200A or More
Working Space
Entrance/
Egress
400A
400A
Copyright 2023, MikeHolt.com
VIOLATION: Service disconnecting means with a combined rating of 1200A or more and where the combined width is over 6 ft requires an entrance not less than 24 in. wide and 6½ ft high at each end of the required working space.

▸Figure 110–99

A single entrance for access to and egress from the required working space is permitted where either of the following conditions are met:

(a) Unobstructed Egress. Where the location permits a continuous and unobstructed way of egress travel. ▸Figure 110–100

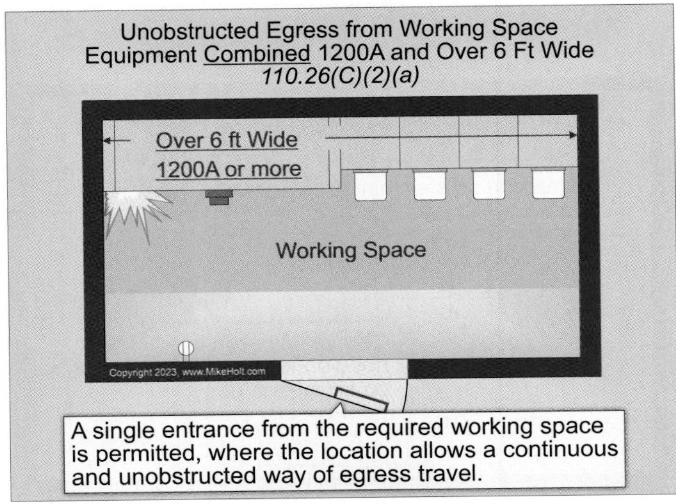

Unobstructed Egress from Working Space
Equipment Combined 1200A and Over 6 Ft Wide
110.26(C)(2)(a)
Over 6 ft Wide
1200A or more
Working Space
Copyright 2023, www.MikeHolt.com
A single entrance from the required working space is permitted, where the location allows a continuous and unobstructed way of egress travel.

▸Figure 110–100

(b) Double Working Space. Where the required working space depth is doubled, and the equipment is located so the edge of the entrance is no closer than the required working space distance required by 110.26(A)(1). ▸Figure 110–101

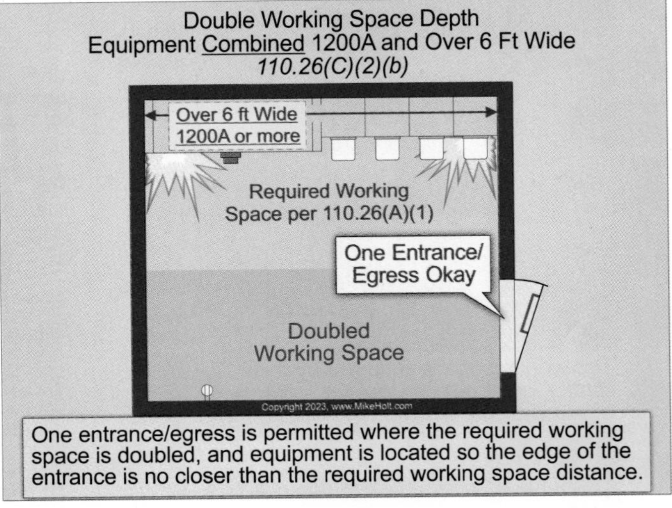

▸Figure 110–101

1st Printing

(3) Fire Exit Hardware on Personnel Doors. Where equipment rated 800A or more contains overcurrent, switching, or control devices is installed, and there is a personnel door(s) intended for entrance to and egress from the working space less than 25 ft from the nearest edge of the working space, the door(s) are required to open at least 90 degrees in the direction of egress and equipped with listed panic or listed fire exit hardware. ▸Figure 110–102

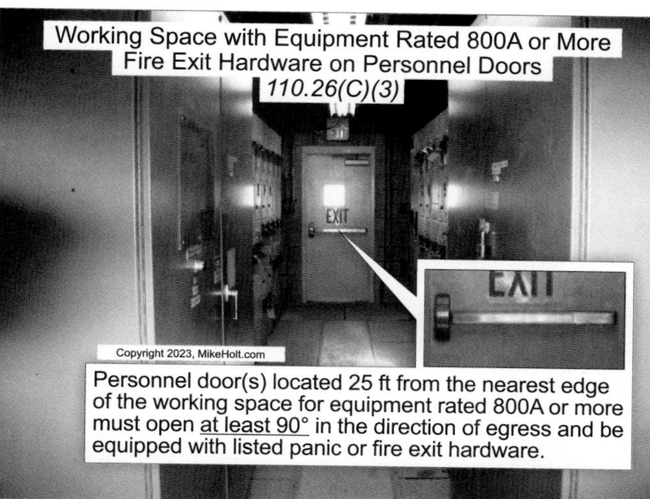

▸Figure 110–102

Author's Comment:

- History has shown that electricians who suffer burns on their hands in electrical arc flash or arc blast events often cannot open doors equipped with knobs that must be turned or doors that must be pulled open.
- Since this requirement is in the *NEC*, electrical contractors are responsible for ensuring panic hardware is installed where required. Some are offended at being held liable for nonelectrical responsibilities, but this rule is designed to save the lives of electricians. For this and other reasons, many construction professionals routinely hold "pre-construction" or "pre-con" meetings to review potential opportunities for miscommunication—before the work begins.

(D) Illumination for Working Space.

Working Space Indoors. Illumination is required for working spaces about service equipment, switchboards, switchgear, enclosed panelboards, or motor control centers installed indoors.

Automatic Means. Illumination for indoor working spaces around service equipment, switchboards, switchgear, enclosed panelboards, or motor control centers cannot be control by automatic means. ▸Figure 110–103

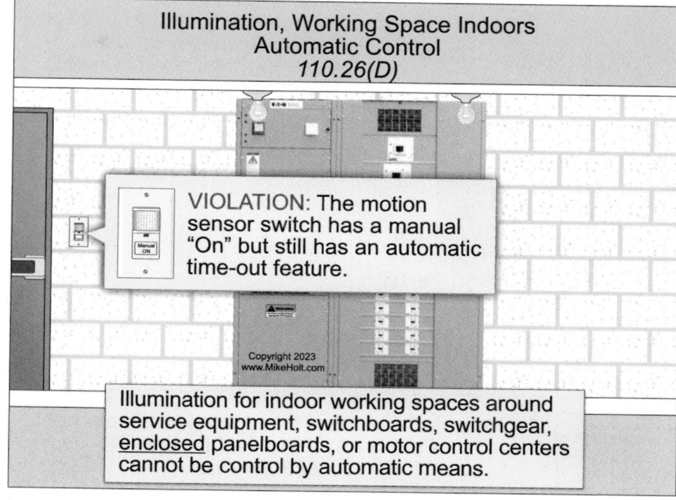

▸Figure 110–103

Author's Comment:

- The *Code* does not identify the minimum foot-candles required to provide proper illumination even though it is essential in electrical equipment rooms for the safety of those qualified to work on such equipment.

(E) Dedicated Electrical Equipment Space. Service equipment, switchboards, panelboards, and motor control centers must have dedicated electrical equipment space and be protected from damage that could result from condensation, leaks, breaks in the foreign systems, or vehicular traffic as follows:

(1) Indoors. Service equipment, switchboards, panelboard enclosures, and motor control centers installed indoors must comply with the following:

(a) Equipment Space. The footprint space (width and depth of the equipment) of the dedicated electrical space extending from the floor to a height of 6 ft above the equipment or to the structural ceiling, whichever is lower, must be dedicated for the electrical installation. ▸Figure 110–104

No piping, ducts, or other equipment foreign to the electrical system can be installed in this dedicated electrical equipment space. ▸Figure 110–105

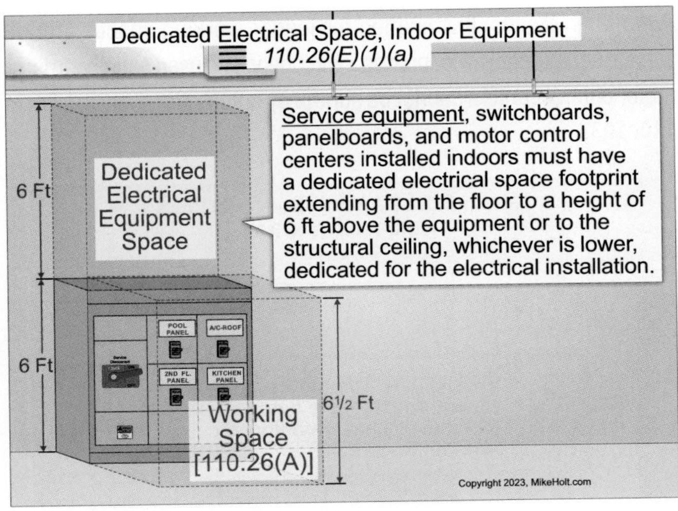

▸Figure 110–104

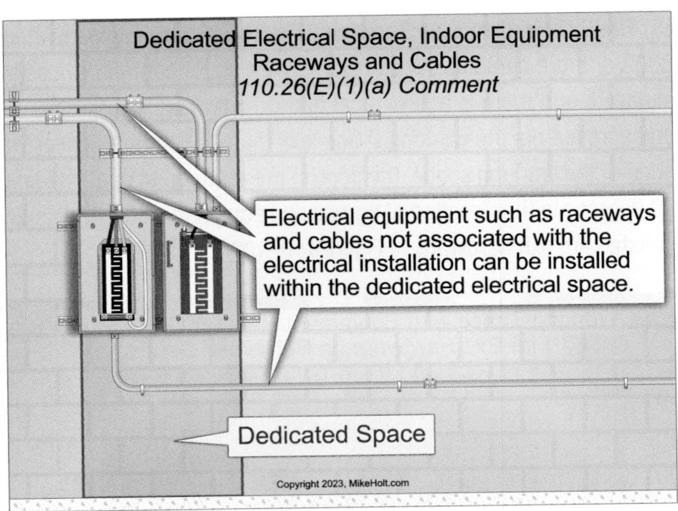

▸Figure 110–106

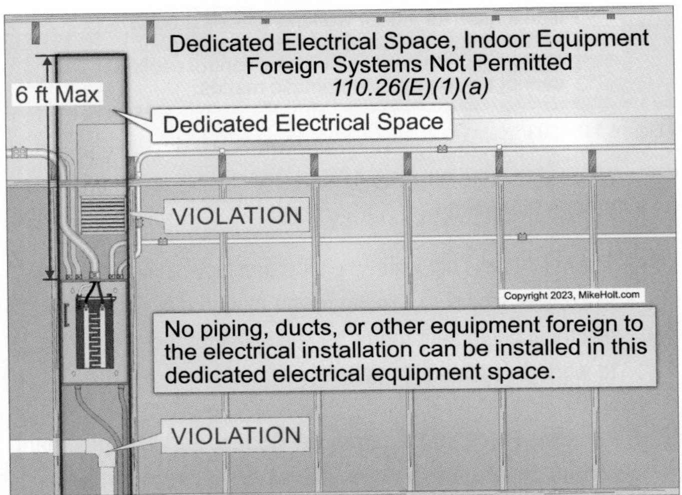

▸Figure 110–105

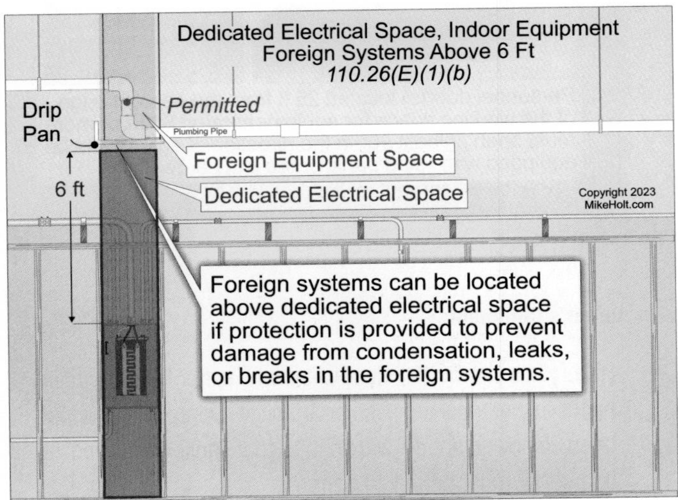

▸Figure 110–107

Author's Comment:

- Electrical equipment such as raceways and cables not associated with the electrical installation can be within the dedicated electrical space. ▸Figure 110–106

Ex: Suspended ceilings with removable panels can be within the dedicated space (6-ft zone).

(b) Foreign Systems. Foreign systems can be located above the dedicated electrical space if protection is installed to prevent damage to the electrical equipment from condensation, leaks, or breaks in the foreign systems. Such protection can be as simple as a drip-pan. ▸Figure 110–107

(c) Sprinkler Protection. Sprinkler protection piping is not permitted in the dedicated space, but the *NEC* does not prohibit sprinklers from spraying water on electrical equipment.

(d) Suspended Ceilings. A dropped, suspended, or similar ceiling is not considered a structural ceiling. ▸Figure 110–108

(2) Outdoor. Outdoor installations for service equipment, switchboards, panelboards, and motor control centers must comply with the following:

(a) Installation Requirements.

(1) Installed in identified enclosures.

(2) Protected from vehicular traffic. ▸Figure 110–109

1st Printing

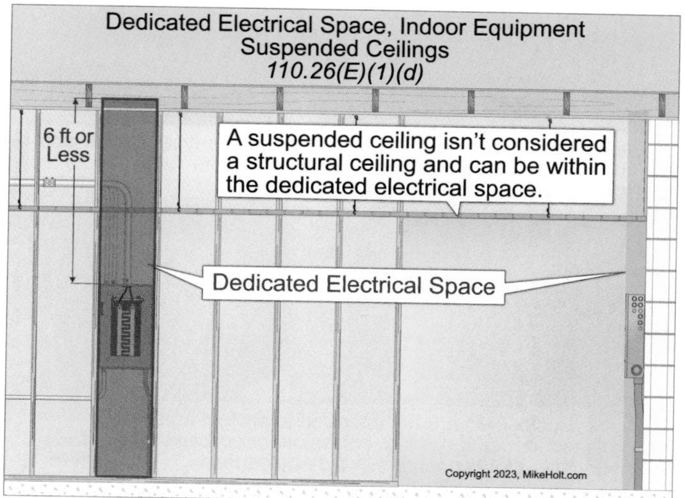

▶Figure 110-108

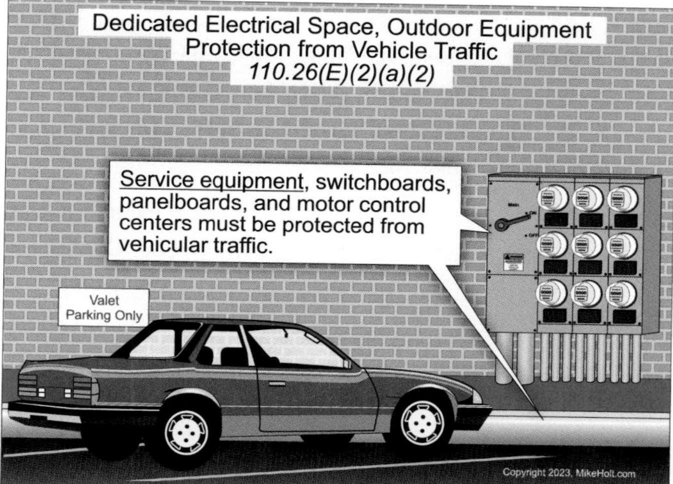

▶Figure 110-109

(3) Protected from accidental spillage or leakage from piping systems.

(b) Working Space. The working clearance space includes the zone described in 110.26(A). Architectural appurtenances (attachments) or other equipment are not permitted within this zone.

(c) Dedicated Equipment Space Outdoors. The footprint space (width and depth of the equipment) of the outdoor dedicated space extending from grade to a height of 6 ft above the equipment must be dedicated for electrical installations. No piping, ducts, or other equipment foreign to the electrical installation can be installed in this dedicated space. ▶Figure 110-110

Ex: Structural overhangs and roof extensions are permitted in this zone.

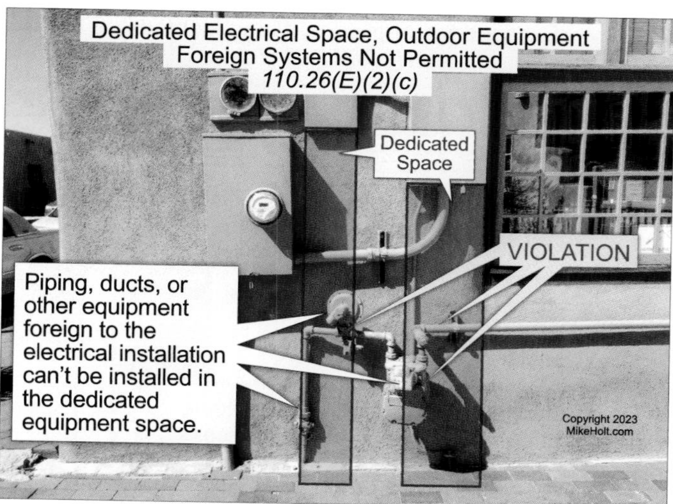

▶Figure 110-110

110.27 Protection Against Physical Damage

(B) Physical Damage. In locations where electrical equipment is likely to be exposed to physical damage, enclosures or guards must be arranged and of such strength as to prevent such damage. ▶Figure 110-111

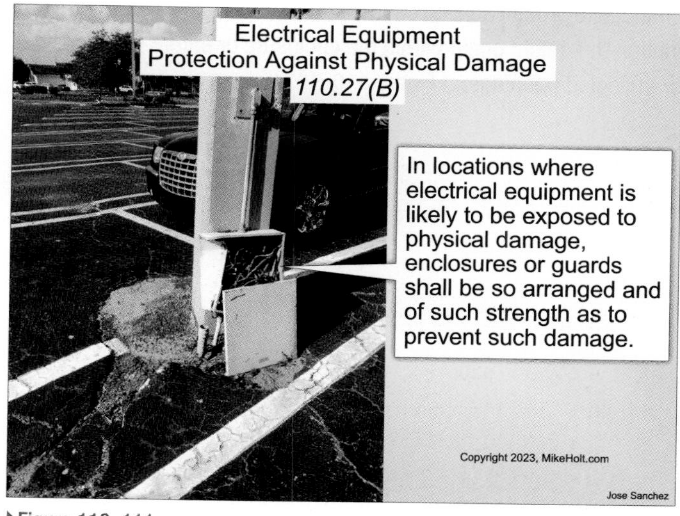

▶Figure 110-111

According to Article 100, "Exposed (as applied to wiring methods)" means on or attached to the surface of a building, or behind panels designed to allow access. ▶Figure 110-112

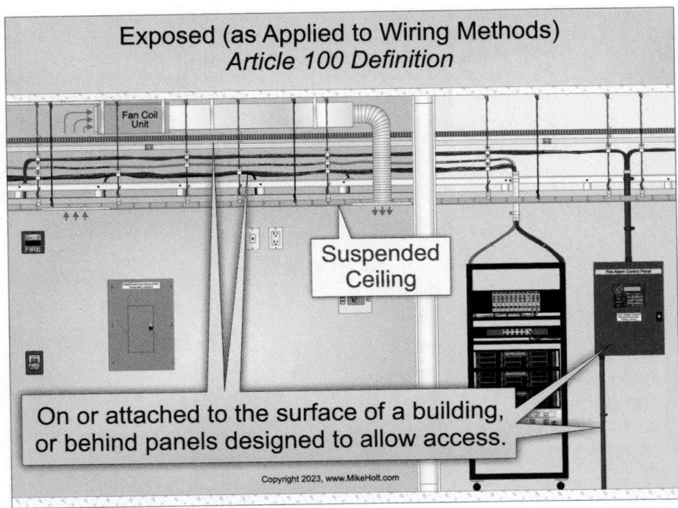
Exposed (as Applied to Wiring Methods)
Article 100 Definition
Fan Coil Unit
Suspended Ceiling
On or attached to the surface of a building, or behind panels designed to allow access.
Copyright 2023, www.MikeHolt.com

▸Figure 110–112

(C) Warning Signs. Electrical rooms must contain warning signs complying with 110.21(B) forbidding unqualified persons to enter.

110.28 NEMA Enclosure Types

Enclosures must be marked with an enclosure-type number and suitable for the location in accordance with Table 110.28. They are not intended to protect against condensation, icing, corrosion, or contamination that might occur within the enclosure or enters via a raceway or unsealed openings. ▸Figure 110–113

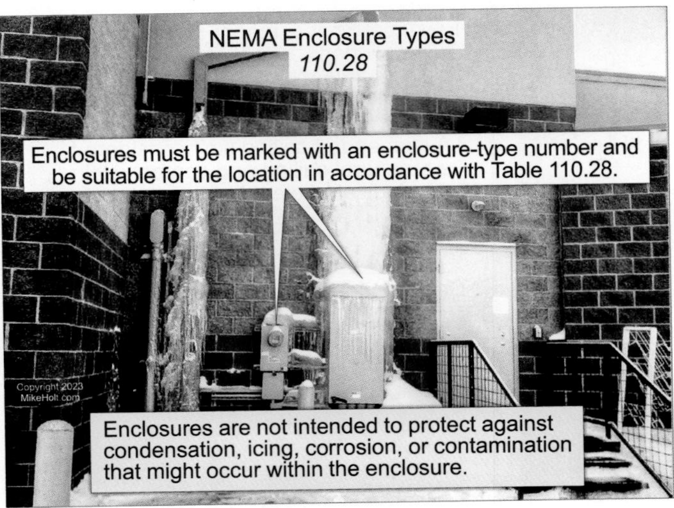
NEMA Enclosure Types
110.28
Enclosures must be marked with an enclosure-type number and be suitable for the location in accordance with Table 110.28.
Copyright 2023 MikeHolt.com
Enclosures are not intended to protect against condensation, icing, corrosion, or contamination that might occur within the enclosure.

▸Figure 110–113

Note 1: Raintight enclosures include Types 3, 3S, 3SX, 3X, 4, 4X, 6, and 6P. Rainproof enclosures are Types 3R and 3RX. Watertight enclosures are Types 4, 4X, 6, and 6P. Driptight enclosures are Types 2, 5, 12, 12K, and 13. Dusttight enclosures are Types 3, 3S, 3SX, 3X, 4, 4X, 5, 6, 6P, 12, 12K, and 13.

Note 3: Dusttight enclosures are suitable for use in hazardous (classified) locations in accordance with 502.10(B)(4), 503.10(A)(2), and 506.15(C)(9).

Note 4: Dusttight enclosures are suitable for use in unclassified locations and in Class II, Division 2; Class III; and Zone 22 hazardous (classified) locations.

Note 5: Some type 4X enclosures may be marked "indoor only."

REVIEW QUESTIONS

Please use the 2023 *Code* book to answer the following questions.

ARTICLE 100—DEFINITIONS

1. Capable of being reached quickly for operation, renewal, or inspections without climbing over or under obstructions, removing obstacles, resorting to portable ladders, or the use of tools (other than keys) is known as "_____."

   (a) accessible (as applied to equipment)
   (b) accessible (as applied to wiring methods)
   (c) accessible, readily (readily accessible)
   (d) all of these

2. The maximum current, in amperes, that a conductor can carry continuously under the conditions of use without exceeding its temperature rating is known as its "_____."

   (a) short-circuit rating
   (b) ground-fault rating
   (c) ampacity
   (d) all of these

3. "_____" means acceptable to the authority having jurisdiction.

   (a) Identified
   (b) Listed
   (c) Approved
   (d) Labeled

4. A device that, when inserted in a receptacle, establishes a connection between the conductors of the attached flexible cord and the conductors connected permanently to the receptacle is known as a(an) "_____."

   (a) attachment plug
   (b) plug cap
   (c) plug
   (d) any of these

5. In many circumstances, the _____ or his or her designated agent assumes the role of the authority having jurisdiction.

   (a) property owner
   (b) developer
   (c) general contractor
   (d) insurance underwriter

6. A "_____" is an area including a sink with one or more of the following: a toilet, urinal, tub, shower, bidet, or similar plumbing fixtures.

   (a) suite
   (b) bathroom
   (c) rest area
   (d) all of these

7. "Bonded" is defined as _____ to establish electrical continuity and conductivity.

   (a) isolated
   (b) guarded
   (c) connected
   (d) separated

8. The connection between two or more portions of the equipment grounding conductor is the definition of a(an) "_____."

   (a) system bonding jumper
   (b) main bonding jumper
   (c) equipment ground-fault jumper
   (d) equipment bonding jumper

9. The circuit conductors between the final overcurrent device protecting the circuit and the outlet(s) are known as "_____ conductors."
   (a) feeder
   (b) branch-circuit
   (c) home run
   (d) main circuit

10. A "_____" consists of two or more ungrounded conductors that have a voltage between them, and a neutral conductor that has equal voltage between it and each ungrounded conductor of the circuit and that is connected to the neutral conductor of the system.
   (a) multi-phase branch circuit
   (b) three-phase lighting supply circuit
   (c) poly-phase branch circuit
   (d) multiwire branch circuit

11. The *NEC* defines a(an) "_____" as a structure that stands alone or that is separated from adjoining structures by fire walls.
   (a) unit
   (b) apartment
   (c) building
   (d) utility

12. A cable routing assembly is composed of single or connected multiple channels as well as associated fittings, forming a structural system to _____ communications wires and cables, optical fiber and data cables; and Class 2, Class 3, and Type PLTC cables; and power-limited fire alarm cables in plenum, riser, and general-purpose applications.
   (a) support
   (b) route
   (c) protect
   (d) support and route

13. A cable tray system is a unit or assembly of units or sections and associated fittings forming a _____ system used to securely fasten or support cables and raceways.
   (a) structural
   (b) flexible
   (c) movable
   (d) secure

14. Type _____ cable is a fabricated assembly of insulated conductors in a flexible interlocked metallic armor.
   (a) AC
   (b) TC
   (c) NM
   (d) MA

15. Coaxial cable is a cylindrical assembly composed of a conductor centered inside a metallic tube or shield, separated by a(an) _____ material and usually covered by an insulating jacket.
   (a) insulating
   (b) conductive
   (c) isolating
   (d) dielectric

16. Type _____ cable is a factory assembly of insulated circuit conductors in an armor of interlocking metal tape, or a smooth or corrugated metallic sheath.
   (a) AC
   (b) MC
   (c) NM
   (d) CMS

17. Type _____ cable is a cable with insulated conductors within an overall nonmetallic jacket.
   (a) AC
   (b) MC
   (c) NM
   (d) TC

18. An "optical fiber cable" is a factory assembly or field assembly of one or more optical fibers having a(an) _____ covering.
   (a) conductive
   (b) nonconductive
   (c) overall
   (d) metallic

19. Type _____ cable is a factory assembly of two or more insulated conductors, with or without associated bare or covered grounding conductors, under a nonmetallic jacket.
   (a) NM
   (b) TC
   (c) SE
   (d) UF

1st Printing

20. A(An) "_____" is a single conductor or multiconductor cable provided with an overall covering, primarily used for services.
(a) service entrance cable
(b) underground feeder cable
(c) tray cable
(d) nonmetallic sheath cable

21. Type _____ is a service-entrance cable, identified for underground use, having a moisture-resistant covering, but not required to have a flame-retardant covering.
(a) SE
(b) NM
(c) UF
(d) USE

22. Type _____ cable is a factory assembly of one or more insulated conductors with an integral or an overall covering of nonmetallic material suitable for direct burial in the earth.
(a) NM
(b) UF
(c) SE
(d) TC

23. A "circuit breaker" is a device designed to open and close a circuit by nonautomatic means and to _____ the circuit automatically on a predetermined overcurrent without damage to itself when properly applied within its rating.
(a) energize
(b) reset
(c) connect
(d) open

24. A Class 2 circuit is defined as the portion of the wiring system between the _____ side of a Class 2 power source and the connected equipment.
(a) load
(b) line
(c) high
(d) low

25. The process, procedures, and testing used to set up and verify the initial performance, operational controls, safety systems, and sequence of operation of electrical devices and equipment, prior to it being placed into active service defines _____.
(a) a field-evaluation
(b) an inspection
(c) equipment documentation
(d) commissioning

26. Wires are considered _____ if rendered inaccessible by the structure or finish of the building.
(a) inaccessible
(b) concealed
(c) hidden
(d) enclosed

27. A separate portion of a conduit or tubing system that provides access through a removable cover(s) to the interior of the system at a junction of two or more sections of the system or at a terminal point of the system defines the term "_____."
(a) junction box
(b) accessible raceway
(c) conduit body
(d) cutout box

28. _____ is a raceway of circular cross section made of a helically wound, formed, interlocked metal strip.
(a) Type MC cable
(b) Type AC cable
(c) LFMC
(d) FMC

29. _____ is a raceway of circular cross section having an outer liquidtight, nonmetallic, sunlight-resistant jacket over an inner flexible metal core.
(a) FMC
(b) LFNMC
(c) LFMC
(d) Vinyl-Clad Type MC

30. A rigid nonmetallic raceway of circular cross section, with integral or associated couplings, connectors, and fittings for the installation of electrical conductors and cables describes _____.
(a) ENT
(b) RMC
(c) IMC
(d) PVC

31. A "continuous load" is a load where the maximum current is expected to continue for _____ or more.

(a) ½ hour
(b) 1 hour
(c) 2 hours
(d) 3 hours

32. The circuit of a control apparatus or system that carries the electric signals directing the performance of the controller but does not carry the main power current defines a "_____."

(a) control circuit
(b) low-voltage circuit
(c) function circuit
(d) performance circuit

33. A "_____" is a device or group of devices that govern, in some predetermined manner, the electric power delivered to the apparatus to which it is connected.

(a) relay
(b) breaker
(c) transformer
(d) controller

34. A dc-to-dc converter is a device that can provide an output _____ voltage and current at a higher or lower value than the input _____ voltage and current.

(a) ac, dc
(b) ac, ac
(c) dc, dc
(d) dc, ac

35. Localization of an overcurrent condition to restrict outages to the circuit or equipment affected, accomplished by the selection and installation of overcurrent protective devices and their ratings or settings is known as _____.

(a) overcurrent protection
(b) interrupting capacity
(c) selective coordination
(d) overload protection

36. A flexible cord is defined as _____ or more flexible insulated conductors enclosed in a flexible covering.

(a) two
(b) three
(c) four
(d) five

37. Areas or enclosures without adequate ventilation, where electrical equipment is located and pool sanitation chemicals are stored, handled, or dispensed is the definition of a _____.

(a) hazardous area
(b) restricted area
(c) corrosive environment
(d) wet location

38. A unit of an electrical system, other than a conductor, which carries or controls electric energy as its principal function is known as a(an) "_____."

(a) raceway
(b) fitting
(c) device
(d) enclosure

39. A(An) _____ is a device, or group of devices, by which the conductors of a circuit can be disconnected from their source of supply.

(a) feeder
(b) enclosure
(c) disconnecting means
(d) conductor interrupter

40. A _____ is a single unit that provides complete and independent living facilities for one or more persons, including permanent provisions for living, sleeping, cooking, and sanitation.

(a) one-family dwelling
(b) two-family dwelling
(c) dwelling unit
(d) multifamily dwelling

41. An automotive-type vehicle for on-road use, such as _____, primarily powered by an electric motor that draws current from a rechargeable storage battery, fuel cell, photovoltaic array, or other source of electric current defines an electric vehicle.

(a) passenger automobiles
(b) buses, trucks, and vans
(c) neighborhood electric vehicles and electric motorcycles
(d) all of these

42. Off-road, self-propelled electric vehicles, such as _____ are not considered electric vehicles.

(a) industrial trucks, hoists, and lifts
(b) golf carts and airline ground support equipment
(c) tractors and boats
(d) all of these

1st Printing

43. Electric vehicle supply equipment includes the conductors and electric vehicle connectors, _____ installed specifically for the purpose of transferring energy between the premises wiring and the electric vehicle.

(a) attachment plugs
(b) fittings
(c) power outlets
(d) all of these

44. Emergency power systems are those systems legally required and classed as emergency by a governmental agency having jurisdiction. These systems are intended to automatically supply illumination and/or power essential for _____.

(a) community activity
(b) safety to human life
(c) public recreation
(d) police and emergency services exclusively

45. "Likely to become energized" is defined as conductive material that could become energized because of _____ or electrical spacing.

(a) improper installation
(b) poor maintenance
(c) the failure of electrical insulation
(d) power surges

46. A(An) _____ is a system consisting of a monitor(s), communications equipment, a controller(s), a timer(s), or other device(s) that monitors and/or controls an electrical load or a power production or storage source.

(a) energy management system
(b) power distribution system
(c) energy storage system
(d) interconnected power production system

47. An energy storage system (ESS) is defined as one or more devices installed as a system capable of storing energy and providing electrical energy into the _____ system or an electric power production and distribution network.

(a) standby
(b) emergency
(c) premises wiring
(d) UPS

48. An ESS(s) (energy storage system) can include but are not limited to _____.

(a) batteries
(b) capacitors
(c) inverters or converters
(d) any of these

49. A(An) _____ at agricultural buildings is where conductive elements are connected together to minimize voltage differences.

(a) voltage gradient
(b) equipotential plane
(c) supplementary grounding system
(d) current dissipation system

50. "Exposed (as applied to _____)," is defined as on or attached to the surface, or behind access panels designed to allow access.

(a) equipment
(b) luminaires
(c) wiring methods
(d) motors

51. The largest amount of current capable of being delivered at a point on the system during a short-circuit condition is the definition of _____.

(a) objectionable current
(b) excessive current
(c) induced current
(d) available fault current

52. The *NEC* defines a "_____" as all circuit conductors between the service equipment, the source of a separately derived system, or other power supply source, and the final branch-circuit overcurrent device.

(a) service
(b) feeder
(c) branch circuit
(d) all of these

53. A(An) _____ that performs field evaluations of electrical or other equipment is known as a "Field Evaluation Body (FEB)."

(a) home inspector
(b) field installer
(c) organization or part of an organization
(d) insurance underwriter

54. Equipment or materials to which has been attached a(an) _____ of an FEB indicating the equipment or materials were evaluated and found to comply with requirements as described in an accompanying field evaluation report is known as "field labeled (as applied to evaluated products)."

(a) symbol
(b) label
(c) other identifying mark
(d) any of these

55. A fountain is defined as an ornamental structure or recreational water feature from which one or more jets or streams of water are discharged into the air, including splash pads, and _____ pools.

(a) ornamental
(b) wading
(c) seasonal
(d) permanently installed

56. A _____ is a building or portion of a building in which one or more self-propelled vehicles can be kept for use, sale, storage, rental, repair, exhibition, or demonstration purposes.

(a) garage
(b) residential garage
(c) service garage
(d) commercial garage

57. A generator is a machine that converts mechanical energy into electrical energy by means of a _____ and alternator and/or inverter.

(a) converter
(b) rectifier
(c) prime mover
(d) turbine

58. Connected (connecting) to ground or to a conductive body that extends the ground connection is called "_____."

(a) equipment grounding
(b) bonded
(c) grounded
(d) all of these

59. A functionally grounded system has an electrical ground reference for operational purposes that is not _____ grounded.

(a) effectively
(b) sufficiently
(c) solidly
(d) any of these

60. A functionally grounded system is often connected to ground through an electronic means internal to an inverter or charge controller that provides _____.

(a) overcurrent protection
(b) ground-fault protection
(c) arc-fault protection
(d) current-limiting properties

61. A(An) "_____" is a device intended for the protection of personnel that functions to de-energize a circuit or portion thereof within an established period of time when a ground-fault current exceeds the values established for a Class A device.

(a) dual-element fuse
(b) inverse time breaker
(c) ground-fault circuit interrupter
(d) safety switch

62. A Class A GFCI trips when the ground-fault current is _____ or higher.

(a) 4 mA
(b) 5 mA
(c) 6 mA
(d) 7 mA

63. A special purpose ground-fault circuit interrupter (SPGFCI) is a device intended for the detection of ground-fault currents, used in circuits with voltage to ground greater than _____, that functions to de-energize a circuit or portion of a circuit within an established period of time when a ground-fault current exceeds the values established for Class C, D, or E devices.

(a) 30V
(b) 60V
(c) 125V
(d) 150V

1st Printing

64. An effective ground-fault current path is an intentionally constructed, low-impedance electrically conductive path designed and intended to carry current during a ground-fault event from the point of a ground fault on a wiring system to _____.
    (a) ground
    (b) earth
    (c) the electrical supply source
    (d) the grounding electrode

65. A system intended to provide protection of equipment from damaging line-to-ground fault currents by causing a disconnecting means to open all ungrounded conductors of the faulted circuit at current levels less than the supply circuit overcurrent device defines "_____."
    (a) ground-fault protection of equipment
    (b) guarded
    (c) personal protection
    (d) automatic protection

66. A(An) _____ is a conductive path(s) that is part of an effective ground-fault current path and connects normally noncurrent-carrying metal parts of equipment together and to the system grounded conductor or to the grounding electrode conductor, or both.
    (a) grounding electrode conductor
    (b) main bonding jumper
    (c) system bonding jumper
    (d) equipment grounding conductor

67. A conducting object through which a direct connection to earth is established is a "_____."
    (a) bonding conductor
    (b) grounding conductor
    (c) grounding electrode
    (d) grounded conductor

68. A conductor used to connect the system grounded conductor, or the equipment to a grounding electrode or to a point on the grounding electrode system, is called the "_____ conductor."
    (a) main grounding
    (b) common main
    (c) equipment grounding
    (d) grounding electrode

69. Health care facilities are defined as buildings or portions of buildings, or mobile enclosures in which human medical, dental, _____, or surgical care are provided.
    (a) psychiatric
    (b) nursing
    (c) obstetrical
    (d) any of these

70. Recognized as suitable for the specific purpose, function, use, environment, and application is the definition of "_____."
    (a) labeled
    (b) identified (as applied to equipment)
    (c) listed
    (d) approved

71. "*In sight from*" or "*within sight from*" is defined as equipment that is visible and not more than _____ from other equipment in sight from that other equipment.
    (a) 10 feet
    (b) 20 feet
    (c) 25 feet
    (d) 50 feet

72. Information and technology equipment and systems are used for creation and manipulation of _____.
    (a) data
    (b) voice
    (c) video
    (d) all of these

73. The operating mode for power production equipment or microgrids that operate in parallel with and are capable of delivering energy to an electric power production and distribution network or other primary source defines a(an) _____ mode.
    (a) hybrid
    (b) inverted
    (c) interactive
    (d) internal

74. The highest current at rated voltage that a device is identified to interrupt under standard test conditions is the "_____."
    (a) interrupting rating
    (b) manufacturer's rating
    (c) interrupting capacity
    (d) withstand rating

75. A device that provides a means to connect intersystem bonding conductors for _____ systems to the grounding electrode system defines the term "intersystem bonding termination."

(a) limited-energy
(b) low-voltage
(c) communications
(d) power and lighting

76. A(An) _____ is equipment that changes dc to ac.

(a) diode
(b) rectifier
(c) transistor
(d) inverter

77. The conductors connected to the dc input of an inverter form the _____.

(a) branch circuit
(b) feeder
(c) inverter input circuit
(d) inverter output circuit

78. The conductors connected to the ac output of an inverter form the _____.

(a) bipolar photovoltaic array
(b) monopole subarray
(c) emergency standby power
(d) inverter output circuit

79. Inverter equipment capable of operating in both interactive and island modes describes a(an) _____ inverter.

(a) multi-purpose
(b) isolated
(c) bidirectional
(d) multimode

80. A(An) _____ inverter is equipment having the capabilities to operate only in island mode.

(a) stand-alone
(b) isolated
(c) bidirectional
(d) independent

81. The operating mode for power production or microgrids that allows energy to be supplied to loads that are disconnected from an electric power production and distribution network or other primary power source defines the term "_____."

(a) island mode
(b) isolation mode
(c) emergency mode
(d) standby mode

82. Equipment or materials to which a label, symbol, or other identifying mark of a product evaluation organization that is acceptable to the authority having jurisdiction has been attached is known as "_____."

(a) listed
(b) labeled
(c) approved
(d) identified

83. A legally required standby system is intended to automatically supply power to _____ (other than those classed as emergency systems) in the event of failure of the normal source.

(a) those systems classed as emergency systems
(b) selected loads
(c) critical branch circuits
(d) essential circuits

84. A "limited care facility" is defined as a building or portion thereof used on a(an) _____ basis for the housing of four or more persons who are incapable of self-preservation because of age; physical limitation due to accident or illness; or limitations such as intellectual disability/developmental disability, mental illness, or chemical dependency.

(a) occasional
(b) 10-hour or less per day
(c) 24-hour
(d) temporary

85. Equipment, materials, or services included in a list published by an organization that is acceptable to the authority having jurisdiction defines the term "_____."

(a) booked
(b) a digest
(c) a manifest
(d) listed

86. A location protected from weather and not subject to saturation with water or other liquids, but subject to moderate degrees of moisture defines a _____ location.

(a) dry
(b) damp
(c) wet
(d) moist

87. A location not normally subject to dampness or wetness but may be temporarily subject to dampness and wetness as in the case of a building under construction defines a _____ location.

(a) dry
(b) damp
(c) moist
(d) wet

88. A location unprotected and exposed to weather, subject to saturation, underground, or in concrete slabs in direct contact with the earth defines a _____ location.

(a) dry
(b) damp
(c) wet
(d) moist

89. Hazardous (classified) locations are defined as those spaces or areas where fire or explosion hazards might exist due to _____.

(a) flammable gases or vapors
(b) combustible dusts
(c) ignitible fibers/flyings
(d) any of these

90. For pools, fountains, and similar installations, the "low-voltage contact limit" is a voltage not exceeding _____.

(a) 15V (RMS) for sinusoidal ac or 21.20V peak for nonsinusoidal ac
(b) 30V for continuous dc
(c) 12.40V peak for dc that is interrupted at a rate of 10 to 200 Hz
(d) all of these

91. A "luminaire" is a complete lighting unit consisting of a light source such as a lamp or lamps, together with the parts designed to position the _____ and connect it to the power supply.

(a) lampholder
(b) light source
(c) fixture
(d) bulb

92. A "wet-niche luminaire" is intended to be installed in a _____ surrounded by water.

(a) transformer
(b) forming shell
(c) hydromassage bathtub
(d) all of these

93. A "manufactured wiring system" is a system containing component parts that are assembled in the process of manufacture and cannot be inspected at the building site without _____.

(a) a permit
(b) a manufacturer's representative present
(c) damage or destruction to the assembly
(d) an engineer's supervision

94. A "_____" is an electric power system capable of operating in island mode and capable of being interconnected to an electric power production and distribution network or other primary source while operating in interactive mode.

(a) tandem system
(b) primary system
(c) microgrid
(d) dual function system

95. An "ac module" is a complete, environmentally protected unit consisting of _____, designed to produce ac power.

(a) solar cells
(b) inverters
(c) other components
(d) all of these

96. A "motor fuel dispensing facility" is that portion of a property where motor fuels are _____ from fixed equipment into the fuel tanks of motor vehicles or marine craft or into approved containers.

(a) stored and dispensed
(b) bought and sold
(c) prepared for consumers
(d) secured and distributed

97. A "neutral conductor" is the conductor connected to the _____ of a system, which is intended to carry current under normal conditions.

(a) grounding electrode
(b) neutral point
(c) intersystem bonding termination
(d) electrical grid

98. The _____ is the "neutral point."

(a) common point on a wye-connection in a polyphase system
(b) midpoint on a single-phase, 3-wire system
(c) midpoint of a single-phase portion of a 3-phase delta system
(d) any of these

99. Any current in excess of the rated current of equipment or the ampacity of a conductor is called "_____."

(a) trip current
(b) fault current
(c) overcurrent
(d) a short circuit

100. An 'overload' is defined as the operation of equipment in excess of normal, full load rating, or of a conductor in excess of its ampacity that, when it persists for a_____, would cause damage or dangerous overheating.

(a) sufficient length of time
(b) short time
(c) long time
(d) none of these

101. A panel, including buses and automatic overcurrent devices, designed to be placed in a cabinet, enclosure, or cutout box and accessible only from the front is known as a "_____."

(a) switchboard
(b) disconnect
(c) panelboard
(d) switchgear

102. A patient "_____" is the location of a patient sleeping bed, or the bed or procedure table of a Category 1 space.

(a) bed location
(b) care area
(c) observation area
(d) sterile area

103. The "patient care space category" is any space of a health care facility where patients are intended to be _____.

(a) admitted
(b) evaluated
(c) registered
(d) examined or treated

104. An "immersion pool" is a pool for ceremonial or ritual immersion of users, which is designed and intended to have its contents _____.

(a) heated
(b) chlorinated
(c) drained or discharged
(d) filtered

105. Permanently installed pools are those that are constructed or installed in the ground or partially in the ground, and all pools installed inside of a building, whether or not served by electrical circuits of any nature.

(a) in the ground
(b) partially in the ground
(c) inside of a building
(d) any of these

106. Pools installed entirely on or above the ground that are intended to be stored when not in use and are designed for ease of relocation, regardless of water depth are considered to be _____.

(a) temporary
(b) storable
(c) portable
(d) exempt from *Code* requirements

107. A "_____" is an enclosed assembly that can include receptacles, circuit breakers, fused switches, fuses, watt-hour meter(s), panelboards and monitoring means identified for marina use.

(a) marina power receptacle
(b) marina outlet
(c) marina power outlet
(d) any of these

108. Electrical generating equipment supplied by any source other than a utility service, up to the source system disconnecting means defines "_____."

(a) a service drop
(b) power production equipment
(c) the service point
(d) utilization equipment

109. The conductors between power production equipment and the service or other premises wiring are known as the "_____."

(a) power source input circuit
(b) power source output conductors
(c) input circuit conductors
(d) output source circuit

1st Printing

110. A "power supply cord" is an assembly consisting of an attachment plug and a length of _____ cord connected to utilization equipment.

(a) heavy duty
(b) hard usage
(c) flexible
(d) light duty

111. An electric utility or another source of power that acts as the main forming and stabilizing source in an electric power system is the "_____ source."

(a) primary
(b) secondary
(c) normal
(d) constant

112. A "PV dc circuit" is any dc conductor in PV source circuits, PV string circuits, and PV _____ converter circuits.

(a) ac-to-dc
(b) dc-to-ac
(c) dc-to-dc
(d) any of these

113. The PV dc circuit conductors between modules in a PV string circuit, and from PV string circuits or dc combiners, to dc combiners, electronic power converters, or a dc PV system disconnecting means are known as the "PV _____ circuit."

(a) source
(b) array
(c) input
(d) output

114. A "PV _____ circuit" is the PV source circuit conductors of one or more series-connected PV modules.

(a) branch
(b) string
(c) combined
(d) grouped

115. A "PV _____" is a complete, environmentally protected unit consisting of solar cells and other components, designed to produce dc power.

(a) interface
(b) battery
(c) module
(d) cell bank

116. The *NEC* defines a(an) "_____" as one who has skills and knowledge related to the construction and operation of the electrical equipment and installations and has received safety training to recognize and avoid the hazards involved.

(a) inspector
(b) master electrician
(c) journeyman electrician
(d) qualified person

117. NFPA 70E, *Standard for Electrical Safety in the Workplace*, provides information to help determine the electrical safety training requirements expected of a(an) "_____."

(a) qualified person
(b) electrical engineer
(c) journeyman electrician
(d) trained individual

118. A "raceway" is an enclosed channel designed expressly for holding _____, with additional functions as permitted in this *Code*.

(a) wires
(b) cables
(c) busbars
(d) any of these

119. A contact device installed at an outlet for the connection of an attachment plug is known as a(an) "_____."

(a) attachment point
(b) tap
(c) receptacle
(d) wall plug

120. A single "receptacle" is a single contact device with no other contact device on the same _____.

(a) circuit
(b) yoke or strap
(c) run
(d) equipment

121. A duplex "receptacle" is an example of a multiple receptacle that has two receptacles on the same _____.

(a) yoke or strap
(b) strap
(c) device
(d) cover plate

122. Article 100 contains only those definitions essential to the application of this *Code*. An article number in parentheses following the definition indicates that the definition only applies to that article.

(a) True
(b) False

123. Electrical equipment that is "sealed" and installed in a hazardous (classified) location is constructed such that the equipment is "sealed" effectively against entry of an external _____ and is not opened during normal operation or for any maintenance activities.

(a) gas
(b) atmosphere
(c) vapor
(d) dust

124. The conductors and equipment connecting the serving utility to the wiring system of the premises served is called a "_____."

(a) branch circuit
(b) feeder
(c) service
(d) service attachment

125. "Service conductors" are the conductors from the service point to the _____.

(a) service disconnecting means
(b) panelboard
(c) switchgear
(d) fire switch

126. The "_____" is the necessary equipment, consisting of a circuit breaker(s) or switch(es) and fuse(s) and their accessories, connected to the serving utility and intended to constitute the main control and disconnect of the serving utility.

(a) service equipment
(b) feeder equipment
(c) feeder disconnect
(d) none of these

127. "_____" is the process of following a manufacturer's set of instructions or applicable industry standards to analyze, adjust, or perform prescribed actions upon equipment with the intention to preserve or restore the operational performance of the equipment.

(a) Maintenance
(b) Inspection
(c) Servicing
(d) Operating Procedure

128. The electrical equipment required to power a floating vessel including, but not limited to, the receptacle and cords is known as "_____."

(a) a marina service
(b) dock power
(c) shore power
(d) ship power

129. A(An) _____ is an abnormal connection (including an arc) of relatively low impedance, whether made accidentally or intentionally, between two or more points of different potential.

(a) ground fault
(b) arc fault
(c) system fault
(d) short circuit

130. The prospective symmetrical fault current at a nominal voltage to which an apparatus or system is able to be connected without sustaining damage exceeding defined acceptance criteria is known as the "_____."

(a) short-circuit current rating
(b) arc-flash rating
(c) overcurrent rating
(d) available fault current

131. A "spa or hot tub" is a hydromassage pool or tub for recreational or therapeutic use, not located in health care facilities, designed for immersion of users, and usually having a _____.

(a) filter
(b) heater
(c) motor-driven blower
(d) all of these

1st Printing

132. A "splash pad" is a fountain intended for recreational use by pedestrians and designed to contain no more than _____ of water depth.

(a) 1 in.
(b) 3 in.
(c) 6 in.
(d) 12 in.

133. A(An) "_____ system" is a system that is not connected to an electric power production and distribution network.

(a) stand-alone
(b) isolated
(c) microgrid
(d) photovoltaic

134. A "structure" is that which is _____, other than equipment.

(a) built
(b) constructed
(c) built or constructed
(d) none of these

135. A "surge-protective device" (SPD) is intended to limit _____ voltages by diverting or limiting surge current and preventing its continued flow while remaining capable of repeating these functions.

(a) spike
(b) transient
(c) high
(d) low

136. A conductor, other than a service conductor, which has overcurrent protection ahead of its point of supply that exceeds the value permitted for similar conductors is known as a "_____."

(a) feeder conductor
(b) service conductor
(c) tap conductor
(d) conductor extension

137. "_____" is an unthreaded thinwall raceway of circular cross section designed for the physical protection and routing of conductors and cables and for use as an equipment grounding conductor when installed utilizing appropriate fittings.

(a) LFNC
(b) EMT
(c) NUCC
(d) RTRC

138. "_____" is a pliable corrugated raceway of circular cross section, with integral or associated couplings, connectors, and fittings that are listed for the installation of electrical conductors.

(a) PVC
(b) ENT
(c) RMC
(d) IMC

139. "_____" is, for grounded circuits, the voltage between the given conductor and that point or conductor of the circuit that is grounded; for ungrounded circuits, the greatest voltage between the given conductor and any other conductor of the circuit.

(a) Line-to-line voltage
(b) Voltage to ground
(c) Phase-to-phase voltage
(d) Neutral to ground voltage

140. A nominal value assigned to a circuit or system for the purpose of conveniently designating its voltage class, such as 120/240V, is called "_____ voltage."

(a) root-mean-square
(b) circuit
(c) nominal
(d) source

141. A(An) "_____" enclosure is constructed or protected so that exposure to the weather will not interfere with successful operation.

(a) weatherproof
(b) weathertight
(c) weather-resistant
(d) all weather

142. "Wireless power transfer equipment" is installed specifically for the purpose of transferring energy between the premises wiring and the electric vehicle without _____ electrical contact.

(a) physical
(b) inductive
(c) magnetic
(d) inductive and magnetic

143. A dc combiner is an enclosure that includes devices used to connect two or more PV system dc circuits in _____.

(a) series
(b) series-parallel
(c) parallel
(d) parallel-series

ARTICLE 110—GENERAL REQUIREMENTS FOR ELECTRICAL INSTALLATIONS

1. General requirements for the examination and approval, installation and use, access to and spaces about electrical conductors and equipment; enclosures intended for personnel entry; and tunnel installations are within the scope of _____.

   (a) Article 800
   (b) Article 300
   (c) Article 110
   (d) Annex J

2. The conductors and equipment required or permitted by this *Code* shall be acceptable only if _____.

   (a) labeled
   (b) listed
   (c) approved
   (d) identified

3. In judging equipment, considerations such as _____ shall be evaluated.

   (a) mechanical strength
   (b) wire-bending and connection space
   (c) arcing effects
   (d) all of these

4. In judging equipment, considerations such as cybersecurity for network-connected _____ to address its ability to withstand unauthorized updates and malicious attacks while continuing to perform its intended safety functionality shall be evaluated.

   (a) normal equipment
   (b) emergency equipment
   (c) standby power equipment
   (d) life safety equipment

5. Equipment that is _____ or identified for a use shall be installed and used in accordance with any instructions included in the listing, labeling, or identification.

   (a) listed, labeled, or both
   (b) listed
   (c) marked
   (d) suitable

6. Product testing, evaluation, and listing (product certification) shall be performed by _____.

   (a) recognized qualified electrical testing laboratories
   (b) the manufacturer
   (c) a qualified person
   (d) an electrical engineer

7. If the conductor material is not specified, the sizes given in the *Code* shall apply to _____ conductors.

   (a) aluminum
   (b) copper-clad aluminum
   (c) copper
   (d) all of these

8. Conductor sizes are expressed in American Wire Gauge (AWG) or in _____.

   (a) inches
   (b) circular mils
   (c) square inches
   (d) cubic inches

9. Completed wiring installations shall be free from _____ other than as required or permitted elsewhere in this *Code*.

   (a) short circuits
   (b) ground faults
   (c) any connections to ground
   (d) all of these

10. Only wiring methods recognized as _____ are included in this *Code*.

    (a) expensive
    (b) efficient
    (c) suitable
    (d) cost effective

11. Equipment intended to interrupt current at _____ levels shall have an interrupting rating at nominal circuit voltage at least equal to the available fault current at the line terminals of the equipment.

    (a) fault
    (b) overcurrent
    (c) overload
    (d) incident energy

12. The _____, and other characteristics of the circuit to be protected shall be selected and coordinated to permit the circuit protective devices used to clear a fault to do so without extensive damage to the electrical equipment of the circuit.

    (a) overcurrent protective devices
    (b) total impedance
    (c) equipment short-circuit current ratings
    (d) all of these

13. Unless identified for use in the operating environment, no conductors or equipment shall be _____ having a deteriorating effect on the conductors or equipment.

    (a) located in damp or wet locations
    (b) exposed to fumes, vapors, liquids, or gases
    (c) exposed to excessive temperatures
    (d) all of these

14. Equipment not _____ for outdoor use and equipment identified only for indoor use such as "dry locations" or "indoor use only," shall be protected against damage from the weather during construction.

    (a) listed
    (b) identified
    (c) suitable
    (d) marked

15. Some _____ can cause severe deterioration of many plastic materials used for insulating and structural applications in equipment.

    (a) cleaning and lubricating compounds
    (b) protective coatings
    (c) paints and enamels
    (d) detergents

16. Electrical equipment shall be installed _____.

    (a) in a professional and skillful manner
    (b) under the supervision of a licensed person
    (c) completely before being inspected
    (d) all of these

17. Unused openings, other than those intended for the operation of equipment, those intended for mounting purposes, or permitted as part of the design for listed equipment shall be _____.

    (a) filled with cable clamps or connectors only
    (b) taped over with electrical tape
    (c) repaired only by welding or brazing in a metal slug
    (d) closed to afford protection substantially equivalent to the wall of the equipment

18. Internal parts of electrical equipment, including busbars, wiring terminals, insulators, and other surfaces, shall not be damaged or contaminated by foreign materials such as _____, or corrosive residues.

    (a) paint, plaster
    (b) cleaners
    (c) abrasives
    (d) any of these

19. Pressure terminal or pressure splicing connectors and soldering lugs shall be _____ for the material of the conductor and shall be properly installed and used.

    (a) listed
    (b) approved
    (c) identified
    (d) all of these

20. Connectors and terminals for conductors more finely stranded than Class B and Class C, as shown in Chapter 9, Table 10, shall be _____ for the specific conductor class or classes.

    (a) listed
    (b) approved
    (c) identified
    (d) all of these

21. Conductors of dissimilar metals shall not be intermixed in a terminal or splicing connector where physical contact occurs between dissimilar conductors unless the device is _____ for the purpose and conditions of use.

    (a) identified
    (b) listed
    (c) approved
    (d) designed

22. Connection of conductors to terminal parts shall ensure a mechanically secure electrical connection without damaging the conductors and shall be made by means of _____.

    (a) solder lugs
    (b) pressure connectors
    (c) splices to flexible leads
    (d) any of these

23. All _____ shall be covered with an insulation equivalent to that of the conductors or with an identified insulating device.

    (a) splices
    (b) joints
    (c) free ends of conductors
    (d) all of these

24. Separately installed pressure connectors shall be used with conductors at the _____ not exceeding the ampacity at the listed and identified temperature rating of the connector.

    (a) voltages
    (b) temperatures
    (c) listings
    (d) ampacities

25. Tightening torque values for terminal connections shall be as indicated on equipment or in installation instructions provided by the manufacturer. An approved means shall be used to achieve the_____ torque value.

    (a) indicated
    (b) identified
    (c) maximum
    (d) minimum

26. Examples of approved means of achieving the indicated _____ values include torque tools or devices such as shear bolts or breakaway-style devices with visual indicators that demonstrate that the proper torque has been applied.

    (a) pressure
    (b) torque
    (c) tightening
    (d) tension

27. On a 4-wire, delta-connected system where the midpoint of one phase winding is grounded, only the conductor or busbar having the higher phase voltage-to-ground shall be durably and permanently marked by an outer finish that is _____ in color.

    (a) black
    (b) red
    (c) blue
    (d) orange

28. Electrical equipment such as switchboards, switchgear, enclosed panelboards, industrial control panels, meter socket enclosures, and motor control centers, which are in other than dwelling units, and are likely to require _____ while energized, shall be field or factory marked to warn qualified persons of potential electric arc-flash hazards.

    (a) examination
    (b) adjustment
    (c) servicing or maintenance
    (d) any of these

29. In other than dwelling units, a permanent arc-flash label shall be field or factory applied to service equipment and feeder supplied equipment rated _____ or more.

    (a) 600A
    (b) 1000A
    (c) 1200A
    (d) 1600A

30. NFPA 70E, *Standard for Electrical Safety in the Workplace*, provides specific criteria for developing arc-flash labels for equipment that provides _____, and so forth.

    (a) nominal system voltage and incident energy levels
    (b) arc-flash boundaries
    (c) minimum required levels of personal protective equipment
    (d) all of these

31. Electrical equipment servicing and electrical preventive maintenance shall be performed by _____ trained in servicing and maintenance of equipment.

    (a) qualified persons
    (b) manufacturer's representatives
    (c) service specialists
    (d) licensed individuals

32. Equipment servicing and electrical preventive maintenance shall be performed in accordance with the original equipment manufacturer's instructions and _____.

(a) information included in the listing information
(b) applicable industry standards,
(c) as approved by the authority having jurisdiction
(d) any of these

33. Equipment that is reconditioned and required by the *Code* to be listed shall be listed or _____ as reconditioned using available instructions from the original equipment manufacturer.

(a) identified
(b) documented
(c) field labeled
(d) certified

34. Where caution, warning, or danger hazard markings such as labels or signs are required by this *Code*, the markings shall be of sufficient durability to withstand the environment involved and warn of these hazards using effective _____.

(a) words
(b) colors
(c) symbols
(d) any combination of words, colors, or symbols

35. Each disconnecting means shall be legibly marked to indicate its purpose unless located and arranged so _____.

(a) that it can be locked out and tagged
(b) it is not readily accessible
(c) the purpose is evident
(d) that it operates at less than 300 volts-to-ground

36. Equipment enclosures for circuit breakers or fuses applied in compliance with the series combination ratings marked on the equipment by the manufacturer in accordance with 240.86(B) shall be _____ to indicate the equipment has been applied with a series combination rating.

(a) legibly marked in the field
(b) inspected and tagged
(c) installed
(d) listed

37. _____ at other than dwelling units shall be legibly field marked with the available fault current, include the date the fault-current calculation was performed, and be of sufficient durability to withstand the environment involved.

(a) Service equipment
(b) Sub panels
(c) Motor control centers
(d) all of these

38. When service equipment is required to be field marked with the available fault current, the value of available fault current for use in determining appropriate minimum short-circuit current ratings of service equipment is available from _____ in published or other forms.

(a) the architect
(b) the engineer
(c) electric utilities
(d) all of these

39. When modifications to the electrical installation occur that affect the available fault current at the service, the available fault current shall be verified or _____ as necessary to ensure the service equipment ratings are sufficient for the available fault current at the line terminals of the equipment.

(a) recalculated
(b) increased
(c) decreased
(d) adjusted

40. If a disconnecting means is required to be lockable open elsewhere in the *NEC*, it shall be capable of being locked in the open position. The provisions for locking shall remain in place with or without _____.

(a) the power off
(b) the lock installed
(c) supervision
(d) a lock-out tag

41. _____, and access to and egress from working space, shall be provided and maintained about all electrical equipment to permit ready and safe operation and maintenance of such equipment.

(a) Ventilation
(b) Unrestricted movement
(c) Circulation
(d) Working space

42. Access to or egress from the required working space about electrical equipment is considered impeded if one or more simultaneously opened equipment doors restrict working space access to be less than _____ wide and 6½ ft high.

(a) 24 in.
(b) 28 in.
(c) 30 in.
(d) 36 in.

43. Working space is required for equipment operating at 1000V, nominal, or less to ground and likely to require _____ while energized.

(a) examination
(b) adjustment
(c) servicing or maintenance
(d) all of these

44. NFPA 70E, *Standard for Electrical Safety in the Workplace*, provides guidance, such as determining severity of potential exposure, planning safe work practices including establishing an electrically _____ work condition, arc-flash labeling, and selecting personal protective equipment.

(a) safe
(b) efficient
(c) grounded
(d) bonded

45. Working space distances for enclosed live parts shall be measured from the _____ of equipment if the live parts are enclosed.

(a) enclosure or opening
(b) front or back
(c) mounting pad
(d) footprint

46. Working space is not required at the back or sides of equipment where all _____ and all renewable, adjustable, or serviceable parts are accessible from the front.

(a) screws
(b) connections
(c) bolts
(d) doors

47. The minimum working space on a circuit for equipment operating at 120V to ground, with exposed live parts on one side and no live or grounded parts on the other side of the working space, is _____.

(a) 1 ft
(b) 3 ft
(c) 4 ft
(d) 6 ft

48. The required working space for access to live parts of equipment operating at 300V to ground, where there are exposed live parts on one side and grounded parts on the other side, is _____.

(a) 3 ft
(b) 3½ ft
(c) 4 ft
(d) 4½ ft

49. The required working space for access to live parts of equipment operating at 300V to ground, where there are exposed live parts on both sides of the workspace is _____.

(a) 3 ft
(b) 3½ ft
(c) 4 ft
(d) 4½ ft

50. The width of the working space shall be not be less than _____ wide, or the width of the equipment, whichever is greater.

(a) 15 in.
(b) 30 in.
(c) 40 in.
(d) 60 in.

51. The minimum height of working spaces shall be clear and extend from the grade, floor, or platform to a height of _____ or the height of the equipment, whichever is greater.

(a) 3 ft
(b) 6 ft
(c) 6½ ft
(d) 7 ft

52. The grade, floor, or platform in the required working space about electrical equipment shall be as level and flat as _____ for the entire required depth and width of the working space.

(a) practical
(b) possible
(c) required
(d) none of these

53. Working space required by Section 110.26 shall not be used for _____.
   (a) storage
   (b) raceways
   (c) lighting
   (d) accessibility

54. When normally enclosed live parts are exposed for inspection or servicing, the working space, if in a passageway or general open space, shall be suitably _____.
   (a) accessible
   (b) guarded
   (c) open
   (d) enclosed

55. For large equipment that contains overcurrent devices, switching devices, or control devices, there shall be one entrance to and egress from the required working space not less than 24 in. wide and _____ high at each end of the working space.
   (a) 5½ ft
   (b) 6 ft
   (c) 6½ ft
   (d) 7 ft

56. For equipment rated 800A or more that contains overcurrent devices, switching devices, or control devices; and where the entrance to the working space has a personnel door(s) less than 25 ft from the nearest edge of the working space, the door shall open at least 90 degrees _____.
   (a) in or out with simple pressure and shall not have any lock
   (b) in the direction of egress and be equipped with listed panic or fire exit hardware
   (c) and be equipped with a locking means
   (d) and be equipped with an electronic opener

57. Illumination shall be provided for all working spaces about service equipment, switchboards, switchgear, enclosed panelboards, or motor control centers _____.
   (a) over 600V
   (b) installed indoors
   (c) rated 1200A or more
   (d) using automatic means of control

58. All service equipment, switchboards, panelboards, and motor control centers shall be _____.
   (a) located in dedicated spaces
   (b) protected from damage
   (c) in weatherproof enclosures
   (d) located in dedicated spaces and protected from damage

59. The minimum height of dedicated equipment space for motor control centers installed indoors is _____ above the enclosure, or to the structural ceiling, whichever is lower.
   (a) 3 ft
   (b) 5 ft
   (c) 6 ft
   (d) 6½ ft

60. A dropped, suspended, or similar ceiling that does not add strength to the building structure shall not be considered a _____ ceiling.
   (a) structural
   (b) secured
   (c) real
   (d) drop

61. All switchboards, switchgear, panelboards, and motor control centers located outdoors shall be _____.
   (a) installed in identified enclosures
   (b) protected from accidental contact by unauthorized personnel or by vehicular traffic
   (c) protected from accidental spillage or leakage from piping systems
   (d) all of these

62. A NEMA Type 1 enclosure is approved for the environmental condition where _____ might be present.
   (a) falling dirt
   (b) falling liquids
   (c) circulating dust
   (d) settling airborne dust

63. Enclosures of switchboards, switchgear, or panelboards that may become ice covered where exposed to sleet may be installed in a _____ enclosure.
   (a) Type 3 or 3R
   (b) Type 3X or RX
   (c) Type 3S or SX
   (d) Type 4 or 4X

64. Enclosure Type 3X for switchboards, switchgear, or panelboards located outdoors are suitable in locations subject to _____.

(a) rain
(b) windblown dust
(c) corrosive agents
(d) any of these

65. A Type 4X enclosure for switchboards, switchgear, or panelboards located indoors is suitable in locations subject to the environmental condition of _____.

(a) falling dirt
(b) falling liquids
(c) corrosive agents
(d) any of these

66. The term "rainproof" is typically used in conjunction with enclosure type(s) _____.

(a) NEMA 3
(b) NEMA 3R and 3RX
(c) NEMA 4
(d) NEMA 4R and 4RX

1st Printing

CHAPTER

5 SPECIAL OCCUPANCIES

Introduction to Chapter 5—Special Occupancies

This chapter covers special occupancies and is the first of three *NEC* chapters that deal with special requirements. A "Special Occupancy" is a location where a facility, or its use, creates conditions that require additional measures to ensure the "practical safeguarding of people and property." Chapter 5 contains 27 articles that address occupancies from aircraft hangers to recreational vehicles. While many of these articles are outside the scope of this material, the following are included:

- **Article 500—Hazardous (Classified) Locations.** Article 500 contains the general requirements applicable to all hazardous (classified) locations. A hazardous (classified) location is an area where the possibility of fire or explosion exists due to the presence of flammable or combustible liquid-produced vapors, flammable gases, combustible dusts, or easily ignitible fibers/flyings.
- **Article 501—Class I Hazardous Locations.** A Class I hazardous (classified) location is an area where flammable or combustible liquid-produced vapors or flammable gases may present the hazard of a fire or explosion.
- **Article 502—Class II Hazardous Locations.** A Class II hazardous (classified) location is an area where the possibility of fire or explosion may exist due to the presence of combustible dust.
- **Article 511—Commercial Garages, Repair and Storage.** These occupancies include locations used for service and repair operations in connection with self-propelled vehicles including passenger automobiles, buses, trucks, and tractors in which flammable liquids or flammable gases are used for fuel or power.
- **Article 514—Motor Fuel Dispensing Facilities.** Article 514 covers gasoline dispensing and service stations where gasoline or other volatile liquids are transferred to the fuel tanks of self-propelled vehicles. Wiring and equipment in the area of service and repair rooms of service stations must comply with the installation requirements in Article 511.
- **Article 517—Health Care Facilities.** This article covers electrical wiring in human health care facilities such as hospitals, nursing homes, limited care facilities, clinics, medical and dental offices, and ambulatory care—whether permanent or movable. It does not apply to animal veterinary facilities.
- **Article 518—Assembly Occupancies.** Article 518 covers buildings or portions of buildings specifically designed or intended for the assembly of 100 or more persons.
- **Article 525—Carnivals, Circuses, Fairs, and Similar Events.** This article covers the installation of portable wiring and equipment for temporary carnivals, circuses, exhibitions, fairs, traveling attractions, and similar functions including wiring in or on structures.
- **Article 547—Agricultural Buildings.** Article 547 covers agricultural buildings or those parts of buildings or adjacent areas where excessive dust or dust with water may accumulate, or where a corrosive atmosphere exists.

• • •

- **Article 550—Mobile Homes, Manufactured Homes, and Mobile Home Parks.** Article 550 covers electrical conductors and equipment within or on mobile and manufactured homes, conductors that connect mobile and manufactured homes to the electrical supply, and the installation of electrical wiring, luminaires, and electrical equipment in or on mobile and manufactured homes.
- **Article 555—Marinas, Boatyards, and Docking Facilities.** This article covers the installation of wiring and equipment in the areas that comprise piers, docks, and other areas in marinas, boatyards for the repair, berthing, launching, storing, or fueling of water crafts.
- **Article 590—Temporary Installations.** Article 590 covers temporary power and lighting for construction, remodeling, maintenance, repair, demolitions, and decorative lighting.

ARTICLE 500

HAZARDOUS (CLASSIFIED) LOCATIONS

Introduction to Article 500—Hazardous (Classified) Locations

This Article contains the general requirements applicable to all hazardous (classified) locations. A hazardous (classified) location is an area where the possibility of fire or explosion exists due to the presence of flammable or combustible liquid-produced vapors, flammable gases, combustible dusts, or easily ignitible fibers/flyings.

Article 500 provides the general rules for Article 501 (Class I Locations), Article 502 (Class II Locations), and Article 503 (Class III Locations). You will notice when studying this article that there are many Informational Notes. Although these notes are not *NEC* requirements [90.5(C)], they contain information that is helpful when trying to understand the context of the related *NEC* rules.

Fire and explosion hazards require three primary components to present a danger. The Fire Triangle (fuel, oxygen, and energy source) helps illustrate the concept of how combustion occurs so we can better understand the reasons behind the *NEC* requirements in Chapter 5. ▶Figure 500–1

- ***Fuel.*** Flammable gases or vapors, combustible dusts, and easily ignitible fibers/flyings.
- ***Oxygen.*** Air and oxidizing atmospheres.
- ***Ignition Source (Heat).*** Electric arcs or sparks, heat-producing equipment such as luminaires and motors, failure of transformers, coils, or solenoids, as well as sparks caused by metal tools dropping on metal surfaces.

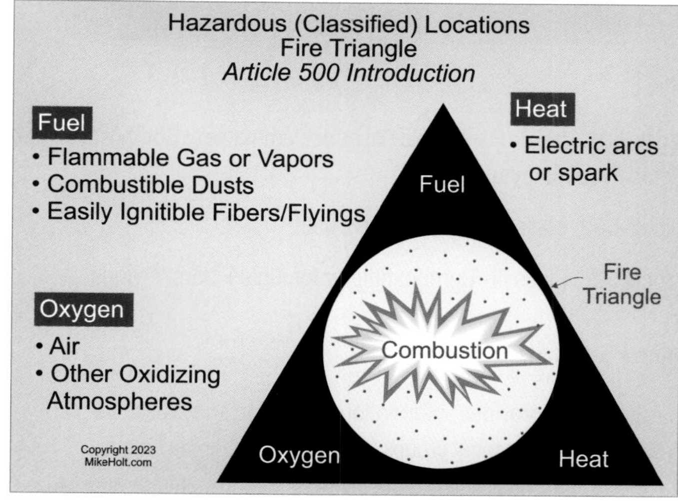

▶Figure 500–1

Many of the illustrations in Chapter 5 use two shades of red to identify a division location (darker red for Division 1 and lighter red to identify Division 2). In some cases, these color schemes are used as a background color to help you tell if the illustration covers Division 1, Division 2, or both (split color background).

500.1 Scope—Articles 500 Through 503

(A) Installations Covered. Article 500 covers area classification and general requirements for electrical equipment and wiring where fire or explosion hazards might exist due to flammable gases, flammable liquid-produced vapors, combustible liquid-produced vapors, combustible dusts, combustible fibers/flyings, or ignitible fibers/flyings. Specific requirements are in: ▶**Figure 500–2**

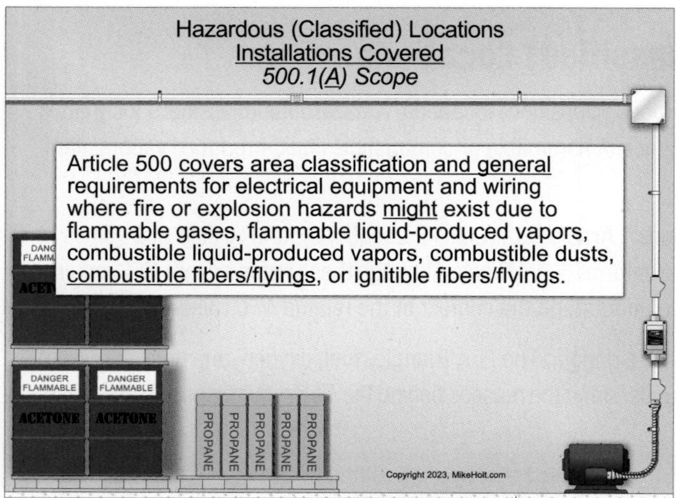
Hazardous (Classified) Locations
Installations Covered
500.1(A) Scope
Article 500 covers area classification and general requirements for electrical equipment and wiring where fire or explosion hazards might exist due to flammable gases, flammable liquid-produced vapors, combustible liquid-produced vapors, combustible dusts, combustible fibers/flyings, or ignitible fibers/flyings.
DANGER FLAMMABLE
ACETONE
PROPANE
Copyright 2023, MikeHolt.com

▶**Figure 500–2**

(1) Article 501. Class I—Flammable Gases or Flammable or Combustible Liquid-Produced Vapors

(2) Article 502. Class II—Combustible Dust

(3) Article 503. Class III—Combustible or Ignitible Fibers/Flyings

Author's Comment:

- Article 500 provides information related to the classifications [500.5], material groups [500.6], protection techniques [500.7], and equipment types [500.8] that are unique and required for Class I, Class II, and Class III locations. Articles 501, 502, and 503 cover the specific wiring requirements in hazardous (classified) areas.

Articles containing installation requirements for hazardous (classified) locations in special occupancies include:

- Article 511. Commercial Garages, Repair and Storage
- Article 514. Motor Fuel Dispensing Facilities

500.4 Documentation

Areas designated as hazardous (classified) locations or determined to be unclassified must be documented on an area classification drawing and other associated documentation. The documentation must be available to the authority having jurisdiction (AHJ) and those who are authorized to design, install, inspect, maintain, or operate the electrical equipment. ▶**Figure 500–3**

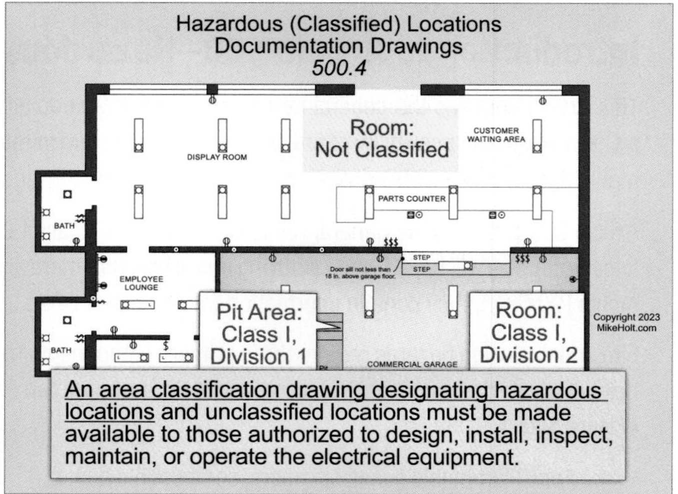
Hazardous (Classified) Locations
Documentation Drawings
500.4
Room:
Not Classified
DISPLAY ROOM
CUSTOMER WAITING AREA
PARTS COUNTER
BATH
EMPLOYEE LOUNGE
STEP
Pit Area:
Class I,
Division 1
COMMERCIAL GARAGE
Room:
Class I,
Division 2
Copyright 2023 MikeHolt.com
An area classification drawing designating hazardous locations and unclassified locations must be made available to those authorized to design, install, inspect, maintain, or operate the electrical equipment.

▶**Figure 500–3**

Author's Comment:

- Proper documentation of hazardous areas assists the designer, installer, and authority having jurisdiction in ensuring adherence to the stringent requirements contained in Articles 501 through 517 of the *Code*. The required classification drawings must indicate the hazardous location area classification(s) and the boundaries between classified and unclassified areas, material group properties such as auto ignition temperatures, and equipment construction suitability.
- Articles 511 through 517, provide established details on the areas that are classified for those occupancies. Additional determination of classified areas is not required for the areas that are classified by those articles. Determining the classification of a specific hazardous area is the responsibility of those who understand the dangers of the products being used such as the fire marshal, plant facility engineer, or insurance underwriter. It is not the responsibility of the electrical designer, electrical contractor, or electrical inspector. Before performing any wiring in or near a hazardous (classified) location, contact the plant facility and design engineer to ensure

1st Printing

that proper installation methods and materials are used. Be sure to review 500.4(B) for additional standards that might need to be consulted.

500.5 Classifications of Hazardous (Classified) Locations

(A) General.

(1) Hazardous (Classified) Locations. Locations are classified according to the properties and concentration of the flammable gases, flammable liquid-produced vapors, combustible liquid-produced vapors, combustible dusts, or combustible or ignitable fibers/flyings that might be present. ▸Figure 500–4

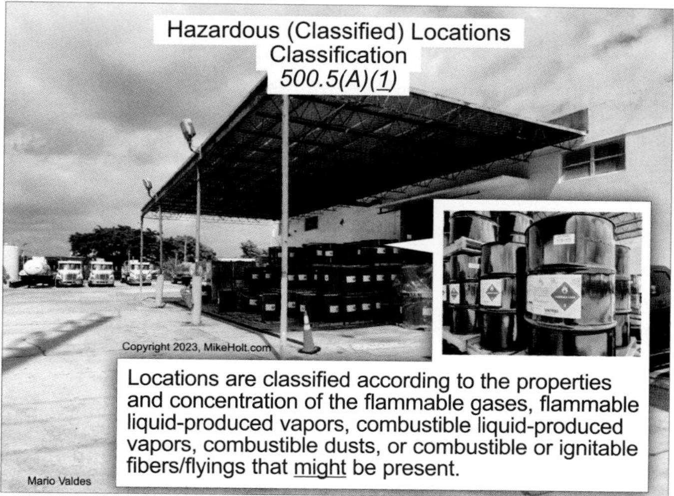

▸Figure 500–4

Each room, section, or area is considered individually in determining its classification. ▸Figure 500–5

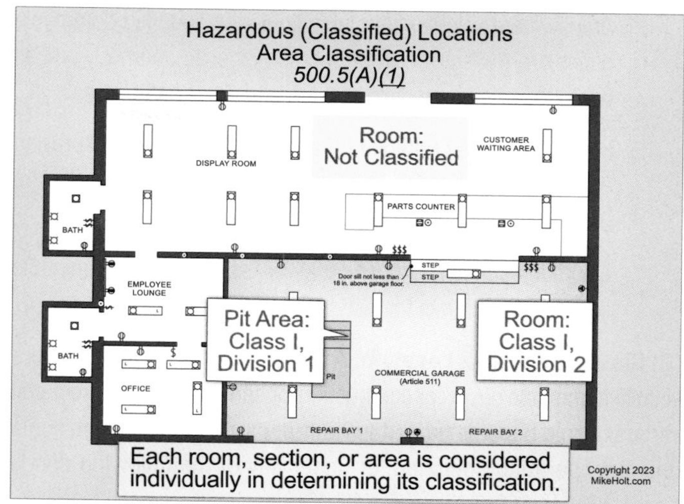

▸Figure 500–5

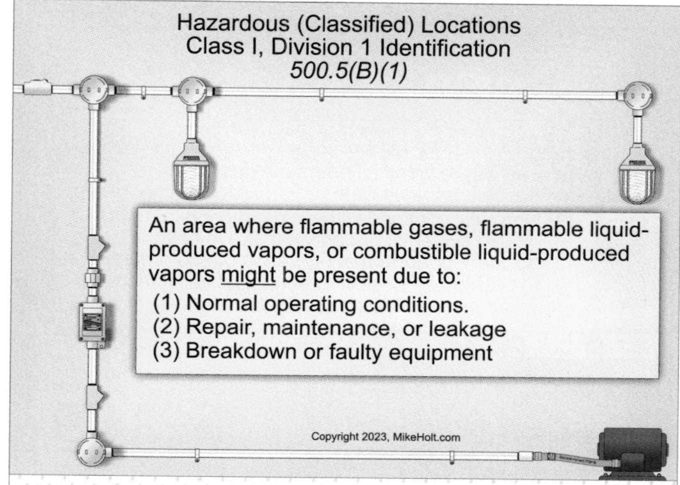

▸Figure 500–6

Note 1: To reduce the need for expensive equipment and expensive wiring methods, locate as much electrical equipment as possible in an unclassified location.

(B) Identification of a Class I Location. A Class I location is an area where flammable gases, flammable liquid-produced vapors, or combustible liquid-produced vapors might be present in quantities sufficient to produce explosive or ignitable mixtures.

(1) Class I, Division 1 Location. A Class I, Division 1 location is a location in which: ▸Figure 500–6

(1) Ignitible concentrations of flammable gases, flammable liquid-produced vapors, or combustible liquid-produced vapors might exist during normal operations, or

(2) Ignitible concentrations of flammable gases, flammable liquid-produced vapors, or combustible liquids above their flash points might exist due to repair or maintenance operations or because of leakage, or

(3) Breakdown or faulty equipment releases ignitable concentrations of flammable gases, flammable liquid-produced vapors, or combustible liquid-produced vapors and the electrical equipment becomes a source of ignition.

Note: Class I, Division 1 locations include:

(1) Areas where volatile flammable liquids or liquefied flammable gases are transferred from one container to another, such as pits or sumps at gasoline storage and dispensing areas.

(2) Interiors of spray booths and areas in the vicinity of spraying and painting operations where volatile flammable solvents are used to coat products with paint or plastics.

(3) Locations containing open tanks or vats of volatile flammable liquids, or dip tanks for parts cleaning or other operations.

(2) Class I, Division 2 Location. A Class 2 location is an area where volatile flammable gases, or combustible or flammable liquid-produced vapors, would become hazardous only in case of an accident, some unusual operating condition, or under any of the following conditions: ▸Figure 500–7

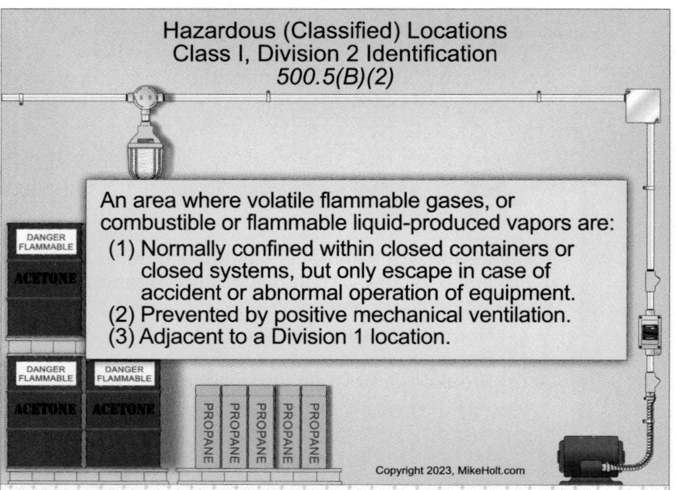

▸Figure 500–7

(1) If flammable gases, flammable liquid-produced vapors, or combustible liquid-produced vapors are handled, processed, or used, but are normally confined within closed containers and the gases would only escape in the case of accidental rupture or breakdown, or in the case of abnormal operation of equipment.

(2) If ignitible concentrations of flammable gases, flammable liquid-produced vapors, or combustible liquid-produced vapors are normally prevented by positive mechanical ventilation but might become hazardous through failure or abnormal operation of the ventilating equipment.

(3) Areas adjacent to a Class I, Division 1 location and to where flammable gases, flammable liquid-produced vapors, or combustible liquid-produced vapors might occasionally be communicated unless prevented by adequate positive-pressure ventilation with effective safeguards against ventilation failure.

Note 1: The quantity of flammable gases, flammable liquid-produced vapors, or combustible liquid-produced vapors that might escape in case of accident, the adequacy of ventilating equipment, the total area involved, and the record of the industry with respect to explosions or fires are all factors that should be taken into consideration.

(C) Identification of a Class II Location. Class II locations are hazardous because of the presence of combustible dust. ▸Figure 500–8

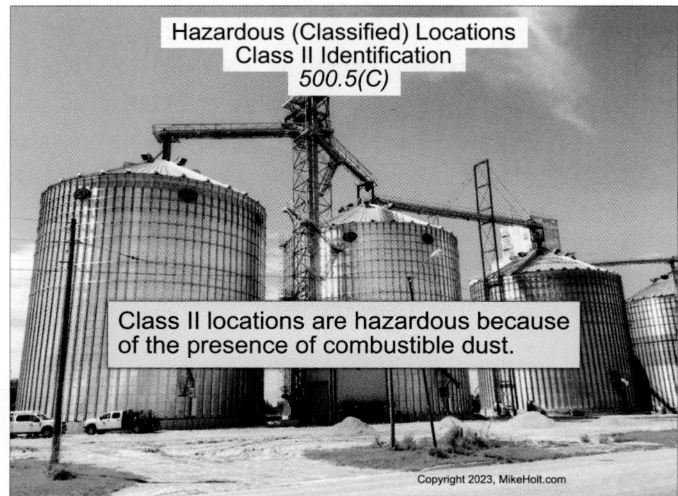

▸Figure 500–8

(1) Class II, Division 1 Location. A Class II, Division 1 location is a location in which:

(1) Under normal operating conditions combustible dust is continuously or periodically suspended in the air in sufficient quantities to produce mixtures that will ignite or explode, or

(2) If faulty equipment releases ignitible mixtures of dust and the equipment becomes a source of ignition, or

(3) In which Group E combustible dusts may be present in quantities sufficient to be hazardous in normal or abnormal operating conditions. All Group E areas are Class II, Division 1 areas. There are no Division 2 areas where combustible metal dusts are handled.

Note: Dusts containing magnesium or aluminum are particularly hazardous, and the use of extreme precautions are necessary to avoid ignition and explosion.

(2) Class II, Division 2 Location. An area where combustible dust would become hazardous under any of the following conditions:

(1) If combustible dust, due to abnormal operations, may be present in the air in quantities sufficient to produce explosive or ignitible mixtures, or

(2) If combustible dust accumulation is normally insufficient to interfere with the normal operation of electrical equipment, but where malfunctioning equipment may result in combustible dust being suspended in the air, or

(3) If combustible dust accumulations on, in, or near electrical equipment could be sufficient to interfere with the safe dissipation of heat from electrical equipment or could be ignitible by abnormal operation or failure of electrical equipment.

Note 1: The quantity of combustible dust that may be present and the adequacy of dust removal systems should be considered when determining the area classification.

(D) Identification of a Class III Location. A Class III location is a location meeting the requirements of 500.5(D)(1)(a) and (D)(2)(b).

(1) Class III, Division 1 Location. A Class III, Division 1 location includes the following:

(a) Combustible Fibers/Flyings. Locations where nonmetal combustible fibers/flyings are in the air under normal operating conditions in quantities sufficient to produce explosive mixtures or where mechanical failure or abnormal operation of machinery or equipment might cause combustible fibers/flyings to be produced and might also provide a source of ignition through simultaneous failure of electrical equipment, through operation of protective devices, or from other causes are classified as Class III, Division 1. Locations where metal combustible fibers/flyings are present must be classified as Class II, Division 1, Group E.

Note 1: Such locations usually include some parts of rayon, cotton, and other textile mills or clothing manufacturing plants as well as facilities that create sawdust and combustible fibers/flyings by pulverizing or cutting wood.

Note 2: Combustible fibers/flyings include flat platelet-shaped particulates, such as metal flakes, and fibrous board such as particle board.

(b) Ignitible Fibers/Flyings. Locations where ignitible fibers/flyings are handled, manufactured, or used are classified as Class III, Division 1.

Note 1: Such locations usually include some parts of rayon, cotton, and other textile mills or clothing manufacturing plants as well as facilities that create sawdust and ignitible fibers/flyings by pulverizing or cutting wood.

Note 2: Ignitible fibers/flyings can include rayon, cotton (including cotton linters and cotton waste), sisal or henequen, istle, jute, hemp, tow, cocoa fiber, oakum, baled waste kapok, Spanish Moss, excelsior, and other materials of similar nature.

(2) Class III, Division 2 Location. A Class III, Division 2 location includes the following:

(a) Combustible Fibers/Flyings. Locations where nonmetal combustible fibers/flyings might be present in the air in quantities sufficient to produce explosive mixtures due to abnormal operations or where accumulations of nonmetal combustible fibers/flyings accumulations are present but are insufficient to interfere with the normal operation of electrical equipment or other apparatus but could, as a result of infrequent malfunctioning of handling or processing equipment, become suspended in the air are classified as Class III, Division 2.

A combustible fiber/flying can produce an explosive mixture when suspended in air.

According to Article 100, "Combustible Fibers/Flyings" are defined as those having any dimension greater than 500 μm in nominal size, which can form an explosive mixture when suspended in air at standard atmospheric pressure and temperature.

(b) Ignitible Fibers/Flyings. Locations where ignitible fibers/flyings are stored or handled, other than in the process of manufacture, are classified as Class III, Division 2.

500.6 Material Groups

For purposes of approval and area classification, air mixtures in hazardous locations must be grouped in accordance with 500.6(A) and (B). ▶Figure 500–9

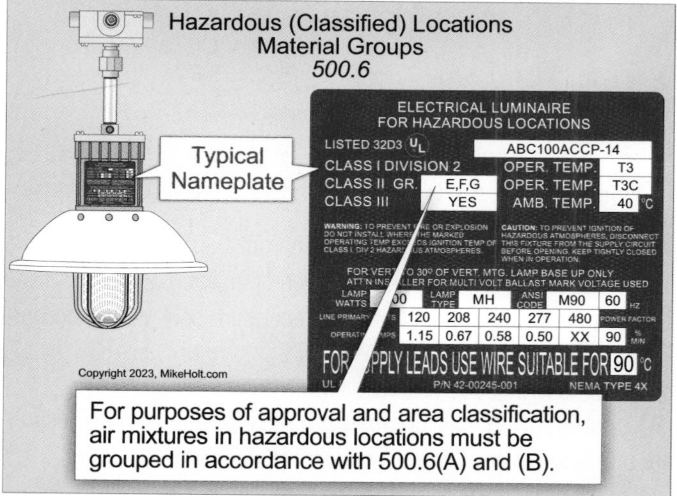

▶Figure 500–9

Author's Comment:

- Refer to 500.6(A) and (B) in the *NEC* to be certain that equipment is listed for the proper group.
- The Cooper Crouse-Hinds *Code Digest* contains a substantial list of different products and their group designations. It can be downloaded from www.coopercrouse-hinds.eu/en/service/brochures.html.

500.7 Protection Techniques

Electrical and electronic equipment in hazardous (classified) locations must be protected by one or more of the techniques in 500.7(A) through (U). Suitability of the protection techniques for specific hazardous (classified) locations are shown in Chapter 9, Table 13.

(A) Explosionproof Equipment. Explosionproof equipment is permitted in any Class I location for which it is identified. ▶Figure 500–10

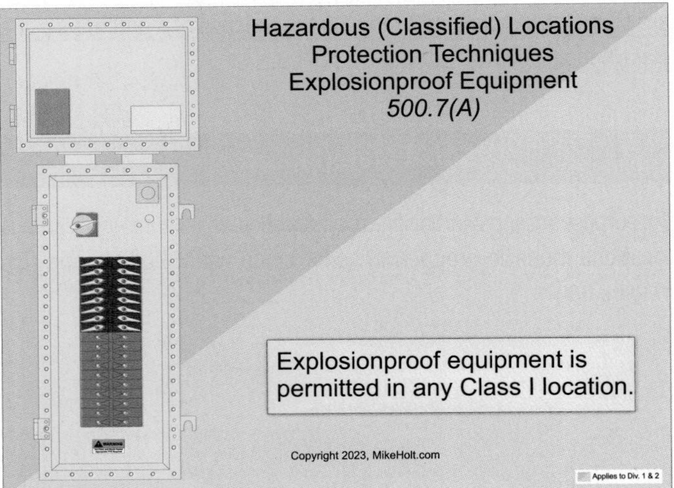

▶Figure 500–10

According to Article 100, "Explosionproof Equipment" is capable of withstanding and containing the force of an internal explosion and designed so the hot gases within the enclosure cool as they escape. ▶Figure 500–11

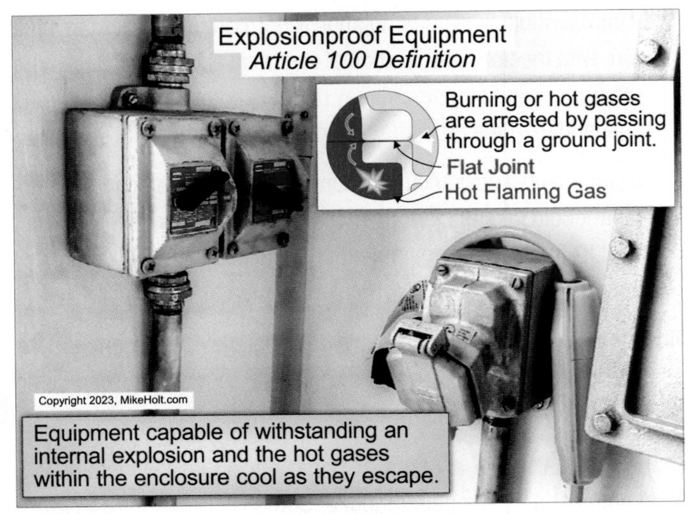

▶Figure 500–11

(B) Dust-Ignitionproof Enclosures. Dust-ignitionproof enclosures are permitted in any Class II location. ▶Figure 500–12

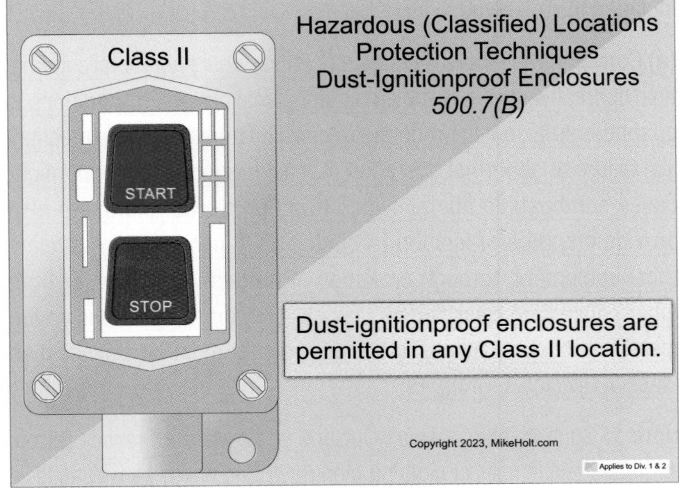

▶Figure 500–12

According to Article 100, "Dust-Ignitionproof" equipment enclosures are designed to exclude dusts and will not permit arcs, sparks, or heat within the enclosure to cause the ignition of exterior dust. ▶Figure 500–13

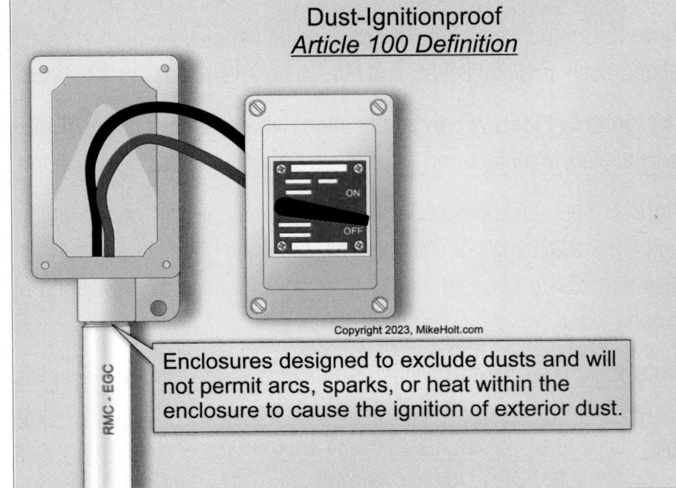

▶Figure 500–13

1st Printing

(C) Dusttight Enclosures. Dusttight enclosures are permitted in Class II, Division 2 or any Class III location. ▸Figure 500–14

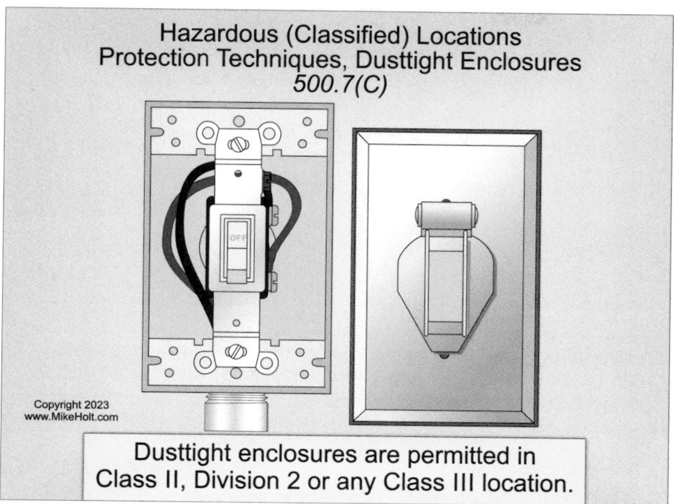

▸Figure 500–14

According to Article 100, "Dusttight Enclosures" are enclosures constructed so that dust will not enter under specified test conditions. ▸Figure 500–15

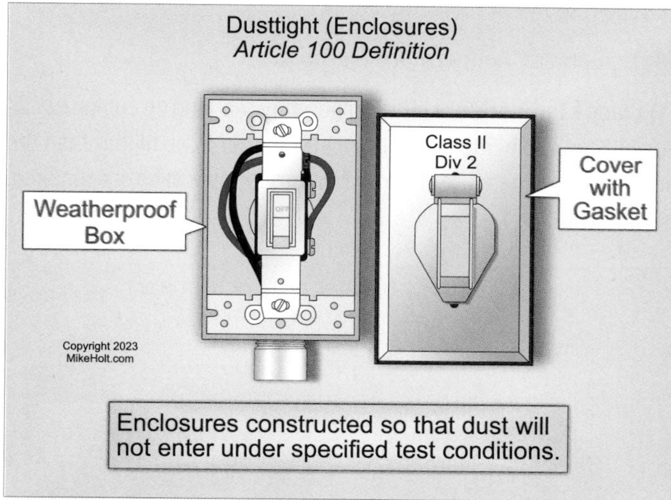

▸Figure 500–15

(D) Purged and Pressurized Systems. Purged and pressurized systems are permitted for equipment in any hazardous (classified) locations for which they are identified. ▸Figure 500–16

According to Article 100, "Purging" is supplying an enclosure with a safe gas at a flow and pressure to sufficiently reduce concentrations of flammable gases, flammable liquid-produced vapors, or combustible liquid-produced vapors to a safe level.

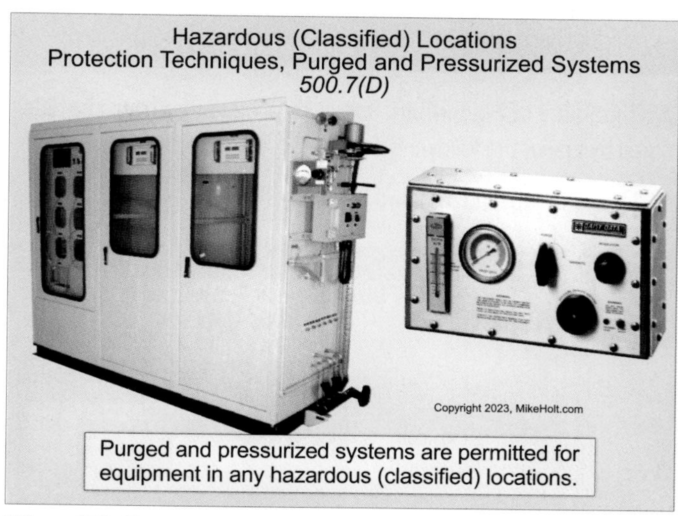

▸Figure 500–16

According to Article 100, "Pressurization" is supplying an enclosure with a safe gas, with or without a continuous flow, with enough pressure to prevent the entrance of combustible dust or ignitible fibers/flyings.

(I) Oil-Immersed Contacts. Oil-immersed make-and-break contacts can be installed in a Class I, Division 2 location.

(J) Hermetically Sealed Contacts. Hermetically sealed contacts can be installed in Class I, Division 2; Class II, Division 2; or Class III locations. ▸Figure 500–17

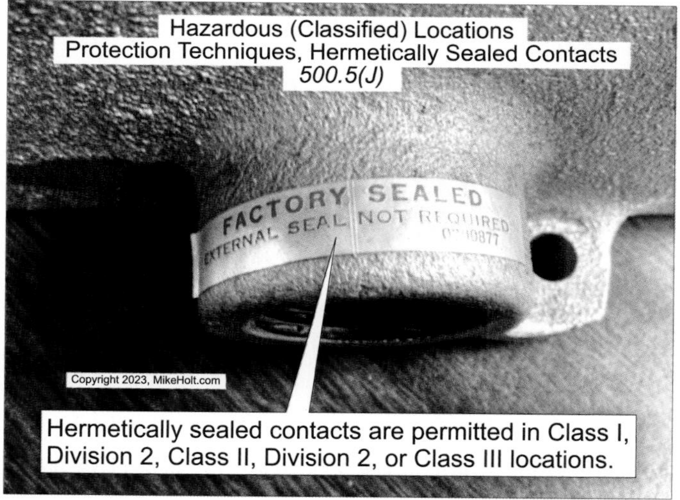

▸Figure 500–17

500.8 Equipment

(A) Suitability of Equipment. Suitability of equipment must be determined by any of the following:

(1) Listing or labeling ▸Figure 500–18

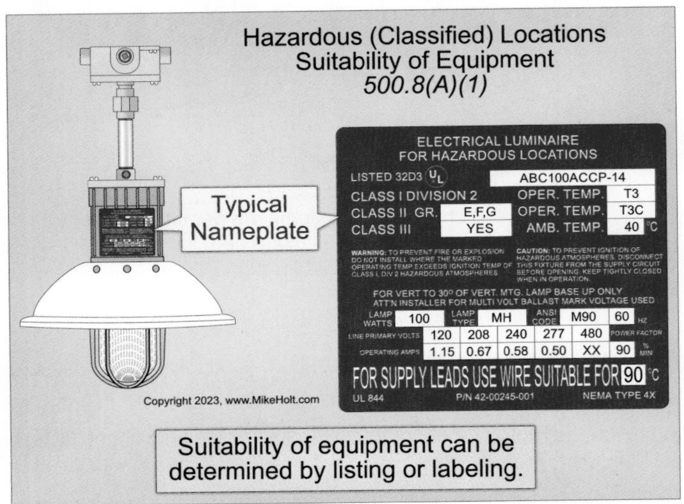

▸Figure 500–18

(2) Field evaluation by a qualified testing laboratory or inspection agency concerned with product evaluation

(3) Evidence acceptable by the authority having jurisdiction such as a manufacturer's self-evaluation or an owner's engineering judgment

Note: Additional documentation might include certificates demonstrating compliance with applicable equipment standards indicating special conditions of use and providing other pertinent information.

(B) Equipment Approval for Class and Properties.

(1) Equipment Identification. Equipment installed in any hazardous (classified) location must be identified for the class and the explosive, combustible, or ignitible properties of the specific gas, vapor, dust, or fibers/flyings that will be present.

(2) Equipment Application. Equipment identified for a Division 1 location is permitted in a Division 2 location of the same class, group, and temperature class.

(3) General-Purpose Equipment. A general-purpose enclosure without make-and-break contacts can be installed in any hazardous (classified) Division 2 location. ▸Figure 500–19

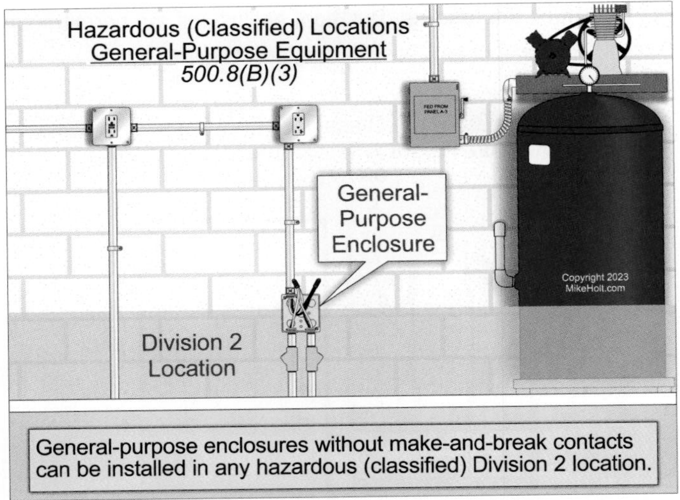

▸Figure 500–19

(C) Equipment Marking.

(4) Equipment Temperature. The marking on equipment must specify the temperature class or operating ambient temperature at 40°C, or at the higher ambient temperature if the equipment is rated and marked for an ambient temperature above 40°C. If provided, the temperature class must be indicated using the temperature class (T codes) shown in Table 500.8(C)(4).

(D) Equipment Temperature Marking.

(1) Class I Temperature. The temperature marking on equipment as specified in Table 500.8(C)(4) is not permitted to be higher than the autoignition temperature of the specific gas or vapor to be encountered. ▸Figure 500–20

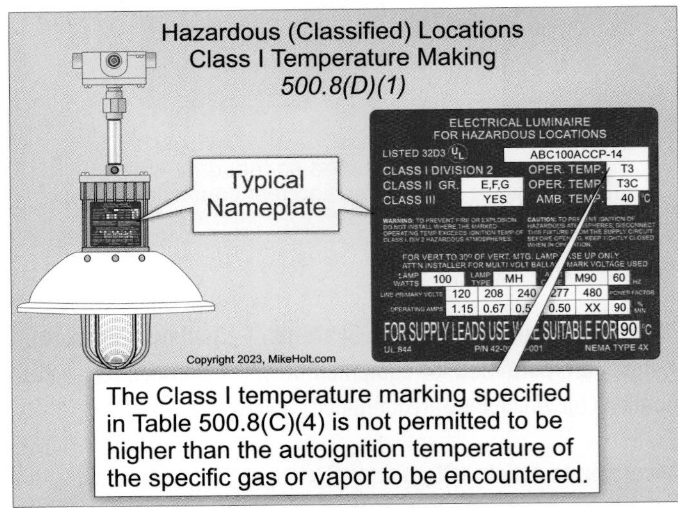

▸Figure 500–20

1st Printing

Table 500.8(C)(4) Classification of Maximum Surface Temperature		
Maximum °C	Temperature °F	Temperature Class (T Code)
450	842	T1
300	572	T2
280	536	T2A
260	500	T2B
230	446	T2C
215	419	T2D
200	392	T3
180	356	T3A
165	329	T3B
160	320	T3C
135	275	T4
120	248	T4A
100	212	T5
85	185	T6

(2) Class II Temperature. Class II equipment must not have exposed surfaces operating at a temperature in excess of the autoignition temperature of the specific dust or metal fiber/flying as contained in Table 500.8(C)(4).

Author's Comment:

- This is accomplished by ensuring that the temperature marking on the equipment (especially luminaires and motors) does not exceed the autoignition temperature of the specific gases, vapors, or types of dust encountered.

(E) Threading. Threaded conduits must be made wrenchtight to prevent arcing when ground-fault current flows through the raceway system, and to ensure the explosionproof or dust-ignitionproof integrity of the raceway system.

(1) Equipment with Threaded Entries. Threaded entries into explosionproof equipment must be made up with at least five threads fully engaged. ▸**Figure 500–21**

Ex: Listed explosionproof equipment with factory NPT entries must be made up with four and one-half threads fully engaged.

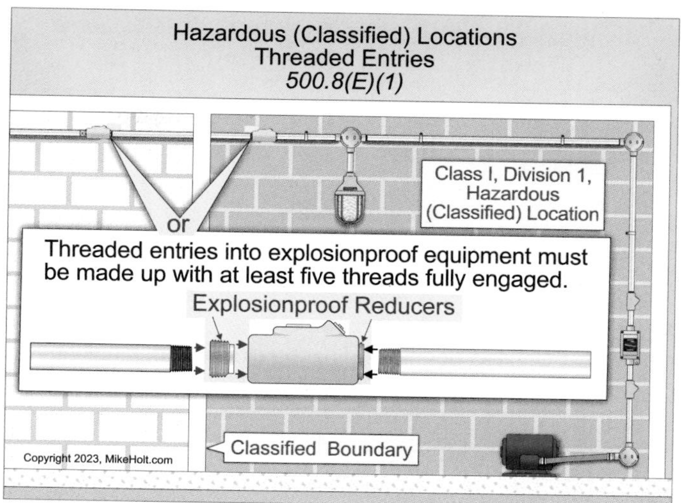

▸**Figure 500–21**

Author's Comment:

- This requirement ensures that if an explosion occurs within a raceway or enclosure, the expanding gas will sufficiently cool as it dissipates through the threads. This prevents hot flaming gases from igniting the surrounding atmosphere of a hazardous (classified) location.
- Remember that it is assumed the flammable atmosphere outside the raceway will seep into the raceway system over time. The goal of the *Code* is to contain any explosion that occurs inside the raceway so the event will not ignite the flammable mixture outside the raceway.

(3) Unused Openings. Unused openings must be closed with blanking elements or close-up plugs listed for the location. Threaded entries must be made up with at least five threads fully engaged [500.8(E)(1)]. ▸**Figure 500–22**

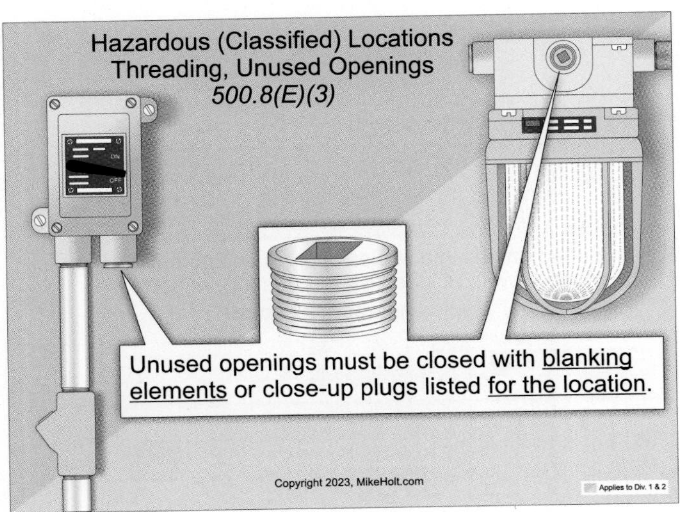
Hazardous (Classified) Locations
Threading, Unused Openings
500.8(E)(3)
Unused openings must be closed with blanking elements or close-up plugs listed for the location.
Copyright 2023, MikeHolt.com
Applies to Div. 1 & 2

▶Figure 500–22

ARTICLE 501

CLASS I HAZARDOUS (CLASSIFIED) LOCATIONS

Introduction to Article 501—Class I Hazardous (Classified) Locations

If an area has sufficient flammable or combustible gases, vapors, or liquids may be present to produce an explosive or ignitible mixture, you have a Class I location. Examples of such locations include some fuel storage areas, certain solvent storage areas, grain processing facilities (where hexane is used), plastic extrusion areas where oil removal is part of the process, refineries, and paint storage areas. Many of these rules are outside of the scope of this material, however, some of the topics we cover include the following:

- Wiring Methods
- Sealing and Drainage
- Grounding and Bonding
- Surge Protection
- Luminaires
- Receptacles and Attachment Plugs

Article 501 consists of three parts:

- Part I. General
- Part II. Wiring
- Part III. Equipment
- Wiring Methods

Part I. General

501.1 Scope

This article covers the electrical equipment and wiring for Class I, Division 1 and Division 2 locations where flammable gases, flammable liquid-produced vapors, or combustible liquid-produced vapors are, or might be, present in the air in quantities sufficient to produce explosive or ignitible mixtures. ▸Figure 501–1

Part II. Wiring

501.10 Wiring Methods

(A) Class I, Division 1.

(1) General. Only the following wiring methods are permitted within a Class I, Division 1 location.

(1) Threaded rigid metal conduit (RMC) or threaded intermediate metal conduit (IMC), including RMC or IMC conduits with supplemental corrosion protection coatings. ▸Figure 501–2

▶Figure 501–1

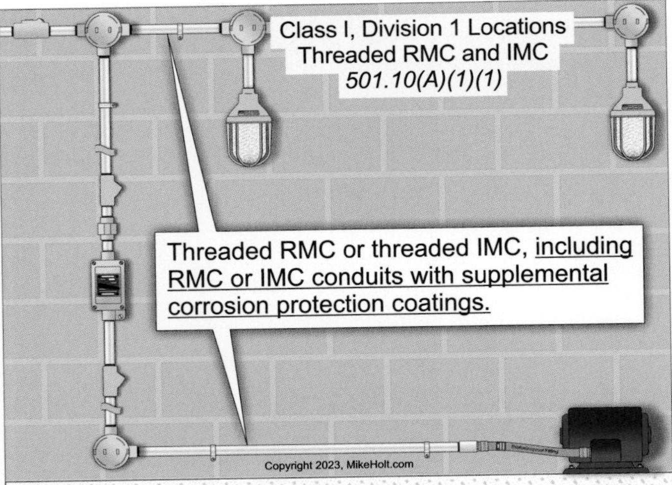

▶Figure 501–2

Author's Comment:

- According to UL Guide Information "DYIX", supplementary corrosion protection is required when ferrous metal raceways are buried in soils having a resistivity of less than 2,000Ω, and at the point where the ferrous metal raceway transitions from concrete encasement to the soil. ▶Figure 501–3

(2) PVC conduit, RTRC conduit, or HDPE conduit, where encased in a concrete envelope a minimum of 2 in. thick and provided with not less than 24 in. of cover measured from the top of the conduit to grade. RMC or IMC conduit must be used for the last 24 in. of the underground run to emergence or to the point of connection to the aboveground raceway. An equipment grounding conductor must be included in the raceway.

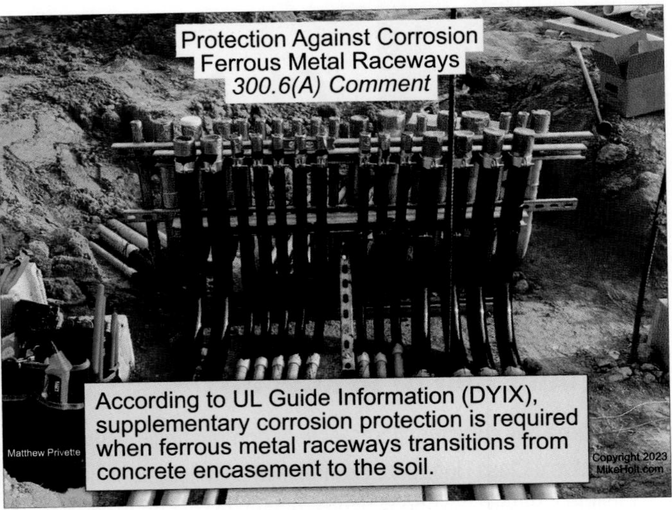

▶Figure 501–3

(2) Class I, Division 1 Flexible Connections. If flexibility is necessary to minimize the transmission of vibration from equipment during operation or to allow for movement after installation during maintenance, the following wiring methods are permitted: ▶Figure 501–4

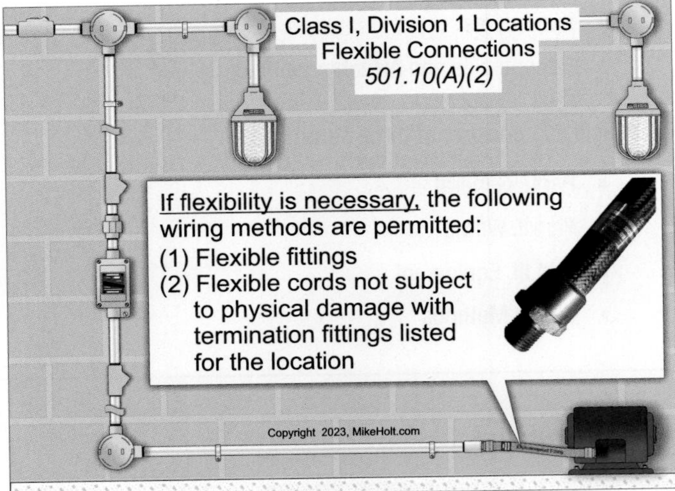

▶Figure 501–4

(1) Flexible fittings listed for the location.

(2) Flexible cords in accordance with 501.140, where the cable is not subject to physical damage and terminates with fittings listed for the location.

(3) Boxes and Fittings. Boxes and fittings must be identified for Class I, Division 1 locations. ▶Figure 501–5

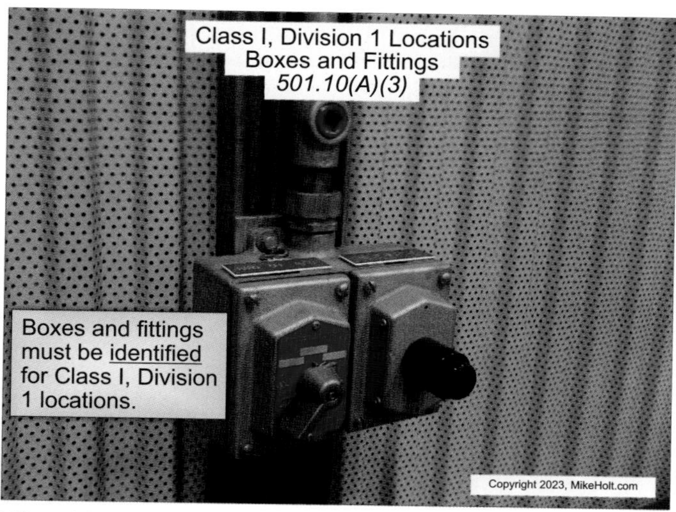

▶Figure 501-5

According to Article 100, "Identified (as applied to equipment)" is defined as suitable for a specific purpose, function, use, environment, or application.

(B) Class I, Division 2.

(1) General. All wiring methods included in Class I, Division 1 locations [501.10(A)] and the following wiring methods are permitted within a Class I, Division 2 location.

(1) Rigid and intermediate metal conduit with listed threaded or threadless fittings, including RMC or IMC conduits with supplemental corrosion protection coatings. ▶Figure 501-6

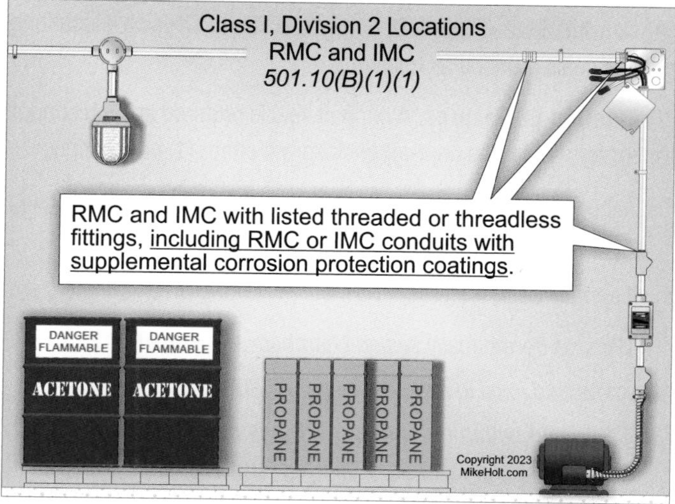

▶Figure 501-6

(2) Enclosed gasketed busways and wireways.

(3) Types PLTC and PLTC-ER cable used for Class 2 power-limited circuits. Type PLTC-ER cable must include an equipment grounding conductor in addition to any drain wire that might be present.

(5) Types MC, MV, TC, or TC-ER cable terminated with listed fittings, including installation in cable tray systems. Type TC-ER cable must include an equipment grounding conductor in addition to any drain wire that might be present.

(6) Where metallic conduit does not provide the corrosion resistance needed for the environment, any of the following wiring methods are permitted:

a. Listed reinforced thermosetting resin conduit (RTRC), factory elbows, and associated fittings, all marked with the suffix "-XW,"

b. PVC-coated rigid metal conduit (RMC), factory elbows, and associated fittings, or

c. PVC-coated intermediate metal conduit (IMC), factory elbows, and associated fittings.

(7) Optical fiber cables can be installed in cable trays or conduits [501.10(B)] and must be sealed in accordance with 501.15. ▶Figure 501-7

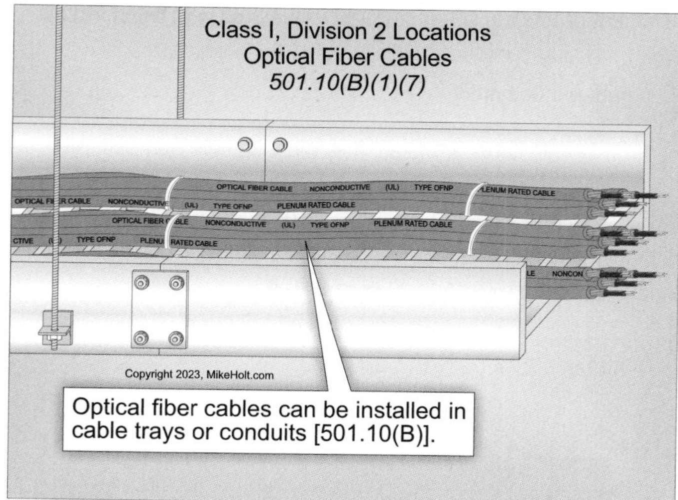

▶Figure 501-7

(2) Class I, Division 2 Flexible Connections. If flexibility is necessary to minimize the transmission of vibration from equipment during operation or to allow for movement after installation during maintenance, the following wiring methods are permitted: ▶Figure 501-8

(1) Listed flexible metal fittings.

(2) Flexible metal conduit with listed fittings and bonded in accordance with 501.30(B).

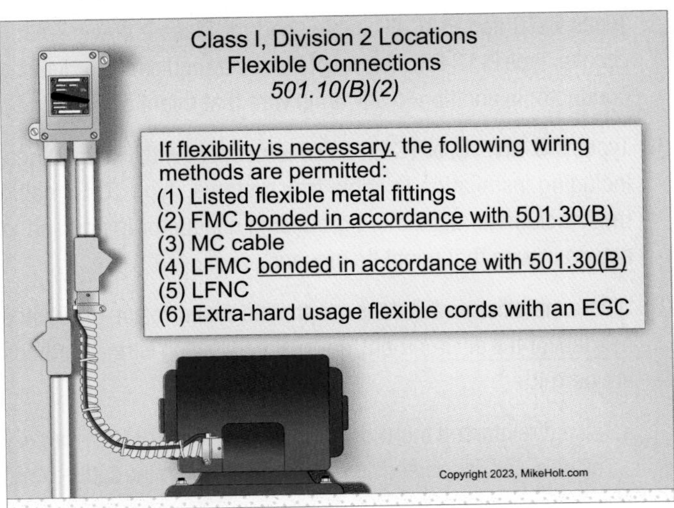

Class I, Division 2 Locations
Flexible Connections
501.10(B)(2)
If flexibility is necessary, the following wiring methods are permitted:
(1) Listed flexible metal fittings
(2) FMC bonded in accordance with 501.30(B)
(3) MC cable
(4) LFMC bonded in accordance with 501.30(B)
(5) LFNC
(6) Extra-hard usage flexible cords with an EGC
Copyright 2023, MikeHolt.com

▸Figure 501–8

(3) Interlocked Type MC cable with listed fittings.

(4) Liquidtight flexible metal conduit with listed fittings and bonded in accordance with 501.30(B).

(5) Liquidtight flexible nonmetallic conduit with listed fittings.

(6) Flexible cords listed for extra-hard usage containing an equipment grounding conductor and terminated with listed fittings.

Author's Comment:

▸ If flexible cords are used, they must comply with 501.140.

(4) Boxes and Fittings. General-purpose enclosures and fittings without make-and-break contacts can be installed in Class I, Division 2 locations [501.115(B)(1)]. ▸**Figure 501–9**

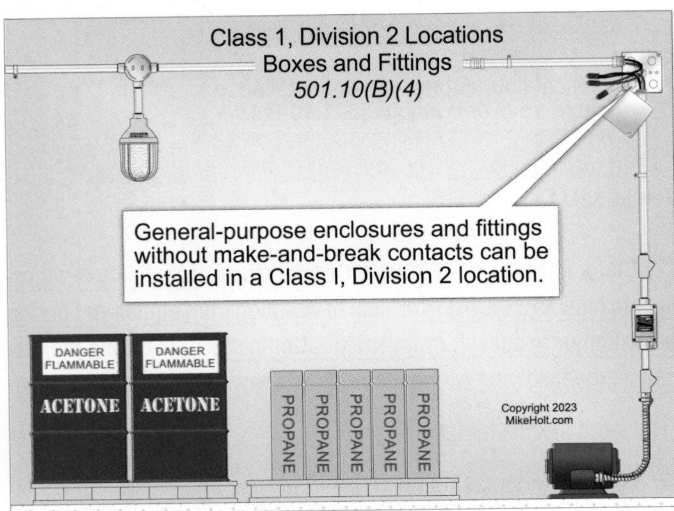

Class 1, Division 2 Locations
Boxes and Fittings
501.10(B)(4)
General-purpose enclosures and fittings without make-and-break contacts can be installed in a Class I, Division 2 location.
DANGER FLAMMABLE
ACETONE
DANGER FLAMMABLE
ACETONE
PROPANE
PROPANE
PROPANE
PROPANE
PROPANE
Copyright 2023 MikeHolt.com

▸Figure 501–9

501.15 Conduit and Cable Seals

Seals for conduit and cable systems must comply with 501.15(A) through (F).

Note 1: Conduit and cable seals must be installed to: ▸**Figure 501–10**

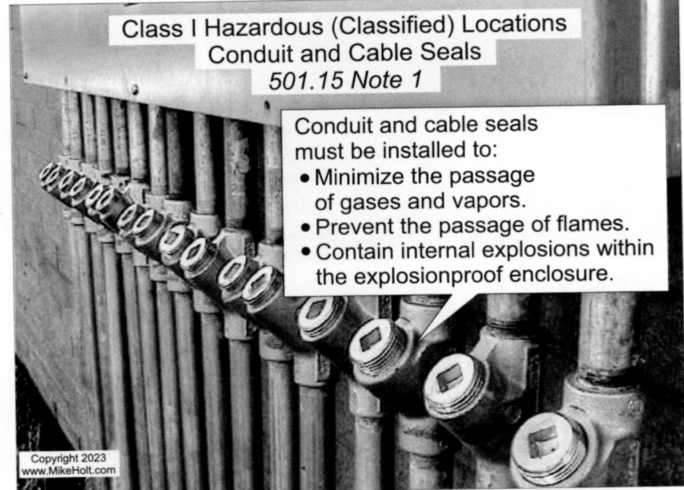

Class I Hazardous (Classified) Locations
Conduit and Cable Seals
501.15 Note 1
Conduit and cable seals must be installed to:
• Minimize the passage of gases and vapors.
• Prevent the passage of flames.
• Contain internal explosions within the explosionproof enclosure.
Copyright 2023 www.MikeHolt.com

▸Figure 501–10

▸ Minimize the passage of gases and vapors from one portion of electrical equipment to another through the conduit or cable.

▸ Prevent the passage of flames from one portion of electrical equipment to another through the conduit or cable.

▸ Contain internal explosions within the explosionproof enclosure.

(A) Conduit Seal—Class I, Division 1. In Class I, Division 1 locations, conduit seals must be as follows:

(1) Entering Enclosures. A conduit seal is required in each conduit that enters an explosionproof enclosure if either (1) or (2) apply:

(1) If the explosionproof enclosure contains make-and-break contacts. ▸**Figure 501–11**

Ex: A conduit seal is not required if the make-and-break contacts are:

(1) Within a hermetically sealed chamber. ▸**Figure 501–12**

(2) Immersed in oil in accordance with 501.115(B)(1)(2).

(3) Contained within an enclosure that is marked "Leads Factory Sealed," "Factory Sealed," "Seal not Required," or the equivalent.

(2) If a trade size 2 or larger conduit enters an explosionproof enclosure containing splices, terminals, or taps. ▸**Figure 501–13**

1st Printing

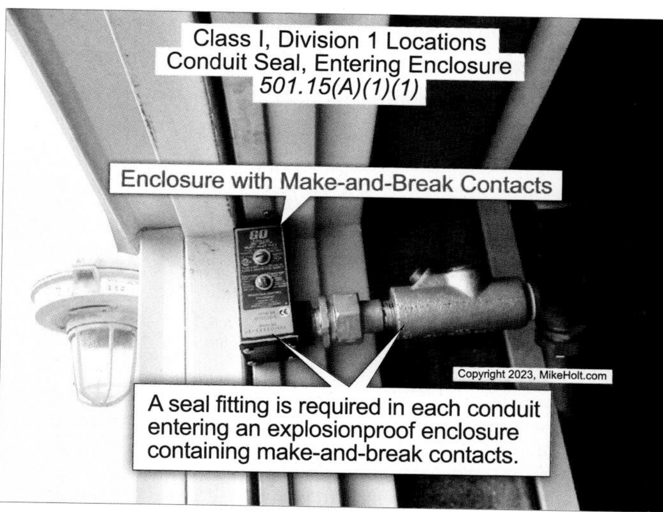

▸Figure 501–11

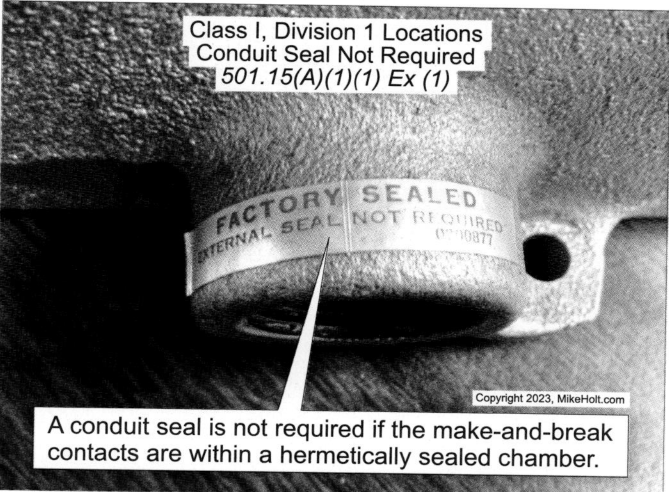

▸Figure 501–12

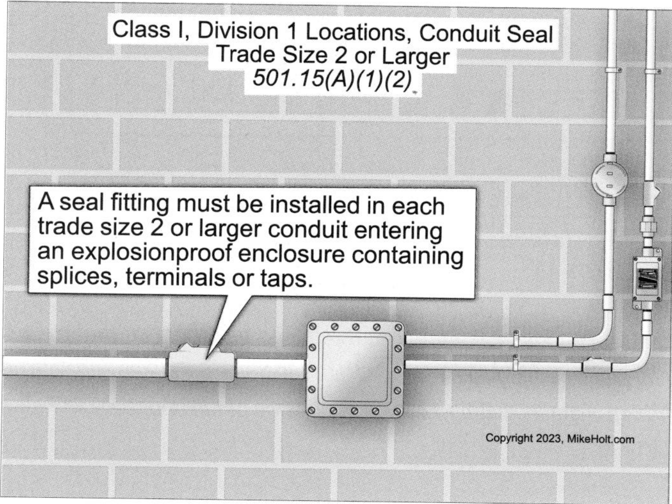

▸Figure 501–13

Author's Comment:

- If a trade size 2 or larger conduit enters an explosionproof enclosure without make-and-break contacts and the conductors pass through without a splice, terminal, or tap a conduit seal is not required.

The conduit seal fitting must be installed within 18 in. of the explosionproof enclosure or as required by the enclosure markings. ▸**Figure 501–14**

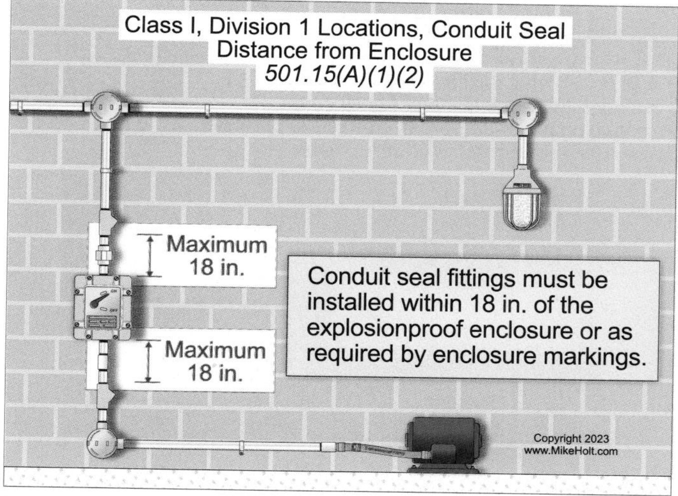

▸Figure 501–14

Only threaded couplings or explosionproof fittings such as unions, reducers, elbows, and capped elbows are permitted between the conduit seal and the explosionproof enclosure. ▸**Figure 501–15**

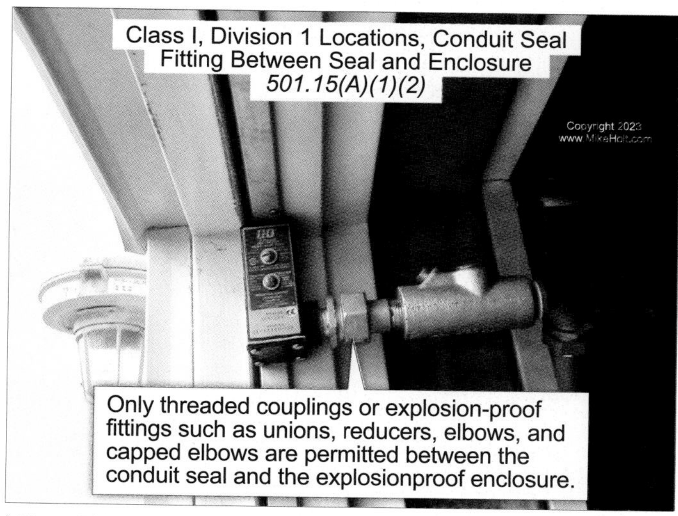

▸Figure 501–15

(2) Pressurized Enclosures. A conduit seal fitting must be installed in each conduit that is not pressurized where the conduit enters a pressurized enclosure. The conduit seal fitting must be installed within 18 in. of the pressurized enclosure.

(3) Between Explosionproof Enclosures. A single conduit seal fitting is permitted between two explosionproof enclosures containing make-and-break contacts if the conduit seal fitting is not more than 18 in. from either of the explosionproof enclosures. ▶Figure 501–16

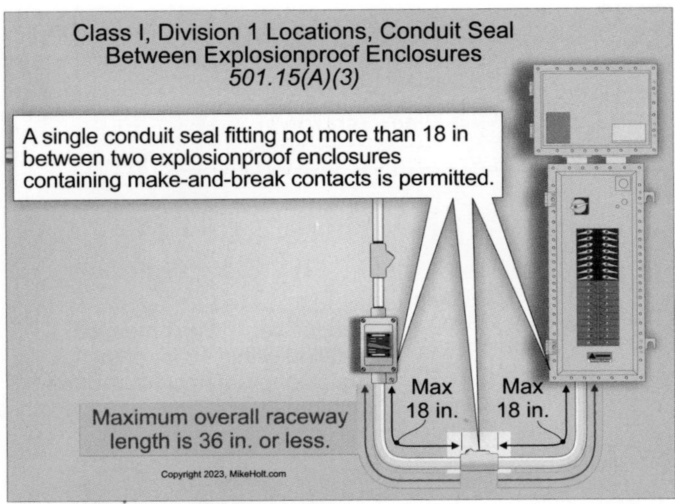

▶Figure 501–16

(4) Class I, Division 1 Boundary Seal. A conduit seal fitting must be installed in each conduit that leaves a Class I, Division 1 location within 10 ft of the Class I, Division 1 location on either side of the boundary. ▶Figure 501–17

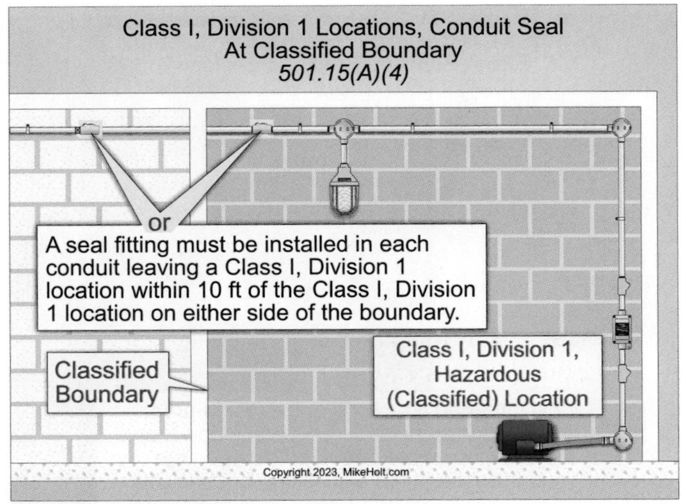

▶Figure 501–17

There must be no fitting between the point at which the conduit leaves the Class I, Division 1 location and the boundary conduit seal fitting, except for a listed explosionproof reducer installed at the conduit seal fitting. ▶Figure 501–18

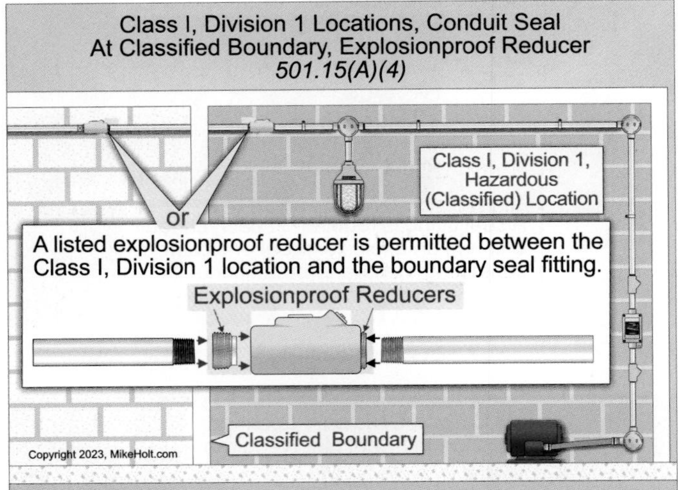

▶Figure 501–18

Where the Class I, Division 1 boundary seal is on a Division 2 area, the Class I, Division 1 wiring method must extend into the Division 2 area boundary seal. ▶Figure 501–19

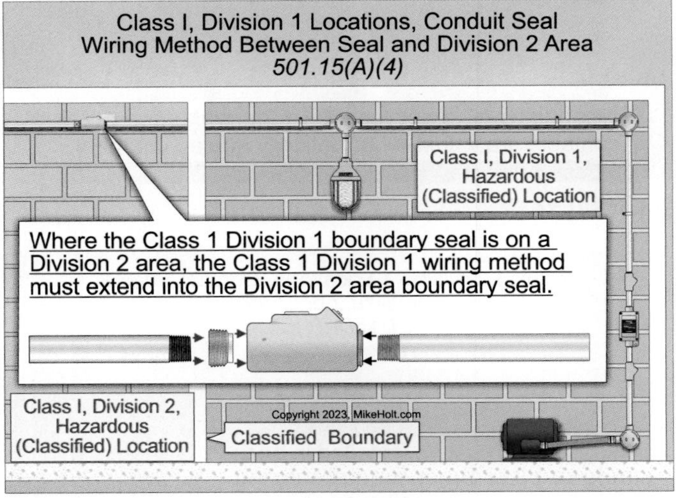

▶Figure 501–19

Ex 1: A conduit seal fitting is not required for a conduit that passes completely through a Class I, Division 1 location unbroken and with no fittings installed within 12 in. of either side of the boundary. ▶Figure 501–20

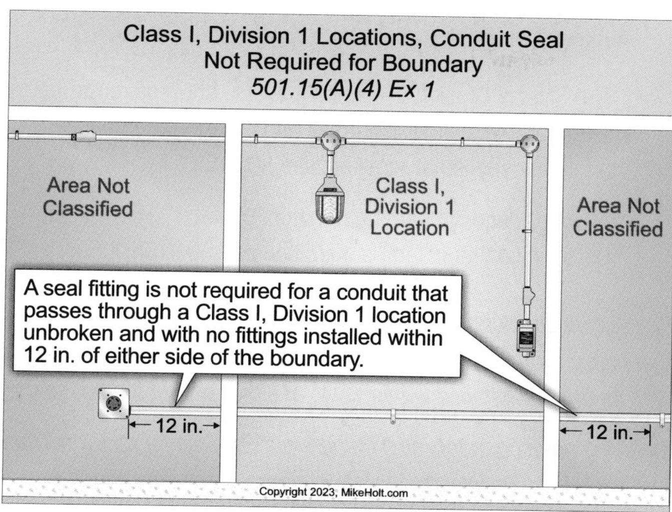

▸Figure 501–20

Ex 2: If the conduit boundary is below grade, the conduit seal can be above grade. There must be no fitting, except for a listed explosionproof reducer installed at the conduit seal fitting, between the conduit seal fitting and the point at which the conduit emerges from below grade. ▸Figure 501–21

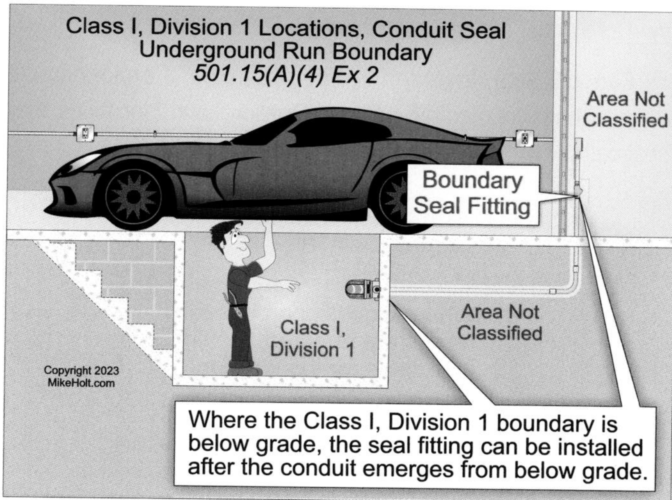

▸Figure 501–21

Author's Comment:

- The wiring method between the conduit seal fitting and the Class I, Division 1 boundary must be rigid metal conduit or intermediate metal conduit [501.10(A)(1)(1)].

(B) Conduit Seal, Class I, Division 2. In Class I, Division 2 locations, conduit seals must be as follows:

(1) Entering Enclosures. A conduit seal fitting must be installed in each conduit entering an explosionproof enclosure containing make-and-break contacts. The seal fitting must be installed within 18 in. of the explosionproof enclosure [501.15(A)(1)(1) and (A)(3)]. The conduit between the seal and enclosure must be rigid or intermediate metal conduit in accordance with 501.10(A)(1)(1). ▸Figure 501–22

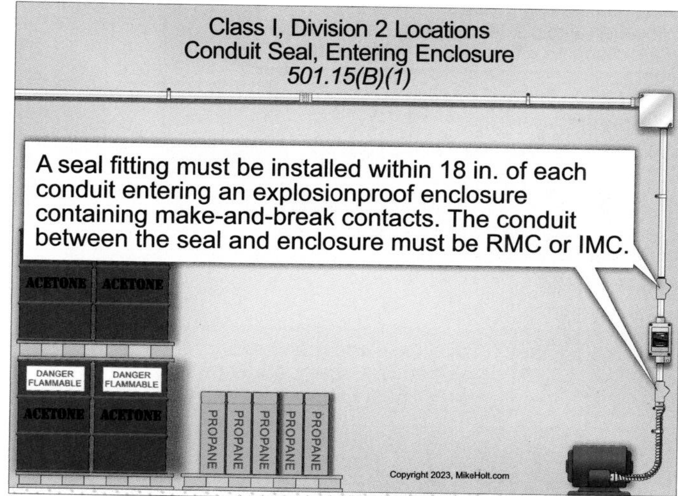

▸Figure 501–22

Author's Comment:

- Threadless connectors are permitted for use on conduits in Class I, Division 2 locations, but they are not permitted to be installed between the conduit seal fitting and an explosionproof enclosure. The raceway between the conduit seal fitting and the explosionproof enclosure must be threaded.

(2) Boundary Seal at Unclassified Location. A conduit seal fitting must be installed in each conduit that leaves a Class I, Division 2 location within 10 ft of the Class I, Division 2 location on either side of the boundary. ▸Figure 501–23

Threaded rigid metal conduit or intermediate metal conduit must be installed between the boundary sealing fitting and the point where the conduit leaves the Class I, Division 2 location. ▸Figure 501–24

No fitting, except for a listed explosionproof reducer installed at the conduit sealing fitting is permitted to be installed between the conduit boundary seal fitting and the point at which the conduit leaves the Class I, Division 2 location.

The Class I, Division 2 boundary seal is not required to be explosionproof, but it must be identified to minimize the passage of gases under normal operating conditions and be accessible. ▸Figure 501–25

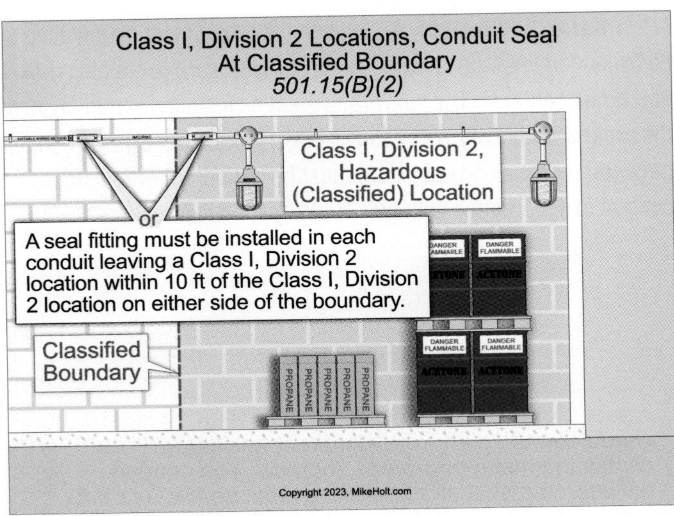

▶Figure 501–23

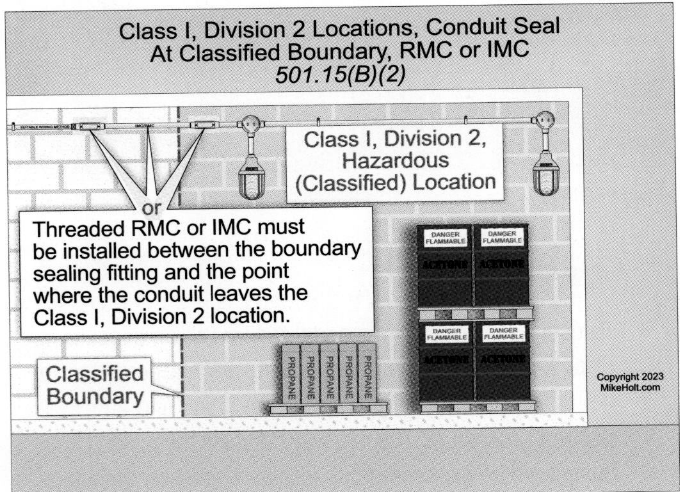

▶Figure 501–24

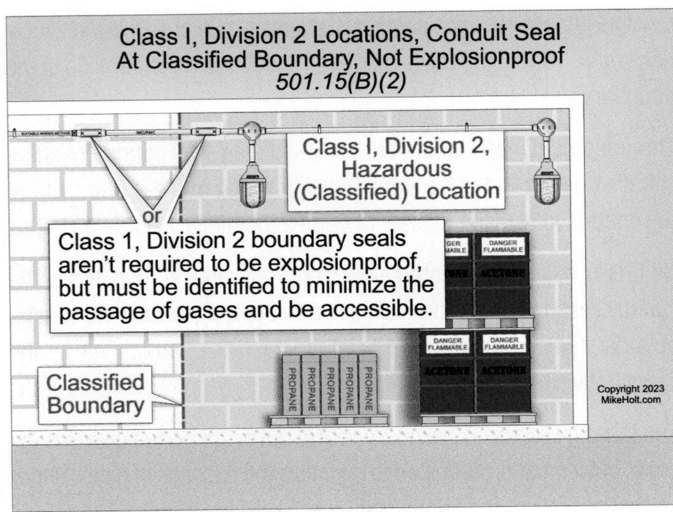

▶Figure 501–25

Author's Comment:

- The Class I, Division 2 boundary seal is not required to be listed for Class I, Division 2 use and an explosionproof seal off compound is not required, see 501.15(C) Ex.
- A type C conduit outlet body using Polywater® FST™ Foam Duct Sealant meets the requirements of 501.15(B)(2).

Ex 1: A conduit boundary seal fitting is not required for a metal raceway that passes completely through the Class I, Division 2 area unbroken with no fittings installed within 12 in. of either side of the boundary.

Ex 2: A conduit boundary seal fitting is not required for raceways that terminate in an unclassified location where the metal conduit transitions to cable trays, ventilated busways, or open wiring if:

(1) The unclassified location is outdoors or the unclassified location is indoors and the conduit system is entirely in one room.

(2) The conduits do not terminate at an enclosure containing an ignition source in normal operation.

Ex 3: A boundary seal fitting is not required for a conduit that passes from an enclosure or a room permitted to use general-purpose equipment as a result of pressurization into a Class I, Division 2 location.

(C) Conduit Seal, Installation Requirements. If explosionproof sealing fittings are required in Class I, Division 1 and 2 locations, they must comply with the following: ▶Figure 501–26

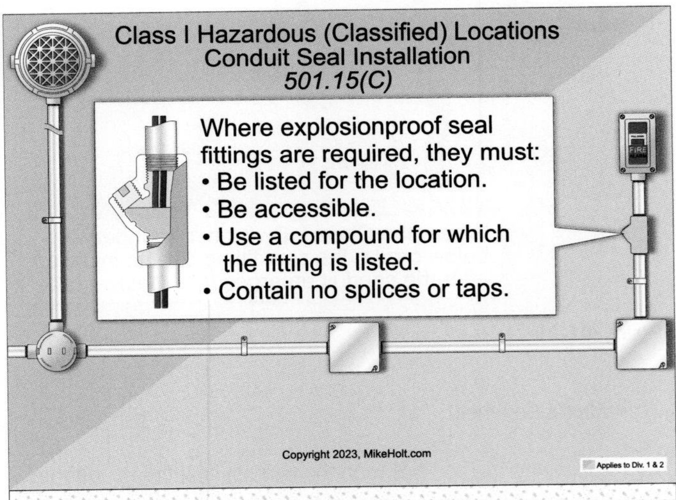

▶Figure 501–26

Ex: A Class I, Division 2 boundary seal that is not required to be explosionproof in accordance with 501.15(B)(2) is not required to comply with the requirements of 501.15(C).

(1) Fittings. Conduit seal fittings must be listed for the location and for the specific sealing compounds and must be accessible.

(2) Compound. Seal off compound(s) must provide a seal, be applied to prohibit the passage of vapors and/or gases and be impervious to the surrounding environment with a melting point of not less than 93°C (200°F).

(3) Thickness of Compounds. Except for listed cable sealing fittings, the thickness of the conduit seal compound installed in completed seals cannot be less than the trade size of the seal fitting, and in no case less than ⅝ in.

(4) Splices and Taps. Splices and taps cannot be made within a conduit seal fitting.

(6) Number of Conductors. The cross-sectional area of conductors is not permitted to exceed 25 percent of the cross-sectional area of rigid metal conduit of the same trade size, unless the seal is specifically identified for a higher percentage fill. ▸Figure 501–27

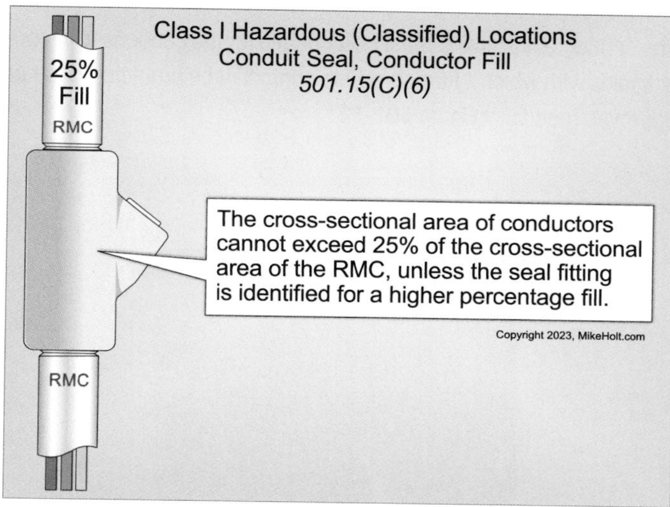

Class I Hazardous (Classified) Locations
Conduit Seal, Conductor Fill
501.15(C)(6)
25% Fill
RMC
The cross-sectional area of conductors cannot exceed 25% of the cross-sectional area of the RMC, unless the seal fitting is identified for a higher percentage fill.
Copyright 2023, MikeHolt.com
RMC

▸Figure 501–27

(D) Cable Seal—Class I, Division 1. In Class I, Division 1 locations, seal fittings must be as follows:

(1) Cable Termination Fittings. Cables must be sealed at all terminations with sealing fittings in accordance with 501.15(C) and installed within 18 in. of the enclosure or as required by the enclosure marking. Only threaded couplings or explosionproof fittings such as unions, reducers, elbows, and capped elbows can be installed between the cable seal fitting and the enclosure.

Type MC-HL cable with a gas/vaportight metallic sheath and a jacketed covering, Type TC-ER-HL cable, and Type IM cable must be sealed with listed termination fittings that permit the sealing compound to surround each individual insulated conductor to minimize the passage of gases or vapors. ▸Figure 501–28

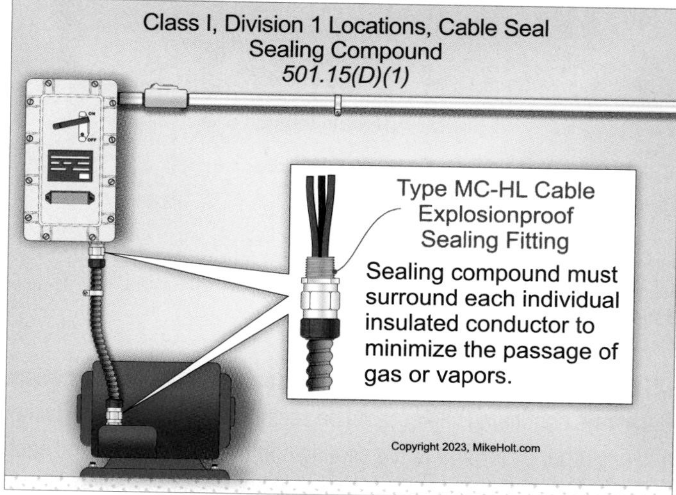

▸Figure 501–28

Author's Comment:

- Type MC-HL is a metal-clad cable with a continuously welded sheath that has extra protection from flammable gases, vapors, or liquids used in hazardous locations. ▸Figure 501–29

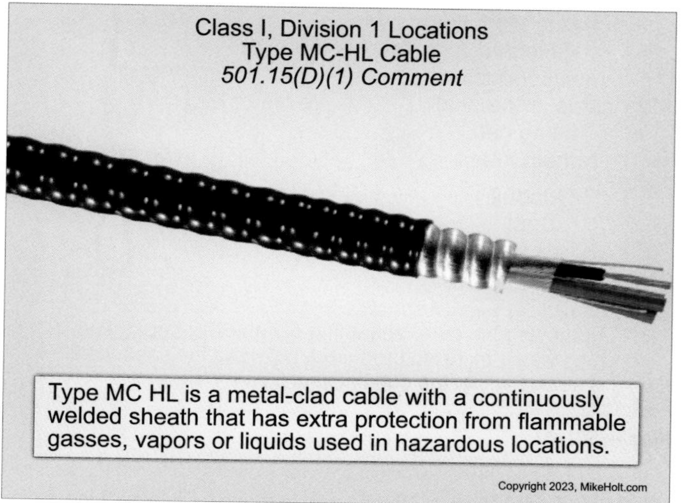

▸Figure 501–29

For shielded cables and twisted-pair cables, removing the shielding material or separating the twisted pairs is not required within the cable seal fitting. ▸Figure 501–30

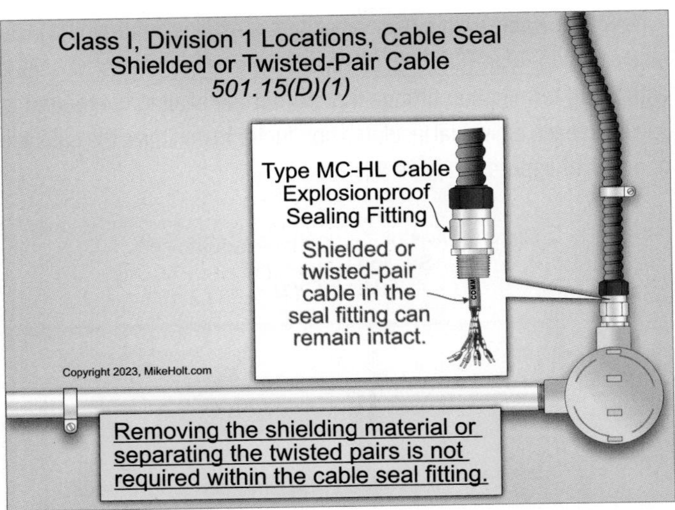

▸Figure 501–30

(2) Cables Capable of Transmitting Gases or Vapors in a Raceway. Raceways containing cables must be sealed after removing the jacket and any other coverings so the sealing compound will surround each individual insulated conductor or optical fiber tube in a manner that minimizes the passage of gases and vapors.

Ex: Removing the outer sheathing of multiconductor cables or separating the twisted pairs is not required, provided the cable core is sealed within the conduit seal fitting. ▸Figure 501–31

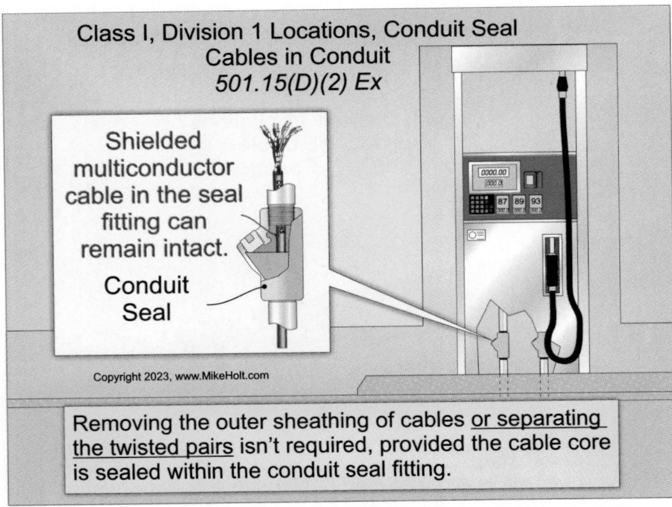

▸Figure 501–31

(E) Cable Seal, Class I, Division 2. In Class I, Division 2 locations, cable seals must be as follows:

Ex: Seals are not required in a Class I, Division 2 location if the cable passes through the location and has an unbroken gas or vaportight sheath.

(1) Multiconductor Cable. Multiconductor or optical fiber cables that enter an explosionproof enclosure must be sealed after removing the jacket and any other coverings so the sealing compound will surround each individual insulated conductor or optical fiber tube to minimize the passage of gases and vapors.

Multiconductor cables or optical fiber cables installed within a raceway must be sealed at the point of entrance into the enclosure in accordance with 501.15(D)(2) or (D)(3).

Ex 2: Removing the shielding material or separating the twisted pairs is not required within the conduit seal fitting.

(4) Cable Seal, Boundary. Cables without a gas/vaportight continuous sheath must be sealed at the boundary of the Class I, Division 2 location in a manner that minimizes the passage of gases or vapors into an unclassified location.

501.20 Conductor Insulation

The conductor insulation must be identified for the condensed vapors or liquids with which it may come into contact or be protected by other approved means. ▸Figure 501–32

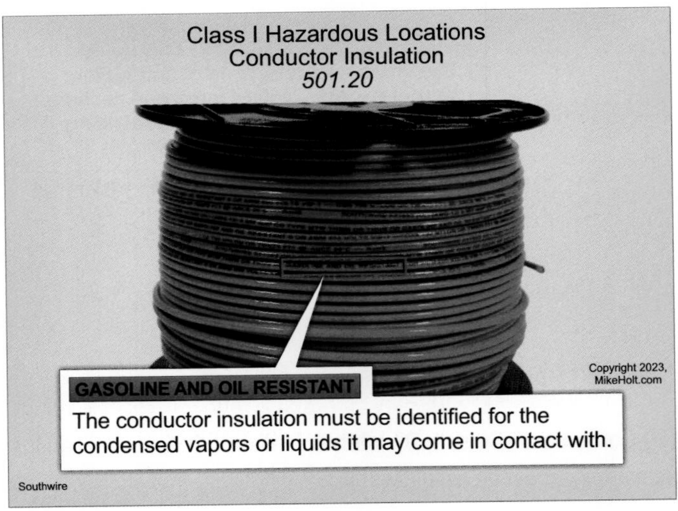

▸Figure 501–32

501.30 Grounding and Bonding

Because of the explosive conditions associated with electrical installations in hazardous (classified) locations [500.5], electrical continuity of metal parts of equipment and raceways must be ensured, regardless of the voltage of the circuit.

1st Printing

(B) Bonding. Bonding must comply with 501.30(B)(1) and (B)(2).

(1) Specific Bonding Means. Bonding in a Class I hazardous (classified) location must comply with the following:

(a) Locknuts are not suitable for bonding purposes in hazardous (classified) locations so bonding jumpers with identified fittings or other approved means of bonding must be used. Such means of bonding apply to all metal conduits between Class I locations and service disconnects or a separately derived system. ▸Figure 501–33

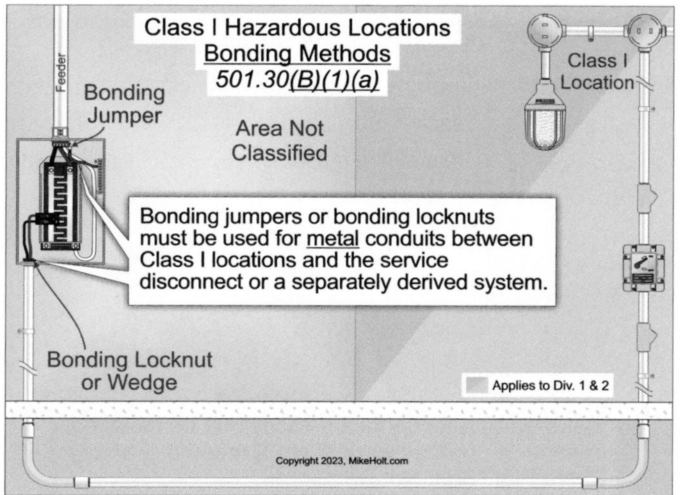

▸Figure 501–33

Author's Comment:

- Regardless of the circuit voltage, the electrical continuity of metal parts of equipment and conduits in hazardous (classified) locations must be ensured by using bonding-type locknuts, wedges, or bushings with bonding jumpers [250.92(B)(4)], whether or not equipment grounding conductors of the wire type are installed in the conduit [250.100]. Threaded couplings and hubs made up wrenchtight provide a suitable low-impedance fault current path [250. 92(B)(2)]. Locknuts alone are not sufficient to serve this purpose.

(2) Flexible Metal Conduit and Liquidtight Flexible Metal Conduit.

(a) Where flexible metal conduit and liquidtight flexible metal conduit are installed as permitted by 501.10(B)(2)(a), the raceway must have an internal or external equipment bonding jumper of the wire type installed in accordance with 250.102(E). ▸Figure 501–34

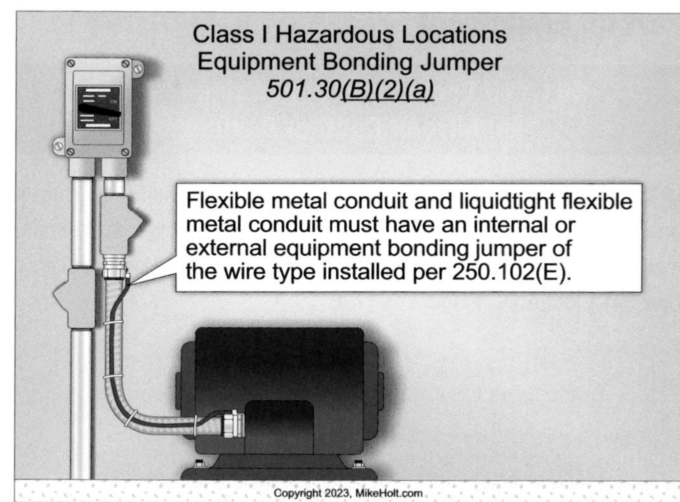

▸Figure 501–34

Author's Comment:

- Load-side bonding jumpers are sized in accordance with Table 250.122 based on the rating of the overcurrent protective device [250.102(D)]. Where installed outside a raceway, the length of bonding jumpers is not permitted to exceed 6 ft and they must be routed with the raceway [250.102(E)(2)]. ▸Figure 501–35

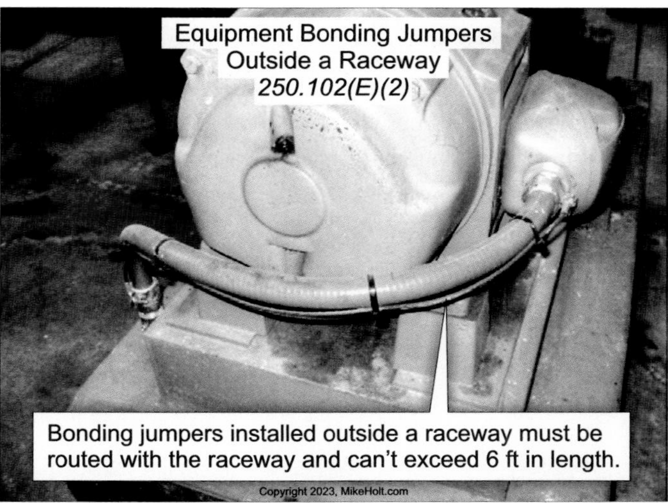

▸Figure 501–35

Part III. Equipment

501.115 Enclosures Containing Make-and-Break Contact Devices

(A) Class I, Division 1. Enclosures containing switches, circuit breakers, motor controllers, fuses, pushbuttons, relays, and similar make-and-break contact devices must be identified for use in a Class I, Division 1 location. ▸Figure 501–36

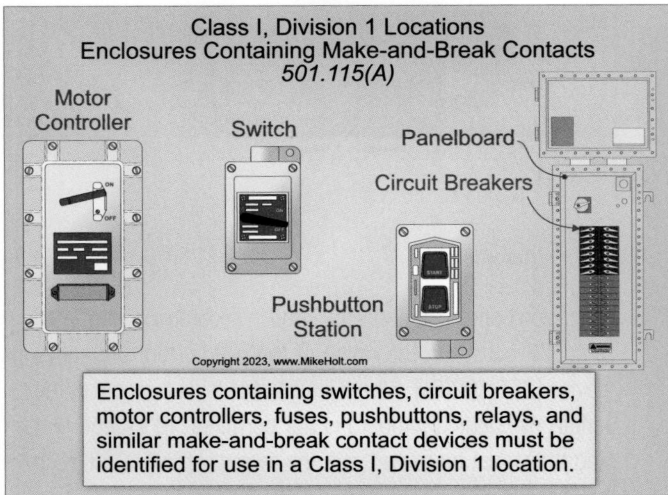

▸Figure 501–36

(B) Class I, Division 2.

(1) Type Required. Enclosures containing switches, circuit breakers, motor controllers, fuses, pushbuttons, relays, and similar make-and-break contact devices must be identified for use in a Class I, Division 2 location in accordance with 501.105(A). ▸Figure 501–37

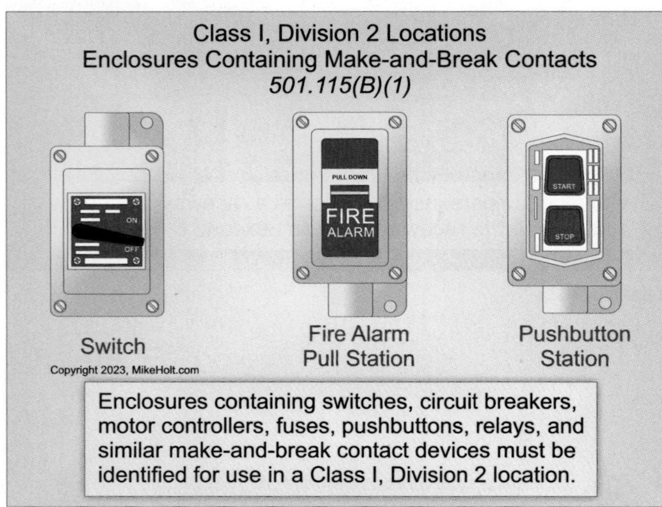

▸Figure 501–37

Make-and-break contact devices can be installed in general-purpose enclosures if any of the following is provided:

(1) The interruption of current occurs within a hermetically sealed chamber.

(2) The make-and-break contacts are oil-immersed.

(3) The interruption of current occurs within an enclosure identified for the location and marked "Leads Factory Sealed," "Factory Sealed," "Seal not Required," or the equivalent. ▸Figure 501–38

▸Figure 501–38

501.125 Motors and Generators

(A) Class I, Division 1. Motors installed in a Class I, Division 1 location must be:

(1) Identified for Class I, Division 1 locations, or

(2) Of the totally enclosed type supplied with positive-pressure ventilation and arranged to automatically de-energize if the air supply fails, or

(3) Of the totally enclosed inert gas-filled type and arranged to automatically de-energize if the gas supply fails.

(B) Class I, Division 2. Motors installed in a Class I, Division 2 location must comply with the following:

(1) Be identified for Class I, Division 2 locations, or

(2) Be identified for Class I, Division 1 locations where make-and-break contacts are present, or

(3) If of the open or nonexplosionproof enclosed type, the motor must not contain any brushes, switching mechanisms, or similar arc-producing devices not identified for use in a Class I, Division 2 location such as squirrel-cage induction motors without arcing devices (three-phase motors).

501.130 Luminaires

(A) Class I, Division 1. Luminaires installed in a Class I, Division 1 location must comply with the following:

(1) Luminaires. Luminaires must be identified for the Class I, Division 1 location. ▸Figure 501-39

▸Figure 501-39

Author's Comment:

- Conduit seals are not required for listed Class I, Division 1 explosionproof luminaires because the lamp compartment is separated or sealed from the wiring compartment in accordance with the listing requirements.

(2) Physical Damage. Luminaires must be protected against physical damage by a suitable guard or by location.

(3) Pendant Luminaires. Pendant luminaires must be suspended by, and supplied through, threaded rigid metal conduit or threaded steel intermediate conduit stems. Threaded joints must be provided with set screws or other means to prevent loosening. Stems longer than 12 in. must be provided with permanent and effective lateral bracing, or with a flexible fitting or connector identified for the Class I, Division 1 location. ▸Figure 501-40

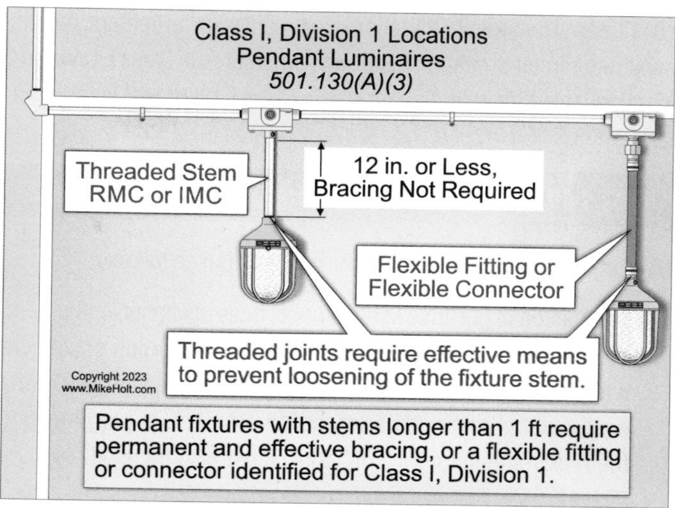

▸Figure 501-40

(4) Boxes and Fittings. Boxes or fittings used to support luminaires must be identified for a Class I location.

(B) Class I, Division 2. Luminaires installed in a Class I, Division 2 location must comply with the following:

(1) Luminaires. If the lamp temperature exceeds 80 percent of the autoignition temperature of the gas or vapor, luminaires must be identified for a Class I, Division 1 location.

(2) Physical Damage. Luminaires must be protected from physical damage by suitable guards or by location.

(3) Pendant Luminaires. Pendant luminaires must be suspended by threaded rigid metal conduit stems, threaded steel intermediate metal conduit stems, or other approved means and threaded joints must be provided with set screws or other means to prevent loosening. Stems longer than 12 in. must be provided with permanent and effective lateral bracing, or an identified flexible fitting or connector must be provided.

(4) Portable Lighting.

(b) Portable lighting equipment must be listed for use in a Class I, Division 1 location, unless the luminaire is mounted on movable stands and connected by a flexible cord as provided in 501.140.

501.135 Utilization Equipment

(A) Class I, Division 1. Utilization equipment such as heaters, motors, switches, circuit breakers, fuses, and luminaires in Class I, Division 1 locations must be identified for use in Class I, Division 1 locations.

(B) Class I, Division 2. Utilization equipment such as heaters, motors, switches, circuit breakers, fuses, and luminaires in Class I, Division 2 locations must be identified for use in Class I, Division 2 locations.

501.140 Flexible Cords, Class I, Divisions 1 and 2

(A) Permitted Uses. Flexible cord is permitted as follows:

(1) Connection of portable lighting or portable utilization equipment. The flexible cord must be attached to the utilization equipment with a cord connector listed for the protection technique of the equipment wiring compartment. An attachment plug meeting the requirements of 501.140(B)(4) must also be used. ▶Figure 501–41

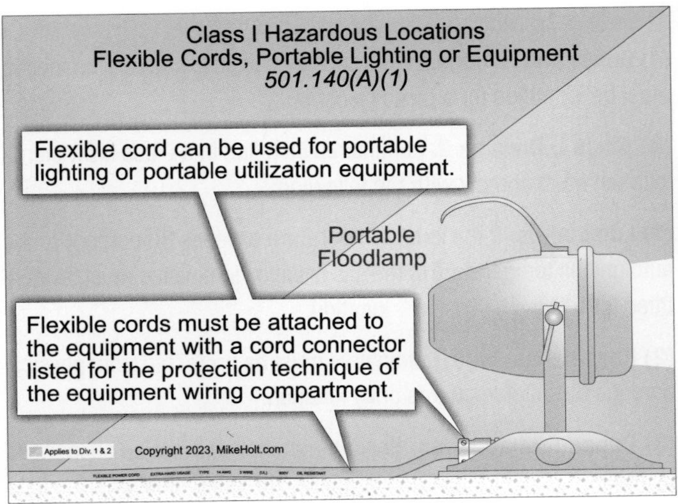
Class I Hazardous Locations
Flexible Cords, Portable Lighting or Equipment
501.140(A)(1)
Flexible cord can be used for portable lighting or portable utilization equipment.
Portable Floodlamp
Flexible cords must be attached to the equipment with a cord connector listed for the protection technique of the equipment wiring compartment.
Applies to Div. 1 & 2
Copyright 2023, MikeHolt.com

▶Figure 501–41

(3) Flexible cords for submersible pumps that can be removed without entering the wet-pit are permitted to be extended from the wet-pit to the power source within a suitable raceway.

(B) Installation. If flexible cords are used, the cords must:

(1) Be listed for extra-hard usage.

(2) Contain an equipment grounding conductor.

(3) Be supported so no tension will be transmitted to the terminal connections.

(4) In Division 1 or Division 2 locations where the boxes, fittings, or enclosures must be explosionproof, the flexible cord must terminate with a flexible cord connector or attachment plug listed for the location, or a listed flexible cord connector installed with a seal that is listed for the location. In Division 2 locations where explosionproof equipment is not required, the flexible cord must terminate with a listed flexible cord connector or listed attachment plug.

(5) Be of continuous length. Where 501.140(A)(5) is applied, cords must be of continuous length from the power source to the temporary portable assembly and from the temporary portable assembly to the utilization equipment.

501.145 Receptacles

Receptacles must be listed for the hazardous (classified) location. ▶Figure 501–42

Class I Hazardous Locations
Receptacles
501.145
CAUTION
TO PREVENT IGNITION OF HAZARDOUS ATMOSPHERES KEEP ALL COVER SCREWS TIGHT DISCONNECT SUPPLY CIRCUIT BEFORE REMOVING SCREWS
RECEPTACLE ASSEMBLY FOR HAZARDOUS LOCATIONS
Copyright 2023, MikeHolt.com
Receptacles must be listed for the hazardous (classified) location.

▶Figure 501–42

Author's Comment:

- Receptacles listed for Class I locations can be any of the following types:
  - **Interlocked Switch Receptacle.** This receptacle contains a built-in rotary switch interlocked with the attachment plug. The switch must be off before the attachment plug can be inserted or removed.
  - **Manual Interlocked Receptacle.** The attachment plug is inserted into the receptacle and then rotated to operate the receptacle's switching contacts.
  - **Delayed Action Receptacle.** This receptacle requires an attachment plug and receptacle constructed so that an electrical arc will be confined within the explosionproof chamber of the receptacle.

ARTICLE 502 CLASS II HAZARDOUS (CLASSIFIED) LOCATIONS

Introduction to Article 502—Class II Hazardous (Classified) Locations

This article covers the requirements for electrical equipment and wiring in Class II, Division 1 and 2 locations where fire or explosion hazards might exist due to the presence of combustible dust. Examples of such locations include flour mills, grain silos, coal bins, wood pulp storage areas, and areas where combustible metals or metal dusts are produced. Many of these rules are outside of the scope of this material, however, some of the topics we cover include the following:

- Wiring Methods
- Grounding and Bonding
- Surge Protection
- Luminaires
- Receptacles and Attachment Plugs

Article 502 consists of three parts:

- Part I. General
- Part II. Wiring
- Part III. Equipment

Part I. General

502.1 Scope

This article covers the requirements for electrical equipment and wiring in Class II, Division 1 and 2 locations where fire or explosion hazards might exist due to the presence of combustible dust. ▶Figure 502–1

Author's Comment:

- Examples of combustible dust include combustible metal dusts, coal, carbon black, charcoal, coke, flour, grain, wood, plastic, and chemicals in the air in quantities sufficient to produce explosive or ignitible mixtures [500.5(C) and 500.8].

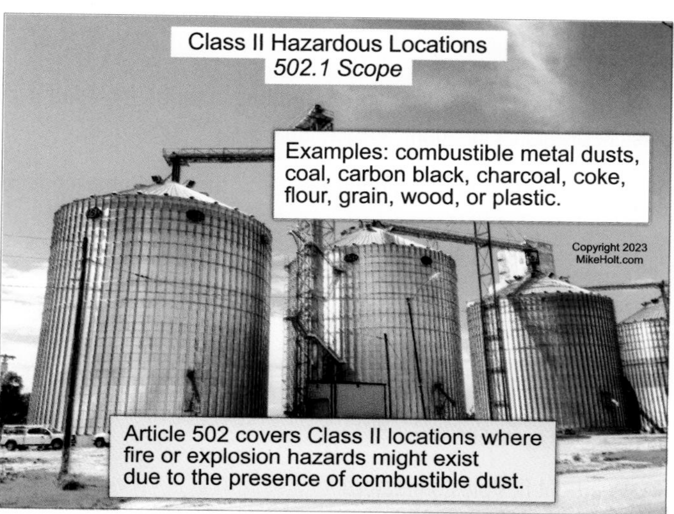

▶Figure 502–1

According to Article 100, "Combustible Dust" is solid particles that are 500 μm (microns) or smaller that can form an explosive mixture when suspended in air at standard atmospheric pressure and temperature.

502.5 Explosionproof Equipment

Explosionproof equipment cannot be installed in a Class II location, unless identified for a Class II location. ▶Figure 502-2

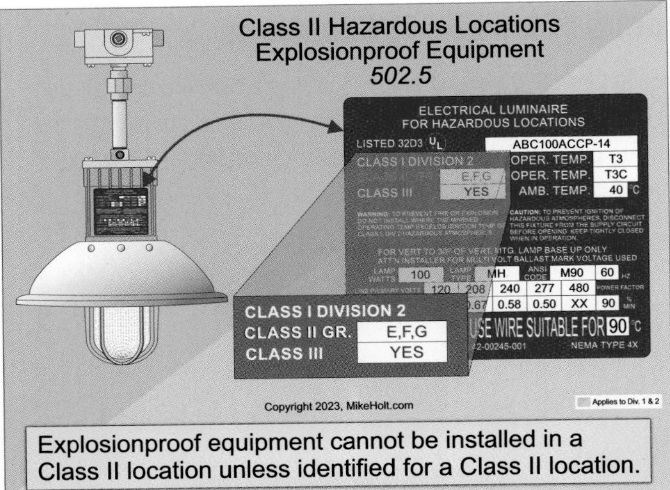

Class II Hazardous Locations
Explosionproof Equipment
502.5
ELECTRICAL LUMINAIRE
FOR HAZARDOUS LOCATIONS
LISTED 32D3
ABC100ACCP-14
OPER. TEMP. T3
OPER. TEMP. T3C
AMB. TEMP. 40 °C
CLASS I DIVISION 2
CLASS II GR. E,F,G
CLASS III YES
USE WIRE SUITABLE FOR 90 °C
NEMA TYPE 4X
Copyright 2023, MikeHolt.com
Applies to Div. 1 & 2
Explosionproof equipment cannot be installed in a Class II location unless identified for a Class II location.

▶Figure 502-2

Part II. Wiring

502.10 Wiring Methods

(A) Class II, Division 1.

(1) General. The following wiring methods can be installed in a Class II, Division 1 location: ▶Figure 502-3

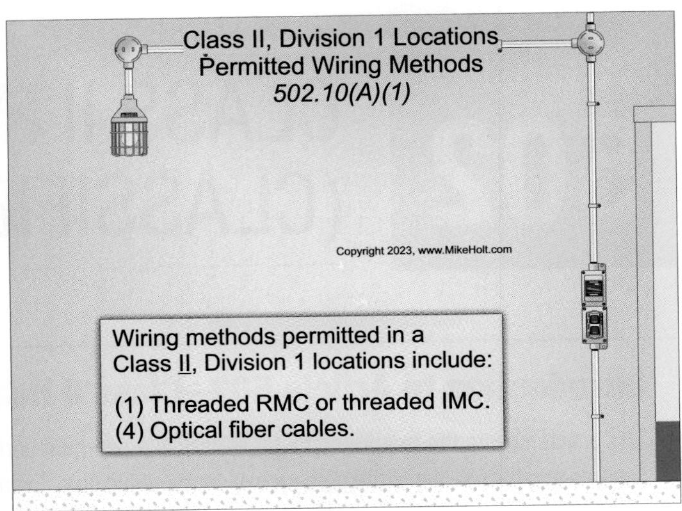

Class II, Division 1 Locations
Permitted Wiring Methods
502.10(A)(1)
Copyright 2023, www.MikeHolt.com
Wiring methods permitted in a Class II, Division 1 locations include:
(1) Threaded RMC or threaded IMC.
(4) Optical fiber cables.

▶Figure 502-3

(1) Threaded rigid metal conduit (RMC) or threaded intermediate metal conduit (IMC).

(4) Optical fiber cable can be installed in RMC or IMC conduits [502.10(A)(1)(1)] and must be sealed in accordance with 502.15.

(2) Flexible Connections. If flexible connections are necessary, any of the following wiring methods are permitted in a Class II, Division 1 location: ▶Figure 502-4

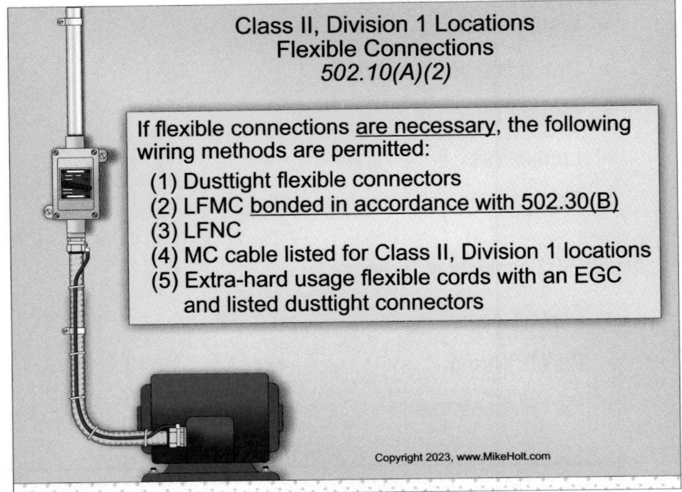

Class II, Division 1 Locations
Flexible Connections
502.10(A)(2)
If flexible connections are necessary, the following wiring methods are permitted:
(1) Dusttight flexible connectors
(2) LFMC bonded in accordance with 502.30(B)
(3) LFNC
(4) MC cable listed for Class II, Division 1 locations
(5) Extra-hard usage flexible cords with an EGC and listed dusttight connectors
Copyright 2023, www.MikeHolt.com

▶Figure 502-4

(1) Dusttight flexible connectors.

(2) Liquidtight flexible metal conduit (LFMC) with listed fittings and bonded in accordance with 502.30(B).

(3) Liquidtight flexible nonmetallic conduit (LFNC) with listed fittings.

(4) Interlocked armor Type MC cable with an impervious jacket and termination fittings listed for Class II, Division 1 locations.

(5) Flexible cords listed for extra-hard usage containing an equipment grounding conductor and terminated with listed dusttight flexible cord connectors. The flexible cords must comply with 502.140.

(3) Boxes and Fittings. Boxes and fittings must be provided with threaded entries and be dusttight. ▶Figure 502-5

(B) Class II, Division 2.

(1) General. In Class II, Division 2 locations, the following wiring methods are permitted: ▶Figure 502-6

1st Printing

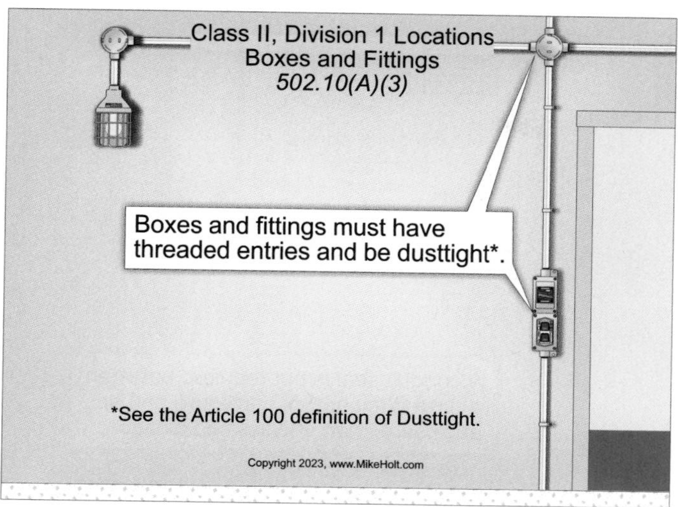

▸Figure 502–5

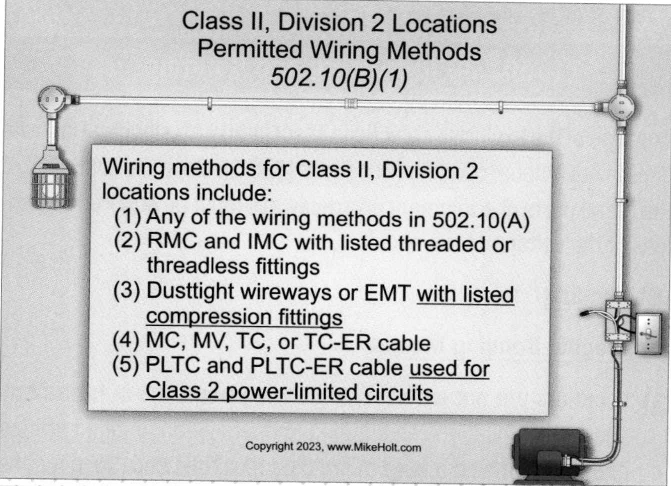

▸Figure 502–6

(1) Any of the wiring methods in 502.10(A).

(2) Rigid metal conduit (RMC) and intermediate metal conduit (IMC) with listed threaded or threadless fittings, including RMC or IMC conduits with supplemental corrosion protection coatings.

(3) Dusttight wireways or electrical metallic tubing (EMT) with listed compression-type connectors or couplings.

(4) Types MC, MV, TC, or TC-ER cable terminated with listed fittings, including installation in cable tray systems. Type TC-ER cable must include an equipment grounding conductor in addition to any drain wire that might be present.

(5) Types PLTC and PLTC-ER cable used for Class 2 power-limited circuits, including installation in cable tray systems. The cable must be terminated with listed fittings. Type PLTC-ER cable must include an equipment grounding conductor in addition to any drain wire that might be present.

(8) Optical fiber cables can be installed in cable trays or RMC or IMC conduits [502.10(B)(1) and (2)] and must be sealed in accordance with 502.15.

(2) Flexible Connections. If flexibility is necessary, wiring methods complying with 502.10(A)(2) are permitted in a Class II, Division 2 location.

(4) Boxes and Fittings. Boxes and fittings in Class II, Division 2 areas must be dusttight. ▸**Figure 502–7**

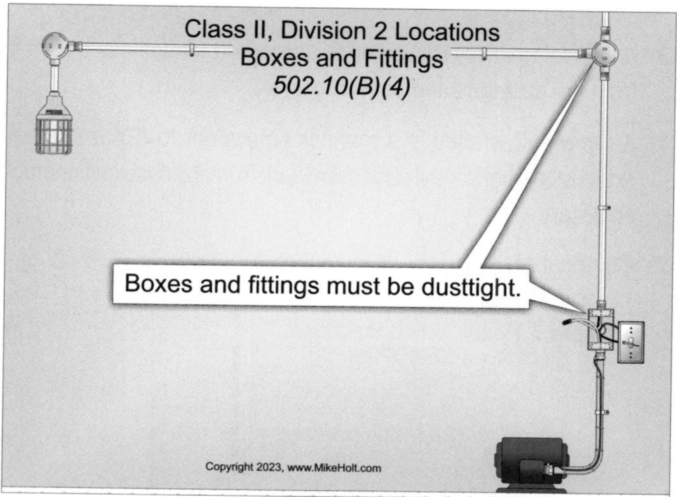

▸Figure 502–7

Author's Comment:

- A standard weatherproof box with a cover and gasket meets this requirement.

502.15 Sealing

In Class II, Division 1 and 2 locations, combustible dust must be prevented from entering the required dust-ignitionproof enclosure from a raceway by any of the following methods:

(1) A permanent and effective seal

(2) A horizontal raceway not less than 10 ft long ▸**Figure 502–8**

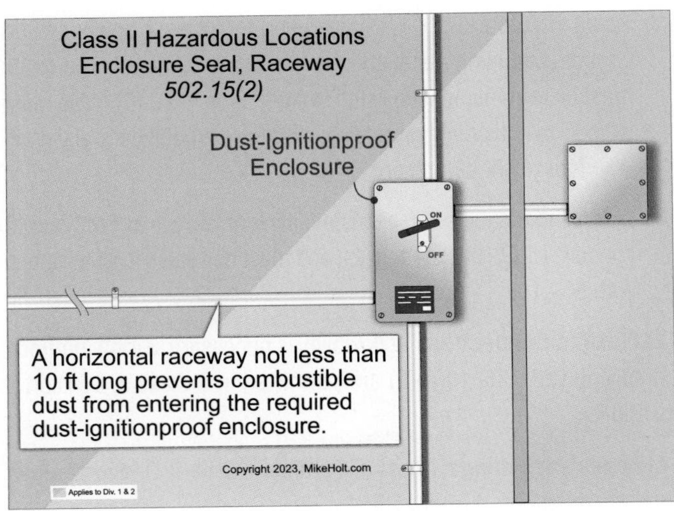
Class II Hazardous Locations
Enclosure Seal, Raceway
502.15(2)
Dust-Ignitionproof Enclosure
A horizontal raceway not less than 10 ft long prevents combustible dust from entering the required dust-ignitionproof enclosure.
Copyright 2023, MikeHolt.com
Applies to Div. 1 & 2

▸Figure 502-8

(3) A vertical raceway that extends downward for not less than 5 ft from the dust-ignitionproof enclosure

(4) A raceway installed in a manner equivalent to (2) or (3) that extends only horizontally and downward from the dust-ignitionproof enclosure

(5) Electrical sealing putty ▸Figure 502-9

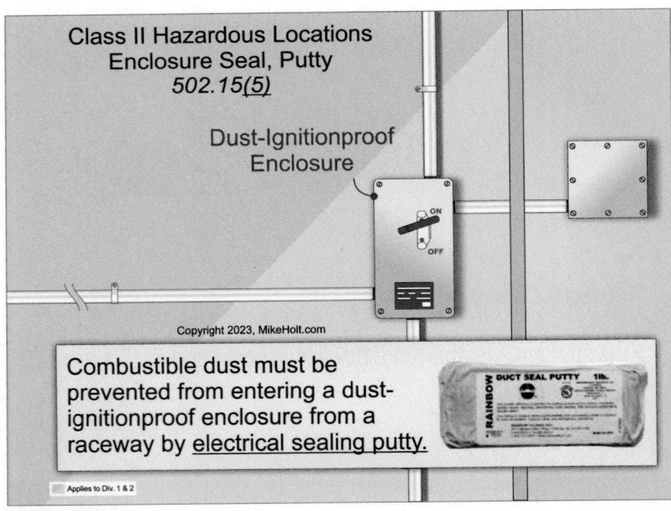
Class II Hazardous Locations
Enclosure Seal, Putty
502.15(5)
Dust-Ignitionproof Enclosure
Copyright 2023, MikeHolt.com
Combustible dust must be prevented from entering a dust-ignitionproof enclosure from a raceway by electrical sealing putty.
DUCT SEAL PUTTY
RAINBOW
Applies to Div. 1 & 2

▸Figure 502-9

A conduit seal is not required between a dust-ignitionproof enclosure and an enclosure in an unclassified location. ▸Figure 502-10

Sealing fittings for Class II locations must be accessible and are not required to be explosionproof.

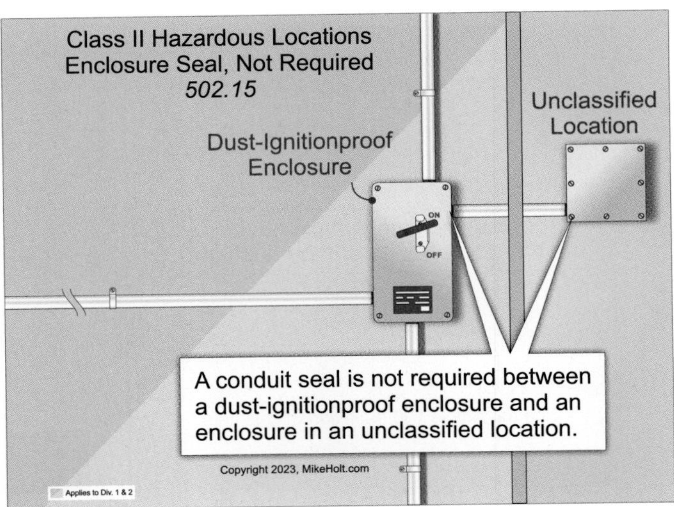
Class II Hazardous Locations
Enclosure Seal, Not Required
502.15
Unclassified Location
Dust-Ignitionproof Enclosure
A conduit seal is not required between a dust-ignitionproof enclosure and an enclosure in an unclassified location.
Copyright 2023, MikeHolt.com
Applies to Div. 1 & 2

▸Figure 502-10

502.30 Grounding and Bonding

Because of the explosive conditions associated with electrical installations in hazardous (classified) locations [500.5], electrical continuity of the metal parts of equipment and raceways must be ensured regardless of the voltage of the circuit.

(B) Bonding.

(1) Specific Bonding Means.

(a) Locknuts are not suitable for bonding purposes in hazardous (classified) locations so bonding jumpers with identified fittings or other approved means of bonding must be used. Such means of bonding apply to all metal raceways between Class II locations and service disconnects or a separately derived system. ▸Figure 502-11

Author's Comment:

- The special bonding requirements for Class II locations are the same as those for 501.30(A) Class I locations [250.94(B)(4)]. Threaded couplings and hubs made up wrenchtight provide a suitable low-impedance fault current path [250. 92(B)(2)].

(2) Flexible Metal Conduit and Liquidtight Flexible Metal Conduit.

(a) Type LFMC. Where flexible metal or liquidtight flexible metal conduit is installed as permitted by 502.10(A)(2), the raceway must have an internal or external equipment bonding jumper of the wire type installed in accordance with 250.102(E). ▸Figure 502-12

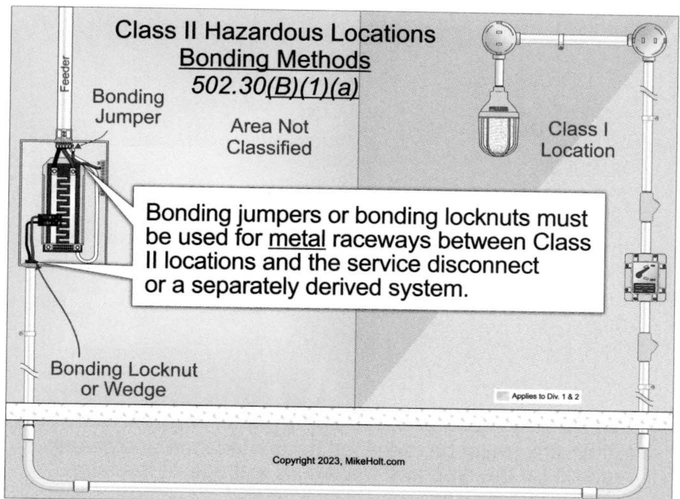

▶Figure 502–11

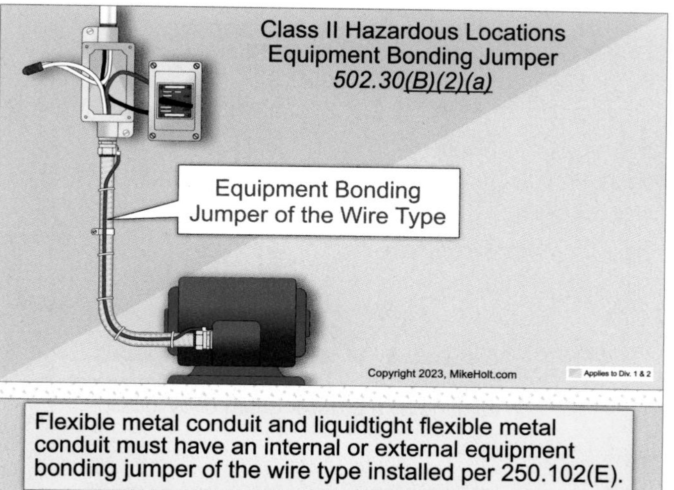

▶Figure 502–12

Author's Comment:

- Load-side bonding jumpers must be sized in accordance with 250.122 based on the rating of the overcurrent protective device [250.102(D)]. Where the bonding jumper is installed outside a raceway, the length of the bonding jumpers is not permitted to exceed 6 ft and they must be routed with the raceway [250.102(E)(2)]. ▶Figure 502–13

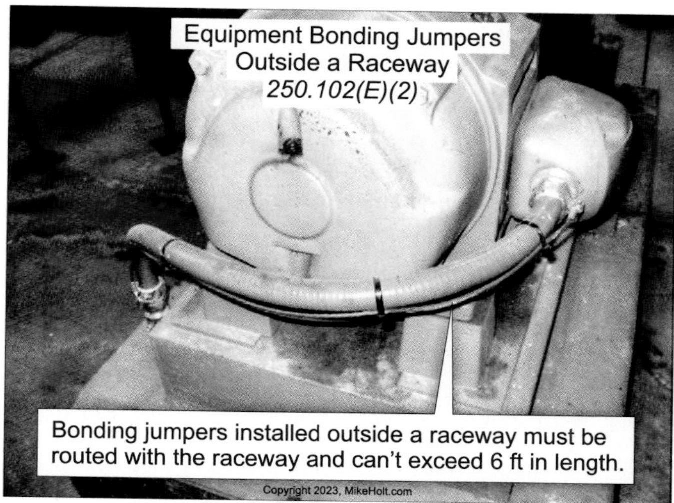

▶Figure 502–13

Part III. Equipment

502.115 Enclosures Containing Make-and-Break Contacts

(A) Class II, Division 1. Enclosures for switches, circuit breakers, motor controllers, fuses, pushbuttons, relays, and similar devices must be identified for a Class II, Division 1 location. ▶Figure 502–14

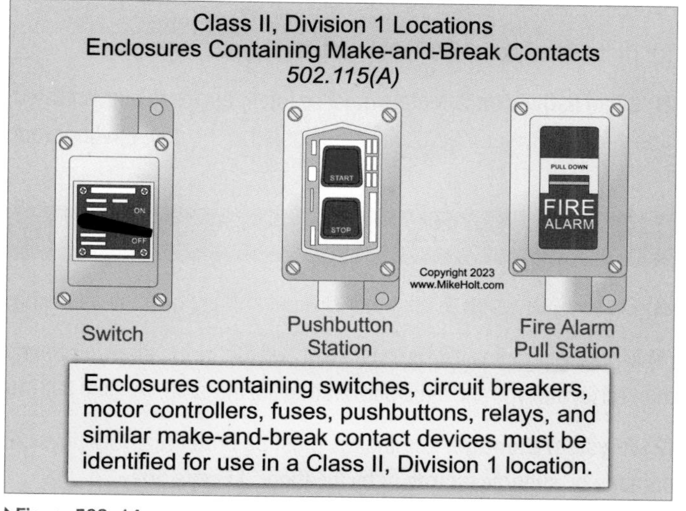

▶Figure 502–14

(B) Class II, Division 2. Enclosures for fuses, switches, circuit breakers, and motor controllers (including pushbuttons, relays, and similar devices) must be dusttight or identified for a Class II, Division 2 location. ▶Figure 502–15

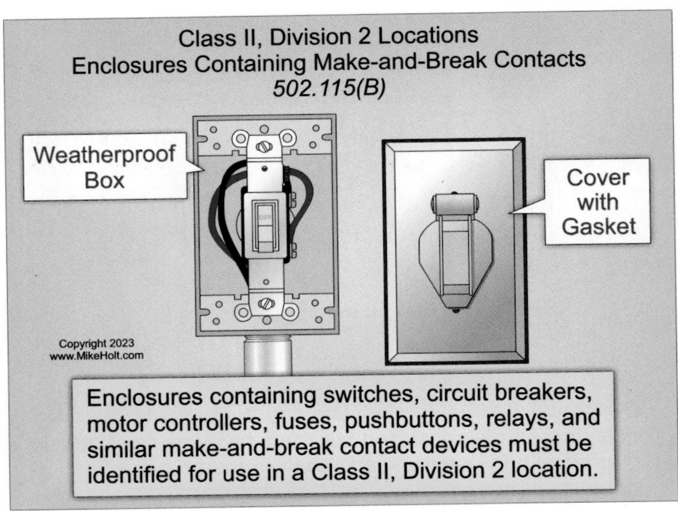

▸Figure 502–15

Author's Comment:

- A standard weatherproof box with a cover and gasket meets this requirement.

502.125 Motors and Generators

(A) Class II, Division 1. Motors must be:

(1) Identified for the location, or

(2) Of the totally enclosed pipe-ventilated type.

(B) Class II, Division 2. Motors must be totally enclosed nonventilated, pipe-ventilated, water-air-cooled, fan-cooled, or be dust-ignitionproof.

502.130 Luminaires

(A) Class II, Division 1. Luminaires must comply with the following:

(1) Marking. Luminaires must be identified for the location and clearly marked for the type and maximum wattage of the lamp. ▸Figure 502–16

(2) Physical Damage. Luminaires must be protected from physical damage by suitable guards or by location. ▸Figure 502–17

(3) Pendant Luminaires. Pendant luminaires must be suspended by threaded rigid metal conduit stems, threaded steel intermediate metal conduit stems, by chains with approved fittings, or by other approved means. ▸Figure 502–18

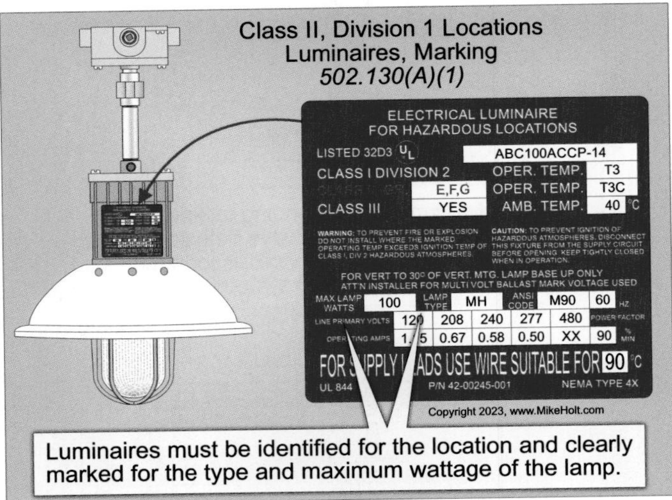

▸Figure 502–16

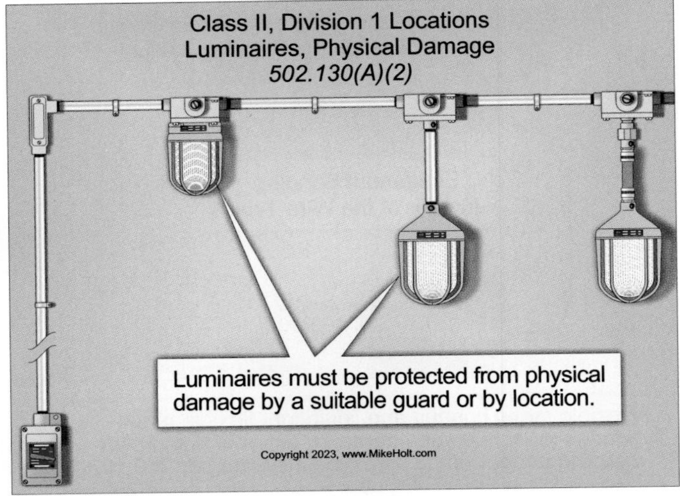

▸Figure 502–17

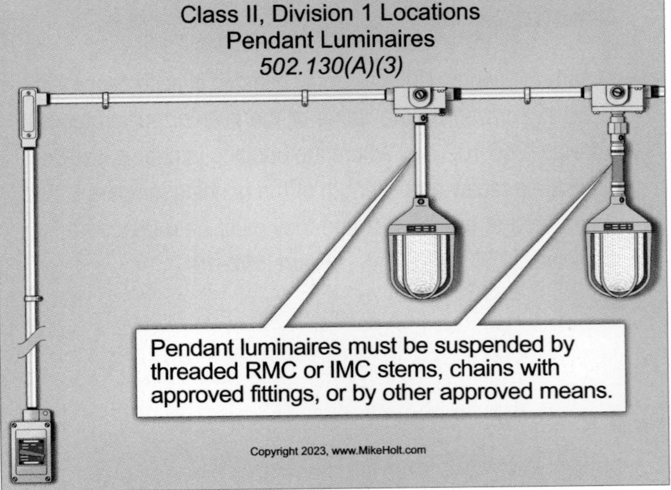

▸Figure 502–18

1st Printing

Threaded joints must be provided with set screws or other effective means to prevent loosening. For stems longer than 1 ft, permanent, effective bracing, or a flexible fitting or connector listed for the Class II, Division 1 location must be provided not more than 1 ft from the point of attachment to the supporting box/fitting.

Flexible cord listed for hard usage is permitted as the wiring between an outlet box/fitting and a pendant luminaire when it contains an equipment grounding conductor and is terminated with fittings that are listed for the location in accordance with 502.10(A)(2)(5).

(4) Supports. Boxes, box assemblies, and fittings used for the support of luminaires must be identified for Class II locations. ▸Figure 502–19

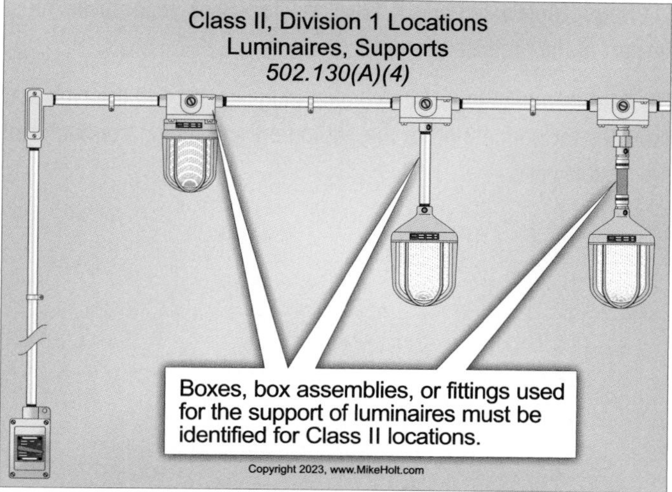
Class II, Division 1 Locations
Luminaires, Supports
502.130(A)(4)
Boxes, box assemblies, or fittings used for the support of luminaires must be identified for Class II locations.
Copyright 2023, www.MikeHolt.com

▸Figure 502–19

(B) Class II, Division 2. Luminaires must comply with the following:

(1) Portable Lighting Equipment. Portable lighting equipment must be identified for the location.

(2) Fixed Lighting. Luminaires must be contained in enclosures that are dusttight or otherwise identified for the location.

(3) Physical Damage. Luminaires must be protected from physical damage by suitable guards or by location.

(4) Pendant Luminaires. Pendant luminaires must be suspended by threaded rigid metal conduit stems, threaded steel intermediate metal conduit stems, by chains with fittings approved by the authority having jurisdiction, or by other means approved by the authority having jurisdiction.

For stems longer than 1 ft, permanent, effective bracing, or a flexible fitting or connector must be provided not more than 1 ft from the point of attachment to the supporting box/fitting. Flexible cord listed for hard usage is permitted as the wiring between an outlet box/fitting and a pendant luminaire when it is terminated with a listed flexible cord connector that maintains the protection technique, but the flexible cord is not permitted to support the luminaire.

502.135 Utilization Equipment

(A) Class II, Division 1. Utilization equipment such as heaters, motors, switches, circuit breakers, and fuses in Class II, Division 1 locations must be identified for use in Class II, Division 1 locations.

(B) Class II, Division 2. Utilization equipment such as heaters, motors, switches, circuit breakers, and fuses in Class II, Division 2 locations must be identified for use in Class II, Division 2 locations.

502.140 Flexible Cords

(A) Permitted Uses. Flexible cord is permitted as follows:

(1) Portable Lighting or Portable Utilization Equipment. The flexible cord must be attached to the equipment with a cord connector listed for the protection technique of the equipment wiring compartment, such as dust-ignitionproof. ▸Figure 502–20

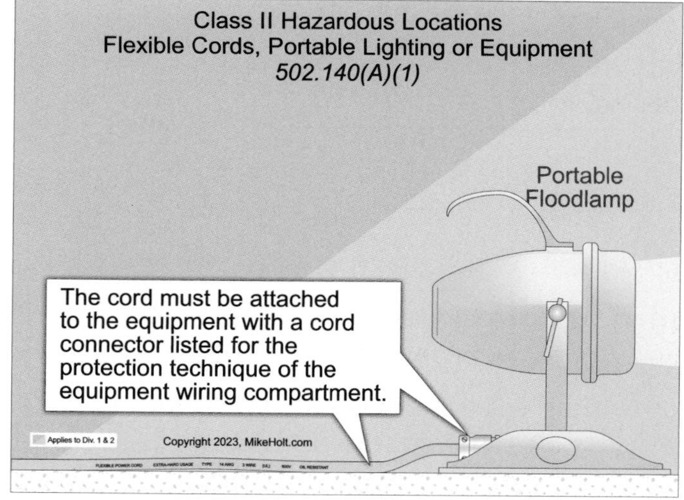
Class II Hazardous Locations
Flexible Cords, Portable Lighting or Equipment
502.140(A)(1)
Portable Floodlamp
The cord must be attached to the equipment with a cord connector listed for the protection technique of the equipment wiring compartment.
Applies to Div. 1 & 2
Copyright 2023, MikeHolt.com

▸Figure 502–20

An attachment plug of the grounding type that complies with 502.145 must also be used.

(B) Installation. Where flexible cords are used, the cords must comply with all the following:

(1) Be of a type listed for extra-hard usage.

(2) Contain an equipment grounding conductor complying with 400.23.

(3) Be supported in such a manner that there will be no tension on the terminal connections.

(4) In Division 1 locations, the flexible cord must terminate with a flexible cord connector listed for the location or a listed flexible cord connector installed with a seal listed for the location. In Division 2 locations, the flexible cord must be terminated with a listed dust-tight flexible cord connector.

502.145 Receptacles and Attachment Plugs

Receptacles and attachment plugs must be identified for the location.

(A) Class II, Division 1.

(1) Receptacles. In Class II, Division 1 locations, receptacles must be part of the premises wiring.

(2) Attachment Plugs. Attachment plugs must be of the type that provides for connection to the equipment grounding conductor of the flexible cord.

(B) Class II, Division 2.

(1) Receptacles. In Class II, Division 2 locations, receptacles must be part of the premises wiring.

(2) Attachment Plugs. Attachment plugs must be of the type that provides for connection to the equipment grounding conductor of the flexible cord.

1st Printing

ARTICLE 511

COMMERCIAL REPAIR AND STORAGE GARAGES

Introduction to Article 511—Commercial Repair and Storage Garages

This article covers the requirements for electrical equipment and wiring in locations used to service and repair vehicles that use volatile flammable liquids or flammable gases for fuel. Take time to refer to the Article 100 definitions used in this article. Often the difference between meeting the requirements of a rule and or misapplying it is a matter of understanding the terms. Many of these rules are outside of the scope of this material, however, some of the topics we cover include the following:

- Scope
- Classification of Hazardous Areas
- Wiring and Equipment

511.1 Scope

Article 511 covers service and repair areas for automobiles, buses, trucks, and tractors in which volatile flammable liquids or flammable gases are used for fuel or power. ▶Figure 511-1

▶Figure 511-1

Author's Comment:

- Installations within the scope of Article 511 include automobile service/repair centers; service/repair garages for commercial vehicles such as trucks and tractors; service/repair garages for fleet vehicles such as cars, buses, and trucks; and shops that service motorcycles and all-terrain vehicles (ATVs).
- This article does not apply to garages used only for diesel fueled or electric vehicle service.

511.3 Classification of Hazardous Areas

General. Where flammable liquids or gaseous fuels are stored, handled, or transferred, electrical wiring and electrical utilization equipment must be designed in accordance with the requirements for Class I, Division 1 or 2 hazardous (classified) locations.

(A) Parking Garages. Parking or storage garages are not required to be classified. ▶Figure 511-2

Commercial Repair and Storage Garages
Parking Garages Not Classified
511.3(A)
Parking or storage garages are not required to be classified.
Copyright 2023 MikeHolt.com

▶Figure 511-2

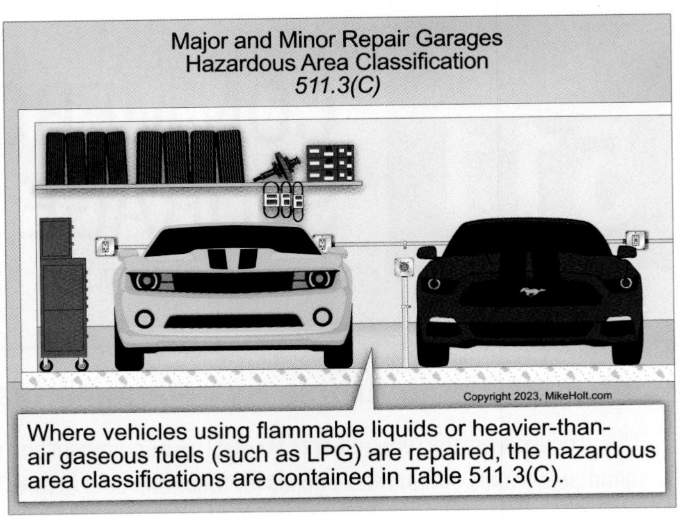
Major and Minor Repair Garages
Hazardous Area Classification
511.3(C)
Copyright 2023, MikeHolt.com
Where vehicles using flammable liquids or heavier-than-air gaseous fuels (such as LPG) are repaired, the hazardous area classifications are contained in Table 511.3(C).

▶Figure 511-3

(B) Repair Garages, With Dispensing. Major and minor repair garages that dispense motor fuels must have the dispensing functions classified in accordance with Table 514.3(B)(1).

According to Article 100, a "Major Repair Garage" is a building or portions of a building where major repairs such as engine overhauls, painting, body and fender work, welding or grinding, and repairs that require draining or emptying the motor vehicle fuel tank are performed on motor vehicles, including associated floor space used for offices, parking, or showrooms.

A "Minor Repair Garage" is a building or portions of a building used for lubrication, inspection, and minor automotive maintenance work such as engine tune-ups, replacement of parts, fluid changes (such as oil, antifreeze, transmission fluid, brake fluid, and air-conditioning refrigerants), brake system repairs, tire rotation, and similar routine maintenance work, including the associated floor space used for offices, parking, or showrooms.

(C) Major and Minor Repair Garages. Where vehicles using flammable liquids or heavier-than-air gaseous fuels (such as LPG) are repaired, the hazardous area classifications are contained in Table 511.3(C). ▶**Figure 511-3,** ▶**Figure 511-4,** ▶**Figure 511-5,** ▶**Figure 511-6,** ▶**Figure 511-7,** ▶**Figure 511-8,** and ▶**Figure 511-9**

Note: NFPA 30A, *Code for Motor Fuel Dispensing Facilities and Repair Garages*, provides information for fire safety at motor fuel dispensing operations and motor vehicle repair facilities.

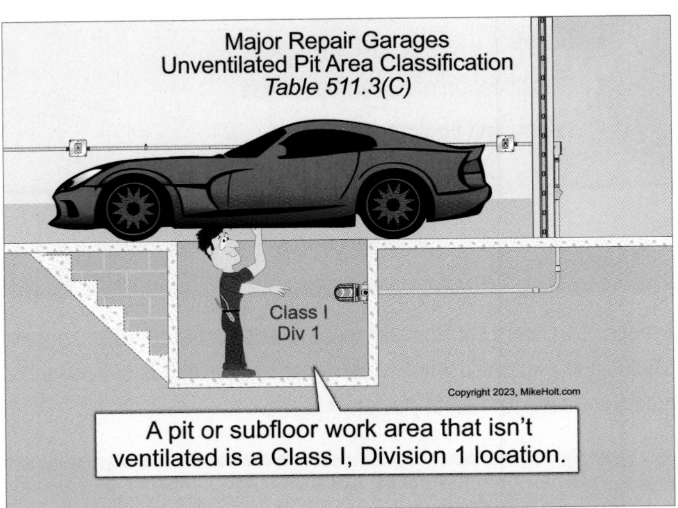
Major Repair Garages
Unventilated Pit Area Classification
Table 511.3(C)
Class I
Div 1
Copyright 2023, MikeHolt.com
A pit or subfloor work area that isn't ventilated is a Class I, Division 1 location.

▶Figure 511-4

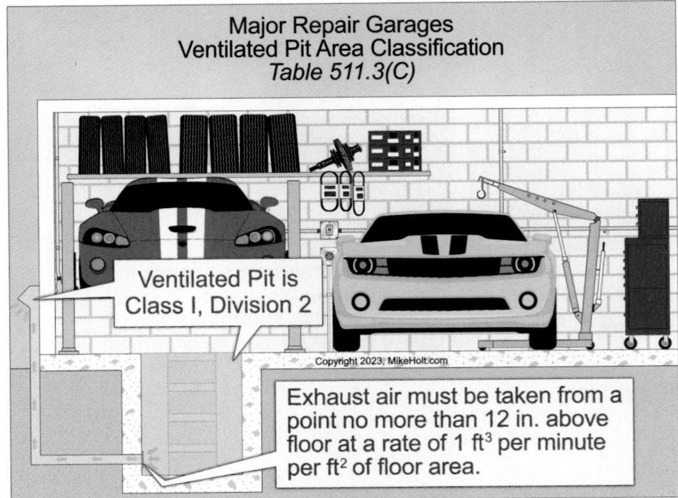
Major Repair Garages
Ventilated Pit Area Classification
Table 511.3(C)
Ventilated Pit is
Class I, Division 2
Copyright 2023, MikeHolt.com
Exhaust air must be taken from a point no more than 12 in. above floor at a rate of 1 ft^3 per minute per ft^2 of floor area.

▶Figure 511-5

1st Printing

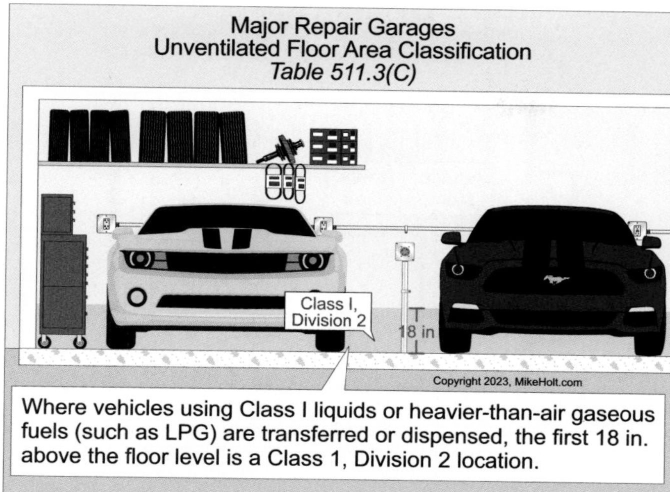

▶Figure 511–6

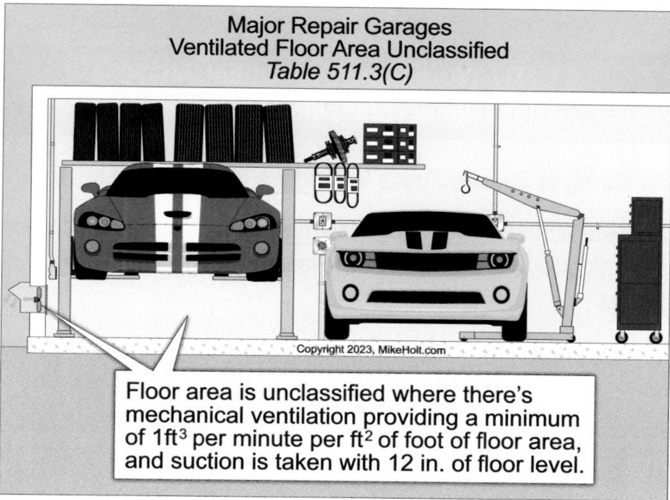

Major Repair Garages
Ventilated Floor Area Unclassified
Table 511.3(C)
Copyright 2023, MikeHolt.com
Floor area is unclassified where there's mechanical ventilation providing a minimum of 1ft³ per minute per ft² of foot of floor area, and suction is taken with 12 in. of floor level.

▶Figure 511–7

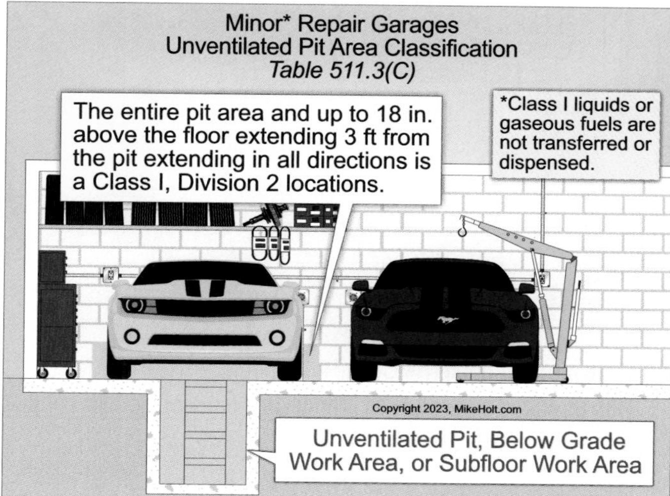

Minor* Repair Garages
Unventilated Pit Area Classification
Table 511.3(C)
The entire pit area and up to 18 in. above the floor extending 3 ft from the pit extending in all directions is a Class I, Division 2 locations.
*Class I liquids or gaseous fuels are not transferred or dispensed.
Copyright 2023, MikeHolt.com
Unventilated Pit, Below Grade Work Area, or Subfloor Work Area

▶Figure 511–8

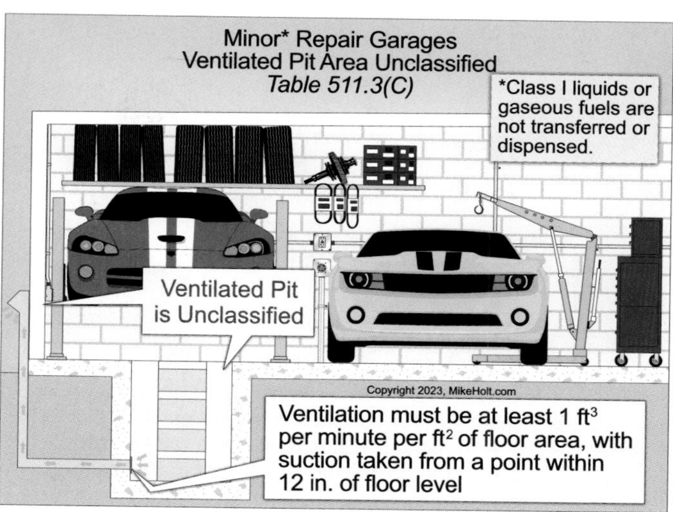

▶Figure 511–9

(D) Major Repair and Storage Garages. Where vehicles using lighter-than-air gaseous fuels (such as hydrogen and natural gas) are repaired or stored, hazardous area classification must be in accordance with Table 511.3(D). ▶Figure 511–10 and ▶Figure 511–11

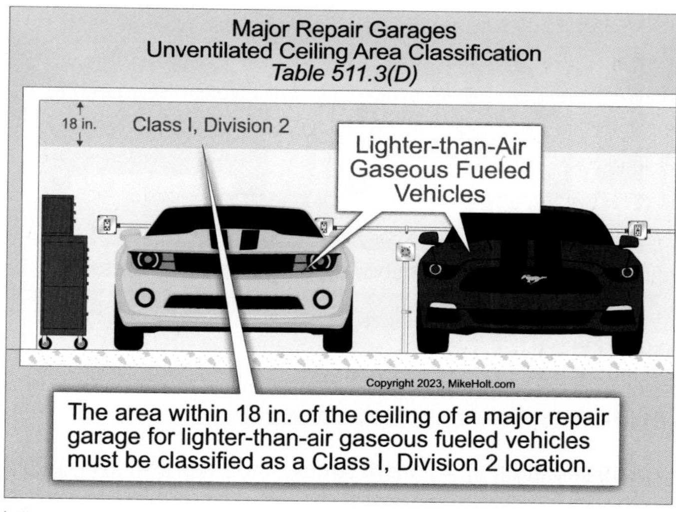

Major Repair Garages
Unventilated Ceiling Area Classification
Table 511.3(D)
18 in.
Class I, Division 2
Lighter-than-Air Gaseous Fueled Vehicles
Copyright 2023, MikeHolt.com
The area within 18 in. of the ceiling of a major repair garage for lighter-than-air gaseous fueled vehicles must be classified as a Class I, Division 2 location.

▶Figure 511–10

Author's Comment:

- Where vehicles using lighter-than-air gaseous fuels (such as hydrogen and natural gas) are repaired or stored in minor repair garages, the hazardous area classification found in Table 511.3(D) is not applicable. ▶Figure 511–12

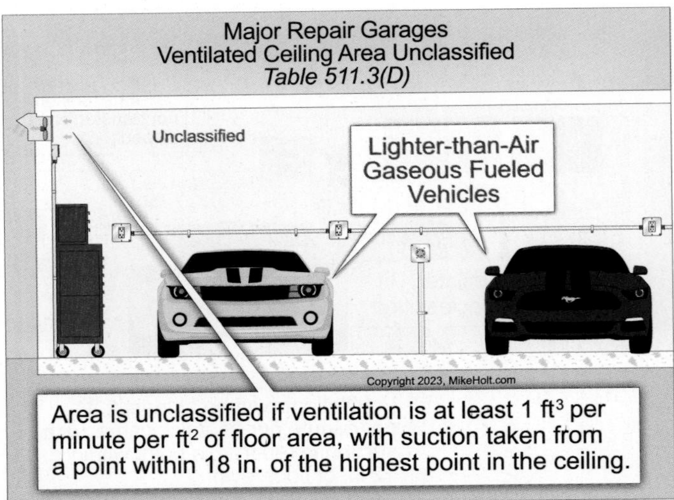

▶Figure 511–11

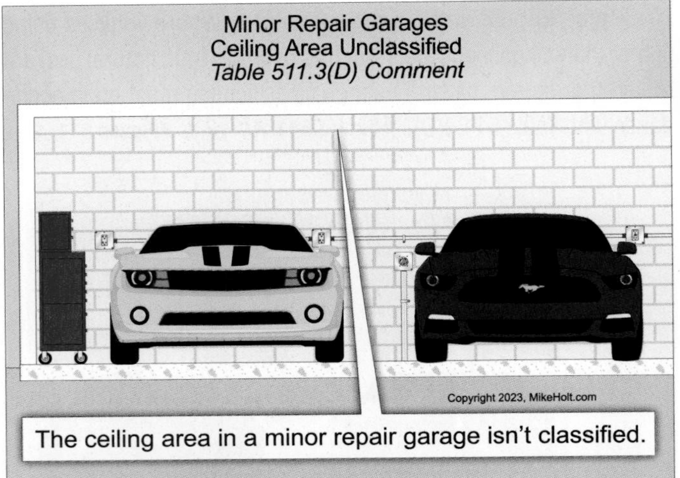

Minor Repair Garages
Ceiling Area Unclassified
Table 511.3(D) Comment
Copyright 2023, MikeHolt.com
The ceiling area in a minor repair garage isn't classified.

▶Figure 511–12

(E) Areas Adjacent to Classified Locations.

(1) Classification of Adjacent Areas. Areas adjacent to classified locations are not classified if mechanically ventilated at a rate of four or more air changes per hour, designed with positive air pressure, or when separated by an unpierced wall, roof, or other solid partition. ▶Figure 511–13

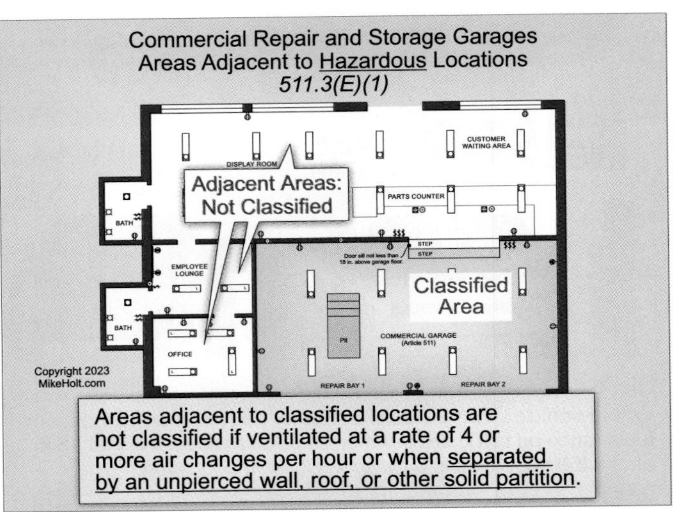

▶Figure 511–13

(2) Alcohol-Based Windshield Washer Fluid. Areas used for the storage, handling, or dispensing into motor vehicles of alcohol-based windshield washer fluid in repair garages are unclassified unless otherwise classified by a provision of 511.3.

511.7 Wiring and Equipment Above Hazardous (Classified) Locations

(A) Wiring in Spaces Above Hazardous (Classified) Locations.

(1) Fixed Wiring. Fixed wiring above hazardous (classified) locations is permitted by one or more of the following wiring methods: ▶Figure 511–14

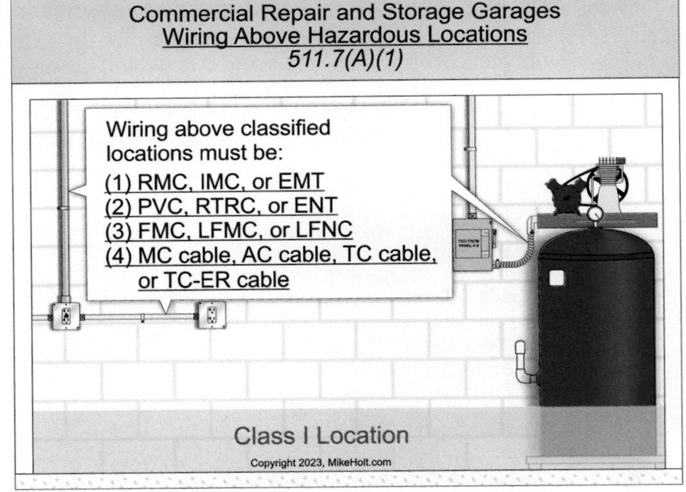

Commercial Repair and Storage Garages
Wiring Above Hazardous Locations
511.7(A)(1)
Wiring above classified locations must be:
(1) RMC, IMC, or EMT
(2) PVC, RTRC, or ENT
(3) FMC, LFMC, or LFNC
(4) MC cable, AC cable, TC cable, or TC-ER cable
Class I Location
Copyright 2023, MikeHolt.com

▶Figure 511–14

(1) Rigid metal conduit (RMC) and intermediate metal conduit (IMC) with threaded or threadless fittings, or electrical metallic conduit (EMT) with listed fittings.

1st Printing

(2) Rigid polyvinyl chloride conduit (PVC), reinforced thermosetting resin conduit (RTRC), or electrical nonmetallic tubing (ENT) with listed fittings.

(3) Flexible metal conduit (FMC), liquidtight flexible metal conduit (LFMC), or liquidtight flexible nonmetallic conduit (LFNC) with listed fittings.

(4) Types MC cable, AC cable, TC cable, or TC-ER cable with listed fittings, including installation in cable trays. Type TC-ER cable must include an equipment grounding conductor in addition to any drain wire.

(2) Pendants (Drop-Cords). For pendants, flexible cord suitable for the type of service and listed for hard usage must be used.

(B) Equipment Above Hazardous (Classified) Locations.

(1) Fixed Electrical Equipment. Fixed electrical equipment must be above the level of any defined hazardous (classified) location or be identified for the location.

(a) Arcing Equipment. Equipment with make-and-break contacts installed less than 12 ft above the floor level must be of the totally enclosed type or constructed to prevent sparks or hot metal particles from escaping.

(b) Fixed Lighting. Luminaires over travel lanes or where exposed to physical damage must be at least 12 ft above the floor level, unless the luminaires are of the totally enclosed type or constructed to prevent sparks or hot metal particles from escaping. ▸Figure 511–15

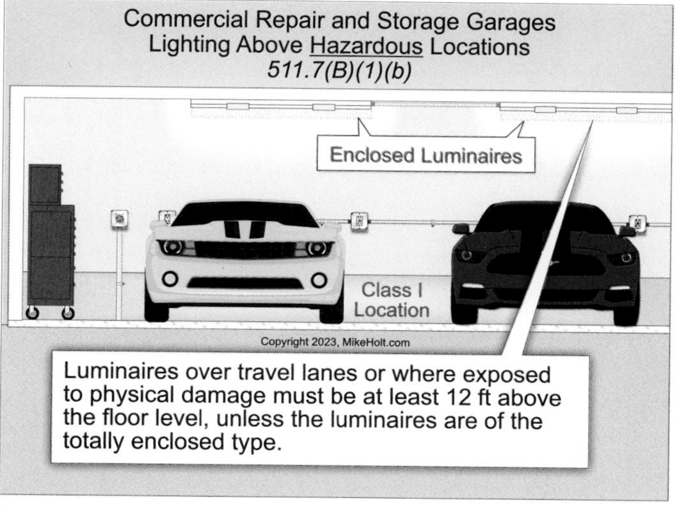
Commercial Repair and Storage Garages
Lighting Above Hazardous Locations
511.7(B)(1)(b)
Enclosed Luminaires
Class I Location
Copyright 2023, MikeHolt.com
Luminaires over travel lanes or where exposed to physical damage must be at least 12 ft above the floor level, unless the luminaires are of the totally enclosed type.

▸Figure 511–15

511.8 Wiring Below Hazardous (Classified) Locations

Wiring below a commercial garage must be one of the following wiring methods:

(1) Threaded rigid metal conduit (RMC) or threaded intermediate metal conduit (IMC) with listed threaded fittings.

(2) PVC conduit, RTRC conduit, or HDPE conduit can be installed below a commercial garage if buried under not less than 2 ft of cover. Threaded rigid metal conduit or threaded intermediate metal conduit must be used when the conduit has less than 2 ft of cover. ▸Figure 511–16

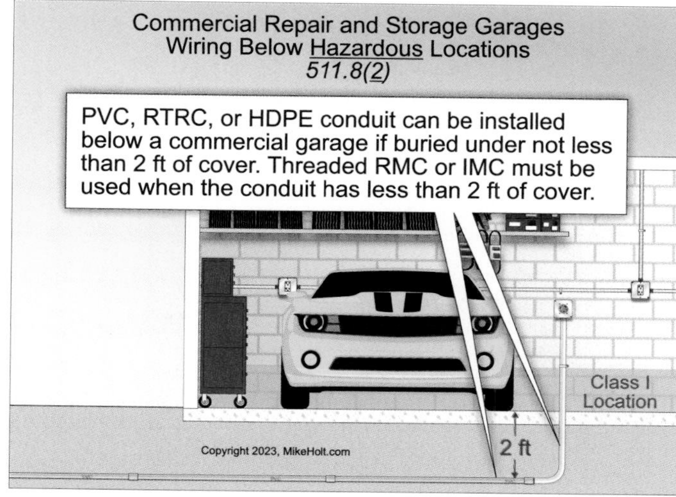
Commercial Repair and Storage Garages
Wiring Below Hazardous Locations
511.8(2)
PVC, RTRC, or HDPE conduit can be installed below a commercial garage if buried under not less than 2 ft of cover. Threaded RMC or IMC must be used when the conduit has less than 2 ft of cover.
Class I Location
2 ft
Copyright 2023, MikeHolt.com

▸Figure 511–16

511.9 Seals

Raceway, cable, and boundary seals must be installed in accordance with 501.15 and apply to the horizontal as well as the vertical boundaries of the defined Class I locations.

511.10 Special Equipment

(A) Battery Charging Equipment. Battery chargers and batteries being charged are not permitted to be within an area classified in accordance with 511.3(B).

511.12 GFCI-Protected Receptacles

GFCI protection for receptacles is required in accordance with 210.8(B). ▶Figure 511–17

Author's Comment:

- GFCI protection is required for receptacles up to 50A, single-phase and receptacles up to 100A, three-phase in accordance with 210.8(B).

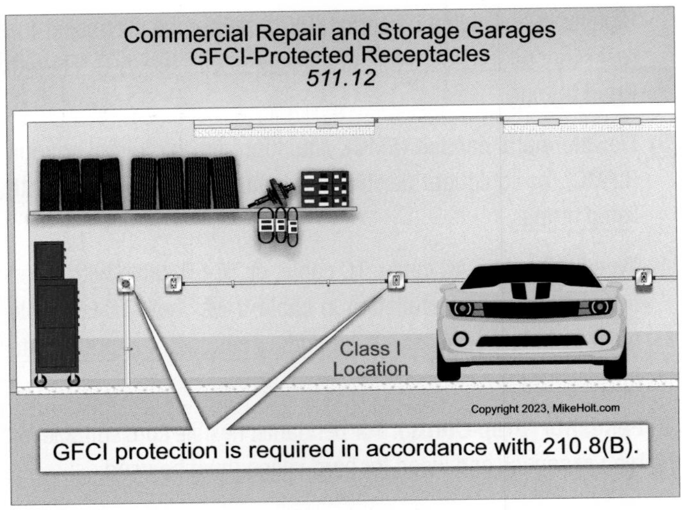

▶Figure 511–17

ARTICLE 514 MOTOR FUEL DISPENSING FACILITIES

Introduction to Article 514—Motor Fuel Dispensing Facilities

This article covers the portion of a facility where fuel is stored and dispensed into the fuel tanks of motor vehicles and marine craft, or into approved containers. Many of these rules are outside of the scope of this material, however, some of the topics we cover include the following:

- Scope
- Classification of Locations
- Wiring and Equipment
- Conduit Seals
- Equipment Bonding

Various tables and diagrams make up about half of this article specifying how to classify a motor fuel dispensing area. While this is the responsibility of the engineer of record, it is helpful to review it so that the specific provisions of this article have context.

Author's Comment:

- Diesel fuel is not a flammable liquid. Therefore, areas associated with diesel dispensing equipment and associated wiring are not required to comply with the hazardous (classified) location requirements of Article 514 [514.3(A)]. However, the other requirements in this article still apply.

514.1 Scope

This article applies to motor fuel dispensing facilities, marine/motor fuel dispensing facilities, motor fuel dispensing facilities inside buildings, and fleet vehicle motor fuel dispensing facilities. ▶Figure 514–1

514.3 Classification of Locations

(A) Unclassified Locations. If the authority having jurisdiction is satisfied that flammable liquids having a flash point below 100°F (such as gasoline) will not be handled, such locations can be unclassified.

(B) Classified Locations.

(1) Class I Locations. Table 514.3(B)(1) must be used to classify motor fuel dispensing facilities and commercial garages where a flammable liquid having a flash point below 100°F is stored, handled, or dispensed.

A Class I location does not extend beyond an unpierced wall, roof, or other solid partition.

(C) Motor Fuel Dispensing Stations in Marinas.

(1) General. Electrical wiring and equipment serving motor fuel dispensing locations must be installed on the side of the wharf, pier, or dock opposite from the fuel piping system. ▶Figure 514–2

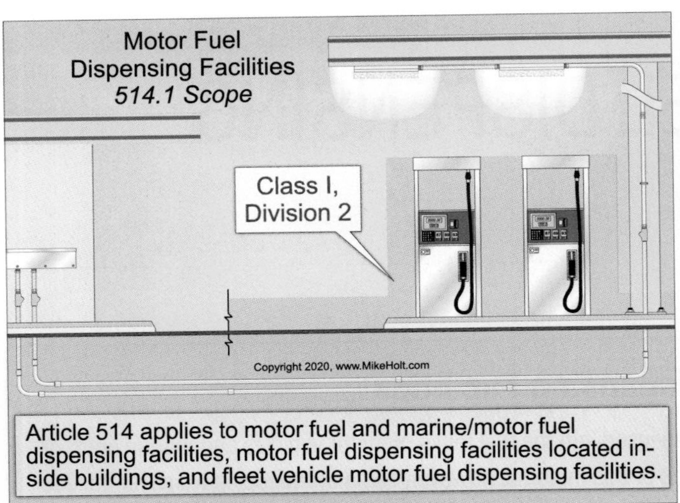

▸Figure 514–1

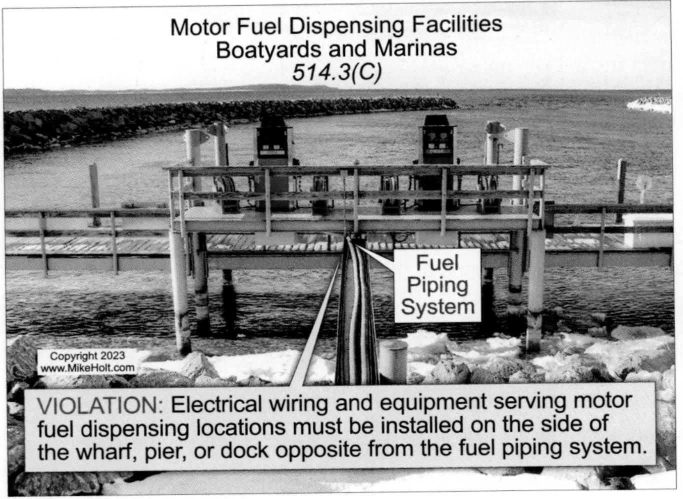

▸Figure 514–2

Author's Comment:

- Electrical wiring and equipment for motor fuel dispensing stations covered by Article 514 in marinas and docking facilities must also comply with Article 555 [555.11].

(b) Area Considered Class I, Division 2.

(1) The area 18 in. above the surface of the dock, pier, or wharf and extending 20 ft horizontally in all directions from the outside edge of the dispenser and down to the water level is considered a Class I, Division 2 location. ▸Figure 514–3

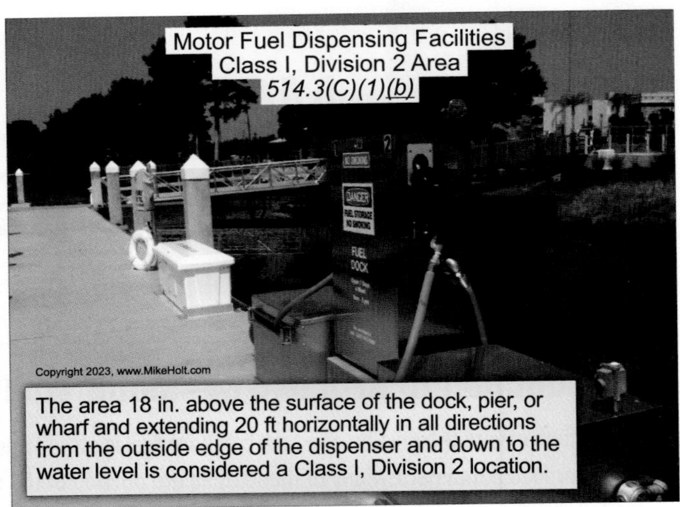

▸Figure 514–3

514.4 Wiring and Equipment Within Hazardous (Classified) Locations

Electrical equipment and wiring within a hazardous (classified) location, as specified in Table 514.3(B)(1), must comply with Article 501.

514.7 Wiring and Equipment Above Hazardous (Classified) Locations

Fixed wiring above a hazardous (classified) location is permitted by one or more of the following: ▸Figure 514–4

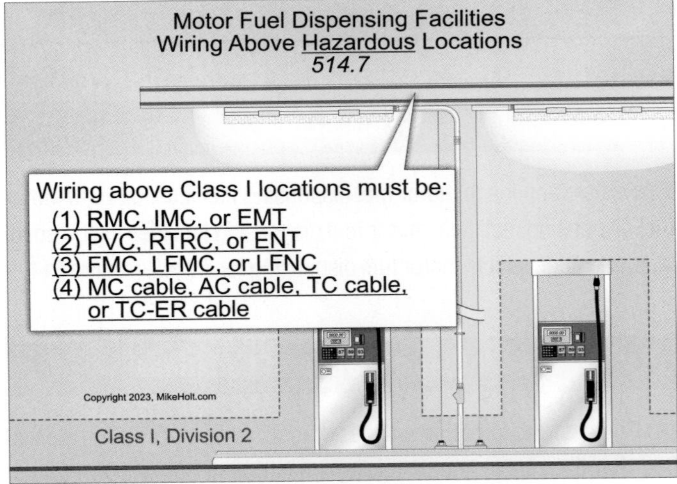

Motor Fuel Dispensing Facilities
Wiring Above Hazardous Locations
514.7
Wiring above Class I locations must be:
(1) RMC, IMC, or EMT
(2) PVC, RTRC, or ENT
(3) FMC, LFMC, or LFNC
(4) MC cable, AC cable, TC cable, or TC-ER cable
Copyright 2023, MikeHolt.com
Class I, Division 2

▸Figure 514–4

(1) Rigid metal conduit (RMC) and intermediate metal conduit (IMC) with threaded or threadless fittings, or electrical metallic conduit (EMT) with fittings.

(2) Rigid polyvinyl chloride conduit (PVC), reinforced thermosetting resin conduit (RTRC), or electrical nonmetallic tubing (ENT) with listed fittings.

(3) Flexible metal conduit (FMC), liquidtight flexible metal conduit (LFMC), or liquidtight flexible nonmetallic conduit (LFNC) with listed fittings.

(4) Types MC cable, AC cable, TC cable, or TC-ER cable with listed fittings, including installation in cable trays. Type TC-ER cable must include an equipment grounding conductor in addition to any drain wire.

514.8 Underground Wiring

(A) Metal Conduit. Wiring beneath a classified location must be installed in threaded rigid metal conduit (RMC) or threaded intermediate metal conduit (IMC) with listed threaded fittings. Electrical conduits below the surface of a Class I, Division 1 or 2 location, as contained in Table 514.3(B)(1) and Table 514.3(B)(2), must be sealed within 10 ft of the point of emergence above grade. ▸Figure 514-5

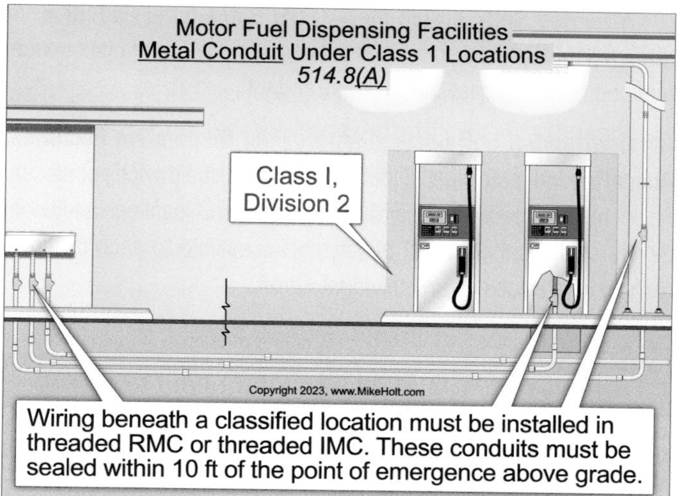
Motor Fuel Dispensing Facilities
Metal Conduit Under Class 1 Locations
514.8(A)
Class I,
Division 2
Copyright 2023, www.MikeHolt.com
Wiring beneath a classified location must be installed in threaded RMC or threaded IMC. These conduits must be sealed within 10 ft of the point of emergence above grade.

▸Figure 514-5

The conduit must not contain any union, coupling, box, or fittings between the conduit seal and the point of emergence above grade.

(C) Nonmetallic Conduit. PVC conduit, RTRC conduit, and HDPE conduit can be installed below a classified location if buried under not less than 2 ft of cover. Threaded rigid metal conduit (RMC) or threaded intermediate metal conduit (IMC) must be used for the last 2 ft of the underground run. ▸Figure 514-6

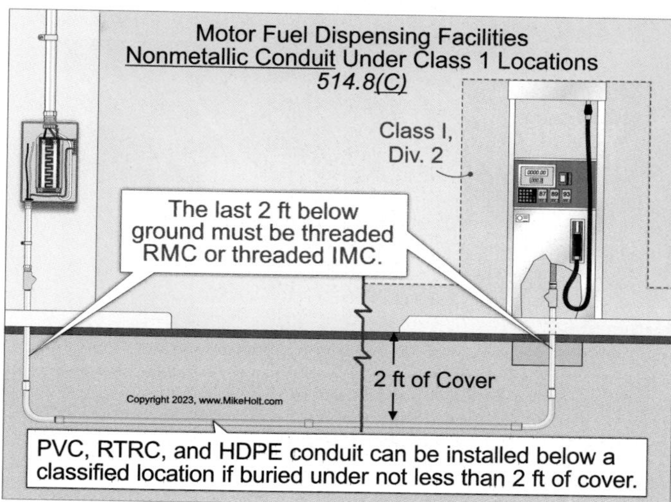
Motor Fuel Dispensing Facilities
Nonmetallic Conduit Under Class 1 Locations
514.8(C)
Class I,
Div. 2
The last 2 ft below ground must be threaded RMC or threaded IMC.
2 ft of Cover
Copyright 2023, www.MikeHolt.com
PVC, RTRC, and HDPE conduit can be installed below a classified location if buried under not less than 2 ft of cover.

▸Figure 514-6

Author's Comment:

- The underground area beneath dispensers is not a classified location, because there is not enough oxygen below ground to create ignition. There may be, however, a substantial amount of gasoline in the earth. Due to this, the *Code* includes requirements that act as though the underground area is classified, meaning that you must follow 514.8 even if you are just passing underneath the area without supplying equipment in the classified location.

514.9 Conduit Seal

(A) At Dispenser. A listed conduit seal fitting must be installed in each raceway run that enters or leaves a dispenser. The conduit seal fitting or listed explosionproof reducer at the seal must be the first fitting after the raceway emerges from the Earth's surface or concrete. ▸Figure 514-7

(B) At Class I Boundary. A listed conduit seal fitting must be installed in each raceway run that leaves a Class I location. ▸Figure 514-8

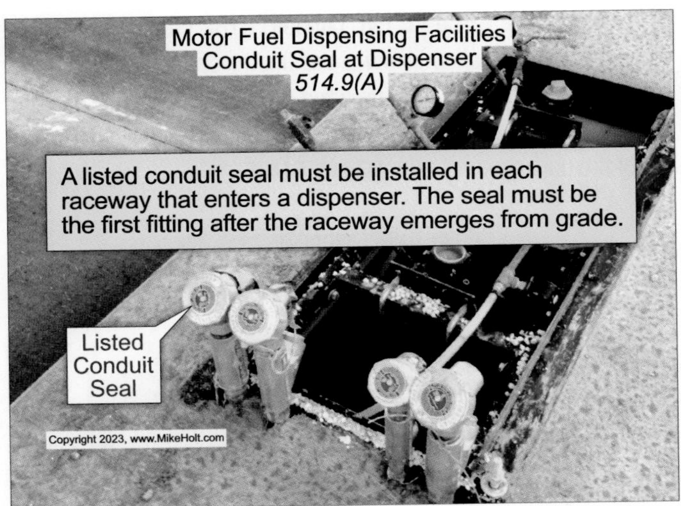

Motor Fuel Dispensing Facilities
Conduit Seal at Dispenser
514.9(A)
A listed conduit seal must be installed in each raceway that enters a dispenser. The seal must be the first fitting after the raceway emerges from grade.
Listed Conduit Seal
Copyright 2023, www.MikeHolt.com

▶Figure 514–7

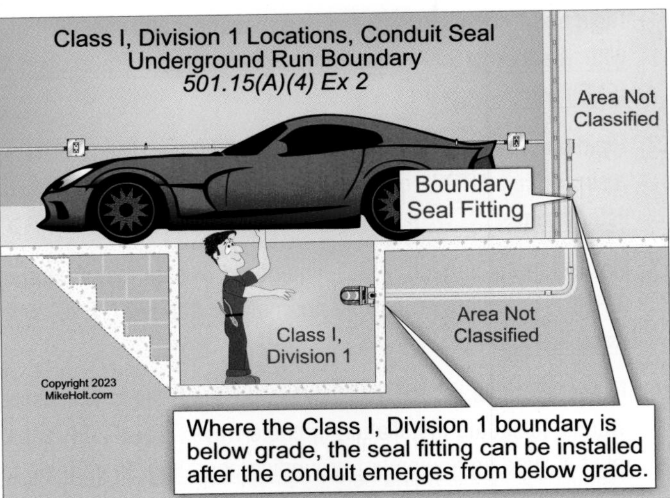

▶Figure 514–9

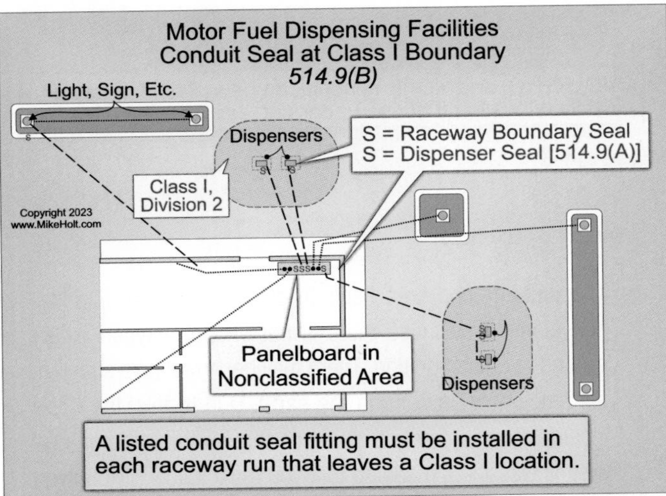

▶Figure 514–8

Author's Comment:

- If the boundary is beneath the ground, the sealing fitting can be installed after the raceway leaves the ground, but there must be no union, coupling, box, or fitting (other than listed explosionproof reducers) at the sealing fitting in the raceway between the sealing fitting and the point at which the raceway leaves the Earth's surface [501.15(A)(4) Ex 2]. ▶**Figure 514–9**

514.11 Circuit Disconnects

(A) Emergency Electrical Disconnects. Fuel dispensing systems must be provided with one or more clearly identified emergency shutoff devices or electrical disconnects. Such devices or disconnects must be installed in approved locations but not less than 20 ft or more than 100 ft from the fuel dispensing devices they serve.

(B) Attended Self-Service Motor Fuel Dispensing Facilities. At attended motor fuel dispensing facilities, the devices or disconnects must be readily accessible to the attendant.

(C) Unattended Self-Service Motor Fuel Dispensing Facilities. At unattended motor fuel dispensing facilities, the devices or disconnects must be readily accessible to patrons and at least one additional device or disconnect must be readily accessible to each group of dispensing devices on an individual island.

514.16 Bonding Requirements

Metal parts of equipment and raceways in Class I locations must be bonded in accordance with 501.30.

1st Printing

HEALTH CARE FACILITIES

Introduction to Article 517—Health Care Facilities

This article covers electrical wiring in health care facilities such as hospitals, nursing homes, limited care and supervisory care facilities, clinics, medical and dental offices, and ambulatory care facilities that provide services to human beings. The requirements of Article 517 do not apply to business offices or waiting rooms, or to animal veterinary facilities. Many of these rules are outside of the scope of this material, however some of the topics we cover include the following:

- Wiring Methods
- Equipment Grounding Conductor for Receptacles and Fixed Electrical Equipment in Patient Care Spaces
- Isolated Ground Receptacles

Article 517 consists of seven parts:

- Part I. General
- Part II. Wiring and Protection
- Part III. Essential Electrical Systems (not covered)
- Part IV. Inhalation Anesthetizing Locations (not covered)
- Part V. Diagnostic Imaging and Treatment Equipment (not covered)
- Part VI. Communications, Signaling Systems, Data Systems, Fire Alarm Systems, and Systems Less than 120V, Nominal (not covered)
- Part VII. Isolated Power Systems (not covered)

Part I. General

517.1 Scope

This article covers electrical wiring in health care facilities such as hospitals, nursing homes, limited care facilities, medical offices, dental offices, and ambulatory care facilities that provide services to human beings. ▸Figure 517–1

According to Article 100, "Health Care Facilities" are buildings, portions of buildings, or mobile enclosures in which medical, dental, psychiatric, nursing, obstetrical, or surgical care is provided for humans. ▸Figure 517–2

Note: Examples of health care facilities include, but are not limited to, hospitals, nursing homes, limited care facilities, medical offices, dental offices, and ambulatory care facilities.

According to Article 100, an "Ambulatory Health Care Occupancy" is an occupancy used to provide services or treatment simultaneously to four or more patients that provides, on an outpatient basis, one or more of the following:

(1) Treatment for patients that renders them incapable of taking action for self-preservation under emergency conditions without the assistance of others.

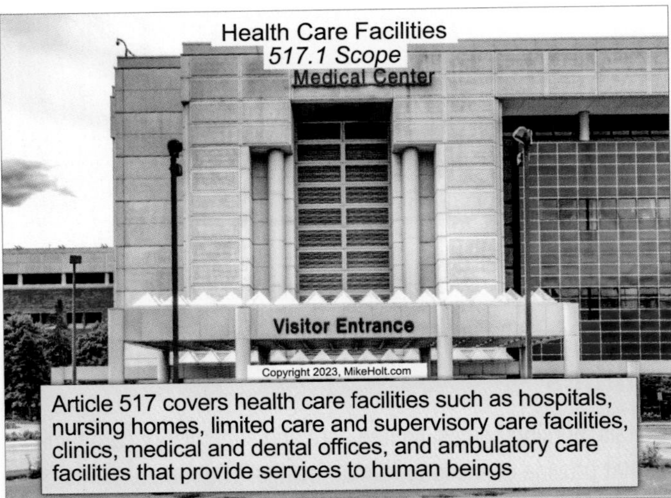
Health Care Facilities
517.1 Scope
Medical Center
Visitor Entrance
Copyright 2023, MikeHolt.com
Article 517 covers health care facilities such as hospitals, nursing homes, limited care and supervisory care facilities, clinics, medical and dental offices, and ambulatory care facilities that provide services to human beings

▶Figure 517–1

Health Care Facilities
Article 100 Definition
Copyright 2023, MikeHolt.com
Buildings, portions of buildings, or mobile enclosures in which medical, dental, psychiatric, nursing, obstetrical, or surgical care is provided for humans.

▶Figure 517–2

(2) Anesthesia that renders the patient incapable of taking action for self-preservation under emergency conditions without the assistance of others.

(3) Treatment for patients who, due to the nature of their injury or illness, are incapable of taking action for self-preservation under emergency conditions without the assistance of others.

According to Article 100, a "Dental Office" is a building or portion of a building in which the following occur:

(1) Examinations and minor treatments or procedures performed under the continuous supervision of a dental professional.

(2) Use of limited to minimal sedation and treatment or procedures that do not render the patient incapable of self-preservation under emergency conditions.

(3) No overnight stays for patients or 24-hour operations.

According to Article 100, a "Hospital" is a building or portion thereof used on a 24-hour basis for the medical, psychiatric, obstetrical, or surgical care of four or more inpatients. ▶**Figure 517–3**

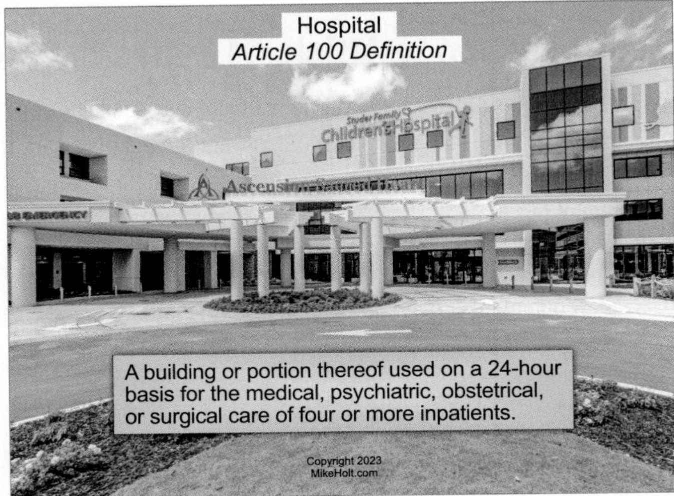
Hospital
Article 100 Definition
A building or portion thereof used on a 24-hour basis for the medical, psychiatric, obstetrical, or surgical care of four or more inpatients.
Copyright 2023
MikeHolt.com

▶Figure 517–3

According to Article 100, a "Limited Care Facility" is a building or an area of a building used for the housing, on a 24-hour basis, of four or more persons who are incapable of self-preservation because of age, physical limitations due to accident or illness, or limitations such as intellectual disability, developmental disability, mental illness, or chemical dependency. ▶**Figure 517–4**

Limited Care Facility
Article 100 Definition
Palm Garden
(352)854-6262
Copyright 2023, MikeHolt.com
A building or an area used for the housing, on a 24-hour basis, of four or more persons who are incapable of self-preservation.

▶Figure 517–4

According to Article 100, a "Medical Office" is a building or part thereof in which the following occur: ▸**Figure 517–5**

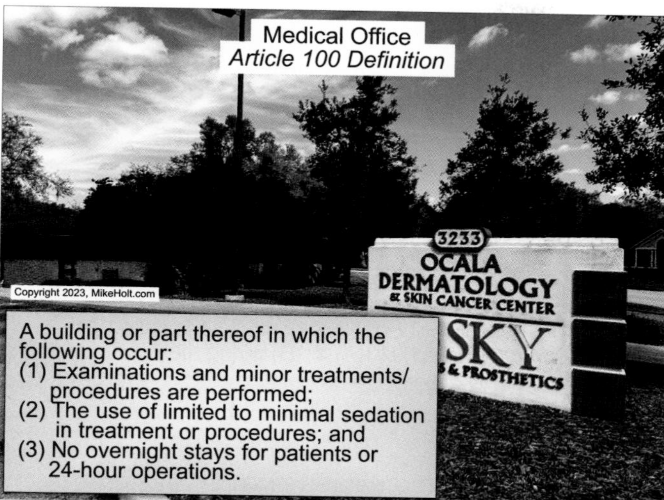
Medical Office
Article 100 Definition
3233
OCALA
DERMATOLOGY
& SKIN CANCER CENTER
SKY
& PROSTHETICS
Copyright 2023, MikeHolt.com
A building or part thereof in which the following occur:
(1) Examinations and minor treatments/procedures are performed;
(2) The use of limited to minimal sedation in treatment or procedures; and
(3) No overnight stays for patients or 24-hour operations.

▸**Figure 517–5**

(1) Examinations and minor treatments/procedures performed under the continuous supervision of a medical professional;

(2) The use of limited to minimal sedation and treatment or procedures that do not render the patient incapable of self-preservation under emergency conditions; and

(3) No overnight stays for patients or 24-hour operations.

According to Article 100, a "Nursing Home" is defined as a building or portion of a building used on a 24-hour basis for the housing and nursing care of four or more persons who, because of mental or physical incapacity, might be unable to provide for their own needs and safety without the assistance of another person. ▸**Figure 517–6**

Author's Comment:

- This article does not apply to animal veterinary facilities.
- Areas of health care facilities not used for the treatment of patients (such as business offices and waiting rooms) are not required to comply with the provisions contained in Article 517.

The requirements contained in Article 517 specify the installation criteria and wiring methods that minimize electrical hazards by adequate low-potential differences only between exposed conductive surfaces that are likely to become energized and those that could be contacted by a patient.

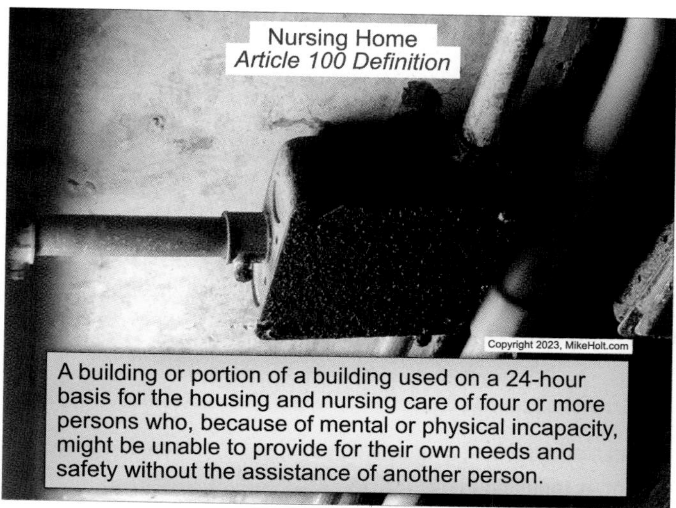
Nursing Home
Article 100 Definition
Copyright 2023, MikeHolt.com
A building or portion of a building used on a 24-hour basis for the housing and nursing care of four or more persons who, because of mental or physical incapacity, might be unable to provide for their own needs and safety without the assistance of another person.

▸**Figure 517–6**

Note 1: In a health care facility, it is difficult to prevent the occurrence of a conductive or capacitive path from the patient's body to some grounded object, because that path might be established accidentally or through instrumentation directly connected to the patient. Other electrically conductive surfaces that might make an additional contact with the patient, or instruments that might be connected to the patient, become possible sources of electric currents that can traverse the patient's body.

Part II. Wiring and Protection

517.10 Applicability

(A) Applicability. Part II applies to patient care spaces.

(B) Not Covered. The requirements contained in Part II of Article 517 do not apply to:

(1) Business offices, corridors, waiting rooms, or similar areas in clinics, medical and dental offices, and outpatient facilities.

(2) Spaces of nursing homes and limited care facilities used exclusively for patient sleeping rooms as determined by the health care facility's governing body.

According to Article 100, a "Health Care Facility's Governing Body" is the person or persons who have the overall legal responsibility for the operation of a health care facility.

(3) Areas used exclusively for:

a. Intramuscular injections (immunizations)

b. Psychiatry and psychotherapy

c. Alternative medicine

d. Optometry

e. Pharmacy services not contiguous to health care facilities

517.12 Wiring Methods

Wiring methods must comply with the Chapter 1 through 4 provisions except as modified in this article.

517.13 Equipment Grounding Conductor for Receptacles and Fixed Electrical Equipment in Patient Care Spaces

Wiring serving patient care spaces, including homeruns, must comply with the requirements of 517.13(A) and (B):

According to Article 100, a "Patient Care Space Category" is any space of a health care facility where patients are intended to be examined or treated. ▸Figure 517-7

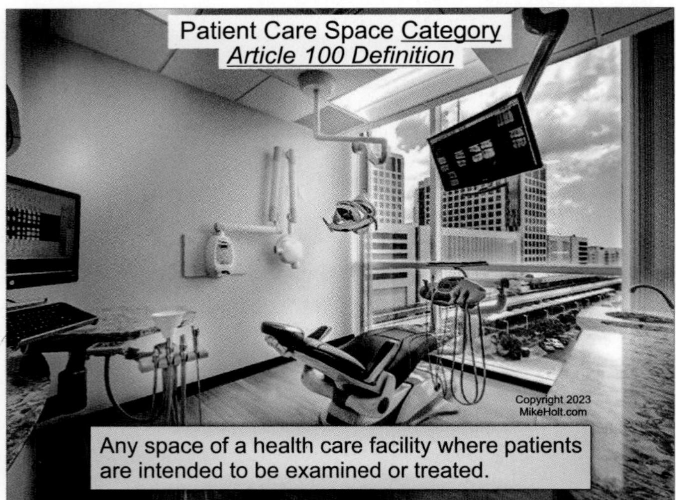

▸Figure 517-7

Note 2: Business offices, corridors, lounges, day rooms, dining rooms, or similar areas are not classified as patient care spaces.

Ex: Luminaires and switches outside the patient care vicinity must be installed in a 517.13(A) or (B) wiring method. ▸Figure 517-8

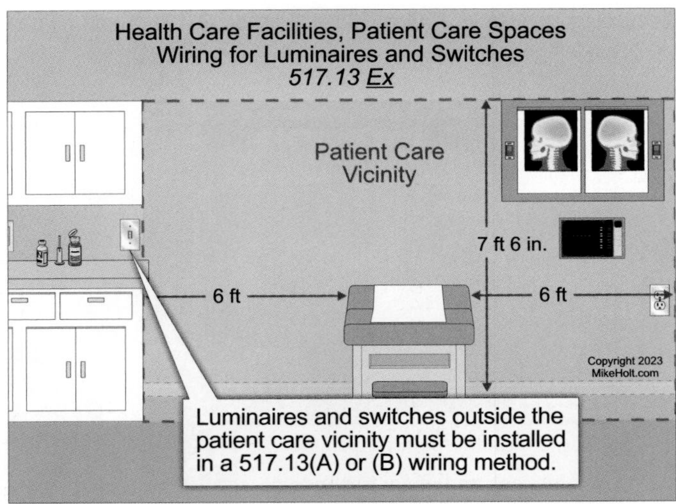

▸Figure 517-8

According to Article 100, a "Patient Care Vicinity" is a space extending vertically to 7 ft 6 in. above the floor and 6 ft horizontally beyond the patient bed, chair, table, treadmill, or other device that supports the patient during examination and treatment. ▸Figure 517-9

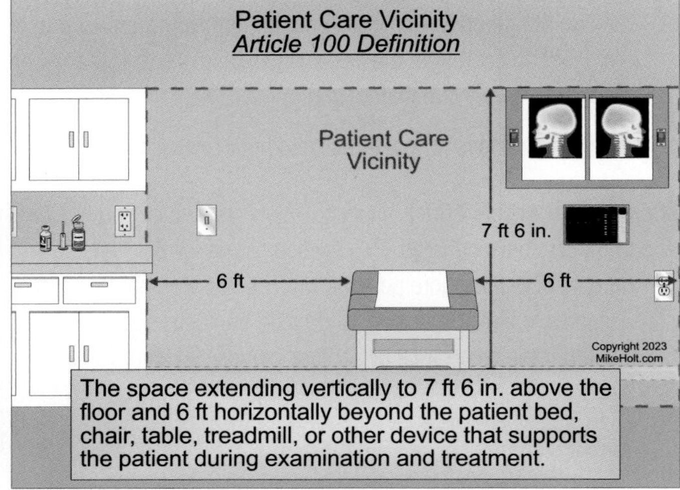

▸Figure 517-9

(A) Wiring Methods—Equipment Grounding Conductor. Branch-circuits serving patient care spaces must be in a metal raceway or metal cable having an armor or sheath that is suitable as an equipment grounding conductor in accordance with 250.118(A). ▸Figure 517-10

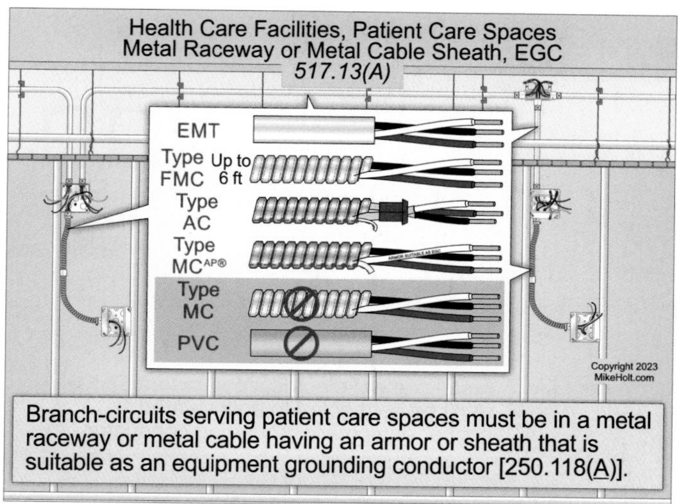

▸Figure 517–10

Author's Comment:

- The metal sheath of traditional Type MC interlocked cable does not qualify as an equipment grounding conductor [250.118(A)(10)(a)]. Therefore, this wiring method cannot be used for circuits in patient care spaces. ▸**Figure 517–11**

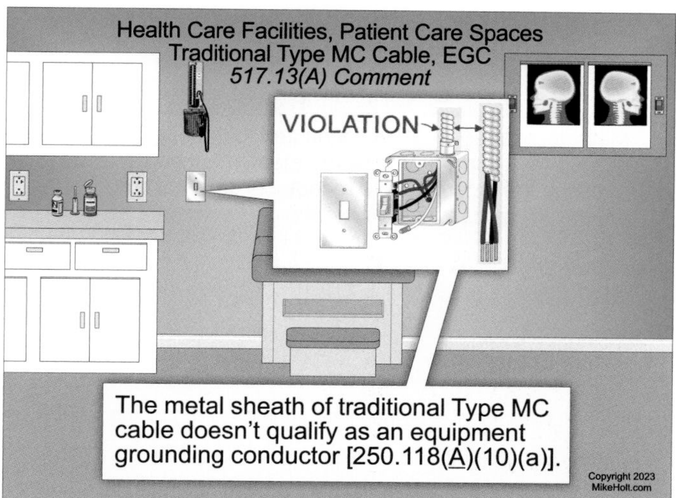

▸Figure 517–11

- The metal armor of Type AC cable qualifies as an equipment grounding conductor [250.118(A)(8)] because it contains an internal bonding strip that is in direct contact with the metal armor of the interlock cable. ▸**Figure 517–12**

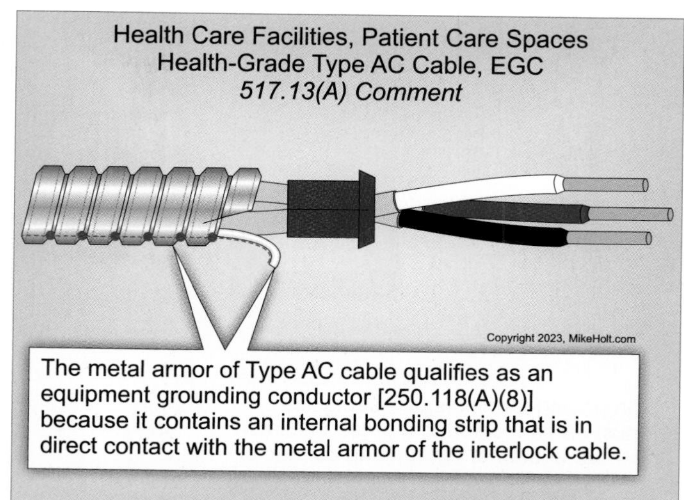

▸Figure 517–12

- The metal sheath of all-purpose Type MC^{AP} cable qualifies as an equipment grounding conductor [250.118(A)(10)(b)] because it contains an internal bonding/grounding conductor that is in direct contact with the metal sheath of the interlock cable. ▸**Figure 517–13**

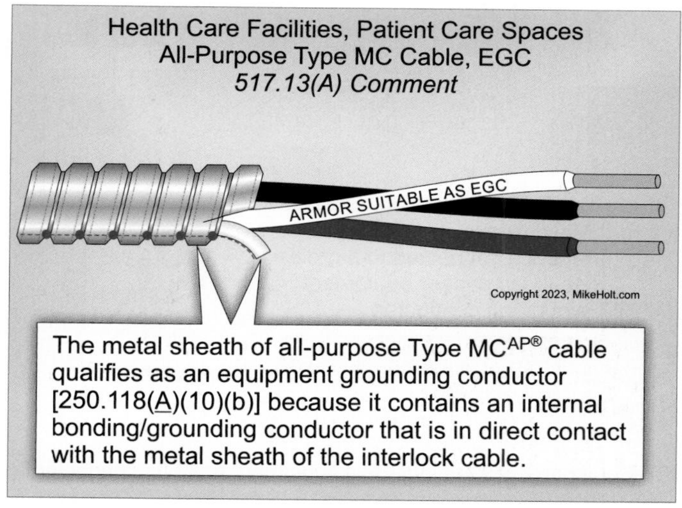

▸Figure 517–13

(B) Wire-Type Equipment Grounding Conductor.

(1) General. An insulated copper equipment grounding conductor with green insulation along its entire length, installed within a suitable wiring method as required in 517.13(A), must be connected to the following:

(1) Grounding terminals of receptacles, other than isolated ground receptacles, must be connected to a green insulated copper equipment grounding conductor. ▸**Figure 517–14**

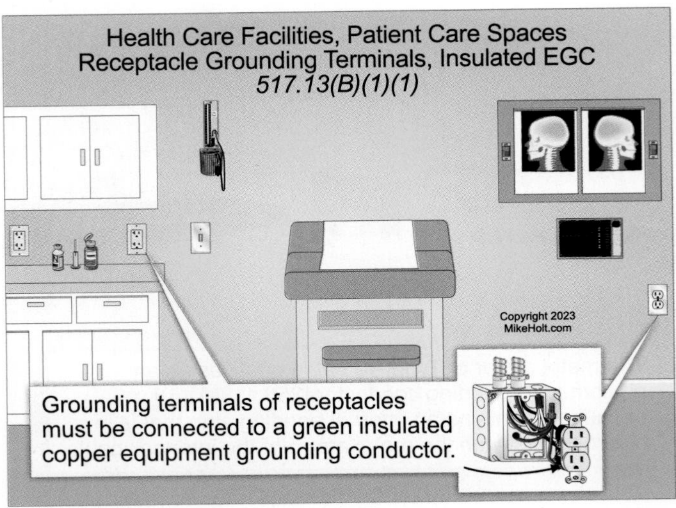

▶Figure 517–14

(2) Metal boxes and enclosures must be connected to a green insulated copper equipment grounding conductor. ▶Figure 517–15

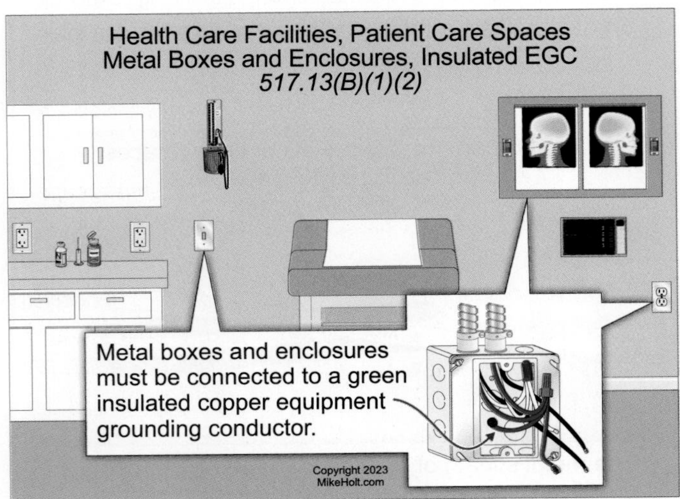

▶Figure 517–15

(3) Metal parts of fixed electrical equipment must be connected to an insulated copper equipment grounding conductor. ▶Figure 517–16

Ex 2: Metal faceplates must be connected to the effective ground-fault current path by the metal mounting screw(s) securing the faceplate to a receptacle or metal box. ▶Figure 517–17

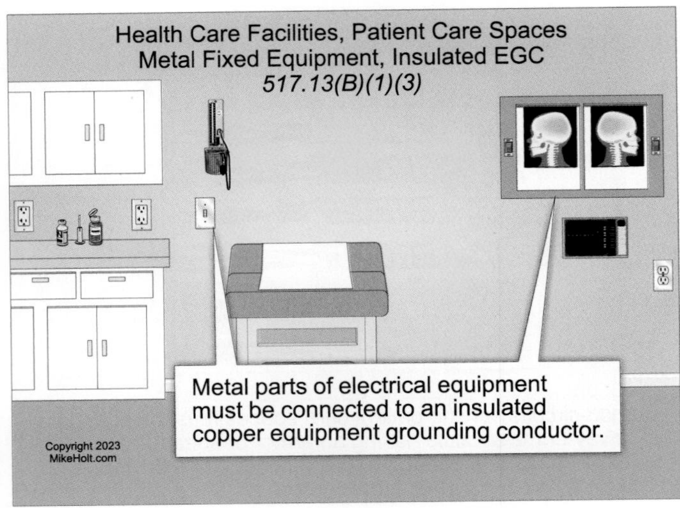

▶Figure 517–16

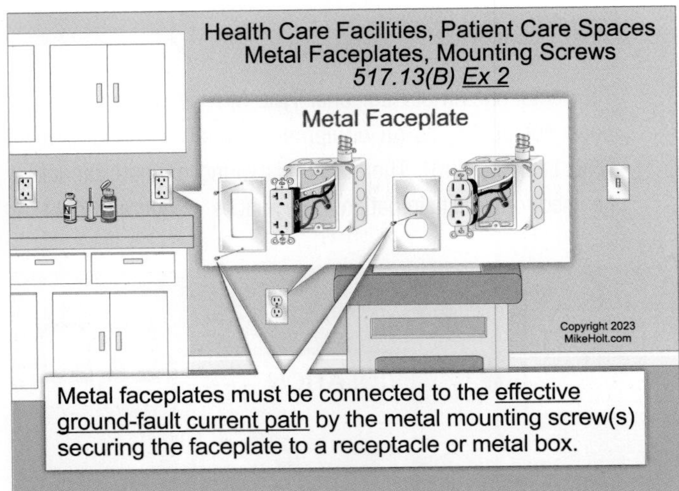

▶Figure 517–17

Author's Comment:

- Often referred to as redundancy, equipment grounding requirements in patient care spaces are based on the concept of two different types of equipment grounding conductors so if there is an installation error, the effective ground-fault current paths are not lost. One effective ground-fault current path is "mechanical" (the wiring method) and the other is of the "wire type." Section 517.13(A) requires the wiring method to be a metal raceway or metal cable that qualifies as an equipment grounding conductor in accordance with 250.118(A)(8) and (10)(b), and Section 517.13(B) requires an insulated copper equipment grounding conductor of the wire type in accordance with 250.118(A)(1).

(2) Sizing. Equipment grounding conductors and equipment bonding jumpers must be sized in accordance with 250.122.

517.16 Isolated Ground Receptacles

(A) Inside Patient Care Vicinity. An isolated ground receptacle must not be installed within a patient care vicinity. ▸Figure 517–18

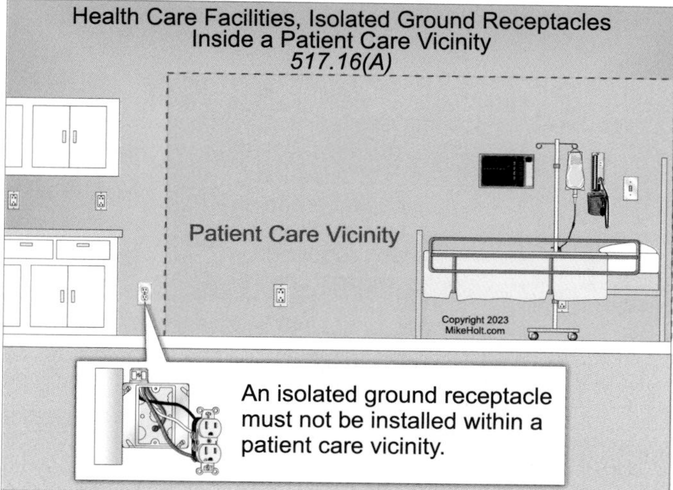

▸Figure 517–18

(B) Outside Patient Care Vicinity. Isolated ground receptacle(s) within the patient care space but outside the patient care vicinity must comply with the following:

(1) The equipment grounding terminal of isolated grounding receptacles must be connected to an insulated equipment grounding conductor in accordance with 250.146(D) and installed in a wiring method described in 517.13(A). The equipment grounding conductor connected to the equipment grounding terminals of the isolated grounding receptacle must have green insulation with one or more yellow stripes along its entire length. ▸Figure 517–19

(2) The insulated equipment grounding conductor required by 517.13(B)(1) must be connected to the metal enclosure containing the isolated ground receptacle in accordance with 517.13(B)(1)(2).

Note 2: Care should be taken in specifying a system containing isolated ground receptacles because the impedance of the effective ground-fault current path is dependent on the equipment grounding conductor(s) and does not benefit from any conduit or building structure in parallel with the equipment grounding conductor.

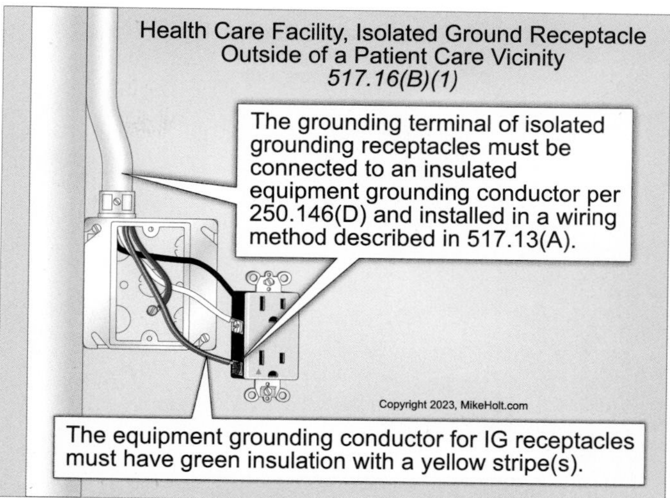

▸Figure 517–19

Author's Comment:

- Use of an isolated equipment grounding conductor does not relieve the requirement for connecting the raceway system and outlet box to an equipment grounding conductor to establish a low-impedance fault current path back to the supply source.
- The equipment grounding conductor of isolated ground receptacles does not provide the benefits of the multiple equipment grounding paths required in 517.13. For that reason, isolated ground receptacles cannot be installed in a patient care vicinity but are allowed in a patient care space where the installation complies with 517.13(A) and (B), if the isolated equipment grounding conductor is identified by green insulation with one or more yellow stripes.

517.18 Category 2 Spaces

(B) Patient Bed Location Receptacles.

According to Article 100, a "Patient Bed Location" is the location of an inpatient sleeping bed. ▸Figure 517–20

(1) Minimum Number. Each patient bed location of a Category 2 space must be provided with a minimum of eight listed and identified hospital grade receptacles. ▸Figure 517–21

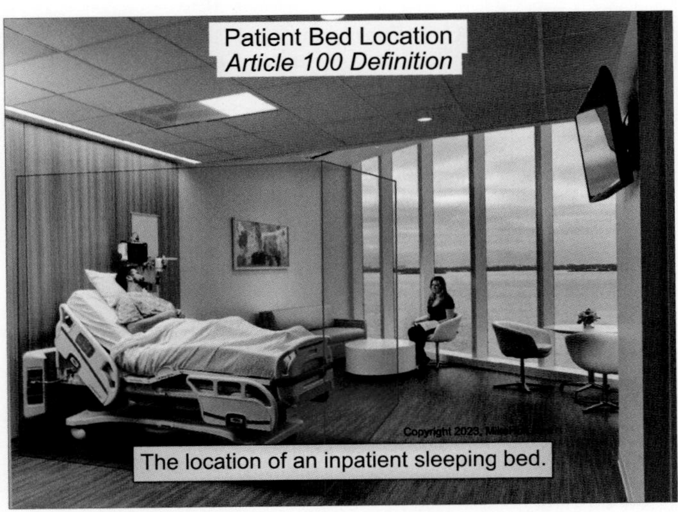

Patient Bed Location
Article 100 Definition
The location of an inpatient sleeping bed.

▶Figure 517–20

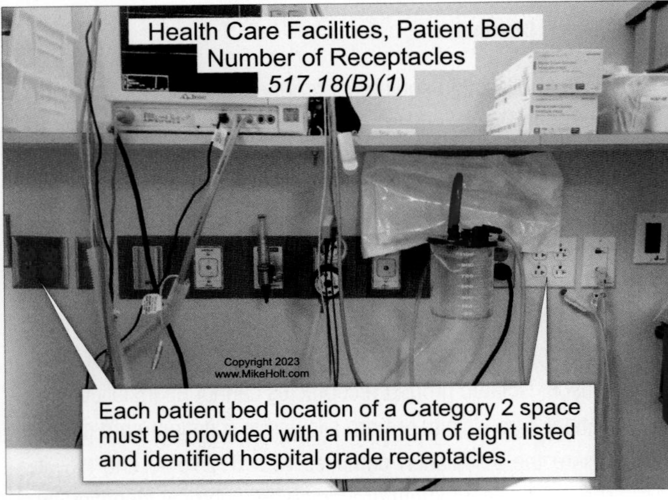

▶Figure 517–21

According to Article 100, "Category 2 Spaces" include, but are not limited to, inpatient bedrooms, dialysis rooms, in vitro fertilization rooms, procedural rooms, and similar rooms.

Author's Comment:

- Hospital grade receptacles are not required in treatment rooms of clinics, medical or dental offices, or outpatient facilities. ▶**Figure 517–22**

▶Figure 517–22

ASSEMBLY OCCUPANCIES

Introduction to Article 518—Assembly Occupancies

This article covers electrical wiring in occupancies commonly called a "Place of Assembly." These are buildings or portions of buildings specifically designed or intended for the assembly of 100 or more people. Many of these rules are outside of the scope of this material, however, some of the topics we cover include the following:

- General Classifications
- Temporary Wiring
- Wiring Methods
- Illumination

A very helpful list can be found in 518.2(A) that identifies many of the types of occupancies these rules apply to.

518.1 Scope

This article covers all buildings or portions of buildings or structures designed or intended for the gathering together of 100 or more persons for purposes such as deliberation, worship, entertainment, eating, drinking, amusement, awaiting transportation, or similar purposes, except for assembly occupancies covered by 520.1. ▶Figure 518–1

Author's Comment:

- Occupancy capacity is determined in accordance with NFPA 101, *Life Safety Code*, or by the applicable building code.

▶Figure 518–1

518.2 General Classifications

(A) Examples. Assembly occupancies include, but are not limited to:

(2) Assembly halls

(3) Auditoriums

(1) Armories

(4) Bowling lanes

(5) Casinos and gaming facilities

(6) Club rooms

(7) Conference rooms

(8) Courtrooms

(9) Dance halls

(10) Dining facilities

(11) Exhibition halls

(12) Gymnasiums

(13) Mortuary chapels

(14) Multipurpose rooms

(15) Museums

(16) Places awaiting transportation

(17) Places of religious worship

(18) Pool rooms

(19) Restaurants

(20) Skating rinks

(B) Multiple Occupancies. Article 518 only applies to that portion(s) of any building with an assembly occupancy of 100 or more persons. ▸Figure 518–2

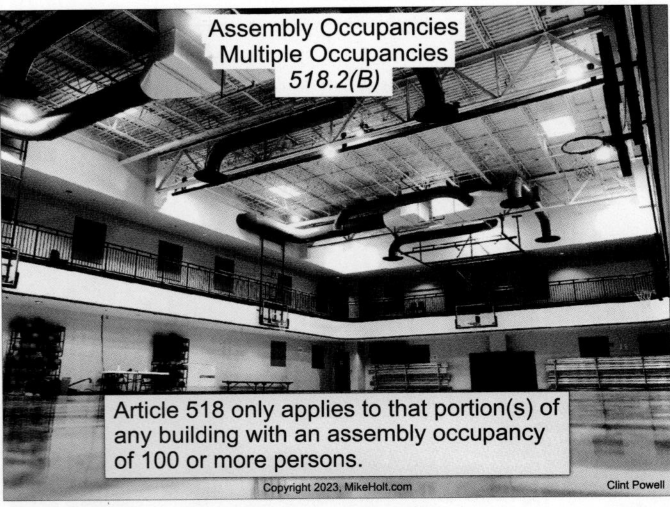

▸Figure 518–2

518.3 Temporary Wiring

Wiring for display booths in exhibit halls can be installed in accordance with Article 590. Approved flexible hard or extra-hard usage cords can be laid on the floor where protected from contact by the public. ▸Figure 518–3

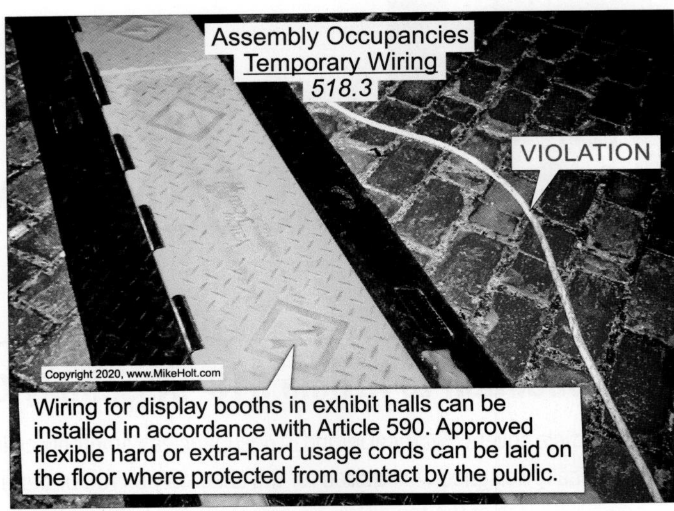

▸Figure 518–3

GFCI protection must be provided in accordance with 210.8(B) for receptacles where required by this *Code*, except for the temporary wiring requirements of 590.6.

Where GFCI protection is by plug-and-cord-connection, the GFCI-protective device must provide a level of protection equivalent to a portable GFCI, whether assembled in the field or at the factory.

518.4 Wiring Methods

(A) General. The wiring methods permitted in places of assembly are limited to the following: ▸Figure 518–4

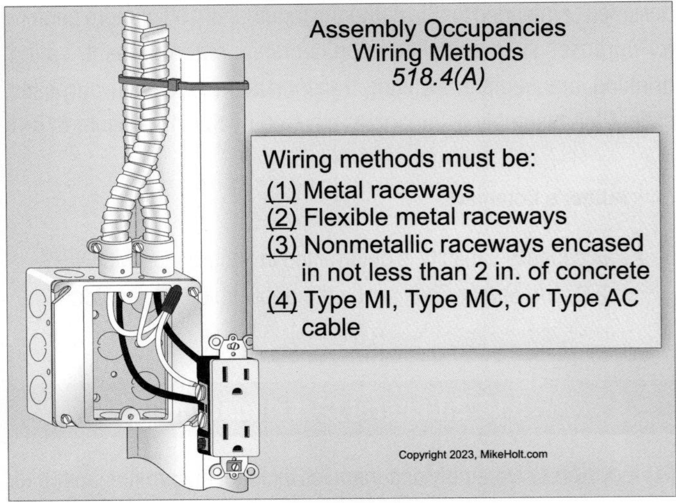

▸Figure 518–4

(1) Metal raceways

(2) Flexible metal raceways

1st Printing

(3) Nonmetallic raceways encased in not less than 2 in. of concrete

(4) Type MI, Type MC, or Type AC cable

(B) Sound Systems, Class 2 Cables, and Coaxial Cables. The following wiring methods are permitted in a place of assembly:

(1) Sound Systems in accordance with 640.9.

(2) Coaxial Cables in accordance with Article 800.

(3) Class 2 Cables in accordance with Article 725, Part III.

(C) Spaces of Nonrated Construction. In addition to the permitted 518.4(A) wiring methods, Type NM cable, electrical nonmetallic tubing, and PVC conduit can be installed in those portions of an assembly occupancy building that are not required to be of fire-rated construction.

Note: Fire-rated construction is the fire-resistive classification used in building codes.

(D) Spaces with Finish Ratings. ENT and PVC can be installed in club rooms, conference and meeting rooms in hotels or motels, courtrooms, dining facilities, restaurants, mortuary chapels, museums, libraries, and places of religious worship where:

(1) Installed concealed within walls, floors, and ceilings that provide a thermal barrier with not less than a 15-minute finish rating. ▸**Figure 518–5**

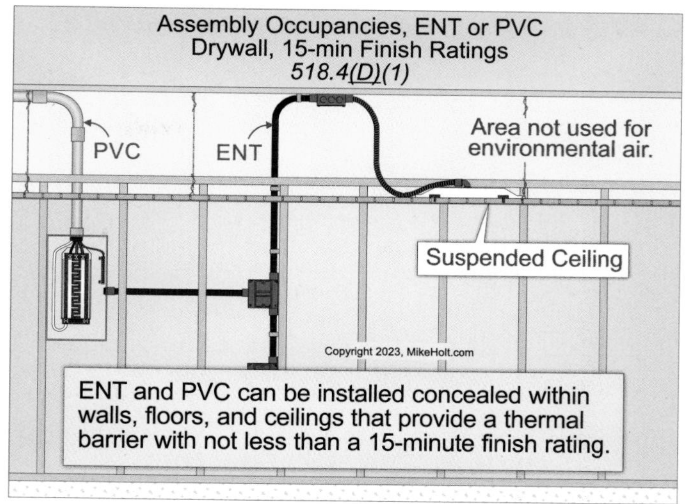
Assembly Occupancies, ENT or PVC
Drywall, 15-min Finish Ratings
518.4(D)(1)
PVC
ENT
Area not used for environmental air.
Suspended Ceiling
Copyright 2023, MikeHolt.com
ENT and PVC can be installed concealed within walls, floors, and ceilings that provide a thermal barrier with not less than a 15-minute finish rating.

▸**Figure 518–5**

(2) Installed above nonplenum [300.22(C)] suspended ceilings where the suspended ceilings provide a thermal barrier with not less than a 15-minute finish rating.

518.6 Illumination

Illumination must be provided for all working spaces about fixed service equipment, switchboards, switchgear, panelboards, or motor control centers installed outdoors that serve assembly occupancies. Control by automatic means only is not permitted. Additional lighting outlets are not required where the workspace is illuminated by an adjacent light source. See 110.26(D).

Notes |

ARTICLE 525 CARNIVALS, CIRCUSES, FAIRS, AND SIMILAR EVENTS

Introduction to Article 525—Carnivals, Circuses, Fairs, and Similar Events

This article covers the installation of portable wiring and equipment for temporary wiring for carnivals, circuses, exhibitions, fairs, traveling attractions, and similar functions, including wiring in or on structures. Many of these rules are outside of the scope of this material, however, some of the topics we cover include the following:

- Scope
- Overhead Conductor Clearances
- Wiring Methods
- Grounding and Bonding

Part I. General

525.1 Scope

Article 525 covers the installation of portable wiring and equipment for carnivals, circuses, exhibitions, fairs, traveling attractions, and similar functions. ▸Figure 525–1

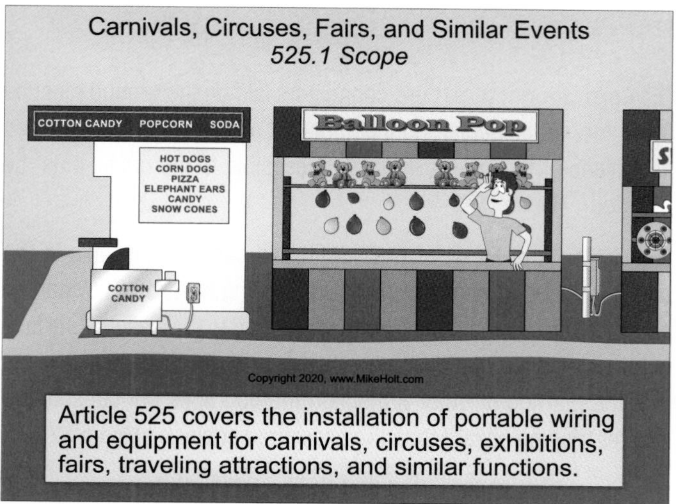

▸Figure 525–1

525.5 Overhead Conductor Clearances

(A) Vertical Clearances. Overhead conductors installed outside tents and concession areas must have a vertical clearance to ground in accordance with 225.18. ▸Figure 525–2

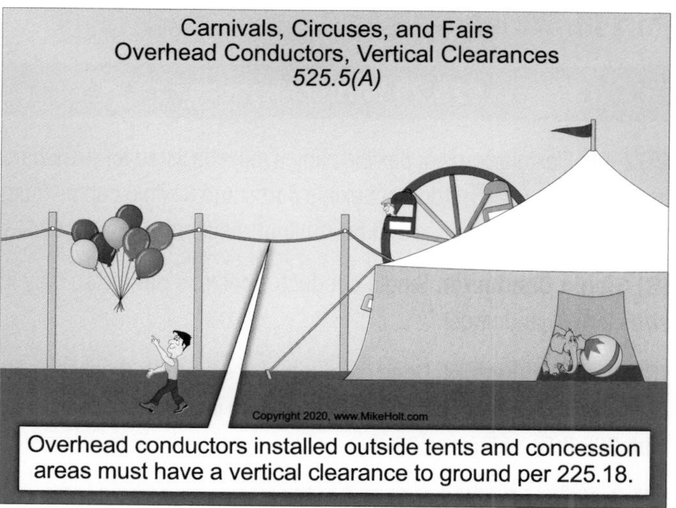

▸Figure 525–2

Author's Comment:

- Section 225.18 includes the following requirements:
  - 10 ft above finished grade, sidewalks, platforms, or projections from which they might be accessible to pedestrians for 120V, 120/208V, 120/240V, or 240V circuits [225.18(1)].
  - 12 ft above residential property and driveways, and those commercial areas not subject to truck traffic for 120V, 120/208V, 120/240V, 240V, 277V, 277/480V, or 480V circuits [225.18(2)].
  - 18 ft over public streets, alleys, roads, parking areas subject to truck traffic, driveways on other than residential property, and other areas traversed by vehicles (such as those used for cultivation, grazing, forestry, and orchards) [225.18(4)].

(B) Clearance to Portable Structures.

(1) Overhead conductors, except for the conductors that supply the amusement ride or attractions, must have a clearance of 15 ft from portable amusement structures.

525.6 Protection of Electrical Equipment

Electrical equipment and wiring for portable structures must be provided with mechanical protection where subject to physical damage.

Part III. Wiring Methods

525.20 Wiring Methods

(A) Type. Flexible cords or flexible cables must be listed for extra-hard usage. Where used outdoors, flexible cords and flexible cables must be listed for wet locations and be sunlight resistant. ▸Figure 525–3

▸Figure 525–3

(B) Single Conductor. Single-conductor cable is permitted only in sizes 2 AWG and larger.

(C) Open Conductors. Open conductors are permitted only as part of a listed assembly or part of festoon lighting installed in accordance with 225.6(B). ▸Figure 525–4

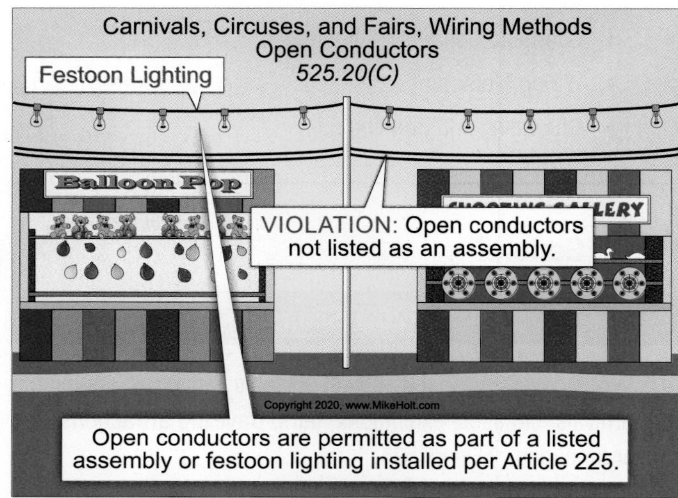

Carnivals, Circuses, and Fairs, Wiring Methods Open Conductors
525.20(C)
Festoon Lighting
Balloon Pop
VIOLATION: Open conductors not listed as an assembly.
Copyright 2020, www.MikeHolt.com
Open conductors are permitted as part of a listed assembly or festoon lighting installed per Article 225.

▸Figure 525–4

(D) Splices. Flexible cords or flexible cables must be continuous without splice or tap between boxes or fittings.

(E) Cord Connectors. Cord connectors laid on the ground must be listed for wet locations. Connectors and cable connections placed in audience traffic paths or areas accessible to the public must be guarded. ▸Figure 525–5

(G) Protection. Flexible cords or flexible cables accessible to the public must be arranged to minimize tripping hazards. They can be covered with nonconductive matting secured to the walkway surface or protected with another approved cable protection method, provided that the matting or other protection method does not constitute a greater tripping hazard than the uncovered cables. ▸Figure 525–6

Burying cables is permitted and the burial depth requirements of 300.5 do not apply.

1st Printing

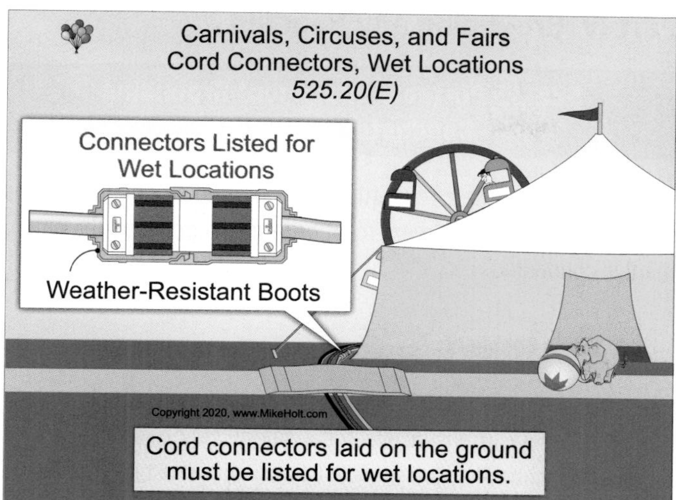

Carnivals, Circuses, and Fairs
Cord Connectors, Wet Locations
525.20(E)
Connectors Listed for Wet Locations
Weather-Resistant Boots
Copyright 2020, www.MikeHolt.com
Cord connectors laid on the ground must be listed for wet locations.

▶Figure 525–5

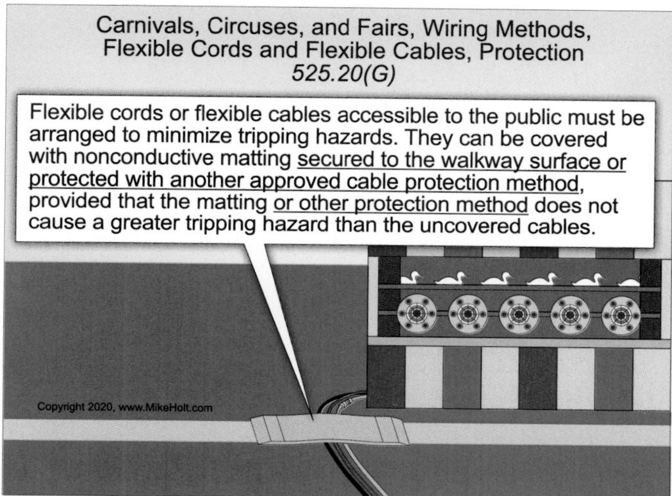

Carnivals, Circuses, and Fairs, Wiring Methods, Flexible Cords and Flexible Cables, Protection
525.20(G)
Flexible cords or flexible cables accessible to the public must be arranged to minimize tripping hazards. They can be covered with nonconductive matting secured to the walkway surface or protected with another approved cable protection method, provided that the matting or other protection method does not cause a greater tripping hazard than the uncovered cables.
Copyright 2020, www.MikeHolt.com

▶Figure 525–6

525.21 Rides, Tents, and Concessions

(A) Disconnecting Means. Each portable structure must have a disconnect that is within sight of, and within 6 ft of, the operator's station and readily accessible to the operator. If accessible to unqualified persons, the disconnect must be lockable.

According to Article 100, "Within Sight" means that it is visible and not more than 50 ft from the location of the equipment.

(B) Inside Tents and Concessions. Electrical wiring for lighting inside tents and concession areas must be securely installed. Where subject to physical damage, the wiring must be provided with mechanical protection [300.4] and lamps must be protected from accidental breakage by a suitable luminaire with a guard.

525.22 Outdoor Portable Distribution or Termination Boxes

(A) Terminal Boxes. Portable distribution and/or terminal boxes installed outdoors must be weatherproof, and the bottom of the enclosure must be not less than 6 in. above the ground.

525.23 GFCI-Protected Receptacles and Equipment

(A) GFCI Protection Required. In addition to the requirements of 210.8(B), GFCI protection must be provided for the following: ▶Figure 525–7

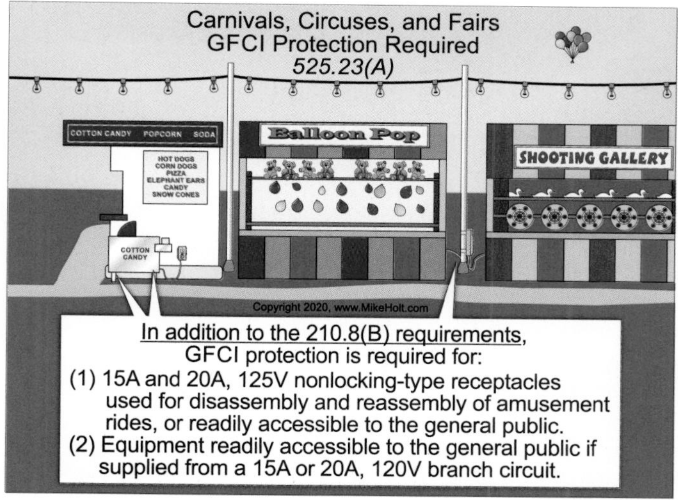

Carnivals, Circuses, and Fairs
GFCI Protection Required
525.23(A)
COTTON CANDY POPCORN SODA
HOT DOGS CORN DOGS PIZZA ELEPHANT EARS CANDY SNOW CONES
Balloon Pop
SHOOTING GALLERY
COTTON CANDY
Copyright 2020, www.MikeHolt.com
In addition to the 210.8(B) requirements, GFCI protection is required for:
(1) 15A and 20A, 125V nonlocking-type receptacles used for disassembly and reassembly of amusement rides, or readily accessible to the general public.
(2) Equipment readily accessible to the general public if supplied from a 15A or 20A, 120V branch circuit.

▶Figure 525–7

(1) 15A and 20A, 125V nonlocking-type receptacles readily accessible to the public or used for disassembly and reassembly of amusement rides and attractions.

(2) Equipment readily accessible to the general public if it is supplied from a 15A or 20A, 120V branch circuit.

GFCI protection can be integral with the attachment plug in the power-supply cord within 12 in. of the attachment plug, or a listed cord set incorporating GFCI protection.

(B) GFCI Protection Not Required. GFCI protection is not required for locking-type receptacles not accessible from grade level.

(C) GFCI Protection Not Permitted. GFCI protection is not permitted for egress lighting.

Author's Comment:

- The purpose of not permitting egress lighting to be GFCI protected is to ensure exit lighting remains energized and stays illuminated.

Part IV. Grounding and Bonding

525.32 Portable Equipment Grounding Conductor Continuity

The continuity of the circuit equipment grounding conductors for portable electrical equipment must be verified each time the equipment is connected.

Author's Comment:

- Verification of circuit equipment grounding conductors is necessary to ensure electrical safety. This rule does not specify how they are verified, what circuits must be verified, how the verification is recorded, or who is required or qualified to perform the verification.

1st Printing

AGRICULTURAL BUILDINGS

Introduction to Article 547—Agricultural Buildings

This article covers buildings, parts of a buildings, or buildings adjacent to areas with accumulations of excessive dust, dust with water, or a corrosive environment. These areas may include poultry, livestock, and fish confinement areas where litter or feed dust may accumulate or where animal excrement may cause corrosive conditions. It also covers areas where livestock with low tolerances to small voltage differences require an equipotential plane. Many of these rules are outside of the scope of this material, however, some of the topics we cover include the following:

- Scope
- Wiring Methods
- Equipment Enclosures, Boxes, Conduit Bodies, and Fittings
- GFCI Protection
- Equipotential Planes

Article 547 consists of three parts:

- Part I. General
- Part II. Installations
- Part III. Distribution

Part I. General

547.1 Scope

Article 547 applies to buildings, parts of a building, or buildings adjacent to areas specified in (A) or (B): ▶Figure 547-1

(A) Excessive Dust and Dust with Water. Buildings or areas where excessive dust and/or dust with water may accumulate such as areas of poultry, livestock, and fish confinement systems where litter or feed dust may accumulate.

▶Figure 547-1

(B) Corrosive Atmosphere. Buildings or areas where a corrosive atmosphere exists, and where the presence of the following conditions exist:

(1) Poultry and animal excrement

(2) Corrosive particles that may combine with water

(3) Areas made damp or wet by periodic washing

Part II. Installations

547.20 Wiring Methods

(A) Wiring Methods. Wiring methods in agricultural buildings are limited to the following: ▸Figure 547–2

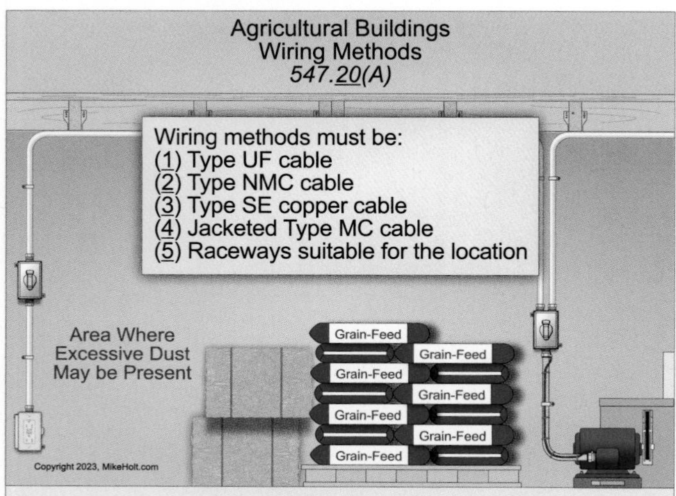

▸Figure 547–2

(1) Type UF cable

(2) Type NMC cable

(3) Type SE copper cable

(4) Jacketed Type MC cable

(5) Raceways suitable for the locations identified in 547.1(A) and (B)

547.22 Equipment Enclosures, Boxes, Conduit Bodies, and Fittings

Equipment enclosures, boxes, conduit bodies, and fittings in areas of agricultural buildings where excessive dust could be present must be designed to minimize the entrance of dust. They must have no openings through which dust can enter the enclosure. ▸Figure 547–3

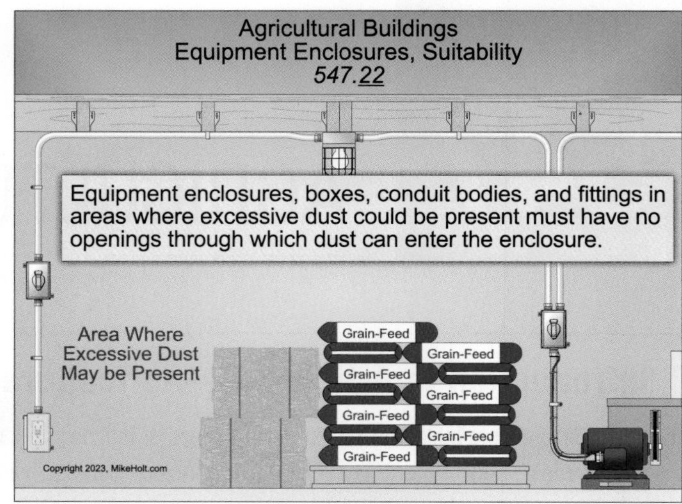

▸Figure 547–3

Author's Comment:

- Weatherproof boxes and covers can be used to meet this requirement.

547.23 Damp or Wet Locations

In damp or wet locations of agricultural buildings, equipment enclosures, boxes, conduit bodies, and fittings must prevent moisture from entering or accumulating within. Boxes, conduit bodies, and fittings must be listed for use in wet locations and enclosures must be weatherproof.

547.24 Corrosive Atmosphere

Where wet dust, excessive moisture, corrosive gases or vapors, or other corrosive conditions could be present in an agricultural building, equipment enclosures, boxes, conduit bodies, and fittings must have corrosion-resistant properties suitable for the conditions.

Note 1: See Table 110.28 for enclosures appropriate for the location.

547.25 Flexible Connections

Where necessary for flexible connections, the following wiring methods are permitted:

(1) Dusttight flexible connectors

(2) Liquidtight flexible metal conduit

(3) Liquidtight flexible nonmetallic conduit

(4) Flexible cord listed for hard usage terminated with listed dust-tight cord connectors

547.26 Physical Protection

Electrical wiring and equipment must be protected where subject to physical damage.

Nonmetallic cables cannot be installed concealed within walls and above ceilings of buildings which are contiguous with or physically adjoined to, livestock confinement areas. ▶Figure 547–4

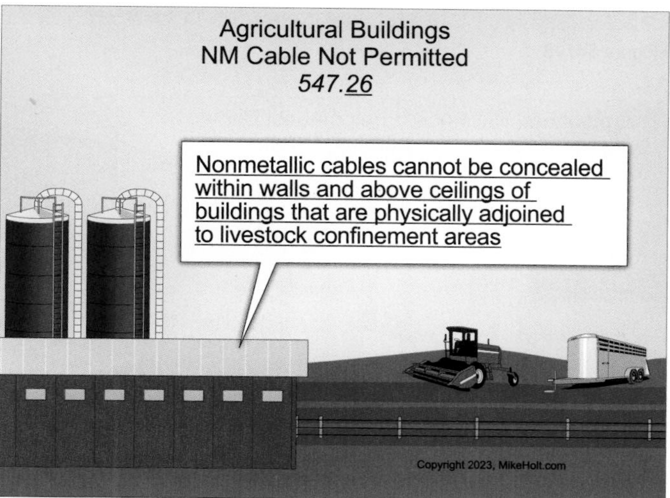
Agricultural Buildings
NM Cable Not Permitted
547.26
Nonmetallic cables cannot be concealed within walls and above ceilings of buildings that are physically adjoined to livestock confinement areas
Copyright 2023, MikeHolt.com

▶Figure 547–4

Note: Rodents often damage nonmetallic cable and conductor insulation within the walls and ceilings of livestock containment areas.

547.27 Equipment Grounding Conductor

Where the equipment grounding conductor is not part of a listed cable assembly, it must be insulated when installed underground. ▶Figure 547–5

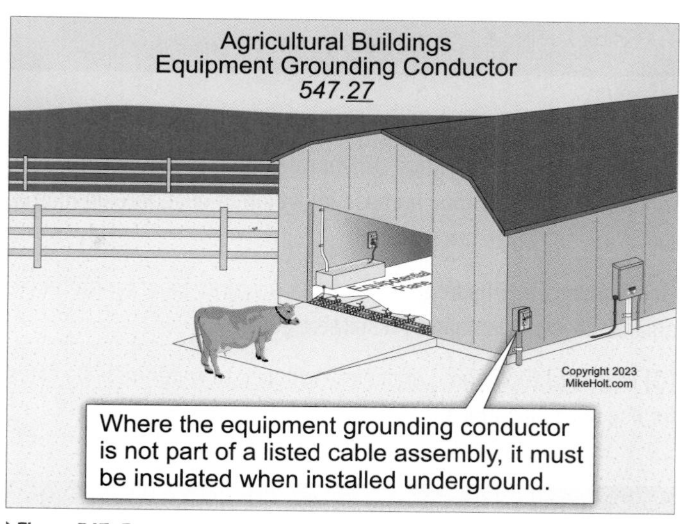
Agricultural Buildings
Equipment Grounding Conductor
547.27
Copyright 2023
MikeHolt.com
Where the equipment grounding conductor is not part of a listed cable assembly, it must be insulated when installed underground.

▶Figure 547–5

547.28 GFCI Protection of Receptacles

GFCI protection is required in accordance with 210.8(B) for 15A and 20A, 125V receptacles, but is not required for receptacles rated 30A or more installed within the following areas: ▶Figure 547–6

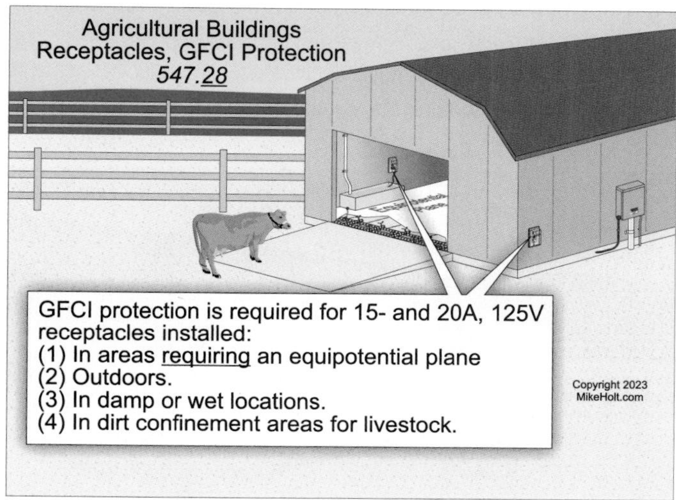
Agricultural Buildings
Receptacles, GFCI Protection
547.28
GFCI protection is required for 15- and 20A, 125V receptacles installed:
(1) In areas requiring an equipotential plane
(2) Outdoors.
(3) In damp or wet locations.
(4) In dirt confinement areas for livestock.
Copyright 2023
MikeHolt.com

▶Figure 547–6

(1) Those requiring an equipotential plane in accordance with 547.44(A)

(2) Outdoors

(3) In damp or wet locations

(4) In dirt confinement areas for livestock

Author's Comment:

- See 210.8(B)(8) for GFCI protection of 250V, 30A and 50A receptacles installed in accessory buildings in adjacent agricultural areas used for storage or maintenance of farm equipment and supplies.

547.31 Luminaires

Luminaires must comply with the following:

(A) Minimize the Entrance of Dust. Luminaires must be installed to minimize the entrance and accumulation of dust, foreign matter, moisture, and corrosive material.

(B) Exposed to Physical Damage. Luminaires must be protected against physical damage by a suitable guard.

(C) Exposed to Water. Luminaires exposed to water must be listed for use in wet locations.

547.44 Equipotential Planes

(A) Where Required. Equipotential planes must be installed as follows:

According to Article 100, a "Equipotential Plane" is conductive elements connected together to minimize voltage differences. ▸Figure 547–7

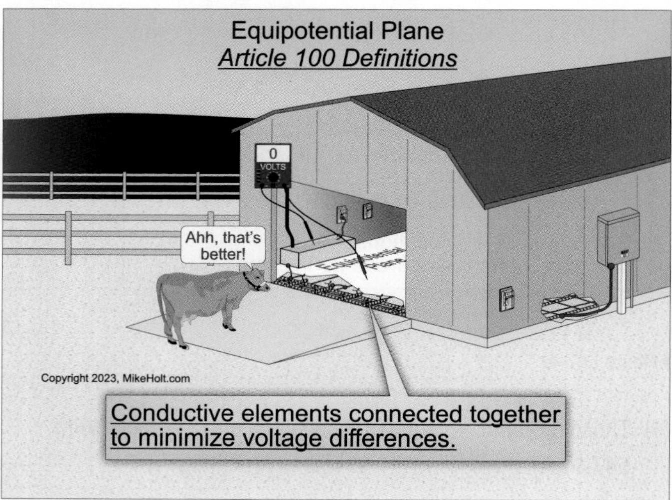

▸Figure 547–7

(1) Indoor Concrete Livestock Confinement Areas. An equipotential plane must be installed in indoor concrete floors where metal electrical equipment is accessible to livestock. ▸Figure 547–8

(2) Outdoor Concrete Livestock Confinement Areas. An equipotential plane must be installed in outdoor concrete slabs where metal electrical equipment is accessible to livestock. ▸Figure 547–9

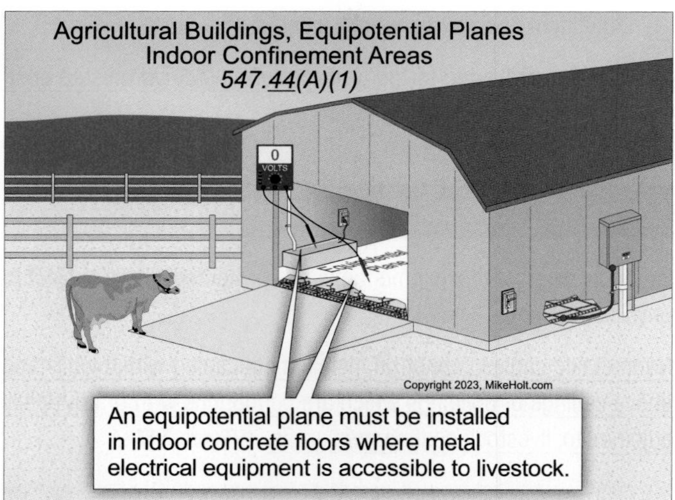

▸Figure 547–8

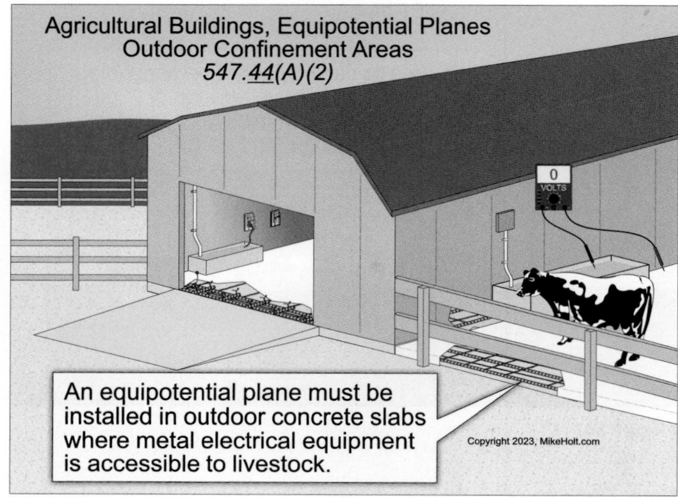

▸Figure 547–9

(B) Bonding. The equipotential plane must be bonded to the grounding electrode system or an equipment grounding terminal in any panelboard of the building's electrical grounding system associated with the equipotential plane by using a solid copper conductor not smaller than 8 AWG. ▸Figure 547–10

Note 1: ASABE Standard EP473.2, *Equipotential Planes in Animal Containment Areas*, provides the recommendation of a voltage gradient ramp at the entrances of agricultural buildings.

Note 2: See the American Society of Agricultural and Biological Engineers (ASABE) EP342.2, *Safety for Electrically Heated Livestock Waterers.*

1st Printing

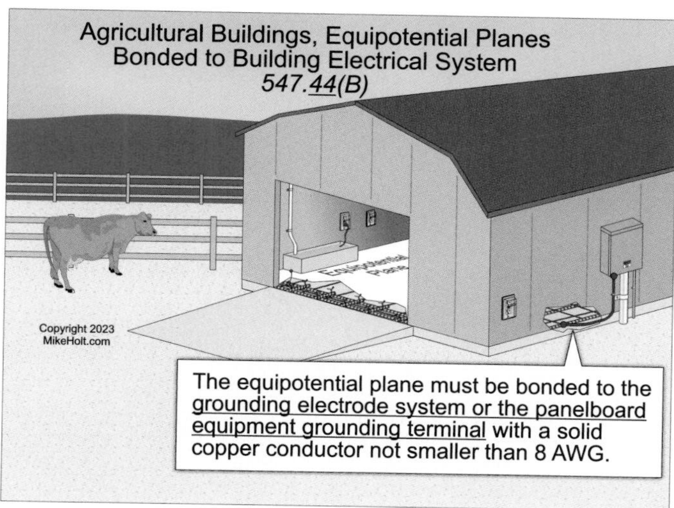
Agricultural Buildings, Equipotential Planes
Bonded to Building Electrical System
547.44(B)
Copyright 2023
MikeHolt.com
The equipotential plane must be bonded to the grounding electrode system or the panelboard equipment grounding terminal with a solid copper conductor not smaller than 8 AWG.

▶Figure 547–10

Author's Comment:

- The bonding requirements contained in Article 547 are unique because of the sensitivity of livestock to small voltage differences, especially in wet or damp concrete animal confinement areas.
- In most instances the voltage difference between metal parts and the Earth will be too low to present a shock hazard to people. However, livestock might detect the voltage difference if they come into contact with the metal parts. Although voltage differences may not be life threatening to the livestock, it has been reported that as little as 0.50V RMS can adversely affect milk production.

1st Printing

1st Printing

ARTICLE 555 MARINAS, BOATYARDS, AND DOCKING FACILITIES

Introduction to Article 555—Marinas, Boatyards, and Docking Facilities

This article covers the installation of wiring and equipment for fixed or floating piers, wharfs, docking facilities, marinas, and boatyards. Fluctuating water levels and the hazard of electric shock drowning (ESD) require special rules to protect the users of these facilities from the hazards that arise from the use of electricity. Many of these rules are outside of the scope of this material, however, some of the topics we cover include the following:

- Scope
- Electrical Datum Plane Distances
- Electric Shock Hazard Sign
- Equipment Grounding Conductor

Article 555 consists of three parts:

- Part I. General
- Part II. Marinas, Boatyards, and Docking Facilities
- Part III. Floating Buildings (not covered)

Part I. General

555.1 Scope

Article 555 covers the installations of wiring and equipment for marinas, boatyards, and docking facilities. ▶Figure 555–1

Marinas, Boatyards, and Docking Facilities
555.1 Scope
Copyright 2023, MikeHolt.com
Article 555 covers the installations of wiring and equipment for marinas, boatyards, and docking facilities.

▶Figure 555–1

According to Article 100, the definition of a "Marina" is a facility, generally on the waterfront, which stores and services boats in berths, on moorings, and in dry storage or dry stack storage. ▶Figure 555–2

A "Boatyard" is a facility used for constructing, repairing, servicing, hauling from the water, storing (on land and in water), and launching of boats (555). ▶Figure 555–3

A "Docking Facility" is a covered or open, fixed, or floating structure that provides access to the water and to which boats are secured. ▶Figure 555–4

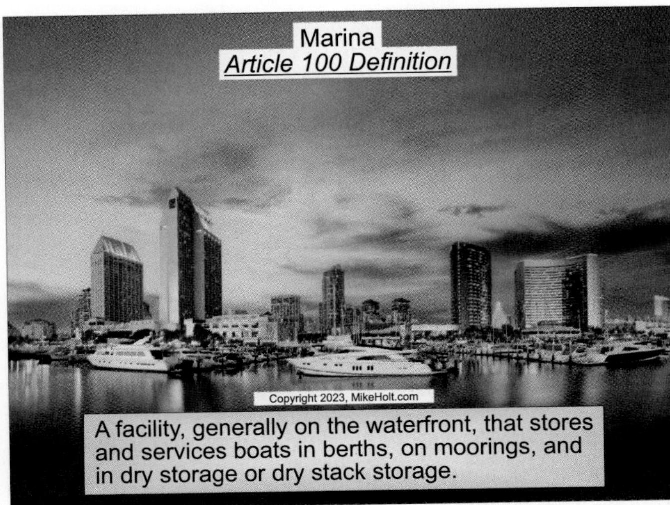
Marina
Article 100 Definition
Copyright 2023, MikeHolt.com
A facility, generally on the waterfront, that stores and services boats in berths, on moorings, and in dry storage or dry stack storage.

▸Figure 555–2

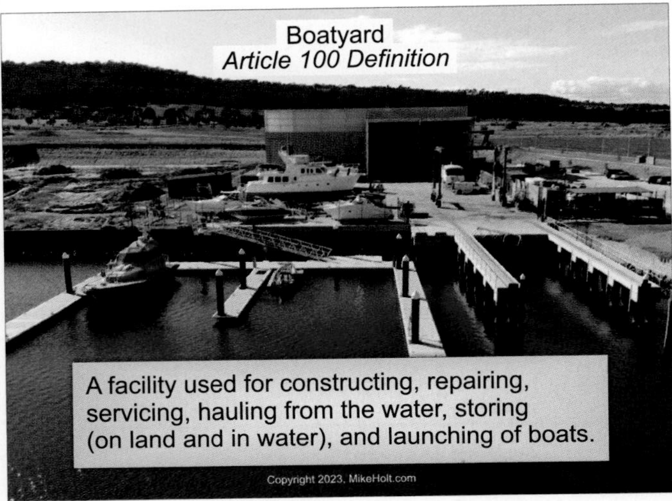
Boatyard
Article 100 Definition
A facility used for constructing, repairing, servicing, hauling from the water, storing (on land and in water), and launching of boats.
Copyright 2023, MikeHolt.com

▸Figure 555–3

Docking Facility
Article 100 Definition
Copyright 2023, MikeHolt.com
Mario Valdes
A fixed or floating structure that provides access to the water and to which boats are secured.

▸Figure 555–4

555.3 Electrical Datum Plane Distances

(A) Floating Pier. A horizontal plane 30 in. above the water level and 12 in. above the level of the deck at the floating pier. ▸**Figure 555–5**

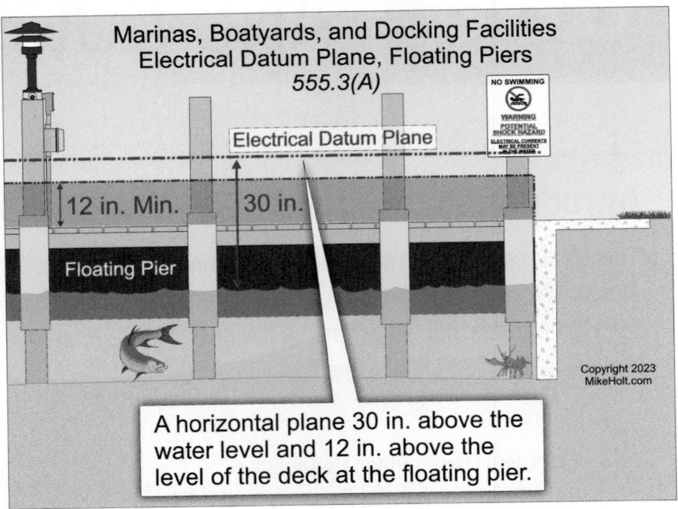
Marinas, Boatyards, and Docking Facilities
Electrical Datum Plane, Floating Piers
555.3(A)
NO SWIMMING
WARNING
POTENTIAL SHOCK HAZARD
Electrical Datum Plane
12 in. Min.
30 in.
Floating Pier
Copyright 2023 MikeHolt.com
A horizontal plane 30 in. above the water level and 12 in. above the level of the deck at the floating pier.

▸Figure 555–5

According to Article 100, a 'Pier' is a structure extending over the water on a fixed or floating structure that provides access to the water. ▸**Figure 555–6**

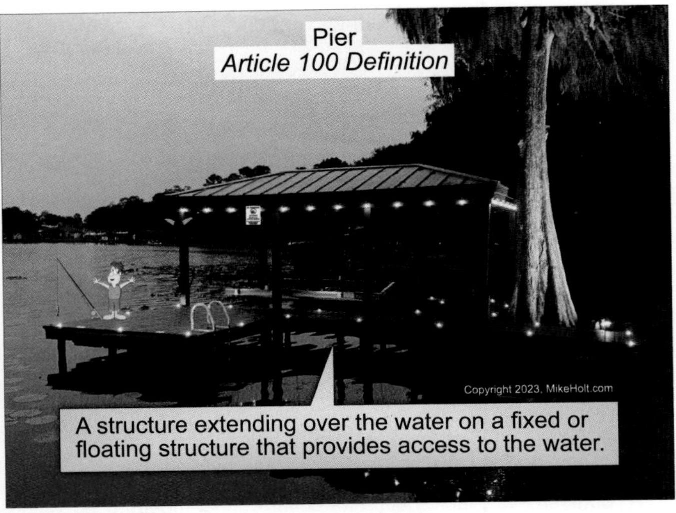
Pier
Article 100 Definition
Copyright 2023, MikeHolt.com
A structure extending over the water on a fixed or floating structure that provides access to the water.

▸Figure 555–6

555.4 Location of Service Equipment

The service equipment for a floating dock or marina must be on land <u>no closer than 5 ft horizontally from</u> the floating structure.

1st Printing

555.7 Transformers

(A) General. Transformers and enclosures must be identified for wet locations.

(B) Replacements. Transformers and enclosures must be identified for wet locations where replacements are made.

555.10 Electric Shock Hazard Sign

A permanent safety sign is required to give notice of electrical shock hazard risks to persons using or swimming near a docking facility, boatyard, or marina. The safety sign must meet all the following requirements: ▸Figure 555-7

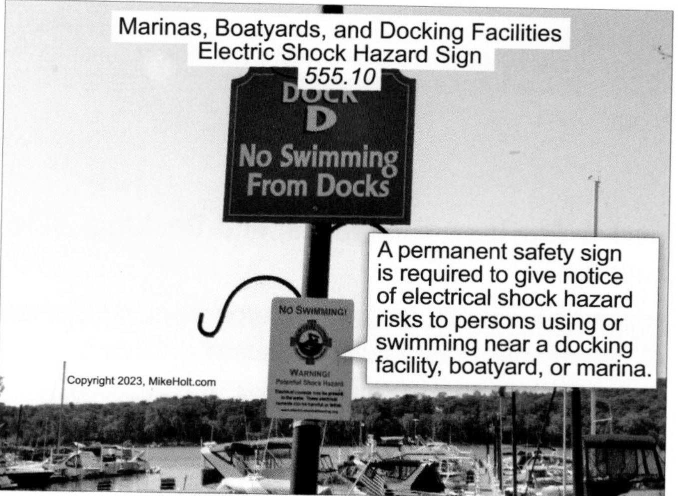
Marinas, Boatyards, and Docking Facilities
Electric Shock Hazard Sign
555.10
DOCK
D
No Swimming
From Docks
A permanent safety sign is required to give notice of electrical shock hazard risks to persons using or swimming near a docking facility, boatyard, or marina.
NO SWIMMING!
WARNING!
Copyright 2023, MikeHolt.com

▸Figure 555-7

(1) The sign must warn of the hazards using effective words, colors, or symbols (or a combination of such) in accordance with 110.21(B)(1) and be of sufficient durability to withstand the environment.

(2) The signs must be clearly visible from all approaches to a marina or boatyard facility.

(3) The signs must state:

WARNING—POTENTIAL SHOCK HAZARD—ELECTRICAL CURRENTS MAY BE PRESENT IN THE WATER.

555.11 Motor Fuel Dispensing Stations—Hazardous (Classified) Locations

Electrical wiring and equipment serving motor fuel dispensing locations must comply with Article 514. ▸Figure 555-8

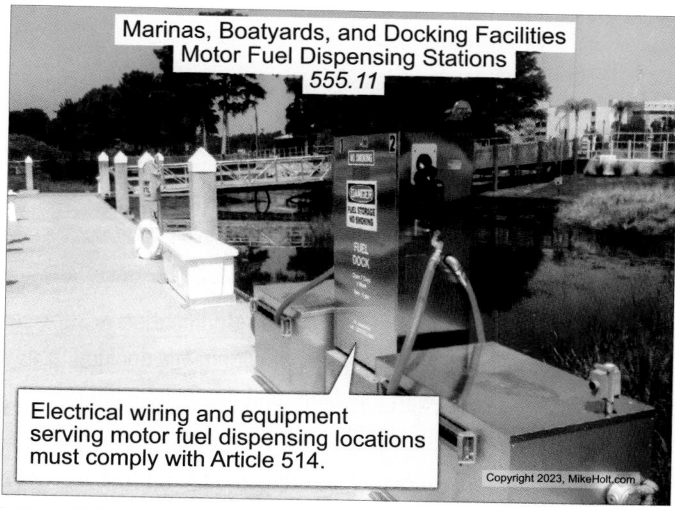
Marinas, Boatyards, and Docking Facilities
Motor Fuel Dispensing Stations
555.11
DANGER
FUEL DOCK
Electrical wiring and equipment serving motor fuel dispensing locations must comply with Article 514.
Copyright 2023, MikeHolt.com

▸Figure 555-8

555.12 Repair Facilities—Hazardous (Classified) Locations

Electrical wiring and equipment at marine craft repair facilities containing flammable or combustible liquids or gases must comply with Article 511. ▸Figure 555-9

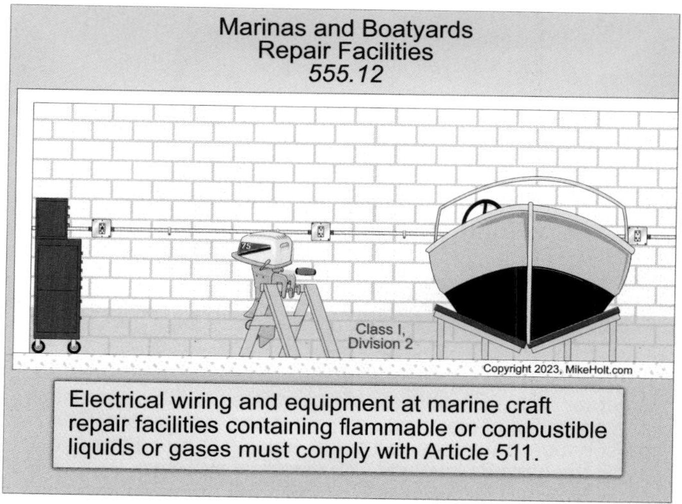
Marinas and Boatyards
Repair Facilities
555.12
Class I,
Division 2
Copyright 2023, MikeHolt.com
Electrical wiring and equipment at marine craft repair facilities containing flammable or combustible liquids or gases must comply with Article 511.

▸Figure 555-9

Author's Comment:

- Important rules in Article 511 to consider include:
  - 511.3–Classification of Hazardous Areas
  - 511.4–Wiring and Equipment in Hazardous (Classified) Locations
  - 511.7–Wiring and Equipment Above Hazardous (Classified) Locations
  - 511.9–Explosionproof Seals
  - 511.12–GFCI-Protected Receptacles

555.15 Replacement of Equipment

Modifications and Replaced Equipment. Modification or replacement of electrical enclosures, devices, or wiring on a docking facility must be in accordance with this *Code* and the installation requires an inspection of the entire circuit.

Repairing Damaged Equipment. Existing equipment that has been damaged must be identified, documented, and repaired by a qualified person to the minimum requirements of the edition of this *Code* to which it was originally installed.

According to Article 100, the definition of qualified persons is "a person with skills and knowledge related to the construction and operation of electrical equipment and installations. This person must have received safety training to recognize and avoid the hazards involved with electrical systems." ▸**Figure 555–10**

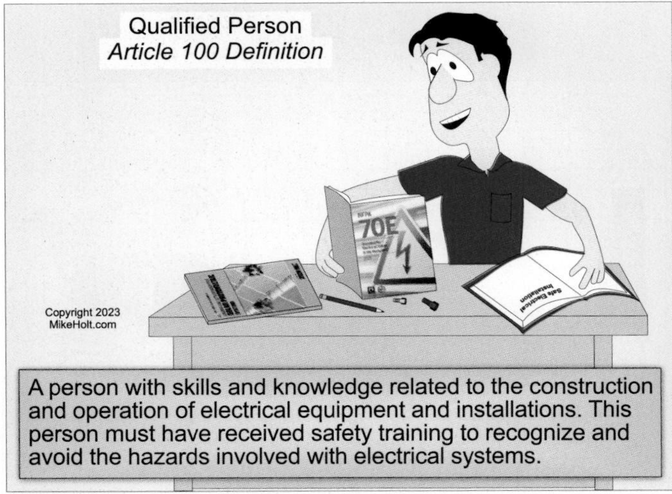

▸**Figure 555–10**

Note: NFPA 303, *Fire Protection Standard for Marinas and Boatyards,* is a resource for guiding the electrical inspection of a marina. ▸**Figure 555–11**

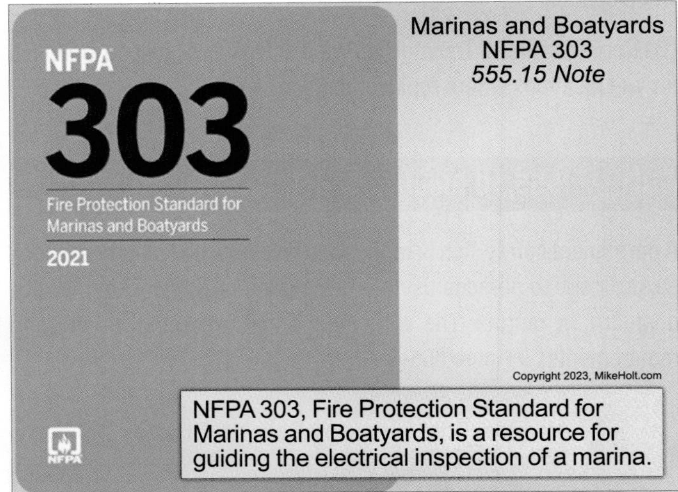

▸**Figure 555–11**

Part II. Marinas, Boatyards, and Docking Facilities

555.30 Electrical Equipment and Connections

(A) New Installation. Electrical equipment (excluding wiring methods) and connections (splices and terminations) not intended for operation while submerged must be located at least 12 in. above the deck of a pier or dock, but not below the electrical datum plane. ▸**Figure 555–12** and ▸**Figure 555–13**

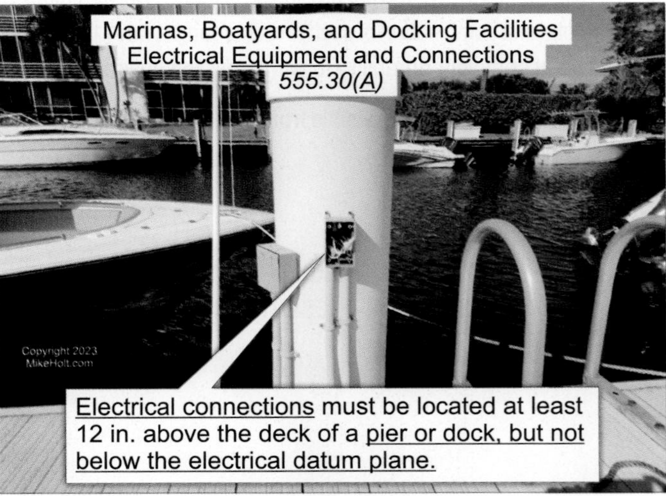

▸**Figure 555–12**

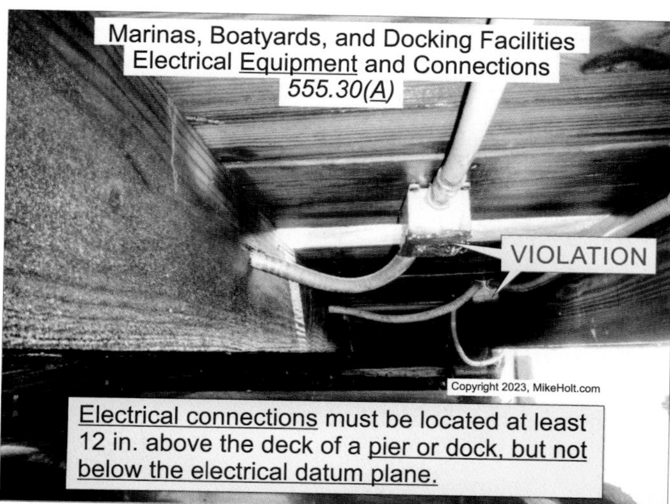
Marinas, Boatyards, and Docking Facilities
Electrical Equipment and Connections
555.30(A)
VIOLATION
Copyright 2023, MikeHolt.com
Electrical connections must be located at least 12 in. above the deck of a pier or dock, but not below the electrical datum plane.

▶Figure 555–13

(B) Replacements. Where equipment is replaced, electrical connections (splices and terminations) must be located at least 12 in. above the deck of a pier or dock but not below the electrical datum plane. ▶Figure 555–14

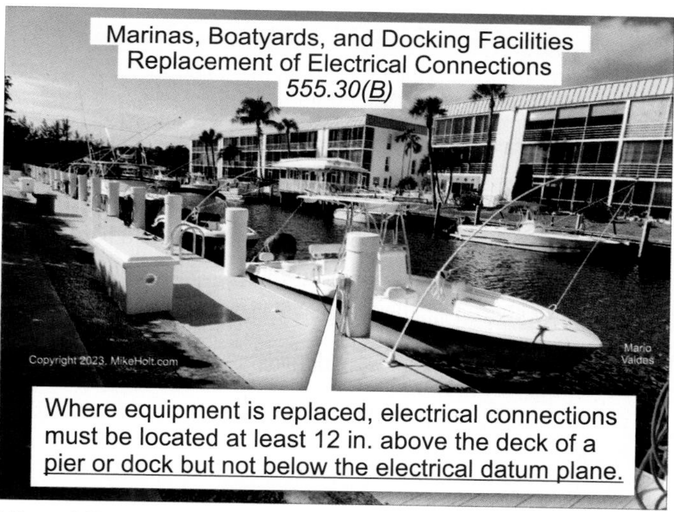
Marinas, Boatyards, and Docking Facilities
Replacement of Electrical Connections
555.30(B)
Copyright 2023, MikeHolt.com
Mario Valdes
Where equipment is replaced, electrical connections must be located at least 12 in. above the deck of a pier or dock but not below the electrical datum plane.

▶Figure 555–14

Author's Comment:

- Sealed wire connector systems are limited to use with Types USE, RHW, XHHW, RW90 EP, RW90, XLPE, or TWU conductors, size 30 AWG through 2,000 kcmil copper or aluminum per the UL Guide Information Sheet for "Sealed Wire Connector Systems (ZMWQ)."

555.33 Receptacles

Receptacles must be mounted not less than 12 in. above the surface of a fixed pier but not below the electrical datum plane. ▶Figure 555–15

Marinas, Boatyards, and Docking Facilities
Receptacles, Fixed Piers
555.33
Copyright 2023, MikeHolt.com
Receptacles must be mounted not less than 12 in. above the surface of a fixed pier but not below the electrical datum plane.

▶Figure 555–15

(A) Shore Power Receptacles.

(1) Enclosures. Shore power receptacles must be part of a listed marina power outlet enclosure listed for wet locations or installed in listed weatherproof enclosures. ▶Figure 555–16

Marinas, Boatyards, and Docking Facilities
Shore Power Receptacles, Enclosure
555.33(A)(1)
Shore power receptacles must be part of a listed marina power outlet enclosure listed for wet locations or installed in listed weatherproof enclosures.
Copyright 2023, MikeHolt.com

▶Figure 555–16

According to Article 100, the definition of "Shore Power" is the electrical equipment required to power a floating vessel including, but not limited to, the receptacle and cords. ▶Figure 555–17

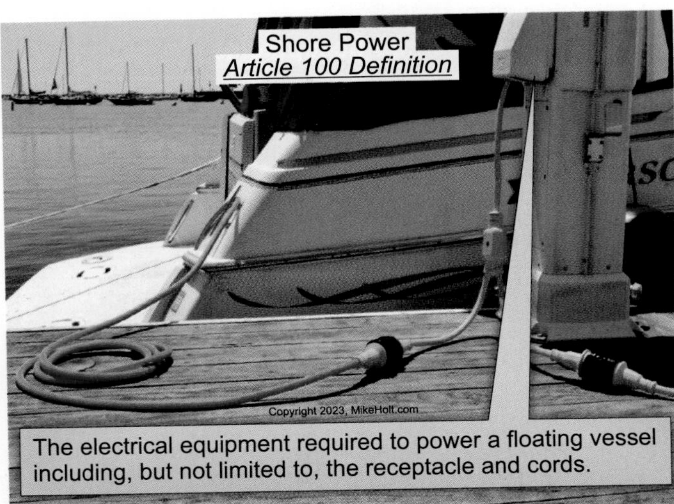
Shore Power
Article 100 Definition
Copyright 2023, MikeHolt.com
The electrical equipment required to power a floating vessel including, but not limited to, the receptacle and cords.

▸Figure 555–17

According to Article 100, the definition of a "Power Outlet, Marina" is an enclosed assembly that can include equipment such as receptacles, circuit breakers, watt-hour meters, and panelboards. ▸Figure 555–18

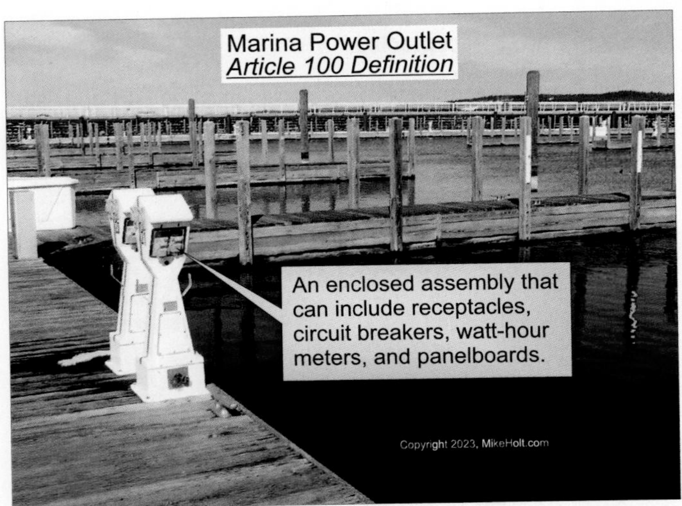
Marina Power Outlet
Article 100 Definition
An enclosed assembly that can include receptacles, circuit breakers, watt-hour meters, and panelboards.
Copyright 2023, MikeHolt.com

▸Figure 555–18

(4) Ratings. Shore power receptacles must be rated at least 30A and must be of the pin and sleeve type if rated 60A or higher.

Author's Comment:

- The rating of the shore power receptacle does not depend on the length of the boat. The *Code* simply sets a minimum rating of 30A and leaves it up to the designer and/or owner to provide the receptacles they deem necessary based on the projected usage of the slips.

(C) Replacement Receptacles. Replacement receptacles must comply with 555.33.

555.34 Wiring Methods and Installation

(A) Wiring Methods.

(1) General. Any Chapter 3 wiring method identified for wet locations containing an insulated equipment grounding conductor is permitted. ▸Figure 555–19

Marinas, Boatyards, and Docking Facilities
Wiring Methods
555.34(A)(1)
Copyright 2023, MikeHolt.com
Any Chapter 3 wiring method identified for wet locations containing a insulated equipment grounding conductor is permitted.

▸Figure 555–19

(2) Portable Power Cables. Sunlight resistant, extra-hard usage cord and extra-hard usage portable power cables listed for use in the environment within which they are installed, are permitted as follows:

(1) As permanent wiring on the underside of piers (floating or fixed).

(2) Where flexibility is necessary as on piers composed of floating sections.

(B) Installation.

(2) Outdoor Branch Circuits and Feeders. Overhead branch-circuit and feeder wiring in locations of the boatyard other than those described in 555.34(B)(1) must be not less than 18 ft above grade. Multiple feeders and branch circuits are permitted for marina installations in accordance with only Part I of Article 225.

(3) Portable Power Cables.

(a) Portable power cables permitted by 555.13(A)(2) must be:

(1) Properly supported.

(2) Located on the underside of the pier.

1st Printing

(3) Securely fastened by nonmetallic clips to structural members other than the deck planking.

(4) Not be subject to physical damage.

(5) Protected against chafing by a permanently installed, oversized sleeve of nonmetallic material when cables pass through structural members.

(b) Where portable power cables are used, there must be a junction box of corrosion-resistant construction with permanently installed terminal blocks on each pier section to which the feeders are connected. A listed marina power outlet employing terminal blocks/bars is permitted in lieu of a junction box. Metal junction boxes and covers, and metal screws and parts that are exposed externally to the boxes, must be of corrosion-resistant materials or protected by material resistant to corrosion.

Author's Comment:

- Portable power cables are specifically listed in Table 400.4 with there usage applicability and this wiring method can be used for branch circuits and feeders.

(4) Protection of Wiring Methods. Rigid metal conduit, intermediate metal conduit, reinforced thermosetting resin conduit (RTRC) listed for aboveground use, or rigid polyvinyl chloride (PVC) conduit suitable for the location must be used to protect wiring to a point at least 8 ft above the docks, decks of piers, and landing stages.

555.35 Ground-Fault Protection (GFPE and GFCI)

Ground-fault protection for docking facilities must be provided in accordance with the following:

(A) GFPE Protection, Feeders. Feeder conductors installed on docking facilities must be provided with GFPEs set to open at trip currents not exceeding 100 mA.

Coordination with the feeder GFPE overcurrent protective device is permitted.

Ex: Transformer secondary conductors of a separately derived system that do not exceed 10 ft, and are installed in a raceway, are permitted to be installed without ground-fault protection. This exception also applies to the supply terminals of the equipment supplied by the transformer secondary conductors.

(B) GFPE and GFCI.

(1) Shore Power Receptacles, GFPE Protection. Shore power receptacles installed in accordance with 555.33(A) must have individual GFPE protection set to open at trip currents not exceeding 30 mA. ▶Figure 555–20

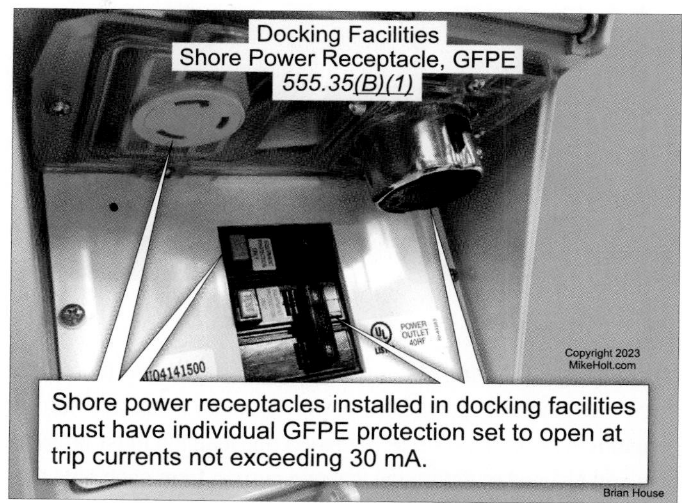

▶Figure 555–20

Author's Comment:

- In accordance with the research study by the American Boat and Yacht Council Foundation, Inc., 30 mA represents an acceptable threshold level for GFPE protection to prevent most electrical shock drowning incidents while remaining practical enough to minimize nuisance tripping.
- If shore power receptacles are replaced, they are required to have GFPE protection [406.4(D)(8)].

(2) Outlets Other than Shore Power, GFCI Protection. GFCI protection is required for docking facility outlets rated 60A and less, single-phase, and 100A and less, three-phase for electrical systems not exceeding 150V to ground.

Ex to (B): Circuits not requiring grounding, not exceeding the low-voltage contact limit, and supplied by listed transformers or power supplies complying with 680.23(A)(2) can be installed without GFCI protection.

(C) Boat Hoist. Boat hoist outlets on docking facilities must be GFCI protected where the circuit voltage does not exceed 240V. ▶Figure 555–21

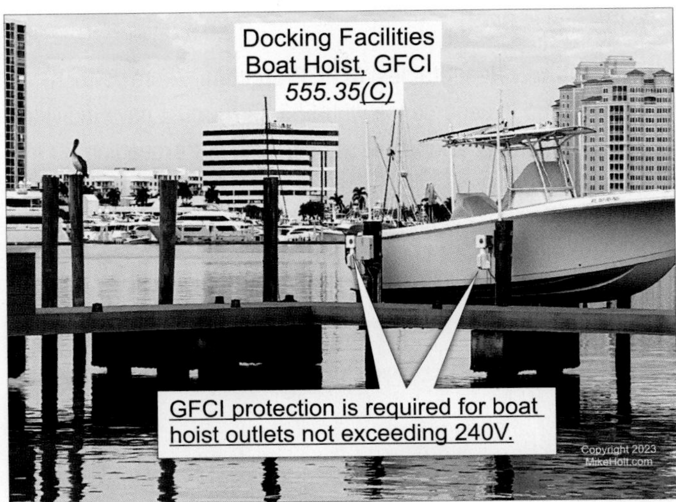

Docking Facilities
Boat Hoist, GFCI
555.35(C)
GFCI protection is required for boat hoist outlets not exceeding 240V.
Copyright 2023
MikeHolt.com

▶Figure 555–21

(D) Leakage Current Measurement Device. Where more than three receptacles supply shore power to boats, a leakage current measurement device for use in marina applications must be available and be used to determine leakage current from each boat that will utilize shore power.

Note 1: Leakage current measurements will provide the capability to determine when an individual boat has defective wiring or other problems contributing to hazardous voltage and current. The use of this test device will allow the facility operator to identify a boat that is creating an electrical hazard. In some cases, a single boat could cause an upstream GFPE device protecting a feeder to trip even though multiple boats are supplied from the same feeder. The use of this test device will help the facility operator prevent a particular boat from contributing to hazardous voltage and current in the marina area.

Note 2: An annual test of each boat with the leakage current measurement device is a prudent step toward determining if a boat has defective wiring that could be contributing hazardous voltage and current. Where the leakage current measurement device reveals that a boat is contributing hazardous voltage and current, repairs should be made to the boat before it is permitted to utilize shore power.

Ex: Where the shore power equipment includes a leakage indicator and leakage alarm, a separate leakage test device is not required.

555.36 Shore Power Receptacle Disconnecting Means

A disconnecting means must be provided for each shore power receptacle in accordance with the following:

(A) Type of Disconnecting Means. A circuit breaker or switch that identifies which shore power receptacle it controls. ▶Figure 555–22

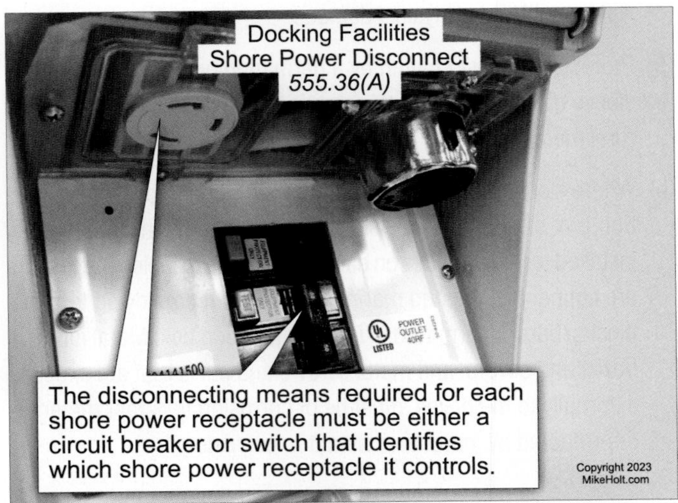

▶Figure 555–22

(B) Location. The shore power receptacle disconnect must be readily accessible and not more than 30 in. from the receptacle it controls. ▶Figure 555–23

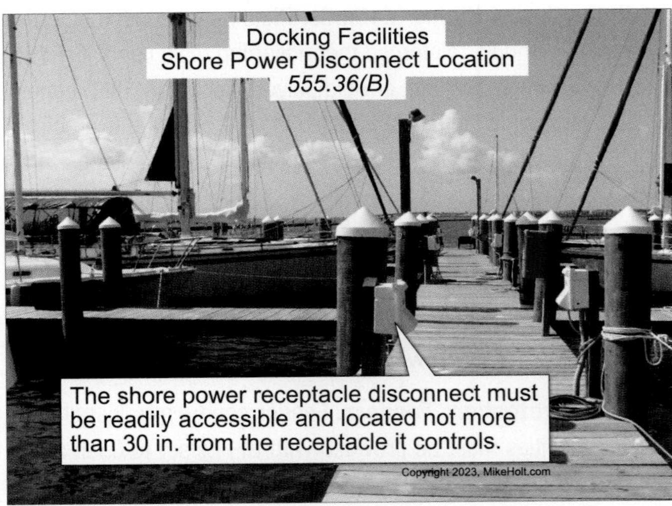

▶Figure 555–23

Author's Comment:

- This shore power receptacle disconnect is intended to eliminate the hazard of someone engaging or disengaging the boat's shore power attachment plug with wet, slippery hands and contacting energized blades.

(C) Emergency Electrical Disconnect. Each marina power outlet or enclosure that provides shore power to boats must have a listed emergency shutoff device or disconnect that is marked "Emergency Shutoff" in accordance with 110.22(A).

The emergency shutoff device or disconnect must be within sight of the marina power outlet, readily accessible, externally operable, and manually resettable. The emergency shutoff device or disconnect must de-energize the power supply to all circuits supplied by the marina power outlet(s). A circuit breaker handle is not permitted to be used for this purpose.

Author's Comment:

- An emergency disconnect within sight of the marina power outlet will provide bystanders with the ability to shutoff power if a swimmer comes in contact with an energized metal boat, dock, or ladder and in cases where it appears that Electric Shock Drowning (ESD) is occurring.

555.37 Equipment Grounding Conductor

(A) Equipment to be Connected to the Equipment Grounding Conductor. The following items in a marina, boatyard, or docking facility must be connected to an equipment grounding conductor of the wire-type run with the circuit conductors:

(1) Metal boxes, metal cabinets, and all other metal enclosures

(2) Metal frames of utilization equipment

(3) Grounding terminals of grounding-type receptacles

(B) Insulated Equipment Grounding Conductor. An insulated equipment grounding conductor, sized in accordance with 250.122 but not smaller than 12 AWG, must be provided for all circuits in a marina, boatyard, or docking facility. ▶Figure 555–24

(C) Feeder Equipment Grounding Conductor. A feeder to a panelboard or distribution equipment must have an insulated equipment grounding conductor [555.37(B)] run from the service to the panelboard or distribution equipment.

(D) Branch-Circuit Equipment Grounding Conductor. The required branch-circuit insulated equipment grounding conductor [555.37(B)] must terminate at a grounding terminal in a panelboard, distribution equipment, or service equipment.

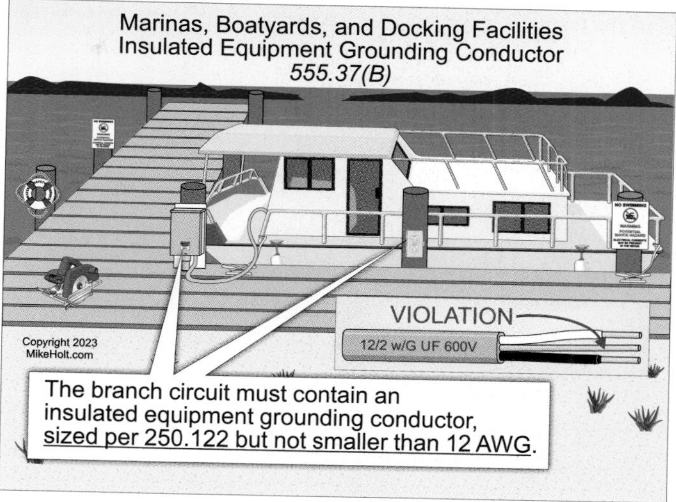
Marinas, Boatyards, and Docking Facilities
Insulated Equipment Grounding Conductor
555.37(B)
VIOLATION
12/2 w/G UF 600V
Copyright 2023
MikeHolt.com
The branch circuit must contain an insulated equipment grounding conductor, sized per 250.122 but not smaller than 12 AWG.

▶Figure 555–24

555.38 Luminaires

(A) General. All luminaires and retrofit kits must be listed and identified for use in their intended environment. Luminaires and their supply connections must be secured to limit damage from watercraft and prevent entanglement of, and interaction with, sea life.

(B) Underwater Luminaires. Luminaires installed below the highest high tide level or electrical datum plane and likely to be periodically submersed must be limited to the following:

(1) Identified as submersible

(2) Operate below the low-voltage contact limit as defined in Article 100

(3) Supplied by a swimming pool transformer in accordance with 680.23(A)(2)

ARTICLE 590 TEMPORARY INSTALLATIONS

Introduction to Article 590—Temporary Installations

This article covers the special requirements for temporary wiring installation and removal for applications such as power for construction, remodeling, maintenance, repair, demolition, decorative lighting, during emergencies, and for tests and experiments. Many of these rules are outside of the scope of this material, however, some of the topics we cover include the following:

- Scope
- Wiring
- Time Constraints
- GFCI Protection

590.1 Scope

Article 590 covers temporary power and lighting installations and removals, including power for construction, remodeling, maintenance, repair, demolition [590.3(A)], decorative lighting [590.3(B)], and during emergencies or for tests and experiments [590.3(C)]. ▸Figure 590-1

Temporary Installations
590.1 Scope
Ramon Ramiro
Copyright 2023, MikeHolt.com
Article 590 applies to temporary electric power and lighting installations.

▸Figure 590-1

Author's Comment:

- Temporary installations for carnivals, circuses, fairs, and similar events must be installed in accordance with Article 525—not Article 590.

590.2 All Wiring Installations

(A) Other Articles. All *NEC* requirements apply to temporary installations unless specifically modified in this article. ▸Figure 590-2

(B) Approval. Temporary wiring methods are acceptable only if approved by the authority having jurisdiction based on the conditions of use and any special requirements of the temporary installation.

Temporary Installations
Other Articles
590.2(A)
Copyright 2023, MikeHolt.com
All NEC requirements apply to temporary installations unless modified by this article.

▶Figure 590–2

590.3 Time Constraints

(A) Construction Period. Electrical power and lighting installations are permitted during the period of construction, remodeling, maintenance, repair, or demolition of buildings, structures, equipment, or similar activities. ▶Figure 590–3

▶Figure 590–3

(B) Decorative Lighting. Decorative holiday lighting is permitted for a period of up to 90 days. ▶Figure 590–4

Author's Comment:

- Decorative lighting used for holiday lighting and similar purposes must be listed [590.5].

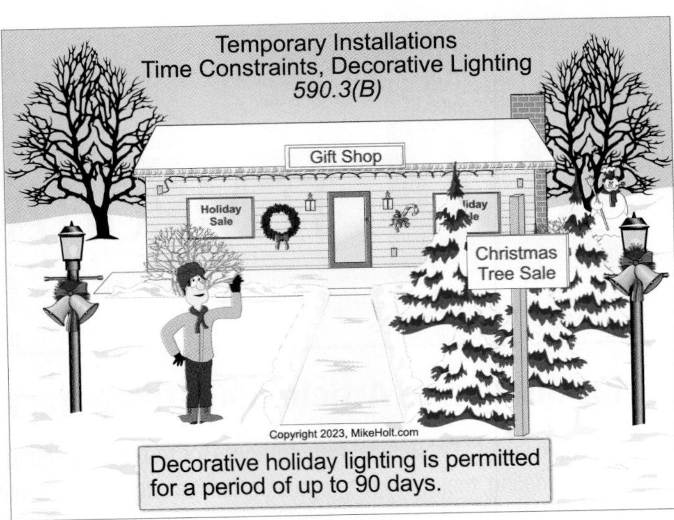

▶Figure 590–4

(C) Emergencies and Experiment Testing. Electrical power and lighting installations are permitted for the duration necessary for emergency and experiment or testing. ▶Figure 590–5 and ▶Figure 590–6

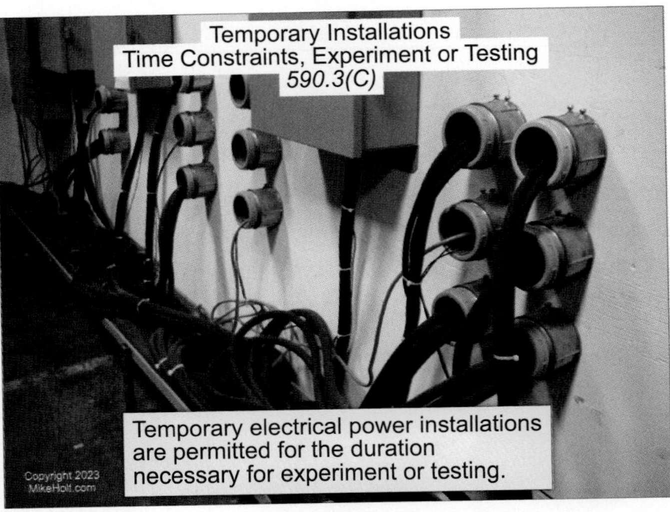

Temporary Installations
Time Constraints, Experiment or Testing
590.3(C)
Copyright 2023 MikeHolt.com
Temporary electrical power installations are permitted for the duration necessary for experiment or testing.

▶Figure 590–5

(D) Removal. Installations must be removed immediately upon the completion of construction. ▶Figure 590–7

590.4 General

(A) Services. Services must be installed in accordance with Parts I through VIII of Article 230 as applicable.

(B) Feeders. Overcurrent protection must be provided in accordance with 240.4, 240.5, 445.12, and 445.13. The following wiring methods are permitted:

1st Printing

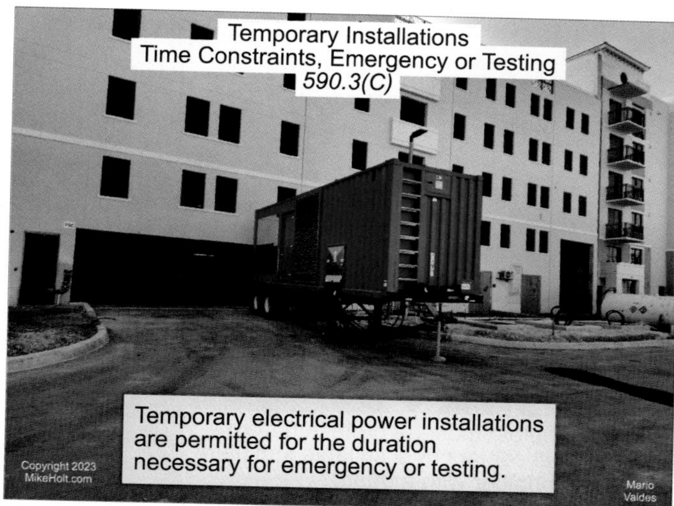
Temporary Installations
Time Constraints, Emergency or Testing
590.3(C)
Temporary electrical power installations are permitted for the duration necessary for emergency or testing.
Copyright 2023 MikeHolt.com
Mario Valdes
▸Figure 590-6

Temporary Installations
Time Constraints, Removal
590.3(D)
VIOLATION
Copyright 2023, MikeHolt.com
Temporary installations must be removed upon the completion of construction.
Ryan Jackson
▸Figure 590-7

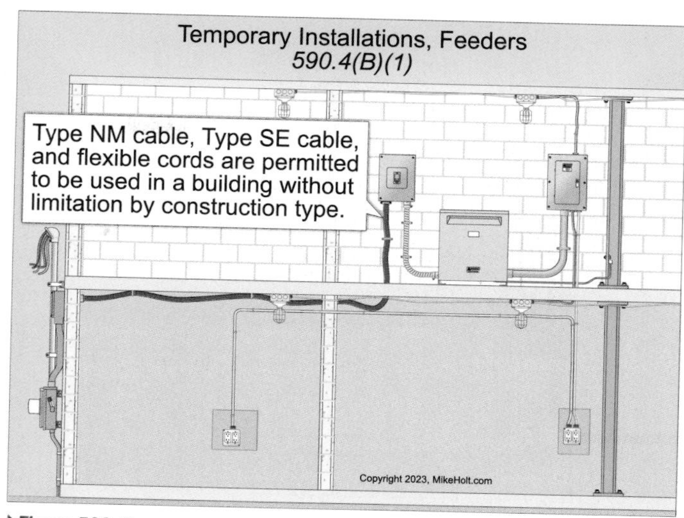
Temporary Installations, Feeders
590.4(B)(1)
Type NM cable, Type SE cable, and flexible cords are permitted to be used in a building without limitation by construction type.
Copyright 2023, MikeHolt.com
▸Figure 590-8

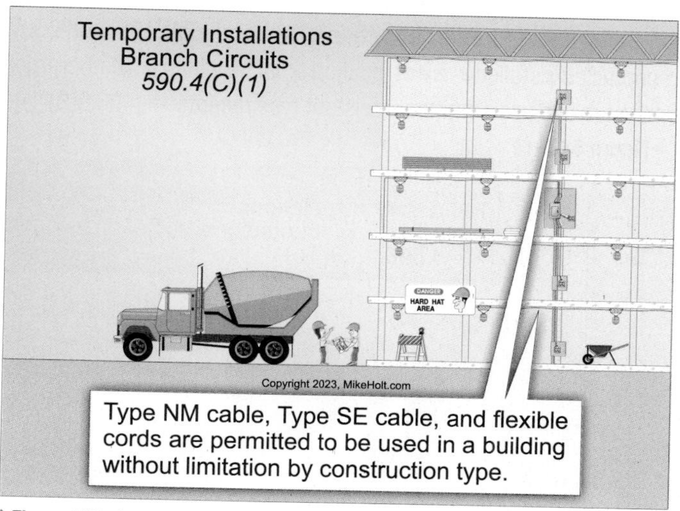
Temporary Installations
Branch Circuits
590.4(C)(1)
Copyright 2023, MikeHolt.com
Type NM cable, Type SE cable, and flexible cords are permitted to be used in a building without limitation by construction type.
▸Figure 590-9

(1) Type NM cable, Type SE cable, and flexible cords are permitted to be used in a building without limitations by construction type. ▸**Figure 590-8**

2) Type SE cable may be installed in a raceway underground.

(C) Branch Circuits. Overcurrent protection must be provided in accordance with 240.4 and 240.5. The following wiring methods are permitted:

(1) Type NM cable, Type SE cable, and flexible cords are permitted to be used in a building without limitations by construction type. ▸**Figure 590-9**

(2) Type SE cable may be installed in a raceway underground.

(D) Receptacles.

(1) Receptacles Not on Lighting Circuit. Receptacles are not permitted on a branch circuit that supplies temporary lighting on a construction site. ▸**Figure 590-10**

Author's Comment:

- This requirement is necessary so illumination is maintained, even when the receptacle's GFCI-protective device opens [590.6].

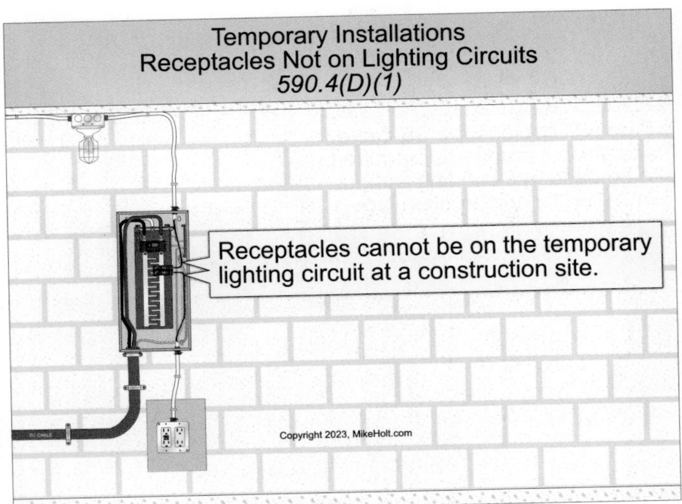

Temporary Installations
Receptacles Not on Lighting Circuits
590.4(D)(1)
Receptacles cannot be on the temporary lighting circuit at a construction site.
Copyright 2023, MikeHolt.com

▶Figure 590–10

(2) Receptacles in Wet Locations. 15A and 20A, 125- and 250V receptacles installed in a wet location must be within a weatherproof enclosure and use a weather-resistant type receptacle [406.9(B)(1)]. ▶Figure 590–11

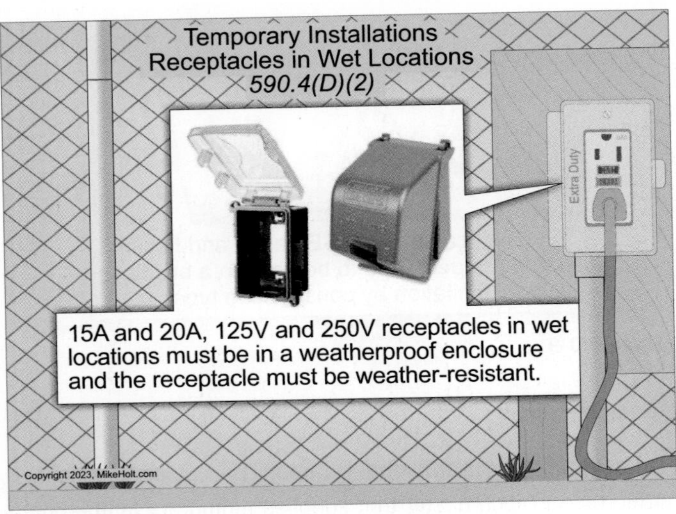

Temporary Installations
Receptacles in Wet Locations
590.4(D)(2)
Extra Duty
15A and 20A, 125V and 250V receptacles in wet locations must be in a weatherproof enclosure and the receptacle must be weather-resistant.
Copyright 2023, MikeHolt.com

▶Figure 590–11

(F) Lamp Protection. Lamps (bulbs) must be protected from accidental contact by a suitable luminaire or lampholder with a guard. ▶Figure 590–12

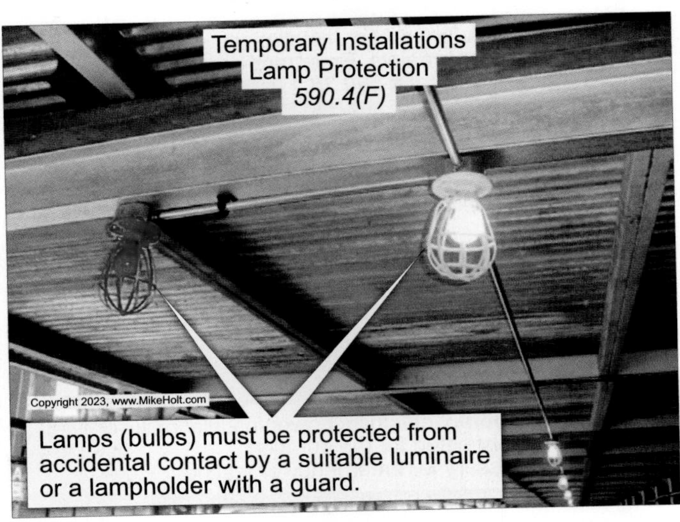

▶Figure 590–12

(G) Splices. A box, conduit body, or other enclosure (with a cover installed) is required for all splices.

Ex 1: On construction sites, a box is not required if the conductors being spliced are from nonmetallic sheathed cables or cords, or metal-sheathed cable assemblies if the grounding continuity can be maintained without the box if:

(1) The circuit conductors being spliced are all from nonmetallic multiconductor cord or cable assemblies, provided the equipment grounding continuity is maintained with or without the box, or

(2) The circuit conductors being spliced are all from metal-sheathed cable assemblies terminated in listed fittings that mechanically secure the cable sheath to maintain effective electrical continuity.

Ex 2: On construction sites, a box is not required for GFCI-protected branch circuits that are permanently installed in framed walls and ceilings and are used to supply temporary power or lighting, the following are permitted:

(1) Splices installed completely inside junction boxes with plaster rings.

(2) Listed pigtail-type lampholders can be installed in ceiling-mounted junction boxes with plaster rings.

(3) Finger safe devices are permitted for supplying and connecting devices.

(H) Protection from Accidental Damage. Cables and flexible cords must be protected from physical damage and from sharp corners and projections when the cables and flexible cords pass through doorways or other pinch points.

(J) Support. Cable assemblies and flexible cords must be supported at intervals that ensure protection from physical damage. Support must be in the form of staples, cable ties, straps, or other similar means designed not to damage the cable or flexible cord assembly. Flexible cords, other than extension cords, are not permitted to lay on the floor or the ground when used as branch circuits or feeders. ▶Figure 590–13

1st Printing

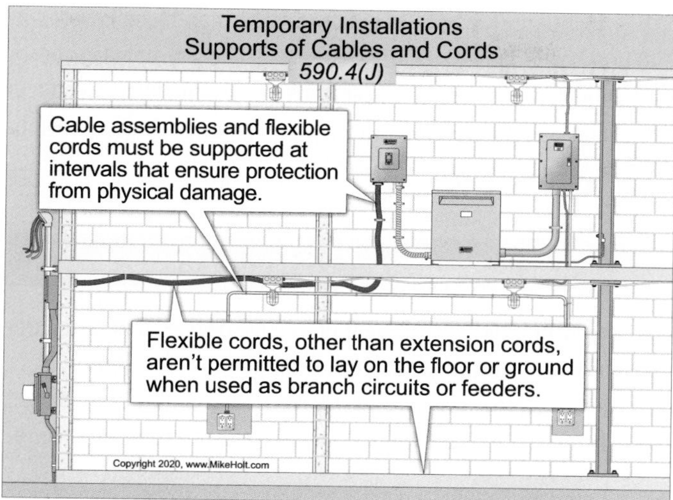
Temporary Installations
Supports of Cables and Cords
590.4(J)
Cable assemblies and flexible cords must be supported at intervals that ensure protection from physical damage.
Flexible cords, other than extension cords, aren't permitted to lay on the floor or ground when used as branch circuits or feeders.
Copyright 2020, www.MikeHolt.com

▸Figure 590–13

Author's Comment:

- The support requirement for temporary cables is determined by the authority having jurisdiction based on the jobsite conditions [590.2(B)].

Vegetation is not permitted to be used to support overhead branch-circuit or feeder conductors. ▸Figure 590–14

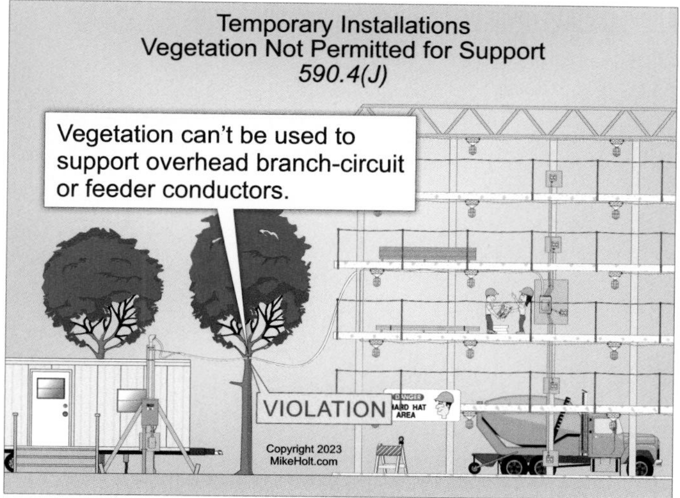
Temporary Installations
Vegetation Not Permitted for Support
590.4(J)
Vegetation can't be used to support overhead branch-circuit or feeder conductors.
VIOLATION
Copyright 2023 MikeHolt.com

▸Figure 590–14

590.5 Listing of Decorative Lighting

Decorative lighting used during holidays and for similar purposes [590.3(B)] must be listed and labeled on the product.

590.6 GFCI Protection for Personnel

(A) Receptacle. GFCI protection is required for receptacles used for construction, remodeling, maintenance, repair, or demolition of buildings, structures, or equipment.

(1) Temporary Receptacles. GFCI protection is required for 15A, 20A, and 30A receptacles used for temporary power and are not part of the permanent wiring of the building. ▸Figure 590–15

Temporary Installations
GFCI Protection of Temporary Receptacles
590.6(A)(1)
GFCI protection is required for 15A, 20A, and 30A receptacles that aren't part of the permanent wiring of the building.
Copyright 2023, MikeHolt.com

▸Figure 590–15

Author's Comment:

- Section 590.6(A) requires 125V and 125/250V, 15A, 20A, and 30A receptacles to have GFCI protection. Section 590.6(B) requires all other receptacles used on temporary installations to be GFCI protected. This simply means all 125V and 125/250V receptacles used for temporary power require GFCI protection.

(2) Permanent Receptacle. GFCI protection is required for 15A, 20A, and 30A receptacles that are part of the permanent wiring of the building and used for temporary power. Listed cord sets or devices incorporating listed ground-fault circuit-interrupter protection for personnel identified for portable use can be used for this purpose. ▸Figure 590–16

(3) Portable Generators 15 kW or Less. GFCI protection is required for 15A, 20A, and 30A, 125V and 250V receptacles that are part of a portable generator rated not greater than 15 kW. ▸Figure 590–17

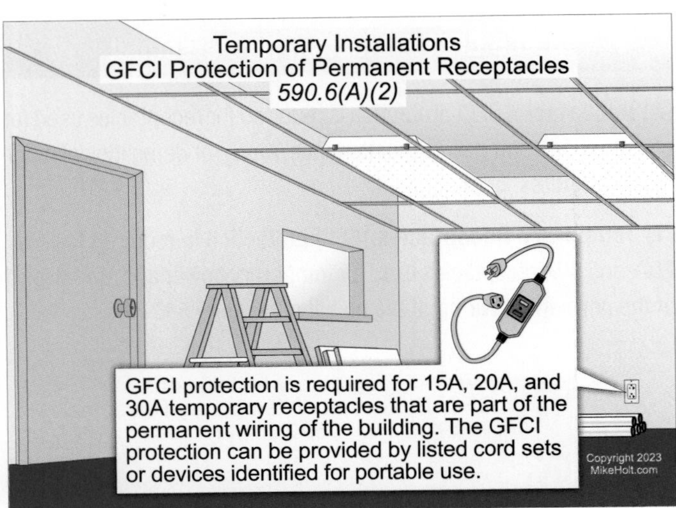
Temporary Installations
GFCI Protection of Permanent Receptacles
590.6(A)(2)
GFCI protection is required for 15A, 20A, and 30A temporary receptacles that are part of the permanent wiring of the building. The GFCI protection can be provided by listed cord sets or devices identified for portable use.
Copyright 2023 MikeHolt.com

▶Figure 590–16

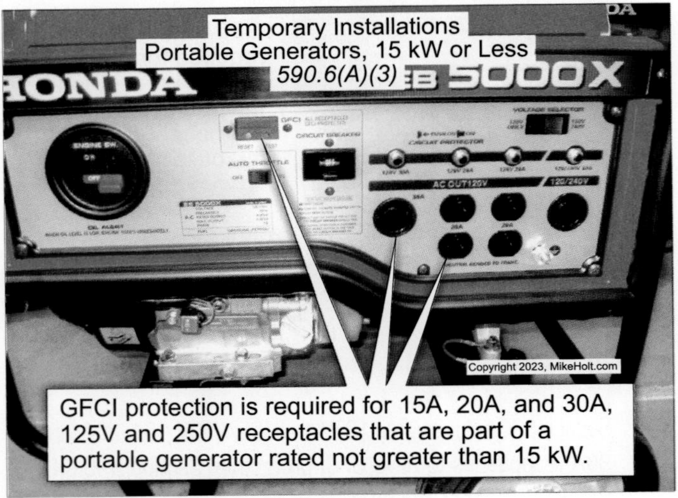
Temporary Installations
Portable Generators, 15 kW or Less
590.6(A)(3)
HONDA
GFCI protection is required for 15A, 20A, and 30A, 125V and 250V receptacles that are part of a portable generator rated not greater than 15 kW.
Copyright 2023, MikeHolt.com

▶Figure 590–17

(B) Other Receptacles. Receptacles other than those covered by 590.6(A)(1) through (A)(3) that supply temporary power used by personnel during construction, remodeling, maintenance, repair, or demolition of buildings, structures, equipment, or similar activities must be GFCI protected.

590.8 Overcurrent Protective Devices

(A) Where Reused. Overcurrent protective devices that have been previously used and are installed in a temporary installation must be examined [110.3(A)] to ensure the devices have been properly installed, properly maintained, and there is no evidence of impending failure.

Author's Comment:

- The phrase "evidence of impending failure" means there is evidence such as arcing, overheating, loose parts, bound equipment parts, visible damage, or deterioration. The phrase "properly maintained" means the equipment has been maintained in accordance with the manufacturers' recommendations and applicable industry codes and standards.

(B) Service Overcurrent Protective Devices. Overcurrent protective devices for 277/480V services with an available fault greater than 10,000A must be of the current-limiting type.

1st Printing

CHAPTER 5

REVIEW QUESTIONS

Please use the 2023 *Code* book to answer the following questions.

ARTICLE 500—HAZARDOUS (CLASSIFIED) LOCATIONS

1. Article _____ covers area classification and general requirements for electrical and electronic equipment and wiring rated at all voltages where fire or explosion hazards might exist due to flammable gases, flammable liquid-produced vapors, combustible liquid-produced vapors, combustible dusts, combustible fibers/flyings, or ignitible fibers/flyings.

   (a) 500
   (b) 501
   (c) 502
   (d) 503

2. Areas designated as hazardous (classified) locations or determined to be unclassified shall be _____ and shall be available to the authority having jurisdiction and those authorized to design, install, inspect, maintain, or operate electrical equipment at these locations.

   (a) cleaned
   (b) documented
   (c) maintained
   (d) all of these

3. Hazardous (classified) locations shall be classified depending on the properties of the _____ that could be present, and the likelihood that a flammable or combustible concentration or quantity is present.

   (a) flammable or combustible liquid-produced vapors
   (b) flammable gases
   (c) combustible dusts or fiber/flyings
   (d) all of these

4. In the layout of electrical installations for hazardous (classified) locations, it is frequently possible to locate much of the equipment in a reduced level of classification or in an _____ location to reduce the amount of special equipment required.

   (a) unclassified
   (b) classified
   (c) Class I
   (d) Class II

5. Class I, Division 1 locations are those areas in which ignitable concentrations of _____ can exist under normal operating conditions.

   (a) combustible dust
   (b) easily ignitable fibers or flyings
   (c) flammable gases or flammable liquid-produced vapors
   (d) pyrotechnics

6. When determining a Class I, Division 2 location, the _____ is(are) a factor(s) that should be considered in determining the classification and extent of the location.

   (a) quantity of flammable material that might escape in case of an accident
   (b) adequacy of ventilating equipment
   (c) record of the industry or business with respect to explosions or fires
   (d) all of these

7. Class II locations are those that are hazardous because of the presence of _____.
   (a) combustible dust
   (b) easily ignitible fibers/flyings
   (c) flammable gases or vapors
   (d) flammable liquids or gases

8. Locations in which combustible dust is in the air under normal operating conditions in quantities sufficient to produce explosive or ignitible mixtures are classified as _____.
   (a) Class I, Division 2
   (b) Class II, Division 1
   (c) Class II, Division 2
   (d) Class III, Division 1

9. A Class II, Division 2 location is a location _____.
   (a) in which combustible dust due to abnormal operations may be present in the air in quantities sufficient to produce explosive or ignitible mixtures
   (b) where combustible dust accumulations are present but are normally insufficient to interfere with the normal operation of electrical equipment but could as a result of infrequent malfunctioning of handling or processing equipment become suspended in the air
   (c) in which combustible dust accumulations on, in, or in the vicinity of the electrical equipment could be sufficient to interfere with the safe dissipation of heat from electrical equipment
   (d) all of these

10. Class III locations are those that are hazardous (classified) because of the presence of _____.
   (a) combustible dust
   (b) combustible nonmetal fibers/flyings
   (c) flammable gases or vapors
   (d) flammable liquids or gases

11. Hazardous (classified) locations where ignitible fibers/flyings are handled, manufactured, or used shall be classified as _____.
   (a) Class I, Division 3
   (b) Class II, Division 2
   (c) Class III, Division 1
   (d) Class III, Division 2

12. Combustible fibers/flyings that may be found in a Class III, _____ hazardous location include flat platelet-shaped particulates, such as metal flakes, and fibrous board, such as particle board.
   (a) Division 1
   (b) Division 2
   (c) Division 3
   (d) Division 4

13. Ignitible fibers/flyings in Class III, Division 1 locations can include _____.
   (a) rayon
   (b) cotton
   (c) cocoa fiber
   (d) any of these

14. A Class III, Division _____ location is where ignitible fibers/flyings are stored or handled but not manufactured.
   (a) 1
   (b) 2
   (c) 3
   (d) all of these

15. Electrical and electronic equipment in hazardous (classified) locations shall be protected by a(an) _____ technique.
   (a) explosionproof
   (b) dust-ignitionproof
   (c) dusttight
   (d) any of these

16. Suitability of identified equipment for use in a hazardous (classified) location shall be determined by _____.
   (a) equipment listing or labeling
   (b) evidence of equipment evaluation from a qualified testing laboratory or inspection agency concerned with product evaluation
   (c) evidence acceptable to the authority having jurisdiction, such as a manufacturer's self-evaluation or an owner's engineering judgment
   (d) any of these

17. Equipment shall be identified not only for the class of hazardous (classified) location, but also for the explosive, combustible, or ignitible properties of the specific _____ present.
   (a) gas or vapor
   (b) dust
   (c) fibers/flyings
   (d) any of these

1st Printing

18. Threaded conduits or fittings installed in hazardous (classified) locations shall be made wrenchtight to _____.

    (a) prevent sparking when a fault current flows through the conduit system
    (b) prevent seepage of gases or fumes
    (c) prevent sag in the conduit runs
    (d) maintain a workmanship like installation

19. In Class I, Division 1 locations, threaded rigid metal conduit entries into explosionproof equipment shall be made up of _____.

    (a) at least five threads fully engaged
    (b) listed pressure fittings
    (c) four threads coated with listed epoxy
    (d) listed threaded bushings

ARTICLE 501—CLASS I HAZARDOUS (CLASSIFIED) LOCATIONS

1. Article 501 covers the requirements for electrical and electronic equipment and wiring for all voltages in Class I, Division 1 and 2 locations, where _____ are or might be present in the air in quantities sufficient to produce explosive or ignitible mixtures.

    (a) flammable gases
    (b) flammable liquid-produced vapors
    (c) combustible liquid-produced vapors
    (d) any of these

2. In Class I, Division 1 locations, the use of threaded rigid metal conduit (RMC) or threaded intermediate metal conduit (IMC), shall be permitted, including RMC or IMC conduit systems with supplemental _____ protection coatings.

    (a) rust
    (b) corrosion
    (c) paint
    (d) none of these

3. Where PVC, RTRC, or HDPE is used in Class I, Division 1 underground locations, the concrete encasement shall be permitted to be omitted where RMC or IMC conduit is used for the last _____ of the underground run to emergence or to the point of connection to the aboveground raceway.

    (a) 12 in.
    (b) 18 in.
    (c) 24 in.
    (d) 30 in.

4. If _____ is necessary to minimize the transmission of vibration from equipment during operation or to allow for movement after installation during maintenance in a Class I, Division 1 location, flexible fittings listed for the location or flexible cord in accordance with 501.140, are permitted if terminated with cord connectors listed for the location.

    (a) flexibility
    (b) mobility
    (c) movement
    (d) none of these

5. Boxes and fittings must be _____ for Class I, Division 1 locations.

    (a) designed
    (b) labeled
    (c) marked
    (d) identified

6. Wiring methods permitted in Class I, Division 1 locations are permitted in Class I, Division 2 locations.

    (a) True
    (b) False

7. _____ is(are) among the wiring methods permitted within a Class I, Division 2 location.

    (a) Enclosed gasketed busways and wireways
    (b) Types MC, MV, TC, or TC-ER cable, including installation in cable tray systems and terminated with listed fittings
    (c) Optical fiber cable Types OFNP, OFCP, OFNR, OFCR, OFNG, OFCG, OFN, and OFC installed in cable trays or any other raceway in accordance with 501.10(B) and sealed in accordance with 501.15
    (d) all of these

8. When provisions for flexibility are necessary in Class I, Division 2 locations, FMC with _____ fittings can be used.

    (a) listed
    (b) identified
    (c) marked
    (d) approved

9. In a Class I, Division 2 location, if flexibility is necessary, _____ is(are) a wiring method(s) permitted.

    (a) listed flexible metal fittings
    (b) flexible metal conduit, liquidtight flexible metal conduit and liquidtight nonmetallic conduit, all with listed fittings
    (c) interlocked armor Type MC cable with listed fittings
    (d) all of these

10. In Class I, Division 2 locations boxes and fittings shall be _____ if required by 501.105(B)(2), 501.115(B)(1), or 501.150(B)(1).
    (a) dustproof
    (b) waterproof
    (c) vaporproof
    (d) explosionproof

11. In Class I hazardous locations, sealing compound shall be used in Type MI cable termination fittings to _____.
    (a) prevent the passage of gas or vapor
    (b) exclude moisture and other fluids from the cable insulation
    (c) limit a possible explosion
    (d) prevent the escape of powder

12. Seals are provided in conduit and cable systems to _____ and prevent the passage of flames from one portion of the electrical installation to another through the conduit.
    (a) minimize the passage of gas or vapor
    (b) exclude moisture and other fluids from the cable insulation
    (c) limit a possible explosion
    (d) prevent the escape of powder

13. In Class I, Division 1 locations, conduit seals shall be installed within _____ from the explosionproof enclosure or as required by the enclosure marking.
    (a) 12 in.
    (b) 18 in.
    (c) 20 in.
    (d) 24 in.

14. In Class I, Division 1 locations, seals shall not be required for conduit entering an enclosure if the switch, circuit breaker, fuse, relay, or resistor is _____.
    (a) enclosed within a chamber hermetically sealed against the entrance of gases or vapors
    (b) immersed in oil in accordance with 501.115(B)(1)(2)
    (c) enclosed within an enclosure, identified for the location, and marked "Leads Factory Sealed," "Factory Sealed," or "Seal not Required," or equivalent
    (d) any of these

15. Class I, Division 1 conduit seals shall be installed if a _____ or larger conduit enters any explosionproof enclosure with splices, terminals, or taps and without a make-and-break contact.
    (a) trade size 1
    (b) trade size 2
    (c) trade size 3
    (d) trade size 4

16. Where two or more explosionproof enclosures that require conduit seals are connected by nipples or runs of conduit not more than _____ long, a single conduit seal in each such nipple connection or run of conduit shall be considered sufficient if the seal is located not more than 18 in. from either enclosure.
    (a) 12 in.
    (b) 18 in.
    (c) 24 in.
    (d) 36 in.

17. A conduit run between a conduit seal and the point at which the conduit leaves a Class I, Division 1 location shall contain no union, coupling, box, or other fitting except for a listed _____ reducer installed at the conduit seal.
    (a) explosionproof
    (b) fireproof
    (c) vaportight
    (d) dusttight

18. A sealing fitting is permitted to be installed within _____ of either side of the boundary where a conduit leaves a Class I, Division 1 location.
    (a) 5 ft
    (b) 6 ft
    (c) 8 ft
    (d) 10 ft

19. For underground conduits in a Class I, Division 1 location where the boundary is below grade, a sealing fitting shall be permitted to be installed _____, and there shall not be any unions, couplings, boxes, or fittings between the sealing fitting and the grade, other than listed explosionproof reducers.
    (a) after the conduit emerges from grade
    (b) before the conduit emerges from grade
    (c) within 10 ft of where the conduit emerges from grade
    (d) if the raceway type is RMC or PVC

20. A conduit seal shall be required in each conduit run leaving a Class I, Division 2 location. The conduit sealing fitting shall be installed on either side of the boundary within _____ of the boundary.

    (a) 1 ft
    (b) 3 ft
    (c) 5 ft
    (d) 10 ft

21. A sealing fitting shall not be required if a metal conduit passes completely through a Class I, Division 2 location if the termination points of the unbroken conduit are located in unclassified locations and it has no fittings installed within _____ of either side of the boundary of the hazardous (classified) location.

    (a) 6 in.
    (b) 12 in.
    (c) 18 in.
    (d) 24 in.

22. The minimum thickness of sealing compound in Class I locations shall not be less than the trade size of the conduit or sealing fitting and, in no case, shall the thickness of the compound be less than _____.

    (a) ⅛ in.
    (b) ¼ in.
    (c) ⅜ in.
    (d) ⅝ in.

23. In Class I, Division 1 and 2 locations, the cross-sectional area of the conductors or optical fiber tubes permitted in a sealing fitting shall not exceed _____ of the cross-sectional area of RMC of the same trade size.

    (a) 25 percent
    (b) 50 percent
    (c) 100 percent
    (d) 125 percent

24. In Class I, Division 1 locations, seals for cables at all terminations shall be installed within _____ of the enclosure or as required by the enclosure marking.

    (a) 6 in.
    (b) 12 in.
    (c) 18 in.
    (d) 20 in.

25. In Class I, Division 1 locations, shielded cables and twisted pair cables that have their conductors sealed in accordance with the instructions provided with their listed fitting, shall not be required to have the shielding material removed or the twisted pairs separated.

    (a) True
    (b) False

26. When installing shielded cables and twisted-pair cables in conduit in a Class I, Division 1 hazardous (classified) location, the removal of shielding material or the separation of the twisted pairs of shielded cables and twisted pair cables isn't required within the conduit seal fitting.

    (a) True
    (b) False

27. Each multiconductor cable installed in conduit in a Class I, Division 1 location shall be considered as a single conductor if the cable is incapable of transmitting _____ through the cable core.

    (a) gases or vapors
    (b) dust
    (c) flyings
    (d) any of these

28. Removal of shielding material and the separation of the twisted pairs of shielded cables and twisted pair cables shall not be required within the conduit seal fitting in a Class I, Division 2 hazardous (classified) location if the conductors are sealed in accordance with instructions provided with a listed fitting to minimize the entrance of gases or vapors and prevent the propagation of flame into the cable core.

    (a) True
    (b) False

29. In Class I locations, the locknut-bushing and double-locknut types of contacts shall not be depended on for _____ purposes.

    (a) bonding
    (b) grounding
    (c) securing
    (d) supporting

30. When FMC or LFMC is used as permitted in Class I, Division 2 locations, it shall include an equipment bonding jumper of the _____ type in compliance with 250.102.

(a) wire
(b) raceway
(c) steel
(d) none of these

31. _____ in Class I, Division 2 locations that are not hermetically sealed or oil-immersed shall be installed in a Class I, Division 1 enclosure.

(a) Circuit breakers
(b) Motor controllers
(c) Switches
(d) any of these

32. Motors, generators, or other rotating electrical machinery identified for Class I, Division 2 locations can be used in Class I, Division 1 locations.

(a) True
(b) False

33. Luminaires installed in Class I, Division 1 locations shall be identified as a complete assembly for the Class I, Division 1 location and shall be clearly marked to indicate the _____ for which it is identified.

(a) maximum wattage of lamps
(b) minimum conductor size
(c) maximum overcurrent protection permitted
(d) all of these

34. Luminaires installed in Class I, Division 1 locations shall be protected from physical damage by a suitable _____.

(a) warning label
(b) pendant
(c) guard or by location
(d) all of these

35. Pendant luminaires in a Class I, Division 1 location shall be suspended by and supplied through threaded rigid metal conduit stems or threaded steel intermediate conduit stems, and threaded joints shall be provided with _____ or other effective means to prevent loosening.

(a) set-screws
(b) welded joints
(c) expansion joints
(d) explosionproof FMC

36. Boxes, box assemblies, or fittings used to support luminaires in Class I, Division 1 locations shall be _____ for Class I locations.

(a) identified
(b) listed
(c) marked
(d) approved

37. Luminaires installed in Class I, Division 2 locations shall be protected from physical damage by a suitable _____.

(a) warning label
(b) pendant
(c) guard or by location
(d) all of these

38. In Class I, Division 1 locations, all utilization equipment shall be _____ for use in a Class I, Division 1 location.

(a) identified
(b) approved
(c) marked
(d) listed

39. Flexible cords are not permitted in Class I locations.

(a) True
(b) False

40. Flexible cords in Class I hazardous (classified) locations shall _____.

(a) be listed as extra-hard usage
(b) contain an equipment grounding conductor
(c) be supported by clamps or other suitable means to avoid tension on the terminals
(d) all of these

41. In Class I, Division 1 or 2 locations where the boxes, fittings, or enclosures are required to be explosionproof, if a flexible cord is used it shall terminate with a cord connector or attachment plug listed for the location, or a listed cord connector installed with a seal that is listed for the location. In Division 2 locations where explosionproof equipment is not required, the cord shall terminate _____.

(a) with irreversible connections
(b) with a listed receptacle
(c) in a splice of any manner
(d) with a listed cord connector or listed attachment plug

42. For Class I locations where 501.140(A)(5) is applied, flexible cords shall be _____ from the power source to the temporary portable assembly and from the temporary portable assembly to the utilization equipment.
    (a) permitted to be spliced
    (b) of continuous length
    (c) installed in a metal raceway
    (d) spliced only using listed splicing kits

ARTICLE 502—CLASS II HAZARDOUS (CLASSIFIED) LOCATIONS

1. Article 502 covers the requirements for electrical and electronic equipment and wiring in Class II, Division 1 and 2 locations where fire or explosion hazards may exist due to _____.
   (a) ignitible gases or vapors
   (b) ignitible fibers/flyings
   (c) combustible dust
   (d) all of these

2. In Class II, Division 1 locations, the use of threaded rigid metal conduit (RMC) or threaded intermediate metal conduit (IMC) shall be permitted, including RMC or IMC conduit systems with supplemental _____ protection coatings.
   (a) rust
   (b) corrosion
   (c) paint
   (d) none of these

3. Where flexibility is necessary, which following wiring method(s) is(are) permitted in a Class II, Division 1 location?
   (a) Dusttight flexible connectors.
   (b) Liquidtight flexible metal conduit with listed fittings.
   (c) Flexible cords listed for extra-hard usage with listed dust-tight cord connectors.
   (d) any of these

4. Boxes and fittings installed in Class II, Division 1 locations shall be provided with threaded bosses for connection to conduit or cable terminations and shall be _____.
   (a) explosionproof
   (b) identified for Class II locations
   (c) dusttight
   (d) weatherproof

5. Raceways permitted as a wiring method(s) in Class II, Division 2 locations include _____.
   (a) RMC and IMC
   (b) PVC
   (c) ENT
   (d) HDPE

6. Boxes and fittings in Class II, Division 2 areas must be _____.
   (a) explosionproof
   (b) sealtight
   (c) vaportight
   (d) dusttight

7. If a raceway provides communication between an enclosure that is required to be dust-ignitionproof and one that is not, suitable means shall be provided to prevent the entrance of dust into the dust-ignitionproof enclosure through the raceway by the use of a _____.
   (a) permanent and effective seal
   (b) horizontal raceway not less than 10 ft long
   (c) vertical raceway that extends downward for not less than 5 ft
   (d) any of these

8. In Class II Locations the locknut-bushing and double-locknut types of contacts shall not be depended on for _____ purposes, but bonding jumpers with identified fittings or other approved means of bonding shall be used.
   (a) bonding
   (b) grounding
   (c) continuity
   (d) any of these

9. Where LFMC is used in a Class II, Division 1 location as permitted in 502.10, it shall _____.
   (a) not be unsupported
   (b) not exceed 6 ft in length
   (c) include an equipment bonding jumper of the wire type
   (d) be listed for use in Class I locations

10. In Class II, Division 1 locations, switches, circuit breakers, motor controllers, and fuses, including pushbuttons, relays, and similar devices shall be provided with enclosures that are _____.
    (a) explosionproof
    (b) identified for the location
    (c) dusttight
    (d) weatherproof

11. In Class II, Division 2 locations, enclosures for fuses, switches, circuit breakers, and motor controllers, including pushbuttons, relays, and similar devices shall be _____.

    (a) dusttight or otherwise identified for the location
    (b) raintight
    (c) rated as Class I, Division 1 explosionproof
    (d) general duty

12. In Class II, Division 1 locations, motors, generators, and other rotating electrical machinery shall be _____.

    (a) listed for the environment
    (b) explosionproof
    (c) general duty
    (d) identified for the location or totally enclosed pipe-ventilated

13. In Class II, Division 2 locations, motors, generators, and other rotating electrical equipment shall be _____.

    (a) totally enclosed nonventilated or pipe-ventilated
    (b) totally enclosed water-air-cooled or fan-cooled
    (c) dust-ignitionproof
    (d) any of these

14. Luminaires installed in Class II, Division 1 locations shall be identified for the location and shall be clearly marked to indicate the _____.

    (a) maximum wattage and type of lamps for which they are designed
    (b) minimum conductor size
    (c) maximum overcurrent protection permitted
    (d) all of these

15. Luminaires installed in Class II, Division 1 locations shall be protected from physical damage by a suitable _____.

    (a) warning label
    (b) pendant
    (c) guard or by location
    (d) all of these

16. Pendant luminaires installed in Class II, Division 1 locations shall be suspended by threaded RMC or steel IMC conduit stems, by chains with approved fittings, or by other approved means. Stems shall be provided with _____ or other effective means to prevent loosening.

    (a) set-screws
    (b) welded joints
    (c) expansion joints
    (d) explosionproof FMC

17. Luminaires for fixed lighting in Class II, Division 2 locations shall be equipped with enclosures that are _____ or otherwise identified for the location.

    (a) dust-ignitionproof
    (b) dusttight
    (c) dustproof
    (d) explosionproof

18. Luminaires for fixed lighting installed in Class II, Division 2 locations shall be protected from physical damage by a suitable _____.

    (a) warning label
    (b) pendant
    (c) guard or by location
    (d) all of these

19. In Class II, Division 2 locations, pendant luminaires can be suspended by _____.

    (a) threaded rigid metal conduit stems
    (b) threaded steel intermediate metal conduit stems
    (c) chains with approved fittings
    (d) any of these

20. Flexible cords used in Class II, Division 1 or 2 locations shall _____, except as permitted for pendant luminaires.

    (a) be listed for hard usage
    (b) be listed for extra-hard usage
    (c) not be permitted
    (d) be Type SJOT or SJOWT

ARTICLE 511—COMMERCIAL REPAIR AND STORAGE GARAGES

1. Article _____ contains the wiring requirements for commercial garages that provide service and repair operations in connection with self-propelled vehicles in which volatile flammable liquids or flammable gases are used for fuel or power.

    (a) 500
    (b) 501
    (c) 511
    (d) 514

2. Parking garages used for parking or storage shall be permitted to be unclassified.

    (a) True
    (b) False

3. In major repair garages where ventilation is not provided, any pit or depression below floor level shall be a Class I, _____ location.
   (a) Division 1
   (b) Division 2
   (c) Division 1 or Division 2
   (d) Division 1 and Division 2

4. For each floor area inside a minor repair garage where ventilation is not provided and Class I liquids or gaseous fuels are not transferred or dispensed, the entire area up to a level of _____ above the floor is considered to be a Class I, Division 2 location.
   (a) 6 in.
   (b) 12 in.
   (c) 18 in.
   (d) 24 in.

5. Any pit for which ventilation is not provided below a minor repair garage floor level is considered to be a Class I, _____ location.
   (a) Division 1
   (b) Division 2
   (c) Division 1 or Division 2
   (d) Division 1 and Division 2

6. In major repair garages where vehicles using lighter-than-air gaseous fuels (such as hydrogen and natural gas) are _____, hazardous area classification guidance is found in Table 511.3(D).
   (a) salvaged for parts
   (b) assembled
   (c) sold to the public
   (d) repaired or stored

7. Areas adjacent to classified locations in commercial garages in which flammable vapors are not likely to be released shall be unclassified where_____.
   (a) mechanically ventilated at a rate of four or more changes per hour
   (b) designed with positive air pressure
   (c) separated by an unpierced wall, roof, or other solid partition
   (d) any of these

8. The area used for _____ of alcohol-based windshield washer fluid in repair garages shall be unclassified.
   (a) storage
   (b) handling
   (c) dispensing into motor vehicles
   (d) any of these

9. Type NM cable is permitted as a fixed wiring method above hazardous classified locations in a commercial garage.
   (a) True
   (b) False

10. Fixed electrical equipment installed in spaces above a hazardous (classified) location in a commercial garage shall be _____.
    (a) well ventilated
    (b) GFPE protected
    (c) GFCI protected
    (d) located above the level of any defined Class I location or identified for the location

11. Fixed lighting in a commercial garage located over lanes on which vehicles are commonly driven shall be located not less than _____ above floor level.
    (a) 10 ft
    (b) 12 ft
    (c) 14 ft
    (d) 16 ft

12. For underground wiring below commercial garages, Type PVC conduit, Type RTRC conduit, and Type HDPE conduit shall be permitted where buried under not less than _____ of cover.
    (a) 1 ft
    (b) 2 ft
    (c) 2½ ft
    (d) 3 ft

13. Battery chargers and their control equipment, and batteries being charged, shall be permitted to be located within locations classified in 511.3.
    (a) True
    (b) False

14. In commercial garages, GFCI protection for personnel shall be provided as required in _____.
    (a) 210.8(A)
    (b) 210.8(B)
    (c) 210.8(C)
    (d) 210.8(D)

ARTICLE 514—MOTOR FUEL DISPENSING FACILITIES

1. Article 514 applies to motor fuel dispensing facilities, marine/motor fuel dispensing facilities, motor fuel dispensing facilities located inside buildings, and _____ vehicle motor fuel dispensing facilities.

   (a) commercial
   (b) hybrid
   (c) military
   (d) fleet

2. In motor fuel dispensing facilities, locations where flammable liquids having a flash point _____, such as gasoline, will not be handled is permitted to be unclassified.

   (a) above 100°F
   (b) below 100°F
   (c) below 86°F
   (d) above 86°F

3. Wiring within dispenser enclosure and all electrical equipment integral with dispensing hose or nozzle of an overhead gasoline dispensing device at a motor fuel dispensing facility is classified as a _____ location.

   (a) Class I, Division 1
   (b) Class I, Division 2
   (c) Class II, Division 1
   (d) Class II, Division 2

4. Underground wiring to motor fuel dispensers shall be installed in _____.

   (a) threaded rigid metal conduit
   (b) threaded steel IMC
   (c) PVC conduit, Type RTRC conduit, and HDPE conduit when buried under not less than 2 ft of cover
   (d) any of these

5. In motor fuel dispensing facilities, all metal raceways, the metal armor or metallic sheath on cables, and all noncurrent-carrying metal parts of fixed and portable electrical equipment _____ shall be grounded and bonded.

   (a) operating at under 600V
   (b) regardless of voltage
   (c) over 300V
   (d) under 50V

ARTICLE 517—HEALTH CARE FACILITIES

1. Article 517 applies to electrical construction and installation criteria in health care facilities that provide services to _____.

   (a) human beings
   (b) animals
   (c) children only
   (d) intellectually challenged persons

2. Wiring methods in healthcare facilities shall comply with Chapters 1 through 4 of the *NEC* except as modified in Article _____.

   (a) 511
   (b) 516
   (c) 517
   (d) 518

3. In patient care spaces, luminaires more than _____ above the floor and switches located outside of the patient care vicinity are permitted to be connected to an equipment grounding return path complying with 517.13(A) or (B).

   (a) 7 ft
   (b) 7½ ft
   (c) 7¾ ft
   (d) 8 ft

4. Branch circuits serving fixed electrical equipment in patient care spaces shall be provided with a(an) _____ by installation in a metal raceway system or a cable having a metallic armor or sheath assembly.

   (a) effective ground-fault current path
   (b) ground-fault current path
   (c) effective current path
   (d) none of these

5. In patient care spaces, metal faceplates shall be connected to an effective ground-fault current path by means of _____ securing the faceplate to a metal yoke or strap of a receptacle or to a metal outlet box.

   (a) ground clips
   (b) rivets
   (c) metal mounting screws
   (d) spot welds

6. In health care facilities, isolated ground receptacles shall be installed in a patient care vicinity.

   (a) True
   (b) False

7. In health care facilities, _____ ground receptacle(s) installed in patient care spaces outside of a patient care vicinity(s) shall comply with 517.16(B)(1) and (2).
   (a) AFCI-protected
   (b) GFCI-protected
   (c) isolated
   (d) all of these

8. Outside of patient care vicinities, the equipment grounding terminals of isolated ground receptacles installed in branch circuits for patient care _____ shall be connected to an insulated equipment grounding conductor in accordance with 250.146(D) installed in a wiring method described in 517.13(A).
   (a) vicinities
   (b) spaces
   (c) bathrooms
   (d) vicinities or spaces

9. Outside of patient care vicinities, the insulated equipment grounding conductor required in 517.13(B)(1) for health care facilities shall be clearly _____ along its entire length by green insulation, with no yellow stripes, and shall not be connected to the grounding terminals of isolated ground receptacles but shall be connected to the box or enclosure indicated in 517.13(B)(1)(2) and to noncurrent-carrying conductive surfaces of fixed electrical equipment indicated in 517.13(B)(1)(3).
   (a) listed
   (b) labeled
   (c) identified
   (d) approved

10. Outside of patient care vicinities, care should be taken in specifying a system containing isolated ground receptacles in health care facilities because the _____ of the effective ground-fault current path is dependent upon the equipment grounding conductor(s) and does not benefit from any conduit or building structure in parallel with the equipment grounding conductor.
   (a) ampacity
   (b) resistance
   (c) effectiveness
   (d) impedance

11. In Category 2 spaces, each patient bed location of health care facilities shall be provided with a minimum of _____ receptacles.
   (a) two
   (b) four
   (c) six
   (d) eight

ARTICLE 518—ASSEMBLY OCCUPANCIES

1. Except for the assembly occupancies explicitly covered by 520.1, Article 518 covers all buildings or portions of buildings or structures designed or intended for the gathering together of _____ or more persons.
   (a) 16
   (b) 50
   (c) 100
   (d) 125

2. Assembly occupancies shall include, but not be limited to, _____.
   (a) conference rooms
   (b) pool rooms
   (c) restaurants
   (d) all of these

3. In assembly occupancies, flexible cables and cords approved for hard or extra-hard usage shall be permitted to be laid on _____ if protected from contact by the general public.
   (a) roofs
   (b) ceilings
   (c) walls
   (d) floors

4. Where ground-fault circuit-interrupter protection for personnel is cord-and-plug-connected to the branch circuit or to the feeder, the ground-fault circuit-interrupter protection shall be listed as _____ ground-fault circuit-interrupter protection.
   (a) suitable
   (b) acceptable
   (c) accessible
   (d) portable

5. The wiring method(s) permitted in an assembly occupancy of fire-rated construction is(are)_____.
   (a) metal raceways
   (b) flexible metal raceways
   (c) Types MI, MC, or AC cables
   (d) all of these

6. In assembly occupancies of fire-rated construction, nonmetallic raceways encased in not less than _____ of concrete shall be permitted.
   (a) 1 in.
   (b) 2 in.
   (c) 3 in.
   (d) 4 in.

7. In assembly occupancies, Type NM cable, ENT, and PVC conduit can be installed in those portions of the building not required to be of _____ construction by the applicable building code.
   (a) Class I, Division 1
   (b) fire-rated
   (c) occupancy-rated
   (d) aboveground

ARTICLE 525—CARNIVALS, CIRCUSES, FAIRS, AND SIMILAR EVENTS

1. Article(s) _____ cover(s) the installation of portable wiring and equipment for carnivals, circuses, fairs, and similar functions.
   (a) 518
   (b) 525
   (c) 590
   (d) all of these

2. Overhead wiring outside of tents and concession areas of carnivals and circuses which are accessible to pedestrians shall maintain a _____ clearance in accordance with 225.18.
   (a) maximum
   (b) minimum
   (c) horizontal
   (d) vertical

3. Portable carnival or circus structures shall be maintained not less than _____ in any direction from overhead conductors operating at 600Vor less.
   (a) 7½ ft
   (b) 10 ft
   (c) 12½ ft
   (d) 15 ft

4. Electrical equipment and wiring methods in or on portable structures for carnivals or circuses shall have mechanical protection where subject to _____.
   (a) public access
   (b) physical damage
   (c) exposure to the weather
   (d) operator access

5. Cord connectors for carnivals, circuses, and fairs shall not be placed in audience traffic paths or within areas accessible to the public unless _____.
   (a) guarded
   (b) labeled
   (c) approved
   (d) identified

6. Flexible _____ accessible to the public at carnivals or circuses shall be permitted to be buried and the requirements of 300.5 shall not apply.
   (a) metallic raceways
   (b) cords and cables
   (c) nonmetallic raceways
   (d) all of these

7. Each portable structure at a carnival, circus, or fair shall be provided with a means to disconnect it from all ungrounded conductors within sight of and within _____ of the operator's station.
   (a) 3 ft
   (b) 6 ft
   (c) 8 ft
   (d) 10 ft

1st Printing

8. Wiring for lighting located inside _____ at carnivals, circuses, and fairs shall be securely installed and, where subject to physical damage, shall be provided with mechanical protection.
   (a) tents and concession areas
   (b) enclosed amusements
   (c) open-air amusements
   (d) all of these

9. Portable distribution and termination boxes installed outdoors at carnivals, circuses, or fairs shall be weatherproof and mounted so the bottom of the enclosure is not less than _____ above the ground.
   (a) 6 in.
   (b) 8 in.
   (c) 10 in.
   (d) 12 in.

10. GFCI protection for personnel shall be provided at carnivals, circuses, and fairs for all 15A and 20A, 125V nonlocking-type receptacles that are readily accessible to _____.
   (a) the general public
   (b) children
   (c) unqualified persons
   (d) event staff

11. For carnivals and fairs, receptacles of the locking type not accessible _____ that only facilitate quick disconnecting and reconnecting of electrical equipment shall not be required to be provided with GFCI protection.
   (a) from grade level
   (b) to the general public
   (c) to unqualified persons
   (d) to event staff

12. The continuity of the _____ conductors at carnivals, circuses, fairs, and similar events shall be verified each time portable electrical equipment is connected.
   (a) equipment grounding
   (b) grounded
   (c) neutral
   (d) phase

ARTICLE 547—AGRICULTURAL BUILDINGS

1. Agricultural buildings where excessive dust and dust with water may accumulate, including all areas of _____ confinement systems where litter dust or feed dust may accumulate shall comply with Article 547.
   (a) poultry
   (b) livestock
   (c) fish
   (d) all of these

2. Agricultural buildings where corrosive atmospheres exist include areas where the following condition(s) exist(s) _____.
   (a) poultry and animal excrement
   (b) corrosive particles which may combine with water
   (c) areas of periodic washing with water and cleansing agents
   (d) all of these

3. The wiring method(s) not permitted to be installed in agricultural buildings is(are) _____.
   (a) Type NM cable
   (b) jacketed Type MC cable
   (c) cable-copper Type SE cable
   (d) all of these

4. Enclosures and fittings installed in areas of agricultural buildings where excessive _____ may be present shall be designed to minimize the entrance of dust and shall have no openings through which dust can enter the enclosure.
   (a) dust
   (b) dirt
   (c) snow
   (d) rain

5. In damp or wet locations of agricultural buildings, equipment enclosures and fittings shall be located or equipped to prevent moisture from _____ within the enclosure, box, conduit body, or fitting.
   (a) entering or accumulating
   (b) draining
   (c) creating a short circuit
   (d) causing damage

6. Where _____ may be present in an agricultural building, enclosures and fittings shall have corrosion-resistance properties suitable for the conditions.

(a) wet dust or excessive moisture
(b) corrosive gases or vapors
(c) other corrosive conditions
(d) any of these

7. Nonmetallic _____ shall not be permitted to be concealed within walls and above ceilings of agricultural building spaces which are contiguous with, or physically adjoined to, livestock confinement areas.

(a) cables
(b) raceways
(c) conduits
(d) conductors

8. All 15A and 20A, 125V, single-phase receptacles installed _____ agricultural buildings shall be GFCI protected.

(a) in areas requiring an equipotential plane of
(b) outdoors of
(c) in dirt confinement areas for livestock in
(d) any of these

9. Luminaires used in agricultural buildings shall _____.

(a) minimize the entrance of dust, foreign matter, moisture, and corrosive material
(b) be protected by a suitable guard if exposed to physical damage
(c) be listed for use in wet locations when exposed to water
(d) all of these

10. A(An) _____ plane shall be installed in all concrete floor confinement areas of livestock buildings, and all outdoor confinement areas with a concrete slab that contains metallic equipment accessible to livestock and that may become energized.

(a) equipotential
(b) electrical datum
(c) neutral-to-earth voltage
(d) elevated

ARTICLE 555—MARINAS, BOATYARDS, AND DOCKING FACILITIES

1. Article 555 covers the installation of wiring and equipment in the areas comprising of _____ and other areas in marinas and boatyards.

(a) fixed or floating piers
(b) floating buildings
(c) wharves and docks
(d) all of these

2. The electrical datum plane for floating piers and boat landing stages shall be a horizontal plane 30 in. above the water level at the floating pier or boat landing stage and a minimum of _____ above the level of the deck

(a) 12 in.
(b) 18 in.
(c) 24 in.
(d) 30 in.

3. Service equipment for a floating building, dock, or marina shall be located on land no closer than _____ horizontally from, and adjacent to, the structure served.

(a) 3 ft
(b) 5 ft
(c) 8 ft
(d) 10 ft

4. Service equipment for a floating building, dock, or marina shall be elevated a minimum of _____ above the electrical datum plane.

(a) 12 in.
(b) 18 in.
(c) 24 in.
(d) 30 in.

5. In marinas, boatyards, and commercial and noncommercial docking facilities, the bottom of enclosures for transformers shall not be located below _____.

(a) 2 ft above the dock
(b) 18 in. above the electrical datum plane
(c) the electrical datum plane
(d) a dock

6. Permanent safety signs shall be installed to give notice of electrical shock hazard risks to persons using or swimming near a boat dock or marina and shall _____.
   (a) comply with 110.21(B)(1) and be of sufficient durability to withstand the environment
   (b) be clearly visible from all approaches to a marina, docking facility, or boatyard facility
   (c) state "WARNING—POTENTIAL SHOCK HAZARD—ELECTRICAL CURRENTS MAY BE PRESENT IN THE WATER."
   (d) all of these

7. When modifications or replacements of _____ are necessary on a docking facility, they shall be required to comply with the requirements of the *NEC*.
   (a) electrical enclosures
   (b) devices
   (c) wiring methods
   (d) all of these

8. Existing electrical equipment on a docking facility that has been damaged shall be _____ by a qualified person to the minimum requirements of the edition of the *NEC* to which it was originally installed.
   (a) identified
   (b) documented
   (c) repaired
   (d) all of these

9. Electrical equipment (excluding wiring methods) and connections in marinas, boatyards, and commercial and noncommercial docking facilities not intended for operation while submerged, shall be located _____.
   (a) at least 12 in. above the deck of a floating structure
   (b) at least 12 in. above the deck of a fixed structure
   (c) not below the electrical datum plane
   (d) all of these

10. Replacement electrical connections at marinas shall be located at least _____ above the deck of a floating or fixed structure.
   (a) 12 in.
   (b) 18 in.
   (c) 24 in.
   (d) 30 in.

11. Receptacles that provide shore power for boats in marinas and docking facilities shall be rated not less than _____.
   (a) 15A
   (b) 20A
   (c) 30A
   (d) 60A

12. Rigid metal conduit, intermediate metal conduit, reinforced thermosetting resin conduit (RTRC) listed for aboveground use, or rigid polyvinyl chloride (PVC) conduit suitable for the location shall be used to protect wiring to a point at least _____ above docks, decks of piers, and landing stages.
   (a) 4 ft
   (b) 6 ft
   (c) 8 ft
   (d) 10 ft

13. Listed GFPE, rated not more than _____, shall be provided for feeders installed on docking facilities.
   (a) 4 mA to 6 mA
   (b) 30 mA
   (c) 75 mA
   (d) 100 mA

14. Listed GFPE, rated not more than _____, shall be provided for receptacles providing shore power at marinas and docking facilities.
   (a) 20 mA
   (b) 30 mA
   (c) 50 mA
   (d) 100 mA

15. Outlets for other than shore power at marinas and docking facilities supplied by branch circuits not exceeding 150V to ground and _____, single-phase, and 150V or less to ground, _____ or less, three- phase, shall be provided with GFCI protection for personnel.
   (a) 15A, 20A
   (b) 20A, 30A
   (c) 30A, 50A
   (d) 60A, 100A

16. Low-voltage circuits not requiring _____, not exceeding the low-voltage contact limit and supplied by listed transformers or power supplies that comply with 680.23(A)(2) shall be permitted to be installed without ground-fault protection at marinas and docking facilities.

    (a) grounding
    (b) bonding
    (c) earthing
    (d) none of these

17. GFCI protection for personnel shall be provided for outlets not exceeding _____ that supply a boat hoist installed at docking facilities.

    (a) 125V
    (b) 150V
    (c) 240V
    (d) 250V

18. Where _____ receptacles supply shore power to boats, a leakage current measurement device for use in marina applications shall be available and be used to determine leakage current from each boat that will utilize shore power.

    (a) two or more
    (b) more than three
    (c) more than four
    (d) more than six

19. Leakage current measurement devices will provide the capability to determine when an individual boat has defective wiring or other problems contributing to hazardous voltage and current and will help the facility operator prevent a particular boat from contributing to hazardous _____ in the marina area.

    (a) voltage
    (b) current
    (c) voltage and current
    (d) none of these

20. A(An) _____ test of each boat with the leakage current measurement device is a prudent step toward determining if a boat has defective wiring that may be contributing hazardous voltage and current in the marina area.

    (a) monthly
    (b) quarterly
    (c) bi-annual
    (d) annual

21. Where the shore power equipment includes a leakage indicator and leakage alarm, a _____ leakage test device shall not be required at marinas and docking facilities.

    (a) separate
    (b) additional
    (c) supplemental
    (d) none of these

22. Disconnecting means for shore power connection(s) shall be provided to _____ each boat from its supply connection(s).

    (a) isolate
    (b) separate
    (c) guard
    (d) control

23. A _____ shall be used to serve as the required shore power receptacle disconnecting means at marinas and docking facilities, and it shall be identified as to which receptacle it controls.

    (a) circuit breaker
    (b) switch
    (c) circuit breaker or fused knife switch
    (d) circuit breaker, switch, or both

24. In marinas, boatyards, and commercial and noncommercial docking facilities, the *NEC* requires a disconnecting means that is readily accessible, located not more than _____ from the receptacle it controls, and located in the supply circuit ahead of the receptacle.

    (a) 12 in.
    (b) 24 in.
    (c) 30 in.
    (d) 36 in.

25. Each marina power outlet or enclosure that provides shore power to boats shall be provided with a listed emergency shutoff device or electrical disconnect that is clearly marked "_____ Shutoff" in accordance with 110.22(A).

    (a) Emergency
    (b) Life-Safety
    (c) Warning
    (d) Hazard

1st Printing

26. Marina equipment grounding conductors shall be of the wire-type, insulated, and sized in accordance with 250.122 but not smaller than _____.
    (a) 14 AWG
    (b) 12 AWG
    (c) 10 AWG
    (d) 8 AWG

27. Where a marina shore power feeder supplies a remote panelboard, an insulated _____ shall extend from a grounding terminal in the service equipment to a grounding terminal in the remote panelboard.
    (a) bonding jumper
    (b) equipment grounding conductor
    (c) grounding electrode conductor
    (d) copper conductor

28. Luminaires and their supply connections shall be secured to structural elements of the marina to limit damage from watercraft and prevent entanglement of and interaction with _____.
    (a) sea life
    (b) swimmers
    (c) fishing lines
    (d) tow lines

29. Luminaires installed at marinas below the highest high tide level or electrical datum plane and likely to be periodically submersed shall be limited to those luminaires that _____.
    (a) are identified as submersible
    (b) operate below the low-voltage contact limit defined in Article 100
    (c) are supplied by an isolating transformer or power supply in accordance with 680.23(A)(2)
    (d) all of these

ARTICLE 590—TEMPORARY INSTALLATIONS

1. The provisions of Article _____ apply to temporary electric power and lighting installations.
    (a) 480
    (b) 555
    (c) 590
    (d) 600

2. Temporary wiring methods shall be acceptable only if _____ based on the conditions of use and any special requirements of the temporary installation.
    (a) listed
    (b) identified
    (c) approved
    (d) any of these

3. Temporary electric power and lighting installations shall be permitted for a period not to exceed 90 days for _____ decorative lighting and similar purposes.
    (a) Christmas
    (b) New Year's
    (c) July 4th
    (d) holiday

4. Temporary electrical power and lighting shall be permitted during emergencies and for _____.
    (a) tests
    (b) experiments
    (c) developmental work
    (d) all of these

5. Temporary wiring shall be _____ immediately upon the completion of construction or purpose for which the wiring was installed.
    (a) disconnected
    (b) removed
    (c) de-energized
    (d) any of these

6. Type(s) _____ cable(s) can be used for temporary feeder installations in any dwelling, building, or structure without any height limitation or limitation by building construction type and without concealment within walls, floors, or ceilings.
    (a) NM
    (b) NMC
    (c) SE
    (d) any of these

7. Type(s) _____ cable(s) shall be permitted to be installed in a feeder raceway in a temporary underground installation.
    (a) NM
    (b) NMC
    (c) SE
    (d) any of these

8. Type(s) _____ cable(s) can be used for temporary branch-circuit installations in any dwelling, building, or structure without any height limitation or limitation by building construction type and without concealment within walls, floors, or ceilings.

    (a) NM
    (b) NMC
    (c) SE
    (d) any of these

9. Type(s) _____ cable(s) shall be permitted to be installed in a branch-circuit raceway in a temporary underground installation.

    (a) NM
    (b) NMC
    (c) SE
    (d) any of these

10. Receptacles on construction sites shall not be installed on _____ that supplies temporary lighting.

    (a) any branch circuit
    (b) the same feeder
    (c) any branch circuit or the same feeder
    (d) any cord or cable

11. All lamps for general illumination at temporary installations shall be protected from accidental contact or breakage by a suitable luminaire or lampholder with a(an) _____.

    (a) box
    (b) cable
    (c) enclosure
    (d) guard

12. A(An) _____ with a cover installed shall be required for all splices at temporary installations.

    (a) box
    (b) conduit body
    (c) enclosure
    (d) any of these

13. For temporary installations on construction sites, a box, conduit body, or other enclosure, with a cover installed, shall be required for all splices except where the circuit conductors being spliced are all from nonmetallic multiconductor _____ assemblies, provided that the equipment grounding continuity is maintained with or without the box.

    (a) listed
    (b) identified
    (c) cord or cable
    (d) feeder and service conductor

14. For temporary installations on construction sites, a box, conduit body, or other enclosure shall not be required if the circuit conductors being spliced are all from _____ terminated in listed fittings that mechanically secure the cable sheath to maintain effective electrical continuity.

    (a) metal-sheathed cable assemblies
    (b) the same power source
    (c) GFCI-protected circuits
    (d) GFPE-protected circuits

15. Flexible cords and flexible cables used for temporary wiring shall _____.

    (a) be protected from accidental damage
    (b) be protected where passing through doorways
    (c) avoid sharp corners and projections
    (d) all of these

16. For temporary installations, cable assemblies, flexible cords, and flexible cables shall be supported by _____ or similar type fittings installed so as not to damage the wiring.

    (a) staples
    (b) cable ties
    (c) straps
    (d) any of these

17. GFCI protection is required for all temporary wiring used for construction, remodeling, maintenance, repair, or demolition of buildings, structures, or equipment from power derived from a(an) _____ or generator.

    (a) electric utility company
    (b) cable or cord
    (c) feeder
    (d) separately derived system

1st Printing

18. All _____, 125V receptacle outlets that are not part of the permanent wiring of the building or structure and are used by personnel for temporary power shall be GFCI protected.
    (a) 15A
    (b) 20A
    (c) 30A
    (d) all of these

19. GFCI protection shall be provided for all _____, single-phase, 15A, 20A, and 30A receptacle outlets installed or existing as part of the permanent wiring of the building or structure and used for temporary electric power.
    (a) 120V
    (b) 125V
    (c) 240V
    (d) 250V

20. For temporary installations, all 125V and 125/250V, single-phase, 15A, 20A, and 30A receptacle outlets that are a part of a _____ or smaller portable generator shall have listed ground-fault circuit-interrupter protection for personnel.
    (a) 5 kW
    (b) 7.50 kW
    (c) 10 kW
    (d) 15 kW

21. When using portable receptacles for temporary wiring installations that are not part of the building or structure, employees shall be protected on construction sites by either ground-fault circuit-interrupters or by the use of a(an) _____.
    (a) insulated conductor program
    (b) double insulated conductor program
    (c) flexible conductor program
    (d) assured equipment grounding conductor program

22. Overcurrent protective devices that have been previously used and are installed in a temporary installation shall be examined to ensure they _____.
    (a) have been properly installed
    (b) have been properly maintained
    (c) show no evidence of impending failure
    (d) all of these

23. Overcurrent protective devices for solidly grounded wye electrical services at temporary installations having an available fault current greater than 10,000A shall _____.
    (a) be provided with GFCI protection
    (b) be current limiting
    (c) be provided with AFCI protection
    (d) provide GFPE protection

CHAPTER

6 SPECIAL EQUIPMENT

Introduction to Chapter 6—Special Equipment

The first four chapters of the *Code* are sequential and form a foundation for each of the subsequent four. Chapter 6, which covers special equipment, is the second of the four *NEC* chapters that deal with special topics. Chapters 5 and 7 focus on special occupancies and special conditions respectively, while Chapter 8 covers communications systems.

What exactly is "Special Equipment"? It is equipment that, by the nature of its use, construction, or by its unique nature creates a need for additional measures to ensure the "safeguarding of people and property" mission of the *NEC*, as stated in Article 90. The *Code* groups the articles in this chapter logically, as you might expect.

- **Article 600—Electric Signs.** This article covers the installation of conductors and equipment for electric signs as defined in Article 100. They include all products and installations that utilize neon tubing, such as signs, decorative elements, skeleton tubing, or art forms.
- **Article 604—Manufactured Wiring Systems.** Article 604 covers field-installed manufactured wiring systems used for branch circuits in accessible areas. The components of a listed manufactured wiring system can be assembled at the jobsite.
- **Article 620—Elevators, Escalators, and Moving Walks.** This article covers electrical equipment and wiring used in connection with elevators, dumbwaiters, escalators, moving walks, wheelchair lifts, and stairway chair lifts.
- **Article 625—Electric Vehicle Power Transfer System.** An electrically powered vehicle needs a dedicated charging circuit and that is where Article 625 comes in. It provides the requirements for the electrical equipment needed to charge automotive-type electric and hybrid vehicles including cars, bikes, and buses.
- **Article 630—Electric Welders.** Electric welding equipment does its job either by creating an electric arc between two surfaces or by heating a rod that melts from overcurrent. Either way results in a hefty momentary current draw. Welding machines come in many shapes and sizes. This article covers electric arc welding and resistance welding apparatus, and other similar welding equipment connected to an electric supply system.
- **Article 640—Audio Signal Amplification and Reproduction Equipment.** Article 640 covers equipment and wiring for audio signal generation, recording, processing, amplification and reproduction, distribution of sound, public address, speech input systems, temporary audio system installations, and electronic musical instruments such as electric organs, electric guitars, and electronic drums/percussion.
- **Article 645—Information Technology Equipment.** This article covers equipment, power-supply wiring, equipment interconnecting wiring, and grounding of information technology equipment and systems including terminal units in an information technology equipment room.

• • •

- **Article 680—Swimming Pools, Spas, Hot Tubs, Fountains, and Similar Installations.** Article 680 covers the installation of bonding and grounding devices for these installations, and the electric wiring and equipment that supply swimming, wading, therapeutic and decorative pools, fountains, hot tubs, spas, and hydromassage bathtubs.
- **Article 690—Solar Photovoltaic (PV) Systems.** This article focuses on reducing the electrical hazards that may arise from installing and operating a solar PV system, to the point where it can be considered safe for property and people. The requirements of the *NEC* Chapters 1 through 4 apply to these installations, except as specifically modified here.
- **Article 691—Large-Scale Solar Photovoltaic (PV) Electric Supply Stations.** Article 691 covers large-scale PV electric supply stations with a generating capacity of 5000 kW or more and not under exclusive utility control.
- **Article 695—Fire Pumps.** This article covers the electric power sources and interconnecting circuits for electric motor-driven fire pumps. It also covers switching and control equipment dedicated to fire pump drivers. Article 695 does not apply to sprinkler system pumps in one- and two-family dwellings or to pressure maintenance (jockey) pumps.

1st Printing

ELECTRIC SIGNS

Introduction to Article 600—Electric Signs

This article covers the special requirements for the installation of conductors, equipment, and field wiring for electric signs. These signs come in many forms and may utilize neon tubing such as decorative elements, skeleton tubing, or art forms. Commercial occupancies often leverage electric signs for aesthetics, identification, or advertising and this article provides the rules governing the installation of this equipment. Many of these rules are outside of the scope of this material, however, some of the topics we cover include the following:

- Listing
- Marking
- Branch Circuits
- Disconnecting Means
- Ballasts, Transformers, Power sources

Part I. General

600.1 Scope

Article 600 covers the installation of conductors, equipment, and field wiring for electric signs. ▸Figure 600–1

▸Figure 600–1

Author's Comment:

- According to Article 100 an "Electric Sign" is defined as any fixed, stationary, or portable self-contained, electrically illuminated utilization equipment with words or symbols designed to convey information or attract attention. ▸Figure 600–2

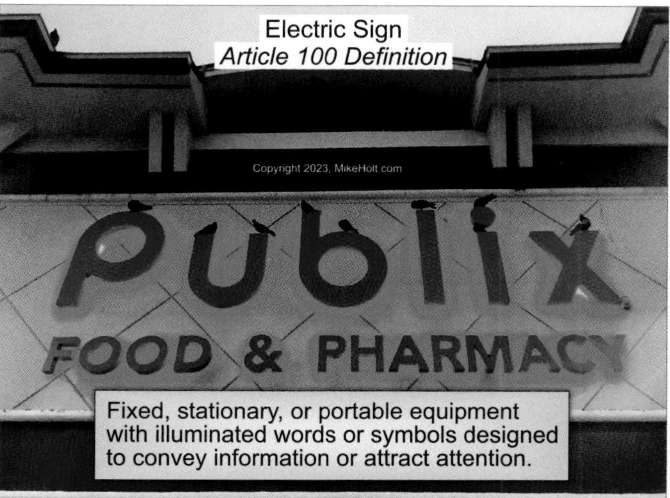

Electric Sign
Article 100 Definition
Copyright 2023, MikeHolt.com
Publix
FOOD & PHARMACY
Fixed, stationary, or portable equipment with illuminated words or symbols designed to convey information or attract attention.

▸Figure 600–2

600.3 Listing

Electric signs and retrofit kits must be listed and labeled and installed in accordance with their instructions. ▸Figure 600–3

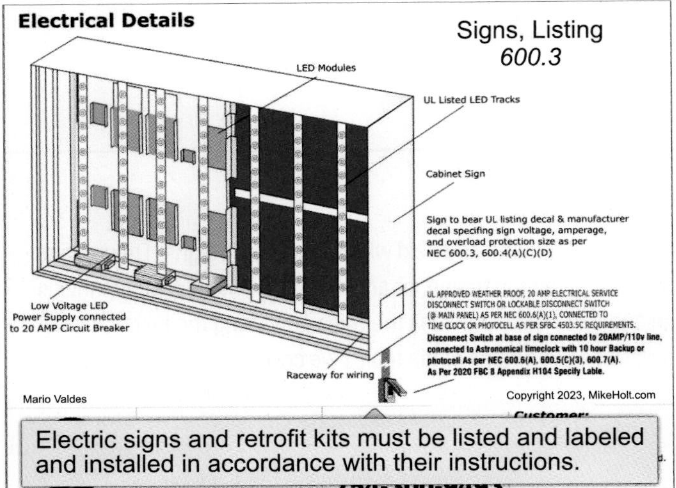

▸Figure 600–3

600.4 Markings

(A) Sign. Sign must be listed, labeled, and marked with the manufacturer's name, trademark, voltage and current ratings, or other means of identification.

(B) Signs with a Retrofitted Illumination System. Signs with a retrofitted illumination system must contain the following:

(1) The sign must be marked that the illumination system has been replaced.

(2) The marking must include the kit provider's and installer's name, logo, or unique identifier.

(3) Signs equipped with tubular light-emitting diode lamps powered by the existing sign sockets must have an additional warning label(s) alerting personnel during relamping that the sign has been modified and that fluorescent lamps are not to be used.

(D) Marking Visibility. The markings required in 600.4(A) and listing labels must be visible after installation and be permanently applied in a location visible prior to servicing. The marking is permitted to be installed in a location not viewed by the public.

600.5 Branch Circuits

(A) Required Sign Outlet. Each commercial building or occupancy accessible to pedestrians must have a sign outlet at the entrance of each tenant space. The outlet must be supplied by a branch circuit rated at least 20A that serves no other loads. ▸Figure 600–4

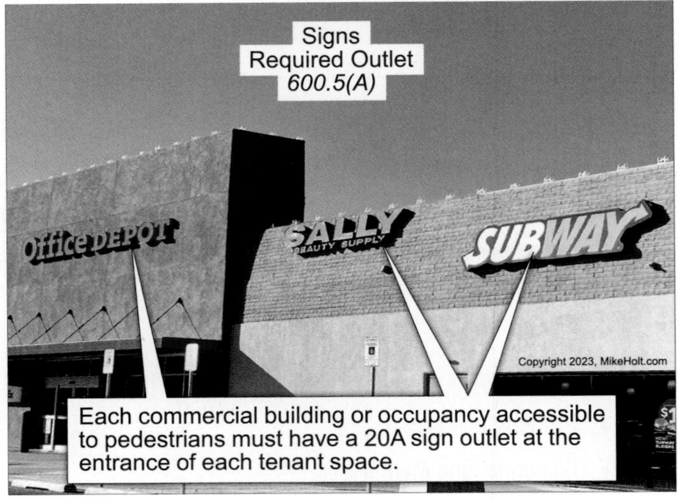

▸Figure 600–4

Ex 1: A sign outlet is not required at entrances intended to be used only by service personnel or employees. ▸Figure 600–5

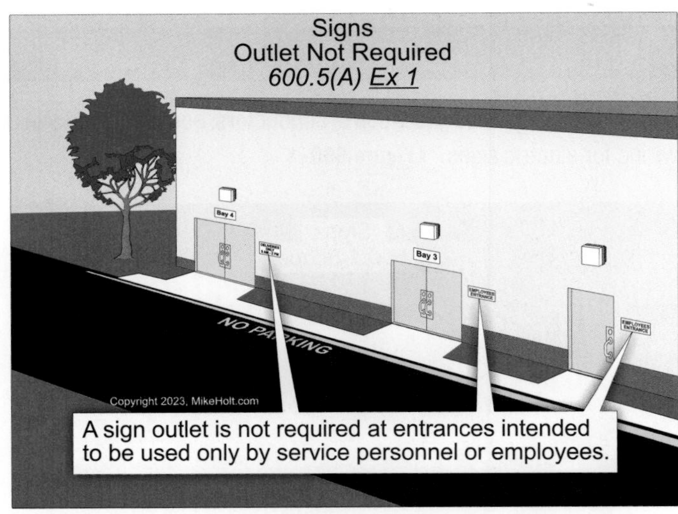

▸Figure 600–5

Ex 2: The required sign branch circuit can supply loads directly related to the control of the sign such as electronic or electromechanical controllers.

(B) Disconnect Marking. A disconnect for a sign or controller is required and it must identity the sign or controller it controls.

Ex: An external disconnect that is mounted on the sign body, sign enclosure, sign pole, or controller is not required to identify the sign it controls.

(C) Branch-Circuit Rating. Branch circuits that supply signs are considered a continuous load for circuit sizing. ▶**Figure 600–6**

▶**Figure 600–6**

(D) Wiring Methods. Wiring methods used to supply signs must comply with 600.5(D)(1), (D)(2), and (D)(3).

(1) Supply. The wiring method used to supply sign must terminate within a sign, a suitable box, a conduit body, or panelboard.

(2) Enclosures as Pull Boxes.

(a) Listed and labeled sign enclosures are permitted as pull or junction boxes for conductors supplying:

(1) Other adjacent signs

(3) Floodlights that are part of a sign

(b) The sign enclosures in 600.5(D)(2)(a) can contain both branch-circuit and secondary conductors.

(c) Listed and labeled neon transformer enclosures are permitted to contain voltages over 1000V, provided the sign disconnect de-energizes all current-carrying conductors in these enclosures.

(3) Metal or Nonmetallic Poles. Metal or nonmetallic poles used to support signs are permitted to enclose supply conductors.

600.6 Disconnecting Means

Disconnect Type. A disconnecting means is required for the circuit conductors to a sign controlled by an externally operable switch or circuit breaker that will open all phase conductors. ▶**Figure 600–7**

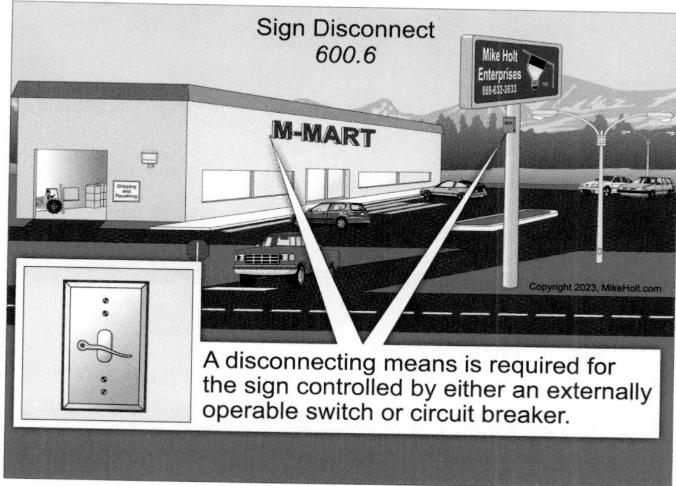

▶**Figure 600–7**

Note: The location of the disconnect is intended to allow service or maintenance personnel and first responders complete and local control of the disconnect.

(A) Disconnect Location. The sign disconnect must be accessible and located in accordance with 600.6(A)(1), (A)(2), or (A)(3). If the sign disconnect is remote from the sign, it must comply with 600.6(A)(4).

(1) At the Point of Entry to a Sign. The sign disconnect must be located where the conductors enter the sign enclosure, sign body, or pole. ▶**Figure 600–8**

Ex 1: A sign disconnect is not required to be at the point the conductors enter a sign enclosure or sign body for conductors that pass through a sign where not accessible and enclosed in a Chapter 3 raceway or metal-jacketed cable.

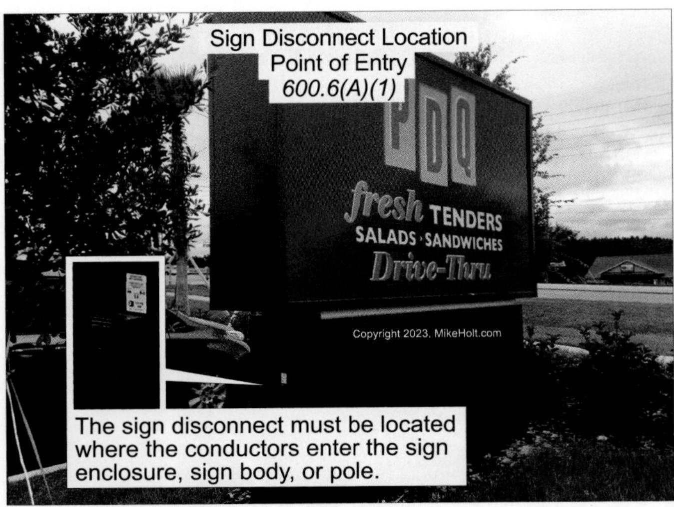

▸Figure 600–8

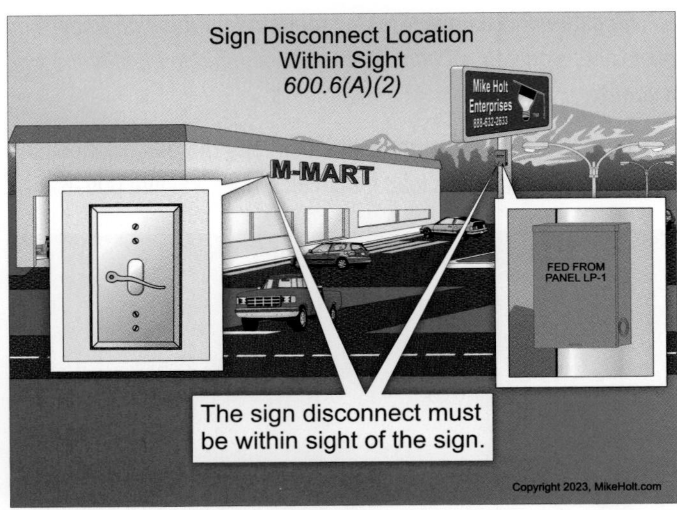

▸Figure 600–9

Ex 2: A sign disconnect is not required to be at the point the conductors enter a sign enclosure or sign body for a feeder that supplies a panelboard within the sign under the following conditions: The feeder conductors must be enclosed where not accessible in a Chapter 3 raceway or metal-jacketed cable, a permanent field-applied danger label that is visible during servicing must be applied to the raceway or metal-clad cable at or near the point of the feeder circuit conductors' entry into the sign enclosure or sign body, and the danger label reads:

DANGER. THIS RACEWAY CONTAINS ENERGIZED CONDUCTORS

The danger label must identify the location of the sign disconnect and the sign disconnect must be capable of being locked in the open position in accordance with 110.25.

(2) Within Sight of the Sign. The sign disconnect must be within sight of the sign. ▸**Figure 600–9**

If the sign disconnect is not within sight of the sign, the disconnect must be capable of being locked in the open position in accordance with 110.25. A permanent field-applied label that identifies the location of the sign disconnect must be placed on the sign where it will be visible during servicing. ▸**Figure 600–10**

According to Article 100, "Within Sight" means equipment that is visible and not more than 50 ft from the location of the other equipment. ▸**Figure 600–11**

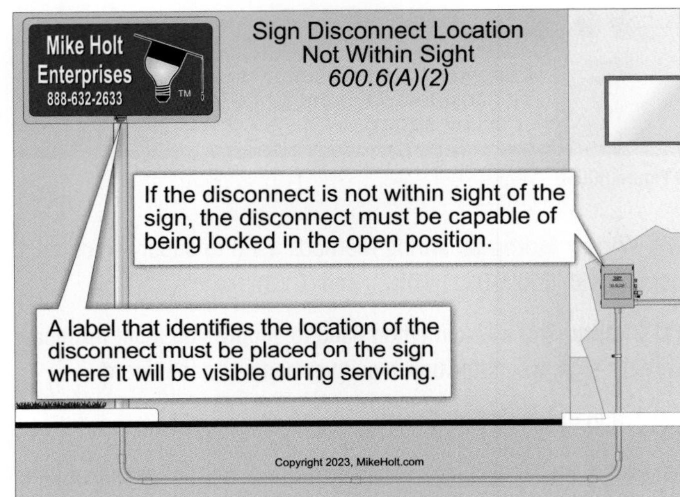

▸Figure 600–10

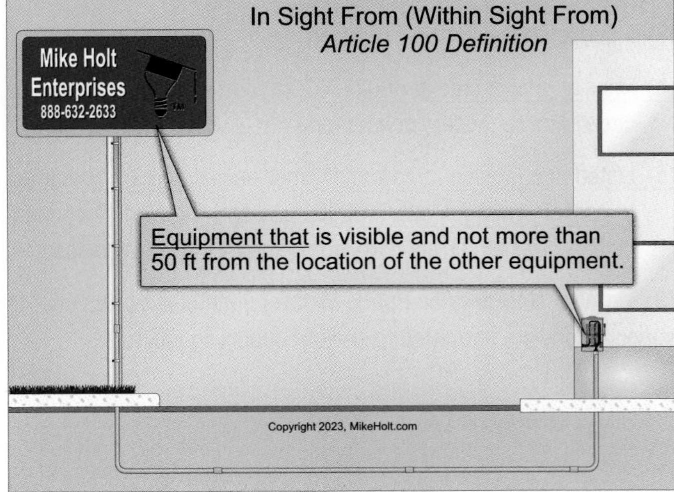

In Sight From (Within Sight From)
Article 100 Definition
Mike Holt Enterprises
888-632-2633
Equipment that is visible and not more than 50 ft from the location of the other equipment.
Copyright 2023, MikeHolt.com

▸Figure 600–11

(3) Controller Disconnect as Sign Disconnect. Sign operated by controllers external to the sign must have a disconnect for the sign controller in accordance with the following:

(1) The controller disconnect must be within sight of or within the controller enclosure.

(2) The controller disconnect must disconnect the sign and the controller from all phase conductors. ▶Figure 600–12

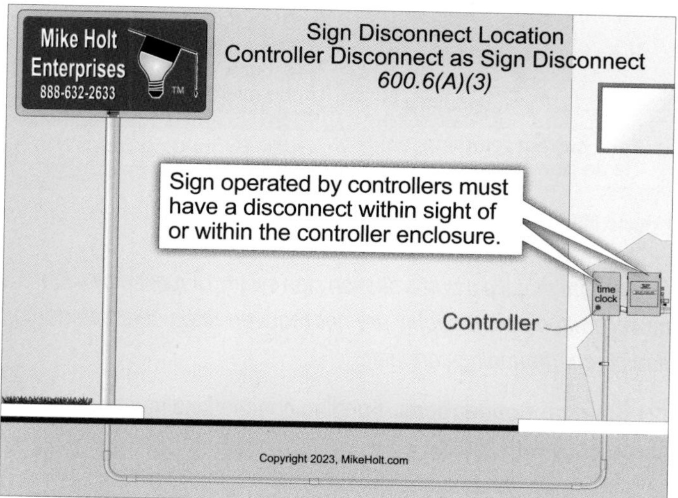
Mike Holt Enterprises 888-632-2633
Sign Disconnect Location
Controller Disconnect as Sign Disconnect
600.6(A)(3)
Sign operated by controllers must have a disconnect within sight of or within the controller enclosure.
time clock
Controller
Copyright 2023, MikeHolt.com

▶Figure 600–12

(3) The controller disconnect must be capable of being locked in the open position in accordance with 110.25.

Ex: Where the controller disconnect is not within sight of the controller, a permanent field-applied label that identifies the location of the controller disconnect must be on the controller where it can be visible during servicing.

(4) Remote Location. If the disconnect is remote from the sign, sign body, or pole, it must be at an accessible location available to first responders and service personnel. ▶Figure 600–13

The location of the disconnect must be marked with a label at the sign location and marked as the disconnect for the sign.

600.7 Grounding and Bonding

(A) Equipment Grounding Conductor and Grounding.

(1) Equipment Grounding Conductor. Metal parts of signs must be connected to the circuit equipment grounding conductor. ▶Figure 600–14

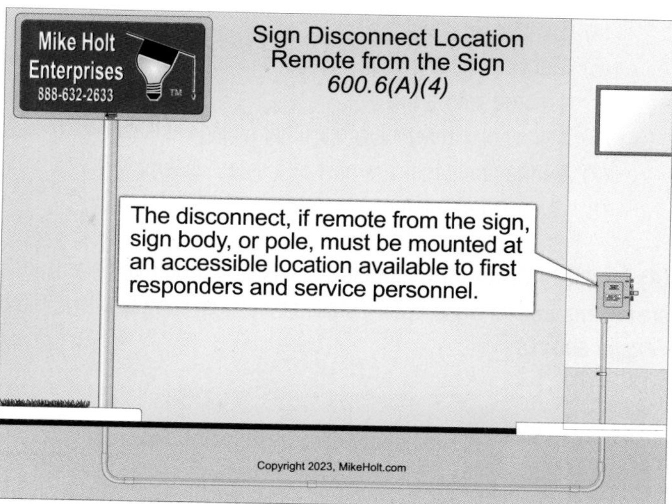
Mike Holt Enterprises 888-632-2633
Sign Disconnect Location
Remote from the Sign
600.6(A)(4)
The disconnect, if remote from the sign, sign body, or pole, must be mounted at an accessible location available to first responders and service personnel.
Copyright 2023, MikeHolt.com

▶Figure 600–13

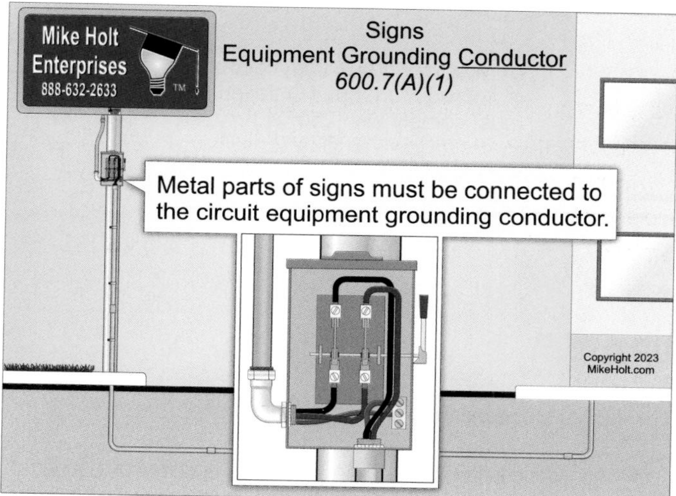
Mike Holt Enterprises 888-632-2633
Signs
Equipment Grounding Conductor
600.7(A)(1)
Metal parts of signs must be connected to the circuit equipment grounding conductor.
Copyright 2023 MikeHolt.com

▶Figure 600–14

(2) Size of Equipment Grounding Conductor. If the equipment grounding conductor is of the wire type, it must be sized in accordance with 250.122.

(3) Connections of Equipment Grounding Conductor. Equipment grounding conductor connections must be made in accordance with 250.130 in a method specified in 250.8.

Author's Comment:

- According to 250.8, equipment grounding conductors of the wire type must terminate in any of the following methods:

  (1) Listed pressure connectors
  (2) Terminal bars
  (3) Pressure connectors listed for grounding and bonding

(4) Exothermic welding
(5) Machine screws that engage at least two threads or are secured with a nut
(6) Self-tapping machine screws that engage at least two threads
(7) Connections that are part of a listed assembly
(8) Other listed means

(4) Auxiliary Grounding Electrode. Auxiliary grounding electrodes are not required for signs, but if installed they must comply with 250.54. ▸**Figure 600–15**

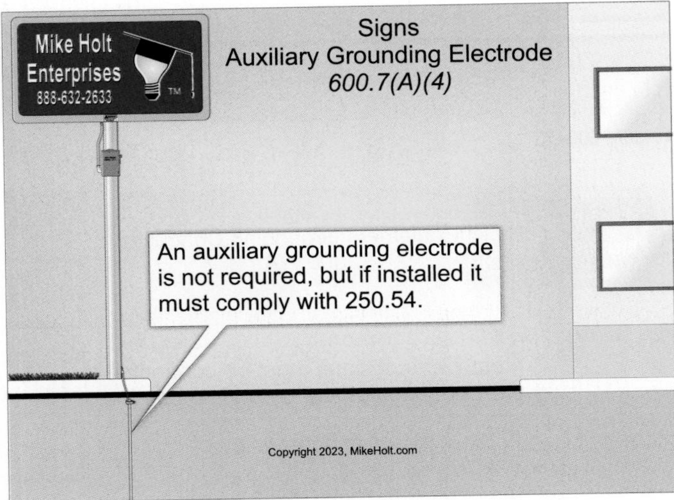

Mike Holt Enterprises 888-632-2633
Signs
Auxiliary Grounding Electrode
600.7(A)(4)
An auxiliary grounding electrode is not required, but if installed it must comply with 250.54.
Copyright 2023, MikeHolt.com

▸**Figure 600–15**

Author's Comment:

- According to 250.54, auxiliary electrodes need not be bonded to the building grounding electrode system, the grounding conductor to the electrode need not be sized in accordance with 250.66, and the contact resistance of the electrode to the Earth is not required to comply with the 25-ohm requirement of 250.53(A)(2) Ex.
- The Earth must not be used as the effective ground-fault current path required by 250.4(A)(4) and 250.4(A)(5). This is because the contact resistance of a grounding electrode to the Earth is high, and very little ground-fault current returns to the electrical supply source via the Earth. The result is the circuit overcurrent protective device will not open and clear a ground fault, so metal parts will remain energized with dangerous step and touch voltage. ▸**Figure 600–16**

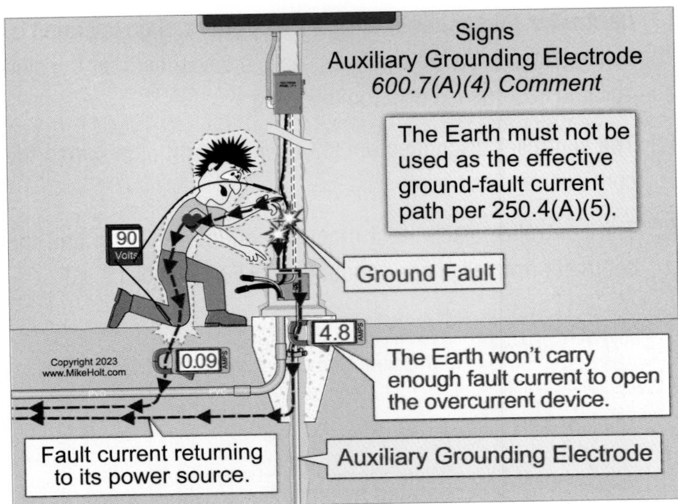

Signs
Auxiliary Grounding Electrode
600.7(A)(4) Comment
The Earth must not be used as the effective ground-fault current path per 250.4(A)(5).
90 Volts
Ground Fault
4.8
0.09
Copyright 2023 www.MikeHolt.com
The Earth won't carry enough fault current to open the overcurrent device.
Fault current returning to its power source.
Auxiliary Grounding Electrode

▸**Figure 600–16**

Ex: Remote metal parts of a section sign system supplied by a Class 2 power-limited power supply are not required to be connected to an equipment grounding conductor.

(B) Bonding.

(1) Metal Parts. Metal parts of sign systems must be bonded together and to the transformer or power-supply equipment grounding conductor.

(2) Bonding Connections. Bonding connections must be made in accordance with 250.8.

Author's Comment:

- According to 250.8, bonding conductors must terminate in any of the following methods:

  (1) Listed pressure connectors
  (2) Terminal bars
  (3) Pressure connectors listed for grounding and bonding
  (4) Exothermic welding
  (5) Machine screws that engage at least two threads or are secured with a nut
  (6) Self-tapping machine screws that engage at least two threads
  (7) Connections that are part of a listed assembly
  (8) Other listed means

(4) Flexible Metal Conduit Length. Listed flexible metal conduit or listed liquidtight flexible metal conduit for secondary circuit conductors for neon tubing can be used as a bonding means if the total length of the flexible metal conduit does not exceed 100 ft.

(7) Bonding Conductors. Bonding conductors installed outside a sign or raceway must be protected from physical damage, installed in accordance with 250.120, sized in accordance with 250.122, and comply with one of the following:

(1) Bonding conductors must be copper and not smaller than 14 AWG.

1st Printing

(2) Bonding conductors must be copper-clad aluminum and not smaller than 12 AWG.

600.9 Location

(A) Vehicles. Signs must be at least 14 ft above areas accessible to vehicles unless protected from physical damage. ▶Figure 600–17

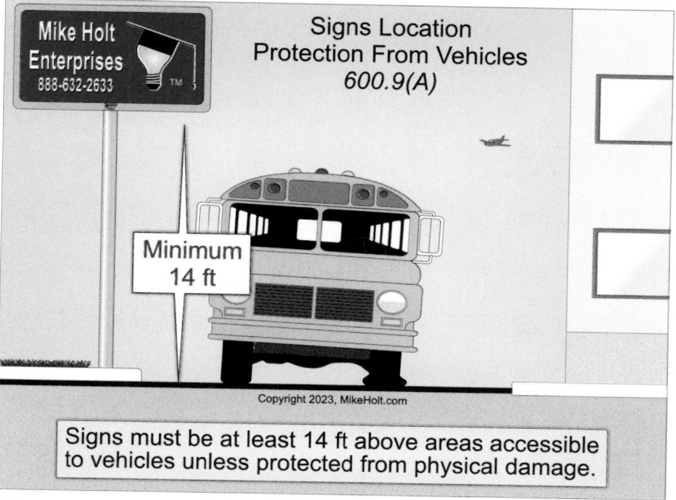

▶Figure 600–17

(B) Pedestrians. Neon tubing used for signs, decorative elements, skeleton tubing, or art forms must be protected from physical damage where readily accessible to pedestrians.

(C) Adjacent to Combustible Materials. Sign systems must be installed so adjacent combustible materials are not subjected to temperatures that exceed 194°F.

(D) Wet Location. Sign systems installed in wet locations must be weatherproof and must have drain holes.

600.21 Ballasts, Transformers, Class 2 Power-Limited Power Sources, and Electronic Power Supplies

Ballasts, transformers, electronic power supplies, and Class 2 power-limited power sources must be self-contained or enclosed in a listed sign body or listed separate enclosure.

(A) Accessibility. Ballasts, transformers, Class 2 power-limited power sources, and electronic power supplies must be securely fastened in place.

(B) Location. The secondary conductors from ballasts, transformers, Class 2 power-limited power sources, and electronic power supplies must be as short as possible.

(D) Working Space. A working space not less than 3 ft high by 3 ft wide by 3 ft deep is required for each ballast, transformer, Class 2 power-limited power source, and electronic power supply if not installed in a sign.

(E) Attic Locations. Ballasts, transformers, Class 2 power-limited power sources, and electronic power supplies are permitted in attics and soffits where an access door (36 in. by 22.50 in. minimum) and a passageway not less than 3 ft high by 2 ft wide with a suitable permanent walkway at least 1 ft wide to the point of entrance for each component is provided.

At least one lighting outlet that contains a switch or is controlled by a wall switch must be installed at the usual point of entrance to these spaces. The lighting outlet must be at or near the equipment requiring servicing.

(F) Suspended Ceilings. Ballasts, transformers, electronic power supplies, and Class 2 power-limited power sources can be above a suspended ceiling, provided the enclosures are securely fastened in place and not connected to the suspended-ceiling grid for support.

Ballasts, transformers, and electronic power supplies installed above a suspended ceiling are not permitted to be connected to the branch-circuit wiring by a flexible cord. ▶Figure 600–18

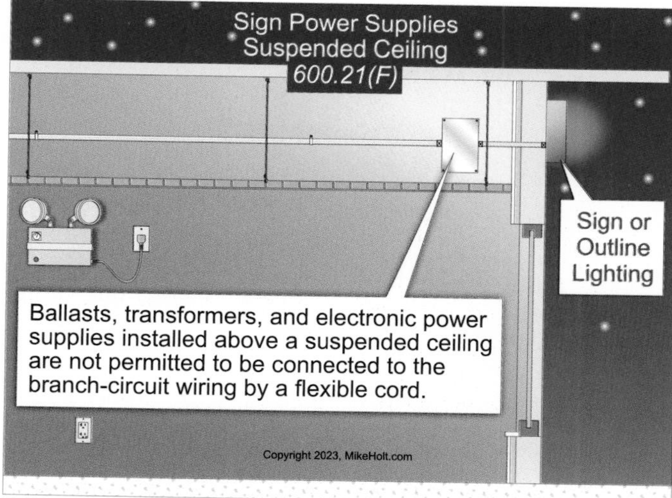

▶Figure 600–18

600.24 Class 2 Power-Limited Power Sources

(A) Listing. Class 2 power-limited power supplies and power sources must be listed for use with electric sign systems or be a component in a listed sign.

(B) Equipment Grounding Conductor. Metal parts of Class 2 power-limited power sources must be connected to the circuit equipment grounding conductor supplying the power source.

1st Printing

ARTICLE 604 MANUFACTURED WIRING SYSTEMS

Introduction to Article 604—Manufactured Wiring Systems

This article covers the installation of field-installed manufactured wiring systems used for the connection of luminaires, utilization equipment, and devices that are assembled by a manufacturer with components which cannot be inspected at the building site without damage to, or destruction of, the component. Many of these rules are outside of the scope of this material, however, some of the topics we cover include the following:

- Scope
- Listing Requirements
- Securing and Supporting

604.1 Scope

Article 604 covers field-installed manufactured wiring systems. ▶Figure 604–1

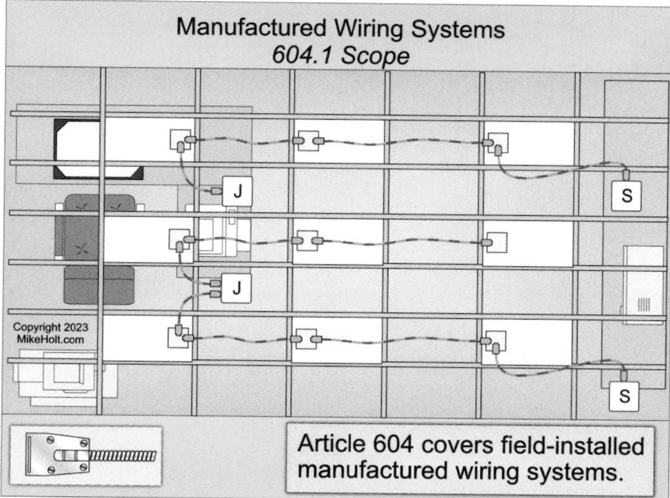

▶Figure 604–1

According to Article 100, a "Manufactured Wiring System" is a system used for the connection of luminaires, utilization equipment, and devices that are assembled by a manufacturer with components which cannot be inspected at the building site without damage to, or destruction of, the component.

Author's Comment:

- Manufactured wiring systems are typically installed in commercial and institutional occupancies because of their ability to be easily installed and relocated as the need arises.

604.6 Listing Requirements

Manufactured wiring systems and associated components must be listed.

604.7 Installation—Securing and Supporting

Type AC and Type MC cable used for manufactured wiring systems must be secured and supported according to the requirements of Article 320 for Type AC cable and Article 330 for Type MC cable. ▶Figure 604–2

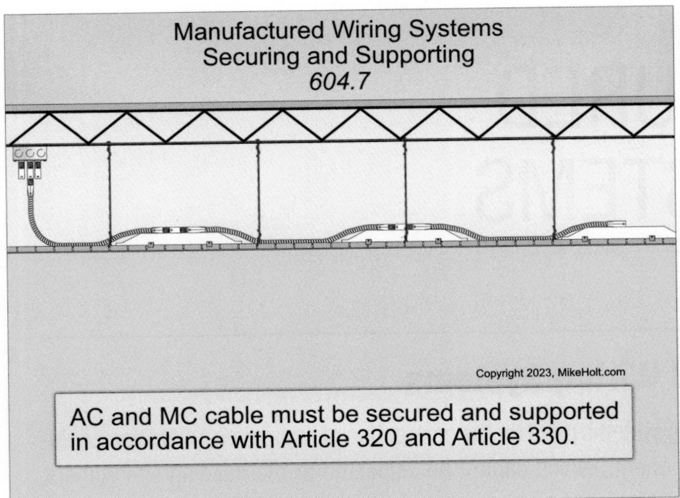
Manufactured Wiring Systems
Securing and Supporting
604.7
Copyright 2023, MikeHolt.com
AC and MC cable must be secured and supported in accordance with Article 320 and Article 330.

▶Figure 604–2

Author's Comment:

- Type AC cable must be secured at intervals not exceeding 4½ ft [320.30(B)], and Type MC cable must be secured at intervals not exceeding 6 ft [330.30(B)].

604.10 Uses Permitted

Manufactured wiring systems can be installed in accessible and dry locations, and in plenum spaces in accordance with 300.22(C). ▶Figure 604–3

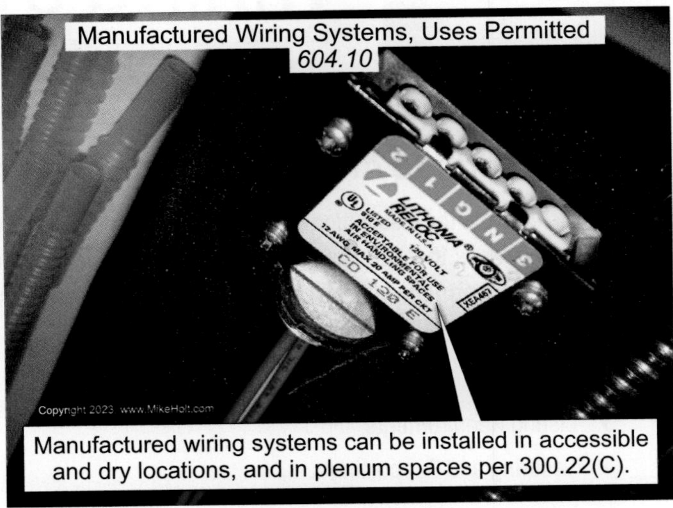
Manufactured Wiring Systems, Uses Permitted
604.10
Copyright 2023 www.MikeHolt.com
Manufactured wiring systems can be installed in accessible and dry locations, and in plenum spaces per 300.22(C).

▶Figure 604–3

ARTICLE

620 ELEVATORS

Introduction to Article 620—Elevators

This article covers the installation of wiring and equipment used with elevators, dumbwaiters, escalators, moving walks, platform lifts, and stairway chairlifts. Due to the design, operation, and frequent maintenance needs for this equipment, there are a variety of special requirements that must be met when they are installed. Many of these rules are outside of the scope of this material, however, some of the topics we cover include the following:

- Scope
- GFCI Protection for Receptacles
- Branch Circuits
- Wiring
- Installation of Conductors
- Disconnecting Means

Article 620 contains these parts:

- Part I. General
- Part II. Conductors
- Part III. Wiring
- Part IV. Installation of Conductors
- Part V. Traveling Cables (Not Covered)
- Part VI. Disconnecting Means and Control
- Parts VII–Part X. (Not Covered)

Part I. General

620.1 Scope

This article covers the installation of electrical equipment and wiring used in connection with elevators, dumbwaiters, escalators, moving walks, platform lifts, and stairway chairlifts. ▶**Figure 620–1**

Author's Comment:

- This material only covers the requirements for elevators, it does not cover the requirements for dumbwaiters, escalators, moving walks, platform lifts, or stairway chairlifts.

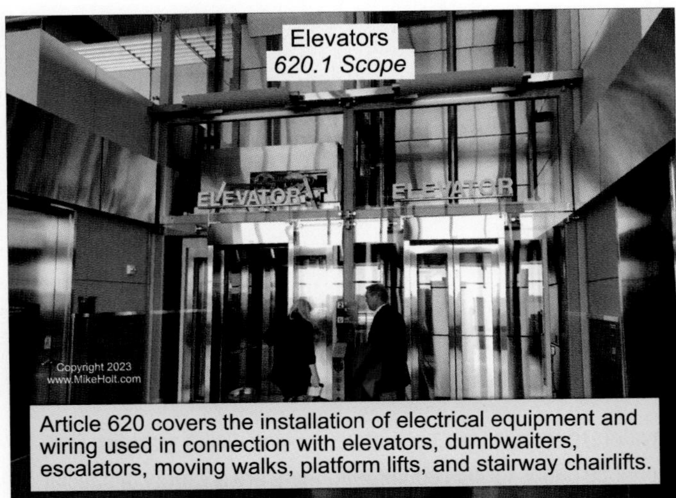

▶Figure 620–1

620.6 GFCI Protection for Receptacles

(A) Pits, Hoistways, and Elevator Cars. Receptacles rated 15A and 20A, 125V in pits, hoistways, and elevator cars must be of the GFCI type. ▶Figure 620–2

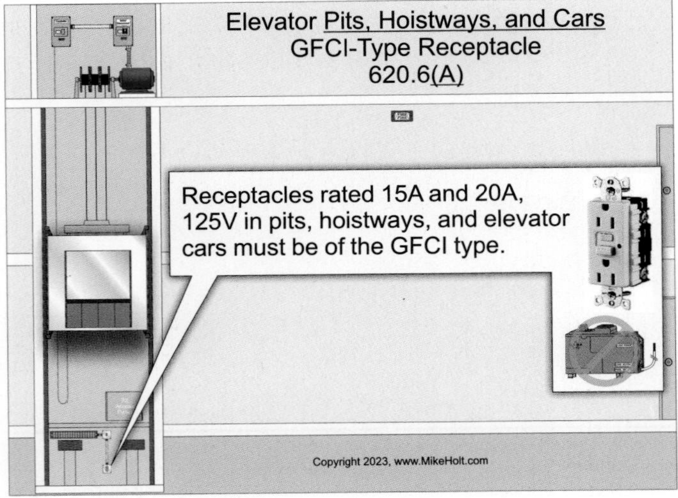

Elevator Pits, Hoistways, and Cars
GFCI-Type Receptacle
620.6(A)
Receptacles rated 15A and 20A, 125V in pits, hoistways, and elevator cars must be of the GFCI type.
Copyright 2023, www.MikeHolt.com

▶Figure 620–2

Author's Comment:

- A worker in an elevator pit area should not have to climb out of the pit to reset the GFCI protection, therefore this rule prohibits the use of a GFCI breaker or GFCI faceless device and requires the receptacle to be of the GFCI type.

(B) Machine Rooms, Control Spaces, Machinery Spaces, Control Rooms, and Truss Interiors. Receptacles rated 15A and 20A, 125V in machine rooms, control spaces, machinery spaces, control rooms, and truss interiors must be GFCI protected. ▶Figure 620–3

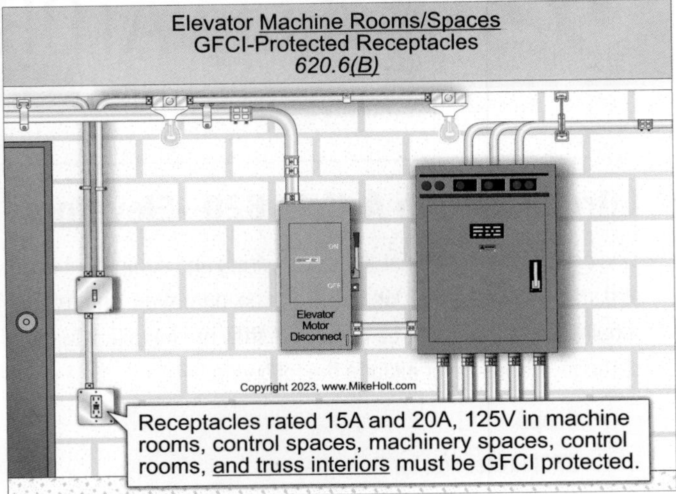

▶Figure 620–3

Author's Comment:

- In elevator machine rooms or spaces, accessibility to reset the GFCI is not as restricted as in pit areas, therefore receptacles in these spaces can be GFCI protected by either a GFCI breaker, GFCI receptacle, or GFCI faceless device.

(C) Sump Pumps. A permanently installed sump pump must be hard wired or supplied by a receptacle that is GFCI protected. ▶Figure 620–4

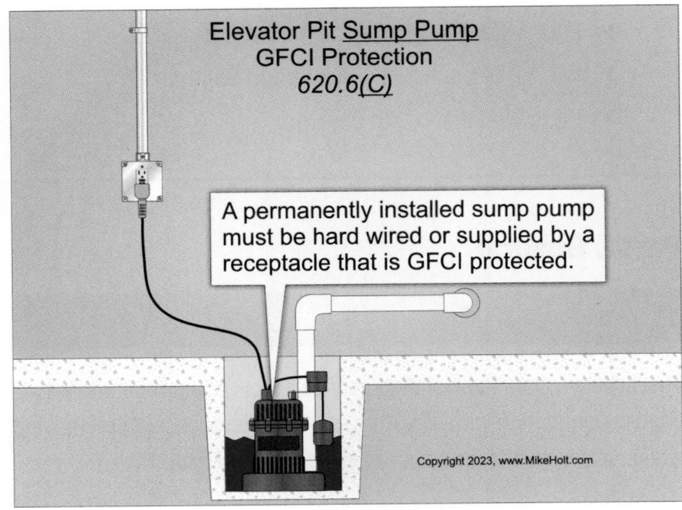

Elevator Pit Sump Pump
GFCI Protection
620.6(C)
A permanently installed sump pump must be hard wired or supplied by a receptacle that is GFCI protected.
Copyright 2023, www.MikeHolt.com

▶Figure 620–4

1st Printing

Part III. Wiring

620.22 Branch Circuits for Elevator Car(s)

(A) Car Light, Receptacles, Auxiliary Lighting, and Ventilation. A separate branch circuit must supply the elevator car lights. This branch circuit is permitted to supply receptacles, alarm devices, emergency responder radio coverage, elevator car ventilation purification systems, monitoring devices not part of the control system, an auxiliary lighting power source, elevator car emergency signaling, communications devices including their associated charging circuits, and ventilation on each elevator car or inside the operation controller.

Where there is no machine room, control room, machinery space, or control space outside the hoistway, the overcurrent protective device must be outside the hoistway and accessible to qualified persons only.

(B) Air-Conditioning and Heating Source. Air-conditioning and heating units must be supplied by a separate branch circuit for each elevator car.

The overcurrent protective device protecting the branch circuit must be in the elevator machine room, control room, machinery space, or control space. If there is no machine room, control room, machinery space, or control space outside the hoistway, the overcurrent protective device must be outside the hoistway and accessible only to qualified persons.

Author's Comment:

- While the air-conditioning and heating must be served by an individual circuit for each elevator car, the branch circuit for the elevator car lights is permitted to serve more than one elevator car. Branch-circuit overcurrent protective devices for elevator cars must be in the elevator machine room.

620.23 Branch Circuits for Machine Room/Machinery Space

(A) Separate Branch Circuits. The branch circuit(s) supplying lighting for machine rooms, control rooms, machinery spaces, control spaces, or truss interiors must be on a separate circuit from the one supplying receptacles. These lighting and receptacle circuits for elevator machine room/spaces may not supply any other load(s). ▸**Figure 620-5**

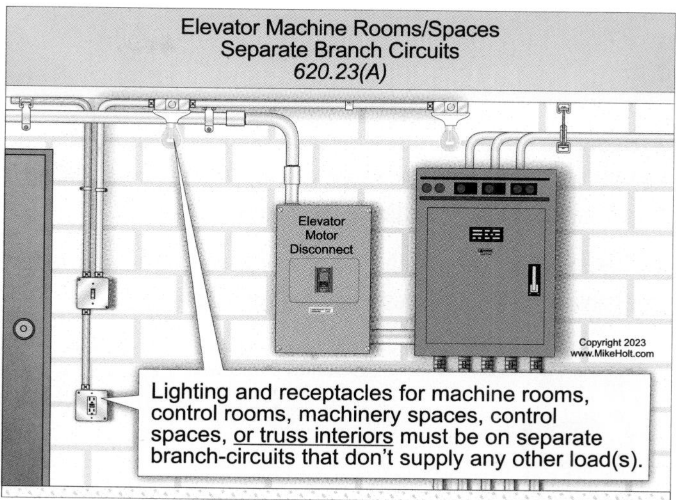

▸**Figure 620-5**

The required lighting in these spaces is not permitted to be connected to the load side of a GFCI.

(B) Light Switch. The switch for machine rooms, control rooms, machinery space, or control space lighting must be located at the point of entry for these areas.

(C) Duplex Receptacle. At least one 125V, single-phase, 15A or 20A duplex receptacle must be installed in each machine room, control room and machinery space, control space, and truss interiors. ▸**Figure 620-6**

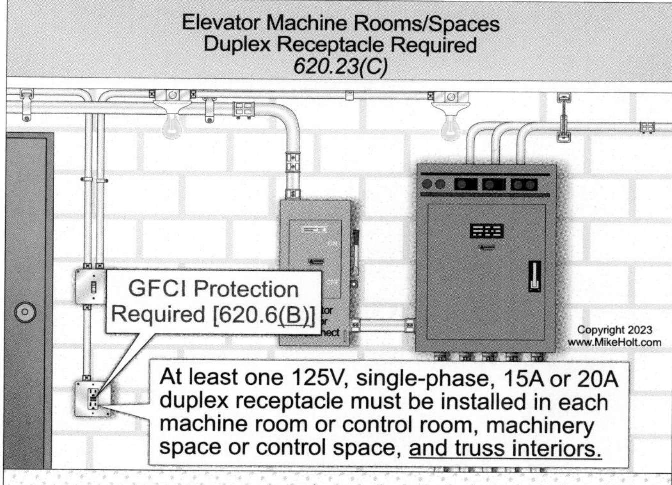

▸**Figure 620-6**

620.24 Branch Circuit for Hoistway Pit Lighting and Receptacles

(A) Separate Branch Circuits. Separate branch circuits must supply the hoistway pit lighting and receptacle(s). The required lighting is not permitted to be connected to the load side of a GFCI.

(B) Light Switch. The switch for hoistway pit lighting must be readily accessible from the pit access door. ▸**Figure 620–7**

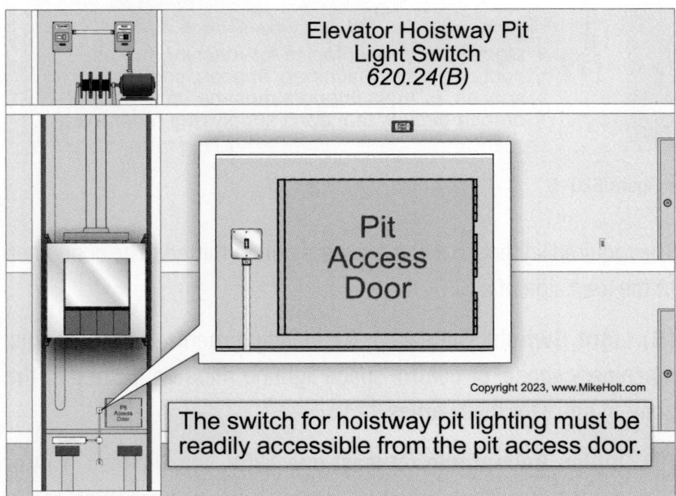
Elevator Hoistway Pit
Light Switch
620.24(B)
Pit
Access
Door
Copyright 2023, www.MikeHolt.com
The switch for hoistway pit lighting must be readily accessible from the pit access door.

▸**Figure 620–7**

(C) Duplex Receptacle. At least one 15A or 20A, 125V duplex GFCI receptacle must be installed in a hoistway pit [620.6(A)]. ▸**Figure 620–8**

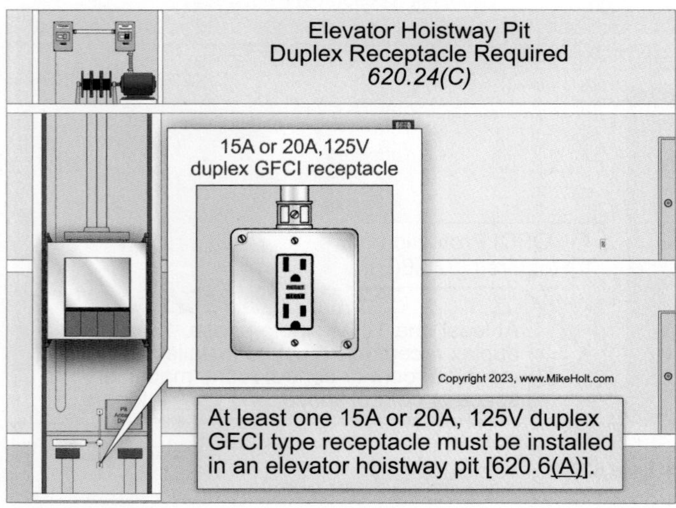
Elevator Hoistway Pit
Duplex Receptacle Required
620.24(C)
15A or 20A,125V
duplex GFCI receptacle
Copyright 2023, www.MikeHolt.com
At least one 15A or 20A, 125V duplex GFCI type receptacle must be installed in an elevator hoistway pit [620.6(A)].

▸**Figure 620–8**

Note 2: In elevator pit areas, receptacles of the GFCI type are required. See 620.6(A).

Part IV. Installation of Conductors

620.37 Wiring in Elevator Hoistways, Control, and Machine Rooms/Spaces

(A) Uses Permitted. The following electrical wiring, raceways, and cables are permitted inside the elevator hoistway, machine room, machinery spaces, control spaces, or control room:

(1) Class 2 power-limited circuits

(2) Communications with the car

(3) Fire detection systems

(4) Pit sump pumps

(5) Branch circuits in accordance with 620.24

(6) Heating, lighting, and ventilating the hoistway

(7) Heating, air-conditioning, lighting, and ventilating the elevator car

Part VI. Disconnecting Means and Control

620.51 Disconnecting Means

A disconnect that opens all phase conductors must be provided for each elevator. The elevator disconnect for the main power supply conductors is not permitted to disconnect power to the branch circuits required in 620.22, 620.23, and 620.24.

(A) Type. The disconnect must be listed and be an enclosed externally operable fused motor-circuit switch or circuit breaker must be capable of being locked in the open position in accordance with 110.25. ▸**Figure 620–9**

(C) Location. The disconnect must be readily accessible to qualified persons.

Author's Comment:

- With advancements in technology, and to save space, many elevators without machine rooms are being installed. The disconnect is located on the elevator itself and is considered readily accessible to qualified persons.

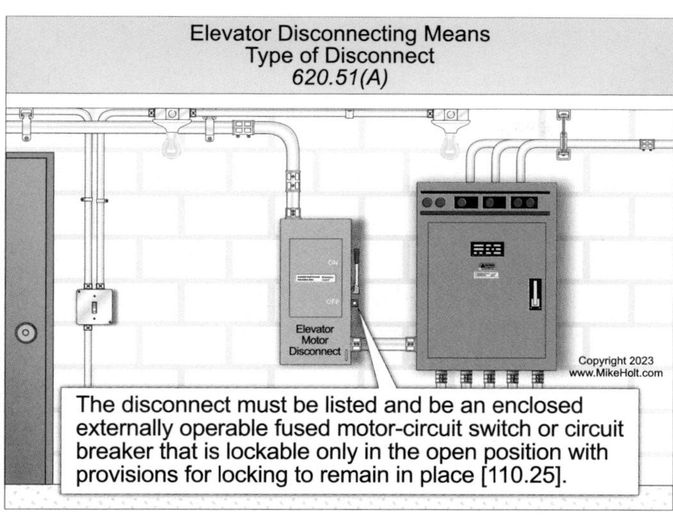
Elevator Disconnecting Means
Type of Disconnect
620.51(A)
Elevator
Motor
Disconnect
Copyright 2023
www.MikeHolt.com
The disconnect must be listed and be an enclosed externally operable fused motor-circuit switch or circuit breaker that is lockable only in the open position with provisions for locking to remain in place [110.25].

▶Figure 620-9

(D) Identification and Signs.

(1) Available Fault Current Marking. Elevator disconnects must be marked in the field with the available fault current at the line terminal and include the date the available fault current calculation was performed. The required field marking must be sufficiently durable to withstand the environment [110.21(B)].

(E) Surge Protection. Where the elevator disconnect is designated as part of an emergency or standby system, surge protection must be provided.

ARTICLE
625
ELECTRIC VEHICLE POWER TRANSFER SYSTEM

Introduction to Article 625—Electric Vehicle Power Transfer System

This article covers the installation of wiring and equipment used to connect electric vehicle power transfer systems to premise wiring. Electric vehicles have evolved over the last decade into not only a load that consumes power, but one that also must be managed and may be used as an interconnected contribute power system. Many of these rules are outside of the scope of this material, however we do cover the following topics in this article:

- Scope
- Electric Vehicle Branch Circuit
- Overcurrent Protection
- Disconnecting Means
- Interactive Equipment
- Wireless Power Transfer Equipment
- GFCI

Part I. General

625.1 Scope

Article 625 covers the installation of conductors and equipment associated with an electric vehicle for the purposes of charging, power export, or bidirectional current flow. ▶Figure 625–1 and ▶Figure 625–2

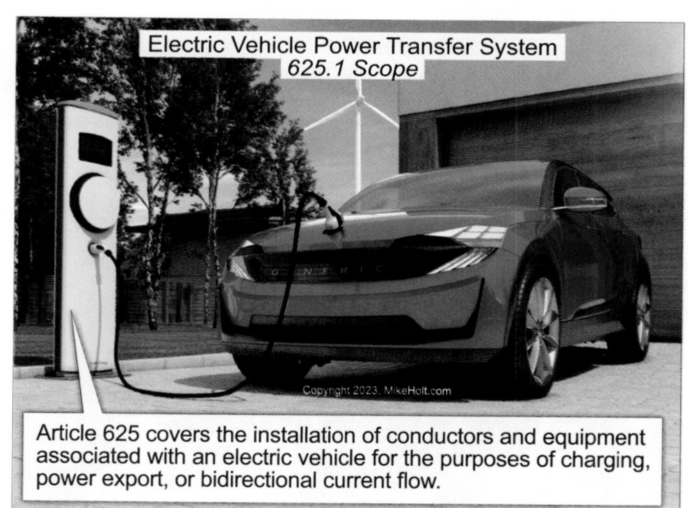

▶Figure 625–1

According to Article 100, "Electric Vehicle" is an on-road use automobile, bus, truck, van, neighborhood electric vehicle and motorcycle primarily powered by an electric motor. ▶Figure 625–3

Note: Off-road, self-propelled electric industrial trucks, hoists, lifts, transports, golf carts, airline ground support equipment, tractors, and boats are not electric vehicles for the purpose of the *NEC*. ▶Figure 625–4

625.6 Listed

Electric vehicle power transfer system equipment for the purposes of charging, power export, or bidirectional current flow must be listed. ▶Figure 625–5

Electric Vehicle Power Transfer System
625.1 Scope
Article 625 covers the installation of conductors and equipment associated with an electric vehicle for the purposes of charging, power export, or bidirectional current flow.
Copyright 2023 MikeHolt.com

▶Figure 625-2

Electric Vehicle
Article 100 Definition
Copyright 2023 www.MikeHolt.com
An on-road use automobile, bus, truck, van, neighborhood vehicle, or motorcycle primarily powered by an electric motor.

▶Figure 625-3

Electric Vehicle
Article 100 Note
CHE • JAGUAR
Electric Motorcars, LLC
Copyright 2023 MikeHolt.com
Off-road, self-propelled electric industrial trucks, hoists, lifts, transports, golf carts, airline ground support equipment, tractors, and boats are not electric vehicles for the purpose of the NEC.

▶Figure 625-4

Electric Vehicle Power Transfer System
Listed Equipment
625.6
BI-DIRECTIONAL CHARGER
Electric vehicle power transfer system equipment for the purposes of charging, power export, or bidirectional current flow must be listed.
Copyright 2023 MikeHolt.com

▶Figure 625-5

Part III. Installation

625.40 Electric Vehicle Branch Circuit

The branch circuit for electric vehicle supply equipment rated greater than 16A or 120V must be supplied by an individual branch circuit. ▶Figure 625-6

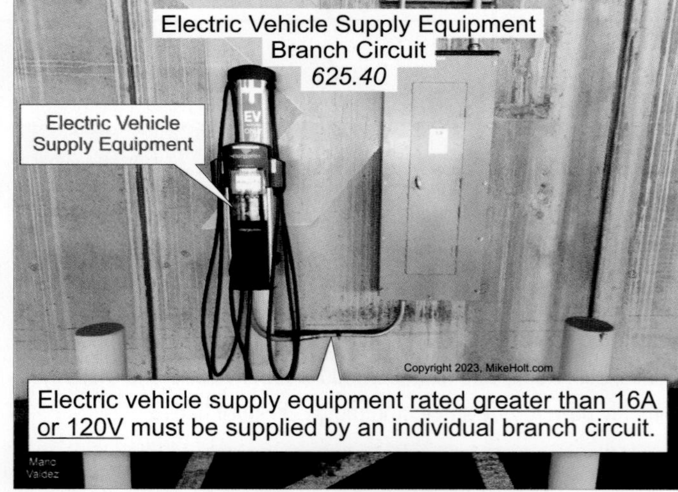
Electric Vehicle Supply Equipment
Branch Circuit
625.40
Electric Vehicle Supply Equipment
Copyright 2023, MikeHolt.com
Electric vehicle supply equipment rated greater than 16A or 120V must be supplied by an individual branch circuit.

▶Figure 625-6

According to Article 100, "Electric Vehicle Supply Equipment (EVSE)" includes the conductors, electric vehicle connectors, attachment plugs, personnel protection system, devices, and power outlets installed for the purpose of transferring energy between the premises wiring and the electric vehicle. ▶Figure 625-7

An "Individual Branch Circuit" is a branch circuit that supplies only one utilization equipment.

1st Printing

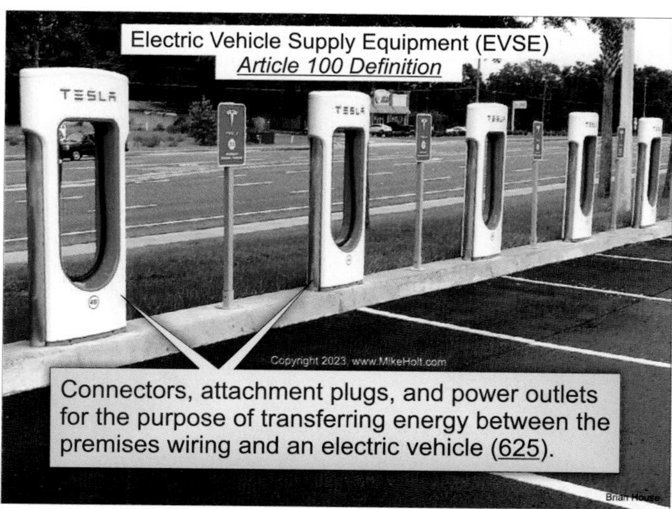
Electric Vehicle Supply Equipment (EVSE)
Article 100 Definition
Connectors, attachment plugs, and power outlets for the purpose of transferring energy between the premises wiring and an electric vehicle (625).
Copyright 2023, www.MikeHolt.com

▸Figure 625–7

Ex: A single branch circuit is permitted to supply more than one electric vehicle supply equipment when the loads are managed by an energy management system in accordance with 625.42(A) or (B).

625.41 Overcurrent Protection

Overcurrent protection must be sized at no less than 125 percent of the electric vehicle supply equipment current rating. ▸**Figure 625–8**

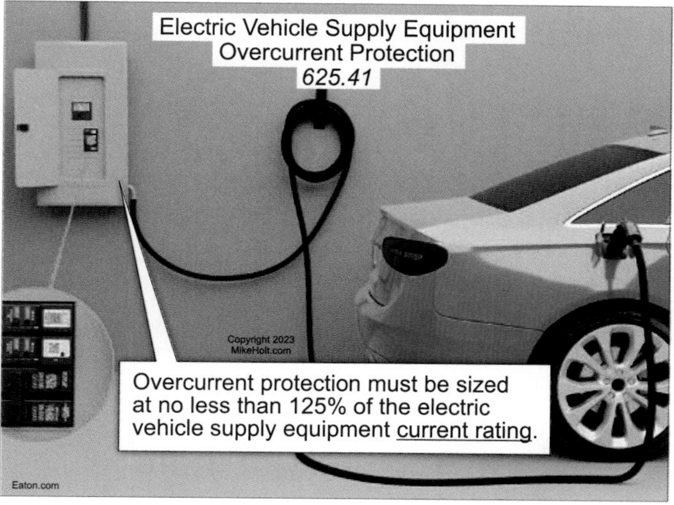
Electric Vehicle Supply Equipment
Overcurrent Protection
625.41
Overcurrent protection must be sized at no less than 125% of the electric vehicle supply equipment current rating.
Copyright 2023 MikeHolt.com
Eaton.com

▸Figure 625–8

▶ Example

Question: *What size overcurrent protection device is required for EVSE (EV Charger) rated 40A?* ▸**Figure 625–9**

(a) 40A *(b) 50A* *(c) 60A* *(d) 70A*

Solution:

The OCPD must have an ampere rating of not less than 50A (40A × 125%).

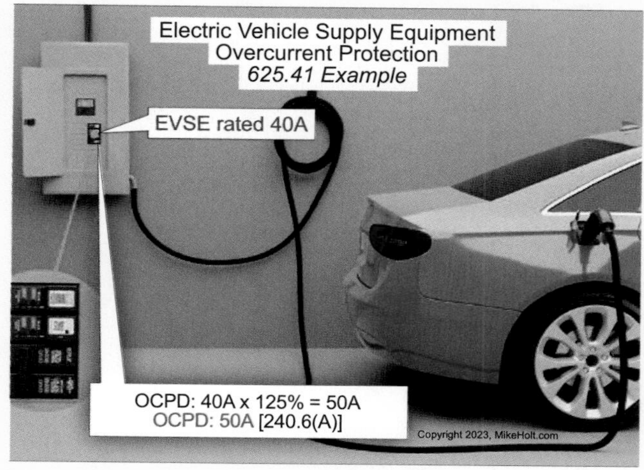
Electric Vehicle Supply Equipment
Overcurrent Protection
625.41 Example
EVSE rated 40A
OCPD: 40A x 125% = 50A
OCPD: 50A [240.6(A)]
Copyright 2023, MikeHolt.com

▸Figure 625–9

Answer: *(b) 50A*

625.42 Load

Electric vehicle supply equipment is considered a continuous load. ▸**Figure 625–10**

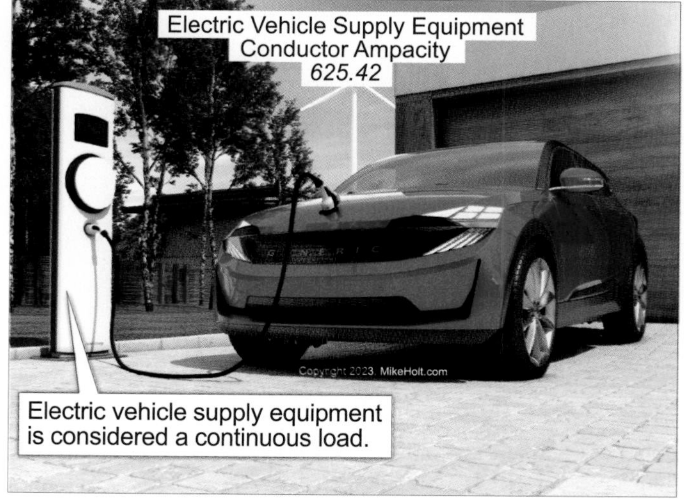
Electric Vehicle Supply Equipment
Conductor Ampacity
625.42
Electric vehicle supply equipment is considered a continuous load.
Copyright 2023, MikeHolt.com

▸Figure 625–10

▶ Conductor Ampacity Example

Question: *What's the minimum conductor ampacity size for an EVSE (EV Charger) rated 40A?* **▸Figure 625–11**

(a) 10 AWG *(b) 8 AWG* *(c) 6 AWG* *(d) 4 AWG*

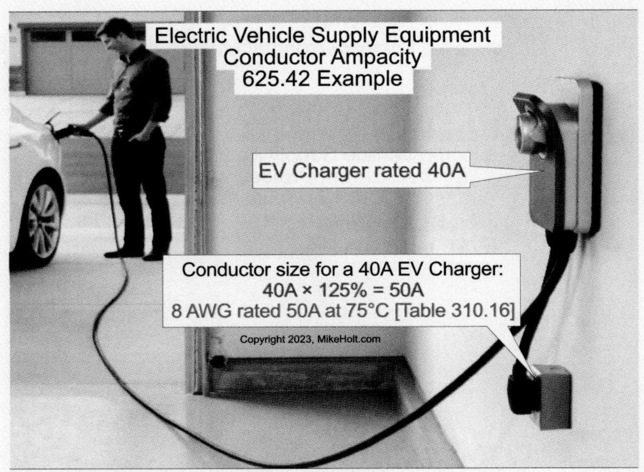
Electric Vehicle Supply Equipment
Conductor Ampacity
625.42 Example
EV Charger rated 40A
Conductor size for a 40A EV Charger:
40A × 125% = 50A
8 AWG rated 50A at 75°C [Table 310.16]
Copyright 2023, MikeHolt.com

▸Figure 625–11

Solution:

The conductor must have an ampacity of not less than 50A (40A × 125%).

8 AWG rated 50A at 75°C [Table 310.16]

Answer: *(b) 8 AWG*

▶ Type NM Cable Example

Question: *What's the minimum type NM cable ampacity size required for an EVSE (EV Charger) rated 40A?* **▸Figure 625–12**

(a) 10 AWG *(b) 8 AWG* *(c) 6 AWG* *(d) 4 AWG*

Solution:

The type NM cable must have an ampacity of not less than 50A (40A × 125%) at 60°C in accordance with 334.80.

6 AWG NM Cable rated 55A at 60°C [Table 310.16]

Answer: *(c) 6 AWG NM Cable*

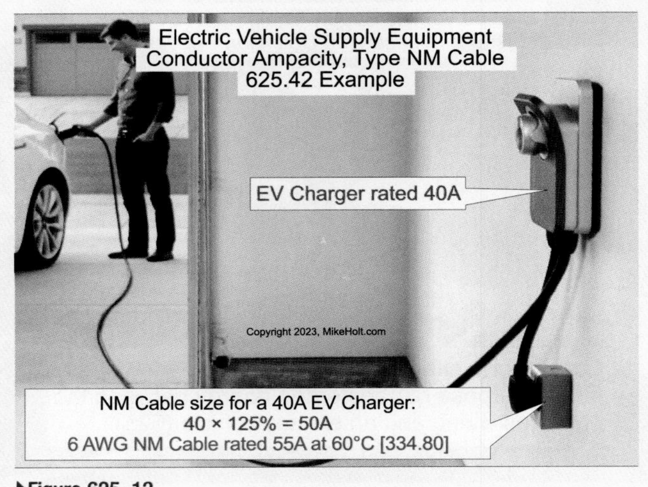
Electric Vehicle Supply Equipment
Conductor Ampacity, Type NM Cable
625.42 Example
EV Charger rated 40A
Copyright 2023, MikeHolt.com
NM Cable size for a 40A EV Charger:
40 × 125% = 50A
6 AWG NM Cable rated 55A at 60°C [334.80]

▸Figure 625–12

(A) Energy Management System. Where an energy management system is used to control the electric vehicle supply equipment, the load is not included when sizing feeders and service conductors in accordance with 750.30(C)(1)(1). **▸Figure 625–13**

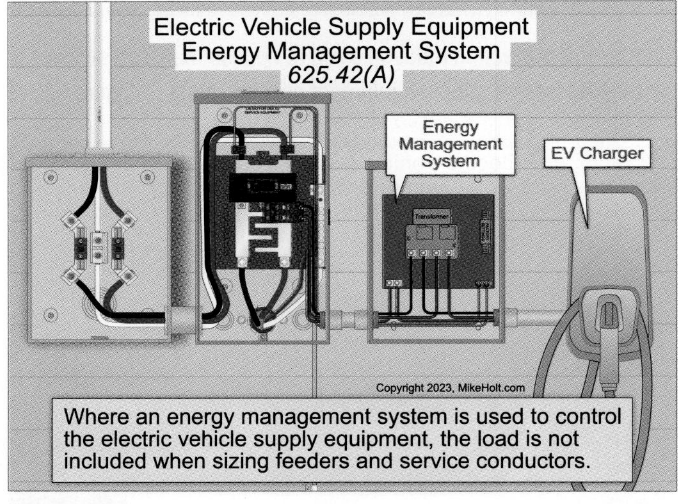
Electric Vehicle Supply Equipment
Energy Management System
625.42(A)
Energy Management System
EV Charger
Transformer
Copyright 2023, MikeHolt.com
Where an energy management system is used to control the electric vehicle supply equipment, the load is not included when sizing feeders and service conductors.

▸Figure 625–13

Author's Comment:

- An EV energy management system prevents the need for a service upgrade to an existing electrical system and EVSE is installed.

(B) Electric Vehicle Supply Equipment with Adjustable Settings. The adjustable ampere setting in accordance with manufacturers of electric vehicle supply equipment must appear on the rating label with sufficient durability to withstand the environment involved.

625.43 Disconnecting Means

Electric vehicle supply equipment (EVSE) rated more than 60A must have a disconnect installed at a readily accessible location. ▶Figure 625–14

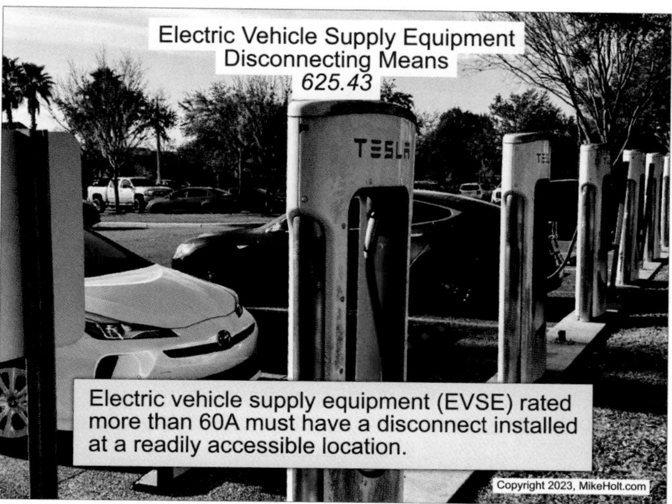
Electric Vehicle Supply Equipment
Disconnecting Means
625.43
Electric vehicle supply equipment (EVSE) rated more than 60A must have a disconnect installed at a readily accessible location.
Copyright 2023, MikeHolt.com

▶Figure 625–14

If the disconnect for the electric vehicle equipment is remote from the electric vehicle supply equipment or wireless power transfer equipment, a plaque must be placed on the equipment denoting the location of the disconnect.

The remote disconnect must be capable of being locked in the open position with provisions for locking to remain in place whether the lock is installed or not in accordance with 110.25.

625.48 Interactive Equipment

Electric vehicle supply equipment that incorporates a power export function as an interactive (grid tied) optional standby system or a bidirectional power feed must be listed and marked as suitable for that purpose. ▶Figure 625–15

When an electric vehicle is used as an optional standby system, the interconnection to premises wiring must be in accordance with Parts I and II of Article 705 apply.

Note 1: See UL 1741, *Inverters, Converters, Controllers and Interconnection System Equipment for Use with Distributed Energy Resources*, for further information on supply equipment.

Note 2: See UL 9741, *Bidirectional Electric Vehicle (EV) Charging System Equipment*, for vehicle interactive (grid tied) systems.

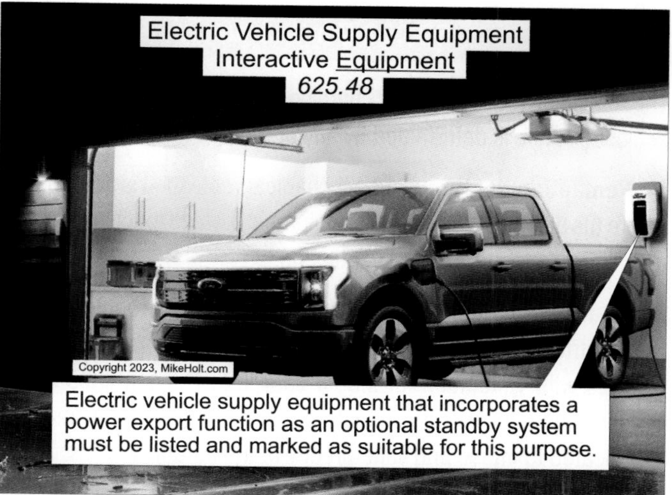
Electric Vehicle Supply Equipment
Interactive Equipment
625.48
Copyright 2023, MikeHolt.com
Electric vehicle supply equipment that incorporates a power export function as an optional standby system must be listed and marked as suitable for this purpose.

▶Figure 625–15

Note 3: See SAE J3072, *Standard for Interconnection Requirements for Onboard, Utility-Interactive Inverter Systems*, for further information.

625.49 Island Mode

Electric vehicle power export equipment and bidirectional electric vehicle supply equipment that incorporate a power export function are permitted to be a part of an interconnected power system operating in island mode.

According to Article 100, "Island Mode" is the operating mode for power production equipment that is disconnected from an electric utility. ▶Figure 625–16

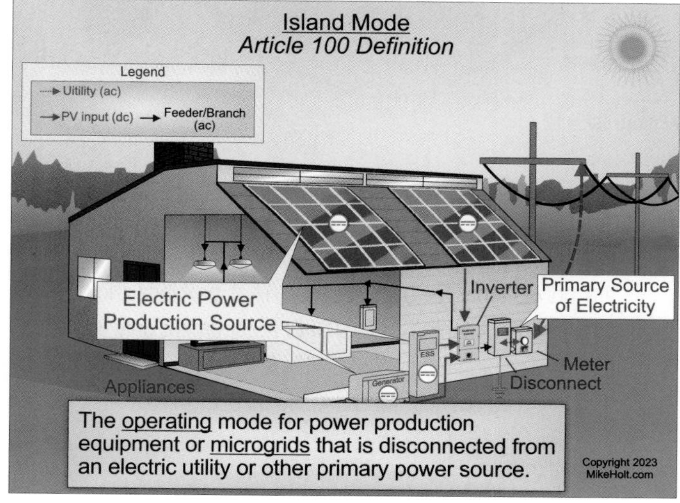
Island Mode
Article 100 Definition
Legend
Utility (ac)
PV input (dc)
Feeder/Branch (ac)
Electric Power Production Source
Inverter
Primary Source of Electricity
Appliances
Meter
Disconnect
The operating mode for power production equipment or microgrids that is disconnected from an electric utility or other primary power source.
Copyright 2023 MikeHolt.com

▶Figure 625–16

625.52 Ventilation

The ventilation requirement for charging an electric vehicle in an indoor enclosed space is determined by any of the following:

(A) Ventilation Not Required. Mechanical ventilation is not required where the electric vehicle supply equipment is listed for charging electric vehicles indoors without ventilation.

(B) Ventilation Required. Mechanical ventilation is required where the electric vehicle supply equipment is listed for charging electric vehicles with ventilation for indoor charging. The ventilation must include both supply and exhaust equipment permanently installed and located to intake and vent directly to the outdoors.

625.54 GFCI

Receptacles for the connection of electric vehicle supply equipment must be GFCI protected. ▸**Figure 625–17**

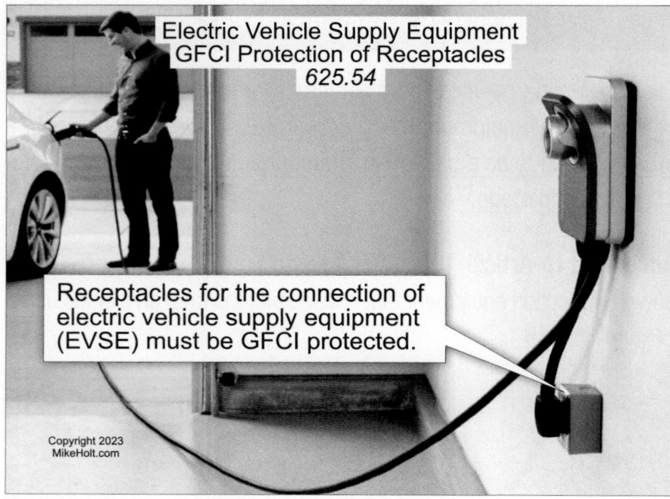
Electric Vehicle Supply Equipment
GFCI Protection of Receptacles
625.54
Receptacles for the connection of electric vehicle supply equipment (EVSE) must be GFCI protected.
Copyright 2023 MikeHolt.com

▸**Figure 625–17**

Author's Comment:

- GFCI breakers or receptacles typically used in dwelling units are not suitable for back feeding. That prohibits their use for a bidirectional EVSE. This GFCI requirement only applies to cord-and-plug-connected EVSE, making hard-wired EVSE the only type suitable for bidirectional use.

Part IV. Wireless Power Transfer Equipment

According to Article 100, "Wireless Power Transfer Equipment (WPTE)" is used to transferring energy between premises wiring and an electric vehicle without physical electrical contact. ▸**Figure 625–18**

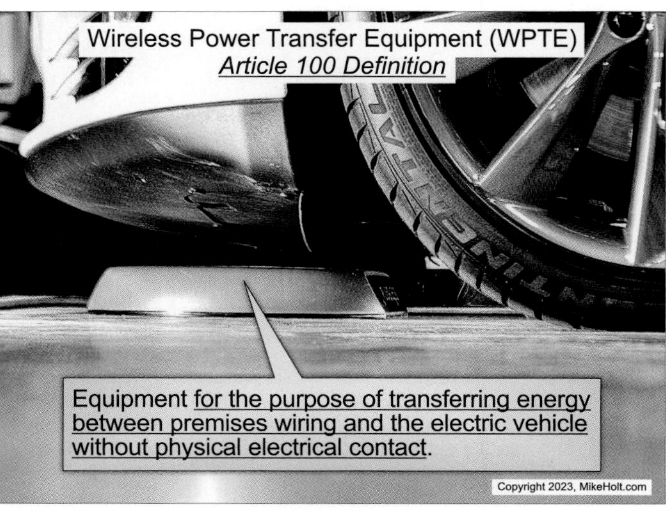
Wireless Power Transfer Equipment (WPTE)
Article 100 Definition
Equipment for the purpose of transferring energy between premises wiring and the electric vehicle without physical electrical contact.
Copyright 2023, MikeHolt.com

▸**Figure 625–18**

625.101 Grounding

The primary pad base plate must be of a nonferrous metal and connected to the circuit equipment grounding conductor unless double-insulated.

625.102 Installation

(A) General. The control pad must comply with 625.102(B). and the primary pad must comply with 625.102(C).

(B) Control Box. The control box enclosure must be suitable for the environment and mounted not less than 18 in. above the floor level for indoor locations or 24 in. above grade level for outdoor locations.

The control box must be mounted in:

(1) Pedestal

(2) Wall or pole

(3) Building or structure

(4) Raised concrete pad

1st Printing

(C) Primary Pad. The primary pad must be secured to the surface or embedded in the surface with its top flush with or below the surface and: ▸Figure 625–19

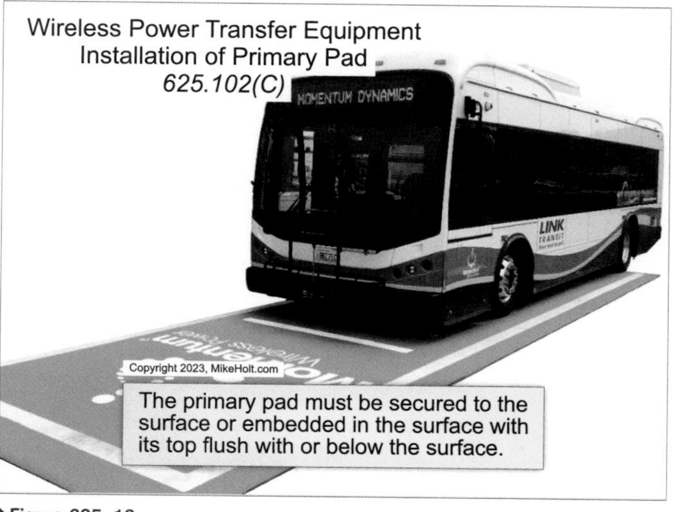
Wireless Power Transfer Equipment
Installation of Primary Pad
625.102(C)
MOMENTUM DYNAMICS
LINK
Copyright 2023, MikeHolt.com
The primary pad must be secured to the surface or embedded in the surface with its top flush with or below the surface.

▸Figure 625–19

(1) Where located in an area requiring snow removal, it must not be located on or above the surface.

Ex: Where installed on private property where snow removal is done manually, the primary pad is permitted to be installed on or above the surface.

(2) The primary pad enclosure must be suitable for the environment; if located in an area subject to severe climatic conditions (e.g. flooding), the enclosure must be suitably for those conditions.

(D) Protection of Cords and Cables to the Primary Pad. The output cable to the primary pad must be secured in place over its entire length for the purpose of restricting its movement and to prevent strain at the connection points. If installed in conditions where drive-over could occur, the cable must be provided with supplemental protection.

(E) Other Wiring Systems. Other wiring systems and fittings specifically listed for use on the WPTE are permitted.

Notes

1st Printing

ARTICLE 630 ELECTRIC WELDERS

Introduction to Article 630—Electric Welders

Article 630 covers the installation of electrical wiring and equipment for electric arc welding and resistance welding equipment connected to an electrical system. Many of these rules are outside of the scope of this material, but we do cover these topics:

- Scope
- Receptacle, GFCI Protection
- Ampacity of Supply Conductors
- Disconnecting Means
- Grounding of Welder Secondary Circuit
- Overcurrent Protection

Article 630 consists of four parts:

- Part I. General
- Part II. Arc Welders
- Part III. Resistance Welders
- Part IV. Welding Cable (Not Covered)

Part I. General

630.1 Scope

Article 630 covers electric arc welding and resistance welding equipment connected to an electrical system. ▸Figure 630-1

Electric Welders
630.1 Scope
Copyright 2023, MikeHolt.com
Article 630 covers electric arc welding and resistance welding equipment.

▸Figure 630-1

630.6 Listing

Welding equipment must be listed.

630.8 Receptacle, GFCI Protection

GFCI protection is required for all 15A and 20A, 125V receptacles used for electrical hand tools or portable lighting equipment installed in work areas where welders are operated. ▸Figure 630-2

Electric Welders
Receptacle, GFCI Protection
630.8
Copyright 2023, MikeHolt.com
GFCI protection is required for 15A and 20A, 125V receptacles used for electrical hand tools or portable lighting equipment installed in work areas where welders are operated.

▸Figure 630–2

Part II. Arc Welders

630.11 Ampacity of Supply Conductors

(A) Individual Arc Welders. The supply conductors for arc welders must have an ampacity of not less than the arc welder nameplate rating. If the nameplate rating is not available, the supply conductors must have an ampacity of not less than the rated primary current multiplied by the factor contained in Table 630.11(A) based on the duty cycle of the arc welder.

Table 630.11(A) Duty Cycle Multiplication Factors for Arc Welders

	Multiplier for Arc Welders	
Duty Cycle	Nonmotor-Generator	Motor-Generator
100	1.00	1.00
90	0.95	0.96
80	0.89	0.91
70	0.84	0.86
60	0.78	0.81
50	0.71	0.75
40	0.63	0.69
30	0.55	0.62
20 or less	0.45	0.55

▸ Individual Nonmotor-Generator Arc Welder Example 1

Question: *A nonmotor-generator arc welder has a primary current rating of 30A with a duty cycle of 30 percent. What is the minimum size branch-circuit conductor permitted to be used for this welder?* **▸Figure 630–3**

(a) 12 AWG *(b) 10 AWG* *(c) 8 AWG* *(d) 6 AWG*

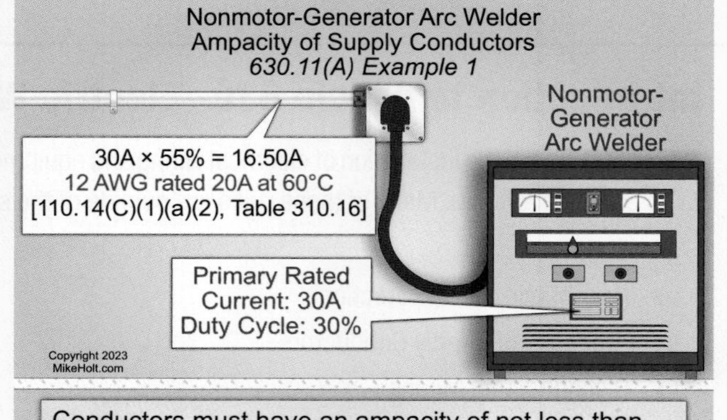
Nonmotor-Generator Arc Welder
Ampacity of Supply Conductors
630.11(A) Example 1
Nonmotor-Generator Arc Welder
30A × 55% = 16.50A
12 AWG rated 20A at 60°C
[110.14(C)(1)(a)(2), Table 310.16]
Primary Rated
Current: 30A
Duty Cycle: 30%
Copyright 2023
MikeHolt.com
Conductors must have an ampacity of not less than the rated primary current multiplied by Table 630.11(A) factor based on the duty cycle of the arc welder.

▸Figure 630–3

Solution:

Demand Load = Primary Rating × Multiplier [Table 630.11(A)]
Demand Load = 30A × 55%
Demand Load = 16.50A

Use 12 AWG rated 20A at 60°C [110.14(C)(1)(a)(2) and Table 310.16].

Answer: *(a) 12 AWG*

▶ Individual Nonmotor-Generator Arc Welder Example 2

Question: *A nonmotor-generator arc welder has a primary current rating of 40A with a duty cycle of 50 percent. What is the minimum size branch-circuit conductor permitted to be used for this welder?* **▸Figure 630–4**

(a) 14 AWG *(b) 12 AWG* *(c) 10 AWG* *(d) 8 AWG*

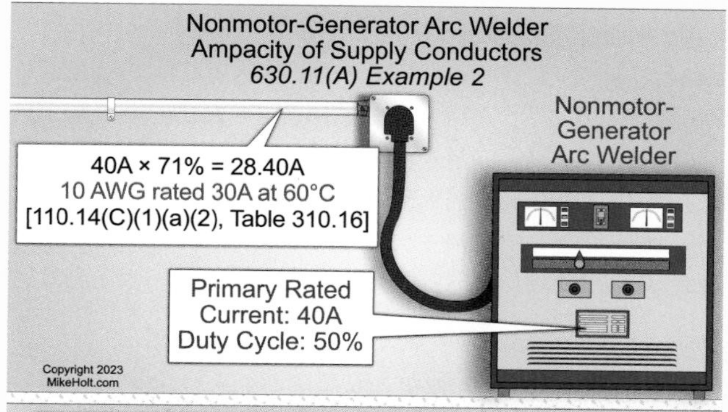

▸Figure 630–4

Solution:

Demand Load = Primary Rating × Multiplier [Table 630.11(A)]

Demand Load = 40A × 71%

Demand Load = 28.40A

Use 10 AWG rated 30A at 60°C [110.14(C)(1)(a)(2) and Table 310.16].

Answer: *(c) 10 AWG*

▶ Individual Motor-Generator Arc Welder Example 1

Question: *A motor-generator arc welder has a primary current rating of 30A with a duty cycle of 30 percent. What is the minimum size branch-circuit conductor permitted to be used for this welder?* **▸Figure 630–5**

(a) 12 AWG *(b) 10 AWG* *(c) 8 AWG* *(d) 6 AWG*

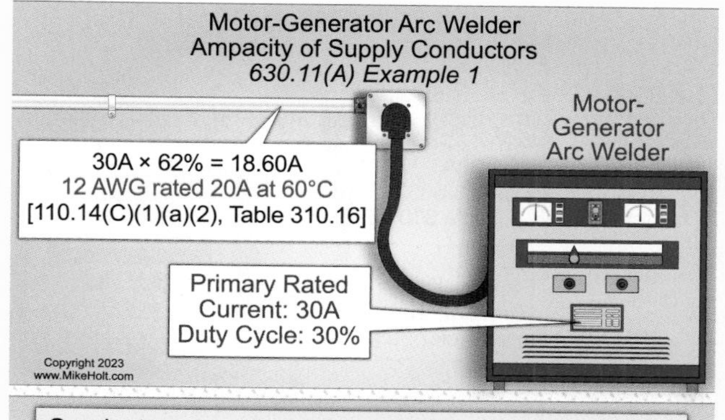

▸Figure 630–5

Solution:

Demand Load = Primary Rating × Multiplier [Table 630.11(A)]

Demand Load = 30A × 62%

Demand Load = 18.60A

Use 12 AWG rated 20A at 60°C [110.14(C)(1)(a)(2) and Table 310.16].

Answer: *(a) 12 AWG*

▶ Individual Motor-Generator Arc Welder Example 2

Question: *A motor-generator arc welder has a primary current rating of 40A with a duty cycle of 50 percent. What is the minimum size branch-circuit conductor permitted to be used for this welder?* **▸Figure 630–6**

(a) 14 AWG (b) 12 AWG (c) 10 AWG (d) 8 AWG

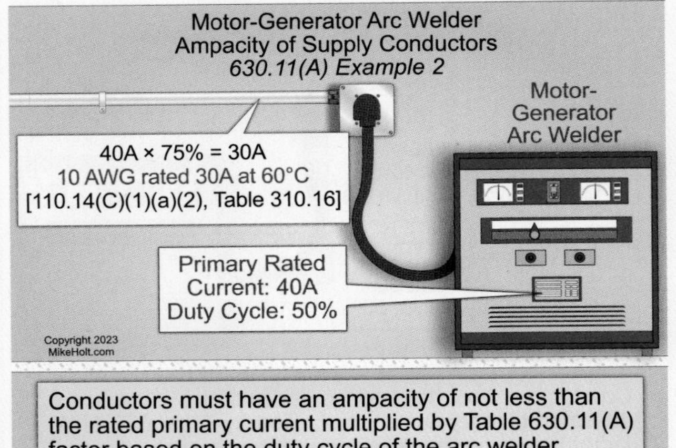

▸Figure 630–6

Solution:

Demand Load = Primary Rating × Multiplier [Table 630.11(A)]

Demand Load = 40A × 75%

Demand Load = 30A

Use 10 AWG rated 30A at 60°C [110.14(C)(1)(a)(2) and Table 310.16].

Answer: *(c) 10 AWG*

(B) Group of Welders. Feeder conductors that supply a group of arc welders must have a minimum ampacity of not less than the sum of the currents as determined in 630.11(A) based on 100 percent of the two largest arc welders, 85 percent for the third largest arc welder, 70 percent for the fourth largest arc welder, and 60 percent for all remaining arc welders.

Author's Comment:

- This calculation method provides an ample margin of safety under high-production conditions.

▶ Group of Arc Welders Example 1

Question: *What is the minimum feeder conductor size for five 30A nonmotor-generator arc welders with a duty cycle of 30 percent?*

(a) 4 AWG (b) 1 AWG (c) 1/0 AWG (d) 2/0 AWG

Solution:

Demand Load = Primary Rating × Multiplier [Table 630.11(A)] × Arc Welder Percentage [630.11(B)]

Welder 1	*30A × 55% = 16.50A × 100%*	*16.50A*
Welder 2	*30A × 55% = 16.50A × 100%*	*16.50A*
Welder 3	*30A × 55% = 16.50A × 85%*	*14.03A*
Welder 4	*30A × 55% = 16.50A × 70%*	*11.55A*
Welder 5	*30A × 55% = 16.50A × 60%*	*+9.90A*
Total Demand Load		*68.61A*

Minimum Conductor Size = 4 AWG rated 70A at 60°C [110.14(C)(1)(a)(2) and Table 310.16]

Answer: *(a) 4 AWG*

▶ Group of Arc Welders Example 2

Question: *What is the minimum feeder conductor size for five 50A nonmotor-generator arc welders with a duty cycle of 50 percent?*

(a) 4 AWG (b) 3 AWG (c) 1/0 AWG (d) 2/0 AWG

Solution:

Demand Load = Primary Rating × Multiplier [Table 630.11(A)] × Arc Welder Percentage [630.11(B)]

Welder 1	*50A × 71% = 35.50A × 100%*	*35.50A*
Welder 2	*50A × 71% = 35.50A × 100%*	*35.50A*
Welder 3	*50A × 71% = 35.50A × 85%*	*30.18A*
Welder 4	*50A × 71% = 35.50A × 70%*	*24.85A*
Welder 5	*50A × 71% = 35.50A × 60%*	*+21.30A*
Total Demand Load		*147.33A*

Minimum Conductor Size = 1/0 AWG rated 150A at 75°C [110.14(C)(1)(b)(2) and Table 310.16]

Answer: *(c) 1/0 AWG*

1st Printing

630.12 Overcurrent Protection

Where the calculated overcurrent protection value does not correspond to the standard protective device ratings in 240.6(A), the next higher standard rating is permitted.

(A) Welders. Each arc welder must have overcurrent protection rated at not more than 200 percent of the maximum rated supply current at the maximum rated output nameplate, or not more than 200 percent of the rated primary current of the arc welder.

(B) Conductors. The conductors must be protected by an overcurrent protective device rated at not more than 200 percent of the conductor ampacity rating in accordance with 110.14(C)(1).

▶ Overcurrent Protection Example

Question: *What is the maximum overcurrent protection rating for 10 AWG, THWN-2 conductors used for a motor generator arc welder with a primary current rating of 30A with a duty cycle of 90 percent?*

(a) 30A *(b) 40A* *(c) 50A* *(d) 60A*

Solution:

Step 1: *Determine Conductor Ampacity:*

Conductor Ampacity = 30A x 90% = 27A [630.11(A)]

10 AWG, THWN-2 is rated 30A at 60°C [110.14(C)(1)(a)(2) and Table 310.16]

Step 2: *Determine Overcurrent Protection size, set to 200 percent of conductor ampacity [630.12(B)]:*

Overcurrent Protection = 27A × 200%
Overcurrent Protection = 54A
Overcurrent Protection = 60A, next size up [240.6(A)]

Answer: *(d) 60A*

630.13 Disconnecting Means

A disconnect is required for each arc welder that is not provided with an integral disconnect and can be a switch, circuit breaker, or listed cord-and-plug connector.

630.15 Grounding of Welder Secondary Circuit

Article 250 does not apply to the secondary circuit conductors of an arc welder consisting of the electrode conductor and the work conductor.

Connecting welder secondary circuits to grounded objects can create parallel paths and can cause objectionable current over equipment grounding conductors.

Caution

CAUTION: The high currents associated with arc welding operations can cause extensive damage to electrical systems and machinery if they stray from the designed closed-loop secondary circuit.

Part III. Resistance Welders

630.31 Ampacity of Supply Conductor

(A) Individual Resistance Welders. To limit voltage drop to a permissible performance value for resistance welders, conductors are usually sized larger than that which is required to prevent overheating.

Author's Comment:

- To avoid cold welds due to insufficient power, follow the equipment voltage ranges stated in the listing or labeling instructions [110.3(B)].

(1) The ampacity of the supply conductors for varied-duty cycle resistance welders is not permitted to be less than 70 percent of the rated primary current for seam and automatically fed resistance welders, and 50 percent of the rated primary current for manually operated resistance welders [630.31(A)(1)].

(2) The supply conductors for resistance welders with a specific duty cycle and nonvarying current levels must have an ampacity of not less than the rated primary current multiplied by the factors in Table 630.31(A)(2), based on the duty cycle of the resistance welder.

Table 630.31(A)(2) Duty Cycle Multiplication Factors for Resistance Welders	
Duty Cycle	Multiplier
30	0.55
25	0.50
20	0.45
15	0.39
10	0.32
7.50	0.27
5 or less	0.22
50	0.71
40	0.63

▶ Individual Resistance Welders Example 1

Question: *What size branch-circuit conductors are required for a 50A resistance welder having a duty cycle of 50 percent?* ▶**Figure 630–7**

(a) 8 AWG *(b) 6 AWG* *(c) 4 AWG* *(d) 2 AWG*

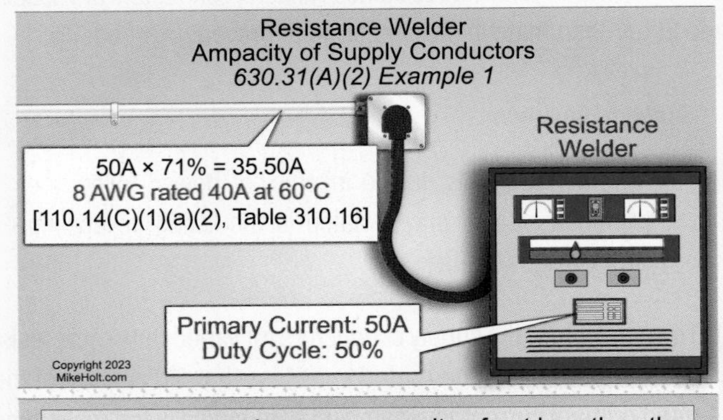
Resistance Welder
Ampacity of Supply Conductors
630.31(A)(2) Example 1
Resistance Welder
50A × 71% = 35.50A
8 AWG rated 40A at 60°C
[110.14(C)(1)(a)(2), Table 310.16]
Primary Current: 50A
Duty Cycle: 50%
Copyright 2023
MikeHolt.com
Conductors must have an ampacity of not less than the rated primary current multiplied by Table 630.31(A)(2) factor based on the duty cycle of the resistance welder.

▶**Figure 630–7**

Solution:

Demand Load = Primary Rating × Multiplier [Table 630.31(A)(2)]

Demand Load = 50A × 71%

Demand Load = 35.50A

Use 8 AWG rated 40A at 60°C [110.14(C)(1)(a)(2) and Table 310.16].

Answer: *(a) 8 AWG*

▶ Individual Resistance Welders Example 2

Question: *What size branch-circuit conductors are required for a 30A resistance welder having a duty cycle of 30 percent?* ▶**Figure 630–8**

(a) 12 AWG *(b) 10 AWG* *(c) 8 AWG* *(d) 6 AWG*

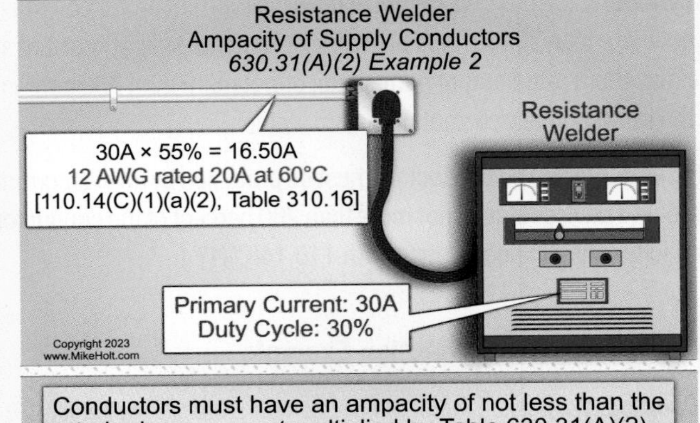
Resistance Welder
Ampacity of Supply Conductors
630.31(A)(2) Example 2
Resistance Welder
30A × 55% = 16.50A
12 AWG rated 20A at 60°C
[110.14(C)(1)(a)(2), Table 310.16]
Primary Current: 30A
Duty Cycle: 30%
Copyright 2023
www.MikeHolt.com
Conductors must have an ampacity of not less than the rated primary current multiplied by Table 630.31(A)(2) factor based on the duty cycle of the resistance welder.

▶**Figure 630–8**

Solution:

Demand Load = Primary Rating × Multiplier [Table 630.31(A)(2)]

Demand Load = 30A × 55%

Demand Load = 16.50A

Use 12 AWG rated 20A at 60°C [110.14(C)(1)(a)(2) and Table 310.16].

Answer: *(a) 12 AWG*

(B) Groups of Resistance Welders. Feeder conductors that supply a group of resistance welders must have an ampacity of not less than the sum of the value determined using 630.31(A)(2) for the largest resistance welder in the group, plus 60 percent of the values determined for all remaining resistance welders [630.31(B)].

1st Printing

▶ Group of Resistance Welders Example 1

Question: *What is the minimum feeder conductor size for five 30A resistance welders with a duty cycle of 30 percent?*

(a) 4 AWG *(b) 3 AWG* *(c) 2 AWG* *(d) 1 AWG*

Solution:

Demand Load = Primary Rating × Multiplier [Table 630.31(A)(2)] × Resistance Welder Percentage [630.31(B)]

Welder 1	*30A × 55% = 16.50A × 100%*	*16.50A*
Welder 2	*30A × 55% = 16.50A × 60%*	*9.90A*
Welder 3	*30A × 55% = 16.50A × 60%*	*9.90A*
Welder 4	*30A × 55% = 16.50A × 60%*	*9.90A*
Welder 5	*30A × 55% = 16.50A × 60%*	*+9.90A*
Total Demand Load		*56.10A*

Minimum Conductor Size = 4 AWG rated 70A at 60°C [110.14(C)(1)(a)(2) and Table 310.16]

Answer: *(a) 4 AWG*

▶ Group of Resistance Welders Example 2

Question: *What is the minimum feeder conductor size for five 50A resistance welders with a duty cycle of 50 percent?*

(a) 4 AWG *(b) 3 AWG* *(c) 2 AWG* *(d) 1 AWG*

Solution:

Demand Load = Primary Rating × Multiplier [Table 630.31(A)(2)] × Resistance Welder Percentage [630.31(B)]

Welder 1	*50A × 71% = 35.50A × 100%*	*35.50A*
Welder 2	*50A × 71% = 35.50A × 60%*	*21.30A*
Welder 3	*50A × 71% = 35.50A × 60%*	*21.30A*
Welder 4	*50A × 71% = 35.50A × 60%*	*21.30A*
Welder 5	*50A × 71% = 35.50A × 60%*	*+21.30A*
Total Demand Load		*120.70A*

Minimum Conductor Size = 1 AWG rated 130A at 75°C [110.14(C)(1)(b)(2) and Table 310.16]

Answer: *(d) 1 AWG*

630.32 Overcurrent Protection

Where the calculated overcurrent protection value does not correspond with the standard protective device ratings in 240.6(A), the next higher standard rating is permitted.

(A) Welders. Each resistance welder must have overcurrent protection set at not more than 300 percent of the rated primary current.

(B) Conductors. Branch-circuit conductors must be protected by an overcurrent protective device rated at not more than 300 percent of the conductor ampacity rating in accordance with 110.14(C)(1).

630.33 Disconnecting Means

A switch or circuit breaker is required to disconnect each resistance welder and its control equipment from the supply circuit.

Notes

ARTICLE 640 AUDIO SIGNAL AMPLIFICATION AND REPRODUCTION EQUIPMENT

Introduction to Article 640—Audio Signal Amplification and Reproduction Equipment

This article covers the installation of electrical wiring and equipment for audio amplification and public address systems. Many of these rules are outside of the scope of this material, however, some of the topics we cover include the following:

- Scope
- Protection of Electrical Equipment
- Access to Electrical Equipment Behind Panels
- Wiring Methods

According to Article 100, "Audio System" is defined as all equipment and interconnecting wiring used to fabricate a fully functional audio signal processing, amplification, and reproduction system.

A "Loudspeaker" is defined as equipment that converts an alternating-current electric signal into an acoustic signal.

Part I. General

640.1 Scope

(A) Covered. Article 640 covers equipment and wiring for permanent and temporary audio sound and public address system installations. ▶Figure 640–1

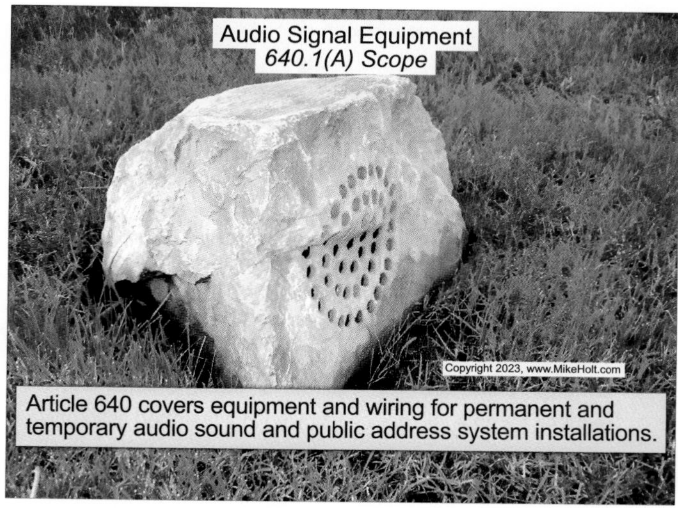

▶Figure 640–1

Audio system locations include restaurants, hotels, business offices, commercial and retail sales environments, churches, schools, auditoriums, theaters, stadiums, and outdoor events such as fairs, festivals, circuses, public events, and concerts.

(B) Not Covered. This article does not cover audio systems for fire and burglary alarms.

640.3 Locations and Other Articles

(A) Spread of Fire or Products of Combustion. Audio circuits (box and wire) installed through fire-resistant-rated walls, partitions, floors, or ceilings must be firestopped to limit the possible spread of fire or products of combustion in accordance with the specific instructions supplied by the manufacturer for the specific type of cable and construction material (drywall, brick, and so on) in accordance with 300.21.

Author's Comment:

- Penetrations into or through fire-resistant-rated walls, floors, partitions, or ceilings must be firestopped using an approved method so the possible spread of fire or products of combustion will not be substantially increased [300.21]. ▶**Figure 640–2**

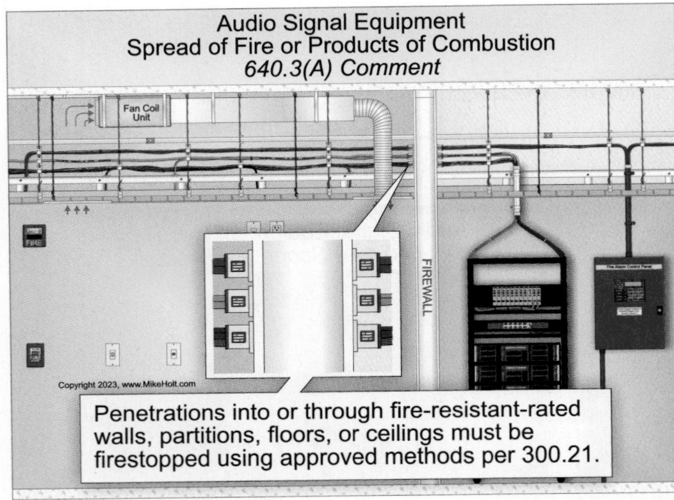

▶**Figure 640–2**

- Although boxes are not required for audio circuits, one is required for an audio device installed in a fire-rated assembly.

(B) Ducts and Plenum Spaces. Audio circuits installed in fabricated ducts for environmental air must comply with 300.22(B), and when installed in plenum spaces, audio circuits must comply with 300.22(C).

Ex 1: Class 2 plenum-rated cables installed in accordance with 722.135(B) can be installed in ducts specifically fabricated for environmental air.

Ex 2: Class 2 plenum-rated cables installed in accordance with 722.135(B) can be installed in plenum spaces.

640.4 Protection of Electrical Equipment

Amplifiers, loudspeakers, and other audio equipment must be located or protected against environmental exposure or physical damage that might cause a fire, shock, or personal hazard.

640.5 Access to Electrical Equipment Behind Panels Designed to Allow Access

Access to equipment is not permitted to be prohibited by an accumulation of audio cables that prevents the removal of suspended-ceiling panels.

640.6 Mechanical Execution of Work

(A) Installation of Audio Cables.

Cable Support, Damage. Exposed audio cables must be supported so the cable will not be damaged by normal building use.

Cable Securement, Fitting. Audio cables must be secured by straps, staples, cable ties, hangers, or similar fittings in a manner that will not damage the cable. ▶**Figure 640–3**

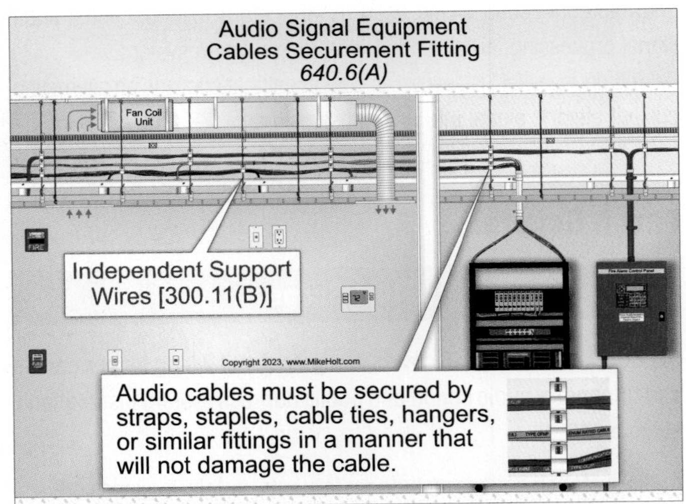

▶**Figure 640–3**

Protection From Physical Damage [300.4]. Audio cables installed parallel or perpendicular to framing members must be protected against damage from penetration by screws or nails by a 1¼ in. separation from the face of the framing member or by a suitable metal plate, in accordance with 300.4(D). ▶**Figure 640–4**

1st Printing

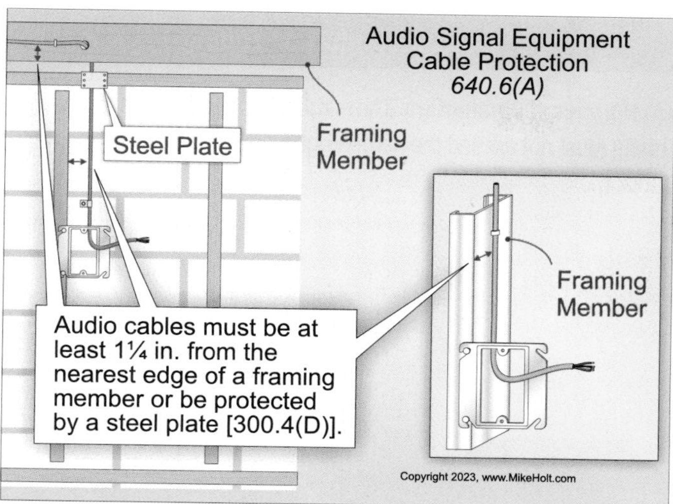
Audio Signal Equipment
Cable Protection
640.6(A)
Steel Plate
Framing Member
Framing Member
Audio cables must be at least 1¼ in. from the nearest edge of a framing member or be protected by a steel plate [300.4(D)].
Copyright 2023, www.MikeHolt.com

▸Figure 640-4

Securing and Supporting [300.11]. Audio cables must be securely fastened in place and the ceiling-support wires, or the ceiling grid, are not permitted to be used to support audio cables [300.11(B)].

(B) Abandoned Audio Cables. The accessible portions of abandoned audio cables must be removed. ▸**Figure 640-5**

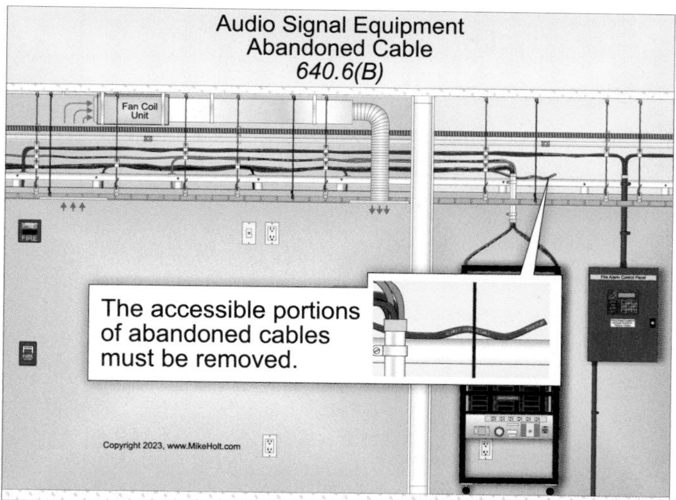
Audio Signal Equipment
Abandoned Cable
640.6(B)
Fan Coil Unit
The accessible portions of abandoned cables must be removed.
Copyright 2023, www.MikeHolt.com

▸Figure 640-5

Author's Comment:

- An abandoned audio distribution cable is one that is not terminated to equipment and not identified for future use with a tag [Article 100].
- This rule does not require the removal of concealed cables abandoned in place, which includes cables in raceways.

According to Article 100, cables in raceways that are concealed are not considered accessible.

(C) Audio Cable Identified for Future Use.

(1) Cable Identification Means. Audio cables identified for future use must be marked with a tag of sufficient durability to withstand the environment involved [110.21(B)].

(2) Cable Tag Criteria. Cable tags must include the following information:

(1) The date the cable was identified for future use.

(2) The date of expected use.

(3) The intended future use of the cable.

640.9 Wiring Methods

(A) Wiring to and Between Audio Equipment.

(1) Branch Circuit. Branch-circuit wiring for audio equipment must comply with Chapters 1 through 4.

(3) Audio Circuits, Output Wiring. Audio output wiring must be installed in accordance with Part II of Article 725.

640.10 Audio Systems Near Bodies of Water

(A) Branch-Circuit Power. Audio equipment supplied by a branch circuit is not permitted to be placed within 5 ft horizontally of the inside wall of a pool, spa, hot tub, or fountain. In addition to the requirements in 210.8(B), the equipment must be supplied by a GFCI-protected branch circuit where required by other articles of the *Code*.

See 680.27(A) for installation of underwater audio equipment.

(B) Class 2 Power-Limited Power Supply. Audio system equipment powered by a listed Class 2 power-limited power supply or an amplifier listed for use with Class 2 wiring, are restricted in their placement near bodies of water by the manufacturer's instructions.

Part II. Permanent Audio System Installations

640.21 Use of Flexible Cords and Flexible Cables

(A) Branch-Circuit Power. Power-supply cords for permanent audio equipment are permitted where the interchange, maintenance, or repair of equipment is facilitated by using a power-supply cord.

(B) Loudspeakers. Cables for loudspeakers must comply with Article 722, and the conductors for outdoor speakers must be identified for the environment.

(C) Between Equipment. Cables for distributing audio signals between equipment must comply with Article 722.

640.23 Conduit or Tubing

(A) Number of Conductors. The number of conductors in a conduit or tubing must not exceed the percentage fill requirements of Chapter 9, Table 1.

ARTICLE 645

INFORMATION TECHNOLOGY EQUIPMENT (ITE)

Introduction to Article 645—Information Technology Equipment (ITE)

This article provides optional wiring methods and materials for information technology equipment (ITE). Information technology rooms often contain huge racks of equipment, raised floors, massive numbers of data and fiber optic cables, and exposed power cords creating special challenges to protect those who use these areas. Many of these rules are outside of the scope of this material, however, some of the topics we cover include the following:

- Scope
- Special Requirements
- Supply Circuits and Interconnecting Cables
- Disconnecting Means
- Equipment Grounding Conductor

645.1 Scope

Article 645 provides optional wiring methods and materials for information technology equipment (ITE) and systems in an information technology equipment room as an alternative to those required in other chapters of this *Code*. ▶**Figure 645–1**

Note 1: An information technology equipment room is an enclosed area specifically designed to comply with the construction and fire protection provisions of NFPA 75, *Standard for the Fire Protection of Information Technology Equipment.*

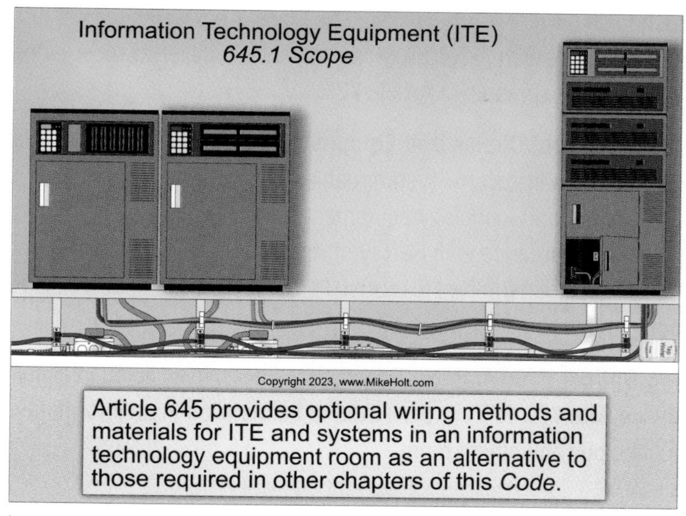

Information Technology Equipment (ITE)
645.1 Scope
Copyright 2023, www.MikeHolt.com
Article 645 provides optional wiring methods and materials for ITE and systems in an information technology equipment room as an alternative to those required in other chapters of this Code.

▶**Figure 645–1**

645.3 Other Articles

Circuits and equipment must comply with 645.3(A) through (I) as applicable.

(A) Spread of Fire or Products of Combustion. Electrical circuits and equipment must be installed in such a way that the spread of fire or products of combustion will not be substantially increased. Openings into or through fire-rated walls, floors, and ceilings for electrical equipment must be firestopped using methods approved by the authority having jurisdiction to maintain the fire-resistance rating of the fire-rated assembly [300.21, 770.26, and 800.26].

(B) Plenum Spaces. The following apply to wiring and cabling in a plenum space above an information technology equipment room:

(1) Wiring must be in accordance with 300.22(C)(1).

(2) Class 2 plenum-rated cables must be installed in accordance with 722.135(B).

(3) Plenum-rated fire alarm cables must be installed in accordance with 760.53(B)(2), 760.135(C), and Table 760.154.

(4) Plenum-rated optical fiber cables must be installed in accordance with 770.113(C) and Table 770.154(a).

(5) Plenum-rated hard-wire telephone cables must be installed in accordance with 800.133(C) and Table 800.154(a).

(6) Plenum-rated coaxial cables must be installed in accordance with 800.113(C) and Table 800.154(a).

(D) Classification of Data Circuits. Data circuits for information technology systems are classified as Class 2 power-limited circuits in accordance with 725.60(A)(4) and must be installed in accordance with the requirements of Article 725.

(E) Fire Alarm Cables and Equipment. Parts I, II, and III of Article 760 apply to fire alarm system cables and equipment installed in an information technology equipment room. Only fire alarm cables listed in accordance with Part IV of Article 760 and listed fire alarm equipment are permitted to be installed in an information technology equipment room.

(H) Optical Fiber Cables. Only optical fiber cables listed in accordance with 770.179 are permitted to be installed in an information technology equipment room.

645.4 Special Requirements

The wiring methods permitted in 645.5 are only permitted where all the following conditions are met:

(1) A disconnect that complies with 645.10 is provided.

(2) A dedicated heating/ventilating/air-conditioning system is provided for the information technology equipment room and is separated from other areas of the occupancy.

(3) The information technology and communications equipment are listed.

(4) The room is occupied and accessible only to persons needed for the maintenance and operation of information technology equipment.

(5) The information technology equipment room is separated from other occupancies by fire-resistant-rated walls, floors, and ceilings with protected openings.

(6) Only electrical equipment and wiring associated with the operation of the information technology room is installed in the room.

645.5 Supply Circuits and Interconnecting Cables

(A) Branch-Circuit Conductors. Branch-circuit conductors for information technology equipment must have an ampacity of not less than 125 percent of the total connected load.

(D) Physical Damage. If exposed to physical damage, power-supply cords, supply circuits, and interconnecting cables must be protected.

(E) Under Raised Floors. Where the area under the raised floor is accessible and openings minimize the entrance of debris beneath the floor, power-supply cords, coaxial cables, connecting cables, interconnecting cables, cord-and-plug connections, and receptacles associated with the information technology equipment can be installed under a raised floor. The installation requirement must comply with (1) through (3) as follows:

(1) Branch-Circuit Wiring Under a Raised Floor. ▸**Figure 645–2**

(a) Branch-circuit wiring under a raised floor must be securely fastened in place in accordance with 300.11.

(b) The following wiring methods are permitted under a raised floor:

(1) Rigid metal conduit

(2) PVC conduit

(3) Intermediate metal conduit

(4) Electrical metallic tubing

(5) Electrical nonmetallic tubing

(6) Metal wireway

(7) Nonmetallic wireway

1st Printing

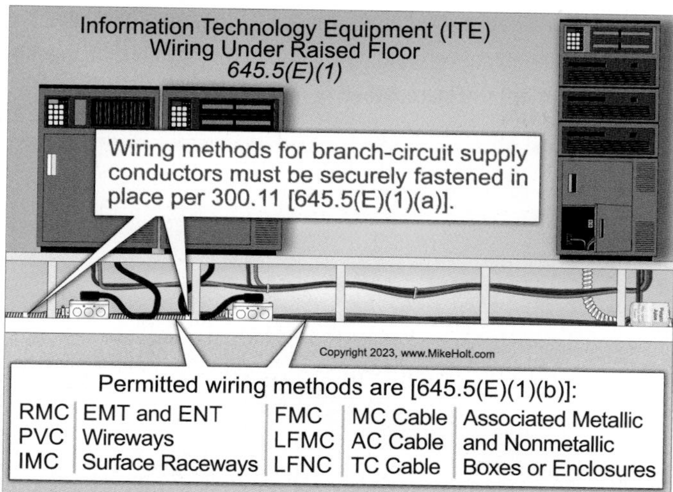

▶Figure 645-2

(8) Surface metal raceway with metal cover

(9) Surface nonmetallic raceway

(10) Flexible metal conduit

(11) Liquidtight flexible metal conduit

(12) Liquidtight flexible nonmetallic conduit

(14) Type MC cable

(15) Type AC cable

(16) Associated metallic and nonmetallic boxes or enclosures

(17) Type TC power and control tray cable

(2) Power-Supply Cords, Data Cables, Interconnecting Cables, and Equipment Grounding Conductors. The following power-supply cords, interconnecting cables, data cables, and equipment grounding conductors are permitted under a raised floor:

(1) Power-supply cords of listed information technology equipment in accordance with 645.5(B).

(2) Interconnecting cables enclosed within a raceway.

(3) Equipment grounding conductors.

(4) Where the air space under a raised floor is protected by an automatic fire suppression system, in addition to wiring installed in accordance with 722.135(B), Types CL2R, CL3R, CL2, and CL3 and substitute cables including CMP, CMR, CM, and CMG installed in accordance with 722.135(E) are permitted under raised floors.

(5) Where the air space under a raised floor is not protected by an automatic fire suppression system, in addition to wiring installed in accordance with 722.135(B), substitute Type CMP cable installed in accordance with 722.135(E) is permitted under raised floors.

(6) Listed Type DP cable.

(3) Installation Requirements for Optical Fiber Cables Under a Raised Floor.

(1) Where the air space under a raised floor is protected by an automatic fire suppression system, optical fiber Types OFNR, OFCR, OFNG, OFCG, OFN, and OFC cables installed in accordance with 770.113(C) are permitted under raised floors.

(2) Where the air space under a raised floor is not protected by an automatic fire suppression system, only optical fiber cables installed in accordance with 770.113(C) are permitted under raised floors.

(F) Securing in Place. Power-supply cords, coaxial cables, connecting cables, and interconnecting cables listed as part of information technology equipment are not required to be secured in place where installed under raised floors. ▶**Figure 645-3**

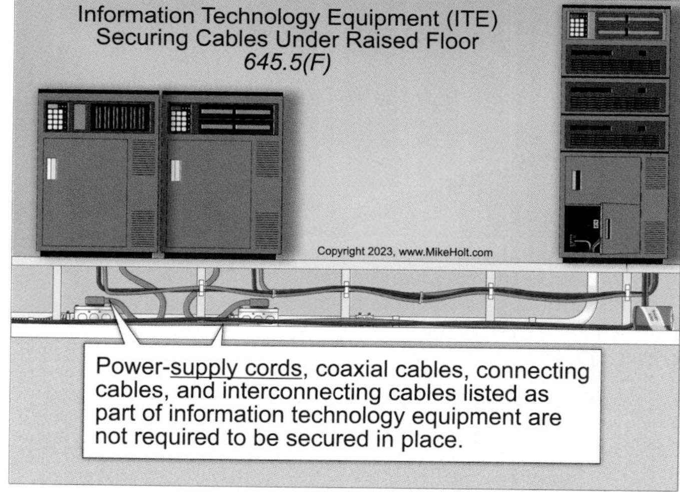

▶Figure 645-3

Raceways and cables under a raised floor not listed as part of information technology equipment must be secured in accordance with 300.11.

645.10 Disconnecting Means

A disconnect is required for electronic equipment in the information technology equipment room and dedicated HVAC systems that serve the room or in designated zones within the room.

(A) Remote Disconnect Controls.

(1) Emergency Access. Remote disconnect controls must be at an approved, readily accessible location.

(2) Disconnect Identification. The remote disconnect means for the control of electronic equipment power and HVAC systems must be grouped and identified. A single means to control both is permitted.

(4) System Operation Continuity. Additional means to prevent unintentional operations of remote disconnect controls are permitted.

645.15 Equipment Grounding and Bonding

Exposed metal parts of an information technology system must be connected to the circuit equipment grounding conductor or be double insulated. ▸**Figure 645–4**

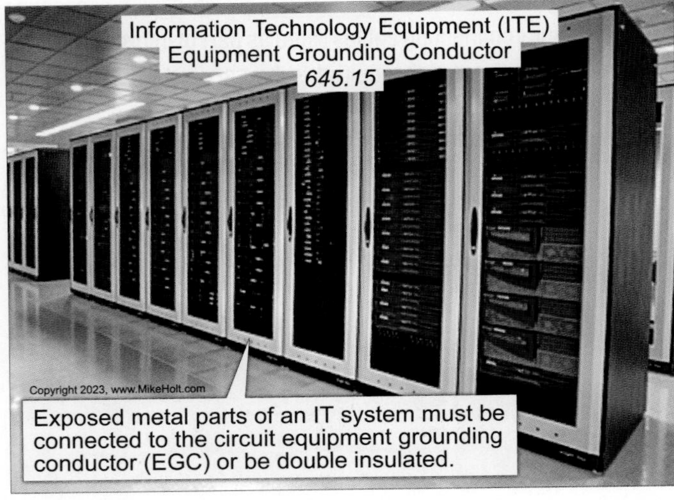

▸**Figure 645–4**

Where signal reference structures are installed, they must be connected to the circuit equipment grounding conductor for the information technology equipment. ▸**Figure 645–5**

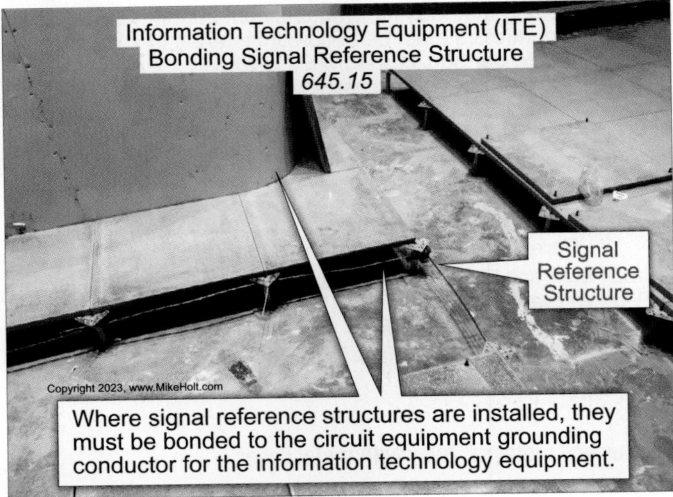

▸**Figure 645–5**

If isolated ground receptacles are installed, they must be connected to an insulated equipment grounding conductor in accordance with 250.146(D) and 406.3(E).

SWIMMING POOLS, HOT TUBS, AND FOUNTAINS

Introduction to Article 680—Swimming Pools, Hot Tubs, and Fountains

This article covers the installation of electrical wiring and equipment for swimming pools, hot tubs, spas, fountains, and hydromassage bathtubs. It is divided into eight parts which only apply to certain types of installations. Be very careful to determine which part(s) of this article apply as identified in the "General" section of each part so you can correctly apply the rules. Many of these rules are outside of the scope of this material, however, some of the topics we cover include the following:

- Bonding and Grounding
- Underwater Pool Luminaires
- Pool Light Junction Boxes, Transformers, or GFCI Enclosures
- Equipotential Bonding
- Hot Tubs
- Fountains

Article 680 consists of eight parts:

- Part I. General Requirements for Pools, Spas, Hot Tubs, and Fountains
- Part II. Permanently Installed Pools
- Part III. Storable Pools
- Part IV. Hot Tubs
- Part V. Fountains
- Part VI. Therapeutic Pools and Tubs (not covered)
- Part VII. Hydromassage Bathtubs
- Part VIII. Electrically Powered Pool Lifts (not covered)

Part I. General Requirements for Pools, Spas, Hot Tubs, and Fountains

680.1 Scope

Article 680 covers the installation of electric wiring and equipment for swimming pools, hot tubs, spas, fountains, and hydromassage bathtubs. ▶Figure 680–1 and ▶Figure 680–2

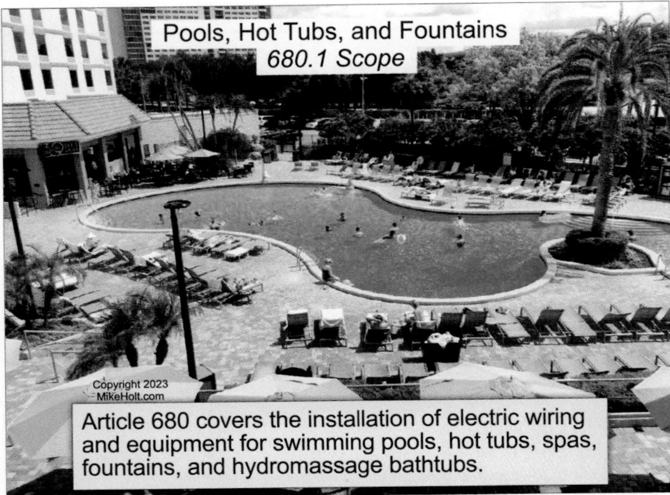

▶Figure 680–1

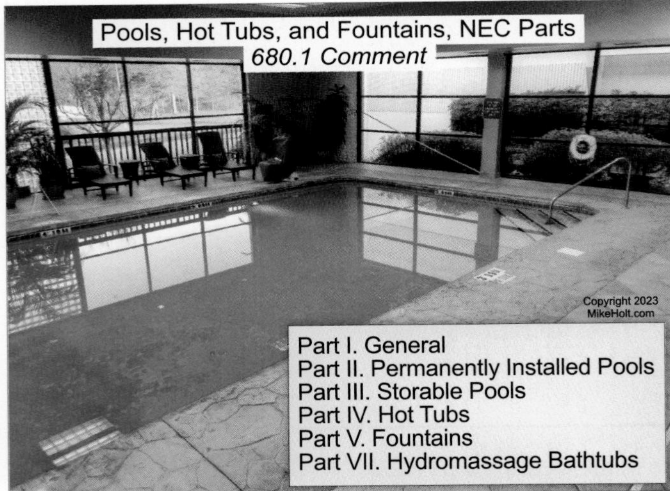

▶Figure 680–2

According to Article 100, a "Pool" is defined as a manufactured or field-constructed equipment designed to contain water on a permanent or semipermanent basis and used for swimming, wading, immersion, or other purposes [680]. ▶Figure 680–3

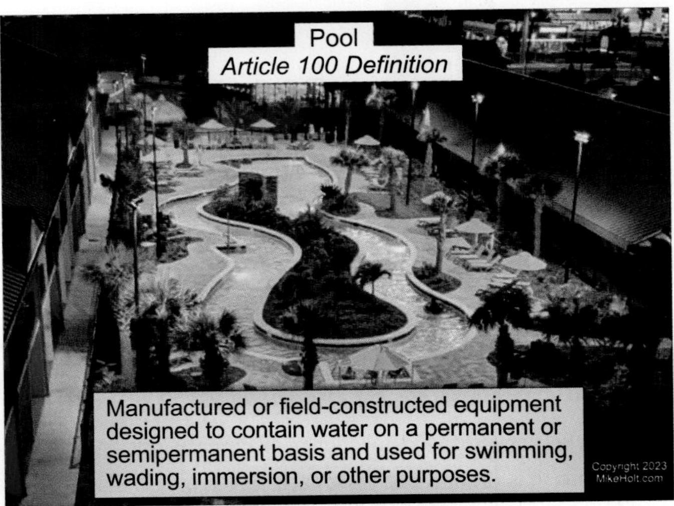

▶Figure 680–3

Author's Comment:

- The definition of a pool includes baptisteries (immersion pools) which must comply with the requirements of Article 680.
- An above ground pool having a maximum water depth greater than 42 in. is considered a permanent pool. See the definition of 'storable pool.'

According to Article 100, a "Spa or Hot Tub" is a recreational or therapeutic hydromassage tub typically not drained after each use (Article 680). ▶Figure 680–4

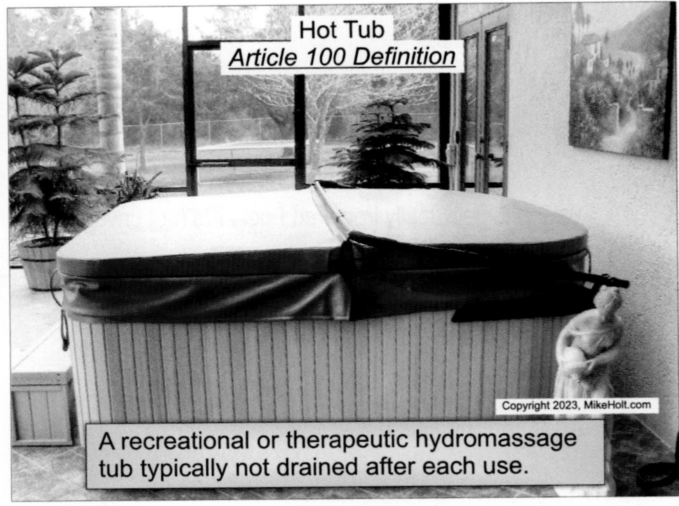

Hot Tub
Article 100 Definition
Copyright 2023, MikeHolt.com
A recreational or therapeutic hydromassage tub typically not drained after each use.

▶Figure 680–4

1st Printing

According to Article 100, a "Fountain" is defined as an ornamental structure or recreational water feature from which one or more jets or streams of water are discharged into the air including splash pads, ornamental pools, display pools, and reflection pools. This definition does not include drinking water fountains or water coolers (Article 680). ▶**Figure 680–5**

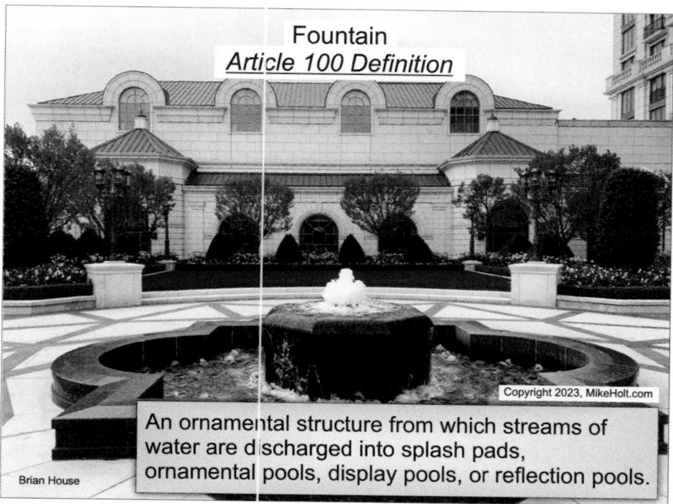

▶**Figure 680–5**

680.4 Inspections After Installation

The authority having jurisdiction is permitted to require periodic inspection and testing for swimming pools and similar bodies of water.

680.5 GFCI and SPGFCI Protection

(A) General. The GFCI and SPGFCI requirements in this Article are in addition to the requirements in 210.8.

(B) GFCI Protection. Where ground fault protection is required in this article for branch circuits rated 150V or less to ground and 60A or less, a GFCI device must be used.

According to Article 100, a "Ground-Fault Circuit Interrupter (GFCI)" is defined as a device intended to protect people by de-energizing a circuit when ground-fault current exceeds the value established for a Class A device. ▶**Figure 680–6**

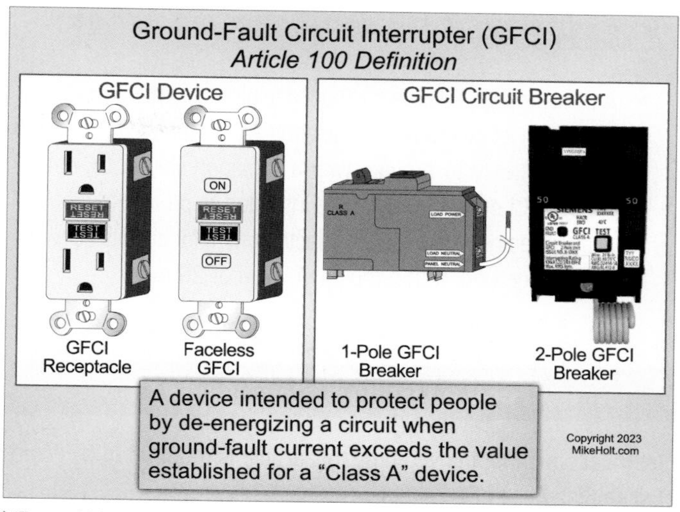

▶**Figure 680–6**

(C) SPGFCI Protection. Where ground-fault protection is required in this article for branch circuits rated over 150V or less to ground, a SPGFCI device must be used.

According to Article 100, a "Special Purpose, Ground-Fault Circuit Interrupter (SPGFCI)" is defined as a device intended to de-energize a 277/480V circuit when the ground-fault current exceeds the values established for a Class C device. ▶**Figure 680–7**

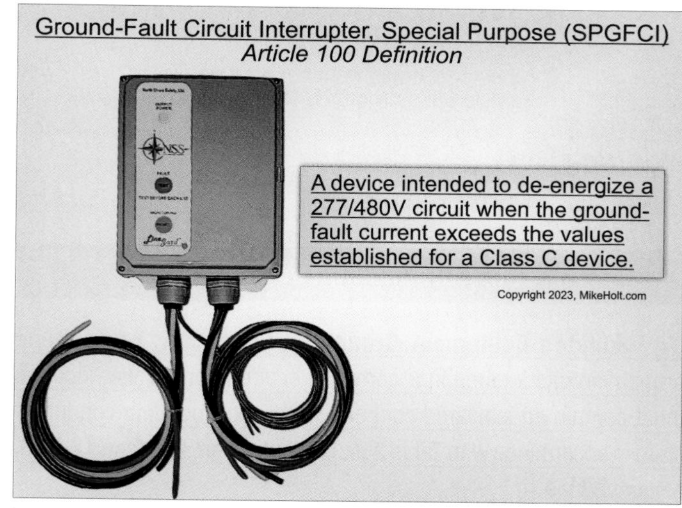

▶**Figure 680–7**

Author's Comment:

- A GFCI protective device is intended to protect humans against maximum let-go levels (muscle contraction) for circuits rated not over 150V to ground, with a trip-open value of 6-mA. An SPGFCI protective device is intended to protect humans against ventricular fibrillation (electrocution) for circuits above 150V to ground, with a trip-open value of 20 mA.

680.6 Listing Requirements

Electrical equipment covered by this article is required to be listed. ▶Figure 680–8

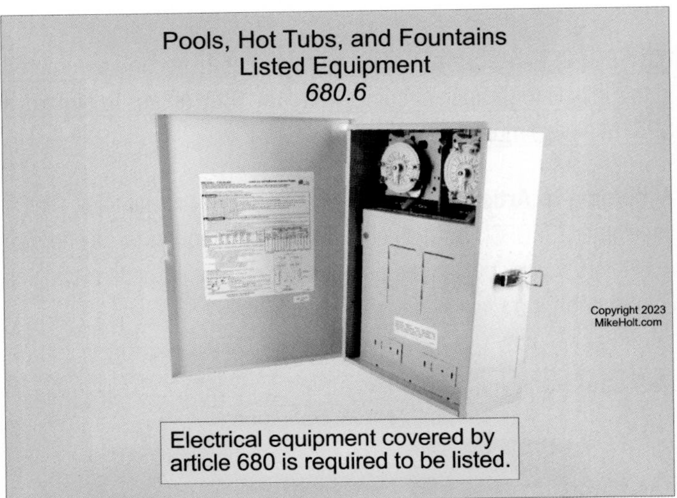

Pools, Hot Tubs, and Fountains
Listed Equipment
680.6
Copyright 2023
MikeHolt.com
Electrical equipment covered by article 680 is required to be listed.

▶Figure 680–8

680.7 Grounding and Bonding

(A) Insulated Equipment Grounding Conductor. Feeders and branch circuits located in a corrosive environment or wet location must contain an insulated copper equipment grounding conductor sized in accordance with Table 250.122, but not smaller than 12 AWG. ▶Figure 680–9

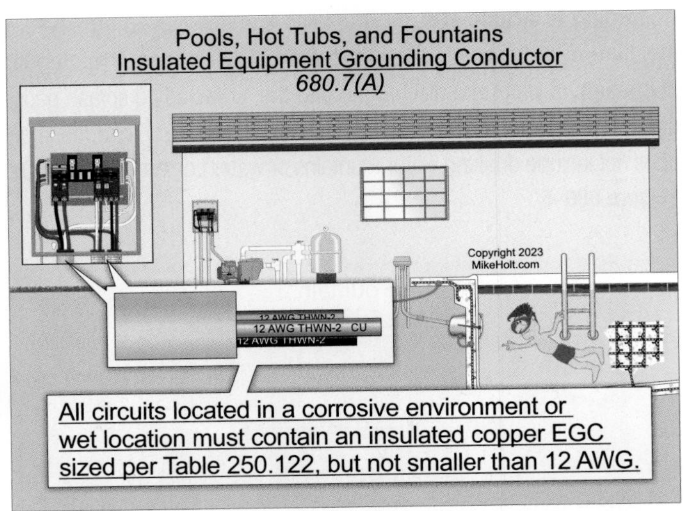

▶Figure 680–9

According to Article 100, a "Corrosive Environment" is defined as areas or enclosures without adequate ventilation where electrical equipment is located and pool sanitation chemicals are stored, handled, or dispensed (Article 680]. ▶Figure 680–10

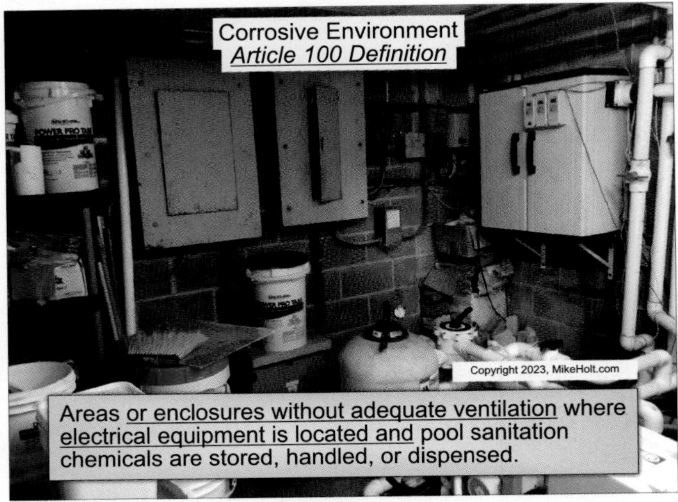

▶Figure 680–10

Note 1: Sanitation chemicals and pool water pose a risk of corrosion (gradually damaging or destroying materials) due to the presence of oxidizers (for example, calcium hypochlorite, sodium hypochlorite, bromine, and chlorinated isocyanurates) and chlorinating agents that release chlorine when dissolved in water.

(B) Cord-and-Plug Connections. Flexible cords must contain an equipment grounding conductor that is an insulated copper conductor sized in accordance with Table 250.122, but not smaller than 12 AWG. The flexible cord must terminate in a grounding-type attachment plug having a fixed grounding contact member.

(C) Terminals. Field-installed terminals in damp or wet locations or corrosive environments must be listed for direct burial use. ▶Figure 680–11

1st Printing

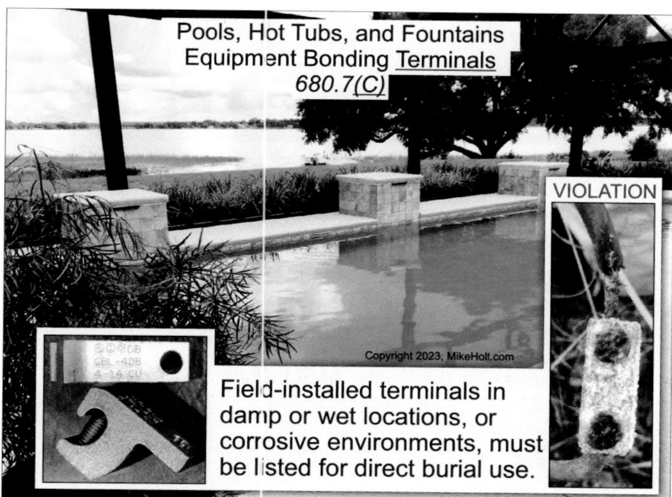
Pools, Hot Tubs, and Fountains
Equipment Bonding Terminals
680.7(C)
VIOLATION
Field-installed terminals in damp or wet locations, or corrosive environments, must be listed for direct burial use.
Copyright 2023, MikeHolt.com

▸Figure 680–11

680.9 Overhead Conductor Clearance

Overhead conductors must meet the clearances from the maximum water level requirements contained in Table 680.9(A). The clearance measurement is taken from the maximum water level. ▸Figure 680–12

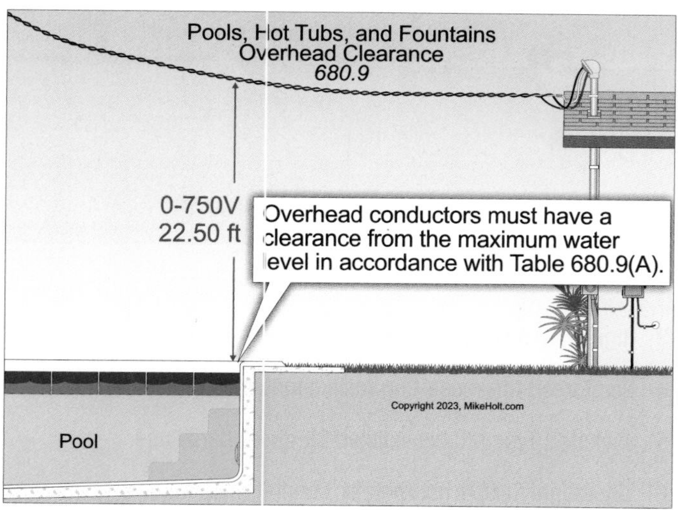
Pools, Hot Tubs, and Fountains
Overhead Clearance
680.9
0-750V
22.50 ft
Overhead conductors must have a clearance from the maximum water level in accordance with Table 680.9(A).
Pool
Copyright 2023, MikeHolt.com

▸Figure 680–12

According to Article 100, "Maximum Water Level," is the highest level that water can reach before it spills out.

(A) Overhead Power Conductors. Exposed overhead power conductors cannot be installed within the clearances contained in Table 680.9(A). ▸Figure 680–13

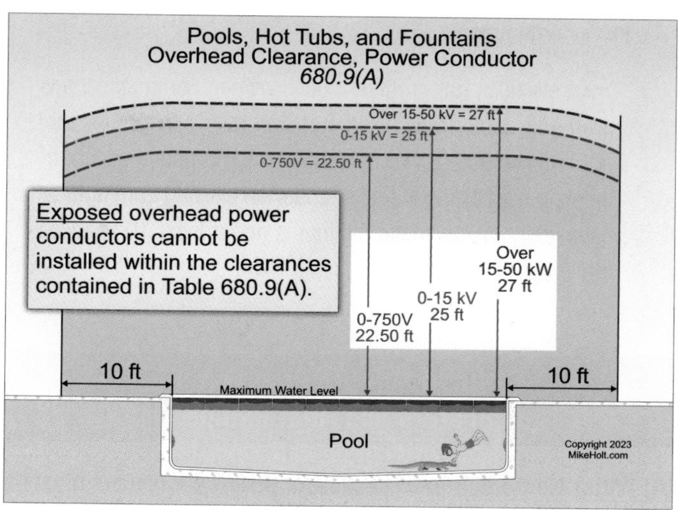
Pools, Hot Tubs, and Fountains
Overhead Clearance, Power Conductor
680.9(A)
Over 15-50 kV = 27 ft
0-15 kV = 25 ft
0-750V = 22.50 ft
Exposed overhead power conductors cannot be installed within the clearances contained in Table 680.9(A).
Over 15-50 kW 27 ft
0-15 kV 25 ft
0-750V 22.50 ft
10 ft
10 ft
Maximum Water Level
Pool
Copyright 2023 MikeHolt.com

▸Figure 680–13

Author's Comment:

- This rule does not prohibit utility-owned overhead service-drop conductors from being installed over a pool, hot tub, or fountain [90.2(D)(5)]. However, it does prohibit a pool, hot tub, or fountain from being installed under an existing service drop that is not at least 22½ ft above the water.

(B) Communications Systems [Chapter 8]. Communications, radio, and television cables within the scope of Chapter 8 cannot be installed less than 10 ft above the maximum water level of swimming and wading pools and diving structures, observation stands, towers, or platforms. ▸Figure 680–14

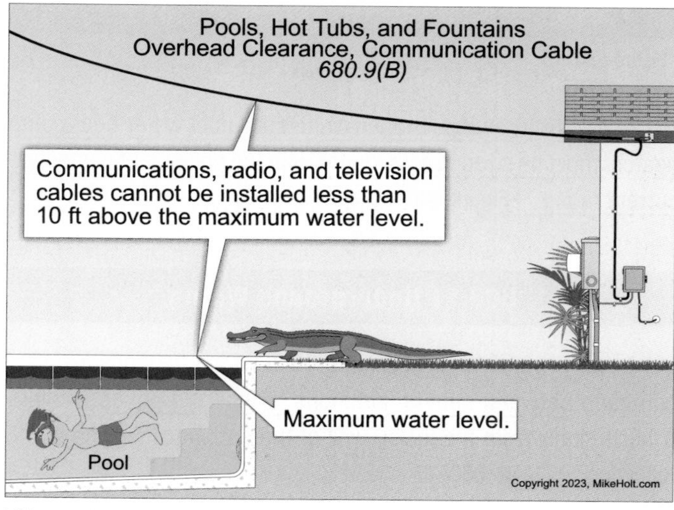
Pools, Hot Tubs, and Fountains
Overhead Clearance, Communication Cable
680.9(B)
Communications, radio, and television cables cannot be installed less than 10 ft above the maximum water level.
Maximum water level.
Pool
Copyright 2023, MikeHolt.com

▸Figure 680–14

Author's Comment:

- This rule does not prohibit a utility-owned communications overhead cable from being installed over a pool, hot tub, or fountain [90.2(B)(4)]. It does prohibit a pool, hot tub, or fountain from being installed under an existing communications utility overhead supply that is not at least 10 ft above the water.

680.10 Electric Pool Water Heaters and Heat Pumps

(A) Water Heaters. Branch-circuits for pool water heaters must be sized at not less than 125 percent of the equipment nameplate current rating. ▶Figure 680–15

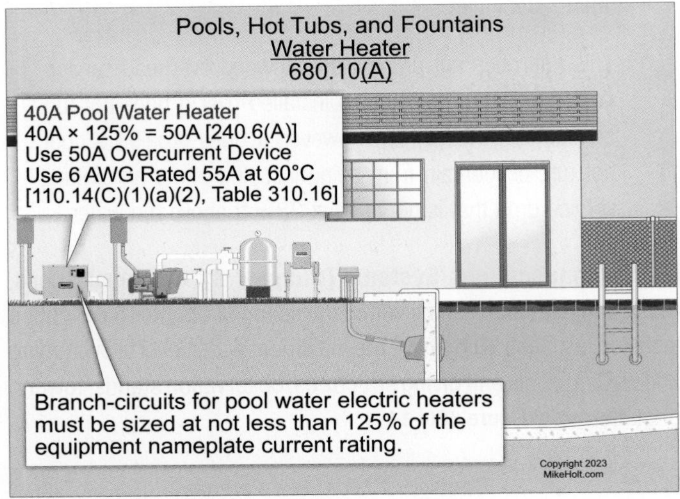
Pools, Hot Tubs, and Fountains
Water Heater
680.10(A)
40A Pool Water Heater
40A × 125% = 50A [240.6(A)]
Use 50A Overcurrent Device
Use 6 AWG Rated 55A at 60°C
[110.14(C)(1)(a)(2), Table 310.16]
Branch-circuits for pool water electric heaters must be sized at not less than 125% of the equipment nameplate current rating.
Copyright 2023 MikeHolt.com

▶Figure 680–15

(B) Water Heat Pump. Branch-circuits for pool water heat pump heaters must be sized in accordance with the equipment nameplate current rating. ▶Figure 680–16

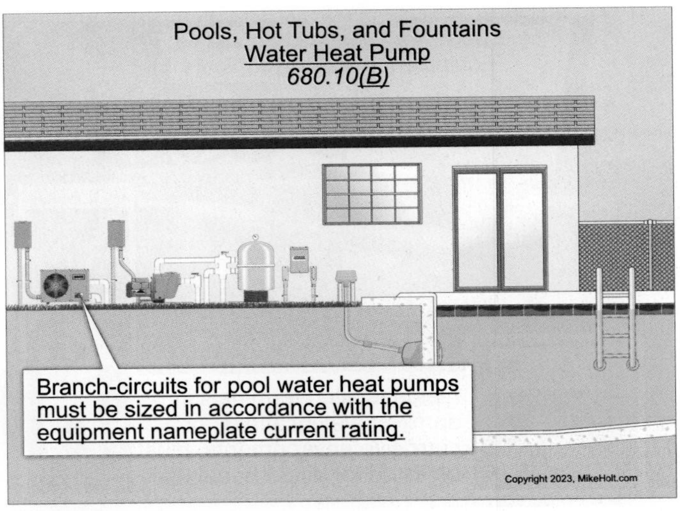
Pools, Hot Tubs, and Fountains
Water Heat Pump
680.10(B)
Branch-circuits for pool water heat pumps must be sized in accordance with the equipment nameplate current rating.
Copyright 2023, MikeHolt.com

▶Figure 680–16

680.11 Underground Wiring

(A) Underground Wiring. Underground wiring methods installed complete between outlets, junctions, or splicing points within 5 ft horizontally from the inside wall of the pool must be one of the following: ▶Figure 680–17

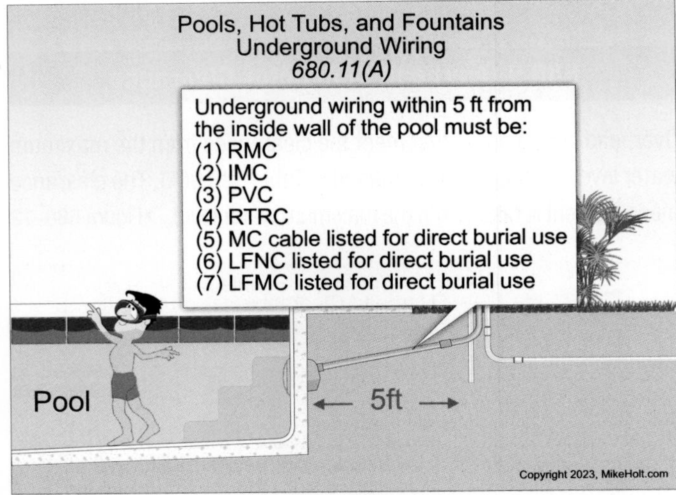
Pools, Hot Tubs, and Fountains
Underground Wiring
680.11(A)
Underground wiring within 5 ft from the inside wall of the pool must be:
(1) RMC
(2) IMC
(3) PVC
(4) RTRC
(5) MC cable listed for direct burial use
(6) LFNC listed for direct burial use
(7) LFMC listed for direct burial use
Pool
5ft
Copyright 2023, MikeHolt.com

▶Figure 680–17

(1) Rigid metal conduit

(2) Intermediate metal conduit

(3) Rigid polyvinyl chloride conduit

(4) Reinforced thermosetting resin conduit

(5) Jacketed Type MC cable listed for direct burial use

(6) Liquidtight flexible nonmetallic conduit listed for direct burial use

(7) Liquidtight flexible metal conduit listed for direct burial use

(B) Wiring Under Pools. Underground wiring beneath pools is permitted for the supply of pool equipment permitted by this article and no other loads.

680.12 Equipment Rooms, Vaults, and Pits

(A) Drainage. Permanently installed pools, hot tubs, or fountain equipment are not permitted to be in rooms, vaults, or pits that do not have drainage that prevents water accumulation during normal operation or maintenance, unless the equipment is rated and identified for submersion.

(B) Receptacles. At least one GFCI-protected 125V, 15A or 20A receptacle must be within the equipment room for permanently installed pools, hot tubs, or fountains. ▸Figure 680–18

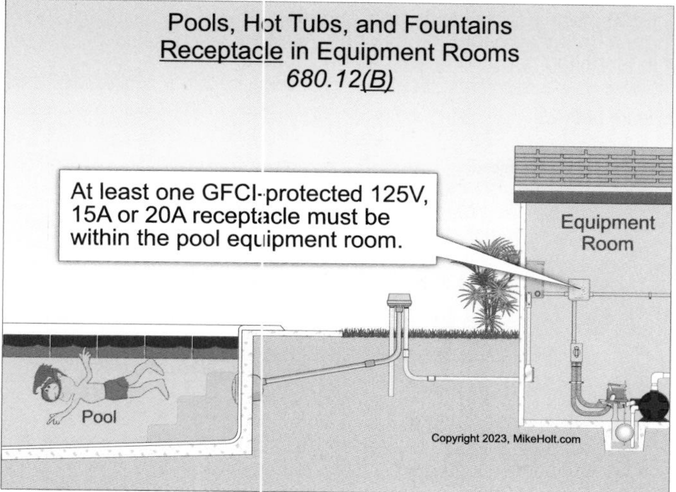

▸Figure 680–18

Receptacles supplied by branch circuits rated 150V or less to ground within an equipment room, vaults, or pits must be GFCI protected.

680.13 Equipment Disconnecting Means

A disconnect is required for pool, hot tub, or fountain equipment. The disconnect must be readily accessible and be within sight and not less than 5 ft from the pool, hot tub, or fountain water, unless separated by a permanently installed barrier. This horizontal distance is measured from the water's edge along the shortest path required to reach the disconnect. ▸Figure 680–19

According to Article 100, "Within Sight" means equipment that it is visible and not more than 50 ft from the location of the other equipment. ▸Figure 680–20

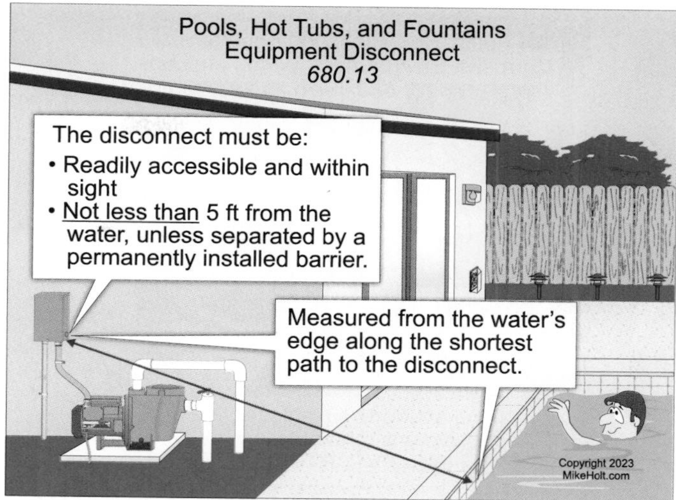

▸Figure 680–19

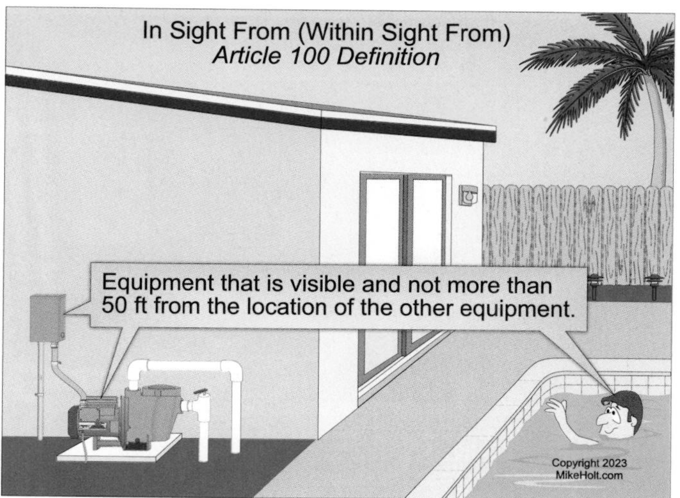

▸Figure 680–20

680.14 Corrosive Environment

(A) Wiring Methods. Wiring methods suitable for use in corrosive environments must be rigid metal conduit, intermediate metal conduit, rigid polyvinyl chloride conduit, reinforced thermosetting resin conduit, or liquidtight flexible nonmetallic conduit. ▸Figure 680–21

According to Article 100, a "Corrosive Environment" is areas or enclosures without adequate ventilation where electrical equipment is located and pool sanitation chemicals are stored, handled, or dispensed (Article 680). ▸Figure 680–22

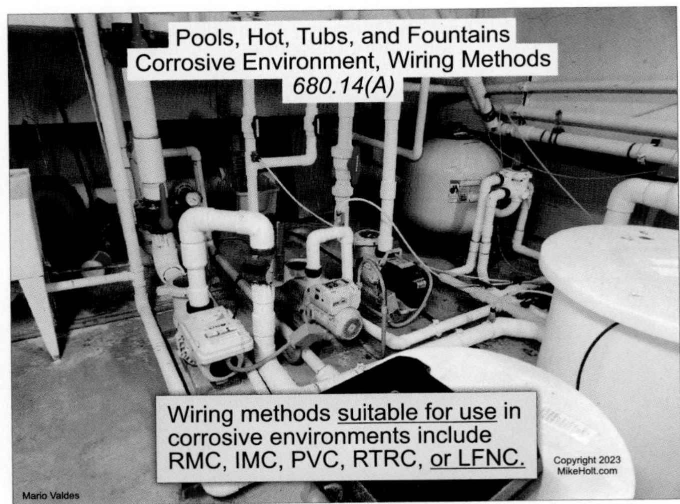
Pools, Hot, Tubs, and Fountains
Corrosive Environment, Wiring Methods
680.14(A)
Wiring methods suitable for use in corrosive environments include RMC, IMC, PVC, RTRC, or LFNC.
Copyright 2023 MikeHolt.com
Mario Valdes

▸Figure 680–21

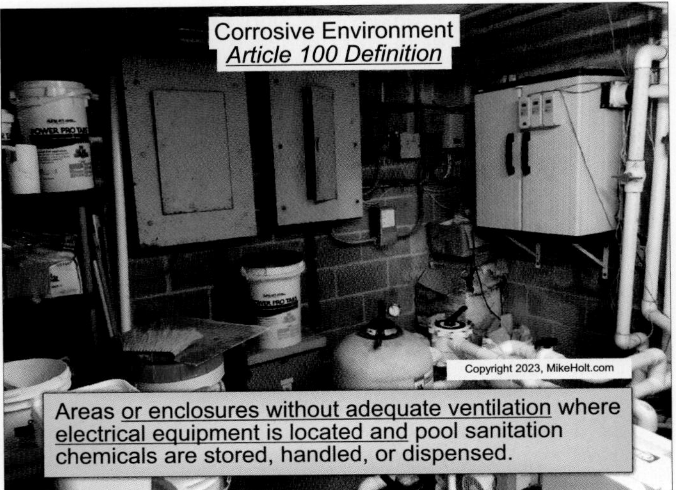
Corrosive Environment
Article 100 Definition
Copyright 2023, MikeHolt.com
Areas or enclosures without adequate ventilation where electrical equipment is located and pool sanitation chemicals are stored, handled, or dispensed.

▸Figure 680–22

Note 1: Sanitation chemicals and pool water pose a risk of corrosion (gradually damaging or destroying materials) due to the presence of oxidizers (for example, calcium hypochlorite, sodium hypochlorite, bromine, and chlorinated isocyanurates) and chlorinating agents that release chlorine when dissolved in water.

(B) Equipment. Equipment in a corrosive pool environment must be suitable for the use or be installed in identified corrosion-resistant enclosures. Equipment listed for use in pools and hot tubs are considered suitable for use in a corrosive pool environment. ▸Figure 680–23 and ▸Figure 680–24

Pools, Hot Tubs, and Fountains
Corrosive Environment, Equipment
680.14(B)
Equipment in a corrosive pool environment must be suitable for the use or be installed in identified corrosion-resistant enclosures.
Copyright 2023, MikeHolt.com

▸Figure 680–23

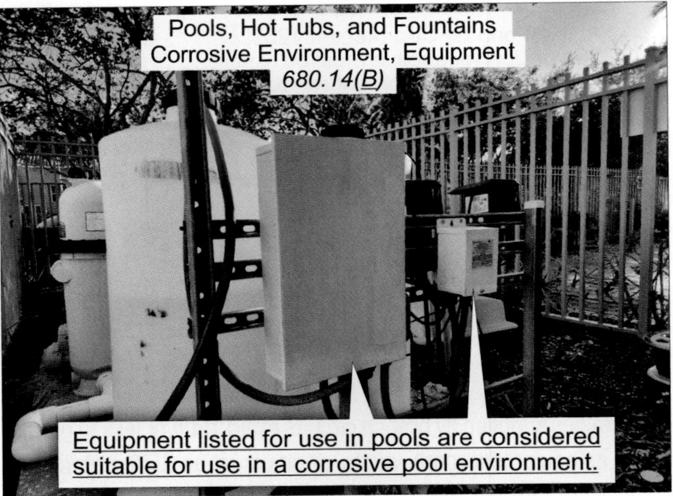
Pools, Hot Tubs, and Fountains
Corrosive Environment, Equipment
680.14(B)
Equipment listed for use in pools are considered suitable for use in a corrosive pool environment.

▸Figure 680–24

Part II. Permanently Installed Pools

680.20 General

The requirements contained in Part I and Part II apply to permanently installed pools as defined by Article 100.

According to Article 100, a "Pool, Permanently Installed" is a pool constructed or installed in the ground or partially in the ground, and pools installed inside of a building (Article 680). ▸Figure 680–25

▸Figure 680–25

680.21 Pool Pump Motors

(A) Wiring Methods. The wiring to a pool pump motor must comply with 680.21(A)(1) or (A)(2).

(1) Flexible Connections. If flexible connections are necessary, liquidtight flexible metal conduit, liquidtight flexible nonmetallic conduit, and Type MC cable suitable for the use are permitted. ▸Figure 680–26

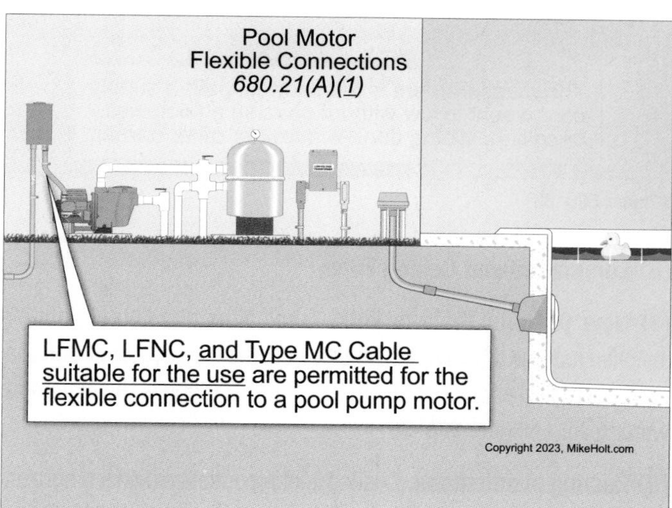

Pool Motor
Flexible Connections
680.21(A)(1)
LFMC, LFNC, and Type MC Cable suitable for the use are permitted for the flexible connection to a pool pump motor.
Copyright 2023, MikeHolt.com

▸Figure 680–26

(C) GFCI and SPGFCI Protection. GFCI protection is required for pool pump motor outlets rated 150V or less to ground and SPGFCI protection is required for pool pump motor outlets rated above 150V to ground. ▸Figure 680–27

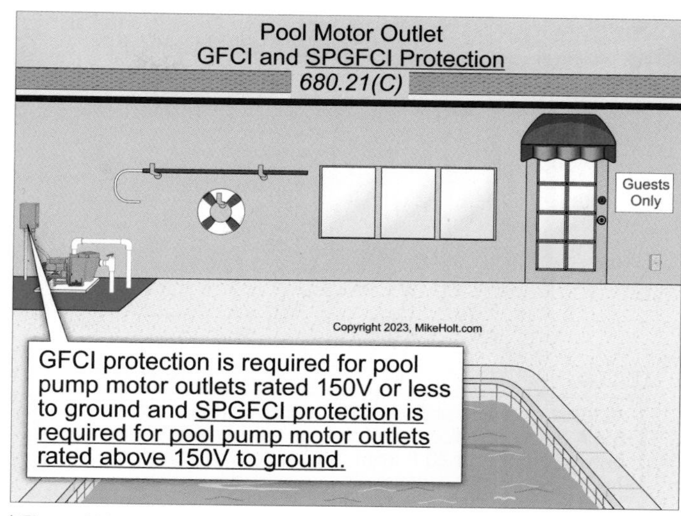

▸Figure 680–27

(D) Pool Pump Motor Replacement. Where a pool pump motor is replaced or repaired, the replacement or repaired pump motor must be provided with GFCI or SPGFCI protection in accordance with 680.5(B) or (C). ▸Figure 680–28

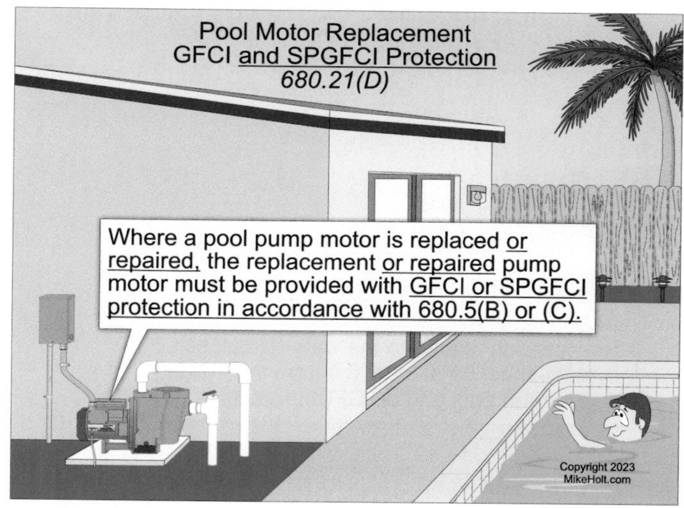

▸Figure 680–28

680.22 Receptacles, Luminaires, and Switches

(A) Receptacles.

(1) Required Receptacle. At least one 15A or 20A, 125V receptacle installed on a general-purpose branch circuit must be not less than 6 ft and not more than 20 ft from the inside wall of a pool. This receptacle must be not more than 6½ ft above the floor, platform, or grade level serving the pool. ▸Figure 680–29

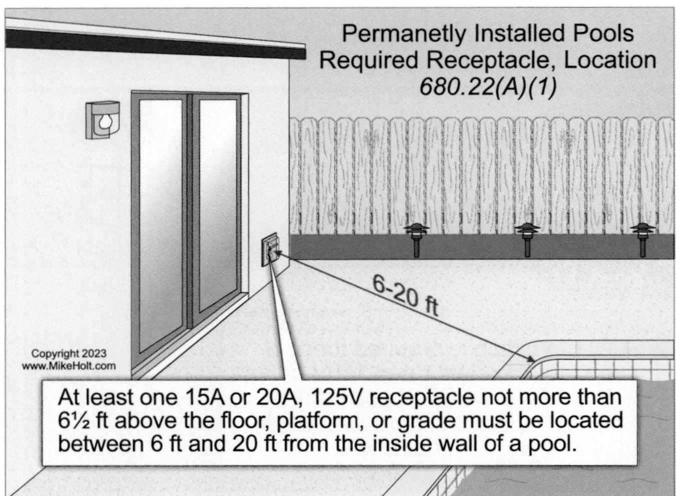

Permanetly Installed Pools
Required Receptacle, Location
680.22(A)(1)
6-20 ft
Copyright 2023
www.MikeHolt.com
At least one 15A or 20A, 125V receptacle not more than 6½ ft above the floor, platform, or grade must be located between 6 ft and 20 ft from the inside wall of a pool.

▸Figure 680–29

(2) Circulation System Receptacle. Receptacles for pool motors or other loads directly related to the circulation system, must be at least 6 ft from the inside walls of the pool and have GFCI protection. ▸**Figure 680–30**

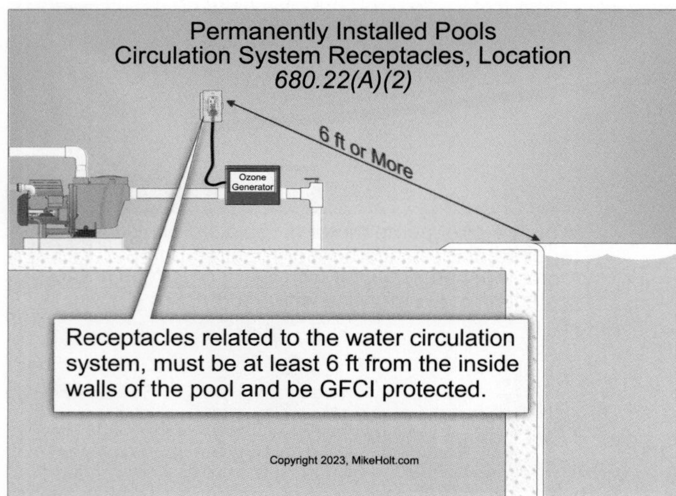

▸Figure 680–30

(3) Other Receptacles. Receptacles for loads not directly related to the circulation system must be not less than 6 ft from the inside walls of a pool. ▸**Figure 680–31**

(4) GFCI. Receptacles rated 125V through 250V, 60A or less within 20 ft of the inside wall of a pool must have GFCI protected.

(5) How to Measure. When measuring receptacle distances from the pool water, the measurement is the shortest path a supply cord would follow without piercing a floor, wall, or ceiling, sliding door, window, or other barrier. ▸**Figure 680–32**

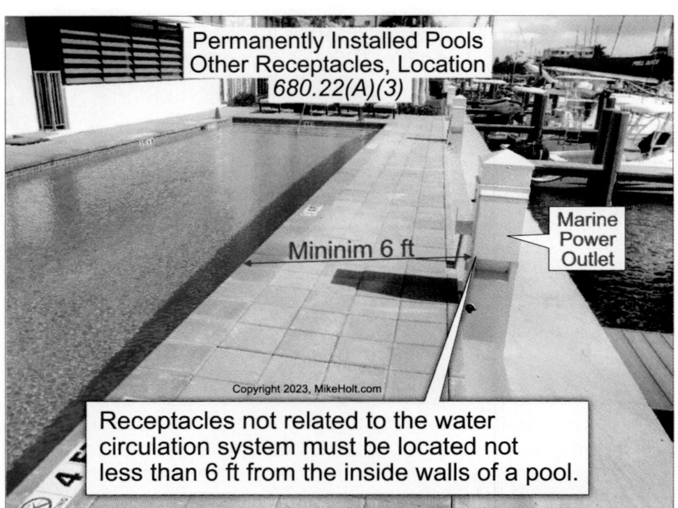

▸Figure 680–31

▸Figure 680–32

(B) Luminaires and Ceiling Fans.

(1) New Outdoor Installations. Luminaires and lighting outlets installed not less than 5 ft horizontally from the inside walls of a permanently installed pool must be not less than 12 ft above the maximum water level. ▸**Figure 680–33**

(3) Existing Installations. Existing lighting outlets within 5 ft horizontally from the inside walls of a permanently installed pool must not be less than 5 ft above the surface of the maximum water level, be rigidly attached to the existing structure, and be GFCI protected. ▸**Figure 680–34**

1st Printing

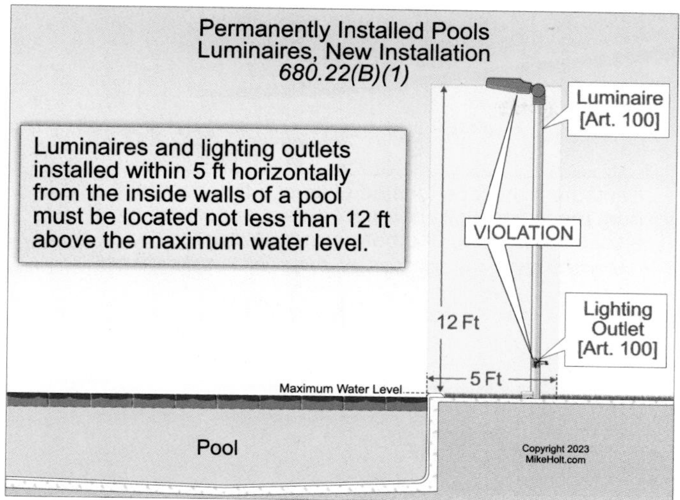

▸Figure 680–33

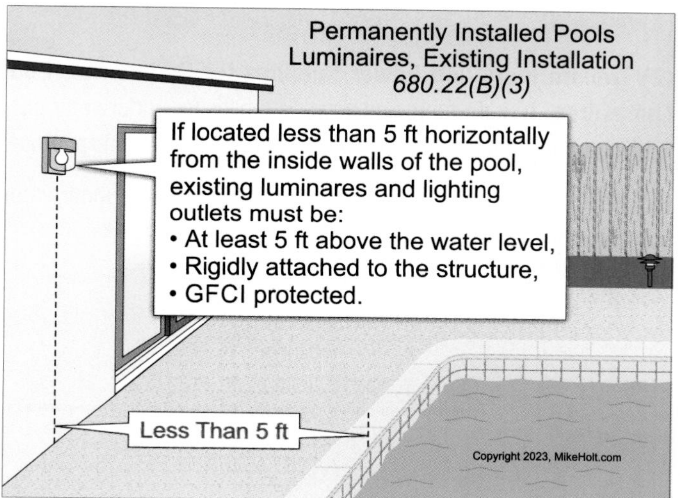

Permanently Installed Pools
Luminaires, Existing Installation
680.22(B)(3)
If located less than 5 ft horizontally from the inside walls of the pool, existing luminares and lighting outlets must be:
• At least 5 ft above the water level,
• Rigidly attached to the structure,
• GFCI protected.
Less Than 5 ft
Copyright 2023, MikeHolt.com

▸Figure 680–34

(4) GFCI and SPGFCI Protection. All luminaires, lighting outlets, and ceiling fans between 5 ft and 10 ft horizontally from the inside walls of a permanently installed pool, and not less than 5 ft above the maximum water, level must have GFCI protection in accordance with 680.5(B) or SPGFCI protection in accordance with 680.5(C). ▸**Figure 680–35**

(6) Low-Voltage Luminaires. Low-voltage lighting systems that are listed, labeled, and identified for swimming pools can be installed without any distance limits to the water. ▸**Figure 680–36**

All other low-voltage lighting must not be installed within 10 ft from the edge of the water in accordance with 411.6(B). ▸**Figure 680–37**

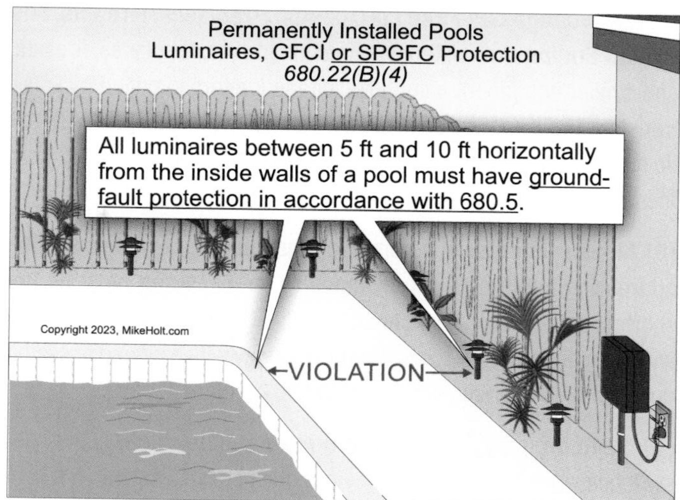

Permanently Installed Pools
Luminaires, GFCI or SPGFC Protection
680.22(B)(4)
All luminaires between 5 ft and 10 ft horizontally from the inside walls of a pool must have ground-fault protection in accordance with 680.5.
Copyright 2023, MikeHolt.com
VIOLATION

▸Figure 680–35

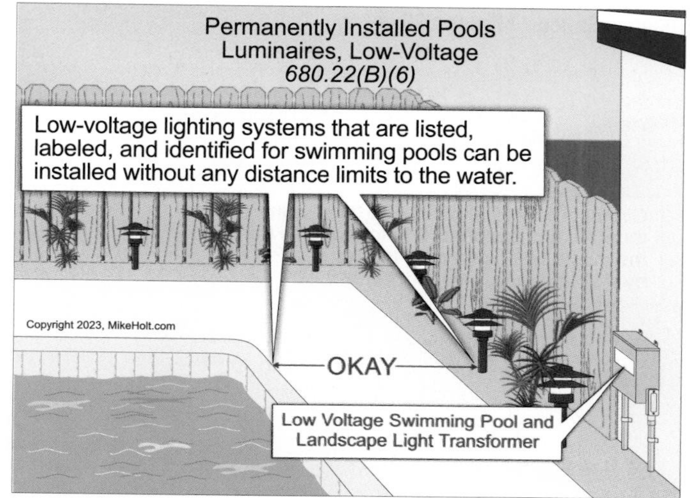

▸Figure 680–36

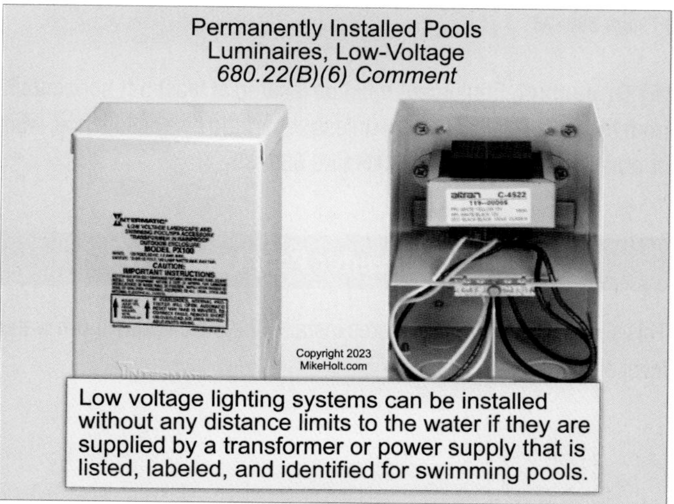

▸Figure 680–37

(7) Low-Voltage Gas-Fired Luminaires, Fireplaces, Fire Pits, and Similar Equipment. Listed gas-fired luminaires, fireplaces, fire pits, and similar equipment using low-voltage ignitors supplied by listed transformers or power supplies that comply with 680.23(A)(2) and do not exceed the low-voltage contact limit can be less than 5 ft from the inside walls of the pool.

(8) Measurements. In determining the dimensions in this section addressing luminaires, the distance to be measured must be the shortest path an imaginary cord connected to the luminaire will follow without piercing a floor, wall, ceiling, doorway with a hinged or sliding door, window opening, or other effective permanent barrier.

(C) Switching Devices. Circuit breakers, time clocks, pool light switches, and other switching devices must be not less than 5 ft horizontally from the inside walls of a pool unless separated by a solid fence, wall, or other permanent barrier that provides at least a 5-ft reach distance. ▸Figure 680–38

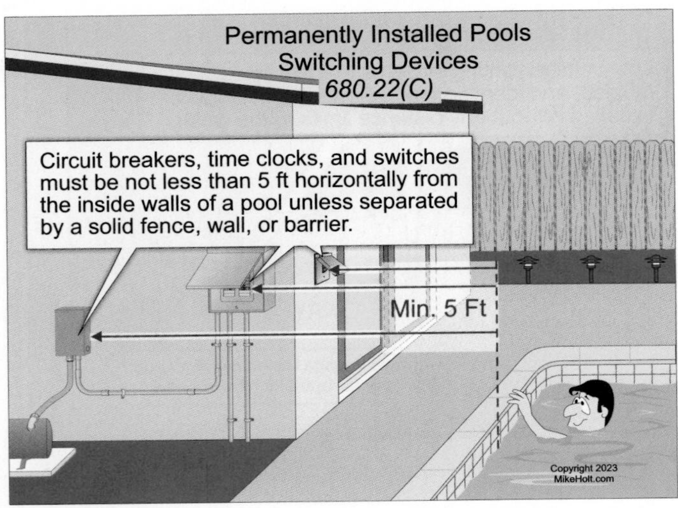

▸Figure 680–38

(E) Equipment. Equipment must be located at least 5 ft horizontally from the inside walls of a pool unless separated by a solid fence, wall, or other permanent barrier. ▸Figure 680–39

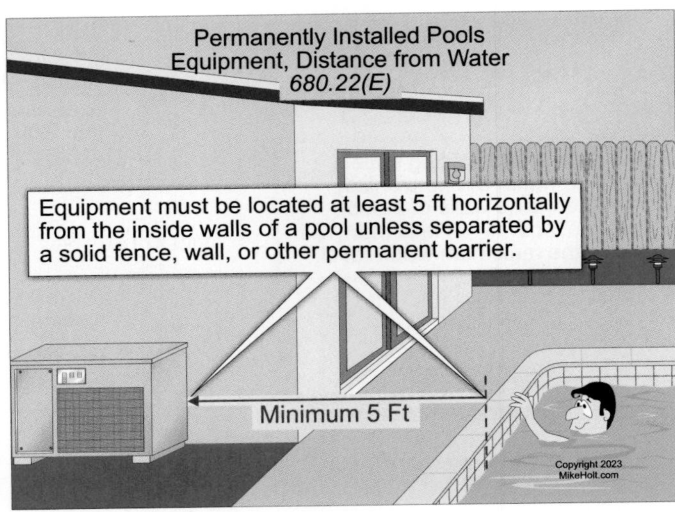

▸Figure 680–39

680.23 Underwater Pool Luminaires

This section covers all luminaires installed below the maximum water level of the pool.

(A) General.

(2) Transformers and Power Supplies for Underwater Pool Luminaires. Transformers and power supplies for underwater pool luminaires must be listed, labeled, and identified for swimming pool use.

(3) GFCI Protection. Branch circuits supplying 120V underwater pool luminaires must be GFCI protected. ▸Figure 680–40

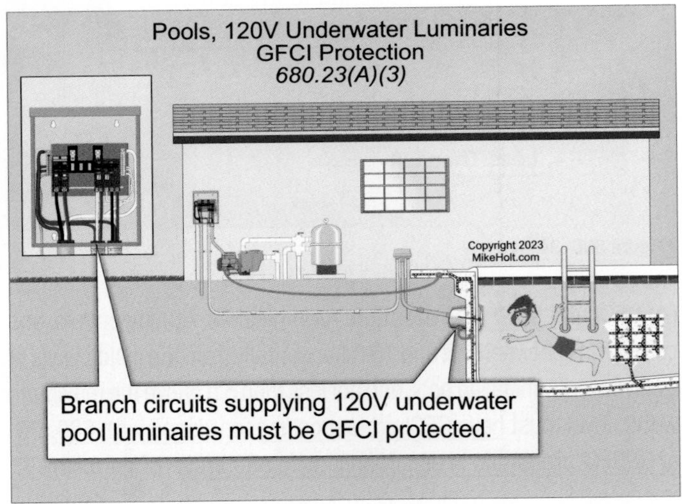

▸Figure 680–40

(5) Wall-Mounted Luminaires. Underwater wall-mounted luminaires must be installed so the top of the luminaire lens is not less than 18 in. below the normal water level. ▸Figure 680–41

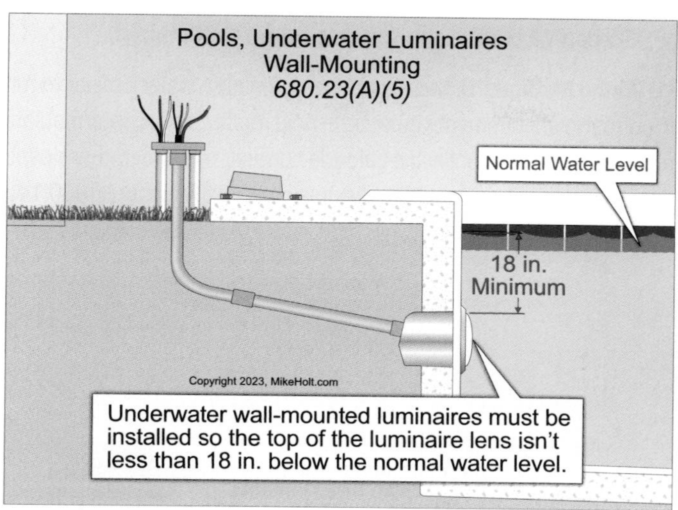

▶Figure 680–41

(B) Wet-Niche Luminaires.

(1) Wet-Niche Forming Shells. Forming shells must be installed for the mounting of all wet-niche underwater luminaires. Forming shells must include provisions for terminating an 8 AWG copper conductor unless the forming shell is part of a listed low-voltage lighting system.

According to Article 100, a "Forming Shell" is defined as a structure designed to support a wet-niche luminaire (Article 680). ▶**Figure 680–42**

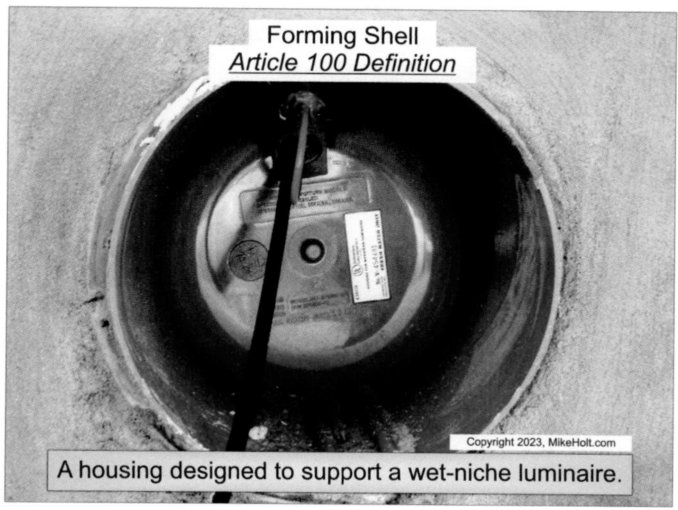

▶Figure 680–42

According to Article 100, a "Luminaire, Wet-Niche" is a luminaire intended to be installed in a forming shell where it will be surrounded by water (Article 680). ▶**Figure 680–43**

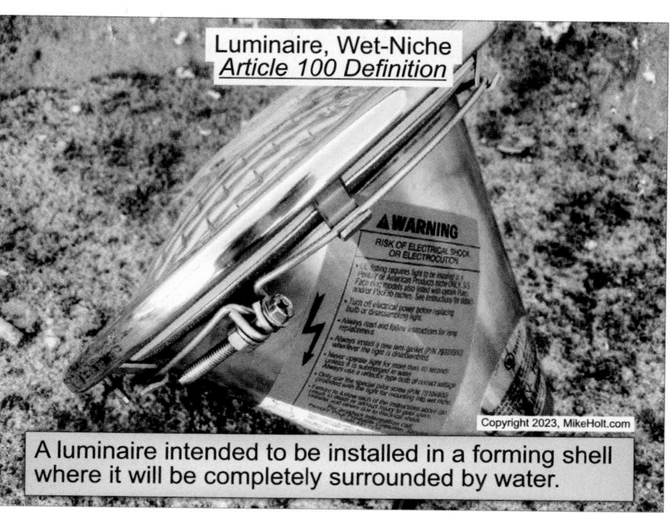

Luminaire, Wet-Niche
Article 100 Definition
WARNING
Copyright 2023, MikeHolt.com
A luminaire intended to be installed in a forming shell where it will be completely surrounded by water.

▶Figure 680–43

(2) Wiring to the Wet-Niche Forming Shell.

(b) PVC Raceway.

120V Wet-Niche Luminaire. A PVC raceway run to the forming shell of a wet-niche luminaire must contain an 8 AWG insulated copper conductor that terminates to the forming shell. ▶**Figure 680–44**

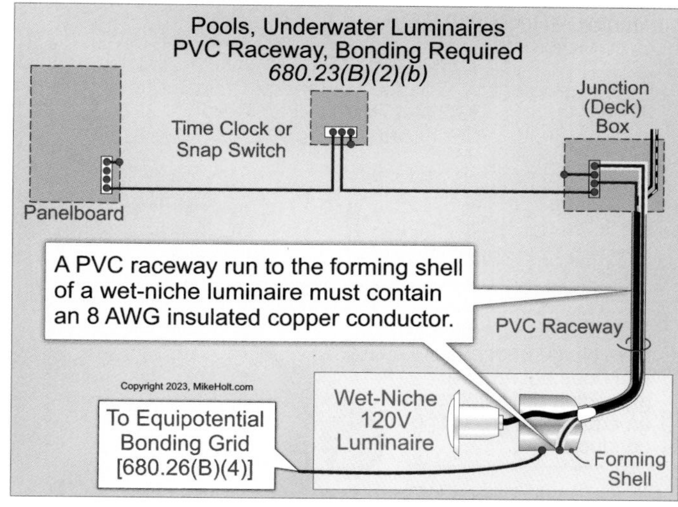

▶Figure 680–44

Low-Voltage Lighting System. A PVC raceway run to the forming shell of a listed low-voltage lighting system that does not require grounding does not require an 8 AWG insulated copper conductor to the forming shell. ▶**Figure 680–45**

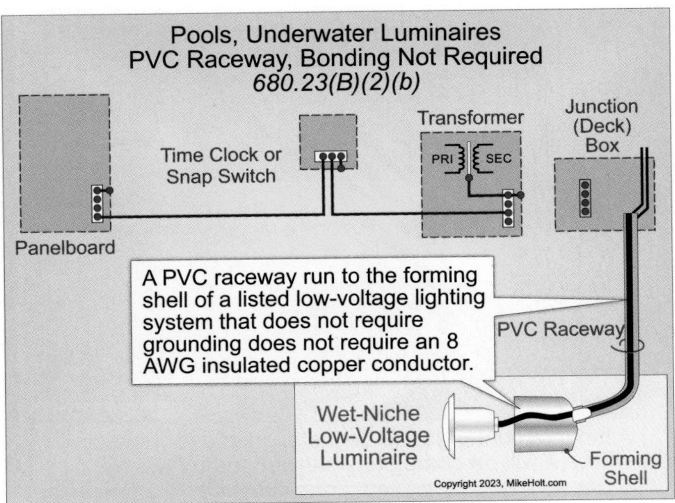
Pools, Underwater Luminaires
PVC Raceway, Bonding Not Required
680.23(B)(2)(b)
Time Clock or
Snap Switch
Transformer
PRI
SEC
Junction
(Deck)
Box
Panelboard
A PVC raceway run to the forming shell of a listed low-voltage lighting system that does not require grounding does not require an 8 AWG insulated copper conductor.
PVC Raceway
Wet-Niche
Low-Voltage
Luminaire
Forming
Shell
Copyright 2023, MikeHolt.com

▶Figure 680–45

The termination of the 8 AWG bonding jumper in the forming shell must be covered with a listed potting compound to protect the connection from the possible deteriorating effects of pool water.

(3) Equipment Grounding Provisions for Cords. The cord or cable supplying a low-voltage underwater luminaire that does not require grounding does not require an insulated copper equipment grounding conductor. ▶**Figure 680–46**

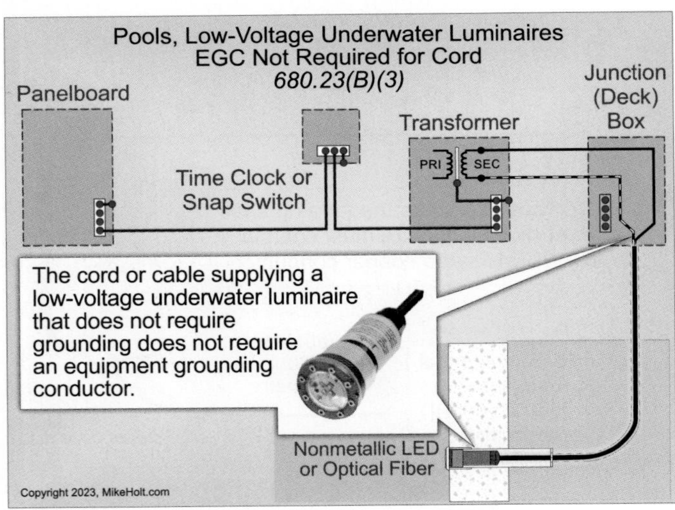
Pools, Low-Voltage Underwater Luminaires
EGC Not Required for Cord
680.23(B)(3)
Panelboard
Junction
(Deck)
Box
Transformer
PRI
SEC
Time Clock or
Snap Switch
The cord or cable supplying a low-voltage underwater luminaire that does not require grounding does not require an equipment grounding conductor.
Nonmetallic LED
or Optical Fiber
Copyright 2023, MikeHolt.com

▶Figure 680–46

(6) Underwater Luminaire Servicing. The location of the forming shell and length of flexible cord for wet-niche pool luminaires must allow for personnel to place the luminaire on the deck for maintenance.

(F) Branch-Circuit Wiring to Underwater Luminaires.

(1) Wiring Methods. Branch-circuit wiring for underwater luminaires run in corrosive environments must be in rigid metal conduit, intermediate metal conduit, rigid polyvinyl chloride conduit, reinforced thermosetting resin conduit, or liquidtight flexible nonmetallic conduit [680.14]. ▶**Figure 680–47**

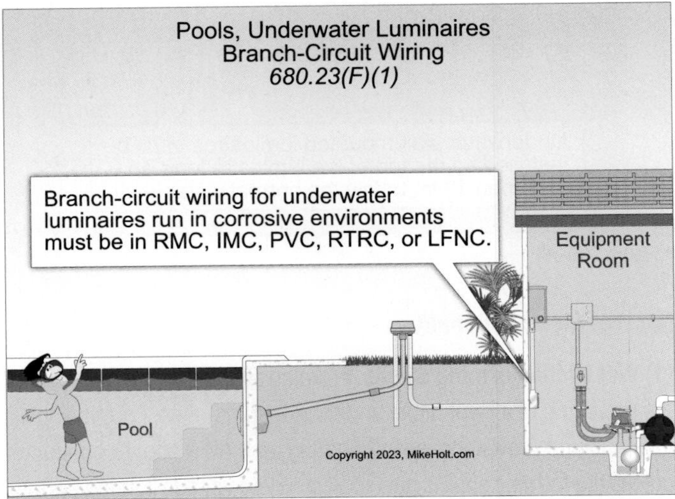
Pools, Underwater Luminaires
Branch-Circuit Wiring
680.23(F)(1)
Branch-circuit wiring for underwater luminaires run in corrosive environments must be in RMC, IMC, PVC, RTRC, or LFNC.
Equipment
Room
Pool
Copyright 2023, MikeHolt.com

▶Figure 680–47

(2) Branch-Circuit Equipment Grounding Conductor.

Wet-Niche 120V Luminaires. An insulated copper equipment grounding conductor not smaller than 12 AWG is required for a wet-niche 120V underwater luminaires. ▶**Figure 680–48**

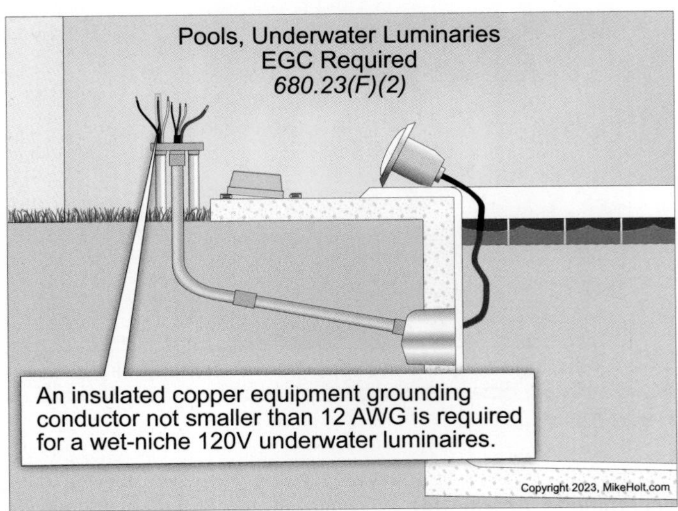
Pools, Underwater Luminaries
EGC Required
680.23(F)(2)
An insulated copper equipment grounding conductor not smaller than 12 AWG is required for a wet-niche 120V underwater luminaires.
Copyright 2023, MikeHolt.com

▶Figure 680–48

Low-Voltage Luminaires. An equipment grounding conductor is not required for a low-voltage underwater luminaires listed as not requiring grounding. ▶**Figure 680–49**

1st Printing

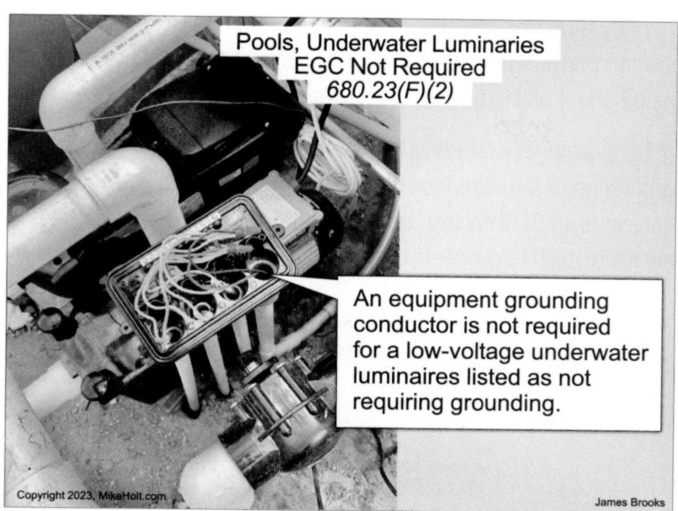

▶Figure 680–49

The circuit equipment grounding conductor for the underwater pool luminaire is not permitted to be spliced, except for the following applications:

(a) If more than one underwater pool luminaire is supplied by the same branch circuit, the circuit equipment grounding conductor can terminate at a listed pool junction box meeting the requirements of 680.24(A).

(b) The circuit equipment grounding conductor can terminate at the grounding terminal of a pool light time clock, listed pool transformer, and pool light junction box. ▶Figure 680–50

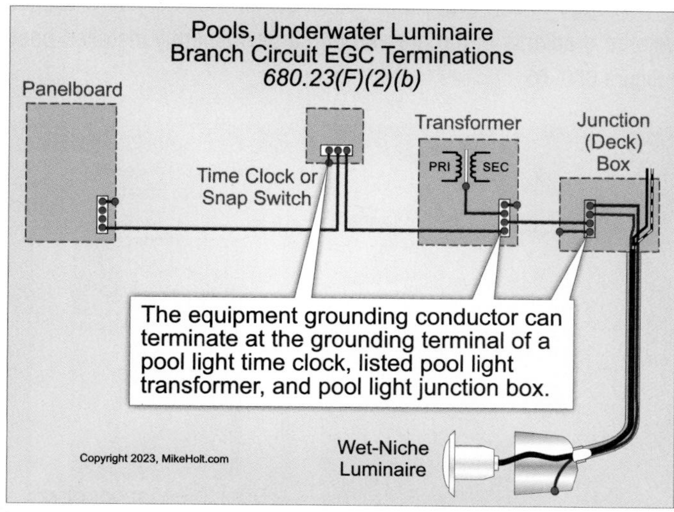

▶Figure 680–50

(3) Conductors. The branch-circuit conductors for the underwater pool luminaire on the load side of a GFCI or transformer used to comply with 680.23(A)(8) are not permitted to occupy raceways or enclosures with other conductors unless the other conductors are:

(1) GFCI protected

(2) Equipment grounding conductors and bonding jumpers as required by 680.23(B)(2)(b)

680.24 Junction Box, Transformer, or GFCI Enclosure

(A) Junction Box. If a junction box is connected to a raceway that extends directly to an underwater pool luminaire forming shell, the junction box must comply with the following:

(1) Construction. The junction box must be listed, labeled, and identified as a swimming pool junction box. ▶Figure 680–51

Pools, Junction Box
Listed
680.24(A)(1)
Copyright 2023
MikeHolt.com
The junction box for an underwater pool luminaire must be listed as a swimming pool junction box.

▶Figure 680–51

(2) Installation.

(a) Vertical Spacing. If the underwater pool luminaire operates at 120V, the junction box must be not less than 4 in. above the ground or pool, or not less than 8 in. above the maximum water level, whichever provides the greater elevation. ▶Figure 680–52

(b) Horizontal Spacing. If the underwater pool luminaire operates at 120V, the junction box must be not less than 4 ft from the inside wall of the pool unless separated by a solid fence, wall, or other permanent barrier. ▶Figure 680–53

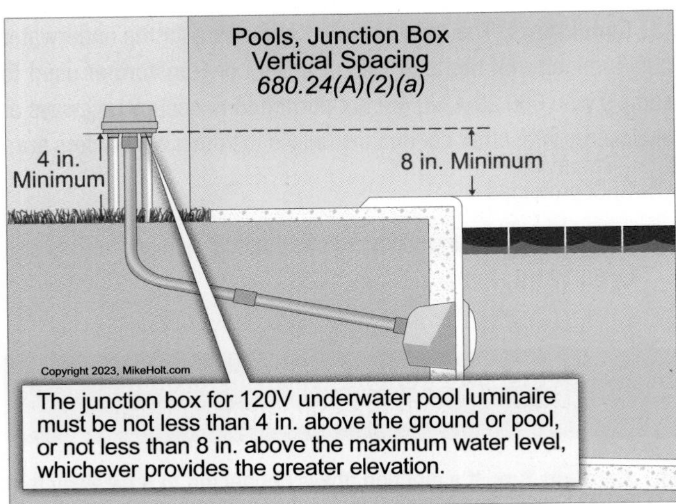
Pools, Junction Box
Vertical Spacing
680.24(A)(2)(a)
4 in. Minimum
8 in. Minimum
Copyright 2023, MikeHolt.com
The junction box for 120V underwater pool luminaire must be not less than 4 in. above the ground or pool, or not less than 8 in. above the maximum water level, whichever provides the greater elevation.

▶Figure 680–52

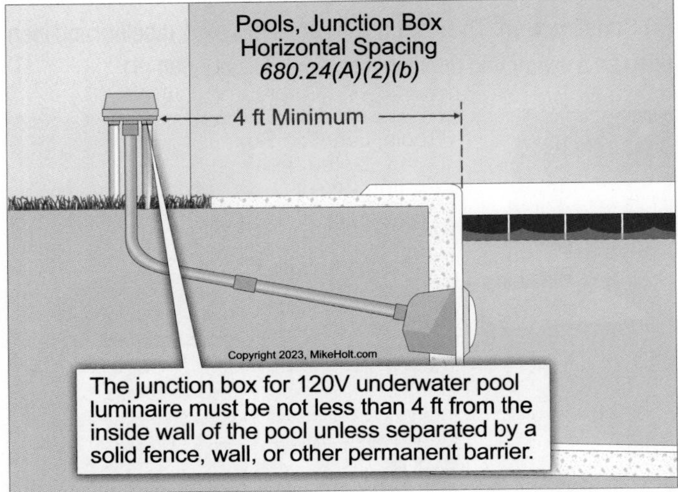
Pools, Junction Box
Horizontal Spacing
680.24(A)(2)(b)
4 ft Minimum
Copyright 2023, MikeHolt.com
The junction box for 120V underwater pool luminaire must be not less than 4 ft from the inside wall of the pool unless separated by a solid fence, wall, or other permanent barrier.

▶Figure 680–53

Author's Comment:

- If conduits are used to support the junction box, the junction box must be supported by two metal conduits threaded wrenchtight into the enclosure according to 314.23(E).

(B) Transformer or GFCI Enclosure. The transformer or GFCI enclosure connected to a raceway that extends directly to an underwater luminaire forming shell must be listed for this purpose.

Author's Comment:

- A pool junction box is still required for the direct connection to an underwater luminaire.

(C) Physical Protection. Junction boxes for underwater luminaires are not permitted to be in a walkway unless afforded protection by being under diving boards or adjacent to fixed structures.

(F) Equipment Grounding Conductor Termination. The equipment grounding of the wire-type required for a junction box, transformer enclosure, or GFCI enclosure for the connection of an underwater pool luminaire must terminate to the panelboard enclosure. ▶Figure 680–54

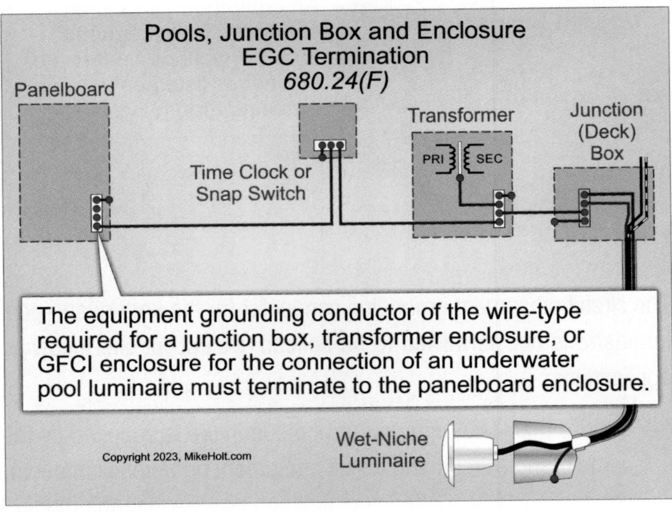
Pools, Junction Box and Enclosure
EGC Termination
680.24(F)
Panelboard
Time Clock or
Snap Switch
Transformer
PRI
SEC
Junction
(Deck)
Box
The equipment grounding conductor of the wire-type required for a junction box, transformer enclosure, or GFCI enclosure for the connection of an underwater pool luminaire must terminate to the panelboard enclosure.
Wet-Niche
Luminaire
Copyright 2023, MikeHolt.com

▶Figure 680–54

680.26 Equipotential Bonding

(A) Voltage Gradients. Equipotential bonding is intended to reduce voltage gradients in the area around a permanently installed pool. ▶Figure 680–55

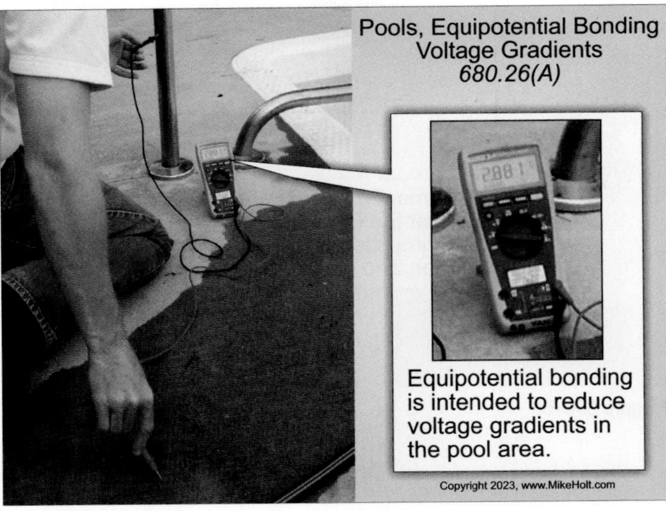
Pools, Equipotential Bonding
Voltage Gradients
680.26(A)
Equipotential bonding is intended to reduce voltage gradients in the pool area.
Copyright 2023, www.MikeHolt.com

▶Figure 680–55

1st Printing

Equipotential bonding must be installed for pools with or without associated electrical equipment related to the pool.

(B) Equipotential Bonded. The parts of a permanently installed pool listed in 680.26(B)(1) through (B)(7) must be bonded together with a solid insulated or bare copper conductor not smaller than 8 AWG using a listed pressure connector, terminal bar, or other listed means in accordance with 250.8(A) [and 680.7]. ▸**Figure 680–56**

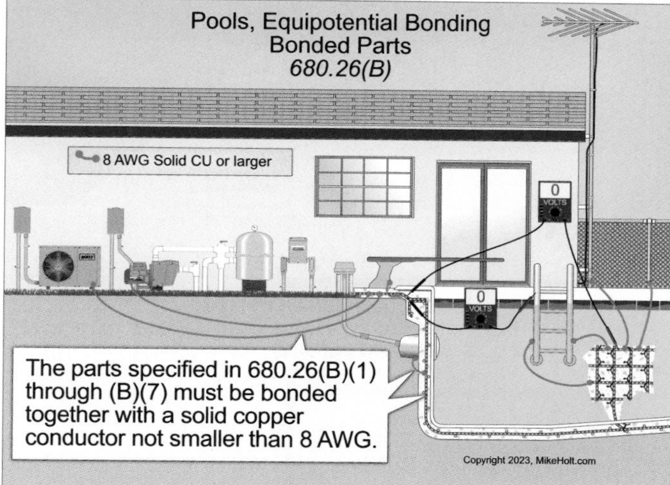

▸**Figure 680–56**

The 8 AWG equipotential bonding conductor is not required to extend (or be attached) to any panelboard, service disconnect, or grounding electrode.

(1) Conductive Pool Shells. Cast-in-place concrete, pneumatically applied or sprayed concrete, and concrete block with painted or plastered coatings must be bonded. Reconstructed conductive pool shells must be bonded.

(a) Structural Reinforcing Steel. Unencapsulated structural reinforcing steel rebar in conductive pool shells must be bonded. ▸**Figure 680–57**

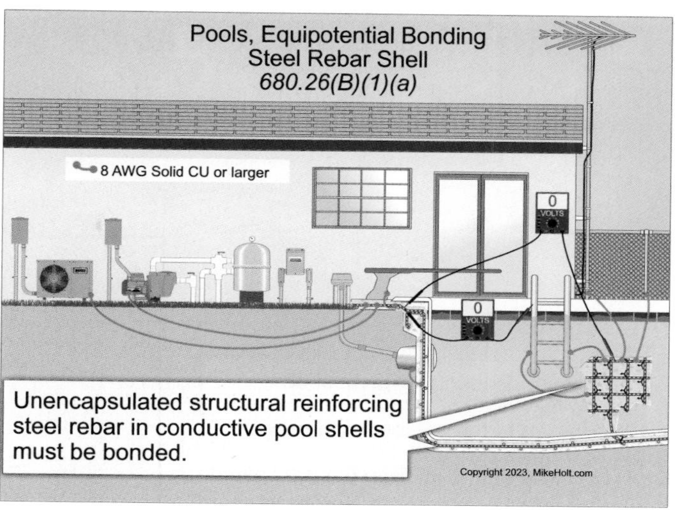

▸**Figure 680–57**

(b) Copper Conductor Grid. Where structural reinforcing steel is encapsulated in a nonconductive compound, a copper conductor grid must be installed as follows: ▸**Figure 680–58**

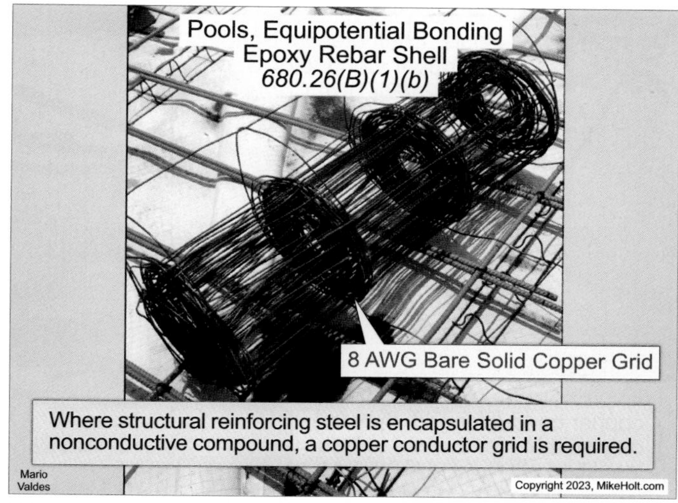

▸**Figure 680–58**

(1) Be constructed of a minimum of 8 AWG bare solid copper conductors bonded to each other at all points of crossing in accordance with 250.8 [and 680.7], or other approved means.

(2) Conform to the contour of the pool.

(3) Be arranged in a 12-in. by 12-in. network of conductors in a uniformly spaced perpendicular grid pattern with a tolerance of 4 in.

(4) Be secured within or under the pool no more than 6 in. from the outer contour of the pool shell. ▸**Figure 680–59**

Author's Comment:

- Encapsulated structural reinforcing steel is used to prevent rebar corrosion and (if used) will make the pool shell insulated, therefore a conductive copper grid is required to bond the pool shell.
- If split bolts are used to bond the copper conductor grid, they are only suitable for 2 wires unless identified otherwise [110.14(A)]. ▸**Figure 680–60**

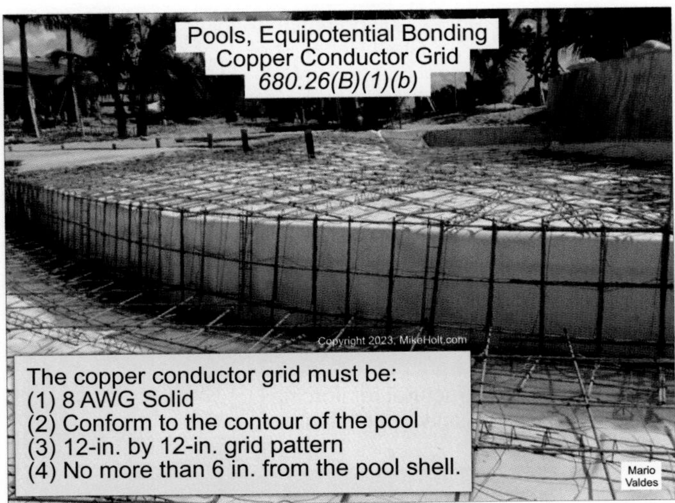

Pools, Equipotential Bonding
Copper Conductor Grid
680.26(B)(1)(b)
The copper conductor grid must be:
(1) 8 AWG Solid
(2) Conform to the contour of the pool
(3) 12-in. by 12-in. grid pattern
(4) No more than 6 in. from the pool shell.
Copyright 2023, MikeHolt.com
Mario Valdes

▸Figure 680–59

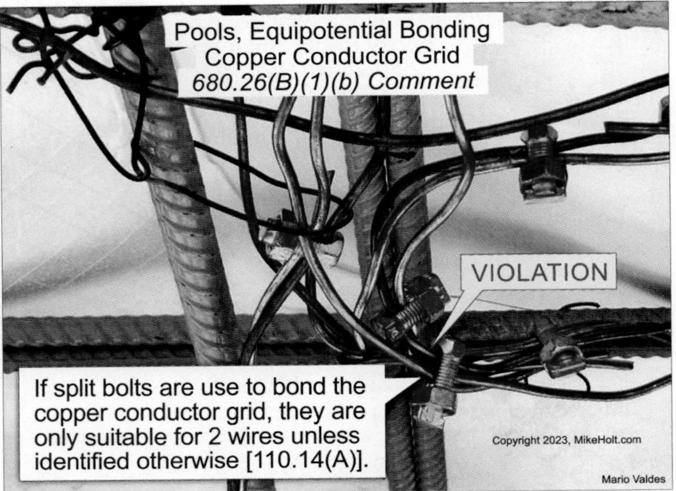

▸Figure 680–60

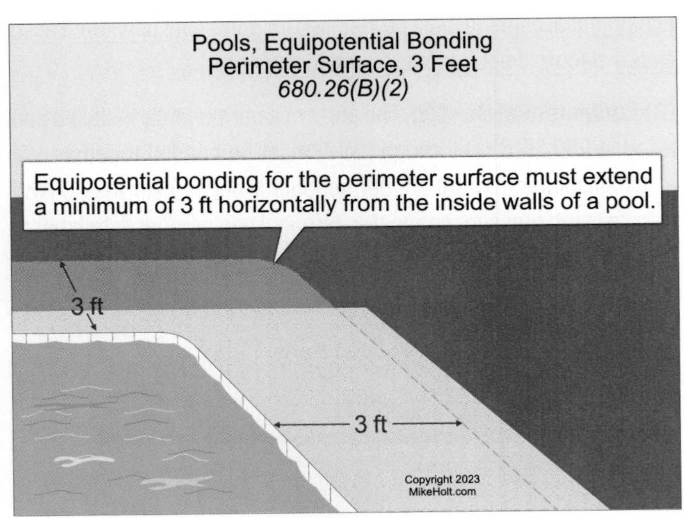

▸Figure 680–61

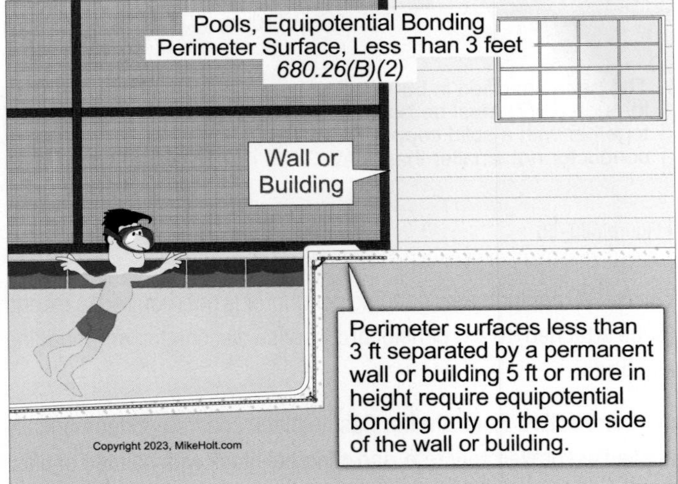

▸Figure 680–62

(2) Perimeter Surfaces. Equipotential bonding for the perimeter surface must extend a minimum of 3 ft horizontally from the inside walls of a pool where not separated by a building or permanent wall 5 ft in height. ▸**Figure 680–61**

Perimeter surfaces less than 3 ft separated by a permanent wall or building 5 ft or more in height require equipotential bonding only on the pool side of the wall or building. ▸**Figure 680–62**

For conductive pool shells, equipotential bonding for perimeter surfaces must be attached to the concrete pool reinforcing steel rebar or copper conductor grid at a minimum of four points uniformly spaced around the perimeter of the pool and be one of the following: ▸**Figure 680–63**

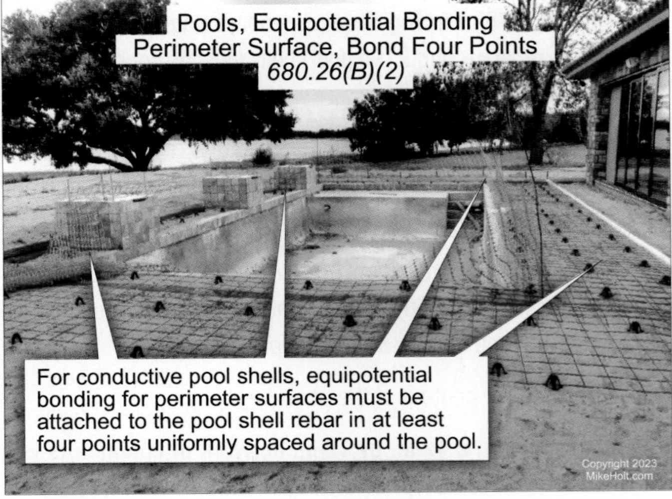

▸Figure 680–63

(a) Structural Reinforcing Steel Rebar. Unencapsulated structural reinforcing steel bonded together by steel tie wires or the equivalent in accordance with 680.26(B)(1)(a). ▶Figure 680–64

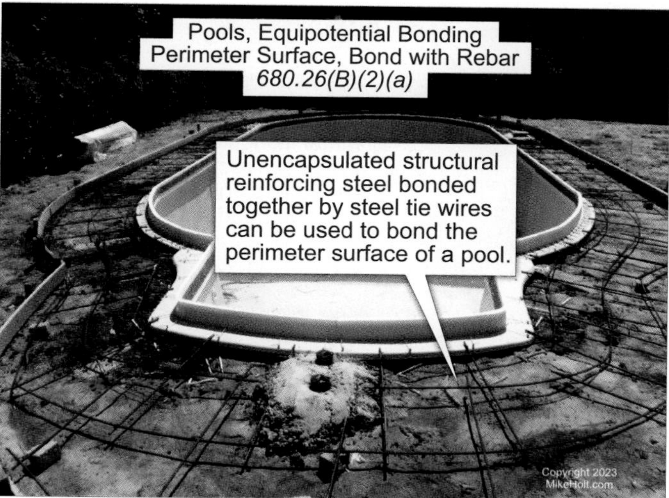

▶Figure 680–64

Author's Comment:

- The *NEC* does not provide a layout requirement for conductive structural steel when used as a perimeter surface equipotential bonding method. ▶Figure 680–65

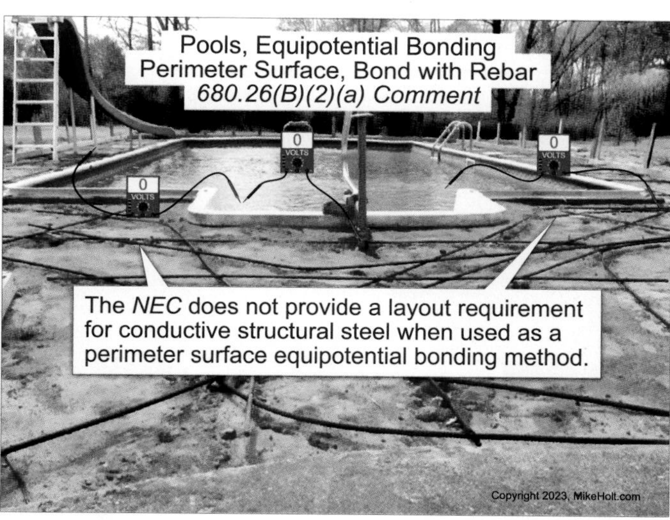

▶Figure 680–65

(b) Copper Ring. Where structural reinforcing steel is not available or is encapsulated in a nonconductive compound, a copper conductor can be used for equipotential perimeter bonding where the following requirements are met: ▶Figure 680–66

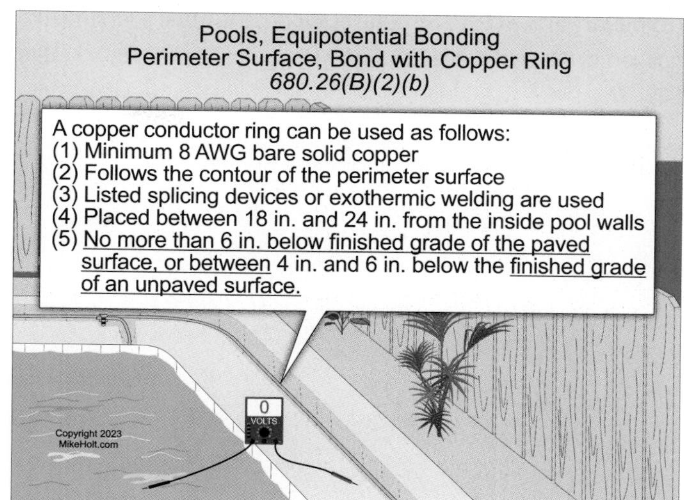

▶Figure 680–66

(1) The copper ring is constructed of 8 AWG bare solid copper or larger.

(2) The copper ring conductor follows the contour of the perimeter surface.

(3) Only listed splicing devices or exothermic welding are used.

(4) The copper ring conductor is placed between 18 in. and 24 in. from the inside walls of the pool.

(5) The copper ring conductor is secured within a paved surface (concrete), no more than 6 in. below finished grade of the paved surface (pavers or concrete), or between 4 in. and 6 in. below the finished grade of an unpaved surface (dirt).

(c) Copper Grid. Where structural reinforcing steel is not available or is encapsulated in a nonconductive compound as an alternate method to a copper ring, a copper grid can be used for perimeter bonding where all the following requirements are met:

(1) The copper grid is constructed of 8 AWG solid bare copper and arranged in a 12-in. by 12-in. network of conductors in a uniformly spaced perpendicular grid pattern with a tolerance of 4 in. in accordance with 680.26(B)(1)(b)(3).

(2) The copper grid follows the contour of the perimeter surface extending 3 ft horizontally beyond the inside walls of the pool.

(3) Only listed splicing devices or exothermic welding are used.

(4) The copper grid is secured within a paved surface (concrete), no more than 6 in. below finished grade of the paved surface (pavers or concrete), or between 4 in. and 6 in. below the finished grade of an unpaved surface (dirt).

(3) Metal Parts of Pool Structure. Metal parts of the pool structure, not part of the pool shell [680.26(B)(1)(a)] must be bonded. ▶Figure 680–67

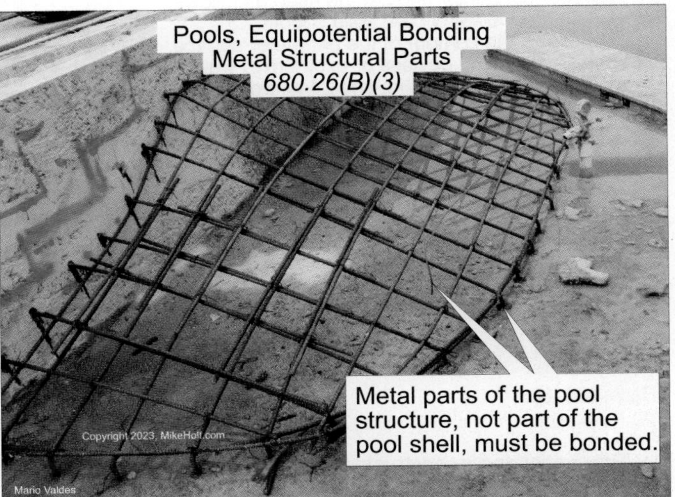
Pools, Equipotential Bonding
Metal Structural Parts
680.26(B)(3)
Metal parts of the pool structure, not part of the pool shell, must be bonded.
Copyright 2023, MikeHolt.com
Mario Valdes

▶Figure 680–67

(4) Metal Forming Shells. All metal forming shells for underwater luminaires must be bonded. ▶Figure 680–68

Pools, Equipotential Bonding
Metal Forming Shells
680.26(B)(4)
Copyright 2023, www.MikeHolt.com
All metal forming shells for underwater luminaires must be bonded.

▶Figure 680–68

Ex: Listed low-voltage lighting are not required to be bonded.

(5) Metal Pool Fittings. Metal fittings attached to the pool structure such as ladders and handrails must be bonded. ▶Figure 680–69

Ex: The following are not required to be bonded:

(1) Isolated parts not over 4 in. in any dimension and not penetrating the pool structure more than1 in.

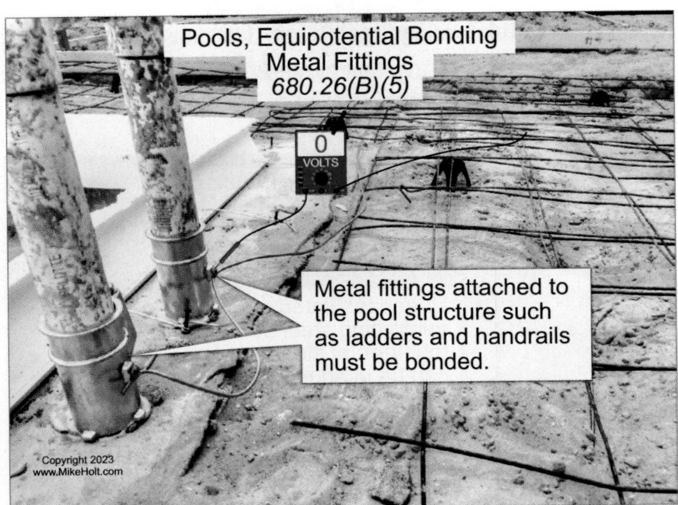
Pools, Equipotential Bonding
Metal Fittings
680.26(B)(5)
0
VOLTS
Metal fittings attached to the pool structure such as ladders and handrails must be bonded.
Copyright 2023
www.MikeHolt.com

▶Figure 680–69

(2) Metallic pool cover anchors in a concrete or masonry deck, 1 in. or less in any dimension and 2 in. or less in length.

(3) Metallic pool cover anchors in a wood or composite deck, 2 in. or less in any dimension and 2 in. or less in length.

(6) Electrical Pool Equipment. Metal parts of the following electrical equipment must be bonded.

(1) Electrically powered pool cover(s)

(2) Pool water circulation, treatment, heating, cooling, or dehumidification equipment ▶Figure 680–70

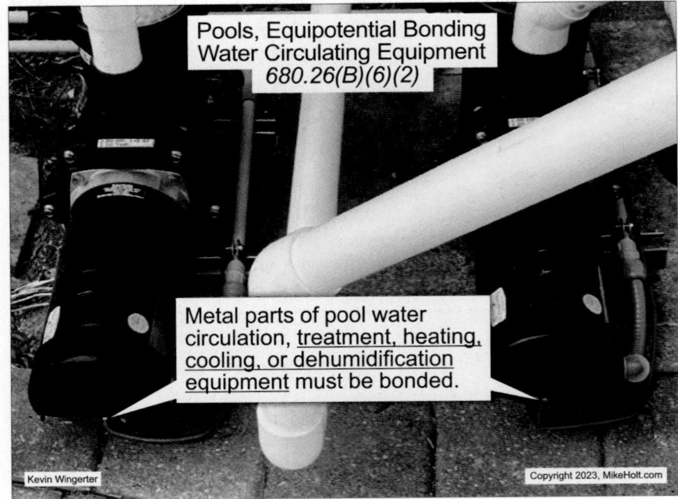
Pools, Equipotential Bonding
Water Circulating Equipment
680.26(B)(6)(2)
Metal parts of pool water circulation, treatment, heating, cooling, or dehumidification equipment must be bonded.
Kevin Wingerter
Copyright 2023, MikeHolt.com

▶Figure 680–70

(3) Other electrical equipment within 5 ft horizontally and 12 ft vertically from the inside walls of the pool, unless separated from the pool by a permanent barrier

1st Printing

(7) Fixed Metal Parts. Fixed metal parts of metal awnings, metal fences, metal doors, and metal window frames within 5 ft horizontally and 12 ft vertically from the inside walls of the pool must be bonded. ▶Figure 680–71

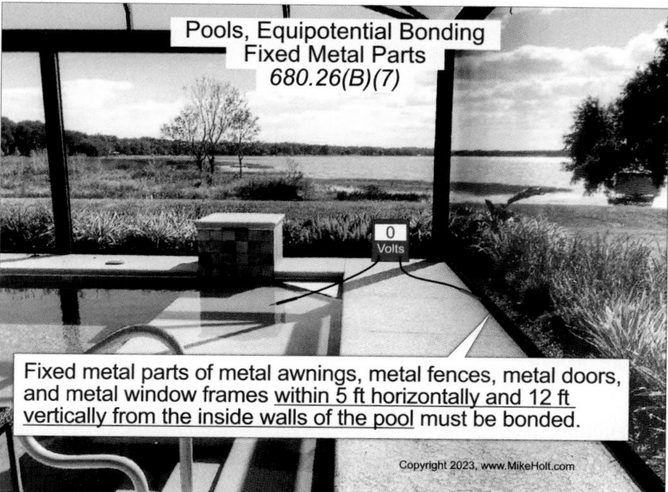

▶Figure 680–71

Ex: Fixed metal parts separated from the pool by a permanent barrier that prevents contact by a person are not required to be bonded. ▶Figure 680–72

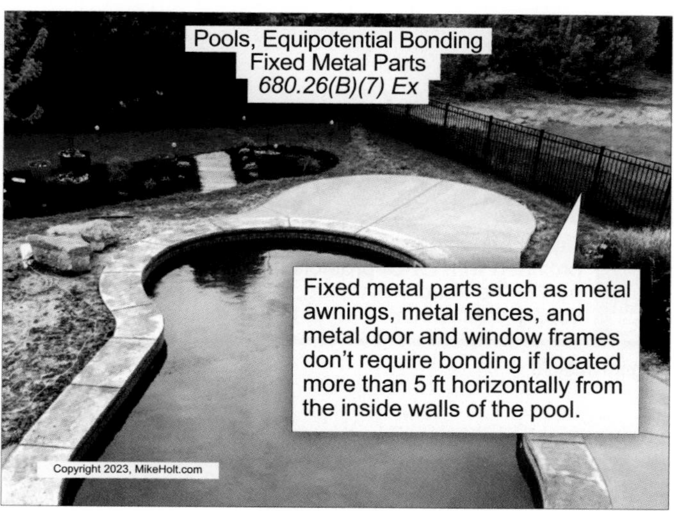

Pools, Equipotential Bonding
Fixed Metal Parts
680.26(B)(7) Ex
Fixed metal parts such as metal awnings, metal fences, and metal door and window frames don't require bonding if located more than 5 ft horizontally from the inside walls of the pool.
Copyright 2023, MikeHolt.com

▶Figure 680–72

(C) Nonconductive Pool Shell. If the water in a vinyl or fiberglass pool shell does not make contact to one of the bonded parts in 680.26(B), a minimum 9 sq in. corrosion-resistant conductive surface in contact with the water must be bonded with a solid copper conductor not smaller than 8 AWG. ▶Figure 680–73

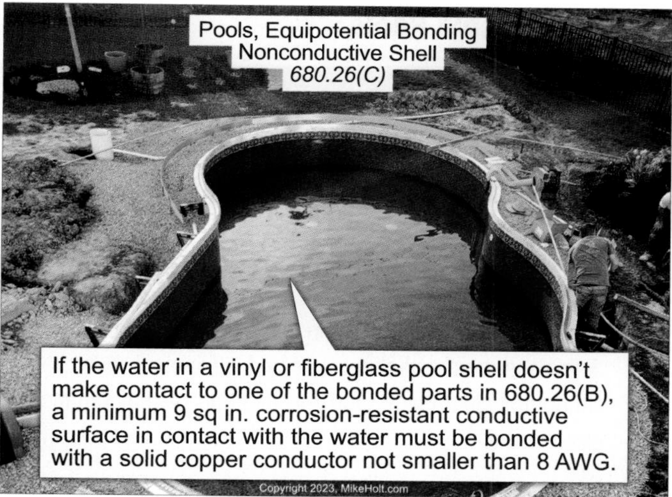

▶Figure 680–73

Author's Comment:

- Where bonded items such as a conductive pool shell, metal ladders, metal rails, or underwater luminaires are in direct contact with the pool water and provide the required surface area, it is not necessary to install a corrosion-resistant conductive device.

680.27 Specialized Equipment

(B) Electrically Operated Covers.

(1) Motors and Controllers. The electric motors, controllers, and wiring for an electrically operated cover must be not less than 5 ft from the inside wall of a permanently installed pool unless separated by a permanent barrier.

(2) GFCI Protection. The branch circuit serving the electric motor and controller circuit must be GFCI protected.

680.28 Gas-Fired Water Heaters

Circuits serving gas-fired swimming pool water heaters operating at 120V must be GFCI protected.

Part III. Storable Pools

680.30 General

Electrical installations for storable pools must comply with Part I as well as Part III of Article 680.

Author's Comment:

- The requirements contained in Part I of Article 680 include definitions, cord-and-plug-connected equipment, overhead conductor clearances, and the location of maintenance disconnects.
- The equipotential bonding requirements contained in 680.26 (Part II of Article 680) do not apply to storable pools, storable spas, storable hot tubs, or storable immersion pools. ▶**Figure 680–74**

▶**Figure 680–74**

According to Article 100, a "Pool, Storable" is a pool installed entirely on or above the ground that is designed for ease of relocation, regardless of water depth (Article 680). ▶**Figure 680–75**

▶**Figure 680–75**

680.31 Pumps

A cord-connected pool filter pump must incorporate an approved system of double insulation or its equivalent and be provided with means for the termination of an equipment grounding conductor for the noncurrent-carrying metal parts of the pump.

Cord-connected pool filter pumps must be provided with GFCI protection that is an integral part of the attachment plug, or in the power-supply cord within 12 in. of the attachment plug. ▶**Figure 680–76**

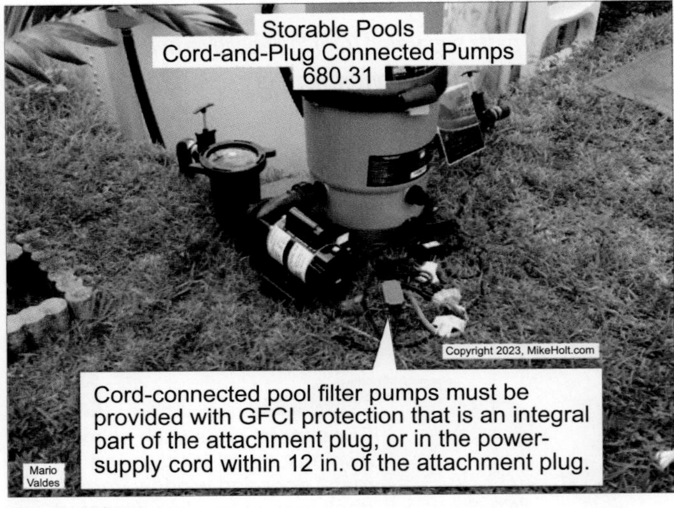

▶**Figure 680–76**

680.32 GFCI Protection

Receptacles rated 125V through 250V, 60A or less located within 20 ft from the inside walls of a storable pool must have GFCI or SPGFCI protection in accordance with 680.5(B) or (C). ▶**Figure 680–77**

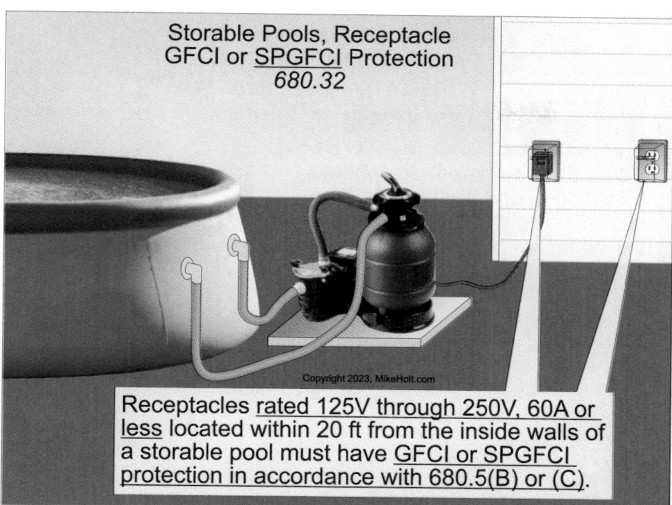
Storable Pools, Receptacle GFCI or SPGFCI Protection 680.32
Copyright 2023, MikeHolt.com
Receptacles rated 125V through 250V, 60A or less located within 20 ft from the inside walls of a storable pool must have GFCI or SPGFCI protection in accordance with 680.5(B) or (C).

▶Figure 680–77

680.34 Receptacle Locations

Receptacles are not permitted to be less than 6 ft from the inside walls of a storable pool. The receptacle distance is measured as the shortest path a flexible cord will follow without passing through a wall, doorway, or window. ▶Figure 680–78

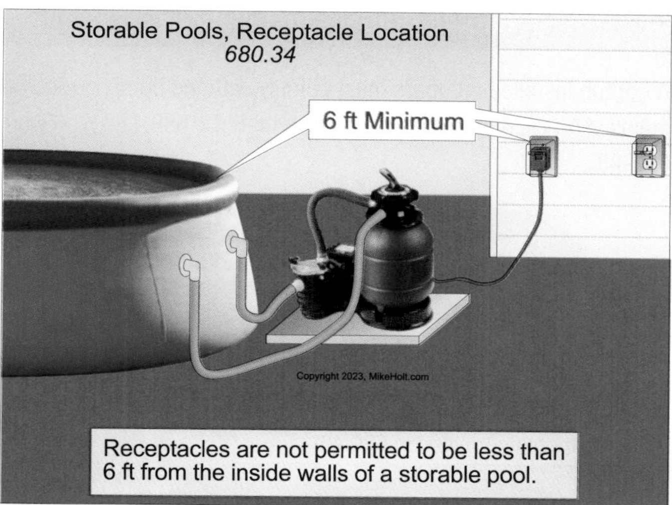
Storable Pools, Receptacle Location 680.34
6 ft Minimum
Copyright 2023, MikeHolt.com
Receptacles are not permitted to be less than 6 ft from the inside walls of a storable pool.

▶Figure 680–78

680.35 Storable Pools

Storable pools must comply with the additional requirements specified in 680.35(A) through (G) of the *Code*.

(A) Cord-Connected Storable Pool Equipment. Storable pool equipment rated 20A, single-phase, 120V or less are permitted to be cord connected if they are GFCI protected.

(B) Pumps. A storable pool pump must be listed, labeled, and identified for swimming pool use. ▶Figure 680–79

Storable Pools Listed Pumps 680.35(B)
A storable pool pump must be listed, labeled, and identified for swimming pool use.
Copyright 2023 MikeHolt.com

▶Figure 680–79

(C) Heaters. If rated 20A or 30A, single-phase, 120V or 250V, the heater must be GFCI protected.

(E) Lighting Outlets. Unless within the low-voltage contact limit, lighting outlets must be not less than 10 ft from the nearest point of an immersion pool.

(F) Switches. Switches, unless they are part of the unit, must be not less than 5 ft from the immersion pool.

(G) Receptacles. All 50A, 250V or less receptacles within 20 ft of the inside wall of a storable pool must be GFCI protected.

Part IV. Hot Tubs

680.40 General

Electrical installations for permanently installed self-contained hot tubs must comply with Part I as well as Part IV of Article 680.

According to Article 100, a "Spa or Hot Tub" is a hydromassage tub designed for recreational or therapeutic use typically not drained after each use (Article 680). ▶Figure 680–80

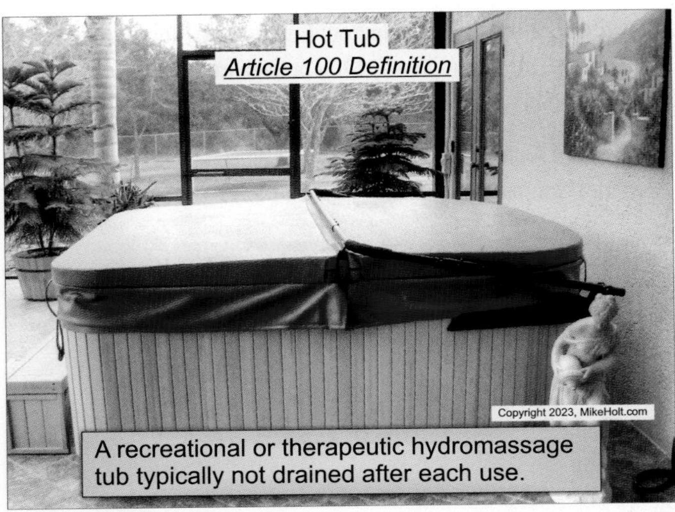

Hot Tub
Article 100 Definition
A recreational or therapeutic hydromassage tub typically not drained after each use.
Copyright 2023, MikeHolt.com

▶Figure 680–80

680.41 Emergency Shutoff Equipment

(A) Emergency Shutoff Switch for Hot Tubs. For other than a one-family dwelling, a labeled emergency hot tub water recirculation and jet system shutoff is required. The emergency shutoff switch must be readily accessible to the users and not less than 5 ft away, adjacent to, and within sight of the hot tub. ▶**Figure 680–81**

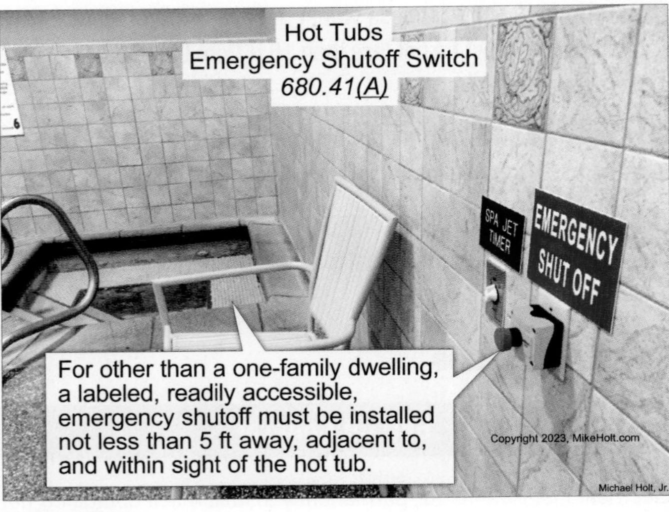

Hot Tubs
Emergency Shutoff Switch
680.41(A)
SPA JET TIMER
EMERGENCY SHUT OFF
For other than a one-family dwelling, a labeled, readily accessible, emergency shutoff must be installed not less than 5 ft away, adjacent to, and within sight of the hot tub.
Copyright 2023, MikeHolt.com
Michael Holt, Jr.

▶Figure 680–81

Author's Comment:

- Either the equipment disconnect [680.13] or a pushbutton that controls a relay can be used to meet the emergency shutoff requirement. ▶**Figure 680–82**

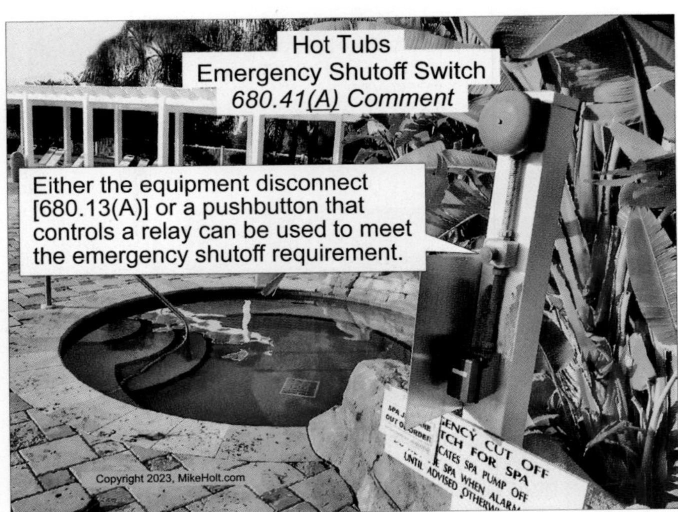

▶Figure 680–82

- The purpose of the emergency shutoff is to protect users from becoming entrapped by the water recirculating system intake. Deaths and injuries have occurred in less than 3 ft of water because individuals became stuck to the water intake opening. This requirement applies to hot tubs installed indoors as well as outdoors.

680.42 Outdoor Installations

A hot tub installed outdoors must comply with the bonding requirements of Article 680 Part II, except as permitted in 680.42(A). ▶**Figure 680–83**

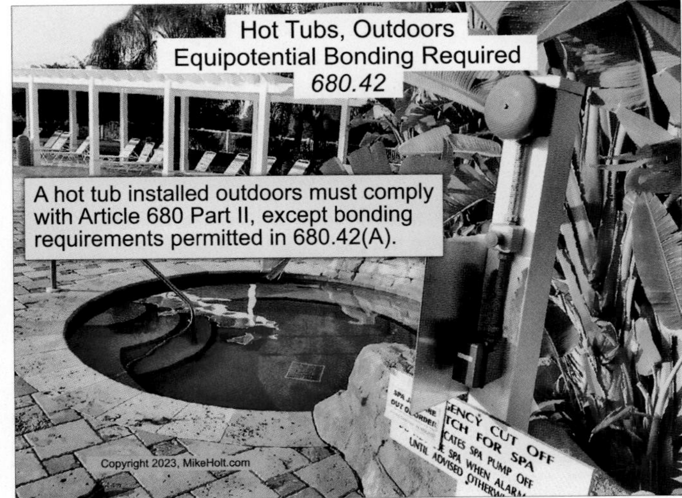

▶Figure 680–83

1st Printing

(B) Equipotential Bonding.

Bonding Required. Equipotential bonding of perimeter surfaces of hot tubs is required in accordance with 680.26.

Bonding Not Required. Bonding for hot tubs is required, unless all the following conditions apply:

(1) The hot tub is listed, labeled, and identified as a self-contained hot tub for aboveground use. ▶**Figure 680–84**

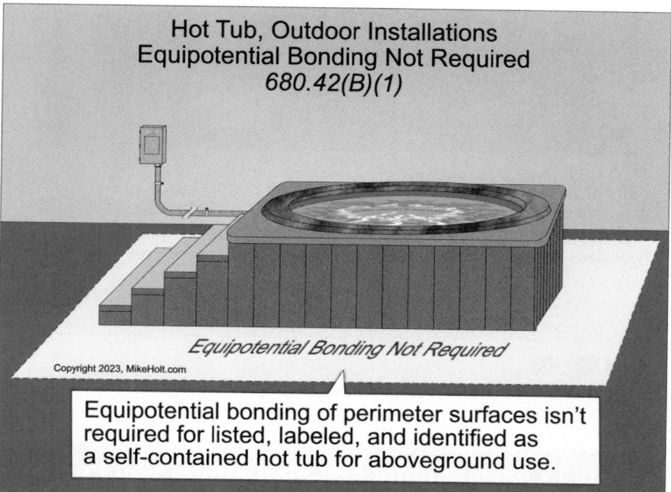

▶**Figure 680–84**

(2) The hot tub is not identified as suitable only for indoor use.

(3) The hot tub is on or above grade.

(4) The top rim of the hot tub is at least 28 in. above any perimeter surface within 30 in. of the hot tub. Nonconductive external steps do not apply to the rim height measurement. ▶**Figure 680–85**

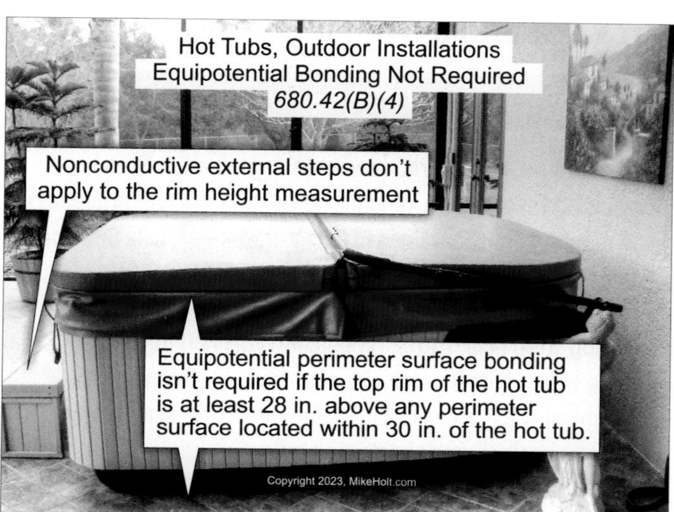

▶**Figure 680–85**

(C) Underwater Luminaires. Wiring to an underwater luminaire in a hot tub must comply with 680.23 or 680.33.

680.43 Indoor Installations

Electrical installations for an indoor hot tub must comply with Parts I and II of Article 680 except as modified by this section.

Indoor installations of spas or hot tubs can be connected by any of the wiring methods contained in Chapter 3.

Ex 2: The equipotential bonding requirements for perimeter surfaces contained in 680.26(B)(2) do not apply to a listed self-contained hot tub installed above an indoor finished floor.

(A) Receptacles. At least one 15A or 20A, 125V receptacle on a general-purpose branch circuit must be not less than 6 ft and not more than 10 ft from the inside wall of a hot tub. ▶**Figure 680–86**

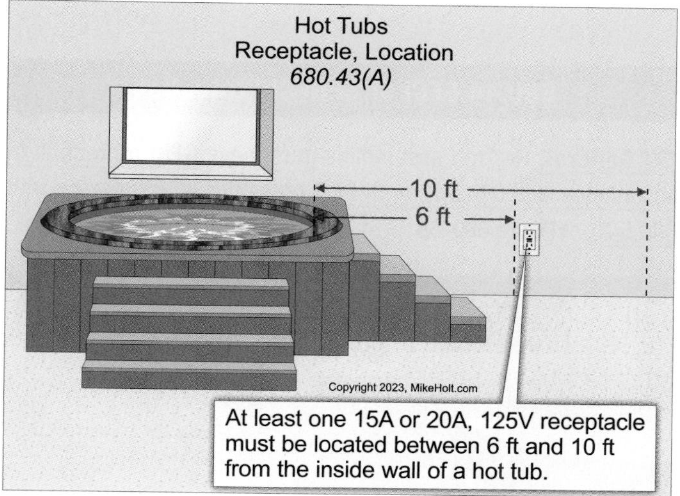

▶**Figure 680–86**

(1) Location. Receptacles must be not less than 6 ft measured horizontally from the inside walls of the hot tub.

(2) GFCI Protection. Receptacles rated 125V through 250V, rated 60A or less within 10 ft of the inside walls of a hot tub must have GFCI protection in accordance with 680.5(B).

(3) Protection, Hot Tub Supply Receptacle. Receptacles that provide power for hot tub equipment must be GFCI protected.

(4) Measurements. In determining the dimensions in this section, the distance to be measured is the shortest path a cord of an appliance connected to the receptacle will follow without piercing a floor, wall, ceiling, doorway with a hinged or sliding door, window opening, or other type of permanent barrier.

(C) Switches. Switches must be at least 5 ft, measured horizontally, from the inside wall of the indoor hot tub. ▶Figure 680–87

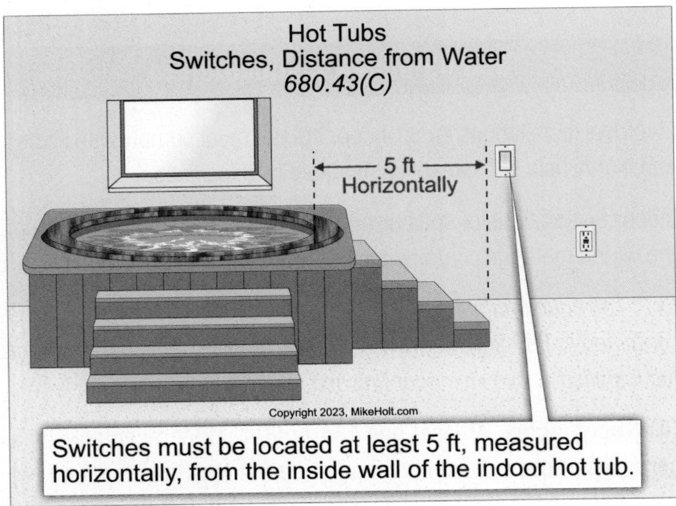

Hot Tubs
Switches, Distance from Water
680.43(C)
5 ft
Horizontally
Copyright 2023, MikeHolt.com
Switches must be located at least 5 ft, measured horizontally, from the inside wall of the indoor hot tub.

▶Figure 680–87

680.44 GFCI or SPGFCI Protection

(A) General. Hot tub assemblies must have GFCI protection in accordance with 680.5(B) or SPGFCI protection in accordance with 680.5(C). ▶Figure 680–88

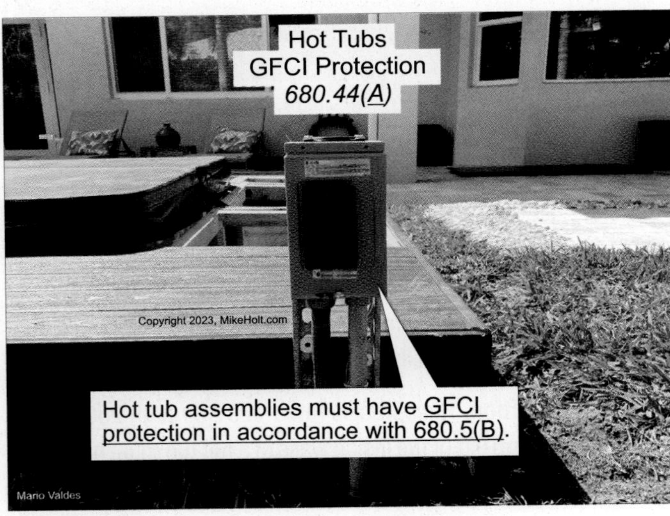

▶Figure 680–88

Author's Comment:

- A two-pole GFCI can protect a 240V hot tub that does not require a neutral. However, the GFCI requires a neutral to operate, so be sure to run a neutral to the hot tub disconnect.

(B) Listed Units. If so marked, a listed self-contained hot tub or a listed packaged equipment assembly that includes integral GFCI protection for all electrical parts, does not require additional GFCI protection. ▶Figure 680–89

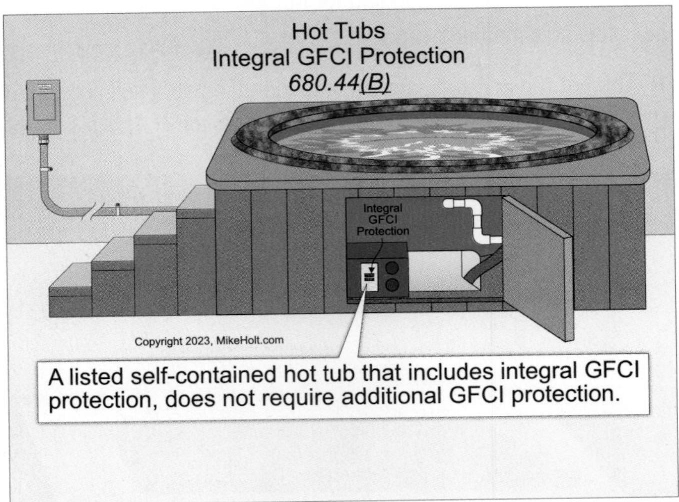

▶Figure 680–89

680.45 Permanently Installed Immersion Pools

Electrical installations at permanently installed immersion pools, whether installed indoors or outdoors, must comply with Parts I, II, and IV of this article, except as modified by section 680.45 and must be connected by the wiring methods of Chapter 3 of the *Code*. Regarding the provisions in Part IV of this article, an immersion pool is considered a hot tub.

Part V. Fountains

680.50 General

The general installation requirements contained in Part I apply to fountains and splash pads intended for recreational use, in addition to those requirements contained in Part V. Part II of Article 680 applies to fountains that have water common to pools.

According to Article 100, a "Fountain" is defined as an ornamental structure or recreational water feature from which one or more jets or streams of water are discharged into the air including splash pads, ornamental pools, display pools, and reflection pools. This definition does not include drinking water fountains or water coolers (Article 680). ▶Figure 680–90

1st Printing

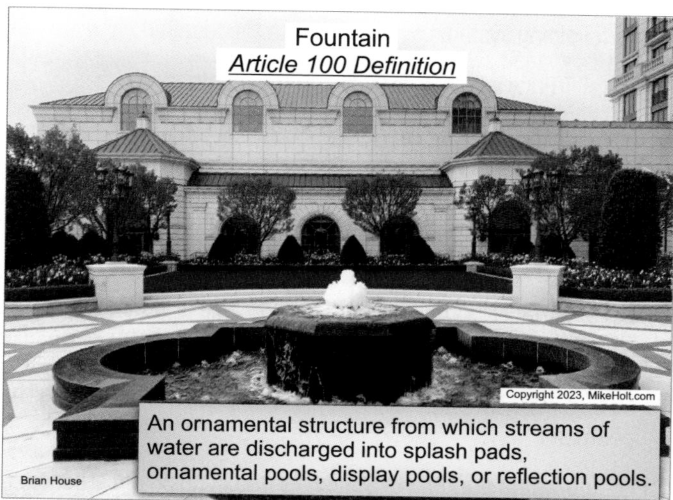

Fountain
Article 100 Definition
An ornamental structure from which streams of water are discharged into splash pads, ornamental pools, display pools, or reflection pools.
Brian House
Copyright 2023, MikeHolt.com

▸Figure 680–90

According to Article 100, a "Splash Pad" is defined as a fountain intended for recreational use by pedestrians with a water depth of 1 in. or less. This definition does not include showers intended for hygienic rinsing prior to use of a pool, spa, or other water feature (Article 680). ▸**Figure 680–91**

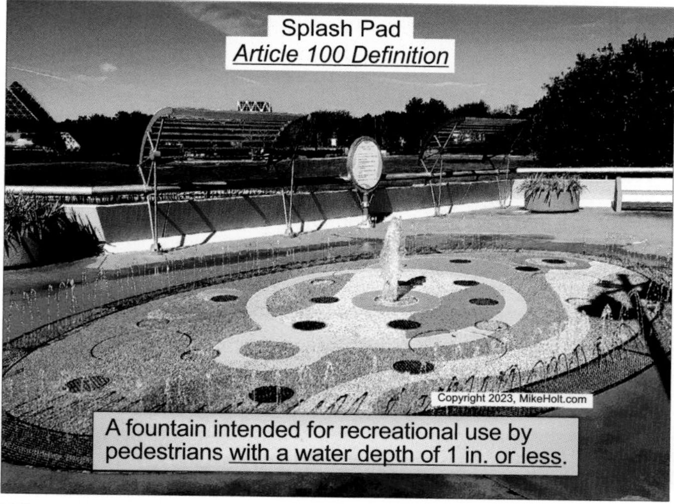

▸Figure 680–91

(A) Additional Requirements.

(2) Splash pads must have equipotential bonding in accordance with 680.26. ▸**Figure 680–92**

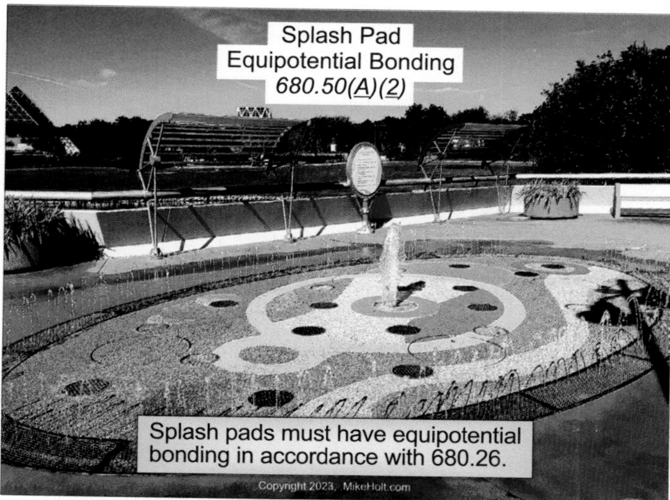

▸Figure 680–92

(B) Equipment Exceeding the Low-Voltage Contact Limit. Fountain equipment with ratings exceeding the low-voltage contact limit must be located at least 5 ft horizontally from the inside walls of a fountain, unless separated from the fountain by a solid fence, wall, or other permanent barrier.

680.51 Luminaires and Submersible Equipment

(A) GFCI Protection. GFCI protection is required for luminaires and submersible equipment unless listed and supplied by a swimming pool transformer in accordance with 680.23(A)(2). ▸**Figure 680–93**

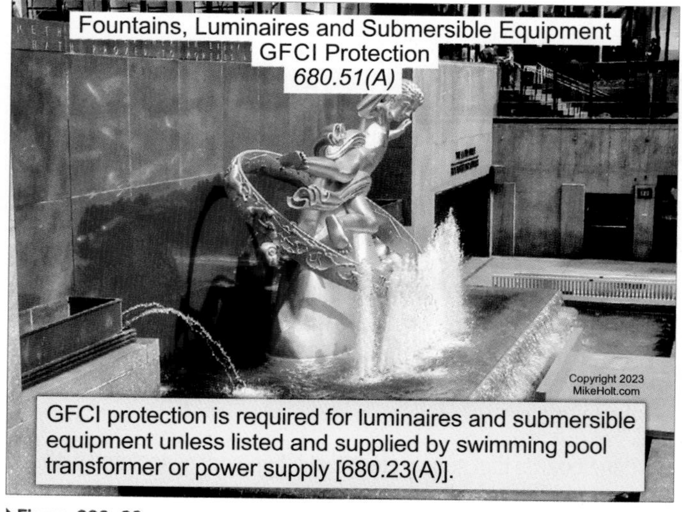

▸Figure 680–93

(C) Luminaire Lenses. Luminaires must be installed so the top of the luminaire lens is below the normal water level unless listed for above-water use. ▶Figure 680–94

Fountains
Luminaire Lenses
680.51(C)
Copyright 2023, www.MikeHolt.com
Luminaires must be installed so the top of the lens is below the normal water level unless listed for above-water use.

▶Figure 680–94

(E) Cords. The maximum length of each exposed flexible cord in a fountain is 10 ft. Power-supply cords that extend beyond the fountain perimeter must be enclosed in a wiring enclosure approved by the authority having jurisdiction.

(F) Servicing. Equipment must be capable of being removed from the water for relamping or for normal maintenance.

(G) Stability. Equipment must be inherently stable or be securely fastened in place.

680.54 Connection to an Equipment Grounding Conductor

(A) Connection to Equipment Grounding Conductor. The following must be connected to the circuit equipment grounding conductor:

(1) Electrical equipment within the fountain or within 5 ft of the inside wall of the fountain.

(2) Electrical equipment associated with the recirculating system of the fountain.

(3) Panelboards that supply electrical equipment associated with the fountain.

(B) Bonding. The following parts must be bonded together with a minimum 8 AWG solid copper conductor and connected to an equipment grounding conductor for a branch circuit supplying fountain equipment:

(1) Metal piping systems associated with the fountain

(2) Metal fittings within or attached to the fountain

(3) Metal parts of electrical equipment associated with the fountain water-circulating system

(4) Metal raceways within 5 ft of the inside wall or perimeter of the fountain and not separated from it by a permanent barrier

(5) Metal surfaces within 5 ft of the inside wall or perimeter of the fountain and not separated from it by a permanent barrier

(6) Electrical equipment within 5 ft from the fountain's inside wall or perimeter

(C) Equipotential Bonding of Splash Pad. For equipotential bonding, the shell of a splash pad is the area where pedestrians walk, bounded by the extent of footing of the splash pad that rises to its exposed surface and its collection basin area. ▶Figure 680–95

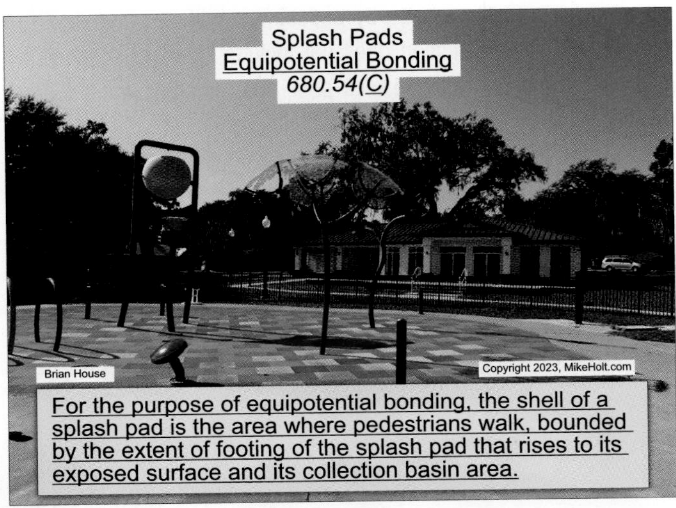
Splash Pads
Equipotential Bonding
680.54(C)
Brian House
Copyright 2023, MikeHolt.com
For the purpose of equipotential bonding, the shell of a splash pad is the area where pedestrians walk, bounded by the extent of footing of the splash pad that rises to its exposed surface and its collection basin area.

▶Figure 680–95

680.55 Methods of Equipment Grounding

(A) Other Requirements. The requirements of 680.7(A), 680.21(A), 680.23(B)(3), 680.23(F)(1) and (2), and 680.24(F) apply to fountains.

(B) Supplied by Flexible Cord. Fountain equipment supplied by a flexible cord must have all exposed metal parts connected to an insulated copper equipment grounding conductor that is an integral part of the cord. ▶Figure 680–96

1st Printing

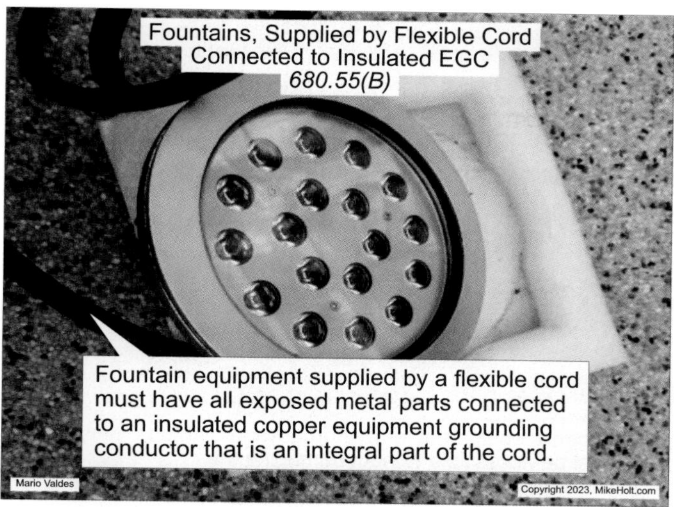
Fountains, Supplied by Flexible Cord
Connected to Insulated EGC
680.55(B)
Fountain equipment supplied by a flexible cord must have all exposed metal parts connected to an insulated copper equipment grounding conductor that is an integral part of the cord.
Mario Valdes
Copyright 2023, MikeHolt.com

▶Figure 680–96

680.56 Cord-and-Plug-Connected Equipment

(A) GFCI Protection. All cord and plug connected equipment for fountains must be GFCI protected.

680.57 Electric Signs in or Adjacent to Fountains

Branch circuits or feeders that supply an electric sign installed within a fountain must be GFCI protected. ▶Figure 680–97

Fountains, Electric Signs
GFCI Protection
680.57
Theater of The Sea
Marine Mammal Park
Islamorada, Florida
Copyright 2023, MikeHolt.com
Brian House
All circuits that supply an electric sign installed within a fountain must be GFCI protected.

▶Figure 680–97

680.58 GFCI Protection of Receptacles

All receptacles rated 125V through 250V, 60A or less within 20 ft of the fountain's edge must have GFCI or SPGFCI protection in accordance with 680.5(B) or (C). ▶Figure 680–98

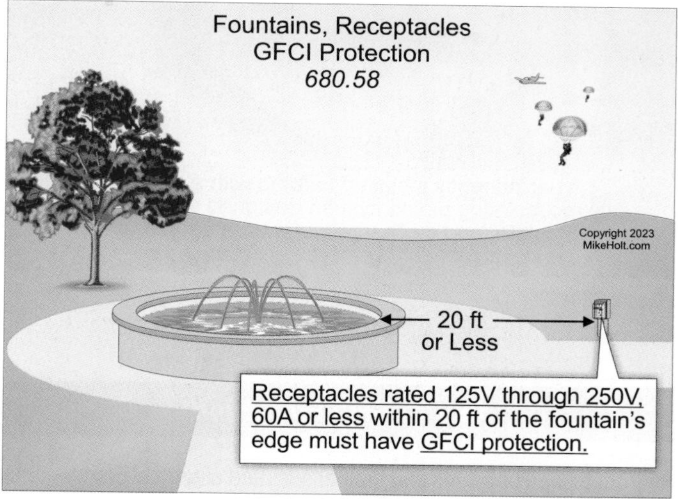
Fountains, Receptacles
GFCI Protection
680.58
Copyright 2023
MikeHolt.com
20 ft
or Less
Receptacles rated 125V through 250V, 60A or less within 20 ft of the fountain's edge must have GFCI protection.

▶Figure 680–98

680.59 GFCI or SPGFCI Protection for Permanently Installed Nonsubmersible Pumps

Outlets supplying permanently installed nonsubmersible pump motors must have GFCI protection in accordance with 680.5(B) or SPGFCI protection in accordance with 680.5(C).

Part VII. Hydromassage Bathtubs

680.70 General

A hydromassage bathtub must only comply with the requirements of Part VII, it is not required to comply with the other parts of this article.

According to Article 100, a "Hydromassage Bathtub" is defined as a permanently installed bathtub with a recirculating piping system designed to accept, circulate, and discharge water after each use. ▶Figure 680–99

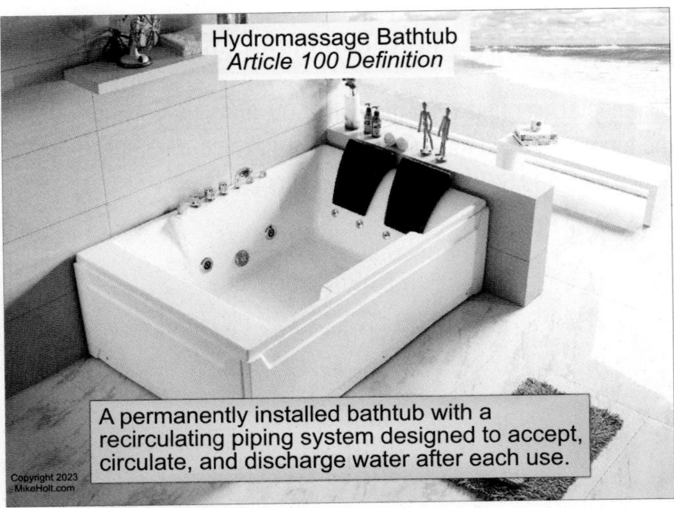
Hydromassage Bathtub
Article 100 Definition
A permanently installed bathtub with a recirculating piping system designed to accept, circulate, and discharge water after each use.
Copyright 2023 MikeHolt.com

▸Figure 680–99

680.71 GFCI Protection

Hydromassage bathtubs and their associated electrical components must be on an individual branch circuit protected by a readily accessible GFCI device. ▸**Figure 680–100**

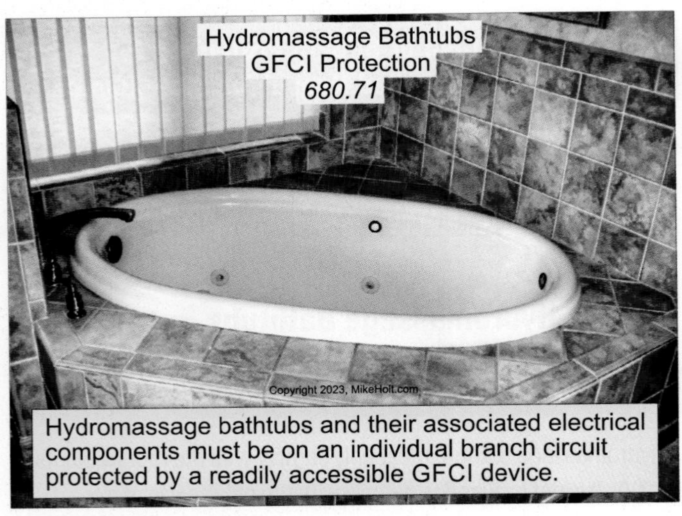
Hydromassage Bathtubs
GFCI Protection
680.71
Copyright 2023, MikeHolt.com
Hydromassage bathtubs and their associated electrical components must be on an individual branch circuit protected by a readily accessible GFCI device.

▸Figure 680–100

All 125V, single-phase receptacles not greater than 30A and within 6 ft horizontally of the inside walls of a hydromassage bathtub must be GFCI protected.

680.73 Accessibility

Electrical equipment for hydromassage bathtubs must be accessible without damaging the building structure or finish and the receptacle must be installed within 1 ft of the opening. ▸**Figure 680–101**

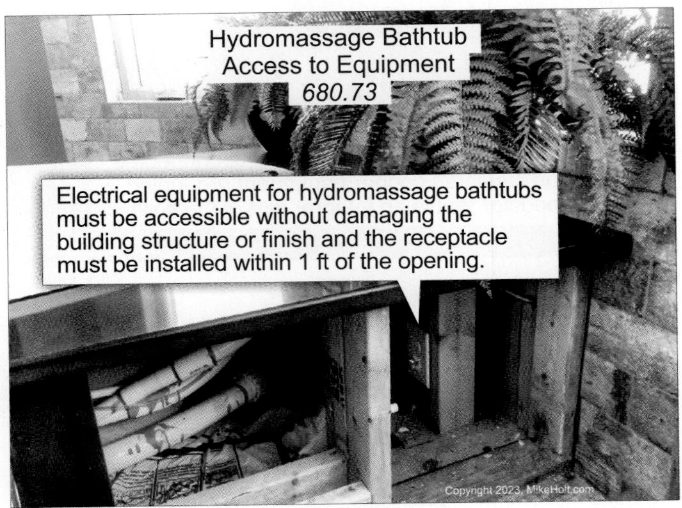
Hydromassage Bathtub
Access to Equipment
680.73
Electrical equipment for hydromassage bathtubs must be accessible without damaging the building structure or finish and the receptacle must be installed within 1 ft of the opening.
Copyright 2023, MikeHolt.com

▸Figure 680–101

680.74 Equipotential Bonding

(A) General. The following parts must be bonded together.

(1) Metal fittings within, or attached to, the hydromassage bathtub structure that are in contact with the circulating water.

(2) Metal parts of electrical equipment associated with the hydromassage bathtub water circulating system, including pump and blower motors.

(3) Metal-sheathed cables, metal raceways, and metal piping within 5 ft of the inside walls of the hydromassage bathtub and not separated from its area by a permanent barrier.

(4) Exposed metal surfaces within 5 ft of the inside walls of the hydromassage bathtub and not separated from it by a permanent barrier.

(5) Metal parts of electrical devices not associated with the hydromassage bathtub within 5 ft from the hydromassage bathtub.

Ex 1: Small conductive surfaces not likely to become energized such as air and water jets, supply valve assemblies, drain fittings not connected to metallic piping, towel bars, mirror frames, and similar nonelectrical equipment not connected to metal framing are not required to be bonded.

Ex 2: Double-insulated motors and blowers are not required to be bonded.

Ex 3: Small conductive surfaces of electrical equipment not likely to become energized, such as the mounting strap or yoke of a listed light switch or receptacle is not required to be bonded.

(B) Bonding Conductor. Metal parts required to be bonded by 680.74(A) must be bonded together using an insulated or bare solid copper conductor not smaller than 8 AWG. Bonding jumpers are not required to be extended or attached to any remote panelboard, service disconnect, or any electrode.

A bonding jumper long enough to terminate on a replacement nondouble-insulated pump or blower motor must be provided, and it must terminate to the equipment grounding conductor of the branch circuit of the motor when a double-insulated circulating pump or blower motor is used.

Notes

ARTICLE
690 SOLAR PHOTOVOLTAIC (PV) SYSTEMS

Introduction to Article 690—Solar Photovoltaic (PV) Systems

This article covers the installation of electrical wiring and equipment for solar photovoltaic systems. Solar PV systems that provide electrical power to an electrical system are a complete industry within the electrical trade and require expert knowledge in electrical, structural, and architectural issues. Many of these rules are outside of the scope of this material, however, some of the topics we cover include the following:

- General Requirements
- Alternating-Current Modules
- Maximum PV System Circuit Voltage
- Overcurrent Protection
- Rapid Shutdown
- Required Disconnects
- Wiring Methods and Materials
- Component Interconnection
- Grounding and Bonding
- Source Connections

Article 690 consists of six parts:

- Part I. General
- Part II. Circuit Requirements
- Part III. Disconnect
- Part IV. Wiring Methods
- Part V. Grounding and Bonding
- Part VI. Source Connections

Part I. General

690.1 Scope

The requirements contained in Article 690 apply to solar photovoltaic (PV) systems other than those covered by Article 691. ▶Figure 690–1

PV Systems
690.1 Scope
Copyright 2023
MikeHolt.com
Article 690 applies to solar photovoltaic (PV) systems other than those covered by Article 691.

▶Figure 690–1

According to Article 100, a "Photovoltaic (PV) System" is the combination of components, circuits, and equipment up to and including the PV system disconnect, that converts solar energy into electrical energy. ▶Figure 690–2

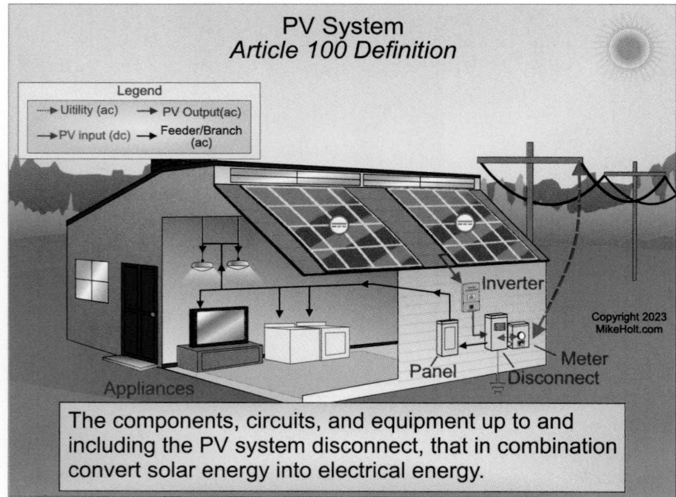

▶Figure 690–2

Note 1: See *NEC* Figure 690.1.

Note 2: Article 691 covers the installation of large-scale PV electric supply stations with an inverter generating capacity of 5000 kW and more, and not under the electric utility control. ▶Figure 690–3

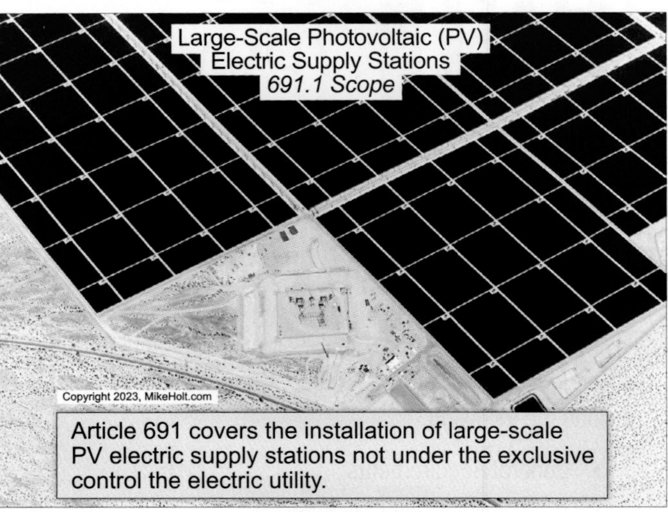

Large-Scale Photovoltaic (PV)
Electric Supply Stations
691.1 Scope
Copyright 2023, MikeHolt.com
Article 691 covers the installation of large-scale PV electric supply stations not under the exclusive control the electric utility.

▶Figure 690–3

According to Article 100, the "Inverter Generating Capacity" is equal to the sum of parallel-connected inverter maximum continuous output power at 40C in watts, kilowatts, volt-amperes, or kilovolt-amperes.

Author's Comment:

- Large-scale PV supply stations have specific design and safety features unique to these facilities and are for the sole purpose of providing electric supply to a system operated by a regulated electric utility.

690.4 General Requirements

(B) Listed or Field Labeled Equipment. Components of the PV system including electronic power converters, inverters, PV modules, ac modules, ac module systems, dc combiners, dc-to-dc converters, PV rapid shutdown equipment, PV hazard control equipment, PV hazard control systems, dc circuit controllers, and charge controllers must be listed or be evaluated for the application and have a field label applied. ▶Figure 690–4

According to Article 100, a "DC Combiner" is an enclosure that includes devices for the parallel connection of two or more PV system dc circuits. ▶Figure 690–5

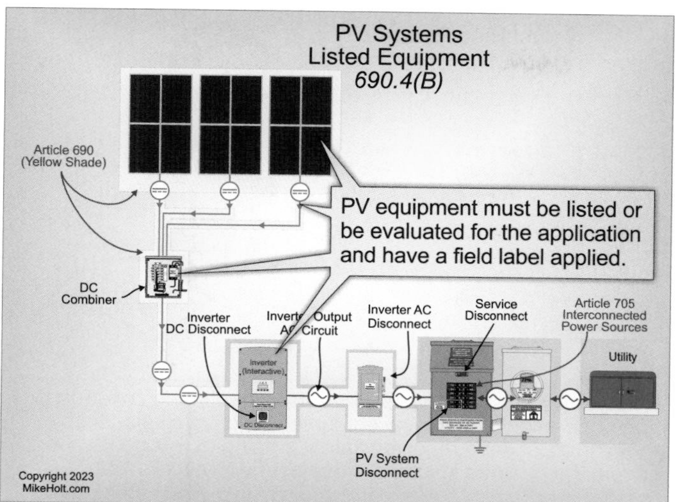

▸Figure 690–4

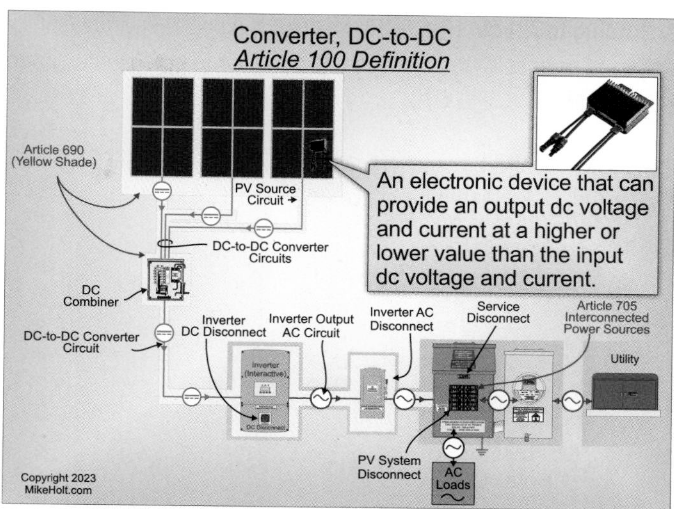

▸Figure 690–6

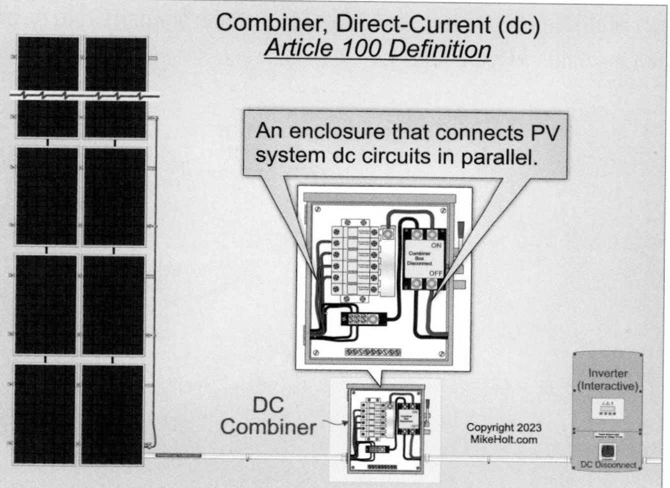

▸Figure 690–5

▸Figure 690–7

According to Article 100, a "DC-to-DC Converter" can provide an output dc voltage and current at a higher or lower value than the input dc voltage and current. ▸**Figure 690–6**

An "Electronic Power Converter" is a device that uses power electronics to convert one form of electrical power into another form of electrical power. Examples of electronic power converters include, but are not limited to, inverters and dc-to-dc converters. ▸**Figure 690–7**

An "Inverter" changes direct current to alternating current. ▸**Figure 690–8**

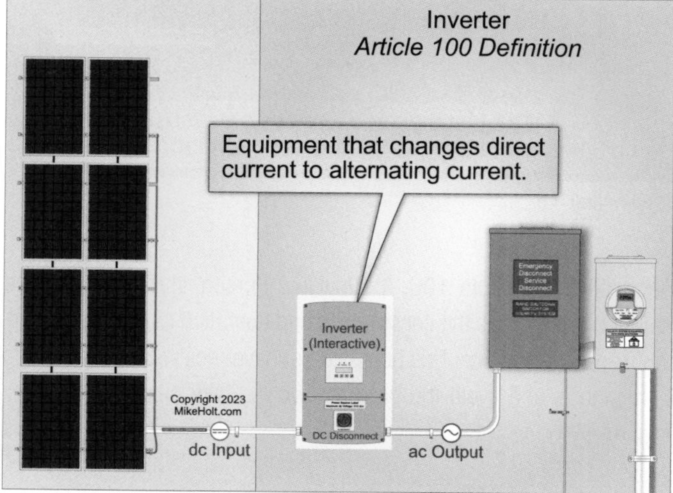

▸Figure 690–8

According to Article 100, A "PV Module" is a unit of environmentally protected solar cells and components designed to produce dc power. ▸**Figure 690–9**

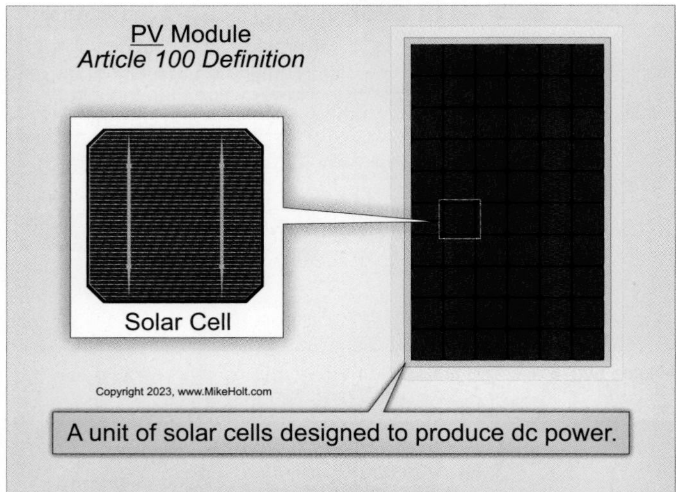
PV Module
Article 100 Definition
Solar Cell
Copyright 2023, www.MikeHolt.com
A unit of solar cells designed to produce dc power.

▸**Figure 690–9**

(C) Qualified Persons. The installation of PV systems must be performed by a qualified person. ▸**Figure 690–10**

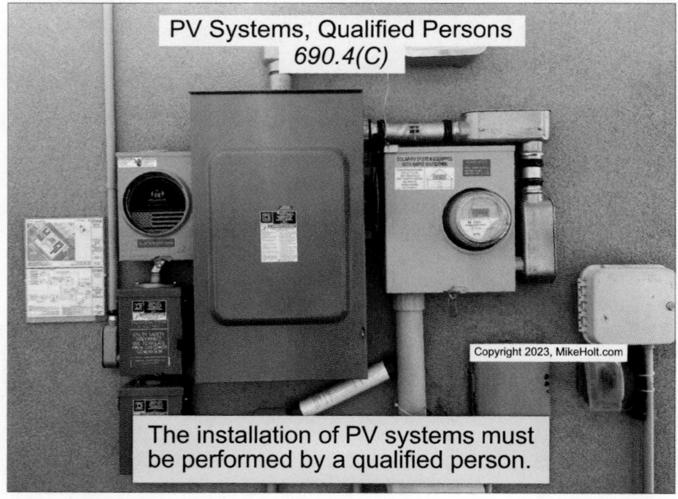
PV Systems, Qualified Persons
690.4(C)
Copyright 2023, MikeHolt.com
The installation of PV systems must be performed by a qualified person.

▸**Figure 690–10**

According to Article 100, a "Qualified Person" has the skills and knowledge related to the construction and operation of electrical equipment and installations. This person must have received safety training to recognize and avoid the hazards involved with electrical systems. ▸**Figure 690–11**

Qualified Person
Article 100 Definition
Copyright 2023 MikeHolt.com
A person with skills and knowledge related to the construction and operation of electrical equipment and installations. This person must have received safety training to recognize and avoid the hazards involved with electrical systems.

▸**Figure 690–11**

(D) Multiple PV Systems. Multiple PV systems are permitted on or in a building. ▸**Figure 690–12**

PV Systems, Buildings
More than One Permitted
690.4(D)
Copyright 2023, MikeHolt.com
Multiple PV systems are permitted on or in a building.

▸**Figure 690–12**

(E) Where Not Permitted. PV system equipment is not permitted to be installed within a bathroom.

(F) Not Readily Accessible. Electronic power converters (inverters and dc-to-dc converters) are not required to be readily accessible and can be mounded on roofs or other areas that are not readily accessible. ▸**Figure 690–13** and ▸**Figure 690–14**

(G) PV Equipment Floating on Bodies of Water. PV equipment floating on or attached to structures floating on bodies of water must be identified as being suitable for the purpose and have wiring methods that allow for expected movement of the equipment. ▸**Figure 690–15**

1st Printing

PV Systems, Electronic Power Converters
Not Readily Accessible
690.4(F)
Electronic power converters (inverters and dc-to-dc converters) are not required to be readily accessible.

▸Figure 690–13

PV Systems, Electronic Power Converters
Not Readily Accessible
690.4(F)
Microinverters
Electronic power converters (inverters and dc-to-dc converters) are not required to be readily accessible.
Andrew Jamshidi Enphase

▸Figure 690–14

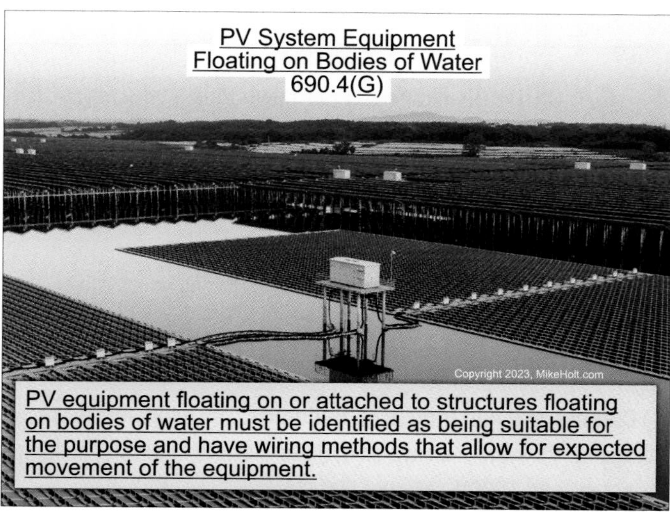
PV System Equipment
Floating on Bodies of Water
690.4(G)
PV equipment floating on or attached to structures floating on bodies of water must be identified as being suitable for the purpose and have wiring methods that allow for expected movement of the equipment.

▸Figure 690–15

Note: PV equipment on bodies of water are subject to increased levels of humidity, corrosion, and mechanical and structural stresses.

690.6 Alternating-Current Modules

According to Article 100, an "AC Module" consists of solar cells, inverters, and other components designed to produce alternating-current power (Article 690). ▸**Figure 690–16**

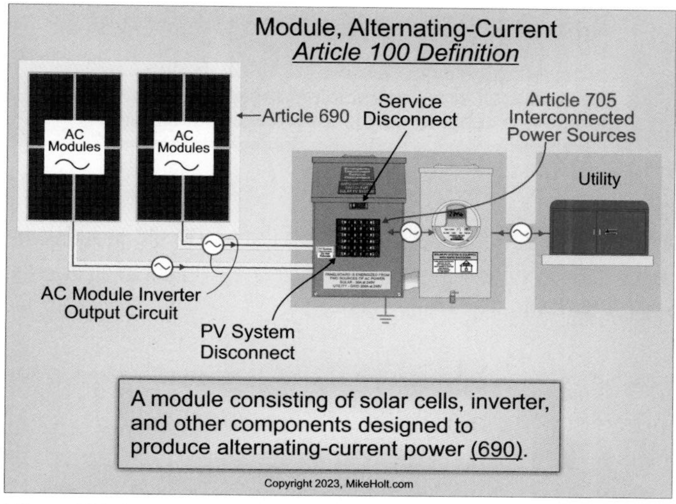
Module, Alternating-Current
Article 100 Definition
AC Modules
AC Modules
Article 690
Service Disconnect
Article 705 Interconnected Power Sources
Utility
AC Module Inverter Output Circuit
PV System Disconnect
A module consisting of solar cells, inverter, and other components designed to produce alternating-current power (690).

▸Figure 690–16

(A) Source (dc) Circuit. The requirements of Article 690 do not apply to the source circuit conductors of an ac module. ▸**Figure 690–17**

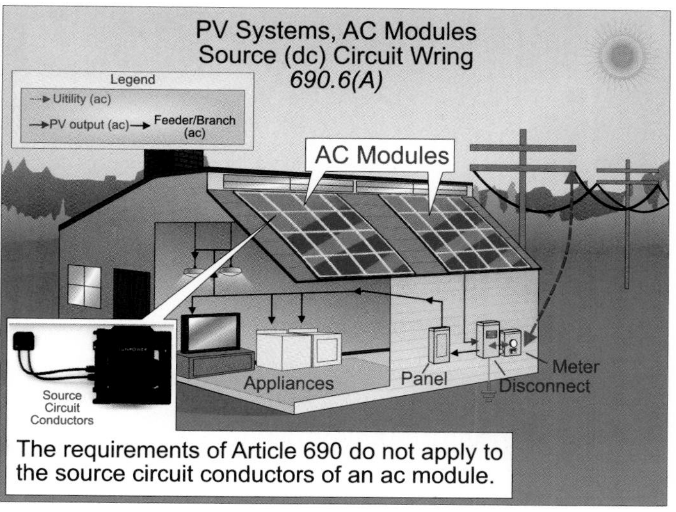
PV Systems, AC Modules
Source (dc) Circuit Wring
690.6(A)
Legend
Uitility (ac)
PV output (ac)
Feeder/Branch (ac)
AC Modules
Source Circuit Conductors
Appliances
Panel
Meter
Disconnect
The requirements of Article 690 do not apply to the source circuit conductors of an ac module.

▸Figure 690–17

(B) Output (ac) Circuit. The ac output circuit conductors for an ac module are considered the inverter ac output circuit. ▸**Figure 690–18**

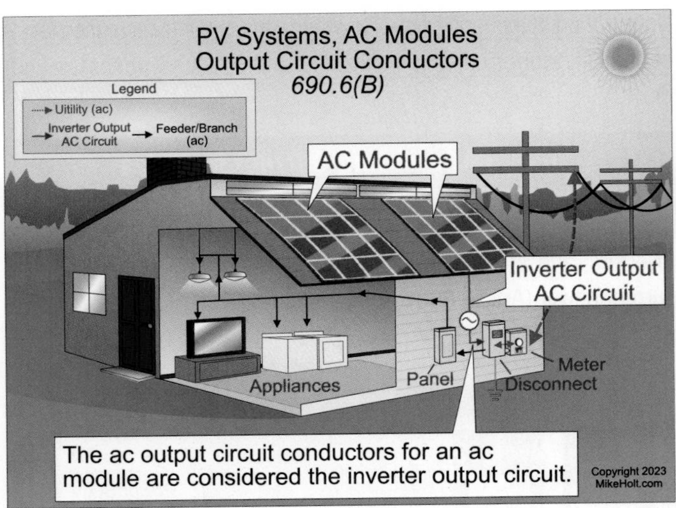

▶Figure 690–18

According to Article 100, an "Inverter Output Circuit" includes the conductors connected to the alternating-current output of an inverter. ▶**Figure 690–19** and ▶**Figure 690–20**

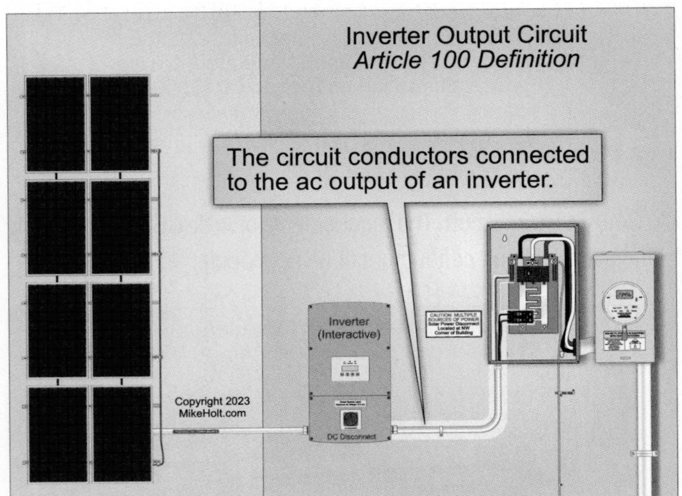

▶Figure 690–19

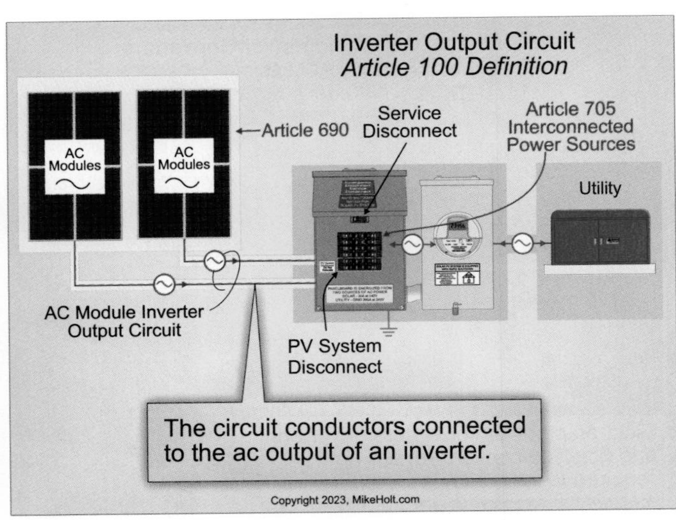

▶Figure 690–20

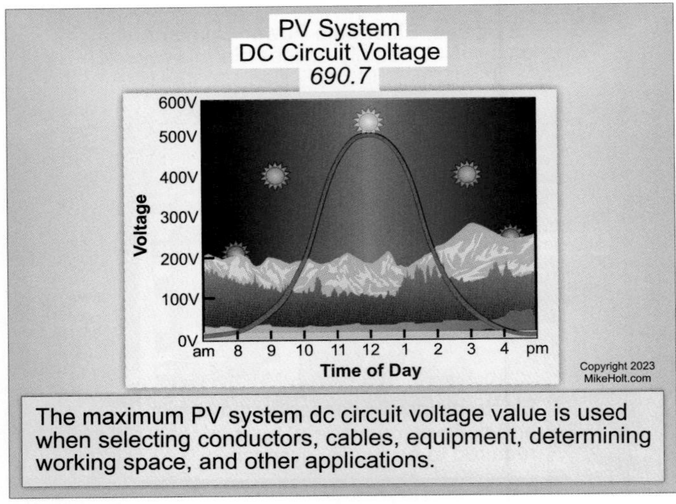

▶Figure 690–21

Caution

CAUTION: Illumination at dawn, dusk, when there is heavy overcast, and even on rainy days is sufficient to produce dangerous dc voltage. ▶**Figure 690–22**

Part II. Circuit Requirements

690.7 Maximum PV System Direct-Current Circuit Voltage

The maximum PV system dc circuit voltage value is used when selecting conductors, cables, equipment, determining working space, and other applications where circuit voltage ratings are used. The maximum PV system dc circuit voltage is the highest voltage between any two conductors of a circuit and must comply with the following: ▶**Figure 690–21**

According to Article 100, a "PV System DC Circuit" consists of any dc conductor in PV source circuits, PV string circuits, and PV dc-to-dc converter circuits. ▶**Figure 690–23**

(1) Commercial and Industrial Buildings. The maximum dc circuit voltage for PV system arrays on commercial and industrial buildings cannot exceed 1000V. ▶**Figure 690–24**

1st Printing

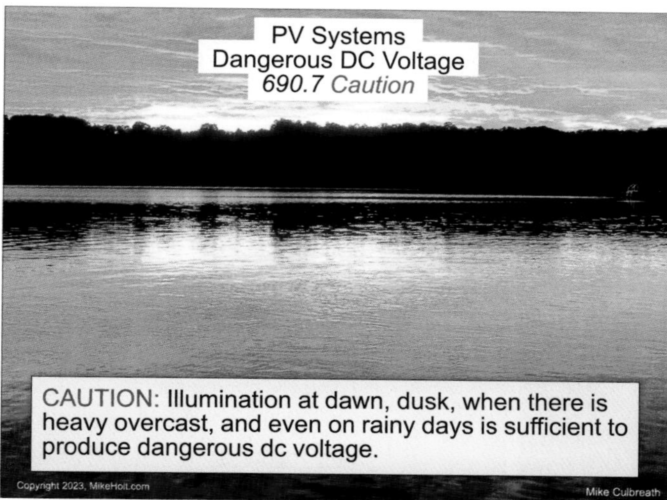

▶Figure 690–22

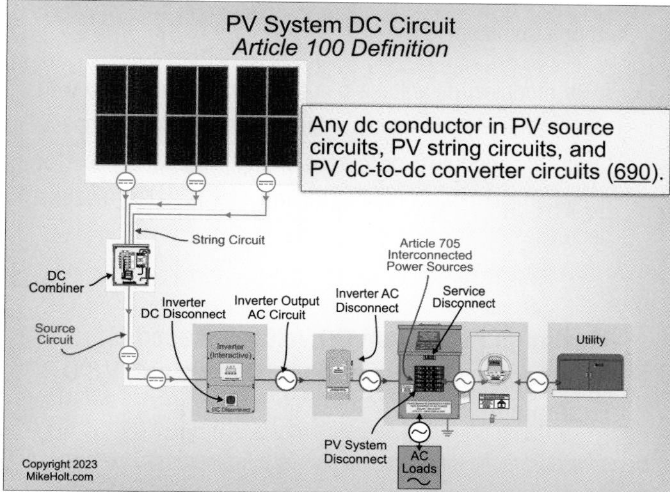

▶Figure 690–23

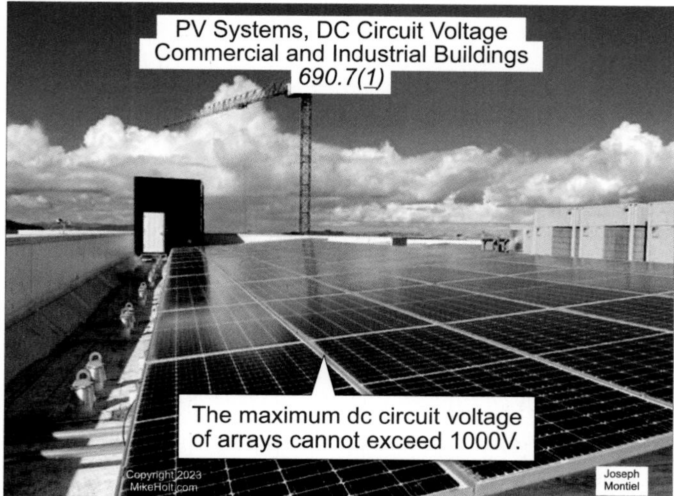

PV Systems, DC Circuit Voltage
Commercial and Industrial Buildings
690.7(1)
The maximum dc circuit voltage of arrays cannot exceed 1000V.
Copyright 2023 MikeHolt.com
Joseph Montiel

▶Figure 690–24

(2) One- and Two-Family Dwellings. The maximum dc circuit voltage for PV systems on one- and two-family dwellings cannot exceed 600V. ▶Figure 690–25

▶Figure 690–25

(3) Over 1000V. PV Systems exceeding 1000V must be installed in accordance with 690.31(G). ▶Figure 690–26

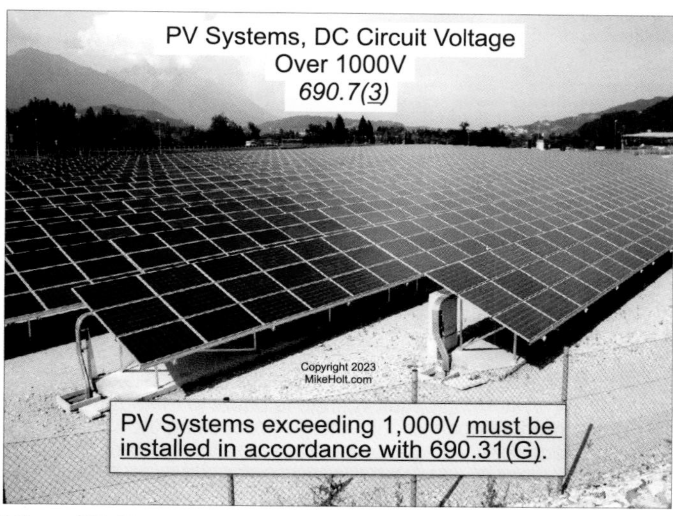

▶Figure 690–26

(A) Calculating PV System Source Circuit Voltage. The maximum calculated PV system dc source circuit voltage is determined by one of the following:

According to Article 100, the "PV Source Circuit" consists of the dc circuit conductors between modules in a PV string and from PV string circuits to dc combiners, electronic power converters, or the PV system dc disconnect (Article 690). ▶Figure 690–27

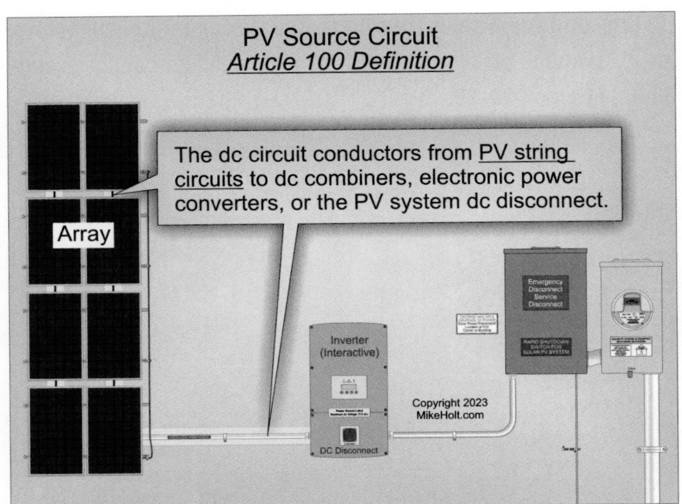

▶Figure 690–27

(1) Manufacturer's Instructions. The PV system dc source circuit voltage is equal to the sum of the series-connected dc modules open-circuit voltage (Voc) in a PV string circuit as corrected for the lowest expected ambient temperature using the manufacturer's voltage temperature coefficient correction. ▶**Figure 690–28**

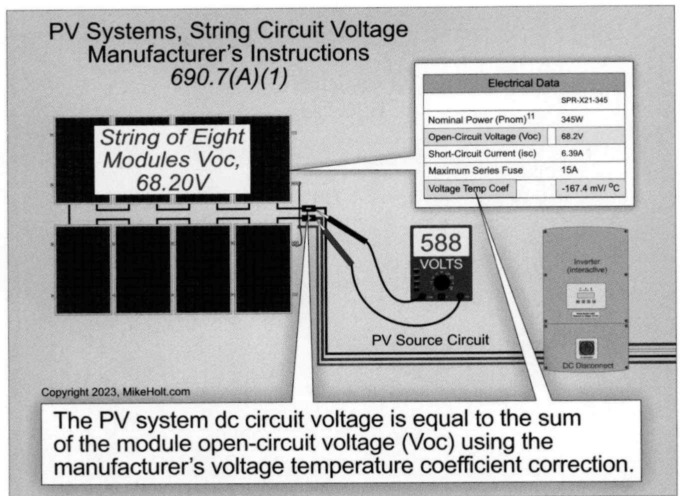

▶Figure 690–28

According to Article 100, a "PV String" circuit consists of the PV source circuit conductors of one or more series-connected PV modules. ▶**Figure 690–29**

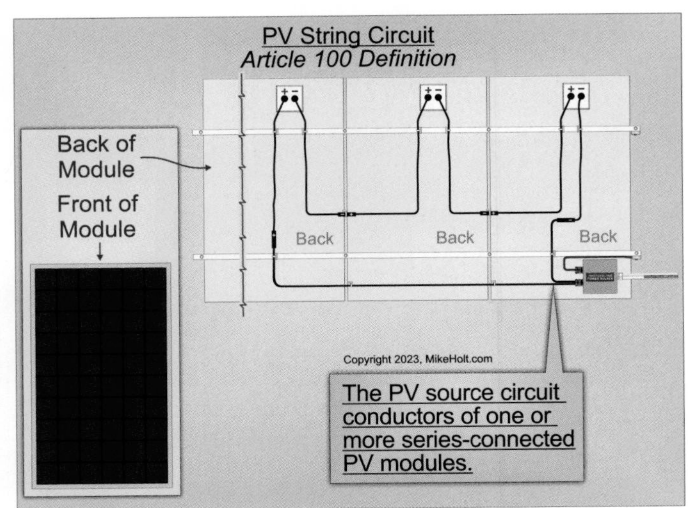

▶Figure 690–29

Author's Comment:

- A PV module's dc voltage has an inverse relationship with temperature, which means that at lower ambient temperatures, the module's dc output voltage increases, and at higher ambient temperatures, the modules' dc voltage output decreases.

▶ Maximum PV System DC Voltage, Based on Manufacturer's Temperature Coefficient, V/°C Example 1

Question: *Using the manufacturer's voltage temperature coefficient of –0.167mV/°C, what is the PV source/string circuit dc voltage for eight modules each rated 68.20 Voc at a temperature of –7°C?* ▶**Figure 690–30**

(a) 539 Vdc *(b) 588 Vdc* *(c) 624 Vdc* *(d) 641 Vdc*

Solution:

PV Voc (V/°C) = Rated Voc + [(Temp.°C–25°C) × Module Coefficient V/°C] × # Modules

PV Circuit Voltage = {68.20 Vdc + [(–7°C–25°C) × –0.167 Vdc/°C]} × 8 modules
PV Circuit Voltage = [68.20 Vdc + (-32°C × –0.167 Vdc/°C)] × 8 modules
PV Circuit Voltage = (68.20 Vdc + 5.344 Vdc) × 8 modules
PV Circuit Voltage = 73.544 Vdc × 8 modules
PV Circuit Voltage = 588 Vdc

Answer: *(b) 588 Vdc*

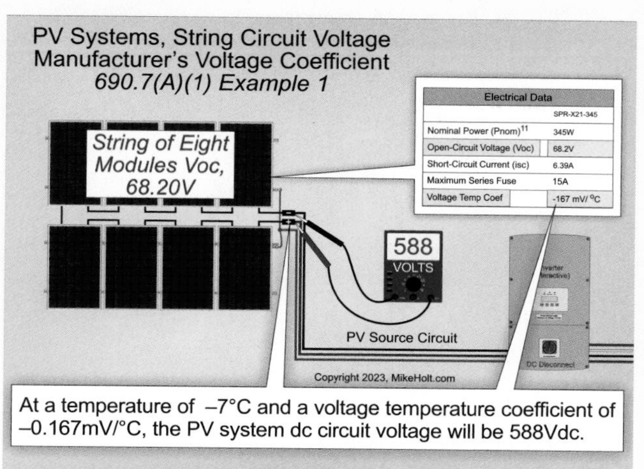

▸Figure 690–30

▸ Maximum PV System DC Voltage, Based on Manufacturer's Temperature Coefficient, V/°C Example 2

Question: *Using the manufacturer's voltage temperature coefficient of -0.167mV/°C, what is the PV source circuit dc voltage for thirteen modules each rated 68.20 Voc at a temperature of -7°C?* **▸Figure 690–31**

(a) 839 Vdc *(b) 888 Vdc* *(c) 924 Vdc* *(d) 956 Vdc*

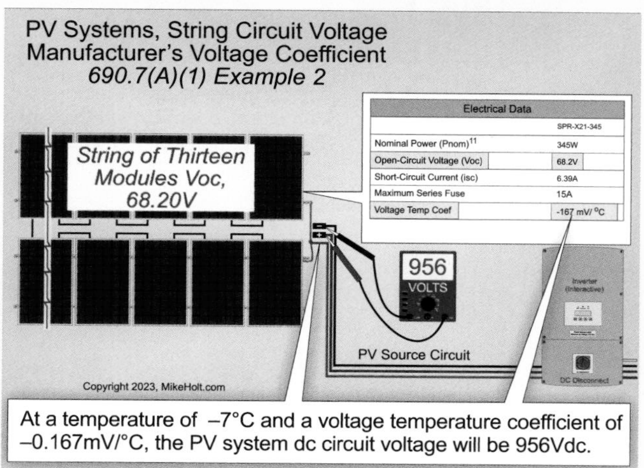

▸Figure 690–31

Solution:

PV Voc (V/°C) = Rated Voc + [(Temp.°C–25°C) × Module Coefficient V/°C] × # Modules

PV Circuit Voltage = {68.20 Vdc + [(-7°C–25°C) × -0.167 Vdc/°C]} × 13 modules

PV Circuit Voltage = [68.20 Vdc + (-32°C × -0.167 Vdc/°C)] × 13 modules

PV Circuit Voltage = (68.20 Vdc + 5.344 Vdc) × 13 modules

PV Circuit Voltage = 73.544 Vdc × 13 modules

PV Circuit Voltage = 956 Vdc

Answer: *(d) 956 Vdc*

Author's Comment:

- See www.SolarABCs.org website to find the low temperature data for a specific location for maximum voltage calculations.

(2) Table of Crystalline and Multicrystalline Modules. The PV system dc source circuit voltage is equal to the sum of the series-connected dc modules' rated open-circuit voltage (Voc) in a PV string circuit as corrected for the lowest expected ambient temperature in accordance with Table 690.7(A).

Table 690.7(A) Voltage Correction Factors for Crystalline and Multicrystalline Silicon Modules

Correction Factors for Ambient Temperatures Below 25°C (77°F) (Multiply the rated open-circuit voltage by the appropriate correction factor shown below.)		
Ambient Temperature (°C)	**Factor**	**Ambient Temperature (°F)**
24 to 20	1.02	76 to 68
19 to 15	1.04	67 to 59
14 to 10	1.06	58 to 50
9 to 5	1.08	49 to 41
4 to 0	1.10	40 to 32
-1 to -5	1.12	31 to 23
-6 to -10	1.14	22 to 14
-11 to -15	1.16	13 to 5
-16 to -20	1.18	4 to -4
-21 to -25	1.20	-5 to -13
-26 to -30	1.21	-14 to -22
-31 to -35	1.23	-23 to -31
-36 to -40	1.25	-32 to -40

▶ Maximum PV System DC Voltage, Based on Table 690.7(A) Temperature Correction [690.7(A)(2)] Example

Question: *Using Table 690.7(A), what is the maximum PV system source circuit dc voltage for twelve crystalline modules each rated 38.30 Voc at a temperature of -7°C?* ▸**Figure 690–32**

(a) 493 Vdc *(b) 513 Vdc* *(c) 524 Vdc* *(d) 541 Vdc*

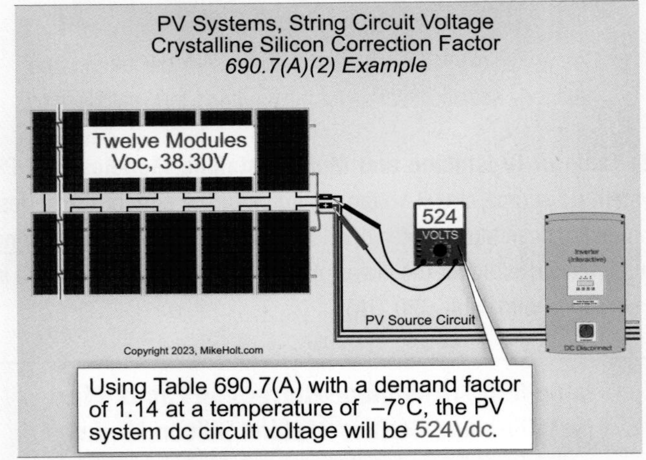

PV Systems, String Circuit Voltage
Crystalline Silicon Correction Factor
690.7(A)(2) Example
Twelve Modules
Voc, 38.30V
524
VOLTS
PV Source Circuit
Copyright 2023, MikeHolt.com
Using Table 690.7(A) with a demand factor of 1.14 at a temperature of –7°C, the PV system dc circuit voltage will be 524Vdc.

▸**Figure 690–32**

Solution:

PV Voc = Module Voc × Table 690.7 Correction Factor × # Modules

PV Circuit Voltage = 38.30 Voc × 1.14 × 12 modules

PV Circuit Voltage = 524 Vdc

Answer: *(c) 524 Vdc*

(3) Engineered Industry Standard Method. For PV systems with an inverter generating capacity of 100 kW or greater, the PV system dc circuit voltage is permitted to be determined by a licensed professional electrical engineer who provides a documented and stamped PV system design using an industry standard method for maximum dc voltage calculation. ▸**Figure 690–33**

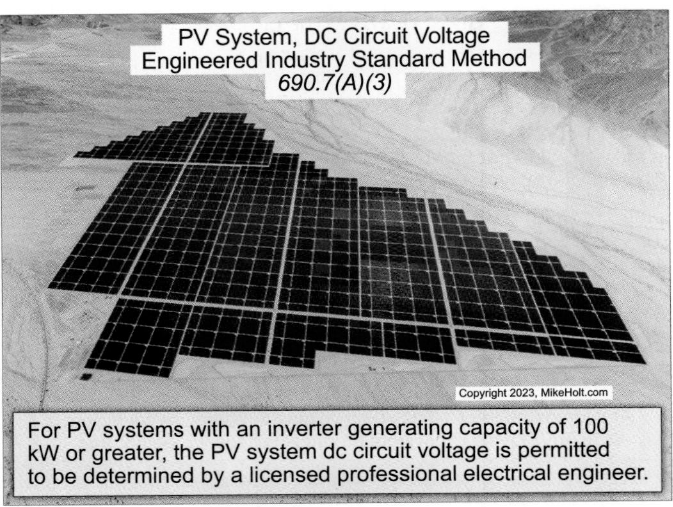

▸**Figure 690–33**

Note 1: One source of lowest-expected ambient temperature design data for various locations is the chapter titled "Extreme Annual Mean Minimum Design Dry Bulb Temperature" found in the *ASHRAE Handbook–Fundamentals.* This temperature data can be used to calculate the maximum voltage.

Note 2: One industry standard method for calculating the PV source and output circuit dc voltage is published by Sandia National Laboratories, reference SAND 2004-3535, *Photovoltaic Array Performance Model.*

(B) Calculating DC-to-DC Converter Circuit Voltage. The dc-to-dc converter circuit voltage is determined by one of the following methods:

According to Article 100, a "DC-to-DC Converter Circuit" consists of the dc circuit conductors connected to the output of dc-to-dc converters. ▸**Figure 690–34**

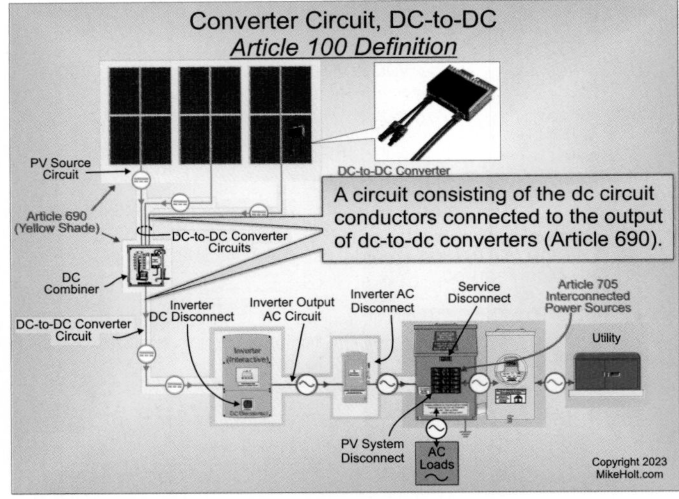

▸**Figure 690–34**

Author's Comment:

- A dc-to-dc converter (optimizer) enables the output circuit voltage to stay within the window that is maximized for direct-current and/or alternating-current power production by the inverter regardless of voltage fluctuations caused by individual module performance or variance in light exposure between modules.

(1) Single DC-to-DC Converter. The output dc voltage for a single dc-to-dc converter (optimizer) is based on the manufactures instructions or equal to the rated output dc voltage of the converter (optimizer). ▶Figure 690–35

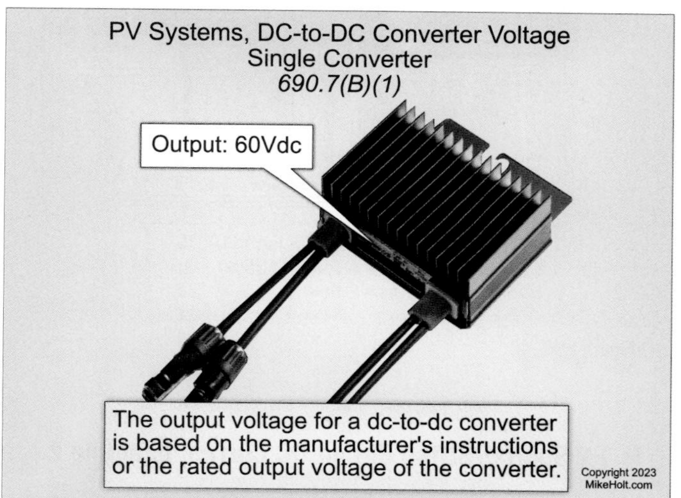

▶Figure 690–35

(2) Series-Connected DC-to-DC Converters. The output dc voltage for multiple dc-to-dc converters connected in series is based on the manufactures instructions or equal to the sum of the rated output voltage of the converters. ▶Figure 690–36

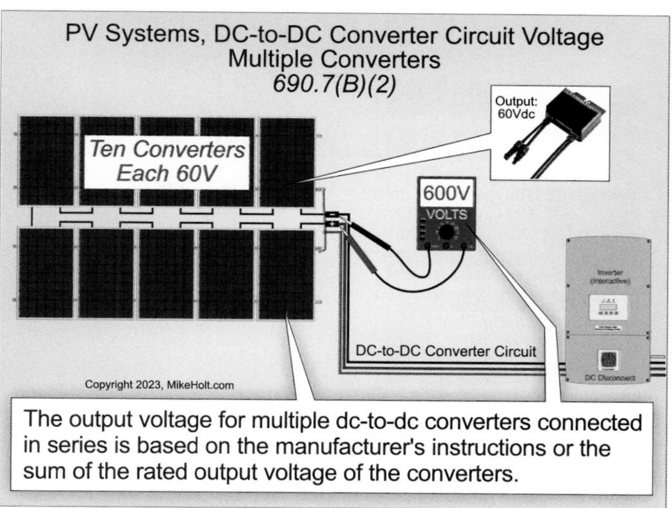

▶Figure 690–36

(D) Marking PV dc Circuit Voltage. A permanent readily visible label indicating the maximum PV system dc circuit voltage, as calculated in accordance with 690.7, must be installed at one of the following locations: ▶Figure 690–37

(1) PV system dc disconnect

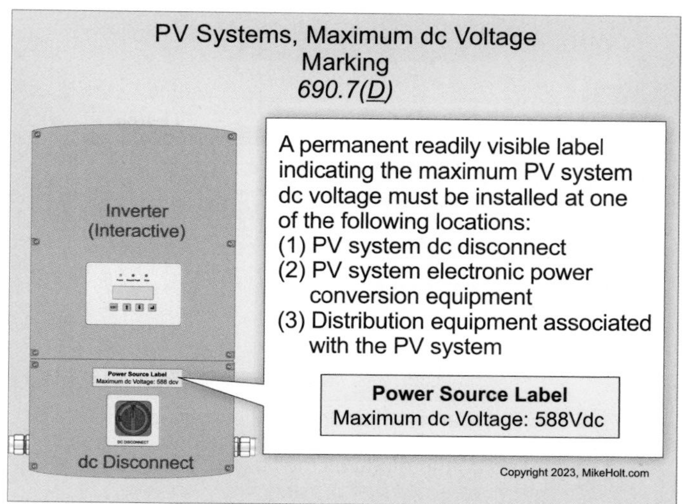

▶Figure 690–37

(2) PV system electronic power converters

(3) Distribution equipment associated with the PV system

690.8 Circuit Current and Conductor Sizing

(A) Calculation of Maximum PV Circuit Current. The maximum PV system current is calculated in accordance with 690.8(A)(1) or (2):

(1) PV System Circuit Current. The maximum PV system circuit current is calculated in accordance with 690.8(A)(1)(a) through (c).

(a) PV System dc Source/String Circuit Current.

(1) PV Systems of Any kW Rating. The maximum PV source/string circuit dc current is equal to the short-circuit current ratings marked on the modules (Isc) multiplied by 125 percent. ▶Figure 690–38

Author's Comment:

- A module can produce more than the rated current when the intensity of the sunlight is greater than the standard used to determine the module's short-circuit rating. This happens when sunlight intensity is affected by altitude, reflection due to snow, refraction through clouds, or low humidity. For this reason, the PV system maximum circuit current is calculated at 125 percent of the module's short-circuit current rating marked on the module's nameplate. This is commonly referred to as an "irradiance factor." ▶Figure 690–39

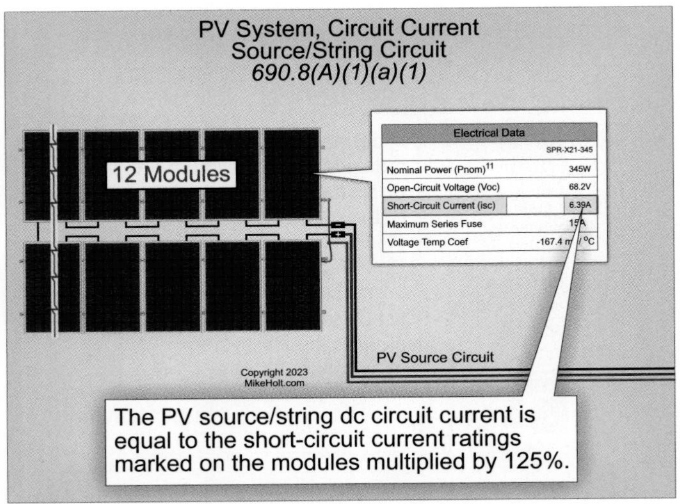

▶Figure 690–38

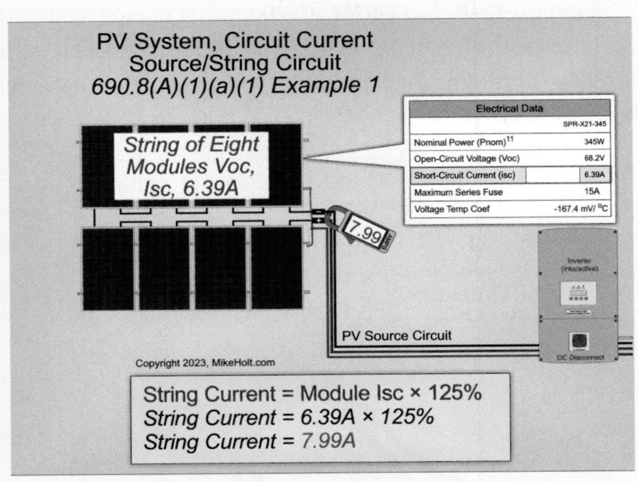

▶Figure 690–40

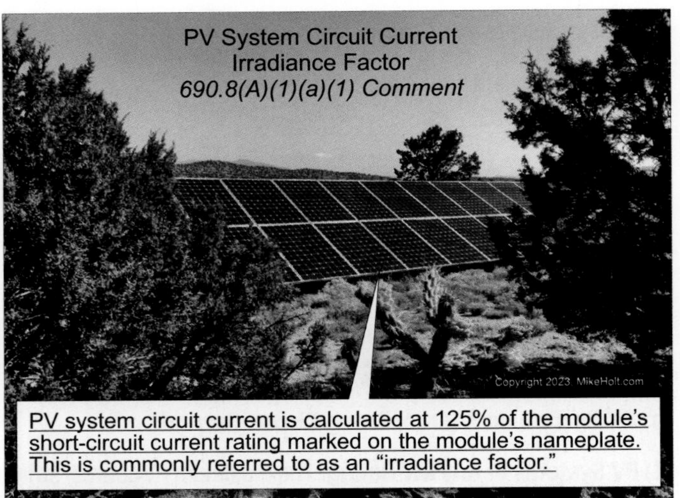

▶Figure 690–39

▶ PV Source/String Circuit DC Current Example 1

Question: *What is the maximum PV string circuit current for 8 series-connected modules having a nameplate short-circuit current (Isc) of 6.39A?* **▶Figure 690–40**

(a) 8A *(b) 9A* *(c) 10A* *(d) 11A*

Solution:

String Circuit Current = Module Isc × 125%

String Circuit Current = 6.39A × 125%

String Circuit Current = 7.99A

Answer: *(a) 8A*

▶ PV Source/String Circuit DC Current Example 2

Question: *What is the maximum circuit current for four PV string circuits of 8 series-connected modules each having a nameplate short-circuit current (Isc) of 6.39A?* **▶Figure 690–41**

(a) 22A *(b) 32A* *(c) 42A* *(d) 52A*

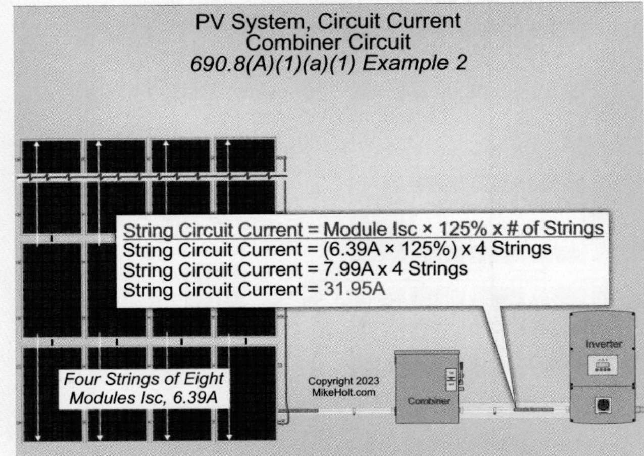

▶Figure 690–41

Solution:

String Circuit Current = Module Isc × 125% × Number of Strings

String Circuit Current = (6.39A × 125%) × 4 Strings

String Circuit Current = 7.99A × 4 Strings

String Circuit Current = 31.95A

Answer: *(b) 32A*

(c) Inverter Output Circuit Current. The inverter output ac circuit current is equal to the continuous output current rating marked on the inverter nameplate. ▶Figure 690–45

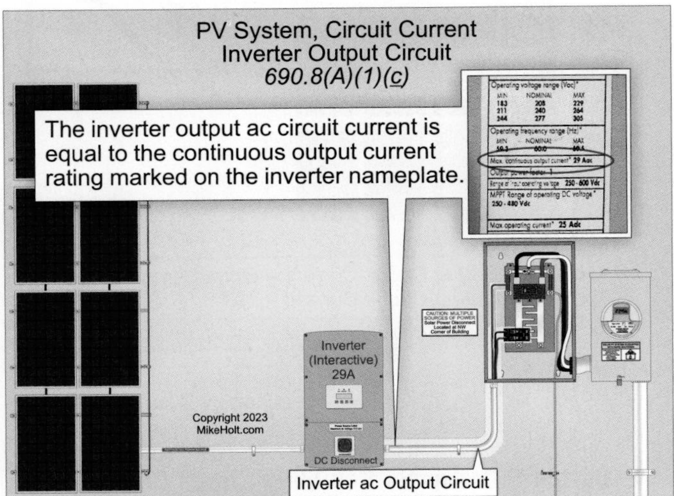

▶Figure 690–45

Note: Modules that can produce electricity when exposed to light on multiple surfaces are labeled with applicable short-circuit currents. Additional guidance is provided in the instructions included with the listing.

(2) Circuits Connected to an Inverter. Where a circuit is protected with an overcurrent protective device not exceeding the conductor ampacity, the maximum current is permitted to be the rated input current of the inverter to which it is connected.

(B) Conductor Sizing. PV circuit conductors must have an ampacity not less than the largest of 690.8(B)(1) or (B)(2).

(1) Conductor Sizing. PV circuit conductors must have an ampacity of not less than 125 percent of the current as determined by 690.8(A). ▶Figure 690–46

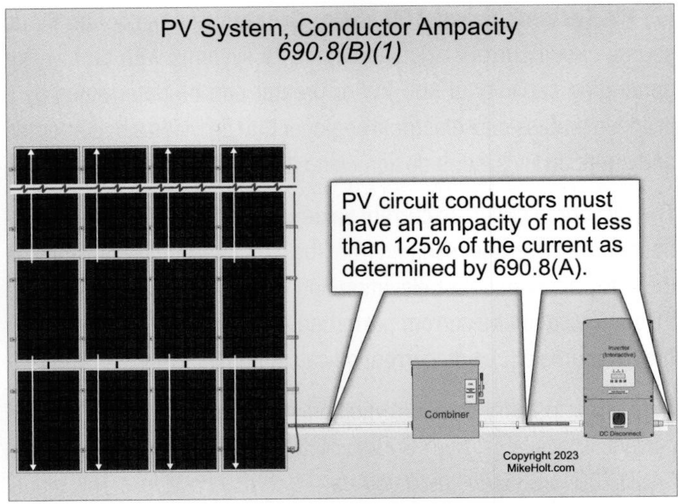

▶Figure 690–46

▶ Source/String Circuit Conductor Ampacity One-String Example

Question: *What is the minimum circuit conductor ampacity for a single string of 8 series-connected modules having a short-circuit current rating (Isc) of 6.39A?* ▶Figure 690–47

(a) 9A *(b) 10A* *(c) 11A* *(d) 12A*

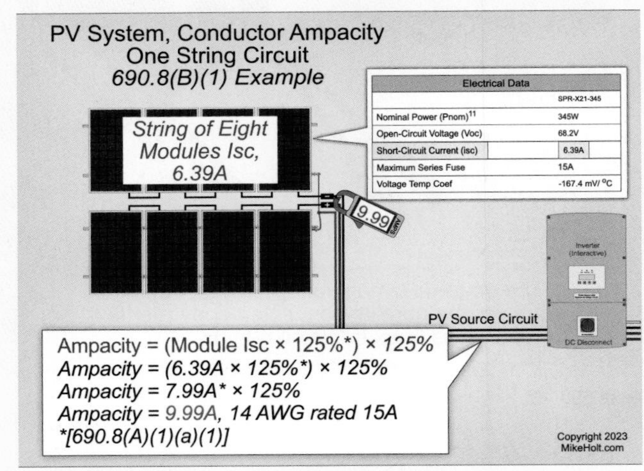

▶Figure 690–47

Solution:

Conductor Ampacity = (Module Isc × 125%)* × 125%

Conductor Ampacity = (6.39A × 125%) × 125%*

Conductor Ampacity = 7.99A × 125%

Conductor Ampacity = 9.99A, 14 AWG rated 15A at 60°C [Table 310.16]

**[690.8(A)(1)(a)]*

Answer: *(b) 10A*

▶ Source/String Circuit Conductor Ampacity Combiner Example

Question: *What is the minimum circuit conductor ampacity required to supply four strings of 8 series-connected modules having a nameplate short-circuit current (Isc) of 6.39A, terminals rated at 75°C?* **▸Figure 690–48**

(a) 25A *(b) 30A* *(c) 35A* *(d) 40A*

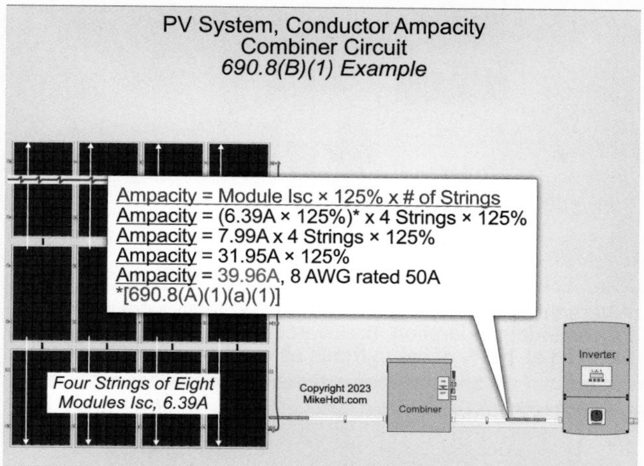

PV System, Conductor Ampacity
Combiner Circuit
690.8(B)(1) Example
Ampacity = Module Isc × 125% x # of Strings
Ampacity = (6.39A × 125%)* x 4 Strings × 125%
Ampacity = 7.99A x 4 Strings × 125%
Ampacity = 31.95A × 125%
Ampacity = 39.96A, 8 AWG rated 50A
*[690.8(A)(1)(a)(1)]
Four Strings of Eight
Modules Isc, 6.39A
Copyright 2023
MikeHolt.com
Combiner
Inverter

▸Figure 690–48

Solution:

Conductor Ampacity = (Module Isc × 125% × 125%) × Number of Strings

Conductor Ampacity = (6.39A × 125% × 125%) × 4 Strings*

Conductor Ampacity = (7.99A × 125%) × 4 Strings

Conductor Ampacity = 9.99A × 4 Strings

Conductor Ampacity = 39.96A, 8 AWG rated 50A at 75°C [Table 310.16]

**[690.8(A)(1)(a)]*

Answer: *(d) 40A*

▶ DC-to-DC Converter Circuit Conductor Ampacity Example

Question: *What is the PV dc-to-dc converter circuit conductor ampacity for each of the two string circuits connected in parallel, each having a nameplate output current rating of 15A?* **▸Figure 690–49**

(a) 18.75A *(b) 19.75A* *(c) 21.50A* *(d) 23.25A*

Solution:

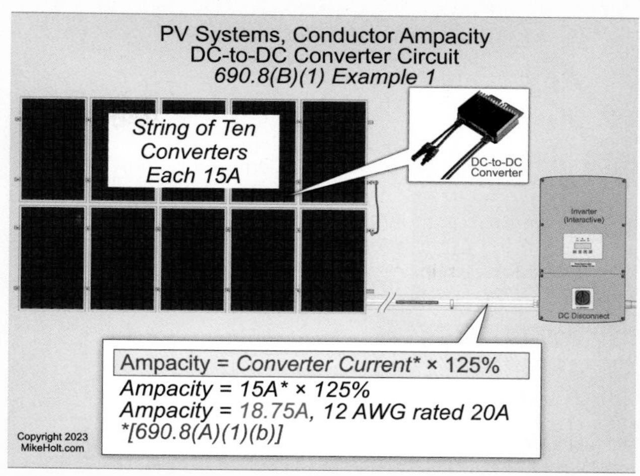

▸Figure 690–49

Conductor Ampacity = DC-to-DC Converter Current* × 125%

*Conductor Ampacity = 15A × 125%**

Conductor Ampacity = 18.75A, 12 AWG rated 20A at 60°C [Table 310.16]

**[690.8(A)(1)(b)]*

Answer: *(a) 18.75A*

▶ DC-to-DC Converter Combiner Circuit Conductor Ampacity Example

Question: *What is the PV dc-to-dc converter circuit current for four string circuits connected in parallel, each having a nameplate output current rating of 15A?* **▸Figure 690–50**

(a) 45A *(b) 55A* *(c) 65A* *(d) 75A*

Solution:

Conductor Ampacity = (DC-to-DC Converter Current* × 125%) × # of Strings

Conductor Ampacity = 15A × 125% × 4 Strings*

Conductor Ampacity = 18.75A × 4 Strings*

Conductor Ampacity = 75A, 4 AWG rated 85A [Table 310.16]

**[690.8(A)(1)(b)]*

Answer: *(d) 75A*

• • •

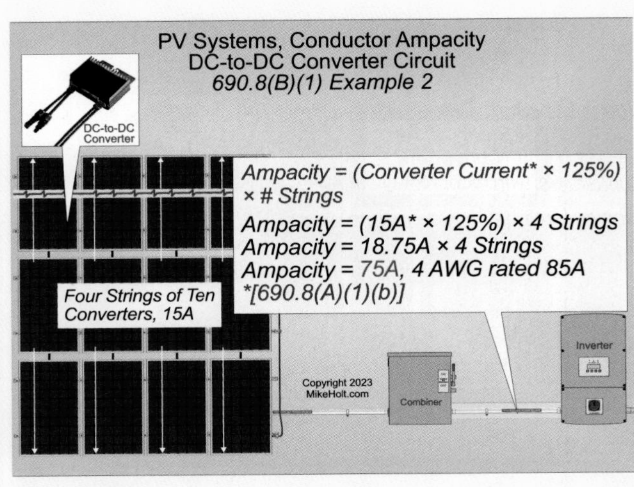

▶Figure 690–50

▶ Inverter Output Circuit Ampacity Example

Question: *What is the minimum inverter ac output circuit conductor ampacity required for inverter rated 24A?* ▶**Figure 690–51**

(a) 20A *(b) 25A* *(c) 30A* *(d) 35A*

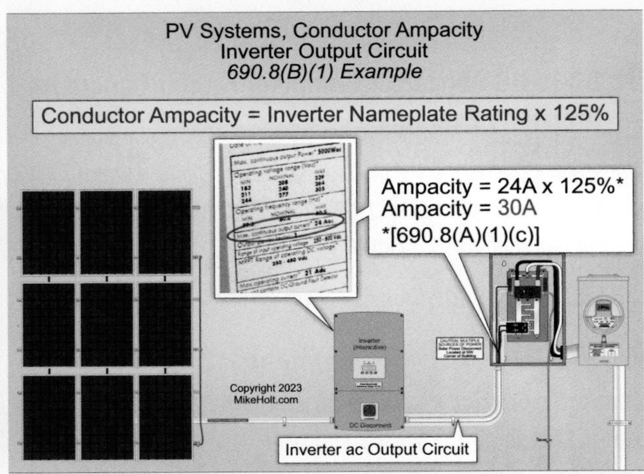

▶Figure 690–51

Solution:

Conductor Ampacity = Inverter Nameplate Rating [690.8(A)(1)(c)] × 125%

Conductor Ampacity = 24A × 125%

Conductor Ampacity = 30A

Answer: *(c) 30A*

Ex: Where the assembly, including the overcurrent protective devices protecting the circuit(s), is listed for operation at 100 percent of its rating, the ampere rating of the overcurrent protective device can be sized to 100 percent of the continuous and noncontinuous loads. ▶**Figure 690–52**

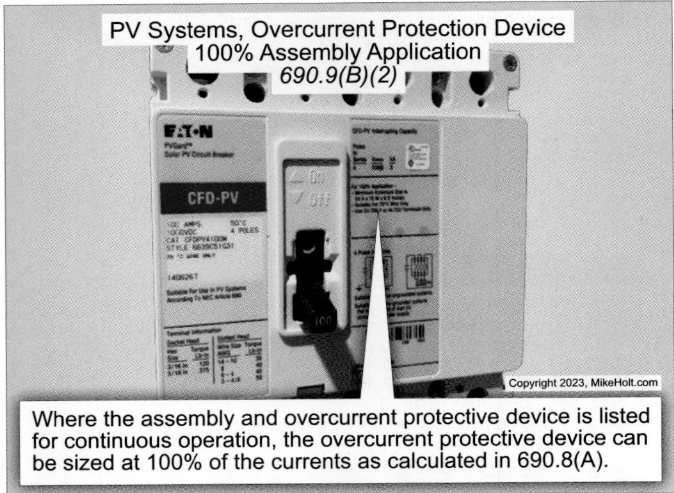

PV Systems, Overcurrent Protection Device
100% Assembly Application
690.9(B)(2)
E:T·N
CFD-PV
Copyright 2023, MikeHolt.com
Where the assembly and overcurrent protective device is listed for continuous operation, the overcurrent protective device can be sized at 100% of the currents as calculated in 690.8(A).

▶Figure 690–52

(2) Conductor Sizing, With Ampacity Correction and/or Adjustment. PV circuit conductors must have an ampacity of not less than 100 percent of the current as determined by 690.8(A) after conductor ampacity correction [Table 310.15(B)(1)(1)] and adjustment [Table 310.15(C)(1)]. ▶**Figure 690–53**

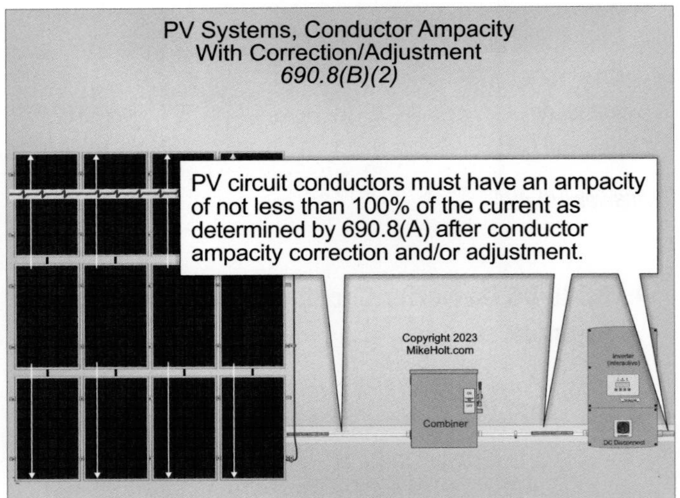

▶Figure 690–53

Author's Comment:

- The Table 310.16 ampacity must be corrected when the ambient temperature is greater than 86°F and adjusted when more than three current-carrying conductors are bundled together. The temperature correction [Table 310.15(B)(1)(1)] and conductor bundling adjustment [Table 310.15(C)(1)] are applied to the conductor ampacity based on the temperature rating of the conductor insulation as contained in Table 310.16, typically in the 90°C column [310.15].

▶ Ampacity with Correction One String Example

Question: *What is the conductor ampacity for a single string of 8 series-connected modules (Isc 6.39) using 14 AWG, USE-2 rated 90°C conductors within a raceway 1 in. above a roof where the ambient temperature is 94°F in accordance with 310.15(B)(1)?* **▶Figure 690–54**

(a) 22A *(b) 24A* *(c) 26A* *(d) 28A*

Solution:

Corrected Ampacity = Table 310.16 Ampacity at 90°C Column × Temperature Correction

14 AWG is rated 25A at 90°C [Table 310.16]

Temperature Correction = 0.96 based on a 94°F ambient temperature [Table 310.15(B)(1)(1)]

Corrected Ampacity = 25A × 96%
Corrected Ampacity = 24A

Note: *14 AWG rated 24A is suitable to supply the 7.99A string load (6.99A × 125%) [690.8(A)(1)(a)(1)]*

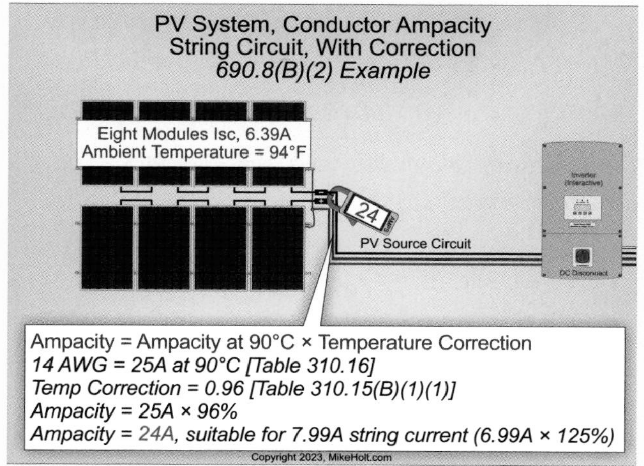

▶Figure 690–54

Answer: *(b) 24A*

▶ Ampacity with Correction/Adjustment Multistring Example

Question: *What is the conductor ampacity for each of four strings of 8 series-connected modules (Isc 6.39) using 14 AWG rated 90°C conductors within a raceway 1 in. above a roof where the ambient temperature is 94°F in accordance with 310.15(B)(1)?* **▶Figure 690–55**

(a) 14.80A *(b) 15.80A* *(c) 16.80A* *(d) 17.80A*

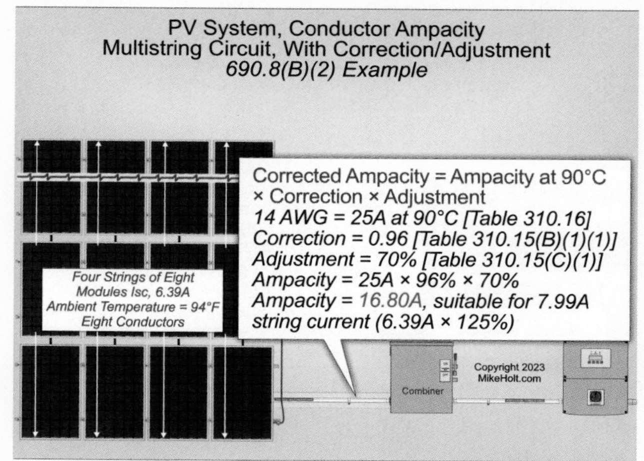

PV System, Conductor Ampacity
Multistring Circuit, With Correction/Adjustment
690.8(B)(2) Example
Four Strings of Eight
Modules Isc, 6.39A
Ambient Temperature = 94°F
Eight Conductors
Corrected Ampacity = Ampacity at 90°C
× Correction × Adjustment
14 AWG = 25A at 90°C [Table 310.16]
Correction = 0.96 [Table 310.15(B)(1)(1)]
Adjustment = 70% [Table 310.15(C)(1)]
Ampacity = 25A × 96% × 70%
Ampacity = 16.80A, suitable for 7.99A
string current (6.39A × 125%)
Combiner
Copyright 2023
MikeHolt.com

▶Figure 690–55

Solution:

Conductor Ampacity = Table 310.16 Ampacity at 90°C Column × Correction × Adjustment

14 AWG is rated 25A at 90°C [Table 310.16].

Temperature Correction = 0.96 based on a 94°F ambient temperature [Table 310.15(B)(1)(1)]

Bundle Adjustment = 70% based on eight current-carrying conductors [Table 310.15(C)(1)]

Conductor Corrected/Adjusted Ampacity = 25A × 96% × 70%
Conductor Corrected/Adjusted Ampacity = 16.80A

Note: 14 AWG, rated 16.80A is suitable to supply the 7.99A string load (6.39A × 125%) [690.8(A)(1)(a)(1)].

Answer: *(c) 16.80A*

▶ Ampacity with Correction Multistring Combiner Output Example

Question: *What is the combiner output conductor ampacity for four input strings of 8 series-connected modules (Isc 6.39) using 8 AWG rated 90°C conductors within a raceway 1 in. above a roof where the ambient temperature is 94°F in accordance with 310.15(B)(1)?* **▸Figure 690–56**

(a) 48.80A (b) 49.80A (c) 51.80A (d) 52.80A

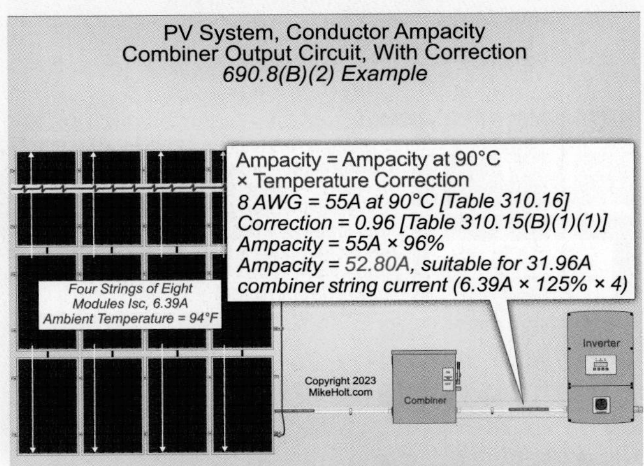

▸Figure 690–56

Solution:

Conductor Ampacity = Table 310.16 Ampacity at 90°C Column × Correction × Adjustment

8 AWG is rated 55A at 90°C [Table 310.16].

Temperature Correction = 0.96 based on a 94°F ambient temperature [Table 310.15(B)(1)(1)]

Corrected Ampacity = 55A × 96%
Corrected Ampacity = 52.80A

Note: *8 AWG, rated 52.80A is suitable to supply the 31.96A combiner string load (6.39A × 125% × 4) [690.8(A)(1)(a)(1)].*

Answer: *(d) 52.80A*

▶ DC-to-DC Converter Circuit Conductor Ampacity with Correction/Adjustment Example

Question: *For an array with dc-to-dc converters having an output current rating of 15A for each dc-to-dc converter circuit, what is the conductor ampacity for eight current-carrying 12 AWG rated 90°C conductors within a raceway 1 in. above a roof where the ambient temperature is 94°F?* **▸Figure 690–57**

(a) 20.20A (b) 21.20A (c) 22.20A (d) 23.20A

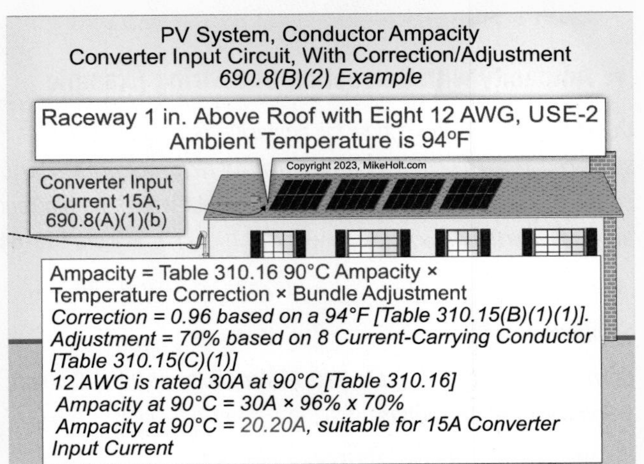

▸Figure 690–57

Solution:

Conductor Ampacity = Table 310.16 Ampacity at 90°C Column × Temperature Correction × Bundle Adjustment

Temperature Correction = 0.96 based on a 94°F ambient temperature [Table 310.15(B)(1)(1)]

Bundle Adjustment = 70% based on eight current-carrying conductors [Table 310.15(C)(1)]

12 AWG is rated 30A at 90°C [Table 310.16].

Conductor Corrected/Adjusted Ampacity = 30A × 96% × 70%
Conductor Corrected/Adjusted Ampacity = 20.16A

Answer: *(a) 20.20A*

▶ DC-to-DC Converter Combiner Circuit Conductor Ampacity with Correction Example

Question: *What is the dc-to-dc converter combiner circuit conductor ampacity for two current-carrying 4 AWG rated 90°C conductors within a raceway 1 in. above a roof where the dc-to-dc converter circuit dc current is 45A and the ambient temperature is 94°F?* **▶Figure 690–58**

(a) 80.20A *(b) 90.20A* *(c) 91.20A* *(d) 92.20A*

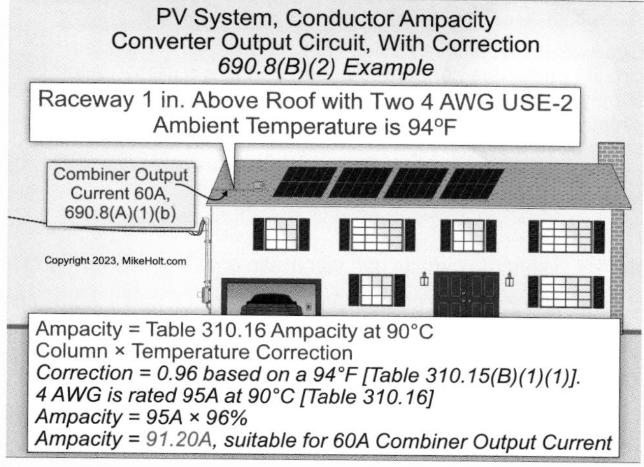
PV System, Conductor Ampacity
Converter Output Circuit, With Correction
690.8(B)(2) Example
Raceway 1 in. Above Roof with Two 4 AWG USE-2
Ambient Temperature is 94°F
Combiner Output
Current 60A,
690.8(A)(1)(b)
Copyright 2023, MikeHolt.com
Ampacity = Table 310.16 Ampacity at 90°C
Column × Temperature Correction
Correction = 0.96 based on a 94°F [Table 310.15(B)(1)(1)].
4 AWG is rated 95A at 90°C [Table 310.16]
Ampacity = 95A × 96%
Ampacity = 91.20A, suitable for 60A Combiner Output Current

▶Figure 690–58

Solution:

Conductor Ampacity = Table 310.16 Ampacity at 90°C Column × Temperature Correction

Temperature Correction = 0.96 based on 94°F ambient temperature [Table 310.15(B)(1)(1)]

4 AWG is rated 95A at 90°C [Table 310.16].

Conductor Corrected Ampacity = 95A × 96%
Conductor Corrected Ampacity = 91.20A

Answer: *(c) 91.20A*

▶ Inverter Output Circuit Conductor Ampacity with Correction Example

Question: *What is the conductor ampacity for two current-carrying 10 AWG conductors rated 90°C supplying a 24A inverter output circuit installed in a location where the ambient temperature is 94°F?* **▶Figure 690–59**

(a) 18.40A *(b) 29.40A* *(c) 38.40A* *(d) 49.40A*

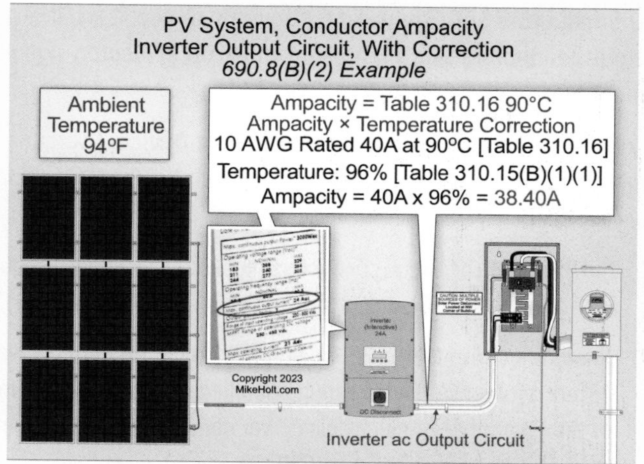
PV System, Conductor Ampacity
Inverter Output Circuit, With Correction
690.8(B)(2) Example
Ambient
Temperature
94°F
Ampacity = Table 310.16 90°C
Ampacity × Temperature Correction
10 AWG Rated 40A at 90°C [Table 310.16]
Temperature: 96% [Table 310.15(B)(1)(1)]
Ampacity = 40A x 96% = 38.40A
Copyright 2023
MikeHolt.com
Inverter ac Output Circuit

▶Figure 690–59

Solution:

Conductor Ampacity = Ampacity at 90°C Column [Table 310.16] × Temperature Correction

Temperature Correction = 0.96 based on a 94°F ambient temperature [Table 310.15(B)(1)(1)]

10 AWG is rated 40A at 90°C [Table 310.16].

Conductor Ampacity at 90°C = 40A × 96%
Conductor Ampacity at 90°C = 38.40A

Answer: *(c) 38.40A*

(D) Parallel-Connected PV String Circuits. Where overcurrent is provided for parallel-connected PV string circuits, the conductor ampacity must not be less than:

(1) The rating of the overcurrent device

(2) The sum of the currents as calculated in 690.8(A)(1)(a) for the other parallel-connected PV string circuits protected by overcurrent device

1st Printing

Author's Comment:

- Parallel-connected PV string circuits typically occur in large-scale PV electric supply stations (solar farms) within the scope of Article 691.

690.9 Overcurrent Protection

(A) Conductors and Equipment. PV system dc circuit and inverter output conductors and equipment must be protected against overcurrent.

(1) Circuits Without Overcurrent Protective Device. Overcurrent protective devices are not required where both the following conditions are met:

(1) The PV system dc circuit conductors must have an ampacity equal to or greater than the dc current in accordance with 690.8(B).

(2) Where the currents from all PV sources do not exceed the overcurrent protective device rating specified by the manufacturer for the PV module or electronic power converters (inverters and dc-to-dc converters). ▶Figure 690–60

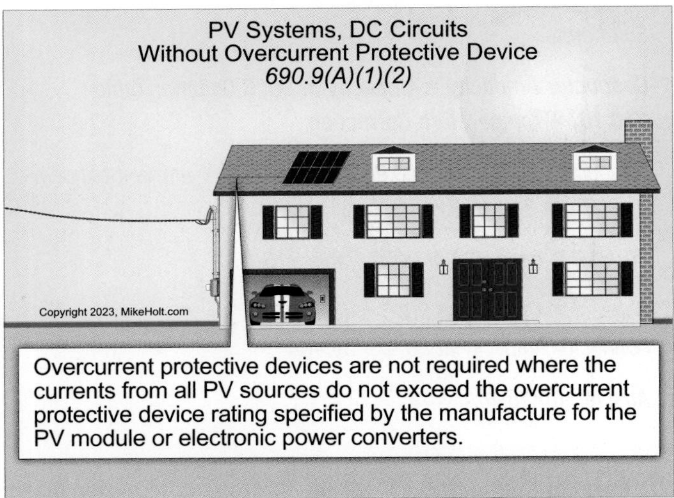

▶Figure 690–60

(2) Overcurrent Protective Device Required. Overcurrent protective devices are required for PV system circuit conductors connected at one end to a current-limited supply and also connected to sources having an available circuit current greater than the ampacity of the conductor at the point of connection to the higher current source. ▶Figure 690–61

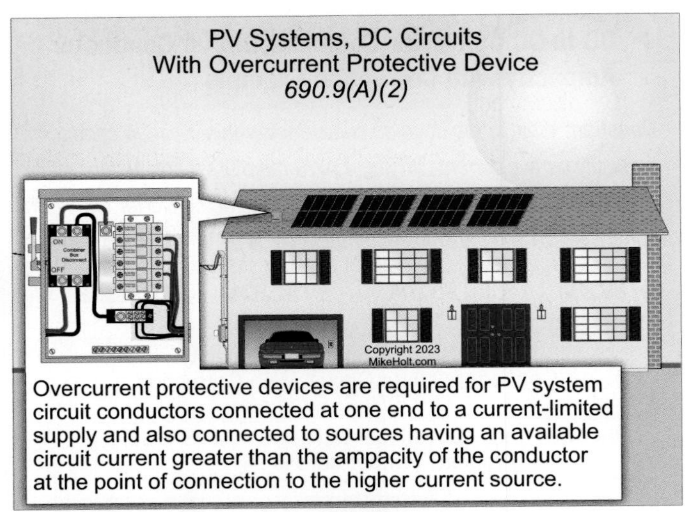

▶Figure 690–61

Note: PV system dc circuits and electronic power converter (inverters and dc-to-dc converters) outputs are current-limited and in some cases do not need overcurrent protection. When these circuits are connected to higher current sources such as parallel-connected PV systems, dc circuits, or energy storage systems the overcurrent protective device is often installed at the higher current source end of the circuit conductor.

(3) Other Circuits. PV circuit conductors that do not comply with 690.9(A)(1) or (A)(2) must have overcurrent protection by one of the following methods:

(1) On Buildings. PV circuit conductors not in a building not longer than 10 ft with overcurrent protection at one end of the circuit.

(2) Within Buildings. PV circuit conductors within a building not longer than 10 ft within a raceway or metal-clad cable with overcurrent protection on one end of the circuit.

(3) Both Ends. PV circuit conductors protected from overcurrent on both ends.

(4) Not On or Within Building. PV circuit conductors not installed on or within buildings are permitted to have overcurrent protection at one end of the circuit if they comply with all the following conditions:

a. The PV system circuit conductors are in metal raceways, metal-clad cables, enclosed metal cable trays, underground, or in pad-mounted enclosures.

b. The PV system circuit conductors terminate to a single circuit breaker or a single set of fuses that limit the current to the ampacity of the conductors.

c. The overcurrent protective device for the conductors is integral with the disconnect or within 10 ft (conductor length) of the disconnect.

d. The disconnect is outside the building or at a readily accessible location nearest the point of entrance of the conductors inside the building. PV circuit conductors are considered outside a building where they are encased or installed under not less than 2 in. of concrete or brick in accordance with 230.6.

(B) Overcurrent Device Ratings. Overcurrent protective devices for PV source (dc) circuits must be listed for PV systems. ▶**Figure 690-62**

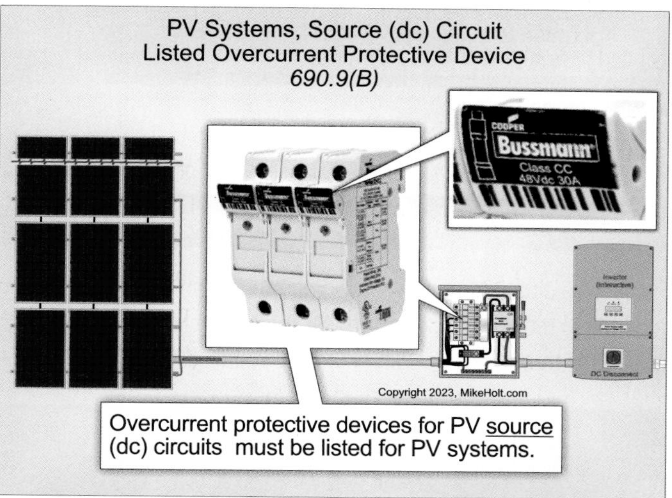

▶**Figure 690-62**

Electronic devices that are listed to prevent backfeed in PV dc circuits are permitted to prevent overcurrent of conductors on the PV array side of the electronic device.

Overcurrent protective devices required by 690.9(A)(2) must comply with one of the following. The next higher standard size overcurrent protective device in accordance with 240.4(B) is permitted.

(1) Overcurrent protective devices for PV circuits must have an ampere rating of not less than 125 percent of the currents as calculated in 690.8(A). ▶**Figure 690-63**

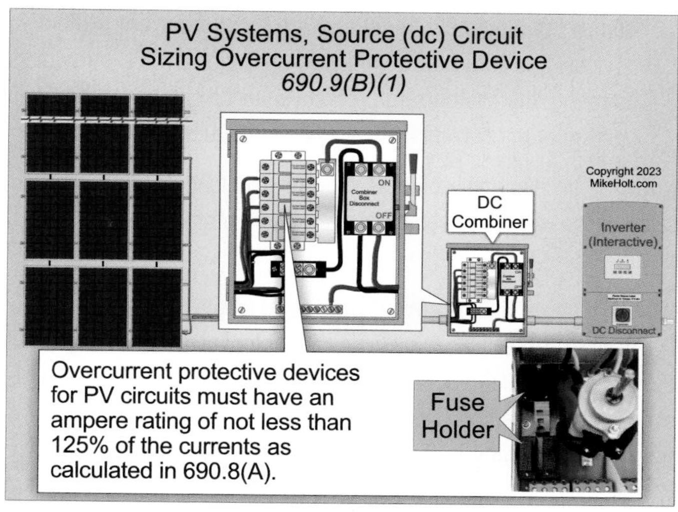

▶**Figure 690-63**

▶ PV System String Overcurrent Protection Device Sizing Example

Question: *What is the minimum size overcurrent protective device current rating required for one string of 8 series-connected modules having a nameplate short-circuit current (Isc) of 6.39A?* ▶**Figure 690-64**

(a) 8A *(b) 9A* *(c) 10A* *(d) 111A*

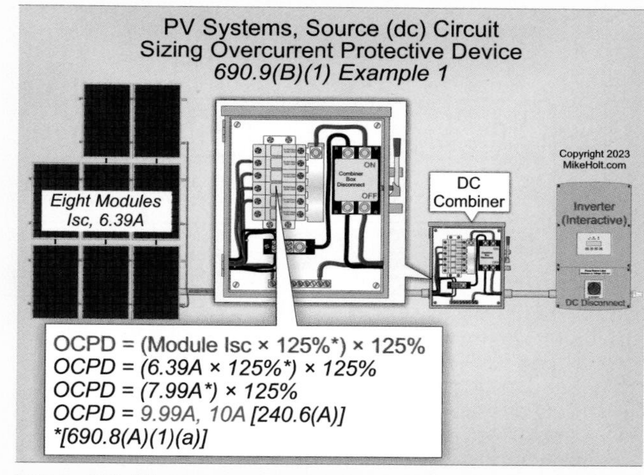

▶**Figure 690-64**

Solution:

OCPD = (Module Isc × 125%*) × 125%

OCPD = (6.39A × 125%) × 125%*

OCPD = (7.99A) × 125%*

OCPD = 9.99A, 10A [240.6(A)]

**[690.8(A)(1)(a)]*

Answer: *(c) 10A*

(2) Where the assembly, together with its overcurrent protective device(s), is listed for continuous operation at 100 percent of its rating, the overcurrent protective device can be sized at 100 percent of the currents as calculated in 690.8(A).

Note: Some electronic devices prevent backfeed current, which in some cases is the only source of overcurrent protection in PV system dc circuits.

(C) PV System Direct-Current Circuits. A single overcurrent protective device on one of the two circuit conductors can be used to protect PV modules and dc-to-dc converter circuit conductors. Where a single overcurrent protective device is used, it must be placed in the same polarity for all circuits within the PV system.

Note: A single overcurrent protective device in either the positive or negative conductors of a functionally grounded PV system provides adequate overcurrent protection.

690.11 Arc-Fault Circuit Protection

PV system dc circuits, on or in a building, operating at 80 Vdc or greater must be protected by a listed PV arc-fault circuit interrupter or other component listed to provide equivalent protection. ▸Figure 690–65

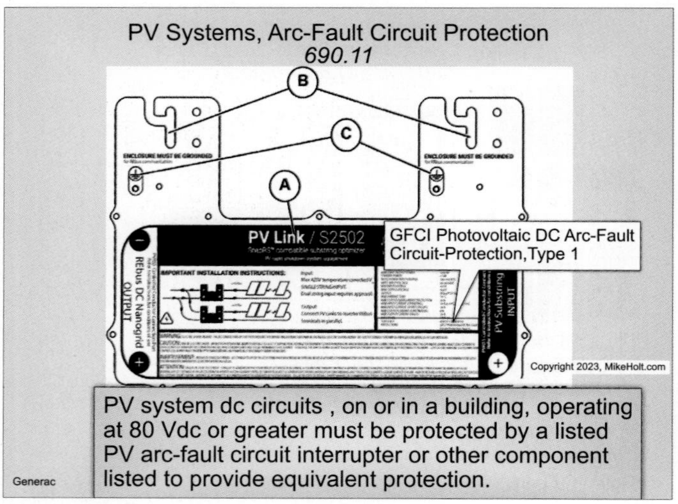

▸Figure 690–65

Ex: Arc fault protection is not required for PV system dc circuits in metal raceways, metal-clad cables, enclosed metal cable trays, or underground if: ▸Figure 690–66

(1) The PV system dc circuits are not installed in or on building or

(2) The PV system dc circuits in or on detached structures whose sole purpose is to support or contain PV system equipment

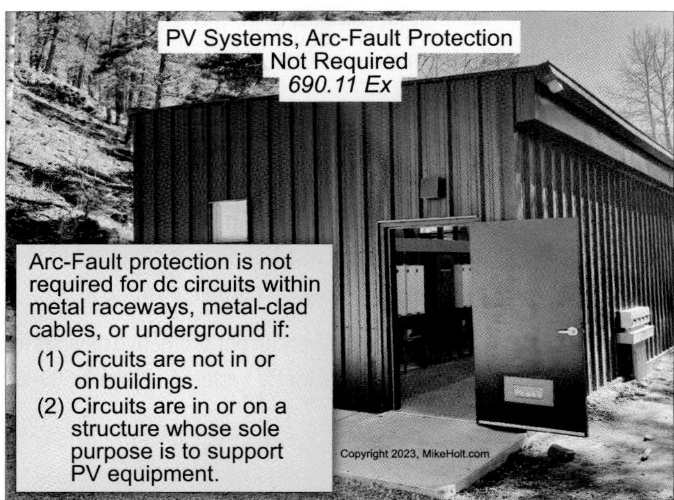

PV Systems, Arc-Fault Protection
Not Required
690.11 Ex
Arc-Fault protection is not required for dc circuits within metal raceways, metal-clad cables, or underground if:
(1) Circuits are not in or on buildings.
(2) Circuits are in or on a structure whose sole purpose is to support PV equipment.
Copyright 2023, MikeHolt.com

▸Figure 690–66

690.12 Rapid Shutdown—PV Circuits on Building

PV system circuits on or in a building must have a rapid shutdown function to reduce shock hazards for firefighters in accordance with 690.12(A) through (D). ▸Figure 690–67 and ▸Figure 690–68

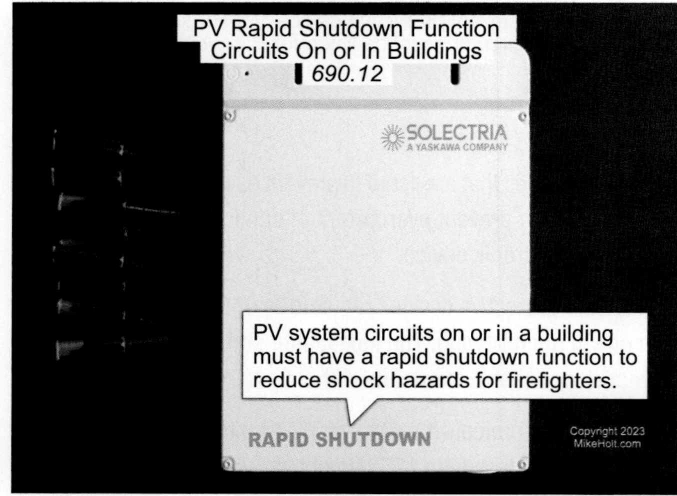

▸Figure 690–67

Ex 1: A rapid shutdown function is not required for ground-mounted PV system conductors that enter buildings whose sole purpose is to house PV system equipment. ▸Figure 690–69

Ex 2: PV equipment and circuits installed on nonenclosed detached structures including, but not limited to, parking shade structures, carports, solar trellises, and similar structures are not required to comply with the rapid shutdown requirements of 690.12. ▸Figure 690–70

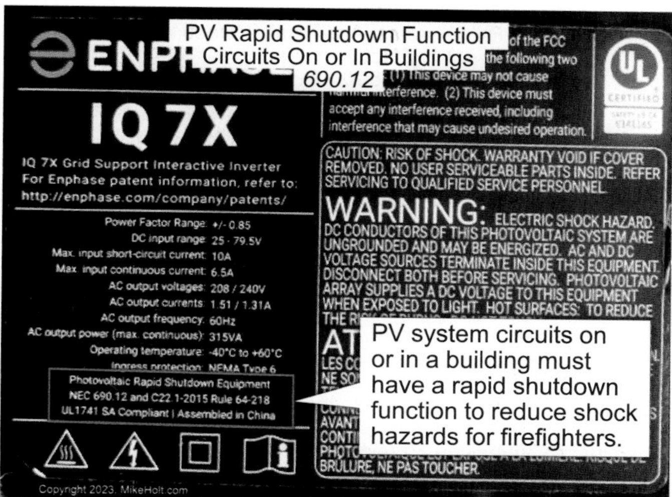
PV Rapid Shutdown Function
Circuits On or In Buildings
690.12
IQ 7X
PV system circuits on or in a building must have a rapid shutdown function to reduce shock hazards for firefighters.
Copyright 2023, MikeHolt.com

▶Figure 690–68

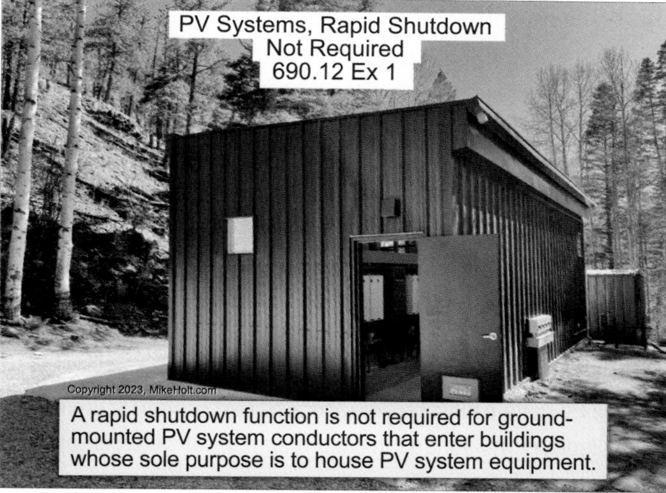
PV Systems, Rapid Shutdown
Not Required
690.12 Ex 1
Copyright 2023, MikeHolt.com
A rapid shutdown function is not required for ground-mounted PV system conductors that enter buildings whose sole purpose is to house PV system equipment.

▶Figure 690–69

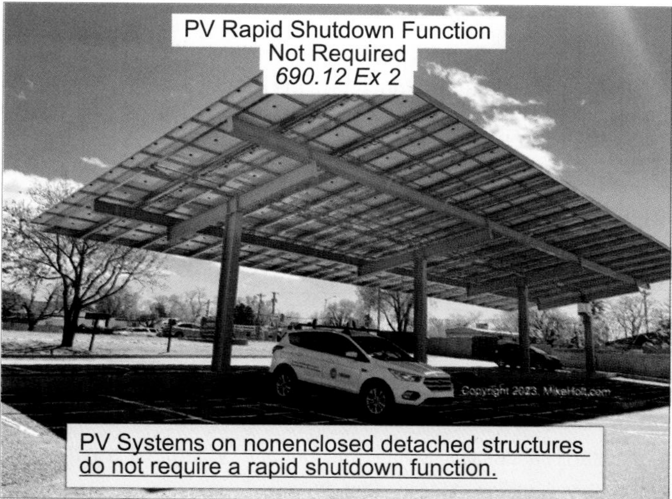
PV Rapid Shutdown Function
Not Required
690.12 Ex 2
Copyright 2023, MikeHolt.com
PV Systems on nonenclosed detached structures do not require a rapid shutdown function.

▶Figure 690–70

(A) Controlled Conductors. The following PV conductors on or in a building located outside of the array boundary as defined in 690.12(B) must be controlled by a rapid shutdown function:

(1) PV system dc circuit conductors ▶**Figure 690–71**

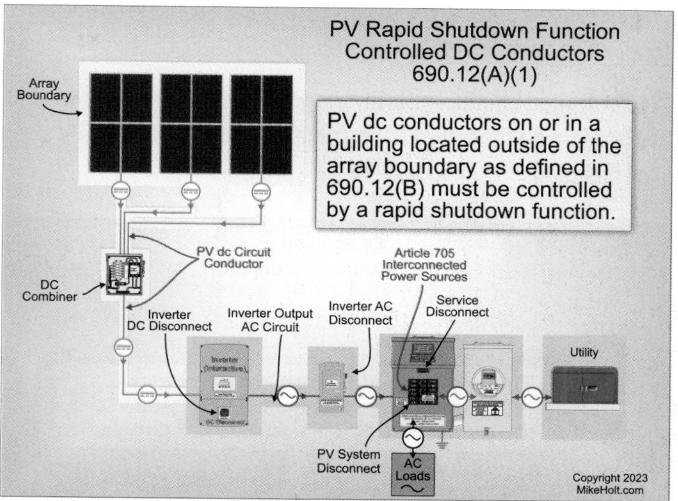
PV Rapid Shutdown Function
Controlled DC Conductors
690.12(A)(1)
Array Boundary
PV dc conductors on or in a building located outside of the array boundary as defined in 690.12(B) must be controlled by a rapid shutdown function.
PV dc Circuit Conductor
Article 705 Interconnected Power Sources
DC Combiner
Inverter DC Disconnect
Inverter Output AC Circuit
Inverter AC Disconnect
Service Disconnect
Utility
PV System Disconnect
AC Loads
Copyright 2023 MikeHolt.com

▶Figure 690–71

(2) Inverter output ac circuits originating from inverters within the array boundary ▶**Figure 690–72**

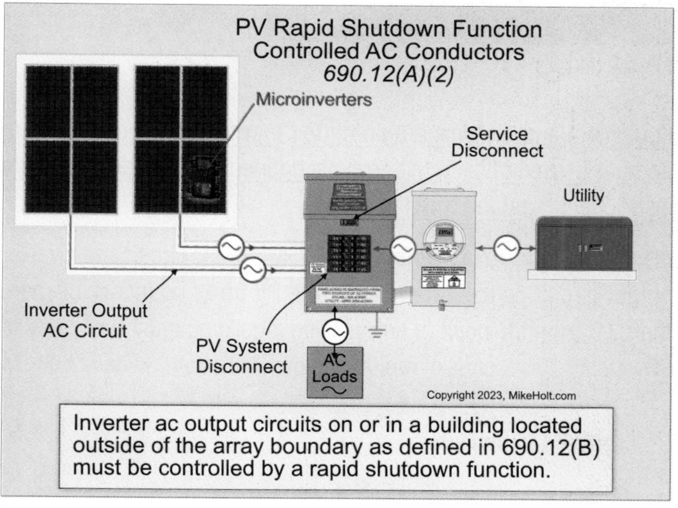
PV Rapid Shutdown Function
Controlled AC Conductors
690.12(A)(2)
Microinverters
Service Disconnect
Utility
Inverter Output AC Circuit
PV System Disconnect
AC Loads
Copyright 2023, MikeHolt.com
Inverter ac output circuits on or in a building located outside of the array boundary as defined in 690.12(B) must be controlled by a rapid shutdown function.

▶Figure 690–72

Note: The rapid shutdown function reduces the risk of electrical shock that dc circuits in a PV system could pose for firefighters. The ac output conductors from PV systems will be either de-energized after shutdown initiation or remain energized if supplied by other sources of power. To prevent PV systems with ac output conductors from remaining energized, they must be controlled by the rapid shutdown function after shutdown initiation.

(2) PV Systems Rated 100 kW or Greater. The maximum PV dc source circuit current calculations for PV systems with an inverter generating capacity of 100 kW or greater can be determined by a licensed professional electrical engineer that provides a documented and stamped PV system design using an industry standard method.

The PV source circuit dc current value is based on the highest three-hour current average resulting from the simulated local irradiance on the array accounting for elevation and orientation. In no case is the PV source circuit dc current permitted to be less than 70 percent of the PV source circuit dc current as calculated in 690.8(A)(1)(a)(1).

Note: One industry standard method for calculating the PV source current is available from Sandia National Laboratories, reference SAND 2004-3535, *Photovoltaic Array Performance Model.* This model is used by the System Advisor Model simulation program provided by the National Renewable Energy Laboratory.

(b) PV DC-to-DC Converter Circuit Current. The dc-to-dc circuit current is equal to the sum of the parallel-connected dc-to-dc converter's continuous output current ratings. ▶Figure 690–42

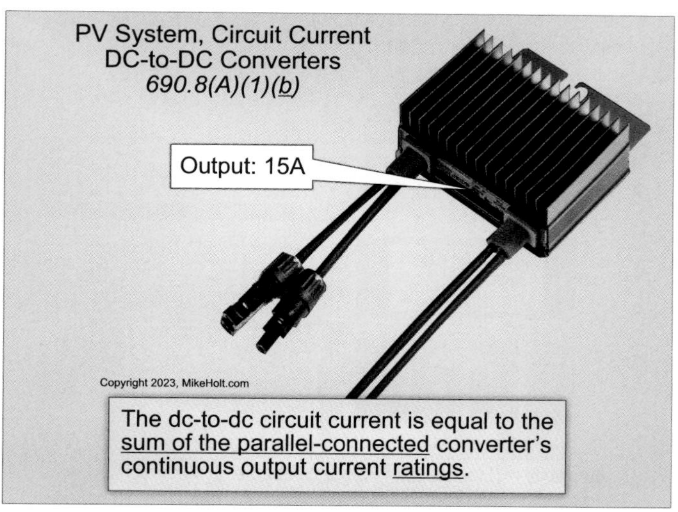

▶Figure 690–42

▶ DC-to-DC Converter Circuit Current Example

Question: *What is the PV dc-to-dc converter output circuit current for a single string, where the nameplate output current rating is 15A?* ▶**Figure 690–43**

(a) 15A *(b) 30A* *(c) 45A* *(d) 60A*

Answer: *(a) 15A*

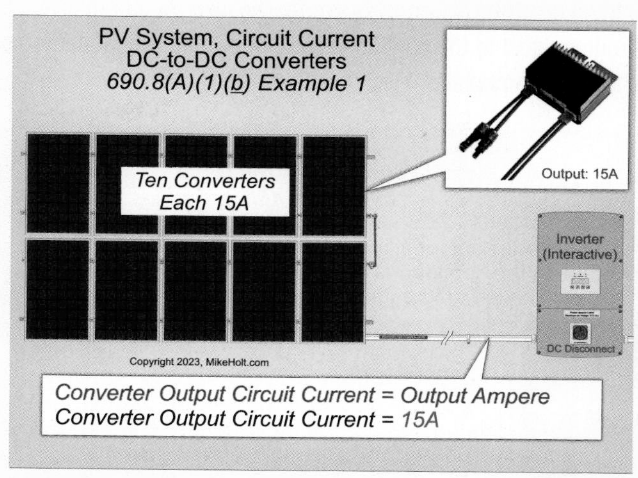

▶Figure 690–43

▶ DC-to-DC Converter Combiner Circuit Current Example

Question: *What is the PV dc-to-dc converter output combiner circuit current for four string circuits connected in parallel, each having a nameplate output current rating of 15A?* ▶**Figure 690–44**

(a) 15A *(b) 30A* *(c) 45A* *(d) 60A*

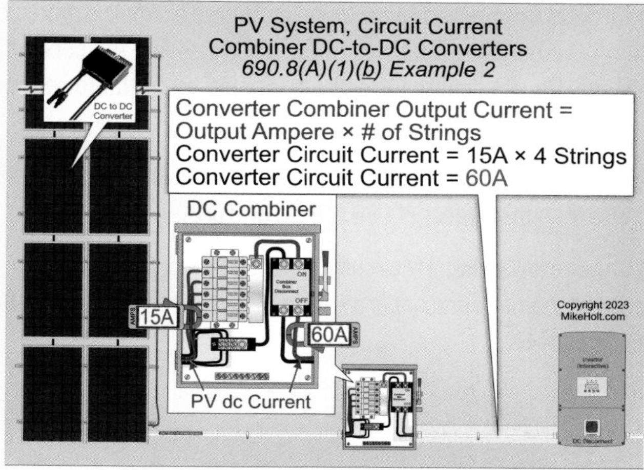

▶Figure 690–44

Solution:

Converter Output Combiner Circuit Current = Output Ampere Rating × Number of Parallel Circuits

Converter Output Combiner Circuit Current = 15A × 4

Converter Output Combiner Circuit Current = 60A

Answer: *(d) 60A*

According to Article 100, "Energize"' means electrically connected to a source of voltage.

Ex: PV system circuits originating within or from arrays not attached to buildings that terminate on the exterior of buildings, and PV system circuits installed in accordance with 230.6, are not considered controlled conductors for rapid shutdown [690.12].

(B) Controlled Limits. The array boundary for a rapid shutdown function is defined as the area 1 ft outside the perimeter of the PV array in all directions. ▶**Figure 690–73**

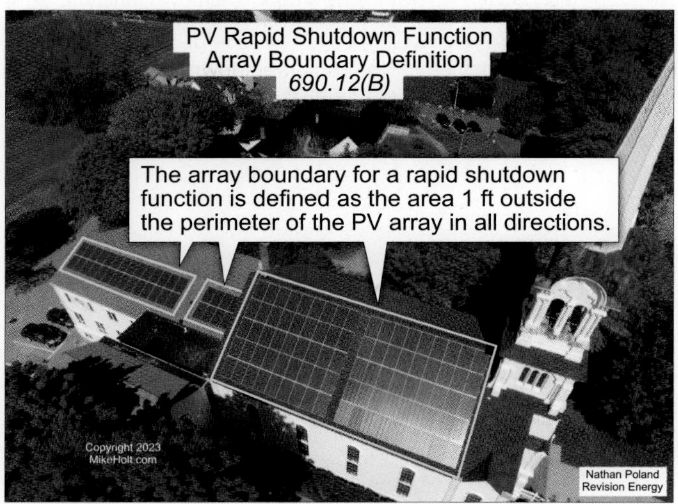

▶**Figure 690–73**

Equipment and systems are permitted to meet the requirements of both inside and outside the array as defined by the manufacturer's instructions included with the listing.

(1) Outside the Array Boundary. PV system dc circuit and inverter output circuit conductors outside the PV array boundary or more than 3 ft from the point of entry inside a building must be limited to 30V within 30 seconds of rapid shutdown initiation. ▶**Figure 690–74**

Author's Comment:

- Thirty seconds provides sufficient time for the dc capacitors of the inverter to discharge to a value of not more than 30V.

(2) Inside the Array Boundary. The PV system rapid shutdown function must comply with one of the following:

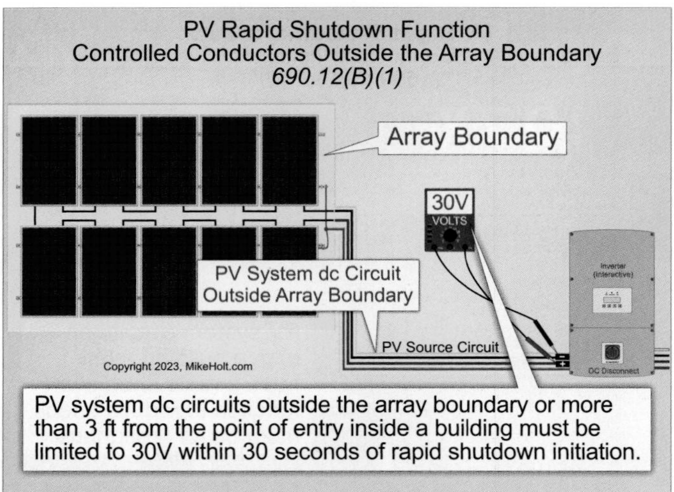

▶**Figure 690–74**

(1) The PV system must provide shock hazard control for firefighters by using a PV hazard control system installed in accordance with the manufacturer's instructions. Where a PV hazard control system requires initiation to transition to a controlled state, the rapid shutdown initiation device [690.12(C)] must perform this initiation.

Note 1: A listed or field-labeled PV hazard control system is comprised of either an individual piece of equipment that fulfills the necessary functions, or multiple pieces of equipment coordinated to perform the functions as described in the manufacturer's instructions to reduce the risk of electric shock hazard for firefighters.

(2) The PV system must provide shock hazard control for firefighters by limiting the voltage inside equipment or between any two conductors of a circuit, or any conductor and ground inside the array boundary to not more than 80V within 30 seconds of rapid shutdown initiation. ▶**Figure 690–75**

(C) Initiation Device. A rapid shutdown initiation device is required to initiate the rapid shutdown function of the PV system. ▶**Figure 690–76**

One- and Two- Family Dwellings. The rapid shutdown function initiation device must be located outside the building at a readily accessible location. ▶**Figure 690–77**

Single PV System. The rapid shutdown initiation must occur by the operation of :

(1) The service disconnect ▶**Figure 690–78**

(2) The PV system disconnect ▶**Figure 690–79**

(3) A readily accessible switch that indicates whether it is in the "off" or "on" position ▶**Figure 690–80**

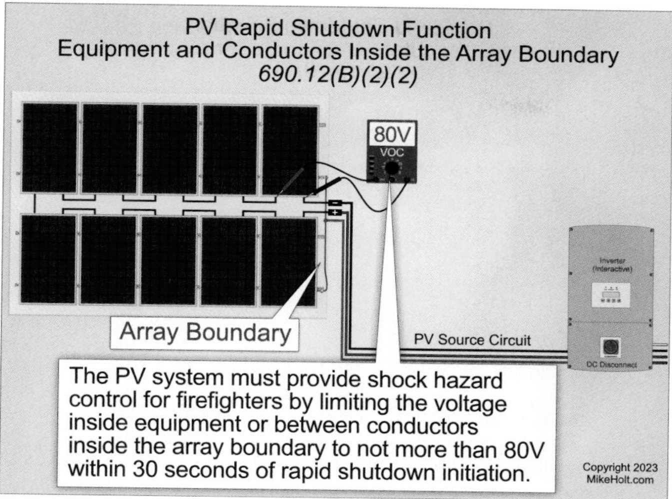

▸**Figure 690–75**

▸**Figure 690–76**

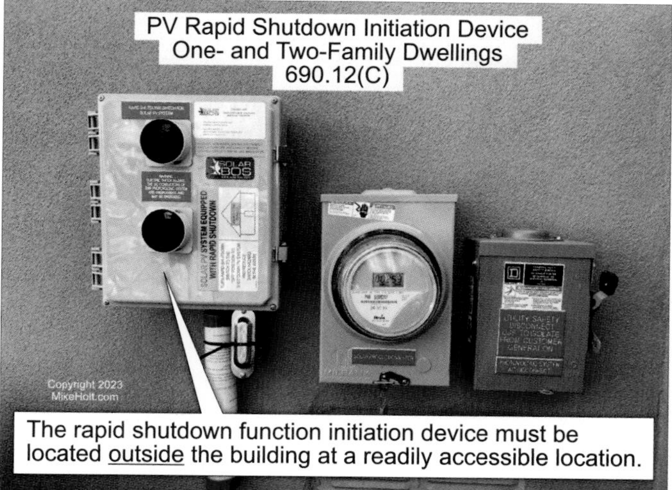

▸**Figure 690–77**

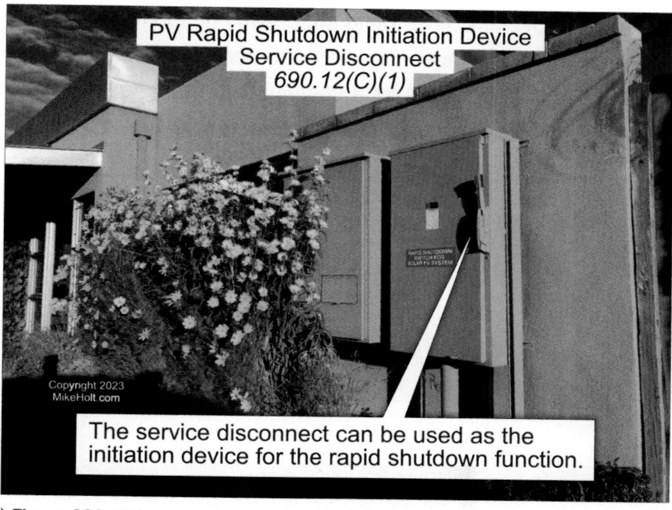

▸**Figure 690–78**

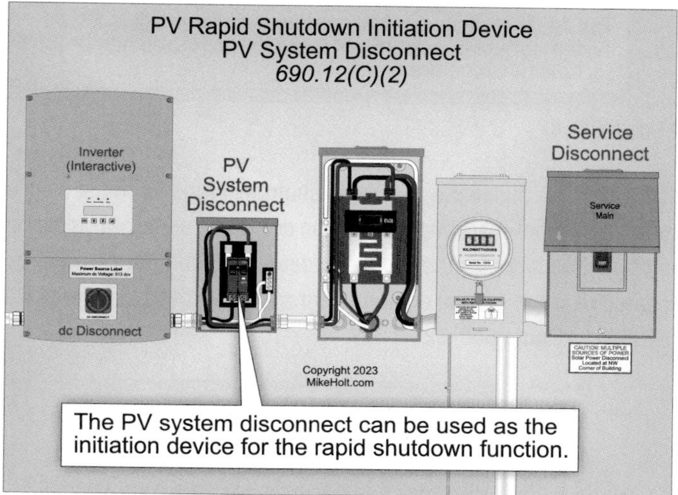

▸**Figure 690–79**

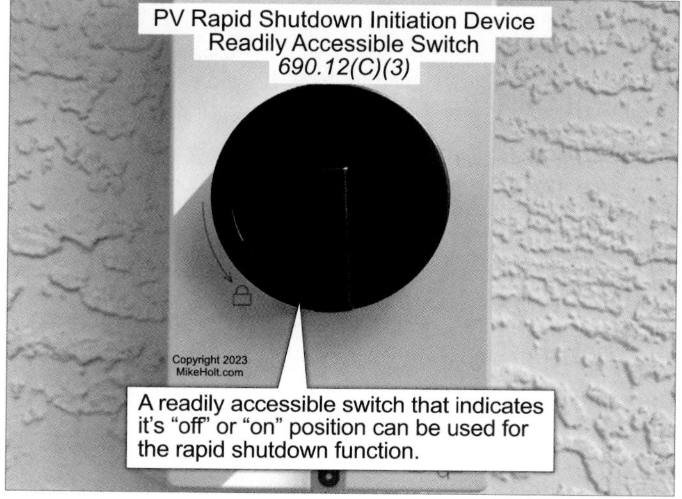

PV Rapid Shutdown Initiation Device
Readily Accessible Switch
690.12(C)(3)
Copyright 2023 MikeHolt.com
A readily accessible switch that indicates it's "off" or "on" position can be used for the rapid shutdown function.

▸**Figure 690–80**

Multiple PV Systems. The rapid shutdown initiation device(s) for multiple PV systems must consist of not more than six switches or six sets of circuit breakers, or a combination of not more than six switches and sets of circuit breakers. ▶**Figure 690–81**

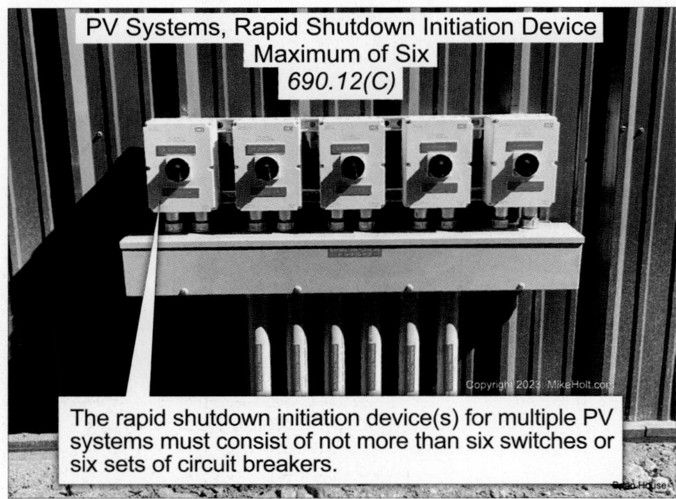

▶**Figure 690–81**

(D) Labels. A building with a rapid shutdown function must have a permanent label indicating the location of all rapid shutdown initiation devices. The label for the rapid shutdown initiation device must be located near the service equipment or at an approved readily visible location. ▶**Figure 690–82**

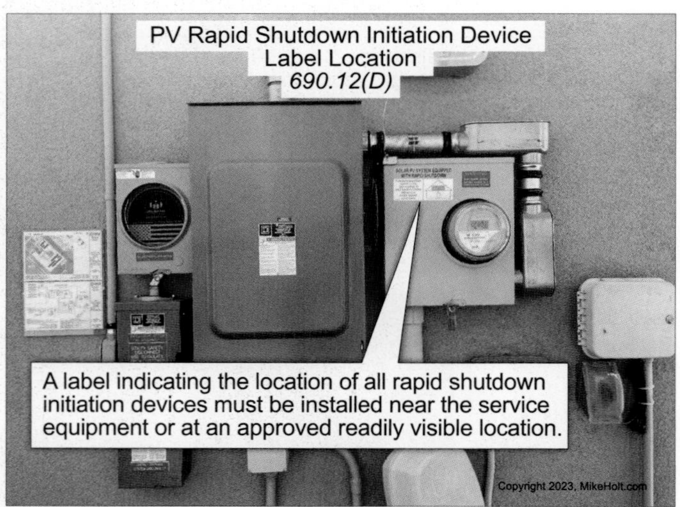

▶**Figure 690–82**

The rapid shutdown initiation device label must include a diagram of the building with a roof and the following words: ▶**Figure 690–83**

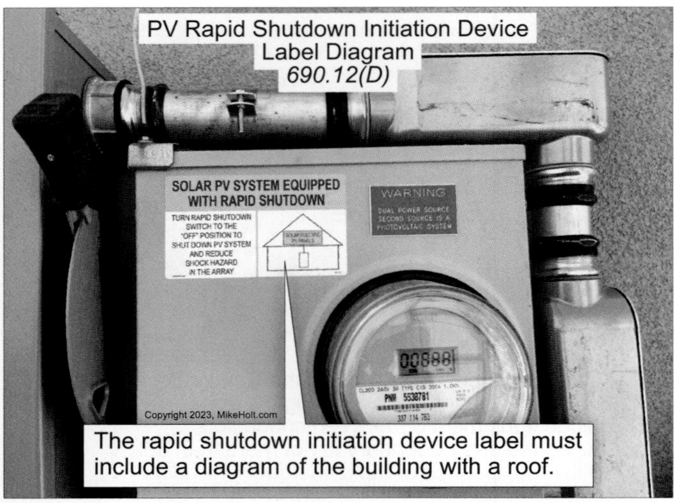

▶**Figure 690–83**

SOLAR PV SYSTEM IS EQUIPPED WITH RAPID SHUTDOWN. TURN RAPID SHUTDOWN SWITCH TO THE "OFF" POSITION TO SHUT DOWN PV SYSTEM AND REDUCE SHOCK HAZARD IN THE ARRAY.

The title "SOLAR PV SYSTEM IS EQUIPPED WITH RAPID SHUTDOWN" must have capitalized characters with a minimum height of 3⁄8 in. All text must be legible and contrast with the background.

Note: See 690.12(D) in the *NEC* for an example.

(1) Buildings with More Than One Rapid Shutdown Type. A building having more than one rapid shutdown type, or a building without a rapid shutdown function, must have a label with a detailed plan view diagram of the roof showing each PV system with a dotted line around areas that remain energized after the rapid shutdown has been initiated.

(2) Rapid Shutdown Switch Label. A rapid shutdown switch must have a label including the following wording with all letters capitalized with a minimum height of 3⁄8 in. in white on a red background located within 3 ft from the rapid shutdown switch. ▶**Figure 690–84**

"RAPID SHUTDOWN SWITCH FOR SOLAR PV SYSTEM"

1st Printing

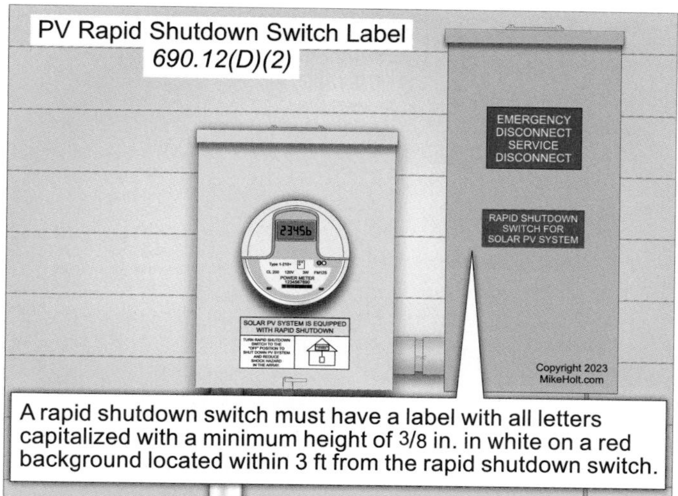
PV Rapid Shutdown Switch Label
690.12(D)(2)
EMERGENCY DISCONNECT SERVICE DISCONNECT
RAPID SHUTDOWN SWITCH FOR SOLAR PV SYSTEM
SOLAR PV SYSTEM IS EQUIPPED WITH RAPID SHUTDOWN
Copyright 2023 MikeHolt.com
A rapid shutdown switch must have a label with all letters capitalized with a minimum height of 3/8 in. in white on a red background located within 3 ft from the rapid shutdown switch.

▶Figure 690–84

Part III. Disconnect

690.13 PV System Disconnect

A readily accessible disconnecting means is required to disconnect power from each PV system permitted by 690.4.

(A) Location.

(1) Readily Accessible. The PV system disconnect must be readily accessible. ▶**Figure 690–85**

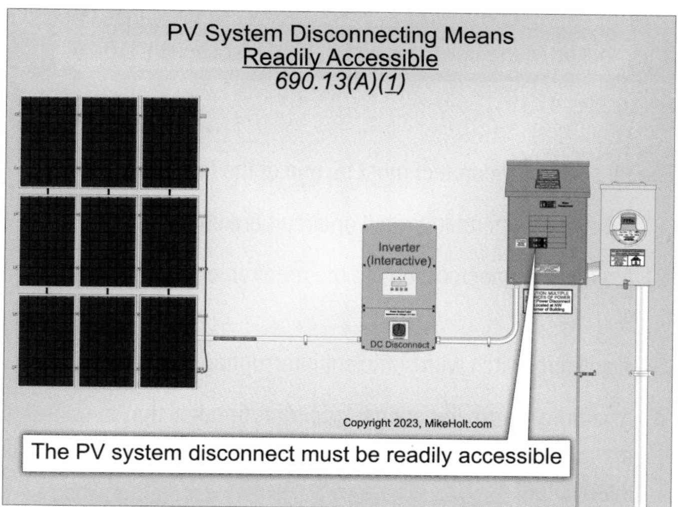
PV System Disconnecting Means
Readily Accessible
690.13(A)(1)
Inverter (Interactive)
DC Disconnect
Copyright 2023, MikeHolt.com
The PV system disconnect must be readily accessible

▶Figure 690–85

(2) Enclosure Door or Cover. The door or hinged cover for the PV system disconnect must be locked or require a tool to open.

(B) Marking. The PV system disconnect must indicate if it is in the open (off) or closed (on) position and be marked "PV SYSTEM DISCONNECT" or equivalent. ▶**Figure 690–86**

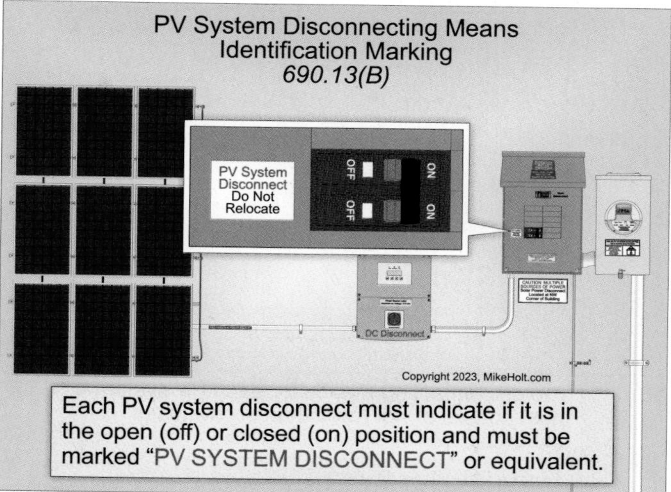
PV System Disconnecting Means
Identification Marking
690.13(B)
PV System Disconnect Do Not Relocate
OFF
ON
DC Disconnect
Copyright 2023, MikeHolt.com
Each PV system disconnect must indicate if it is in the open (off) or closed (on) position and must be marked "PV SYSTEM DISCONNECT" or equivalent.

▶Figure 690–86

Where the line and load terminals of the PV system disconnect may be energized when the disconnect is in the open (off) position, the disconnect must be marked with the following or equivalent: ▶**Figure 690–87**

WARNING—ELECTRIC SHOCK HAZARD
TERMINALS ON THE LINE AND LOAD SIDES MAY
BE ENERGIZED IN THE OPEN POSITION

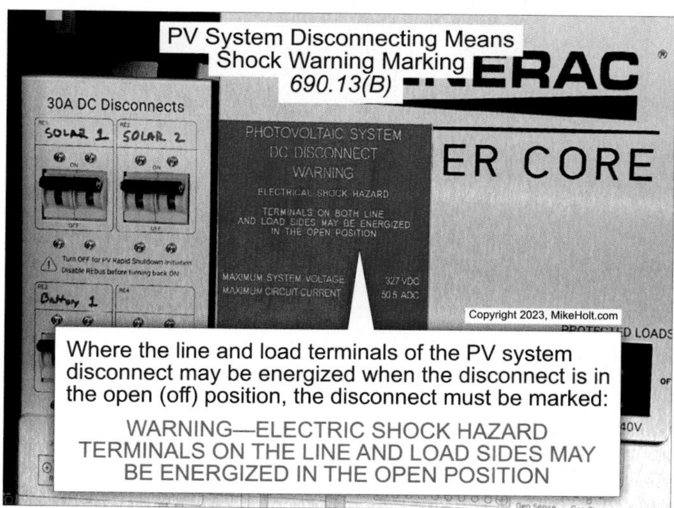
PV System Disconnecting Means
Shock Warning Marking
690.13(B)
30A DC Disconnects
PHOTOVOLTAIC SYSTEM
DC DISCONNECT
WARNING
ELECTRICAL SHOCK HAZARD
TERMINALS ON BOTH LINE AND LOAD SIDES MAY BE ENERGIZED IN THE OPEN POSITION
MAXIMUM SYSTEM VOLTAGE
MAXIMUM CIRCUIT CURRENT
ER CORE
Copyright 2023, MikeHolt.com
Where the line and load terminals of the PV system disconnect may be energized when the disconnect is in the open (off) position, the disconnect must be marked:
WARNING—ELECTRIC SHOCK HAZARD
TERMINALS ON THE LINE AND LOAD SIDES MAY BE ENERGIZED IN THE OPEN POSITION

▶Figure 690–87

The warning markings on the disconnect must be permanently affixed and have sufficient durability to withstand the environment involved [110.21(B)].

(C) Maximum Number of Disconnects. The disconnecting means for each PV system must consist of not more than six switches and/or six sets of circuit breakers. ▸Figure 690–88

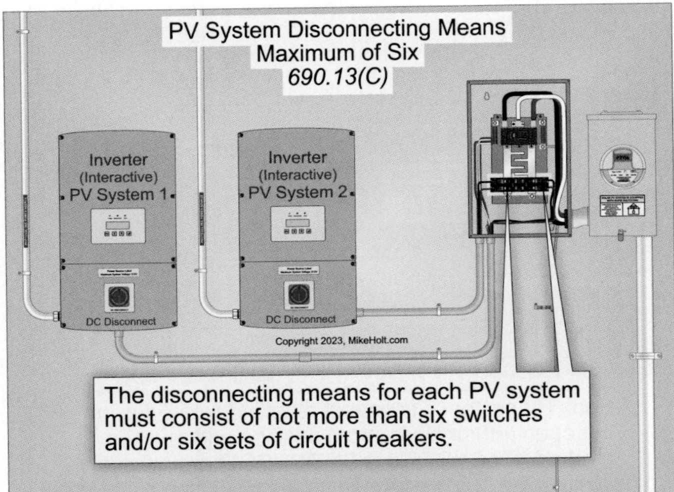

▸Figure 690–88

A single PV system disconnect is permitted for the combined ac output of one or more microinverters or ac modules. ▸Figure 690–89

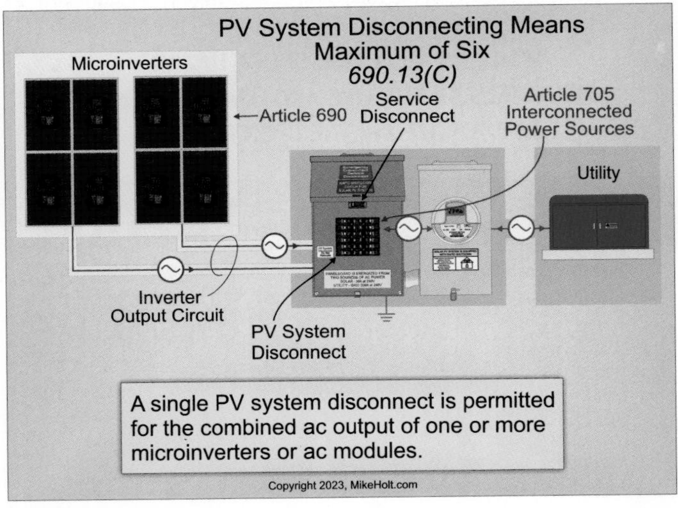

▸Figure 690–89

Note: This requirement of a maximum of six PV system disconnects does not limit the number of PV systems on a premises [690.4(D)].

(D) Ratings. The PV system disconnect must be rated for the circuit current, the available fault current, and voltage. ▸Figure 690–90

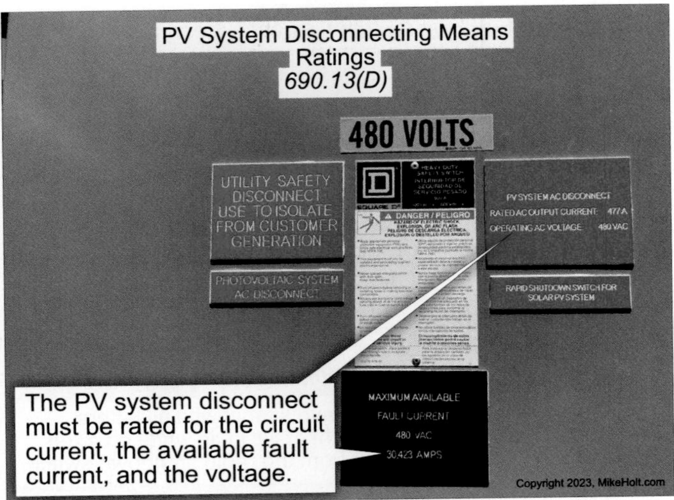

▸Figure 690–90

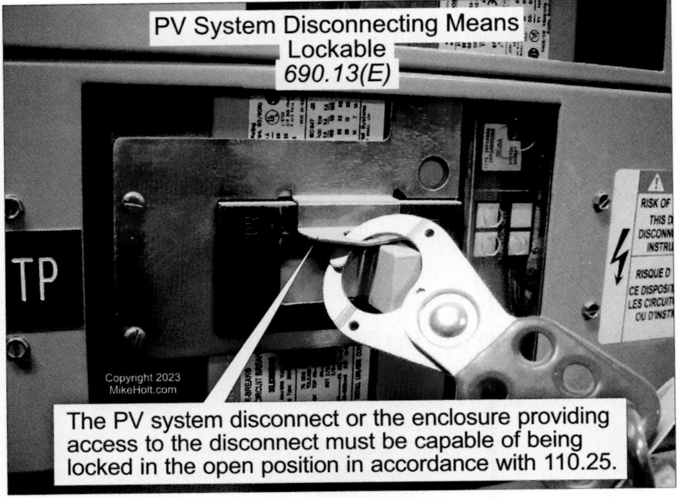

▸Figure 690–91

(E) Type of Disconnect. The PV system disconnect or the enclosure providing access to the disconnect must be capable of being locked in the open position in accordance with 110.25. ▸Figure 690–91

The PV system disconnect must be one of the following types:

(1) A manually operable switch or circuit breaker

(2) A mating connector meeting the requirements of 690.33(D)(1) or (D)(3)

(3) A pull-out switch with sufficient interrupting rating

(4) A remote-controlled switch or circuit breaker that is operable manually and is opened automatically when control power is interrupted

(5) A device listed or approved for the intended application

Note: Circuit breakers marked "line" and "load" may not be suitable for backfeed or reverse current applications. ▸Figure 690–92

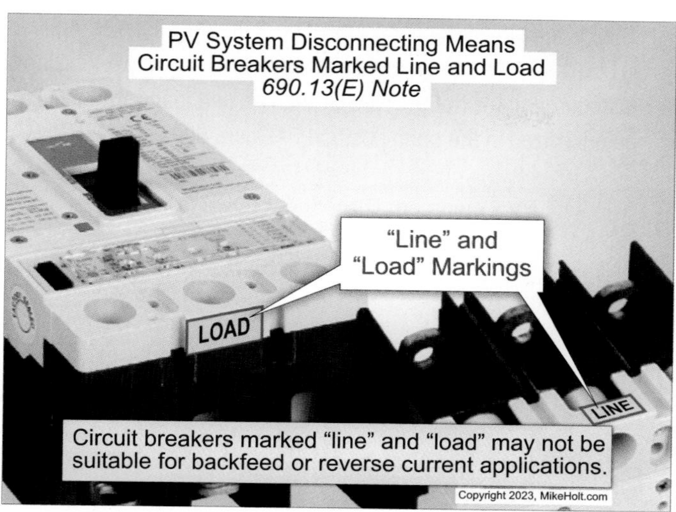

▸Figure 690-92

690.15 PV Equipment Disconnect/Isolating Device

An equipment disconnect or isolating device must be provided for ac PV modules, fuses, dc-to-dc converters, and inverters in accordance with the following: ▸**Figure 690-93**

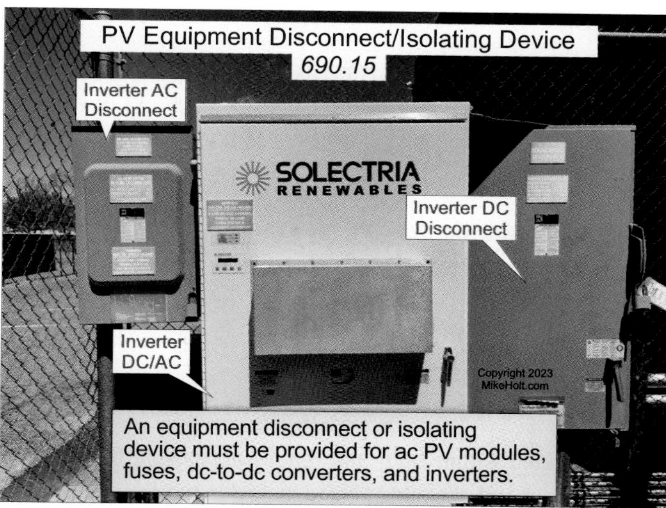

▸Figure 690-93

(A) PV Equipment Disconnecting Means. Where disconnects are required to isolate equipment, the disconnect must be one of the following types:

(1) Over 30A Circuits (load-break). A disconnect in accordance with 690.15(C).

(2) Isolating Device (not load-break). An isolating device that is part of listed equipment.

(3) Not over 30A Circuits (not load-break). An isolating device in accordance with 690.15(B).

(B) PV Equipment Isolating Device (not load-break). An isolating device not rated for interrupting the circuit current must be marked "Do Not Disconnect Under Load" or "Not for Current Interrupting."

Isolating devices must be one of the following types:

(1) A mating connector meeting the requirements of 690.33 if listed and identified for use with specific equipment ▸**Figure 690-94**

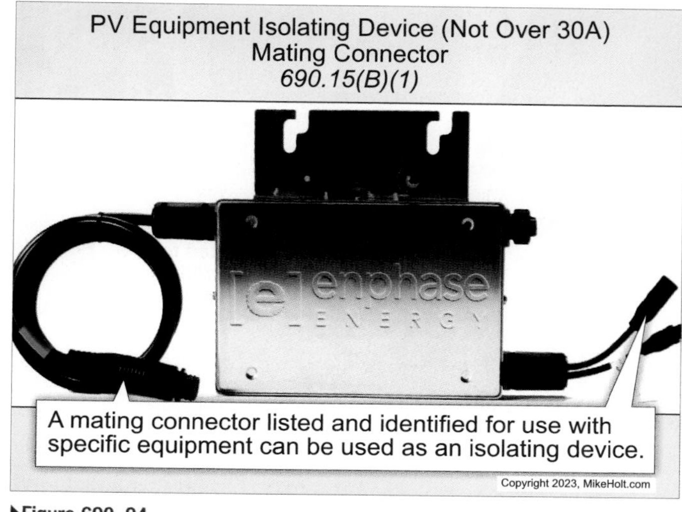

▸Figure 690-94

(2) A finger-safe fuse holder ▸**Figure 690-95**

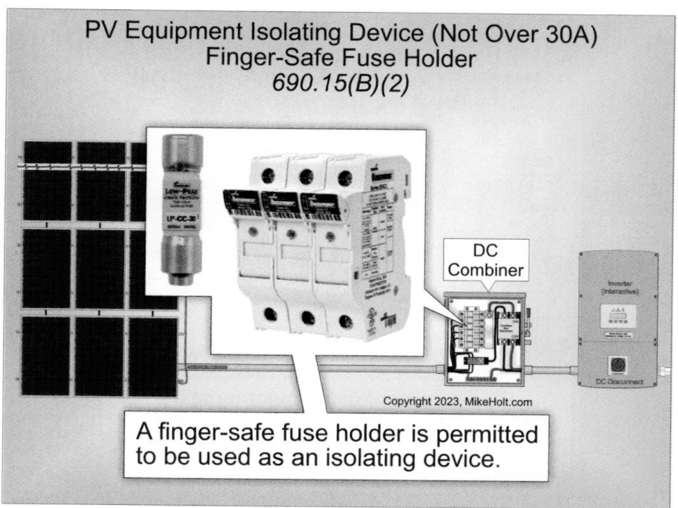

PV Equipment Isolating Device (Not Over 30A)
Finger-Safe Fuse Holder
690.15(B)(2)
DC
Combiner
Copyright 2023, MikeHolt.com
A finger-safe fuse holder is permitted to be used as an isolating device.

▸Figure 690-95

(3) A device that requires a tool to place it in the open (off) position

(4) A device listed for the intended application

(C) PV Equipment Disconnecting Means (load-break). A PV equipment disconnect must comply with all the following:

(1) The PV equipment disconnect must be rated for the circuit current, the available fault current, and voltage. ▸Figure 690–96

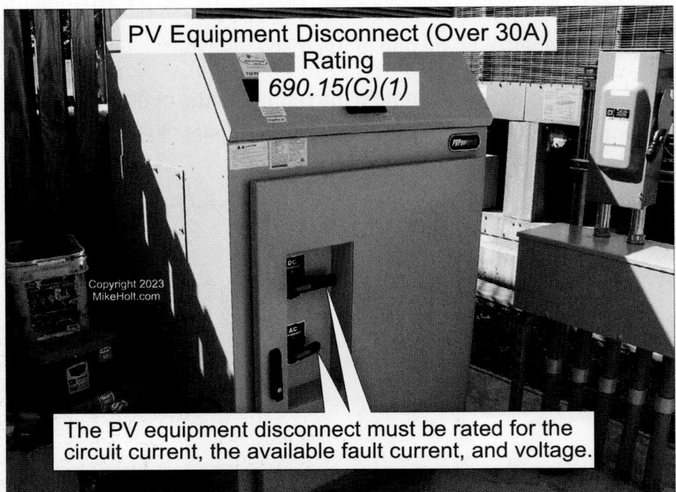
PV Equipment Disconnect (Over 30A)
Rating
690.15(C)(1)
Copyright 2023
MikeHolt.com
The PV equipment disconnect must be rated for the circuit current, the available fault current, and voltage.

▸Figure 690–96

(2) The PV equipment disconnect must simultaneously disconnect all current-carrying circuit conductors to which it is connected.

(3) The PV equipment disconnect must be externally operable without exposing the operator to contact with energized parts and indicate whether it is in the open (off) or closed (on) position. ▸Figure 690–97

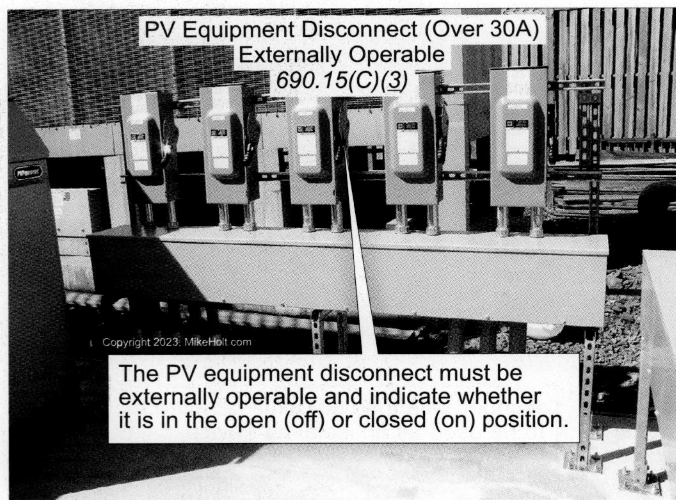
PV Equipment Disconnect (Over 30A)
Externally Operable
690.15(C)(3)
Copyright 2023, MikeHolt.com
The PV equipment disconnect must be externally operable and indicate whether it is in the open (off) or closed (on) position.

▸Figure 690–97

(4) The PV equipment disconnect must be of the same type as required in 690.13(E). An equipment disconnect must have a warning label in accordance with 690.13(B) if the line and load terminals can be energized in the open position. ▸Figure 690–98

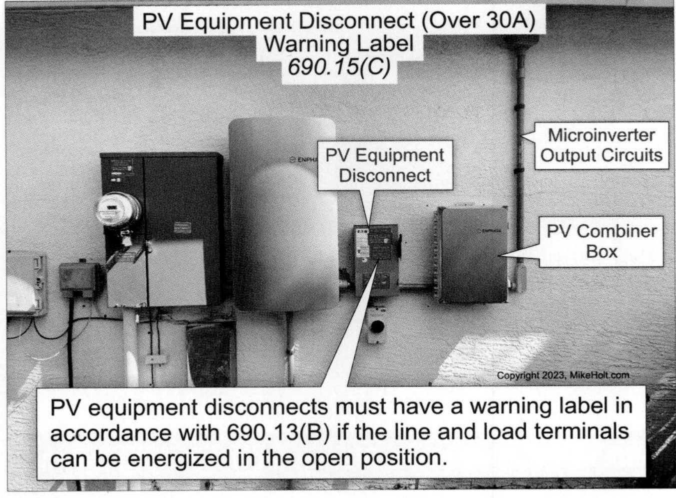
PV Equipment Disconnect (Over 30A)
Warning Label
690.15(C)
Microinverter Output Circuits
PV Equipment Disconnect
PV Combiner Box
Copyright 2023, MikeHolt.com
PV equipment disconnects must have a warning label in accordance with 690.13(B) if the line and load terminals can be energized in the open position.

▸Figure 690–98

The warning markings on the disconnect must be permanently affixed and have sufficient durability to withstand the environment involved [110.21(B)].

Note: A common installation practice is to terminate the dc circuit conductors on the line side of a disconnect which will de-energize load-side terminals, blades, and fuses when the disconnect is in the open position.

(D) Location and Control. PV equipment isolating devices and equipment disconnects for PV equipment must comply with any one of the following:

(1) Located within the PV equipment

(2) Located within sight and readily accessible from the PV equipment

(3) Not located within sight and readily accessible from the PV equipment and capable of being locked in the open position in accordance with 110.25

(4) Remote-control with one of the following:

a. The disconnect and their controls are within the same equipment.

b. The disconnect must be capable of being locked in the open position in accordance with 110.25 and the location of the controls are marked on the disconnect.

Part IV. Wiring Methods

690.31 Wiring Methods and Materials

(A) Wiring Systems.

(1) Serviceability. Where wiring devices with integral enclosures are used, a sufficient length of cable must be provided to facilitate replacement.

(2) Where Readily Accessible. PV system dc circuit conductors operating at over 30V that are readily accessible to unqualified persons must be guarded, or installed within a raceway, in multiconductor jacketed cable, or Type MC cable. ▶Figure 690-99 and ▶Figure 690-100

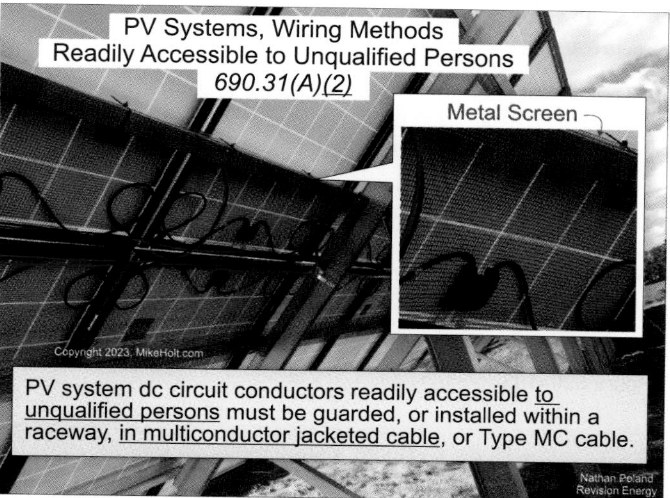

▶Figure 690-99

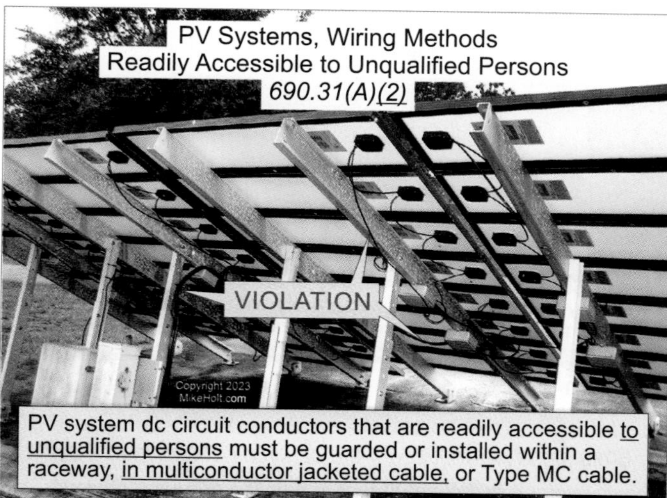

▶Figure 690-100

(3) Conductor Ampacity. PV circuit conductors with insulation rated at 105°C and 125°C can have their ampacities determined by Table 690.31(A)(3)(1) and corrected by Table 690.31(A)(3)(2).

Table 690.31(A)(3)(1) Conductor Ampacity, Not More Than Three Current-Carrying Conductors in Raceway, Cable, or Earth, with Ambient Temperature of 30°C (86°F)

Wire Size AWG	PVC, CPE, XLPE 105°C	XLPE, EPDM 125°C
14	29	31
12	36	39
10	46	50
8	64	69
6	81	87
4	109	118
3	129	139
2	143	154
1	168	181
1/0	193	208
2/0	229	247
3/0	263	284
4/0	301	325

Table 690.31(A)(3)(2) Correction Factors

Ambient Temperature (°C)	Temperature Rating of Conductor		Ambient Temperature (°F)
	105°C (221°F)	125°C (257°F)	
31–35	0.97	0.97	87–95
36–40	0.93	0.95	96–104
41–45	0.89	0.92	105–113
46–50	0.86	0.89	114–122
51–55	0.82	0.86	123–131

(4) Special Equipment. Wiring systems specifically listed for PV systems are permitted.

See 110.14(C) for conductor temperature limitations due to termination provisions.

(B) Identification and Grouping.

(1) Mixing Conductors of Different Systems.

PV System Direct-Current Circuit Conductors. PV system dc circuit conductors are permitted to be installed in the same enclosure, cable, or raceway with other PV system dc circuit conductors, unless prohibited by equipment listing.

PV System Alternating-Current Circuit Conductors. PV system dc circuit conductors are not permitted to be installed in the same enclosure, cable, or raceway with inverter ac output circuit conductors or other conductors unless separated by a barrier or partition.

Ex. Where all conductors or cables have an insulation rating equal to at least the maximum circuit voltage applied to any conductor:

(1) Multiconductor jacketed ac cables can in the same enclosure with dc circuits where all circuits serve the PV system.

(2) Inverter output ac circuits can be in the same enclosure or wireway with PV system dc circuits that are identified and grouped in accordance with 690.31(B)(2) and (B)(3). ▸**Figure 690–101**

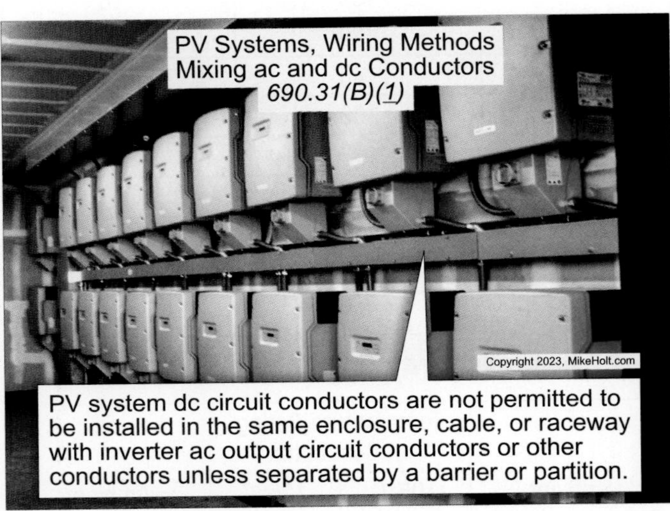

▸**Figure 690–101**

(3) Multiconductor jacketed cable, Type MC cable, or listed wiring harnesses identified for the application can be in the same enclosure or raceway with non-PV system circuits.

(2) Polarity Identification of Direct-Current Conductors. PV system dc circuit conductors must have all termination, connection, and splice points permanently identified for polarity by color coding, marking tape, tagging, or in accordance with 690.31(B)(2)(a) and (B)(2)(b). ▸**Figure 690–102**

(a) Conductors must be identified by an approved permanent marking means such as labeling, sleeving, or shrink-tubing that is suitable for the conductor size.

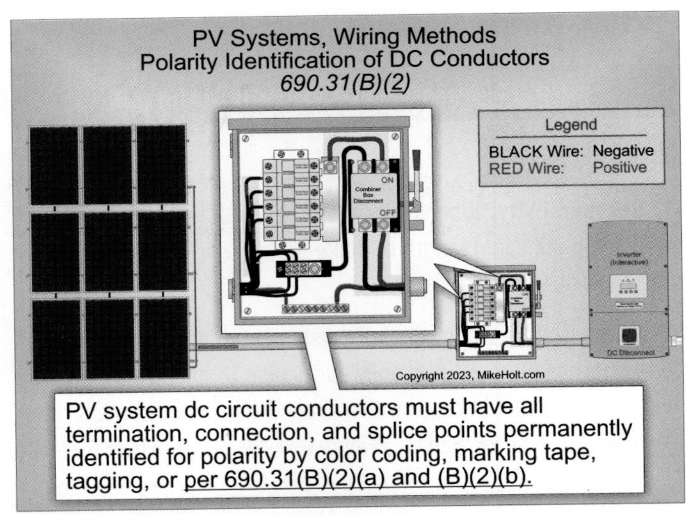

▸**Figure 690–102**

(b) The positive sign (+) or the word "POSITIVE" or "POS" for the positive conductor and the negative sign (−) or the word "NEGATIVE" or "NEG" for the negative conductor. Polarity marking must be durable and be of a color other than green, white, gray, or red.

(3) Grouping of Conductors. PV system dc and ac conductors in the same enclosure or wireway must be grouped separately with cable ties or similar means at least once and at intervals not to exceed 6 ft. ▸**Figure 690–103**

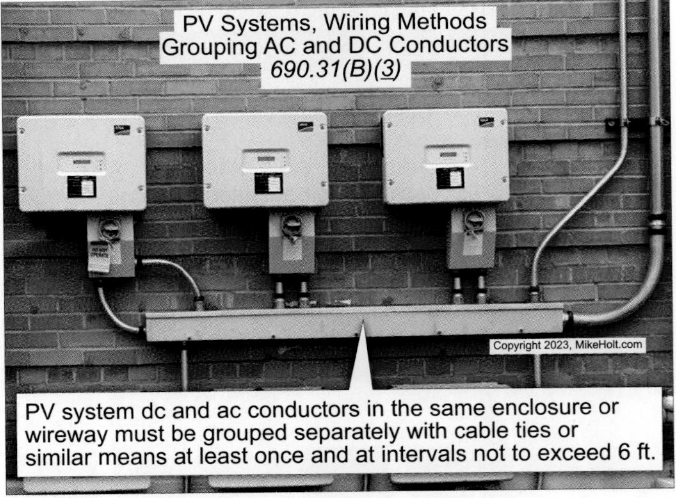

▸**Figure 690–103**

Ex: Grouping is not required if the dc circuit enters from a cable or raceway unique to the circuit that makes the grouping obvious.

(C) Cables. Type PV wire, Type PV cable, and Type DG cable must be listed.

1st Printing

(1) Single Conductor Cable, Exposed. Single conductor cables for PV systems must comply with 690.31(C)(1)(a) through (C)(1)(c).

(a) Cable Types. Single conductor cables within the PV array that are exposed outdoors must be one of the following types: ▸Figure 690–104

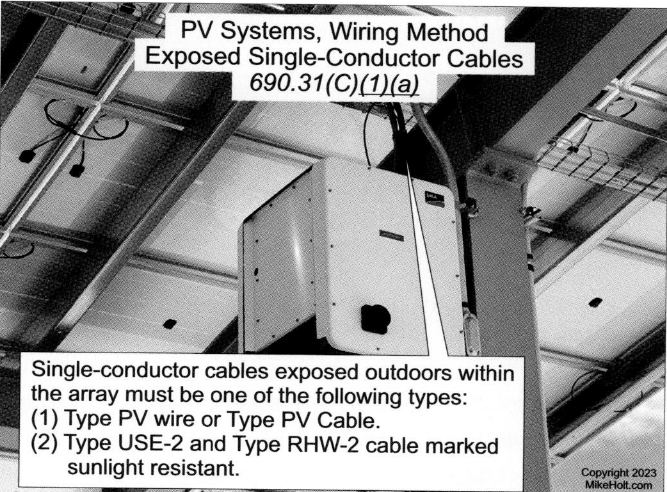

▸Figure 690–104

(1) Type PV wire or Type PV cable

(2) Type USE-2 and Type RHW-2 cable marked sunlight resistant

(b) Support, Cables 8 AWG and Smaller. Exposed cables 8 AWG or smaller must be supported and secured at intervals not to exceed 24 in. by cable ties, straps, hangers, or similar fittings listed and identified for securement and support in outdoor locations.

(c) Support, Cables Larger than 8 AWG. Exposed cables larger than 8 AWG must be supported and secured at intervals not to exceed 54 in. by cable ties, straps, hangers, or similar fittings listed and identified for securement and support in outdoor locations.

(2) Cable Tray. Single-conductor Type PV wire, Type PV cable, or Type DG cable can be installed in cable trays in outdoor locations.

Where installed in uncovered cable trays, the ampacity of single-conductor PV wire smaller than 1/0 AWG and the adjustment factors for 1/0 AWG single-conductor cables in 392.80(A)(2) can be used.

Where single-conductor PV wire smaller than 1/0 AWG is installed in ladder ventilated trough cable trays, the following apply:

(1) All single conductors must be installed in a single layer.

(2) Conductors that are bound together to comprise each circuit pair can be installed in other than a single layer.

(3) The sum of the diameters of all single-conductor cables must not exceed the cable tray width.

(3) Multiconductor Jacketed Cable. Where a multiconductor jacketed cable is part of a listed PV assembly, the cable must be installed in accordance with the manufacturer's instructions. ▸Figure 690–105

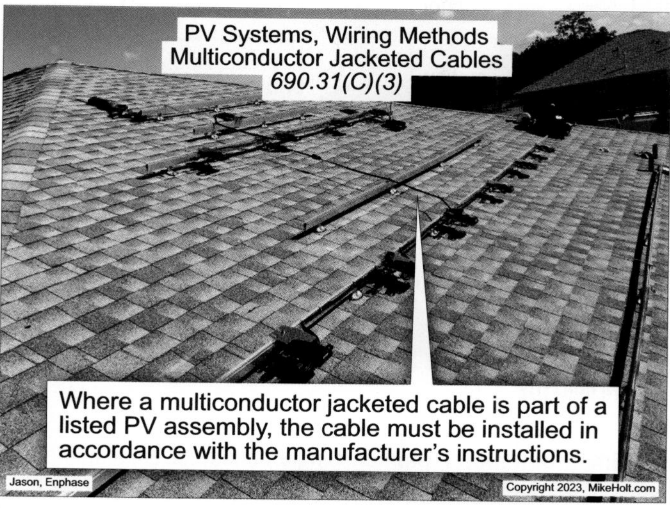

▸Figure 690–105

(4) Flexible Cords and Cables for Tracking PV Arrays. Flexible cords connected to moving parts of tracking PV arrays must be installed in accordance with Article 400, be identified as hard-service cord or portable power cable, be suitable for extra-hard usage, and be listed for outdoor use, water resistant, and sunlight resistant. ▸Figure 690–106

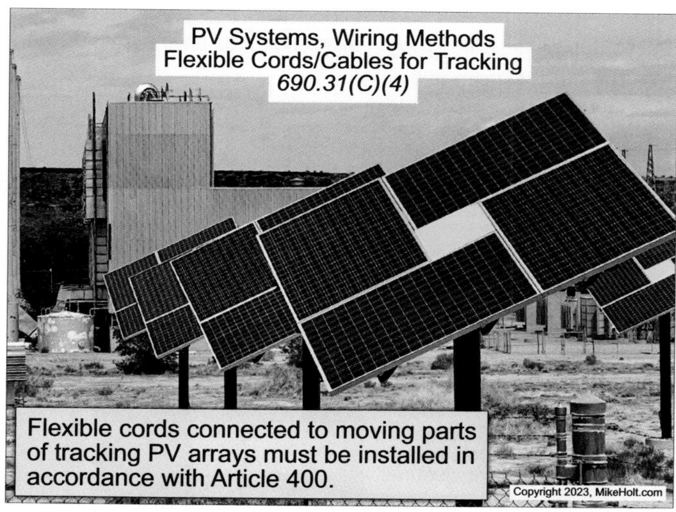

▸Figure 690–106

(5) Flexible, Fine-Stranded Cables. Flexible, finely-stranded cables must terminate on terminals, lugs, devices, or connectors identified for the use of finely stranded conductors in accordance with 110.14. ▸Figure 690–107

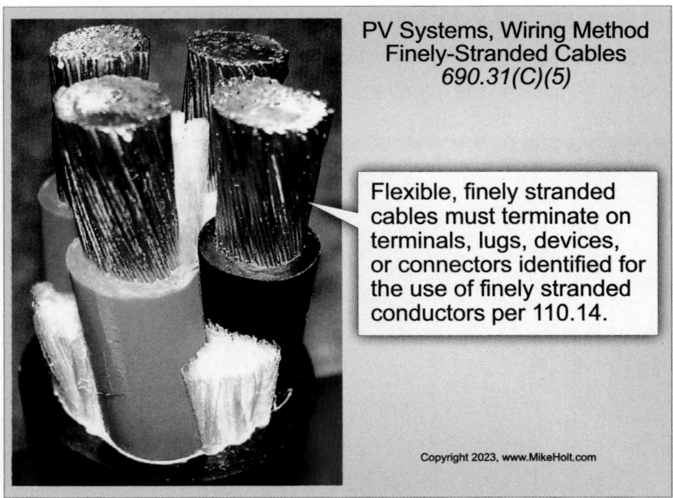

▸Figure 690–107

(6) Small-Conductor Cables. Single conductor cables listed for outdoor use that are sunlight resistant and moisture resistant in sizes 16 AWG and 18 AWG are permitted for module interconnections where the cables have an ampacity for the load.

(D) PV System Direct-Current Circuits On or In Buildings. Wiring methods for PV system dc circuits on or in buildings must comply with the following additional requirements:

(1) Metal Raceways and Enclosures. PV system dc circuit conductors inside a building must be installed in a metal raceway, Type MC cable that complies with 250.118(A)(10)(b) and metal enclosures. ▸**Figure 690–108** and ▸**Figure 690–109**

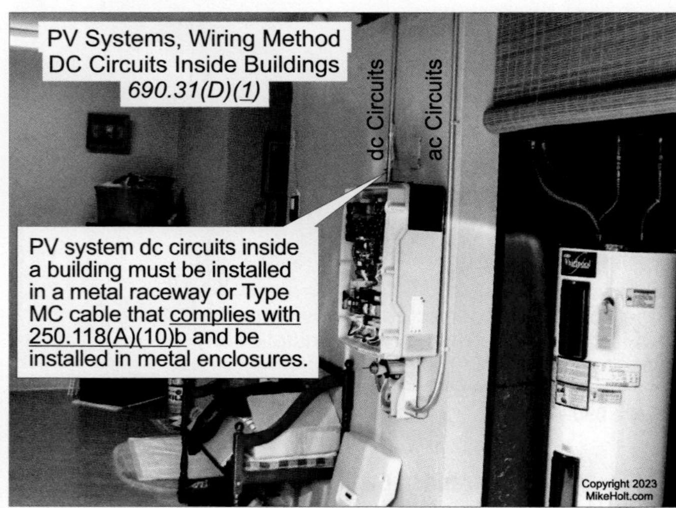

PV Systems, Wiring Method
DC Circuits Inside Buildings
690.31(D)(1)
dc Circuits
ac Circuits
PV system dc circuits inside a building must be installed in a metal raceway or Type MC cable that complies with 250.118(A)(10)b and be installed in metal enclosures.
Copyright 2023 MikeHolt.com

▸Figure 690–108

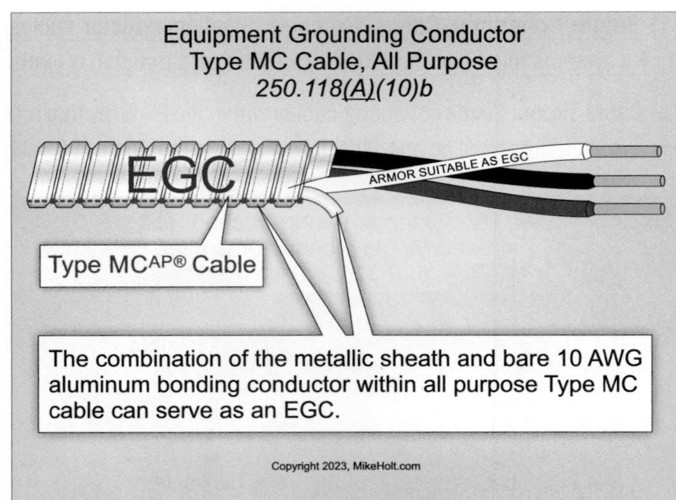

Equipment Grounding Conductor
Type MC Cable, All Purpose
250.118(A)(10)b
EGC
ARMOR SUITABLE AS EGC
Type MCAP® Cable
The combination of the metallic sheath and bare 10 AWG aluminum bonding conductor within all purpose Type MC cable can serve as an EGC.
Copyright 2023, MikeHolt.com

▸Figure 690–109

Ex: PV hazard control system conductors that are installed for a rapid shutdown application in accordance with 690.12(B)(2)(1) can be provided with (or listed for use with) nonmetallic enclosures, nonmetallic raceways, and nonmetallic cables at the point of penetration of the building.

(2) Marking and Labeling. Unless located and arranged so the purpose is evident, the following wiring methods and enclosures on or in buildings containing PV system dc circuit conductors must be marked with a permanent label containing the words "PHOTOVOLTAIC POWER SOURCE" or "SOLAR PV DC CIRCUIT." ▸**Figure 690–110**

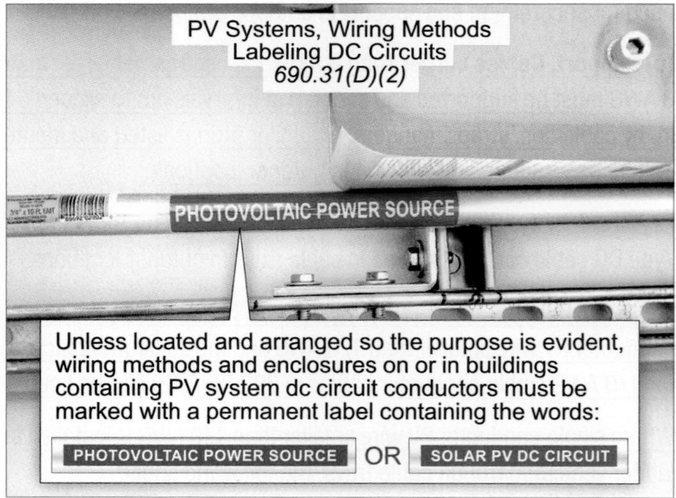

▸Figure 690–110

(1) Exposed raceways, cable trays, and other wiring methods

(2) Covers or enclosures of pull boxes and junction boxes

(3) Conduit bodies having unused openings

The label must be visible after installation. The letters must be capitalized and be a minimum height of ⅜ in. in white on a red background. ▶Figure 690–111

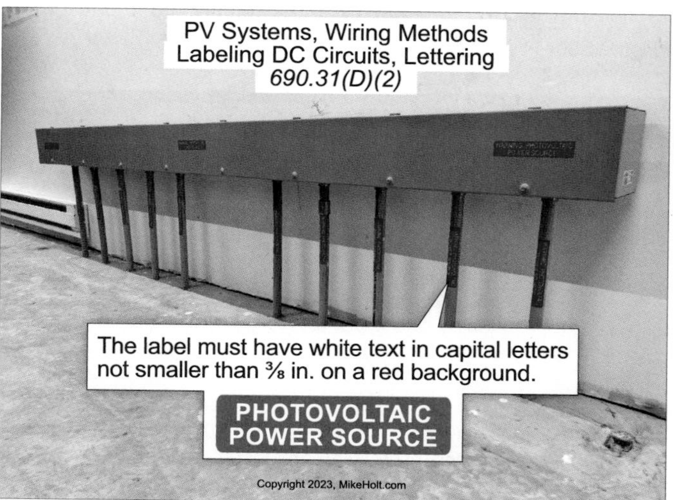

▶Figure 690–111

Labels must appear on every section of the wiring system that is separated by enclosures, walls, partitions, ceilings, or floors. Spacing between labels is not permitted to be more than 10 ft, and the label must be suitable for the environment. ▶Figure 690–112

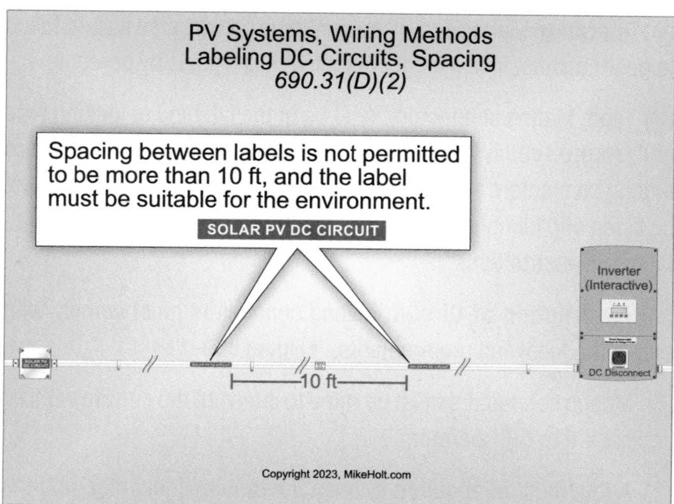

▶Figure 690–112

(F) Wiring Methods and Mounting Systems. Roof-mounted PV array mounting systems are permitted to be held in place with an approved means other than those required by 110.13 and must utilize wiring methods that allow for any expected movement of the array.

Note: Expected movement of unattached PV arrays is often included in structural calculations.

(G) Over 1000V Direct Current. PV system dc circuits greater than 1000V: ▶Figure 690–113

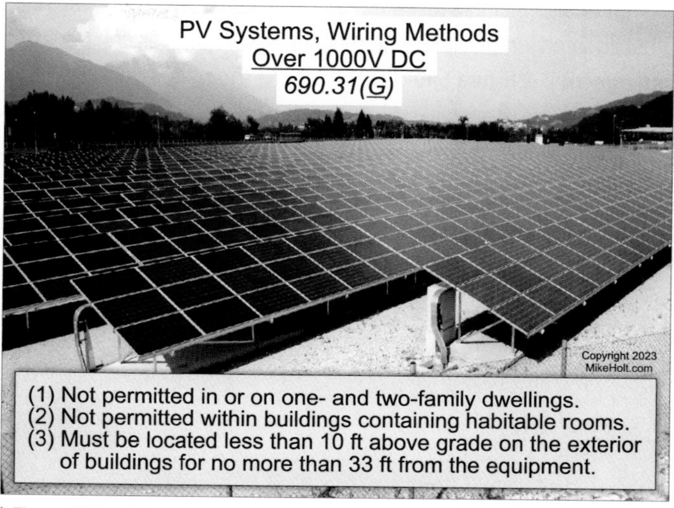

▶Figure 690–113

(1) Are not permitted on or in one- and two-family dwellings.

(2) Are not permitted within buildings containing habitable rooms.

(3) Must be located less than 10 ft above grade on the exterior of buildings and cannot be attached to the building surface for more than 33 ft from the equipment.

According to Article 100, "Habitable Room" is defined as a room for living, sleeping, eating, or cooking, excluding bathrooms, toilet rooms, closets, hallways, storage or utility spaces, and similar areas. ▶Figure 690–114

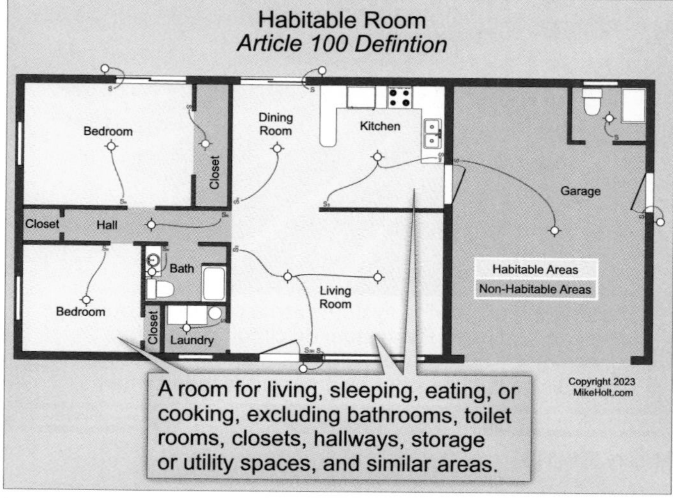

▶Figure 690–114

690.32 Component Interconnections

Fittings and connectors for PV systems with concealed wiring methods must be listed for the on-site interconnection of modules or other array components. ▶Figure 690–115

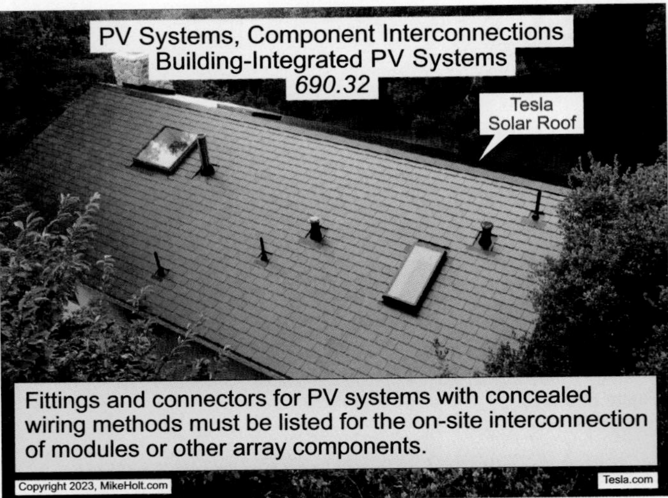

▶Figure 690–115

Author's Comment:

- Building-integrated PV systems are a part of the buildings structure and have PV system dc circuit conductors concealed by built-up, laminate, or membrane roofing materials as well as solar shingle and facade systems. ▶Figure 690–116

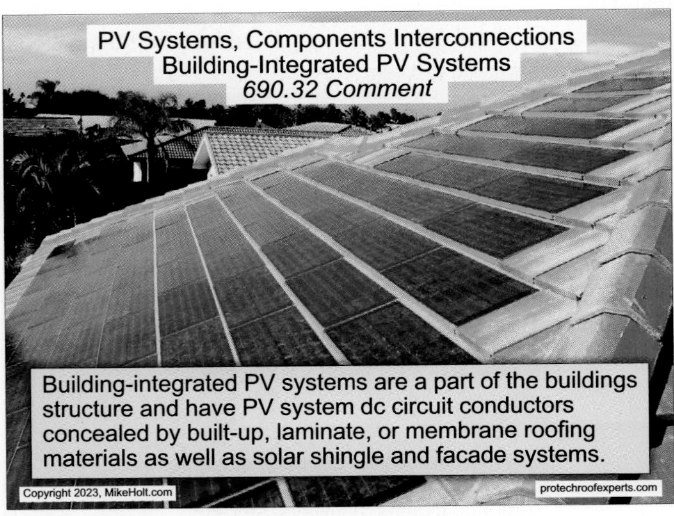

▶Figure 690–116

690.33 Connectors (Mating)

Mating connectors, other than listed connectors for building-integrated PV systems as covered in 690.32, must comply with the following: ▶Figure 690–117

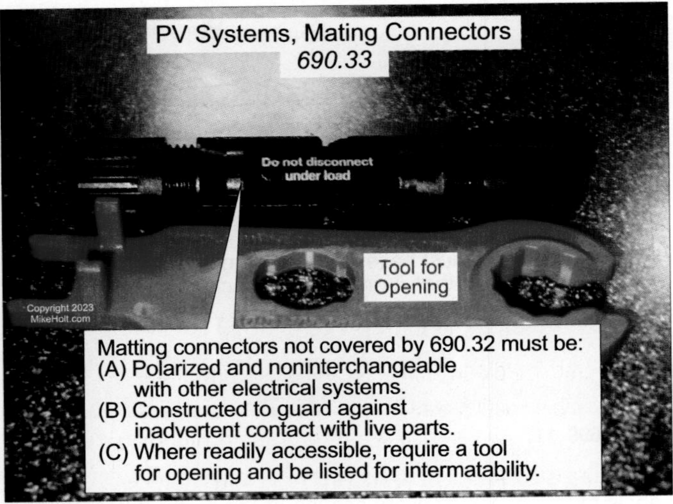

▶Figure 690–117

(A) Configuration. Mating connectors must be polarized and be noninterchangeable with other electrical systems on the premises.

(B) Guarding. Mating connectors must be constructed and installed to guard against inadvertent contact with live parts by persons.

(C) Type. Mating connectors must be of the latching or locking type and, where readily accessible, require a tool for opening. Where mating connectors are not of the identical type and brand, they must be listed and identified for intermatability as described in the manufacturer's instructions.

(D) Interruption of Circuit. Mating connectors must comply with one of the following requirements. ▶Figure 690–118

(1) Mating connectors must be rated to interrupt the current without hazard to the operator.

(2) A tool must be required to open the mating connector, and the mating connectors must be marked "DO NOT DISCONNECT UNDER LOAD" OR "NOT FOR CURRENT INTERRUPTING."

(3) Mating connectors supplied as part of listed equipment must be used in accordance with instructions provided with the listed connected equipment.

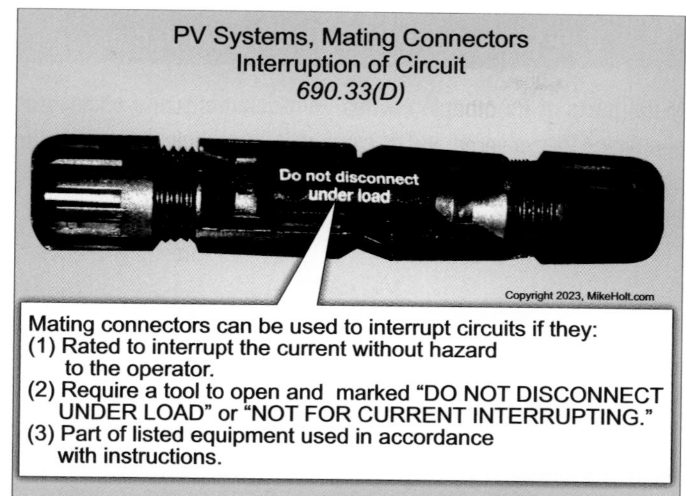

▸Figure 690–118

Note: Some listed equipment, such as micro-inverters, are evaluated to make use of mating connectors as disconnect devices even though the mating connectors are marked as "DO NOT DISCONNECT UNDER LOAD" OR "NOT FOR CURRENT INTERRUPTING." ▸**Figure 690–119**

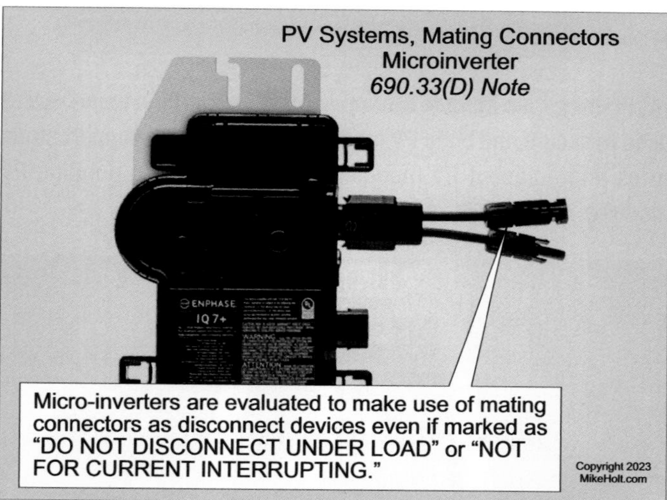

▸Figure 690–119

690.34 Access to Boxes

Junction, pull, and outlet boxes are permitted to be behind PV modules. ▸**Figure 690–120**

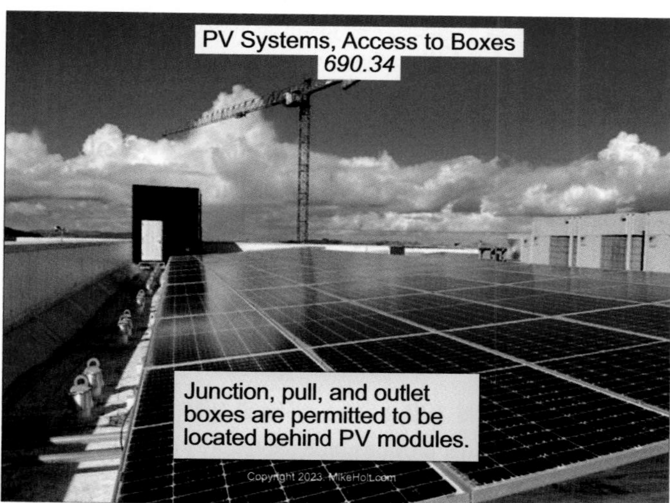

▸Figure 690–120

Part V. Grounding and Bonding

690.41 PV System DC Circuit Grounding and Protection

(A) PV System DC Circuit Grounding Configurations. One or more of the following system configurations are required for PV system dc circuits:

(1) 2-wire circuits with one functionally grounded conductor

(2) Bipolar circuits according to 690.7(C) with a functional ground reference (center tap)

(3) Circuits not isolated from the grounded inverter output circuit (functionally grounded inverter)

(4) Ungrounded circuits

(5) Solidly grounded circuits as permitted in 690.41(B)

(6) Circuits protected by equipment listed and identified for the use

Author's Comment:

- Typically, inverters installed today are of the "not isolated from the grounded inverter output circuit" type [690.41(A)(3)]. These PV systems are known as a "functionally grounded inverters."

According to Article 100, a "Functionally Grounded" is a PV system that has an electrical ground reference for operational purposes that is not solidly grounded.

Note: A functionally grounded PV system is often connected to ground through an electronic means that is internal to an inverter or charge controller which provides ground-fault protection.

(B) DC Ground-Fault Detector-Interrupter (GFDI) Protection. PV system dc circuits that exceed 30 volts or 8 amperes must be provided with GFDI protection to reduce fire hazards as follows:

Note: If GFDI is not included in the dc-to-dc converter, then the installation manual must provide a warning statement that indicates GFDI is not included.

According to Article 100, a "Ground-Fault Detector-Interrupter, dc (GFDI)" is a device that provides protection for PV system dc circuits by detecting a ground fault and could interrupt the fault path in the dc circuit.

(1) Ground-Fault Detection. The GFDI device or system must be detect ground fault(s) in the PV system dc circuits, and be listed for providing GFDI protection. For dc-to-dc converters not listed as providing GFDI protection, where required, listed GFDI protection equipment identified for the combination of the dc-to- dc converter and the GFDI device must be installed to protect the circuit.

Note: Some dc-to-dc converters without integral GFDI protection on their input (source) side can prevent other GFDI protection equipment from properly functioning on portions of PV system dc circuits.

(2) Faulted Circuits. The faulted circuits must be controlled by one of the following methods:

(1) The current-carrying conductors of the faulted circuit must be automatically disconnected.

(2) The device providing GFDI protection fed by the faulted circuit must automatically cease to supply power to output circuits and interrupt the faulted PV system dc circuits from the ground reference in a functionally grounded system.

Author's Comment:

- Inverters listed to UL 1741 have been tested and listed for ground-fault protection. They will automatically stop supplying power to output circuits and will interrupt the PV system dc circuits from ground reference.

690.43 Equipment Grounding Conductor

Metal parts of PV module frames, PV equipment, and enclosures containing PV system ac and dc conductors must be connected to the circuit equipment grounding conductor in accordance with 690.43(A) through (D). ▶Figure 690–121

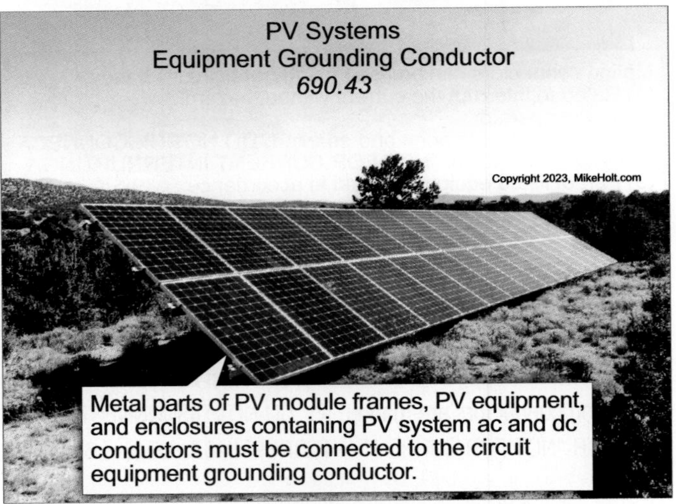

▶Figure 690–121

(A) Photovoltaic Module Mounting Systems and Devices. Devices used to secure and bond PV module frames to metal support structures and adjacent PV modules must be listed for bonding PV modules. ▶Figure 690–122

▶Figure 690–122

Note: UL 2703 is the *Standard for Mounting Systems, Mounting Devices, Clamping/Retention Devices, and Ground Lugs for Use with Flat-Plate Photovoltaic Modules*.

(B) Bonding Equipment to Metal Support Structure. Metal support structures listed, labeled, and identified for bonding and grounding metal parts of PV systems can be used to bond PV equipment to the metal support structure. ▸Figure 690–123

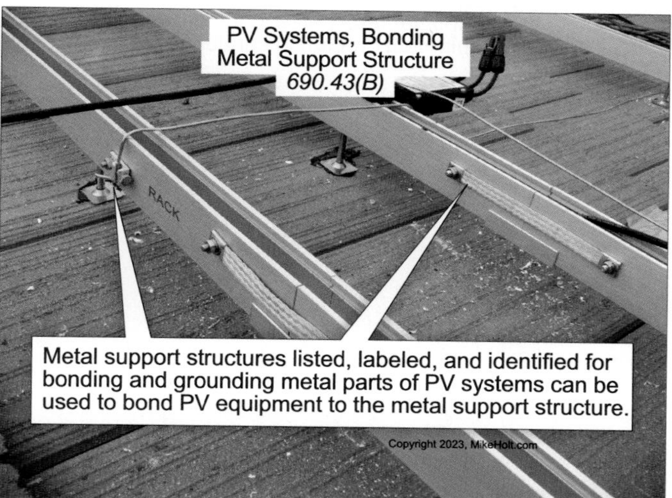
PV Systems, Bonding
Metal Support Structure
690.43(B)
RACK
Metal support structures listed, labeled, and identified for bonding and grounding metal parts of PV systems can be used to bond PV equipment to the metal support structure.
Copyright 2023, MikeHolt.com

▸Figure 690–123

(C) Equipment Grounding Conductor Location. Equipment grounding conductors are permitted to be run separately from the PV circuit conductor within the PV array. ▸Figure 690–124

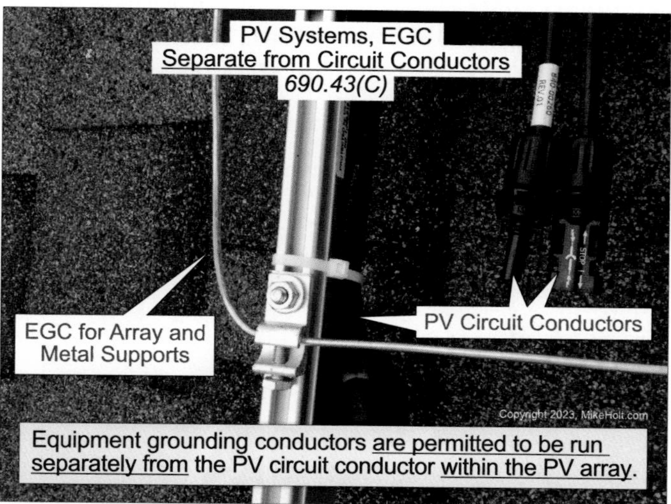
PV Systems, EGC
Separate from Circuit Conductors
690.43(C)
EGC for Array and
Metal Supports
PV Circuit Conductors
Copyright 2023, MikeHolt.com
Equipment grounding conductors are permitted to be run separately from the PV circuit conductor within the PV array.

▸Figure 690–124

Where PV system circuit conductors leave the vicinity of the PV array, equipment grounding conductors must comply with 250.134.

(D) Bonding Over 250V. The bonding bushing and bonding jumper requirements contained in 250.97 for circuits over 250V to ground do not apply to metal raceways and metal cables containing PV system dc circuit conductors. ▸Figure 690–125

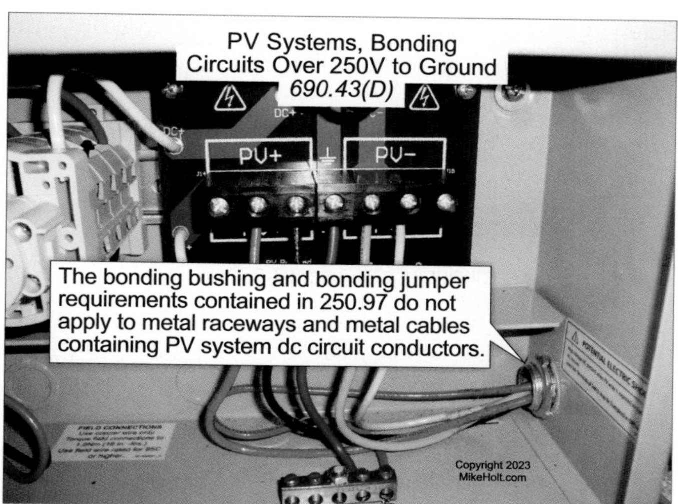
PV Systems, Bonding
Circuits Over 250V to Ground
690.43(D)
PV+
PV–
The bonding bushing and bonding jumper requirements contained in 250.97 do not apply to metal raceways and metal cables containing PV system dc circuit conductors.
Copyright 2023
MikeHolt.com

▸Figure 690–125

690.45 Size of Equipment Grounding Conductors

Equipment grounding conductors for PV system circuits must be sized in accordance with 250.122 based on the rating of the circuit overcurrent protective device. ▸Figure 690–126

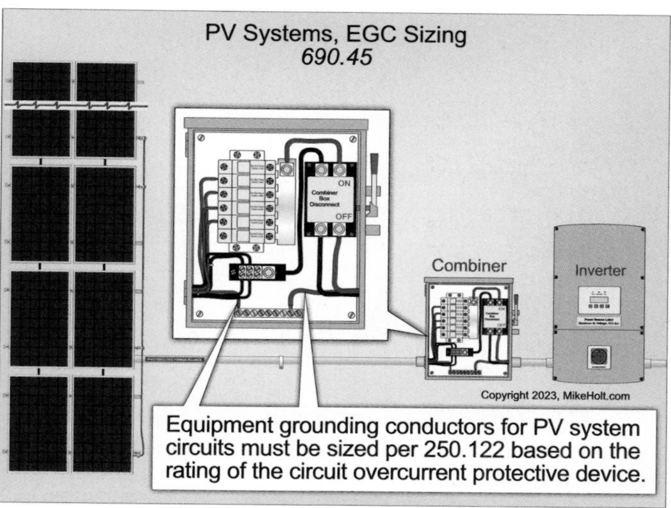
PV Systems, EGC Sizing
690.45
ON
OFF
Combiner
Inverter
Copyright 2023, MikeHolt.com
Equipment grounding conductors for PV system circuits must be sized per 250.122 based on the rating of the circuit overcurrent protective device.

▸Figure 690–126

Where no overcurrent protective device is required [690.9(A)(1)], the equipment grounding conductor for the PV system dc circuit must be sized in accordance with Table 250.122 based on an assumed overcurrent protective device for the circuit sized in accordance with 690.9(B).

Equipment grounding conductors for PV system dc and ac circuits are not required to be increased in size to address voltage-drop considerations. ▸Figure 690–127

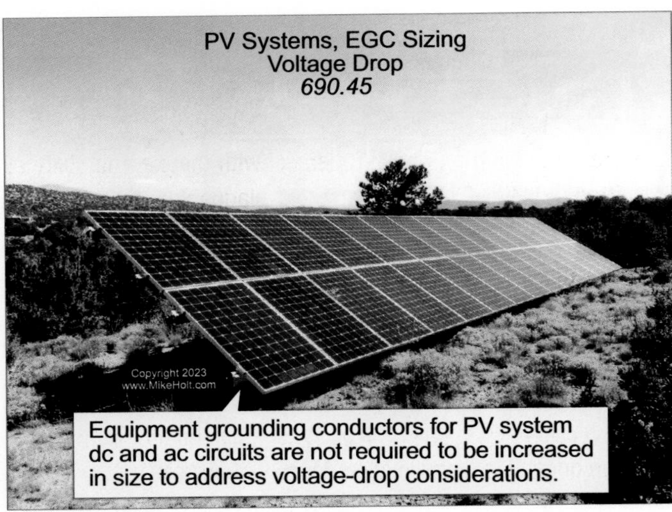
PV Systems, EGC Sizing
Voltage Drop
690.45
Copyright 2023
www.MikeHolt.com
Equipment grounding conductors for PV system dc and ac circuits are not required to be increased in size to address voltage-drop considerations.

▶Figure 690–127

690.47 Grounding Electrode System

(A) Required Grounding Electrode System. A building or structure supporting a PV system must have a grounding electrode system installed. ▶Figure 690–128

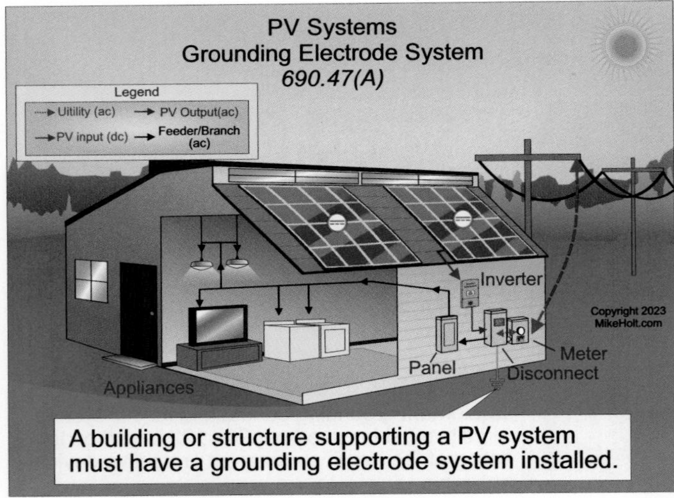
PV Systems
Grounding Electrode System
690.47(A)
Legend
Uitility (ac)
PV Output(ac)
PV input (dc)
Feeder/Branch (ac)
Inverter
Copyright 2023
MikeHolt.com
Meter
Panel
Disconnect
Appliances
A building or structure supporting a PV system must have a grounding electrode system installed.

▶Figure 690–128

(1) Grounding PV Systems. PV systems are grounded when the PV inverter output ac circuit equipment grounding conductor terminates to the distribution equipment grounding conductor terminal. ▶Figure 690–129

Note: Most PV systems are functionally grounded rather than solidly grounded.

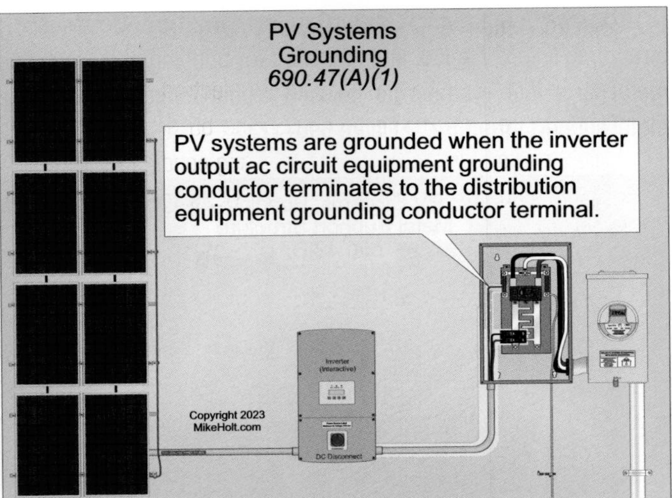
PV Systems
Grounding
690.47(A)(1)
PV systems are grounded when the inverter output ac circuit equipment grounding conductor terminates to the distribution equipment grounding conductor terminal.
Copyright 2023
MikeHolt.com
DC Disconnect

▶Figure 690–129

Author's Comment:

- A functionally grounded system is one that has an electrical ground reference for operational purposes that is not solidly grounded. It is often connected to ground through an electronic means that is internal to an inverter or charge controller that provides ground-fault protection.

(B) Auxiliary Grounding Electrode. Auxiliary grounding electrodes, in accordance with 250.54 are permitted to be connected to the PV module frame(s) or support structure. ▶Figure 690–130

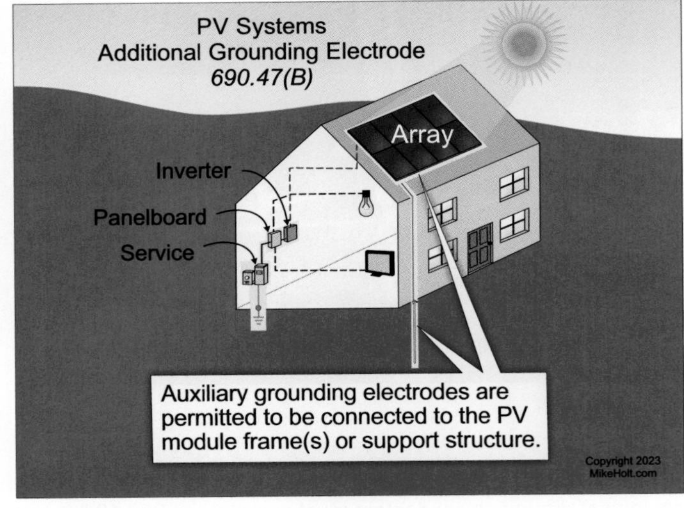
PV Systems
Additional Grounding Electrode
690.47(B)
Array
Inverter
Panelboard
Service
Auxiliary grounding electrodes are permitted to be connected to the PV module frame(s) or support structure.
Copyright 2023
MikeHolt.com

▶Figure 690–130

1st Printing

Author's Comment:

- According to 250.54, if an auxiliary electrode is installed, it is not required to be bonded to the building grounding electrode system, to have the grounding conductor sized to 250.66, nor must it comply with the 25Ω single ground rod requirement of 250.53(A)(2) Ex.

Caution

CAUTION: An auxiliary electrode may cause PV system equipment failures by providing a path for lightning to travel through electronic equipment. ▶**Figure 690–131**

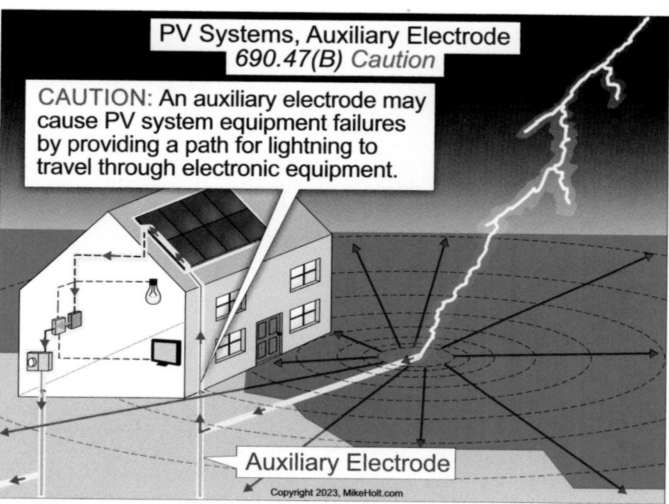
PV Systems, Auxiliary Electrode
690.47(B) Caution
CAUTION: An auxiliary electrode may cause PV system equipment failures by providing a path for lightning to travel through electronic equipment.
Auxiliary Electrode
Copyright 2023, MikeHolt.com

▶**Figure 690–131**

Part VI. Source Connections

690.56 Identification of Power Sources

Where a PV System operates in parallel with the electric utility as permitted by Article 705, a permanent plaque, label, or directory must be installed at the service disconnect location in accordance with 705.10.

690.59 Connection to Other Power Sources

PV systems connected in parallel with the electric utility must have the interconnection made in accordance with Article 705.

Notes

1st Printing

ARTICLE
691

LARGE-SCALE PHOTOVOLTAIC (PV) ELECTRIC SUPPLY STATIONS

Introduction to Article 691—Large-Scale Photovoltaic (PV) Electric Supply Stations

This article covers the installation of electrical wiring and equipment for large-scale photovoltaic systems. Large-scale photovoltaic (PV) electric supply stations require a careful documented review of the design by an engineer to ensure safe operation and compliance with the applicable electrical standards and industry practices. Many of these rules are outside of the scope of this material, however, some of the topics we cover include the following:

- Special Requirements for Large-Scale PV Electric Supply Stations
- Equipment
- Engineered Design
- Fire Mitigation
- Fence Bonding and Grounding

691.1 Scope

Article 691 covers the installation of large-scale PV electric supply stations not under control of an electric utility. ▸Figure 691–1

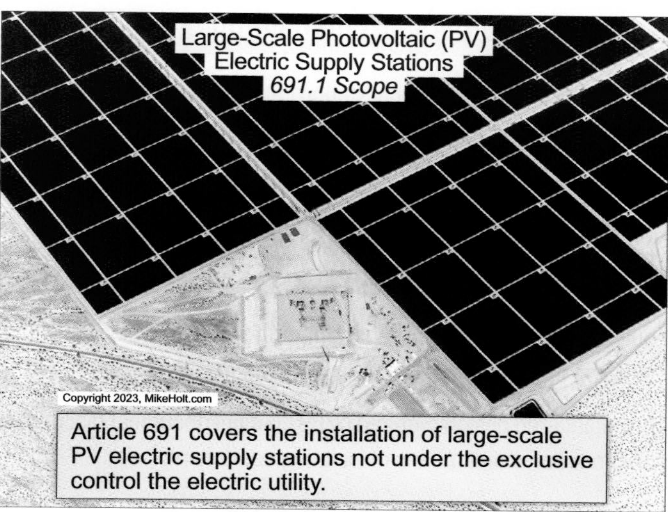
Large-Scale Photovoltaic (PV)
Electric Supply Stations
691.1 Scope
Copyright 2023, MikeHolt.com
Article 691 covers the installation of large-scale PV electric supply stations not under the exclusive control the electric utility.

▸Figure 691–1

Note 1: Facilities covered by this article have specific design and safety features unique to large-scale PV facilities outlined 691.4 and are operated for the sole purpose of providing electric supply to a system operated by a regulated electric utility for the transfer of electric energy.

691.4 Special Requirements for Large-Scale PV Electric Supply Stations

Large-scale PV electric supply stations are only permitted to be accessible to authorized personnel and must comply with the following requirements:

(1) Electrical circuits and equipment must be maintained and operated by qualified person.

(2) PV electric supply stations must be restricted in accordance with 110.31 and have field-applied hazard markings that are permanently affixed and have sufficient durability to withstand the environment involved [110.21(B)].

(3) The connection between the PV electric supply and the electric utility system must be through medium- or high-voltage switch gear, substations, switchyards, or similar methods whose sole purpose is to interconnect the two systems.

(4) Loads within the PV electric supply station must only be used to power auxiliary equipment for the generation of the PV power.

(5) Large-scale PV electric supply stations are not permitted to be installed on buildings.

(6) The station is monitored from a central command center.

(7) The station has an inverter generating capacity of not less than 5000 kW.

Note 2: Some individual sites with capacities less than 5000 kW are operated as part of a group of facilities with a total generating capacity of much greater than 5000 kW.

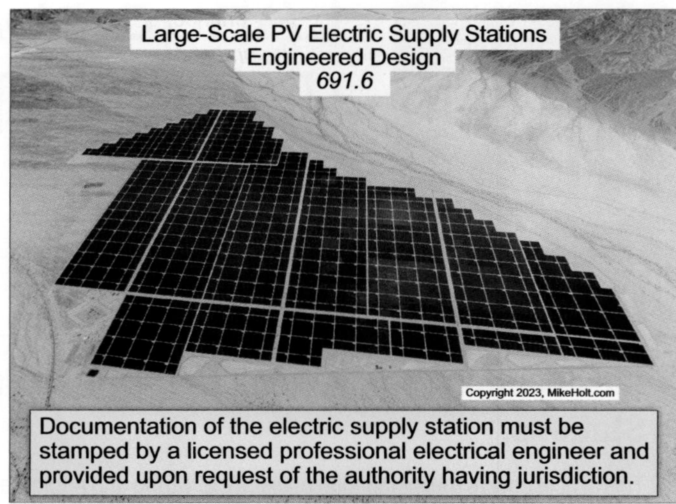
Large-Scale PV Electric Supply Stations
Engineered Design
691.6
Copyright 2023, MikeHolt.com
Documentation of the electric supply station must be stamped by a licensed professional electrical engineer and provided upon request of the authority having jurisdiction.

▸Figure 691–2

691.5 Equipment

All electrical equipment must be approved for installation by one of the following:

(1) Listing and labeling

(2) Be evaluated for the application and have a field label applied

(3) Where products complying with 691.5(1) or (2) are not available, by engineering review validating that the electrical equipment is evaluated and tested to relevant standards or industry practice

691.6 Engineered Design

Documentation of the electric supply station must be stamped by a licensed professional electrical engineer and provided upon request of the authority having jurisdiction. Additional stamped independent engineering reports by a licensed professional electrical engineer detailing compliance of the design with applicable electrical standards and industry practice must be provided upon request of the authority having jurisdiction. ▸Figure 691–2

This documentation must include details of the conformance of the design with Article 690 and any alternative methods to Article 690, or other articles of the *NEC*.

691.7 Conformance of Construction to Engineered Design

Documentation by a licensed professional electrical engineer that the construction of the electric supply station conforms to the electrical engineered design must be provided upon request of the authority having jurisdiction. Additional stamped independent engineering reports by a licensed professional electrical engineer detailing that the construction conforms with this *Code*, applicable standards, and industry practice must be provided upon request of the authority having jurisdiction. This independent engineer must be retained by the system owner or installer.

691.8 Direct-Current Operating Voltage

Large-scale PV electric supply station calculations must be included in the documentation required in 691.6.

691.9 Disconnect for Isolating Photovoltaic Equipment

Equipment disconnects are not required to be within sight of equipment and may be remote from the equipment.

The engineered design required by 691.6 must document disconnection procedures and means of isolating equipment.

1st Printing

For information on electrical system maintenance, see NFPA 70B, *Recommended Practice for Electrical Equipment Maintenance.* For information on written procedures and conditions of maintenance, including lockout/tagout procedures, see NFPA 70E, *Standard for Electrical Safety in the Workplace.*

Buildings whose sole purpose is to house and protect supply station equipment are not required to include a rapid shutdown function to reduce shock hazard for firefighters [690.12]. Written standard operating procedures must be available at the site detailing necessary shutdown procedures in the event of an emergency.

691.10 Fire Mitigation

PV systems that do not provide arc-fault protection as required by 690.11 must include details of fire mitigation plans to address dc arc faults in the documentation required in 691.6.

Fire mitigation plans are typically reviewed by the local fire agency and include topics such as access roads within the facility.

691.11 Fence Bonding and Grounding

Fence grounding requirements and details must be included in the documentation required in 691.6.

Note: See 250.194 for fence bonding and grounding requirements for PV systems that operate at more than 1000V between conductors. Grounding requirements for other portions of electric supply station fencing are assessed based on the presence of overhead conductors, proximity to generation and distribution equipment, and associated step and touch potential.

Notes

ARTICLE

695 FIRE PUMPS

Introduction to Article 695—Fire Pumps

This article covers the installation of electrical wiring and equipment for fire pumps. The general philosophy behind most *Code* requirements is to provide circuit protection that will disconnect power before allowing the conductors to overheat and become damaged, however, article 695 departs from this philosophy. A fire pump motor must keep running no matter what since it supplies water to a facility's fire protection piping. Many of these rules are outside of the scope of this material, however, some of the topics we cover include the following:

- Electric Power Source(s)
- Continuity of Power
- Transformers
- Power Wiring
- Fire Pump Controller Voltage Drop
- Equipment Location
- Surge Protection

695.1 Scope

(A) Covered. Article 695 covers the installation of: ▶**Figure 695–1**

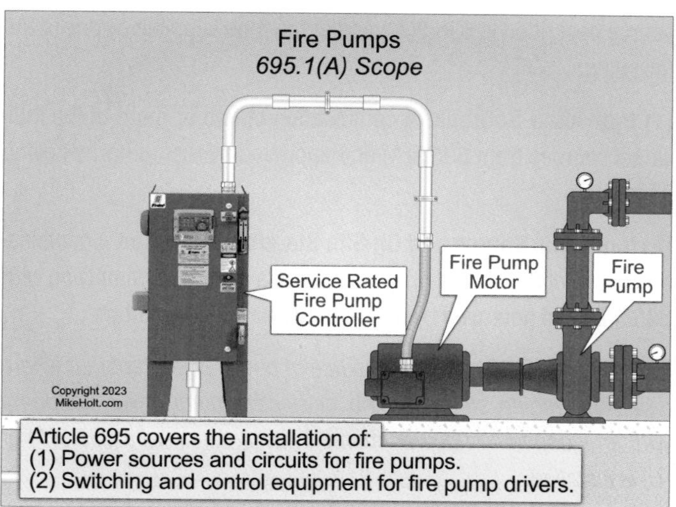

▶**Figure 695–1**

(1) Electric power sources and interconnecting circuits for fire pumps.

(2) Switching and control equipment dedicated to fire pump drivers.

(B) Not Covered. Article 695 does not cover:

(1) Performance, maintenance, testing, and the internal wiring of the components of the system.

(2) The installation of pressure maintenance (jockey or makeup) pumps.

Note: Article 430 governs the installation of pressure maintenance (jockey or makeup) pumps, whether they are supplied by the fire pump or not.

(3) Transfer equipment upstream of the fire pump transfer switch(es).

Author's Comment:

- Fire pump installations should be designed by qualified experts in the field due to the critical importance of professionally designed systems. Fire pump installations can interconnect with other systems such as backup power systems and sprinkler systems. Generally, the electrician or electrical contractor doing a fire pump installation will not be doing any calculations but following a set of specifications provided for the job.

(4) Water pumps installed in one- and two-family dwellings and used for fire suppression.

695.3 Electric Power Source(s)

(A) Individual Sources. Power to fire pump motors must be supplied by a reliable source with the capacity to carry the locked-rotor current of the fire pump motor(s), pressure maintenance pump motors, and the full-load current of any associated fire pump equipment. Specifically permitted reliable sources of power include:

(1) Separate Remote Service. A separate service for the fire pump remote from the normal service to minimize unintentional interruption [230.72(B)] or a connection ahead of, but not within, the service disconnect [230.82(5)]. ▸Figure 695–2

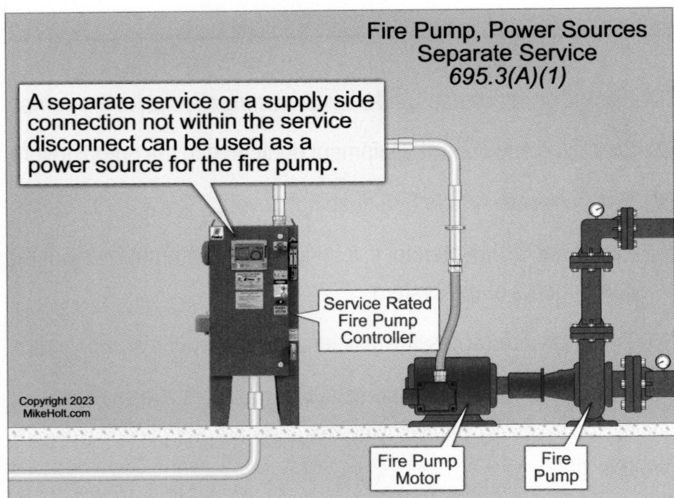
Fire Pump, Power Sources
Separate Service
695.3(A)(1)
A separate service or a supply side connection not within the service disconnect can be used as a power source for the fire pump.
Service Rated Fire Pump Controller
Fire Pump Motor
Fire Pump
Copyright 2023 MikeHolt.com

▸Figure 695–2

Author's Comment:

- To minimize unintentional interruption, the service disconnect for the fire pump system must be remote from the other power system service disconnects [230.72(B)]. Generally, the pump feeder tap termination point is situated ahead of the main service disconnect(s) and the fire pump disconnect is within sight of fire pump itself.

(2) On-Site Power. An on-site power generator located and protected to minimize damage by fire.

See NFPA 20, *Standard for the Installation of Stationary Pumps for Fire Protection,* for guidance on the determination of electric power source reliability. ▸Figure 695–3

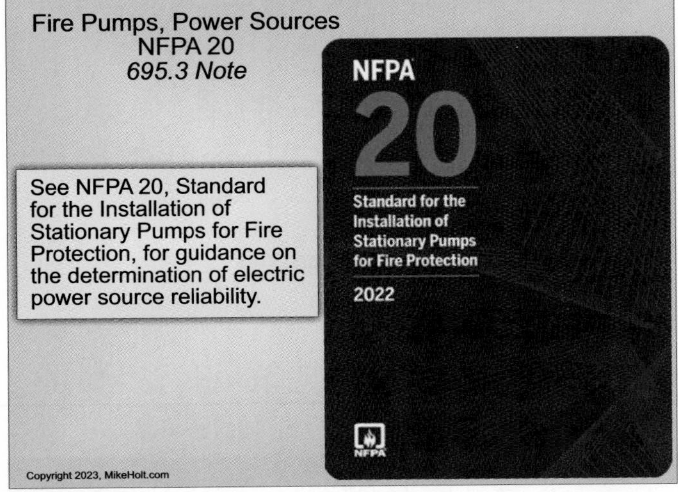
Fire Pumps, Power Sources
NFPA 20
695.3 Note
See NFPA 20, Standard for the Installation of Stationary Pumps for Fire Protection, for guidance on the determination of electric power source reliability.
NFPA
20
Standard for the Installation of Stationary Pumps for Fire Protection
2022
NFPA
Copyright 2023, MikeHolt.com

▸Figure 695–3

(B) Multiple Sources. If reliable power cannot be obtained from a source described in 695.3(A), power must be supplied by any of the following:

(1) Individual Sources. A combination of two or more of the individual sources from 695.3(A) and approved by the authority having jurisdiction.

(2) Individual Source and On-Site Standby Generator. A combination of one of the sources in 695.3(A) and a generator complying with 695.3(D) and approved by the authority having jurisdiction.

Ex to (1) and (2): An alternate source of power is not required where a backup, engine, steam turbine, or electric motor driven fire pump with an independent power source in accordance with 695.3(A) or (C) is installed.

(F) Transfer of Power. Transfer of power to the fire pump controller must take place within the pump room.

695.4 Continuity of Power

(B) Connection Through Disconnect and Overcurrent Device.

(1) Number of Disconnecting Means.

(a) A single means of disconnect is permitted to be installed between the fire pump electric supply and:

(1) A listed fire pump controller, or

(2) A listed fire pump power transfer switch, or

(3) A listed combination fire pump controller/power transfer switch.

(2) Overcurrent Device Selection.

(a) Individual Sources. Overcurrent protection for individual sources must comply with the following:

(1) The overcurrent protective device(s) must have an ampere rating to carry indefinitely the sum of the locked-rotor current of the largest fire pump motor and 100 percent of the full-load current of the other pump motors and fire pump's accessory equipment. ▶Figure 695-4

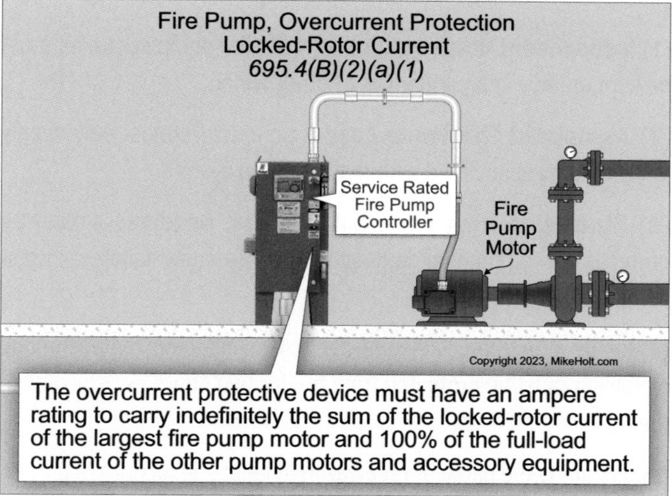

▶Figure 695-4

Author's Comment:

- **Motor Locked-Rotor Current (LRC).** If the rotating part of the motor winding (armature) becomes jammed so it cannot rotate, no counter-electromotive force (CEMF) will be produced in the motor winding. This results in a decrease in conductor impedance to the point that it is effectively a short circuit. The motor then operates at locked-rotor current (often six times the full-load ampere rating) depending on the motor's *Code* letter rating [430.7(B)]. This condition will cause the motor winding to overheat and be destroyed if the current is not quickly reduced or removed. ▶Figure 695-5

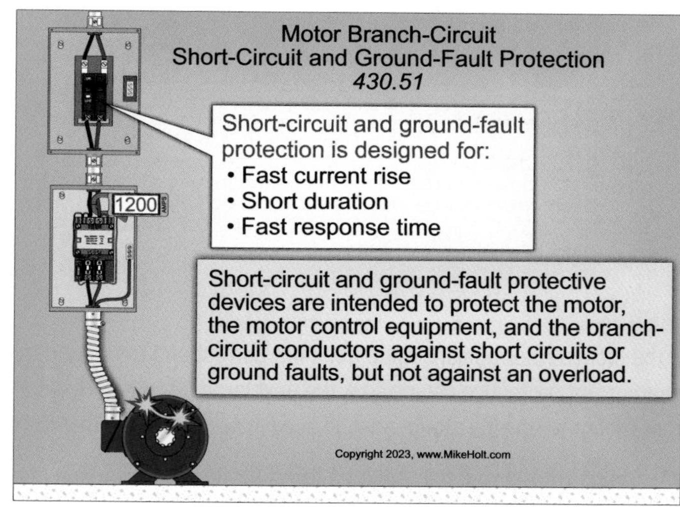

Motor Branch-Circuit
Short-Circuit and Ground-Fault Protection
430.51
1200
Short-circuit and ground-fault protection is designed for:
• Fast current rise
• Short duration
• Fast response time
Short-circuit and ground-fault protective devices are intended to protect the motor, the motor control equipment, and the branch-circuit conductors against short circuits or ground faults, but not against an overload.
Copyright 2023, www.MikeHolt.com

▶Figure 695-5

▶ Fire Pump Overcurrent Size Example

Question: *What size overcurrent protective device is required for a 25 hp, 460V, three-phase fire pump motor that has a locked-rotor current rating of 183A where the circuit conductors are 8 AWG?* ▶**Figure 695-6**

(a) 100A *(b) 200A* *(c) 250A* *(d) 300A*

Solution:

The overcurrent protective device(s) must be selected or set to carry indefinitely the locked-rotor current of the fire pump motor [695.4(B)(2)(a)(1) and 240.6(A)].

Locked-Rotor Current = 183A
Protection Size = 200A

Answer: *(b) 200A*

The branch-circuit conductors are sized at no less than 125 percent of the motor's FLC [695.6(B)(1)(1) and Table 430.250].

Branch-Circuit Conductor = 34A × 125%
Branch-Circuit Conductor = 42.50A

8 AWG is rated 50A at 75°C [110.14)(C)(1)(a)(3) and Table 310.16].

• • •

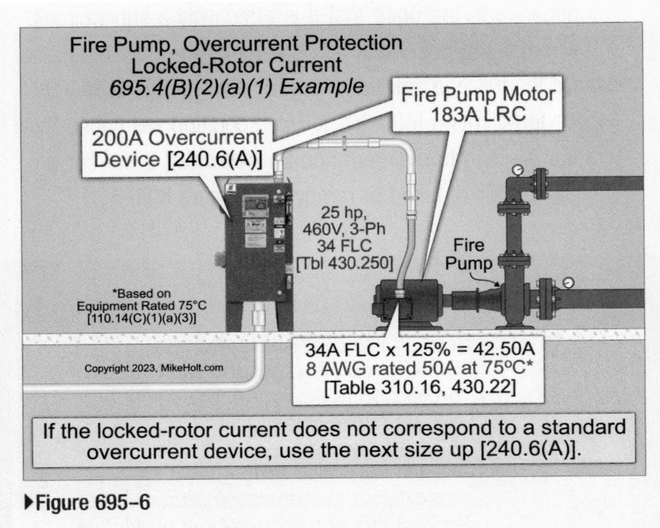

▶Figure 695–6

If the locked-rotor current value does not correspond to a standard overcurrent protective device size, the next larger standard overcurrent protective device rating must be used in accordance with 240.6.

(2) Overcurrent protection must be listed for fire pump service and must not:

a. Open within 2 minutes at 600 percent of the full-load current of the pump motor(s).

b. Open with a re-start locked-rotor current of 24 times the full-load current of the pump motor(s).

c. Open within 10 minutes at 300 percent of the full-load current of the pump motor(s).

d. Have a field adjustable trip setting.

(b) On-Site Standby Generators. Overcurrent protective devices between an on-site standby generator and a fire pump controller must be sized in accordance with 430.62, based on the largest rating or setting of the short-circuit and ground-fault device for the largest motor FLC and the sum of other motors on the feeder.

695.5 Transformers

(A) Size. If a transformer supplies an electric fire pump motor, it must be sized at no less than 125 percent of the sum of the fire pump motor(s) and pressure maintenance pump(s) motor loads, and 100 percent of the ampere rating of the fire pump's accessory equipment.

(B) Overcurrent Protection. The primary overcurrent protective device(s) must be sized to carry indefinitely the sum of the locked-rotor current of the fire pump motor(s) and pressure maintenance pump motor(s), and 100 percent of the ampere rating of the fire pump's accessory equipment. Secondary overcurrent protection is not permitted. The requirement to carry the locked-rotor current indefinitely does not apply to fire pump motor conductors.

695.6 Power Wiring

(A) Supply Conductors.

(1) Services.

Outside. Service conductors must be physically routed outside buildings.

Inside. Where service conductors are run inside a building, they must be encased in 2 in. of concrete or brick [230.6].

Ex: Supply conductors within a fire pump room are not required to be encased in 2 in. of concrete or brick as required by 230.6(1) or (2).

See 250.24(D) for routing the grounded conductor to the service equipment.

(2) Feeders. Fire pump controller supply conductors must comply with all the following:

(1) Independent Routing. Conductors to fire pump controller must be kept entirely independent of all other wiring.

(2) Associated Fire Pump Loads. Conductors must only supply loads directly associated with the fire pump system.

(3) Protection from Potential Damage. Conductors must be protected from potential damage by fire, structural failure, or operational accident.

(4) Inside a Building. Fire pump controller conductors routed through a building must be protected from fire for two hours by using any of the following methods:

(a) Encasing the cable or raceway in at least 2 in. of concrete.

(b) Using a cable or raceway that is part of a listed fire-resistive cable system.

(c) Using a cable or raceway that is protect by a listed electrical circuit protective system.

Ex: The conductors between an electrical equipment room and fire pump room are not required to have two-hour fire protection unless otherwise required in 700.10(D). ▶**Figure 695–7**

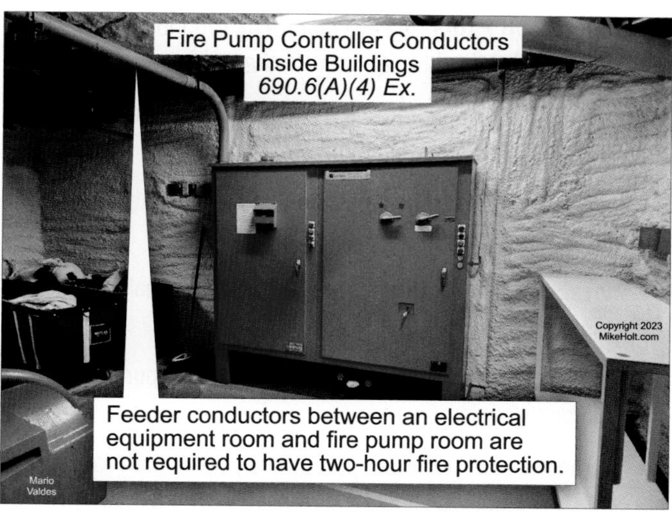

▶Figure 695–7

(B) Conductor Ampacity.

(1) Fire Pump Motors and Other Equipment. Conductors supplying a fire pump motor(s) pressure maintenance pump(s), and associated fire pump accessory equipment, must have a minimum ampacity of not less than the sum of the following:

(1) 125 percent of the sum of the fire pump motor(s) and pressure maintenance motor(s) full-load current(s), and

(2) 100 percent of the associated fire pump accessory equipment full-load current(s).

(2) Fire Pump Motors Only. Conductors supplying only a fire pump motor must have a minimum ampacity of not less than 125 percent of the motor full-load current rating in accordance with 430.22 and must comply with the voltage-drop requirements in 695.7. ▶**Figure 695–8**

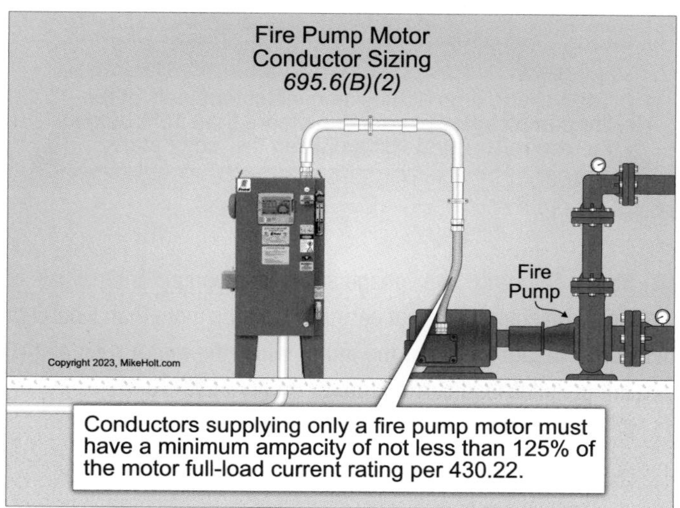

▶Figure 695–8

▶ Fire Pump Conductor Size Example

Question: *What size conductor is required for a 25 hp, 460V, three-phase fire pump motor with terminals rated 75°C, a locked-rotor current of 183A, and with circuit overcurrent protection set to 200A?* ▶**Figure 695–9**

(a) 8 AWG *(b) 6 AWG* *(c) 4 AWG* *(d) 3 AWG*

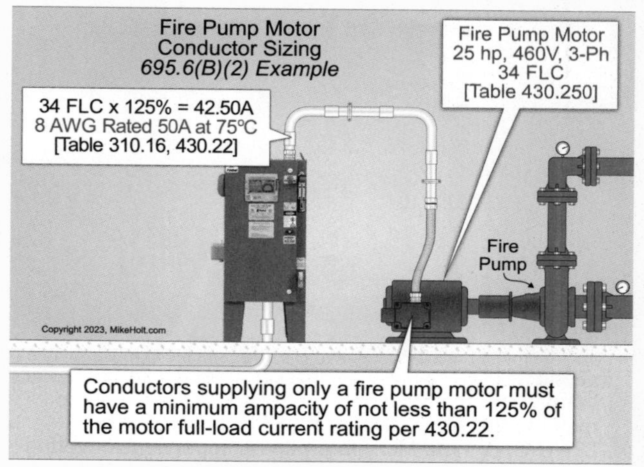

▶Figure 695–9

Solution:

A 25 hp, 460V, Three-Phase Motor FLC = 34A [Table 430.250].

Determine the branch-circuit conductor at 125 percent of the motor's FLC [Table 430.250 and 695.6(B)(1)(1)].

Branch-Circuit Conductor = 34A × 125%
Branch-Circuit Conductor = 42.50A

Use an 8 AWG conductor rated 50A at 75°C [110.14)(C)(1)(a)(3) and Table 310.16].

Answer: *(a) 8 AWG*

The overcurrent protective device(s) must be selected or set to carry indefinitely the locked-rotor current of the fire pump motor [695.4(B)(2)(a)(1)].

Locked-Rotor Current = 218A
Protection Size = 250A

(C) Overload Protection. Circuits for fire pumps must not have overload protection and must be protected against short circuits only.

(D) Pump Wiring.

(1) Wiring Methods. Wiring from the fire pump controllers to the fire pump motors must be in rigid metal conduit, intermediate metal conduit, electrical metallic tubing, liquidtight flexible metal conduit, liquidtight flexible nonmetallic conduit Type LFNC-B, or listed Type MC cable with an impervious covering. ▶Figure 695–10

Fire Pumps, Wiring Methods
695.6(D)(1)
Copyright 2023
MikeHolt.com
Mario
Valdes
Wiring from the fire pump controllers to the fire pump motors must be in RMC, IMC, EMT, LFMC, Type LFNC-B, or Type MC cable with an impervious covering.

▶Figure 695–10

(2) Fittings. Fittings must be listed for use in wet locations. ▶Figure 695–11

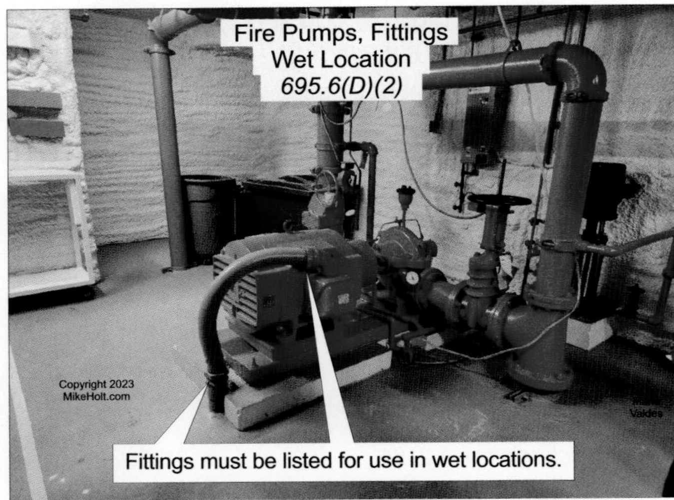
Fire Pumps, Fittings
Wet Location
695.6(D)(2)
Copyright 2023
MikeHolt.com
Fittings must be listed for use in wet locations.

▶Figure 695–11

(3) Connections. The connections in the motor terminal box must be made with a listed device. Twist-on, insulation-piercing type, and soldered wire connectors are not allowed.

(G) Ground-Fault Protection of Equipment. Ground-fault protection of equipment (GFPE) is not permitted in the fire pump power circuit.

(J) Terminations. Where raceways or cables are terminated at a fire pump controller, the following requirements apply:

(1) Raceway or cable fittings must be listed and identified for use in wet locations.

(2) The raceway or cable fittings must be at least equal to that of the fire pump controller.

(3) The instructions of the manufacturer of the fire pump controller must be followed.

(4) Alterations to the fire pump controller, other than raceway or cable terminations, must be approved by the authority having jurisdiction.

695.7 Fire Pump Controller Voltage Drop

(A) Motor Starting. The voltage at the line contact terminals of the fire pump controller is not permitted to drop more than 15 percent below the controller-rated voltage when the motor starts. ▶Figure 695–12

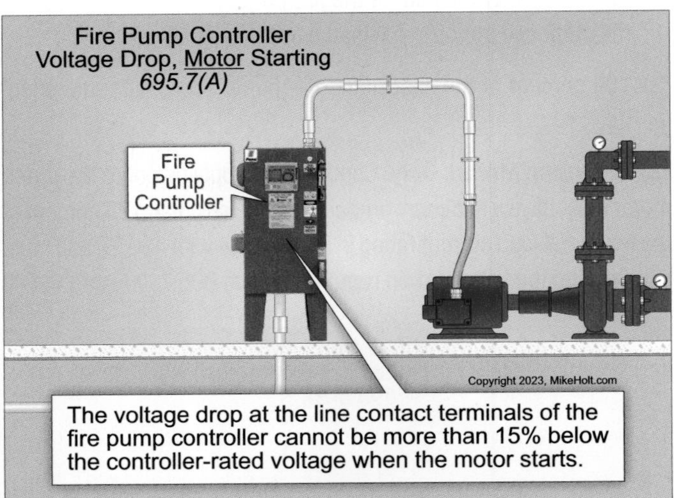
Fire Pump Controller
Voltage Drop, Motor Starting
695.7(A)
Fire
Pump
Controller
Copyright 2023, MikeHolt.com
The voltage drop at the line contact terminals of the fire pump controller cannot be more than 15% below the controller-rated voltage when the motor starts.

▶Figure 695–12

(D) Motor Running. The voltage at the load contactor terminals of the fire pump controller is not permitted to drop more than 5 percent below the voltage rating of the motor when the motor runs at 115 percent of its full-load current rating. ▶Figure 695–13

1st Printing

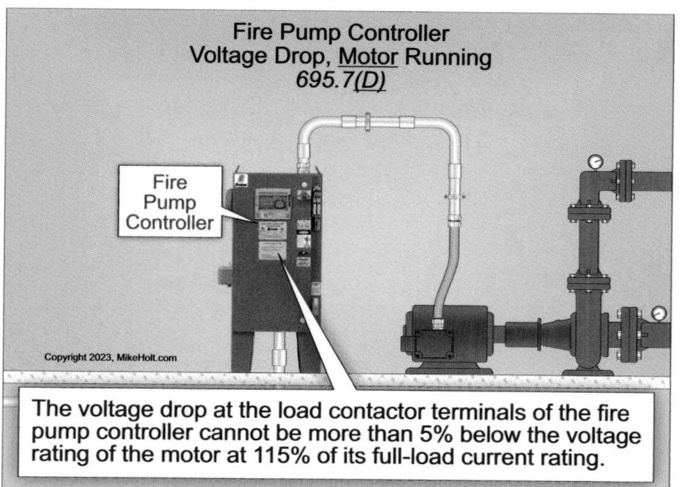

▸Figure 695–13

Author's Comment:

- Sizing conductors for fire pump circuits to account for start-up and running voltage drop because of low power factor during start-up must be performed by a qualified person—typically, an electrical engineer.

695.10 Listed Equipment

Diesel engine fire pump controllers, electric fire pump controllers, electric motors, fire pump power transfer switches, foam pump controllers, and limited-service controllers must be listed for fire pump service. ▸**Figure 695–14**

Fire Pumps
Listed Equipment
695.10
Copyright 2023
MikeHolt.com
Fire pump controllers, electric fire pump motors, and fire pump power transfer switches must be listed.
Mario Valdes

▸Figure 695–14

695.12 Equipment Location

(E) Protection Against Pump Water. Fire pump controller and power transfer switches must be located or protected so they are not damaged by water escaping from pumps or pump connections.

695.14 Control Wiring

(E) Wiring Methods. Control wiring must be in rigid metal conduit, intermediate metal conduit, liquidtight flexible metal conduit, electrical metallic tubing, liquidtight flexible nonmetallic conduit, or Type MC cable with an impervious covering.

695.15 Surge Protection

A listed surge-protective device must be installed in or on the fire pump controller. ▸**Figure 695–15**

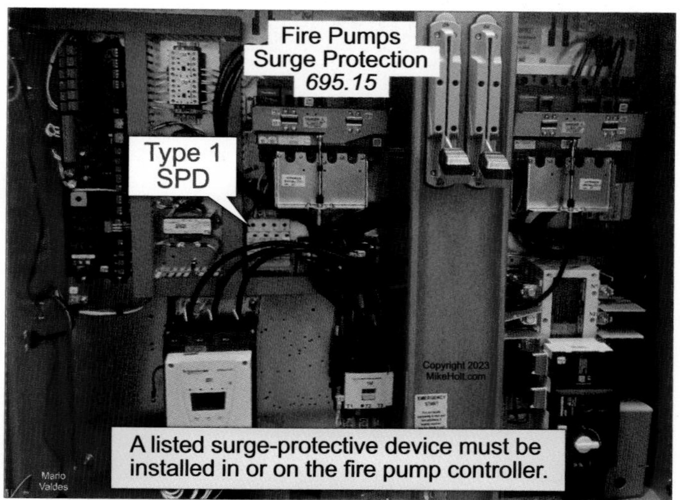

▸Figure 695–15

Notes

CHAPTER 6

REVIEW QUESTIONS

Please use the 2023 *Code* book to answer the following questions.

ARTICLE 600—ELECTRIC SIGNS

1. Article 600 covers the installation of conductors, equipment, and field wiring for _____, and outline lighting, regardless of voltage.
   (a) electric signs
   (b) retrofit kits
   (c) neon tubing
   (d) all of these

2. Fixed, mobile, or portable electric signs, section signs, outline lighting, photovoltaic powered signs, and retrofit kits shall be _____ and installed in conformance with that listing, unless otherwise approved by special permission.
   (a) marked
   (b) assembled
   (c) identified for the location
   (d) listed and labeled

3. Signs and outline lighting systems shall be listed and labeled and marked with the _____.
   (a) manufacturer's name, trademark, or other means of identification
   (b) input voltage
   (c) current rating
   (d) all of these

4. For signs with a retrofitted illumination system, the sign shall be marked that the illumination system has been _____.
   (a) replaced
   (b) modified
   (c) refurbished
   (d) updated

5. Signs with a retrofitted illumination system equipped with tubular light-emitting diode lamps powered by the existing sign sockets shall include a label alerting the service personnel that the sign has been modified and also include a warning not to install _____ lamps.
   (a) incandescent
   (b) fluorescent
   (c) LED
   (d) all of these

6. The markings and listing labels required for signs and outline lighting systems, shall be visible after installation and shall be permanently applied in a location visible prior to _____.
   (a) servicing
   (b) maintenance
   (c) servicing or maintenance
   (d) none of these

7. Each commercial building and occupancy accessible to pedestrians shall have at least one sign outlet in an accessible location at each entrance to each tenant space supplied by a branch circuit rated at least _____.
   (a) 15A
   (b) 20A
   (c) 30A
   (d) 40A

8. A sign or outline lighting outlet shall not be required at commercial building or occupancy entrances for _____ that are intended to be used only by service personnel or employees.
   (a) deliveries
   (b) service corridors
   (c) service hallways
   (d) any of these

9. A disconnecting means for a sign, outline lighting system, or controller shall be marked to identify the _____, outline lighting system, or controller it controls.
   (a) branch circuit
   (b) feeder
   (c) sign
   (d) all of these

10. Branch circuits that supply signs shall be considered to be _____ loads for the purposes of calculations.
   (a) continuous
   (b) separate
   (c) combined
   (d) dynamic

11. Where sign enclosures might be used as pull boxes, listed and labeled neon transformer boxes shall be permitted to contain multiple voltages over _____.
   (a) 277V
   (b) 480V
   (c) 600V
   (d) 1000V

12. Metal or nonmetallic poles used to support signs are permitted to enclose _____.
   (a) supply conductors
   (b) surge-protective devices
   (c) lightning arresters
   (d) overcurrent protective devices

13. Each sign and outline lighting system circuit supplying a sign, outline lighting system, or skeleton tubing shall be controlled by an externally operable switch or circuit breaker that opens all _____ conductors and controls no other load.
   (a) ungrounded
   (b) grounded
   (c) equipment grounding
   (d) all of these

14. The location of the sign and outline lighting system disconnect is intended to allow service or maintenance personnel and _____ complete and local control of the disconnecting means.
   (a) security personnel
   (b) emergency personnel
   (c) first responders
   (d) local jurisdictional personnel

15. The disconnect for a sign or outline lighting shall be located at the point the feeder circuit or branch circuits supplying a sign or outline lighting system enters a _____.
   (a) sign enclosure
   (b) sign body
   (c) pole in accordance with 600.5(D)(3)
   (d) any of these

16. A sign disconnect shall not be required for branch circuits or feeder conductors passing through the sign where not accessible and enclosed in a Chapter 3 _____ raceway or metal-jacketed cable identified for the location.
   (a) listed
   (b) labeled
   (c) identified
   (d) approved

17. A disconnect shall not be required at the point of entry to a sign enclosure or sign body for branch-circuit or feeder conductors that supply internal _____ in a sign enclosure or sign body.
   (a) switchboards
   (b) switchgears
   (c) panelboards
   (d) any of these

18. Where the disconnecting means is out of the line of sight from any section of a sign or outline lighting able to be energized, the disconnecting means shall be _____ in accordance with 110.25.
   (a) secured
   (b) bolted
   (c) lockable
   (d) visible when installed

1st Printing

19. A permanent field-applied marking identifying the location of the disconnecting means shall be applied to the sign in a location visible during _____.
    (a) installation
    (b) repair
    (c) retrofitting
    (d) servicing

20. Where the disconnecting means for a sign or outline lighting is not located within sight of the _____, a permanent field-applied marking identifying the location of the disconnecting means shall be applied to the controller in a location visible during servicing.
    (a) controller
    (b) branch circuit
    (c) feeder
    (d) photocell

21. The disconnecting means, if located remote from the sign, sign body, or pole shall be mounted at a(an) _____ location available to first responders and service personnel.
    (a) available
    (b) accessible
    (c) readily accessible
    (d) visible

22. Metal equipment of signs, outline lighting, and skeleton tubing systems shall be grounded by connection to the _____ of the supply branch circuit(s) or feeder using the types of equipment grounding conductors specified in 250.118.
    (a) grounding electrode conductor
    (b) equipment grounding conductor
    (c) neutral conductor
    (d) ground rod

23. Listed flexible metal conduit or listed liquidtight flexible metal conduit that encloses the secondary sign circuit conductor from a transformer or power supply for use with neon tubing is permitted as a bonding means if the total accumulative length of the conduit in the secondary sign circuit does not exceed _____.
    (a) 10 ft
    (b) 25 ft
    (c) 50 ft
    (d) 100 ft

24. Bonding conductors installed outside of a sign or raceway used for the bonding connections of the noncurrent-carrying metal parts of signs shall be protected from physical damage and shall be copper not smaller than _____.
    (a) 14 AWG
    (b) 12 AWG
    (c) 8 AWG
    (d) 6 AWG

25. Bonding conductors installed outside of a sign or raceway used for the bonding connections of the noncurrent-carrying metal parts of signs, shall be protected from physical damage and are permitted to be copper-clad aluminum not smaller than _____.
    (a) 14 AWG
    (b) 12 AWG
    (c) 8 AWG
    (d) 6 AWG

26. The bottom of sign and outline lighting system equipment shall be at least _____ above areas accessible to vehicles unless protected from physical damage.
    (a) 12 ft
    (b) 14 ft
    (c) 16 ft
    (d) 18 ft

27. Neon tubing, other than _____, readily accessible to pedestrians shall be protected from physical damage.
    (a) those in Class I, Division 1 locations
    (b) listed, dry location, portable signs
    (c) fixed equipment
    (d) wet location portable signs

28. Signs and outline lighting systems shall be installed so that adjacent combustible materials are not subjected to temperatures in excess of _____.
    (a) 60°C
    (b) 75°C
    (c) 90°C
    (d) 105°C

29. A working space not less than 3 ft high by 3 ft wide by _____ deep is required for each ballast, transformer, electronic power supply, and Class 2 power source where not installed in a sign.

(a) 2 ft
(b) 3 ft
(c) 4 ft
(d) 6 ft

30. At least one lighting outlet containing a switch or controlled by a wall switch shall be installed in in attic spaces containing ballasts for electric signs with the _____ located at the usual point of entry to these spaces.

(a) receptacle
(b) switch
(c) point of control
(d) luminaire

31. Ballasts, transformers, electronic power supplies, and Class 2 power sources for signs can be located above a suspended ceiling, provided the enclosures are securely fastened in place and are _____.

(a) effectively bonded
(b) not dependent on the suspended-ceiling grid for support
(c) rated at not more than 300V
(d) effectively grounded

ARTICLE 604—MANUFACTURED WIRING SYSTEMS

1. Article _____ applies to field-installed wiring using off-site manufactured subassemblies for branch circuits, remote-control circuits, signaling circuits, and communications circuits in accessible areas.

(a) 600
(b) 604
(c) 605
(d) 610

2. Manufactured wiring systems and associated components shall be _____.

(a) listed
(b) labeled
(c) identified
(d) approved

3. Manufactured wiring systems shall be _____ in accordance with the applicable cable or conduit article for the cable or conduit type employed.

(a) secured
(b) supported
(c) secured and supported
(d) strapped and tied

ARTICLE 620—ELEVATORS

1. Article 620 covers the installation of electrical equipment and wiring used in connection with elevators, dumbwaiters, escalators, moving walks, platform lifts, and _____.

(a) stairway chairlifts
(b) pool lifts
(c) boat hoists
(d) all of these

2. Each 15A and 20A, 125V receptacle installed in pits, in hoistways, on the cars of elevators and dumbwaiters associated with wind turbine tower elevators, on the platforms or in the runways and machinery spaces of platform lifts and stairway chairlifts, and in escalator and moving walk wellways shall be _____.

(a) on a GFCI-protected circuit
(b) of the GFCI type
(c) provided with GFPE protection
(d) current limiting

3. All 125V, single-phase, 15A and 20A receptacles installed in _____ for elevators, dumbwaiters, escalators, moving walks, lifts, and chairlifts shall have Class A ground-fault circuit-interrupter protection for personnel.

(a) machine rooms
(b) control spaces
(c) control rooms
(d) all of these

4. A(An) _____ branch circuit shall supply the elevator car lights and shall be permitted to supply receptacles (for alarm devices, emergency responder radio coverage (ERRC), car ventilation purification systems, and monitoring devices not part of the control system), auxiliary lighting power sources, car emergency signaling, communications devices (including their associated charging circuits), and ventilation on each elevator car.

   (a) GFCI-protected
   (b) AFCI-protected
   (c) multiwire
   (d) separate

5. The overcurrent device protecting the branch circuit supplying the air-conditioning and heating units on each elevator car shall be located in the elevator _____, or control space.

   (a) machine room
   (b) control room
   (c) machinery space
   (d) any of these

6. The branch circuit(s) supplying the lighting for an elevator machine room/machinery space shall be separate from the branch circuit(s) supplying the receptacles and shall not be connected to the load side of a(an) _____.

   (a) local subpanel
   (b) SWD-type circuit breaker
   (c) HID-type circuit breaker
   (d) GFCI

7. A(An) _____ shall be located at the point of entry to an elevator machine room, control room, machinery space or control space.

   (a) directory
   (b) lighting switch
   (c) control circuit disconnecting means
   (d) emergency exit map

8. At least _____ 125V, single-phase, 15A or 20A, duplex receptacle(s) shall be provided in each elevator machine room and elevator machinery space.

   (a) one
   (b) two
   (c) three
   (d) four

9. Separate _____ shall supply the elevator hoistway pit lighting and receptacles and the required lighting shall not be connected to the load side of a ground-fault circuit interrupter.

   (a) feeders
   (b) subpanels
   (c) emergency systems
   (d) branch circuits

10. The lighting switch for elevator hoistway pits shall be readily accessible from the _____.

   (a) pit access door
   (b) elevator car
   (c) floor of the pit
   (d) machinery room

11. At least _____ 125V, single-phase, 15A or 20A, duplex receptacle(s) shall be provided in the elevator hoistway pit.

   (a) one
   (b) two
   (c) three
   (d) four

12. Electrical wiring, raceways, and cables used directly in connection with an elevator shall be permitted inside the hoistway, machine rooms, control rooms, machinery spaces, and control spaces, including wiring for _____.

   (a) communications with the car
   (b) fire detection systems
   (c) pit sump pumps
   (d) any of these

13. A single means for disconnecting all ungrounded main power supply conductors for each _____ shall be provided and be designed so that no pole can be operated independently.

   (a) elevator or dumbwaiter
   (b) escalator or moving walk
   (c) platform lift or stairway chairlift
   (d) any of these

14. The disconnecting means for an elevator or escalator shall be an enclosed externally operable circuit breaker or fused motor circuit switch that is _____ in accordance with 110.25.

   (a) capable of interrupting six times the locked-rotor current
   (b) lockable only in the open position
   (c) inherently protected
   (d) suitable for use as service equipment

15. The disconnecting means for an elevator shall be located where it is _____ to qualified persons.
    (a) accessible
    (b) readily accessible
    (c) disclosed only
    (d) accessible only with a key

ARTICLE 625—ELECTRIC VEHICLE POWER TRANSFER SYSTEM

1. Article 625 covers the electrical conductors and equipment connecting an electric vehicle to premises wiring for the purposes of ____.
    (a) charging
    (b) power export
    (c) bidirectional current flow
    (d) any of these

2. Electric vehicle power transfer system equipment for the purposes of charging, power export, or bidirectional current flow shall be _____.
    (a) listed
    (b) labeled
    (c) identified
    (d) all of these

3. Each outlet installed for the purpose of supplying EVSE (electric vehicle supply equipment) greater than _____ or 120V charging electric vehicles shall be supplied by an individual branch circuit.
    (a) 12A
    (b) 16A
    (c) 18A
    (d) 20A

4. Overcurrent protection for circuits supplying electric vehicle supply (EVSE) and wireless power transfer (WPTE) equipment shall have a current rating of not less than _____ of the maximum load of the electric vehicle supply equipment.
    (a) 100 percent
    (b) 110 percent
    (c) 125 percent
    (d) 150 percent

5. Electric vehicle charging loads shall be considered to be a(an) _____ load.
    (a) noncontinous
    (b) hard
    (c) extended
    (d) continuous

6. Services and feeders for EVSE shall be sized in accordance with the product ratings unless the overall rating of the installation can be limited through _____.
    (a) an energy management system (EMS) that provides load management of the EVSE
    (b) EVSE that has an ampere adjustment means with restricted access
    (c) ampere adjustments that are in accordance with the manufacturer's instructions
    (d) all of these

7. For electric vehicle supply and wireless power transfer equipment (EVSE and WPTE) more than _____ or more than 150V to ground, the disconnecting means shall be provided and installed in a readily accessible location.
    (a) 20A
    (b) 30A
    (c) 50A
    (d) 60A

8. Where a disconnecting means for EVSE and WPTE is required and installed remote from the equipment, a plaque shall be installed _____ denoting the location of the disconnecting means.
    (a) adjacent to the equipment
    (b) on the equipment
    (c) within 3 ft of the equipment
    (d) within sight of the equipment

9. Electric vehicle supply equipment _____ as suitable for charging electric vehicles indoors without ventilation is permitted indoors.
    (a) listed
    (b) labeled
    (c) identified
    (d) all of these

10. Where the equipment is listed for charging electric vehicles that require ventilation for _____ charging, mechanical ventilation, such as a fan, shall be provided.
   (a) outdoor
   (b) indoor
   (c) exterior
   (d) any of these

11. All receptacles installed for the connection of electric vehicle charging shall have _____.
   (a) arc-fault circuit-interrupter protection
   (b) ground-fault circuit-interrupter protection
   (c) current-limiting protection
   (d) ground-fault protection for equipment

ARTICLE 630—ELECTRIC WELDERS

1. Article _____ covers apparatus for electric arc welding, resistance welding, plasma cutting, and other similar welding and cutting process equipment that is connected to an electrical supply system.
   (a) 600
   (b) 620
   (c) 630
   (d) 680

2. All welding and cutting power equipment under the scope of Article 630 shall be _____.
   (a) identified
   (b) labeled
   (c) listed
   (d) approved

3. All 125V, 15A and 20A receptacles for electrical hand tools or portable lighting equipment, supplied by single-phase branch circuits rated _____ or less to ground, installed in work areas where welders are operated shall have ground-fault circuit-interrupter protection for personnel.
   (a) 125V
   (b) 150V
   (c) 240V
   (d) 250V

4. The ampacity of the supply conductors to an individual electric arc welder shall not be less than the _____ current value of the nameplate rating.
   (a) effective
   (b) instantaneous
   (c) peak
   (d) none of these

5. The minimum ampacity of conductors feeding a group of welders shall be based on the individual currents determined in 630.11(A) as the sum of _____ of the two largest welders, plus 85 percent of the third largest welder, plus 70 percent of the fourth largest welder, plus 60 percent of all remaining welders.
   (a) 100 percent
   (b) 115 percent
   (c) 125 percent
   (d) 175 percent

6. An arc welder shall have overcurrent protection rated or set at not more than _____ of the rated primary current of the welder.
   (a) 100 percent
   (b) 125 percent
   (c) 150 percent
   (d) 200 percent

7. A disconnecting means shall be provided in the supply circuit for each arc welder not equipped with _____.
   (a) a governor
   (b) a shunt-trip device
   (c) an integral disconnect
   (d) GFCI protection

8. The required ampacity for the supply conductors for a resistance welder with a duty cycle of 15 percent and a primary current of 21A is _____.
   (a) 5.67A
   (b) 6.72A
   (c) 8.19A
   (d) 9.45A

9. Each resistance welder shall have an overcurrent device rated or set at not more than _____ of the rated primary current of the welder.
   (a) 80 percent
   (b) 100 percent
   (c) 125 percent
   (d) 300 percent

10. Conductors that supply one or more resistance welders shall be protected by an overcurrent device rated or set at not more than _____ of the conductor ampacity.

(a) 80 percent
(b) 100 percent
(c) 125 percent
(d) 300 percent

11. A _____ shall be provided to disconnect each resistance welder and its control equipment from the supply circuit.

(a) contactor
(b) relay
(c) magnetic starter
(d) switch or circuit breaker

ARTICLE 640—AUDIO SIGNAL AMPLIFICATION AND REPRODUCTION EQUIPMENT

1. Electronic organs or other electronic musical instruments are included in the scope of Article _____.

(a) 640
(b) 641
(c) 650
(d) 680

2. For audio signal processing, amplification, and reproduction equipment, 300.22(B) shall apply to _____ installed in ducts specifically fabricated for environmental air.

(a) speakers
(b) Class 3 circuits
(c) circuits and equipment
(d) only power-limited circuits

3. Class 2 and Class 3 cables for audio signal processing, amplification, and reproduction equipment installed in accordance with 722.135(B) shall be permitted to be installed in ducts specifically fabricated for _____.

(a) environmental air
(b) processed air
(c) heat exchange air
(d) none of these

4. Class 2 and Class 3 cables for audio signal processing, amplification, and reproduction equipment installed in accordance with 722.135(B) shall not be permitted to be installed in other spaces used for environmental air (plenums).

(a) True
(b) False

5. Amplifiers, loudspeakers, and other equipment shall be located or protected so as to guard against environmental exposure or physical damage that might cause _____.

(a) a fire
(b) shock
(c) a personal hazard
(d) all of these

6. Exposed audio cables shall be secured by _____ or similar fittings designed and installed so as not to damage the cable.

(a) straps
(b) staples
(c) hangers
(d) any of these

7. The accessible portion of abandoned audio distribution cables shall be _____.

(a) removed
(b) tagged
(c) secured
(d) disconnected

8. Audio cables identified for future use shall be marked with a tag of sufficient durability to withstand _____.

(a) moisture
(b) humidity
(c) the environment involved
(d) temperature fluctuations

9. Audio system equipment supplied by branch-circuit power shall not be located within _____ horizontally of the inside wall of a pool, spa, hot tub, fountain, or prevailing tidal high-water mark.

(a) 18 in.
(b) 2 ft
(c) 5 ft
(d) 10 ft

1st Printing

ARTICLE 645—INFORMATION TECHNOLOGY EQUIPMENT (ITE)

1. Article 645 covers _____ and grounding of information technology equipment and systems in an information technology equipment room.

   (a) equipment
   (b) power-supply wiring
   (c) interconnecting wiring
   (d) all of these

2. Section(s) 300.21, 770.26, and 800.26 shall apply to penetrations of the _____ information technology room boundary.

   (a) rated-resistant
   (b) flame-resistant
   (c) smoke-resistant
   (d) fire-resistant

3. Wiring and cabling in other spaces used for environmental air (plenums) above an information technology equipment room must comply with _____.

   (a) wiring methods [300.22(C)(1)]
   (b) Class 2, Class 3, and PLTC cables [722.135(B)]
   (c) fire alarm systems [760.53(B)(2), 760.135(C), and Table 760.154]
   (d) all of these

4. Wiring and cabling in other spaces used for environmental air (plenums) above an information technology equipment room must comply with _____.

   (a) optical fiber cables [770.113(C) and Table 770.154(a)]
   (b) communications circuits [800.133(C) and Table 800.154(a)]
   (c) CATV and radio distribution systems [820.113(C) and Table 800.154(a)]
   (d) all of these

5. Article 645 does not apply unless an information technology equipment room contains _____.

   (a) a disconnecting means complying with 645.10
   (b) a separate heating/ventilating/air-conditioning (HVAC) system
   (c) separation by fire-resistance-rated walls, floors, and ceilings
   (d) all of these

6. Branch-circuit conductors for data processing equipment in information technology equipment rooms shall have an ampacity not less than _____ of the total connected load.

   (a) 80 percent
   (b) 100 percent
   (c) 125 percent
   (d) the sum

7. In information technology equipment rooms, where exposed to physical damage, _____ shall be protected.

   (a) power-supply cords
   (b) branch-circuit supply conductors
   (c) interconnecting cables
   (d) all of these

8. Where the area under the floor is accessible and openings minimize the entrance of debris beneath the floor, _____, and receptacles associated with the information technology equipment is permitted.

   (a) power-supply cords and communication cables
   (b) connecting and interconnecting cables
   (c) cord-and-plug connections
   (d) all of these

9. Information technology equipment branch-circuit supply conductors under a raised floor are permitted to be installed only in EMT.

   (a) True
   (b) False

10. General purpose Type _____ cables are permitted within the raised floor area of an information technology equipment room if installed in accordance with 722.135(E).

    (a) CMR
    (b) CM
    (c) CMG
    (d) CL2, CM, or CMG

11. Interconnecting cables under raised floors that support information technology equipment shall be listed Type _____ cable having adequate fire-resistant characteristics suitable for use under raised floors of an information technology equipment room.

    (a) RF
    (b) UF
    (c) LS
    (d) DP

12. Which of the following are permitted under raised floors of information technology equipment rooms for the support of information technology equipment?
    (a) Power-supply cords of listed information technology equipment in accordance with 645.5(B).
    (b) Interconnecting cables enclosed in a raceway.
    (c) Equipment grounding conductors.
    (d) all of these

13. In addition to optical fiber cables installed in accordance with 770.113(C), Types OFNR, OFCR, OFNG, OFCG, OFN, and OFC shall be permitted _____ raised floors of an information technology equipment room.
    (a) under
    (b) above
    (c) on top
    (d) none of these

14. Power-supply cords, communications cables, connecting cables, interconnecting cables, and associated boxes, connectors, plugs, and receptacles that are listed as part of, or for, information technology equipment shall not be required to be secured in place where installed _____.
    (a) above suspended ceilings
    (b) exposed on interior walls
    (c) under raised floors
    (d) exposed on exterior walls

15. An approved means shall be provided to disconnect power to all electronic equipment in the information technology equipment room or in designated zones within the room. There shall also be a similar approved means to disconnect the power to all _____ serving the room or designated zones.
    (a) dedicated HVAC systems
    (b) lighting circuits
    (c) audio systems
    (d) all of these

16. In information technology rooms, the remote disconnect controls shall be located at approved locations _____ in case of fire to authorized personnel and emergency responders.
    (a) accessible
    (b) readily accessible
    (c) secured
    (d) restricted

17. The remote disconnect means for the control of electronic equipment power and HVAC systems in information technology equipment rooms, shall be _____.
    (a) grouped
    (b) identified
    (c) grouped and identified
    (d) none of these

18. Exposed noncurrent-carrying metal parts of an information technology system shall be _____.
    (a) GFPE protected
    (b) inaccessible to unqualified personnel
    (c) GFCI protected
    (d) bonded to an equipment grounding conductor or double insulated

ARTICLE 680—SWIMMING POOLS, SPAS, HOT TUBS, FOUNTAINS, AND SIMILAR INSTALLATIONS

1. The construction and installation requirements of electrical wiring for, and equipment in or adjacent to, all swimming, wading, therapeutic, and decorative pools are covered in Article _____.
    (a) 555
    (b) 600
    (c) 680
    (d) 690

2. After the completion of permanently installed swimming pools, the authority having jurisdiction shall be permitted to require _____ inspection and testing.
    (a) seasonal
    (b) monthly
    (c) periodic
    (d) annual

3. Where required in Article 680, ground-fault protection of receptacles and outlets on branch circuits rated 150V or less to ground and _____ or less, single- or three-phase, shall be provided with a Class A GFCI.
    (a) 20A
    (b) 30A
    (c) 50A
    (d) 60A

4. Where required in Article 680, ground-fault protection of receptacles and outlets on branch circuits operating at voltages above 150V to ground, shall be provided with _____ protection not to exceed 20 mA.

   (a) Class A GFCI
   (b) GFPE
   (c) SPGFCI
   (d) current-limiting overcurrent

5. All electrical equipment and products covered by Article 680 shall be _____.

   (a) identified
   (b) labeled
   (c) listed
   (d) approved

6. Feeders and branch circuits installed in a corrosive environment or wet location near swimming pools shall contain an insulated copper EGC sized in accordance with Table 250.122, but not smaller than _____.

   (a) 12 AWG
   (b) 10 AWG
   (c) 8 AWG
   (d) 6 AWG

7. Field-installed terminals for swimming pools in damp or wet locations or corrosive environments shall be composed of copper, copper alloy, or stainless steel and shall be _____ for direct burial use.

   (a) identified
   (b) labeled
   (c) listed
   (d) approved

8. Overhead conductors and open overhead wiring not in _____ shall comply with the minimum clearances given in Table 680.9(A).

   (a) tubing
   (b) a conduit
   (c) a cable
   (d) a raceway

9. Overhead conductors for communications, radio, and television coaxial cable shall be located no less than _____ above the maximum water level of swimming and wading pools, diving structures, and observation stands, towers, or platforms.

   (a) 40 ft
   (b) 30 ft
   (c) 20 ft
   (d) 10 ft

10. All electric pool water heaters shall have the heating elements subdivided into loads not exceeding _____ and protected at not over 60A.

    (a) 20A
    (b) 35A
    (c) 48A
    (d) 60A

11. The ampacity of the branch-circuit conductors and the rating or setting of overcurrent protective devices for electrically powered swimming pool heat pumps and chillers using the circulating water system shall be sized _____.

    (a) to comply with the nameplate
    (b) not greater than 35A
    (c) at 125 percent of its rating
    (d) less than 60A

12. Underground wiring within 5 ft horizontally from the inside wall of the pool _____.

    (a) shall be permitted
    (b) shall not be permitted
    (c) shall be required
    (d) none of these

13. Underground wiring shall not be permitted under a pool unless this wiring is necessary to supply pool equipment.

    (a) True
    (b) False

14. Electric swimming pool equipment shall not be installed in vaults or pits that do not have drainage that prevents water accumulation during normal operation or maintenance unless the equipment is _____ and identified for submersion.

    (a) rated
    (b) listed
    (c) marked
    (d) approved

15. At least _____ GFCI-protected 125V, 15A or 20A receptacle(s) on a general-purpose circuit shall be located within a pool equipment room.

    (a) one
    (b) two
    (c) three
    (d) four

16. The maintenance disconnecting means required for swimming pool equipment shall be _____ and at least 5 ft from the water's edge, unless separated by a permanently installed barrier.

    (a) secured
    (b) at least 24 in. above the highest water level of the pool
    (c) capable of being locked in the open position
    (d) readily accessible and within sight from its equipment

17. Rigid metal conduit, intermediate metal conduit, rigid polyvinyl chloride conduit, reinforced thermosetting resin conduit, and liquidtight flexible nonmetallic conduit shall be considered to be resistant to the _____ environments that may be present in or about the areas covered by Article 680.

    (a) dry
    (b) damp
    (c) wet
    (d) corrosive

18. Equipment listed for pool and spa use shall be considered _____ for use in corrosive environments.

    (a) suitable
    (b) appropriate
    (c) acceptable
    (d) any of these

19. Outlets serving pool motors on branch circuits rated above 150V to ground and 60A or less shall be provided with _____ protection.

    (a) SPGFCI
    (b) GFCI
    (c) shunt-trip
    (d) current-limiting

20. Where a pool pump motor is replaced or repaired, the replacement or repaired pump motor shall be provided with _____.

    (a) new branch-circuit wiring
    (b) a new bonding jumper
    (c) GFCI protection
    (d) GFPE protection

21. A 125V receptacle shall be installed a minimum of _____ and a maximum of 20 ft from the inside wall of a permanently installed pool.

    (a) 3 ft
    (b) 6 ft
    (c) 8 ft
    (d) 12 ft

22. GFCI-protected receptacles that provide power for water-pump motors related to the circulation and sanitation system of a pool shall be located not less than _____ from the inside walls of the pool.

    (a) 3 ft
    (b) 6 ft
    (c) 8 ft
    (d) 12 ft

23. All receptacles rated 125V through 250V, 60A or less, located within _____ of the inside walls of a pool shall have GFCI protection.

    (a) 6 ft
    (b) 8 ft
    (c) 10 ft
    (d) 20 ft

24. Luminaires installed above new outdoor pools or the area extending _____ horizontally from the inside walls of the pool shall be installed at a height of not less than 12 ft above the maximum water level of the pool.

    (a) 3 ft
    (b) 5 ft
    (c) 10 ft
    (d) 12 ft

25. Listed low-voltage gas-fired luminaires, decorative fireplaces, fire pits, and similar equipment using low-voltage ignitors that do not require grounding and are supplied by listed transformers or power supplies that comply with 680.23(A)(2) with outputs that do not exceed the low-voltage contact limit shall be permitted to be located less than _____ from the inside walls of the pool.

    (a) 3 ft
    (b) 5 ft
    (c) 10 ft
    (d) 12 ft

1st Printing

26. Switching devices shall be at least _____ horizontally from the inside walls of a pool unless separated from the pool by a solid fence, wall, or other permanent barrier.

    (a) 3 ft
    (b) 5 ft
    (c) 10 ft
    (d) 12 ft

27. Equipment in or around pool areas with ratings exceeding the low-voltage contact limit shall be located at least _____ horizontally from the inside walls of a pool unless separated from the pool by a solid fence, wall, or other permanent barrier.

    (a) 5 ft
    (b) 8 ft
    (c) 10 ft
    (d) 20 ft

28. Transformers and power supplies used for the supply of underwater luminaires for swimming pools, together with the transformer or power-supply enclosure, shall be listed, labeled, and identified for _____ use.

    (a) damp location
    (b) wet location
    (c) outdoor location
    (d) swimming pool and spa

29. For permanently installed pools, a GFCI shall be installed in the branch circuit supplying luminaires operating at more than the low-voltage _____.

    (a) setting
    (b) listing
    (c) contact limit
    (d) trip limit

30. Wet-niche luminaires shall be installed with the top of the luminaire lens not less than _____ below the normal water level of the pool.

    (a) 6 in.
    (b) 12 in.
    (c) 18 in.
    (d) 24 in.

31. When PVC is run from a pool light forming shell to a pool junction box, an 8 AWG _____ bonding jumper shall be installed in the raceway.

    (a) solid bare
    (b) solid insulated copper
    (c) stranded insulated copper
    (d) solid or stranded insulated copper

32. Wet-niche luminaires installed in swimming pools shall be removable from the water for inspection, relamping, or other maintenance. The luminaire maintenance location shall be accessible _____.

    (a) while the pool is drained
    (b) without entering the pool water
    (c) during construction
    (d) all of these

33. Where branch-circuit wiring on the supply side of enclosures and junction boxes connected to conduits run to underwater luminaires are installed in _____ environments, the wiring method of that portion of the branch circuit shall be in accordance with 680.14.

    (a) dry
    (b) damp
    (c) wet
    (d) corrosive

34. A pool light junction box connected to a conduit that extends directly to a forming shell shall be _____ for this use.

    (a) listed
    (b) identified
    (c) labeled
    (d) all of these

35. The pool light junction box shall be located not less than _____, measured from the inside of the bottom of the box, above the ground level or pool deck, or not less than 8 in. above the maximum pool water level, whichever provides the greater elevation.

    (a) 4 in.
    (b) 6 in.
    (c) 8 in.
    (d) 12 in.

36. The pool light junction box shall be located not less than _____ from the inside wall of the pool, unless separated from the pool by a solid fence, wall, or other permanent barrier

(a) 2 ft
(b) 3 ft
(c) 4 ft
(d) 6 ft

37. The _____ of a pool light junction box, transformer enclosure, or other enclosure in the supply circuit to a wet-niche or no-niche luminaire and the field-wiring chamber of a dry-niche luminaire shall be connected to the equipment grounding terminal of the panelboard.

(a) equipment grounding jumper
(b) grounded conductors
(c) grounding terminals
(d) ungrounded conductors

38. The equipotential bonding required by 680.26(B)and (C) to reduce _____ gradients in the pool area shall be installed only for pools with associated electrical equipment related to the pool.

(a) current
(b) voltage
(c) resistance
(d) power

39. The parts specified in 680.26(B)(1) through (B)(7) shall be bonded together using solid copper conductors, insulated, covered, or bare, not smaller than _____.

(a) 12 AWG
(b) 10 AWG
(c) 8 AWG
(d) 6 AWG

40. Reconstructed pool shells shall meet the equipotential bonding requirements of section 680.26.

(a) True
(b) False

41. For equipotential bonding of permanently installed pools, the perimeter surface to be bonded shall be considered to extend for _____ horizontally beyond the inside walls of the pool and shall include unpaved surfaces and other types of paving.

(a) 3 ft
(b) 5 ft
(c) 10 ft
(d) 12 ft

42. Where a copper grid is used for the purposes of equipotential bonding around pool perimeter surfaces, the copper grid shall be secured within or below a paved surface, but no more than _____ below finished grade.

(a) 2 in.
(b) 4 in.
(c) 6 in.
(d) 8 in.

43. For perimeter equipotential bonding of permanently installed pools, where conductive pool shell structural reinforcing steel is not available or is encapsulated in a nonconductive compound, a copper ring shall be utilized where _____.

(a) a minimum 8 AWG bare solid copper conductor is provided and follows the contour of the perimeter surface
(b) only listed splicing devices or exothermic welding are used
(c) the conductor is 18 in. to 24 in. from the inside wall of the pool and 4 to 6 in. below the finished grade
(d) all of these

44. All fixed metal parts where located no greater than _____ horizontally of the inside walls of the pool shall be bonded unless separated by a permanent barrier.

(a) 4 ft
(b) 5 ft
(c) 8 ft
(d) 10 ft

45. All fixed metal parts where located no greater than _____ vertically above the maximum water level of the pool, observation stands, towers, or platforms, or any diving structures, shall be bonded.

(a) 6 ft
(b) 8 ft
(c) 10 ft
(d) 12 ft

46. The electric motors, controllers, and wiring for an electrically operated pool cover shall be located at least _____ from the inside wall of the pool or separated from the pool by a permanent barrier.

(a) 5 ft
(b) 6 ft
(c) 10 ft
(d) 20 ft

1st Printing

47. The electric motor and controller for an electrically operated pool cover shall be _____.

(a) GFCI protected
(b) AFCI protected
(c) GFPE protected
(d) current limited

48. Circuits serving gas-fired swimming pool and spa water heaters operating at voltages above the low-voltage contact limit shall be provided with _____ protection.

(a) GFCI
(b) AFCI
(c) combined AFCI/GFCI
(d) a gas valve emergency shut-off

49. All receptacles rated 125V through 250V, 60A or less, located within _____ of the inside walls of a storable pool, storable spa, or storable hot tub shall have GFCI protection or SPGFCI protection in accordance with 680.5(B) or (C) as applicable.

(a) 8 ft
(b) 10 ft
(c) 15 ft
(d) 20 ft

50. Receptacles shall be located not less than _____ from the inside walls of a storable pool, storable spa, or storable hot tub.

(a) 5 ft
(b) 6 ft
(c) 15 ft
(d) 20 ft

51. For permanently installed spas or hot tubs in other than one-family dwellings, a clearly labeled emergency shutoff or control switch for the purpose of stopping the motor(s) that provides power to the recirculation system and jet system shall be installed at a point _____ to the users and, not less than 5 ft away, adjacent to, and within sight of the spa or hot tub.

(a) accessible
(b) readily accessible
(c) available
(d) of the pneumatic type and accessible

52. Where spas or hot tubs are installed indoors, the equipotential bonding requirements for perimeter surfaces in 680.26(B)(2) shall not apply to a listed self-contained spa or hot tub installed above a finished floor.

(a) True
(b) False

53. At least one 15A or 20A, 125V receptacle on a general-purpose branch circuit shall be located a minimum of _____ and a maximum of 10 ft from the inside wall of a spa or hot tub installed indoors.

(a) 18 in.
(b) 2 ft
(c) 6 ft
(d) 7 ft 6 in.

54. Receptacles rated 125V through 250V, _____ or less located within 10 ft of the inside walls of an indoor spa or hot tub, shall have GFCI protection or SPGFCI protection in accordance with 680.5(B) or (C) as applicable.

(a) 20A
(b) 30A
(c) 60A
(d) 100A

55. Switches shall be located at least _____, measured horizontally, from the inside walls of an indoor spa or hot tub.

(a) 4 ft
(b) 5 ft
(c) 7 ft 6 in.
(d) 12 ft

56. The outlet(s) that supplies a _____ shall have GFCI protection or SPGFCI protection in accordance with 680.5(B) or (C) as applicable except as otherwise provided in 680.44.

(a) self-contained spa or hot tub
(b) packaged spa or hot tub equipment assembly
(c) field-assembled spa or hot tub
(d) all of these

57. Permanently installed fountains shall comply with Part(s) I and V of Article 680. Fountains that have water common to a pool shall also comply with Part(s) _____ of Article 680.

(a) II
(b) III
(c) IV
(d) all of these

58. Permanently installed fountains intended for recreational use by pedestrians, including _____, shall also comply with the requirements in 680.26.

    (a) splash pads
    (b) hot tubs
    (c) spas
    (d) all of these

59. Permanently installed fountain equipment with ratings exceeding the low-voltage contact limit shall be located at least _____ horizontally from the inside walls of a spa or hot tub, unless separated from the spa or hot tub by a solid fence, wall, or other permanent barrier.

    (a) 3 ft
    (b) 5 ft
    (c) 6 ft
    (d) 10 ft

60. The maximum exposed length of a fountain cord shall be limited to _____.

    (a) 5 ft
    (b) 10 ft
    (c) 12 ft
    (d) 15 ft

61. Luminaires installed in a fountain shall _____.

    (a) be removable from the water for relamping or normal maintenance
    (b) not have a metal housing
    (c) be permitted to be installed embedded in the concrete
    (d) be permitted to require draining of the fountain for maintenance or relamping

62. Metal piping systems associated with a fountain shall be bonded to the equipment grounding conductor of the _____.

    (a) branch circuit supplying the fountain
    (b) bonding grid
    (c) fountain's equipotential plane
    (d) grounding electrode system

63. Electrical equipment for fountains that is supplied by a flexible cord shall have all exposed noncurrent-carrying metal parts grounded by an insulated copper equipment grounding conductor that is an integral part of the _____.

    (a) cord
    (b) feeder circuit
    (c) branch circuit
    (d) fountain

64. All electrical equipment for fountains, including power-supply cords, shall be _____ protected.

    (a) AFCI
    (b) GFCI
    (c) current-limiting
    (d) GFPE

65. Electric signs installed within a fountain or within _____ of the fountain edge shall have GFCI protection.

    (a) 2 ft
    (b) 5 ft
    (c) 6 ft
    (d) 10 ft

66. All receptacles rated 125V through 250V, 60A or less, located within _____ of a fountain edge shall have GFCI protection or SPGFCI protection in accordance with 680.5(B) or (C) as applicable.

    (a) 8 ft
    (b) 10 ft
    (c) 15 ft
    (d) 20 ft

67. Outlets supplying all permanently installed nonsubmersible pump motors for fountains shall have _____ protection.

    (a) AFCI and GFCI
    (b) GFPE
    (c) AFCI and GFPE
    (d) GFCI or SPGFCI

68. Hydromassage bathtubs and their associated electrical components shall be on an individual branch circuit(s) and protected by a(an) _____ GFCI.

    (a) exposed
    (b) accessible
    (c) readily accessible
    (d) concealed

69. Hydromassage bathtub electrical equipment shall be _____ without damaging the building structure or building finish.

    (a) readily accessible
    (b) accessible
    (c) within sight
    (d) installed

70. For hydromassage bathtubs, small conductive surfaces not likely to become energized, such as air and water jets, supply valve assemblies, and drain fittings not connected to metallic piping, and towel bars, mirror frames, and similar nonelectrical equipment not connected to _____ shall not be required to be bonded.

    (a) metal framing
    (b) nonmetallic framing
    (c) metal gas piping
    (d) any of these

71. Where installed for hydromassage bathtubs, double-insulated _____ shall not be bonded.

    (a) motors and blowers
    (b) cords
    (c) cables
    (d) fittings

72. Where installed for hydromassage bathtubs, small conductive surfaces of electrical equipment not likely to become energized, such as the mounting strap or yoke of a listed light switch or receptacle that is grounded, shall not be required to be bonded.

    (a) True
    (b) False

73. Where installed for hydromassage bathtubs, _____ shall be bonded together.

    (a) all exposed metal surfaces that are within 5 ft of the inside walls of the tub and not separated from the tub area by a permanent barrier
    (b) small conductive surfaces such as towel bars and mirror frames
    (c) double-insulated motors
    (d) mounting straps or yokes of listed light switches or receptacles

74. The 8 AWG solid bonding jumper required for equipotential bonding in the area of hydromassage bathtubs shall not be required to be extended to any _____.

    (a) remote panelboard
    (b) service equipment
    (c) electrode
    (d) any of these

ARTICLE 690—SOLAR PHOTOVOLTAIC (PV) SYSTEMS

1. Article 690 applies to solar _____ systems, including the array circuit(s), inverter(s), and controller(s) for such systems.

    (a) photoconductive
    (b) PV
    (c) photogenic
    (d) photosynthesis

2. All equipment intended for use in PV systems shall be listed or be _____ for the application and have a field label applied.

    (a) identified
    (b) marked
    (c) approved
    (d) evaluated

3. Where multiple PV systems are in or on a single building or structure remotely located from each other, a directory in accordance with 705.10 shall be provided at each PV system _____.

    (a) disconnecting means
    (b) array
    (c) collector
    (d) inverter

4. PV system equipment and disconnecting means shall not be installed in bathrooms, unless listed for the application.

    (a) True
    (b) False

5. Electronic power converters and their associated devices installed on PV systems can be mounted on roofs or other areas where they are not _____ accessible.

    (a) readily
    (b) easily
    (c) relatively
    (d) any of these

6. PV equipment floating on or attached to structures floating on bodies of water shall be _____ and shall utilize wiring methods that allow for any expected movement of the equipment.
   (a) designed for the purpose
   (b) listed for the purpose
   (c) identified as being suitable for the purpose
   (d) approved by marina authorities

7. The requirements of Article _____ pertaining to PV source circuits shall not apply to ac modules or ac module systems. The PV source circuit, conductors, and inverters shall be considered as internal components of an ac module or ac module system.
   (a) 660
   (b) 670
   (c) 680
   (d) 690

8. In PV systems, the output of an ac module or an ac module system is considered a(an) _____ output circuit.
   (a) inverter
   (b) module
   (c) PV
   (d) subarray

9. For calculating maximum PV source circuit voltage, one source for lowest-expected _____ temperature design data for various locations is the chapter titled Extreme Annual Mean Minimum Design Dry Bulb Temperature found in the ASHRAE *Handbook—Fundamentals*.
   (a) ambient
   (b) average
   (c) medium
   (d) any of these

10. For crystalline and multicrystalline silicon modules, the PV system voltage ambient temperature correction is _____ if the ambient temperature is 20°C.
   (a) 1.02
   (b) 1.04
   (c) 1.06
   (d) 1.08

11. The maximum dc voltage for a PV source circuit is permitted to be calculated in accordance with the sum of the PV module-rated open-circuit voltage of the series-connected modules in the PV string circuit _____ for the lowest expected ambient temperature using the open-circuit voltage temperature coefficients in accordance with the instructions included in the listing or labeling of the module.
   (a) corrected
   (b) adjusted
   (c) demanded
   (d) none of these

12. For crystalline and multicrystalline silicon modules, the maximum dc source circuit voltage is equal to the sum of the PV module rated open-circuit voltage of the _____-connected modules in the PV string circuit corrected for the lowest expected ambient temperature using the correction factors provided in Table 690.7(A).
   (a) parallel
   (b) series
   (c) series-parallel
   (d) multiwire

13. For a PV system source circuit with an inverter generating capacity of _____ or greater, the maximum dc voltage is permitted to be a documented and stamped PV system design, using an industry standard method maximum voltage calculation provided by a licensed professional electrical engineer.
   (a) 25 kW
   (b) 50 kW
   (c) 75 kW
   (d) 100 kW

14. For PV dc-to-dc converter circuits connected to the output of a single dc-to-dc converter, the _____ shall be determined in accordance with the instructions included in the listing or labeling of the dc-to-dc converter.
   (a) minimum voltage
   (b) minimum current
   (c) maximum voltage
   (d) maximum current

1st Printing

15. A permanent readily visible label indicating the highest maximum dc voltage in a PV system, calculated in accordance with 690.7, shall be provided by the installer at the _____.
    (a) dc PV system disconnecting means
    (b) PV system electronic power conversion equipment
    (c) distribution equipment associated with the PV system
    (d) any of these

16. For circuit sizing and current calculation of PV systems, the maximum PV source current is equal to the sum of the short-circuit current ratings of the PV modules connected in _____ multiplied by 125 percent.
    (a) series
    (b) parallel
    (c) series-parallel
    (d) multiwire

17. For circuit sizing and current calculation of PV systems, the maximum PV inverter output circuit current is equal to the inverter _____ output current rating.
    (a) average
    (b) peak
    (c) continuous
    (d) intermittent

18. For circuit sizing calculations of PV systems without adjustment and/or correction factors, the minimum conductor size must have an ampacity not less than the maximum currents calculated in 690.8(A) multiplied by _____.
    (a) 75 percent
    (b) 100 percent
    (c) 125 percent
    (d) 150 percent

19. Overcurrent protection for PV system dc circuit conductors and equipment shall not be required where the _____.
    (a) conductors have sufficient ampacity for the maximum circuit current
    (b) currents from all sources do not exceed the maximum overcurrent protective device rating specified for the PV module or electronic power converter
    (c) conductors have a short-circuit rating above the available fault current
    (d) conductors have sufficient ampacity for the maximum circuit current and the currents from all sources do not exceed the maximum overcurrent protective device rating specified for the PV module or electronic power converter

20. For PV systems where overcurrent protection is required on one end and the circuit conductor is also connected to a source having an available maximum current greater than the ampacity of the circuit conductor, the circuit conductors shall be protected from overcurrent at the point of connection to _____ current source(s).
    (a) the lower
    (b) the higher
    (c) either
    (d) both

21. Overcurrent devices used in PV source circuits shall be _____ for use in PV systems.
    (a) identified
    (b) approved
    (c) recognized
    (d) listed

22. Overcurrent devices for PV source circuits shall be sized not less than _____ of the maximum currents calculated in 690.8(A).
    (a) 80 percent
    (b) 100 percent
    (c) 125 percent
    (d) 250 percent

23. The overcurrent device rating for a PV source circuit assembly that, together with its overcurrent device(s), is listed for continuous operation at 100 percent of its rating shall be permitted to be used at _____ of its rating.
    (a) 100 percent
    (b) 125 percent
    (c) 225 percent
    (d) 150 percent

24. Overcurrent devices for PV system dc circuits shall be readily accessible.
    (a) True
    (b) False

25. Photovoltaic systems with PV system dc circuits operating at _____ dc or greater between any two conductors shall be protected by a listed PV arc-fault circuit interrupter, or other system components listed to provide equivalent protection.
    (a) 30V
    (b) 50V
    (c) 80V
    (d) 120V

26. PV system dc circuits that utilize metal-clad cables installed _____ shall be permitted without AFCI protection where the circuits are not installed in or on buildings.
    (a) in metal raceways
    (b) in enclosed metal cable trays
    (c) underground
    (d) any of these

27. PV system dc circuits that utilize metal-clad cables installed _____ shall be permitted without AFCI protection where the circuits are located in or on detached structures whose sole purpose is to support or contain PV system equipment.
    (a) in metal raceways
    (b) in enclosed metal cable trays
    (c) underground
    (d) any of these

28. PV system circuits installed on or in buildings shall include _____ to reduce shock hazard for firefighters.
    (a) ground-fault circuit protection
    (b) arc-fault circuit protection
    (c) a rapid shutdown function
    (d) automated power transfer

29. Ground-mounted PV system circuits that _____ buildings, of which the sole purpose is to house PV system equipment, shall not be required to comply with the 690.12 requirements for rapid shutdown.
    (a) enter
    (b) pass through
    (c) enter or pass through
    (d) none of these

30. PV equipment and circuits installed on nonenclosed _____ structures including but not limited to parking shade structures, carports, solar trellises, and similar structures shall not be required to comply with the 690.12 requirements for rapid shutdown.
    (a) detached
    (b) attached
    (c) fixed
    (d) separate

31. PV system circuits originating within or from arrays not attached to buildings that terminate on the _____ of buildings shall not be considered controlled conductors for the purposes of requiring a rapid shutdown function.
    (a) exterior
    (b) interior
    (c) inside
    (d) none of these

32. The rapid shutdown function reduces the risk of electrical shock that dc circuits in a PV system could pose for _____.
    (a) personnel
    (b) employees
    (c) firefighters
    (d) installers

33. The requirements for the controlled conductors that are part of the rapid shutdown of a PV system shall apply to _____.
    (a) PV system dc circuits
    (b) inverter output circuits originating from inverters located within the array boundary
    (c) PV system ac circuits
    (d) PV system dc circuits and inverter output circuits originating from inverters located within the array boundary

34. For the purpose of a PV system rapid shutdown system, the term array boundary as used in 690.12(B) is defined as _____ from the array in all directions.
    (a) 1 ft
    (b) 3 ft
    (c) 5 ft
    (d) 50 ft

35. For the purpose of a PV system rapid shutdown system, equipment and systems shall be permitted to meet the requirements of both inside and outside the array as defined by the _____.
    (a) manufacturer's instructions included with the listing
    (b) installer
    (c) inspector
    (d) local utility

36. For PV system rapid shutdown systems, controlled conductors located outside the array boundary or more than 3 ft from the point of entry inside a building shall be limited to not more than _____ within 30 seconds of rapid shutdown initiation.

(a) 80V
(b) 50V
(c) 30V
(d) 15V

37. The PV system rapid shutdown function shall provide shock hazard control for firefighters by limiting the highest voltage inside equipment or between any two conductors of a circuit or any conductor and ground inside array boundary to not more than 80V within _____ of rapid shutdown initiation.

(a) 30 seconds
(b) 45 seconds
(c) 60 seconds
(d) 90 seconds

38. For PV system rapid shutdown systems, the rapid shutdown initiation device off position shall indicate that the rapid shutdown function has been _____ for all PV systems connected to that device.

(a) initiated
(b) locked out
(c) disconnected
(d) activated

39. For one-family and two-family dwellings, the rapid shutdown initiation device(s) where required, shall be located at a(an) _____ location outside the building.

(a) accessible
(b) secured
(c) public
(d) readily accessible

40. For a single PV system, the rapid shutdown initiation shall occur by the operation of which of the following devices?

(a) The service disconnecting means.
(b) The PV system disconnecting means.
(c) A readily accessible switch that plainly indicates whether it is in the off or on position.
(d) any of these

41. Buildings with PV systems having rapid shutdown shall have a permanent label located at each service equipment location to which the PV systems are connected or at an approved readily visible location and shall indicate the location of _____.

(a) overcurrent protection devices
(b) utility connections
(c) non-utility power sources
(d) rapid shutdown initiation devices

42. The required label for buildings with PV systems having rapid shutdown shall be titled "SOLAR PV SYSTEM IS EQUIPPED WITH RAPID SHUTDOWN" in capitalized letters at least _____ high.

(a) ¼ in.
(b) 5⁄16 in.
(c) ⅜ in.
(d) ½ in.

43. For buildings that have PV systems with more than one rapid shutdown type or PV systems with no rapid shutdown, a detailed plan view diagram of the roof shall be provided showing each different PV system with a dotted line around areas that remain _____ after rapid shutdown is initiated.

(a) energized
(b) de-energized
(c) grounded
(d) none of these

44. For buildings with rapid shutdown, the rapid shutdown switch shall have a label that reads "RAPID SHUTDOWN SWITCH FOR SOLAR PV SYSTEM" installed within _____ of the switch.

(a) 3 ft
(b) 6 ft
(c) 10 ft
(d) 25 ft

45. A means is required to disconnect the PV system from all wiring systems including power systems, energy storage systems, and utilization equipment and its associated premises wiring.

(a) True
(b) False

46. The PV system disconnecting means shall be installed at a(an) _____ location.

(a) guarded
(b) accessible
(c) protected
(d) readily accessible

47. Where PV system disconnecting means of systems above _____ are readily accessible to unqualified persons, any enclosure door or hinged cover that exposes live parts when open shall be locked or require a tool to open.

    (a) 30V
    (b) 120V
    (c) 240V
    (d) 600V

48. The PV system disconnecting means shall plainly indicate whether in the open (off) or closed (on) position and be _____ "PV SYSTEM DISCONNECT" or equivalent.

    (a) listed as a
    (b) approved as a
    (c) permanently marked
    (d) temporarily marked

49. The PV system disconnecting means shall have ratings sufficient for the _____ that is available at the terminals of the PV system disconnect.

    (a) maximum circuit current
    (b) available fault current
    (c) voltage
    (d) all of these

50. For PV systems, means shall be provided to _____ ac PV modules, fuses, dc-to-dc converters, inverters, and charge controllers from all conductors that are not solidly grounded.

    (a) disconnect
    (b) open
    (c) close
    (d) turn off

51. Where a disconnect is required to _____ PV system equipment, the equipment disconnecting means shall be installed in accordance with 690.15(C).

    (a) open
    (b) isolate
    (c) close
    (d) open or close

52. Where a disconnect is required to isolate PV system equipment, the disconnecting means shall be permitted to be an isolating device as part of listed equipment where an interlock or similar means _____ the opening of the isolating device under load.

    (a) prevents
    (b) prohibits
    (c) facilitates
    (d) any of these

53. Where a disconnect is required to isolate PV system equipment with a maximum circuit current of _____ or less, an isolating device shall be installed in accordance with 690.15(B).

    (a) 15A
    (b) 20A
    (c) 30A
    (d) 50A

54. An isolating device for PV system equipment shall which of the following?

    (a) A mating connector meeting the requirements of 690.33 and listed and identified for use with specific equipment.
    (b) A finger-safe fuse holder or an isolating switch that requires a tool to place the device in the open (off) position.
    (c) An isolating device listed for the intended application.
    (d) any of these

55. The PV system equipment disconnecting means shall have ratings sufficient for the _____ that is available at the terminals of the PV system disconnect.

    (a) maximum circuit current
    (b) available fault current
    (c) voltage
    (d) all of these

56. Where PV source and output circuits operating at over 30V are installed in readily accessible locations, circuit conductors shall be guarded or installed in _____.

    (a) MC cable
    (b) multiconductor jacketed cable
    (c) a raceway
    (d) any of these

57. Where not otherwise allowed in an equipment's listing, PV system dc circuits shall not occupy the same equipment wiring enclosure, cable, or raceway as other non-PV systems, or inverter output circuits, unless separated from other circuits by a _____.

    (a) barrier
    (b) partition
    (c) barrier or partition
    (d) none of these

58. PV system dc circuits shall not occupy the same equipment wiring enclosure, cable, or raceway as other non-PV systems, or inverter output circuits, unless the PV system dc circuits are separated from other circuits by a barrier or _____.

    (a) partition
    (b) sleeve
    (c) double insulation
    (d) shield

59. PV system dc circuit conductors that rely on other than color coding for polarity identification shall be identified by an approved permanent marking means such as _____.

    (a) labeling
    (b) sleeving
    (c) shrink-tubing
    (d) any of these

60. PV system dc circuit conductor marking means for nonsolidly grounded positive conductors shall include imprinted plus signs (+) or the word POSITIVE or POS durably marked on insulation of a color other than _____.

    (a) green
    (b) white
    (c) gray
    (d) all of these

61. PV system dc circuit conductors shall have polarity identification at all termination, connection, and splice points by _____.

    (a) color coding
    (b) marking tape
    (c) tagging or other approved means
    (d) all of these

62. Where ac and dc conductors of PV systems occupy the same junction box, pull box, or wireway, the ac and dc conductors shall be grouped separately by cable ties or similar means at least once and at intervals not to exceed _____.

    (a) 1 ft
    (b) 3 ft
    (c) 6 ft
    (d) 10 ft

63. The requirement for grouping PV system conductors is not required if the circuit enters from a cable or raceway unique to the circuit that makes the grouping obvious.

    (a) True
    (b) False

64. Single-conductor PV system cables with _____ insulation marked sunlight resistant can be used to connect photovoltaic modules in outdoor locations within the PV array.

    (a) THHN
    (b) USE-2
    (c) RHW-2
    (d) USE-2 and RHW-2

65. Single-conductor PV wire or cable of all sizes shall be permitted in cable trays installed in outdoor locations, provided that the cables are supported at intervals not to exceed _____ and secured at intervals not to exceed 54 in.

    (a) 12 in.
    (b) 24 in.
    (c) 36 in.
    (d) 48 in.

66. Flexible cords and flexible cables, where connected to moving parts of tracking PV _____, shall comply with Article 400.

    (a) systems
    (b) arrays
    (c) cells
    (d) modules

67. Where inside buildings, PV system dc circuits that exceed 30V or 8A shall be contained in _____.

    (a) metal raceways
    (b) MC cable that complies with 250.118(10)
    (c) metal enclosures
    (d) any of these

68. Labels or markings of PV system raceways and enclosures shall be suitable for the environment and be placed with a maximum of _____ of spacing.

(a) 5 ft
(b) 10 ft
(c) 20 ft
(d) 25 ft

69. Which of the following wiring methods and enclosures that contain photovoltaic power source conductors shall be marked "PHOTOVOLTAIC POWER SOURCE"?

(a) Exposed raceways, cable trays, and other wiring methods.
(b) The covers or enclosures of pull boxes and junction boxes.
(c) Conduit bodies in which any of the available conduit openings are unused.
(d) all of these

70. Equipment and wiring methods containing PV system dc circuits with a maximum voltage greater than 1,000V shall not be permitted _____.

(a) on or in single-family dwellings
(b) on or in two-family dwellings
(c) within buildings containing habitable rooms
(d) all of these

71. Equipment and wiring methods containing PV system dc circuits with a maximum voltage greater than 1000V, where installed on the exterior of buildings, shall be located not less than _____ above grade.

(a) 8 ft
(b) 10 ft
(c) 12 ft
(d) 15 ft

72. Fittings and connectors that are intended to be concealed at the time of on-site assembly, where _____ for such use, shall be permitted for on-site interconnection of PV modules or other array components.

(a) approved
(b) identified
(c) marked
(d) listed

73. Mating connectors used in PV source circuits shall be polarized and shall have a configuration that are _____ with receptacles in other electrical systems on the premises.

(a) noninterchangeable
(b) interchangeable
(c) compatible
(d) none of these

74. Mating connectors that are readily accessible and that are used in PV source circuits operating at over 30V dc or 15V ac shall require a _____ for opening.

(a) special access code
(b) lock combination
(c) password
(d) tool

75. Mating connectors used for PV circuits shall _____.

(a) be rated for the interrupting current with no risk of injury or hazard
(b) require a tool to open and be marked
(c) be supplied as part of the listed equipment
(d) any of these

76. Junction, pull, and outlet boxes located behind modules or panels shall be so installed that the wiring contained in them can be rendered accessible directly or by displacement of a module(s) or panel(s) secured by removable fasteners and connected _____.

(a) in a raceway
(b) by a flexible wiring system
(c) in PVC
(d) in RMC

77. Exposed noncurrent-carrying metal parts of PV module frames, electrical equipment, and conductor enclosures of PV systems shall be connected to a(an) _____.

(a) grounding jumper
(b) bonding jumper
(c) equipment grounding conductor
(d) grounding jumper or bonding jumper

1st Printing

78. Devices and systems used for mounting PV modules that are also used for bonding module frames shall be _____ for bonding PV modules.

    (a) listed
    (b) labeled
    (c) identified
    (d) all of these

79. _____ conductors shall be permitted to be run separately from the PV system conductors within the PV array.

    (a) Bonding
    (b) Alternating-current
    (c) Surge protective
    (d) Equipment grounding

80. The bonding requirements contained in 250.97 shall apply only to solidly grounded PV system circuits operating over _____ to ground.

    (a) 30V
    (b) 60V
    (c) 120V
    (d) 250V

81. Equipment grounding conductors for PV system circuits shall be sized in accordance with _____.

    (a) 250.4
    (b) 250.66
    (c) 250.102
    (d) 250.122

82. For PV systems that are not solidly grounded, the _____ for the output of the PV system, where connected to associated distribution equipment connected to a grounding electrode system, shall be permitted to be the only connection to ground for the system.

    (a) equipment grounding conductor
    (b) grounding conductor
    (c) grounded conductor
    (d) any of these

ARTICLE 691—LARGE-SCALE PHOTOVOLTAIC (PV) ELECTRIC SUPPLY STATIONS

1. Article _____ covers the installation of large-scale PV electric supply stations not under exclusive utility control.

    (a) 690
    (b) 691
    (c) 694
    (d) 695

2. Large-scale PV systems that do not provide arc-fault protection shall include details of fire mitigation plans to address _____ in the documentation required in 691.6.

    (a) dc arc faults
    (b) dc and ac arc faults
    (c) dc ground faults
    (d) dc and ac ground faults

3. According to 691.1, facilities covered by Article 691 have specific design and safety features unique to large-scale _____ facilities outlined in 691.4 and are operated for the sole purpose of providing electric supply to a system operated by a regulated utility for the transfer of electric energy.

    (a) industrial
    (b) electrical
    (c) distribution
    (d) PV

4. The electrical circuits and equipment of large-scale PV electric supply stations shall be maintained and operated only by _____ persons.

    (a) qualified
    (b) authorized
    (c) utility
    (d) operational

5. Access to large-scale PV electric supply stations shall be _____ in accordance with 110.31.

    (a) allowed
    (b) restricted
    (c) permitted
    (d) none of these

6. The electrical loads within a large-scale PV electric supply station shall only be used to power auxiliary equipment for the _____ of the PV power.
   (a) distribution
   (b) storage
   (c) generation
   (d) regulation

7. _____ PV electric supply stations are permitted to be installed on buildings.
   (a) Isolated
   (b) Large-scale
   (c) Island mode
   (d) Interconnected

8. Electrical equipment for large-scale PV electric supply stations shall only be approved for installation by _____.
   (a) listing and labeling
   (b) being evaluated for the application and having a field label applied
   (c) qualified personnel
   (d) listing and labeling or by being evaluated for the application and having a field label applied

9. Engineering documentation of large-scale electric supply stations shall include details of conformance of the design with _____.
   (a) Article 250
   (b) Article 690
   (c) Article 702
   (d) Article 710

10. Documentation by a licensed professional _____ that the construction of the large-scale PV electric supply station conforms to the electrical engineered design shall be provided upon request of the authority having jurisdiction
    (a) PV installer
    (b) electrician
    (c) electrical engineer
    (d) electrical inspector

11. The engineered design required for large-scale PV electric supply stations, shall document _____ procedures and means of isolating equipment.
    (a) disconnection
    (b) maintenance
    (c) inspection
    (d) installation

12. Buildings whose sole purpose is to house and protect large-scale PV supply station equipment shall not be required to comply with 690.12. Written standard _____ shall be available at the site detailing necessary shutdown procedures in the event of an emergency.
    (a) guidelines
    (b) operating procedures
    (c) documentation
    (d) any of these

13. Fire mitigation plans, where required for large-scale PV systems, are typically reviewed by the _____ and include topics such as access roads within the facility.
    (a) electrical inspector
    (b) civil engineer
    (c) local fire agency
    (d) forestry service

ARTICLE 695—FIRE PUMPS

1. Article 695 covers the installation of the electric power sources and interconnecting circuits, and the switching and control equipment dedicated to drivers for _____.
   (a) generators
   (b) fire pumps
   (c) alarm systems
   (d) large-scale solar arrays

2. The requirements for _____ are not covered by Article 695.
   (a) the installation of pressure maintenance pumps
   (b) fire pump controllers
   (c) fire pump disconnects
   (d) all of these

3. Power to fire pump motors shall be capable of carrying indefinitely the _____ when connected to the power supply.
   (a) sum of the locked-rotor current of the fire pump motor(s)
   (b) locked-rotor current of the pressure maintenance pump motors
   (c) full-load current of any associated fire pump equipment
   (d) all of these

1st Printing

4. When a fire pump is supplied by an individual source, the _____ shall be rated to carry indefinitely the sum of the locked-rotor current of the largest fire pump motor and the full-load current of all of the other pump motors and accessory equipment.
   (a) overcurrent protective device(s)
   (b) pump motor conductors
   (c) pump motor controllers
   (d) source supply conductors

5. Transformers that supply a fire pump motor shall be sized no less than _____ of the sum of the fire pump motor(s) and pressure maintenance pump motors, and 100 percent of associated fire pump accessory equipment.
   (a) 100 percent
   (b) 125 percent
   (c) 250 percent
   (d) 300 percent

6. The primary overcurrent protective device for a transformer supplying a fire pump shall carry the sum of the locked-rotor current of the fire pump motor(s), pressure maintenance pump motor(s), and the full-load current of associated fire pump accessory equipment _____.
   (a) for 15 minutes
   (b) for 45 minutes
   (c) for 3 hours
   (d) indefinitely

7. Fire pump supply conductors on the load side of the final disconnecting means and overcurrent device(s) that are inside (routed through) a building shall be protected from fire for 2 hours using _____.
   (a) a cable or raceway encased in a minimum 2 in. of concrete
   (b) a cable or raceway part of a listed fire-resistive cable system
   (c) a cable or raceway protected by a listed electrical circuit protective system
   (d) any of these

8. Feeder conductors supplying fire pump motors and accessory equipment shall have a _____ ampacity in accordance with 430.22 and shall comply with the voltage-drop requirements in 695.7.
   (a) maximum
   (b) minimum
   (c) permitted
   (d) none of these

9. All wiring from the controllers to the fire pump motors shall be in _____, listed Type MC cable with an impervious covering, or Type MI cable.
   (a) rigid or intermediate metal conduit
   (b) electrical metallic tubing (EMT)
   (c) liquidtight flexible metallic or nonmetallic conduit
   (d) any of these

10. Ground-fault protection of equipment shall _____ in any fire pump power circuit.
   (a) not be installed
   (b) be provided
   (c) be permitted
   (d) be listed

11. Unless the requirements of 695.7(B) or (C) are met, the voltage at the line terminals of a fire pump motor controller shall not drop more than _____ below the controller's normal rated voltage under motor-starting conditions.
   (a) 5 percent
   (b) 10 percent
   (c) 15 percent
   (d) 20 percent

12. When a fire pump motor operates at 115 percent of its full-load current rating, the supply voltage at the load terminals of the fire pump controller shall not drop more than _____below the voltage rating of the motor connected to those terminals.
   (a) 5 percent
   (b) 10 percent
   (c) 15 percent
   (d) 20 percent

13. All electric motor-driven fire pump control wiring shall be in _____.
   (a) rigid metal conduit or intermediate metal conduit
   (b) liquidtight flexible metal conduit, electrical metallic tubing, or liquidtight flexible nonmetallic conduit
   (c) listed Type MC cable with an impervious covering or Type MI cable
   (d) any of these

14. A(An) _____ surge protective device shall be installed in or on the fire pump controller.
    (a) listed
    (b) labeled
    (c) identified
    (d) approved

CHAPTER

7 SPECIAL CONDITIONS

Introduction to Chapter 7—Special Conditions

Chapter 7, which covers special conditions, is the third of the *NEC* chapters that deal with specific topics. Chapters 5 and 6 cover special occupancies, and special equipment, respectively. Remember, the first four chapters of the *Code* are sequential and form a foundation for each of the subsequent three. Chapter 8 which covers hard-wired telephones and coaxial cable is not subject to the requirements of Chapters 1 through 7 except where the requirements are specifically referenced there.

What exactly is a "Special Condition"? It is a situation that does not fall under the category of special occupancies or special equipment but creates a need for additional measures to ensure the "safeguarding of people and property" mission of the *NEC* as stated in 90.2(C).

- **Article 700—Emergency Systems.** This article covers the installation, operation, and maintenance of emergency systems consisting of circuits and equipment intended to supply power for illumination, fire detection, elevators, fire pumps, public safety, industrial processes where current interruption would produce serious life safety or health hazards, and similar functions.
- **Article 701—Legally Required Standby Systems.** This article covers the installation, operation, and maintenance of legally required standby systems consisting of circuits and equipment intended to supply illumination or power when the normal electrical supply is interrupted to aid in firefighting, rescue operations, control of health hazards, and similar operations.
- **Article 702—Optional Standby Systems.** This article covers permanently installed and portable optional standby power systems intended to supply power where life safety does not depend on the performance of the system.
- **Article 705—Interconnected Electric Power Production Sources.** This article covers the installation of electric power production sources (PV, ESS, generator) operating in parallel with the primary source of power (electric utility).
- **Article 706—Energy Storage Systems.** This article applies to energy storage systems that have a capacity greater than 1 kWh that can operate in stand-alone (off-grid) or interactive (grid tied) mode with other electric power production sources to provide electrical energy to the premises wiring system.
- **Article 710—Stand-Alone Systems.** This article covers electric power production systems operating in island (off-grid) mode not connected to an electric utility.
- **Article 722—Cables for Power-Limited Circuits.** This article combines common cabling requirements for Class 2 power-limited circuits [Article 725] and power-limited fire alarm circuits [Article 760].

• • •

- **Article 724—Class 1 Power-Limited Circuits.** This article covers Class 1 circuits, maximum of 1000 VA at 30V, that are power-limited and provides alternative requirements for minimum conductor sizes, overcurrent protection, insulation requirements, wiring methods, and materials. A Class 1 circuit is the wiring system between the load side of a Class 1 power source and the connected equipment.
- **Article 725—Class 2 Power-Limited Circuits.** This article contains the requirements for Class 2 power-limited circuits, maximum of 100 VA at 30Vthat are not an integral part of a device or appliance. These circuits extend between the load side of a power-limited power source or transformer and the connected Class 2 power-limited equipment.
- **Article 760—Fire Alarm Systems.** This article covers the installation of wiring and equipment for fire alarm systems. It includes fire detection and alarm notification, voice, guard's tour, sprinkler waterflow, and sprinkler supervisory systems.
- **Article 770—Optical Fiber Cables.** Article 770 covers the installation of optical fiber cables which transmit signals using light. It also contains the installation requirements for raceways that contain optical fiber cables, and rules for composite cables (hybrid cables) that combine optical fibers with current-carrying metallic conductors.

1st Printing

ARTICLE 700 EMERGENCY SYSTEMS

Introduction to Article 700—Emergency Systems

This article covers the installation, operation, and maintenance of emergency systems consisting of circuits and equipment intended to supply power for illumination, fire detection, elevators, fire pumps, public safety, industrial processes where current interruption would produce serious life safety or health hazards, and similar functions. The authority having jurisdiction makes the determination as to whether such a system is necessary for a given facility and what it must be connected to it. Many of these rules are outside of the scope of this material, however, some of the topics we cover include the following:

- Scope
- Tests and Maintenance
- Capacity and Rating
- Signals
- Surge Protection
- Wiring to Emergency Loads
- Sources of Power
- Emergency Illumination
- Selective Coordination

Article 700 consists of six parts:

- Part I. General
- Part II. Circuit Wiring
- Part III. Sources of Power
- Part IV. Emergency System Circuits for Lighting and Power
- Part V. Control (Not Covered)
- Part VI. Overcurrent Protection

Part I. General

700.1 Scope

Article 700 covers the installation, operation, and maintenance of emergency systems consisting of circuits and equipment intended to supply illumination and power when the normal electrical supply is interrupted. ▶Figure 700–1

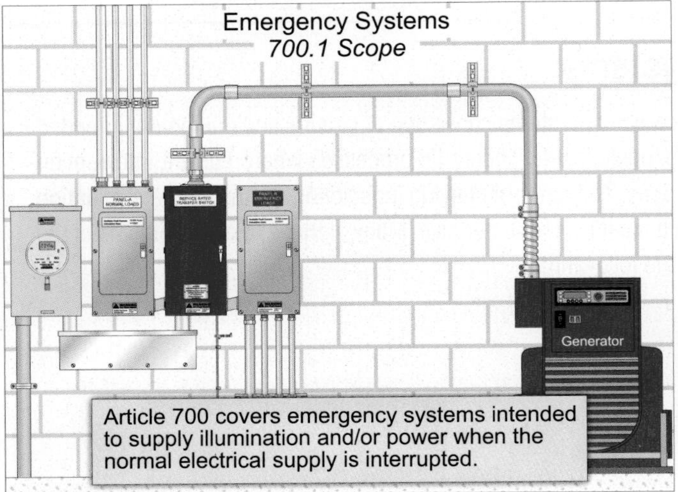

▶Figure 700–1

According to Article 100, "Emergency Systems" are those systems required and classed as emergency by a governmental agency having jurisdiction. These systems are intended to automatically supply illumination and/or power essential for safety to human life. ▶Figure 700–2

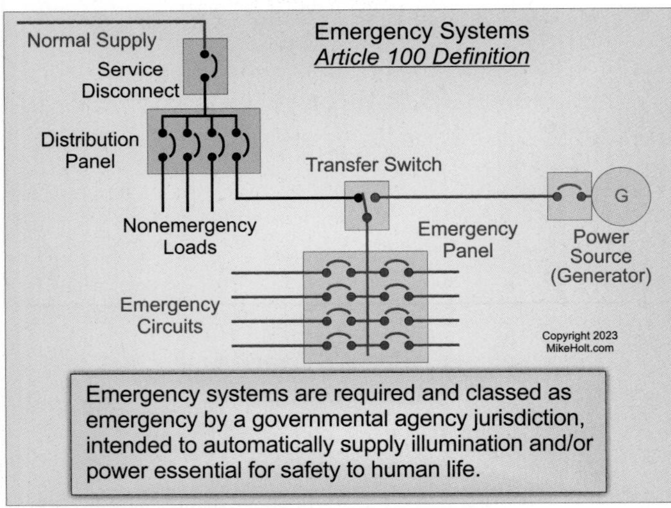

▶Figure 700–2

Note 1: Emergency systems are generally installed in places of assembly where artificial illumination is required for safe exiting and for panic control in buildings subject to occupancy by large numbers of persons such as hotels, theaters, sports arenas, health care facilities, and similar institutions. Emergency systems may also provide power for such functions as ventilation where essential to maintain life, fire detection and alarm systems, elevators, fire pumps, public safety announcing systems, industrial processes where current interruption would produce serious life safety or health hazards, and similar functions.

Note 4: For specific locations of emergency lighting requirements, see NFPA 101, *Life Safety Code.* ▶Figure 700–3

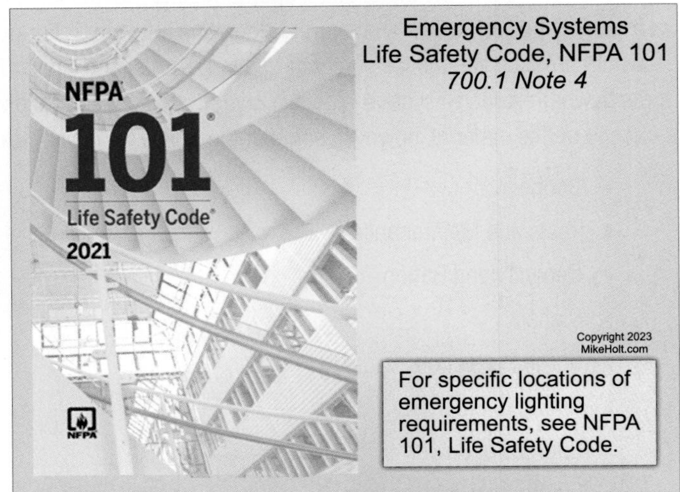

▶Figure 700–3

Author's Comment:

- According to NFPA 101, *Life Safety Code*, emergency power systems are generally installed where artificial illumination is required for safe exiting and for panic control in buildings subject to occupancy by large numbers of people. Some examples are high-rise buildings, jails, sports arenas, schools, health care facilities, and similar structures.

Note 5: For specific performance requirements of emergency power systems, see NFPA 110, *Standard for Emergency and Standby Power Systems.* ▶Figure 700–4

1st Printing

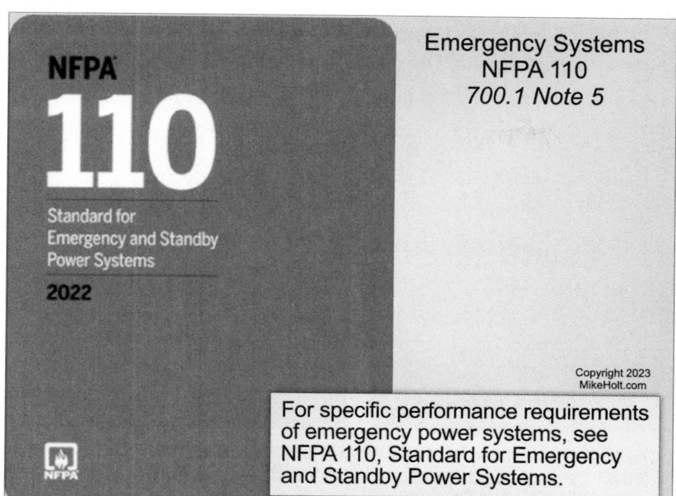
NFPA
110
Standard for
Emergency and Standby
Power Systems
2022
Emergency Systems
NFPA 110
700.1 Note 5
Copyright 2023
MikeHolt.com
For specific performance requirements of emergency power systems, see NFPA 110, Standard for Emergency and Standby Power Systems.

▶Figure 700–4

700.3 Tests and Maintenance

(A) Commissioning Witness Test. To ensure the emergency power system meets or exceeds the original installation specifications, the authority having jurisdiction must conduct or witness the commissioning of the emergency power system upon completion.

Note: See NECA 90, *Standard for Commissioning Building Electrical Systems.*

According to Article 100, "Commissioning" is the process, procedures, and testing used to set up and verify the initial performance, operational controls, safety systems, and sequence of operation of electrical devices and equipment prior to them being placed into active service.

(B) Periodic Testing. Emergency power systems must be periodically tested on a schedule approved by the authority having jurisdiction to ensure adequate maintenance has been performed and the systems are in proper operating condition.

Author's Comment:

- Running the emergency power system under its anticipated load and making sure power is transferred within 10 seconds is often considered an acceptable method of operational testing.

(C) Maintenance. Emergency system equipment must be maintained in accordance with manufacturer's instructions and industry standards.

(D) Written Record. A written record of the acceptance test, periodic testing, and maintenance must be kept.

Author's Comment:

- The *NEC* does not specify the required record retention period.

700.4 Capacity and Rating

(A) Capacity. An emergency power system must have adequate system capacity in accordance with Article 220 or by another approved method.

The system capacity must be sufficient for the rapid load changes and transient power and energy requirements associated with any expected loads.

(B) Selective Load Management. The electric power production system is permitted to supply emergency, legally required standby, and optional standby system loads where a load management system includes automatic selective load pickup and load shedding to ensure adequate power to the following:

(1) Emergency circuits

(2) Legally required standby circuits

(3) Optional standby circuits

700.5 Transfer Switch

(A) General. Transfer switches must be automatic, listed, marked for emergency use, and approved by the authority having jurisdiction. ▶Figure 700–5

(C) Automatic Transfer Switches. Automatic transfer switches must be able to be electrically operated and mechanically held.

(E) Use. Transfer switches for emergency systems are only permitted to supply emergency loads. ▶Figure 700–6

Author's Comment:

- Multiple transfer switches are required where a single generator is used to supply emergency loads, legally required standby loads, and optional loads.

(F) Documentation. The short-circuit current rating of the transfer switch must be field marked on the exterior of the transfer switch.

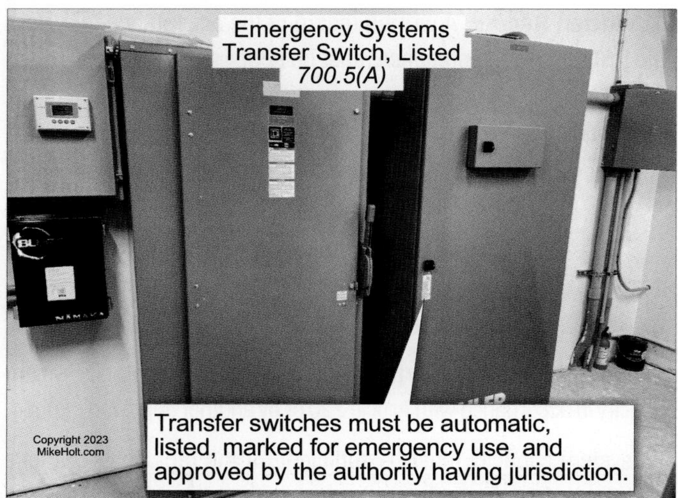

▶Figure 700–5

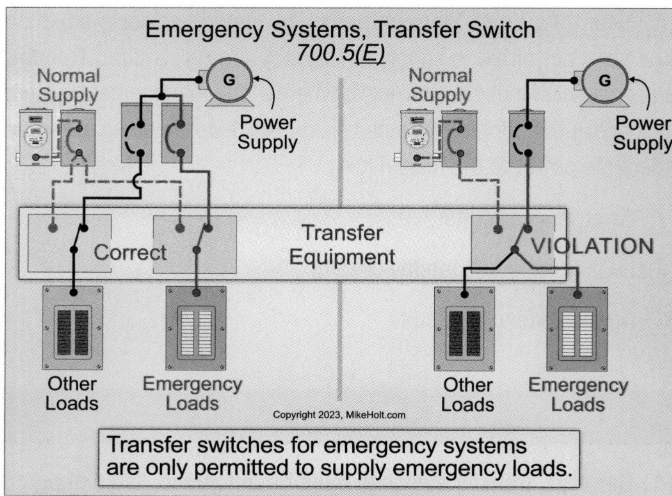

▶Figure 700–6

700.6 Signals

Audible, visual, and facility or network remote annunciation signaling devices must be installed where applicable for the purposes of: ▶**Figure 700–7**

(A) Malfunction Signal. To indicate a malfunction of the emergency source of power.

(B) Carrying Load Signal. To indicate that the emergency source is carrying load.

(C) Storage Battery Charging Malfunction Signal. To indicate that the battery charger is not functioning.

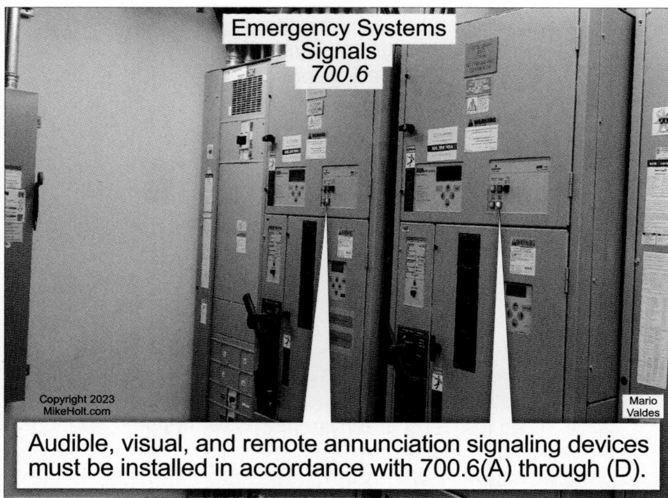

Emergency Systems
Signals
700.6
Copyright 2023 MikeHolt.com
Mario Valdes
Audible, visual, and remote annunciation signaling devices must be installed in accordance with 700.6(A) through (D).

▶Figure 700–7

(D) Ground-Fault Signal. To indicate a ground fault in a 4-wire, three-phase, 277/480V wye-connected system rated 1000A or more.

700.7 Signs

(A) Emergency Sources. A sign must be placed at service equipment indicating the type and location of each on-site emergency power source. ▶**Figure 700–8**

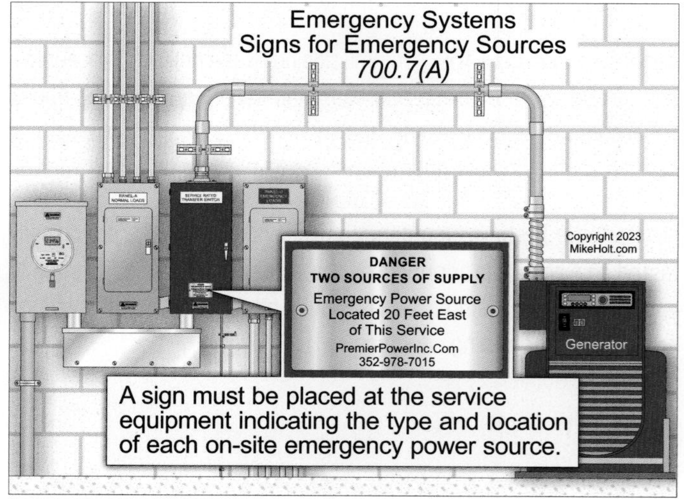

Emergency Systems
Signs for Emergency Sources
700.7(A)
Copyright 2023 MikeHolt.com
DANGER
TWO SOURCES OF SUPPLY
Emergency Power Source
Located 20 Feet East
of This Service
PremierPowerInc.Com
352-978-7015
Generator
A sign must be placed at the service equipment indicating the type and location of each on-site emergency power source.

▶Figure 700–8

700.8 Surge Protection

A listed surge-protective device must be installed for all emergency system switchgear, switchboards, and panelboards. ▶**Figure 700–9**

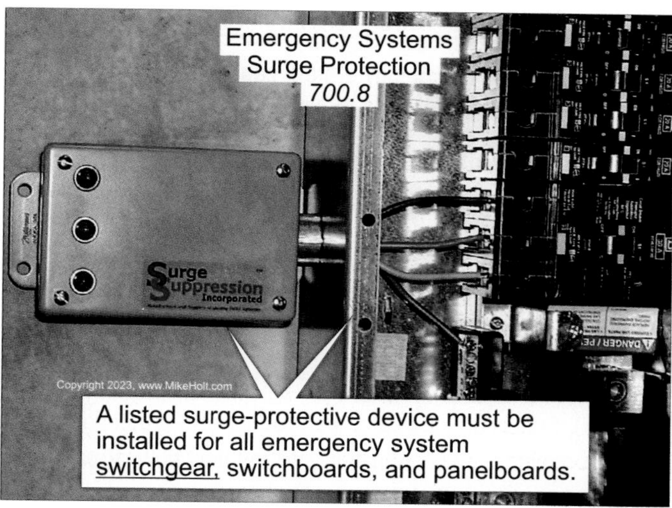

▸Figure 700–9

Part II. Circuit Wiring

700.10 Wiring to Emergency Loads

(A) Identification. Components of the emergency system must be marked so they are easily identified as part of the emergency system.

(1) Boxes, enclosures, transfer switches, generators, and panels containing emergency circuits must be marked as a component of an emergency system. ▸Figure 700–10

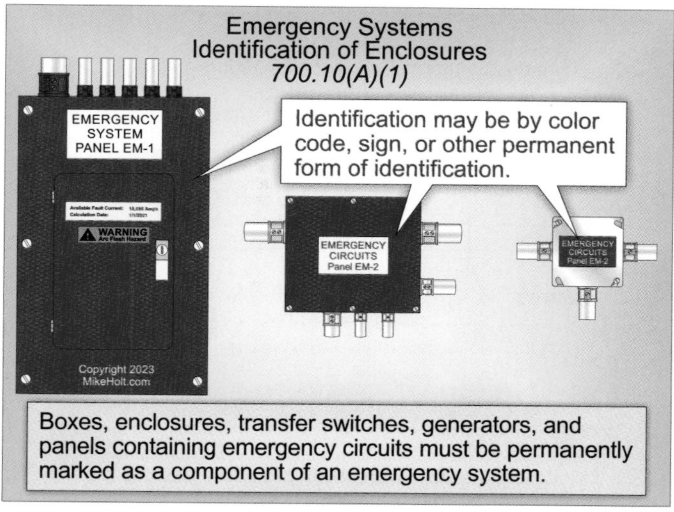

▸Figure 700–10

Author's Comment:

▸ The marking required by this section for enclosures, cables, and raceways can be by any approved method that identifies the component(s) as part of the emergency system, such as the words "Emergency System," "Emergency Circuits," or by color code such as the use of a red raceway or box cover. Colored raceways and fittings are permitted but not required.

(2) Cable and raceways must be marked as part of the emergency system at intervals not exceeding 25 ft. ▸Figure 700–11

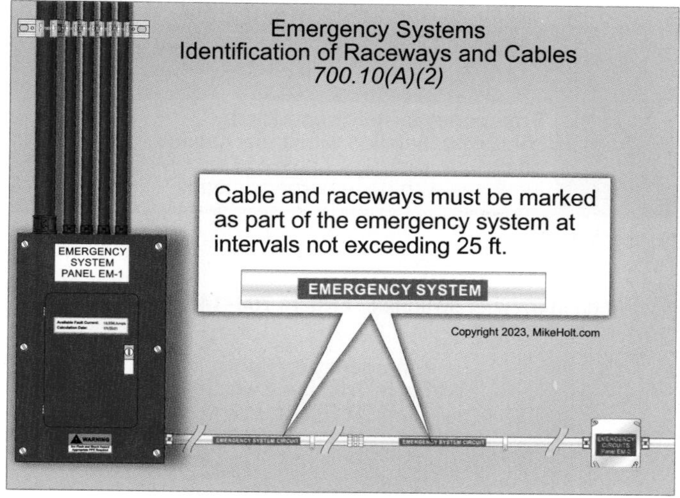

▸Figure 700–11

Receptacles connected to the emergency system must be identified by having a distinctive color or marking on either the receptacle or cover plate. ▸Figure 700–12

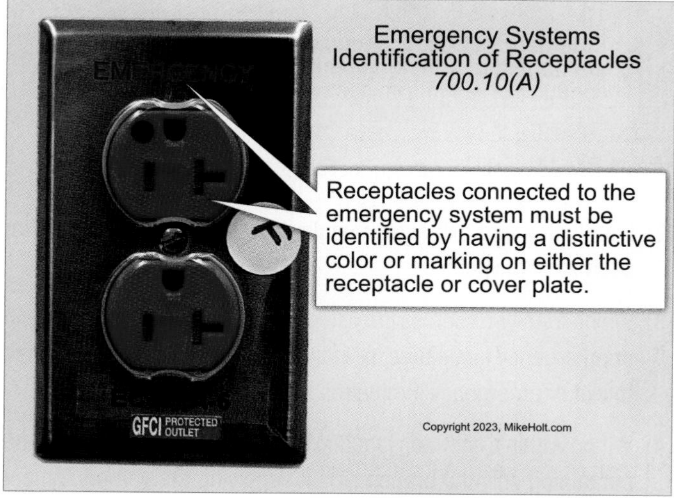

▸Figure 700–12

(B) Independent Wiring. Emergency system conductors cannot be installed within any cabinet, enclosure, raceway, cable, or luminaire with nonemergency loads, except for the following: ▶Figure 700–13

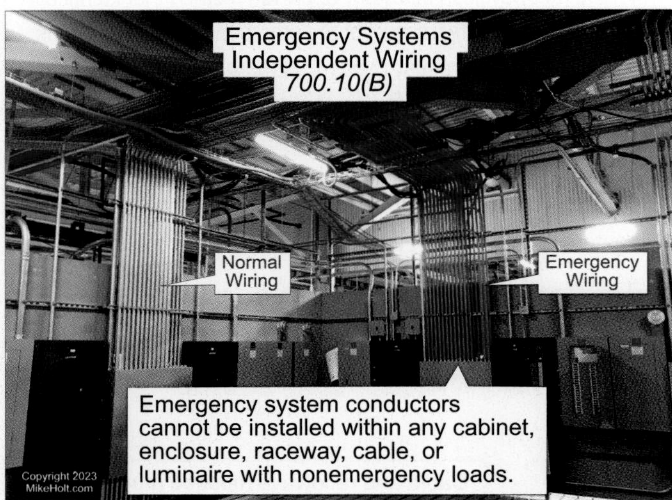

▶Figure 700–13

(1) Wiring in transfer switches. ▶Figure 700–14

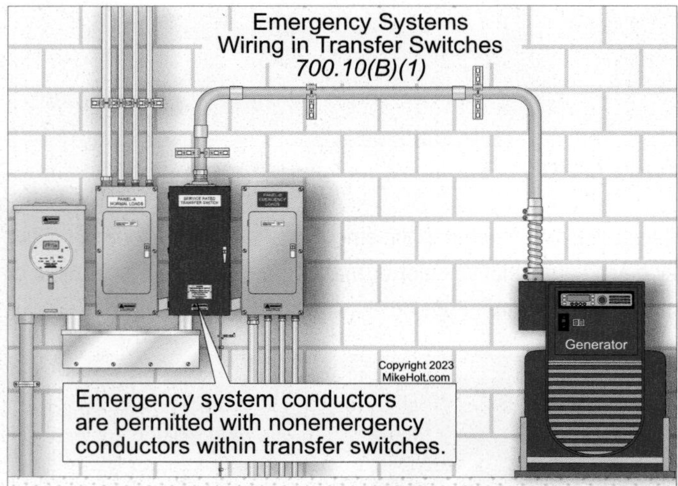

▶Figure 700–14

(2) Luminaires and exit signs supplied from emergency and other sources of power.

(3) Wiring from two sources in a listed load control relay supplying exit or emergency luminaires, or in a common junction box attached to exit or emergency luminaires.

(4) Wiring within a common junction box attached to unit equipment, containing only the branch circuit supplying the unit equipment and the emergency circuit supplied by the unit equipment.

(5) Wiring within a traveling cable to an elevator.

(6) Wiring from an emergency system can supply emergency and other loads in accordance with the following:

a. Where the emergency and nonemergency loads are in separate vertical switchboard or switchgear sections or individual disconnects mounted in separate enclosures.

b. Where the bus is:

(i) Supplied by a feeder without overcurrent protection at the source.

(ii) Supplied by a feeder with overcurrent protection that is selectively coordinated with the next downstream overcurrent protective device in the nonemergency system.

c. Emergency circuits are not permitted to originate from the same vertical switchgear section, vertical switchboard section, panelboard, or individual disconnect enclosure as other circuits.

d. It is permitted to utilize single or multiple feeders to supply distribution equipment between an emergency source and the point where the emergency loads are separated from all other loads.

e. At the emergency power source, such as a generator, multiple integral overcurrent protective devices are permitted to supply a designated emergency or a designated nonemergency load, provided there is complete separation between emergency and nonemergency loads beginning immediately after the overcurrent protective device line-side connections. ▶Figure 700–15

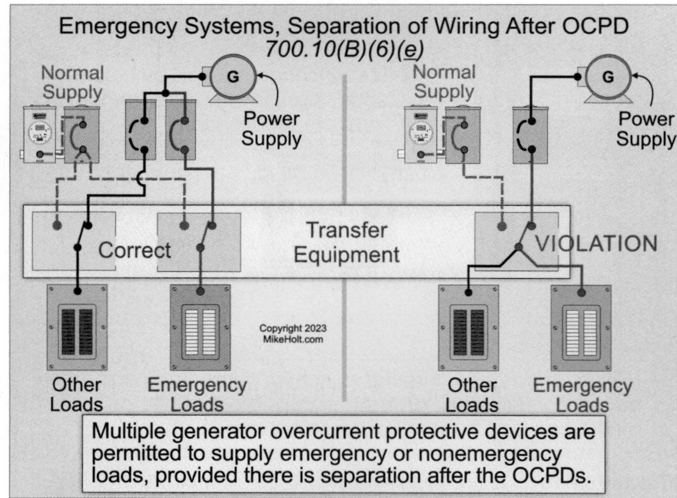

▶Figure 700–15

Wiring of two or more emergency circuits supplied from the same source can be installed in the same raceway, cable, box, or cabinet.

Author's Comment:

- Separation of the circuits served by a generator source for emergency circuits may be accomplished by running feeders from a single generator to individual overcurrent protective devices, or to a distribution switchboard that separates emergency circuits in different vertical sections from other loads.

(C) Wiring Design and Location. Emergency wiring circuits must be designed and located to minimize the hazards that might cause failure due to flooding, fire, icing, vandalism, and other adverse conditions.

700.11 Wiring, Class 2-Powered Emergency Lighting Systems

(A) General. Line voltage supply wiring and Class 2 power-limited emergency lighting control devices must comply with 700.10.

Class 2 power-limited emergency circuits must comply with 700.11(B) through (D).

(B) Identification. Class 2 power-limited emergency circuits must be marked so they will be readily identified as a component of an emergency circuit or system by the following methods:

(1) All boxes and enclosures for Class 2 power-limited emergency circuits must be marked as a component of an emergency circuit or system.

(2) Exposed cable, cable tray, or raceways systems must be marked to be identified as a component of an emergency circuit or system within 3 ft of each connector and at intervals not to exceed 25 ft.

(C) Separation of Circuits. Class 2 power-limited emergency circuits must be wired in a listed, jacketed cable or with one of the wiring methods of Chapter 3. If installed alongside nonemergency Class 2 power-limited circuits that are bundled, Class 2 power-limited emergency circuits must be bundled separately. If installed alongside nonemergency Class 2 power-limited circuits that are not bundled, Class 2 power-limited emergency circuits must be separated by a nonconductive sleeve or nonconductive barrier from all other Class 2 power-limited circuits. Separation from other circuits must comply with 725.136.

(D) Protection. Wiring must comply with the requirements of 300.4 and be installed in a raceway, armored or metal-clad cable, or cable tray.

Ex 1: Section 700.11(D) does not apply to wiring that does not exceed 6 ft in length and that terminates at an emergency luminaire or an emergency lighting control device.

Ex 2: Section 700.11(D) does not apply to locked rooms or locked enclosures that are accessible only to qualified persons.

Note: Locked rooms accessible only to qualified persons include locked telecommunications rooms, locked electrical equipment rooms, or other access-controlled areas.

Part III. Sources of Power

700.12 General Requirements

Emergency power must be available within 10 seconds in the event of failure of the normal power to the building. ▸Figure 700–16

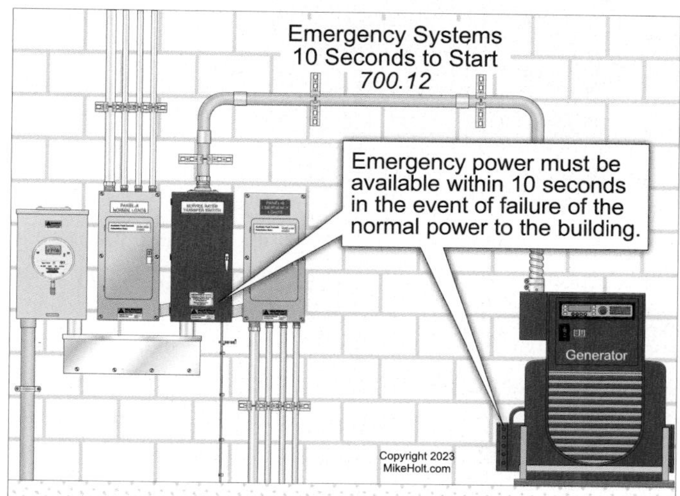
Emergency Systems
10 Seconds to Start
700.12
Emergency power must be available within 10 seconds in the event of failure of the normal power to the building.
Generator
Copyright 2023
MikeHolt.com

▸Figure 700–16

The emergency power supply must be any of the following:

(A) Power Source Considerations. In selecting an emergency source of power, consideration must be given to the occupancy and the type of service to be rendered, whether of minimum duration, as for evacuation of a theater, or longer duration, as for supplying emergency power and lighting due to an indefinite period of current failure from trouble either inside or outside the building.

(B) Equipment Design and Location. Equipment must be designed and located to minimize the hazards that might cause complete failure due to flooding, fires, icing, and vandalism.

(C) Supply Duration. The emergency power source must be of suitable rating and capacity to supply and maintain the total load for the duration determined by the system design. In no case can the duration be less than 2 hours of system operation unless used for emergency illumination in 700.12(C)(4) or unit equipment in 700.12(I).

Note: For information on classification of emergency power supply systems, see NFPA 110, *Standard for Emergency and Standby Power Systems.* ▸Figure 700–17

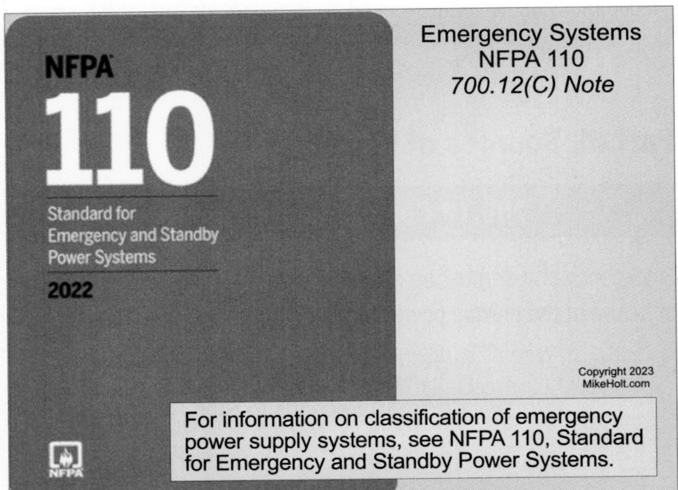

▸Figure 700–17

(4) Storage Battery and UPS Systems. Storage batteries and uninterruptible power supply (UPS) systems used to supply emergency illumination must be of suitable rating and capacity to supply and maintain the total load for a period of not less than 90 minutes, without the voltage applied to the load falling below 87½ percent of the nominal voltage. Automotive-type batteries are not permitted for this purpose. Automatic battery charging means must be provided.

Author's Comment:

- Uninterruptible power supplies (UPS) generally include a rectifier, a storage battery, and an inverter to convert direct-current (dc) to alternating-current (ac).

(D) Generators.

(1) Prime Mover-Driven. A generator approved by the authority having jurisdiction and sized in accordance with 700.4 is permitted as the emergency power source if it has means to automatically start the prime mover when the normal power source fails.

(E) Stored-Energy Power Supply Systems.

(1) Types. Stored-energy power supply systems must be one of the following types:

(1) Uninterruptible power supply (UPS)

(2) Fuel cell system

(3) Energy storage system

(4) Storage battery

(5) Other approved equivalent stored energy sources that comply with 700.12

(F) Separate Service. A separate service is permitted as the emergency power source where approved by the authority having jurisdiction [230.2(A)] and the following: ▸Figure 700–18

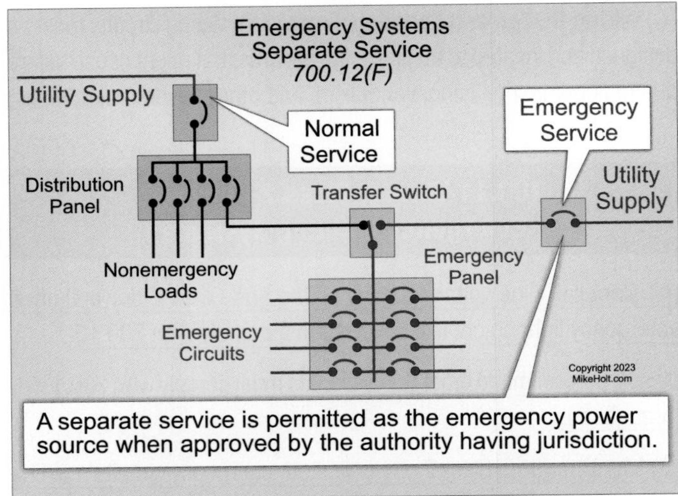

▸Figure 700–18

(1) Separate service conductors are installed from the electric utility.

(2) The emergency service conductors are electrically and physically remote from other service conductors to minimize the possibility of simultaneous interruption of supply.

Author's Comment:

- To minimize the possibility of simultaneous interruption, the service disconnect for the emergency system must be located remotely from the other power system's service disconnect [230.72(B)].

(H) Battery-Equipped Emergency Luminaires.

(1) Listing. All battery-equipped emergency luminaires must be listed.

(2) Installation of Battery-Equipped Emergency Luminaires.

(1) Battery-equipped emergency luminaires must be fixed in place (not portable).

(2) Wiring to each luminaire must be installed in accordance with any Chapter 3 wiring method, or a cord-and-plug connection with a flexible cord not more than 3 ft in length. Flexible cord, with or without a plug, for unit equipment is permitted for battery-equipped emergency luminaires installed in accordance with 410.62(C)(1). ▶Figure 700–19

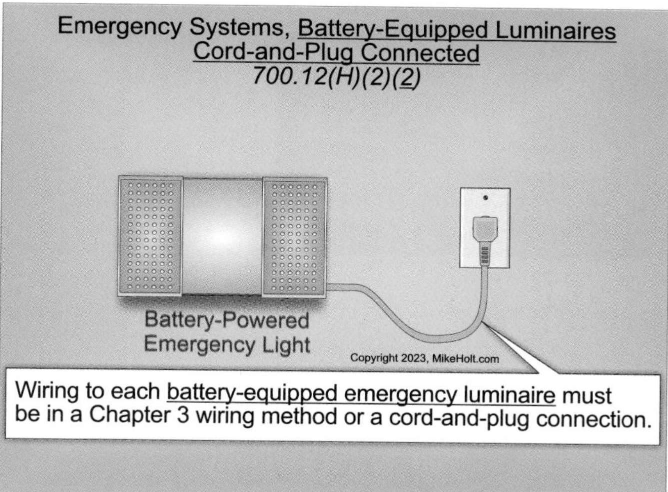

Emergency Systems, Battery-Equipped Luminaires
Cord-and-Plug Connected
700.12(H)(2)(2)
Battery-Powered
Emergency Light
Copyright 2023, MikeHolt.com
Wiring to each battery-equipped emergency luminaire must be in a Chapter 3 wiring method or a cord-and-plug connection.

▶Figure 700–19

(3) The branch-circuit(s) wiring that supplies battery-equipped emergency luminaires must be one of the following:

a. The branch circuit serving the normal lighting in the area, with a connection ahead of any local switches. ▶Figure 700–20

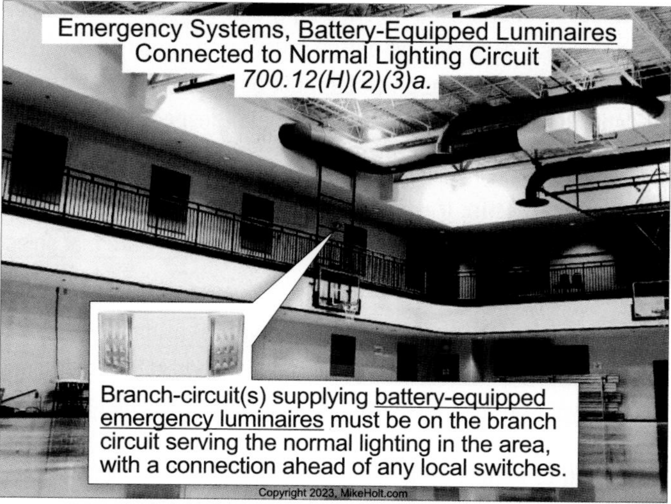

▶Figure 700–20

b. The branch circuits serving the normal lighting in the area, if that branch circuit is equipped with means to monitor the status of the area's normal lighting branch circuit ahead of any local switches.

c. A separate branch circuit originating from the same panelboard as the normal lighting circuits that is provided with a lock-on feature.

Author's Comment:

- There are two reasons why the battery-equipped emergency luminaire (battery pack) unit equipment must be connected ahead of the switch controlling the normal area lighting: (1) in the event of a power loss to the lighting circuit, the battery-equipped emergency luminaire lighting packs will activate and provide emergency lighting for people to exit the building, and (2) the battery-equipped emergency luminaire will not turn on when the switch controlling normal lighting is turned off.

(4) The branch circuit that feeds the battery-equipped emergency luminaires must be clearly identified at the distribution panel.

Author's Comment:

- Identification and marking must be in accordance with 110.22(A) and 408.4(A).

(6) Power for remote luminaries providing the exterior lighting of an exit door can be supplied by the battery-equipped emergency luminaires serving the area immediately inside the exit door.

Part IV. Emergency System Circuits for Lighting and Power

700.15 Loads on Emergency Branch Circuits

Emergency circuits must only supply emergency loads.

700.16 Emergency Illumination

(A) General. Emergency illumination include means of egress lighting, illuminated exit signs, and all other luminaires specified as necessary to provide the required illumination.

(B) System Reliability. Emergency illumination must be designed and installed so that the failure of any illumination source will not leave in total darkness any space that requires emergency illumination.

Emergency lighting control devices installed in emergency lighting systems must be listed for use in those systems. See 700.12(F).

Note: See 700.23 through 700.26 for applications for emergency system control devices.

(D) Disconnecting Means. When an emergency system is installed, emergency illumination is required for an indoor service disconnect. ▸**Figure 700–21**

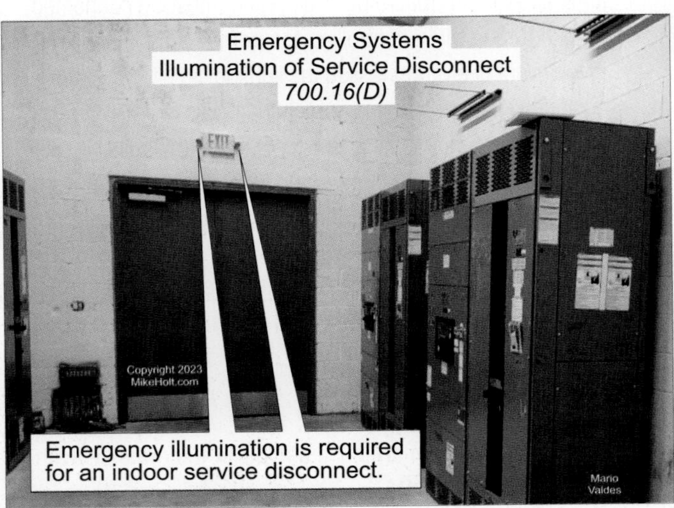

Emergency Systems
Illumination of Service Disconnect
700.16(D)
EXIT
Copyright 2023
MikeHolt.com
Emergency illumination is required for an indoor service disconnect.
Mario Valdes

▸**Figure 700–21**

700.19 Multiwire Branch Circuits

Multiwire branch circuits are not permitted to supply emergency system circuits. ▸**Figure 700–22**

700.27 Class 2 Powered Emergency Lighting Systems

Devices that combine control signals with Class 2 emergency power on a single circuit must be listed as emergency lighting control devices.

Note: An example of a device combining control signals with Class 2 emergency power sources is a Power over Ethernet (PoE) switch.

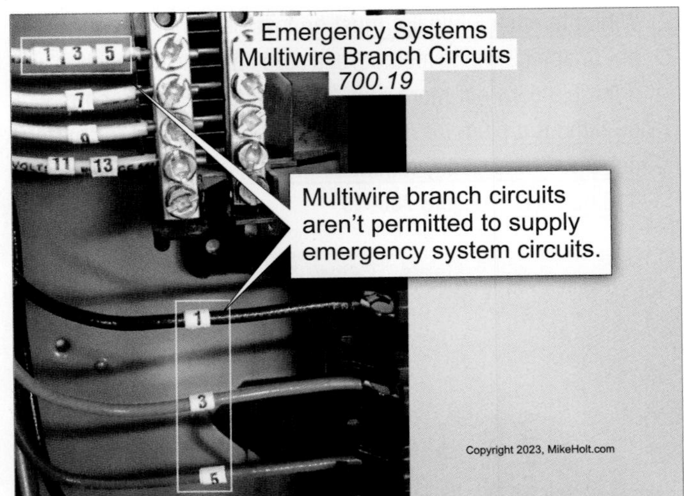

▸**Figure 700–22**

Part VI. Overcurrent Protection

700.30 Accessibility

The branch-circuit overcurrent protective devices for emergency circuits must be accessible to authorized persons only.

700.32 Selective Coordination

(A) General. Overcurrent devices for emergency power systems must be selectively coordinated with all supply-side and load-side overcurrent protective devices. The design must be made by an engineer or similarly qualified person and it must be documented and made available to those authorized to design, install, inspect, maintain, and operate the system. ▸**Figure 700–23**

(B) Replacements. If emergency system overcurrent protective devices are replaced, they must be reevaluated to ensure that selective coordination is maintained.

(C) Modifications. If modifications, additions, or deletions to the emergency system(s) occur, selective coordination of the emergency system overcurrent protective devices must be re-evaluated.

According to Article 100, "Selective Coordination" means the overcurrent protection scheme confines the interruption to a specific area rather than to the whole system. For example, if a short circuit or ground fault occurs with selective coordination, the only breaker/fuse that will open is the one protecting just the branch circuit involved. Without selective coordination, an entire floor of a building can go dark.

 1st Printing

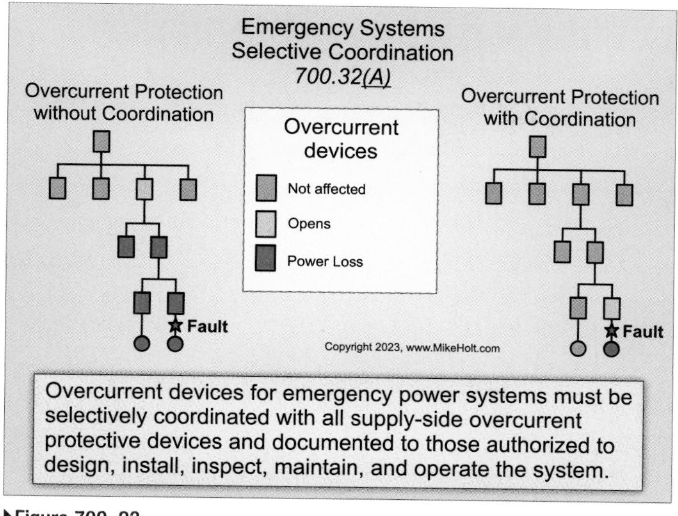
Emergency Systems
Selective Coordination
700.32(A)
Overcurrent Protection without Coordination
Overcurrent Protection with Coordination
Overcurrent devices
Not affected
Opens
Power Loss
Fault
Fault
Copyright 2023, www.MikeHolt.com
Overcurrent devices for emergency power systems must be selectively coordinated with all supply-side overcurrent protective devices and documented to those authorized to design, install, inspect, maintain, and operate the system.

▶Figure 700–23

Note: See the *NEC* Note Figure 700.32(C) for an example of how emergency system overcurrent protective devices (OCPDs) selectively coordinate with all supply-side OCPDs.

NEC Note Figure 700.32(C) Emergency System Selective Coordination

- OCPD D selectively coordinates with OCPDs C, F, E, B, and A.
- OCPD C selectively coordinates with OCPDs F, E, B, and A.
- OCPD F selectively coordinates with OCPD E.
- OCPD B is not required to selectively coordinate with OCPD A because OCPD B is not an emergency system OCPD.

Notes

ARTICLE 701 LEGALLY REQUIRED STANDBY SYSTEMS

Introduction to Article 701—Legally Required Standby Systems

This article covers the installation, operation, and maintenance of legally required standby systems consisting of circuits and equipment intended to supply illumination or power when the normal electrical supply is interrupted to aid in firefighting, rescue operations, control of health hazards, and similar operations. Many of these rules are outside of the scope of this material, however, some of the topics we cover include the following:

- Scope
- Commissioning and Maintenance
- Capacity and Rating
- Transfer Switches
- Wiring
- Sources of Power
- Selective Coordination

Article 701 consists of four parts:

- Part I. General
- Part II. Circuit Wiring
- Part III. Sources of Power
- Part IV. Overcurrent Protection

Part I. General

701.1 Scope

Article 701 covers the installation, operation, and maintenance of legally required standby systems consisting of circuits and equipment intended to supply illumination or power when the normal electrical supply is interrupted. ▸Figure 701–1

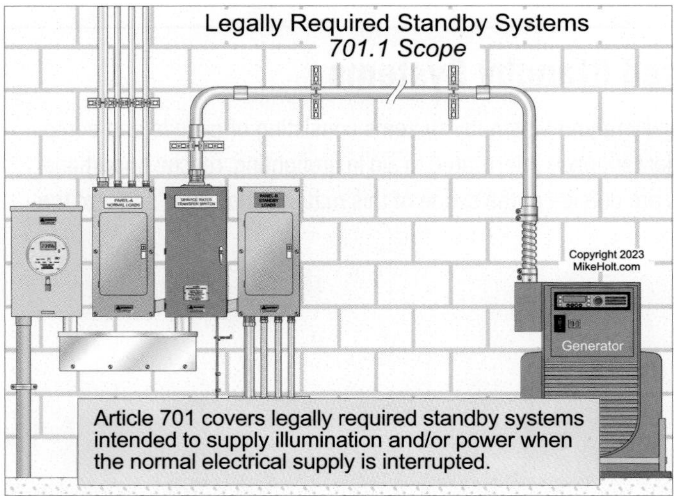
Legally Required Standby Systems
701.1 Scope
Copyright 2023
MikeHolt.com
Generator
Article 701 covers legally required standby systems intended to supply illumination and/or power when the normal electrical supply is interrupted.

▸Figure 701–1

According to Article 100, "Legally Required Standby Systems" are classified as legally required by a governmental agency, intended to automatically supply power to selected loads in the event of failure of the normal power source. ▸Figure 701–2

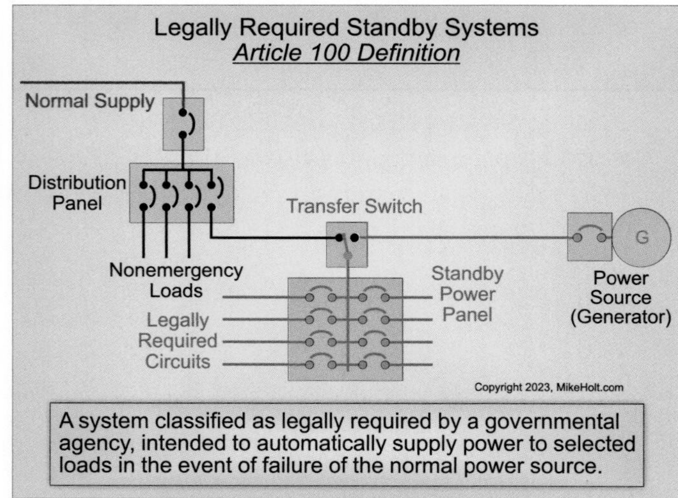
Legally Required Standby Systems
Article 100 Definition
Normal Supply
Distribution Panel
Transfer Switch
G
Nonemergency Loads
Legally Required Circuits
Standby Power Panel
Power Source (Generator)
Copyright 2023, MikeHolt.com
A system classified as legally required by a governmental agency, intended to automatically supply power to selected loads in the event of failure of the normal power source.

▸Figure 701–2

Note 4: Legally required standby systems typically supply loads such as heating and refrigeration systems, ventilation and smoke removal systems, sewage disposal, lighting systems, and industrial processes that, when stopped, could create hazards or hamper rescue or fire-fighting operations.

Author's Comment:

- Legally required standby systems provide electric power to aid in firefighting, rescue operations, control of health hazards, and similar operations.

701.3 Commissioning and Maintenance

(A) Commissioning or Witness Test. To ensure that the legally required standby system meets or exceeds the original installation specifications, the authority having jurisdiction must conduct or witness the commissioning of the legally required system upon completion of the installation.

(B) Periodic Testing. Legally required standby systems must be periodically tested in a manner approved by the authority having jurisdiction to ensure adequate maintenance has been performed and the systems are in proper operating condition.

Author's Comment:

- Running the legally required standby system under the loads of the facility to make sure power transfers within 60 seconds is often considered an acceptable method of operational testing.

(C) Maintenance. Legally required standby system equipment must be maintained in accordance with the manufacturer's instructions and industry standards.

(D) Written Record. A written record must be kept of all required tests and maintenance.

Author's Comment:

- The *NEC* does not specify the required record retention period.

701.4 Capacity and Rating

(A) Rating. Equipment for a legally required standby system must be suitable for the available fault current at its terminals.

(B) Capacity. The alternate power supply must have adequate capacity in accordance with Parts I through IV of Article 220 or by another approved method. The system capacity must be sufficient for the rapid load changes, and transient power and energy requirements associated with any expected loads.

(C) Load Management. The legally required standby alternate power supply can supply legally required standby and optional standby system loads if there is adequate capacity, or where a load management system includes automatic selective load pickup and load shedding is provided that will ensure adequate power to the legally required standby system circuits.

701.5 Transfer Switches

(A) General. Transfer switches must be automatic, listed, and marked for emergency system or legally required standby system use. Meter-mounted transfer switches are not permitted for legally required standby system use.

(C) Automatic Transfer Switches. Automatic transfer switches must be able to be electrically operated and mechanically held.

(D) Documentation. The short-circuit current rating of the transfer switch must be field marked on the exterior of the transfer switch.

701.6 Signals

Audible and visual signal devices must be installed where practicable for the purposes of:

(A) Malfunction Signals. To indicate a malfunction of the standby source of power.

(B) Carrying Load Signals. To indicate that the standby source is carrying load.

(C) Battery Charging Malfunction Signals. To indicate that the battery charger is not functioning.

(D) Ground-Fault Signals. To indicate a ground fault in a 4-wire, three-phase, 277/480V wye-connected system rated 1000A or more.

701.7 Signs

(A) Mandated Standby. A sign must be placed at the service-entrance equipment indicating the type and location of on-site legally required standby power systems. ▸Figure 701–3

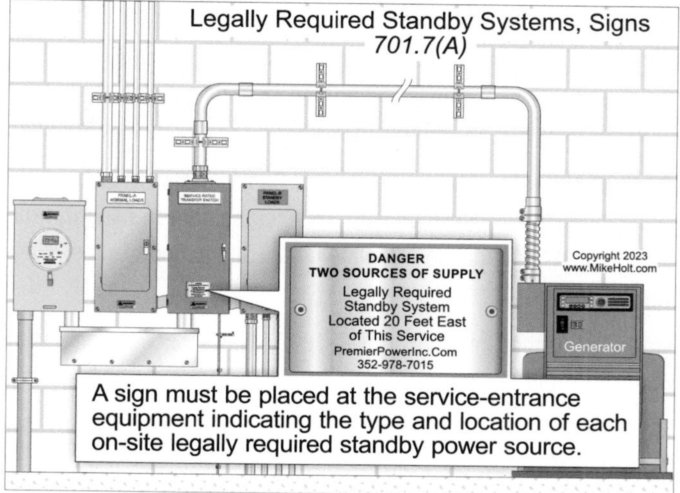
Legally Required Standby Systems, Signs
701.7(A)
DANGER
TWO SOURCES OF SUPPLY
Legally Required
Standby System
Located 20 Feet East
of This Service
PremierPowerInc.Com
352-978-7015
Copyright 2023
www.MikeHolt.com
Generator
A sign must be placed at the service-entrance equipment indicating the type and location of each on-site legally required standby power source.

▸Figure 701–3

Part II. Circuit Wiring

701.10 Wiring

(A) General. Legally required standby system wiring is permitted to be in the same raceways, boxes, and cabinets with other general wiring.

Author's Comment:

- Unlike wiring for emergency systems, which must be kept entirely independent of other wiring, the wiring for legally required standby systems may be installed with other (normal) wiring because legally required standby system loads are not essential for life safety.

Part III. Sources of Power

701.12 General Requirements

If the normal supply fails, legally required standby power must be available within 60 seconds. The supply system for the legally required standby power supply is permitted to be one or more of the following:

(A) Power Source Considerations. In selecting a legally required standby source of power, consideration must be given to the type of service to be rendered, whether of short-time duration or long duration.

(B) Equipment Design and Location. Consideration must be given to the location or design, or both, of all equipment to minimize the hazards that might cause complete failure due to floods, fires, icing, and vandalism.

Note: For further information, see ANSI/IEEE 493, *Recommended Practice for the Design of Reliable Industrial and Commercial Power Systems*.

(D) Generator Set.

(1) Prime Mover-Driven. A generator approved by the authority having jurisdiction and sized in accordance with 701.4 is permitted as the legally required power source if it has the means to automatically start the prime mover on failure of the normal power source.

(E) Stored-Energy Power Supply Systems.

(1) Types. Stored-energy power supply systems must consist of one the following types:

(1) Uninterruptible power supply

(2) Fuel cell system

(3) Energy storage system

(4) Storage battery

(5) Other approved equivalent stored energy sources that comply with 701.12

(F) Separate Service. An additional service is permitted as the legally required power source where approved by the authority having jurisdiction [230.2(A)] and the following additional requirements:

(1) Separate service conductors are installed from the electric utility.

(2) The legally required service conductors must be electrically and physically remote from other service conductors to minimize the possibility of simultaneous interruption of supply.

Author's Comment:

- To minimize the possibility of simultaneous interruption, the service disconnect for the legally required power system must be remotely located from the other power system's service disconnect [230.72(B)].

(G) Connection Ahead of Service Disconnecting Means. If approved by the authority having jurisdiction, connection ahead of, but not within, the same cabinet, enclosure, or vertical switchboard or switchgear section is permitted as the legally required power source. See 230.82(5) for additional information. ▸Figure 701–4

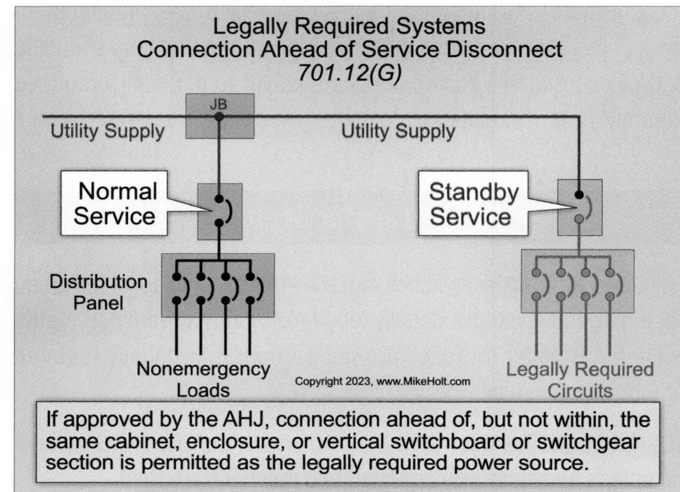

▸Figure 701–4

To minimize the possibility of simultaneous interruption, the disconnect for the legally required power system must be remotely located from other power system service disconnects.

Part IV. Overcurrent Protection

701.30 Accessibility

The branch-circuit overcurrent protective devices for legally required standby circuits must be accessible to authorized persons only.

1st Printing

701.32 Selective Coordination

(A) General. Overcurrent devices for legally required standby systems must be selectively coordinated with all supply-side and load-side overcurrent protective devices. The design must be made by an engineer or similarly qualified person and it must be documented and made available to those authorized to design, install, inspect, maintain, and operate the system.

According to Article 100, "Selective Coordination" means the overcurrent protection scheme confines the interruption to a specific area rather than to the whole system. For example, if a short circuit or ground fault occurs with selective coordination, the only breaker/fuse that will open is the one protecting just the branch circuit involved. Without selective coordination, an entire floor of a building can go dark.

(B) Replacements. If legally required standby system overcurrent protective devices are replaced, they must be re-evaluated to ensure selective coordination is maintained.

(C) Modifications. If modifications, additions, or deletions to the legally required standby system(s) occur, selective coordination is required of the legally required system(s).

Note: See the *NEC* Note Figure 701.32(C) for an example of how legally required standby system overcurrent protective devices (OCPDs) selectively coordinate with all supply-side OCPDs.

Notes |

ARTICLE
702

OPTIONAL STANDBY SYSTEMS

Introduction to Article 702—Optional Standby Systems

This article covers the installation requirements for permanent and portable optional standby power systems intended to supply power where life safety does not depend on the system's performance. You will see these systems in facilities where the loss of electricity can cause economic loss, business interruptions, or personal inconvenience. Many of these rules are outside of the scope of this material, however, some of the topics we cover include the following:

- Capacity and Rating
- Interconnection or Transfer Equipment
- Wiring

Article 702 consists of two parts:

- Part I. General
- Part II. Wiring

Part I. General

702.1 Scope

Article 702 covers permanently installed and portable optional standby power systems. ▶Figure 702–1

According to Article 100, "Optional Standby System" is a system intended to supply power where life safety does not depend on the performance of the system. ▶Figure 702–2 and ▶Figure 702–3

Author's Comment:

- Optional standby systems are typically installed to provide an alternate source of electric power for industrial and commercial buildings, farms, and residences to serve loads such as heating and refrigeration systems, data processing, and industrial processes that when stopped during any power outage can cause discomfort, economic loss, serious interruption of the process, damage to product or the like.

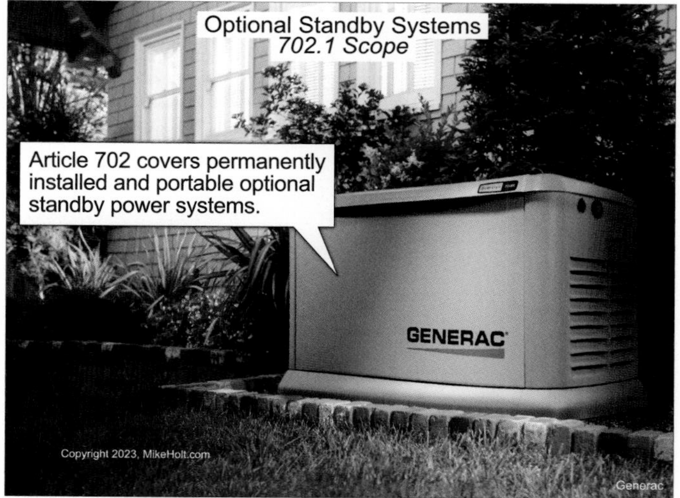
Optional Standby Systems
702.1 Scope
Article 702 covers permanently installed and portable optional standby power systems.
GENERAC
Copyright 2023, MikeHolt.com
Generac

▶Figure 702–1

- Article 702 also covers portable and trailer- or vehicle-mounted generators that might be used for a dwelling. ▶Figure 702–4

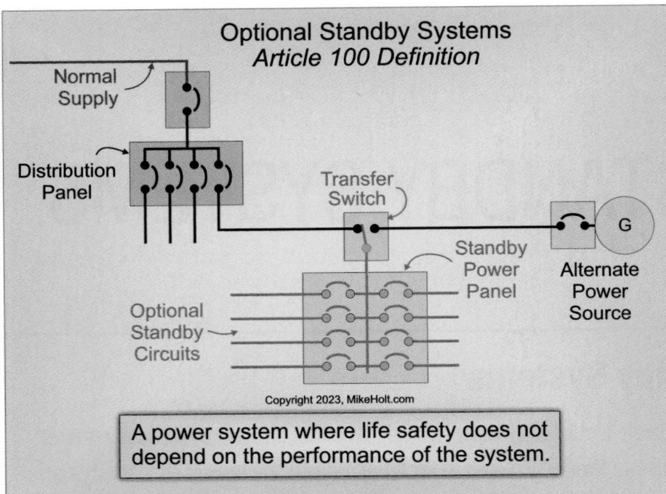

▸Figure 702–2

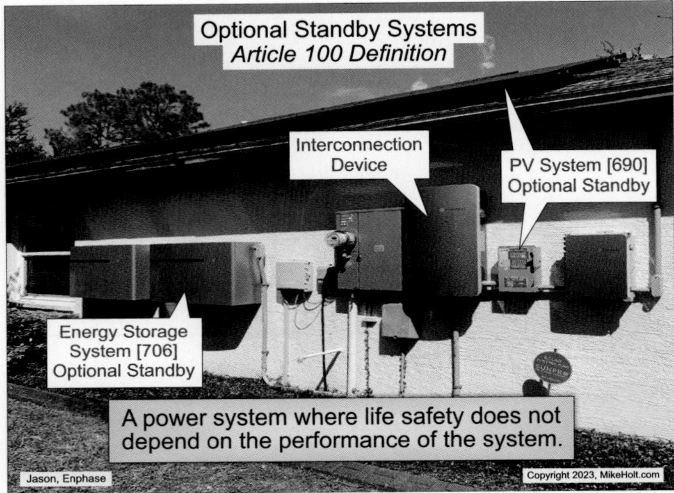

▸Figure 702–3

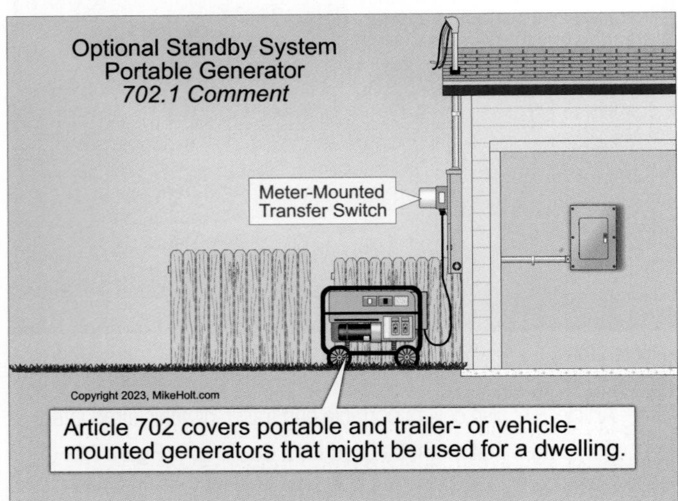

▸Figure 702–4

702.4 Capacity and Rating

(A) System Capacity.

(1) Manual and Nonautomatic Load Connection. If the connection of the loads to the optional standby system is manual or nonautomatic, the optional standby system must be sized to supply all the loads selected by the user intended to be operated at one time. ▸**Figure 702–5**

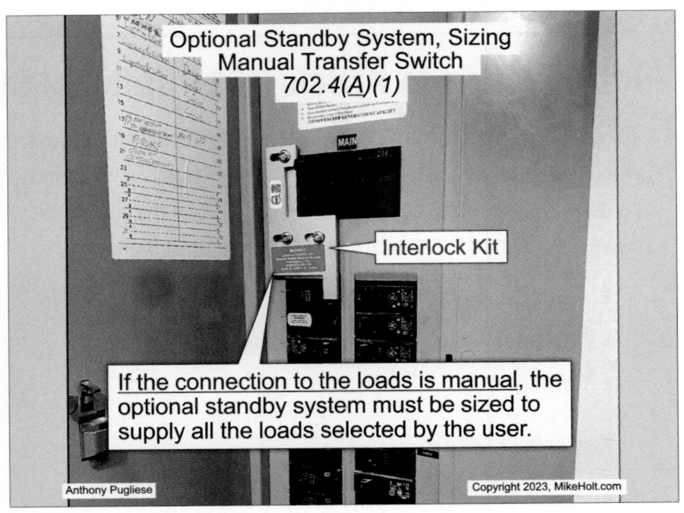

Optional Standby System, Sizing
Manual Transfer Switch
702.4(A)(1)
MAIN
Interlock Kit
If the connection to the loads is manual, the optional standby system must be sized to supply all the loads selected by the user.
Anthony Pugliese
Copyright 2023, MikeHolt.com

▸Figure 702–5

Note: Manual and nonautomatic transfer switches require human intervention.

(2) Automatic Load Connection. If the connection for a load to the optional standby system is automatic, the optional standby system must be sized as follows:

(a) Full Load. The optional standby source must be capable of supplying the full load that is automatically connected as determined by Article 220 or another approved method. ▸**Figure 702–6**

Author's Comment:

- For existing facilities, the demand data for one year or the average power demand for a 15-minute period over a minimum of 30 days can be used to size the electric power source [220.87]. ▸**Figure 702–7**

(b) Energy Management System (EMS). Where a system is employed in accordance with 750.30 that will automatically manage the connected load, the standby source must have a capacity sufficient to supply the maximum load that will be connected by the EMS. ▸**Figure 702–8**

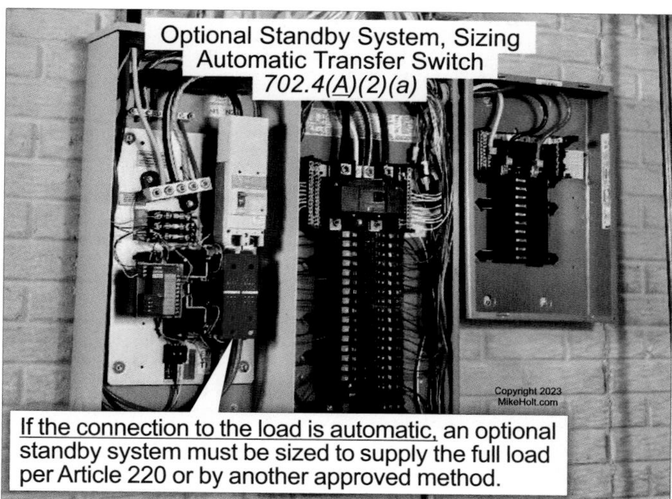
Optional Standby System, Sizing
Automatic Transfer Switch
702.4(A)(2)(a)
Copyright 2023
MikeHolt.com
If the connection to the load is automatic, an optional standby system must be sized to supply the full load per Article 220 or by another approved method.

▶Figure 702-6

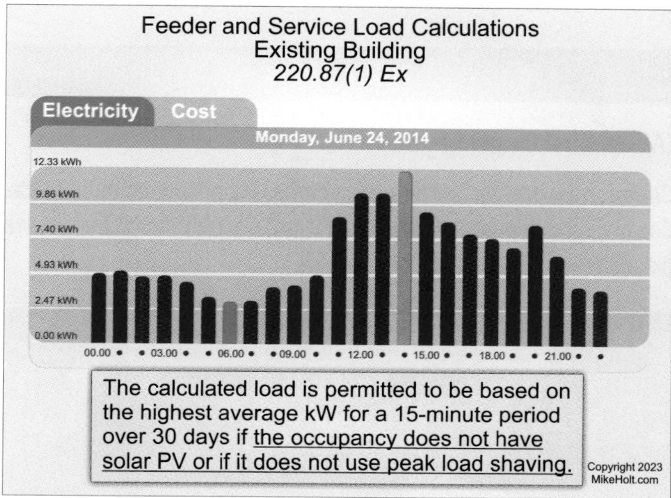
Feeder and Service Load Calculations
Existing Building
220.87(1) Ex
Electricity
Cost
Monday, June 24, 2014
12.33 kWh
9.86 kWh
7.40 kWh
4.93 kWh
2.47 kWh
0.00 kWh
00.00
03.00
06.00
09.00
12.00
15.00
18.00
21.00
The calculated load is permitted to be based on the highest average kW for a 15-minute period over 30 days if the occupancy does not have solar PV or if it does not use peak load shaving.
Copyright 2023
MikeHolt.com

▶Figure 702-7

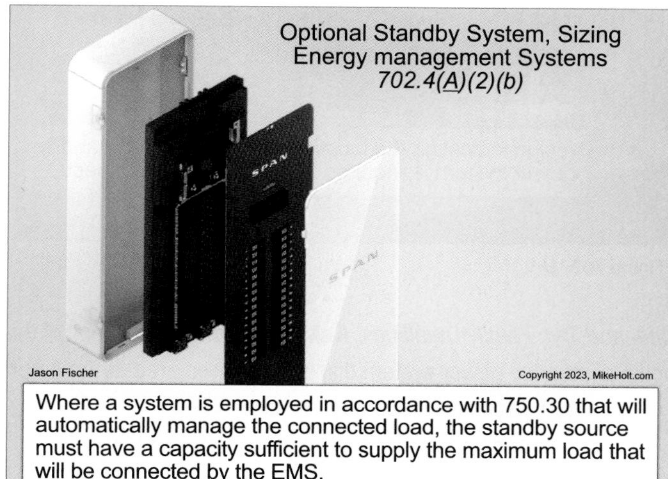
Optional Standby System, Sizing
Energy management Systems
702.4(A)(2)(b)
Jason Fischer
Copyright 2023, MikeHolt.com
Where a system is employed in accordance with 750.30 that will automatically manage the connected load, the standby source must have a capacity sufficient to supply the maximum load that will be connected by the EMS.

▶Figure 702-8

702.5 Interconnection Equipment or Transfer Equipment

(A) General. Interconnection equipment or a transfer equipment is required for the connection of an optional standby system to premises wiring. ▶**Figure 702-9** and ▶**Figure 702-10**

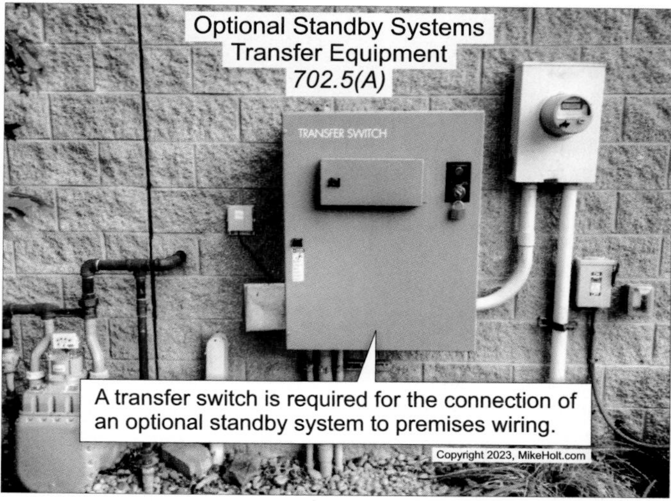
Optional Standby Systems
Transfer Equipment
702.5(A)
TRANSFER SWITCH
A transfer switch is required for the connection of an optional standby system to premises wiring.
Copyright 2023, MikeHolt.com

▶Figure 702-9

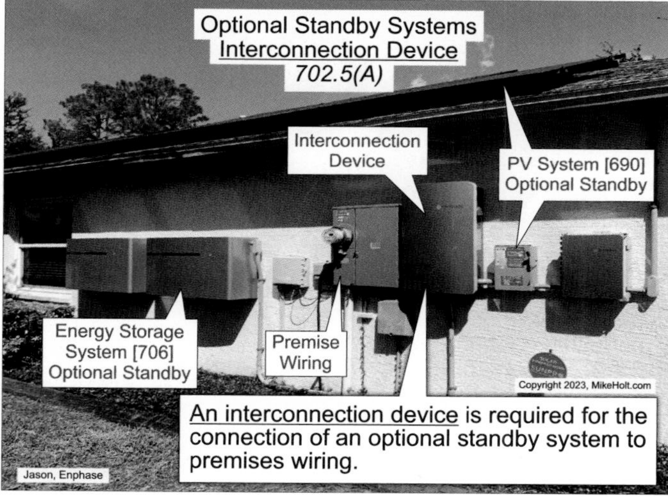
Optional Standby Systems
Interconnection Device
702.5(A)
Interconnection Device
PV System [690]
Optional Standby
Energy Storage
System [706]
Optional Standby
Premise
Wiring
Copyright 2023, MikeHolt.com
An interconnection device is required for the connection of an optional standby system to premises wiring.
Jason, Enphase

▶Figure 702-10

According to Article 100, a "Transfer Switch" is an automatic or nonautomatic device used to transfer loads from one power source to another. ▶**Figure 702-11**

Interconnection equipment and transfer switch must be listed and installed to prevent the inadvertent interconnection of all sources of supply.

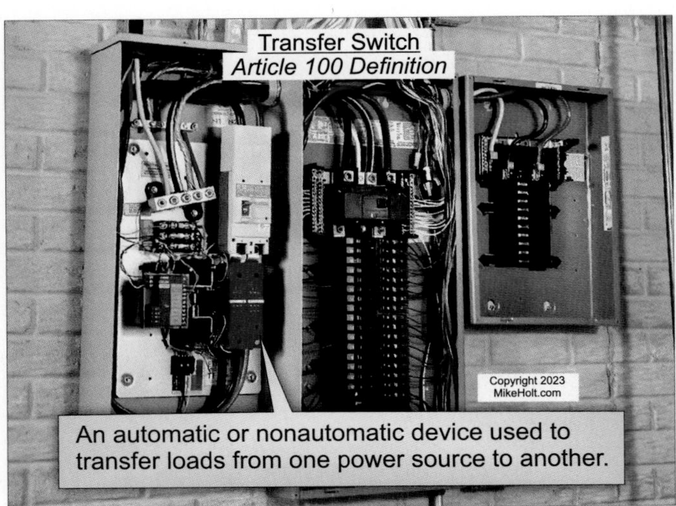
Transfer Switch
Article 100 Definition
Copyright 2023
MikeHolt.com
An automatic or nonautomatic device used to transfer loads from one power source to another.

▸Figure 702–11

(B) Meter-Mounted Transfer Switches. A listed meter-mounted transfer switch installed between the electric utility meter and the meter enclosure in accordance with 230.82(11) must be listed. ▸**Figure 702–12**

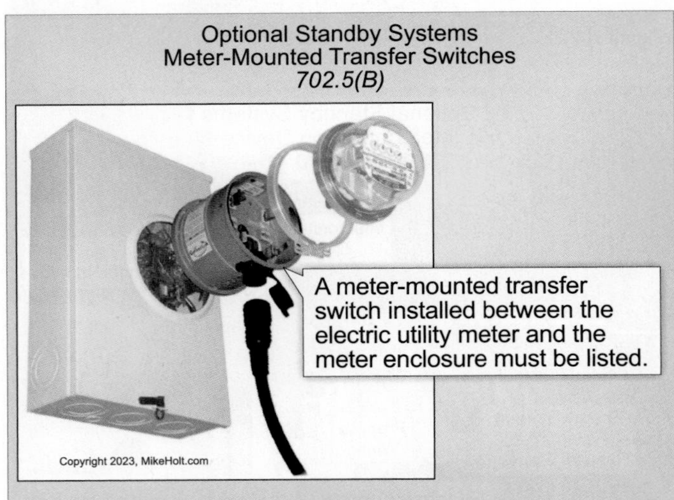
Optional Standby Systems
Meter-Mounted Transfer Switches
702.5(B)
A meter-mounted transfer switch installed between the electric utility meter and the meter enclosure must be listed.
Copyright 2023, MikeHolt.com

▸Figure 702–12

(C) Documentation. In other than dwelling units, the short-circuit current rating of the transfer equipment, based on the specific overcurrent protective device type and settings protecting the transfer equipment, must be field marked on the exterior of the transfer equipment.

(D) Parallel Installation. Optional standby systems installed in parallel with other power production sources must comply with Parts I or II of Article 705. ▸**Figure 702–13**

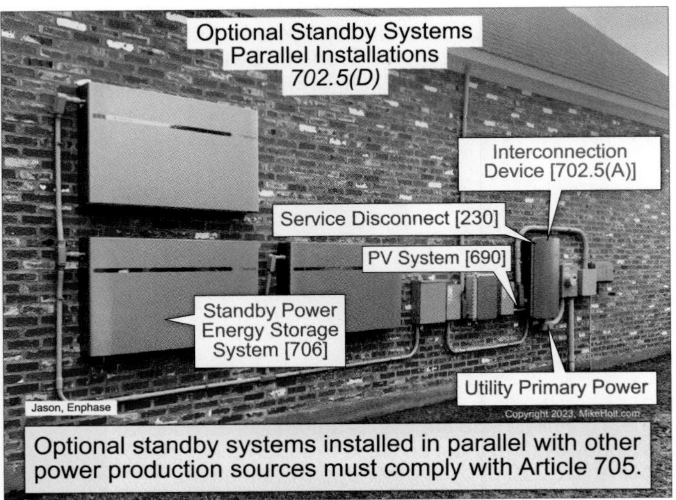
Optional Standby Systems
Parallel Installations
702.5(D)
Interconnection Device [702.5(A)]
Service Disconnect [230]
PV System [690]
Standby Power Energy Storage System [706]
Utility Primary Power
Jason, Enphase
Copyright 2023, MikeHolt.com
Optional standby systems installed in parallel with other power production sources must comply with Article 705.

▸Figure 702–13

702.7 Signs

(A) Optional Power Sources.

Commercial and Industrial Installations. A sign indicating the location of each optional standby power system is required at the service disconnect. ▸**Figure 702–14**

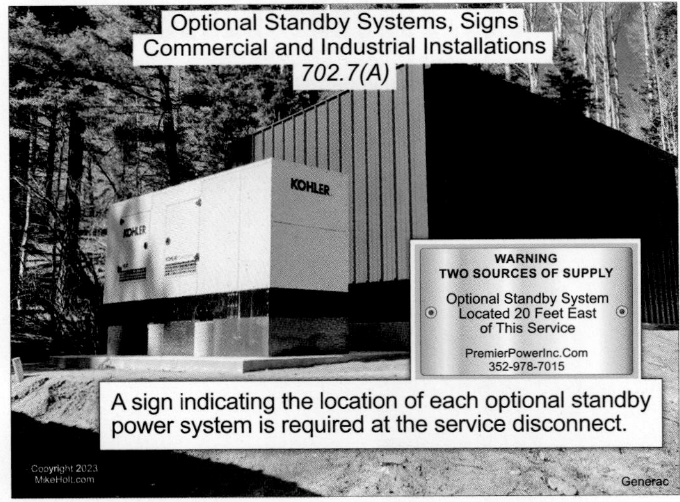
Optional Standby Systems, Signs
Commercial and Industrial Installations
702.7(A)
KOHLER
WARNING
TWO SOURCES OF SUPPLY
Optional Standby System
Located 20 Feet East
of This Service
PremierPowerInc.Com
352-978-7015
A sign indicating the location of each optional standby power system is required at the service disconnect.
Copyright 2023
MikeHolt.com
Generac

▸Figure 702–14

One- and Two-Family Dwellings. A sign indicating the location of the optional standby power system disconnect is required at the emergency shutoff disconnect [230.85]. ▸**Figure 702–15**

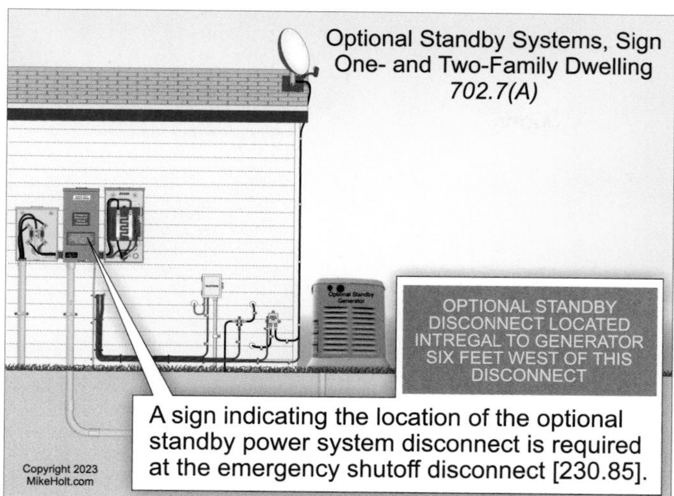

▸Figure 702–15

(C) Power Inlet. Where a power inlet is used for the connection of a portable generator, a warning sign must be placed near the power inlet to indicate the type of generator permitted to be connected to the inlet. The warning sign must state: ▸Figure 702–16

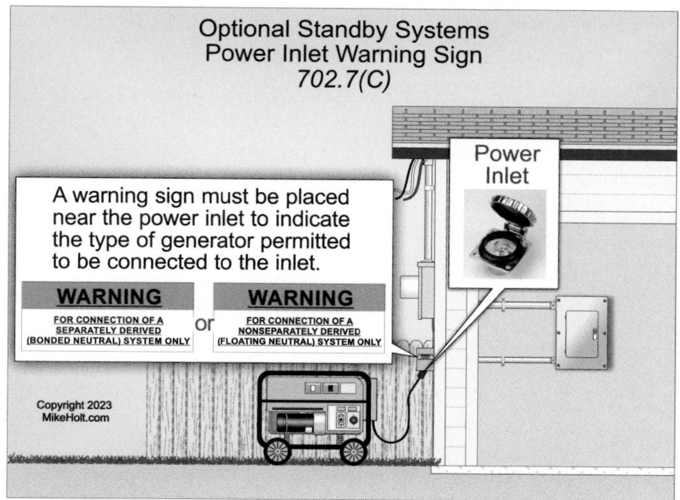

▸Figure 702–16

WARNING—FOR CONNECTION OF A SEPARATELY DERIVED (BONDED NEUTRAL) SYSTEM ONLY

or

WARNING—FOR CONNECTION OF A NONSEPARATELY DERIVED (FLOATING NEUTRAL) SYSTEM ONLY

Part II. Circuit Wiring

702.10 Wiring

Optional standby system wiring can occupy the same raceways, cables, enclosures, and cabinets with other wiring.

702.12 Outdoor Generators

(B) Flanged Inlet. The flanged inlet for a portable generator must be located outside a building or structure. ▸Figure 702–17

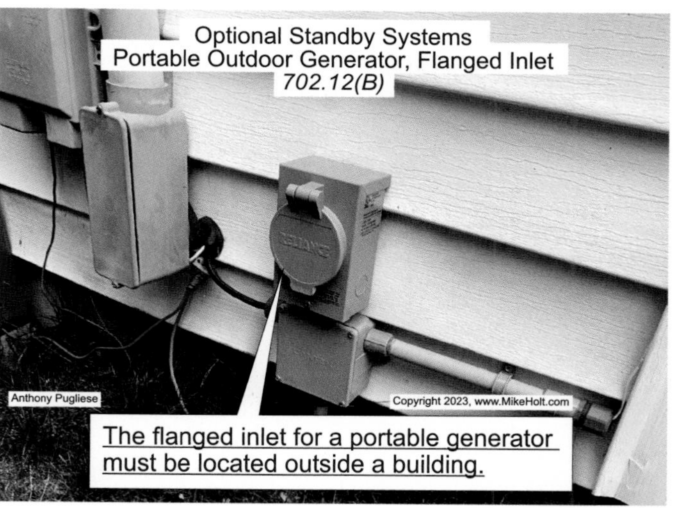

Optional Standby Systems
Portable Outdoor Generator, Flanged Inlet
702.12(B)
Anthony Pugliese
Copyright 2023, www.MikeHolt.com
The flanged inlet for a portable generator must be located outside a building.

▸Figure 702–17

Notes

INTERCONNECTED ELECTRIC POWER PRODUCTION SOURCES

Introduction to Article 705—Interconnected Electric Power Production Sources

This article covers the installation of electric power production sources (PV, ESS, EV, generator) operating in parallel with the primary source of power (electric utility). Many of these rules are outside of the scope of this material, however, some of the topics we cover include the following:

- Scope
- Equipment Approval
- System Installation
- Identification of Parallel Power Production Sources
- Service and Load Side Connection
- Energy Management Systems
- Wiring
- Overcurrent Protection
- Microgrid Systems

Article 705 consists of two parts:

- Part I. General
- Part II. Microgrid Systems

Part I. General

705.1 Scope

This article covers the installation of electric power production sources (PV, ESS, generator) operating in parallel with the primary source of power (electric utility). ▸**Figure 705–1** and ▸**Figure 705–2**

Note 1: The primary source of power typically includes the electric utility or it can be an on-site power source.

According to Article 100, "Power Production Equipment" is electrical generating equipment up to the system disconnect supplied by any source of electrical power (PV, ESS, generator) other than the electric utility. Examples of power production equipment include such items as generators, PV Systems, and energy storage systems. ▸**Figure 705–3** and ▸**Figure 705–4**

A "Primary Source" is the main source of power in an electric power system.

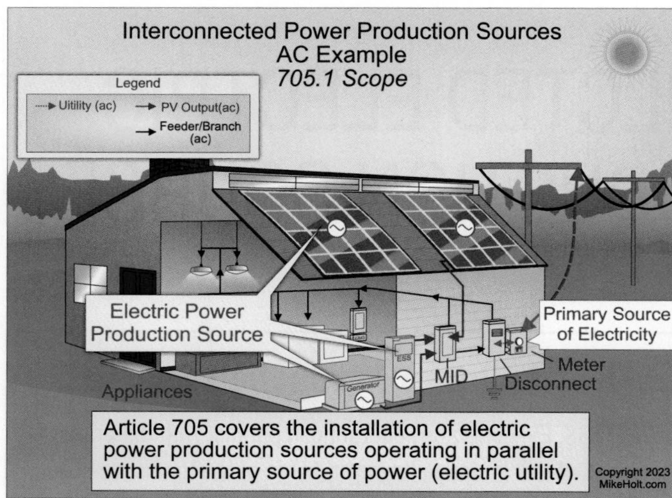

▸Figure 705–1

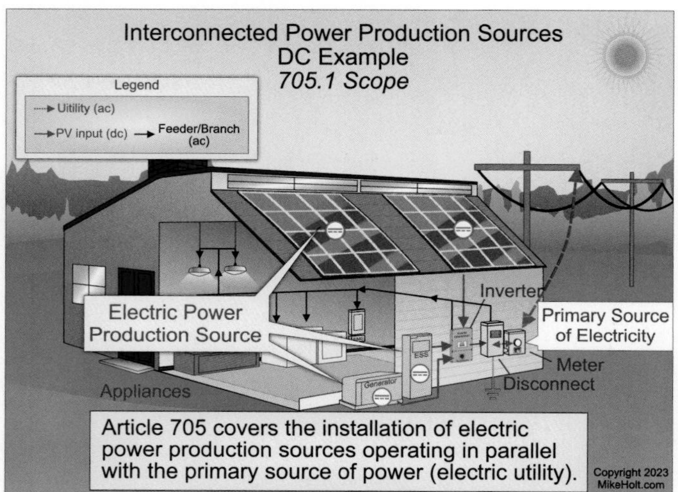

▸Figure 705–2

▸Figure 705–3

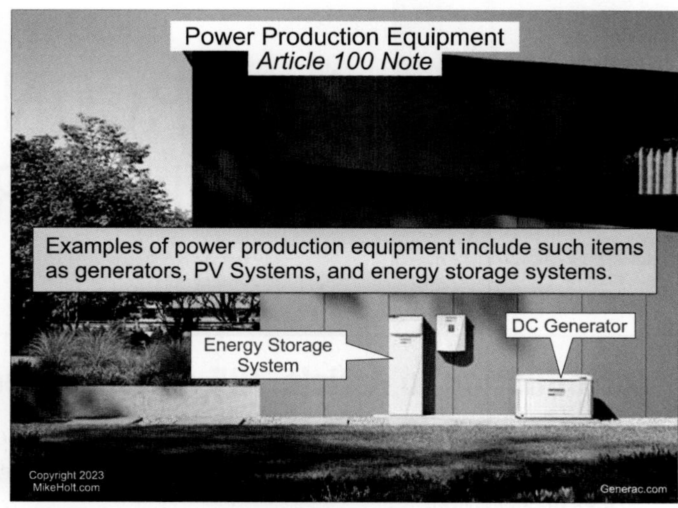

▸Figure 705–4

705.6 Equipment Approval

Interconnection devices and interactive (grid tied) equipment operating in parallel with power production sources (PV, ESS, generator) must be listed for the required interactive (grid tied) function. ▸**Figure 705–5**, ▸**Figure 705–6**, ▸**Figure 705–7**, and ▸**Figure 705–8**

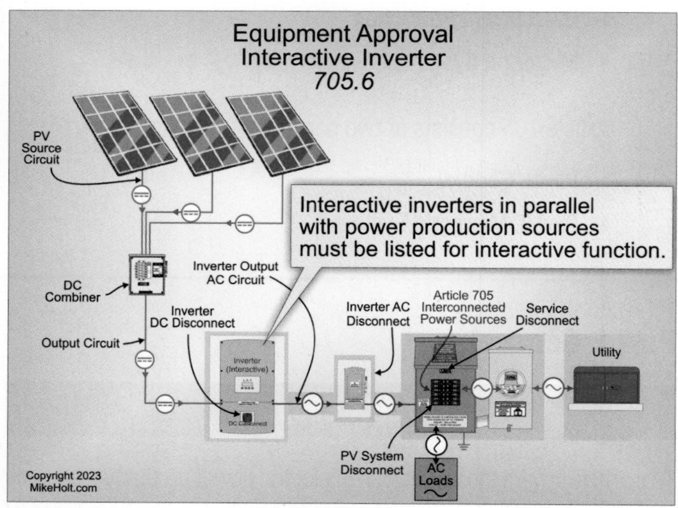

▸Figure 705–5

Note 2: An interactive (grid tied) function is common in microgrid interconnect devices (MID), power control systems, interactive (grid tied) inverters, and ac energy storage systems. ▸**Figure 705–9**

1st Printing

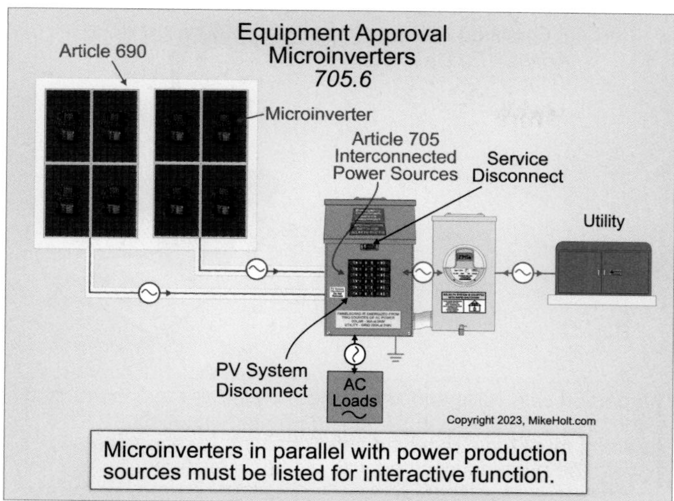
Equipment Approval
Microinverters
705.6
Article 690
Microinverter
Article 705
Interconnected
Power Sources
Service
Disconnect
Utility
PV System
Disconnect
AC
Loads
Copyright 2023, MikeHolt.com
Microinverters in parallel with power production sources must be listed for interactive function.

▸**Figure 705-6**

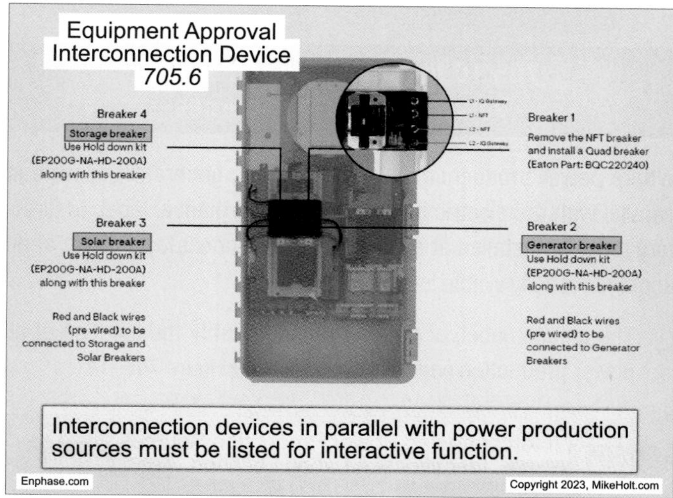
Equipment Approval
Interconnection Device
705.6
Breaker 4
Storage breaker
Use Hold down kit (EP200G-NA-HD-200A) along with this breaker
Breaker 3
Solar breaker
Use Hold down kit (EP200G-NA-HD-200A) along with this breaker
Red and Black wires (pre wired) to be connected to Storage and Solar Breakers
Breaker 1
Remove the NFT breaker and install a Quad breaker (Eaton Part: BQC220240)
Breaker 2
Generator breaker
Use Hold down kit (EP200G-NA-HD-200A) along with this breaker
Red and Black wires (pre wired) to be connected to Generator Breakers
Interconnection devices in parallel with power production sources must be listed for interactive function.
Enphase.com
Copyright 2023, MikeHolt.com

▸**Figure 705-7**

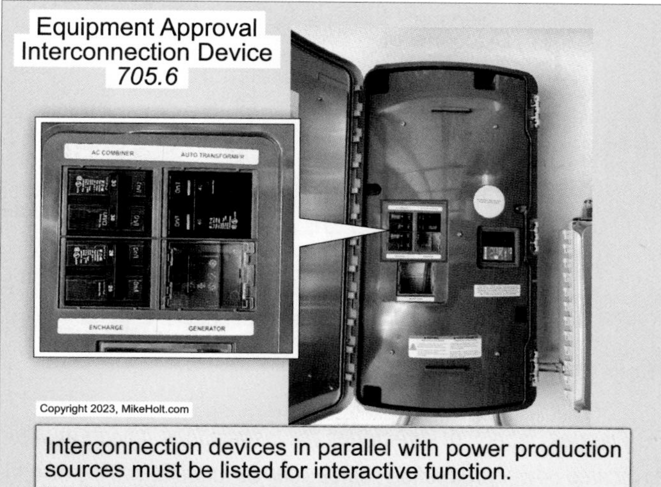
Equipment Approval
Interconnection Device
705.6
AC COMBINER
AUTO TRANSFORMER
ENCHARGE
GENERATOR
Copyright 2023, MikeHolt.com
Interconnection devices in parallel with power production sources must be listed for interactive function.

▸**Figure 705-8**

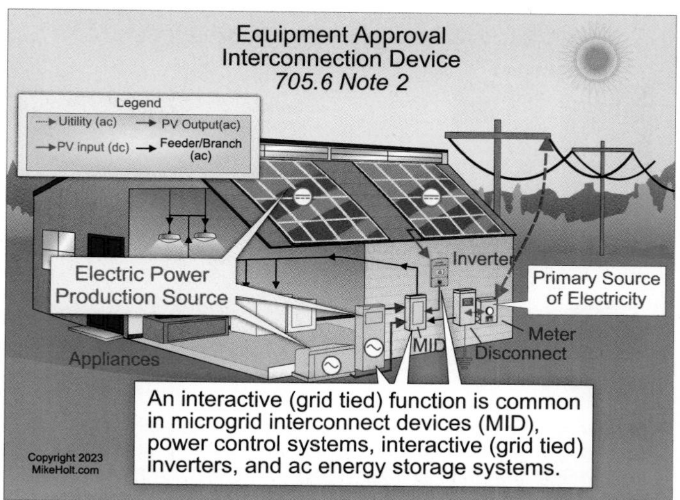
Equipment Approval
Interconnection Device
705.6 Note 2
Legend
Utility (ac)
PV Output(ac)
PV input (dc)
Feeder/Branch (ac)
Electric Power
Production Source
Appliances
Inverter
MID
Primary Source
of Electricity
Meter
Disconnect
An interactive (grid tied) function is common in microgrid interconnect devices (MID), power control systems, interactive (grid tied) inverters, and ac energy storage systems.
Copyright 2023
MikeHolt.com

▸**Figure 705-9**

According to Article 100, "Interactive Mode" means the operating mode where power production equipment or a microgrid are in parallel with each other and the electric utility. ▸**Figure 705-10**

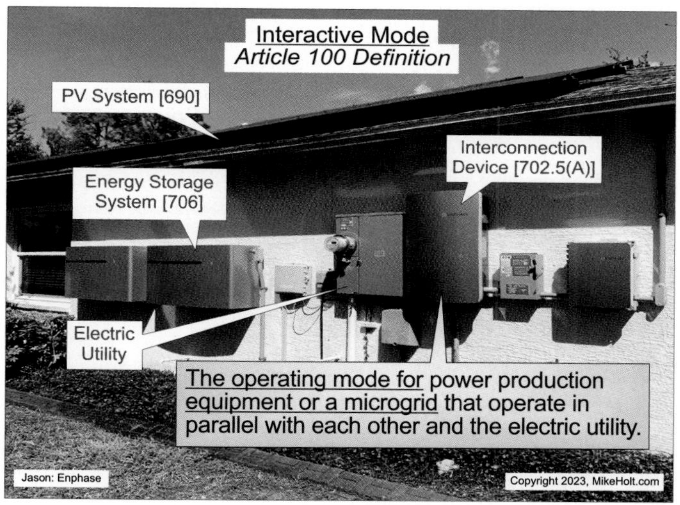
Interactive Mode
Article 100 Definition
PV System [690]
Energy Storage
System [706]
Interconnection
Device [702.5(A)]
Electric
Utility
The operating mode for power production equipment or a microgrid that operate in parallel with each other and the electric utility.
Jason: Enphase
Copyright 2023, MikeHolt.com

▸**Figure 705-10**

Author's Comment:

- A listed interactive (grid tied) power production source automatically stops exporting power upon loss of electric utility voltage and cannot be reconnected until the voltage has been restored. Interactive (grid tied) inverters can automatically or manually resume exporting power to the electric utility once the electric utility source is restored [705.40]. ▸**Figure 705-11**

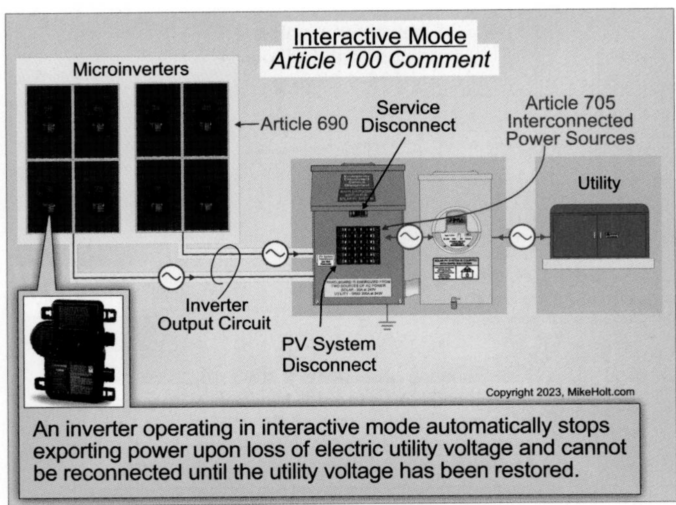
Interactive Mode
Article 100 Comment
Microinverters
Article 690
Service Disconnect
Article 705 Interconnected Power Sources
Utility
Inverter Output Circuit
PV System Disconnect
Copyright 2023, MikeHolt.com
An inverter operating in interactive mode automatically stops exporting power upon loss of electric utility voltage and cannot be reconnected until the utility voltage has been restored.

▶Figure 705-11

Qualified Person
Article 100 Definition
Copyright 2023 MikeHolt.com
A person with skills and knowledge related to the construction and operation of electrical equipment and installations. This person must have received safety training to recognize and avoid the hazards involved with electrical systems.

▶Figure 705-13

705.8 System Installation

The installation of power production sources (PV, ESS, generator) in parallel with the electric utility must be performed by a qualified person. ▶**Figure 705-12**

Interconnected Power Production Sources
Qualified Persons
705.8
PV System [690]
Interconnection Device [702.5(A)]
Energy Storage System [706]
Electric Utility
The installation of power production sources in parallel with the electric utility must be performed by a qualified person.
Jason: Enphase
Copyright 2023, MikeHolt.com

▶Figure 705-12

According to Article 100, a "Qualified Person" has the skills and knowledge related to the construction and operation of electrical equipment and installations. This person must have received safety training to recognize and avoid the hazards involved with electrical systems [Article 100]. ▶**Figure 705-13**

705.10 Identification of Parallel Power Production Sources

Where power production sources (PV, ESS, generator) operate in parallel with the electric utility, a permanent plaque, label, or directory must be installed at each service disconnect location, or at an approved readily visible location as follows:

(1) The plaque, label, or directory must identify the location of all power production source disconnects. ▶**Figure 705-14**

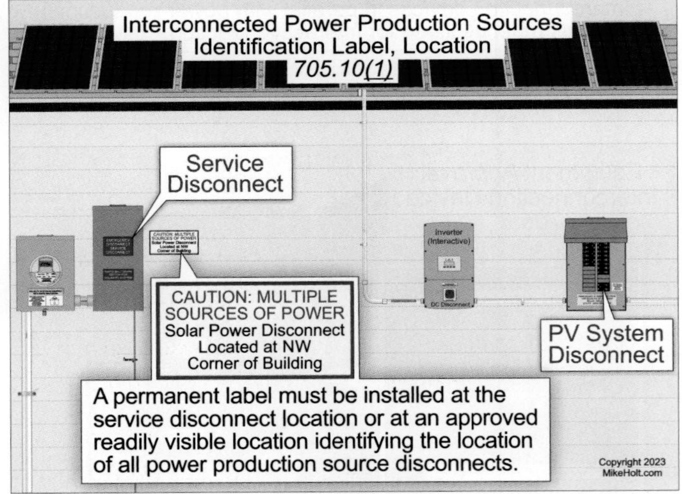
Interconnected Power Production Sources
Identification Label, Location
705.10(1)
Service Disconnect
CAUTION: MULTIPLE SOURCES OF POWER
Solar Power Disconnect
Located at NW
Corner of Building
PV System Disconnect
A permanent label must be installed at the service disconnect location or at an approved readily visible location identifying the location of all power production source disconnects.
Copyright 2023 MikeHolt.com

▶Figure 705-14

Ex: Plaques, labels, or directories for installations having multiple co-located power production sources can be identified as a group(s). A plaque or directory is not required for each power source.

Author's Comment:

- The exception to 705.10 infers that where there is only one service disconnect location, only one plaque or directory is required at the service disconnect indicating the location of the other power production sources.

(2) The plaque, label, or directory must indicate the emergency telephone numbers of any off-site entities servicing the power source systems.

(3) The plaque, label, or directory must be marked with the wording "CAUTION: MULTIPLE SOURCES OF POWER." The marking must be affixed and have sufficient durability to withstand the environment involved [110.21(B)]. ▶Figure 705–15

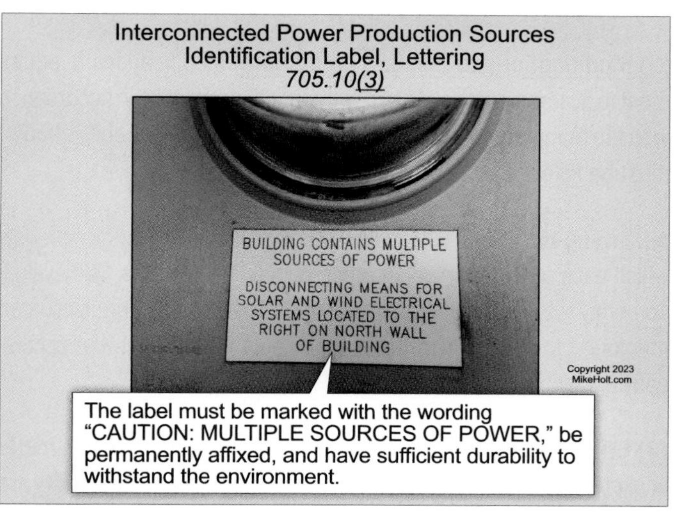
Interconnected Power Production Sources
Identification Label, Lettering
705.10(3)
BUILDING CONTAINS MULTIPLE SOURCES OF POWER
DISCONNECTING MEANS FOR SOLAR AND WIND ELECTRICAL SYSTEMS LOCATED TO THE RIGHT ON NORTH WALL OF BUILDING
Copyright 2023 MikeHolt.com
The label must be marked with the wording "CAUTION: MULTIPLE SOURCES OF POWER," be permanently affixed, and have sufficient durability to withstand the environment.

▶Figure 705–15

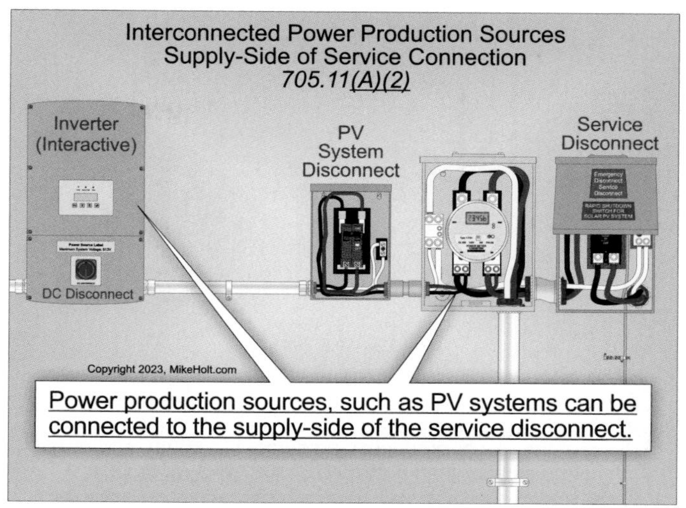
Interconnected Power Production Sources
Supply-Side of Service Connection
705.11(A)(2)
Inverter (Interactive)
PV System Disconnect
Service Disconnect
DC Disconnect
Copyright 2023, MikeHolt.com
Power production sources, such as PV systems can be connected to the supply-side of the service disconnect.

▶Figure 705–16

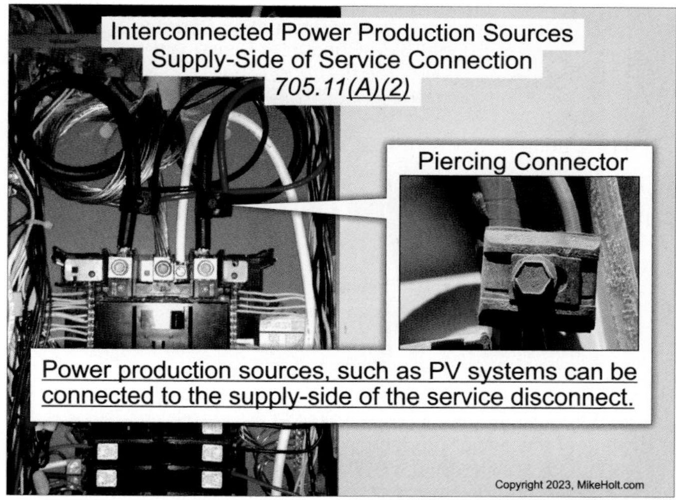
Interconnected Power Production Sources
Supply-Side of Service Connection
705.11(A)(2)
Piercing Connector
Power production sources, such as PV systems can be connected to the supply-side of the service disconnect.
Copyright 2023, MikeHolt.com

▶Figure 705–17

705.11 Service Connection

(A) Utility Connections. Power production sources can be connected to the electric utility as follows:

(1) Power production sources, such as PV and energy storage systems can be directly connected to the electric utility by a separate service.

(2) Power production sources, such as PV systems can be connected to the supply-side of the service disconnect. ▶Figure 705–16 and ▶Figure 705–17

(3) To an additional set of service entrance conductors in accordance with 230.40 Ex 5.

(B) Conductor Sizing. Power production source supply-side conductors must comply with all the following: ▶Figure 705–18 and ▶Figure 705–19

(1) Power production source supply-side conductors must have an ampacity of not less than 125 percent of the continuous current rating of the power production equipment, see 705.28.

(2) Power production source supply-side conductors must not be smaller than 6 AWG copper or 4 AWG aluminum or copper-clad aluminum.

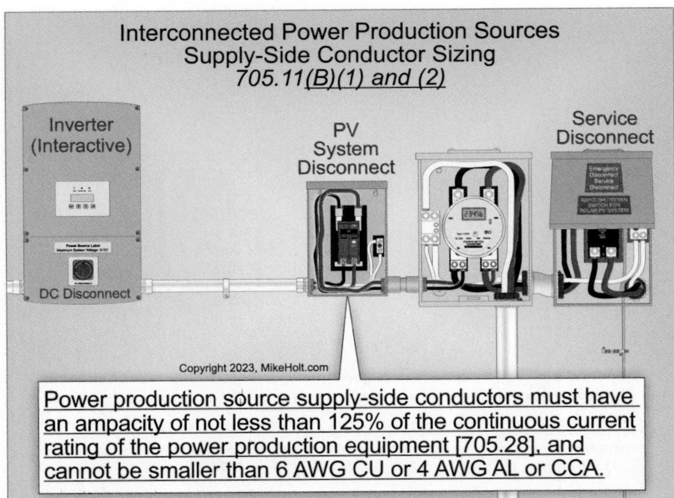

▶Figure 705–18

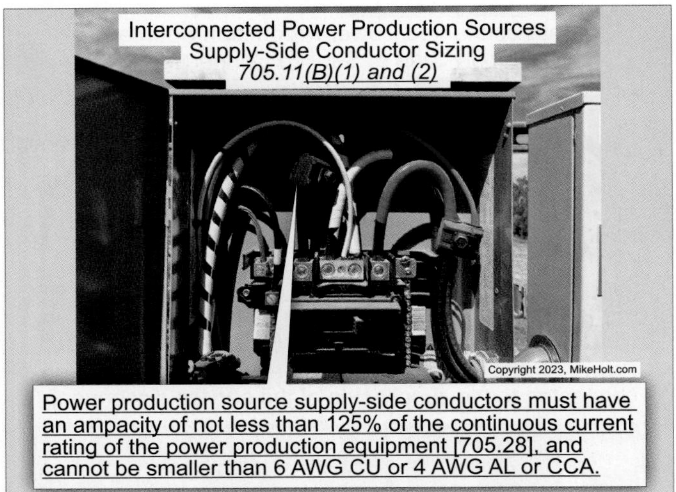

▶Figure 705–19

(C) Supply-Side Connections. Connection to service conductors must comply with the following:

(1) Conductor Splices or Taps. Splices and taps to service conductors must be in accordance with 230.46.

Author's Comment:

- According to 230.46, pressure connectors, devices for splices and tap connections, and power distribution blocks installed on service conductors must be listed and marked "suitable for use on the line side of the service equipment" or equivalent. ▶Figure 705–20

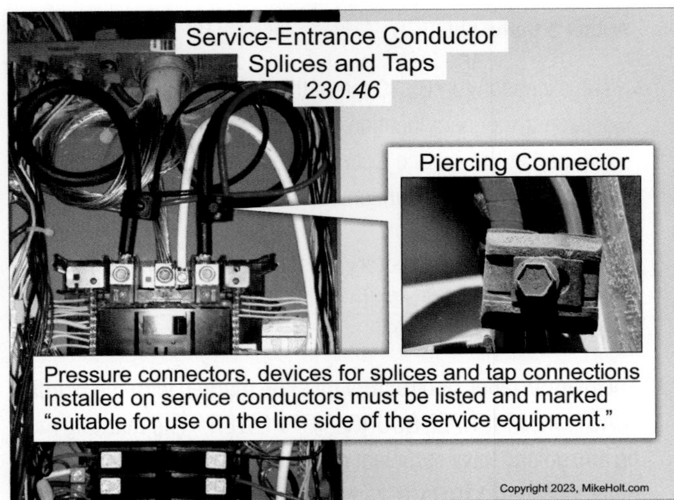

▶Figure 705–20

(2) Modifications to Existing Equipment. Modifications to equipment to accommodate supply-side connections must be in accordance with the manufacturer's instructions or the equipment modification(s) must be field evaluated and be field labeled.

According to Article 100, "Field Labeled" is equipment or materials which have a label, symbol, or other identifying mark of a field evaluation body (FEB) indicating the equipment or materials were evaluated and found to comply with the requirements described in the accompanying field evaluation report.

(3) Utility Meter Enclosure. Supply-side connections within meter socket enclosures under the exclusive control of the electric utility are only permitted where approved by the electric utility. ▶Figure 705–21

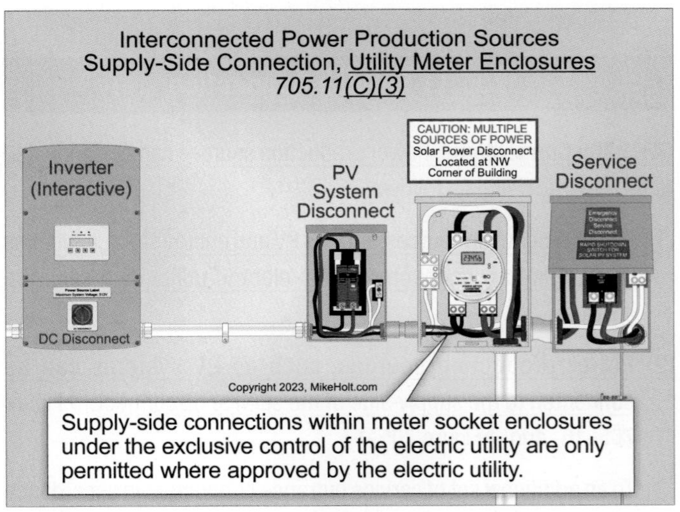

▶Figure 705–21

(D) Power Production Source Disconnect. A disconnecting means in accordance with Article 230, Parts VI through VIII must be provided to disconnect the power production source supply conductor. ▶Figure 705–22

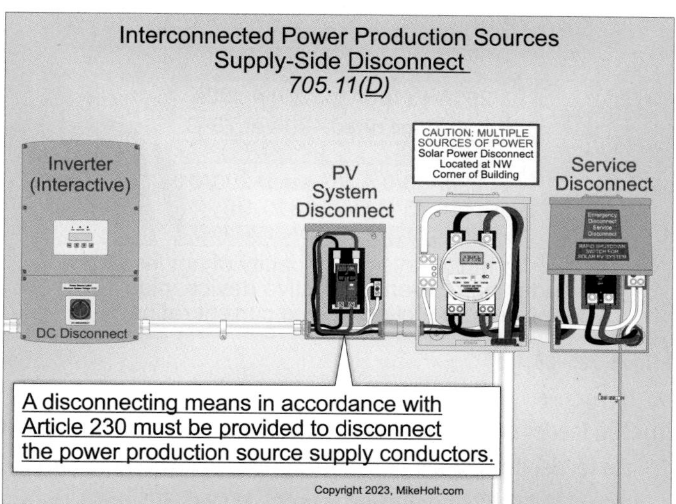

▶Figure 705–22

(E) Bonding and Grounding. Metal enclosures, metal raceways, and cable methods containing supply-side conductors must be bonded in accordance with Article 250, Parts II through V and VIII. ▶Figure 705–23

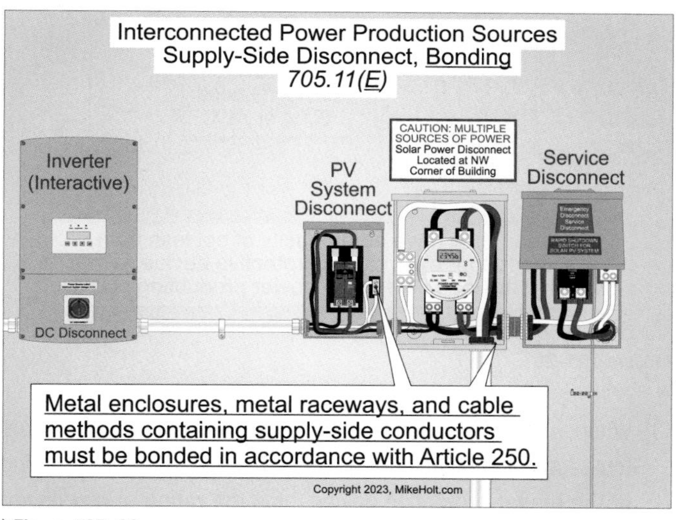

▶Figure 705–23

(F) Overcurrent Protection. Supply-side conductors terminating to the power production disconnect must have overcurrent protection in accordance with Article 230, Part VII. ▶Figure 705–24

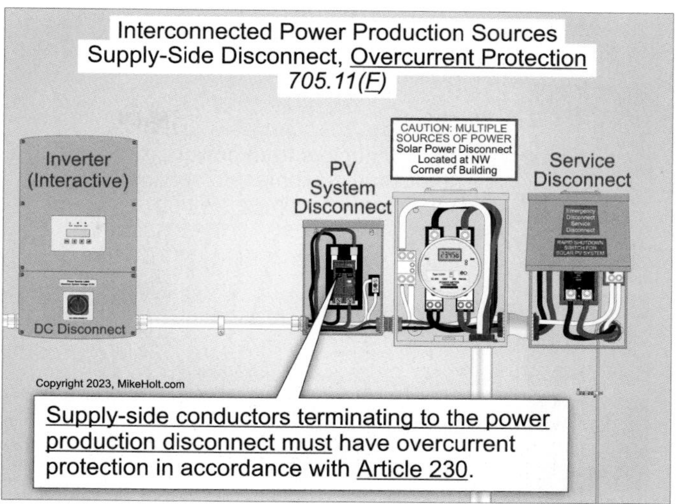

▶Figure 705–24

705.12 Load-Side Source Connection

Electric power production source (PV, ESS, generator) output conductors can be connected to the feeder or feeder equipment (load-side of service disconnect). ▶Figure 705–25

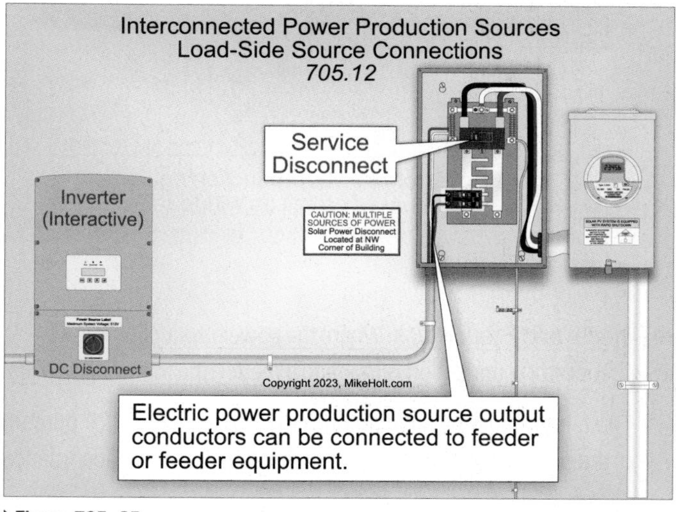

▶Figure 705–25

According to Article 100, "Power Production Source Output Conductors" are the conductors from the power production equipment to premises wiring or service equipment. ▶Figure 705–26 and ▶Figure 705–27

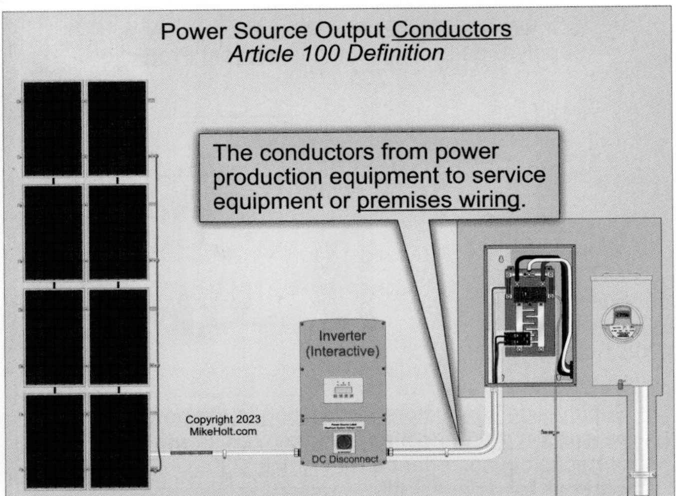

▸Figure 705-26

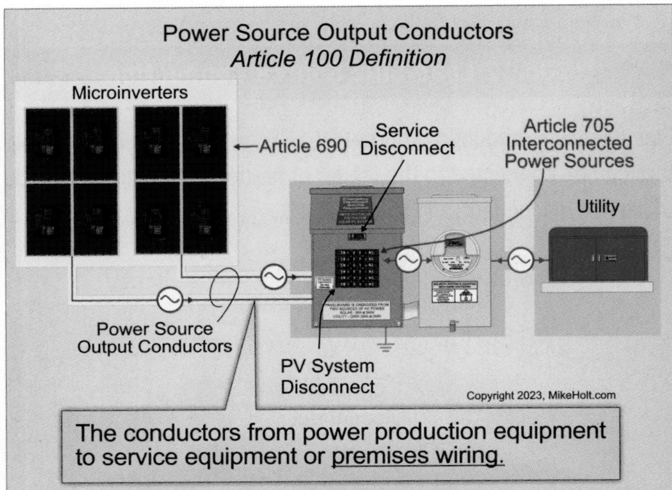

▸Figure 705-27

(A) Feeder and Feeder Taps. Where the power production source (PV, ESS, generator) connection is made to a feeder, the following applies:

(1) The feeder must have an ampacity of not less than 125 percent of the power production source nameplate current in accordance with 705.28(A).

(2) Where a power production source connection is made to a feeder at a location that is not at the opposite end of the feeder overcurrent protective device, that portion of the feeder on the load side of the power source connection must have an ampacity as follows:

(a) The feeder must have an ampacity of not less than the feeder overcurrent protective device, plus 125 percent of the power production source current rating. ▸Figure 705-28

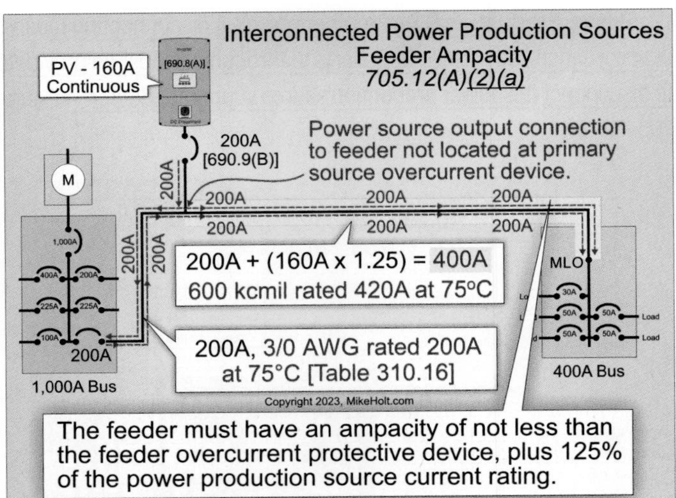

▸Figure 705-28

(b) The feeder must have an ampacity of not less than 100 percent the feeder overcurrent protective device rating placed at the load side of the power production source. ▸Figure 705-29

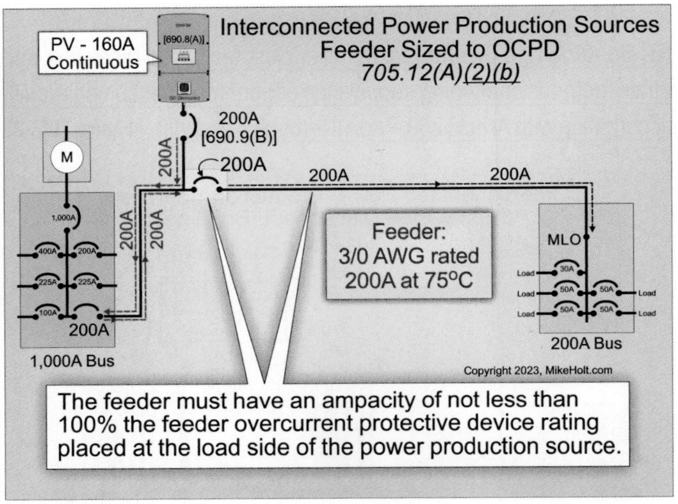

▸Figure 705-29

(3) Where a tap connection is made to a feeder, the tap conductors must have an ampacity of not less than one-third of the rating of the feeder protective device, plus the rating of any power production source overcurrent protective device connected to the feeder. ▸Figure 705-30

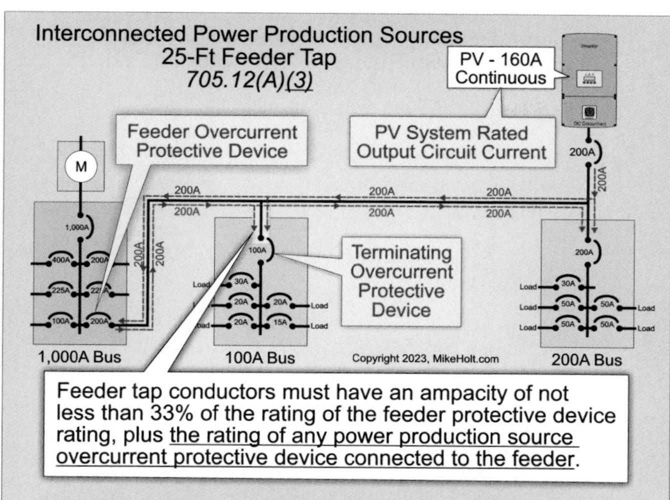

Interconnected Power Production Sources
25-Ft Feeder Tap
705.12(A)(3)
PV - 160A Continuous
Feeder Overcurrent Protective Device
PV System Rated Output Circuit Current
Terminating Overcurrent Protective Device
1,000A Bus
100A Bus
200A Bus
Copyright 2023, MikeHolt.com
Feeder tap conductors must have an ampacity of not less than 33% of the rating of the feeder protective device rating, plus the rating of any power production source overcurrent protective device connected to the feeder.

▸Figure 705–30

▸ Feeder Tap—25-Foot Example

Question: *What size tap conductor, not more than 25 ft long made from a 200A-protected feeder supplied with an inverter having an ac current rating of 160A is required to a 100A overcurrent protective device?* ▸**Figure 705–31**

(a) 3 AWG *(b) 2 AWG* *(c) 1 AWG* *(d) 1/0 AWG*

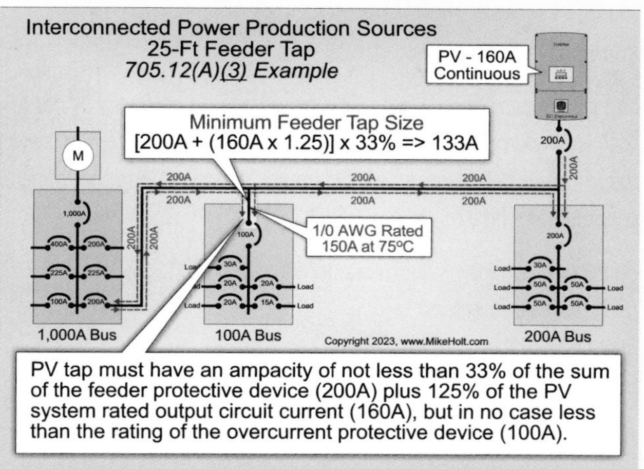

Interconnected Power Production Sources
25-Ft Feeder Tap
705.12(A)(3) Example
PV - 160A Continuous
Minimum Feeder Tap Size
[200A + (160A x 1.25)] x 33% => 133A
1/0 AWG Rated 150A at 75ºC
1,000A Bus
100A Bus
200A Bus
Copyright 2023, www.MikeHolt.com
PV tap must have an ampacity of not less than 33% of the sum of the feeder protective device (200A) plus 125% of the PV system rated output circuit current (160A), but in no case less than the rating of the overcurrent protective device (100A).

▸Figure 705–31

Solution:

PV system taps not longer than 25 ft must have an ampacity of not less than 33 percent of the feeder overcurrent protective device rating (200A) plus 125 percent of the PV system rated current (160A), but in no case less than the rating of the terminating overcurrent protective device (100A) [240.21(B)(2)].

Feeder Tap Conductor Ampacity = > [200A + (160A × 125%)] × 33%, but not less than 100A

Feeder Tap Conductor Ampacity = > (200A + 200A) × 33%, but not less than 100A

Feeder Tap Conductor Ampacity = > 400A × 33%, but not less than 100A

Feeder Tap Conductor Ampacity = > 133A, but no less than 100A

Feeder Conductor Size = 1/0 AWG rated 150A at 75°C [Table 310.16]

Answer: *(d) 1/0 AWG*

(B) Panelboard Busbar Ampere Rating. Where the power production source (PV, ESS, generator) connection is made to distribution equipment with no specific listing and instructions for combining multiple sources, one of the following methods (B)(1) through (B)(6) must be used:

(1) Overcurrent Protection Device, Anywhere. Where the power production source (PV, ESS, generator) connection is made to a circuit breaker in a panelboard, the panelboard busbar must have an ampere rating of not less than the rating of the panelboard overcurrent protective device, plus 125 percent of the power production source current rating in accordance with 705.28. ▸**Figure 705–32**

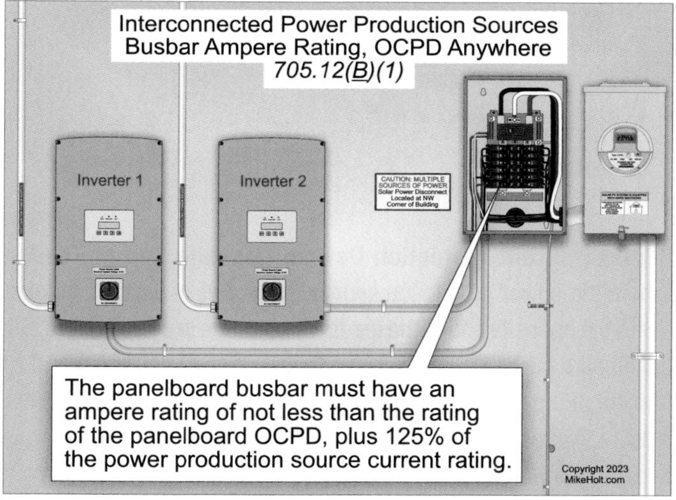

Interconnected Power Production Sources
Busbar Ampere Rating, OCPD Anywhere
705.12(B)(1)
Inverter 1
Inverter 2
The panelboard busbar must have an ampere rating of not less than the rating of the panelboard OCPD, plus 125% of the power production source current rating.
Copyright 2023 MikeHolt.com

▸Figure 705–32

▶ Panelboard Busbar Ampere Rating Example

Question: *What is the minimum busbar ampere rating for a panelboard protected by a 150A overcurrent protective device if it is supplied by two interactive inverters each having an output current rating of 20A?* **▸Figure 705–33**

(a) 200A *(b) 250A* *(c) 260A* *(d) 300A*

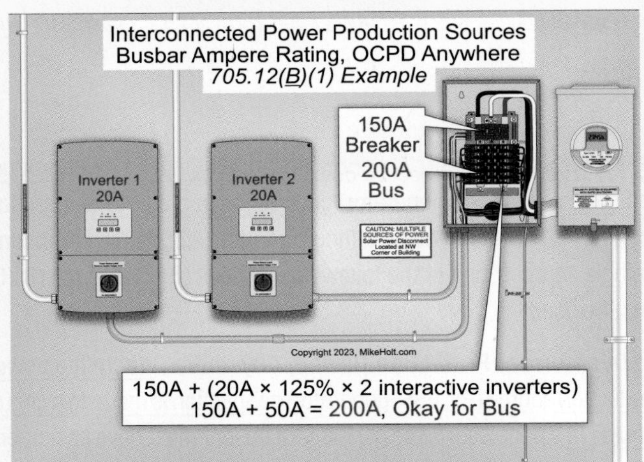

▸Figure 705–33

Solution:

Minimum Busbar Ampere Rating = >150A + (20A × 125% × 2 interactive inverters)
Minimum Busbar Ampere Rating = >150A + 50A
Minimum Busbar Ampere Rating = >200A

Answer: *(a) 200A*

(2) Overcurrent Protection Device, Opposite End of Feeder. Where the power production source terminates in a circuit breaker at not the opposite end of the feeder termination in a panelboard, the panelboard busbar must have an ampere rating of not less than 120 percent of the sum of the panelboard overcurrent protective device, plus 125 percent of the power production source current rating in accordance with 705.28. **▸Figure 705–34**

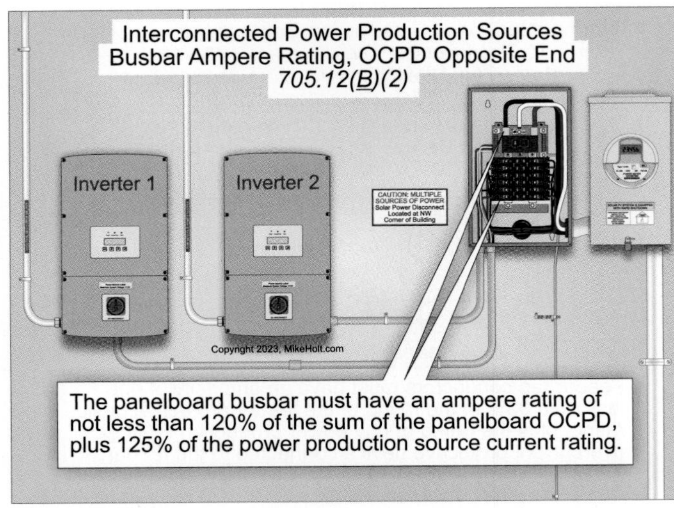

▸Figure 705–34

▶ Panelboard Busbar Ampere Rating—Opposite Feeder Termination Example

Question: *Can a 200A rated panelboard protected by a 175A overcurrent protective device be supplied by two interactive inverters where each has an output current rating of 24A and are opposite the feeder termination?* **▸Figure 705–35**

(a) Yes *(b) No*

Solution:

The panelboard busbar ampacity must have an ampacity of not less than 120 percent of the panelboard overcurrent protective device rating, plus 125 percent of the power source(s) current rating in accordance with 705.28.

Panelboard Busbar × 120% => 175A + (24A × 125% × 2 interactive inverters)
200A × 120% = >175A + 60A
240A = >235A

Answer: *(a) Yes*

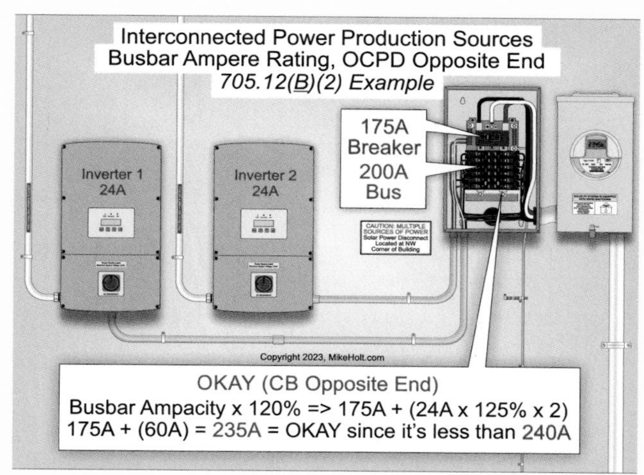

▸Figure 705–35

Where the power production source terminates in a circuit breaker at the opposite end of the feeder termination in a panelboard, a warning label with sufficient durability to withstand the environment involved [110.21(B)] must be applied to the distribution equipment next to the power production source backfed breaker and read: ▸Figure 705–36

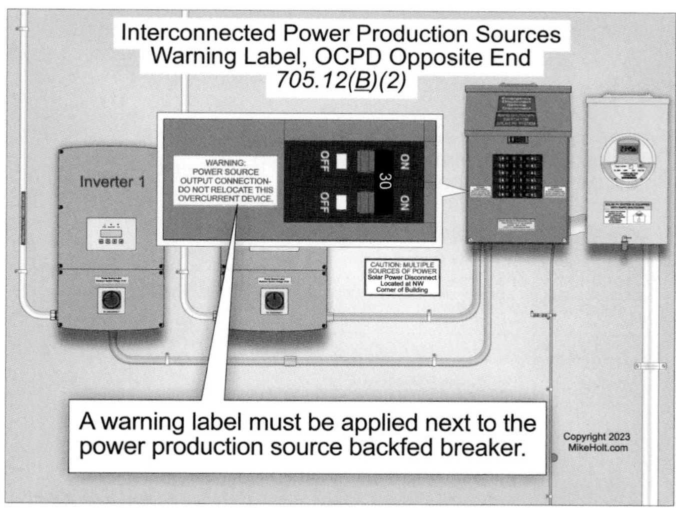

▸Figure 705–36

WARNING—POWER SOURCE OUTPUT DO NOT RELOCATE THIS OVERCURRENT DEVICE

(3) Sum of Overcurrent Protection Devices. The panelboard busbar must have an ampere rating of not less than the sum of the ampere ratings of all overcurrent protective devices in the panelboard, exclusive of the feeder overcurrent protective device protecting the panelboard. ▸Figure 705–37

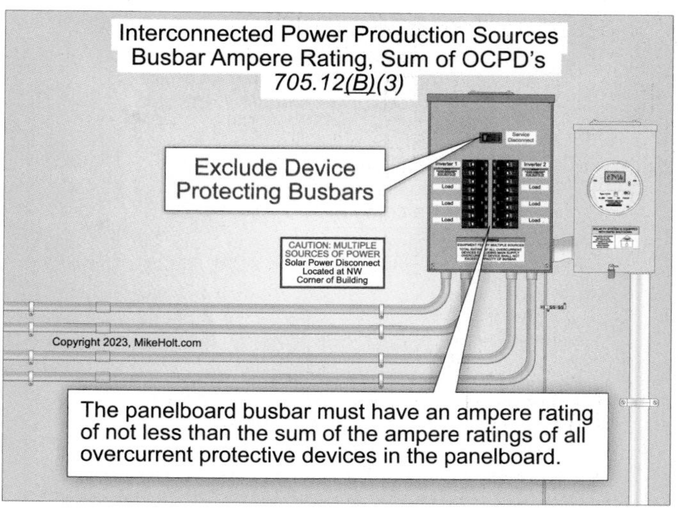

▸Figure 705–37

▸ Panelboard Busbar Ampere Rating—Sum of Breakers Not to Exceed Busbar Ampere Rating Example 1

Question: *What is the minimum busbar ampere rating for a panelboard containing two 30A, two-pole circuit breakers and six 20A, two-pole circuit breakers?* ▸**Figure 705–38**

(a) 12A *(b) 140A* *(c) 180A* *(d) 210A*

Solution:

The panelboard busbar ampacity must have an ampere rating of not less than the sum of the ampere ratings of all the overcurrent protective devices, exclusive of the overcurrent protective device protecting the panelboard busbar.

Panelboard Busbar = >(30A × 2) + (20A × 6)
Panelboard Busbar = >60A + 120A
Panelboard Busbar = 180A

Answer: *(c) 180A*

• • •

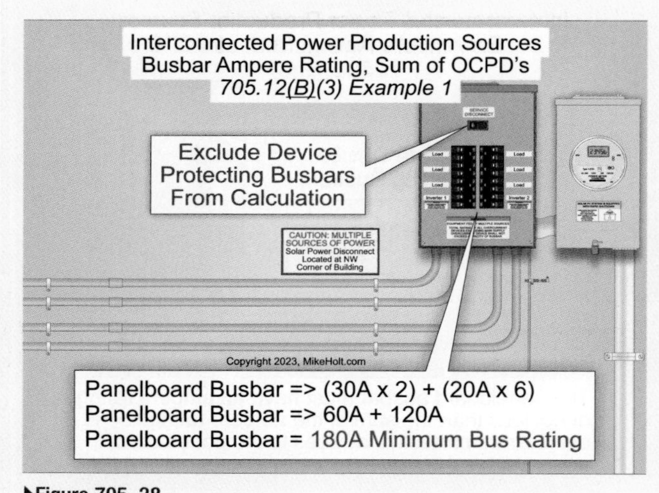

▸Figure 705–38

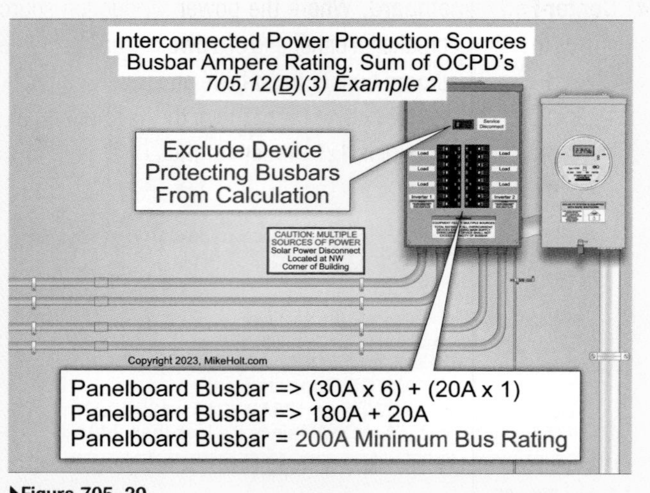

▸Figure 705–39

▸ Panelboard Busbar Ampere Rating—Sum of Breakers Not to Exceed Busbar Ampere Rating Example 2

Question: *What is the minimum busbar ampere rating for a panelboard containing six 30A, two-pole circuit breakers and one 20A, one-pole circuit breaker?* **▸Figure 705–39**

(a) 125A (b) 150A (c) 175A (d) 200A

Solution:

The panelboard busbar ampere rating must be equal to or greater than the sum of the ampere ratings of all the overcurrent protective devices on the panelboard busbar.

Panelboard Busbar = >(30A × 6) + (20A × 1)
Panelboard Busbar = >180A + 20A
Panelboard Busbar = 200A

Answer: *(d) 200A*

Where the panelboard busbar is sized to the sum of the ampere ratings of all overcurrent protective devices in the panelboard, a warning label with sufficient durability to withstand the environment involved [110.21(B)] must be applied to the distribution equipment and read: **▸Figure 705–40**

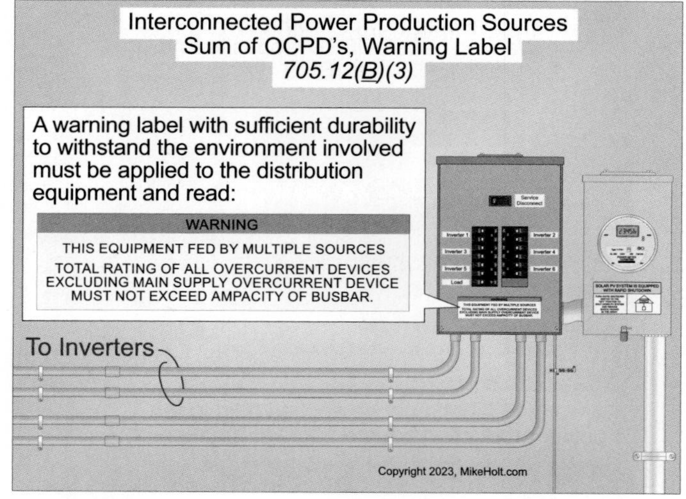

▸Figure 705–40

WARNING—EQUIPMENT FED BY MULTIPLE SOURCES. TOTAL RATING OF ALL OVERCURRENT DEVICES EXCLUDING MAIN SUPPLY OVERCURRENT DEVICE MUST NOT EXCEED AMPACITY OF BUSBAR.

1st Printing

(4) Center-Fed Panelboard. Where the power production source terminates to a circuit breaker at either end of a dwelling unit center-fed panelboard, the panelboard busbar must have an ampere rating not less than 120 percent of the sum of the rating of the panelboard overcurrent protective device, plus 125 percent of the power production source current. ▶**Figure 705–41**

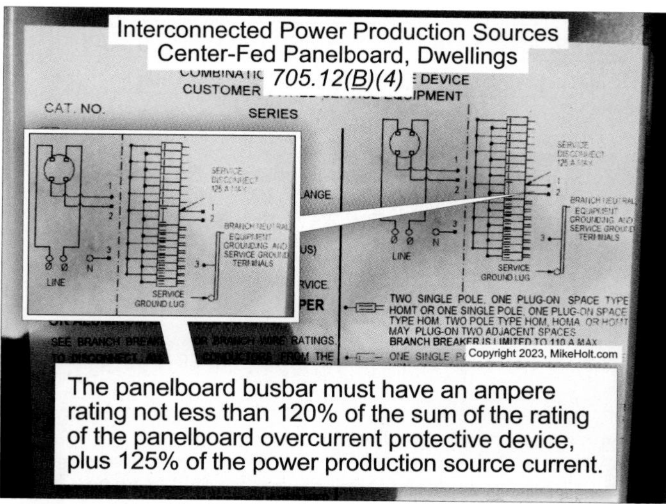

▶**Figure 705–41**

(5) Feed-Through Connections. Where the power production source terminates to feed-through connections in a panelboard, the power production source conductors must be sized in accordance with 705.12(A).

Where an overcurrent protective device is installed at either end of feed-through conductors, panelboard busbars on either side of the feed-through conductors can be sized in accordance with 705.12(B)(1) through (3).

(6) Engineering Supervision. Other connections are permitted where designed under engineering supervision that includes available fault-current and busbar load calculations.

705.13 Energy Management Systems

An energy management system [750.30] is permitted to limit current on the busbars and conductors that are supplied by power production sources (PV, ESS, generator). ▶**Figure 705–42**

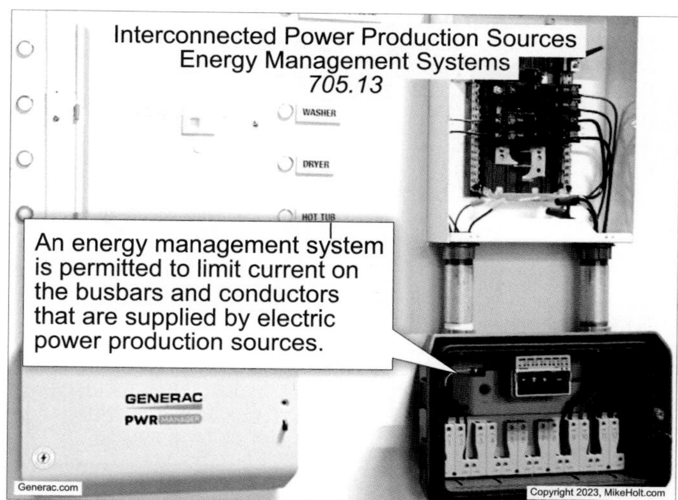

▶**Figure 705–42**

According to Article 100, an "Energy Management System" consisting of monitor(s), communications equipment, controller(s), timer(s), or other device(s) that monitors and/or controls an electrical load or a power production or storage source. ▶**Figure 705–43** and ▶**Figure 705–44**

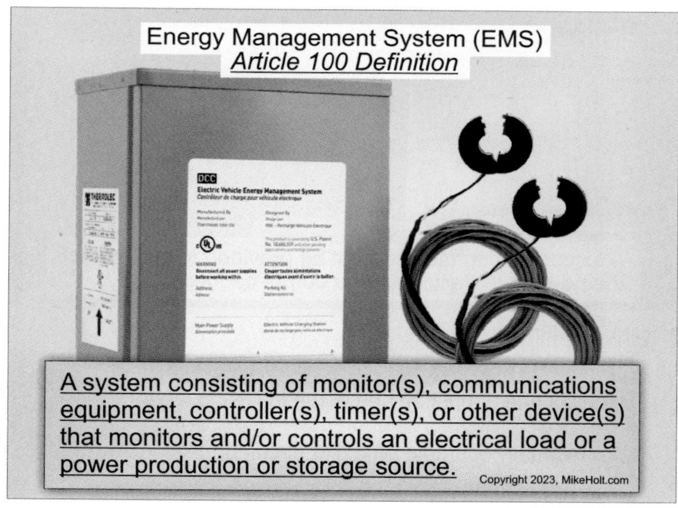

▶**Figure 705–43**

705.20 Power Production Source Disconnect

A disconnecting means must be provided to disconnect the power production source output conductors (PV, ESS, generator) and comply with the following: ▶**Figure 705–45**

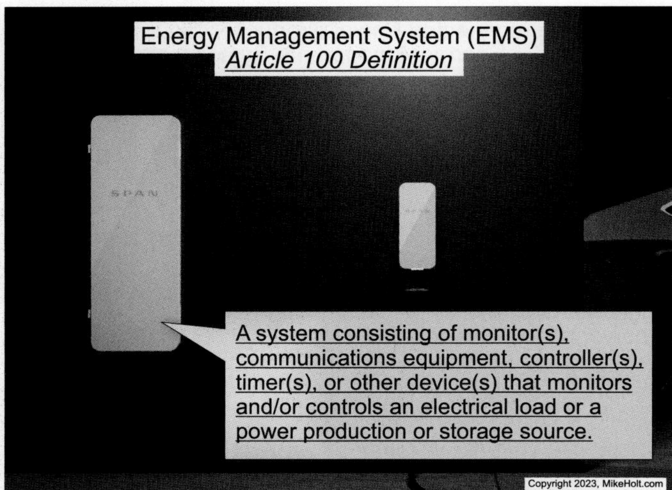
Energy Management System (EMS)
Article 100 Definition
A system consisting of monitor(s), communications equipment, controller(s), timer(s), or other device(s) that monitors and/or controls an electrical load or a power production or storage source.
Copyright 2023, MikeHolt.com

▶Figure 705–44

Interconnected Power Production Sources
Output Circuit Disconnect
705.20
Copyright 2023, MikeHolt.com
A disconnecting means must be provided to disconnect the power production source output conductors.

▶Figure 705–45

(1) The disconnect must be one of the following types:

a. A manually operable switch or circuit breaker

b. A load-break-rated pull-out switch

c. A remote-controlled switch or circuit breaker capable of being operated manually and opened automatically when control power is interrupted

d. A device listed for the intended application

(2) Simultaneously open all ungrounded conductors of the circuit.

(3) Be readily accessible.

(4) Be externally operable.

(5) Indicate if it is in the open (off) or closed (on) position.

(6) Have ratings sufficient for the circuit current, available fault current, and voltage at the terminals.

(7) Where line and load terminals are capable of being energized in the open position, the disconnect must be marked. ▶Figure 705–46

WARNING: ELECTRIC SHOCK HAZARD
TERMINALS ON THE LINE AND LOAD SIDES MAY
BE ENERGIZED IN THE OPEN POSITION.

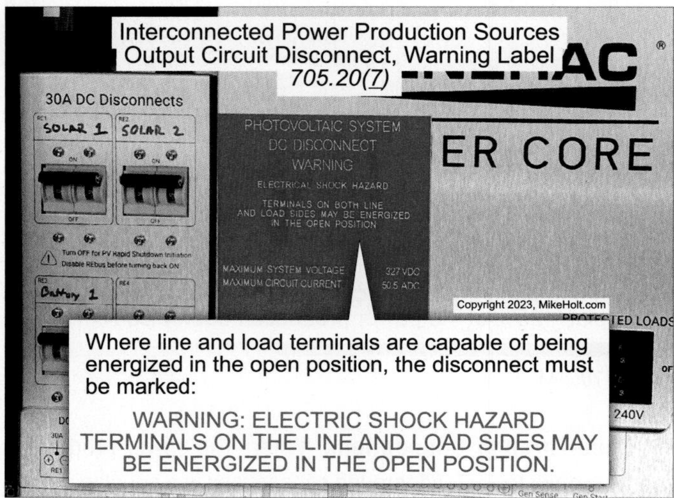
Interconnected Power Production Sources
Output Circuit Disconnect, Warning Label
705.20(7)
30A DC Disconnects
SOLAR 1
SOLAR 2
PHOTOVOLTAIC SYSTEM
DC DISCONNECT
WARNING
ELECTRICAL SHOCK HAZARD
TERMINALS ON BOTH LINE AND LOAD SIDES MAY BE ENERGIZED IN THE OPEN POSITION
MAXIMUM SYSTEM VOLTAGE
MAXIMUM CIRCUIT CURRENT
327 VDC
50.5 ADC
ER CORE
Copyright 2023, MikeHolt.com
Where line and load terminals are capable of being energized in the open position, the disconnect must be marked:
WARNING: ELECTRIC SHOCK HAZARD
TERMINALS ON THE LINE AND LOAD SIDES MAY
BE ENERGIZED IN THE OPEN POSITION.
240V

▶Figure 705–46

Note: With interconnected power sources, some switches and fuses are capable of being energized from both directions.

705.25 Wiring Methods

Power source output conductors must comply with 705.25(A) through (C).

(A) General. In addition to Chapter 3 raceways and cables, wiring methods and fittings listed for use with power production equipment are permitted. ▶Figure 705–47

(B) Flexible Cords and Cables. Flexible cords used to connect moving parts of power production equipment, or where used for ready removal for maintenance and repair, must be listed and identified as Type DG cable, suitable for extra-hard usage, and be water resistant. Cables exposed to sunlight must be sunlight resistant.

Flexible, finely-stranded cables must terminate on terminals, lugs, devices, or connectors identified for the use of finely stranded conductors in accordance with 110.14(A). ▶Figure 705–48

1st Printing

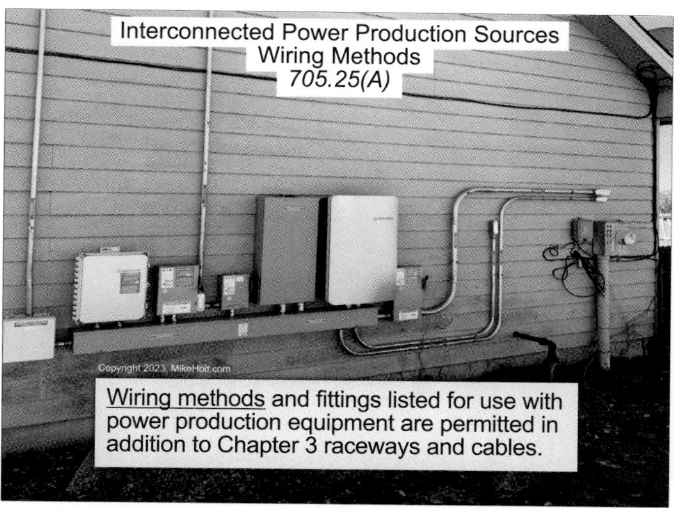
Interconnected Power Production Sources
Wiring Methods
705.25(A)
Wiring methods and fittings listed for use with power production equipment are permitted in addition to Chapter 3 raceways and cables.
Copyright 2023, MikeHolt.com

▶Figure 705–47

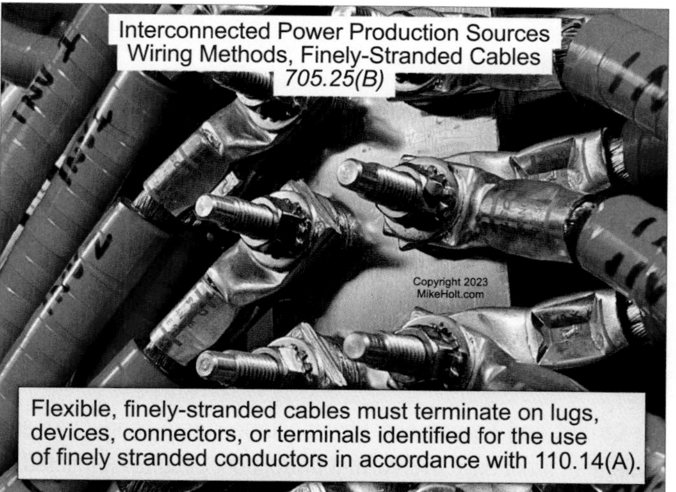
Interconnected Power Production Sources
Wiring Methods, Finely-Stranded Cables
705.25(B)
Copyright 2023 MikeHolt.com
Flexible, finely-stranded cables must terminate on lugs, devices, connectors, or terminals identified for the use of finely stranded conductors in accordance with 110.14(A).

▶Figure 705–48

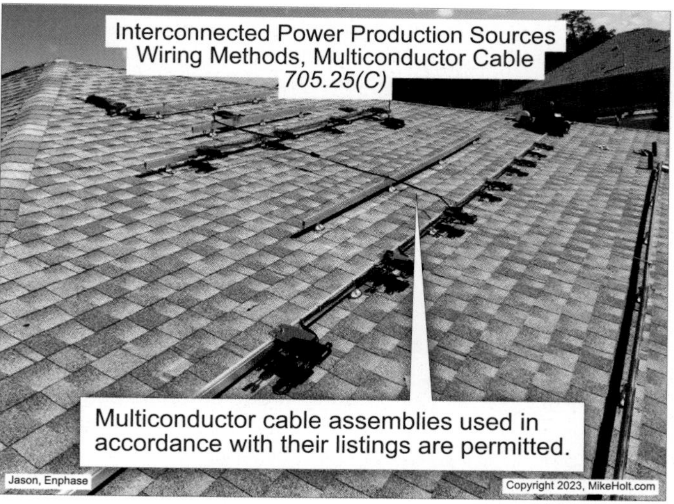
Interconnected Power Production Sources
Wiring Methods, Multiconductor Cable
705.25(C)
Multiconductor cable assemblies used in accordance with their listings are permitted.
Jason, Enphase
Copyright 2023, MikeHolt.com

▶Figure 705–49

Interconnected Power Production Sources
Power Source Output Current
705.28(A)(1)
ESS = 16A
PV - Three Strings 16A Each
ESS = 16A
ESS = 16A
PV = 48A
ESS = 48A
Copyright 2023, MikeHolt.com
The power source output current is equal to the sum of the output current of the power production equipment nameplate current rating.

▶Figure 705–50

(C) Multiconductor Cable Assemblies. Multiconductor cable assemblies used in accordance with their listings are permitted. ▶**Figure 705–49**

Note: An ac module harness is one example of a multiconductor cable assembly.

705.28 Output Current and Circuit Sizing

(A) Power Source Output Current.

(1) Equipment Nameplate. The power source output current of power production equipment (PV, ESS, generator) is equal to the sum of the output current of the power production equipment nameplate current rating. ▶**Figure 705–50**

(2) Energy Management System. The power source output current of all interconnected power production equipment is equal to the current setting of the energy management system [750.30]. ▶**Figure 705–51**

(B) Power Source Conductor Ampacity. Power production source (PV, ESS, generator) conductors must have an ampacity as follows: ▶**Figure 705–52**

(1) One hundred twenty-five percent of the power production equipment nameplate current rating [705.28(A)]

Ex 1: If the assembly, including the overcurrent protective devices protecting the circuit, is listed for operation at 100 percent, the conductors can be sized at not less than the calculated current of 705.28(A).

Power Source Output Current
Energy Management System
705.28(A)(2)
The power source output current of all interconnected power production equipment is equal to the current setting of the energy management system.
Copyright 2023, MikeHolt.com

▸Figure 705–51

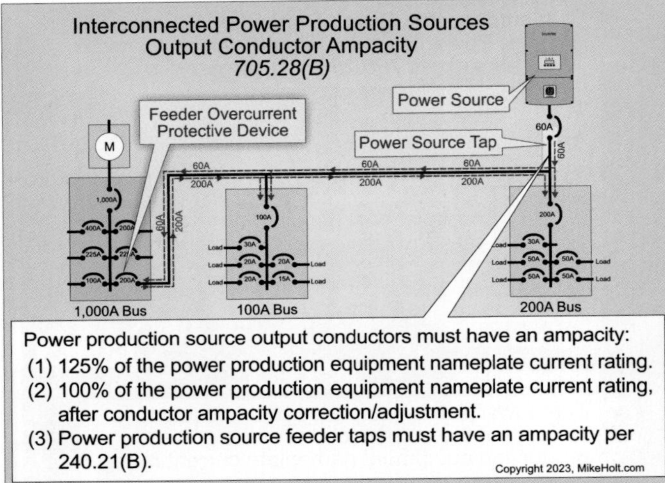

Interconnected Power Production Sources
Output Conductor Ampacity
705.28(B)
Power Source
Feeder Overcurrent Protective Device
Power Source Tap
1,000A Bus
100A Bus
200A Bus
Power production source output conductors must have an ampacity:
(1) 125% of the power production equipment nameplate current rating.
(2) 100% of the power production equipment nameplate current rating, after conductor ampacity correction/adjustment.
(3) Power production source feeder taps must have an ampacity per 240.21(B).
Copyright 2023, MikeHolt.com

▸Figure 705–52

Ex 2: Where a circuit is connected at both its supply and load ends to separately installed pressure connections as covered in 110.14(C)(2), the ampacity of the conductors can be sized at not less than the calculated current of 705.28(A). No portion of the circuit can extend into an enclosure.

(2) One hundred percent of the power production equipment nameplate current rating, after conductor ampacity correction and/or adjustment [310.15 and 705.28(A)]

(3) Power production source feeder taps [705.12(A)(3)] must have an ampacity in accordance with 240.21(B)

(C) Neutral Conductors. Neutral conductors must be sized as follows:

(1) Line-to-Neutral Power Sources. The neutral conductor to a single-phase line-to-neutral power production source must have an ampacity of not less than the current calculated in 705.28(A).

(2) Instrumentation, Voltage or Phase Detection. A neutral conductor used solely for instrumentation, voltage detection, or phase detection can be sized in accordance with Table 250.102(C)(1). ▸**Figure 705–53**

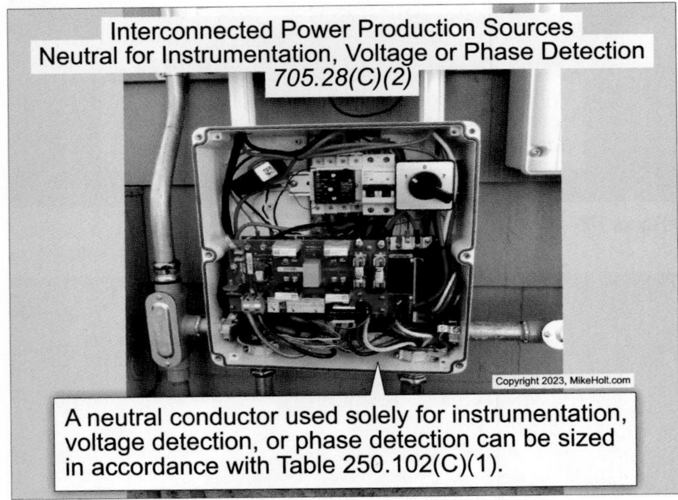

Interconnected Power Production Sources
Neutral for Instrumentation, Voltage or Phase Detection
705.28(C)(2)
A neutral conductor used solely for instrumentation, voltage detection, or phase detection can be sized in accordance with Table 250.102(C)(1).
Copyright 2023, MikeHolt.com

▸Figure 705–53

705.30 Overcurrent Protection

(A) Circuit and Equipment. Power source output conductors and equipment must have overcurrent protection. Circuits connected to more than one electrical source must have overcurrent protection from all sources.

(B) Overcurrent Device Ratings. The overcurrent protective device for power production source (PV, ESS, or generator) conductors must have an ampere rating of not less than 125 percent of the power production equipment nameplate current [705.28(A)].

▶ Example

Question: *What size overcurrent protective device is required for the power source output circuit conductors installed to an inverter with a nameplate ampere rating of 30A?* ▶**Figure 705-54**

(a) 20A *(b) 30A* *(c) 40A* *(d) 50A*

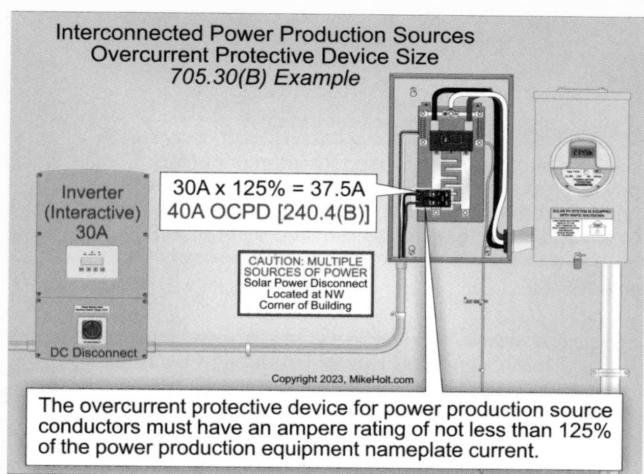

▶**Figure 705-54**

Solution:

OCPD = 30A × 125% [705.30(B)]
OCPD = 37.5A
OCPD = 40A [240.4(B) and 240.6]

Answer: *(c) 40A*

Ex: Where the assembly, together with its overcurrent protective device(s) is listed for continuous operation at 100 percent of its rating, the overcurrent protective device is permitted to be sized at 100 percent of the current calculated in 705.28(A). ▶**Figure 705-55**

▶**Figure 705-55**

(C) Marking. Equipment containing overcurrent devices supplied from multiple power production sources must be marked to indicate the presence of all sources of power. ▶**Figure 705-56** and ▶**Figure 705-57**

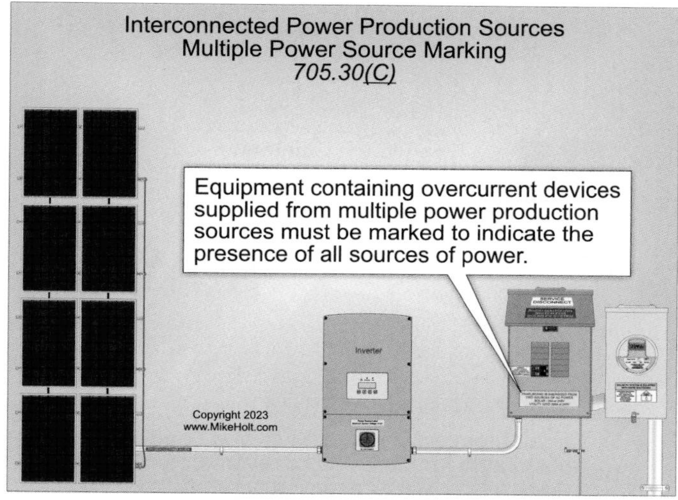

▶**Figure 705-56**

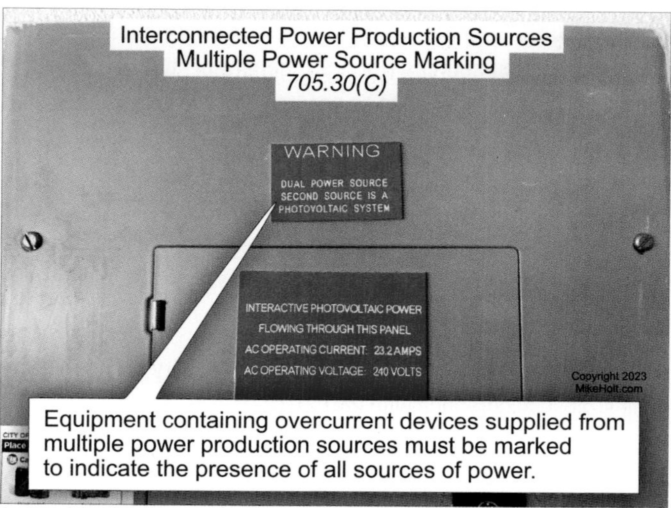

▶**Figure 705-57**

(D) Suitable for Backfeed. Circuit breakers not marked "line" and "load" are suitable for backfeed or reverse current. ▶**Figure 705-58**

Circuit breakers marked "line" and "load" are not suitable for backfeed or reverse current. ▶**Figure 705-59**

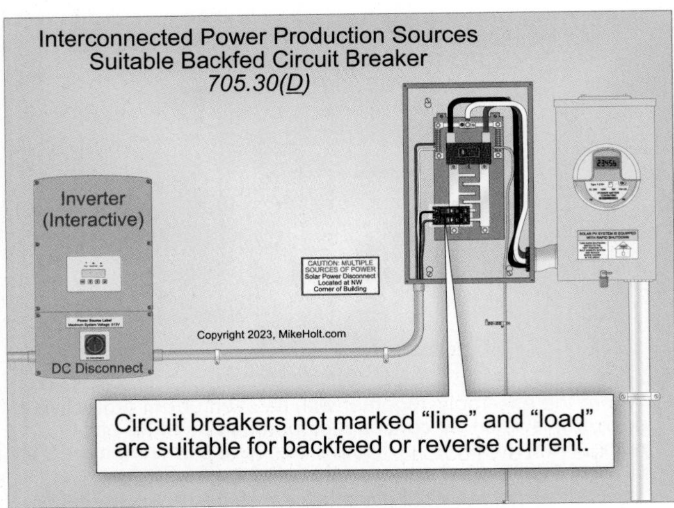
Interconnected Power Production Sources
Suitable Backfed Circuit Breaker
705.30(D)
Inverter
(Interactive)
CAUTION: MULTIPLE SOURCES OF POWER Solar Power Disconnect Located at NW Corner of Building
Copyright 2023, MikeHolt.com
DC Disconnect
Circuit breakers not marked "line" and "load" are suitable for backfeed or reverse current.

▸Figure 705-58

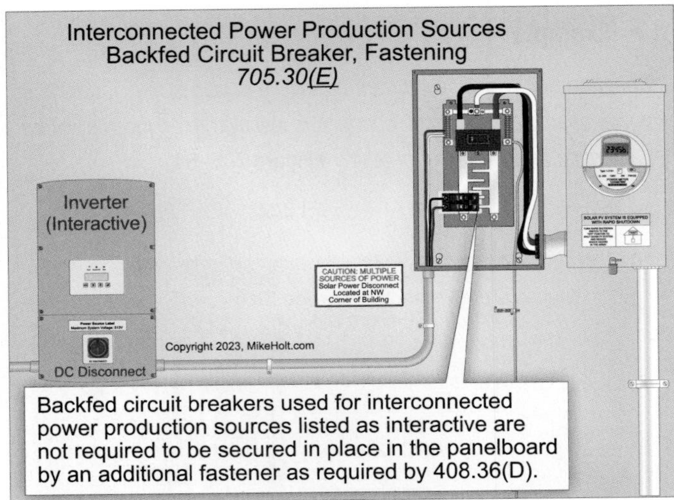
Interconnected Power Production Sources
Backfed Circuit Breaker, Fastening
705.30(E)
Inverter
(Interactive)
CAUTION: MULTIPLE SOURCES OF POWER Solar Power Disconnect Located at NW Corner of Building
Copyright 2023, MikeHolt.com
DC Disconnect
Backfed circuit breakers used for interconnected power production sources listed as interactive are not required to be secured in place in the panelboard by an additional fastener as required by 408.36(D).

▸Figure 705-60

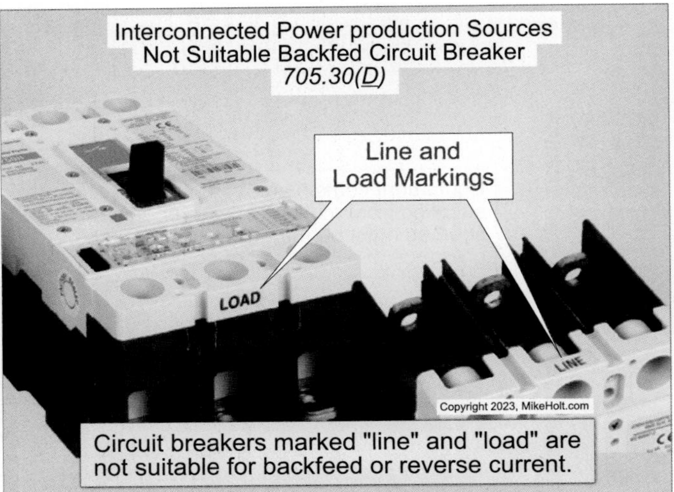
Interconnected Power production Sources
Not Suitable Backfed Circuit Breaker
705.30(D)
Line and
Load Markings
LOAD
LINE
Copyright 2023, MikeHolt.com
Circuit breakers marked "line" and "load" are not suitable for backfeed or reverse current.

▸Figure 705-59

Interconnected Power Production Sources
Power Transformers
705.30(F)
The primary side of a transformer is the side with a source of power that has the highest available fault current.
Copyright 2023, MikeHolt.com

▸Figure 705-61

(E) Fastening. Backfed circuit breakers used for interconnected power production sources (PV, ESS, generator) that are listed as interactive are not required to be secured in place in the panelboard by an additional fastener as required by 408.36(D). ▸**Figure 705-60**

(F) Transformers.

(1) Overcurrent Protection. The side of a transformer with a source of power on each side that has the highest available fault current is considered the primary side. ▸**Figure 705-61**

(2) Secondary Conductors. Transformer secondary conductors are to be sized in accordance with 240.21(C).

705.32 Ground-Fault Protection

Where ground-fault protection of equipment is installed in ac circuits as required else where in this *Code*, the output of interconnected power production equipment must be connected to the supply side of the ground-fault protection equipment.

Ex: Connection of power production equipment shall be permitted to be made to the load side of ground-fault protection equipment where installed in accordance with 705.11 or where there is ground-fault.

1st Printing

705.40 Loss of Primary Source

The output of power production equipment (PV, ESS, generator) must automatically disconnect from the primary source when the primary source loses a phase conductor and reconnect when the primary source is restored.

Ex: A listed interactive inverter must automatically cease exporting power when one or more of the phases of the primary source opens and is not required to automatically disconnect all phase conductors from the primary source. ▶**Figure 705-62**

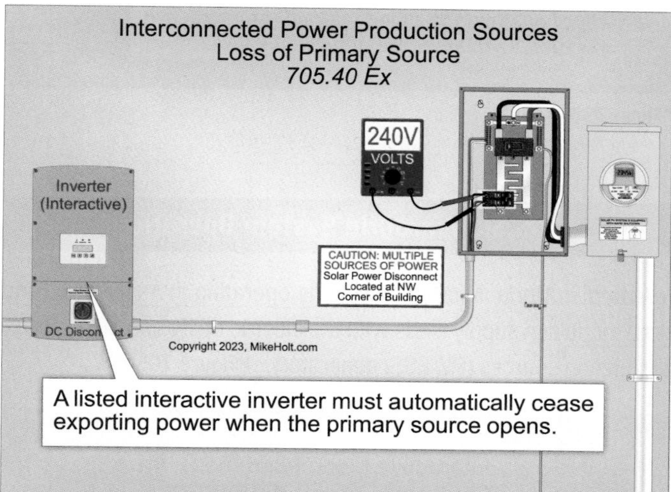

Interconnected Power Production Sources
Loss of Primary Source
705.40 Ex
240V
VOLTS
Inverter (Interactive)
CAUTION: MULTIPLE SOURCES OF POWER Solar Power Disconnect Located at NW Corner of Building
DC Disconnect
Copyright 2023, MikeHolt.com
A listed interactive inverter must automatically cease exporting power when the primary source opens.

▶**Figure 705-62**

Author's Comment:

- If the primary source phase conductor opens, an interactive (grid tied) inverter stops exporting power and remains de-energized until the primary source power is restored. ▶**Figure 705-63**

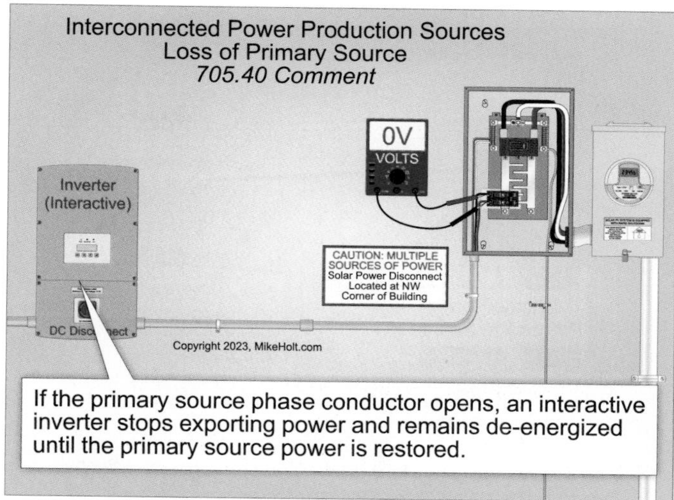

Interconnected Power Production Sources
Loss of Primary Source
705.40 Comment
0V
VOLTS
Inverter (Interactive)
CAUTION: MULTIPLE SOURCES OF POWER Solar Power Disconnect Located at NW Corner of Building
DC Disconnect
Copyright 2023, MikeHolt.com
If the primary source phase conductor opens, an interactive inverter stops exporting power and remains de-energized until the primary source power is restored.

▶**Figure 705-63**

Note 1: Risks to electric utility personnel and equipment could occur if an interactive (grid tied) power production source is set to operate in the island mode. Special detection methods are required to determine if an electric utility supply system outage has occurred and whether there should be automatic disconnection. When the electric utility supply system is restored, special detection methods are typically required to limit exposure of power production sources to out-of-phase reconnection.

Multimode power production equipment is permitted to operate in island mode to supply loads that have been disconnected from the electric utility. ▶**Figure 705-64**

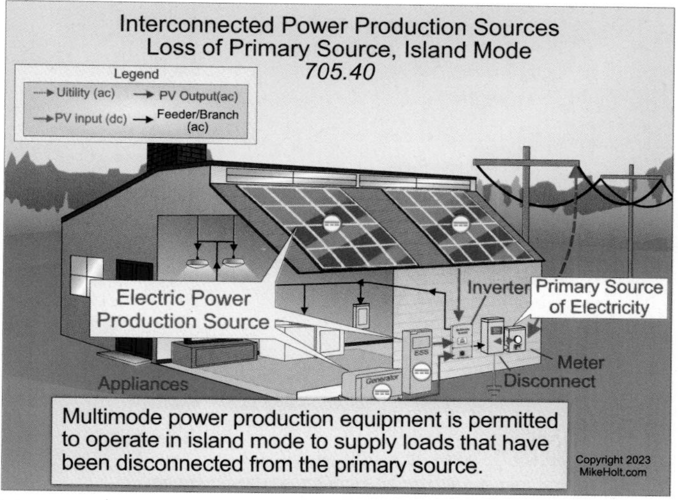

Interconnected Power Production Sources
Loss of Primary Source, Island Mode
705.40
Legend
Utility (ac)
PV Output(ac)
PV input (dc)
Feeder/Branch (ac)
Electric Power Production Source
Inverter
Primary Source of Electricity
Meter
Disconnect
Appliances
Generator
Multimode power production equipment is permitted to operate in island mode to supply loads that have been disconnected from the primary source.
Copyright 2023 MikeHolt.com

▶**Figure 705-64**

According to Article 100, "Island Mode" is the operating mode for power production equipment or a microgrid that is disconnected from an electric utility. ▶**Figure 705-65**

"Multimode Inverter's" are listed to operate in both interactive (grid tied) and island mode. ▶**Figure 705-66**

705.45 Unbalanced Interconnections

(A) Single-Phase. Single-phase inverters must be placed on the electrical system so that unbalanced system voltage at the electric utility service disconnect is not more than three percent.

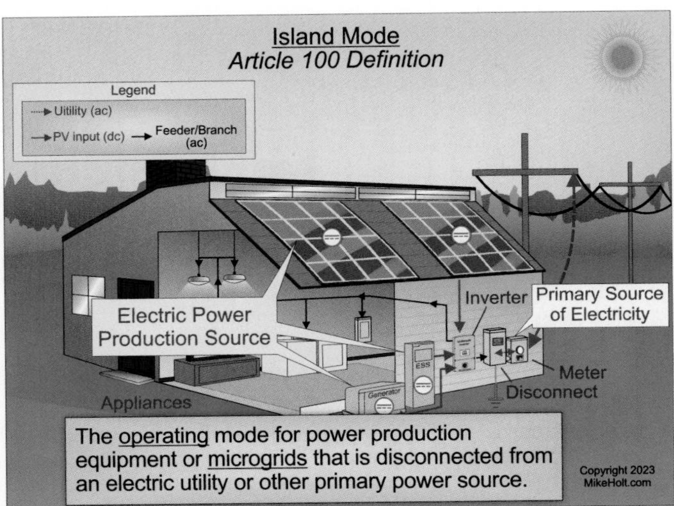

▸Figure 705-65

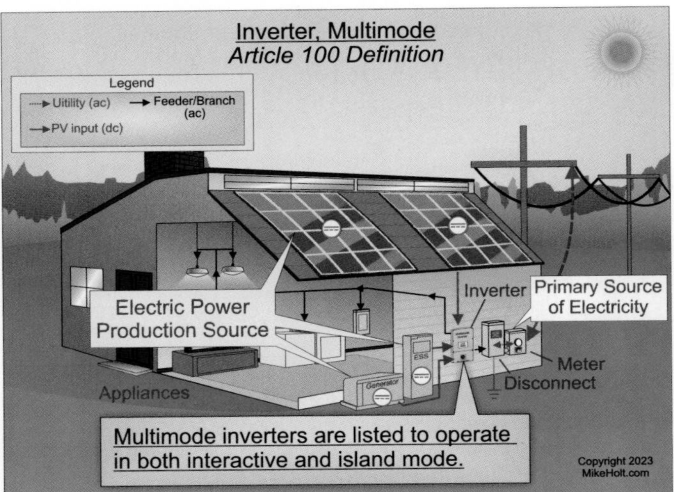

▸Figure 705-66

(B) Three-Phase. Three-phase inverters must have all phases automatically de-energized upon loss of, or unbalanced voltage in one or more phases unless the inverter is designed so significant unbalanced voltages will not result.

Part II. Microgrid Systems

According to Article 100, a "Microgrid" is a collection of power production sources that are capable of operating in island (off-grid) or interactive (grid-tied) mode with the electric utility. Examples of microgrid power sources include photovoltaic systems, energy storage systems, generators, electric vehicles that are used as a source of supply. ▸**Figure 100-67**

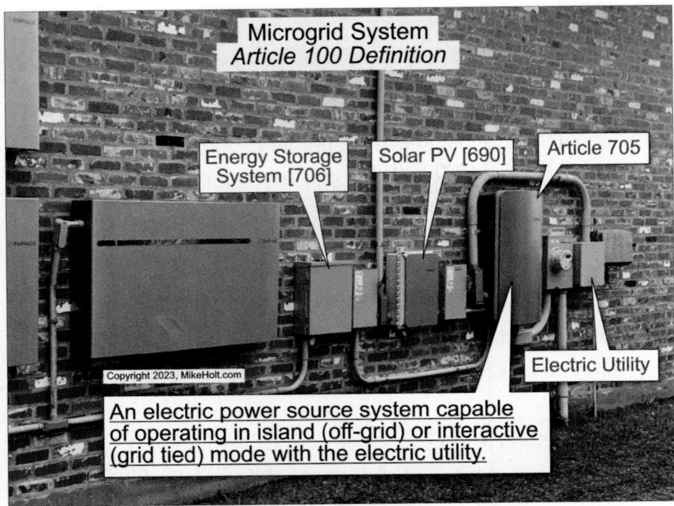

▸Figure 705-67

705.50 Microgrid System Operation

Interactive Mode. Microgrid systems operating in interactive (grid tied) mode can supply loads with the electric utility and other power production sources (PV, ESS, generator). ▸**Figure 705-68**

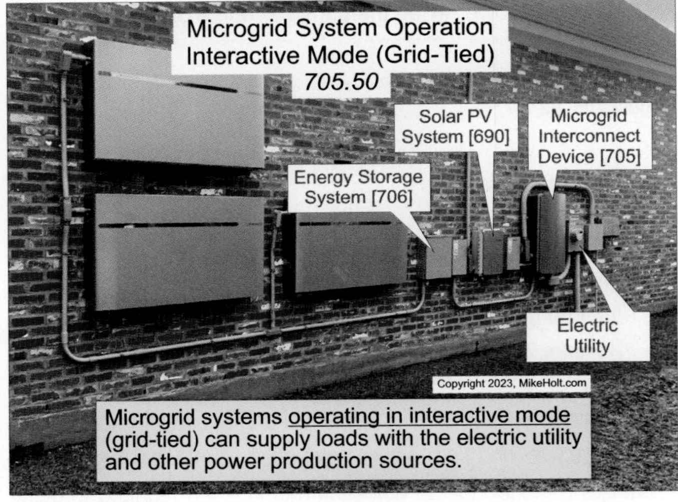

▸Figure 705-68

According to Article 100, "Interactive Mode" is the operating mode for power production equipment or a microgrid that operates in parallel with and can deliver power to the electric utility. ▸**Figure 705-69**

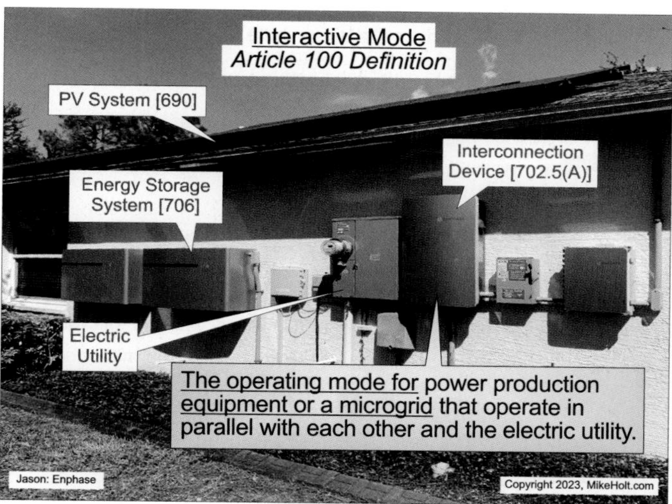

▶Figure 705-69

Author's Comment:

- A listed interactive (grid tied) inverter automatically stops exporting power upon loss of electric utility voltage and cannot be reconnected until the voltage has been restored. Interactive (grid tied) inverters can automatically or manually resume exporting power to the electric utility once the electric utility source is restored.

Island Mode. Microgrid systems operating in island (off-grid) mode can supply loads with other power production sources (PV, ESS, generator) that have been disconnected from the electric utility. ▶**Figure 705-70**

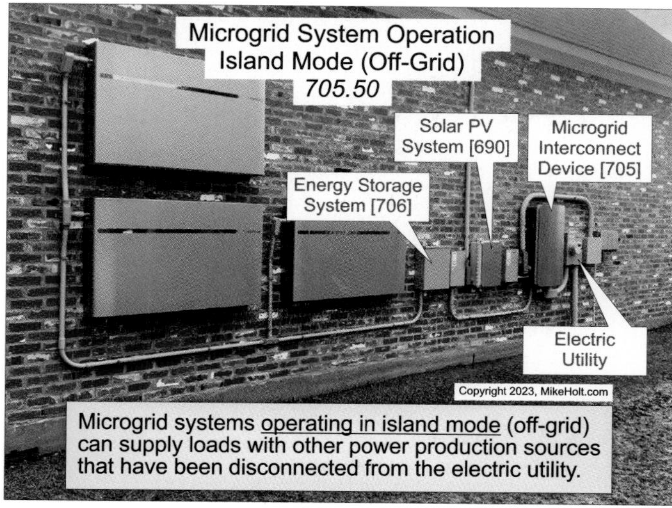

▶Figure 705-70

According to Article 100, "Island Mode" is the operating mode for power production equipment or a microgrid that is disconnected from an electric utility or other primary power source. ▶**Figure 705-71**

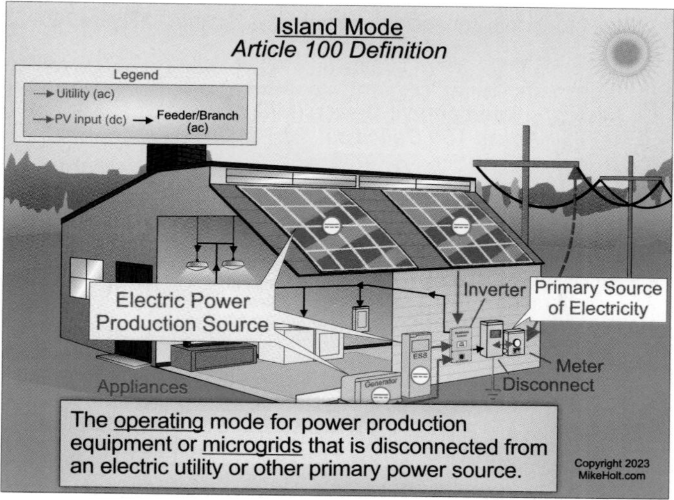

▶Figure 705-71

705.60 Connections to the Primary Source

Connections of the microgrid to the primary source must be in accordance with 705.11, 705.12, or 705.13. ▶**Figure 705-72**

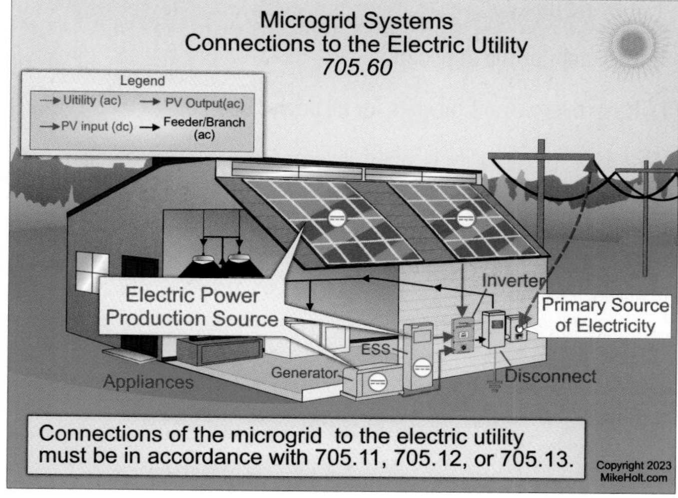

▶Figure 705-72

705.70 Microgrid Interconnect Devices (MID)

According to Article 100, a "Microgrid Interconnect Device (MID)" is a device that enables a microgrid system to disconnect from and reconnect to an interconnected primary power source. ▸**Figure 705–73**

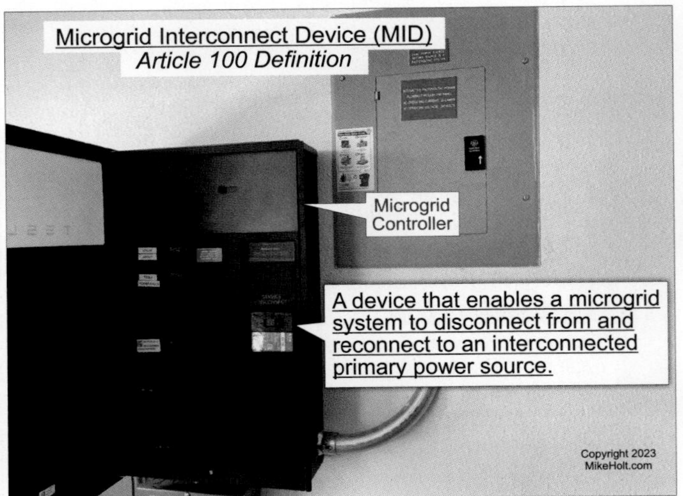
Microgrid Interconnect Device (MID)
Article 100 Definition
Microgrid Controller
A device that enables a microgrid system to disconnect from and reconnect to an interconnected primary power source.
Copyright 2023 MikeHolt.com

▸**Figure 705–73**

A microgrid interconnect device must comply with the following: ▸**Figure 705–74**

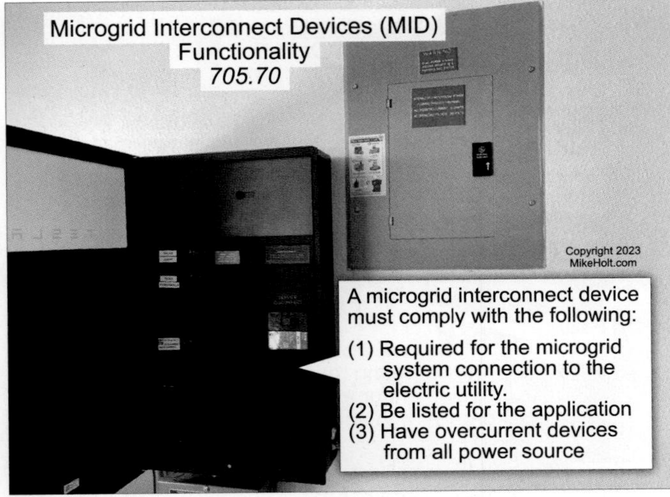
Microgrid Interconnect Devices (MID) Functionality 705.70
Copyright 2023 MikeHolt.com
A microgrid interconnect device must comply with the following:
(1) Required for the microgrid system connection to the electric utility.
(2) Be listed for the application
(3) Have overcurrent devices from all power source

▸**Figure 705–74**

(1) Required for the connection between a microgrid system and the electric utility

(2) Be listed for the application

(3) Have overcurrent devices for all power source

Note: MID functionality is often incorporated in an interactive (grid tied) or multimode inverter, energy storage system, or similar device identified for interactive (grid tied) operation.

705.76 Microgrid Control System (MCS)

Microgrid control systems must comply with the following:

(1) Coordinate interaction between multiple power sources

(2) Be evaluated for the application and have a field label applied, or be listed, or be designed under engineering supervision

(3) Monitor and control microgrid power production

(4) Monitor and control transitions with the electric utility

Note: MID functionality is often incorporated in an interactive (grid tied) or multimode inverter, energy storage system, or similar device identified for interactive (grid tied) operation.

1st Printing

ARTICLE 706 ENERGY STORAGE SYSTEMS

Introduction to Article 706—Energy Storage Systems

This article applies to energy storage systems that have a capacity greater than 1 kWh that can operate in stand-alone (off-grid) or interactive (grid tied) mode with other electric power production sources to provide electrical energy to the premises wiring system. Energy storage systems can have many components including batteries, capacitors, inverters or converters to change voltage levels or to make a change between an alternating-current or a direct-current system. Many of these rules are outside of the scope of this material, however, some of the topics we cover include the following:

- Scope
- Qualified Personnel
- Listing
- Commissioning and Maintenance
- Disconnect Requirements
- ESS in Parallel with Other Sources of Power
- General Installation Requirements

Article 706 consists of four parts:

- Part I. General
- Part II. Disconnect
- Part III. Installation Requirements
- Part IV. Energy Storage System Circuit Requirements

Part I. General

706.1 Scope

This article applies to energy storage systems that have a capacity greater than 1 kWh that can operate in stand-alone (off-grid) or interactive (grid tied) mode with other electric power production sources. ▸**Figure 706–1**

According to Article 100, an "Energy Storage Systems" (ESS) has one or more devices installed as a system capable of storing energy and providing electrical energy to the premises wiring system. ▸**Figure 706–2**

706.3 Qualified Personnel

The installation and maintenance of energy storage system must be performed by a qualified person. ▸**Figure 706–3**

According to Article 100, a "Qualified Person" has the skills and knowledge related to the construction and operation of electrical equipment and installations. This person must have received safety training to recognize and avoid the hazards involved with electrical systems. ▸**Figure 706–4**

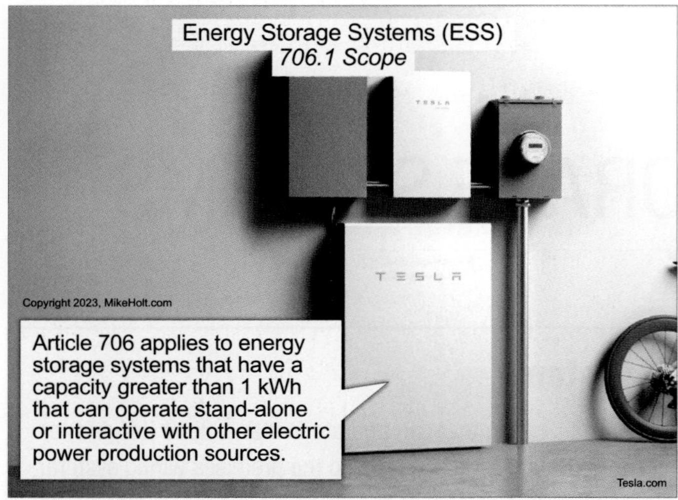

▶**Figure 706–1**

Energy Storage Systems (ESS)
Article 100 Definition
Devices capable of storing energy and providing electrical energy to the premises wiring system.
Copyright 2023, MikeHolt.com
Francisco Cruz

▶**Figure 706–2**

▶**Figure 706–3**

▶**Figure 706–4**

706.4 System Nameplate Requirements

Energy storage systems must have the following marked on a nameplate. ▶**Figure 706–5** and ▶**Figure 706–6**

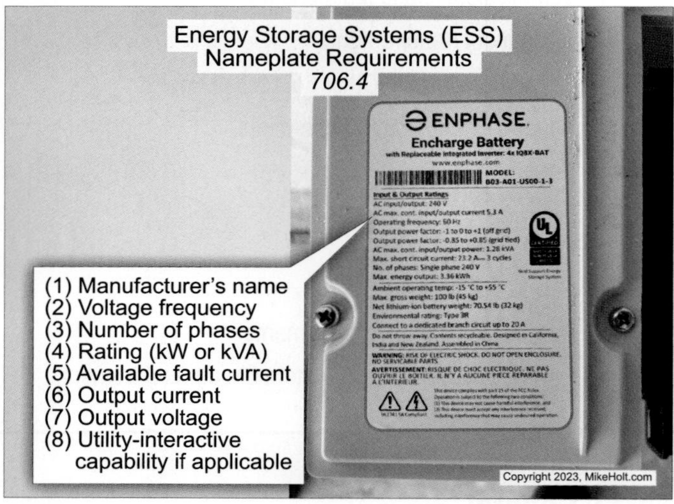

▶**Figure 706–5**

(1) Manufacturer's name

(2) Rated frequency

(3) Number of phases

(4) Rating (kW or kVA)

(5) Available fault current of ESS

(6) Input and output current

(7) Input and output voltage

(8) Utility-interactive capability if applicable

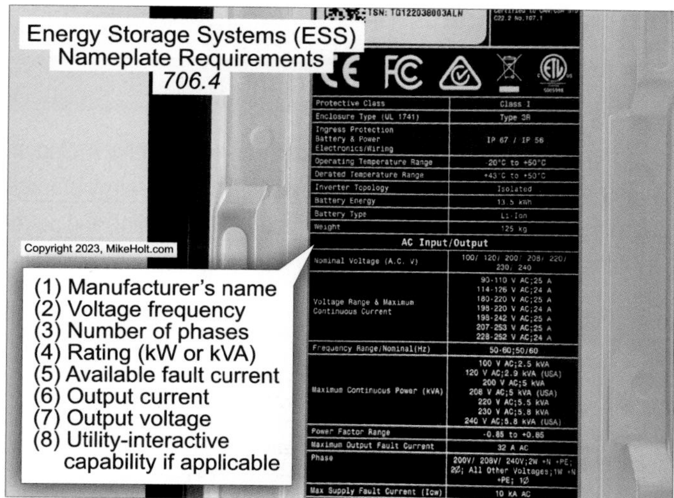
Energy Storage Systems (ESS)
Nameplate Requirements
706.4
Copyright 2023, MikeHolt.com
(1) Manufacturer's name
(2) Voltage frequency
(3) Number of phases
(4) Rating (kW or kVA)
(5) Available fault current
(6) Output current
(7) Output voltage
(8) Utility-interactive capability if applicable

▶Figure 706-6

706.5 Listing

Energy storage systems must be listed. ▶Figure 706-7

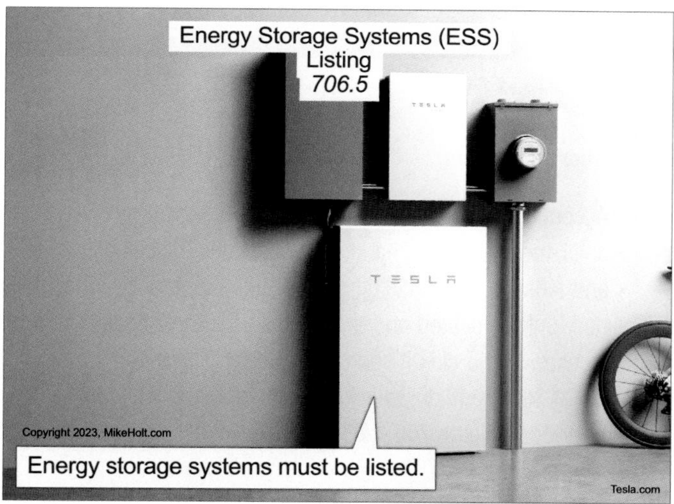
Energy Storage Systems (ESS)
Listing
706.5
TESLA
Copyright 2023, MikeHolt.com
Energy storage systems must be listed.
Tesla.com

▶Figure 706-7

Author's Comment:

- Although the *Code* does not identify the specific standard used to list energy storage systems, updated building and fire codes are more specific and now increasingly require a UL 9540, *Standard for Energy Storage Systems and Equipment*, listing for these systems. Annex A of the *NEC* provides references to product safety standards that the Code-Making Panels believe are generally relevant to each article.

706.6 Multiple Systems

Multiple energy storage systems are permitted on <u>the same premises</u>.

Author's Comment:

- As with PV systems, energy storage systems may be composed of multiple pieces of equipment assembled into a single system, or each piece of equipment may be considered an energy storage system on its own. The best way to identify an energy storage system is to look for a nameplate and review the instructions, both of which are part of the equipment's listing.

706.7 Commissioning and Maintenance

<u>**(A) Commissioning.** For other than one- and two-family dwellings, energy storage systems must be commissioned upon installation.</u> ▶Figure 706-8

Energy Storage Systems (ESS)
Commissioning
706.7(A)
Copyright 2023, MikeHolt.com
For other than one- and two-family dwellings, ESS must be commissioned upon installation.

▶Figure 706-8

<u>**Note:** For information related to the commissioning of ESS, see NFPA 855, *Standard for the Installation of Stationary Energy Storage Systems*.</u>

According to Article 100, "Commissioning" is the process, procedures, and testing used to set up and verify the initial performance, operational controls, safety systems, and sequence of operation of electrical devices and equipment prior to them being placed into active service.

(B) Maintenance. For other than one- and two-family dwellings, energy storage systems must be maintained in proper and safe operating condition in accordance with manufacturer and industry standards. A written record of repairs and replacements must be kept. ▶**Figure 706–9**

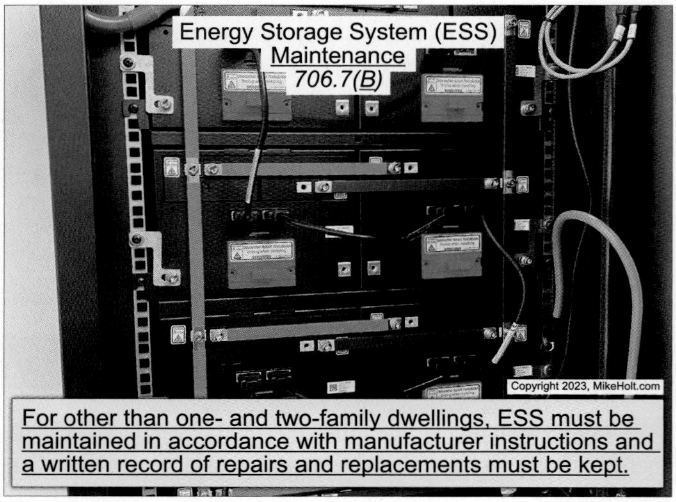

▶**Figure 706–9**

Note: For information related to general electrical equipment maintenance and developing an effective electrical preventive maintenance program, see NFPA 70B, *Recommended Practice for Electrical Equipment Maintenance*, or ANSI/NETA ATS-2017, *Standard for Acceptance Testing Specifications for Electrical Power Equipment and Systems.* ▶**Figure 706–10**

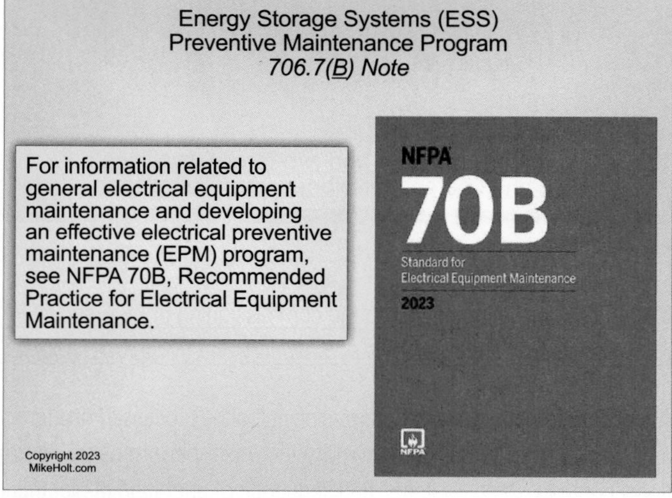
Energy Storage Systems (ESS)
Preventive Maintenance Program
706.7(B) Note
For information related to general electrical equipment maintenance and developing an effective electrical preventive maintenance (EPM) program, see NFPA 70B, Recommended Practice for Electrical Equipment Maintenance.
NFPA
70B
Standard for Electrical Equipment Maintenance
2023
NFPA
Copyright 2023 MikeHolt.com

▶**Figure 706–10**

Part II. Disconnect

706.15 Disconnect

(A) Energy Storage System Disconnecting Means. A disconnecting means must be provided to disconnect the energy storage system from other sources of power, utilization equipment, and premises wiring. ▶**Figure 706–11**

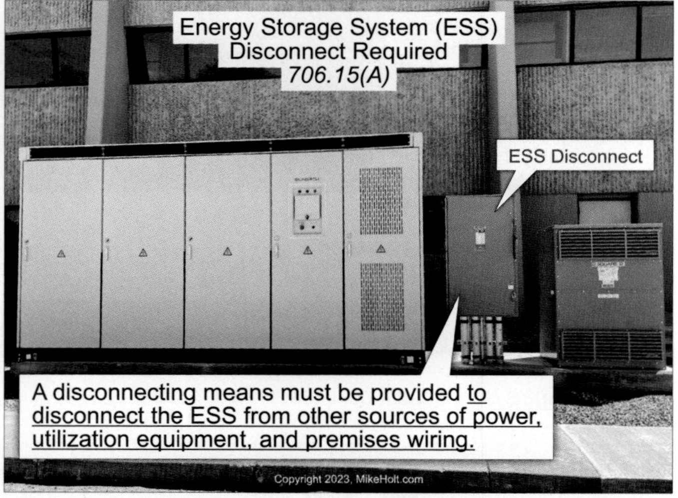
Energy Storage System (ESS)
Disconnect Required
706.15(A)
ESS Disconnect
A disconnecting means must be provided to disconnect the ESS from other sources of power, utilization equipment, and premises wiring.
Copyright 2023, MikeHolt.com

▶**Figure 706–11**

Author's Comment:

- According to 110.22, in other than one- or two-family dwelling units, the disconnect marking must include the identification and location of the circuit source that supplies the disconnect unless located and arranged so the identification and location of the circuit source is evident. The marking must be of sufficient durability to withstand the environment involved. ▶**Figure 706–12**

(B) Disconnect Location and Control. The energy storage system disconnect must be readily accessible and comply with one of the following: ▶**Figure 706–13**

(1) The disconnect is located within the energy storage system.

(2) The disconnect is located within sight and not more than 10 ft from the energy storage system.

(3) Where the disconnect is not located within sight of the energy storage system, the disconnect, or the enclosure providing access to the disconnect, must be capable of being locked in the open position in accordance with 110.25.

1st Printing

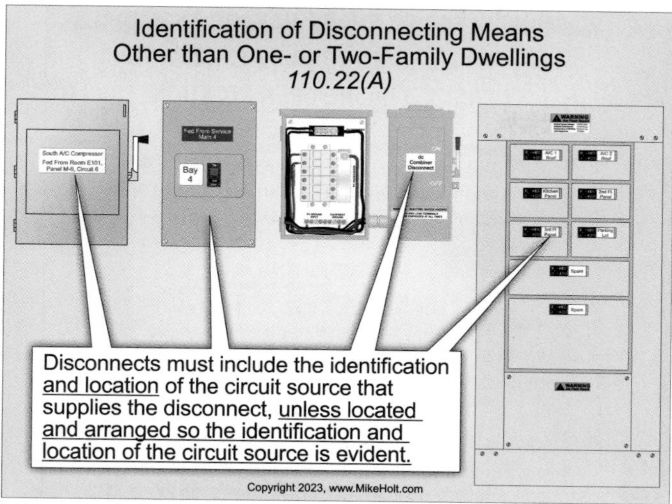

▸Figure 706–12

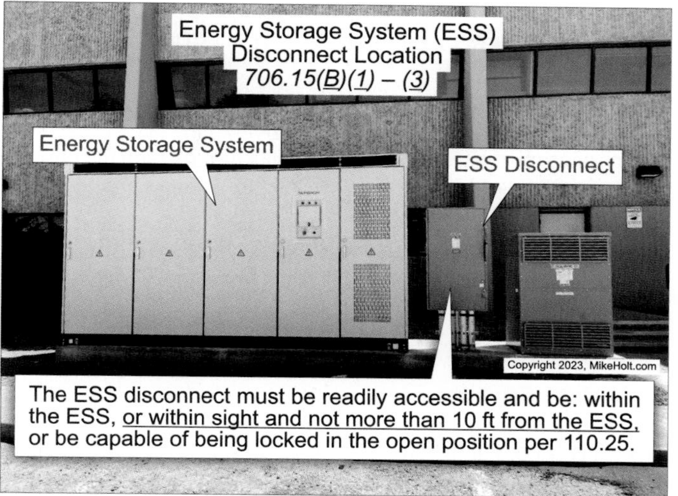

▸Figure 706–13

One- and Two-Family Dwellings. The energy storage system must include an emergency shutdown function to cease the export of power from the energy storage system to premises wiring. The initiation device for the energy storage system emergency shutdown function must be located at a readily accessible location outside the building. ▸**Figure 706–14**

The energy storage system emergency shutdown initiation device must plainly indicate whether if it is in the "off" or "on" position.

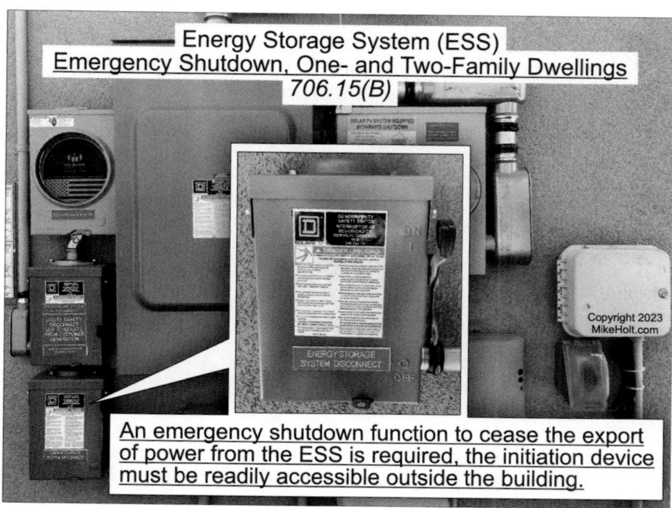

▸Figure 706–14

Author's Comment:

- It is important to note that the requirements in 706.15(A) can be met with disconnects that are integral to the listed energy storage system equipment. Since an energy storage system application may have multiple individual energy storage system units, each may require a disconnect, but this does not necessarily mean each will require a separate disconnect switch adjacent to the units. Many energy storage system manufacturers will choose to incorporate a means of disconnect into their energy storage system units. These disconnects will be evaluated during the system's listing.

(C) Disconnect Marking. The energy storage system disconnect must plainly indicate whether it is in the open (off) or closed (on) position and be marked: ▸**Figure 706–15**

"ENERGY STORAGE SYSTEM DISCONNECT"

For other than one- and two-family dwellings, the energy storage system disconnect must be legibly marked to indicate the following: ▸**Figure 706–16**

(1) The nominal system voltage

(2) The available fault current of the ESS

(3) An arc-flash label applied in accordance with acceptable industry practice

(4) The date the calculation was performed

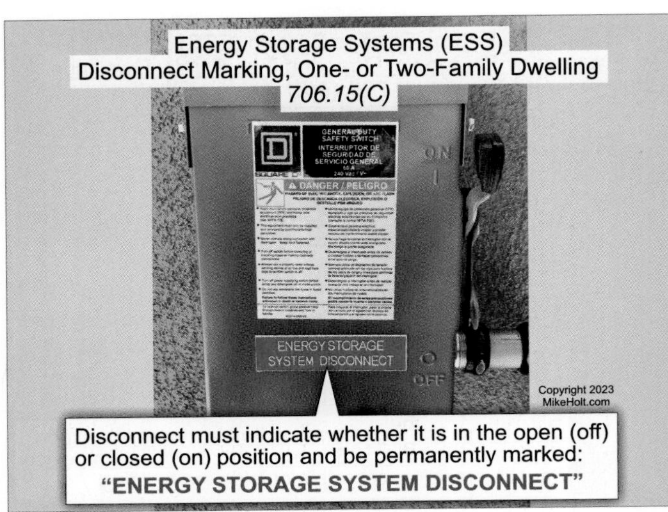

▶Figure 706–15

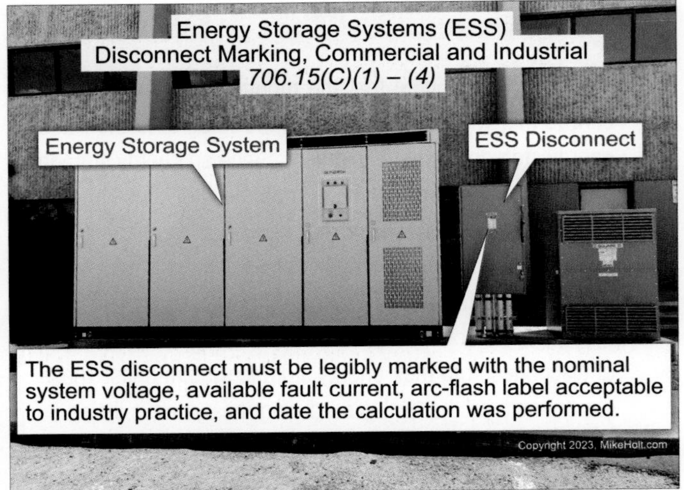

Energy Storage Systems (ESS)
Disconnect Marking, Commercial and Industrial
706.15(C)(1) – (4)
Energy Storage System
ESS Disconnect
The ESS disconnect must be legibly marked with the nominal system voltage, available fault current, arc-flash label acceptable to industry practice, and date the calculation was performed.
Copyright 2023, MikeHolt.com

▶Figure 706–16

Note 1: Industry practices for equipment labeling are described in NFPA 70E, *Standard for Electrical Safety in the Workplace*. This standard provides specific criteria for developing arc-flash labels for equipment that provides nominal system voltage, incident energy levels, arc-flash boundaries, minimum required levels of personal protective equipment, and so forth.

Note 2: ESS electronics could include inverters or other types of power conversion equipment.

If line and load terminals within the energy storage system disconnect could be energized in the open position, the disconnect must be marked: ▶**Figure 706–17**

WARNING ELECTRIC SHOCK HAZARD TERMINALS ON THE LINE AND LOAD SIDES MAY BE ENERGIZED IN THE OPEN POSITION

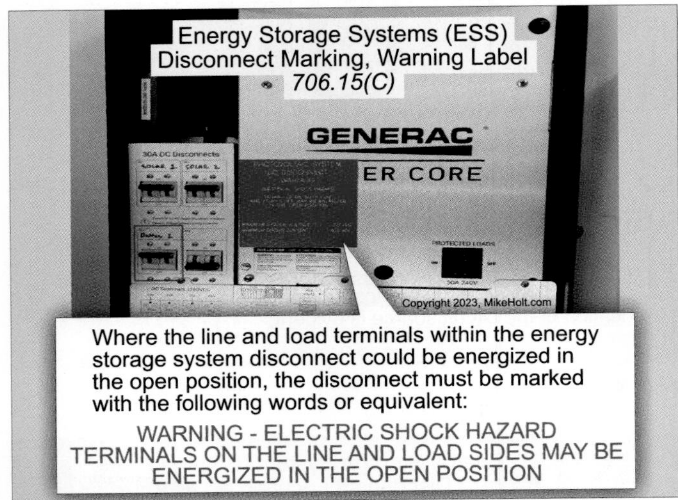

▶Figure 706–17

The marking must have sufficient durability to withstand the environment involved [110.21(B)].

(D) Partitions Between Components. Where energy storage system circuits pass through a wall, floor, or ceiling, a readily accessible disconnect within sight of the energy storage system is required.

Author's Comment:

- It is important to note that 706.15(D) will not apply to every energy storage system application where circuit conductors travel through walls, floors, or ceilings. This section is for those applications (typically large ones) where the battery is in one room and other equipment that is part of the energy storage system is in another. In those cases, a disconnect must be in the room containing the battery. This does not apply to situations where the entire energy storage system is in one room and the output circuit from the energy storage system connects to other systems in other rooms. In those cases, the disconnect location requirements in 706.15(A) are all that apply.

(E) Disconnecting Means for Batteries. Where the battery of the energy storage system is separate from the electronics and subject to field servicing, the following applies:

Note: Batteries could include an enclosure, battery monitoring and controls, or other related battery components.

(1) Disconnecting Means. A readily accessible disconnect is required within sight of the battery.

Note: See 240.21(H) for information on the location of the overcurrent protective device for battery conductors.

(3) Remote Activation. Where the battery disconnect is provided with remote controls and the controls are not within sight of the battery, the battery disconnect must be capable of being locked in the open position in accordance with 110.25, and the location of the controls must be field marked on the battery disconnect.

(4) Notification. The battery disconnect must be legibly marked to withstand the environment involved and include:

(1) Nominal battery voltage

(2) Available fault current

Note 1: Battery equipment suppliers can provide information about available fault current on any battery model.

(3) An arc-flash label in accordance with acceptable industry practice

Note 2: See NFPA 70E -2021, *Standard for Electrical Safety in the Workplace*, for assistance in determining the severity of potential exposure, planning safe work practices, determining arc-flash labeling, and selecting personal protective equipment.

(4) Date the calculation was performed

706.16 ESS in Parallel with Other Sources of Power

ESS in parallel with other sources of power must comply with the following: ▶Figure 706–18

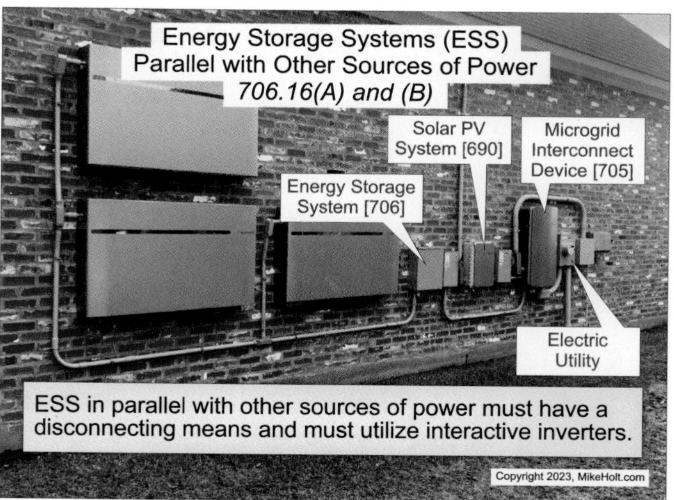

▶Figure 706–18

(A) Disconnect. All sources of power must have a disconnecting means.

(B) Interactive Inverter. All sources of power must utilize interactive (grid tied) inverters.

(C) Loss of Interactive System Power. Upon loss of the electric utility power, the interactive (grid tied) inverter must automatically disconnect from the electric utility in accordance with 705.40.

(D) Unbalanced Interconnections. Unbalanced ac connections must comply with 705.45.

(E) Parallel with Other Sources of Power. The parallel connection of the energy storage system to other sources of power must be in accordance with 705.12.

(F) Stand-Alone Operation. Where the ESS is operating in stand-alone (off-grid) mode, the requirements of 710.15 apply.

Part III. Installation Requirements

706.20 General Installation Requirements

(C) Spaces About Energy Storage Systems.

(1) The working space for energy storage systems must comply with 110.26. ▶Figure 706–19 and ▶Figure 706–20

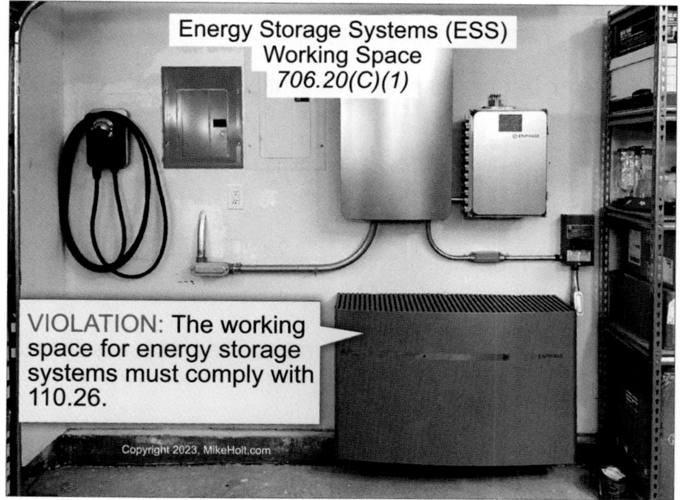

▶Figure 706–19

(2) Energy storage systems must be spaced apart in accordance with the manufacturer's instructions.

▸Figure 706–20

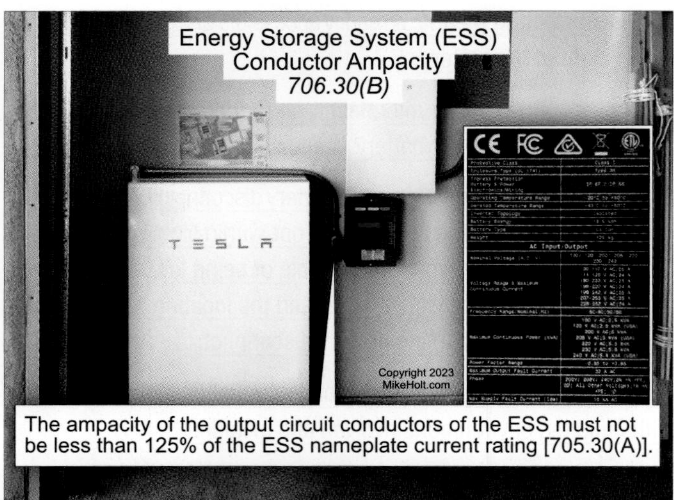

Energy Storage System (ESS)
Conductor Ampacity
706.30(B)
TESLA
Copyright 2023 MikeHolt.com
The ampacity of the output circuit conductors of the ESS must not be less than 125% of the ESS nameplate current rating [705.30(A)].

▸Figure 706–21

Note: Additional space may be needed to accommodate energy storage system hoisting equipment, tray removal, or spill containment.

Part IV. Energy Storage System Circuit Requirements

706.30 Circuit Current Rating

(A) Circuit Current Rating. The maximum current for an energy storage system is as follows:

(1) Nameplate-Rated Circuit Current. The rated current indicated on the energy storage system nameplate.

(2) Inverter Output Current. The continuous inverter output ac current rating.

(3) Inverter Input Current. The continuous inverter input dc current at the lowest input voltage.

(4) Inverter Utilization Output Circuit Current. The continuous inverter output ac current rating.

(5) DC-to-DC Converter Output Current. The continuous dc-to-dc converter's nameplate current rating.

(B) Conductor Ampacity. The ampacity of the output circuit conductors of the energy storage system(s) to the wiring system supplying the load must not be less than 125 percent of the current rating of the energy storage system in accordance with 705.30(A) or the rating of the overcurrent protective device [706.31]. ▸**Figure 706–21**

▸ Example

Question: *What is the minimum size ampacity conductor required for an energy storage system with a nameplate current rating of 25A?* ▸**Figure 706–22**

(a) 12 AWG *(b) 10 AWG* *(c) 8 AWG* *(d) 6 AWG*

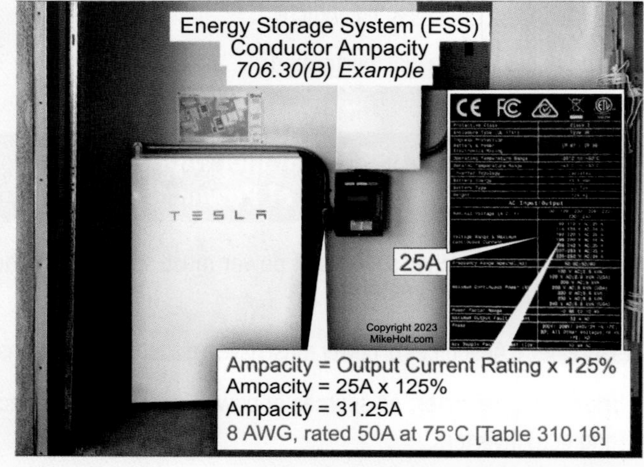

▸Figure 706–22

Solution:

Conductor Ampacity = Output Current Rating × 125%

Conductor Ampacity = 25A × 125%

Conductor Ampacity = 31.25A, 8 AWG rated 50A [Table 310.16]

Answer: *(c) 8 AWG*

706.31 Overcurrent Protection

(A) Circuits and Equipment. Overcurrent protective devices must be in accordance with 706.31(B) through (F).

(B) Overcurrent Device Ratings. Overcurrent protective devices must have an ampere rating of not less than 125 percent of the current marked on the energy storage system nameplate [706.30(A)] ▶**Figure 706-23**

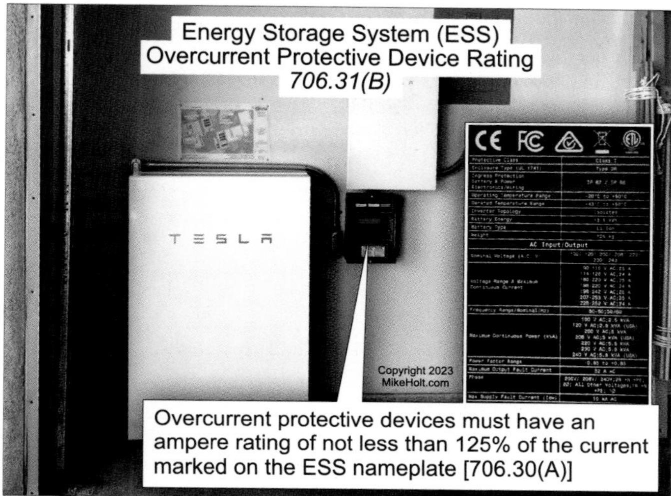
Energy Storage System (ESS)
Overcurrent Protective Device Rating
706.31(B)
TESLA
Copyright 2023
MikeHolt.com
Overcurrent protective devices must have an ampere rating of not less than 125% of the current marked on the ESS nameplate [706.30(A)]

▶**Figure 706-23**

▶ Example

Question: *What size overcurrent protective device ampere rating is required for an energy storage system with a nameplate current of 25A marked on the equipment?* ▶**Figure 706-24**

(a) 25A *(b) 30A* *(c) 35A* *(d) 40A*

Solution:

OCPD = Nameplate Current Rating × 125%

OCPD = 25A × 125%

OCPD = 31.25A, use 35A breaker or fuse [240.6]

Answer: *(c) 35A*

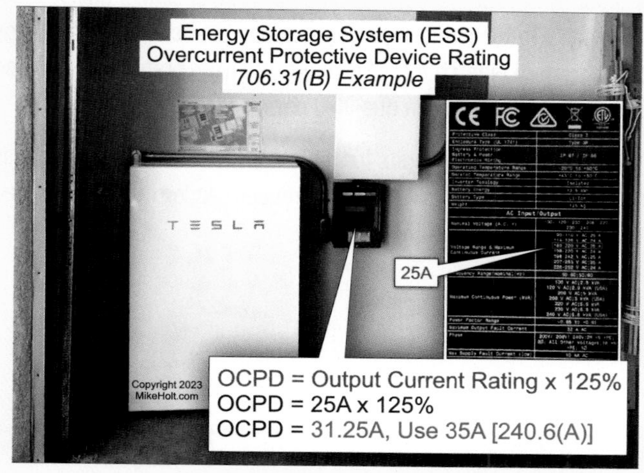
Energy Storage System (ESS)
Overcurrent Protective Device Rating
706.31(B) Example
TESLA
25A
Copyright 2023
MikeHolt.com
OCPD = Output Current Rating x 125%
OCPD = 25A x 125%
OCPD = 31.25A, Use 35A [240.6(A)]

▶**Figure 706-24**

Ex: Where the assembly (including the overcurrent protective devices) is listed for operation at 100 percent of its rating, the ampere rating of the overcurrent protective devices is permitted to be not less than the currents calculated in 706.30(B).

(C) Listing. Overcurrent protective devices used for dc circuits must be listed for direct current application.

(D) Current Limiting. Current-limiting overcurrent protective devices must be installed for each energy storage system dc output circuit. ▶**Figure 706-25**

Energy Storage System (ESS)
Current-Limiting OCPD
706.31(D)
Current-limiting overcurrent protective devices must be installed for each energy storage system dc output circuit.
Copyright 2023
MikeHolt.com

▶**Figure 706-25**

Ex: Where current-limiting overcurrent protection is provided for the dc output circuits, additional current-limiting overcurrent protective devices are not required.

(E) Disconnect for Fuses. A switch, pullouts, or similar device must be provided to disconnect power to fuses associated with energy storage system when the fuse is energized from both directions and is accessible to other than qualified persons.

(F) Location. Where circuits from the energy storage systems pass through a wall, floor, or ceiling; overcurrent protection must be provided at the energy storage component.

Author's Comment:

- As with 706.15(D), this one will not apply to every energy storage system application where circuit conductors travel through walls, floors, or ceilings. This section is for those applications (typically large ones) where the battery is in one room and other equipment that is part of that energy storage system is in another room.

STAND-ALONE SYSTEMS

Introduction to Article 710—Stand-Alone Systems

This article covers electric power production systems operating in island (off-grid) mode not connected to an electric utility. Many of these rules are outside of the scope of this material, however, some of the topics we cover include the following:

- Scope
- Equipment Approval
- Identification of Power Sources
- Stand-Alone Inverter Input Circuit Current
- Wiring

710.1 Scope

This article covers electric power production systems, such as Solar PV, energy storage systems (ESS), and/or generator not connected to an electric utility. ▶**Figure 710–1**

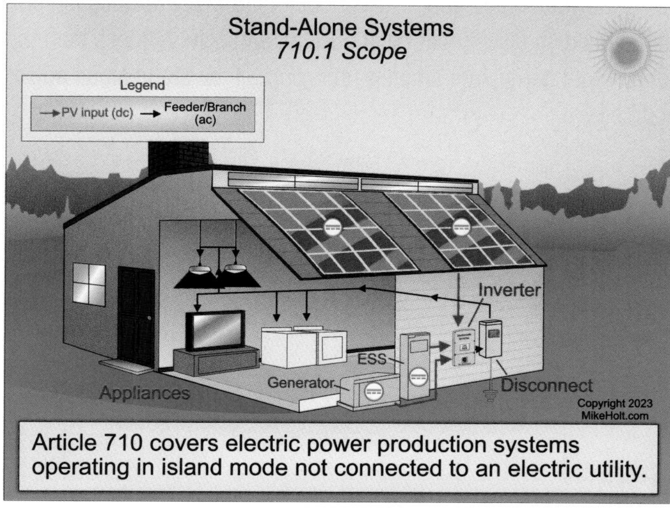

▶**Figure 710–1**

According to Article 100, a "Stand-Alone System" is an electrical power system that is not interconnected to the electric utility power system.

"Island Mode" is the operating mode for power production equipment or a microgrid that is disconnected from an electric utility or other primary power source. ▶**Figure 710–2**

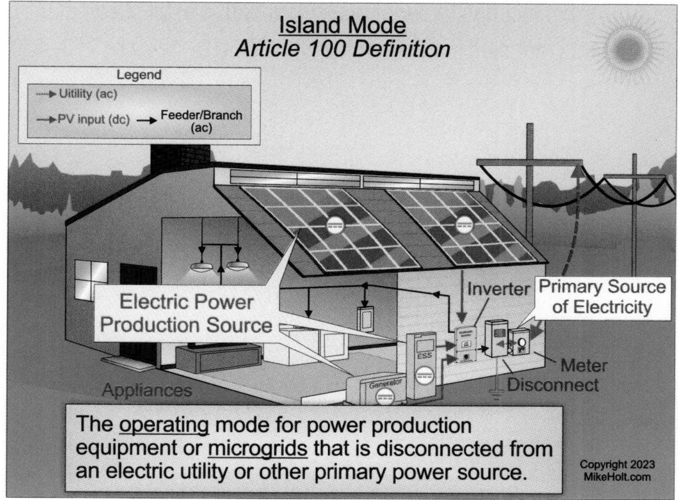

▶**Figure 710–2**

Note: Stand-alone systems can include any combination of PV, ESS, and/or a generator.

710.6 Equipment Approval

Stand-alone (off-grid) power production equipment must be listed for use in island (off-grid) mode. ▶Figure 710–3

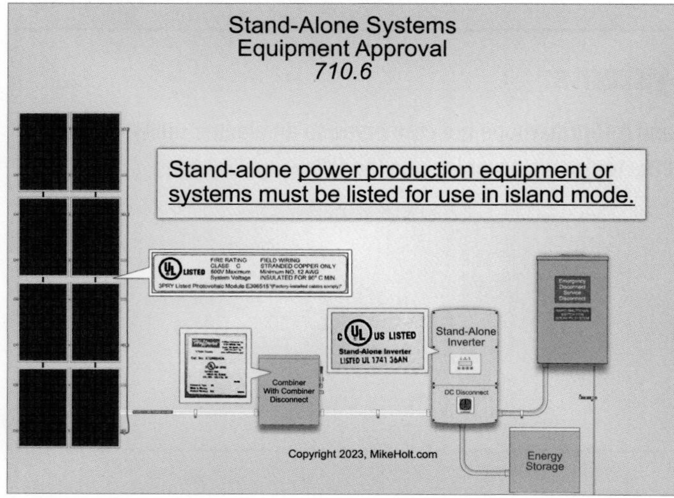
Stand-Alone Systems
Equipment Approval
710.6
Stand-alone power production equipment or systems must be listed for use in island mode.
Stand-Alone Inverter
Combiner With Combiner Disconnect
DC Disconnect
Energy Storage
Copyright 2023, MikeHolt.com

▶Figure 710–3

710.10 Identification of Power Sources

A sign is required at the power source disconnect or other approved readily visible location that identifies the location of all power source disconnects installed in accordance with 705.10. ▶Figure 710–4

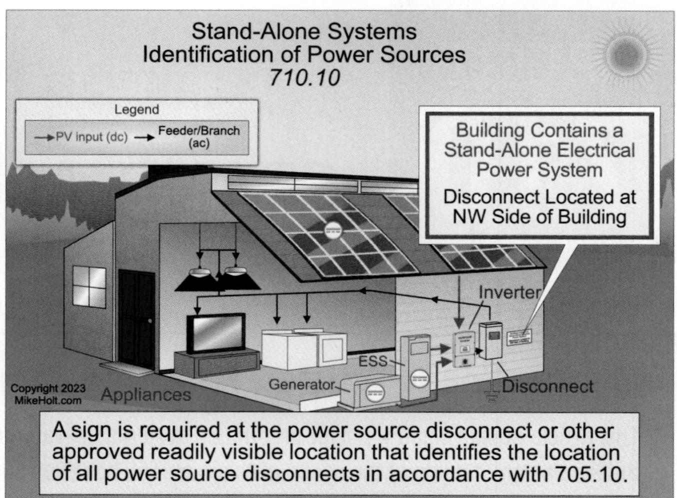
Stand-Alone Systems
Identification of Power Sources
710.10
Legend
PV input (dc)
Feeder/Branch (ac)
Building Contains a Stand-Alone Electrical Power System
Disconnect Located at NW Side of Building
Inverter
ESS
Generator
Appliances
Disconnect
Copyright 2023 MikeHolt.com
A sign is required at the power source disconnect or other approved readily visible location that identifies the location of all power source disconnects in accordance with 705.10.

▶Figure 710–4

710.12 Stand-Alone Inverter Input Circuit Current

The maximum stand-alone (off-grid) inverter input circuit current occurs when the inverter is producing rated power at the lowest input voltage.

710.15 Wiring

(A) Power Supply Capacity. The power supply of a stand-alone (off-grid) system must have a capacity of not less than the largest single load.

(B) Conductor Ampacity. The conductors from the power source(s) to the building disconnect must have an ampacity not less than the total output nameplate ampere ratings of all the stand-alone power source(s).

1st Printing

CABLES FOR POWER-LIMITED CIRCUITS

Introduction to Article 722—Cables for Power-Limited Circuits

Article 722—Cables for Power-Limited Circuits. This article contains the cabling requirements that are common to Class 2 power-limited circuits [Article 725] and power-limited fire alarm circuits [Article 760]. Power limited circuits are not considered a fire or electric shock hazard which allows some additional flexibility in the wiring methods and installation practices. Many of these rules are outside of the scope of this material, however, some of the topics we cover include the following:

- Scope
- Electrical Equipment Behind Access Panels
- Abandoned Cable
- Installation of Power-Limited Cables
- Listing Requirements

Part I. General

722.1 Scope

This article covers the general requirements for the installation Class 2 power-limited cables [Article 725] and power-limited fire alarm cables [Article 760]. ▶Figure 722–1

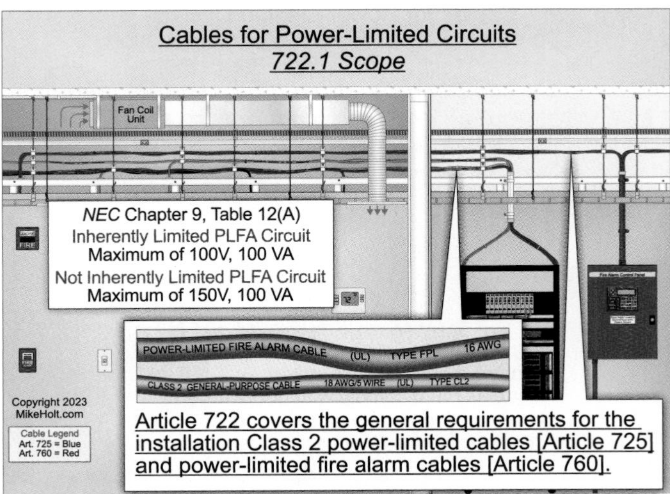

▶Figure 722–1

According to Article 100, a "Class 2 Power-Limited Circuit" is the portion of the wiring system between the load side of a power-limited power source or transformer and the connected Class 2 power-limited equipment. ▶Figure 722–2

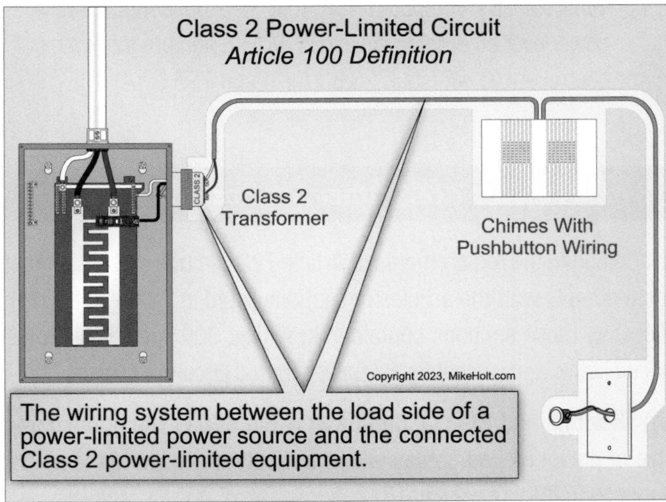

▶Figure 722–2

According to Article 100, a "Power-Limited Fire Alarm Circuit" is defined as a fire alarm circuit powered by a power-limited source. ▶Figure 722–3

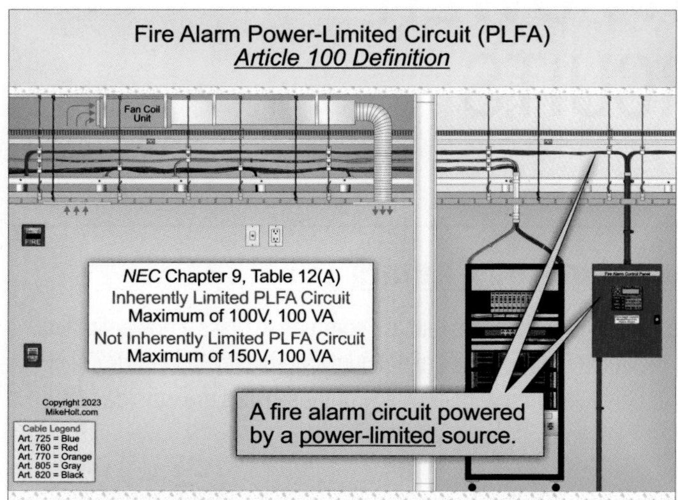

▶Figure 722–3

Author's Comment:

- Class 2 power-limited circuits are rendered safe by limiting the power source to 100 VA for circuits operating at 30V or less, and the current to 5 mA for circuits over 30V [725.60(A) and Chapter 9, Table 11(A)].
- Class 2 power-limited circuits typically include wiring for low-energy, low-voltage loads such as thermostats, programmable controllers, burglar alarms, and security systems. This type of circuit also includes twisted-pair or coaxial cable that interconnects computers for local area networks (LANs), power over ethernet applications (POEs), and programmable controller I/O circuits [725.60(A)(3) and 725.60(A)(4)].

722.3 Other Articles

In addition to the requirements of Article 722, circuits and equipment must comply with the articles or sections listed in 722.3(A) through (O). Only those sections contained in Article 300 specifically referenced below apply to cables for power-limited circuits. ▶Figure 722–4

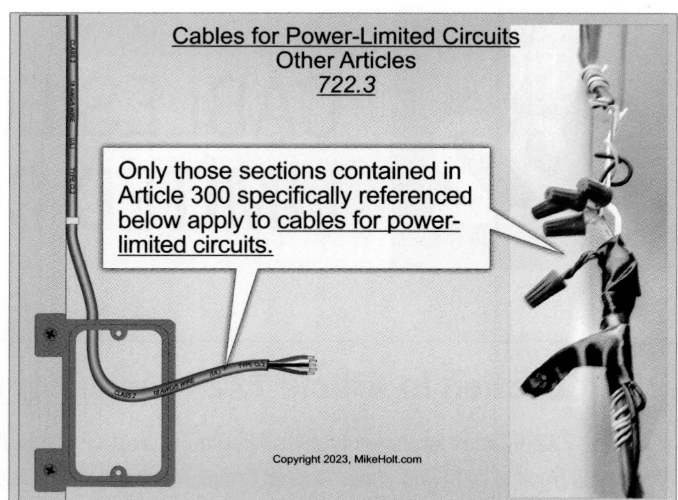

▶Figure 722–4

(A) Number and Size of Cables in a Raceway. The number and size of power-limited cables within a raceway are limited in accordance with 300.17. ▶Figure 722–5

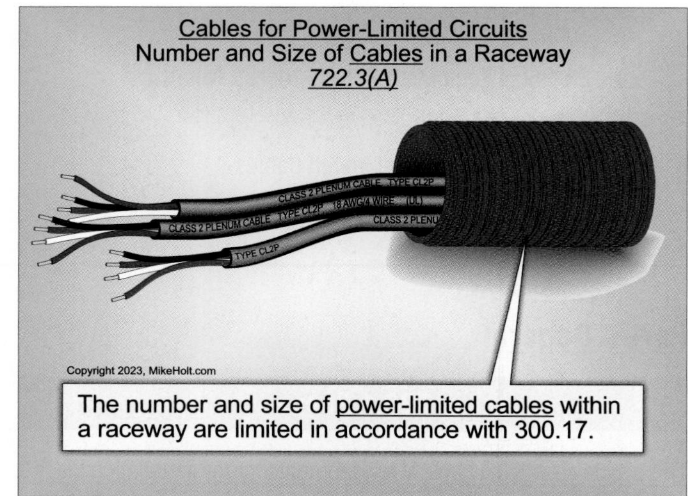

▶Figure 722–5

(B) Spread of Fire or Products of Combustion. Installation of power-limited circuits must comply with 300.21. ▶Figure 722–6

▶Figure 722–6

Author's Comment:

- Electrical circuits and equipment must be installed in such a way that the spread of fire or products of combustion will not be substantially increased. Openings into or through fire-resistive walls, floors, and ceilings for electrical equipment must be firestopped using methods approved by the authority having jurisdiction to maintain the fire-resistance rating of the fire-resistive assembly [300.21]. ▸**Figure 722–7**

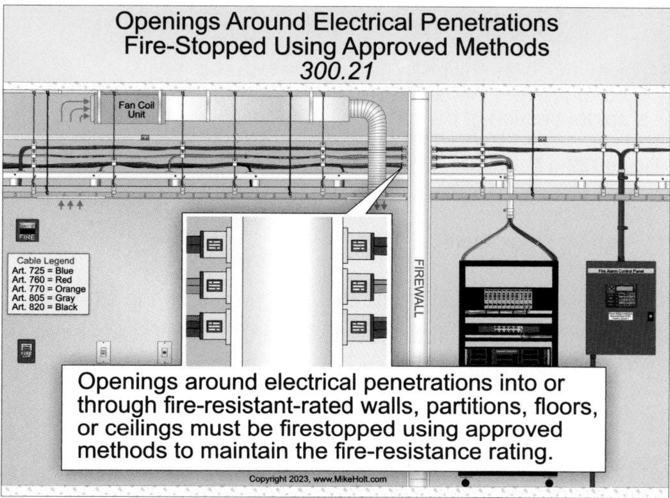

Openings Around Electrical Penetrations
Fire-Stopped Using Approved Methods
300.21
Fan Coil Unit
Cable Legend
Art. 725 = Blue
Art. 760 = Red
Art. 770 = Orange
Art. 805 = Gray
Art. 820 = Black
FIREWALL
Openings around electrical penetrations into or through fire-resistant-rated walls, partitions, floors, or ceilings must be firestopped using approved methods to maintain the fire-resistance rating.
Copyright 2023, www.MikeHolt.com

▸**Figure 722–7**

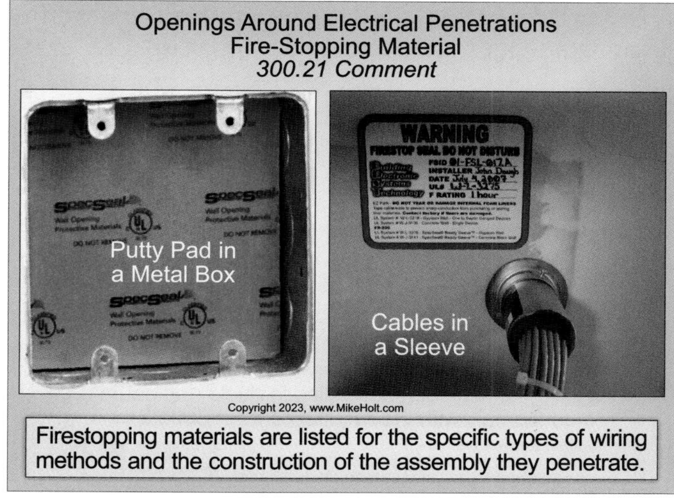

▸**Figure 722–8**

- Boxes installed in fire-resistive assemblies must be listed for the purpose. If steel boxes are used, they must be secured to the framing member, so cut-in type boxes are not permitted. "Putty pads" are typically installed on the exterior of the box, but many manufacturers have listed inserts for box interiors. Firestopping materials are listed for the specific types of wiring methods and the construction of the assembly they penetrate. ▸**Figure 722–8**

- Outlet boxes must have a horizontal separation of not less than 24 in. when installed on opposites sides in a fire-resistive assembly, unless an outlet box is listed for closer spacing or protected by fire-resistant "putty pads" in accordance with manufacturer's instructions. Building codes also have restrictions on penetrations on opposite sides of a fire-resistive wall. ▸**Figure 722–9** and ▸**Figure 722–10**

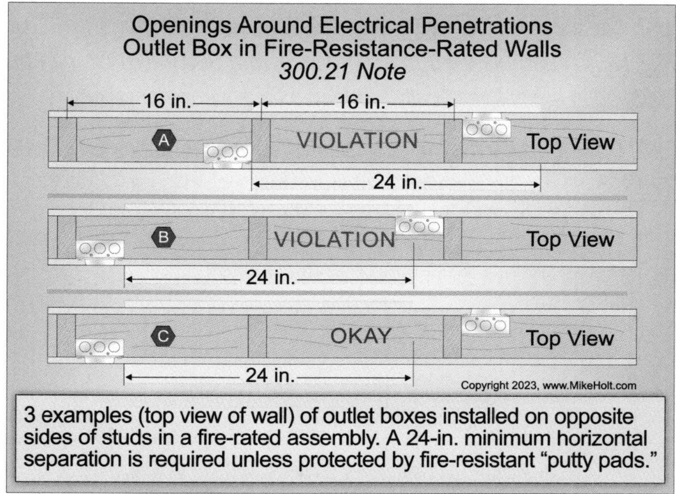

▸**Figure 722–9**

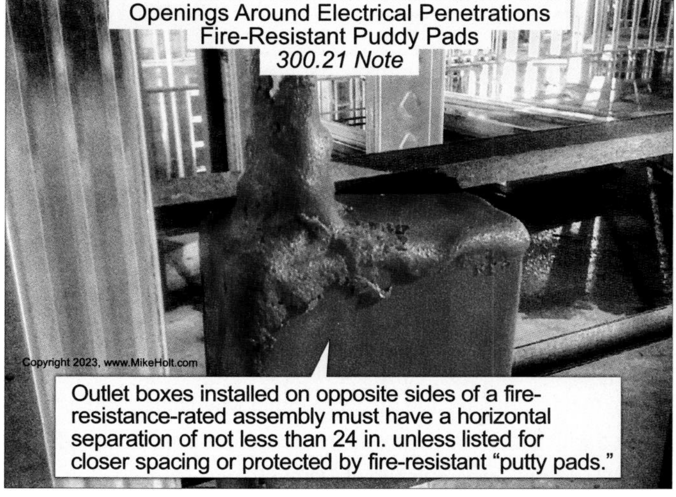

▸**Figure 722–10**

(C) Ducts and Plenum Spaces. Power-limited circuits installed in ducts or plenums must comply with 300.22. ▸**Figure 722–11**

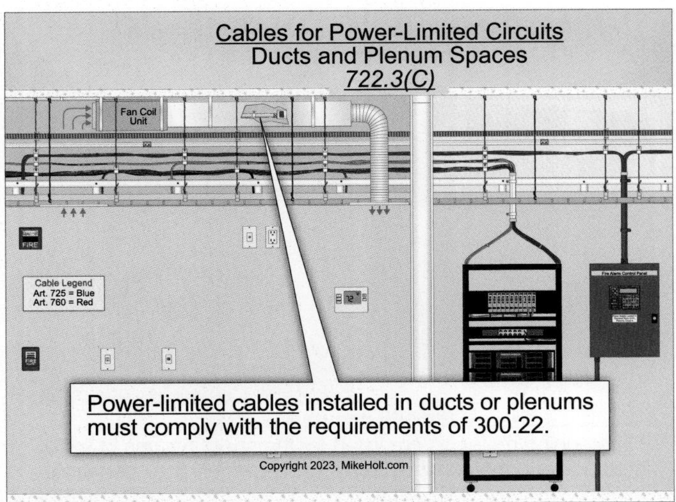

▸Figure 722–11

Ex 1: Class 2 power-limited cables selected in accordance with Table 722.135(B) and installed in accordance with 300.22(B) Ex, can be installed in ducts specifically fabricated for environmental air.

Ex 2: Class 2 power-limited cables selected in accordance with Table 722.135(B) can be installed in plenum spaces. ▸**Figure 722–12**

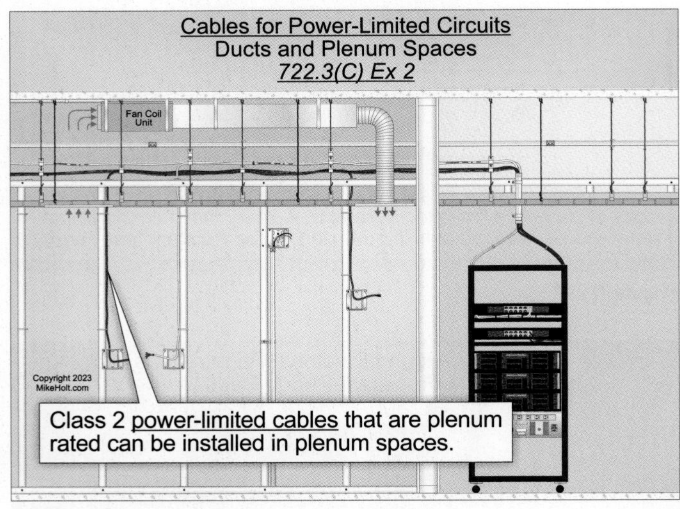

▸Figure 722–12

(E) Cable Trays. Power-limited circuits in cable trays must be installed in accordance with Parts I and II of Article 392.

(G) Raceways Exposed to Different Temperatures. If a raceway is subjected to different temperatures, and where condensation is known to be a problem, the raceway with power-limited cables must be filled with a material approved by the authority having jurisdiction that will prevent the circulation of warm air to a colder section of the raceway [300.7(A)]. ▸**Figure 722–13**

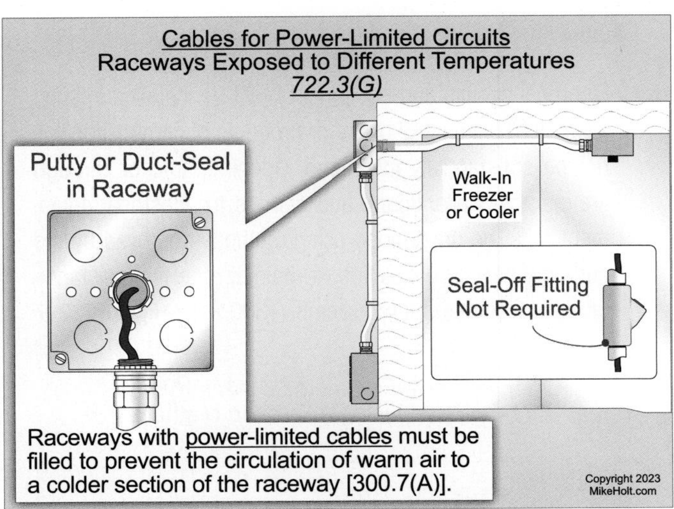

▸Figure 722–13

Author's Comment:

- This raceway seal is one that is approved by the authority having jurisdiction to prevent the circulation of warm air to a cooler section of the raceway and is not the same thing as an explosionproof seal.

(J) Corrosive, Damp, or Wet Locations. Where installed in corrosive, damp, or wet locations, Class 2 cables must be identified for the location in accordance with 110.11 and 310.10(F). Cables installed in underground raceways [300.5(B)] or in raceways aboveground in wet locations [300.9] must be identified for wet locations. Where corrosion may occur, the requirements of 300.6 must be used.

(O) Specific Requirements. As appropriate, the installation of wires and cables must also comply with the requirements of the following:

(1) Class 2 cables—Part II of Article 725

(3) Fire alarm cables—Part III of Article 760

722.21 Electrical Equipment Behind Access Panels

Access to equipment cannot be prohibited by an accumulation of power-limited cables that prevents the removal of suspended-ceiling panels. ▸**Figure 722–14**

722.24 Mechanical Execution of Work

(A) General. Cables for power-limited circuits must be installed in a neat and workmanlike manner. ▸**Figure 722–15**

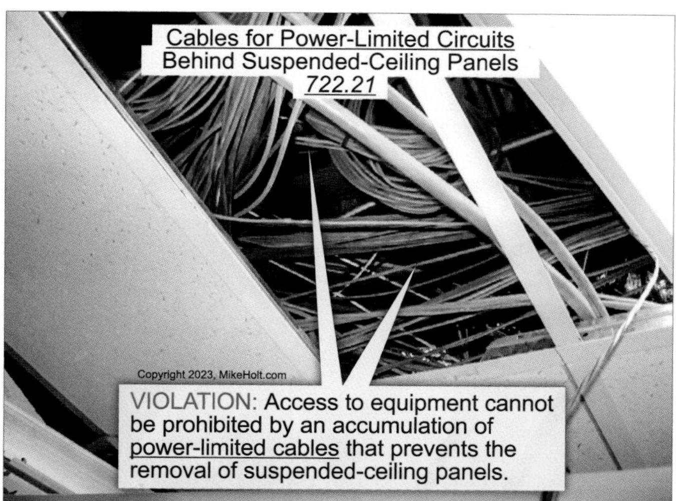

▶Figure 722–14

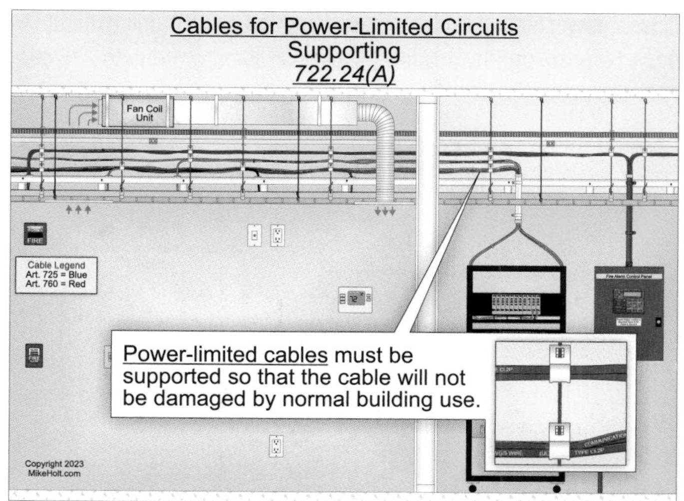

▶Figure 722–16

▶Figure 722–15

▶Figure 722–17

Cable Support. Exposed power-limited cables must be supported by the structural components of the building so the cable will not be damaged by normal building use. ▶**Figure 722–16**

Cable Securement. Power-limited cables must be secured by straps, staples, hangers, listed cable ties identified for securement and support, or similar fittings designed and installed in a manner that will not damage the cable. ▶**Figure 722–17**

Protection From Physical Damage [300.4]. Power-limited cables installed through or parallel to framing members or furring strips must be protected where they are likely to be penetrated by nails or screws by installing the wiring method so it is not less than 1¼ in. from the nearest edge of the framing member or furring strips, or by protecting it with a ¹⁄₁₆ in. thick steel plate or equivalent [300.4(A) and (D)]. ▶**Figure 722–18**

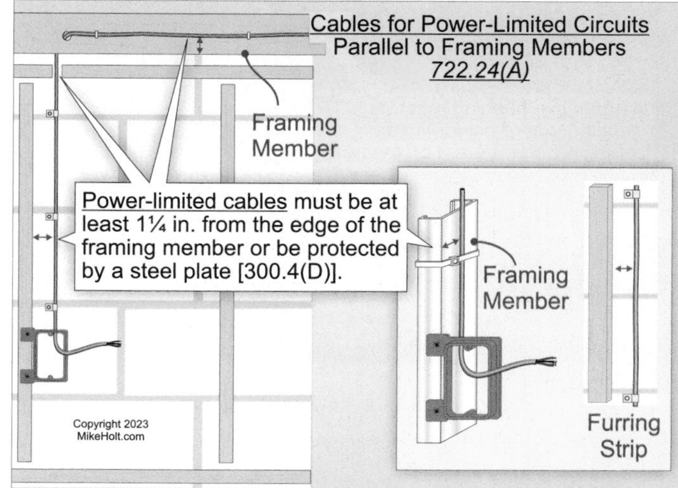

▶Figure 722–18

Class 2 power-limited cables installed through metal framing members must be protected by a listed bushing or listed grommets. ▶Figure 722–19

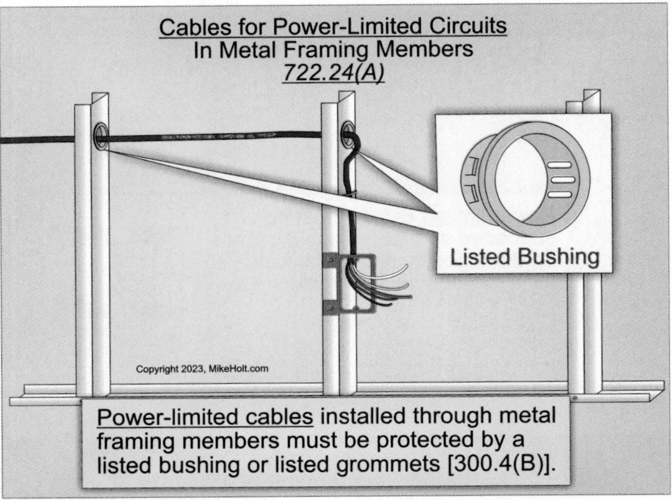
Cables for Power-Limited Circuits
In Metal Framing Members
722.24(A)
Listed Bushing
Copyright 2023, MikeHolt.com
Power-limited cables installed through metal framing members must be protected by a listed bushing or listed grommets [300.4(B)].

▶Figure 722–19

Securing and Supporting [300.11]. Ceiling-support wires or the ceiling grid is not permitted to support raceways or cables. Independent support wires secured at both ends can be used to support raceways or cables.

Protective Bushing at Raceway [300.15(C)]. A bushing must be installed where power-limited cables emerge from raceways. ▶Figure 722–20

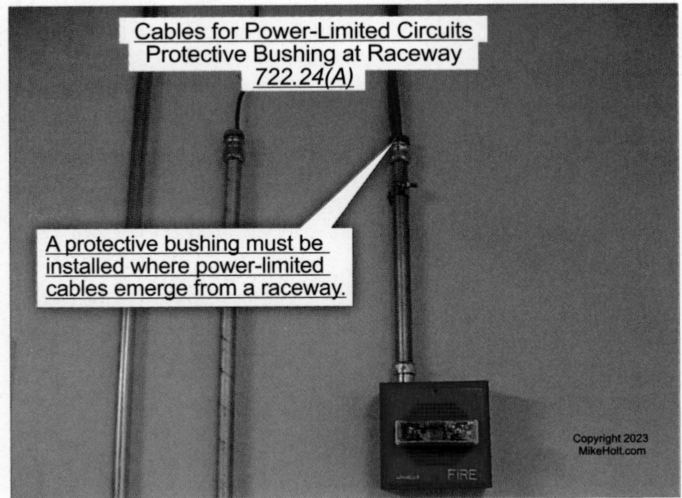
Cables for Power-Limited Circuits
Protective Bushing at Raceway
722.24(A)
A protective bushing must be installed where power-limited cables emerge from a raceway.
FIRE
Copyright 2023 MikeHolt.com

▶Figure 722–20

Cable Ties [300.22(C)]. Nonmetallic cable ties used to secure and support power limited cables in plenum spaces must be listed as having low smoke and heat release properties in accordance with 300.22(C). ▶Figure 722–21

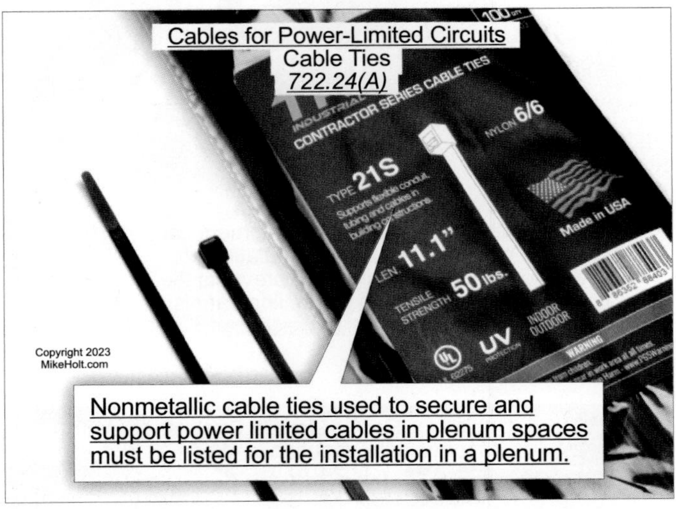
Cables for Power-Limited Circuits
Cable Ties
722.24(A)
CONTRACTOR SERIES CABLE TIES
NYLON 6/6
TYPE 21S
LEN. 11.1"
TENSILE STRENGTH 50 lbs.
UV
INDOOR OUTDOOR
Made in USA
Copyright 2023 MikeHolt.com
Nonmetallic cable ties used to secure and support power limited cables in plenum spaces must be listed for the installation in a plenum.

▶Figure 722–21

Note 2: Paint, plaster, cleaners, abrasives, corrosive residues, or other contaminants can result in an undetermined alteration of Class 2 cable properties.

(B) Support of Cables. Power-limited cables are not permitted to be strapped, taped, or attached by any means to the exterior of any raceway. ▶Figure 722–22 and ▶Figure 722–23

Ex 1: Power-limited cables can be supported by the raceway that supplies power to equipment controlled by a Class 2 power-limited circuit [300.11(C)(2)]. ▶Figure 722–24

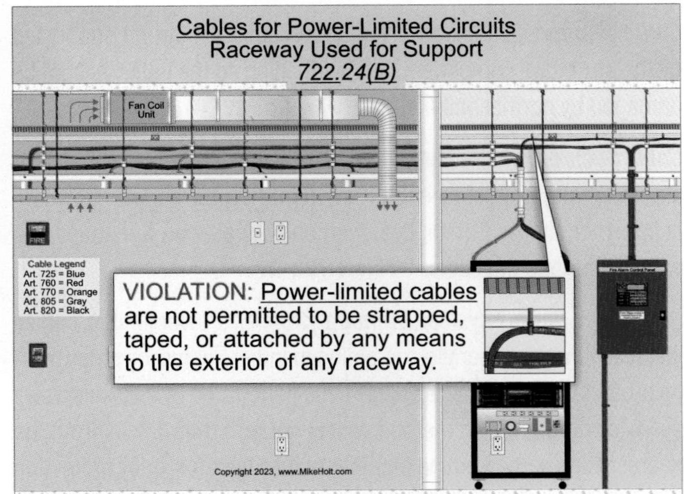
Cables for Power-Limited Circuits
Raceway Used for Support
722.24(B)
Fan Coil Unit
Cable Legend
Art. 725 = Blue
Art. 760 = Red
Art. 770 = Orange
Art. 805 = Gray
Art. 820 = Black
VIOLATION: Power-limited cables are not permitted to be strapped, taped, or attached by any means to the exterior of any raceway.
Copyright 2023, www.MikeHolt.com

▶Figure 722–22

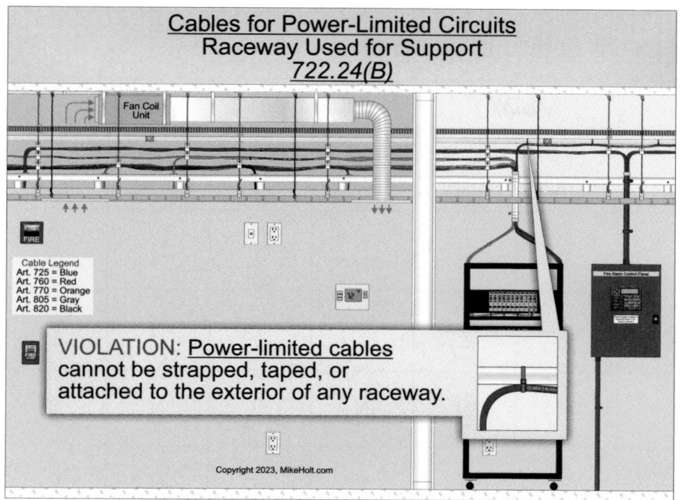

▸Figure 722–23

▸Figure 722–25

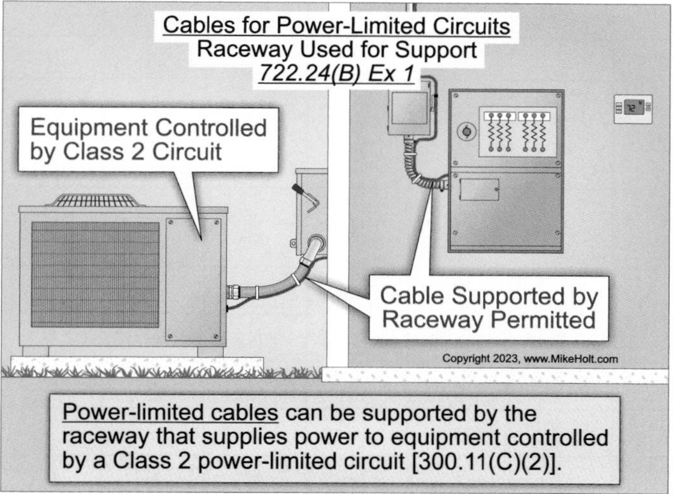

▸Figure 722–24

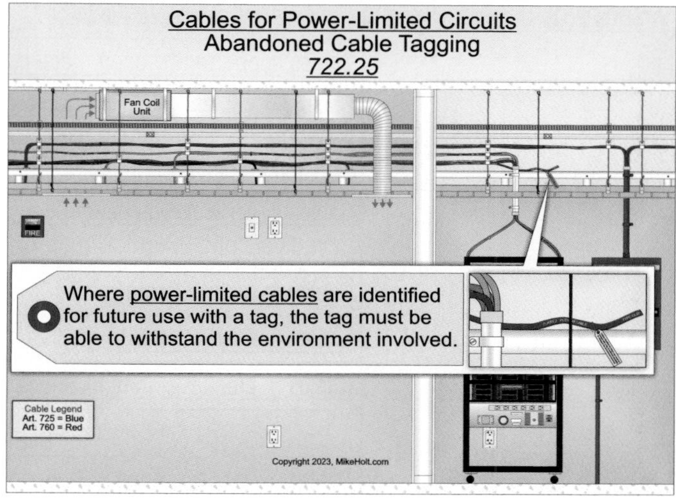

▸Figure 722–26

722.25 Abandoned Cable

To limit the spread of fire or products of combustion within a building, the accessible portions of abandoned power-limited cables must be removed. ▸Figure 722–25

According to Article 100, "Abandoned Cable" is defined as a cable that is not terminated at equipment other than a termination fitting or a connector and is not identified for future use with a tag.

Where power-limited cables are identified for future use with a tag, the tag must be able to withstand the environment involved. ▸**Figure 722–26**

722.135 Installation of Power-Limited Cables

The installation of cables must comply with the following:

(A) Listing. Power-limited cables installed in buildings must be listed.

(B) Cables in Buildings. The installation of cables must comply with Table 722.135(B).

Table 722.135(B) Installation of Listed Cables in Buildings								
Applications		Cable Type[1]						
		Plenum	Riser	General Purpose	Limited Use	Under Carpet	PLTC
In ducts specifically fabricated for environmental air as described in 300.22(B)2	Cables in lengths as short as practicable to perform the required function	Y	N	N	N	N	N
	In a metal raceway that complies with 300.22(B)	Y	Y	Y	Y	N	Y
In plenum space as described in 300.22(C)	Cables in other spaces used for environmental air	Y	N	N	N	N	N
	Cables in a metal raceway that complies with 300.22(C)	Y	Y	Y	Y	N	Y
	Cables in plenum communications raceways	Y	N	N	N	N	N
	Cables supported by open metal cable trays	Y	N	N	N	N	N
	Cables or cables installed in raceways supported by solid bottom metal cable trays with solid metal covers	Y	Y	Y	Y	N	Y
In risers and vertical runs	Cables in vertical runs penetrating one or more floors and in vertical runs in a shaft	Y	Y	N	N	N	N
	Cables in metal raceways	Y	Y	Y	Y	N	Y
	Cables in fireproof shafts	Y	Y	Y	N	N	Y
	Cables in plenum communications raceways	Y	Y	N	N	N	N
	Cables in riser communications raceways	Y	Y	N	N	N	N
	Cables in one- and two-family dwellings	Y	Y	Y	Y[3]	N	Y
Cables installed in metal raceways in a riser having firestops at each floor[2]	Cables	Y	Y	Y	Y	N	Y
	Cables in plenum communications raceways	Y	Y	Y	Y	N	Y
	Cables in riser communications raceways	Y	Y	Y	Y	N	Y
	Cables in general purpose communications raceways	Y	Y	Y	Y	N	Y
In fireproof riser shafts having firestops at each floor[2]	Cables in plenum communications raceways	Y	Y	Y	N	N	Y
	Cables in riser communications raceways	Y	Y	Y	N	N	Y

Table 722.135(B) Installation of Listed Cables in Buildings (continued)

Applications		Cable Type[1]					
		Plenum	Riser	General Purpose	Limited Use	Under Carpet	PLTC
In cable trays	Cables in general-purpose communications raceways	Y	Y	Y	N	N	Y
	Outdoors	N	N	N	N	N	Y
	Cables, or cables in plenum, riser, or general-purpose communications raceways, installed indoors	Y	Y	Y	N	N	Y
In cross-connect arrays	Cables, and cables in plenum, riser, or general-purpose communications raceways	Y	Y	Y	N	N	Y
In one-, two-, and multifamily dwellings, and in building locations other than the locations covered above	Cables	Y	Y	Y	Y[3]	N	Y
	Cables in plenum, riser, or general-purpose communications raceways, or raceways recognized in Chapter 3	Y	Y	Y	Y	N	Y
	Cables in nonconcealed spaces	Y	Y	Y	Y[4]	Y	Y
	Under carpet, floor covering, modular flooring, and planks	N	N	N	N	Y	N

[1]*"N" indicates that the cable type is not permitted to be installed in the application. "Y" indicates that the cable type can be installed in the application, subject to any limitations described in this article or the articles described in 722.3(O).*

[2]*In 300.22(B), cables are permitted in ducts specifically fabricated for environmental air only if directly associated with the air distribution system.*

[3]*Limited-use cable can be installed only in one-, two-, and multifamily dwellings and only if the cable is smaller in diameter than 0.25 in.*

[4]*The exposed length of cable must not exceed 10 ft.*

(D) In Hoistways. Power-limited cables in hoistways must be installed in rigid metal conduit, rigid nonmetallic conduit, intermediate metal conduit, liquidtight flexible nonmetallic conduit, or electrical metallic tubing.

(E) Cable Substitutions. Cable substitutions can be made in accordance with Table 722.135(E) and the installation requirements of the articles described in 722.3(O) must also apply.

Table 722.135(E) Cable Substitutions

Cable Type	Permitted Substitutions
CL3P	CMP
CL2P	CMP, CL3P
CL3R	CMP, CL3P, CMR
CL2R	CMP, CL3P, CL2P, CMR, CL3R
PLTC	None
CL3	CMP, CL3P, CMR, CL3R, CMG, CM, PLTC
CL2	CMP, CL3P, CL2P, CMR, CL3R, CL2R, CMG, CM, PLTC, CL3
CL3X	CMP, CL3P, CMR, CL3R, CMG, CM, PLTC, CL3, CMX
CL2X	CMP, CL3P, CL2P, CMR, CL3R, CL2R, CMG, CM, PLTC, CL3, CL2, CMX, CL3X
FPLP	CMP
FPLR	CMP, FPLP, CMR
FPL	CMP, FPLP, CMR, FPLR, CMG, CM
OFNP	None
OFCP	OFNP
OFNR	OFNP
OFCR	OFNP, OFCP, OFNR
OFNG, OFN	OFNP, OFNR
OFCG, OFC	OFNP, OFCP, OFNR, OFCR, OFNG, OFN
CMUC	None

(H) Bundling of 4-Pair POE Cables. Section 725.144 applies to 4-pair cables are used to transmit power and data to a powered device.

Part II. Listing Requirements

722.179 Listing and Marking of Power-Limited Cables

Power-limited cables installed in buildings must be listed in accordance with 722.179(A) and marked in accordance with 722.179(B) or (C). ▸Figure 722–27

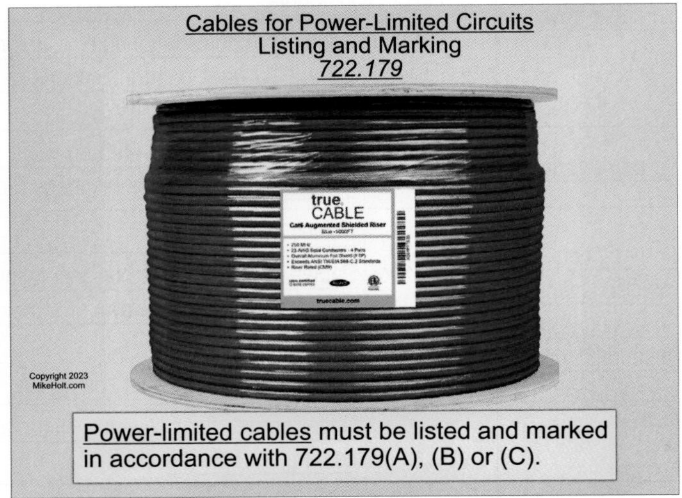

Cables for Power-Limited Circuits
Listing and Marking
722.179
true CABLE
truecable.com
Copyright 2023
MikeHolt.com
Power-limited cables must be listed and marked in accordance with 722.179(A), (B) or (C).

▸Figure 722–27

(A) Listing. Power-limited cables installed as wiring methods within buildings must be listed as resistant to the spread of fire and other criteria in accordance with 722.179(A)(1) through (A)(16).

(1) Plenum-Rated Cable. Plenum-rated cable must be listed as suitable for use in ducts, plenums, and other space for environmental air. They must be listed as having adequate fire-resistant and low-smoke producing characteristics. Refer to Table 722.179(B) for plenum cable types. ▸Figure 722–28

(2) Riser-Rated Cable. Riser-rated cable must be listed as suitable for use in a vertical run in a shaft, or from floor to floor, and must be listed as having fire-resistant characteristics capable of preventing the carrying of fire from floor to floor.

(3) General-Purpose Rated Cable. General-purpose rated cable must be listed as resistant to the spread of fire and as suitable for general-purpose use, except for risers, ducts, plenums, and other space used for environmental air, and must be listed as resistant to the spread of fire.

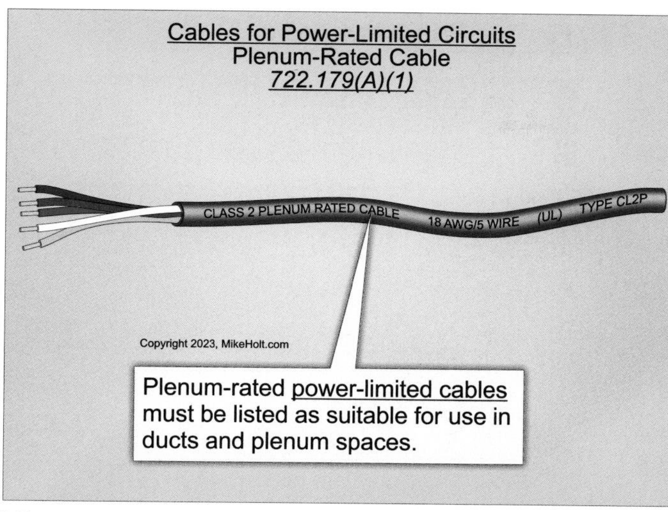
Cables for Power-Limited Circuits
Plenum-Rated Cable
722.179(A)(1)
CLASS 2 PLENUM RATED CABLE
18 AWG/5 WIRE
(UL)
TYPE CL2P
Copyright 2023, MikeHolt.com
Plenum-rated power-limited cables must be listed as suitable for use in ducts and plenum spaces.

▸Figure 722–28

(4) Alternative General-Purpose Cable. Alternative general-purpose optical fiber cable must be listed as suitable for general-purpose use, except for risers and plenums, and must also be resistant to the spread of fire.

(5) Limited-Use Cable. Limited-use cable must be listed as suitable for use in dwellings and raceways and must be listed as resistant to the spread of flame.

(6) Type PLTC. Type PLTC nonmetallic-sheathed, power-limited tray cable must be listed as being suitable for cable trays, resistant to the spread of fire, and sunlight- and moisture-resistant. Type PLTC cable used in a wet location must be listed for use in wet locations and marked "wet" or "wet location."

(9) Limited Power (LP) Cable. Limited power (LP) cables must be listed as suitable for carrying power and data circuits up to a specified current for each conductor. The cables must be marked with the suffix "-LP (XXA)" where "XXA" designates that current limit is amperes per conductor.

Note: An example of the marking on a Class 2 cable with an LP rating is "CL2-LP (0.60A) 75°C 23 AWG 4-pair," which indicates it is a 4-pair plenum cable with 23 AWG conductors, a temperature rating of 75°C, and a current limit of 0.60A per conductor.

(11) Wet Locations. Cable used in a wet location must be listed for use in wet locations and be marked "wet" or "wet location" or have a moisture-impervious metal sheath.

ARTICLE 724

CLASS 1 POWER-LIMITED CIRCUITS

Introduction to Article 724—Class 1 Power-Limited Circuits

This article covers Class 1 circuits, which are limited to a maximum of 1000 VA at 30V. This allows for alternative requirements for minimum conductor sizes, overcurrent protection, insulation types, wiring methods, and materials. A Class 1 circuit is the wiring system between the load side of a Class 1 power source and the connected equipment. Many of these rules are outside of the scope of this material, however, some of the topics we cover include the following:

- Scope
- Circuit Identification
- Power Sources
- Overcurrent Protection
- Wiring Methods
- Conductors of Different Circuits in Same Cable, Cable Tray, Enclosure, or Raceway

Part I. General

724.1 Scope

This article covers Class 1 power-limited circuits, not more than 1000 VA at 30V [724.40] that are not an integral part of a device or utilization equipment. ▸**Figure 724–1**

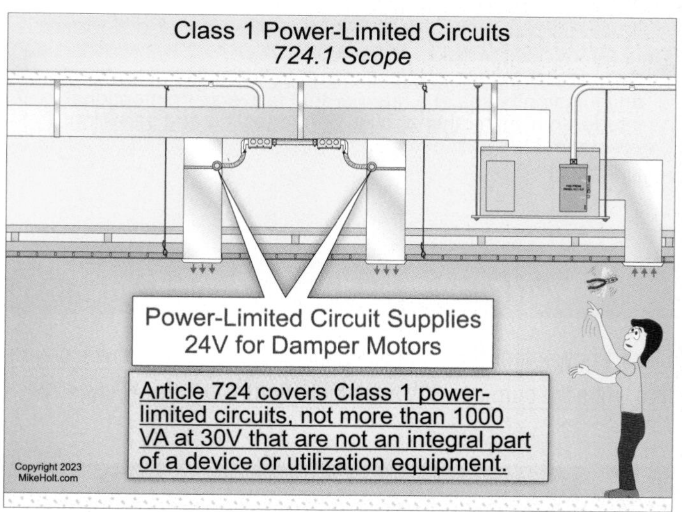
Class 1 Power-Limited Circuits
724.1 Scope
Power-Limited Circuit Supplies
24V for Damper Motors
Article 724 covers Class 1 power-limited circuits, not more than 1000 VA at 30V that are not an integral part of a device or utilization equipment.
Copyright 2023
MikeHolt.com

▸**Figure 724–1**

According to Article 100, a "Class 1 Power-Limited Circuit" is the wiring system between the load side of a Class 1 power-limited power source and the connected equipment. ▸**Figure 724–2**

724.30 Class 1 Circuit Identification

Class 1 power-limited circuits must be identified at terminal and junction box locations in a manner that prevents unintentional interference with other circuits during testing and servicing. ▸**Figure 724–3**

Class 1 Power-Limited Circuit
Article 100 Definition
The wiring system between the load side of a Class 1 power-limited power source and the connected equipment.
120 VAC
24 VDC
Jennifer Martin
Copyright 2023, MikeHolt.com

▸Figure 724–2

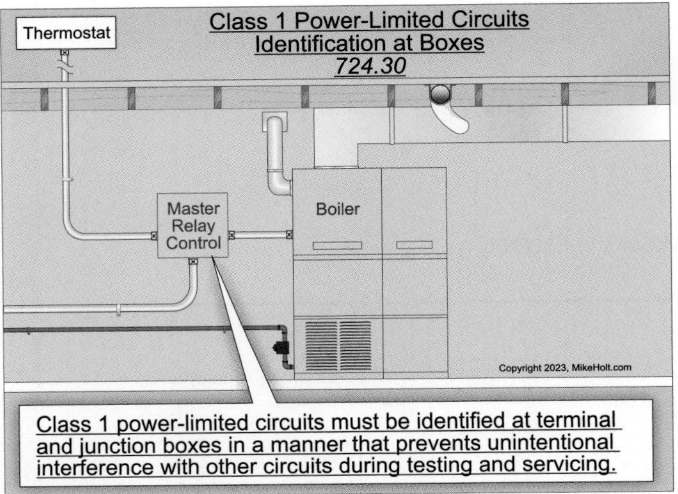
Thermostat
Class 1 Power-Limited Circuits
Identification at Boxes
724.30
Master Relay Control
Boiler
Copyright 2023, MikeHolt.com
Class 1 power-limited circuits must be identified at terminal and junction boxes in a manner that prevents unintentional interference with other circuits during testing and servicing.

▸Figure 724–3

724.40 Class 1 Power Source

Class 1 power-limited circuits must be supplied from a power source that limits the output to 30V at no more than 1000 VA. ▸Figure 724–4

724.43 Class 1 Circuit Overcurrent Protection

Overcurrent protection for conductors 14 AWG and larger must be in accordance with the conductor ampacity in accordance with 110.14(C)(1) and Table 310.16. Overcurrent protection for 18 AWG conductors is not permitted to exceed 7A, and for 16 AWG conductors, overcurrent protection is not permitted to exceed 10A.

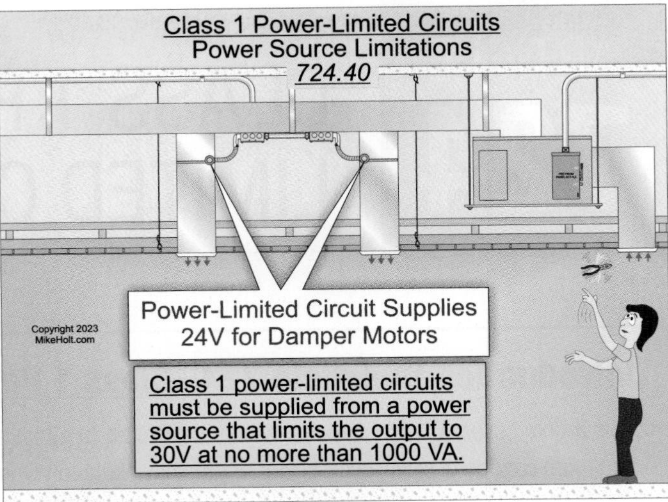
Class 1 Power-Limited Circuits
Power Source Limitations
724.40
Copyright 2023 MikeHolt.com
Power-Limited Circuit Supplies 24V for Damper Motors
Class 1 power-limited circuits must be supplied from a power source that limits the output to 30V at no more than 1000 VA.

▸Figure 724–4

724.45 Class 1 Circuit Overcurrent Protective Device Location

(A) Point of Supply. Overcurrent protective devices must be at the point where the conductor to be protected receives its supply.

(D) Primary Side of Transformer. Class 1 circuit conductors supplied by a transformer having only a 2-wire secondary can be protected by the primary overcurrent protective device in accordance with 450.3(B), provided the primary overcurrent protective device does not exceed the value determined by multiplying the secondary conductor ampacity by the secondary-to-primary transformer voltage ratio. ▸Figure 724–5

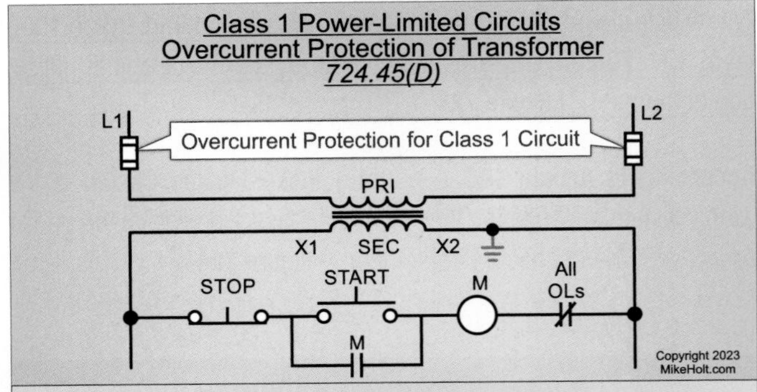
Class 1 Power-Limited Circuits
Overcurrent Protection of Transformer
724.45(D)
L1
L2
Overcurrent Protection for Class 1 Circuit
PRI
X1
SEC
X2
STOP
START
M
All OLs
M
Copyright 2023 MikeHolt.com
Class 1 circuit conductors supplied by a transformer having only a 2-wire secondary can be protected by the primary overcurrent protective device sized per 450.3(B), provided the primary overcurrent protective device does not exceed the value determined by multiplying the secondary conductor ampacity by the secondary-to-primary transformer voltage ratio.

▸Figure 724–5

724.46 Class 1 Circuit Wiring Methods

Class 1 power-limited circuits must be installed in accordance with Part I of Article 300 and be installed in a suitable Chapter 3 wiring method. ▶Figure 724-6

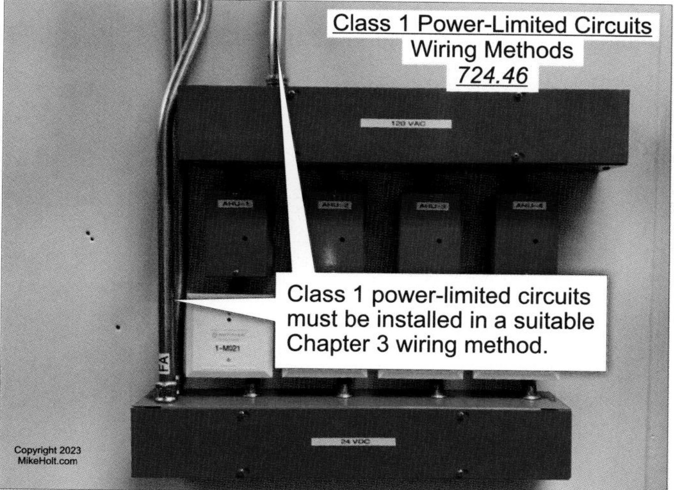
Class 1 Power-Limited Circuits
Wiring Methods
724.46
Class 1 power-limited circuits must be installed in a suitable Chapter 3 wiring method.
Copyright 2023 MikeHolt.com

▶Figure 724-6

724.48 Conductors of Different Circuits in Same Cable, Cable Tray, Enclosure, or Raceway

(A) Class 1 Power-Limited Circuits with Other Class 1 Power-Limited Circuits. Two or more Class 1 power-limited circuits can be installed in the same cable, enclosure, or raceway provided all conductors are insulated for the maximum voltage of any conductor.

(B) Class 1 Power-Limited Circuits with Power Circuits. Class 1 power-limited circuits can be installed with electrical power conductors under the following conditions:

(1) In a Cable, Enclosure, or Raceway. Class 1 power-limited circuits can be in the same cable, enclosure, or raceway with power-supply circuits if the equipment powered is functionally associated with the Class 1 circuit.

Class 1 power-limited circuits can be installed together with the conductors of electric light, and power, where separated by a barrier.

724.49 Class 1 Circuit Conductors

(A) Size and Use. Conductors of sizes 18 AWG and 16 AWG installed within a raceway, enclosure, or listed cable are permitted if they do not supply a load that exceeds the ampacities given in Table 402.5. Conductors 14 AWG and larger must meet the ampacities given in Table 310.16.

(B) Insulation. Class 1 circuit conductors must have at least a 600V insulation rating.

724.51 Number of Conductors in a Raceway

(A) Class 1 Circuit Conductors. Raceways must be large enough to permit the installation and removal of conductors without damaging conductor insulation as limited by 300.17. ▶Figure 724-7

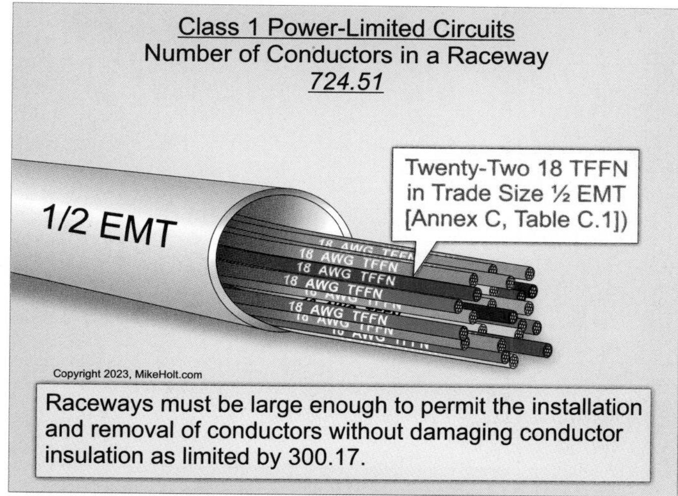
Class 1 Power-Limited Circuits
Number of Conductors in a Raceway
724.51
1/2 EMT
Twenty-Two 18 TFFN in Trade Size ½ EMT [Annex C, Table C.1])
18 AWG TFFN
Copyright 2023, MikeHolt.com
Raceways must be large enough to permit the installation and removal of conductors without damaging conductor insulation as limited by 300.17.

▶Figure 724-7

Author's Comment:

- When all conductors within a raceway are the same size and insulation, the number of conductors permitted can be found in Annex C for the raceway type [Chapter 9, Notes to Tables, Note 1].
- For conductors not included in Chapter 9 (such as multiconductor cable), the actual dimensions must be used. If one multiconductor cable is used inside a raceway, the single-conductor percentage fill area must be used [Chapter 9, Notes to Tables, Note 5 and 9].

ARTICLE 725

CLASS 2 POWER-LIMITED CIRCUITS

Introduction to Article 725—Class 2 Power-Limited Circuits

This article contains the requirements for Class 2 power-limited circuits, maximum of 100 VA at 30Vthat are not an integral part of a device or appliance. These circuits extend between the load side of a power-limited power source or transformer and the connected Class 2 power-limited equipment. These circuits are commonly used for burglar alarms, access control, sound, nurse call, intercoms, some computer networks, some lighting dimmer controls, and some low-voltage industrial controls. Many of these rules are outside of the scope of this material, however, some of the topics we cover include the following:

- Scope
- Safety-Control Equipment
- Circuit Requirements
- Wiring Methods
- Separation from Power Conductors
- Conductors of Different Circuits in Same Cable, Enclosure, Cable Tray, and Raceway
- Bundling Cables Transmitting Power and Data

Part I. General

725.1 Scope

Article 725 covers the requirements for Class 2 power-limited circuits, maximum 100 VA at 30V [725.60], that are not an integral part of a device or utilization equipment. ▸**Figure 725–1**

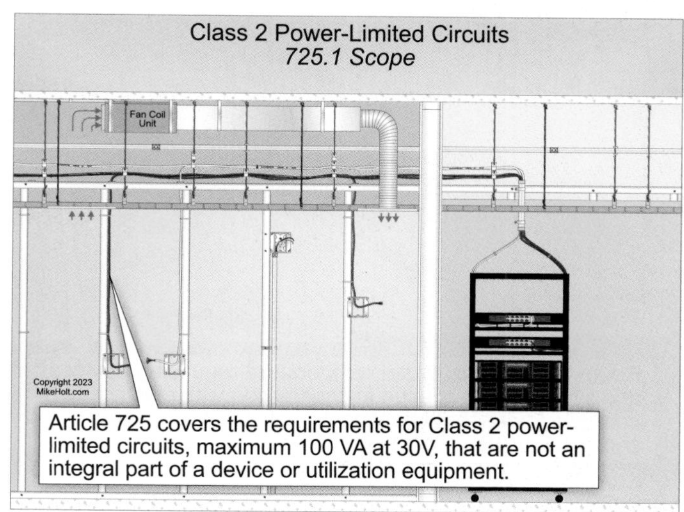

▸**Figure 725–1**

According to Article 100, a "Class 2 Power-Limited Circuit" is the portion of the wiring system between the load side of a power-limited power source or transformer and the connected Class 2 power-limited equipment. ▸**Figure 725–2**

Note 1: These circuits have electrical power and voltage limitations that differentiate them from electrical power circuits. Alternative requirements are given regarding minimum conductor sizes, overcurrent protection, insulation requirements, and wiring methods and materials.

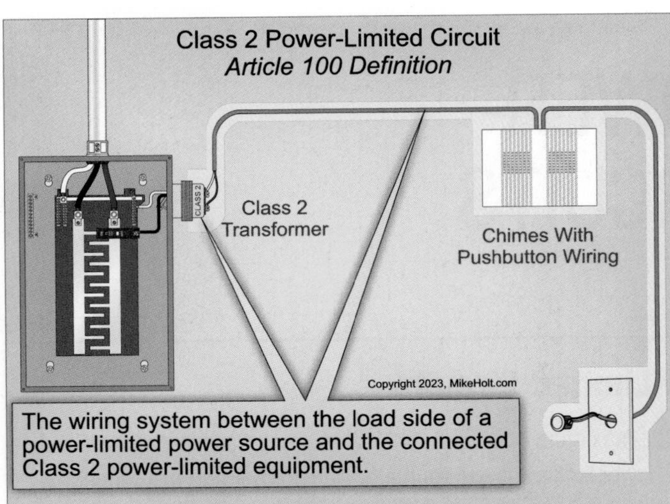

▸Figure 725–2

725.31 Safety-Control Equipment

Where damage to power-limited circuits can result in a failure of safety-control equipment that would introduce a direct fire or life hazard, the power-limited circuits must be installed in accordance with 724.31.

Room thermostats, water temperature regulating devices, and similar controls used in conjunction with electrically controlled household heating and air-conditioning are not considered safety-control equipment. ▸Figure 725–3

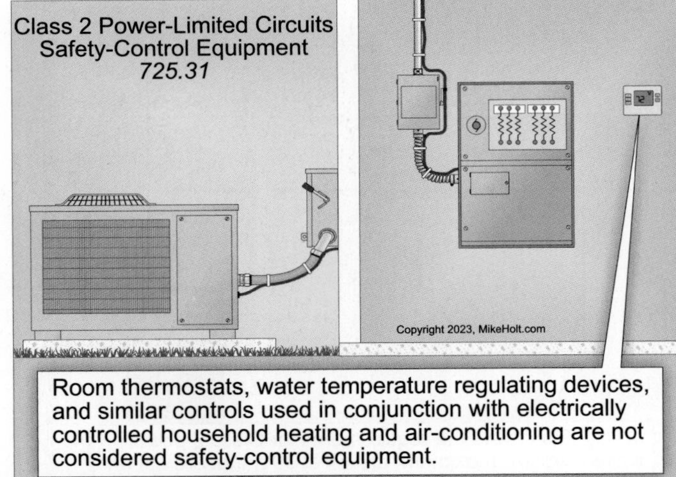

▸Figure 725–3

Part II. Class 2 Circuit Requirements

725.60 Power Sources for Class 2 Circuits

(A) Power Source. The power source for a Class 2 circuit must be as follows:

(1) A listed Class 2 transformer ▸Figure 725–4

Class 2 Power-Limited Circuits
Power Source, Transformer
725.60(A)(1)
Copyright 2023, MikeHolt.com
Transformers used as a Class 2 power source must be listed.

▸Figure 725–4

(2) A listed Class 2 power source

(3) Equipment listed as a Class 2 power source

Ex 2: Where a circuit has an energy level at or below the limits established in Chapter 9, Tables 11(A) and 11(B), the equipment is not required to be listed as a Class 2 power transformer, power supply, or power source.

(4) Listed audio/video information technology equipment (computers) and industrial equipment limited-power circuits ▸Figure 725–5

(5) A battery source or battery source system listed and identified as Class 2

(C) Marking. Equipment supplying Class 2 circuits must be durably marked to indicate each circuit that is a Class 2 circuit. The power sources for power-limited circuits in 725.60(A)(3) and power-limited circuits for listed audio/video equipment, listed information technology equipment, and listed industrial equipment in 725.60(A)(4) must have a label indicating the maximum voltage and rated current output per conductor for each connection point on the power source. Where multiple connection points have the same rating, a single label can be used.

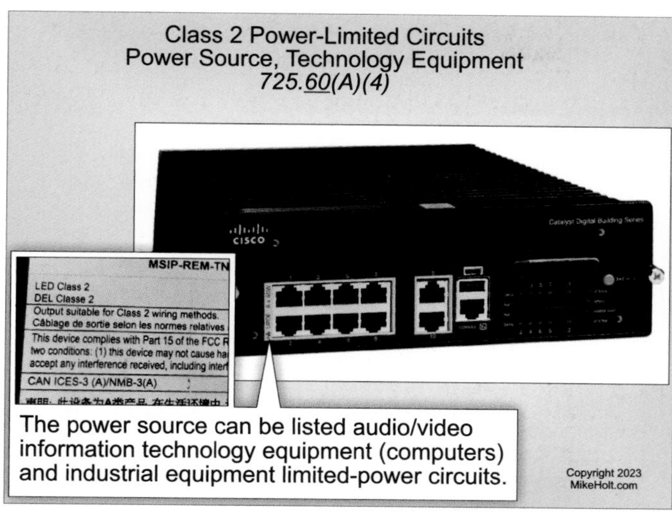

▶Figure 725–5

Note 1: The rated current for power sources covered in 725.144 is the output current per conductor the power source is designed to deliver to an operational load at normal operating conditions, as declared by the manufacturer.

725.127 Wiring Methods on Supply Side of the Class 2 Power Source

Conductors and equipment on the supply side of the Class 2 power source must be installed in accordance with Chapters 1 through 4. ▶Figure 725–6

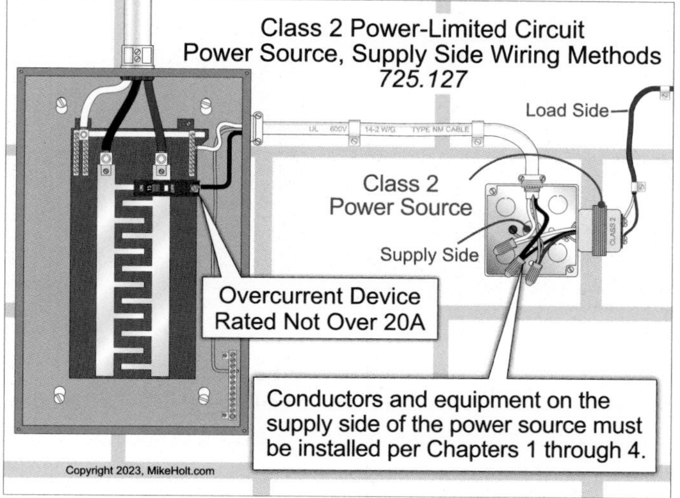

▶Figure 725–6

725.130 Wiring Methods on Load Side of the Class 2 Power Source

(B) Class 2 Wiring Methods. Class 2 circuits are permitted to use Class 2 wiring of the type in 722.179 if installed in accordance with 725.136 through 725.144. ▶Figure 725–7

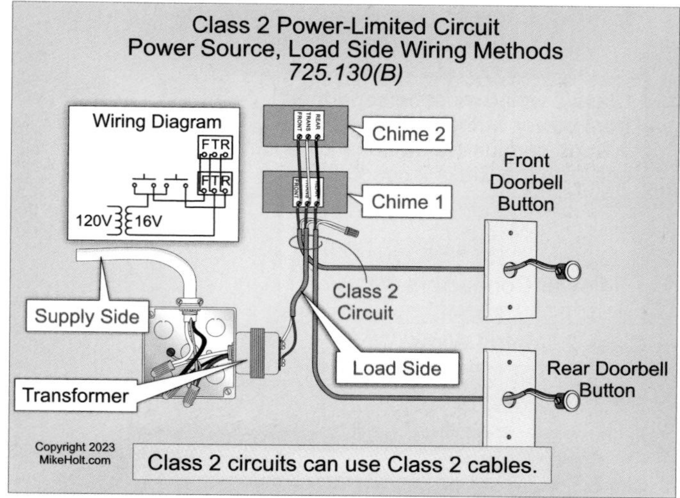

▶Figure 725–7

725.136 Separation from Power Conductors

(A) Enclosures, Raceways, or Cables. Class 2 cables are not permitted in any enclosure or raceway with power and Class 1 power-limited circuits, except as permitted in (B) through (I). ▶Figure 725–8

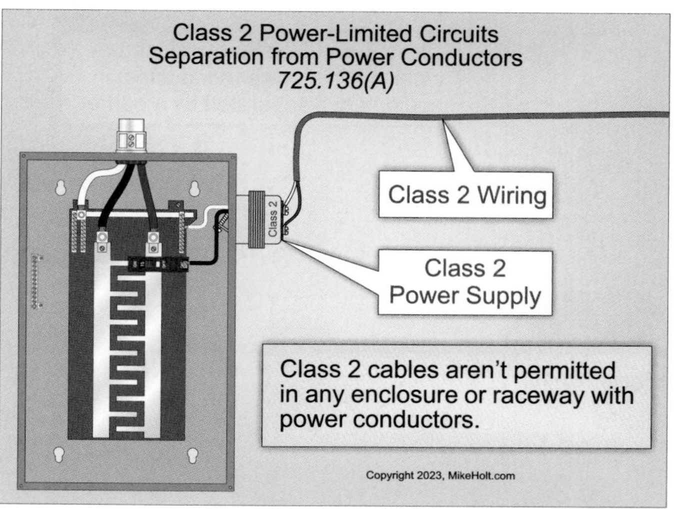

▶Figure 725–8

Author's Comment:

- Class 2 wiring must be separated from power wiring so the higher-voltage conductors do not accidentally energize the Class 2 conductors. ▶Figure 725-9

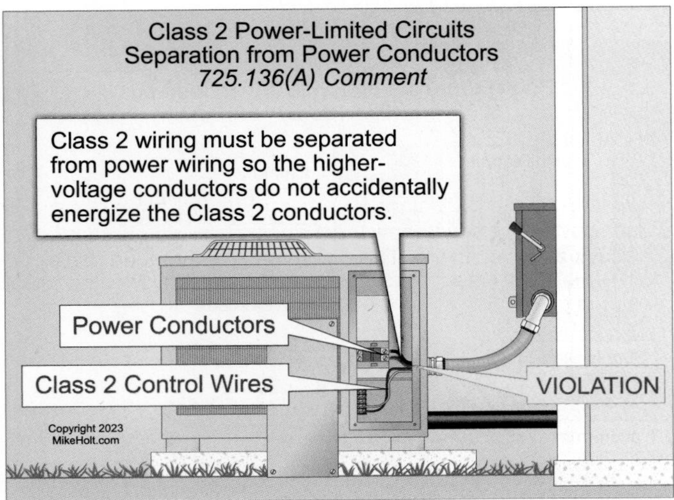

Class 2 Power-Limited Circuits
Separation from Power Conductors
725.136(A) Comment
Class 2 wiring must be separated from power wiring so the higher-voltage conductors do not accidentally energize the Class 2 conductors.
Power Conductors
Class 2 Control Wires
VIOLATION
Copyright 2023 MikeHolt.com

▶Figure 725-9

(B) Separated by Barriers. Class 2 circuit conductors can be installed with power conductors and Class 1 conductors if separated by a barrier. ▶Figure 725-10 and ▶Figure 725-11

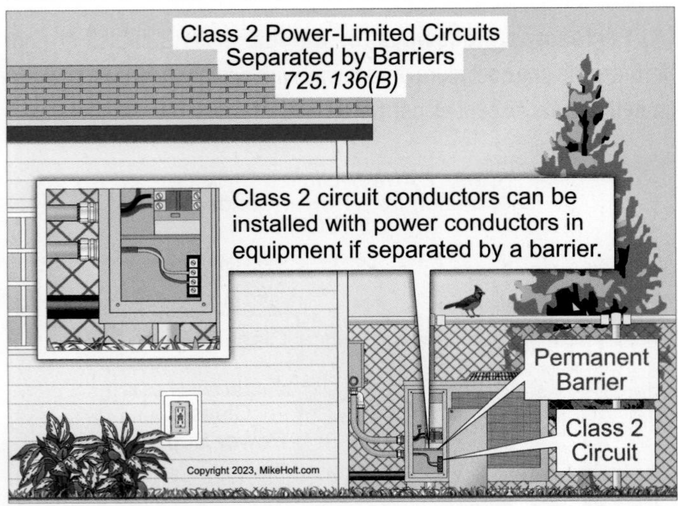

Class 2 Power-Limited Circuits
Separated by Barriers
725.136(B)
Class 2 circuit conductors can be installed with power conductors in equipment if separated by a barrier.
Permanent Barrier
Class 2 Circuit
Copyright 2023, MikeHolt.com

▶Figure 725-10

Author's Comment:

- Separation is required to prevent a fire or shock hazard that can occur from a short between the Class 2 circuits and the higher-voltage circuits.

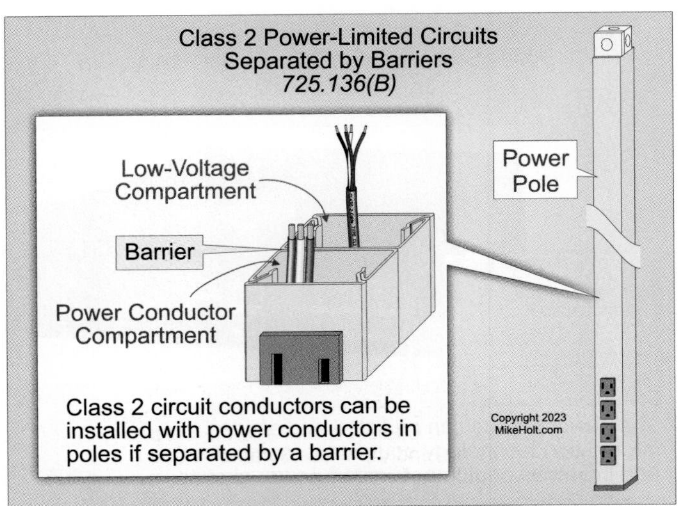

Class 2 Power-Limited Circuits
Separated by Barriers
725.136(B)
Low-Voltage Compartment
Barrier
Power Conductor Compartment
Power Pole
Class 2 circuit conductors can be installed with power conductors in poles if separated by a barrier.
Copyright 2023 MikeHolt.com

▶Figure 725-11

(D) Associated Systems Within Enclosures. Class 2 circuit conductors can be installed in compartments, enclosures, and outlet boxes with electric light and power circuits where (1) or (2) applies:

(1) Class 2 circuit conductors can be installed with power conductors where routed to maintain a minimum of ¼ in. separation. ▶Figure 725-12

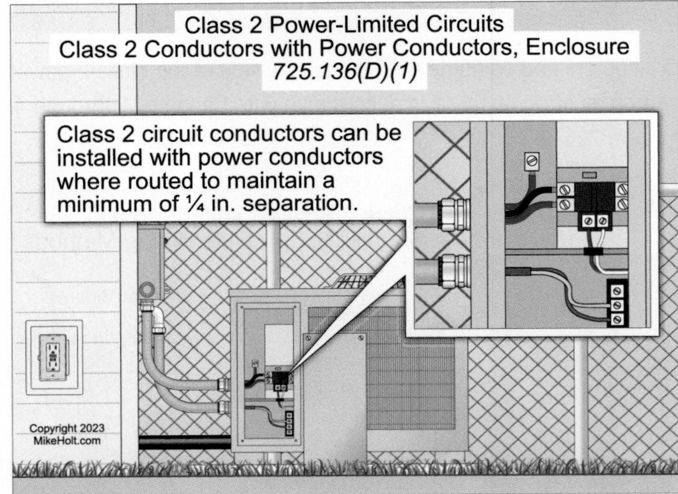

Class 2 Power-Limited Circuits
Class 2 Conductors with Power Conductors, Enclosure
725.136(D)(1)
Class 2 circuit conductors can be installed with power conductors where routed to maintain a minimum of ¼ in. separation.
Copyright 2023 MikeHolt.com

▶Figure 725-12

(2) Class 2 circuit conductors can be installed with power conductors within associated equipment operating at not over 150V to ground, if the Class 2 circuits are contained in a Class 3 cable, and the Class 2 circuit conductors extending beyond the Class 3 cable maintain a minimum of ¼ in. separation from the power conductors. ▶Figure 725-13

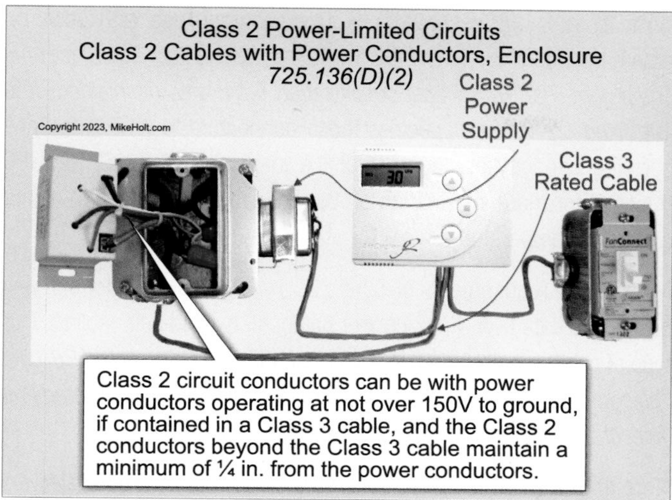
Class 2 Power-Limited Circuits
Class 2 Cables with Power Conductors, Enclosure
725.136(D)(2)
Class 2 Power Supply
Class 3 Rated Cable
Copyright 2023, MikeHolt.com
Class 2 circuit conductors can be with power conductors operating at not over 150V to ground, if contained in a Class 3 cable, and the Class 2 conductors beyond the Class 3 cable maintain a minimum of ¼ in. from the power conductors.

▸Figure 725–13

(G) Cable Trays. Class 2 circuit conductors can be installed with power conductors in cable trays if separated by a barrier or where the Class 2 circuits are installed in Type MC cable. ▸**Figure 725–14**

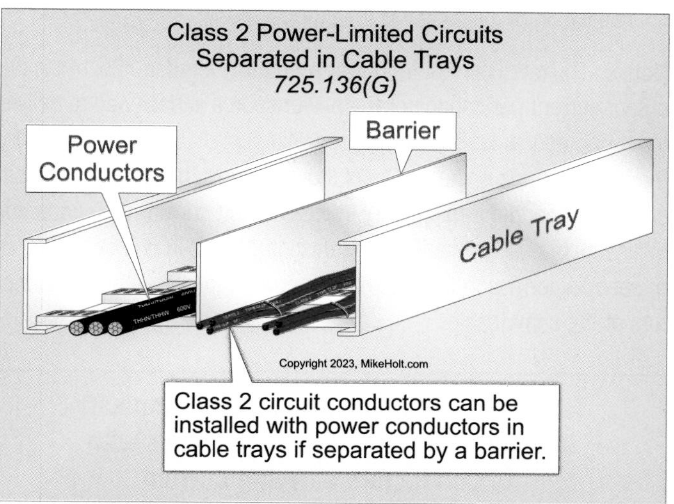
Class 2 Power-Limited Circuits
Separated in Cable Trays
725.136(G)
Power Conductors
Barrier
Cable Tray
Copyright 2023, MikeHolt.com
Class 2 circuit conductors can be installed with power conductors in cable trays if separated by a barrier.

▸Figure 725–14

(I) Other Applications. Class 2 circuit conductors cannot be installed in the same raceway or cable with power conductors unless:

(1) The Class 2 circuits are contained within a nonmetallic-sheathed cable. ▸**Figure 725–15** and ▸**Figure 725–16**

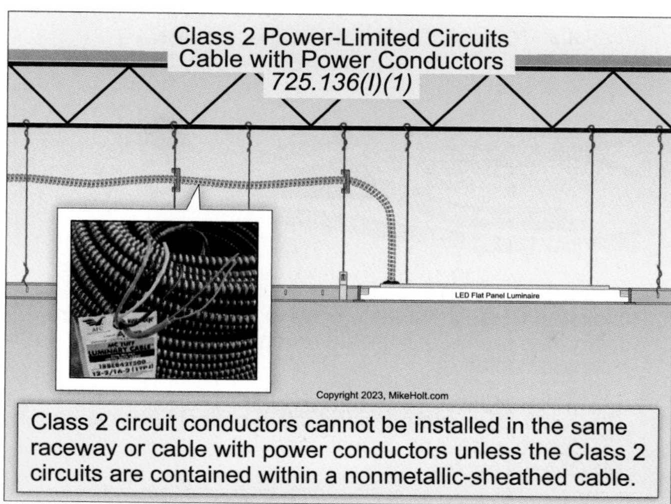
Class 2 Power-Limited Circuits
Cable with Power Conductors
725.136(I)(1)
LED Flat Panel Luminaire
Copyright 2023, MikeHolt.com
Class 2 circuit conductors cannot be installed in the same raceway or cable with power conductors unless the Class 2 circuits are contained within a nonmetallic-sheathed cable.

▸Figure 725–15

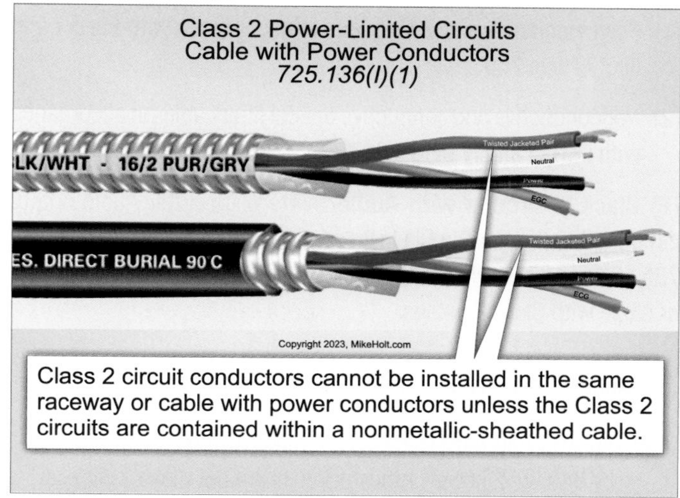
Class 2 Power-Limited Circuits
Cable with Power Conductors
725.136(I)(1)
LK/WHT - 16/2 PUR/GRY
Twisted Jacketed Pair
Neutral
Power
EGC
ES. DIRECT BURIAL 90°C
Copyright 2023, MikeHolt.com
Class 2 circuit conductors cannot be installed in the same raceway or cable with power conductors unless the Class 2 circuits are contained within a nonmetallic-sheathed cable.

▸Figure 725–16

725.139 Conductors of Different Circuits in Same Cable, Enclosure, Cable Tray, and Raceway

(A) Class 2 Conductors. Class 2 circuit conductors can be in the same cable, enclosure, or raceway with other Class 2 circuit conductors.

(E) Class 2 Cables with Other Cables. Jacketed Class 2 cables can be in the same enclosure, cable tray, raceway, as jacketed cables of any of the following. ▸**Figure 725–17**

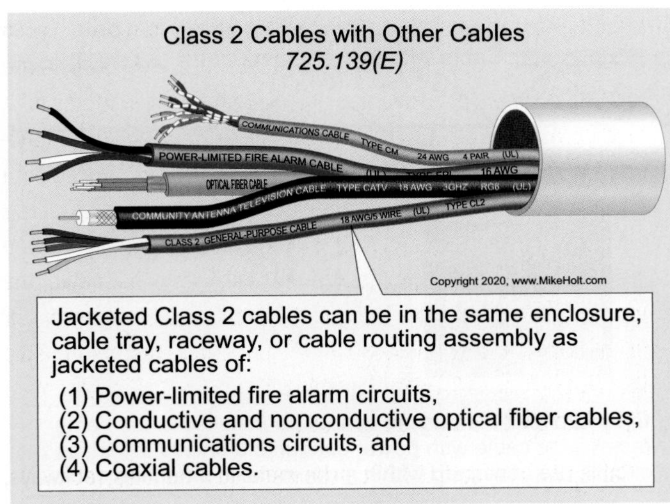
Class 2 Cables with Other Cables
725.139(E)
COMMUNICATIONS CABLE TYPE CM 24 AWG 4 PAIR (UL)
POWER-LIMITED FIRE ALARM CABLE
16 AWG
OPTICAL FIBER CABLE
COMMUNITY ANTENNA TELEVISION CABLE TYPE CATV 18 AWG 3GHZ RG6 (UL)
CLASS 2 GENERAL-PURPOSE CABLE 18 AWG/5 WIRE (UL) TYPE CL2
Copyright 2020, www.MikeHolt.com
Jacketed Class 2 cables can be in the same enclosure, cable tray, raceway, or cable routing assembly as jacketed cables of:
(1) Power-limited fire alarm circuits,
(2) Conductive and nonconductive optical fiber cables,
(3) Communications circuits, and
(4) Coaxial cables.

▸Figure 725–17

(1) Power-limited fire alarm circuits in accordance with Parts I and III of Article 760.

(2) Nonconductive and conductive optical fiber cables in accordance with Parts I and IV of Article 770.

(F) Class 2 Circuits with Audio System Circuits. Audio output circuits [640.9(C)] using Class 2 wiring methods in accordance with 725.133 and 725.154 are not permitted to be installed in any raceway, or cable with Class 2 cables.

Author's Comment:

- Audio circuits must use a Class 2 wiring method when required by 640.9(C), however these circuits are not Class 2 circuits!

725.144 Bundling Cables Transmitting Power and Data

This section applies to Class 2 circuits that transmit power and data to a powered device over listed cabling. Section 300.11 and Parts I and III of Article 725 apply to Class 2 circuits that transmit power and data.

Conductors that carry power and data must be copper and the current is not permitted to exceed the current limitation of the connectors.

Note 1: An example of cables that transmit power and data include closed-circuit TV cameras (CCTV).

Note 2: The 8P8C connector is in widespread use with powered communications systems. IEC 60603-7, *Connectors for Electronic Equipment—Part 7-1: Detail specification for 8-way, unshielded, free and fixed connectors*, specifies these connectors to have a current-carrying capacity per contact of 1A maximum at 60°C. See IEC 60603-7 for more information on current-carrying capacity at higher and lower temperatures.

Note 3: The requirements of Table 725.144 were derived for carrying power and data over 4-pair copper balanced twisted-pair cabling. This type of cabling is described in ANSI/TIA 568-C.2, *Commercial Building Telecommunications Cabling Standard—Part 2: Balanced Twisted-Pair Telecommunications Cabling and Components.*

Note 4: See TIA-TSB-184-A, *Guidelines for Supporting Power Delivery Over Balanced Twisted-Pair Cabling*, for information on installation and management of balanced twisted-pair cabling supporting power delivery.

Note 5: See ANSI/NEMA C137.3, *American National Standard for Lighting Systems—Minimum Requirements for Installation of Energy Efficient Power over Ethernet (PoE) Lighting Systems*, for information on installation of cables for PoE lighting systems.

Note 6: The rated current for power sources covered in 725.144 is the output current per conductor the power source is designed to deliver to an operational load at normal operating conditions, as declared by the manufacturer. In the design of these systems, the actual current in any given conductor might vary from the rated current per conductor by as much as 20 percent. An increase in current in one conductor is offset by a corresponding decrease in current in one or more conductors of the same cable.

Table 725.144 Copper Conductor Ampacity in 4-Pair Class 2 Power/Data Cables with All Conductors Carrying Current
See *NEC* Table 725.144 for details.

Table 725.144 Note 1: For bundle sizes over 192 cables, or for conductor sizes smaller than 26 AWG, ampacities can be determined by qualified personnel under engineering supervision.

Table 725.144 Note 2: Where only half of the conductors in each cable are carrying current, the values in the table can be increased by a factor of 1.40.

1st Printing

Note 1 to Table 725.144: Elevated cable temperatures can reduce a cable's data transmission performance. For information on practices for 4-pair balanced twisted-pair cabling, see TIA-TSB-184-A and 6.4.7, 6.6.3, and Annex G of ANSI/TIA-568-C.2, which provide guidance on adjustments for operating temperatures between 20°C and 60°C.

Note 2 to Table 725.144: The per-contact current rating of connectors can limit the maximum current below the ampacity shown in Table 725.144.

(A) Use of 4-Pair Class 2 Cables to Transmit Power and Data. Where Types CL3P, CL2P, CL3R, CL2R, CL3, or CL2 4-pair cables transmit power and data, the rated current per conductor of the power source is not permitted to exceed the ampacities in Table 725.144 at an ambient temperature of 30°C. For ambient temperatures above 30°C, the correction factors in Table 310.15(B)(1)(1) must be applied.

Ex: Compliance with Table 725.144 is not required for conductors 24 AWG or larger and the rated current per conductor of the power source does not exceed 0.30A.

Note: One example of the use of Class 2 cables is a network of closed-circuit TV cameras using 24 AWG, 60°C rated, Type CL2R, Category 5e balanced twisted-pair cabling.

(B) Use of Class 2-LP Cables to Transmit Power and Data. Types CL3P-LP, CL2P-LP, CL3R-LP, CL2R-LP, CL3-LP, or CL2-LP cables are permitted to supply power to equipment from a power source with a rated current per conductor up to the marked current limit immediately following the suffix "-LP" and are permitted to transmit data to the equipment. Where the number of bundled LP cables is 192 or less and the selected ampacity of the cables in accordance with Table 725.144 exceeds the marked current limit of the cable, the ampacity determined from the table is permitted to be used. For ambient temperatures above 30°C, the correction factors of Table 310.15(B)(1)(1) or 310.15(B)(2) applies. The Class 2-LP cables must comply with the following, as applicable:

(1) Cables with the suffix "-LP" can be installed in bundles, raceways, cable trays, and communications raceways.

(2) Cables with the suffix "-LP" and a marked current limit must follow the substitution hierarchy of 722.1135(E) in the *NEC* for the cable type without the suffix "-LP" and without the marked current limit.

(3) System design is permitted by qualified persons under engineering supervision.

Note: An example of a limited-power (LP) cable is a cable marked Type CL2-LP 23 AWG 4-pair Class 2 cable rated 75°C with an LP current rating of 0.60A per conductor.

Notes

FIRE ALARM SYSTEMS

Introduction to Article 760—Fire Alarm Systems

This article covers the installation of wiring and equipment for fire alarm systems. It includes fire detection and alarm notification, voice, guard's tour, sprinkler waterflow, and sprinkler supervisory systems. Many of these rules are outside of the scope of this material, however, some of the topics we cover include the following:

- Scope
- Access to Electrical Equipment Behind Panels Designed to Allow Access
- Abandoned Cables
- Circuit Identification
- Supply-Side Overvoltage Protection
- Fire Alarm Circuit Requirements
- Wiring Methods
- Separation from Power Conductors

Part I. General

760.1 Scope

Article 760 covers the installation of circuit wiring and equipment for fire alarm systems. ▶**Figure 760–1**

▶**Figure 760–1**

According to Article 100, a "Fire Alarm Circuit" is the wiring connected to equipment powered and controlled by the fire alarm system. ▶**Figure 760–2**

Author's Comment:

- Residential smoke alarm systems, including interconnecting wiring, are not covered by Article 760 because they are not powered by a fire alarm system as defined in NFPA 72, *National Fire Alarm and Signaling Code*.

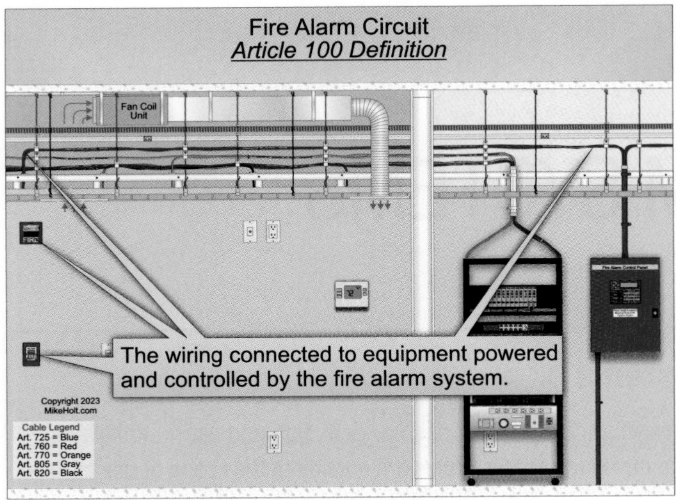

▶Figure 760–2

Note 1: Fire alarm systems include fire detection and alarm notification, guard's tour, sprinkler waterflow, and sprinkler supervisory systems. Other circuits that might be controlled or powered by the fire alarm system include building safety functions, elevator capture, elevator shutdown, door release, smoke doors and damper control, fire doors and damper control, and fan shutdown.

Note 2: NFPA 72, *National Fire Alarm and Signaling Code,* provides the requirements for the selection, installation, performance, use, testing, and maintenance of fire alarm systems. ▶**Figure 760–3**

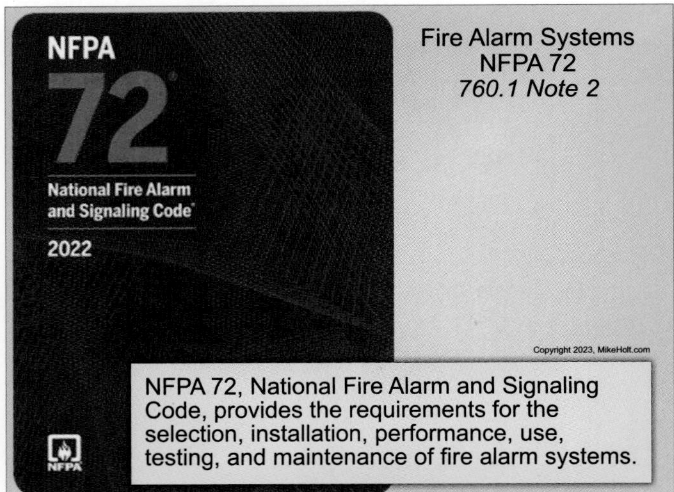

▶Figure 760–3

Author's Comment:

- Building control circuits associated with the fire alarm system, such as elevator capture and fan shutdown, must comply with Article 725 [760.3(D)]. Article 760 applies if these components are powered and directly controlled by the fire alarm system.
- NFPA 101, *Life Safety Code*, or the local building code specifies when and where a fire alarm system is required.

760.3 Other Articles

Fire alarm circuits and equipment must comply with 760.3(A) through (O). Only those sections contained in Article 300 specifically referenced below apply to fire alarm systems.

(A) Spread of Fire or Products of Combustion. Installation of fire alarm circuits must comply with 300.21. ▶**Figure 760–4**

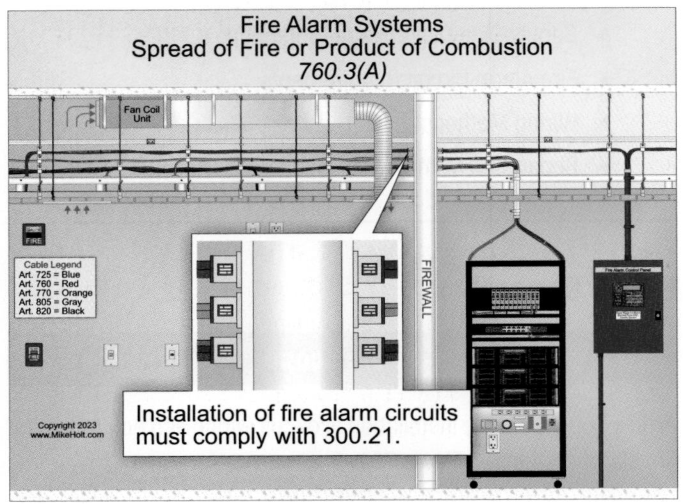

▶Figure 760–4

(B) Ducts and Plenum Spaces. Fire alarm cables installed in ducts or plenum spaces must comply with 300.22. ▶**Figure 760–5**

Ex 1: Power-limited fire alarm cables selected in accordance with Table 760.154 and installed in accordance with 760.135(B) and 300.22(B) Ex can be installed in ducts specifically fabricated for environmental air.

Ex 2: Power-limited fire alarm cables selected in accordance with Table 760.154 and installed in accordance with 760.135(C) can be installed in plenum spaces.

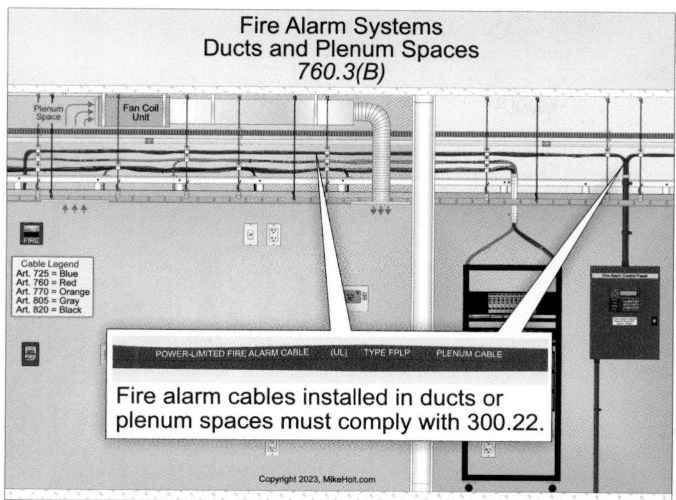

▸Figure 760–5

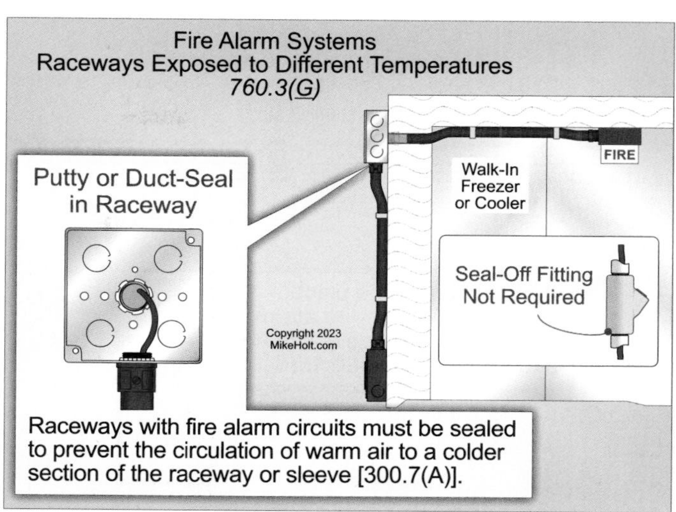

▸Figure 760–6

(C) Corrosive, Damp, or Wet Locations. Fire alarm circuits installed in corrosive, damp, or wet locations must be identified for use in the operating environment [110.11], must be of materials suitable for the environment in which they are to be installed, and must be of a type suitable for the application [300.5(B), 300.6, 300.9, and 310.10(F)].

(D) Building Control Circuits. Building control systems with Class 2 circuits (elevator capture, fan shutdown, and so on) associated with the fire alarm system, but not controlled and powered by the fire alarm system, must be installed in accordance with Article 725.

(G) Raceways or Sleeves Exposed to Different Temperatures. If a raceway or sleeve is subjected to different temperatures, and where condensation is known to be a problem, the raceway or sleeve must be filled with a material approved by the authority having jurisdiction that will prevent the circulation of warm air to a colder section of the sleeve or raceway in accordance with 300.7(A). ▸**Figure 760–6**

(I) Installation Cables in a Raceway. Raceways must be large enough to permit the installation and removal of cables without damaging conductor insulation [300.17]. ▸**Figure 760–7**

Author's Comment:

- When all conductors within a raceway are the same size and insulation, the number of conductors permitted can be found in Annex C for the raceway type.
- For conductors not included in Chapter 9 (such as multiconductor cable), the actual dimensions must be used. If one multiconductor cable is used inside a raceway the single-conductor percentage fill area must be used [Chapter 9, Notes to Tables, Note 5 and 9].

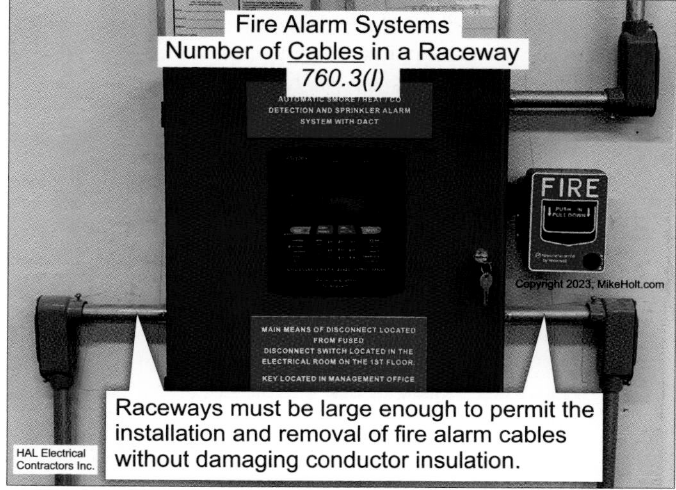

▸Figure 760–7

(J) Protective Bushing at Raceway. When a raceway is used for the support or protection of cables, a bushing is required to reduce the potential for abrasion and must be placed at the location the cables exit the raceway in accordance with 300.15(C). ▸**Figure 760–8**

(O) Cables for Power-Limited Fire Alarm (PLFA) Circuits. The listing and installation of cables for power-limited fire alarm circuits must comply with Part III of this article and Parts I and II of Article 722. ▸**Figure 760–9**

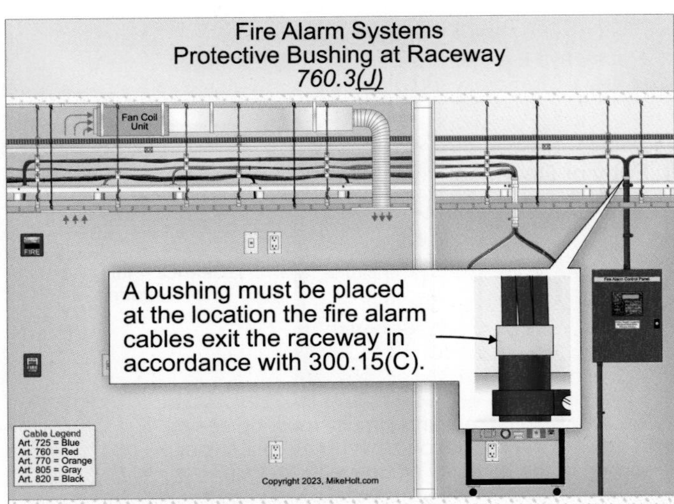

▸Figure 760–8

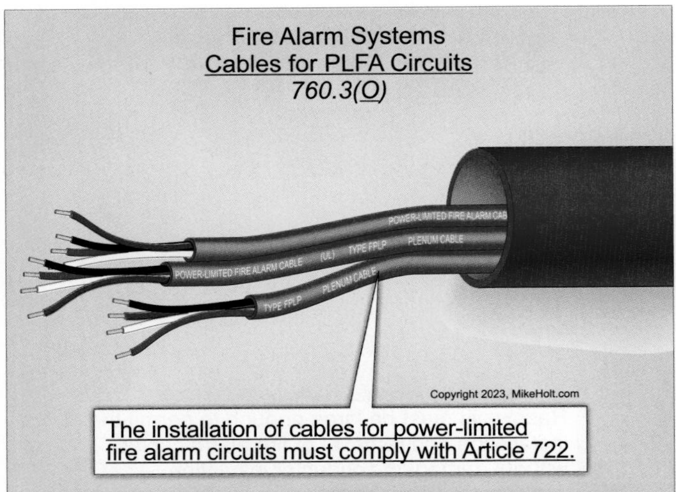

▸Figure 760–9

760.21 Access to Electrical Equipment Behind Panels Designed to Allow Access

Access to equipment cannot be prohibited by an accumulation of cables that prevents the removal of suspended-ceiling panels.

760.24 Mechanical Execution of Work

(A) General. Fire alarm circuits must be installed in a neat and workmanlike manner.

Cable Support. Exposed fire alarm cables must be supported by the structural components of the building so the cable(s) will not be damaged by normal building use. ▸**Figure 760–10**

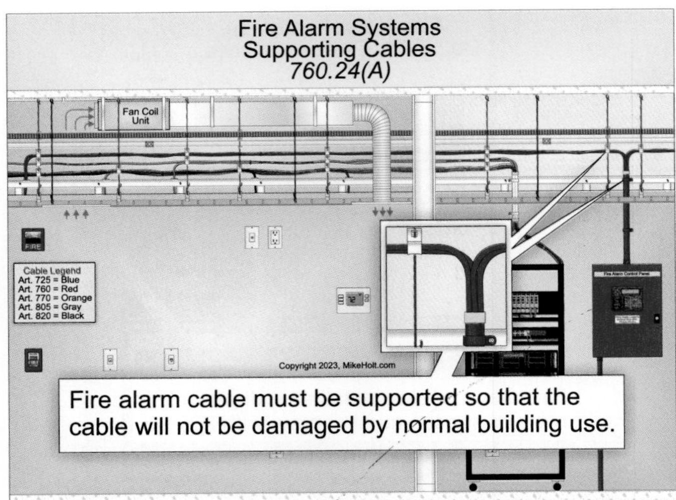

▸Figure 760–10

Cable Securement. Fire alarm cables must be secured by hardware including straps, staples, hangers, listed cable ties identified for securement and support, or similar fittings designed and installed in a manner that will not damage the cable. ▸**Figure 760–11**

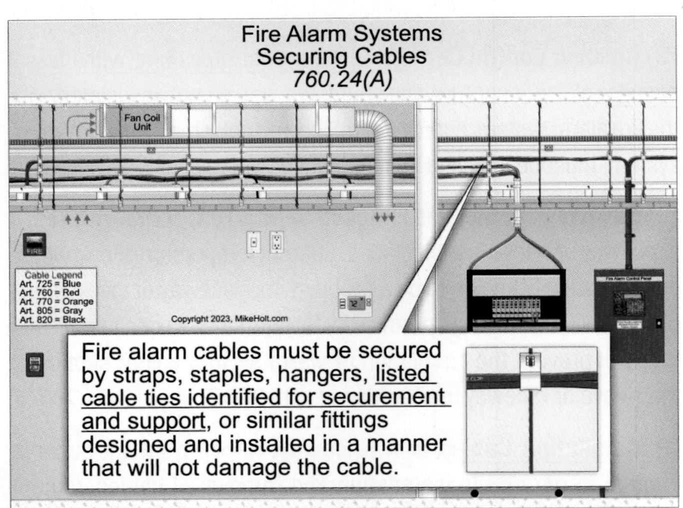

▸Figure 760–11

Protection From Physical Damage [300.4]. Fire alarm cables installed through or parallel to framing members or furring strips must be protected where they are likely to be penetrated by nails or screws by installing the wiring method so it is not less than 1¼ in. from the nearest edge of the framing member or furring strips, or by protecting it with a $\frac{1}{16}$ in. thick steel plate or equivalent [300.4(A) and (D)]. ▸**Figure 760–12**

1st Printing

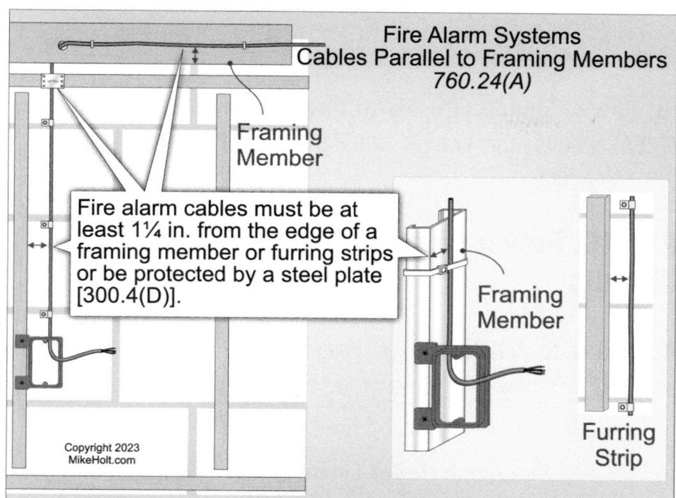

Fire Alarm Systems
Cables Parallel to Framing Members
760.24(A)
Framing Member
Fire alarm cables must be at least 1¼ in. from the edge of a framing member or furring strips or be protected by a steel plate [300.4(D)].
Framing Member
Furring Strip
Copyright 2023 MikeHolt.com

▸Figure 760-12

Securing and Supporting [300.11]. Ceiling-support wires or the ceiling grid is not permitted to support raceways or cables. Independent support wires secured at both ends can be used to support raceways or cables. Raceways and cables can be supported by independent support wires attached to the suspended ceiling in accordance with 300.11(B) [760.130(B)]. ▸**Figure 760-13**

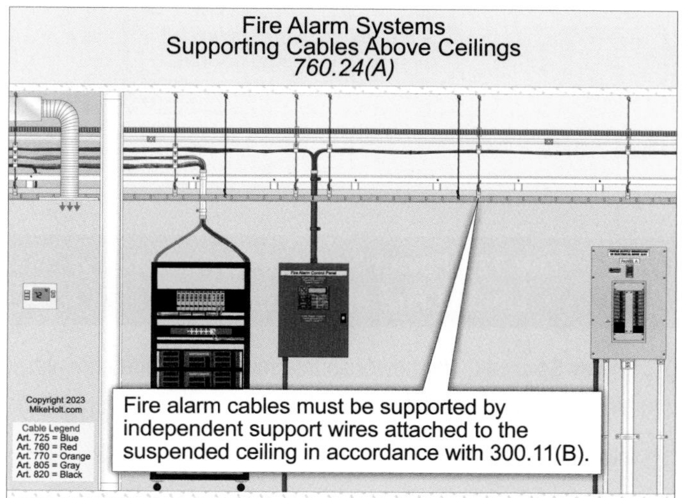

▸Figure 760-13

Note: Paint, plaster, cleaners, abrasives, corrosive residues, or other contaminants might result in an undetermined alteration of PLFA and NPLFA cable properties.

760.25 Abandoned Cables

To limit the spread of fire or products of combustion within a building, abandoned fire alarm cables must be removed. ▸**Figure 760-14**

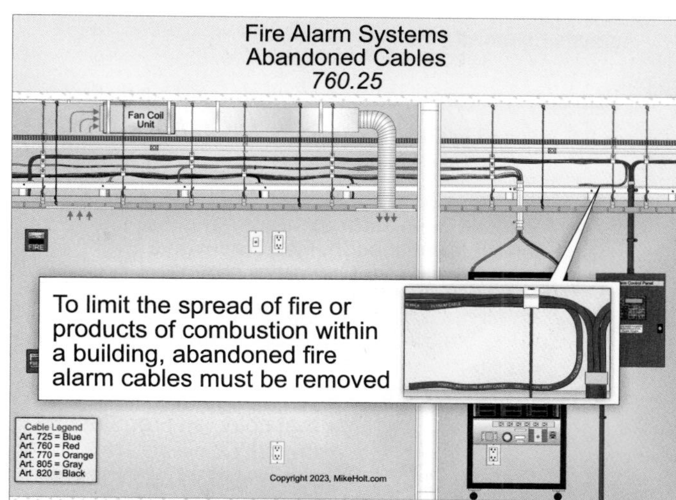

▸Figure 760-14

According to Article 100, "Abandoned Cable" is defined as a cable that is not terminated at equipment other than a termination fitting or a connector and is not identified for future use with a tag.

Where cables are identified for future use with a tag, the tag must be able to withstand the environment involved.

760.30 Fire Alarm Circuit Identification

Fire alarm circuits must be identified at terminal and junction boxes. ▸**Figure 760-15**

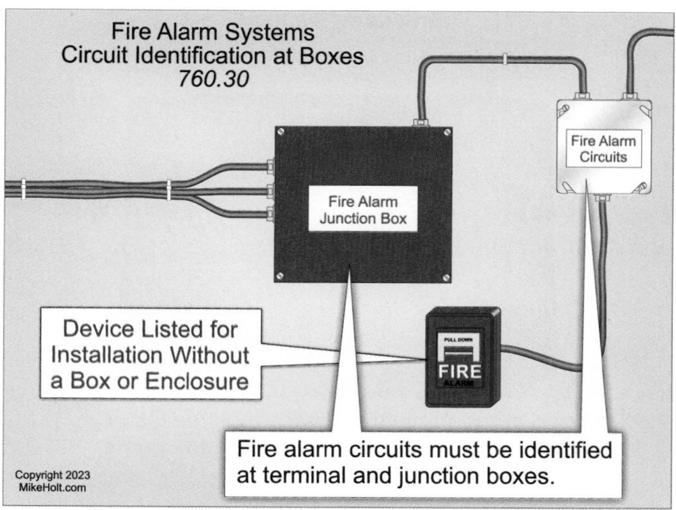

▸Figure 760-15

The identification must be in such a manner that will help to prevent unintentional signals on the fire alarm system circuits during testing and servicing of other systems.

Author's Comment:

- Red raceways and fittings are sometimes used, but that color is not required by the *NEC*. ▸**Figure 760–16**

▸**Figure 760–16**

760.33 Supply-Side Overvoltage Protection

A listed surge-protective device must be installed on the supply side of a fire alarm control panel in accordance with Part II of Article 242. ▸**Figure 760–17**

▸**Figure 760–17**

760.35 Fire Alarm Circuit Requirements

(B) Power-Limited Fire Alarm Circuits. Power-limited fire alarm (PLFA) circuits must comply with Parts I and III of this article.

Part III. Power-Limited Fire Alarm (PLFA) Circuits

According to Article 100, a "Power-Limited Fire Alarm" circuit is powered by a power-limited source. ▸**Figure 760–18**

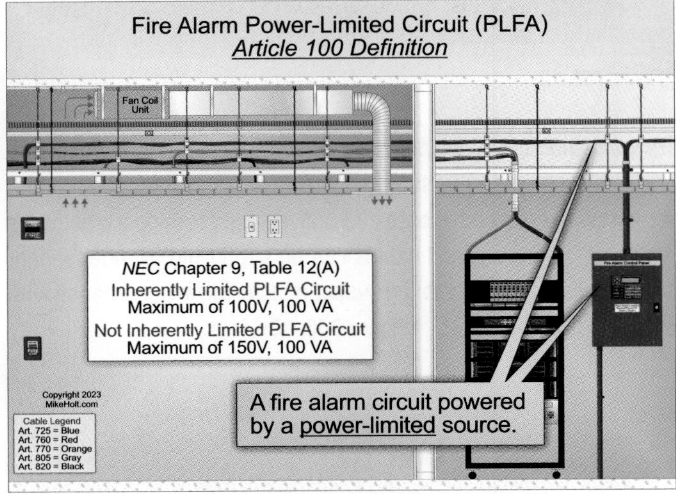

▸**Figure 760–18**

760.121 Power Sources for Power-Limited Fire Alarm Equipment

(A) Power Sources. The power source for power-limited fire alarm equipment must be one of the following:

(1) A listed PLFA transformer

(2) A listed PLFA power supply

(3) Listed equipment marked to identify the PLFA power source

(B) Branch Circuit. Power-limited fire alarm equipment must comply with the following: ▸**Figure 760–19**

(1) The branch circuit supplies no other loads.

(2) The branch circuit is not GFCI or AFCI protected.

1st Printing

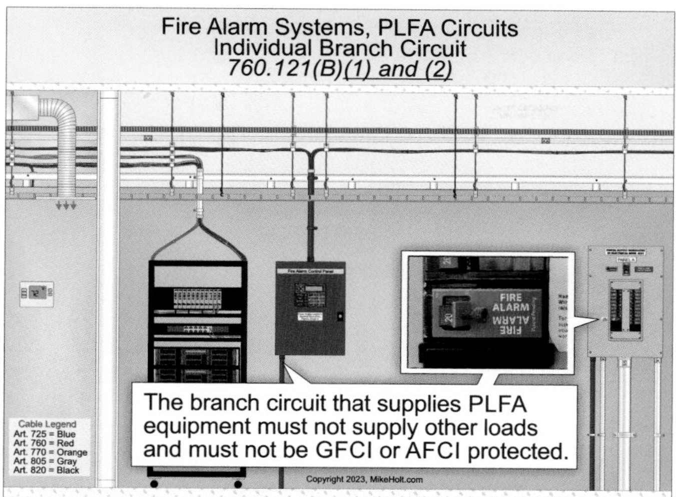

▸Figure 760–19

(3) The location of the branch-circuit overcurrent protective device for the power-limited fire alarm equipment must be identified at the fire alarm control unit. ▸Figure 760–20

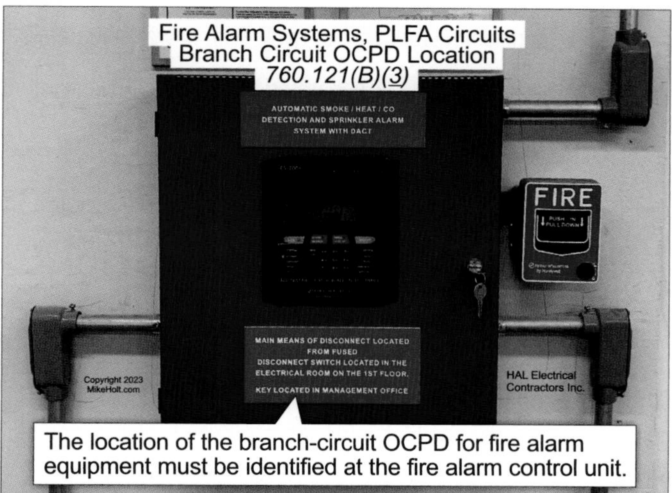

▸Figure 760–20

(4) The branch-circuit disconnect must be identified in red, be accessible only to qualified personnel, and be identified as the "FIRE ALARM CIRCUIT." The red identification must not damage the overcurrent protective device or obscure any manufacturer's markings. ▸Figure 760–21

(5) The fire alarm branch-circuit disconnect is permitted to be secured in the closed (on) position. ▸Figure 760–22

Note: GFCI protection is not required for receptacles in dwelling-unit unfinished basements that supply power for fire alarm systems. See 210.8(A)(5) Ex.

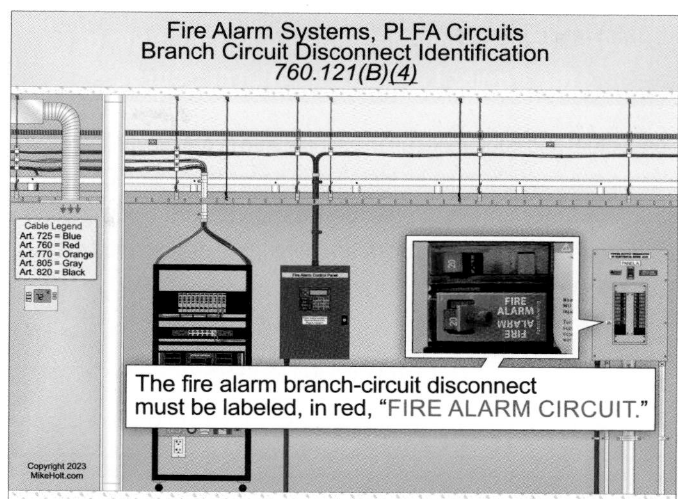

▸Figure 760–21

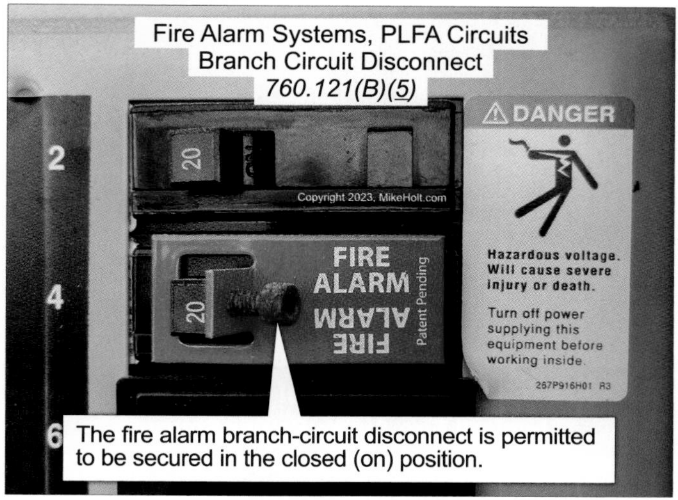

▸Figure 760–22

760.124 Marking

Fire alarm equipment supplying power-limited fire alarm cable circuits must be durably marked to indicate each circuit that is a power-limited fire alarm circuit.

760.127 Wiring Methods on Supply Side of the Power-Limited Fire Alarm Source

Conductors and equipment on the supply side of the power-limited fire alarm power supply must be installed in accordance with Chapters 1 through 4. Transformers or other devices supplied from power-supply conductors must be protected by an overcurrent device rated not over 20A. ▶**Figure 760–23**

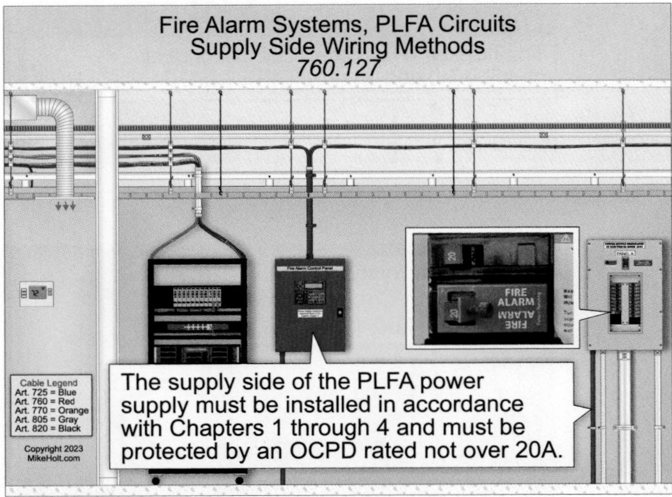

▶**Figure 760–23**

760.130 Load Side of the Power-Limited Fire Alarm Power Source

(B) PLFA Wiring Methods and Materials.

(1) Cable splices and terminations of power-limited fire alarm conductors must be made in listed fittings, boxes, enclosures, fire alarm devices, or utilization equipment [110.3(B) and 300.15]. ▶**Figure 760–24**

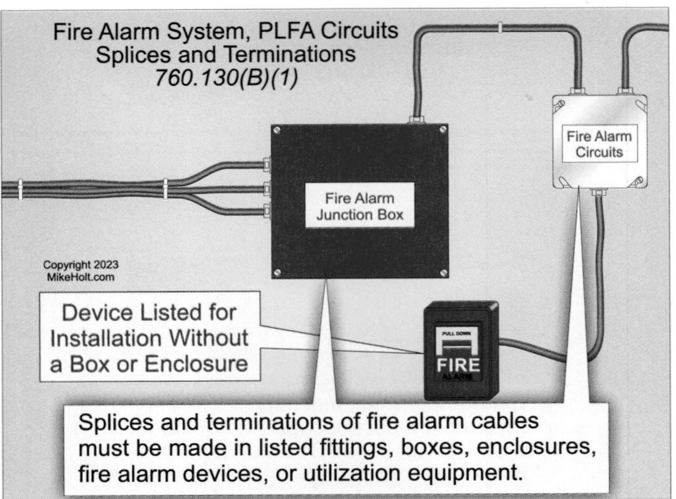

Fire Alarm System, PLFA Circuits
Splices and Terminations
760.130(B)(1)
Fire Alarm Circuits
Fire Alarm Junction Box
Copyright 2023
MikeHolt.com
Device Listed for Installation Without a Box or Enclosure
FIRE
Splices and terminations of fire alarm cables must be made in listed fittings, boxes, enclosures, fire alarm devices, or utilization equipment.

▶**Figure 760–24**

Where installed exposed, cables shall be adequately supported and installed such that maximum protection against physical damage is afforded. Where located within 7 ft of the floor, cables must be securely fastened in an approved manner at intervals of not more than 18 in.

(2) Passing Through a Floor or Wall. Cables shall be installed in metal raceways or rigid nonmetallic conduit where passing through a floor or wall to a height of 7 ft above the floor, unless adequate protection can be afforded by building construction such as detailed in 760.130(B)(1) or unless an equivalent solid guard is provided.

760.136 Separation from Power Conductors

(A) General. Power-limited fire alarm cables are not permitted to be placed in any enclosure, raceway, or cable with power conductors.

(B) Separated by Barriers. If separated by a barrier, power-limited fire alarm circuits are permitted with power conductors.

Author's Comment:

- Separation is required to prevent a fire or shock hazard that can occur from a short between the fire alarm circuit and the higher-voltage circuits.

(D) Associated Systems. Power-limited fire alarm conductors can be installed with power conductors where introduced solely to connect to equipment associated with power circuit conductors, and:

(1) A minimum of ¼ in. separation is maintained from the power-limited fire alarm conductors from the power conductors.

760.143 Support of PLFA Cables

Power-limited fire alarm cables are not permitted to be strapped, taped, or attached to the exterior of any raceway as a means of support. ▶**Figure 760–25**

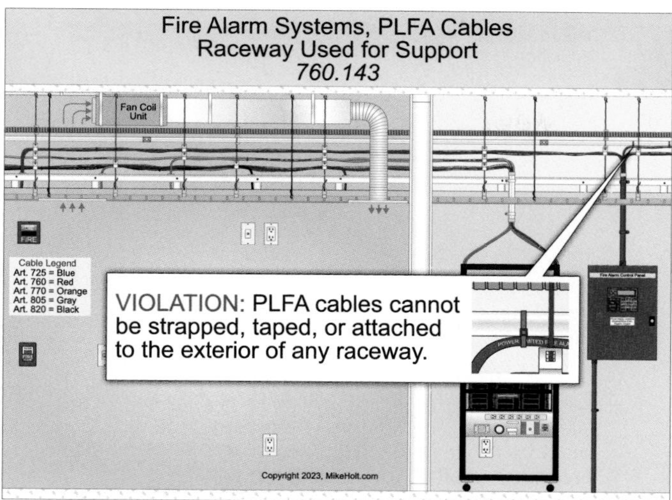
Fire Alarm Systems, PLFA Cables
Raceway Used for Support
760.143
Fan Coil Unit
Cable Legend
Art. 725 = Blue
Art. 760 = Red
Art. 770 = Orange
Art. 805 = Gray
Art. 820 = Black
VIOLATION: PLFA cables cannot be strapped, taped, or attached to the exterior of any raceway.
Copyright 2023, MikeHolt.com

▸**Figure 760–25**

OPTICAL FIBER CABLES

Introduction to Article 770—Optical Fiber Cables

Article 770 covers the installation of optical fiber cables which transmit signals using light. It also contains the installation requirements for raceways that contain optical fiber cables, and rules for composite cables (hybrid cables) that combine optical fibers with current-carrying metallic conductors. Many of these rules are outside of the scope of this material, however, some of the topics we cover include the following:

- Scope
- Access to Electrical Equipment Behind Panels Designed to Allow Access
- Abandoned Cable
- Spread of Fire or Products of Combustion
- Installation of Optical Fiber Cables and Electrical Conductors

Part I. General

770.1 Scope

Article 770 covers the installation of optical fiber cables but does not cover the construction of optical fiber cables. ▶**Figure 770–1**

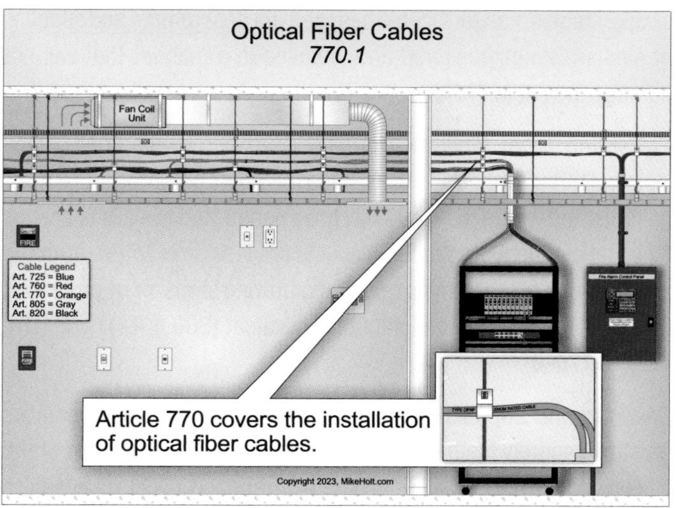

▶**Figure 770–1**

According to Article 100, an "Optical Fiber Cable" is an assembly of optical fibers having an overall covering. ▶**Figure 770–2**

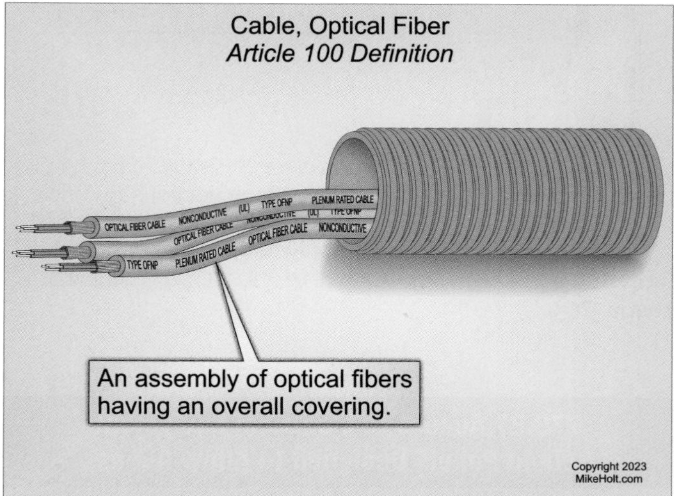

▶**Figure 770–2**

Note: A field-assembled optical fiber cable is an assembly of one or more optical fibers within a jacket. The jacket is installed like a raceway into which the optical fibers are inserted.

Author's Comment:

- The growth of high-tech applications and significant technological development of optical fibers and the equipment used to send and receive light pulses has increased the use of optical fibers. Since optical fiber cable is not affected by electromagnetic interference, there has been a large growth in its uses in voice, data transfer, data processing, and computer control of machines and processes.

770.3 Other Articles

Only those sections in Article 300 referenced in Article 770 apply to optical fiber cables.

Author's Comment:

- Article 770 does not reference 300.15, so boxes are not required for splices or terminations of optical fiber cable. ▸**Figure 770–3**

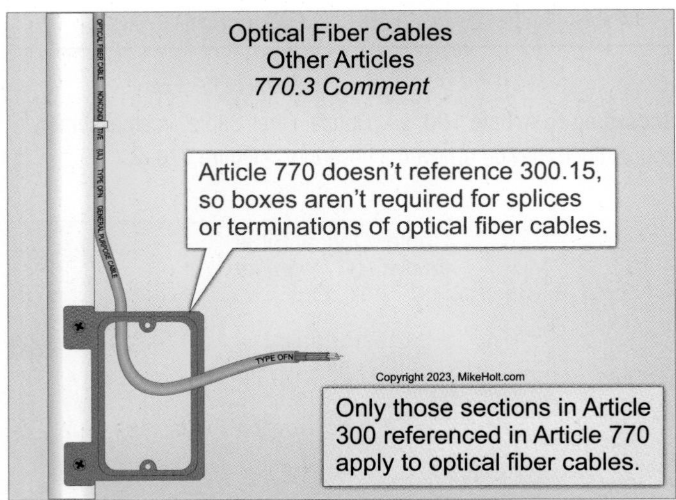

▸**Figure 770–3**

770.21 Access to Electrical Equipment Behind Panels Designed to Allow Access

Access to equipment is not permitted to be denied by an accumulation of optical fiber cables that prevents the removal of suspended-ceiling panels.

Author's Comment:

- Cables must be located so suspended-ceiling panels can be moved to provide access to electrical equipment.

770.24 Mechanical Execution of Work

(A) General. Optical fiber cables must be installed in a neat and workmanlike manner.

Cable Support, Damage. Exposed optical fiber cables must be supported by the structural components of the building so the cables will not be damaged by normal building use. ▸**Figure 770–4**

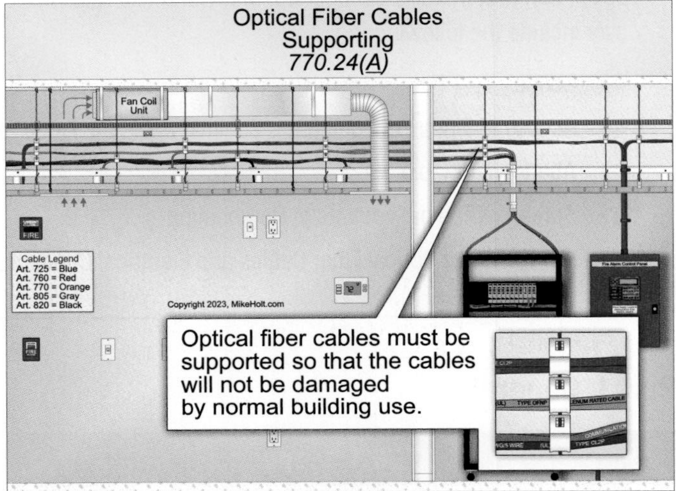

▸**Figure 770–4**

Cable Securement, Fitting. Optical fiber cable must be secured by straps, staples, hangers, cable ties listed for securement and support, or similar fittings designed and installed in a manner that will not damage the cable. ▸**Figure 770–5**

Protection From Physical Damage [300.4]. Optical fiber cables installed through or parallel to framing members or furring strips must be protected where they are likely to be penetrated by nails or screws by installing the wiring method so it is not less than 1¼ in. from the nearest edge of the framing member or furring strips, or by protecting it with a ¹⁄₁₆ in. thick steel plate or equivalent [300.4(A)(1) and (D)]. ▸**Figure 770–6**

Securing and Supporting [300.11]. Optical fiber cable assemblies must be securely fastened in place. The ceiling-support wires or the ceiling grid are not permitted to be used to support optical fiber cables [300.11(B)]. ▸**Figure 770–7**

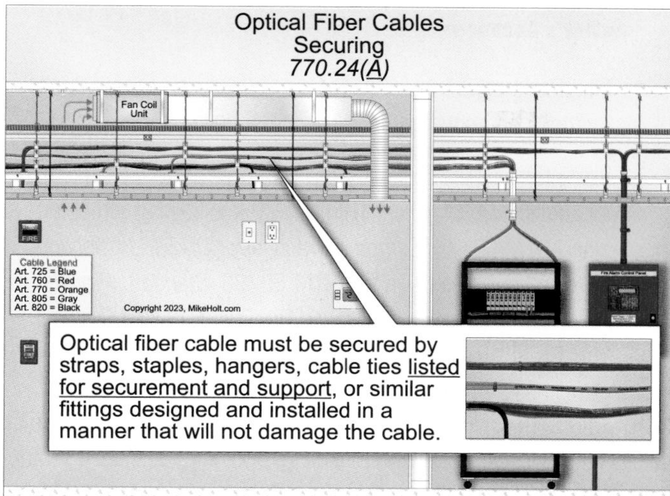

▶Figure 770–5

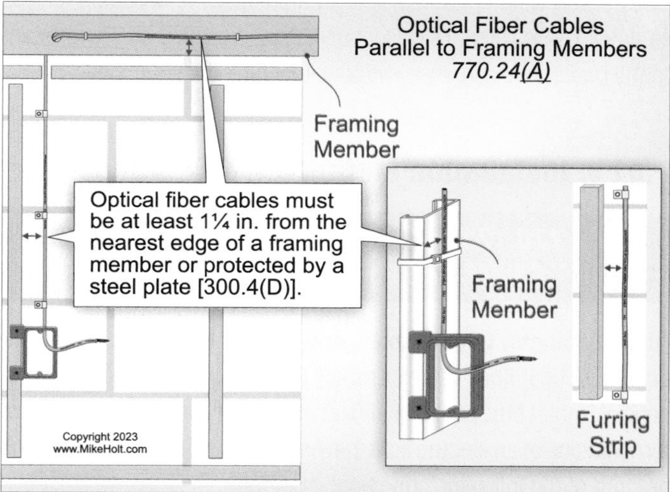

▶Figure 770–6

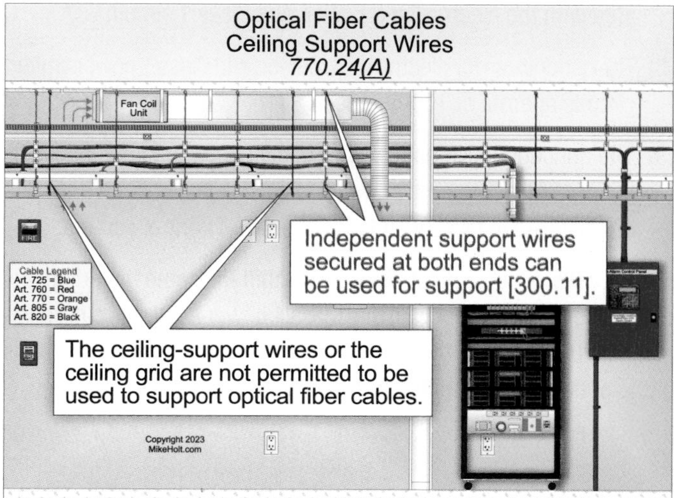

▶Figure 770–7

Cable Ties, Plenum Rated. Cable ties used to secure or support optical fiber cables in plenums must be listed for use in a plenum space in accordance with 800.170. ▶**Figure 770–8**

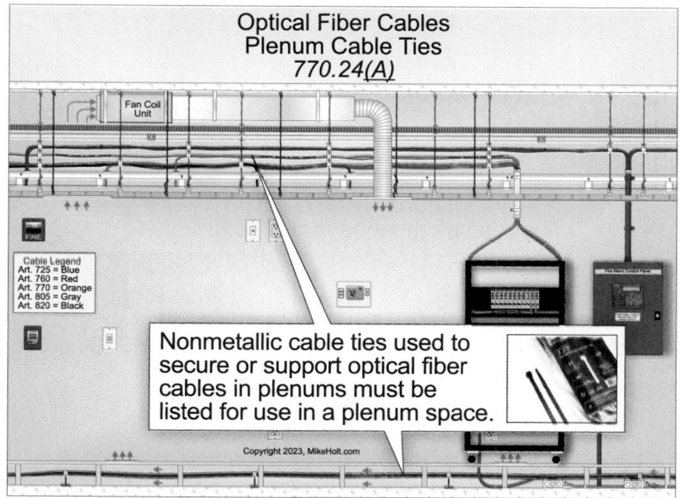

▶Figure 770–8

Note 1: Industry practices are described in ANSI/NECA/FOA 301, *Standard for Installing and Testing Fiber Optic Cables;* ANSI/TIA-568.0-D, *Generic Telecommunications Cabling for Customer Premises;* and ANSI/TIA 568.3-D, *Optical Fiber Cabling and Components Standard.*

Note 3: Paint, plaster, cleaners, abrasives, corrosive residues, or other contaminants can result in an undetermined alteration of optical fiber cable properties.

770.25 Abandoned Cable

To limit the spread of fire or products of combustion within a building, abandoned optical fiber cables must be removed. ▶**Figure 770–9**

Where cables are identified for future use with a tag, the tag must be able to withstand the environment involved. ▶**Figure 770–10**

770.26 Spread of Fire or Products of Combustion

Optical fiber cables must be installed in such a way that the spread of fire or products of combustion will not be substantially increased. Openings in fire-resistant-rated walls, floors, and ceilings for optical fiber cables must be firestopped using methods approved by the authority having jurisdiction to maintain the fire-resistance rating of the fire-resistive assembly. ▶**Figure 770–11**

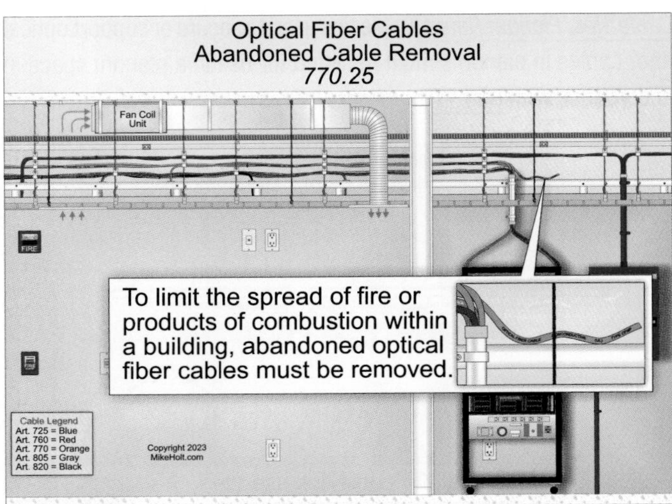

▸**Figure 770-9**

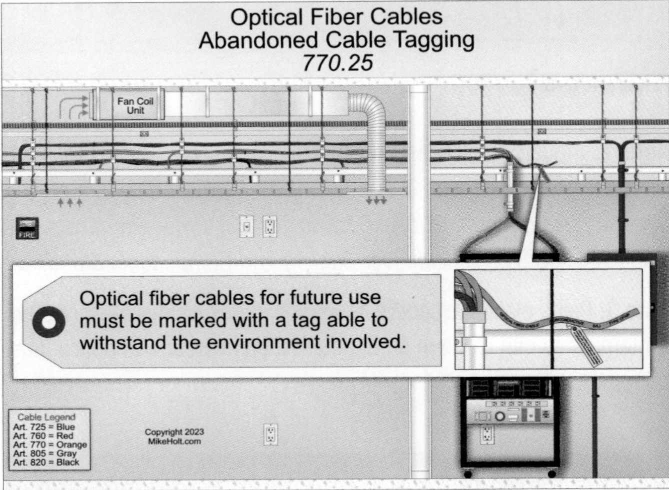

▸**Figure 770-10**

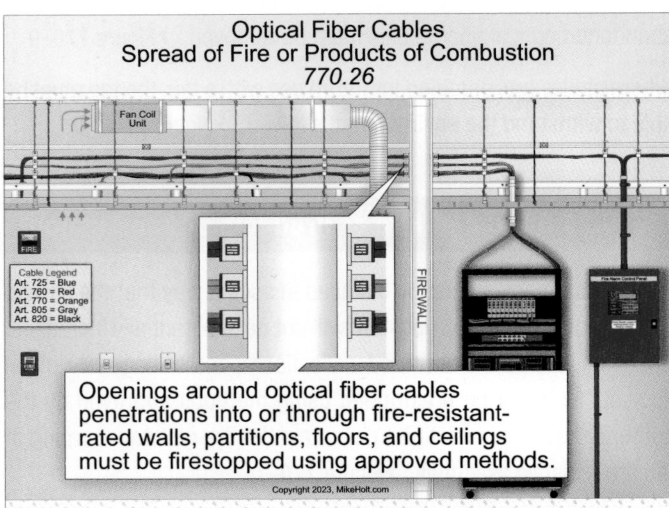

▸**Figure 770-11**

Author's Comment:

- Firestop material is listed for the specific types of wiring methods and construction structures.
- Visit International Firestop Council's website (www.firestop.org) for additional information on firestop system training complying with ASTM E2174, *Standard Practice for On-Site Inspection of Installed Firestops*, and ASTM E2393, *Standard Practice for On-Site Inspection of Installed Fire Resistive Joint Systems and Perimeter Fire Barriers.*

Note: Directories of electrical construction materials published by qualified testing laboratories contain many listing installation restrictions necessary to maintain the fire-resistive rating of assemblies. Outlet boxes must have a horizontal separation of not less than 24 in. when installed on opposites sides in a fire-resistive assembly, unless an outlet box is listed for closer spacing or protected by fire-resistant "putty pads" in accordance with manufacturer's instructions.

Part V. Installation Methods Within Buildings

770.133 Installation of Optical Fiber Cables and Electrical Conductors

(B) In Cabinets, Outlet Boxes, and Similar Enclosures. Nonconductive optical fiber cables are not permitted to occupy the same cabinet, outlet box, panel, or similar enclosure housing the electrical terminations of an electric light, power, and Class 1 circuit unless one or more of the following conditions exist:

(1) The nonconductive optical fiber cables are functionally associated with the electric light, power, and Class 1 circuit.

(2) The conductors for electric light, power, and Class 1 power-limited circuits operate at 1000V or less.

(3) The nonconductive optical fiber cables and the electrical terminations of electric light, power, and Class 1 power-limited circuits are installed in factory- or field-assembled control centers.

Same Cable. When optical fibers are within the same hybrid optical cable for electric light, power, and Class 1 power-limited circuits operating at 1000V or less, they can be installed only where the functions of the optical fibers and the electrical conductors are associated.

1st Printing

Same Raceway. Optical fibers in hybrid optical fiber cables containing only current-carrying conductors for electric light, power, or Class 1 power-limited circuits rated 1000V or less are permitted to occupy the same cabinet, cable tray, outlet box, panel, raceway, or other termination enclosure with conductors for electric light, power, or Class 1 power-limited circuits operating at 1000V or less.

Notes

CHAPTER 7

REVIEW QUESTIONS

Please use the 2023 *Code* book to answer the following questions.

ARTICLE 700—EMERGENCY SYSTEMS

1. Article _____ applies to the electrical safety of the installation, operation, and maintenance of emergency systems intended to supply, distribute, and control electricity for illumination, power, or both, to required facilities when the normal electrical supply or system is interrupted.

    (a) 500
    (b) 600
    (c) 700
    (d) 800

2. Emergency systems are generally installed in places of assembly where artificial illumination is required for safe exiting and for panic control in buildings subject to occupancy by large numbers of persons, such as _____ and similar institutions.

    (a) hotels
    (b) theaters and sports arenas
    (c) health care facilities
    (d) all of these

3. The _____ shall conduct or witness a test of the complete emergency system upon installation and periodically afterward.

    (a) electrical engineer
    (b) authority having jurisdiction
    (c) qualified person
    (d) manufacturer's representative

4. Emergency system equipment shall be maintained in accordance with _____.

    (a) the authority having jurisdiction
    (b) UL listing(s)
    (c) manufacturer instructions and industry standards
    (d) OSHA regulations

5. A _____ record shall be kept of required tests and maintenance on emergency systems.

    (a) written
    (b) typed
    (c) emailed
    (d) stored

6. An emergency system shall have adequate _____ in accordance with Article 220 or by another approved method.

    (a) lighting
    (b) capacity
    (c) voltage
    (d) power

7. An emergency system's capacity shall be sufficient for the _____ and transient power and energy requirements associated with any expected loads.

    (a) demand load current
    (b) rapid load changes
    (c) peak-demand current
    (d) shaved-load current

8. For emergency systems, transfer equipment shall be _____ for emergency use and approved by the authority having jurisdiction.
   (a) automatic
   (b) listed
   (c) marked
   (d) all of these

9. Automatic transfer switches for emergency systems shall be _____.
   (a) able to be remotely operated
   (b) able to be locked in the "closed" position
   (c) permitted to be reconditioned
   (d) electrically operated and mechanically held

10. An emergency transfer switch for emergency systems shall supply only _____.
   (a) emergency loads
   (b) computer equipment
   (c) UPS equipment
   (d) all of these

11. Where used for emergency systems, the short-circuit current rating of the transfer equipment, based on the specific overcurrent protective device type and settings protecting the transfer equipment, shall be field marked on the _____ of the transfer equipment.
   (a) exterior
   (b) top
   (c) interior
   (d) underside

12. In locations containing an emergency system, a _____ shall be placed at the service-entrance equipment indicating the type and location of each on-site emergency power source.
   (a) sign
   (b) label
   (c) marking
   (d) plaque

13. A listed _____ protective device shall be installed in or on all emergency systems switchgear, switchboards and panelboards.
   (a) surge
   (b) GFCI
   (c) AFCI
   (d) GFPE

14. Emergency circuits shall be permanently marked so they will be readily identified as a _____ of an emergency circuit or system.
   (a) segment
   (b) section
   (c) component
   (d) critical branch

15. All boxes and enclosures (including transfer switches, generators, and power panels) for emergency circuits shall be _____ marked as a component of an emergency circuit or system.
   (a) approved and
   (b) permanently
   (c) legibly
   (d) luminescent and

16. Wiring from an emergency source or emergency source distribution overcurrent protection to emergency loads shall be kept independent of all other wiring and equipment except in _____.
   (a) transfer equipment enclosures
   (b) exit or emergency luminaires supplied from two sources
   (c) listed load control relays supplying exit or emergency luminaires, or a common junction box, attached to exit or emergency luminaires supplied from two sources
   (d) all of these

17. Emergency circuit wiring power sources, such as a generator or multiple integral overcurrent protective devices shall each be permitted to supply a designated emergency or a designated nonemergency load, provided that there is complete _____ between emergency and nonemergency loads.
   (a) labeling
   (b) distinction
   (c) separation
   (d) identification

18. If wiring from an emergency source is used to supply emergency and other loads, then _____ switchgear sections or switchboard sections, with or without a common bus, or individual disconnects mounted in separate enclosures shall be used to separate emergency loads from all other loads.
   (a) separate vertical
   (b) separate horizontal
   (c) combined vertical and horizontal
   (d) identified

19. Wiring from an emergency source to supply emergency and other (nonemergency) loads shall be permitted if the common bus of separate sections of the switchgear, separate sections of the switchboard, or the individual enclosures are supplied by single or multiple feeders with or without _____.

    (a) overcurrent protection at the source
    (b) ground-fault protection at the source
    (c) a current-limiting device at the source
    (d) load-shaving monitoring

20. Emergency systems circuit wiring shall be designed and located to minimize the hazards that might cause failure because of _____.

    (a) flooding
    (b) fire
    (c) icing
    (d) all of these

21. Line voltage supply wiring and installation of _____ emergency lighting control devices shall comply with 700.10 while Class 2 emergency circuits shall comply with 700.11(B) through (D).

    (a) Class 1
    (b) Class 2
    (c) Class 3
    (d) Class 4

22. All boxes and enclosures for _____ emergency circuits shall be permanently marked as a component of an emergency circuit or system unless the intent of such circuits is obvious.

    (a) Class 1
    (b) Class 2
    (c) Class 3
    (d) Class 4

23. Exposed cable, cable tray, or raceway systems shall be permanently marked to be identified as a component of an emergency circuit or system within _____ of each connector.

    (a) 12 in.
    (b) 18 in.
    (c) 2 ft
    (d) 3 ft

24. If installed alongside nonemergency Class 2 circuits that are bundled, Class 2 emergency circuits shall be _____ separately.

    (a) tagged
    (b) color-coded
    (c) bundled
    (d) labeled

25. Wiring of Class 2 emergency circuits shall comply with the requirements of 300.4 and be installed in a(an) _____.

    (a) raceway
    (b) armored-cable or metal-clad cable
    (c) cable tray
    (d) any of these

26. Wiring protection requirements for Class 2 emergency circuits shall not apply to wiring that do not exceed _____ in length and that terminate at an emergency luminaire or an emergency lighting control device

    (a) 2 ft
    (b) 3 ft
    (c) 4 ft
    (d) 6 ft

27. Wiring protection requirements for Class 2 emergency circuits shall not apply to locked rooms or locked enclosures that are accessible only to _____.

    (a) qualified persons
    (b) staff
    (c) maintenance personnel
    (d) licensed individuals

28. Emergency system sources of power shall be such that, in the event of failure of the normal supply to, or within, the building or group of buildings concerned, emergency lighting, emergency power, or both shall be available within the time required for the application but not to exceed _____.

    (a) 5 seconds
    (b) 10 seconds
    (c) 30 seconds
    (d) 60 seconds

29. Emergency equipment for emergency systems shall be _____ and located so as to minimize the hazards that might cause complete failure due to flooding, fires, icing, and vandalism.
    (a) approved
    (b) listed
    (c) installed
    (d) designed

30. The emergency power source shall be of suitable rating and capacity to supply and maintain the total load for the duration determined by the system design and in no case shall the duration be less than _____ of system operation unless used for emergency illumination in 700.12(C)(4) or unit equipment in 700.12(H).
    (a) 1 hour
    (b) 1½ hour
    (c) 2 hours
    (d) 3 hours

31. Storage batteries and UPS used to supply emergency illumination shall maintain the total load for a minimum period of _____, without the voltage applied to the load falling below 87½ percent of nominal voltage.
    (a) 1 hour
    (b) 1½ hour
    (c) 2 hours
    (d) 2½ hours

32. Battery-equipped emergency luminaires shall be on the same branch circuit that serves the normal lighting in the area and connected _____ any local switches.
    (a) with
    (b) ahead of
    (c) after
    (d) downstream of

33. Battery-equipped emergency luminaires shall be on the same or a different branch circuit as that serving the normal lighting in the area if that circuit is equipped with means to _____ the status of that area's normal lighting branch circuit ahead of any local switches.
    (a) alert to
    (b) indicate
    (c) monitor
    (d) react to

34. In emergency systems, no appliances or lamps, other than those specified as required for emergency use, shall be supplied by _____.
    (a) emergency lighting circuits
    (b) multiwire branch circuits
    (c) HID-rated circuit breakers
    (d) only load-shaved circuits

35. Emergency lighting systems shall be designed and _____ so that the failure of any illumination source cannot leave in total darkness any space that requires emergency illumination.
    (a) installed
    (b) listed
    (c) inspected
    (d) labeled

36. The emergency system branch circuit serving emergency lighting and power circuits shall be permitted to be part of a multiwire branch circuit.
    (a) True
    (b) False

37. Emergency system(s) overcurrent protective devices shall be selectively coordinated with all _____ overcurrent protective devices.
    (a) supply-side
    (b) load-side only
    (c) downstream
    (d) reconditioned

38. Where emergency system(s) OCPDs are replaced, they shall be _____ to ensure selective coordination is maintained with all supply-side and load-side OCPDs.
    (a) inspected
    (b) identified
    (c) re-evaluated
    (d) arranged

39. Where _____ to the emergency system(s) occur, selective coordination of the emergency system(s) OCPDs with all supply-side and load-side OCPDs shall be re-evaluated.
    (a) modifications
    (b) additions
    (c) deletions
    (d) any of these

ARTICLE 701—LEGALLY REQUIRED STANDBY SYSTEMS

1. Article 701 applies to the electrical safety of the installation, operation, and maintenance of _____ systems.

    (a) emergency
    (b) legally required standby
    (c) optional standby
    (d) dwelling-unit standby

2. The branch-circuit overcurrent devices in legally required standby system circuits shall be accessible only to _____.

    (a) the authority having jurisdiction
    (b) authorized persons
    (c) the general public
    (d) qualified persons

3. The _____ shall conduct or witness the commissioning of the complete legally required standby system upon installation.

    (a) electrical engineer
    (b) authority having jurisdiction
    (c) qualified person
    (d) manufacturer's representative

4. Legally required standby systems shall be tested _____ on a schedule and in a manner approved by the authority having jurisdiction to ensure the systems are maintained in proper operating condition.

    (a) monthly
    (b) quarterly
    (c) annually
    (d) periodically

5. Legally required standby system equipment shall be maintained in accordance with _____.

    (a) UL listing(s)
    (b) local emergency services requirements
    (c) manufacturer instructions and industry standards
    (d) local jurisdictional requirements

6. A _____ record shall be kept of required tests and maintenance on legally required standby systems.

    (a) written
    (b) typed
    (c) emailed
    (d) stored

7. Legally required standby system equipment shall be suitable for _____ at its terminals.

    (a) the available fault current
    (b) the maximum overload current only
    (c) the minimum fault current
    (d) a one-hour rating

8. A legally required standby system shall have adequate capacity in accordance with Article _____ or by another approved method.

    (a) 210
    (b) 220
    (c) 230
    (d) 700

9. Transfer equipment for legally required standby systems shall be _____.

    (a) automatic
    (b) listed
    (c) marked for emergency system or legally required standby use
    (d) all of these

10. Automatic transfer switches on legally required standby systems shall be electrically operated and _____ held.

    (a) electrically
    (b) mechanically
    (c) gravity
    (d) any of these

11. Where used for legally required standby systems, the short-circuit current rating of the transfer equipment, based on the specific overcurrent protective device type and settings protecting the transfer equipment, shall be field marked on the _____ of the transfer equipment.

    (a) exterior
    (b) top
    (c) interior
    (d) underside

12. Audible and visual signal devices shall be provided, where practicable, for legally required standby systems to indicate _____.

    (a) a malfunction of the standby source
    (b) that the standby source is carrying load
    (c) that the battery charger is not functioning
    (d) all of these

13. A sign shall be placed at the service entrance indicating the _____ of each on-site legally required standby power source.
    (a) capacity
    (b) date of last testing
    (c) manufacturer
    (d) type and location

14. Legally required standby system wiring can occupy the same raceways, cables, boxes, and cabinets with other general-purpose wiring.
    (a) True
    (b) False

15. Where a legally required standby source of power is installed, the transition time from the instant of failure of the normal power source to the emergency generator source shall not exceed _____.
    (a) 10 seconds
    (b) 20 seconds
    (c) 30 seconds
    (d) 60 seconds

16. Where approved by the authority having jurisdiction, connections ahead of and not within the same cabinet, enclosure, vertical switchgear section, or vertical switchboard section as the _____ disconnecting means shall be permitted for legally required standby systems.
    (a) emergency
    (b) service
    (c) optional
    (d) all of these

17. Legally required standby system overcurrent protective devices (OCPDs) shall be _____ with all supply-side and load-side OCPDs.
    (a) series rated
    (b) selectively coordinated
    (c) installed in parallel
    (d) labeled in accordance

18. Where legally required standby system OCPDs are replaced, they shall be _____ to ensure selective coordination is maintained with all supply-side and load-side OCPDs.
    (a) inspected
    (b) identified
    (c) re-evaluated
    (d) arranged

19. Where _____ to legally required standby systems occur, selective coordination of the legally required standby system OCPDs with all supply-side and load-side OCPDs shall be re-evaluated.
    (a) modifications
    (b) additions
    (c) deletions
    (d) any of these

ARTICLE 702—OPTIONAL STANDBY SYSTEMS

1. Article 702 applies to _____ optional standby systems.
   (a) temporarily installed
   (b) portable
   (c) readily accessible
   (d) the installation and operation of

2. Optional standby system wiring is permitted to occupy the same _____ with other general wiring.
   (a) raceways
   (b) cables
   (c) boxes and cabinets
   (d) all of these

3. If the connection of load is manual or nonautomatic, an optional standby system shall have adequate _____ for the supply of all equipment intended to be operated at one time.
   (a) ventilation
   (b) supervision
   (c) fuel supply
   (d) capacity and rating

4. Manual and nonautomatic transfer equipment for optional standby systems require _____ intervention.
   (a) human
   (b) animal
   (c) electrician
   (d) inspector

5. Where automatic transfer equipment is used, an optional standby system shall be capable of supplying _____.
   (a) the full load that is automatically connected
   (b) all equipment where life safety is dependent
   (c) all emergency and egress lighting
   (d) all fire and security systems

6. Optional standby system interconnection or transfer equipment shall be designed and installed so as to prevent the inadvertent interconnection of _____ of supply in any operation of the equipment.
   (a) the normal source
   (b) the standby source
   (c) all sources
   (d) none of these

7. Meter-mounted optional standby system transfer switches installed between the _____ and the meter enclosure shall be listed meter-mounted transfer switches.
   (a) service connection point
   (b) utility meter
   (c) utility transformer
   (d) cold sequence disconnect

8. A sign shall be placed at the service-entrance equipment for other than one- and two-family dwellings that indicates the _____ of each on-site optional standby power source.
   (a) installer
   (b) date of installation
   (c) date of last testing
   (d) type and location

9. For _____ dwelling units, a sign shall be placed at the disconnecting means required in 230.85 that indicates the location of each permanently installed on-site optional standby power source disconnect or means to shut down the prime mover as required in 445.19(C).
   (a) apartment
   (b) guest suite
   (c) multi-family
   (d) one- and two-family

10. Where a power inlet is used for an optional standby system's temporary connection to a portable generator, a warning sign shall be placed near the inlet to indicate the _____ that the system is capable of, based on the wiring of the transfer equipment.
   (a) type of fuel supply
   (b) type of derived system
   (c) type of GFCI protection
   (d) temporary power supply time

11. For optional standby purposes, a portable generator rated 15 kW or less is installed using a flanged inlet or other cord-and-plug-type connection, the flanged inlet or other cord-and-plug-type connection shall be located _____ of a building or structure.
   (a) outside
   (b) inside
   (c) outside or inside
   (d) none of these

ARTICLE 705—INTERCONNECTED ELECTRIC POWER PRODUCTION SOURCES

1. Article 705 covers the installation of one or more electric power production sources operating in parallel with a(an) _____ source(s) of electricity.
   (a) secondary
   (b) alternate
   (c) primary
   (d) stand-alone

2. The output of interactive electric power production sources equipment shall be _____ disconnected from all ungrounded conductors of the primary source when one or more of the phases of the primary source to which it is connected opens.
   (a) manually
   (b) automatically
   (c) manually or automatically
   (d) manually and automatically

3. Interconnected electric power production sources microgrid systems shall be capable of operating in interactive mode with a primary source of power, or electric utility, or other electric power production and distribution network and shall be permitted to disconnect from other sources and operate in _____ mode.
   (a) automated
   (b) emergency
   (c) isolated
   (d) island

4. Interconnection and interactive equipment intended to connect to or operate in parallel with power production sources shall be listed for the required interactive function or be _____ for the interactive function and have a field label applied, or both.

   (a) tested
   (b) evaluated
   (c) approved
   (d) licensed

5. Installations of one or more interconnected electrical power production sources operating in parallel with a primary source(s) of electricity shall be performed only by _____.

   (a) qualified persons
   (b) utility company persons
   (c) the authority having jurisdiction
   (d) utility company persons or the authority having jurisdiction

6. For interconnected electric power production source(s), a permanent _____, denoting the location of each power source disconnecting means for the building or structure, shall be installed at each service equipment location or at an approved readily visible location.

   (a) label
   (b) plaque
   (c) directory
   (d) any of these

7. Interconnected power production installations with multiple co-located power production sources shall be permitted to be _____ as a group(s).

   (a) identified
   (b) labeled
   (c) marked
   (d) all of these

8. Interconnected electric power production source(s) are permitted to be connected to the _____ side of the service disconnecting means in accordance with 230.82(6).

   (a) line
   (b) supply
   (c) source
   (d) any of these

9. For interconnected electric power production sources connected to a service, the ampacity of the _____ connected to the power production source service disconnecting means shall not be less than the sum of the power production source maximum circuit current in 705.28(A).

   (a) service conductors
   (b) power production source output current
   (c) service disconnect rating
   (d) sum of all overcurrent protective devices

10. For interconnected electric power production source(s) connected to a service, the service conductors connected to the power production source service disconnecting means shall be sized in accordance with 705.28 and not be smaller than _____ copper.

   (a) 8 AWG
   (b) 6 AWG
   (c) 4 AWG
   (d) 3 AWG

11. A disconnecting means in accordance with Parts VI through VIII of Article 230 shall be provided to _____ all ungrounded conductors of an interconnected electric power production source from the conductors of other systems.

   (a) coordinate
   (b) disconnect
   (c) protect
   (d) all of these

12. Interconnected electric power production source metal enclosures, metal wiring methods, and metal parts associated with the service connected to a power production source shall be _____ in accordance with Parts II through V and VIII of Article 250.

   (a) installed
   (b) grounded
   (c) bonded
   (d) protected

13. The rating of the overcurrent protective device of the interconnected electric power production source service disconnecting means shall be used to determine if _____ is required in accordance with 230.95.

   (a) ground-fault protection of equipment
   (b) arc-fault protection
   (c) surge protection
   (d) lightning protection

14. The output of an interconnected electric power source shall be permitted to be connected to the _____ side of the service disconnecting means of the other source(s) at any distribution equipment on the premises.
    (a) load
    (b) bottom
    (c) top
    (d) line

15. Where the interconnected electric power production source output connection is made to a feeder at a location other than the opposite end of the feeder from the primary source overcurrent device, that portion of the feeder on the load side of the power source output connection shall be protected by a(an) _____.
    (a) feeder ampacity not less than the sum of the primary source overcurrent device and 125 percent of the power source output circuit current
    (b) overcurrent device at the load side of the power source connection point rated not greater than the ampacity of the feeder
    (c) feeder ampacity not less than the sum of the primary source overcurrent device and 125 percent of the power source output circuit current, or an overcurrent device at the load side of the power source connection point rated not greater than the ampacity of the feeder
    (d) none of these

16. Where interconnected electric power production source output connections are made at busbars, the sum of _____ of the power source(s) output circuit current and the rating of the overcurrent device protecting the busbar shall not exceed the busbar ampere rating.
    (a) 100 percent
    (b) 110 percent
    (c) 115 percent
    (d) 125 percent

17. Where two interconnected electric power production sources are located at opposite ends of a busbar that contains loads, the sum of 125 percent of the power-source(s) output circuit current and the rating of the overcurrent device protecting the busbar shall not exceed _____ of the busbar ampere rating.
    (a) 100 percent
    (b) 115 percent
    (c) 120 percent
    (d) 125 percent

18. When determining the ampere rating of busbars associated with load-side source connections of interconnected electric power production sources, one can use the sum of the ampere ratings of all overcurrent devices on _____, both load and supply devices, excluding the rating of the overcurrent device protecting the busbar, but shall not exceed the ampacity of the busbar.
    (a) metering equipment
    (b) panelboards
    (c) switchgear
    (d) all of these

19. Where interconnected electric power production source output connections are made at either end of a _____ panelboard in dwellings, it shall be permitted where the sum of 125 percent of the power-source(s) output circuit current and the rating of the overcurrent device protecting the busbar does not exceed 120 percent of the busbar ampere rating.
    (a) front-fed
    (b) back-fed
    (c) center-fed
    (d) none of these

20. Interconnected electric power production source connections shall be permitted on busbars of panelboards that supply _____ connected to feed-through conductors.
    (a) power distribution blocks
    (b) terminals
    (c) lugs
    (d) none of these

21. An emergency management system (EMS), in accordance with 705.30, shall be permitted to limit current and loading on the busbars and conductors supplied by the output of one or more interconnected electric power production sources or _____ sources.
    (a) utility power
    (b) energy storage
    (c) stand-alone power
    (d) all of these

22. Means shall be provided to disconnect power source output circuit conductors of interconnected electric power production source equipment from conductors of other systems. The disconnecting means shall be a _____.

    (a) manually operable switch or circuit breaker
    (b) load-break-rated pull-out switch
    (c) device listed or approved for the intended application
    (d) any of these

23. Wiring methods and fittings _____ for use with interconnected electric power production source systems shall be permitted in addition to the general wiring methods and fittings permitted elsewhere in this Code.

    (a) marked
    (b) labeled
    (c) identified
    (d) listed

24. Fused disconnects at interconnected electric power production source output connections are considered suitable for _____ unless otherwise marked.

    (a) backfeed
    (b) current limiting
    (c) current adjustment
    (d) slash rating

25. Listed plug-in-type circuit breakers backfed from interconnected electric power production sources that are listed and identified as _____ shall not require a fastener as required by 408.36(D).

    (a) interactive
    (b) active
    (c) reactive
    (d) interactive or active

26. In accordance with Article 705, for the purpose of overcurrent protection, the primary side of transformers with sources on each side shall be the side connected to the largest source of _____ current.

    (a) available fault
    (b) short-circuit
    (c) output power source
    (d) available fault current or short-circuit

27. For interconnected electric power production sources systems, risks to personnel and equipment associated with the primary source could occur if an interactive electric power production source can operate as an intentional _____.

    (a) island
    (b) power production system
    (c) primary source of power
    (d) none of these

28. For interconnected electric power production source system(s), single-phase power sources in interactive systems shall be connected to three-phase power systems in order to limit unbalanced voltages at the point of interconnection to not more than _____.

    (a) 2 percent
    (b) 3 percent
    (c) 5 percent
    (d) 10 percent

ARTICLE 706—ENERGY STORAGE SYSTEMS

1. Article 706 applies to all energy storage systems (ESS) having a capacity greater than _____ that may be stand-alone or interactive with other electric power production sources.

    (a) 1 kWh
    (b) 2 kWh
    (c) 5 kWh
    (d) 10 kWh

2. The installation and maintenance of energy storage system (ESS) equipment and all associated wiring and interconnections shall be performed only by _____.

    (a) qualified persons
    (b) ESS specialists
    (c) licensed electricians
    (d) maintenance personnel

3. Each energy storage system (ESS) shall be provided with a nameplate plainly visible after installation and marked with the _____.

    (a) rated frequency
    (b) number of phases (if ac)
    (c) rating in kW or kVA
    (d) all of these

4. Energy storage systems shall be _____.
   - (a) labeled
   - (b) identified for their use
   - (c) listed
   - (d) classified

5. Means shall be provided to _____ the energy storage system (ESS) from all wiring systems, including other power systems, utilization equipment, and its associated premises wiring
   - (a) disconnect
   - (b) shut down
   - (c) turn off
   - (d) eliminate

6. The disconnecting means for energy storage systems (ESS) shall be readily accessible and shall be located within sight and within _____ from the ESS.
   - (a) 3 ft
   - (b) 5 ft
   - (c) 10 ft
   - (d) 25 ft

7. Where the disconnecting means for energy storage systems cannot be located within sight of the ESS, the disconnecting means, or the enclosure providing access to the disconnecting means, shall be capable of being _____ in accordance with 110.25.
   - (a) locked
   - (b) labeled
   - (c) installed remotely
   - (d) identified

8. In cases where the battery is separate from the energy storage system (ESS) electronics, the batteries could include an enclosure, battery monitoring and controls, or other related battery components.
   - (a) True
   - (b) False

9. In cases where the battery is separate from the energy storage system (ESS) electronics and is subject to field servicing, a disconnecting means shall be readily accessible and located _____ the battery.
   - (a) adjacent to
   - (b) within 3 ft of
   - (c) within sight of
   - (d) within 25 ft of

10. For required notification and marking purposes for energy storage systems (ESS) for available fault current derived from the stationary battery system, _____ can provide information about available fault current on any particular battery model.
    - (a) UL listings
    - (b) battery equipment suppliers
    - (c) equipment labeling
    - (d) the design engineer

11. Where controls to activate the energy storage system (ESS) battery disconnecting means are used and are not located within sight of the battery, the location of the controls shall be marked _____.
    - (a) on the batteries
    - (b) adjacent to the batteries
    - (c) on the disconnecting means
    - (d) in a secure location

12. Energy storage system (ESS) battery disconnecting means shall be legibly marked in the field and shall include the _____.
    - (a) nominal battery voltage
    - (b) available fault current and arc-flash label
    - (c) date the calculation was performed
    - (d) all of these

13. The energy storage system (ESS) inverter output circuit maximum current shall be _____.
    - (a) the inverter continuous output current rating
    - (b) the inverter continuous input current rating
    - (c) 110 percent of the inverter continuous output current rating
    - (d) 125 percent of the inverter continuous input current rating

14. Overcurrent protective devices, where required, shall be rated in accordance with Article 240 and the rating provided on systems serving the energy storage system (ESS) shall be not less than _____ of the maximum currents calculated in 706.30(A).
    - (a) 110 percent
    - (b) 115 percent
    - (c) 125 percent
    - (d) 167 percent

ARTICLE 710—STAND-ALONE SYSTEMS

1. Article 710 covers electric power production systems that operate in _____ and not connected to an electric utility supply.
   (a) island mode
   (b) standby mode
   (c) tandem mode
   (d) generating mode

2. According to the scope of 710.1, stand-alone systems often include a single or a compatible interconnection of sources such as _____.
   (a) engine generators
   (b) solar PV or wind
   (c) ESS or batteries
   (d) all of these

3. All stand-alone power production equipment or systems shall be approved for use _____.
   (a) as legally required standby power
   (b) as optional standby power
   (c) in island mode
   (d) as supplemental power on demand

4. A permanent _____ shall be installed at a building supplied by a stand-alone system at each service equipment location or at an approved readily visible location and shall denote the location of each power source disconnect for the building or be grouped with other plaques or directories for other on-site sources.
   (a) plaque
   (b) label
   (c) directory
   (d) any of these

5. Power supply to premises wiring systems fed by stand-alone or isolated microgrid power sources is permitted to have _____ than the calculated load.
   (a) less capacity
   (b) greater capacity
   (c) 120 percent greater capacity
   (d) 125 percent greater capacity

6. The circuit conductors between a stand-alone source and a _____ shall be sized based on the sum of the output ratings of the stand-alone source(s).
   (a) distribution panel
   (b) building or structure disconnect
   (c) calculated load
   (d) demand load

ARTICLE 722—CABLES FOR POWER-LIMITED CIRCUITS

1. Article _____ covers the general requirements for the installation of single- and multiple-conductor cables used in Class 2 and Class 3 power-limited circuits, power-limited fire alarm (PLFA) circuits, Class 4 fault-managed power circuits, and optical fiber installations.
   (a) 722
   (b) 723
   (c) 724
   (d) 725

2. Power-limited circuits installed in _____ shall comply with 300.22.
   (a) ducts
   (b) plenums
   (c) other space used for environmental air
   (d) any of these

3. A bushing shall be installed where power-limited cables _____ from raceways used for mechanical support or protection.
   (a) emerge
   (b) enter
   (c) exit
   (d) any of these

4. Nonmetallic ______ and other nonmetallic cable accessories used to secure and support power-limited cables in other spaces used for environmental air (plenums) shall be listed as having low smoke and heat release properties
   (a) wires
   (b) hangars
   (c) straps
   (d) cable ties

5. Power-limited fire alarm cables shall not be strapped, taped, or attached by any means to the exterior of any conduit or other raceway as a means of _____.
   (a) support
   (b) securement
   (c) strapping
   (d) all of these

6. The accessible portion of abandoned power-limited cables shall be _____.
   (a) removed
   (b) replaced
   (c) repaired
   (d) any of these

7. Power-limited cables installed in buildings shall be _____.
   (a) identified
   (b) marked
   (c) labeled
   (d) listed

8. Class 2, Class 3, and Type PLTC power-limited cables, installed as wiring methods within buildings, shall be listed as resistant to the spread of _____ and other criteria in accordance with 722.179(A)(1) through (A)(16).
   (a) fire
   (b) water
   (c) smoke
   (d) dust

9. Power-limited plenum cable shall be listed as suitable for use in ducts, plenums, and other space for environmental air and shall be listed as having adequate fire-resistant and _____ producing characteristics.
   (a) medium-smoke
   (b) high-smoke
   (c) low-smoke
   (d) no-smoke

10. Riser power-limited cable shall be listed as suitable for use in a vertical run in a shaft or from _____ and shall be listed as having fire-resistant characteristics capable of preventing the carrying of fire from floor to floor.
   (a) floor to wall
   (b) up to bottom
   (c) wall to wall
   (d) floor to floor

11. Cable used in a wet location shall be listed for use in wet locations and be marked "wet" or "wet location" or have a moisture-impervious _____ sheath.
   (a) metal
   (b) plastic
   (c) fiberglass
   (d) any of these

ARTICLE 724—CLASS 1 POWER-LIMITED CIRCUITS

1. Article _____ covers Class 1 circuits, including power-limited Class 1 remote-control and signaling circuits that are not an integral part of a device or utilization equipment.
   (a) 722
   (b) 723
   (c) 724
   (d) 725

2. Class 1 power-limited circuits shall be _____ at terminal and junction locations in a manner that prevents unintentional interference with other circuits during testing and servicing.
   (a) grouped
   (b) identified
   (c) taped
   (d) isolated

3. Class 1 circuits installed in ducts, _____, and other spaces used for environmental air shall comply with 300.22.
   (a) plenums
   (b) air-conditioning units
   (c) suspended ceilings
   (d) any of these

4. Bushings shall be installed for Class 1 power-limited circuits where cables emerge from raceways used for _____ support or protection in accordance with 300.15(C).
   (a) mechanical
   (b) electrical
   (c) extra
   (d) none of these

5. Class 1 power-limited circuits shall be supplied from a source with a rated output of not more than _____ and 1000 VA.
   (a) 12V
   (b) 24V
   (c) 30V
   (d) 50V

6. Class 1 power-limited circuit overcurrent protection shall not exceed _____ for 18 AWG conductors and _____ for 16 AWG.
   (a) 7A, 10A
   (b) 8A, 10A
   (c) 9A, 12A
   (d) 10A, 15A

7. Power-supply conductors and Class 1 power-limited circuit conductors can occupy the same cable, enclosure, or raceway without a barrier _____.
   (a) only where the equipment powered is functionally associated
   (b) where the circuits involved are not a mixture of ac and dc
   (c) under no circumstances
   (d) only where the equipment is essential for life safety

8. Class 1 circuits and power-supply circuits are permitted to be installed together with the conductors of _____ where separated by a barrier.
   (a) electric light
   (b) power
   (c) nonpower-limited fire alarm
   (d) all of these

ARTICLE 725—CLASS 2 POWER-LIMITED CIRCUITS

1. Article _____ covers power-limited circuits, including power-limited remote-control and signaling circuits, that are not an integral part of a device or of utilization equipment.
   (a) 722
   (b) 724
   (c) 725
   (d) 726

2. Class 2 and Class 3 circuits installed in _____, plenums, or other space used for environmental air shall comply with 300.22.
   (a) ducts
   (b) air-conditioning units
   (c) suspended ceilings
   (d) any of these

3. The listing and installation of cables for Class 2 and Class 3 circuits shall comply with Part I and Part II of Article _____.
   (a) 300
   (b) 722
   (c) 760
   (d) 770

4. Where damage to power-limited circuits can result in a failure of safety-control equipment that would introduce a direct fire or life _____, the power-limited circuits shall be installed in accordance with 724.31.
   (a) hazard
   (b) threat
   (c) situation
   (d) none of these

5. The power source for a Class 2 circuit shall be _____.
   (a) a listed Class 2 transformer
   (b) a listed Class 2 power supply
   (c) other listed equipment marked to identify the Class 2 power source
   (d) any of these

6. _____ audio/video information technology, communications, and industrial equipment limited-power circuits are permitted to be used as the power source for a Class 2 or a Class 3 circuit.
   (a) Listed
   (b) Labeled
   (c) Identified
   (d) Approved

7. Equipment supplying Class 2 or Class 3 circuits shall be durably marked where plainly visible to indicate _____.
   (a) each circuit that is a Class 2 or Class 3 circuit
   (b) the circuit VA rating
   (c) the size of conductors serving each circuit
   (d) all of these

8. Use of _____ wiring methods for Class 2 and Class 3 circuits on the load side of the power source shall be permitted.
   (a) Class 1
   (b) Class 2
   (c) Class 3
   (d) Class 4

1st Printing

9. Conductors of Class 2 and Class 3 circuits on the load side of the power source shall be _____ in accordance with 722.179.
   (a) bare
   (b) covered
   (c) insulated
   (d) all of these

10. Cables and conductors of Class 2 and Class 3 circuits _____ be placed with conductors of electric light, power, Class 1, nonpower-limited fire alarm circuits, and medium power network-powered broadband communications circuits.
   (a) shall be permitted to
   (b) shall not
   (c) shall
   (d) shall be required to

11. As a general rule, open conductors of Class 2 and Class 3 signaling circuits shall be separated by at least _____ from conductors of electric power and light.
   (a) 2 in.
   (b) 4 in.
   (c) 6 in.
   (d) 8 in.

12. Sections 725.144(A) and (B) shall apply to _____ circuits that transmit power and data to a powered device over listed cabling.
   (a) all
   (b) Class 1, 2, and 3
   (c) Class 2 and 3
   (d) low-voltage

13. For the purposes of bundling cables transmitting power and data, the requirements of 300.11 and Parts I and III of Article 725 shall apply to Class 2 and Class 3 circuits that transmit power and data. The conductors that carry power for the data circuits shall be _____.
   (a) copper
   (b) copper-clad aluminum
   (c) aluminum
   (d) any of these

14. For the purposes of bundling cables transmitting power and data, one example of the use of cables for Class 2 or Class 3 circuits that transmit power and data is the connection of _____.
   (a) closed-circuit TV cameras (CCTV)
   (b) antennas
   (c) coaxial cable
   (d) none of these

15. Where the bundling of cables transmitting power and data are concerned, the 8P8C connector is in widespread use with powered communications systems using Class 2 or Class 3 circuits and these connectors are typically rated at _____ maximum.
   (a) 0.50A
   (b) 1.00A
   (c) 1.20A
   (d) 1.30A

16. When using Table 725.144, bundle sizes over _____ cables, or conductor sizes smaller than 26 AWG, ampacities shall be permitted to be determined by qualified personnel under engineering supervision.
   (a) 129
   (b) 178
   (c) 187
   (d) 192

17. Where only half of the conductors in each cable are carrying current, the values in Table 725.144 shall be permitted to be increased by a factor of _____.
   (a) 1
   (b) 1.2
   (c) 1.4
   (d) 1.6

18. Where Types CL3P, CL2P, CL3R, CL2R, CL3, or CL2 transmit power and data, the rated current per conductor of the power source shall not exceed the ampacities in Table 725.144 at an ambient temperature of _____.
   (a) 30°C
   (b) 60°C
   (c) 75°C
   (d) 90°C

19. One example of the use of Class 2 cables is a network of closed-circuit TV cameras using 24 AWG, 60°C rated, Type _____, Category 5e balanced twisted-pair cabling.

 (a) CL2R
 (b) PLTC
 (c) OCFN
 (d) Type MC cable

ARTICLE 760—FIRE ALARM SYSTEMS

1. Article 760 covers the requirements for the installation of wiring and equipment of _____.

 (a) communications systems
 (b) antennas
 (c) fire alarm systems
 (d) fiber optics

2. Fire alarm systems include _____.

 (a) fire detection and alarm notification
 (b) guard's tour
 (c) sprinkler waterflow
 (d) all of these

3. Fire alarm circuits shall be identified at all terminal and junction locations in a manner that helps prevent unintentional signals on fire alarm system circuits during _____ of other systems.

 (a) installation
 (b) testing and servicing
 (c) renovations
 (d) all of these

4. _____ fire alarm cables installed in ducts, plenums, or other spaces used for environmental air shall comply with 300.22.

 (a) Fire rated
 (b) Metal-clad
 (c) Power-limited and nonpower-limited
 (d) Line-voltage

5. _____ fire alarm cables selected in accordance with Table 760.154 and installed in accordance with 722.135 and 300.22(B) Ex, shall be permitted to be installed in ducts specifically fabricated for environmental air.

 (a) Power-limited
 (b) Nonpower-limited
 (c) Power-limited and nonpower-limited
 (d) Line-voltage

6. The number and _____ of fire alarm cables and conductors shall comply with 300.17.

 (a) cross-sectional area
 (b) diameter
 (c) size
 (d) none of these

7. Fire alarm circuit cables and conductors installed exposed on the surface of ceilings and sidewalls shall be supported by _____, hangers, or similar fittings designed and installed so as not to damage the cable.

 (a) straps
 (b) staples
 (c) cable ties
 (d) any of these

8. Where abandoned fire alarm cables are identified for future use with a tag, the tag shall be of sufficient durability to withstand _____.

 (a) the environment involved
 (b) heat
 (c) moisture
 (d) sunlight

9. A listed _____ shall be installed on the supply side of a fire alarm control panel in accordance with Part II of Article 242.

 (a) current-limiting device
 (b) selectively coordinated device
 (c) surge-protective device (SPD)
 (d) current transformer

10. The branch circuit supplying power-limited fire alarm equipment shall not be supplied through _____ circuit interrupters.

 (a) ground-fault
 (b) arc-fault
 (c) ground-fault or arc-fault
 (d) none of these

11. The fire alarm circuit disconnecting means for a power-limited fire alarm system shall _____.

 (a) have red identification
 (b) be accessible only to qualified personnel
 (c) be identified as "FIRE ALARM CIRCUIT"
 (d) all of these

1st Printing

12. A _____alarm branch-circuit disconnecting means shall be permitted to be secured in the "on" position.
    (a) fire
    (b) security
    (c) smoke
    (d) all of these

13. _____ protection is not required for receptacles in dwelling-unit unfinished basements that supply power for fire alarm systems.
    (a) SPD
    (b) AFCI
    (c) GFCI
    (d) any of these

14. Fire alarm equipment supplying power-limited fire alarm circuits shall be durably marked where plainly visible to indicate each circuit that is _____.
    (a) supplied by a nonpower-limited fire alarm circuit
    (b) a power-limited fire alarm circuit
    (c) a fire alarm circuit
    (d) supervised

15. The maximum breaker size on the supply side of a fire alarm transformer is _____.
    (a) 5A
    (b) 10A
    (c) 15A
    (d) 20A

16. Cable splices or terminations in power-limited fire alarm systems shall be made in listed _____ or utilization equipment.
    (a) fittings
    (b) boxes or enclosures
    (c) fire alarm devices
    (d) any of these

17. Power-limited fire alarm circuit cables and conductors shall not be placed in any cable, cable tray, compartment, enclosure, manhole, _____, or similar fitting with conductors of electric light, power, Class 1, nonpower-limited fire alarm circuits, and medium-power network-powered broadband communications circuits.
    (a) outlet box
    (b) device box
    (c) raceway
    (d) any of these

18. Power-limited fire alarm circuit conductors are permitted to be _____ to the exterior of any conduit or other raceway as a means of support.
    (a) strapped
    (b) taped
    (c) attached by any means
    (d) none of these

ARTICLE 770—OPTICAL FIBER CABLES

1. Article 770 covers the installation of optical fiber cables. This article does not cover the construction of _____ cables.
    (a) coaxial
    (b) tray
    (c) optical fiber
    (d) industrial trolley

2. Access to electrical equipment shall not be denied by an accumulation of optical fiber cables that _____ the removal of panels, including suspended-ceiling panels.
    (a) prevent
    (b) hinder
    (c) block
    (d) require

3. Optical fiber cables installed _____ on the surface of ceilings and walls shall be supported by the building structure in such a manner that the cable will not be damaged by normal building use.
    (a) exposed
    (b) in raceways
    (c) hidden
    (d) exposed and concealed

4. Paint, plaster, cleaners, abrasives, corrosive residues, or other contaminants may result in an undetermined alteration of optical fiber cable _____.
    (a) usefulness
    (b) voltage
    (c) properties
    (d) reliability

5. The _____ portion of abandoned optical fiber cables shall be removed.

    (a) accessible
    (b) exposed
    (c) concealed
    (d) salvageable

6. Openings around penetrations of optical fiber cables and communications raceways through fire-resistant-rated walls, partitions, floors, or ceilings shall be _____ using approved methods to maintain the fire-resistance rating.

    (a) closed
    (b) opened
    (c) draft stopped
    (d) firestopped

7. Nonconductive optical fiber cables _____ permitted to occupy the same cabinet, outlet box, panel, or similar enclosure housing the electrical terminations of an electric light, power, Class 1, non-power-limited fire alarm, or medium-power network-powered broadband communications circuit.

    (a) shall be
    (b) shall not be
    (c) any of these
    (d) none of these

8. Nonconductive optical fiber cables shall not be permitted to occupy the same _____ or similar enclosure unless the nonconductive optical fiber cables are functionally associated with the electric circuits.

    (a) cabinet
    (b) outlet box
    (c) panel
    (d) any of these

CHAPTER

8 COMMUNICATIONS SYSTEMS

Introduction to Chapter 8—Communications Systems

Chapter 8 covers the wiring requirements communications circuits such as hard-wired telephones, radio and TV antennas, satellite dishes, and CATV systems. ▶Figure 8–1

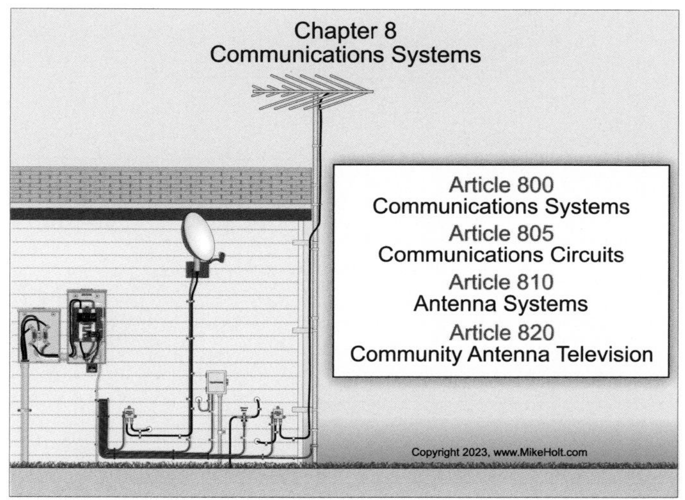

▶Figure 8–1

The communications systems covered in this chapter pose little to no risk from fire or electric shock and have some unique installation methods and rules that need special consideration when applying installation rules. None of the requirements contained in Chapters 1 through 7 apply to chapter 8, except where specifically referenced [90.3]. It's good to remember that communications equipment and wiring under the exclusive control of communications utilities located outdoors, or in building spaces used exclusively for such installations, are exempt from the NEC [90.2(D)(4)].

This material only covers the following articles contained in Chapter 8:

- **Article 800—General Requirements for Communications Systems.** This article covers general requirements for the installation of coaxial cable [Article 800], hard-wired telephones [Article 805], and radio distribution systems [Article 820].
- **Article 810—Radio and Television Antenna Equipment.** This article covers antenna systems for radio and television receiving equipment, amateur radio transmitting and receiving equipment, and certain features of transmitter safety. It also addresses antennas such as multi-element, vertical rod, and dish, and the wiring and cabling connecting them to the equipment.

Notes

1st Printing

GENERAL REQUIREMENTS FOR COMMUNICATIONS SYSTEMS

Introduction to Article 800—General Requirements for Communications Systems

This article contains the general requirements applicable to all installations of coaxial cable [Article 800], hard-wired telephones [Article 805], and radio distribution systems [Article 820]. Many of these requirements mirror those contained in Article 722. Take special not that Article 810 is not included within the scope of this chapter. Many of these rules are outside of the scope of this material, however, some of the topics we cover include the following:

- Scope
- Access to Electrical Equipment Behind Panels Designed to Allow Access
- Abandoned Cable
- Spread of Fire or Products of Combustion
- Separation from Lightning Conductors
- Wiring
- Applications of Listed Communications Wires, Coaxial Cables, and Raceways

Article 800 consists of five parts:

- Part I. General
- Part II. Wires and Cables Outside and Entering Buildings
- Part III. Grounding Methods
- Part IV. Installation Methods Within Buildings
- Part V. Listing Requirements

Part I. General

800.1 Scope

Article 800 covers general requirements for hard-wired telephones [Article 805] and Coaxial Cable [Article 820]. ▶Figure 800–1

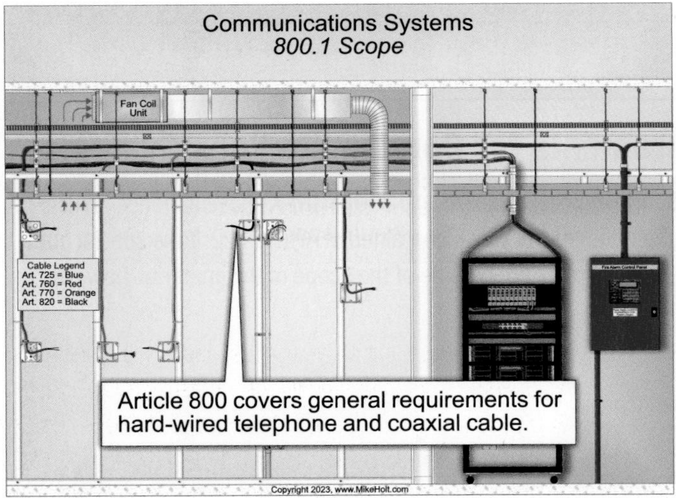

▶Figure 800–1

800.3 Other Articles

Only those sections of Chapters 1 through 7 referenced in this article apply to Chapter 8. ▶Figure 800–2

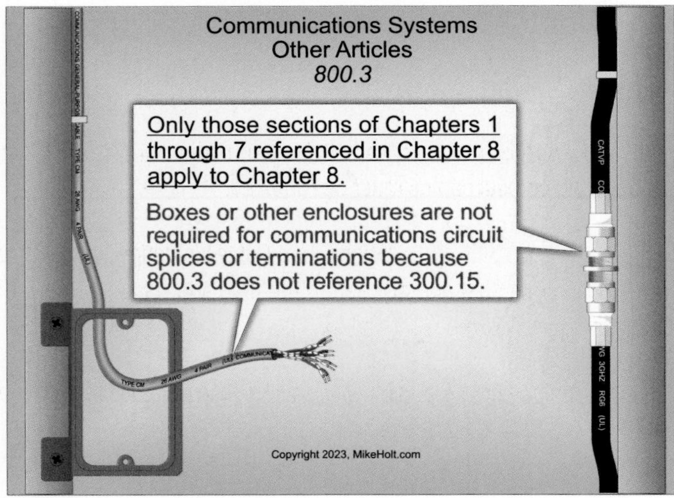

▶Figure 800–2

(A) Output Circuits. As appropriate for the services provided, the output circuits derived from a network-powered broadband communications system's network interface unit (NIU) or from a premises-powered broadband communications system's network terminal must comply with the requirements of the following:

(1) Class 2 power-limited circuits—Part II of Article 725 and Parts I and II of Article 722

(2) Power-limited fire alarm circuits—Part III of Article 760

(3) Optical fiber cables—Part V of Article 770

(B) Hazardous (Classified) Locations. For circuits and equipment installed in a location classified in accordance with 500.5, the applicable requirements of Chapter 5 apply.

(C) Wiring in Ducts for Dust or Vapor Removal. The requirements of 300.22(A) apply.

(D) Equipment in Plenum Spaces. Equipment installed in plenum spaces must comply with 300.22(C)(3).

Author's Comment:

- According to 300.22(C)(3), electrical equipment with a metal enclosure, or a nonmetallic enclosure listed for use in an air-handling space, can be installed in a plenum space.

(E) Installation and Use. Communications equipment must be installed and used according to manufacturers' instructions in accordance with 110.3(B).

(F) Optical Fiber Cable. Where optical fiber cable is used to provide a communications circuit within a building, Article 770 applies.

800.21 Access to Electrical Equipment Behind Panels Designed to Allow Access

Access to equipment must not be prohibited by an accumulation of coaxial cables that prevents the removal of suspended-ceiling panel.

800.24 Mechanical Execution of Work

(A) General. Equipment and cabling must be installed in a neat and workmanlike manner. ▶Figure 800–3

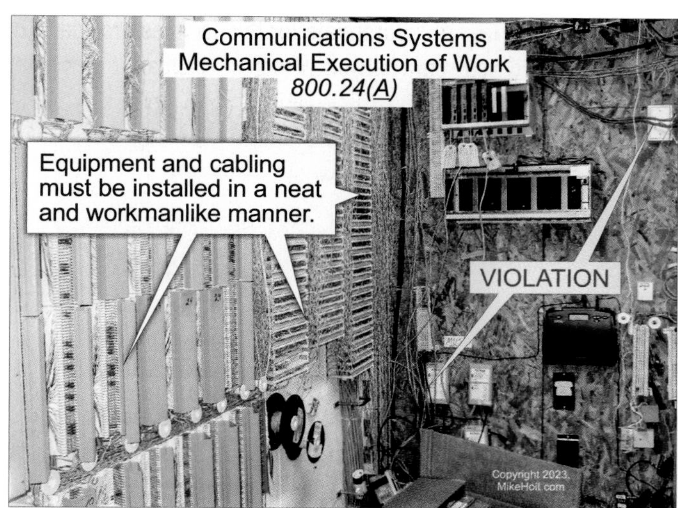
Communications Systems
Mechanical Execution of Work
800.24(A)
Equipment and cabling must be installed in a neat and workmanlike manner.
VIOLATION
Copyright 2023, MikeHolt.com

▸Figure 800–3

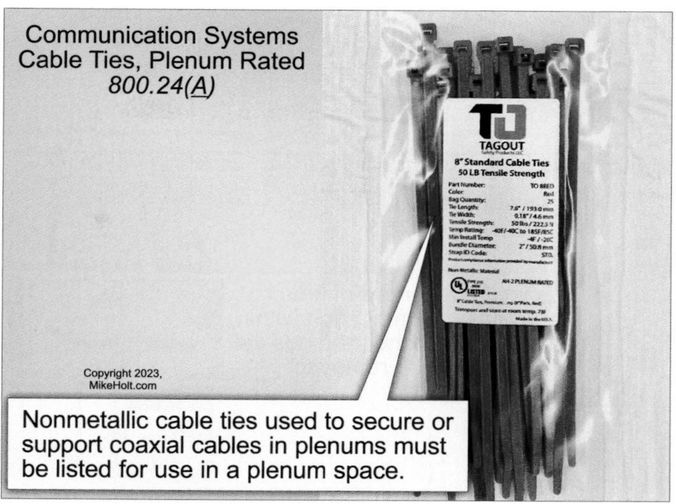
Communication Systems
Cable Ties, Plenum Rated
800.24(A)
TAGOUT
8" Standard Cable Ties
50 LB Tensile Strength
Copyright 2023, MikeHolt.com
Nonmetallic cable ties used to secure or support coaxial cables in plenums must be listed for use in a plenum space.

▸Figure 800–4

Cable Support, Damage. Exposed coaxial cables must be supported by the structural components of the building so the cable will not be damaged by normal building use.

Cable Securement, Fitting. Coaxial cables must be secured by straps, staples, hangers, cable ties listed and identified for securement and support, or similar fittings designed and installed in a manner that will not damage the cable.

Protection From Physical Damage [300.4]. Coaxial cables installed through or parallel to framing members or furring strips must be protected where they are likely to be penetrated by nails or screws by installing the wiring method so it is not less than 1¼ in. from the nearest edge of the framing member or furring strips, or by protecting it with a ¹⁄₁₆ in. thick steel plate or equivalent [300.4(A)(1) and (D)].

Securing and Supporting [300.11]. Communications raceways and coaxial cable assemblies must be securely fastened in place. The ceiling-support wires or the ceiling grid are not permitted to be used to support coaxial cables [300.11(B)].

Cable Ties, Plenum Rated. Cable ties used to secure or support coaxial cables in plenums must be listed for use in a plenum space in accordance with 800.170. ▸Figure 800–4

Note 1: Accepted industry practices are described in ANSI/TIA-568, *Commercial Building Telecommunications Infrastructure Standard*; ANSI/TIA-569-D, *Telecommunications Pathways and Spaces*; ANSI/TIA-570-C, *Residential Telecommunications Infrastructure Standard*; ANSI/TIA-1005-A, *Telecommunications Infrastructure Standard for Industrial Premises*; ANSI/TIA-1179, *Healthcare Facility Telecommunications Infrastructure Standard*; ANSI/TIA-4966, *Telecommunications Infrastructure Standard for Educational Facilities*; and other ANSI-approved installation standards.

Note 3: Paint, plaster, cleaners, abrasives, corrosive residues, or other contaminants may result in an undetermined alteration of wire and cable properties.

800.25 Abandoned Cable

To limit the spread of fire or products of combustion within a building, abandoned coaxial cables must be removed. ▸Figure 800–5

According to Article 100, "Abandoned Cable" is defined as a cable that is not terminated at equipment other than a termination fitting or a connector and is not identified for future use with a tag.

Where cables are identified for future use with a tag, the tag must be able to withstand the environment involved.

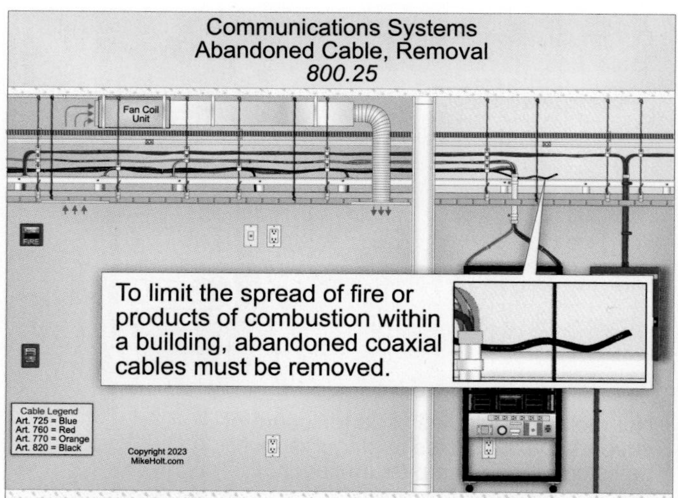

▶Figure 800–5

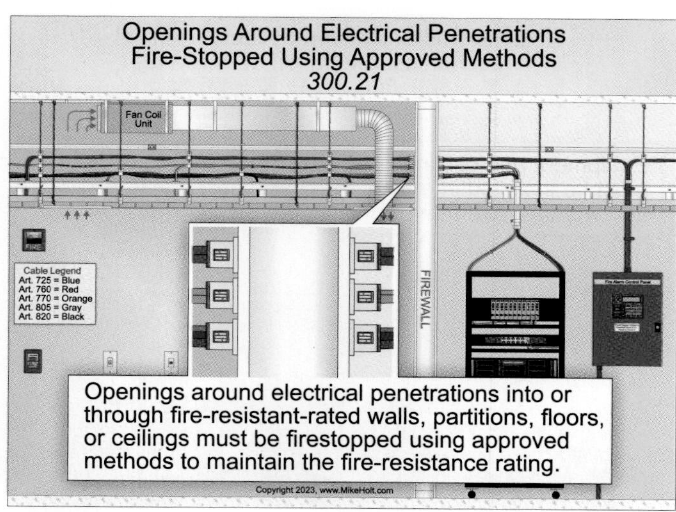

▶Figure 800–6

800.26 Spread of Fire or Products of Combustion

Coaxial cables must be installed in such a way that the spread of fire or products of combustion will not be substantially increased.

Openings into or through fire-resistant-rated walls, floors, and ceilings for electrical equipment must be firestopped using methods approved by the authority having jurisdiction to maintain the fire-resistance rating of the fire-rated assembly.

Author's Comment:

- Electrical circuits and equipment must be installed in such a way that the spread of fire or products of combustion will not be substantially increased. Openings into or through fire-resistive walls, floors, and ceilings for electrical equipment must be firestopped using methods approved by the authority having jurisdiction to maintain the fire-resistance rating of the fire-resistive assembly [300.21]. ▶**Figure 800–6**
- Boxes installed in fire-resistive assemblies must be listed for the purpose. If steel boxes are used, they must be secured to the framing member, so cut-in type boxes are not permitted. "Putty pads" are typically installed on the exterior of the box, but many manufacturers have listed inserts for box interiors. Firestopping materials are listed for the specific types of wiring methods and the construction of the assembly they penetrate. ▶**Figure 800–7**

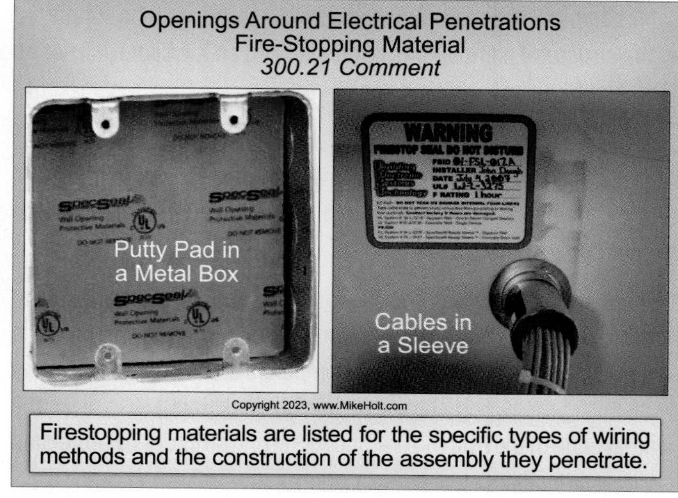

▶Figure 800–7

- Outlet boxes must have a horizontal separation of not less than 24 in. when installed on opposites sides in a fire-resistive assembly, unless an outlet box is listed for closer spacing or protected by fire-resistant "putty pads" in accordance with manufacturer's instructions. Building codes also have restrictions on penetrations on opposite sides of a fire-resistive wall. ▶**Figure 800–8** and ▶**Figure 800–9**

1st Printing

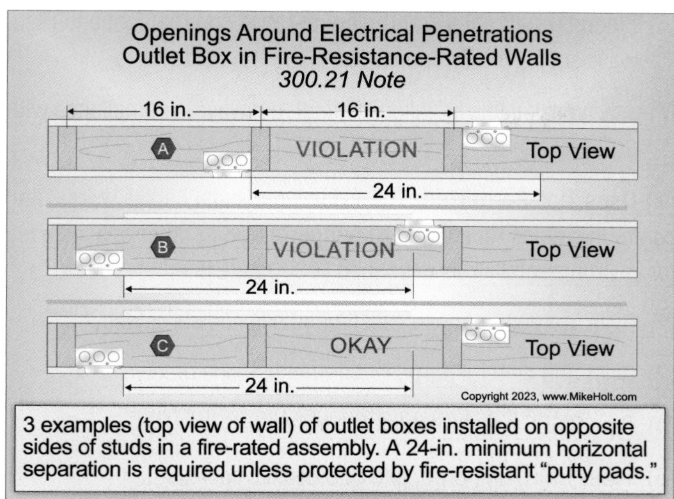
Openings Around Electrical Penetrations
Outlet Box in Fire-Resistance-Rated Walls
300.21 Note
16 in.
16 in.
A
VIOLATION
Top View
24 in.
B
VIOLATION
Top View
24 in.
C
OKAY
Top View
24 in.
Copyright 2023, www.MikeHolt.com
3 examples (top view of wall) of outlet boxes installed on opposite sides of studs in a fire-rated assembly. A 24-in. minimum horizontal separation is required unless protected by fire-resistant "putty pads."

▶Figure 800–8

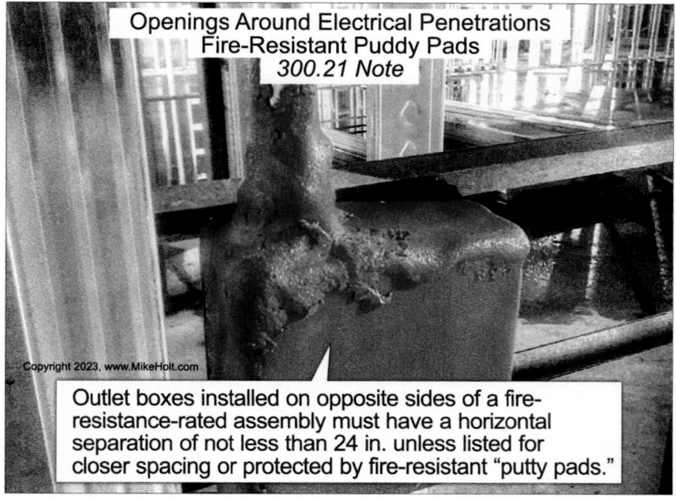
Openings Around Electrical Penetrations
Fire-Resistant Puddy Pads
300.21 Note
Copyright 2023, www.MikeHolt.com
Outlet boxes installed on opposite sides of a fire-resistance-rated assembly must have a horizontal separation of not less than 24 in. unless listed for closer spacing or protected by fire-resistant "putty pads."

▶Figure 800–9

Part II. Wires and Cables Outside and Entering Buildings

800.53 Separation from Lightning Conductors

Where practicable <u>on buildings</u>, a separation of not less than 6 ft must be maintained between communications circuits <u>or coaxial cables</u> and lightning protection conductors.

Part IV. Installation Methods Within Buildings

800.110 Raceways

(A) Types of Raceways.

(1) Chapter 3 Raceways. Cables can be installed in any Chapter 3 raceway. ▶Figure 800–10

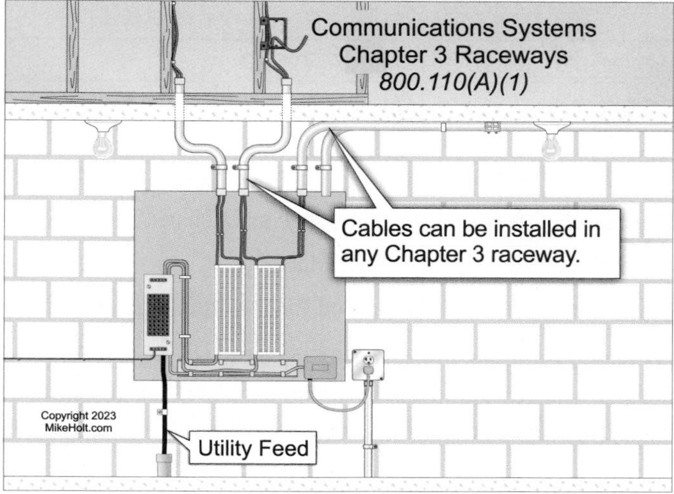
Communications Systems
Chapter 3 Raceways
800.110(A)(1)
Cables can be installed in any Chapter 3 raceway.
Copyright 2023 MikeHolt.com
Utility Feed

▶Figure 800–10

Author's Comment:

- Coaxial cable is not required to be installed in a Chapter 3 raceway, but when it is, it must be installed in accordance with the Chapter 3 requirements for that raceway.

(2) Communications Raceways. Coaxial cables can be installed in communications raceways selected using Table 800.154(b), listed in accordance with 800.182, and installed in accordance with 800.113 and 362.24 through 362.56 where the requirements for electrical nonmetallic tubing (ENT) apply.

(B) Raceway Fill for Communications Wires and Cables. The raceway fill limitations of 300.17 do not apply to coaxial cables installed within a raceway.

800.113 Installation of Communications Wires, Cables, and Raceways

<u>Types of cables used by this section are identified in Table 800.113.</u>

Table 800.113 Cables Used for Communications Circuits	
	Listed Cable Types
Plenum cables	CMP, CATVP, BLP, OFNP, OFCP
Riser cables	CMR, CATVR, BMR, BLR, OFNR, OFCR
General-purpose cables	CMG, CM, CATV, BM, BL, OFNG, OFN, OFCG, OFC
Limited-use cables	CMX, CATVX, BLX
Undercarpet	CMUC
Underground	BMU, BLU

(A) Listing. Coaxial cables in buildings must be installed in accordance with the limitations of the listing.

(B) Ducts Specifically Fabricated for Environmental Air.

(1) Uses Permitted. The following coaxial cables are permitted in ducts specifically fabricated for environmental air as described in 300.22(B) if they are directly associated with the air distribution system:

(1) Plenum-rated cables up to 4 ft in length

(2) Any type of cable in a metal raceway in accordance with 300.22(B)

(2) Uses Not Permitted. The following coaxial cables are not permitted in ducts specifically fabricated for environmental air as described in 300.22(B):

(1) Plenum, riser, and general-purpose communications raceways

(3) Riser, general-purpose, and limited-use cables

(4) Type CMUC cables and wires

(5) Types BMU and BLU cables

(6) Communications wires

(7) Hybrid power and communications cables

(C) Plenum Spaces.

(1) Uses Permitted. The following coaxial cables are permitted to be installed in plenum spaces as described in 300.22(C):

(1) Plenum-rated cables

(2) Plenum-rated communications raceways

(4) Plenum-rated cables installed in plenum-rated communications raceways

(6) Plenum-rated cables and plenum-rated communications raceways supported by open metal cable tray systems

(7) Any type of cable installed in metal raceways in compliance with 300.22(C)

(2) Uses Not Permitted. The following coaxial cables, wires, and communications raceways are not permitted in other spaces used for environmental air as described in 300.22(C):

(1) Riser, general-purpose, and limited-use coaxial cables

(2) Riser and general-purpose communications raceways

(4) Type CMUC coaxial cables and wires

(5) Types BMR, BM, BMU, and BLU coaxial cables

(6) Communications wires

(7) Hybrid power and coaxial cables

800.133 Installation of Coaxial Cables and Equipment

(A) In Raceways, Cable Trays, Boxes, and Enclosures.

(1) Permitted with Other Circuits. Coaxial cables are permitted in the same raceway, cable tray, box, or enclosure with jacketed coaxial cables of any of the following: ▸Figure 800–11

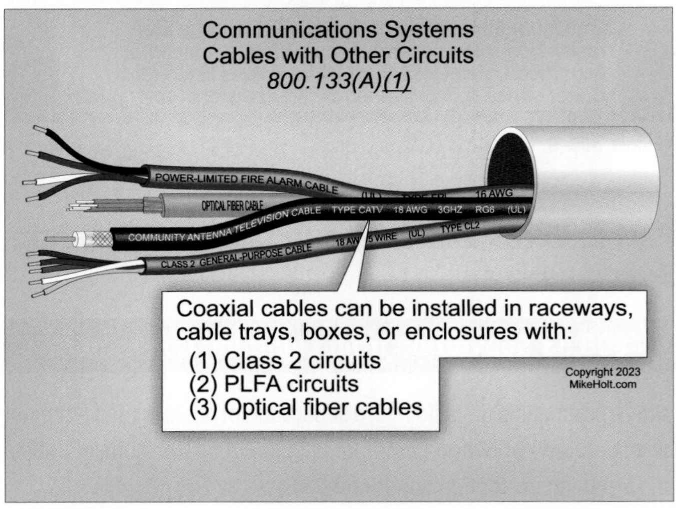

▸Figure 800–11

(1) Class 2 power-limited circuits in compliance with Article 725

(2) Power-limited fire alarm systems in compliance with Parts I and III of Article 760

(3) Nonconductive and conductive optical fiber cables in compliance with Parts I and V of Article 770

(3) Separation from Power Conductors. Coaxial cables are not permitted to be placed in any raceway, compartment, outlet box, junction box, or similar fitting with conductors of electric power or Class 1 power-limited circuits.

Ex 1: Coaxial cables are permitted in the same enclosure with power conductors if separated by a barrier. ▶Figure 800–12

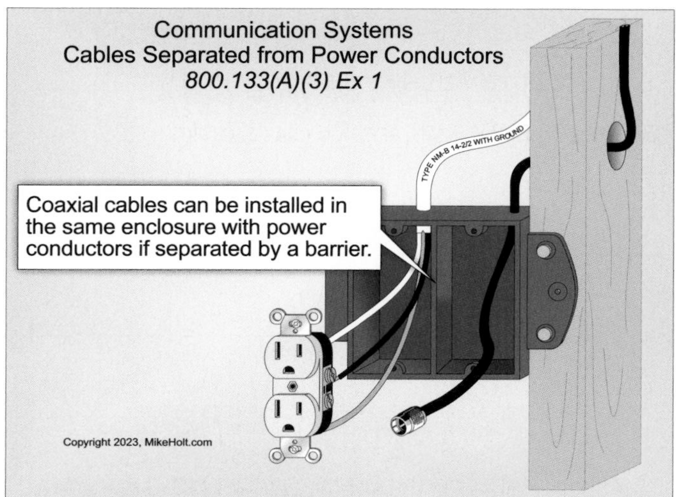

Communication Systems
Cables Separated from Power Conductors
800.133(A)(3) Ex 1
Coaxial cables can be installed in the same enclosure with power conductors if separated by a barrier.
TYPE NM-B 14-2/2 WITH GROUND
Copyright 2023, MikeHolt.com

▶Figure 800–12

Ex 2: Power conductors that supply coaxial cable distribution equipment must maintain ¼ in. of separation from coaxial cables within the enclosure.

(B) Separation from Power Conductors. Coaxial cables must be separated by at least 2 in. from conductors of any electric light, power, and Class 1 power-limited circuits.

Ex 1: Coaxial cables are not required to have a 2-in. separation from a Chapter 3 wiring method. ▶Figure 800–13

(C) Support of Coaxial Cables. Coaxial cables are not permitted to be strapped, taped, or attached by any means to the exterior of any raceway as a means of support.

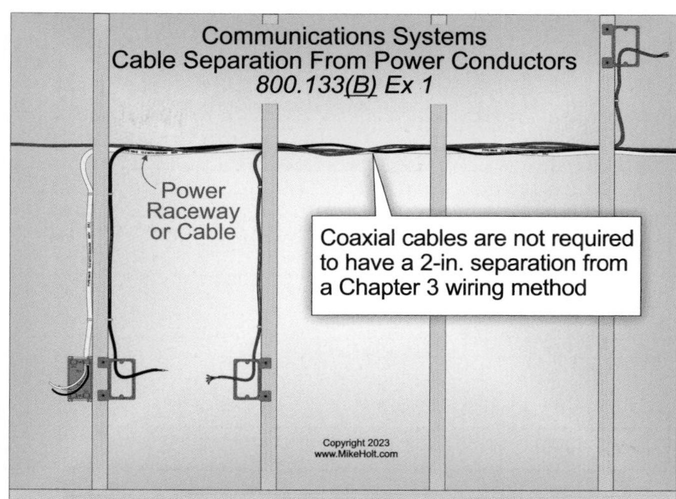

▶Figure 800–13

800.154 Applications of Listed Communications Wires, Coaxial Cables, and Raceways

Permitted and nonpermitted applications of listed communications wires, coaxial cables, coaxial cables and raceways, must be in accordance with one of the following:

(1) Listed communications wires and coaxial cables as indicated in Table 800.154(a)

(2) Listed communications raceways as indicated in Table 800.154(b)

The permitted applications are subject to the installation requirements of 800.110 and 800.113.

800.170 Plenum Cable Ties

Cable ties intended for use in plenum space, in accordance with 300.22(C), must be listed as having low smoke and heat release properties.

ARTICLE 810 ANTENNA SYSTEMS

Introduction to Article 810—Antenna Systems

This article covers antenna systems and the wiring and cabling associated with that equipment. Unlike other articles in this chapter, Article 810 is not covered by the general rules in Article 800. As a result, it stands completely alone in the *Code* unless a rule here references a specific rule elsewhere in the *NEC*. Many of these rules are outside of the scope of this material, however, some of the topics we cover include the following:

- Scope
- Avoid Contact with Conductors of Other Systems
- Metal Antenna Supports—Bonding
- Clearances
- Antenna Discharge Unit
- Bonding Conductors and Grounding Electrode Conductors

Article 810 consists of four parts:

- Part I. General
- Part II. Receiving Equipment—Antenna Systems
- Part III. Amateur and Citizen Band Transmitting and Receiving Stations
- Part IV. Interior Installation – Transmitting Stations

Part I. General

810.1 Scope

Article 810 covers antenna systems for radio and television receiving equipment, and amateur and citizen band radio transmitting and receiving equipment. It also covers antennas such as wire-strung type, multi-element, vertical rod, flat, or parabolic. ▸**Figure 810–1**

Author's Comment:

- Article 810 covers:
  - Antennas that receive local television signals.
  - Satellite antennas which are often referred to as satellite dishes.
  - Roof-mounted antennas for AM/FM/XM radio reception.
  - Amateur radio transmitting and receiving equipment, including HAM radio equipment (a noncommercial [amateur] communications system). ▸**Figure 810–2**

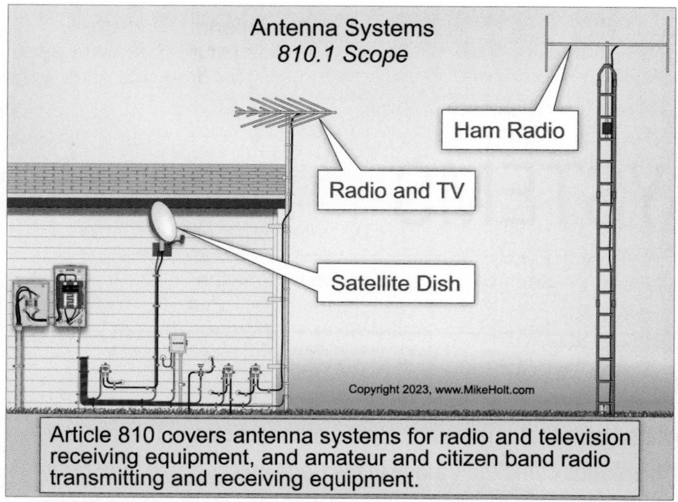
Antenna Systems
810.1 Scope
Ham Radio
Radio and TV
Satellite Dish
Copyright 2023, www.MikeHolt.com
Article 810 covers antenna systems for radio and television receiving equipment, and amateur and citizen band radio transmitting and receiving equipment.

▸Figure 810–1

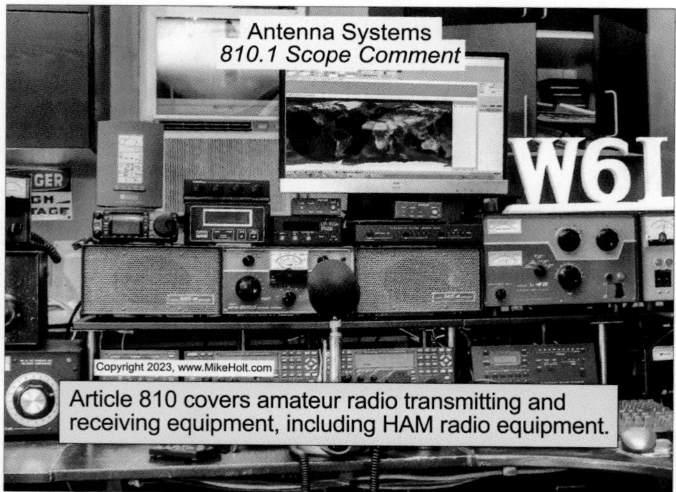
Antenna Systems
810.1 Scope Comment
W6L
Copyright 2023, www.MikeHolt.com
Article 810 covers amateur radio transmitting and receiving equipment, including HAM radio equipment.

▸Figure 810–2

810.3 Other Articles

(2) Coaxial cables must be installed in accordance with Article 800. ▸Figure 810–3

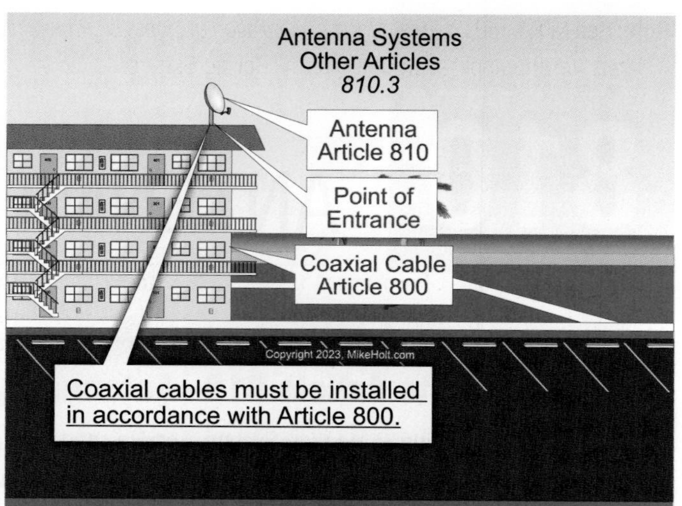
Antenna Systems
Other Articles
810.3
Antenna
Article 810
Point of
Entrance
Coaxial Cable
Article 800
Copyright 2023, MikeHolt.com
Coaxial cables must be installed in accordance with Article 800.

▸Figure 810–3

Author's Comment:

- According to the *National Electrical Code Handbook*, "One of the leading causes of electrical shock and electrocution is the accidental contact of radio, television, and amateur radio transmitting and receiving antennas, and equipment with light or power conductors. Extreme caution should therefore be exercised during this type of installation, and periodic visual inspections should be conducted thereafter."

Part II. Receiving Equipment—Antenna Systems

810.13 Avoid Contact with Conductors of Other Systems

Outdoor antennas and lead-in conductors must be kept at least 2 ft away from exposed electric power conductors to avoid the possibility of accidental contact.

810.15 Metal Antenna Supports—Bonding

Outdoor masts and metal structures that support antennas must be bonded in accordance with 810.21. ▸Figure 810–4

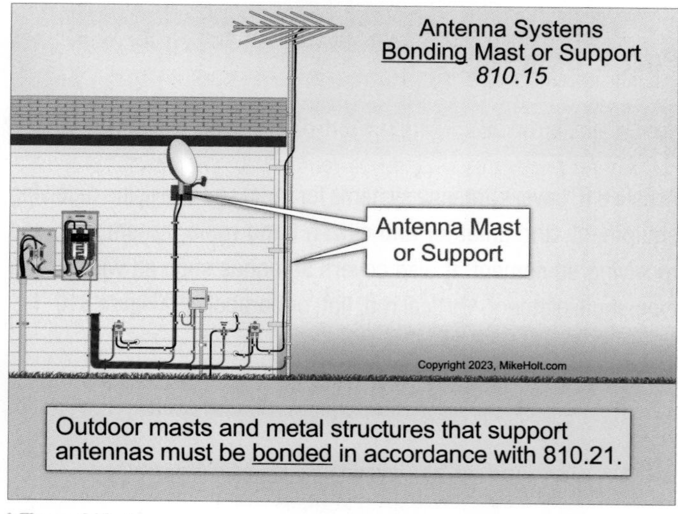
Antenna Systems
Bonding Mast or Support
810.15
Antenna Mast
or Support
Copyright 2023, MikeHolt.com
Outdoor masts and metal structures that support antennas must be bonded in accordance with 810.21.

▸Figure 810–4

Note: See NFPA 780, *Standard for the Installation of Lightning Protection Systems*, for the application of the term "Rolling Sphere."

810.18 Clearances

(A) Outside of Buildings.

Clearance From Power Conductors. Lead-in conductors attached to buildings must be installed so they cannot swing closer than 2 ft to the conductors of circuits of 250V or less, or closer than 10 ft to the conductors of circuits of over 250V.

Clearance From Lightning Protection System. Lead-in conductors must be kept at least 6 ft away from the lightning protection system. ▸Figure 810–5

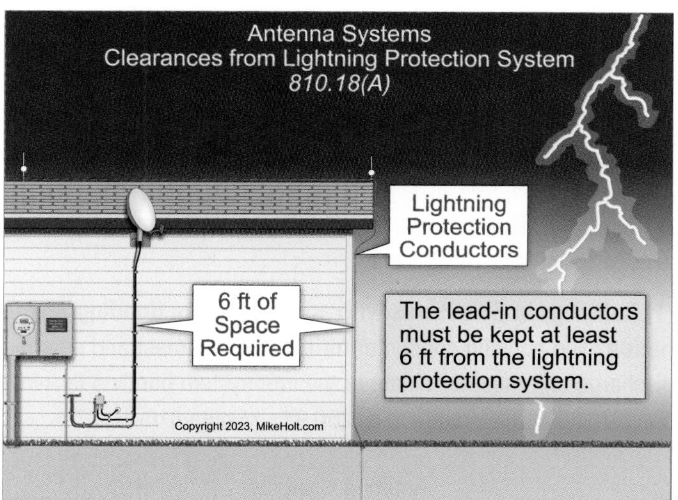

▸Figure 810–5

Underground Clearances. Underground antenna lead-in conductors must maintain a separation of not less than 12 in. from electric power conductors.

Ex: Separation of antenna cables from power conductors is not required where the underground antenna lead-in conductors or the electric power conductors are installed in raceways or metal cable armor. ▸Figure 810–6

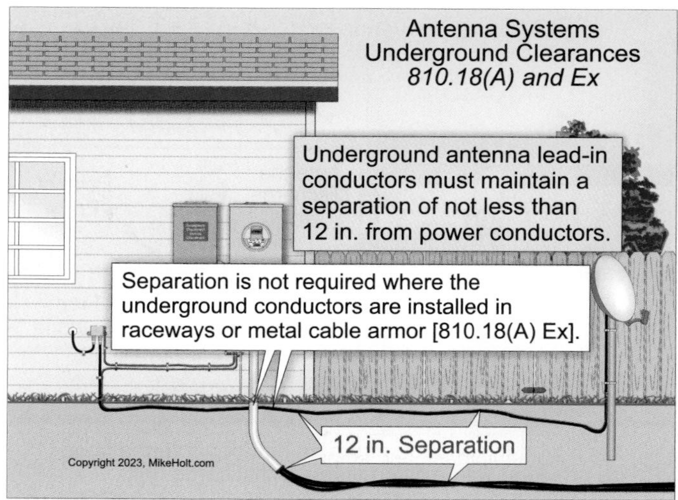

▸Figure 810–6

(B) Indoors. Indoor antenna and lead-in conductors are not permitted to be less than 2 in. from electric power conductors, unless one of the following applies:

(1) The other conductors are in metal raceways or cable armor.

(2) The indoor antennas and indoor lead-ins are separated from other conductors by a firmly fixed nonconductor.

(C) Boxes. Antenna lead-in conductors can be in the same box or enclosure with power conductors if separated by a barrier. ▸Figure 810–7

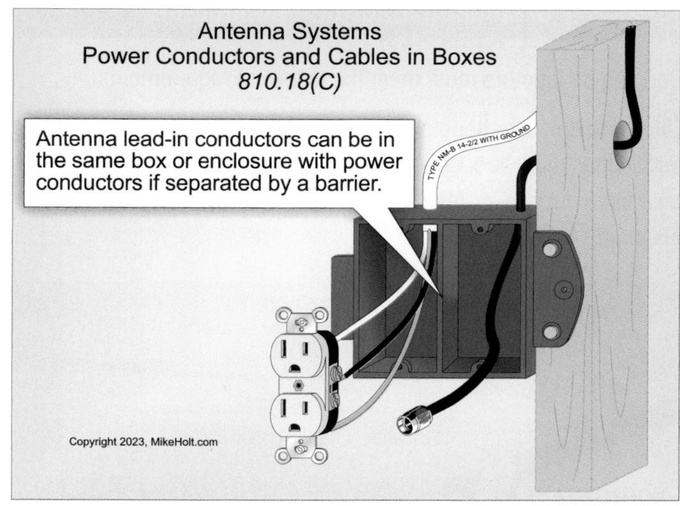

▸Figure 810–7

810.20 Antenna Discharge Unit

(A) Listed. Each lead-in conductor from an outdoor antenna must be provided with a listed antenna discharge unit. ▸Figure 810–8

(B) Location. The antenna discharge unit must be outside or inside the building, nearest the point of entrance, but not near combustible material.

(C) Bonding. The antenna discharge unit must be bonded in accordance with 810.21.

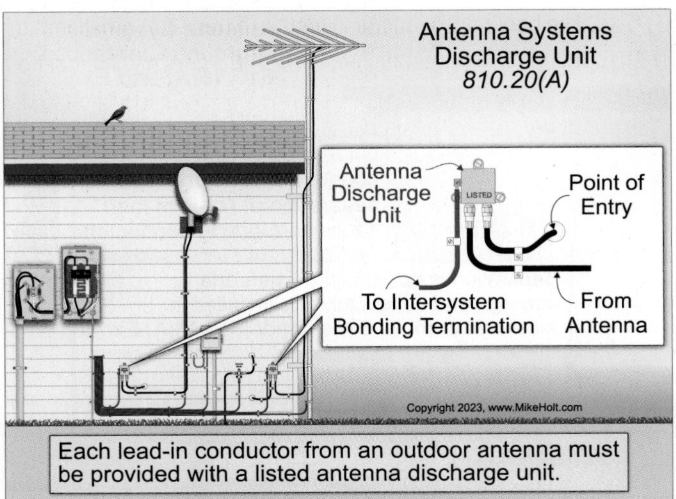
Antenna Systems
Discharge Unit
810.20(A)
Antenna
Discharge
Unit
Point of
Entry
To Intersystem
Bonding Termination
From
Antenna
Copyright 2023, www.MikeHolt.com
Each lead-in conductor from an outdoor antenna must be provided with a listed antenna discharge unit.

▸Figure 810–8

810.21 Bonding Conductors and Grounding Electrode Conductors

Bonding conductors must meet the following requirements:

(A) Material. The bonding conductor to the intersystem bonding termination must be copper, copper-clad aluminum, copper-clad steel, aluminum, bronze, or other corrosion-resistant conductive material. ▸Figure 810–9

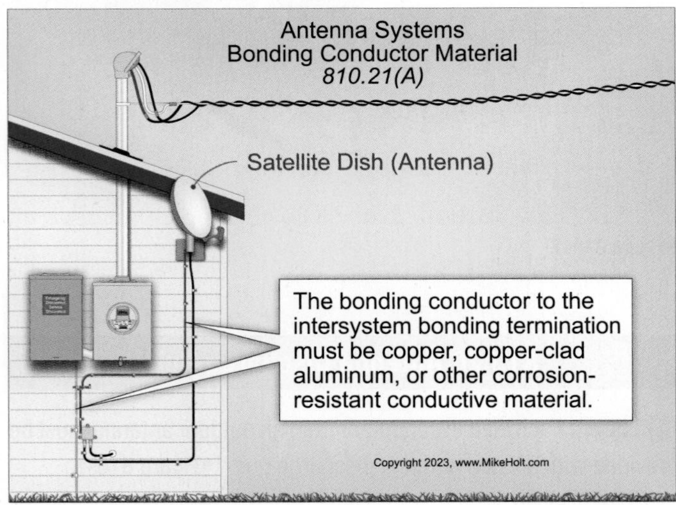
Antenna Systems
Bonding Conductor Material
810.21(A)
Satellite Dish (Antenna)
The bonding conductor to the intersystem bonding termination must be copper, copper-clad aluminum, or other corrosion-resistant conductive material.
Copyright 2023, www.MikeHolt.com

▸Figure 810–9

If aluminum or copper-clad aluminum is used, the bonding conductor must not be installed outside within 18 in. from the Earth, or if subject to corrosive conditions.

(B) Insulation. Insulation on bonding conductors is not required.

(C) Supports. The bonding conductor must be securely fastened in place.

(D) Physical Protection. Bonding conductors must be mechanically protected where subject to physical damage. Where installed in a metal raceway, both ends of the raceway must be bonded to the contained conductor.

Author's Comment:

- Installing the bonding conductor in PVC conduit is a better practice.

(E) Run in Straight Line. The bonding conductor must be run in as straight a line as practicable.

Author's Comment:

- Lightning does not like to travel around corners or through loops, which is why the bonding conductor must be run as straight as practicable.

(F) Bonding Terminations. The bonding conductor must terminate in accordance with the following:

(1) Buildings or Structures with an Intersystem Bonding Termination. The bonding conductor for the antenna mast and antenna discharge unit must terminate to the intersystem bonding termination [Article 100] as required by 250.94. ▸Figure 810–10

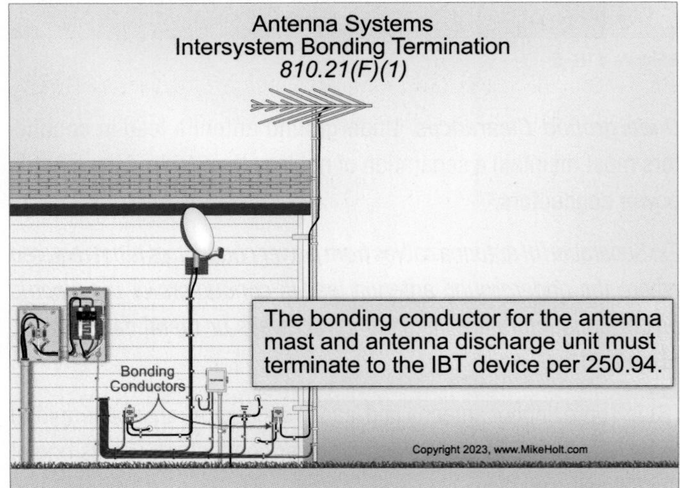
Antenna Systems
Intersystem Bonding Termination
810.21(F)(1)
The bonding conductor for the antenna mast and antenna discharge unit must terminate to the IBT device per 250.94.
Bonding
Conductors
Copyright 2023, www.MikeHolt.com

▸Figure 810–10

(2) Buildings or Structures without an Intersystem Bonding Termination. If the building or structure has no intersystem bonding termination, the bonding conductor must be connected to the nearest accessible grounding location on one of the following:

(1) The grounding electrode system as covered in 250.50

(2) The service accessible means external to the building as covered in 250.94

(3) The nonflexible metal service raceway. ▶Figure 810–11

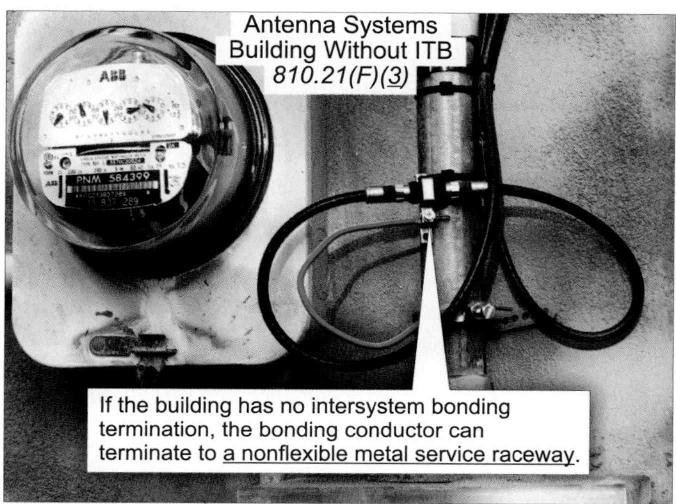

▶Figure 810–11

(4) The service disconnect enclosure

(5) The grounding electrode conductor or the grounding electrode conductor metal enclosures of the service disconnect

(6) The grounded interior metal water piping systems, within 5 ft from its point of entrance to the building, as covered in 250.68(C)(1).

Author's Comment:

- Section 250.68(C)(1) permits interior metal water piping within 5 ft from the point of entrance to a building to extend or interconnect bonding jumpers to grounding electrodes.

An intersystem bonding termination device must not interfere with the opening of an equipment enclosure and must be mounted on nonremovable parts. An intersystem bonding termination device cannot be mounted on a door or cover even if the door or cover is nonremovable.

(G) Inside or Outside Building. The bonding conductor can be installed either inside or outside the building.

(H) Size. The bonding conductor is not permitted to be smaller than 10 AWG copper, 8 AWG aluminum, or 17 AWG copper-clad steel or bronze. ▶Figure 810–12

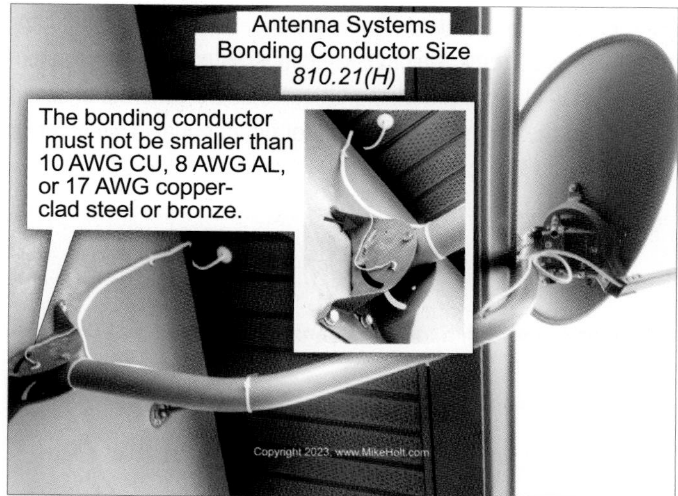

▶Figure 810–12

(J) Bonding of Electrodes. A ground rod installed for the antenna system must be bonded to the building's power grounding electrode system with a minimum 6 AWG copper conductor. ▶Figure 810–13

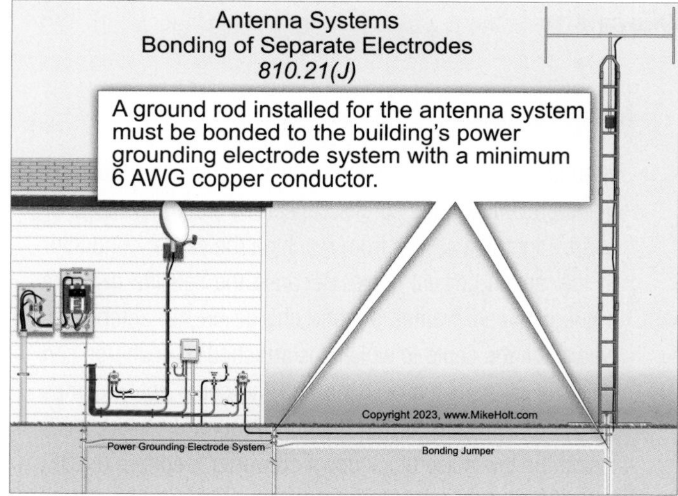

▶Figure 810–13

Author's Comment:

- A separate grounding electrode is not required for radio and TV equipment, but if it is installed, then it must be bonded to the building's power grounding electrode system with a minimum 6 AWG copper conductor.

- Bonding of electrodes helps reduce induced voltage differences between the power and communications systems during lightning events.

(K) Electrode Connection. Termination of the bonding conductor must be by exothermic welding, listed lugs, listed pressure connectors, or listed clamps. Grounding fittings that are concrete-encased or buried in the Earth must be listed for direct burial in accordance with 250.70. ▶Figure 810–14

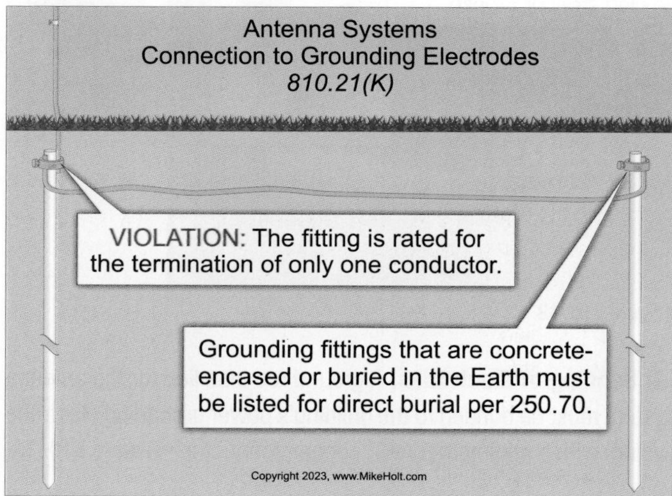
Antenna Systems
Connection to Grounding Electrodes
810.21(K)
VIOLATION: The fitting is rated for the termination of only one conductor.
Grounding fittings that are concrete-encased or buried in the Earth must be listed for direct burial per 250.70.
Copyright 2023, www.MikeHolt.com

▶Figure 810–14

Author's Comment:

- Grounding the lead-in antenna coaxial cables and the mast helps prevent voltage surges caused by static discharge or nearby lightning strikes from reaching the center conductor of the lead-in coaxial cable. Because the satellite dish sits outdoors, wind creates a static charge on the antenna as well as on the cable to which it is attached. This charge can build up on both the antenna and the cable until it jumps across an air space, often passing through the electronics inside the low noise block down converter feedhorn (LNBF) or receiver. Connecting the antenna and/or satellite dish to the building's grounding electrode system (grounding) helps dissipate this static charge.
- Nothing can prevent damage from a direct lightning strike, but grounding with proper surge protection can help reduce damage to the satellite dish and other equipment from nearby lightning strikes.

Part III. Amateur and Citizen Band Transmitting and Receiving Stations—Antenna Systems

810.51 Other Sections

In addition to complying with Part III, antenna systems for amateur and citizen band transmitting and receiving stations must comply with 810.11 through 810.15.

810.57 Antenna Discharge Units—Transmitting Stations

Each lead-in conductor for outdoor antennas must be provided with an antenna discharge unit or other suitable means to drain static charges from the antenna system.

Ex 1: If the lead-in conductor is protected by a continuous metallic shield that is bonded in accordance with 810.58, an antenna discharge unit or other suitable means is not required.

Ex 2: If the antenna is bonded in accordance with 810.58, an antenna discharge unit or other suitable means is not required.

810.58 Bonding Conductors and Grounding Electrode Conductors—Amateur and Citizen Band Transmitting and Receiving Stations

Bonding conductors must comply with 810.58(A) through 810.58(C).

(A) Other Sections. Bonding conductors for amateur and citizen band transmitting and receiving stations must comply with 810.21(A) through 810.21(C).

(B) Size of Protective Bonding Conductor. The protective bonding conductor for transmitting stations must be as large as the lead-in but not smaller than 10 AWG copper, bronze, or copper-clad steel.

(C) Size of Operating Bonding Conductor. The operating bonding conductor for transmitting stations must be at least 14 AWG copper or its equivalent.

CHAPTER

8

REVIEW QUESTIONS

Please use the 2023 *Code* book to answer the following questions.

ARTICLE 800—GENERAL REQUIREMENTS FOR COMMUNICATIONS SYSTEMS

1. Only those sections of _____ referenced in Chapter 8 shall apply to Chapter 8.

   (a) Chapters 1 through 4
   (b) Chapters 2 and 3
   (c) Chapters 1 through 7
   (d) the Annexes

2. For communications circuit wiring in _____, the requirements of 300.22(A) shall apply.

   (a) underfloor spaces
   (b) suspended-ceiling spaces
   (c) plenums
   (d) ducts for dust or loose stock, or for vapor removal

3. For communications circuit wiring in _____, the requirements of 300.22(C)(3) shall apply.

   (a) spaces used for environmental air
   (b) ducts for dust
   (c) ducts for loose stock
   (d) ducts for vapor removal

4. Where _____ cable is used to provide a communications circuit within a building, Article 770 shall apply

   (a) coaxial
   (b) fire alarm
   (c) low-voltage
   (d) optical fiber

5. Communications cable ties intended for use in other space used for environmental air (plenums) shall be _____ as having low smoke and heat release properties.

   (a) listed
   (b) labeled
   (c) identified
   (d) approved

6. For communications systems, access to electrical equipment shall not be denied by an accumulation of _____ that prevent(s) the removal of suspended-ceiling panels.

   (a) routers
   (b) amplifiers
   (c) ductwork
   (d) wires and cables

7. Communications cables installed _____ on the surface of ceilings and sidewalls shall be supported by the building structure in such a manner that the cable will not be damaged by normal building use.

   (a) in raceways
   (b) in conduit
   (c) hidden
   (d) exposed

8. For communications systems, plenum _____ and other nonmetallic cable accessories used to secure and support cables in other spaces used for environmental air (plenums) shall be listed as having low smoke and heat release properties in accordance with 800.17.
   (a) fittings
   (b) hangars
   (c) straps
   (d) cable ties

9. The _____ portions of abandoned communications cables shall be removed.
   (a) accessible
   (b) exposed
   (c) concealed
   (d) damaged

10. Openings around penetrations of communications cables, communications raceways, and cable routing assemblies through fire-resistant-rated walls, partitions, floors, or ceilings shall be _____ using approved methods to maintain the fire resistance rating.
   (a) closed
   (b) opened
   (c) draft stopped
   (d) firestopped

11. Where practicable on buildings, a separation of at least _____ shall be maintained between lightning protection conductors and all communications wires and cables and CATV-type coaxial cables.
   (a) 1 ft
   (b) 2 ft
   (c) 3 ft
   (d) 6 ft

12. Wires and cables for communications systems shall be permitted to be installed in any raceway included in _____.
   (a) Chapter 3
   (b) Chapter 8
   (c) Article 300
   (d) Article 800

13. The raceway fill requirements of Chapters 3 and 9 shall apply to _____-power network-powered broadband communications cables.
   (a) low
   (b) medium
   (c) high
   (d) multiconductor

14. Cables used for communications circuits, communications wires, cable routing assemblies, and communications raceways installed in buildings shall be _____ and installed in accordance with the limitations of the listing.
   (a) marked
   (b) labeled
   (c) identified
   (d) listed

15. Communications wires and cables and CATV-type _____ cables shall not be strapped, taped, or attached by any means to the exterior of any raceway as a means of support.
   (a) camera
   (b) coaxial
   (c) internet
   (d) telephone

16. Type _____ communications plenum cables shall be listed as being suitable for use in ducts, plenums, and other spaces used for environmental air.
   (a) CMR
   (b) CMG
   (c) CMX
   (d) CMP

ARTICLE 810—ANTENNA SYSTEMS

1. Article _____ covers antenna systems for radio and television receiving equipment, amateur and citizen band radio transmitting and receiving equipment, and certain features of transmitter safety.
   (a) 680
   (b) 700
   (c) 810
   (d) 840

2. _____ that connect antennas to equipment shall comply with the appropriate article of Chapter 8.
   (a) Equipment grounding conductors
   (b) Coaxial cables
   (c) Power conductors
   (d) Tuning cables

3. Masts and metal structures supporting antennas shall be grounded or bonded in accordance with 810.21, unless the antenna and its related supporting mast or structure are within a zone of protection defined by a _____ radius rolling sphere.
   (a) 75-ft
   (b) 100-ft
   (c) 125-ft
   (d) 150-ft

4. NFPA 780, *Standard for the Installation of Lightning Protection Systems*, provides information for the application of the term "_____" as used in 810.15.
   (a) air terminals
   (b) zone protection
   (c) rolling sphere
   (d) copper rod

5. Underground antenna conductors for radio and television receiving station equipment shall be separated at least _____ from any light, power, or Class 1 circuit conductors.
   (a) 12 in.
   (b) 18 in.
   (c) 5 ft
   (d) 6 ft

6. Indoor antennas and indoor lead-ins shall not be run nearer than _____ to conductors of other wiring systems in the premise.
   (a) 2 in.
   (b) 3 in.
   (c) 4 in.
   (d) 6 in.

7. Indoor antennas and indoor lead-ins shall be permitted to occupy the same box or enclosure with conductors of other wiring systems where separated from such other conductors by _____.
   (a) insulation rated at the highest voltage present
   (b) an effective permanently installed barrier
   (c) at least 2 in of separation
   (d) at least 4 in of separation

8. Receiving station antenna discharge units shall be located outside the building or inside the building between the point of entrance of the lead-in and the radio set or transformers and as near as practicable to the _____.
   (a) entrance of the conductors to the building
   (b) intersystem bonding termination
   (c) grounding electrode system
   (d) any of these

9. The bonding conductor or grounding electrode conductor for a radio/television receiving station antenna system shall be protected where subject to physical damage, and where installed in a metal raceway, both ends of the raceway shall be bonded to the _____ conductor.
   (a) contained
   (b) grounded
   (c) ungrounded
   (d) largest

10. The bonding conductor or grounding electrode conductor for an antenna mast or antenna discharge unit for radio and television equipment shall be run to the _____ in as straight a line as practicable.
   (a) lightning arrester
   (b) surge-protective device
   (c) grounding electrode
   (d) main electrical disconnect enclosure

11. If the building or structure served has an intersystem bonding termination, the bonding conductor for the radio and television equipment antenna mast or antenna discharge unit, shall be connected to the _____.
   (a) main electrical disconnect enclosure
   (b) grounding electrode
   (c) surge protective device
   (d) intersystem bonding termination

12. For antenna systems, an intersystem bonding termination device shall not be mounted on a door or cover even if the door or cover is _____.
   (a) plastic
   (b) removable
   (c) nonremovable
   (d) fiberglass

13. The bonding conductor or grounding electrode conductor for radio and television receiving station antenna discharge units shall not be smaller than _____.

    (a) 10 AWG copper
    (b) 8 AWG aluminum
    (c) 17 AWG copper-clad steel or bronze
    (d) any of these

14. If a separate grounding electrode is installed for the radio and television receiving station equipment, it shall be bonded to the building's electrical power grounding electrode system with a bonding jumper not smaller than _____.

    (a) 10 AWG
    (b) 8 AWG
    (c) 6 AWG
    (d) 1/0 AWG

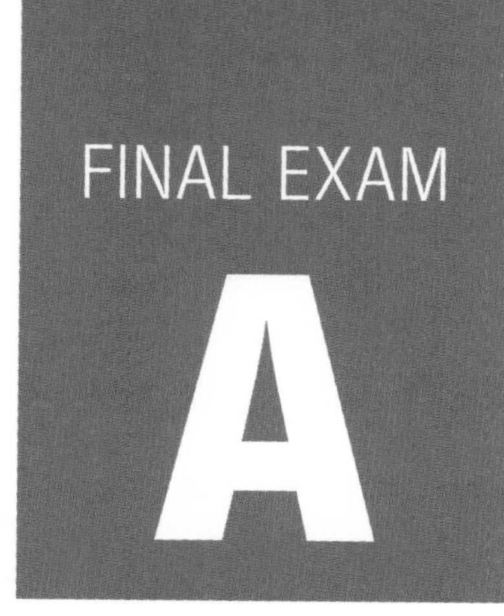

FINAL EXAM A—STRAIGHT ORDER

Please use the 2023 *Code* book to answer the following questions.

1. The purpose of the *NEC* is for _____.
   (a) it to be used as a design manual
   (b) use as an instruction guide for untrained persons
   (c) the practical safeguarding of persons and property
   (d) interacting with inspectors

2. Installations used to export electric power from vehicles to premises wiring or for _____ current flow is covered by the *NEC*.
   (a) emergency
   (b) primary
   (c) bidirectional
   (d) secondary

3. The *Code* does not cover installations under the exclusive control of an electric utility such as _____.
   (a) service drops or service laterals
   (b) electric utility office buildings
   (c) electric utility warehouses
   (d) electric utility garages

4. By special permission, the authority having jurisdiction may waive *NEC* requirements or approve alternative methods where equivalent _____ can be achieved and maintained.
   (a) safety
   (b) workmanship
   (c) installations
   (d) job progress

5. In the *NEC*, the word(s) _____ indicate a mandatory requirement.
   (a) shall
   (b) shall not
   (c) shall be permitted
   (d) shall or shall not

6. Capable of being reached quickly for operation, renewal, or inspections without climbing over or under obstructions, removing obstacles, resorting to portable ladders, or the use of tools (other than keys) is known as _____.
   (a) accessible (as applied to equipment)
   (b) accessible (as applied to wiring methods)
   (c) accessible, readily (readily accessible)
   (d) all of these

7. The connection between two or more portions of the equipment grounding conductor is the definition of a(an) _____.
   (a) system bonding jumper
   (b) main bonding jumper
   (c) equipment ground-fault jumper
   (d) equipment bonding jumper

8. The circuit conductors between the final overcurrent device protecting the circuit and the outlet(s) are known as _____ conductors.
   (a) feeder
   (b) branch-circuit
   (c) home run
   (d) main circuit

9. _____ cable is a cable with insulated conductors within an overall nonmetallic jacket.
   (a) AC
   (b) MC
   (c) NM
   (d) TC

10. _____ cable is a factory assembly of one or more insulated conductors with an integral or an overall covering of nonmetallic material suitable for direct burial in the earth.
   (a) NM
   (b) UF
   (c) SE
   (d) TC

11. Emergency power systems are those systems legally required and classed as emergency by a governmental agency having jurisdiction. These systems are intended to automatically supply illumination and/or power essential for _____.
   (a) community activity
   (b) safety to human life
   (c) public recreation
   (d) police and emergency services exclusively

12. The largest amount of current capable of being delivered at a point on the system during a short-circuit condition is the definition of _____.
   (a) objectionable current
   (b) excessive current
   (c) induced current
   (d) available fault current

13. Connected (connecting) to ground or to a conductive body that extends the ground connection is called _____.
   (a) equipment grounding
   (b) bonded
   (c) grounded
   (d) all of these

14. An effective ground-fault current path is an intentionally constructed, low-impedance electrically conductive path designed and intended to carry current during a ground-fault event from the point of a ground fault on a wiring system to _____.
   (a) ground
   (b) earth
   (c) the electrical supply source
   (d) the grounding electrode

15. Inverter equipment capable of operating in both interactive and island modes describes a(an) _____ inverter.
   (a) multi-purpose
   (b) isolated
   (c) bidirectional
   (d) multimode

16. A(An) _____ is equipment that changes dc to ac.
   (a) diode
   (b) rectifier
   (c) transistor
   (d) inverter

17. The operating mode for power production or microgrids that allows energy to be supplied to loads that are disconnected from an electric power production and distribution network or other primary power source defines the term _____.
   (a) island mode
   (b) isolation mode
   (c) emergency mode
   (d) standby mode

18. A wet-niche luminaire is intended to be installed in a _____ surrounded by water.
   (a) transformer
   (b) forming shell
   (c) hydromassage bathtub
   (d) all of these

19. Any current in excess of the rated current of equipment or the ampacity of a conductor is called _____.
   (a) trip current
   (b) fault current
   (c) overcurrent
   (d) a short circuit

20. A patient _____ is the location of a patient sleeping bed, or the bed or procedure table of a Category 1 space.
   (a) bed location
   (b) care area
   (c) observation area
   (d) sterile area

21. Permanently installed pools are those that are constructed or installed in the ground or partially in the ground, and all pools installed inside of a building, whether or not served by electrical circuits of any nature.
    (a) in the ground
    (b) partially in the ground
    (c) inside of a building
    (d) any of these

22. A raceway is an enclosed channel designed expressly for holding _____, with additional functions as permitted in this *Code*.
    (a) wires
    (b) cables
    (c) busbars
    (d) any of these

23. _____ is an unthreaded thinwall raceway of circular cross section designed for the physical protection and routing of conductors and cables and for use as an equipment grounding conductor when installed utilizing appropriate fittings.
    (a) LFNC
    (b) EMT
    (c) NUCC
    (d) RTRC

24. _____ is a pliable corrugated raceway of circular cross section, with integral or associated couplings, connectors, and fittings that are listed for the installation of electrical conductors.
    (a) PVC
    (b) ENT
    (c) RMC
    (d) IMC

25. General requirements for the examination and approval, installation and use, access to and spaces about electrical conductors and equipment; enclosures intended for personnel entry; and tunnel installations are within the scope of _____.
    (a) Article 800
    (b) Article 300
    (c) Article 110
    (d) Annex J

26. Some _____ can cause severe deterioration of many plastic materials used for insulating and structural applications in equipment.
    (a) cleaning and lubricating compounds
    (b) protective coatings
    (c) paints and enamels
    (d) detergents

27. NFPA 70E, *Standard for Electrical Safety in the Workplace*, provides specific criteria for developing arc-flash labels for equipment that provides _____, and so forth.
    (a) nominal system voltage and incident energy levels
    (b) arc-flash boundaries
    (c) minimum required levels of personal protective equipment
    (d) all of these

28. Electrical equipment servicing and electrical preventive maintenance shall be performed by _____ trained in servicing and maintenance of equipment.
    (a) qualified persons
    (b) manufacturer's representatives
    (c) service specialists
    (d) licensed individuals

29. Equipment servicing and electrical preventive maintenance shall be performed in accordance with the original equipment manufacturer's instructions and _____.
    (a) information included in the listing information
    (b) applicable industry standards,
    (c) as approved by the authority having jurisdiction
    (d) any of these

30. Each disconnecting means shall be legibly marked to indicate its purpose unless located and arranged so _____.
    (a) that it can be locked out and tagged
    (b) it is not readily accessible
    (c) the purpose is evident
    (d) that it operates at less than 300 volts-to-ground

31. The minimum height of working spaces shall be clear and extend from the grade, floor, or platform to a height of _____ or the height of the equipment, whichever is greater.
    (a) 3 ft
    (b) 6 ft
    (c) 6½ ft
    (d) 7 ft

32. All switchboards, switchgear, panelboards, and motor control centers located outdoors shall be _____.
    (a) installed in identified enclosures
    (b) protected from accidental contact by unauthorized personnel or by vehicular traffic
    (c) protected from accidental spillage or leakage from piping systems
    (d) all of these

33. A NEMA Type 1 enclosure is approved for the environmental condition where _____ might be present.
    (a) falling dirt
    (b) falling liquids
    (c) circulating dust
    (d) settling airborne dust

34. Hazardous (classified) locations shall be classified depending on the properties of the _____ that could be present, and the likelihood that a flammable or combustible concentration or quantity is present.
    (a) flammable or combustible liquid-produced vapors
    (b) flammable gases
    (c) combustible dusts or fiber/flyings
    (d) all of these

35. In the layout of electrical installations for hazardous (classified) locations, it is frequently possible to locate much of the equipment in a reduced level of classification or in an _____ location to reduce the amount of special equipment required.
    (a) unclassified
    (b) classified
    (c) Class I
    (d) Class II

36. A Class III, Division _____ location is where ignitible fibers/flyings are stored or handled but not manufactured.
    (a) 1
    (b) 2
    (c) 3
    (d) all of these

37. Threaded conduits or fittings installed in hazardous (classified) locations shall be made wrenchtight to _____.
    (a) prevent sparking when a fault current flows through the conduit system
    (b) prevent seepage of gases or fumes
    (c) prevent sag in the conduit runs
    (d) maintain a workmanship like installation

38. A sealing fitting is permitted to be installed within _____ of either side of the boundary where a conduit leaves a Class I, Division 1 location.
    (a) 5 ft
    (b) 6 ft
    (c) 8 ft
    (d) 10 ft

39. Removal of shielding material and the separation of the twisted pairs of shielded cables and twisted pair cables shall not be required within the conduit seal fitting in a Class I, Division 2 hazardous (classified) location if the conductors are sealed in accordance with instructions provided with a listed fitting to minimize the entrance of gases or vapors and prevent the propagation of flame into the cable core.
    (a) True
    (b) False

40. In Class I, Division 1 locations, all utilization equipment shall be _____ for use in a Class I, Division 1 location.
    (a) identified
    (b) approved
    (c) marked
    (d) listed

41. For Class I locations where 501.140(A)(5) is applied, flexible cords shall be _____ from the power source to the temporary portable assembly and from the temporary portable assembly to the utilization equipment.
    (a) permitted to be spliced
    (b) of continuous length
    (c) installed in a metal raceway
    (d) spliced only using listed splicing kits

1st Printing

42. Boxes and fittings installed in Class II, Division 1 locations shall be provided with threaded bosses for connection to conduit or cable terminations and shall be _____.
    (a) explosionproof
    (b) identified for Class II locations
    (c) dusttight
    (d) weatherproof

43. In Class II Locations the locknut-bushing and double-locknut types of contacts shall not be depended on for _____ purposes, but bonding jumpers with identified fittings or other approved means of bonding shall be used.
    (a) bonding
    (b) grounding
    (c) continuity
    (d) any of these

44. In Class II, Division 2 locations, enclosures for fuses, switches, circuit breakers, and motor controllers, including pushbuttons, relays, and similar devices shall be _____.
    (a) dusttight or otherwise identified for the location
    (b) raintight
    (c) rated as Class I, Division 1 explosionproof
    (d) general duty

45. The area used for _____ of alcohol-based windshield washer fluid in repair garages shall be unclassified.
    (a) storage
    (b) handling
    (c) dispensing into motor vehicles
    (d) any of these

46. In commercial garages, GFCI protection for personnel shall be provided as required in _____.
    (a) 210.8(A)
    (b) 210.8(B)
    (c) 210.8(C)
    (d) 210.8(D)

47. In health care facilities, _____ ground receptacle(s) installed in patient care spaces outside of a patient care vicinity(s) shall comply with 517.16(B)(1) and (2).
    (a) AFCI-protected
    (b) GFCI-protected
    (c) isolated
    (d) all of these

48. The wiring method(s) permitted in an assembly occupancy of fire-rated construction is(are) _____.
    (a) metal raceways
    (b) flexible metal raceways
    (c) Types MI, MC, or AC cables
    (d) all of these

49. Article(s) _____ cover(s) the installation of portable wiring and equipment for carnivals, circuses, fairs, and similar functions.
    (a) 518
    (b) 525
    (c) 590
    (d) all of these

50. Cord connectors for carnivals, circuses, and fairs shall not be placed in audience traffic paths or within areas accessible to the public unless _____.
    (a) guarded
    (b) labeled
    (c) approved
    (d) identified

51. Enclosures and fittings installed in areas of agricultural buildings where excessive _____ may be present shall be designed to minimize the entrance of dust and shall have no openings through which dust can enter the enclosure.
    (a) dust
    (b) dirt
    (c) snow
    (d) rain

52. Nonmetallic _____ shall not be permitted to be concealed within walls and above ceilings of agricultural building spaces which are contiguous with, or physically adjoined to, livestock confinement areas.
    (a) cables
    (b) raceways
    (c) conduits
    (d) conductors

53. Luminaires used in agricultural buildings shall _____.
    (a) minimize the entrance of dust, foreign matter, moisture, and corrosive material
    (b) be protected by a suitable guard if exposed to physical damage
    (c) be listed for use in wet locations when exposed to water
    (d) all of these

54. For temporary installations on construction sites, a box, conduit body, or other enclosure, with a cover installed, shall be required for all splices except where the circuit conductors being spliced are all from nonmetallic multiconductor _____ assemblies, provided that the equipment grounding continuity is maintained with or without the box.

(a) listed
(b) identified
(c) cord or cable
(d) feeder and service conductor

55. When using portable receptacles for temporary wiring installations that are not part of the building or structure, employees shall be protected on construction sites by either ground-fault circuit-interrupters or by the use of a(an) _____.

(a) insulated conductor program
(b) double insulated conductor program
(c) flexible conductor program
(d) assured equipment grounding conductor program

56. Article 600 covers the installation of conductors, equipment, and field wiring for _____, and outline lighting, regardless of voltage.

(a) electric signs
(b) retrofit kits
(c) neon tubing
(d) all of these

57. Each sign and outline lighting system circuit supplying a sign, outline lighting system, or skeleton tubing shall be controlled by an externally operable switch or circuit breaker that opens all _____ conductors and controls no other load.

(a) ungrounded
(b) grounded
(c) equipment grounding
(d) all of these

58. Bonding conductors installed outside of a sign or raceway used for the bonding connections of the noncurrent-carrying metal parts of signs, shall be protected from physical damage and are permitted to be copper-clad aluminum not smaller than _____.

(a) 14 AWG
(b) 12 AWG
(c) 8 AWG
(d) 6 AWG

59. Article _____ applies to field-installed wiring using off-site manufactured subassemblies for branch circuits, remote-control circuits, signaling circuits, and communications circuits in accessible areas.

(a) 600
(b) 604
(c) 605
(d) 610

60. Where a disconnecting means for EVSE and WPTE is required and installed remote from the equipment, a plaque shall be installed _____ denoting the location of the disconnecting means.

(a) adjacent to the equipment
(b) on the equipment
(c) within 3 ft of the equipment
(d) within sight of the equipment

61. All welding and cutting power equipment under the scope of Article 630 shall be _____.

(a) identified
(b) labeled
(c) listed
(d) approved

62. Conductors that supply one or more resistance welders shall be protected by an overcurrent device rated or set at not more than _____ of the conductor ampacity.

(a) 80 percent
(b) 100 percent
(c) 125 percent
(d) 300 percent

63. Class 2 and Class 3 cables for audio signal processing, amplification, and reproduction equipment installed in accordance with 722.135(B) shall be permitted to be installed in ducts specifically fabricated for _____.

(a) environmental air
(b) processed air
(c) heat exchange air
(d) none of these

64. Exposed audio cables shall be secured by _____ or similar fittings designed and installed so as not to damage the cable.

(a) straps
(b) staples
(c) hangers
(d) any of these

65. Article 645 does not apply unless an information technology equipment room contains _____.
    (a) a disconnecting means complying with 645.10
    (b) a separate heating/ventilating/air-conditioning (HVAC) system
    (c) separation by fire-resistance-rated walls, floors, and ceilings
    (d) all of these

66. The ampacity of the branch-circuit conductors and the rating or setting of overcurrent protective devices for electrically powered swimming pool heat pumps and chillers using the circulating water system shall be sized _____.
    (a) to comply with the nameplate
    (b) not greater than 35A
    (c) at 125 percent of its rating
    (d) less than 60A

67. Luminaires installed above new outdoor pools or the area extending _____ horizontally from the inside walls of the pool shall be installed at a height of not less than 12 ft above the maximum water level of the pool.
    (a) 3 ft
    (b) 5 ft
    (c) 10 ft
    (d) 12 ft

68. Listed low-voltage gas-fired luminaires, decorative fireplaces, fire pits, and similar equipment using low-voltage ignitors that do not require grounding and are supplied by listed transformers or power supplies that comply with 680.23(A)(2) with outputs that do not exceed the low-voltage contact limit shall be permitted to be located less than _____ from the inside walls of the pool.
    (a) 3 ft
    (b) 5 ft
    (c) 10 ft
    (d) 12 ft

69. All fixed metal parts where located no greater than _____ vertically above the maximum water level of the pool, observation stands, towers, or platforms, or any diving structures, shall be bonded.
    (a) 6 ft
    (b) 8 ft
    (c) 10 ft
    (d) 12 ft

70. Where spas or hot tubs are installed indoors, the equipotential bonding requirements for perimeter surfaces in 680.26(B)(2) shall not apply to a listed self-contained spa or hot tub installed above a finished floor.
    (a) True
    (b) False

71. Permanently installed fountains intended for recreational use by pedestrians, including _____, shall also comply with the requirements in 680.26.
    (a) splash pads
    (b) hot tubs
    (c) spas
    (d) all of these

72. For crystalline and multicrystalline silicon modules, the PV system voltage ambient temperature correction is _____ if the ambient temperature is 20°C.
    (a) 1.02
    (b) 1.04
    (c) 1.06
    (d) 1.08

73. For circuit sizing calculations of PV systems without adjustment and/or correction factors, the minimum conductor size must have an ampacity not less than the maximum currents calculated in 690.8(A) multiplied by _____.
    (a) 75 percent
    (b) 100 percent
    (c) 125 percent
    (d) 150 percent

74. For PV systems where overcurrent protection is required on one end and the circuit conductor is also connected to a source having an available maximum current greater than the ampacity of the circuit conductor, the circuit conductors shall be protected from overcurrent at the point of connection to _____ current source(s).
    (a) the lower
    (b) the higher
    (c) either
    (d) both

75. For PV system rapid shutdown systems, controlled conductors located outside the array boundary or more than 3 ft from the point of entry inside a building shall be limited to not more than _____ within 30 seconds of rapid shutdown initiation.

(a) 80V
(b) 50V
(c) 30V
(d) 15V

76. Where a disconnect is required to _____ PV system equipment, the equipment disconnecting means shall be installed in accordance with 690.15(C).

(a) open
(b) isolate
(c) close
(d) open or close

77. An isolating device for PV system equipment shall which of the following?

(a) A mating connector meeting the requirements of 690.33 and listed and identified for use with specific equipment.
(b) A finger-safe fuse holder or an isolating switch that requires a tool to place the device in the open (off) position.
(c) An isolating device listed for the intended application.
(d) any of these

78. Equipment and wiring methods containing PV system dc circuits with a maximum voltage greater than 1000V shall not be permitted _____.

(a) on or in single-family dwellings
(b) on or in two-family dwellings
(c) within buildings containing habitable rooms
(d) all of these

79. Exposed noncurrent-carrying metal parts of PV module frames, electrical equipment, and conductor enclosures of PV systems shall be connected to a(an) _____.

(a) grounding jumper
(b) bonding jumper
(c) equipment grounding conductor
(d) grounding jumper or bonding jumper

80. Large-scale PV systems that do not provide arc-fault protection shall include details of fire mitigation plans to address _____ in the documentation required in 691.6.

(a) dc arc faults
(b) dc and ac arc faults
(c) dc ground faults
(d) dc and ac ground faults

81. When a fire pump is supplied by an individual source, the _____ shall be rated to carry indefinitely the sum of the locked-rotor current of the largest fire pump motor and the full-load current of all of the other pump motors and accessory equipment.

(a) overcurrent protective device(s)
(b) pump motor conductors
(c) pump motor controllers
(d) source supply conductors

82. Feeder conductors supplying fire pump motors and accessory equipment shall have a _____ ampacity in accordance with 430.22 and shall comply with the voltage-drop requirements in 695.7.

(a) maximum
(b) minimum
(c) permitted
(d) none of these

83. Article _____ applies to the electrical safety of the installation, operation, and maintenance of emergency systems intended to supply, distribute, and control electricity for illumination, power, or both, to required facilities when the normal electrical supply or system is interrupted.

(a) 500
(b) 600
(c) 700
(d) 800

84. Wiring of Class 2 emergency circuits shall comply with the requirements of 300.4 and be installed in a(an) _____.

(a) raceway
(b) armored-cable or metal-clad cable
(c) cable tray
(d) any of these

85. Battery-equipped emergency luminaires shall be on the same branch circuit that serves the normal lighting in the area and connected _____ any local switches.

(a) with
(b) ahead of
(c) after
(d) downstream of

86. Legally required standby system overcurrent protective devices (OCPDs) shall be _____ with all supply-side and load-side OCPDs.

(a) series rated
(b) selectively coordinated
(c) installed in parallel
(d) labeled in accordance

87. Interconnected power production installations with multiple co-located power production sources shall be permitted to be _____ as a group(s).

(a) identified
(b) labeled
(c) marked
(d) all of these

88. The rating of the overcurrent protective device of the interconnected electric power production source service disconnecting means shall be used to determine if _____ is required in accordance with 230.95.

(a) ground-fault protection of equipment
(b) arc-fault protection
(c) surge protection
(d) lightning protection

89. When determining the ampere rating of busbars associated with load-side source connections of interconnected electric power production sources, one can use the sum of the ampere ratings of all overcurrent devices on _____, both load and supply devices, excluding the rating of the overcurrent device protecting the busbar, but shall not exceed the ampacity of the busbar.

(a) metering equipment
(b) panelboards
(c) switchgear
(d) all of these

90. Listed plug-in-type circuit breakers backfed from interconnected electric power production sources that are listed and identified as _____ shall not require a fastener as required by 408.36(D).

(a) interactive
(b) active
(c) reactive
(d) interactive or active

91. The installation and maintenance of energy storage system (ESS) equipment and all associated wiring and interconnections shall be performed only by _____.

(a) qualified persons
(b) ESS specialists
(c) licensed electricians
(d) maintenance personnel

92. For required notification and marking purposes for energy storage systems (ESS) for available fault current derived from the stationary battery system, _____ can provide information about available fault current on any particular battery model.

(a) UL listings
(b) battery equipment suppliers
(c) equipment labeling
(d) the design engineer

93. Where controls to activate the energy storage system (ESS) battery disconnecting means are used and are not located within sight of the battery, the location of the controls shall be marked _____.

(a) on the batteries
(b) adjacent to the batteries
(c) on the disconnecting means
(d) in a secure location

94. Energy storage system (ESS) battery disconnecting means shall be legibly marked in the field and shall include the _____.

(a) nominal battery voltage
(b) available fault current and arc-flash label
(c) date the calculation was performed
(d) all of these

95. For the purposes of bundling cables transmitting power and data, the requirements of 300.11 and Parts I and III of Article 725 shall apply to Class 2 and Class 3 circuits that transmit power and data. The conductors that carry power for the data circuits shall be _____.

(a) copper
(b) copper-clad aluminum
(c) aluminum
(d) any of these

96. Fire alarm equipment supplying power-limited fire alarm circuits shall be durably marked where plainly visible to indicate each circuit that is _____.

(a) supplied by a nonpower-limited fire alarm circuit
(b) a power-limited fire alarm circuit
(c) a fire alarm circuit
(d) supervised

97. The maximum breaker size on the supply side of a fire alarm transformer is _____.

(a) 5A
(b) 10A
(c) 15A
(d) 20A

98. For communications circuit wiring in _____, the requirements of 300.22(A) shall apply.

(a) underfloor spaces
(b) suspended-ceiling spaces
(c) plenums
(d) ducts for dust or loose stock, or for vapor removal

99. The raceway fill requirements of Chapters 3 and 9 shall apply to _____-power network-powered broadband communications cables.

(a) low
(b) medium
(c) high
(d) multiconductor

100. If a separate grounding electrode is installed for the radio and television receiving station equipment, it shall be bonded to the building's electrical power grounding electrode system with a bonding jumper not smaller than _____.

(a) 10 AWG
(b) 8 AWG
(c) 6 AWG
(d) 1/0 AWG

1st Printing

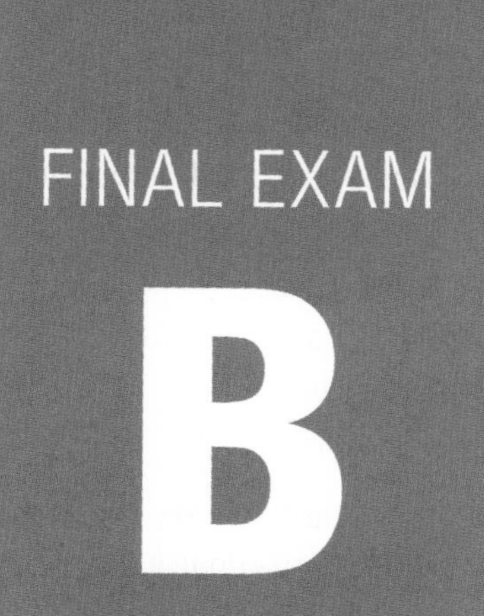

FINAL EXAM B— RANDOM ORDER

Please use the 2023 *Code* book to answer the following questions.

1. Separately installed pressure connectors shall be used with conductors at the _____ not exceeding the ampacity at the listed and identified temperature rating of the connector.
   (a) voltages
   (b) temperatures
   (c) listings
   (d) ampacities

2. Internal parts of electrical equipment, including busbars, wiring terminals, insulators, and other surfaces, shall not be damaged or contaminated by foreign materials such as _____, or corrosive residues.
   (a) paint, plaster
   (b) cleaners
   (c) abrasives
   (d) any of these

3. Seals are provided in conduit and cable systems to _____ and prevent the passage of flames from one portion of the electrical installation to another through the conduit.
   (a) minimize the passage of gas or vapor
   (b) exclude moisture and other fluids from the cable insulation
   (c) limit a possible explosion
   (d) prevent the escape of powder

4. Flexible cords and flexible cables, where connected to moving parts of tracking PV _____, shall comply with Article 400.
   (a) systems
   (b) arrays
   (c) cells
   (d) modules

5. Installations of communications equipment under the exclusive control of communications utilities located outdoors or in building spaces used exclusively for such installations _____ covered by the *NEC*.
   (a) are
   (b) are sometimes
   (c) are not
   (d) may be

6. Areas or enclosures without adequate ventilation, where electrical equipment is located and pool sanitation chemicals are stored, handled, or dispensed is the definition of a _____.
   (a) hazardous area
   (b) restricted area
   (c) corrosive environment
   (d) wet location

7. Flexible cords are not permitted in Class I locations.
   (a) True
   (b) False

8. For interconnected electric power production source(s) connected to a service, the service conductors connected to the power production source service disconnecting means shall be sized in accordance with 705.28 and not be smaller than _____ copper.

   (a) 8 AWG
   (b) 6 AWG
   (c) 4 AWG
   (d) 3 AWG

9. Engineering documentation of large-scale electric supply stations shall include details of conformance of the design with _____.

   (a) Article 250
   (b) Article 690
   (c) Article 702
   (d) Article 710

10. Where only half of the conductors in each cable are carrying current, the values in Table 725.144 shall be permitted to be increased by a factor of _____.

    (a) 1
    (b) 1.2
    (c) 1.4
    (d) 1.6

11. In Class I, Division 1 locations, seals shall not be required for conduit entering an enclosure if the switch, circuit breaker, fuse, relay, or resistor is _____.

    (a) enclosed within a chamber hermetically sealed against the entrance of gases or vapors
    (b) immersed in oil in accordance with 501.115(B)(1)(2)
    (c) enclosed within an enclosure, identified for the location, and marked Leads Factory Sealed, Factory Sealed, or Seal not Required, or equivalent
    (d) any of these

12. A(An) _____ surge protective device shall be installed in or on the fire pump controller.

    (a) listed
    (b) labeled
    (c) identified
    (d) approved

13. Flexible cords and flexible cables used for temporary wiring shall _____.

    (a) be protected from accidental damage
    (b) be protected where passing through doorways
    (c) avoid sharp corners and projections
    (d) all of these

14. Where PVC, RTRC, or HDPE is used in Class I, Division 1 underground locations, the concrete encasement shall be permitted to be omitted where RMC or IMC conduit is used for the last _____ of the underground run to emergence or to the point of connection to the aboveground raceway.

    (a) 12 in.
    (b) 18 in.
    (c) 24 in.
    (d) 30 in.

15. A dc-to-dc converter is a device that can provide an output _____ voltage and current at a higher or lower value than the input _____ voltage and current.

    (a) ac, dc
    (b) ac, ac
    (c) dc, dc
    (d) dc, ac

16. The bonding requirements contained in 250.97 shall apply only to solidly grounded PV system circuits operating over _____ to ground.

    (a) 30V
    (b) 60V
    (c) 120V
    (d) 250V

17. Article _____ covers antenna systems for radio and television receiving equipment, amateur and citizen band radio transmitting and receiving equipment, and certain features of transmitter safety.

    (a) 680
    (b) 700
    (c) 810
    (d) 840

18. In cases where the battery is separate from the energy storage system (ESS) electronics, the batteries could include an enclosure, battery monitoring and controls, or other related battery components.
    (a) True
    (b) False

19. Fixed lighting in a commercial garage located over lanes on which vehicles are commonly driven shall be located not less than _____ above floor level.
    (a) 10 ft
    (b) 12 ft
    (c) 14 ft
    (d) 16 ft

20. Cable used in a wet location shall be listed for use in wet locations and be marked wet or wet location or have a moisture-impervious _____ sheath.
    (a) metal
    (b) plastic
    (c) fiberglass
    (d) any of these

21. A listed _____ shall be installed on the supply side of a fire alarm control panel in accordance with Part II of Article 242.
    (a) current-limiting device
    (b) selectively coordinated device
    (c) surge-protective device (SPD)
    (d) current transformer

22. Suitability of identified equipment for use in a hazardous (classified) location shall be determined by _____.
    (a) equipment listing or labeling
    (b) evidence of equipment evaluation from a qualified testing laboratory or inspection agency concerned with product evaluation
    (c) evidence acceptable to the authority having jurisdiction, such as a manufacturer's self-evaluation or an owner's engineering judgment
    (d) any of these

23. PV system dc circuits shall not occupy the same equipment wiring enclosure, cable, or raceway as other non-PV systems, or inverter output circuits, unless the PV system dc circuits are separated from other circuits by a barrier or _____.
    (a) partition
    (b) sleeve
    (c) double insulation
    (d) shield

24. Ground-fault protection of equipment shall _____ in any fire pump power circuit.
    (a) not be installed
    (b) be provided
    (c) be permitted
    (d) be listed

25. Electrical equipment (excluding wiring methods) and connections in marinas, boatyards, and commercial and noncommercial docking facilities not intended for operation while submerged, shall be located _____.
    (a) at least 12 in. above the deck of a floating structure
    (b) at least 12 in. above the deck of a fixed structure
    (c) not below the electrical datum plane
    (d) all of these

26. When PVC is run from a pool light forming shell to a pool junction box, an 8 AWG _____ bonding jumper shall be installed in the raceway.
    (a) solid bare
    (b) solid insulated copper
    (c) stranded insulated copper
    (d) solid or stranded insulated copper

27. Connectors and terminals for conductors more finely stranded than Class B and Class C, as shown in Chapter 9, Table 10, shall be _____ for the specific conductor class or classes.
    (a) listed
    (b) approved
    (c) identified
    (d) all of these

28. All service equipment, switchboards, panelboards, and motor control centers shall be _____.
    (a) located in dedicated spaces
    (b) protected from damage
    (c) in weatherproof enclosures
    (d) located in dedicated spaces and protected from damage

29. Automatic transfer switches on legally required standby systems shall be electrically operated and _____ held.
    (a) electrically
    (b) mechanically
    (c) gravity
    (d) any of these

30. Buildings whose sole purpose is to house and protect large-scale PV supply station equipment shall not be required to comply with 690.12. Written standard _____ shall be available at the site detailing necessary shutdown procedures in the event of an emergency.
    (a) guidelines
    (b) operating procedures
    (c) documentation
    (d) any of these

31. Electrical generating equipment supplied by any source other than a utility service, up to the source system disconnecting means defines _____.
    (a) a service drop
    (b) power production equipment
    (c) the service point
    (d) utilization equipment

32. All receptacles rated 125V through 250V, 60A or less, located within _____ of a fountain edge shall have GFCI protection or SPGFCI protection in accordance with 680.5(B) or (C) as applicable.
    (a) 8 ft
    (b) 10 ft
    (c) 15 ft
    (d) 20 ft

33. Pools installed entirely on or above the ground that are intended to be stored when not in use and are designed for ease of relocation, regardless of water depth are considered to be _____.
    (a) temporary
    (b) storable
    (c) portable
    (d) exempt from *Code* requirements

34. A PV _____ circuit is the PV source circuit conductors of one or more series-connected PV modules.
    (a) branch
    (b) string
    (c) combined
    (d) grouped

35. Areas adjacent to classified locations in commercial garages in which flammable vapors are not likely to be released shall be unclassified where_____.
    (a) mechanically ventilated at a rate of four or more changes per hour
    (b) designed with positive air pressure
    (c) separated by an unpierced wall, roof, or other solid partition
    (d) any of these

36. Luminaires installed in Class I, Division 2 locations shall be protected from physical damage by a suitable _____.
    (a) warning label
    (b) pendant
    (c) guard or by location
    (d) all of these

37. For communications systems, access to electrical equipment shall not be denied by an accumulation of _____ that prevent(s) the removal of suspended-ceiling panels.
    (a) routers
    (b) amplifiers
    (c) ductwork
    (d) wires and cables

38. A separate portion of a conduit or tubing system that provides access through a removable cover(s) to the interior of the system at a junction of two or more sections of the system or at a terminal point of the system defines the term _____.
    (a) junction box
    (b) accessible raceway
    (c) conduit body
    (d) cutout box

39. In sight from or within sight from is defined as equipment that is visible and not more than _____ distant from other equipment is in sight from that other equipment. (*TC Note to CK: Please italicize in sight from.)
    (a) 10 feet
    (b) 20 feet
    (c) 25 feet
    (d) 50 feet

40. A single receptacle is a single contact device with no other contact device on the same _____.
    (a) circuit
    (b) yoke or strap
    (c) run
    (d) equipment

41. Rigid metal conduit, intermediate metal conduit, reinforced thermosetting resin conduit (RTRC) listed for aboveground use, or rigid polyvinyl chloride (PVC) conduit suitable for the location shall be used to protect wiring to a point at least _____ above docks, decks of piers, and landing stages.
    (a) 4 ft
    (b) 6 ft
    (c) 8 ft
    (d) 10 ft

42. Fixed electrical equipment installed in spaces above a hazardous (classified) location in a commercial garage shall be _____.
    (a) well ventilated
    (b) GFPE protected
    (c) GFCI protected
    (d) located above the level of any defined Class I location or identified for the location

43. Where inside buildings, PV system dc circuits that exceed 30V or 8A shall be contained in _____.
    (a) metal raceways
    (b) MC cable that complies with 250.118(10)
    (c) metal enclosures
    (d) any of these

44. A Type 4X enclosure for switchboards, switchgear, or panelboards located indoors is suitable in locations subject to the environmental condition of _____.
    (a) falling dirt
    (b) falling liquids
    (c) corrosive agents
    (d) any of these

45. The enforcement of the *NEC* is the responsibility of the authority having jurisdiction, who is responsible for _____.
    (a) making interpretations of rules
    (b) approval of equipment and materials
    (c) granting special permission
    (d) all of these

46. Type(s) _____ cable(s) can be used for temporary branch-circuit installations in any dwelling, building, or structure without any height limitation or limitation by building construction type and without concealment within walls, floors, or ceilings.
    (a) NM
    (b) NMC
    (c) SE
    (d) any of these

47. For communications circuit wiring in _____, the requirements of 300.22(C)(3) shall apply.
    (a) spaces used for environmental air
    (b) ducts for dust
    (c) ducts for loose stock
    (d) ducts for vapor removal

48. Overcurrent devices used in PV source circuits shall be _____ for use in PV systems.
    (a) identified
    (b) approved
    (c) recognized
    (d) listed

49. Where a disconnect is required to isolate PV system equipment with a maximum circuit current of _____ or less, an isolating device shall be installed in accordance with 690.15(B).
    (a) 15A
    (b) 20A
    (c) 30A
    (d) 50A

50. Overcurrent devices for PV system dc circuits shall be readily accessible.

    (a) True
    (b) False

51. Nonmandatory information relative to the use of the *NEC* is provided in informative annexes and are _____.

    (a) included for information purposes only
    (b) not enforceable requirements of the *Code*
    (c) enforceable as a requirement of the *Code*
    (d) included for information purposes only and are not enforceable requirements of the *Code*

52. When the *Code* uses _____, it indicates the actions are allowed but not required.

    (a) shall or shall not
    (b) shall not be permitted
    (c) shall be permitted
    (d) none of these

53. If the *Code* requires new products that may not yet be available at the time the *NEC* is adopted, the _____ can allow products that comply with the most recent previous edition of the *Code* adopted by the jurisdiction.

    (a) electrical engineer
    (b) master electrician
    (c) authority having jurisdiction
    (d) none of these

54. Information and technology equipment and systems are used for creation and manipulation of _____.

    (a) data
    (b) voice
    (c) video
    (d) all of these

55. All equipment intended for use in PV systems shall be listed or be _____ for the application and have a field label applied.

    (a) identified
    (b) marked
    (c) approved
    (d) evaluated

56. Likely to become energized is defined as conductive material that could become energized because of _____ or electrical spacing.

    (a) improper installation
    (b) poor maintenance
    (c) the failure of electrical insulation
    (d) power surges

57. Indoor antennas and indoor lead-ins shall be permitted to occupy the same box or enclosure with conductors of other wiring systems where separated from such other conductors by _____.

    (a) insulation rated at the highest voltage present
    (b) an effective permanently installed barrier
    (c) at least 2 in of separation
    (d) at least 4 in of separation

58. Where PV source and output circuits operating at over 30V are installed in readily accessible locations, circuit conductors shall be guarded or installed in _____.

    (a) MC cable
    (b) multiconductor jacketed cable
    (c) a raceway
    (d) any of these

59. Receptacles on construction sites shall not be installed on _____ that supplies temporary lighting.

    (a) any branch circuit
    (b) the same feeder
    (c) any branch circuit or the same feeder
    (d) any cord or cable

60. The PV system equipment disconnecting means shall have ratings sufficient for the _____ that is available at the terminals of the PV system disconnect.

    (a) maximum circuit current
    (b) available fault current
    (c) voltage
    (d) all of these

61. The disconnecting means, if located remote from the sign, sign body, or pole shall be mounted at a(an) _____ location available to first responders and service personnel.

    (a) available
    (b) accessible
    (c) readily accessible
    (d) visible

62. In Class I, Division 1 locations, seals for cables at all terminations shall be installed within _____ of the enclosure or as required by the enclosure marking.
    (a) 6 in.
    (b) 12 in.
    (c) 18 in.
    (d) 20 in.

63. Equipment or materials to which has been attached a(an) _____ of an FEB indicating the equipment or materials were evaluated and found to comply with requirements as described in an accompanying field evaluation report is known as field labeled (as applied to evaluated products).
    (a) symbol
    (b) label
    (c) other identifying mark
    (d) any of these

64. In Class I, Division 1 locations, the use of threaded rigid metal conduit (RMC) or threaded intermediate metal conduit (IMC), shall be permitted, including RMC or IMC conduit systems with supplemental _____ protection coatings.
    (a) rust
    (b) corrosion
    (c) paint
    (d) none of these

65. Article 695 covers the installation of the electric power sources and interconnecting circuits, and the switching and control equipment dedicated to drivers for _____.
    (a) generators
    (b) fire pumps
    (c) alarm systems
    (d) large-scale solar arrays

66. For electric vehicle supply and wireless power transfer equipment (EVSE and WPTE) more than _____ or more than 150V to ground, the disconnecting means shall be provided and installed in a readily accessible location.
    (a) 20A
    (b) 30A
    (c) 50A
    (d) 60A

67. In Class II, Division 2 locations, pendant luminaires can be suspended by _____.
    (a) threaded rigid metal conduit stems
    (b) threaded steel intermediate metal conduit stems
    (c) chains with approved fittings
    (d) any of these

68. In judging equipment, considerations such as _____ shall be evaluated.
    (a) mechanical strength
    (b) wire-bending and connection space
    (c) arcing effects
    (d) all of these

69. Article 517 applies to electrical construction and installation criteria in health care facilities that provide services to _____.
    (a) human beings
    (b) animals
    (c) children only
    (d) intellectually challenged persons

70. In Class I, Division 1 locations, threaded rigid metal conduit entries into explosionproof equipment shall be made up of _____.
    (a) at least five threads fully engaged
    (b) listed pressure fittings
    (c) four threads coated with listed epoxy
    (d) listed threaded bushings

71. The required working space for access to live parts of equipment operating at 300V to ground, where there are exposed live parts on both sides of the workspace is _____.
    (a) 3 ft
    (b) 3½ ft
    (c) 4 ft
    (d) 4½ ft

72. For permanently installed pools, a GFCI shall be installed in the branch circuit supplying luminaires operating at more than the low-voltage _____.
    (a) setting
    (b) listing
    (c) contact limit
    (d) trip limit

73. Wireless power transfer equipment is installed specifically for the purpose of transferring energy between the premises wiring and the electric vehicle without ____ electrical contact.

(a) physical
(b) inductive
(c) magnetic
(d) inductive and magnetic

74. Feeders and branch circuits installed in a corrosive environment or wet location near swimming pools shall contain an insulated copper EGC sized in accordance with Table 250.122, but not smaller than _____.

(a) 12 AWG
(b) 10 AWG
(c) 8 AWG
(d) 6 AWG

75. A functionally grounded system is often connected to ground through an electronic means internal to an inverter or charge controller that provides _____.

(a) overcurrent protection
(b) ground-fault protection
(c) arc-fault protection
(d) current-limiting properties

76. Completed wiring installations shall be free from _____ other than as required or permitted elsewhere in this *Code*.

(a) short circuits
(b) ground faults
(c) any connections to ground
(d) all of these

77. Class I, Division 1 locations are those areas in which ignitable concentrations of _____ can exist under normal operating conditions.

(a) combustible dust
(b) easily ignitable fibers or flyings
(c) flammable gases or flammable liquid-produced vapors
(d) pyrotechnics

78. All receptacles installed for the connection of electric vehicle charging shall have _____.

(a) arc-fault circuit-interrupter protection
(b) ground-fault circuit-interrupter protection
(c) current-limiting protection
(d) ground-fault protection for equipment

79. Overcurrent protective devices for solidly grounded wye electrical services at temporary installations having an available fault current greater than 10,000A shall _____.

(a) be provided with GFCI protection
(b) be current limiting
(c) be provided with AFCI protection
(d) provide GFPE protection

80. In other than dwelling units, a permanent arc-flash label shall be field or factory applied to service equipment and feeder supplied equipment rated _____ or more.

(a) 600A
(b) 1,000A
(c) 1,200A
(d) 1,600A

81. _____ that connect antennas to equipment shall comply with the appropriate article of Chapter 8.

(a) Equipment grounding conductors
(b) Coaxial cables
(c) Power conductors
(d) Tuning cables

82. Equipment grounding conductors for PV system circuits shall be sized in accordance with _____.

(a) 250.4
(b) 250.66
(c) 250.102
(d) 250.122

83. Where two or more explosionproof enclosures that require conduit seals are connected by nipples or runs of conduit not more than _____ long, a single conduit seal in each such nipple connection or run of conduit shall be considered sufficient if the seal is located not more than 18 in. from either enclosure.

(a) 12 in.
(b) 18 in.
(c) 24 in.
(d) 36 in.

84. In patient care spaces, metal faceplates shall be connected to an effective ground-fault current path by means of _____ securing the faceplate to a metal yoke or strap of a receptacle or to a metal outlet box.
   (a) ground clips
   (b) rivets
   (c) metal mounting screws
   (d) spot welds

85. The prospective symmetrical fault current at a nominal voltage to which an apparatus or system is able to be connected without sustaining damage exceeding defined acceptance criteria is known as the _____.
   (a) short-circuit current rating
   (b) arc-flash rating
   (c) overcurrent rating
   (d) available fault current

86. Section(s) 300.21, 770.26, and 800.26 shall apply to penetrations of the _____ information technology room boundary.
   (a) rated-resistant
   (b) flame-resistant
   (c) smoke-resistant
   (d) fire-resistant

87. Where approved by the authority having jurisdiction, connections ahead of and not within the same cabinet, enclosure, vertical switchgear section, or vertical switchboard section as the _____ disconnecting means shall be permitted for legally required standby systems.
   (a) emergency
   (b) service
   (c) optional
   (d) all of these

88. Means shall be provided to disconnect power source output circuit conductors of interconnected electric power production source equipment from conductors of other systems. The disconnecting means shall be a _____.
   (a) manually operable switch or circuit breaker
   (b) load-break-rated pull-out switch
   (c) device listed or approved for the intended application
   (d) any of these

89. Flexible cords used in Class II, Division 1 or 2 locations shall _____, except as permitted for pendant luminaires.
   (a) be listed for hard usage
   (b) be listed for extra-hard usage
   (c) not be permitted
   (d) be SJOT or SJOWT

90. The markings and listing labels required for signs and outline lighting systems, shall be visible after installation and shall be permanently applied in a location visible prior to _____.
   (a) servicing
   (b) maintenance
   (c) servicing or maintenance
   (d) none of these

91. Signs and outline lighting systems shall be installed so that adjacent combustible materials are not subjected to temperatures in excess of _____.
   (a) 60°C
   (b) 75°C
   (c) 90°C
   (d) 105°C

92. Class 2 and Class 3 cables for audio signal processing, amplification, and reproduction equipment installed in accordance with 722.135(B) shall not be permitted to be installed in other spaces used for environmental air (plenums).
   (a) True
   (b) False

93. Fittings and connectors that are intended to be concealed at the time of on-site assembly, where _____ for such use, shall be permitted for on-site interconnection of PV modules or other array components.
   (a) approved
   (b) identified
   (c) marked
   (d) listed

94. Exposed (as applied to _____), is defined as on or attached to the surface, or behind access panels designed to allow access.
   (a) equipment
   (b) luminaires
   (c) wiring methods
   (d) motors

95. Article 620 covers the installation of electrical equipment and wiring used in connection with elevators, dumbwaiters, escalators, moving walks, platform lifts, and _____.
    (a) stairway chairlifts
    (b) pool lifts
    (c) boat hoists
    (d) all of these

96. When normally enclosed live parts are exposed for inspection or servicing, the working space, if in a passageway or general open space, shall be suitably _____.
    (a) accessible
    (b) guarded
    (c) open
    (d) enclosed

97. For each floor area inside a minor repair garage where ventilation is not provided and Class I liquids or gaseous fuels are not transferred or dispensed, the entire area up to a level of _____ above the floor is considered to be a Class I, Division 2 location.
    (a) 6 in.
    (b) 12 in.
    (c) 18 in.
    (d) 24 in.

98. For underground conduits in a Class I, Division 1 location where the boundary is below grade, a sealing fitting shall be permitted to be installed _____, and there shall not be any unions, couplings, boxes, or fittings between the sealing fitting and the grade, other than listed explosionproof reducers.
    (a) after the conduit emerges from grade
    (b) before the conduit emerges from grade
    (c) within 10 ft of where the conduit emerges from grade
    (d) if the raceway type is RMC or PVC

99. For PV systems, means shall be provided to _____ ac PV modules, fuses, dc-to-dc converters, inverters, and charge controllers from all conductors that are not solidly grounded.
    (a) disconnect
    (b) open
    (c) close
    (d) turn off

100. 1Each energy storage system (ESS) shall be provided with a nameplate plainly visible after installation and marked with the _____.
    (a) rated frequency
    (b) number of phases (if ac)
    (c) rating in kW or kVA
    (d) all of these

INDEX

F

1st Printing

ABOUT THE AUTHOR

Mike Holt—Author

Mike Holt
Founder and President
Mike Holt Enterprises
Groveland, Florida

Mike Holt is an author, businessman, educator, speaker, publisher and *National Electrical Code* expert. He has written hundreds of electrical training books and articles, founded three successful businesses, and has taught thousands of electrical *Code* seminars across the U.S. and internationally. His dynamic presentation style, deep understanding of the trade, and ability to connect with students are some of the reasons that he is one of the most sought-after speakers in the industry.

His company, Mike Holt Enterprises, has been serving the electrical industry for almost 50 years, with a commitment to creating and publishing books, videos, online training, and curriculum support for electrical trainers, students, organizations, and electrical professionals. His devotion to the trade, coupled with the lessons he learned at the University of Miami's MBA program, have helped him build one of the largest electrical training and publishing companies in the United States.

Mike is committed to changing lives and helping people take their careers to the next level. He has always felt a responsibility to provide education beyond the scope of just passing an exam. He draws on his previous experience as an electrician, inspector, contractor and instructor, to guide him in developing powerful training solutions that electricians understand and enjoy. He is always mindful of how hard learning can be for students who are intimidated by school, by their feelings towards learning, or by the complexity of the *NEC*. He's mastered the art of simplifying and clarifying complicated technical concepts and his extensive use of illustrations helps students apply the content and relate the material to their work in the field. His ability to take the intimidation out of learning is reflected in the successful careers of his students.

Mike's commitment to pushing boundaries and setting high standards extends into his personal life as well. He's an eight-time Overall National Barefoot Waterski Champion. Mike has more than 20 gold medals, many national records, and has competed in three World Barefoot Tournaments. In 2015, at the tender age of 64, he started a new adventure—competitive mountain bike racing and at 65 began downhill mountain biking. Every day he continues to find ways to motivate himself, both mentally and physically.

Mike and his wife, Linda, reside in New Mexico and Florida, and are the parents of seven children and seven grandchildren. As his life has changed over the years, a few things have remained constant: his commitment to God, his love for his family, and doing what he can to change the lives of others through his products and seminars.

Special Acknowledgments

My Family. First, I want to thank God for my godly wife who's always by my side and for my children.

My Staff. A personal thank you goes to my team at Mike Holt Enterprises for all the work they do to help me with my mission of changing peoples' lives through education. They work tirelessly to ensure that, in addition to our products meeting and exceeding the educational needs of our customers, we stay committed to building life-long relationships throughout their electrical careers.

The National Fire Protection Association. A special thank you must be given to the staff at the National Fire Protection Association (NFPA), publishers of the *NEC*—in particular, Jeff Sargent for his assistance in answering my many *Code* questions over the years. Jeff, you're a "first class" guy, and I admire your dedication and commitment to helping others understand the *NEC*.

ABOUT THE ILLUSTRATOR

Mike Culbreath—Illustrator

Mike Culbreath
Graphic Illustrator
Alden, Michigan

Mike Culbreath has devoted his career to the electrical industry and worked his way up from apprentice electrician to master electrician. He started working in the electrical field doing residential and light commercial construction, and later did service work and custom electrical installations. While working as a journeyman electrician, he suffered a serious on-the-job knee injury. As part of his rehabilitation, Mike completed courses at Mike Holt Enterprises, and then passed the exam to receive his Master Electrician's license. In 1986, with a keen interest in continuing education for electricians, he joined the staff to update material and began illustrating Mike Holt's textbooks and magazine articles.

Mike started with simple hand-drawn diagrams and cut-and-paste graphics. Frustrated by the limitations of that style of illustrating, he took a company computer home to learn how to operate some basic computer graphics software. Realizing that computer graphics offered a lot of flexibility for creating illustrations, Mike took every computer graphics class and seminar he could to help develop his skills. He's worked as an illustrator and editor with the company for over 30 years and, as Mike Holt has proudly acknowledged, has helped to transform his words and visions into lifelike graphics.

Originally from South Florida, Mike now lives in northern lower Michigan where he enjoys hiking, kayaking, photography, gardening, and cooking; but his real passion is his horses. He also loves spending time with his children Dawn and Mac and his grandchildren Jonah, Kieley, and Scarlet.

ABOUT THE MIKE HOLT TEAM

There are many people who played a role in the production of this textbook. Their efforts are reflected in the quality and organization of the information contained in this textbook, and in its technical accuracy, completeness, and usability.

Technical Writing

Mario Valdes is the Technical Content Editor and works directly with Mike to ensure that content is technically accurate, relatable, and valuable to all electrical professionals. He plays an important role in gathering research, analyzing data, and assisting Mike in the writing of the textbooks. He reworks content into different formats to improve the flow of information and to ensure expectations are being met in terms of message, tone, and quality. He edits illustrations and proofreads content to "fact-check" each sentence, title, and image structure. Mario enjoys working in collaboration with Mike and Brian to enhance the company's brand image, training products, and technical publications.

Editorial and Production

Brian House is part of the content team that reviews our material to make sure it's ready for our customers. He also coordinates the team that constructs and reviews this textbook and its supporting resources to ensure its accuracy, clarity, and quality.

Toni Culbreath worked tirelessly to proofread and edit this publication. Her attention to detail and her dedication is irreplaceable. A very special thank you goes out to Toni (Mary Poppins) Culbreath for her many years of dedicated service.

Cathleen Kwas handled the design, layout, and typesetting of this book. Her desire to create the best possible product for our customers is greatly appreciated, and she constantly pushes the design envelope to make the product experience just a little bit better.

Vinny Perez and **Eddie Anacleto** have been a dynamic team. They have taken the best instructional graphics in the industry to the next level. Both Eddie and Vinny bring years of graphic art experience to the pages of this book and have been a huge help updating and improving the content, look, and style our graphics.

Dan Haruch is an integral part of the video recording process and spends much of his time making sure that the instructor resources created from this product are the best in the business. His dedication to the instructor and student experience is much appreciated.

Video Team

Special thank you to **Peter Furrow**, owner of Earth Electric Inc. of Cape Canaveral, Florida, for attending this video recording as a guestand contributing his time and energy to help us.

The following special people provided technical advice in the development of this textbook as they served on the video team along with author **Mike Holt.**

Vince Della Croce
Business Development Manager, Licensed Electrical Inspector, Plans Examiner, Master Electrician
vincent.della_croce@siemens.com
Port Saint Lucie, Florida

Vince Della Croce began his career in IBEW Local Union #3, New York City as a helper, and progressed to journeyman and foreman electrician, before relocating to Florida. He's licensed by the State of Florida as a Master Electrician and Electrical Inspector and Plans Examiner.

He holds an Associate of Science degree in Electronic Engineering and Electrical Maintenance Technology from Penn Foster College and represents Siemens in the role of Business Development Manager with a focus on supporting electrical inspectors throughout the country.

Vince serves the IAEI Florida Chapter and IAEI Southern Section as Education Chairman. He was an alternate member of Code-Making Panels 7 and 12 for the 2017 *NEC*. He is an alternate member of Code-Making Panel 17 for the 2023 *NEC*. Vince is also a principal technical committee member of NFPA 73, 78, 99, and 1078.

Vince has two sons. The oldest is serving the community as a police sergeant and holds a Master's Degree in Business Administration. The youngest is working as a business developer and holds a Bachelor's Degree in Marketing.

Daniel Brian House
Vice President of Digital and Technical Training
Mike Holt Enterprises, Instructor, Master Electrician
Brian@MikeHolt.com
Ocala, Florida

Brian House is Vice President of Digital and Technical Training at Mike Holt Enterprises, and a Certified Mike Holt Instructor. He is a permanent member of the video teams, on which he has served since the 2011 *Code* cycle. Brian has worked in the trade since the 1990s in residential, commercial and industrial settings. He opened a contracting firm in 2003 that designed energy-efficient lighting retrofits, explored "green" biomass generators, and partnered with residential PV companies in addition to traditional electrical installation and service.

In 2007, Brian was personally selected by Mike for development and began teaching seminars for Mike Holt Enterprises after being named a "Top Gun Presenter" in Mike's Train the Trainer boot camp. Brian travels around the country teaching electricians, instructors, military personnel, and engineers. His experience in the trenches as an electrical contractor, along with Mike Holt's instructor training, gives him a teaching style that is practical, straightforward, and refreshing.

Today, as Vice President of Digital and Technical Training at Mike Holt Enterprises, Brian leads the apprenticeship and digital product teams. They create cutting-edge training tools, and partner with in-house and apprenticeship training programs nationwide to help them reach the next level. He is also part of the content team that helps Mike bring his products to market, assisting in the editing of the textbooks, coordinating the content and illustrations, and assuring the technical accuracy and flow of the information.

Brian is high energy, with a passion for doing business the right way. He expresses his commitment to the industry and his love for its people in his teaching, working on books, and developing instructional programs and software tools.

Brian and his wife Carissa have shared the joy of their four children and many foster children during 25 years of marriage. When not mentoring youth at work or church, he can be found racing mountain bikes or SCUBA diving with his kids. He's passionate about helping others and regularly engages with the youth of his community to motivate them into exploring their future.

Eric Stromberg, P.E.
Electrical Engineer, Instructor
Eric@MikeHolt.com
Los Alamos, New Mexico

Eric Stromberg has a bachelor's degree in Electrical Engineering and is a professional engineer. He started in the electrical industry when he was a teenager helping the neighborhood electrician. After high school, and a year of college, Eric worked for a couple of different audio companies, installing sound systems in a variety of locations from small buildings to baseball stadiums. After returning to college, he worked as a journeyman wireman for an electrical contractor.

After graduating from the University of Houston, Eric took a job as an electronic technician and installed and serviced life safety systems in high-rise buildings. After seven years he went to work for Dow Chemical as a power distribution engineer. His work with audio systems had made him very sensitive to grounding issues and he took this experience with him into power distribution. Because of this expertise, Eric became one of Dow's grounding subject matter experts. This is also how Eric met Mike Holt, as Mike was looking for grounding experts for his 2002 Grounding vs. Bonding video.

Eric taught the *National Electrical Code* for professional engineering exam preparation for over 20 years, and has held continuing education teacher certificates for the states of Texas and New Mexico. He was on the electrical licensing and advisory board for the State of Texas, as well as on their electrician licensing exam board. Eric now consults for a Department of Energy research laboratory in New Mexico, where he's responsible for the electrical standards as well as assisting the laboratory's AHJ.

Eric's oldest daughter lives with her husband in Zurich, Switzerland, where she teaches for an international school. His son served in the Air Force, has a degree in Aviation logistics, and is a pilot and owner of an aerial photography business. His youngest daughter is a singer/songwriter in Los Angeles.

Mario Valdes, Jr.
Technical Content Editor Mike Holt Enterprises, Electrical Inspector, Electrical Plans Examiner, Master Electrician
Mario@MikeHolt.com
Ocala, Florida

Mario Valdes, Jr. is a member of the technical team at Mike Holt Enterprises, working directly with Mike Holt in researching, re-writing, and coordinating content, to assure the technical accuracy of the information in the products. He is a permanent member of the video teams, on which he has served since the 2017 *Code* cycle.

Mario is licensed as an Electrical Contractor, most recently having worked as an electrical inspector and plans examiner for an engineering firm in South Florida. Additionally, he was an Electrical Instructor for a technical college, teaching students pursuing an associate degree in electricity. He taught subjects such as ac/dc fundamentals, residential and commercial wiring, blueprint reading, and electrical estimating. He brings to the Mike Holt team a wealth of knowledge and devotion for the *NEC*.

He started his career at 16 years old in his father's electrical contracting company. Once he got his Florida State contractor's license, he ran the company as project manager and estimator. Mario's passion for the *NEC* prompted him to get his inspector and plans review certifications and embark on a new journey in electrical *Code* compliance. He's worked on complex projects such as hospitals, casinos, hotels and multi-family high rise buildings. Mario is very passionate about educating electrical professionals about electrical safety and the *National Electrical Code*.

Mario's a member of the IAEI, NFPA, and ICC, and enjoys participating in the meetings; he believes that by staying active in these organizations he'll be ahead of the game, with cutting-edge knowledge pertaining to safety codes.

When not immersed in the electrical world Mario enjoys fitness training. He resides in Pembroke Pines, Florida with his beautiful family, which includes his wife and his two sons. They enjoy family trip getaways to Disney World and other amusement parks.

1st Printing